Index to the 1800 Massachusetts Federal Census
for the County of
Hampshire

Rebecca M. Sullivan
Deborah Lee Larsson

Index to the 1800 Massachusetts Federal Census
for the County of
Hampshire

October 2014

ISBN: 978-1503059108

FOREWARD:

This is the seventh volume of several containing the heads of household that were enumerated in the 1800 United States Federal Census in Massachusetts. Our seventh volume is comprised of those towns in Hampshire County. In order to make it easy for the researcher, towns are alphabetized, followed by an alphabetical index of Hampshire county.

We have made every attempt at correctly transcribing each town. However, many of these documents are torn, covered with ink, tape marks, rips and poor handwriting. Spelling errors have been left as they were originally written. Any names & enumerations illegible are denoted with an asterisk.

This book should be used as a guide and research aid. When possible the actual image should be obtained for proper verification and citation. Visit the National Archives website to find out more on how to obtain census images. www.archives.gov/research/census.

In order to get all of the information on one page to make for easy reading we had to reduce the size of the font.

Drop us a line, we'd love to hear what you're researching: rsulli1219@aol.com

Becky & Deb
October 2014

Check out our other books:

INDEX

INDEX

INDEX

Hampshire County

Hampshire County Stats

Microfilm Reel Number: M32-15

Town:	Page Numbers:	Enumerated By:
Amherst	289-296	Charles Phelps
Ashfield	337-346	William Bull
Barnardston	76-80	Unknown
Belchertown	203-212	Unknown
Blanford	175-182	Unknown
Brimfield	269-275	Unknown
Buckland	325-331	William Bull
Charlemont	191-194	Hugh M. Clallan
Chester	143-150	David Shepard
Chesterfield	19-25	Levi Lyman
Colrain	184-190	Unknown
Conway	56-61	Unknown
Cummington	303-305	Unknown
Deerfield	51-55	Unknown
Easthampton	134-137	Unknown
Gill	85-88	Unknown
Goshen	309-312	Unknown
Granby	252-255	Unknown
Granville East Society	527-533	Unknown
Granville Middle Society	165-167	Unknown
Granville West Society	168-170	Jacob Bates
Greenfield	71-76	Caleb Clap
Greenwich	218-224	Unknown
Hadley	285-289	Unknown
Hatfield	11-14	Unknown
Hawley	331-335	William Bull
Heath	195-198	Unknown
Holland	278-280	Unknown
Leverett	113-117	Joshua Green
Leyden	80-84	Caleb Clap

Hampshire County Stats

Microfilm Reel Number: M32-15

Town:	Page Numbers:	Enumerated By:
Longmeadow	91-95	Unknown
Ludlow	255-258	Unknown
Middlefield	155-159	Unknown
Monson	262-268	Unknown
Montague	65-68	Unknown
Montgomery	159-162	Unknown
New Salem	96-104	Unknown
Northampton	2-11	Unknown
Northfield	27-31	Unknown
Norwich	151-154	Unknown
Orange	41-43	Unknown
Palmer	258-262	Unknown
Pelham	213-217	Unknown
Plainfield	306-309	Unknown
Rowe	198-201	Unknown
Russell	137-139	James Taylor
Shelburne	319-325	William Bull
Shutesbury	108-118	Unknown
South Brimfield	275-278	Unknown
South Hadley	248-251	Unknown
Southampton	128-133	James Taylor
Southwick	358-361	Unknown
Springfield	239-248	Unknown
Sunderland	282-283	Charles Phelps
Ware	225-228	Unknown
Warwick	36-40	Unknown
Wendell	105-108	Joshua Green
West Springfield	349-357	Unknown
Westfield	118-128	James Taylor
Westhampton	15-18	Unknown

Hampshire County Stats

Microfilm Reel Number: M32-15

Town:	Page Numbers:	Enumerated By:
Whately	44-48	John Williams
Wilbraham	232-238	Unknown
Williamsburg	441-448	Unknown
Worthington	297-302	Ezra Starkweather

TOWN	PG#	LN#	HEADS OF HOUSEHOLD LAST NAME	FIRST NAME	FREE WHITE MALES under 10	10 to 16	16 to 26	26 to 45	45 and over	FREE WHITE FEMALES under 10	10 to 16	16 to 26	26 to 45	45 and over	TOTAL ALL OTHER	TOTAL SLAVES	TOTALS	DISTRICT/ TOWNSHIP	NOTES
Amherst	289	1	Bothwood	Solomon			1	2	2	1			3	2			11		
Amherst	289	2	Clark	Simeon	1	1		1	1	1			3	1			9		
Amherst	289	3	Clark	Judah			1					1	1				3		
Amherst	289	4	Cutter	Robert			4		1		1	2		2			10		
Amherst	289	5	Perry	Jonathan		1	1	1		4		2		1			10		
Amherst	289	6	Strong	Simeon Esq		1	3		1			1	1	1	1		9		
Amherst	289	7	Coleman	Seth			2		1		1	1		1	1		7		
Amherst	289	8	Billings	Joel		1	3		1			1		1			7		
Amherst	289	9	Boman	William	1	1	1		1		1	2		1			8		
Amherst	289	10	Bixbee	Rufus			1			1		1					3		
Amherst	289	11	Goodale	Isaac		1			1			1		1			4		
Amherst	289	12	Goodale	Thomas			1	1			1	1	1				5		
Amherst	289	13	Fillmore	William	2		1					1					4		
Amherst	289	14	Baker	Isaac		1		1				1					3		
Amherst	289	15	Hastings	Elijah	1		1		1		2	1	2				8		
Amherst	289	16	Henderson	Timothy	2	2	2	1		1			1	1			10		
Amherst	289	17	Cook	Martin	1	1		1			1		1				5		
Amherst	289	18	Hendricks	James				1			1	1					3		
Amherst	289	19	Smith	Moses	1			1		2			1				5		
Amherst	290	1	Cowles	Levi				1			1		1	1			4		
Amherst	290	2	Cowles	Oliver	1			1		1			1				4		
Amherst	290	3	Cowles	Simeon	3	1	1		1	1	1	2	1				11		
Amherst	290	4	Dickinson	Nathaniel			1		2			1		2			6		
Amherst	290	5	Stephens	Phinehas	2			1	1	1			1				5		
Amherst	290	6	Smith	Jonathan			1					1					2		
Amherst	290	7	Smith	Noah			1	1				3		1			6		
Amherst	290	8	Smith	David	1		1	1		1			1	2			7		
Amherst	290	9	Smith	Elijah			1			2			1				4		
Amherst	290	10	Ingram	John	1	1	1	1		2	1	1	1				9		
Amherst	290	11	Bond	Solomon	1		1				1		1				4		
Amherst	290	12	Green	Timothy			1										1		
Amherst	290	13	Ingram	Samuel			1			1	1		1				4		
Amherst	290	14	Elmer	Elijah	1	1			1	1	2		1				7		
Amherst	290	15	Carpenter	Richard	1			1	2			1		1			7		
Amherst	290	16	Cowles	David			3	1	1				1	1			7		
Amherst	290	17	Cowles	Hannah			1					1	2	1			5		
Amherst	290	18	Eastman	Ebenezer	1	1	3	1	1		2	1		1			11		
Amherst	290	19	Ingram	David	1			1			1	1		2			6		
Amherst	290	20	Ingram	Nathan	1		1						1				3		
Amherst	290	21	Eastman	Joseph		1	2		1		1			1			6		
Amherst	290	22	Dickinson	Ruth	1		2					1		1			5		
Amherst	290	23	Clark	Elisha			1			2			1				4		
Amherst	290	24	Dickinson	John			4	1		2			1				8		
Amherst	290	25	Marsh	Jonathan	2	1	2		1		1	2		1			10		
Amherst	290	26	Cushman	Epraim	1			1	1	3	2	1	1				9		
Amherst	290	27	Dickinson	Azariah	3	1			1	1			1	1			8		
Amherst	290	28	Marshal	Isaac			2	1	2			2		2			9		
Amherst	290	29	Ingram	Ebenezer	3		1	1		2	1	1	1				10		
Amherst	290	30	Rood	Abigal									1				1		
Amherst	290	31	Smith	Friend	1		1	1		3		1	1				8		
Amherst	290	32	Rowe	Abel	1		2					2					5		
Amherst	290	33	Scott	Israel	1		1	1		2			1				6		
Amherst	290	34	Clark	Nathan	2			1					1				4		
Amherst	290	35	Kellogg	Elijah	1		1						1				3		
Amherst	290	36	Hawley	Moses				1					3				4		
Amherst	290	37	Kellogg	Ephraim	3		2	1	1	3		1	1	1			13		
Amherst	290	38	Kellogg	Joseph	1	2			1	1	2		1	1			9		
Amherst	290	39	Dickinson	Eli			1			1			1				3		
Amherst	291	1	Kellogg	John	1	1		1		3	1		1				8		
Amherst	291	2	Perkins	Nathan	1			1			1	1					4		
Amherst	291	3	Dickinson	William	3	1	1			1	1		1				8		
Amherst	291	4	Warner	Josiah		1	1	3	2		1			1			9		
Amherst	291	5	Youngs	Mercy										1			1		
Amherst	291	6	Pratt	Matthew		2			1			1		1			5		
Amherst	291	7	Pratt	Ebenezer	1			1		2		1					5		
Amherst	291	8	Hawley	Zachariah	3	1	1	1	1		2	1		1			11		
Amherst	291	9	Green	Larkin			1			1			1				3		
Amherst	291	10	Hawley	Zachariah Jun	1		1						1				3		
Amherst	291	11	Kimbal	Benjamin	3			1					1				5		
Amherst	291	12	Morton	Joseph	1	1	1		1		1			1			6		
Amherst	291	13	Stutson	Hgideon	1	1		1		3	2		1				9		
Amherst	291	14	Belding	Hezekiah			1	1	1		1		1				5		
Amherst	291	15	Dickinson	Asa	2	2		1	1	1		4		1			12		
Amherst	291	16	Dickinson	Elihu	2			1	1			1					5		
Amherst	291	17	Beffel	Apahel			1	1			1	1					4		
Amherst	291	18	Parker	Eli	2		1		1	2	2	1	1				10		
Amherst	291	19	Parker	Eli Junr	2			1		2	2	1	1				9		
Amherst	291	20	Kellogg	Daniel	3	1			2				2	2			10		
Amherst	291	21	Lewis	Elisha			1	1		1		2					8		

11

TOWN	PG#	LN#	HEADS OF HOUSEHOLD		FREE WHITE MALES					FREE WHITE FEMALES					TOTAL ALL OTHER	TOTAL SLAVES	TOTALS	DISTRICT/ TOWNSHIP	NOTES
			LAST NAME	FIRST NAME	under 10	10 to 16	16 to 26	26 to 45	45 and over	under 10	10 to 16	16 to 26	26 to 45	45 and over					
Amherst	291	22	Hubbard	Hannah		1			1		3			1			6		
Amherst	291	23	Dickinson	Seth	2			1		3	1		1				8		
Amherst	291	24	Nash	Moses	4		1						1				6		
Amherst	291	25	Ayer	Amos	1				1	1	1	1					6		
Amherst	291	26	Blodget	Asahel	2		1	1					1	1			6		
Amherst	291	27	Williams	Catharine									1				1		
Amherst	291	28	Garnwell	Samuel	1		1						1				3		
Amherst	291	29	Adams	Eliphalet	1		1			1	1	1					5		
Amherst	291	30	Blodget	David	3		1				2	3	1	1			11		
Amherst	291	31	Dickinson	Medard	2	1	1	1		1	3		1				10		
Amherst	291	32	Dickinson	Noah	1			1						1			3		
Amherst	291	33	Winslow	Amasa	1		1			2			1				5		
Amherst	291	34	Dickinson	Zimri			1			1			1				3		
Amherst	291	35	Wilkinson	George		1	2		1	3		1	1				9		
Amherst	291	36	Billings	Aaron	3		2	1		2	1		1				10		
Amherst	291	37	Dickinson	Gad		1		1					1				3		
Amherst	291	38	Standley	Edward A	3		1	1		2			1				8		
Amherst	291	39	Dickinson	Simeon		1	1	1					1	2			6		
Amherst	292	1	Montague	Luke			1										1		
Amherst	292	2	Clapp	Oliver		1	1	1						1			4		
Amherst	292	3	Watson	Joseph	4		1			1			1				7		
Amherst	292	4	Blair	Joseph	1		1					1					3		
Amherst	292	5	Watson	David			1						1				2		
Amherst	292	6	Mattson	Ebenezer Jun		2		1			1		1		1		6		
Amherst	292	7	Dickinson	Simeon Jun			1						1				2		
Amherst	292	8	Nash	Eunie		1				2			1				4		
Amherst	292	9	Dickinson	Elisha	2	1	1		1	1	2	1		2			11		
Amherst	292	10	Dickinson	Joseph		1		1	1	1		2		1			7		
Amherst	292	11	Pebbles	Francis	2		1						1				4		
Amherst	292	12	Church	Joseph Junr	3	2		1		1	1		1	1			10		
Amherst	292	13	Church	Joseph				1					1				2		
Amherst	292	14	Dickinson	Ebenezer		1		2		6			2	1			12		
Amherst	292	15	Eastman	John	1	2	1		1	2	1	2	1				11		
Amherst	292	16	Mattson	Ebenezer				1						1			2		
Amherst	292	17	Baker	Enos	2		1	1		2			1				7		
Amherst	292	18	Baker	Elijah				1						1			2		
Amherst	292	19	Baker	Martin	1		1			1			1				4		
Amherst	292	20	Smith	Stephen		1	1	1				1		1			5		
Amherst	292	21	Montague	Zebina		1	1	1		1		1		1			6		
Amherst	292	22	Edwards	Phillip	1	2	1			1			1				6		
Amherst	292	23	Draper	Ichabod Revnd		1		1		1		1					4		
Amherst	292	24	Edwards	Nathaniel			1	1					2	1			5		
Amherst	292	25	Hastings	Moses	3	1	1	1			2	3	1	1			13		
Amherst	292	26	Dickinson	Silas	1		1			2	1	1					6		
Amherst	292	27	Pomeroy	Simeon	2	2	2	1		1		1					9		
Amherst	292	28	Peck	Joseph P		1						1					2		
Amherst	292	29	Thayer	Josiah	2	3	2	1			1		1	1			11		
Amherst	292	30	Dickinson	Nahan	1		2	1	1			2		1			8		
Amherst	292	31	Morton	John			2							1			4		
Amherst	292	32	Pomeroy	David	1	1		1	1	3	1		1				10		
Amherst	292	33	Hastings	Thomas	1		2	1			2	1	1				8		
Amherst	292	34	Hastings	Samuel		1	1	1			2		1				6		
Amherst	292	35	Williams	Justus		1	1	1	1	1	1		1				7		
Amherst	292	36	Williams	John		1	1	1	1			1	1				6		
Amherst	292	37	Nash	Reuben	2	1	1		1	2	1	1	1				10		
Amherst	292	38	Dickinson	Stephen	2			1		1		1					5		
Amherst	292	39	Church	Giles	3		2	1			1	1	1	1			10		
Amherst	292	40	Burnham	James	2	1	1	1		1	2		1				8		
Amherst	292	41	Cooley	Daniel	1	1	1	1		1		1					6		
Amherst	293	1	Potter	Joseph	1	2		1			1	1	1	1			8		
Amherst	293	2	Cowles	Enos		1			1		2	1		2			7		
Amherst	293	3	McMaster	Joshua	2	1	1	1					1				6		
Amherst	293	4	Dickinson	Jonathan	1	2		1	1	1			1				7		
Amherst	293	5	Smith	Benjamin		1		1	1	1	1		1	1			7		
Amherst	293	6	Smith	Timothy	2	1		1			1		1				6		
Amherst	293	7	Coleman	Seth Junr	1		1			1		1					4		
Amherst	293	8	Smith	Nath Alexander		1		1				1		1			4		
Amherst	293	9	Moody	Rufus	1		1	1					1				4		
Amherst	293	10	Moody	Jonathan		1	1		1	1			1				6		
Amherst	293	11	Hubbard	Elihu	1	3		1		2	1	1	1				10		
Amherst	293	12	Warner	Jonathan	1	3	1		1	3	1		1				11		
Amherst	293	13	Moody	Asahel		1	2		1	2			1	1			8		
Amherst	293	14	Moody	Silas	3		1			1			1				6		
Amherst	293	15	Duglass	Joseph	2		1			2			1				6		
Amherst	293	16	Smith	Chester	1		1						1				3		
Amherst	293	17	Kellogg	Jonathan	1	2		1	1				1	2			8		
Amherst	293	18	Smith	Elisha	1				1		1	2	1				6		
Amherst	293	19	Coye	Wyllis			1			3			1				5		
Amherst	293	20	Holmes	Samuel	2					2							6		

12

TOWN	PG#	LN#	HEADS OF HOUSEHOLD		FREE WHITE MALES					FREE WHITE FEMALES					TOTAL ALL OTHER	TOTAL SLAVES	TOTALS	DISTRICT/ TOWNSHIP	NOTES
			LAST NAME	FIRST NAME	under 10	10 to 16	16 to 26	26 to 45	45 and over	under 10	10 to 16	16 to 26	26 to 45	45 and over					
Amherst	293	21	Dickinson	Judah	2		1	1	1		1		1	1			8		
Amherst	293	22	Dickinson	Perez			1	1		2	2	1					7		
Amherst	293	23	Franklin	Nathan	1			1		1		2	1	1			7		
Amherst	293	24	Goodale	David	2		1		1			1		2			7		
Amherst	293	25	Dickinson	Salomon	3	2		1		3	1		1				11		
Amherst	293	26	Searl	Elisha				1						1			2		
Amherst	293	27	Robbins	Isaac	2			1		3	1	1	1	1			10		
Amherst	293	28	Smith	Ethan		2		2			1		2	1			8		
Amherst	293	29	Robbins	Joseph			1	1				1	1				4		
Amherst	293	30	Flemming	James	1			2	1	3		2	1	2			12		
Amherst	293	31	Warner	Jacob					1	2	2			1			6		
Amherst	294	1	Howard	Jonathan				1		1			4	1			7		
Amherst	294	2	Smith	Sarah	2	3	1			1		1		1			9		
Amherst	294	3	Smith	Asa	1	1		1		3			1				7		
Amherst	294	4	Moody	Medad		1			1			1	1	1			5		
Amherst	294	5	Green	Clark			1			1		1					4		
Amherst	294	6	Eloner	Simeon		2			1	1		3		1			8		
Amherst	294	7	Lee	Henry	1				1		1	3		1			7		
Amherst	294	8	Moody	Elihu	1	1		1		2			1				6		
Amherst	294	9	Green	Zara	1		1						1				3		
Amherst	294	10	Moody	Lemuel	1			2	1			1	1				6		
Amherst	294	11	White	Jewel	2			1		1	1		1				6		
Amherst	294	12	Moody	Joel		1		1	1	1		2		1			7		
Amherst	294	13	Fish	Stephen	2	2	3		1	2		1		1			12		
Amherst	294	14	Lee	John	1	2	1		1	1	2	1		1			10		
Amherst	294	15	Nelson	Benja		2	1		1		1			1			6		
Amherst	294	16	Dana	Amariah	1	2			1	2	1	1		1			9		
Amherst	294	17	Green	Timothy	1	1			1	3	1	2		1			10		
Amherst	294	18	Merrick	James			2	1			1	1		1			6		
Amherst	294	19	Moody	Eldad					1				1				2		
Amherst	294	20	Rice	William	3	1		1		2			1				8		
Amherst	294	21	Kellogg	Martin Jun	1		1						1				3		
Amherst	294	22	Smith	Ithamar	2		1	1		2	2		1				9		
Amherst	294	23	Smith	Eleazer		1		1		1			1	1			5		
Amherst	294	24	Zale	Elijah	1		1						1				3		
Amherst	294	25	Abby	Mason	2		1	1		1	1		1				7		
Amherst	294	26	Kellogg	Martin		1			1	2	2		1				7		
Amherst	294	27	Cowles	Reuben	2	1			1	1	1	1	1				8		
Amherst	294	28	Clark	Simeon Jun		1		1		1	2		1				6		
Amherst	294	29	Clark	Irena	3					1	1		1				6		
Amherst	294	30	Smith	Arad		1						1					2		
Amherst	294	31	Smith	Samuel	1			1		2	1	1	1	1			8		
Amherst	294	32	Chase	Ral*			1			1		1			1		4		
Amherst	296	1	Bottwood	Wlliam	1		1	1		3	1		1	1			9		
Amherst	296	2	Billings	John	3			1	1	6		1	3	1			16		
Amherst	296	3	Dickinson	Elijah		1	1	1	1	1		1	1	1			8		
Amherst	296	4	Parsons	Gideon	3	1		1		2	1		1				9		
Amherst	296	5	Parsons	David Revd	2	2			1	3	2	1	1	1			13		
Amherst	296	6	Warner	Elisha	1			1					1				3		
Amherst	296	7	Warner	David		1			1		1		1				4		
Amherst	296	8	Merrils	Calvin	4		3	1	1	1		2	1	1			14		

TOWN	PG#	LN#	LAST NAME	FIRST NAME	FWM under 10	FWM 10 to 16	FWM 16 to 26	FWM 26 to 45	FWM 45 and over	FWF under 10	FWF 10 to 16	FWF 16 to 26	FWF 26 to 45	FWF 45 and over	TOTAL ALL OTHER	TOTAL SLAVES	TOTALS	DISTRICT/ TOWNSHIP	NOTES
Ashfield	337	1	Alden	Barnabas		1	2	1		4	1	1	2	1			13		
Ashfield	337	2	Alden	David Junr	1	1		1		3	2		1				9		
Ashfield	337	3	Aldrich	Solomon	3	2		1		1	1		1				9		
Ashfield	337	4	Aldrich	Benjm	3	1		1		1			1				7		
Ashfield	337	5	Annible	Saml Jr				1		1		1					3		
Ashfield	337	6	Allis	Lemuel		1	2		1	2	1		1				8		
Ashfield	337	7	Andrews	Otis	2			1		2			1				6		
Ashfield	337	8	Alden	John	2	1		1	1	4	1	1	1	1			13		
Ashfield	337	9	Alden	Ebenz				1					1				2		
Ashfield	337	10	Alden	Henry	1			1		2			1				5		
Ashfield	337	11	Amiden	Mary			1					1		1			3		
Ashfield	337	12	Amible	Barnabas	2			1		2		1					6		
Ashfield	337	13	Andrews	James	3		2		1	1	2		1				10		
Ashfield	337	14	Allis	Abel			1	1				2		1			5		
Ashfield	337	15	Bartlett	Sarah	1		1				1			1			4		
Ashfield	337	16	Bemont	John			1	1				3		1			6		
Ashfield	337	17	Bemont	Phinehas	3			1			2		1				7		
Ashfield	337	18	Bemont	John Junr	3	1		1		1			1				7		
Ashfield	337	19	Benton	Bezer	1	1		1			1		1				5		
Ashfield	337	20	Bemont	Reuben	3	1		1			1		1				7		
Ashfield	337	21	Belding	Saml Jr		1		1			1			1			4		
Ashfield	338	1	Belding	Daniel	6	1	2		1	1	2	3					16		
Ashfield	338	2	Bachelor	Saml	1		1		1			1	1	1			5		
Ashfield	338	3	Belding	John	3		1	1		2	2		1				10		
Ashfield	338	4	Bishop	Joseph			1			1		1					3		
Ashfield	338	5	Burnet	Archibald	1	1	1		1	2	2			1			9		
Ashfield	338	6	Bronson	Roger	1			1		1		1					4		
Ashfield	338	7	Burton	Saml				1					1				2		
Ashfield	338	8	Butler	Davis	1		1		1	1		1		1			6		
Ashfield	338	9	Brown	Leml	3	1		1		2			1				8		
Ashfield	338	10	Balding	Ebenz		1		1	1		1		1	1			6		
Ashfield	338	11	Brant	Zebulon		1		1		1	1		1				5		
Ashfield	338	12	Briggs	Jasper	2			1					1				4		
Ashfield	338	13	Bracket	Benjm	3	1		1		2	1		1				9		
Ashfield	338	14	Bassett	Elisha		2	1	1				1		1			6		
Ashfield	338	15	Bassett	Lot	3	1	1	1		2	2		1				11		
Ashfield	338	16	Barber	Elisha															Enumeration left blank
Ashfield	338	17	Baldwin	David		1		1				2		1			5		
Ashfield	338	18	Baldwin	David Jr	1		1			2			1				5		
Ashfield	338	19	Baldwin	Jonathan	3			1					1				5		
Ashfield	338	20	Baldwin	John	1			1		2			1				5		
Ashfield	338	21	Blake	Silas	2			1		1			1				5		
Ashfield	338	22	Baker	Allen			3										3		
Ashfield	338	23	Bardwell	Saml				1						1			2		
Ashfield	338	24	Borthwick	Peter		1				1		1					3		
Ashfield	338	25	Bemont	Sama	3			1		1			1				6		
Ashfield	338	26	Blotchet	Aaron		1				2		1					4		
Ashfield	338	27	Cranston	Elisha Jr	1	1	4		1	3	1		1				12		
Ashfield	338	28	Clark	Silas	1		3	1		2		1	1				9		
Ashfield	338	29	Cross	Stephen	1	1	1		1	3	1		1				9		
Ashfield	338	30	Cranston	Asa	2	2		1		1		1	1				8		
Ashfield	338	31	Cranston	Abner	2			1		2	1		1				7		
Ashfield	339	1	Church	Caleb	1	1			1			1		1			5		
Ashfield	339	2	Cook	Levi	3	2		2	1	1	1	1	1	1			13		
Ashfield	339	3	Collins	Joseph	1		2	1				1					5		
Ashfield	339	4	Crudenton	Isaac		1		1					1	1			4		
Ashfield	339	5	Cross	John	1	1		1		1	1	2		2			9		
Ashfield	339	6	Cross	Cephas	1		1	2		4	1		1				10		
Ashfield	339	7	Clark	Alvin	2	1		1					1				5		
Ashfield	339	8	Case	James	2			1		2		1		1			7		
Ashfield	339	9	Carr	Amos	2	2		1				1					6		
Ashfield	339	10	Cranston	Jonathan	3	1		1	1	2	2	1		1			12		
Ashfield	339	11	Cranston	David	1	1		1		1			1				5		
Ashfield	339	12	Church	Caleb Jr			1						1				2		
Ashfield	339	13	Clough	Calvin	2	1	1	1		1		1	1				8		
Ashfield	339	14	Church	Seth		1						1					2		
Ashfield	339	15	Cobb	Priscilla		1	1			1				1			4		
Ashfield	339	16	Dickinson	David		2	1			1		1					5		
Ashfield	339	17	Divol	Josiah	2	1	1			2			1				7		
Ashfield	339	18	Dyer	Benjm	2			1		1			1				5		
Ashfield	339	19	Dyer	Jesse	1			1					1				3		
Ashfield	339	20	Damon	Edward	1				1	3	2		1				8		
Ashfield	339	21	Drake	Josiah	1		1	1					1				4		
Ashfield	339	22	Dunbar	Jerimiah	1	1	1	1		3			1				8		
Ashfield	339	23	Davis	Sylvester	1			1				1					3		
Ashfield	339	24	Darby	Saml	1		1					1					3		
Ashfield	339	25	Eldridge	Levi	1	1	3		1	2	2		2				12		
Ashfield	339	26	Eldridge	Eli	1		1	1			2		1	1			7		
Ashfield	339	27	Ellis	John		1		1				1	1	1			5		
Ashfield	339	28	Ellis	David	1	1		1		1	2		1	2			9		
Ashfield	339	29	Elmore	Saml	2	1		1		1			1				6		
Ashfield	340	1	Elmore	Gad	3	1		1		1	1	1					9		
Ashfield	340	2	Elmore	Saml Junr	2	1		1		1			1				6		
Ashfield	340	3	Elmore	Zenas	2			1		1			1				5		
Ashfield	340	4	Eldridge	Saml	3			1		2			2				8		
Ashfield	340	5	Ellis	Jonathan		1			1			1	1				6		
Ashfield	340	6	Eages	Stephen	1			1		1		1					4		
Ashfield	340	7	Frary	Moses	1	3	1		1	3	1	3	1				14		
Ashfield	340	8	Flower	Lamrock	2	1	1	1	1	1	2		1	1			11		
Ashfield	340	9	Flower	Willm	1		2				3	2	1				9		

14

TOWN	PG#	LN#	LAST NAME	FIRST NAME	FREE WHITE MALES					FREE WHITE FEMALES					TOTAL ALL OTHER	TOTAL SLAVES	TOTALS	DISTRICT/ TOWNSHIP	NOTES
					under 10	10 to 16	16 to 26	26 to 45	45 and over	under 10	10 to 16	16 to 26	26 to 45	45 and over					
Ashfield	340	10	Field	Zachariah	4	1		3		1	1		1				11		
Ashfield	340	11	Ford	John	2			1					1				4		
Ashfield	340	12	Fuller	Josiah	2	2		1		3	1		1				10		
Ashfield	340	13	Fuller	Solomon	1	1	1	2		1	1	1	1				9		
Ashfield	340	14	Fuller	Luke				1					1				2		
Ashfield	340	15	Foster	Willm				1	1		1	1		1			5		
Ashfield	340	16	Foster	Lewis			1		1			1		1			4		
Ashfield	340	17	Forbush	Ebenz		1		1		3			1				6		
Ashfield	340	18	Flower	George	2			1		1			1				5		
Ashfield	340	19	Flower	Willm Junr	3					1		1					5		
Ashfield	340	20	Forbush	Thomas				1		3			1				5		
Ashfield	340	21	Gray	Robert		1	1		1	1	1	1	1				7		
Ashfield	340	22	Gray	Jonathan	1	1			1	3	1		1				8		
Ashfield	340	23	Guilford	Saml	1		2	1		2	3		1				10		
Ashfield	341	1	Graves	Randal	3	2		1		1	1		1				9		
Ashfield	341	2	Goodwin	Eldad F.	2		1	1		3	2	1	1				11		
Ashfield	341	3	Graves	Dorus	1		2					1					4		
Ashfield	341	4	Goodwin	Uriah		1		1						1			3		
Ashfield	341	5	Howes	Saml				1					1				2		
Ashfield	341	6	Howes	Anthony		1	1			1		2		1			7		
Ashfield	341	7	Howes	Joshua		1	1							1			3		
Ashfield	341	8	Hosford	Dudley	1			1		2			1				5		
Ashfield	341	9	Hall	Saml	1	1	1		1	1		3		1			9		
Ashfield	341	10	Hall	Nathaniel	2	1			1	2			1				7		
Ashfield	341	11	Hall	Joseph	5	1	1	1				2					10		
Ashfield	341	12	Hall	Reuben	2	1	1		1		1	2		1			9		
Ashfield	341	13	Howes	Zachariah	2	1	2		1	2	2		1				11		
Ashfield	341	14	Howes	Ezekiel	4			1		1			1				7		
Ashfield	341	15	Howes	Mark	1	1	1	1		2			1				7		
Ashfield	341	16	Howes	Joseph	3			1		1		1	1				7		
Ashfield	341	17	Holbut	Reuben	1	2		1	1	2			1				8		
Ashfield	341	18	Howes	Kimbal		1	1		1	1	3		1				8		
Ashfield	341	19	Howes	Barnabas	1		1						1				3		
Ashfield	341	20	Hubbard	Samuel	2		1						1				4		
Ashfield	341	21	Howard	Abijah	1			1					1				3		
Ashfield	341	22	Howes	Heaman	5			1		1			1				8		
Ashfield	341	23	Hill	Solomon				1		2			1				4		
Ashfield	341	24	Hammond	Timothy					1	1	1		1				4		
Ashfield	342	1	Jordan	Edmund	1			1		1	1		1				5		
Ashfield	342	2	King	John			1		1					1			3		
Ashfield	342	3	King	Enoch	2	2		1		2	2		1				10		
Ashfield	342	4	Kellogg	Daniel	1					1		1					3		
Ashfield	342	5	Kilburn	Jacob	4	1	1		1	1	1			1			10		
Ashfield	342	6	Kelley	Abner	1		3		1	1	1			1			8		
Ashfield	342	7	Knotton	Joshua	2			1		2	1		1	1			8		
Ashfield	342	8	Keyes	Stephen		1			1					1			3		
Ashfield	342	9	Kellogg	Saml				1		1		1	1				4		
Ashfield	342	10	Lyon	Aaron		1			1				1	1			4		
Ashfield	342	11	Lyon	David	3	1		1		2		1	1				9		
Ashfield	342	12	Loomis	Jonah	2			1		1			1				5		
Ashfield	342	13	Lilly	Jonathan			1	1				1		1			4		
Ashfield	342	14	Lilly	Bethniel	5	2		1		1			1				10		
Ashfield	342	15	Lilly	Eliakim	3			1		2			1				7		
Ashfield	342	16	Lilly	Foster	2			1					1				4		
Ashfield	342	17	Mighells	Nathl				1		2			1				4		
Ashfield	342	18	Moody	Saml	1		1						1				3		
Ashfield	342	19	McGinster	Augustus	2			1		2			1				6		
Ashfield	342	20	Mighells	Daniel			2		1			1	1				5		
Ashfield	342	21	Mighells	John	2	2		1		1			1				7		
Ashfield	342	22	Merrill	Stephen	2				1				1				4		
Ashfield	343	1	Mantor	John L.	1	1		1		1			1	1			6		
Ashfield	343	2	Mantor	Jeremiah		1		1				1		1			4		
Ashfield	343	3	Mansfield	Paxson	3			1					1				5		
Ashfield	343	4	Norton	Selah	3		1		1	2	3			1			11		
Ashfield	343	5	Newton	Asa	2	2		1		2		1	1				9		
Ashfield	343	6	Newton	George			1			1			1				3		
Ashfield	343	7	Putney	Jedediah			2						1				3		
Ashfield	343	8	Porter	Simeon			1						1				2		
Ashfield	343	9	Porter	Nehemiah				1				1		1			3		
Ashfield	343	10	Porter	John	1	1	1		1		2	1		1			8		
Ashfield	343	11	Porter	Joseph	2	3	1	1					1	1			11		
Ashfield	343	12	Porter	John 2d	1		1			2			1				5		
Ashfield	343	13	Porter	Saml	2		1		1	1	3		1				9		
Ashfield	343	14	Phillips	Caleb	2	1		1		3	1	2	1				11		
Ashfield	343	15	Phillips	Saml	2	2		1		2			1				8		
Ashfield	343	16	Putney	Elisha		1			1	1	1	2		1			7		
Ashfield	343	17	Putney	Ebenz	1			1		2			1				5		
Ashfield	343	18	Patrick	John	1					2			1				4		
Ashfield	343	19	Patrick	Silas	1		2	1	2	1			1	1			9		
Ashfield	343	20	Perkins	Timothy	2	2		1		1			1				7		
Ashfield	343	21	Packard	Caleb	3	1		1		1	2	1	1				10		
Ashfield	343	22	Parker	Elisha		2	1		1	1				1			6		
Ashfield	343	23	Phillips	Phillip	2			1			1		2				6		
Ashfield	343	24	Phillips	Abner	1	1		1	1	2			1	1			8		
Ashfield	343	25	Phillips	Elijah	1	2		1		3	1		1	1			10		
Ashfield	343	26	Phillips	Simeon	2			1				1					4		
Ashfield	343	27	Phillips	Vesparian	1	2	1		1		1	1		2			9		
Ashfield	344	1	Phillips	Spencer	2				1	1	2			1			7		
Ashfield	344	2	Phillips	David					1				1				3		
Ashfield	344	3	Porter	Asa	4			1		1			1				7		

TOWN	PG#	LN#	LAST NAME	FIRST NAME	FREE WHITE MALES					FREE WHITE FEMALES					TOTAL ALL OTHER	TOTAL SLAVES	TOTALS	DISTRICT/ TOWNSHIP	NOTES
					under 10	10 to 16	16 to 26	26 to 45	45 and over	under 10	10 to 16	16 to 26	26 to 45	45 and over					
Ashfield	344	4	Porter	Joshua	2			1		1			1				5		
Ashfield	344	5	Perry	John	2			1	1	1			2				7		
Ashfield	344	6	Paine	Elijah	2		1	1		1	1		1				7		
Ashfield	344	7	Paine	Joseph R.				1				1		1			3		
Ashfield	344	8	Phillips	Thomas		1	1	1			1	1		1			6		
Ashfield	344	9	Phillips	Israel				1		1		1					3		
Ashfield	344	10	Paine	Joseph Junr	2			1		2		1					6		
Ashfield	344	11	Perkins	Abiezer	2		3	1		1		1	1				9		
Ashfield	344	12	Putney	Jedediah				1									1		
Ashfield	344	13	Phillips	David	3			1					1				5		
Ashfield	344	14	Phillips	Saml	1			1		2		1					5		
Ashfield	344	15	Parker	Sylvanus	2			1		2			1				6		
Ashfield	344	16	Perkins	Eliab	2	1	1		1	1		1					7		
Ashfield	344	17	Ranney	George	1	1	1		1		1	3		1			9		
Ashfield	344	18	Ranney	Thomas		1	1	1				1		1			5		
Ashfield	344	19	Ranney	Francis	1	1	1	1		1	1	3		1			10		
Ashfield	344	20	Rude	Sebrus		1	1	1	1	2	1		1	1			9		
Ashfield	344	21	Rogers	Joshua				1		2			1	1			5		
Ashfield	344	22	Rogers	Benjm		1		1	1			1		1			5		
Ashfield	344	23	Richards	Calvin	3			1		2	2	1	1				10		
Ashfield	344	24	Richmond	Zephh	3			1		1			1				6		
Ashfield	344	25	Ranney	Saml	1			1				1					3		
Ashfield	344	26	Sears	Jonathan		1	2	2	1	1	3	1		1			12		
Ashfield	344	27	Sears	Paul	2	1			1	3	2	1	1				11		
Ashfield	344	28	Sears	Roland	2	3	1		1	1		2		1			11		
Ashfield	344	29	Sears	Enos		2		1		1	1	2		1			8		
Ashfield	344	30	Selden	Asa		1		1		2			1				5		
Ashfield	345	1	Stowell	Caleb	1	1		1		2	2		1				8		
Ashfield	345	2	Stowell	David	2			1		1			1				5		
Ashfield	345	3	Smith	David	1	1		1		3			1				7		
Ashfield	345	4	Smith	Chipman	3		1	1		1	2		1	1			10		
Ashfield	345	5	Smith	Martin	1		1			2			1				5		
Ashfield	345	6	Smith	Elijah			1		1	1		1		1			5		
Ashfield	345	7	Smith	Jonathan Junr	4		1		1	1	1		1				9		
Ashfield	345	8	Stoching	Joseph				1						1			2		
Ashfield	345	9	Stoching	Abraham	1	1	1	1	1	1			1	1			8		
Ashfield	345	10	Stoching	Amos	1		2	1		3			1				8		
Ashfield	345	11	Sherwin	John				1						1			2		
Ashfield	345	12	Sherwin	Nathl	2	1		1	1	2	1		1	1			10		
Ashfield	345	13	Smith	Ehiliab Junr				1			1			1			3		
Ashfield	345	14	Smith	Ehiliab 3d	2			1		2			1				6		
Ashfield	345	15	Smith	Jeduthan	3	1		1	1	3			1	1			11		
Ashfield	345	16	Sadler	John		1		1		2	1	1	1				7		
Ashfield	345	17	Sheppard	Isaac	1	1	1		1	1	1		1				7		
Ashfield	345	18	Sheppard	Isaac Junr	1	1		1		1	1		1				6		
Ashfield	345	19	Sears	Peter		1		1						1			3		
Ashfield	345	20	Standish	Israel		1		1				1		1			4		
Ashfield	345	21	Sadler	Joshua	2	2		1		2	1		1				9		
Ashfield	345	22	Smith	Ebenz	2			1		1		1					5		
Ashfield	345	23	Savage	Abraham	3	2	1	1		1	1	1	1	1			12		
Ashfield	345	24	Smith	Joseph	1		1		1					1			4		
Ashfield	345	25	Smith	Abner	2				2	3	2		1	1			11		
Ashfield	345	26	Sears	seth				1						1			2		
Ashfield	345	27	Sadler	Noah	2	1		1		2	1		1				8		
Ashfield	345	28	Sanderson	Elnathan	2	1			1	1	1		1				7		
Ashfield	345	29	Sanderson	Morcena	1			1		1		1					4		
Ashfield	345	30	Taylor	John	1	1	1	1		2	3		1				10		
Ashfield	345	31	Toby	Elijah	1			1					1				3		
Ashfield	345	32	Taylor	Ebenz			1	1				2	1				5		
Ashfield	345	33	Tower	Thomas	3	1	1		1	2	2		1				11		
Ashfield	345	34	Taylor	Ezekiel	2	1		1		2			1				7		
Ashfield	345	35	Taylor	Stephen	3			1		1			1				6		
Ashfield	345	36	Taylor	Isaiah	2			1		2			1				6		
Ashfield	345	37	Usher	James	1	1			1	2		1		1			7		
Ashfield	346	1	Vincent	David	2			1		2			1				6		
Ashfield	346	2	Vincent	Joseph	2			1		1			1				5		
Ashfield	346	3	Warner	Thos Capt.	2	2		1		3	1	1	1				11		
Ashfield	346	4	Warren	Joseph			2		1		1			2			6		
Ashfield	346	5	Warren	Joseph Junr	2	1		1		3	1		1				9		
Ashfield	346	6	Warren	Timothy	2			1		1	2		1				7		
Ashfield	346	7	Warren	Stephen	1	1			1	3	2	2	1				11		
Ashfield	346	8	Williams	Ephm Esq	3	2	6	1				3	1				16		
Ashfield	346	9	Ward	Elijah	2			1		2			1				6		
Ashfield	346	10	Ward	Caleb	3	2			1		1	2	1				10		
Ashfield	346	11	Williams	Apollos	3				1	2		1	1				8		
Ashfield	346	12	White	Thomas		1	2	1		3		1	1				9		
Ashfield	346	13	Wait	Elijah		1		1									2		
Ashfield	346	14	Wait	Seth Junr	1			1	1	2			1	1			7		
Ashfield	346	15	Ward	Moses	1			1		2			1				5		
Ashfield	346	16	Ward	Alexander	3	1		1		3	2		1				11		
Ashfield	346	17	Weeks	David				1				1		1			3		
Ashfield	346	18	Williams	David	1		2					1					4		
Ashfield	346	19	Wait	Gad	5	1		1		1	1		1				10		
Ashfield	346	20	Ward	Phinehas		1	3	1		3	2		1				11		

TOWN	PG#	LN#	HEADS OF HOUSEHOLD		FREE WHITE MALES					FREE WHITE FEMALES					TOTAL ALL OTHER	TOTAL SLAVES	TOTALS	DISTRICT/ TOWNSHIP	NOTES
			LAST NAME	FIRST NAME	under 10	10 to 16	16 to 26	26 to 45	45 and over	under 10	10 to 16	16 to 26	26 to 45	45 and over					
Barnardston	76	1	Allen	Anna							1			1			2		
Barnardston	76	2	Allen	Jonathan	4	1		1					1				7		
Barnardston	76	3	Alger	Simon		1	1		1	1			1	1			6		
Barnardston	76	4	Allis	Thomas				1						1			2		
Barnardston	76	5	Alexander	George				1			1	1					3		
Barnardston	76	6	Aldridge	Joseph	2			1		1			1	1			6		
Barnardston	76	7	Allen	Joseph	1	1		1		2	1		1				7		
Barnardston	76	8	Burnett	Joseph		1			1			3	1				7		
Barnardston	76	9	Briggs	Zadoch	3	1		1		1	2	2	1				11		
Barnardston	76	10	Bogg	Israel	3		1		1	1	3	1	1				11		
Barnardston	77	11	Burnham	Elisha			1	1			2			1			5		
Barnardston	77	12	Brooks	John		1		1					1	1			4		
Barnardston	77	13	Burk	Lovina	1	2	1	1			1		1	2			9		
Barnardston	77	14	Cushman	Rachael	1	1	3				2			1			8		
Barnardston	77	15	Chapen	Zalmuna	3			1	1	1			1	1			8		
Barnardston	77	16	Chapen	Caleb Junr	5	1		1					1				8		
Barnardston	77	17	Connabell	Jonathan			2			1	1						4		
Barnardston	77	18	Chapen	Joel				1						1			2		
Barnardston	77	19	Chapen	Hezekiah		1			1	1	1			1			5		
Barnardston	77	20	Chapen	Israel	2	1		1			1		1				6		
Barnardston	77	21	Cushman	Artimas		1		1		4	1	2		1			10		
Barnardston	77	22	Cook	Amasa		2		1		1		1		1			6		
Barnardston	77	23	Connabell	John		2		1		2	3	1		3			12		
Barnardston	77	24	Chapen	Joel Junr	2			1					1				4		
Barnardston	77	25	Cooley	Oliver				1		2			1				4		
Barnardston	77	26	Denio	Joseph		1		1	1	1			1	2			7		
Barnardston	77	27	Darling	Elind		1		1		3		1					6		
Barnardston	77	28	Dickenson	Arias	3	1	1					1		1			8		
Barnardston	77	29	Dewey	Thomas	1		1			1		1					4		
Barnardston	77	30	Dean	David	2			1		1			1				5		
Barnardston	77	31	Edwards	Thomas		2	1		1			3		1			8		
Barnardston	77	32	Frizell	Michael	1			1		3			1				6		
Barnardston	77	33	Fox	Noah	3	1	1	1		3		2	1				13		
Barnardston	77	34	Field	Jesse	1		1		1	2	2	3	1	2			13		
Barnardston	77	35	Flagg	Samuel	1		1	1		2	1		1				7		
Barnardston	77	36	Fox	William	3	2	1		1	4	1	1		1			14		
Barnardston	77	37	Foster	Ezekiel				1			1		1				3		
Barnardston	77	38	Green	Samuel	2	1		1		3	3		1				11		
Barnardston	77	39	Green	Woodbridge		1		1			1	1	1				5		
Barnardston	77	40	Gould	Gideon		1		1		2	2		1				7		
Barnardston	77	41	Gilbert	Joshua			1			2			1				4		
Barnardston	77	42	Gould	Oliver	2	1	1	1		1		1	1				8		
Barnardston	77	43	Gilbert	Thoma	2	2		1		1			1				7		
Barnardston	78	1	Horsley	Thomas	2		1						1				4		
Barnardston	78	2	Harvey	Peter			1	1				1		1			4		
Barnardston	78	3	Hale	John	2		1	1		1	1		1				7		
Barnardston	78	4	Hale	Israel	2	2		1		1			2				8		
Barnardston	78	5	Hamilton	John	2		1	1		1			1				6		
Barnardston	78	6	Hale	Elizer	2		1			2			1				6		
Barnardston	78	7	Hale	Samuel		1		1		3	1		1				7		
Barnardston	78	8	Hastings	Samuel			2		1			1	2	1			7		
Barnardston	78	9	Hale	Chilab			1	1		1				1			4		
Barnardston	78	10	Hodge	Levi		2	2	1		3	2		1				11		
Barnardston	78	11	Hale	Elijah	2	2		1		1	1		1				8		
Barnardston	78	12	Hill	Jabez	4	1		1		1			1				8		
Barnardston	78	13	Hale	Daniel	1			1				1					3		
Barnardston	78	14	Johnson	Joseph	2			1		1			1				5		
Barnardston	78	15	Kinsley	Elijah				1						1			2		
Barnardston	78	16	Kinsley	Gamaliel	2			1		1			1				5		
Barnardston	78	17	Lomis	Daniel				1				1		1			3		
Barnardston	78	18	Loveland	Thomas				1		1				1			3		
Barnardston	78	19	Moorey	George	1		1					1					3		
Barnardston	78	20	Nickerson	Edward	2	2		1		1			1				7		
Barnardston	78	21	Nickerson	Covel				1						1			2		
Barnardston	78	22	Newcomb	William	1		1					1					3		
Barnardston	78	23	Nichols	Nathan	2			1		1	1		1				6		
Barnardston	78	24	Newcomb	Hezekiah	1	2	2		1		1	3		1			11		
Barnardston	78	25	Newcomb	William	4	2	2		1		1			1			11		
Barnardston	78	26	Nightingale	Ebenezer	1		1			1	1		1				6		
Barnardston	78	27	Pinks	John	4			1		1		1		1			8		
Barnardston	78	28	Parmenter	Elias	1	1	1	1		1		2	3	1			11		
Barnardston	78	29	Pursile	Ezra	1	1	2		1	1			1	1			8		
Barnardston	78	30	Parmenter	Jason				1					1	1			3		
Barnardston	78	31	Parks	Jonathan	2		1	1		2			1				7		
Barnardston	78	32	Parks	Reuben		1	2	1		1				1			6		
Barnardston	78	33	Ritter	John	1	2		1		2	1	1	1				9		
Barnardston	78	34	Ryther	David	3	1		1	1	2	1		1	1			11		
Barnardston	79	1	Ryther	David Junr	3		1	1		2		1					8		
Barnardston	79	2	Ryther	Peter			2				1	1					5		

17

TOWN	PG#	LN#	LAST NAME	FIRST NAME	FREE WHITE MALES					FREE WHITE FEMALES					TOTAL ALL OTHER	TOTAL SLAVES	TOTALS	DISTRICT/ TOWNSHIP	NOTES
					under 10	10 to 16	16 to 26	26 to 45	45 and over	under 10	10 to 16	16 to 26	26 to 45	45 and over					
Barnardston	79	3	Root	Samuel	3	1		1	1	2			1				9		
Barnardston	79	4	Rogers	Nathan	1		1					1					3		
Barnardston	79	5	Robinson	Hulda			1			2	1	1					5		
Barnardston	79	6	Shelden	Jonathan	1		1		1	2		1		1			7		
Barnardston	79	7	Slate	Joseph			1		1	2		1		1			6		
Barnardston	79	8	Slate	Daniel					1	1			1	1			4		
Barnardston	79	9	Slate	Joseph Junr	1			1		2			1				5		
Barnardston	79	10	Shelden	Timothy				1		2		1	1				5		
Barnardston	79	11	Severence	David				1		2		1	1				5		
Barnardston	79	12	Smith	Joseph	2	1	3		1		2	1	1				11		
Barnardston	79	13	Scott	Elihu	2	1		1		1			1	1			7		
Barnardston	79	14	Slate	Jonathan		1	1		1			2		1			6		
Barnardston	79	15	Scott	Moses			1		1	2	2	1		1			8		
Barnardston	79	16	Slate	Israel	2	1		1		3	2		1				10		
Barnardston	79	17	Sprague	Asa			2					1	1	1			5		
Barnardston	79	18	Shelden	Asad	3			1		1		1		1			7		
Barnardston	79	19	Shelden	Elisha	2	1		1		1	2		1		1		9		
Barnardston	79	20	Shelden	Amasa		1		1	1				2				5		
Barnardston	79	21	Squires	Medad	2		2	1		1			1	1			8		
Barnardston	79	22	Snow	Prince	1	1	1	1	1	1		1		1			8		
Barnardston	79	23	Slate	Zebediah	3	2	1	1		1		2	1				11		
Barnardston	79	24	Scott	Rufus	1		1					1					3		
Barnardston	79	25	Severence	John				1					1				2		
Barnardston	79	26	Streeter	Pearly	2	1		1		3			1				8		
Barnardston	79	27	Silner	Samuel Junr	4	1	2		1		1	2		1			12		
Barnardston	79	28	Sanderson	Joseph	1		2	1			1	1					6		
Barnardston	79	29	Smith	Moses				1		1			1				3		
Barnardston	79	30	Tyler	John	2	2		1		2	1		1				9		
Barnardston	79	31	Tyler	James	1		1			1		3					6		
Barnardston	79	32	Warner	Ichabod			1		1			1		1			4		
Barnardston	79	33	Warner	Pliny	2			1				1					4		
Barnardston	79	34	Warner	Joel			1			1		1					3		
Barnardston	79	35	Warner	Roswell			1			1		1					3		
Barnardston	80	1	Webster	Stephen				1				1	1				3		
Barnardston	80	2	Webster	Stephen Junr	3	1		1		2	1		1				9		
Barnardston	80	3	Wright	Abner	1	2	3		1			1		1			9		
Barnardston	80	4	Wright	Job			1		1		1	3		1			7		
Barnardston	80	5	Wright	Nehemiah	3			1					1				5		
Barnardston	80	6	Wilcox	Timothy	2			1			1			1			5		
Barnardston	80	7	Warner	Joseph	2	1			1	2	2	1		1			10		

TOWN	PG#	LN#	LAST NAME	FIRST NAME	FREE WHITE MALES under 10	10 to 16	16 to 26	26 to 45	45 and over	FREE WHITE FEMALES under 10	10 to 16	16 to 26	26 to 45	45 and over	TOTAL ALL OTHER	TOTAL SLAVES	TOTALS	DISTRICT/ TOWNSHIP	NOTES
Belchertown	203	1	Burbank	John	1			1		1	1	1					5		
Belchertown	203	2	Bicknal	Timo	1			1		1		1					4		
Belchertown	203	3	Dearing	Theodore					1			1					2		
Belchertown	203	4	Welch	Solomon	2			1		1			1				5		
Belchertown	203	5	Brown	Thomas 2d				1					1	1			3		
Belchertown	203	6	Gates	John	3			1		1			1				6		
Belchertown	203	7	Blackman	Jona Jewett											1		1		
Belchertown	203	8	Butler	Stephen				1		1		1	1				4		
Belchertown	203	9	Williams	Moses	1		1			1			1				4		
Belchertown	203	10	Barton	Reuben Jr	1			1		2			1				5		
Belchertown	203	11	Jinks	David	1			1			1		1				4		
Belchertown	203	12	Jinks	Thomas				1		1		1					3		
Belchertown	204	1	Ranger	Ephraim			1			2		1					4		
Belchertown	204	2	Blair	Joseph	2			1		2	2		1				8		
Belchertown	204	3	Church	John	2			1		2			1				6		
Belchertown	204	4	Ingram	Joseph	2			1		1			2				6		
Belchertown	204	5	Preston	Justus	1		1			1			1				4		
Belchertown	204	6	Bardwell	Martin Jr	1		1						1				3		
Belchertown	204	7	Thayer	Elijah	5	1		1					3	1			11		
Belchertown	204	8	Goodale	Elisha				1						1			2		
Belchertown	204	9	Buxton	Wm			1	1		3				1			6		
Belchertown	204	10	Adams	Wm	1	1		1				1	1				5		
Belchertown	204	11	Bartlett	David		1		1				1		2			5		
Belchertown	204	12	Bridgeman	Oliver		1	2	1			2		1				7		
Belchertown	204	13	Bridgeman	Joseph	1		3	1		1	2	2	1				11		
Belchertown	204	14	Billings	Benja			2	1	2		2	1		2			10		
Belchertown	204	15	Bardwell	Jona Jewett		2		1		4		2	1				10		
Belchertown	204	16	Billings	Joseph Jr	2	2		1	1	2		1	2	1			12		
Belchertown	204	17	Bissell	Ebenz	2			1		1			1				5		
Belchertown	204	18	Bartlett	Phillip		1											1		
Belchertown	204	19	Brown	Nathan Capt	3	1		1		1	1		1		1		9		
Belchertown	204	20	Brown	Robt	1	1		1		3	1	1	1				9		
Belchertown	204	21	Brown	Charles Lieut	2			1		2			1				6		
Belchertown	204	22	Bliss	Ebenz			2	1	1		1	1		1			7		
Belchertown	204	23	Bridgeman	Wright	1		2	1					1				5		
Belchertown	204	24	Bailey	John		1		1		1			1				4		
Belchertown	204	25	Chapman	Wm Lt	2	2	1	1					1				7		
Belchertown	204	26	Currier	Samuel	2			1		1			1				5		
Belchertown	204	27	Clough	Amasa	3	1	1	1	1	1	1	2	1	1			13		
Belchertown	204	28	Clough	Benja			2	1		2			1				6		
Belchertown	204	29	Chase	Timothy	2	1		1		3	1		1				9		
Belchertown	204	30	Clark	Eleazr Capt	1	2	2	1			1	1	1				9		
Belchertown	204	31	Clark	Caleb				1						3			4		
Belchertown	204	32	Converse	James		2	2	1		1				1			7		
Belchertown	204	33	Dunbar	Azel Lt	1		1	1		1	1		2				7		
Belchertown	204	34	Dunbar	Robert		1		1				1		1			4		
Belchertown	204	35	Dwight	Justus	1	1		1	1	1	1		1				7		
Belchertown	204	36	Draper	Seth			2	1					1				4		
Belchertown	205	1	Dwight	Henry	3		3		1	1		1		1			10		
Belchertown	205	2	Dodge	Caleb				1						1			2		
Belchertown	205	3	Dodge	Zebulon	2	1	1	1		4	1	1	1				12		
Belchertown	205	4	Eaton	Walter	1			1					1				3		
Belchertown	205	5	Eaton	Marion	2	1	2	1		2			1				9		
Belchertown	205	6	Field	Lemuel	2	1			1	2	2	1					9		
Belchertown	205	7	Fobes	Abner	1			1		2	1	1	1	1			8		
Belchertown	205	8	Graves	Perez Lt		1	1	1		1	1		1				6		
Belchertown	205	9	Giles	Thomas Wid		1							1				2		
Belchertown	205	10	Gates	Thos Asa Lt.		2	1	1		3	1	2	1				11		
Belchertown	205	11	Graves	Dwight	1	1	1	1				1	1	1			7		
Belchertown	205	12	Gilbert	Timothy	2			1		1		1	1	1			7		
Belchertown	205	13	Gilbert	John Maj	2	1	2		1	3	1		1				11		
Belchertown	205	14	Drake	Jonah	1			1				1		1			4		
Belchertown	205	15	Green	Joel Capt			1	1			1	4					8		
Belchertown	205	16	Goodale	Nathanl	1		1	1				1	1	1			6		
Belchertown	205	17	Hannemon	Elijah	1			1		2			1				5		
Belchertown	205	18	Hannemon	Rachel Wd				1				1					2		
Belchertown	205	19	Hunt	John	1	1		1			1			1			5		
Belchertown	205	20	Hannemon	Wm	2			1		1			1				5		
Belchertown	205	21	Holland	Park Esq				1		1	2		2				6		
Belchertown	205	22	Holland	Jonas	2			1		2			1				6		
Belchertown	205	23	Haskell	Jeremiah			1		1		2	1		1			6		
Belchertown	205	24	Hathaway	Thomas	1	2		1					1				5		
Belchertown	205	25	Hewlet	Thomas	2		1							1			4		
Belchertown	205	26	Hunting	Amos	2			1		2		2	1				8		
Belchertown	205	27	Hunting	Elisha	2	1		1	1				1				6		
Belchertown	205	28	Hanks	James	2	1		1	1	4		1	1	1			12		
Belchertown	205	29	Hanks	Ebenz	3	1		1		1		1	1				8		
Belchertown	205	30	Howard	Jona		1		1					1				3		
Belchertown	205	31	Howe	Sylvanus Lt	1		1	1		1		1					8		

TOWN	PG#	LN#	LAST NAME	FIRST NAME	FREE WHITE MALES under 10	10 to 16	16 to 26	26 to 45	45 and over	FREE WHITE FEMALES under 10	10 to 16	16 to 26	26 to 45	45 and over	TOTAL ALL OTHER	TOTAL SLAVES	TOTALS	DISTRICT/ TOWNSHIP	NOTES
Belchertown	205	32	Howe	Ester Doct		2	1		1		1	2		1			8		
Belchertown	205	33	Hannemon	Moses Jr			1	2	1			1	1				6		
Belchertown	205	34	Bush	Hezekiah Esq			1					1		1			3		
Belchertown	205	35	Hewlet	Mason Lt				1			1			1			3		
Belchertown	206	1	Hannemon	Phinehas		2	2		1	1				1			7		
Belchertown	206	2	Hannemon	Caleb	1				1	1			1				4		
Belchertown	206	3	Ingals	Samuel			1	3	1		1	3		1			10		
Belchertown	206	4	Kentfield	Shubal	1			1		2			1				5		
Belchertown	206	5	Kentfield	Ebenz	3	1		1		3	2		1				11		
Belchertown	206	6	Keith	Zadock	2	1	3				1	3	1				11		
Belchertown	206	7	Keith	Simeon		2	2	1	1	2				1			9		
Belchertown	206	8	Knowlton	Roswell	2	1			1	2			1				7		
Belchertown	206	9	Kentfield	Jonathan				1	1	1	2		1				6		
Belchertown	206	10	Kentfield	David 2d	1		1			1		1					4		
Belchertown	206	11	Keith	Joseph		1	1					1					3		
Belchertown	206	12	Luden	Enos	1	1		1		1			1	1			6		
Belchertown	206	13	Lincoln	Enos		1	1			1		1					4		
Belchertown	206	14	Lovel	Silas	1			1	1	1				1			5		
Belchertown	206	15	Mason	Amos	1	1		1		1		1	1	1			7		
Belchertown	206	16	Manley	Reuben	2	1	1	1		2	2		1				10		
Belchertown	206	17	Newhall	Nathan	1		1		1	1		1		1			6		
Belchertown	206	18	Pratt	Micah	1			1		1	1	2		1			7		
Belchertown	206	19	Lincoln	Ebenz	2			1		1			1				5		
Belchertown	206	20	Hill	Ebenz				1						1			2		
Belchertown	206	21	Peeso	John		1		1		2	1		1				6		
Belchertown	206	22	Packard	Abram	1	2	1		1	1				2			8		
Belchertown	206	23	Pettingall	Stephen	1		1		1	2			1	1			7		
Belchertown	206	24	Pettingall	Nathaniel		1	1		1		1	1		1			6		
Belchertown	206	25	Pettingall	Paul				1		3				1			5		
Belchertown	206	26	Packard	Solomon				1									1		
Belchertown	206	27	Pratt	David Capt	3	2	1		1	1	1	2		1			12		
Belchertown	206	28	Pratt	Jabez		1		1			1	1	1				5		
Belchertown	206	29	Prentice	Moses				1			1	3		1			6		
Belchertown	206	30	Read	Joseph	2	3			1		2	1	1				10		
Belchertown	206	31	Robinson	Israel				1						1			2		
Belchertown	206	32	Robbins	Samuel	1	1	1		1	1	1			1			7		
Belchertown	206	33	Ruggles	Mary Wd		1	1							1			3		
Belchertown	206	34	Rider	Daniel	4			1		1			1				7		
Belchertown	206	35	Randell	Joseph	1	1		1	1	1		2		1			8		
Belchertown	206	36	Randell	Nehemiah	3			1		1		1					6		
Belchertown	207	1	Randell	Israel	2	2	1	1	1			1		1			9		
Belchertown	207	2	Smith	Daniel Lt		1	1		1	1				1			5		
Belchertown	207	3	Smith	Amasa Maj	4			1	1	1	1		1	2			11		
Belchertown	207	4	Shumway	David	2	2			1	1	1	1		1			9		
Belchertown	207	5	Shumway	Solomon		1		1	1	1	1	2		2			9		
Belchertown	207	6	Baker	William Jr	1		3		1		1			1			7		
Belchertown	207	7	Shumway	Nathan	3			1	1		1	1	1				8		
Belchertown	207	8	Shumway	Penwell			1										1		
Belchertown	207	9	Shumway	Cyrel		2	1		1	2				1			7		
Belchertown	207	10	Stebbins	Giddeon Capt		1	1	2	1	1		4		1			11		
Belchertown	207	11	Smith	Hezekiah				1					2	1			4		
Belchertown	207	12	Shaw	William			3		1	1				1			6		
Belchertown	207	13	Shaw	Elias			1			1		1					3		
Belchertown	207	14	Torrance	Wm		1	1		1			1		2			6		
Belchertown	207	15	Thayer	John	2	2		1		2	2			1			10		
Belchertown	207	16	Thayer	Reuben	2	2		1		2		1	1				9		
Belchertown	207	17	Town	Solomon	2	1		1		1	1		1				7		
Belchertown	207	18	Warner	Phinehas	2			1		2			1	1			7		
Belchertown	207	19	Warner	Seth				1						1			2		
Belchertown	207	20	Warner	Titus	2			1		1			1				5		
Belchertown	207	21	Ward	John		3	1		1	1		1		1			8		
Belchertown	207	22	Wood	Ichabod	2			1		2	1		1				7		
Belchertown	207	23	Wood	Solomon				1		3			1				5		
Belchertown	207	24	Wood	Sylvanus	1			1		1		1					4		
Belchertown	207	25	Steel	John			1										1		
Belchertown	207	26	Wilson	Nathan	2			1					1				4		
Belchertown	207	27	Wilson	Thomas Lt		2		1		2	2	1		2			10		
Belchertown	207	28	Williams	Justus				1					2				3		
Belchertown	207	29	Ward	Samuel		1		1		1				2			5		
Belchertown	207	30	Wood	Zeanon		1	1							1			3		
Belchertown	207	31	Wilson	Asa	1	2	1	1		3	1		1				10		
Belchertown	207	32	Wilson	Reuben	1	1		1		3	1		1				8		
Belchertown	207	33	Ward	Ebenzr	3			1					1				5		
Belchertown	207	34	Weeks	Holland	2		1		1	2		1	1				9		
Belchertown	207	35	Warner	Ebenz				1			1		1	1			4		
Belchertown	207	36	Washburn	Eliab	3			1		1		1					6		
Belchertown	207	37	Fisher	Joseph	1	3			1	2			1	1			9		
Belchertown	208	1	Sanford	Ichabod	1	1	5	1			1	1					10		
Belchertown	208	2	Shumway	Stephen	1					3	2	2	1				10		

TOWN	PG#	LN#	LAST NAME	FIRST NAME	M under 10	M 10–16	M 16–26	M 26–45	M 45+	F under 10	F 10–16	F 16–26	F 26–45	F 45+	TOTAL ALL OTHER	TOTAL SLAVES	TOTALS	DISTRICT/ TOWNSHIP	NOTES
Belchertown	208	3	Bartlett	Solomon	1	1			1	1	1		1				6		
Belchertown	208	4	Fox	Isaac					1					1			2		
Belchertown	208	5	Atwood	John	2			1		1			1				5		
Belchertown	208	6	Allen	Edmond Capt	1	2	2		1	4		3	1				14		
Belchertown	208	7	Abbott	James	2		2	1		2	1		1				9		
Belchertown	208	8	Parson	Eldad	2	2		1	1	2	1	2					11		
Belchertown	208	9	Button	Elias	1	1	2		1	2	1		1				9		
Belchertown	208	10	Barker	Nathl		2			1			1	1	1			6		
Belchertown	208	11	Barnabas	Nathan	3			1		1	1			1			7		
Belchertown	208	12	Bardwell	Elijah Capt	2	1	1		1	2		3	1				11		
Belchertown	208	13	Bardwell	Simeon	3	1	1		1	2			1				9		
Belchertown	208	14	Bartlett	Isaac	2			1			1	1	1				6		
Belchertown	208	15	Barton	Reuben				1					1				2		
Belchertown	208	16	Brown	Thomas	1		1	1					2	1			6		
Belchertown	208	17	Baret	Smith	2	1			1	1	1		1				7		
Belchertown	208	18	Bibbee	James			1	1	1					1			4		
Belchertown	208	19	Bardwell	Martin			1		1	2	2			1			7		
Belchertown	208	20	Baggs	Noble		1	1		1			4		1			8		
Belchertown	208	21	Bicknal	Wm			1		1		1			1			4		
Belchertown	208	22	Cowl	Amasa		1		1		1			1				4		
Belchertown	208	23	Clark	Wm				1		1			1				3		
Belchertown	208	24	Clark	Enos		2	1	1	1	1		1		1			8		
Belchertown	208	25	Cleaveland	Freeman	2			1		1		1	1				6		
Belchertown	208	26	Comstock	Jacob Jr		1	1		1			1		1			5		
Belchertown	208	27	Clark	Phinehas B.				1	1	1		1					4		
Belchertown	208	28	Cleaveland	Jesse			1		1				1				3		
Belchertown	208	29	Newhall	Theodore			1		1	1	1		1				5		
Belchertown	208	30	Dagget	Samuel			1		1				1	1			4		
Belchertown	208	31	Taylor	Will		1			1	1				1			4		
Belchertown	208	32	Freeman	John black man											6		6		
Belchertown	208	33	Hannemon	Solomon			1		1	1			1				4		
Belchertown	208	34	Capen	Purchase	2	2	3		1	1	1		1				11		
Belchertown	208	35	Cowls	John Lt	1	2	1	1		1		1	1				8		
Belchertown	208	36	Cowl	Joshua	1			1				1					3		
Belchertown	208	37	Cowl	John Capt	2	2	2	1	1	1	1		1	1			12		
Belchertown	208	38	Cowl	Josiah	2	1		1		1			1	1			7		
Belchertown	208	39	Smith	Thomas	2	1		1		2	1		1				8		
Belchertown	209	1	Biglow	Samuel					1				1				2		
Belchertown	209	2	Billings	Stephen	1			1				1					3		
Belchertown	209	3	Dwight	Samuel	2			1		2	3		1	1			10		
Belchertown	209	4	Davis	Aaron	3			1		2			1				7		
Belchertown	209	5	Davis	Moses	2	1		1		2			1				7		
Belchertown	209	6	Davis	Samuel			2	1		1			1				5		
Belchertown	209	7	Dale	Joshua		1	2	1		1			1				6		
Belchertown	209	8	Fairfield	Thaddeus		4	1	1				3					10		
Belchertown	209	9	Forward	Justus Revd	2		1	1	2	1	3		1				11		
Belchertown	209	10	Green	Ebenz Sargt			1			2			1	1			5		
Belchertown	209	11	Guy	Amasa	2		2			2	2	1	1				10		
Belchertown	209	12	Howard	Silas	1		1	1		3	2			1	1		10		
Belchertown	209	13	Fay	Benajah	1			1		1		1					4		
Belchertown	209	14	Jinks	Lawrence		2	2	1			1			1			7		
Belchertown	209	15	Kentfield	Erstus	2			1		2			1				6		
Belchertown	209	16	Kentfield	Josiah	2	1	1	1		1	1		1	1			9		
Belchertown	209	17	Lemmen	Saml	4	1	2		1	2		1					11		
Belchertown	209	18	Lemmon	John			1										1		
Belchertown	209	19	Leach	Oywal	1	1	1						1	1			5		
Belchertown	209	20	Grout	Jona Esq			1										1		
Belchertown	209	21	Lyman	Giles			1	1		2			1				5		
Belchertown	209	22	Lyman	Jona		1		1				2					4		
Belchertown	209	23	Lyman	Aron Doct		1		1		5			1				8		
Belchertown	209	24	McIntosh	John		1			1	1			1				4		
Belchertown	209	25	Moody	Jacob Jr	1			1		3			1				6		
Belchertown	209	26	Morgan	Titus			1						1				2		
Belchertown	209	27	Morse	Asa	1			1	1	2		1		1			7		
Belchertown	209	28	Mark	Nathaniel	1				1	1				1			4		
Belchertown	209	29	More	Noah	1			1		1			1				4		
Belchertown	209	30	Mason	Richard			1		1					1			3		
Belchertown	209	31	Nichols	Elijah			1	1		3			1				6		
Belchertown	209	32	Ashley	Saml		1		1				1		1			4		
Belchertown	209	33	Gray	Eliphalet	2			1		2	1		1				7		
Belchertown	209	34	Owens	Eliazr	4	2		1				1	1				9		
Belchertown	209	35	Olds	Justin		1	1		1	2	1	1		1			8		
Belchertown	209	36	Moor	George			1			2		1					4		
Belchertown	209	37	Phelps	Martin Doct	1	1			1	2	1	1	1				8		
Belchertown	209	38	Phelps	Eliakim Capt	1	1	2		1	2	1		1				9		
Belchertown	209	39	Phelps	Benjamin	1	1		1		1	1		1				6		
Belchertown	209	40	Perkins	Samuel		1	1		1				3	1			7		
Belchertown	209	41	Perkins	Samuel Jr				1					1				2		
Belchertown	210	1	Phelps	Noah			1			1			1				3		

TOWN	PG#	LN#	LAST NAME	FIRST NAME	FREE WHITE MALES under 10	10 to 16	16 to 26	26 to 45	45 and over	FREE WHITE FEMALES under 10	10 to 16	16 to 26	26 to 45	45 and over	TOTAL ALL OTHER	TOTAL SLAVES	TOTALS	DISTRICT/ TOWNSHIP	NOTES
Belchertown	210	2	Porter	Daniel		1			1		1			1			4		
Belchertown	210	3	Preston	Jacob Jr	1	1			1			1	2		1			7		
Belchertown	210	4	Root	Orlando			2		1			1	1	1			6		
Belchertown	210	5	Root	Darius			1			1		1					3		
Belchertown	210	6	Root	Elisha					1		1	1	1				4		
Belchertown	210	7	Root	Remembrance	1			1		1		1					4		
Belchertown	210	8	Rice	Timothy		2			1			3		1			7		
Belchertown	210	9	Randell	Jotham	2			1					1				4		
Belchertown	210	10	Robinson	Josiah Jr				1			1	1	1				4		
Belchertown	210	11	Rice	Nathan		1		1					1				3		
Belchertown	210	12	Rhodes	Thaddeus			1	1		1		1		1			5		
Belchertown	210	13	Scranton	Samuel	1		1		1	1	1	2		2			9		
Belchertown	210	14	Shong	Phinehas Capt	1	1	2	1		2	2	1	1	1			12		
Belchertown	210	15	Simmington	Michael	2			1		2			1				6		
Belchertown	210	16	Stary	Caleb	1	1		1		2			1				6		
Belchertown	210	17	Squire	Daniel			1		1					1			3		
Belchertown	210	18	Smith	James		1	1		1			1	1				5		
Belchertown	210	19	Sherbrook	Ephraim		1			1	1	1	2		1			7		
Belchertown	210	20	Smith	Jonathan	1		1		1	1				1			5		
Belchertown	210	21	Shumway	Asa	1			1	1			2	1	1			8		
Belchertown	210	22	Stary	Isaac Capt	1	1	1		1			1		1			6		
Belchertown	210	23	Hunt	Abner	2			1		2			1				6		
Belchertown	210	24	Stary	Moses	2			1		2			1				6		
Belchertown	210	25	Wilson	Chester			1										1		
Belchertown	210	26	Shaw	Daniel	2	3	1		1	4		2	1				14		
Belchertown	210	27	Torry	Ezra		2			1			2		1			6		
Belchertown	210	28	Town	Jona Capt	1	1		2				1	1				6		
Belchertown	210	29	Thompson	James	1		1	1	1		2	1		1			8		
Belchertown	210	30	Turner	Samuel			1	1		2		1	1				6		
Belchertown	210	31	Town	Amasa	2	1			1								4		
Belchertown	210	32	Bardwell	Joseph	1	1	1		1	1	1	2		1			9		
Belchertown	210	33	Willis	Solomon		1			1		1		1				4		
Belchertown	211	1	Whitman	James	1	1		1		1	1		1				6		
Belchertown	211	2	Willis	Abisha	1				1			1	1				4		
Belchertown	211	3	Walker	Josiah	3		1						1				5		
Belchertown	211	4	Woodward	Ephraim	2			1		2	1		1				7		
Belchertown	211	5	Worthington	David	2			1				3	1				7		
Belchertown	211	6	Worthington	Wm		1			1		1	3		1			7		
Belchertown	211	7	Clifford	Samuel	1	1		1		3	2		1				9		
Belchertown	211	8	Witt	Ivory	4			1		2	2	1	1				11		
Belchertown	211	9	Wood	Zephiniah		1	1				1	2		2			7		
Belchertown	211	10	Walker	Hezekiah	2	2		1		2		1	1	1			10		
Belchertown	211	11	Walker	Silas	3			1		1		1					6		
Belchertown	211	12	Whitney	Ebenz	2		1		1		1			1			6		
Belchertown	211	13	Walker	James Jr	4	2		1			2			1			10		
Belchertown	211	14	Walker	Jason Lt			1			1		1					3		
Belchertown	211	15	Walker	Jas Capt		1		1						1			3		
Belchertown	211	16	Howe	Hannah Wd										1			1		
Belchertown	211	17	Olds	David			1						1	1			3		
Belchertown	211	18	Kentfield	David	3	1			1	5	1	1	1				13		
Belchertown	211	19	Woodward	Elisha	1			1				1					3		
Belchertown	211	20	Bowden	Benja		1			1	1	1		1				5		
Belchertown	211	21	Shumway	Whitney	1			1		2			1				5		
Belchertown	211	22	Jewett	Jedidiah				1						1			2		
Belchertown	211	23	Torrance	Jeduthene	1		1			1		1					4		
Belchertown	211	24	Shaw	Elias			1					1					2		
Belchertown	211	25	Banister	Abner C.	1		1			1		2					5		
Belchertown	211	26	Phelps	Dudley	1			1			1		1				4		
Belchertown	211	27	Eddy	Hezekiah			1	1					1				3		
Belchertown	211	28	Walker	Nathaniel	1			1					1				3		
Belchertown	211	29	Dwight	Jonathan			1	1									2		
Belchertown	211	30	Rhoades	Aaron	1	1		1		2			1				6		
Belchertown	211	31	Burnham	Reuben	1			1		2			1				5		
Belchertown	211	32	Haydin	Moses				1		2		1					6		
Belchertown	212	1	Hallow	Richard P.	3	2	3	1		1	1		1				12		
Belchertown	212	2	Whitney	Dorothy	1						1	2		1			5		
Belchertown	212	3	Blackmar	David	1	1		1		3			1				7		
Belchertown	212	4	Ames	Robert		1			1			1		1			4		
Belchertown	212	5	Hayden	Moses								1		1			2		
Belchertown	212	6	Allen	Nathan	4			1				1		1			7		

TOWN	PG#	LN#	HEADS OF HOUSEHOLD LAST NAME	FIRST NAME	FREE WHITE MALES under 10	10 to 16	16 to 26	26 to 45	45 and over	FREE WHITE FEMALES under 10	10 to 16	16 to 26	26 to 45	45 and over	TOTAL ALL OTHER	TOTAL SLAVES	TOTALS	DISTRICT/ TOWNSHIP	NOTES
Blanford	175	1	Beard	James		1		1	1		1		1				7		
Blanford	175	2	Bruce	Jesse	3	1		1			1	1		1			8		
Blanford	175	3	Anderson	James	3	1		1		1		1	1				8		
Blanford	175	4	Kirkland	Elias			1		1	2	1			1			6		
Blanford	175	5	Phillip	Eliphalet	2	2		1	1	2	1		1				10		
Blanford	175	6	Taggard	Benjamin	1	1		1		3			1				7		
Blanford	175	7	Gibbs	Samuel	2	1		1		2			1	1			8		
Blanford	175	8	Gibbs	Ephraim	2	2		1	1	3	1	1	1	1			13		
Blanford	175	9	Frisley	Chandler			1					1					2		
Blanford	175	10	Blair	Timothy		1			1				1				3		
Blanford	175	11	Stewart	Moses	2	2		1		1	1		1				8		
Blanford	175	12	Collister	John	1	1		1		2	1	1	1				8		
Blanford	175	13	Brewster	Vial											3		3		
Blanford	175	14	Jones	Jethro											5		5		
Blanford	175	15	Jones	Jethro Junr											5		5		
Blanford	175	16	Jones	Jason											4		4		
Blanford	175	17	Wheeler	John			1		1	5	3		1				11		
Blanford	175	18	McConoughey	Saml				1		3			1				5		
Blanford	175	19	Goodwin	Thomas	2	1			1	1	1	2		1			9		
Blanford	175	20	Cannon	Elisha				1		1		1					3		
Blanford	175	21	Tray	Giles	1	2		1		1		1	1	1			8		
Blanford	175	22	Sinnet	John	1			1		2			1				5		
Blanford	175	23	Hamilton	Hugh	2	1		1		1			1				6		
Blanford	175	24	Osborn	Jonathan				1		3			1				5		
Blanford	175	25	Blair	George	3	1			1	3	1		1				10		
Blanford	175	26	Blair	George Jun	2		1						1				4		
Blanford	175	27	Boies	Rufus			1			1			1				3		
Blanford	175	28	Boies	Gardner			1						1				2		
Blanford	175	29	Hill	Joseph		1		1		3	1		1				7		
Blanford	175	30	Scott	William			2	1		2	1		1	1			8		
Blanford	175	31	Boies	Joel	3	2			1			1	1				8		
Blanford	175	32	Higgins	Nathaniel			1	1	1	1		1					5		
Blanford	175	33	Guil	Martin				1		1			1				3		
Blanford	175	34	Gibbs	Elijah	2	1		2		1	1		1				8		
Blanford	175	35	Blair	John	2	1	2		2	1	1	1					10		
Blanford	175	36	Hunt	Joseph	2	1	1	1			1	2		1			9		
Blanford	176	1	Blair	Alexr			1		1	1	1		1				5		
Blanford	176	2	Knox	Elijah	2			1				1					4		
Blanford	176	3	Jackson	Ezra	1	1		1		3			1				7		
Blanford	176	4	Bartlett	Ebenezer			2	1	1	2			1				7		
Blanford	176	5	Knox	John	1		3		1	1	1	2		1			10		
Blanford	176	6	Ranney	Abner		4	2	2	1		1	1		1			12		
Blanford	176	7	Warren	Noah		1		1		1			1				4		
Blanford	176	8	Granger	John M.	4	2	1		1	1		1					10		
Blanford	176	9	Rockwell	Amasa	2			1		1			1				5		
Blanford	176	10	Blair	Adam	2	1			1	1	2		1				8		
Blanford	176	11	Hunter	Samuel	1					2	1		1				6		
Blanford	176	12	Moore	James	1		1	1		2			1	1			7		
Blanford	176	13	Lloyd	William	1			1	1			1		1			5		
Blanford	176	14	Boies	Reuben		2			1		1	2		2	1		9		
Blanford	176	15	Williams	John	2			1		1	1		1				6		
Blanford	176	16	Pease	Abner	1	1		1		1	1		1				6		
Blanford	176	17	Blair	Rufus	2	1	2	1	1		1		1	1			10		
Blanford	176	18	Boies	David	2	1	3			1	1	1		1			10		
Blanford	176	19	Boies	Samuel	1	3	2		1	2	1		1				11		
Blanford	176	20	Blair	David		1	2		1			1		1			6		
Blanford	176	21	Blair	Asa	2	1	2		1	1	1		1				9		
Blanford	176	22	Willson	Andrew	4			1		1			1				7		
Blanford	176	23	Boies	William	2	1		1	1		1		1				7		
Blanford	176	24	Stewart	Solomon			1		1					1			3		
Blanford	176	25	Babcock	James	2			1		2			1				6		
Blanford	176	26	Cannon	William I.	1	1		1		3	2		1				9		
Blanford	176	27	Knox	Oliver	2		1		1	1	3	2		1			11		
Blanford	176	28	Ferguson	Samuel	1	1		1	1				2	1			7		
Blanford	176	29	Boies	Saml	2	1		1	2	4	1	2	1	1			15		
Blanford	176	30	Wales	Henry	1			1			1	1	1				5		
Blanford	176	31	Burster	Joseph B	1			1		3	2		1				8		
Blanford	176	32	Conoughey	David	1			1		1	2	1	1				7		
Blanford	176	33	Osborn	Alexander	1	1		1					1				4		
Blanford	176	34	Boies	Samuel	2	1		1	1	4			1	1			11		
Blanford	176	35	Hamilton	John	1	1	1			1		1	1				7		
Blanford	176	36	Blair	Isaac		2	2		1	1		2					9		
Blanford	176	37	Cochran	John	1		2		1	2	2	4		1			13		
Blanford	176	38	Osborn	David	2			1					1				4		
Blanford	176	39	Thompson	Sanford		1	1			1		1	1				5		
Blanford	177	1	Freeman	James	2	1		1			1		1	1			7		
Blanford	177	2	Cannon	Martin	1			1		3		2	1				8		
Blanford	177	3	Sloper	Samuel	1	1	1		1	1		2	1	1			9		
Blanford	177	4	Curtis	Jeremiah	2			1		2			1				6		
Blanford	177	5	Watson	John	1	3	2		1	1	3			1			12		
Blanford	177	6	Frary	Jonathan			2	1	1			3					8		
Blanford	177	7	Farnham	Reuben	1	2	1		2	2	1			2			11		
Blanford	177	8	Knox	John 2nd	4	1		1		2	1		1				10		
Blanford	177	9	Bates	Lemuel	1	2		1		2		1	1				8		
Blanford	177	10	Weller	David		1	1		1			3		1			7		
Blanford	177	11	Bowers	Benjamin	2		1	1				3		1			9		
Blanford	177	12	Bunnel	Jonathan	1		1		1	1			1				5		
Blanford	177	13	Morgan	Simeon	3	2	1	1		1			1				9		
Blanford	177	14	Reed	Thomas	1	1	1			1		1					5		
Blanford	177	15	Waterman	Ebenezer	1		1		3			1					6		

TOWN	PG#	LN#	LAST NAME	FIRST NAME	FREE WHITE MALES under 10	10 to 16	16 to 26	26 to 45	45 and over	FREE WHITE FEMALES under 10	10 to 16	16 to 26	26 to 45	45 and over	TOTAL ALL OTHER	TOTAL SLAVES	TOTALS	DISTRICT/ TOWNSHIP	NOTES
Blanford	177	16	Hall	David		3	1	1			1		1				7		
Blanford	177	17	Hall	Jonathan		1	2	1		1			1	1			7		
Blanford	177	18	Smith	Jeddiah		2	2		1		2	1		1			9		
Blanford	177	19	Moore	Thomas	1	1	1		1	2	2	2	1				11		
Blanford	177	20	Guile	Levi	2	1		1		3			1				8		
Blanford	177	21	Lloyd	Robert			2		1	2		1	1	1			8		
Blanford	177	22	Loyd	John	2		1	1				1	1				6		
Blanford	177	23	Diver	Daniel	1	2		1	1	3	1	2		1			12		
Blanford	177	24	Card	Daniel			1							1			2		
Blanford	177	25	Moore	Samuel	5	1		1			1	1					9		
Blanford	177	26	Nice	George	2	2			1	2			1				8		
Blanford	177	27	Harden	Joel	1	1	1	1		2			1	1			8		
Blanford	177	28	Herring	Benjamin	3				1	2	2	1					9		
Blanford	177	29	Hamilton	Ephraim			1	1	1				2	1			6		
Blanford	178	1	Hamilton	James			1			2			1				4		
Blanford	178	2	Hamilton	Francis	1		1						1				3		
Blanford	178	3	Phelps	Philip	2	2	2		1	4		2		1			14		
Blanford	178	4	Lloyd	James	3		1		1	2	1		1				9		
Blanford	178	5	Shepded	Marian	1					2		1	1	1			6		
Blanford	178	6	Loyd	James Jun	2	1		1		1			1				6		
Blanford	178	7	Shepded	Jonathan	2	2		1			1	1	2				9		
Blanford	178	8	Boies	John			2		1				1				4		
Blanford	178	9	Walker	Elisha		1	1	1					1	1			5		
Blanford	178	10	Shepded	Elijah	4	1		1		1	1		1				9		
Blanford	178	11	Henry	James		1						1					2		
Blanford	178	12	Knox	David	1			1		2	1		1				6		
Blanford	178	13	Frost	John	2	2		1		1	1		1				8		
Blanford	178	14	Brown	James				1		2			1				4		
Blanford	178	15	Cannon	Isaac	1			1		2	1		2				7		
Blanford	178	16	Blair	Enoch	3			1		1			1				6		
Blanford	178	17	Blair	John	3	1		1			1	2					8		
Blanford	178	18	Sanderson	Trial	2			1		2	1		1				7		
Blanford	178	19	Gibbs	Silas	1			1		1			1				4		
Blanford	178	20	Gibbs	Israel		2		1					1	1			5		
Blanford	178	21	Brown	William 2nd	1			1		4	1		1				8		
Blanford	178	22	White	Joel		1		1		3	1		1				7		
Blanford	178	23	Knox	Samuel		1		1		1	2		1				6		
Blanford	178	24	Knox	Eli		1					1						2		
Blanford	178	25	Brown	William		1	1	1					1				3		
Blanford	178	26	Gibbs	Isaac	1	1	1		1			1		1			6		
Blanford	178	27	Smith	John	1			1		1			1				5		
Blanford	178	28	Almy	Job		1		1				1	1				4		
Blanford	178	29	Smith	Samuel				1						1			2		
Blanford	178	30	Twaddle	Daniel	1			1		1				1			5		
Blanford	178	31	Smith	Robert	3	1		1		1	1		1				8		
Blanford	178	32	Stewart	William	2	2		1		3		2		1			11		
Blanford	178	33	Knox	David	1		1	1		2	1		1				7		
Blanford	178	34	Ferguson	John	1	2		1		2	1	1		1			9		
Blanford	178	35	Boies	Elias			1						1				2		
Blanford	178	36	Beard	Joseph		1		1		1	2		1				6		
Blanford	178	37	Gibbs	Levi	1	1	1			1		1					5		
Blanford	178	38	Felton	Seth	2			1		2			1				6		
Blanford	178	39	Gibbs	Nathaniel	2			1		2			1				6		
Blanford	178	40	Sinnet	James	4	1		1		2			1				9		
Blanford	178	41	Bois	Margaret		1				1	2		1				5		
Blanford	178	42	Carter	John	2	1		1			1	2	1				8		
Blanford	178	43	Carter	Elias		1		1			1	1		1			5		
Blanford	179	1	Morton	John	2	1		1		1			1				6		
Blanford	179	2	Cochran	Cornelus		1		1					1				3		
Blanford	179	3	Stewart	Nathan	1	2		1		1	1		1				7		
Blanford	179	4	Savage	John		1		1					1				3		
Blanford	179	5	Gorham	Glass	4			1		1			1				7		
Blanford	179	6	Knox	Levi	1			1		1	1		1				5		
Blanford	179	7	Knox	William	2		1		1	1	2			1			8		
Blanford	179	8	Girder	Samuel				1					1				2		
Blanford	179	9	Parks	Roger	1		3		1		1	1		1			8		
Blanford	179	10	Slade	James				1					1				2		
Blanford	179	11	San*	David	1	1		1		3	1	3		1			12		
Blanford	179	12	Crooks	John	2	2		1			1			1			7		
Blanford	179	13	Cannon	Samuel		1		1		1	1	1					5		
Blanford	179	14	Brown	Jane						1		1		1	1		3		
Blanford	179	15	Reed	Amos	3	2	1	1		1	2	1					11		
Blanford	179	16	Gleason	William				1		1		1	1				4		
Blanford	179	17	Culver	Asa	2	2	1		1		1	1	1	1			10		
Blanford	179	18	Stow	Ebenezer		1	1			1			2		1		6		
Blanford	179	19	Falley	Daniel	3		2	1					1				7		
Blanford	179	20	Lindsley	Joseph				1		3			1				5		
Blanford	179	21	Lindsley	Moses	2			1	1		2		1				7		
Blanford	179	22	Lindsley	William		2			1	4			1				8		
Blanford	179	23	Crooks	James	2	1		1		2			1				7		
Blanford	179	24	Michel	Moses	1	2	1		1	2	1		1				9		
Blanford	179	25	Canada	David	3	2	2		1	1		1		1			11		
Blanford	179	26	Osborn	John	2			1		1			1				5		
Blanford	179	27	Ferguson	Solomon				1			1		1				3		
Blanford	179	28	Freeland	Joseph	2			1		2	2	2	1				10		
Blanford	179	29	Freeland	William			1			3			1				5		
Blanford	179	30	Gilbert	Edmund	4	1		1				1	1				8		
Blanford	179	31	Buttolph	Star		1				3			1				6		
Blanford	179	32	Beard	John			1	1			1		1				6		
Blanford	179	33	Knox	William		1		1	1	1			1	1			6		

TOWN	PG#	LN#	LAST NAME	FIRST NAME	FREE WHITE MALES					FREE WHITE FEMALES					TOTAL ALL OTHER	TOTAL SLAVES	TOTALS	DISTRICT/ TOWNSHIP	NOTES
					under 10	10 to 16	16 to 26	26 to 45	45 and over	under 10	10 to 16	16 to 26	26 to 45	45 and over					
Blanford	179	34	Mitchel	William	2		1		1			1	1	1			7		
Blanford	179	35	Johnson	Jonas	1			1		2			1				5		
Blanford	180	1	Osborn	Luke			2		1			1		1			5		
Blanford	180	2	Ring	Robert		1	1		1		2	1		1			7		
Blanford	180	3	McGomery	Wm		1	1		1					1			4		
Blanford	180	4	Nimmocks	Mary	1			1					2	1			5		
Blanford	180	5	Waterman	Asael	3		1			2	1		1				8		
Blanford	180	6	Noble	Solomon	3	1		1					1				6		
Blanford	180	7	Button	Perry	3	1		1					1				6		
Blanford	180	8	Canada	John Jr	4		1		2	1	1	1	1				11		
Blanford	180	9	Shepard	Sarah	1								1	1			3		
Blanford	180	10	Badger	Joseph Revd	1	2			1	2	1		1				8		
Blanford	180	11	Hayse	Jacob		1	1		1	1			1				5		
Blanford	180	12	Knox	Elijah	2	2	1	1		3	1		1				11		
Blanford	180	13	Canada	John	4		1	1	1	1	2		1				11		
Blanford	180	14	Crooks	William		1		1	1			1		1			5		
Blanford	180	15	King	James				1	1	1		1		1			5		
Blanford	180	16	Backett	John	1	2	1		1	3		1		1			10		
Blanford	180	17	Fox	Joseph	1	1		1		3		1					7		
Blanford	180	18	Bishop	Joseph	1			1		4		1	1				8		
Blanford	180	19	Dayton	Giles Jr		1	1		1			2		1			6		
Blanford	180	20	Henery	Samuel	1			1	1	1	1	1		1			7		
Blanford	180	21	Fowler	Medad	2	1	1		1	2	1		1				9		
Blanford	180	22	Dayton	Giles	1	1	1		1			2		1			7		
Blanford	181	1	Butler	David	2			1		1	1		1				6		
Blanford	181	2	Hstings	John	1			1					1				3		
Blanford	181	3	Hamilton	David		2			1	3	1	2		1			10		
Blanford	181	4	Ferguson	Dorothy	1		2							1			4		
Blanford	181	5	Blair	Jacob			1	2		1		1		1			6		
Blanford	181	6	Knox	William		2	2		1	1		3		1			10		
Blanford	181	7	Cannon	Nathan	1	2	1	1		3	1		1	1			11		
Blanford	181	8	Pheland	John	2		1	1		1	1		1				7		
Blanford	181	9	Coe	Gad	3	1		1		1			1				7		
Blanford	181	10	King	Elisha	1		1					1					3		
Blanford	181	11	Canada	William		1	2		1		1			1			6		
Blanford	181	12	White	John	1	1		1		3			1				7		
Blanford	181	13	Woodbridge	Wil	3	2		1		1	1	1	1				10		
Blanford	181	14	Bridgen	Thomas			1			3			1				5		
Blanford	181	15	Baker	John	2		1					1					4		
Blanford	181	16	Sizer	Anthony	1	1		1		3			1				7		
Blanford	181	17	Harfield	Elizabeth		1	2			2	1	1	1				8		
Blanford	181	18	Farnham	Elisha	1	1		1		2	2		1				8		
Blanford	181	19	Latimer	Aholiab	3			1		1			1				6		
Blanford	181	20	Knox	Seth		1	2		1	1	2	2	1	1			11		
Blanford	181	21	Ashman	Eli P	1		1	1				2					5		
Blanford	181	22	Bennet	Judah		1		1					1				3		
Blanford	181	23	Atwater	Russel	5		2	1	1				1	1			11		
Blanford	181	24	Blair	Robert Jun	1	1			1	2		3	1	1			10		
Blanford	181	25	Hatch	Timothy	2	1	3	1		1	1		1				10		
Blanford	181	26	Gillmore	Thomas	1			1		1		1					4		
Blanford	181	27	Simons	Timothy		1		1		1			1				4		
Blanford	181	28	Adkins	David		1	1		1	1	3		1				8		
Blanford	181	29	Blair	Reuben	2		1	1		1	1		1				7		
Blanford	181	30	Noble	John	1	1			1				1				4		
Blanford	181	31	Hanning	David			1	1		2	2		1				7		
Blanford	182	1	Bishop	Jesse	1		1			4		1		2			9		
Blanford	182	2	Fox	Joseph	1	1		1		2	1	1	1				8		
Blanford	182	3	Brackett	John	1	2	1	1		3		1	1				10		
Blanford	182	4	Pratt	John	1			1			1		1	1			5		
Blanford	182	5	Johnson	William	1	1			1	3	1	1	1				9		
Blanford	182	6	Morrison	Alexander	1	1			1	2	2		1				8		
Blanford	182	7	Merrit	Asa	2	2		1		1			1				7		
Blanford	182	8	Boies	Levi	1			1		3		1	1				7		
Blanford	182	9	Knox	Nathan Esq	2	2		1		2	1		1				9		
Blanford	182	10	Gorham	John		1	1		1					1			4		
Blanford	182	11	Nobles	Elihu			1			4		1	1				8		
Blanford	182	12	Babcock	John		1		2	1		1			1			6		
Blanford	182	13	Webster				1		1			1					3		First name left blank
Blanford	182	14	Pelton	Thomas				1		6		1	1				9		
Blanford	182	15	Scott	Benjamin	2	1		1		1			1				6		
Blanford	182	16	Hall	John	1	1		1		2		3	1				9		
Blanford	182	17	Harskill	Philip	1	1			1	1	1	2		1			8		
Blanford	182	18	King	Esop	1	1		1		1			1				5		
Blanford	182	19	Shepard	Oliver	3			1		1			1				6		
Blanford	182	20	Sperry	Elihu Jr		1	2		1	3		1		2			10		
Blanford	182	21	Blair	Jacob			1					1					2		
Blanford	182	22	Ingraham	David	2			1		1			1				5		
Blanford	182	23	Latimer	Jacob				1		2			1				4		
Blanford	182	24	Sperry	Elihu		1		1	1	2		1		2			8		

TOWN	PG#	LN#	LAST NAME	FIRST NAME	FREE WHITE MALES under 10	10 to 16	16 to 26	26 to 45	45 and over	FREE WHITE FEMALES under 10	10 to 16	16 to 26	26 to 45	45 and over	TOTAL ALL OTHER	TOTAL SLAVES	TOTALS	DISTRICT/ TOWNSHIP	NOTES
Brimfield	269	1	Ward	Samuel Dexter				1		2		1					4		
Brimfield	269	2	Charles	Thomas			1		1	1	1		1				5		
Brimfield	269	3	Collins	Lewis		1		1					1	1			4		
Brimfield	269	4	Aspinwall	Prince	1	1	1	1	1		1	2	1				9		
Brimfield	269	5	Morgan	Joseph Jr	2	2	5	1		1		1	1				13		
Brimfield	269	6	Ward	Christopher				1		1	1		1				4		
Brimfield	269	7	Morgan	Joseph		1			1	1				1			4		
Brimfield	269	8	Brown	Jonathan		1	2		1		1	2		1			8		
Brimfield	269	9	Williams	Persis Wd		2	1			1	1			1			6		
Brimfield	269	10	Barrows	Gershom Capt.		1			1					1			3		
Brimfield	269	11	Hubbard	John B				1						1			2		
Brimfield	269	12	Stebbins	Zerah				1									1		
Brimfield	269	13	Stebbins	Levi		1		1					1	2			5		
Brimfield	269	14	Stebbins	Abijah			1			1	1		1				4		
Brimfield	269	15	Hartley	Edward		1		1		1				1			4		
Brimfield	269	16	Salisbury	Benjamin		1		1		1		1	1				5		
Brimfield	269	17	Goss	John A				1		1			1				3		
Brimfield	269	18	Brown	Bartholomew	1	1	2	1	1		1	1	1	1			10		
Brimfield	269	19	Bliss	Thomas	1	2	4	1	1	1		1	3	1			14		
Brimfield	269	20	Hubbard	Simeon	1		1	1	1	1	2	1	1				9		
Brimfield	269	21	Bliss	Aaron	1		1	2				1	1				6		
Brimfield	269	22	Miller	Ebenezer				1						1			2		
Brimfield	269	23	Tyler	Nathan			1			1			1				3		
Brimfield	269	24	Miller	Benjamin				1			1	1		1			4		
Brimfield	269	25	Hubbard	Jonathan	1		1	1	1			2		1			7		
Brimfield	269	26	Hoar	Joseph Capt.	1	1	2		1	1	1		1				8		
Brimfield	269	27	Liveny	John				1									1		
Brimfield	269	28	Hoar	Solomon	1		1	1		3		1	1				8		
Brimfield	269	29	Hoar	David	1	1		1		3	1	1	1				9		
Brimfield	269	30	Bishop	Richard		2	1		1		2	1		2			9		
Brimfield	269	31	Hubbard	Thomas	1		1	1		3	1		1				8		
Brimfield	269	32	Winslow	Shubael Dr		1		1	1	1		2		1			6		
Brimfield	269	33	Blair	Oliver	1	1	1			2		1					6		
Brimfield	269	34	Webber	Amasa	1			1		1			1				4		
Brimfield	269	35	Bugbee	Ebenezer				1				1					2		
Brimfield	269	36	Blackmore	Willard				1		1		1					3		
Brimfield	269	37	Farrel	Josiah		1	1		1			1		1			5		
Brimfield	269	38	Powers	Isaac		1			1					1			3		
Brimfield	269	39	Powers	Stephen	1	1	1	1		1		1	1				7		
Brimfield	270	1	Powers	Eli			2			1		1					4		
Brimfield	270	2	Shaw	Samuel	3			1		1	1		1				7		
Brimfield	270	3	Ward	Stephen				1		2			1				4		
Brimfield	270	4	Brooks	Sylvanus		1		1		3	1		1				7		
Brimfield	270	5	Blodgett	Jonas Dr	1		3		1	1	2			1			9		
Brimfield	270	6	Shaw	Joshua	1			1		1			1				4		
Brimfield	270	7	Patrick	Reuben Capt	1	1	1	2		3	1	1	1				11		
Brimfield	270	8	Nutting	Jonathan		1	2		1			1		1			6		
Brimfield	270	9	Nutting	James		1	1		1	2	2		1				8		
Brimfield	270	10	Hitchcock	Nathaniel			2		1	2	2		1				8		
Brimfield	270	11	Frost	Daniel		1	4					2		1			8		
Brimfield	270	12	Dunham	Benjamin	1			1		3			1				6		
Brimfield	270	13	Dunham	Joseph			1	1		1				1			4		
Brimfield	270	14	Dunham	Joseph Jr	1	1		1		2	1	1					7		
Brimfield	270	15	Hitchcock	Joseph Dr				1						1			2		
Brimfield	270	16	Hitchcock	Ezra	1	1	1	1		1	1	1					7		
Brimfield	270	17	Nichols	Stephen				1		1				1			3		
Brimfield	270	18	Nichols	Daniel	5			1		1			1				8		
Brimfield	270	19	Nichols	Lois Wido		1						1		1			3		
Brimfield	270	20	Sherman	John Jr	1			1		2			1				5		
Brimfield	270	21	Hitchcock	Mary Wido		1	2			1		2		2			8		
Brimfield	270	22	Stebbins	Benja Capt		2	1						1				4		
Brimfield	270	23	Stebbins	Uriah	3			1		1			1				6		
Brimfield	270	24	Stebbins	Abner Jr	2	1		1		4	2		1				11		
Brimfield	270	25	Stebbins	Abner			1	1					1	1			4		
Brimfield	270	26	Smith	Abel			1							1			3		
Brimfield	270	27	Smith	Royal		1		1						1			3		
Brimfield	270	28	Nichols	Jabez Capt		1	2		1	1	1	3		1			10		
Brimfield	270	29	Darling	Asa	1					1			1				3		
Brimfield	270	30	Forgate	Daniel		1	1	1		1	1		1				6		
Brimfield	270	31	Bugbee	Calvin	3			1			1		1				6		
Brimfield	270	32	Marrick	Benjamin	1		2		1		1	2	1				8		
Brimfield	270	33	Fenton	John	1	1	3	1		3			1	1			11		
Brimfield	270	34	Bacon	James				1		1		2		1			5		
Brimfield	270	35	Bacon	Amasa	1		1					1					3		
Brimfield	270	36	Nichols	Asher			2		1	1			1				5		
Brimfield	270	37	Annis	Molley Wd						2	1		1				4		
Brimfield	270	38	Nichols	John	1	2			1	3	1		1				9		
Brimfield	270	39	Blashfield	Jno Jr			1	1					1				3		
Brimfield	270	40	Gardner	Jno Jr	3			1				2		1			8		

TOWN	PG#	LN#	LAST NAME	FIRST NAME	M under 10	M 10 to 16	M 16 to 26	M 26 to 45	M 45 and over	F under 10	F 10 to 16	F 16 to 26	F 26 to 45	F 45 and over	TOTAL ALL OTHER	TOTAL SLAVES	TOTALS	DISTRICT/ TOWNSHIP	NOTES
Brimfield	270	41	Hunter	Samuel				2						2			4		
Brimfield	270	42	Faye	Thomas	2	1	1		1	2	1			1			9		
Brimfield	270	43	Faye	Uriah		1			1					1			3		
Brimfield	270	44	Blodgett	Daniel	1			1					1				3		
Brimfield	271	1	Collins	Daniel	3	1		1		1			1				7		
Brimfield	271	2	Ballow	Peter		1			1		1			2			5		
Brimfield	271	3	Pierce	Subbiness			1	1		2		1					5		
Brimfield	271	4	Williams	Thomas	2			1		1			1				5		
Brimfield	271	5	Ward	Amasa				1				2		1			4		
Brimfield	271	6	Sprague	Hosea	2	1		1		2			1				7		
Brimfield	271	7	Lumbard	Thomas				1						1			2		
Brimfield	271	8	Lumbard	Thomas Jun	2			1		1		1	1				6		
Brimfield	271	9	Lumbard	Gideon	2		1	1		3	1		1				9		
Brimfield	271	10	Ayres	Thomas	4			1		1	1		1				8		
Brimfield	271	11	Bond	John			1		1			1	1	1			5		
Brimfield	271	12	Graves	Joseph	1	1			1					1			4		
Brimfield	271	13	Graves	Peter		2	1		1			1		1			6		
Brimfield	271	14	Ellinwood	Thomas			1		1				1	1			4		
Brimfield	271	15	Blashfield	John				1						1			2		
Brimfield	271	16	Hutchinson	Eleazer				1						1			2		
Brimfield	271	17	Blashfield	Luke				1		1				1			3		
Brimfield	271	18	Charles	Levi		1	1						1				3		
Brimfield	271	19	Charles	Aaron Capt	1			1	1			1		1			5		
Brimfield	271	20	Charles	Arunah			1				1	1					3		
Brimfield	271	21	Bond	Mark				2						1			3		
Brimfield	271	22	Bond	Rowlandson	1		1			1		1					4		
Brimfield	271	23	Tucker	Jos				1						1			2		
Brimfield	271	24	Hitchcock	Medad Capt	1		3	1		2	2	1	1				11		
Brimfield	271	25	Brown	Isachar Deacn	1	1	1	1				1		1			6		
Brimfield	271	26	Brown	Isachar Jr				1		2				1			4		
Brimfield	271	27	Nichols	Zadok	1	1	2		1	1	1	1		1			9		
Brimfield	271	28	Nichols	Samuel Capt		1	1		1			1		2			6		
Brimfield	271	29	Nichols	Abner			1						1				2		
Brimfield	271	30	Crouch	Ephraim	2			1		1			1				5		
Brimfield	271	31	Davidson	Nthl Majr					1					1			2		
Brimfield	271	32	Danielson	Benja			1						1				2		
Brimfield	271	33	Henry	Jonas											8		8		
Brimfield	271	34	Eaton	William Capt		2	2			3	1	1	1				10		
Brimfield	271	35	Bailes	Lemuel	1		2			3	2	3	1				13		
Brimfield	271	36	Hitchcock	Noah		1		1		1		1		1			5		
Brimfield	271	37	Hitchcock	Jesse	1	1	2	1		3		1	1				10		
Brimfield	271	38	Hitchcock	Enos	1			1		1	1	1					5		
Brimfield	271	39	Bliss	Ichabod				1		3	1	2	1				8		
Brimfield	271	40	Charles	Simeon	1		1	1		1		2	1				7		
Brimfield	271	41	Warren	Philemon	1		2	1		2			2				8		
Brimfield	271	42	Moor	John	1			1			1	1	1				5		
Brimfield	272	1	Greenhill	Joel	2	2			1	2	2	1	1				11		
Brimfield	272	2	Pynchon	Stephen Esq			1			1		1					3		
Brimfield	272	3	Dudley	Joseph			1										1		
Brimfield	272	4	Moor	James	1			1		2				1			5		
Brimfield	272	5	Arms	Polly Wd	1					1				1			3		
Brimfield	272	6	Brown	Archelaus	2		1		1	1	2	1	1				9		
Brimfield	272	7	Russell	Abigail Wd							1	1		1			3		
Brimfield	272	8	Hitchcock	Gad	1			1		2			1				5		
Brimfield	272	9	Cooley	Thomas			1						1				2		
Brimfield	272	10	Guthrie	Saml Doct	2		1	1		1			1				6		
Brimfield	272	11	Holbrook	Zenas	3			1	1					1			6		
Brimfield	272	12	Holbrook	Nicholas		1		1		2		1		1			6		
Brimfield	272	13	Morgan	Abner Esq			2	1		1	1	1	1				7		
Brimfield	272	14	Moffartt	Joseph Doct		1		1						1			3		
Brimfield	272	15	Brown	Clark Revd	1	1		1				1	1	1			6		
Brimfield	272	16	Morgan	Jacob	2	1		1		3		1	1				9		
Brimfield	272	17	Morgan	Daniel	1			1		1			1				4		
Brimfield	272	18	Sherman	Jona Capt				1						1			2		
Brimfield	272	19	Sherman	Benjamin	1			1		1		1					4		
Brimfield	272	20	Bement	John			1			1		1					3		
Brimfield	272	21	Bement	Jesse				1				1		1			3		
Brimfield	272	22	Hitchcock	Samuel	1		1					1					3		
Brimfield	272	23	Hitchcock	Peter			1						1				2		
Brimfield	272	24	Sherman	Thomas	2	1	2	1			1	1	1	1			10		
Brimfield	272	25	Morgan	Pearly	1			1		2		1					5		
Brimfield	272	26	Morgan	Enoch	1	1		1		2		1	1	1			8		
Brimfield	272	27	Sherman	Belsey Wido	2		2			1	1	1		1			8		
Brimfield	272	28	Charles	Nehemiah		1	1			1	1	1	1				6		
Brimfield	272	29	Partridge	Frederick			1			2			1				4		
Brimfield	272	30	Pierce	Seth	1	1	2		1			1		1			7		
Brimfield	272	31	Blashfield	Alfred		1	1			2			1	1			6		
Brimfield	272	32	Butterworth	William	1			1		3		1	1				7		
Brimfield	272	33	Morgan	Aaron Maj		1	2		1	1		1		1			7		

TOWN	PG#	LN#	LAST NAME	FIRST NAME	FREE WHITE MALES					FREE WHITE FEMALES					TOTAL ALL OTHER	TOTAL SLAVES	TOTALS	DISTRICT/ TOWNSHIP	NOTES
					under 10	10 to 16	16 to 26	26 to 45	45 and over	under 10	10 to 16	16 to 26	26 to 45	45 and over					
Brimfield	272	34	Morgan	Justin			1						1				2		
Brimfield	272	35	Bugbee	David			1		1	2	1		2				7		
Brimfield	272	36	Sesions	Saml Capt	1	1	1	1	1	1		2					8		
Brimfield	272	37	Abbot	Zebadiah	2	1			1	2	2			2			10		
Brimfield	272	38	Blashfield	Betty										1			1		
Brimfield	272	39	Wheelock	Henry	4		1	1		1			2	1			10		
Brimfield	272	40	Tarbill	Elijah	2		1		1		1	1		1			7		
Brimfield	272	41	Clark	Eliphalet	2	2		1		2			1				8		
Brimfield	272	42	Bates	Elisha			1			2			1				4		
Brimfield	273	1	Bates	Rufus	2			1		1		1	1				6		
Brimfield	273	2	Berly	Lynel	2			1		3		1	1				8		
Brimfield	273	3	Allen	Elijah	2		1	1		3			1				8		
Brimfield	273	4	Lumbard	Joseph Jr		1	1		1		1			1			5		
Brimfield	273	5	Mason	Oliver		1		1				2		1			5		
Brimfield	273	6	Alllen	Caleb	2			1		1		1	1				6		
Brimfield	273	7	Rockwell	John				1		2			1				4		
Brimfield	273	8	Bates	Moses	2			1		1			1	1			6		
Brimfield	273	9	Bates	Samuel Lt		1			1			1		1			4		
Brimfield	273	10	Bates	Samuel Junr			1			1		1					3		
Brimfield	273	11	Bullard	David	1	2		1				1		1			6		
Brimfield	273	12	Draper	George		1								1			2		
Brimfield	273	13	Blashfield	Ozeon Capt	1	1	1		1	3	1	1	2				11		
Brimfield	273	14	Burt	Daniel		1	2		1	2		1	1				8		
Brimfield	273	15	Janes	Orsamus			4	1			1	1		1			8		
Brimfield	273	16	Tarbill	Elijah Junr			2			1		1					4		
Brimfield	273	17	Janes	Pheny	1	1		1		1	1		1				6		
Brimfield	273	18	Till	James											2		2		
Brimfield	273	19	Allen	Alfred	2	1		1		1			1				6		
Brimfield	273	20	Janes	Cyrus	3		1	1			1	1	1				8		
Brimfield	273	21	Charles	Abraham		1		1	1			1					4		
Brimfield	273	22	Janes	William Junr		1		1		4	1	1	1				9		
Brimfield	273	23	Bond	Bailey		1	1						1				3		
Brimfield	273	24	Janes	William				1						1			2		
Brimfield	273	25	Draper	Isaac		1		1		1	1	2		1			7		
Brimfield	273	26	Lumbard	Joseph				1						1			2		
Brimfield	273	27	Lumbard	David	3			1		2	1	1	1				9		
Brimfield	273	28	Lumbard	Aaron	2	2		1		2	1	1	1				10		
Brimfield	273	29	Charles	Nathanl	1	1		1		2			1				6		
Brimfield	273	30	Draper	John				1						2			3		
Brimfield	273	31	Baker	Joseph		1		1		4			1				7		
Brimfield	273	32	Partridge	Joseph	2		1	1		1			1				6		
Brimfield	273	33	Baxter	John				1		1			1				3		
Brimfield	273	34	Scott	John				1					1	1			3		
Brimfield	273	35	Russell	Titus	1	1		1		1			1	2			7		
Brimfield	273	36	Townley	Reuben			2		2		1			2			7		
Brimfield	273	37	Fairbanks	Ebenz Deacn			2	1	1			1		1			6		
Brimfield	273	38	Fairbanks	Henry	1			1		1			1				4		
Brimfield	273	39	Fairbanks	Joseph	2			1		1			1				5		
Brimfield	273	40	Fay	Levi	2		1	1		1	2		1				8		
Brimfield	273	41	Barrows	Joel	4			1					1				6		
Brimfield	273	42	Faye	Jonathan		1	2		1		1	2		1			8		
Brimfield	273	43	Sherman	Barzilla	1			1	1	1			1	2			7		
Brimfield	273	44	Parker	James	1			1		3			1				6		
Brimfield	273	45	Bennett	Jonathan	1			1		1			1				4		
Brimfield	274	1	Hitchcock	Abijah	2			1					1				4		
Brimfield	274	2	Adams	Nathl	1	1		1		1	2			1			7		
Brimfield	274	3	Hitchcock	Danl	3	1		1		1	2		2				10		
Brimfield	274	4	Hitchcock	Elijah			2		1		1	1		1			6		
Brimfield	274	5	Gleason	Jason	2	1	1	1		1			1				7		
Brimfield	274	6	Howard	Asa	2			1		2			1				6		
Brimfield	274	7	Sesions	Alex Col		1	3		1		1	1		1			8		
Brimfield	274	8	Chapin	Rufus	2		1	1					1				5		
Brimfield	274	9	Haynes	Samuel				1									1		
Brimfield	274	10	Morgan	Jona		1	1			1			1	1			6		
Brimfield	274	11	Stone	Thomas	2	1		1					1				5		
Brimfield	274	12	Haynes	Daniel		1	1	2	2	1		2		1			10		
Brimfield	274	13	Bates	Simeon		1	1		1			3		1			7		
Brimfield	274	14	Hibbard	Alpheus			1			1		2					4		
Brimfield	274	15	Danielson	Luther	3	1		1		1	1		1				8		
Brimfield	274	16	Browning	James				1				1					2		
Brimfield	274	17	Dennison	George				1					1				2		
Brimfield	274	18	Howard	Samuel	1			1					1				3		
Brimfield	274	19	Browning	Joseph Esq				1		1			1	1	1		4		
Brimfield	274	20	Bond	Nathan	2		1					1					4		
Brimfield	274	21	Browning	Davis	1	1		1		2	1		1				7		
Brimfield	274	22	Anderson	Margaret Wd			1						1				2		
Brimfield	274	23	Parker	Nathaniel	5	1	1	1				1	1				10		
Brimfield	274	24	Anderson	Amasa	2			1					1				4		
Brimfield	274	25	Thompson	Jonathan Lt					1					1			2		

TOWN	PG#	LN#	HEADS OF HOUSEHOLD		FREE WHITE MALES					FREE WHITE FEMALES					TOTAL ALL OTHER	TOTAL SLAVES	TOTALS	DISTRICT/ TOWNSHIP	NOTES
			LAST NAME	FIRST NAME	under 10	10 to 16	16 to 26	26 to 45	45 and over	under 10	10 to 16	16 to 26	26 to 45	45 and over					
Brimfield	274	26	Thompson	Sylvanus	2	1	1		1	1	2		1				9		
Brimfield	274	27	Haynes	Jonas		1		1	1			3	1				7		
Brimfield	274	28	Aikins	John				1		1		1					3		
Brimfield	274	29	Charles	Aaron Jr		1	1		1		1		1				5		
Brimfield	274	30	Shaw	George		1			1				1				3		
Brimfield	274	31	Shaw	Daniel	2		1	2		1			1				7		
Brimfield	274	32	Nelson	Benjamin	1	1	2	1			2	1		1			9		
Brimfield	274	33	Haynes	Joseph	3		1		1	3	3		1				12		
Brimfield	275	1	Wales	Oliver	2		3		1	1			1	1			9	South Brimfield	
Brimfield	275	2	Young	David Doct		1	1	1		1		1	1				6	South Brimfield	
Brimfield	275	3	Wales	Shubael				1		2				2			5	South Brimfield	
Brimfield	275	4	Rogers	Joseph		1	1		1		1			1			5	South Brimfield	
Brimfield	275	5	Winchester	Aaron	4	2		1					1				8	South Brimfield	
Brimfield	275	6	Underwood	Eliha	1	2	2		1	1		1		1			9	South Brimfield	
Brimfield	275	7	Holbridge	William	1	1	1		1		2	1		1			8	South Brimfield	
Brimfield	275	8	Fletcher	Amos	2			1		2			1				6	South Brimfield	
Brimfield	275	9	Underwood	Alpheus	1		1					1					3	South Brimfield	
Brimfield	275	10	Stewart	Paul		2		1		3	1		1	1			9	South Brimfield	
Brimfield	275	11	Stewart	James			1	1			1	1	1				5	South Brimfield	
Brimfield	275	12	Munger	Samuel				1			2		1				4	South Brimfield	
Brimfield	275	13	Munger	Cyrus	3	1	1		1	1	1		1				9	South Brimfield	
Brimfield	275	14	Green	Amos		1	1		1		2						5	South Brimfield	
Brimfield	275	15	Munger	Amasa		1	1			2	2		1				7	South Brimfield	
Brimfield	275	16	Munger	John				1					1				2	South Brimfield	
Brimfield	275	17	White	Nathan Capt	1	1	1	1		1	1	1	1				8	South Brimfield	
Brimfield	275	18	Rogers	Oliver	2			1		2	1		1				7	South Brimfield	
Brimfield	275	19	Needham	David Capt	2	2	1		1	3		1	1				11	South Brimfield	
Brimfield	275	20	Moulton	Ebenezer	2	1			1	3		1	1				9	South Brimfield	
Brimfield	275	21	Dawson	Diminicus	2	1	2		1	1	1	2		1			11	South Brimfield	

29

Table headers — HEADS OF HOUSEHOLD (LAST NAME, FIRST NAME); FREE WHITE MALES (under 10, 10 to 16, 16 to 26, 26 to 45, 45 and over); FREE WHITE FEMALES (under 10, 10 to 16, 16 to 26, 26 to 45, 45 and over); TOTAL ALL OTHER; TOTAL SLAVES; TOTALS; DISTRICT/TOWNSHIP; NOTES.

TOWN	PG#	LN#	LAST NAME	FIRST NAME	M <10	M 10-16	M 16-26	M 26-45	M 45+	F <10	F 10-16	F 16-26	F 26-45	F 45+	TOTAL ALL OTHER	TOTAL SLAVES	TOTALS	DISTRICT/ TOWNSHIP	NOTES
Buckland	325	1	Allen	Joseph		1		1		1		2					5		
Buckland	325	2	Ames	John	1		4	1		3		1	1				11		
Buckland	325	3	Allis	Stephen	2	1	2	1			2		1				9		
Buckland	325	4	Abby	Reuben	2			1					1				4		
Buckland	325	5	Annible	Edward	1			1		2	2	1	1				8		
Buckland	325	6	Blackmer	Rowland					1	1				1			3		
Buckland	325	7	Butler	James		1	2		1	4	2	1	1				12		
Buckland	325	8	Belding	Saml	2			2		1			1				6		
Buckland	325	9	Brackey	Saml		1		1		2			1				5		
Buckland	325	10	Ballard	Joseph	1	1		1				2					5		
Buckland	325	11	Ballard	Benjm			1			2			1				4		
Buckland	325	12	Blackmer	John H.	1	2		1		2	1		1				8		
Buckland	326	1	Brooks	Jabez		1		1		1		1					4		
Buckland	326	2	Brooks	Alpheus			2	1		5			1				9		
Buckland	326	3	Bachelor	Nathan	1			1				1	1				4		
Buckland	326	4	Bullard	John Jr	1			1					1				3		
Buckland	326	5	Bracket	James	2			1					1				4		
Buckland	326	6	Butler	Peter	2				1	2			1				6		
Buckland	326	7	Boyden	Elijah			1		1	1	1	1					5		
Buckland	326	8	Bullard	John				1				1					2		
Buckland	326	9	Chapin	Japhet	2	2		1	1	3		1	1				11		
Buckland	326	10	Chilson	Joseph					1	1	1			1			4		
Buckland	326	11	Colman	Gershom		1	1	1						1			4		
Buckland	326	12	Colman	Nathl		1					1	2					5		
Buckland	326	13	Cook	Nathan				1	1	3	1	1		1			8		
Buckland	326	14	Cross	Jeduthan	1			1		3		1	1				7		
Buckland	326	15	Cook	Josiah Junr	1	2		2		1		1	1	1			9		
Buckland	326	16	Carter	Elias	1		2	2		1	2		1				10		
Buckland	326	17	Clark	John			1										1		
Buckland	326	18	Carter	Sama		1		1		1	1			1			5		
Buckland	326	19	Benjm	Carter	2			1		3			1				7		
Buckland	326	20	Carter	Elisha		1	1	1		2	1		1				7		
Buckland	326	21	Clark	Robert		1		1				1		1			4		
Buckland	326	22	Clark	James	1			1		3			1				6		
Buckland	326	23	Carter	Elias Jr	3			1		3			1				8		
Buckland	326	24	Carter	Elijah				1		2			1				4		
Buckland	326	25	Clark	Robert Jr	2		1					1							
Buckland	326	26	Cook	Abel		1	2	1		3			1				8		
Buckland	326	27	Cobb	Josiah Junr	2			1		2		1					6		
Buckland	327	1	Drake	Josiah				1						1			5		
Buckland	327	2	Davis	Josiah	2	2		1		4	1		1				44		
Buckland	327	3	Drake	Jehiel	2		1			2		1					6		
Buckland	327	4	Edson	Jesse			2	1		1			1	1			6		
Buckland	327	5	Eddy	Peletiah		1	1	1					1				4		
Buckland	327	6	Ellis	John	1		1		1	3	2	2		1			11		
Buckland	327	7	Ellis	Benjm	1	2	1		1	1		2		1			9		
Buckland	327	8	Ellis	Stephen			1			1		1					3		
Buckland	327	9	Fuller	George	1			1		1		1					5		
Buckland	327	10	Fuller	Eli	1		1		1	3		1	1				8		
Buckland	327	11	Furbush	Thomas					1		1	1		1			4		
Buckland	327	12	Fessenden	Wyman	1			1				1					3		
Buckland	327	13	Flower	Joseph						3	2	1	1				7		
Buckland	327	14	Forbes	Edward	1	1		1		1		1					5		
Buckland	327	15	Forbes	Jotham	3			1		1		1	1				7		
Buckland	327	16	Fuller	Thankful		1						1					2		
Buckland	327	17	Fay	Nathan	1		1	1		3	3			1			10		
Buckland	327	18	Grant	John					1	1	1	1	1				5		
Buckland	327	19	Graham	Zenas			2	1		1		1					5		
Buckland	327	20	Hosley	David			2										2		
Buckland	327	21	Hastings	Solomon	3	1		1		2			1				8		
Buckland	327	22	Holden	Elihu	2			1		2		1	1				7		
Buckland	328	1	Harvey	Jonathan	2			1		2	2			2			9		
Buckland	328	2	Hathway	Josiah	2		2	1		3		1	1				10		
Buckland	328	3	Harris	Sarah									1				1		
Buckland	328	4	Hinkley	Solomon	3			1		1			1				6		
Buckland	328	5	Hook	Willm Capt.					1		1		1				3		
Buckland	328	6	Judd	Asahel	2			1					1	1			5		
Buckland	328	7	Jones	Alfred	1		1	1				1	1	1			6		
Buckland	328	8	Jones	Willm	1	1	2		1	2	1		1				9		
Buckland	328	9	Johnson	David	2			1		1	1		1				6		
Buckland	328	10	Johnson	Josiah		1	3		1	5	1	1		1			13		
Buckland	328	11	Jones	Abraham	2	1			1		1	1	1				7		
Buckland	328	12	Jennings	Ephraim		1	2		2	1				2			8		
Buckland	328	13	Jones	Rufus	2		1					1					4		
Buckland	328	14	Jones	Erastus	2		1										3		
Buckland	328	15	Jones	Bidear	3			1					1				5		
Buckland	328	16	Knowles	Seth	5			1		1	1		1				9		
Buckland	328	17	Kilburn	Saml			1		1	1	2			1			6		
Buckland	328	18	Lyon	Nathan		1		1			1	1					5		

30

TOWN	PG#	LN#	LAST NAME	FIRST NAME	FREE WHITE MALES					FREE WHITE FEMALES					TOTAL ALL OTHER	TOTAL SLAVES	TOTALS	DISTRICT/ TOWNSHIP	NOTES
					under 10	10 to 16	16 to 26	26 to 45	45 and over	under 10	10 to 16	16 to 26	26 to 45	45 and over					
Buckland	328	19	Leonard	Calvin	1			1		1		1		1			5		
Buckland	328	20	Leonard	Ichabod	2			1				1	1				5		
Buckland	328	21	Lazeel	Calvin	2	2		1		2			1				8		
Buckland	328	22	Lachey	James	2	1		1		1	1	1		1			8		
Buckland	328	23	Lazeel	Robert	3			1		2	1	1	2	1			11		
Buckland	328	24	Leonard	Ziba	3	1		1		1	1		1				8		
Buckland	328	25	Locke	John	2			1		2	2		1	1			9		
Buckland	328	26	Lyon	Aaron		1		1		3	2		1				8		
Buckland	328	27	Merril	Jesse				1		1	1	1	1				5		
Buckland	329	1	Matthewson	Philip	1			1		1	1		1				5		
Buckland	329	2	Nitt	Adam M.	1	2		1		1	1		1				7		
Buckland	329	3	May	Oliver		1		1					1				3		
Buckland	329	4	Nims	John	3		1		1	2	2	4	1				14		
Buckland	329	5	Nichols	Asa			1			1		1	1				4		
Buckland	329	6	Nelson	Stephen		1			1	3			1				6		
Buckland	329	7	Nichols	Saml			1			1		1					3		
Buckland	329	8	Nichols	Joseph	2		1			1			1				5		
Buckland	329	9	Pelton	Cale	3			1					1				5		
Buckland	329	10	Perkins	Edmund	3		1	1	1	2		1	1	2			12		
Buckland	329	11	Pomroy	Enos	3	1	1	1		2	1	1	1				11		
Buckland	329	12	Putnam	Willm	1	2		1		2			1				7		
Buckland	329	13	Potter	Joseph	1	1			1	1		1	1				6		
Buckland	329	14	Prince	Saml	2	1	1	1		1	1	1	1				9		
Buckland	329	15	Perkins	Rufus	3		1	1		1	3		1				10		
Buckland	329	16	Rood	Thaddeus	4			1		2			1				8		
Buckland	329	17	Reniff	George	4			1		2			1				8		
Buckland	329	18	Ruddock	Edward	3		1			1			1				6		
Buckland	329	19	Rawson	Moses		1	1		1	2	1		1				7		
Buckland	329	20	Smith	Elisha	1	1		1			1	1		1			6		
Buckland	329	21	Sprague	Benjm	3			1		3	1	3	1				12		
Buckland	329	22	Shaw	Simeon	1		1		1		1	1		1			6		
Buckland	329	23	Smith	Lemuel			1	1				1		1			4		
Buckland	329	24	Smith	Saml	2		1			1			1				5		
Buckland	329	25	Sprague	Jonathan				1						1			2		
Buckland	329	26	Sprague	Jonathan Jr	2			1		3			1				7		
Buckland	329	27	Savage	Abraham	3	2	1	1		1	1	1	1	1			12		
Buckland	329	28	Smith	Abel		1		1				1		1			4		
Buckland	330	1	Shephard	Joseph		1		1		2				2			6		
Buckland	330	2	Spalding	Josiah Rev.		1		1		2	2		1				7		
Buckland	330	3	Shaw	Benjm	1	1		1		1	1	2	1				9		
Buckland	330	4	Sheldon	Saml			1					1					2		
Buckland	330	5	Smith	Enos	1	1	2		1	1			1				7		
Buckland	330	6	Truesdel	Saml				1		1				1			3		
Buckland	330	7	Truesdel	Leml	1		1			1		1					4		
Buckland	330	8	Thayer	Elijah		1		1			2		1				5		
Buckland	330	9	Thayer	Elijah Jr	1		1						1				3		
Buckland	330	10	Tryon	Josiah		1	1						1				3		
Buckland	330	11	Tryon	Timothy	1			1		1			1				4		
Buckland	330	12	Taylor	Joshua Jr	2			1		2	4		1				10		
Buckland	330	13	Taylor	Willm	1	2		1		2	2		1				9		
Buckland	330	14	Townsley	Dan	3			1		2			1				7		
Buckland	330	15	Taylor	Leml	2		3		1	1		2		1			10		
Buckland	330	16	Taylor	Saml Esq			2	1	1		1	3		1			9		
Buckland	330	17	Taylor	Saml Junr	2	1		1		1		1					6		
Buckland	330	18	Taylor	Enos	2	1		1		1		1					6		
Buckland	330	19	Trowbridge	Daniel	3	1	1	1		1	1	1	1				10		
Buckland	330	20	Toby	Isaac	1	2			1	2	1	1		1			9		
Buckland	330	21	Trow	Benjm	1			1		3			1				6		
Buckland	330	22	Taylor	Barnabas		1		1				1	1				4		
Buckland	330	23	Thompson	Saml				1				1		1			3		
Buckland	330	24	Webber	Abner	1					1			1				3		
Buckland	330	25	Webber	John	1		2		1	2	1			1			8		
Buckland	330	26	Ward	John	1			1	1	3	2		1	1			10		
Buckland	330	27	Woodard	James	1	1	1		1		2	1		1			8		
Buckland	330	28	White	Zebulon				1			1	1		1			4		
Buckland	330	29	Ware	Michael		1		1	1	1			1	1			6		
Buckland	331	1	Ware	Michael Jr	2			1		2			1				6		
Buckland	331	2	Woodard	Daniel	2			1		2			1				6		
Buckland	331	3	Weeks	Elijah	2			1		1			1				5		
Buckland	331	4	Ward	Luke	1			1		2		1		1			6		
Buckland	331	5	Wood	Amos	2	1	1	1	1	1		1	1	1			10		
Buckland	331	6	Ward	Jeremiah	2			1	1	1	1		1	1			8		
Buckland	331	7	Whitney	Jacob	1			1				1	1				4		
Buckland	331	8	Whitney	Willm	2	2			2	1	1		2				10		
Buckland	331	9	Wilder	Gardner	1		3		1		1	3		1			10		
Buckland	331	10	White	Levi	3	1		1					1				6		
Buckland	331	11	Wood	John			1		1	1		1	1				5		
Buckland	331	12	Woodard	Henry	3	1		1		2	1		1	1			10		
Buckland	331	13	Wilkie	John				1				1	1				3		

31

TOWN	PG#	LN#	HEADS OF HOUSEHOLD		FREE WHITE MALES					FREE WHITE FEMALES					TOTAL ALL OTHER	TOTAL SLAVES	TOTALS	DISTRICT/ TOWNSHIP	NOTES
			LAST NAME	FIRST NAME	under 10	10 to 16	16 to 26	26 to 45	45 and over	under 10	10 to 16	16 to 26	26 to 45	45 and over					
Buckland	331	14	Walker	Job	2			1		1			1				5		
Buckland	331	15	Wilkie	John Jun			1			2	1						4		
Buckland	331	16	Ware	Ariel	2			1		1			1				5		
Buckland	331	17	Ward	John 2d			1										1		
Buckland	331	18	Wade	Amos Capt.	2	2	1		1		1		1				8		
Buckland	331	19	Wade	Amos Junr	2	2	1		1		1		1				8		

TOWN	PG#	LN#	HEADS OF HOUSEHOLD		FREE WHITE MALES					FREE WHITE FEMALES					TOTAL ALL OTHER	TOTAL SLAVES	TOTALS	DISTRICT/ TOWNSHIP	NOTES
			LAST NAME	FIRST NAME	under 10	10 to 16	16 to 26	26 to 45	45 and over	under 10	10 to 16	16 to 26	26 to 45	45 and over					
Charlemont	191	1	Cobb	Elisha			1		1		1			1			4		
Charlemont	191	2	Cobb	Nathanael			1			1		1					3		
Charlemont	191	3	Crosby	Jonathan	3	1		1		2			1				8		
Charlemont	191	4	Chambers	John				1		3			1				5		
Charlemont	191	5	Dyer	James				1		1	1			1			4		
Charlemont	191	6	Fuller	John		1	1			2			1				5		
Charlemont	191	7	Field	Joseph	1			1			1		1				4		
Charlemont	191	8	Fales	James	3	1		1		1		2	1	1			10		
Charlemont	191	9	Fales	Jeremiah				1		1			1				3		
Charlemont	191	10	Flagg	Benoni	2	1		1	1	1	1	1	1				10		
Charlemont	191	11	Ford	Samuel	4	2		1			1		1				9		
Charlemont	191	12	Foster	Amos	1	1		1		2		1					6		
Charlemont	191	13	Green	Sarah	2	1				2	1	2	1				9		
Charlemont	191	14	Gould	Jeremiah				1						1			2		
Charlemont	191	15	Gould	Aaron	1	2	2	1		3	1		1	1			12		
Charlemont	191	16	Giles	Edward			1	1		2			1	1			6		
Charlemont	191	17	Giles	Edward Jun	1			1		4			1				7		
Charlemont	191	18	Graves	Jesse		1	2	1			1			1			6		
Charlemont	192	1	Gould	Nathan			1	1						1			3		
Charlemont	192	2	Gray	James		1		1		3	1		1				7		
Charlemont	192	3	Green	Ebenezer	2			1		1			1				5		
Charlemont	192	4	Graves	Ebenezer	1	1		1		1			1				5		
Charlemont	192	5	Gould	Benjamin	1			1		4		1					7		
Charlemont	192	6	Hastings	Jonathan			2		1	2	2			1			8		
Charlemont	192	7	Hill	Samuel	4			1		1	1			1			8		
Charlemont	192	8	Hawks	Gershom		1			1			2		1			5		
Charlemont	192	9	Hawks	Joshua		2			1	2	1	1		1			8		
Charlemont	192	10	Hawks	Jared	3	2	3		1	1			2		1		13		
Charlemont	192	11	Hartwell	Jonathan				1		2	2	1					6		
Charlemont	192	12	Hawks	Rufus	2	1		1			2	1		1			8		
Charlemont	192	13	Hawks	Ephraim	3	1	1		1	1		2	1		1		11		
Charlemont	192	14	Hawks	Elihu	3		1		1		1	1	1				8		
Charlemont	192	15	Hawks	Jonathan	2	1	1		1	2		1	2	1			11		
Charlemont	192	16	Hawks	Israel	4	1		1					1				7		
Charlemont	192	17	Hartwell	William		1		1				2		1			5		
Charlemont	192	18	Hunt	Jacob	2	1	1		1		1		1				7		
Charlemont	192	19	Hall	John	1	1	2		1	2	2	1		1			11		
Charlemont	192	20	Hawks	Jared Jur			1				2	1					4		
Charlemont	192	21	Kindrick	John			1			3			1				5		
Charlemont	192	22	Johnson	Billy				1		2	1		1				5		
Charlemont	192	23	Leonard	Jonas	5			1					1				7		
Charlemont	192	24	Leggett	William	2		1			1			1				5		
Charlemont	192	25	Leggett	Thomas	1		1	1		1			1				5		
Charlemont	192	26	Leggett	Robert			2		1				1	1			5		
Charlemont	192	27	Kellogg	Ebenezer				1				1					2		
Charlemont	192	28	McFarling	Ephraim	1		1	1		2			1				6		
Charlemont	192	29	Mitchel	Asaph	2			1		1			1				5		
Charlemont	192	30	Montague	Ebenezer	1			1		2		1	1				6		
Charlemont	192	31	Mayhew	Freeburn		3	2		1	1	1	1	1	1			11		
Charlemont	192	32	Nichels	Thomas Jur	2			1			1		1				5		
Charlemont	192	33	Nash	Joseph	1		1	1		1		1	1				6		
Charlemont	192	34	Nichels	Thomas		1	3		1		1			1			7		
Charlemont	192	35	Nichels	James	1			1		2			1				5		
Charlemont	192	36	Nichels	Asa	4			1					1				6		
Charlemont	193	1	Parker	James		1		1		2			1				5		
Charlemont	193	2	Parker	Samuel		1	4		1	1				1			8		
Charlemont	193	3	Pierce	Josiah	2	2			1	2			1				8		
Charlemont	193	4	Pike	Elisha	1	1		1		4			1				8		
Charlemont	193	5	Parsons	Azariah				1		2			1				4		
Charlemont	193	6	Parsons	Noah	1			1					1				3		
Charlemont	193	7	Phips	George	2	1			1	2		1					7		
Charlemont	193	8	Rice	Joel	2	1		1		2			1				7		
Charlemont	193	9	Riddle	Samuel	2			1		1	1		1				6		
Charlemont	193	10	Rice	David				1				1					2		
Charlemont	193	11	Rice	Catherine			1							1			2		
Charlemont	193	12	Rice	Ezra			1							1			2		
Charlemont	193	13	Rice	Calvin		1		1			1		1				4		
Charlemont	193	14	Rice	Aaron Jur	4			1	1		2		1	1			10		
Charlemont	193	15	Rice	John		1	1	1		2		1					8		
Charlemont	193	16	Rice	Joseph	1	1		1		2	1		1				7		
Charlemont	193	17	Rice	Martin	2	2	1		1	1	2	1	1				11		
Charlemont	193	18	Rice	Luke	1			1				1	1				4		
Charlemont	193	19	Rice	Artemas	1	1	1		1	2	1		1	1			9		
Charlemont	193	20	Rice	Aaron					1			1		1			3		
Charlemont	193	21	Rice	Silvanus Jur	2			1				1					4		
Charlemont	193	22	Rice	Samuel	1	2	1		1	2	1	3	1				12		
Charlemont	193	23	Rice	Ruth			1				2			1			4		
Charlemont	193	24	Rudd	Zebbeus	2	2		2	1	2			1	1			11		
Charlemont	193	25	Rudd	Nathanael	1												3		

TOWN	PG#	LN#	HEADS OF HOUSEHOLD		FREE WHITE MALES					FREE WHITE FEMALES					TOTAL ALL OTHER	TOTAL SLAVES	TOTALS	DISTRICT/ TOWNSHIP	NOTES
			LAST NAME	FIRST NAME	under 10	10 to 16	16 to 26	26 to 45	45 and over	under 10	10 to 16	16 to 26	26 to 45	45 and over					
Charlemont	193	26	Rudd	Andrew		2		1			1		1				5		
Charlemont	193	27	Rogers	Oren	1			1		1	1						4		
Charlemont	193	28	Rice	Silvanus			3	1						1			5		
Charlemont	193	29	Stearns	Levi			2	1		2	1		1				7		
Charlemont	193	30	Shippy	Peter				2						2			4		
Charlemont	193	31	Shippy	Christopher	2		1	1		2	1			1			8		
Charlemont	193	32	Smith	Andrew		2		1		4	1	1	1				10		
Charlemont	193	33	Shurtleaf	Silas				1			1	1		1			4		
Charlemont	194	1	Scott	Consider			2			1		1					4		
Charlemont	194	2	Steel	Elijah	1			1		2			1				5		
Charlemont	194	3	Stearns	Timothy	1		1			1		1					4		
Charlemont	194	4	Swan	Josiah		1	2	1				1		1			6		
Charlemont	194	5	Stanford	Moses		1	1	1		1	1			1			6		
Charlemont	194	6	Shurtleaf	James	3			1		1		1					6		
Charlemont	194	7	Taylor	Sarah							1			1			2		
Charlemont	194	8	Taylor	Tertius	1	1	1		1			1	1	2			8		
Charlemont	194	9	Taylor	Rufus	2			1		3			1				7		
Charlemont	194	10	Tinney	Josiah			1		1	2		1		1			6		
Charlemont	194	11	Upton	Joseph			1	1		1		1					4		
Charlemont	194	12	Upton	Elias	4			1		1			1				7		
Charlemont	194	13	Upton	Abiathar				1		3			1				5		
Charlemont	194	14	Upton	Josiah	1	2		1		1	2		1				8		
Charlemont	194	15	Upton	Nathanael	1			1					1				3		
Charlemont	194	16	White	Jonathan				1									1		
Charlemont	194	17	White	Josiah		1		1		1			1				4		
Charlemont	194	18	Wilder	Abel	2			1		2	1		1				7		
Charlemont	194	19	Wheelock	Abijah	3	1		1		2			1				8		
Charlemont	194	20	William	William		2	3		1			1	3		1		11		
Charlemont	194	21	Young	Henry			1			1		1					3		
Charlemont	194	22	Young	Robert	3			1		1			1				6		

TOWN	PG#	LN#	HEADS OF HOUSEHOLD		FREE WHITE MALES					FREE WHITE FEMALES					TOTAL ALL OTHER	TOTAL SLAVES	TOTALS	DISTRICT/ TOWNSHIP	NOTES
			LAST NAME	FIRST NAME	under 10	10 to 16	16 to 26	26 to 45	45 and over	under 10	10 to 16	16 to 26	26 to 45	45 and over					
Chester	143	1	Hamelton	David	1	1		1		2	1		1				7		
Chester	143	2	Bigalow	John	4			1		2	1		1				9		
Chester	143	3	Quigley	William	2	2	1		2			3	1				11		
Chester	143	4	Hamelton	John	3			1		1	2		1				8		
Chester	143	5	Gamwell	John Jr	2			1					1				4		
Chester	143	6	Bell	Abraham	3				1		2		1				7		
Chester	143	7	Moor	William Lieut		1	4	1			1			1			8		
Chester	143	8	Hamilton	James Deac				1				1		1			3		
Chester	143	9	Hamilton	Lemuel	1		1					1					3		
Chester	143	10	Quigley	Adam	1		1	1					1	1			5		
Chester	143	11	Bell	Aaron Junr	1		1			1		2					5		
Chester	143	12	Quigley	James	3			1		1	1		1				7		
Chester	143	13	James	John Capt	1	2			1	2	1		1	1			9		
Chester	143	14	Eldar	William	1	3		1		3	1		1	2			12		
Chester	143	15	Hollon	Simon E. Capt	3		1	1		2	2		1				10		
Chester	143	16	Pelton	Tabor	1	1		1		4			1				8		
Chester	143	17	Pike	Samuel				1		4			1				6		
Chester	143	18	Noney	James	1	2	3	1		2	1	2		2			14		
Chester	143	19	Colton	Chauncy	1		1			1	1						4		
Chester	143	20	Cobb	John			1			1			1				3		
Chester	143	21	Matthews	Gideon		3		1					1				5		
Chester	143	22	Matthews	Edmond	2		1			2			1				6		
Chester	144	1	Matthews	Gideon Deac	1		1			1			1		1		5		
Chester	144	2	Matthews	Samuel Deac				1		1		1	1				4		
Chester	144	3	Smith	John Deac				1			1		1				3		
Chester	144	4	Smith	John Junr			1				1	1					3		
Chester	144	5	Carpenter	Ebenezer		1											1		
Chester	144	6	Smith	Isaac	1		1		1			1					4		
Chester	144	7	Johnson	Ely	3		1					1					5		
Chester	144	8	Foot	William	2	2		1	1		1		1				8		
Chester	144	9	Corvel	Lemuel		1		1		3			1				6		
Chester	144	10	Hollon	William Doct			1						1				2		
Chester	144	11	Shepard	Mather			1	1		1		2					5		
Chester	144	12	Bascom	Aaron Revd	1	1	1	1			2	1	1				8		
Chester	144	13	Eminom	Sylvester	1			1					1				3		
Chester	144	14	Shepard	David		1	1	1	1		2	1		1			8		
Chester	144	15	Smith	Daniel 2d	2		1	1		1	1		1	1			8		
Chester	144	16	Kendall	David	2					1	1		1				5		
Chester	144	17	Williston	Consider	2	1						2					5		
Chester	144	18	Seischo	Joseph	1		1						1				3		
Chester	144	19	Forbes	Agnes		2								1			3		
Chester	144	20	Sacket	Washam		2							1				3		
Chester	144	21	Phelps	Seth Lieut	1	3	1			2	1		1				9		
Chester	144	22	Henry	Samuel Lieut	1		1			1	1		1				5		
Chester	144	23	Eldar	John Deac	1		1	1					1				4		
Chester	144	24	Campbell	Matthew	1	1	1			1		1			1		6		
Chester	144	25	Cross	David	2	1		1		2	1		2				9		
Chester	144	26	Hambelton	Nathan Capt		1			1	1			1				6		
Chester	144	27	Slayton	Ebenezer	3	1	2	1		1	1	1	1				11		
Chester	144	28	Ingraham	Jedediah	1		1			1			1				4		
Chester	144	29	Campbell	James	1	2	1		1	2			1	1			9		
Chester	144	30	Toogood	William Capt		2		1						1			4		
Chester	144	31	Willcox	Elisha Capt	1	2		1			1			2			7		
Chester	144	32	Smith	Joab	3			1		1	2		1				8		
Chester	144	33	Smith	Abner Lieut	1	2			1		2	1		3			10		
Chester	144	34	Egelston	Jerusha Wd								1	1	1			3		
Chester	144	35	Arnsworth	Edward	1			1		2			1				5		
Chester	144	36	Drake	Abraham	3	1		1		2			1				8		
Chester	144	37	Wait	Josiah	1				1	1				1			4		
Chester	144	38	Eldar	Thomas	2	1	1		1			2					7		
Chester	144	39	Eldar	Thomas Junr	1			1					1				3		
Chester	144	40	Smith	William 2d				1		3			1				5		
Chester	145	1	Ayres	Asa	1			1		2	1		1				6		
Chester	145	2	Judd	Selethiel	4			1		1	1		1				8		
Chester	145	3	Taylor	Amos		1			1		1	2		1			6		
Chester	145	4	Taylor	William	2			1					1				4		
Chester	145	5	Collins	William	1	1	1	1		2			1	1			8		
Chester	145	6	Taylor	Edward	3			1		2			1				7		
Chester	145	7	Prentice	Asahel	1			1				1	1				4		
Chester	145	8	Prentice	Joseph	1			1		2		1					5		
Chester	145	9	Faning	Elisha	1	2		1		2	1	1	1				9		
Chester	145	10	Stephens	John	1		2		1	1			1	1			7		
Chester	145	11	Fellows	Jacob					1		1			1			3		
Chester	145	12	Beamiss	Sylvester	1	1	2	1		3	1		1				10		
Chester	145	13	Beamiss	Nathaniel	3			1					1				5		
Chester	145	14	Miller	Ephraim Lieut			1		1		1			1			4		
Chester	145	15	Miller	Samuel	1			1		1			1				4		
Chester	145	16	Miller	Ephraim Junr	1			1					1				3		
Chester	145	17	Holton	William	5			1					1				7		

35

| TOWN | PG# | LN# | HEADS OF HOUSEHOLD | | FREE WHITE MALES | | | | | FREE WHITE FEMALES | | | | | TOTAL ALL OTHER | TOTAL SLAVES | TOTALS | DISTRICT/ TOWNSHIP | NOTES |
			LAST NAME	FIRST NAME	under 10	10 to 16	16 to 26	26 to 45	45 and over	under 10	10 to 16	16 to 26	26 to 45	45 and over					
Chester	145	18	Ladd	John	3	1		1		2	2		1				10		
Chester	145	19	White	Elijah			1			1		1		1			4		
Chester	145	20	Collins	Calvin	4	1		1				1					7		
Chester	145	21	Fleming	James	1			1			1	1					4		
Chester	145	22	Bush	Enoch Lieut	1			1		2	1		1				6		
Chester	145	23	Leonard	Josiah	2				1			1		1			5		
Chester	145	24	Henry	Jonas		1	2		1	2	2	1		1			10		
Chester	145	25	Henry	James	1		1					1					3		
Chester	145	26	Shepard	Charles	2			1		1	1		1		1		7		
Chester	145	27	Fay	Sarah Wd	2	1	1				1		1	2			8		
Chester	145	28	Dewey	John	2			1		1			1				5		
Chester	145	29	Vanderburgh	John											1		1		
Chester	145	30	Bush	Oliver		1		1		1			1				4		
Chester	145	31	Dewey	Stephen	2			1		2			1				6		
Chester	145	32	Barker	Abijah	1	1		1	1	1		2		1			8		
Chester	145	33	Sanderson	Silvanus Lt	2	2	1		1	2			2				10		
Chester	145	34	Bacon	Timothy		1			1	1	2		1				6		
Chester	145	35	Alexander	Nathaniel Capt	1	1			1	1	2	2		1			9		
Chester	145	36	Walton	Andrew			2		1	1				1			5		
Chester	145	37	Johnson	Benjamin			1	1						1			3		
Chester	145	38	Noble	Warham			1						1				2		
Chester	145	39	Clark	Orrin	2			1					1				4		
Chester	145	40	Skinner	Augustus	2	1		1		2			1				7		
Chester	145	41	Squire	Ezekiel				1					1				2		
Chester	146	1	Squire	Ezekiel Junr	3		1	1					1				6		
Chester	146	2	Wood	James	1			1		1	2	1					6		
Chester	146	3	Tanner	Clark	1	1		1		4			1				8		
Chester	146	4	Riley	Julias	1	3	1		1	1		2		1			10		
Chester	146	5	Smith	Robert				1						1			2		
Chester	146	6	Smith	Jesse		1		1		3			1				6		
Chester	146	7	Church	Richard	3			1		3			1				8		
Chester	146	8	Eastman	Benjamin		1	1	1				1	1				5		
Chester	146	9	Pease	James	1			1		1		1					4		
Chester	146	10	Day	Abraham	2			1		1		1					5		
Chester	146	11	day	Irena Wd		1	1	1					1				4		
Chester	146	12	Wharfield	Reuben	3	2		1		2		1	1				10		
Chester	146	13	Pomeroy	Joseph	4	2		1		1	1		1				10		
Chester	146	14	Belding	Othniel	1	1		1		2	1	1	1				8		
Chester	146	15	Belding	Amos	1		1					1					3		
Chester	146	16	Taylor	John	1			1		1			1				4		
Chester	146	17	Fobes	Nathan	3	2	1	1		1	1		1				10		
Chester	146	18	Whitt	Abner	3	2	1	1		1	1		1				10		
Chester	146	19	Claps	Eliakim Ens	2			1		2	1		1		1		8		
Chester	146	20	French	Samuel				1		1				1			3		
Chester	146	21	French	Asahel			1					1					2		
Chester	146	22	Cox	James				1						1			2		
Chester	146	23	Cox	Polly Carpus	2			1		2			1				6		
Chester	146	24	French	Ozias Capt	1	1	1	1		3	1		1				9		
Chester	146	25	Pomeroy	Luther Capt	1			1		3	3		1				9		
Chester	146	26	Freeman	Brewster	3			1		1	1		1				7		
Chester	146	27	Freeman	Silas						1		1			1		3		
Chester	146	28	Freeman	Silas Junr	1			1		4			1				7		
Chester	146	29	Elliss	Noah		1		1					1	1			4		
Chester	146	30	Slayton	Asa Lieut		2		1	1		2			1			7		
Chester	146	31	Miner	Rufus	1			1		3			1				6		
Chester	146	32	Stephenson	Eli			1			1			1				3		
Chester	146	33	Elliss	Samuel		1	1	1					1				4		
Chester	146	34	Lunnon	William				1					1				2		
Chester	146	35	Hiscock	Noah	2			1		2			1				6		
Chester	146	36	Bigalow	James		1		1		3	2		1				8		
Chester	146	37	Grayham	David			2			1		1					4		
Chester	146	38	Bush	Gerthom		1		1					1				3		
Chester	147	1	Rust	Joseph Ashley		1				1	1	1					4		
Chester	147	2	Bigalow	Daniel	1			1		2		1	1				6		
Chester	147	3	Sandford	Daniel	3			1		2			1				7		
Chester	147	4	Wood	Nathan	1		1		1			1		1			5		
Chester	147	5	Cady	Asa Lieut.		1	1		1	1	1	1					6		
Chester	147	6	Webber	Jonatha H.		1						2		1			5		
Chester	147	7	Wait	Jonathan	3		1	1			2	2		1			10		
Chester	147	8	Blackman	Elijah Maj	1		2		1		1			1			6		
Chester	147	9	Searles	Zenas	1	2	1	1		3			2				10		
Chester	147	10	Sizer	William Capt	1	2	2	1	1		2	1	1	1			12		
Chester	147	11	Sizer	William Ens			1			1		1		1			4		
Chester	147	12	Sizer	John	1		1						1				3		
Chester	147	13	Plum	Charles	1	1			2		1			1			6		
Chester	147	14	Plum	Comfort	1		1						1				3		
Chester	147	15	Lee	Enoch	2		2	1		1	2		1				9		
Chester	147	16	Miller	Jonathan		1			1		1	1		1			5		
Chester	147	17	Miller	Jonathan Junr	1			1									3		

TOWN	PG#	LN#	LAST NAME	FIRST NAME	under 10	10 to 16	16 to 26	26 to 45	45 and over	under 10	10 to 16	16 to 26	26 to 45	45 and over	TOTAL ALL OTHER	TOTAL SLAVES	TOTALS	DISTRICT/TOWNSHIP	NOTES
					FREE WHITE MALES					FREE WHITE FEMALES									
Chester	147	18	Gillmon	William	2	3	1	1		2			1				10		
Chester	147	19	Parsons	Gideon		1		1		1	1	1			1		6		
Chester	147	20	Parsons	Thadeus				1		1		1					3		
Chester	147	21	Clark	John Scott	2			1		1	1		1				6		
Chester	147	22	Chase	Christopher	3			1		1			1				6		
Chester	147	23	Smith	John	2	1	1		1	2	1		1				9		
Chester	147	24	Carlisle	John			1	1		1	1	1		1			6		
Chester	147	25	Smith	William	2	1		1			1	2	1				8		
Chester	147	26	Williams	John	2			1		2			1	1			7		
Chester	147	27	Lyman	Stephen Junr			1						1				2		
Chester	147	28	Lyman	Crispus	3		1						1				5		
Chester	147	29	Lyman	Stephen Deacn		1	2		1			1		1			6		
Chester	147	30	Lyman	Timothy		1	1		1	1	1		1				6		
Chester	147	31	Mann	Nathan				1		2			1	1			5		
Chester	147	32	Goodwill	Nathaniel	2		1	1		2		2					8		
Chester	147	33	Bell	James	1	1	1	1		2	1	1					8		
Chester	147	34	Pomeroy	Amasa	1	1		1		1		3	1				8		
Chester	147	35	Abbot	Lois Wd		2	1			3	1	1	1	1			10		
Chester	147	36	Parmenter	Deacn John N.		2	1		1			2		1			7		
Chester	147	37	Abbot	Ebenezer	2		1		1	1	3	1	1				10		
Chester	148	1	Abbot	Joseph			1		1	1	2		1				6		
Chester	148	2	Abbot	Abial	2	1	1		1	2	2		1				10		
Chester	148	3	Bell	Aaron			2		1					1			4		
Chester	148	4	Ingall	Zadoc	2	1	1	1		1	1		1				8		
Chester	148	5	Bell	William	1		1		1	1		1		1			6		
Chester	148	6	Bell	Justus			1			3	1		1				6		
Chester	148	7	Tinker	Silas	1	3	1		1			3		1			10		
Chester	148	8	Tinker	Rufus	3	2		1			1		1				8		
Chester	148	9	Brass	Garret	3			1					1				6		
Chester	148	10	Wright	Joshua	1	1		1	1	2			1				8		
Chester	148	11	Gamwell	John	2	2	2		1	1	1	1		1			11		
Chester	148	12	Johnson	Jesse Deacn		1		1		1	2		1				6		
Chester	148	13	Johnson	Isaac	1			1				1					3		
Chester	148	14	Bates	Reuben	3			1		1		1	1				7		
Chester	148	15	Stone	William	1		1	1			1		1				5		
Chester	148	16	Rust	Justin	2			1		1	1		1				6		
Chester	148	17	Smith	John 2d			1			1			1				3		
Chester	148	18	Kelso	Lucretia		1							1				2		
Chester	148	19	Winchel	Grove	1		1	1		1		1		1			6		
Chester	148	20	Smith	Daniel		2	1			3	1	1	1				9		
Chester	148	21	Gibson	Roger	2			1		1	1		1				6		
Chester	148	22	Geer	Lylsby	4		1			1		1					7		
Chester	148	23	Tinker	Sylvester		1						1					2		
Chester	148	24	Falley	Richard	1	1		1		2			1				6		
Chester	148	25	Tanner	Silas	1		1					1					3		
Chester	148	26	Culver	Charles	1	1	2		1	2			1				8		
Chester	148	27	Gillmore	James	1	3	1		1	2		1	1				10		
Chester	148	28	Ensign	Seamour		1											1		
Chester	148	29	Soule	Elizabeth	2						1	1	1				5		
Chester	148	30	Cook	Perley		1		1		3	2						7		
Chester	148	31	Scott	William	1	1		1		1	1		1				6		
Chester	148	32	Scott	James	1	1		1		1			1				5		
Chester	148	33	Seaward	Joel					1					1			2		
Chester	149	1	Seaward	Nathan	1			1	1	3	1		1				8		
Chester	149	2	Seaward	Joel Junr	1		2	1		2		1	1				8		
Chester	149	3	Elsworth	Jonathan			1			1	1	1					4		
Chester	149	4	Stiles	Samuel Lieut	4	1		1		1	2		1				10		
Chester	149	5	Stiles	Ashbel					1	1	1		1				4		
Chester	149	6	Jackson	John	1			1		1			2				5		
Chester	149	7	Henry	John		1						2					3		
Chester	149	8	Moor	Samuel	1		1		1	2	1		2				8		
Chester	149	9	Kelso	John Capt		1		1			1	1	1				5		
Chester	149	10	Kelso	James		1						1					2		
Chester	149	11	Henry	Andrew	1	1	1		1	2	1	1					8		
Chester	149	12	Bidlake	Jonathan	1		1					1					3		
Chester	149	13	Bascom	James	4	1		1			1		1				8		
Chester	149	14	Wilcox	James	1						1		1				3		
Chester	149	15	Plum	Jacob		1				3	1						5		
Chester	149	16	Carpenter	Benjamin	3			1		1			1				6		
Chester	149	17	Bell	Samuel	1	1	1		1	1	2		2				9		
Chester	149	18	Hamilton	John Lieut	3	1	1			2	1	1	1				10		
Chester	149	19	Quigley	Hugh	3	1		1		3		1	1				10		
Chester	149	20	Gamwell	Samuel					1					1			2		
Chester	149	21	Mehanna	John	2		1			1			1				5		
Chester	149	22	Hotchkis	Jotham	2		1			3		2	1				9		
Chester	149	23	Egelston	Oliver	3		1			1			1				6		
Chester	149	24	Collins	Nathaniel	2	1		1		3			1				8		
Chester	149	25	Combs	Nathaniel	1			1		2			1				5		
Chester	149	26	Herrin	Samuel	1	1		1		2	2	1		1			9		

TOWN	PG#	LN#	LAST NAME	FIRST NAME	FREE WHITE MALES					FREE WHITE FEMALES					TOTAL ALL OTHER	TOTAL SLAVES	TOTALS	DISTRICT/ TOWNSHIP	NOTES
					under 10	10 to 16	16 to 26	26 to 45	45 and over	under 10	10 to 16	16 to 26	26 to 45	45 and over					
Chester	149	27	Herrin	Solomon				1		2		1					4		
Chester	149	28	Hancock	Lewis	1			1		3	3		1				9		
Chester	149	29	Sanderson	Elnathan			1							1			2		
Chester	149	30	Otis	Samuel	1			1		1		1					4		
Chester	149	31	Procter	Josiah	3				1				1	1			6		
Chester	149	32	Griffen	Silas	4			1		1			1				7		
Chester	150	1	Wright	Bazaleel	1	2	1	1		2			1				8		
Chester	150	2	Carter	John	1	1		1		1	1		1				6		
Chester	150	3	Melvin	James			2		1		1			1			5		
Chester	150	4	Moor	Hiram	2	2			1	3	1		1				10		
Chester	150	5	Culver	Asahel		1	1					1	1				4		
Chester	150	6	White	William	2			1		1			1		1		6		
Chester	150	7	Wait	Seth	1		1			2		1					5		
Chester	150	8	Wright	Lewis	1			1		3	2		2	2			11		
Chester	150	9	Carlisle	William	1			1		3			1				6		
Chester	150	10	Cooley	Timothy	2	1		1		2	2		1				9		
Chester	150	11	Cooley	Seneca			1			1		1					3		
Chester	150	12	Clark	Simon		1		1				1					3		

TOWN	PG#	LN#	LAST NAME	FIRST NAME	FREE WHITE MALES					FREE WHITE FEMALES					TOTAL ALL OTHER	TOTAL SLAVES	TOTALS	DISTRICT/ TOWNSHIP	NOTES
					under 10	10 to 16	16 to 26	26 to 45	45 and over	under 10	10 to 16	16 to 26	26 to 45	45 and over					
Chesterfield	19	1	Shaw	Asa		1			1			1		1			4		
Chesterfield	19	2	Duncan	William	1	1	1		1	3	2			1			10		
Chesterfield	19	3	Bates	Abner					1			2		1			4		
Chesterfield	19	4	Bates	Abner Jun	2			1		1		1					5		
Chesterfield	19	5	Bates	John			1			1		1					3		
Chesterfield	19	6	Beswick	Charles				1			1	1	1				4		
Chesterfield	19	7	Beswick	Charles Jr	2			1		3		1					7		
Chesterfield	19	8	Cogswell	Hezekiah	2			1		2		1					6		
Chesterfield	19	9	Cogswell	Ezra				1			2		1				4		
Chesterfield	19	10	Baker	Elisha	1			1		2	1		1				6		
Chesterfield	19	11	Billings	Levett				1		1	1	1		1			5		
Chesterfield	19	12	Britt	Ebenz			1			1			1				3		
Chesterfield	19	13	King	Isaac			1					1	1				3		
Chesterfield	19	14	Knight	Joshua		1	1		1		2	1	1				7		
Chesterfield	19	15	Rhoades	Joseph	1	1	1	2	1	1	2	1	1				11		
Chesterfield	19	16	Rhoades	Samuel		1	1		1		1		1				5		
Chesterfield	19	17	Wilder	Jabez		1	1		1		2			1			6		
Chesterfield	19	18	Edwards	Oliver	2		1	1		2	2		1				9		
Chesterfield	19	19	Cushing	Abel	1	1		1		3			1				7		
Chesterfield	20	1	Warner	Joel	4	1		1	1		1		1				9		
Chesterfield	20	2	Rice	Alvin		1	1			1		1					4		
Chesterfield	20	3	Clap	Amasa	1	2	2		1		1		2				9		
Chesterfield	20	4	Clap	Paul			1			2	1	1					5		
Chesterfield	20	5	Ewell	John		2	1	1		1	1	1					7		
Chesterfield	20	6	Ewell	Malachi			1			1		1					3		
Chesterfield	20	7	Wilder	Abel	1	1	1	1			1	1					6		
Chesterfield	20	8	Sylvester	Luke				2					2				4		
Chesterfield	20	9	Bates	Benjamin		1		1			1						4		
Chesterfield	20	10	Bates	Benjamin Jr	2			1		1		1					5		
Chesterfield	20	11	Baker	Seth	2			1		1		1					5		
Chesterfield	20	12	Baker	Thaddeus		1		1		2			1				5		
Chesterfield	20	13	Baker	Stephen				1				1	1				3		
Chesterfield	20	14	Baker	Thomas			1					1					2		
Chesterfield	20	15	Baker	Lemuel			1					1					2		
Chesterfield	20	16	Bates	Caleb	1	1		1		2	2		1				8		
Chesterfield	20	17	White	Consider			1	1		4	1	1	1				9		
Chesterfield	20	18	Bailey	Joseph S.			1					1					2		
Chesterfield	20	19	Wills	Josiah	2			1		1	1						5		
Chesterfield	20	20	Merrick	Joseph			1	1		2	1	1	1				7		
Chesterfield	20	21	Sylvester	George H	1		1	1		1			1				5		
Chesterfield	20	22	Parsons	Benja		1		1		1			1				4		
Chesterfield	20	23	Starkweather	Robert Jr	1	1	1	1		2			1				7		
Chesterfield	20	24	Shaddock	Samuel		1	1		1		1			1			5		
Chesterfield	20	25	Stephenson	John				1					1				2		
Chesterfield	20	26	Stephenson	John Jun	2	1		1		3	1		1				9		
Chesterfield	20	27	Beldon	Jonathan		1		1		3	1			1			7		
Chesterfield	20	28	Robinson	Zebulon			2	1		1	1		1				6		
Chesterfield	20	29	Vining	Ebenezer	2	1	1			3	1	1	1				10		
Chesterfield	20	30	Lawrence	Iasel	1			1		1			1				4		
Chesterfield	20	31	Robbins	Jesse											3		3		
Chesterfield	20	32	Geer	Joseph	2	1	1	1			1	1	1				8		
Chesterfield	20	33	Drake	James	2			1			2						5		
Chesterfield	20	34	Fiske	Josiah			1		1	1	1		1				5		
Chesterfield	20	35	Bonney	Luke		3	1		1	1		1	1				8		
Chesterfield	21	1	Metcalf	Phineas	1			1		3		1					6		
Chesterfield	21	2	Drake	Noah	2		1	1		3	2	1	1	1			12		
Chesterfield	21	3	Phelps	Spencer		1	1		1	1		1	1				6		
Chesterfield	21	4	Bissell	Noah		1	2		1	3	2	1					10		
Chesterfield	21	5	Howard	Mark	1			1		2	2		1				7		
Chesterfield	21	6	Allen	Timothy				1						1			2		
Chesterfield	21	7	Buck	Mathew				1						1			2		
Chesterfield	21	8	Cleaveland	Samuel	3			1		2	2		1				9		
Chesterfield	21	9	Joslyn	Abraham	1		2		1	2	2		1				9		
Chesterfield	21	10	Bryant	Nathaniel			1		1			1		2			5		
Chesterfield	21	11	Buck	Daniel	4	3		1		2	1	1	1				13		
Chesterfield	21	12	Sylvester	Nathaniel		1	3		1	2	2						9		
Chesterfield	21	13	Robinson	Zebulon	2			1		2		1	1				7		
Chesterfield	21	14	Mills	Thomas				1				1					2		
Chesterfield	21	15	Cowing	John	1	2		1		5			1	1			11		
Chesterfield	21	16	Cowing	Reuben	3			1		1	1		1				7		
Chesterfield	21	17	Thayer	Joel	1	1	1					1	1				5		
Chesterfield	21	18	Meech	Dennis	2	1		1		1	2		1		1		9		
Chesterfield	21	19	Sylvester	Nehemiah	1		2		1	2	2	2		1			11		
Chesterfield	21	20	Sylvester	Gershom	1	1		1		1			1				5		
Chesterfield	21	21	Phinney	Ephraim	1				1		2	1		1			6		
Chesterfield	21	22	Patch	Thomas	3				1	3			1				8		
Chesterfield	21	23	Patch	Ephraim					1			2		1			4		
Chesterfield	21	24	Cole	Amariah		1	3	1	1	3	2	1	1				13		
Chesterfield	21	25	Cole	Consider	2	2		1		1							8		

TOWN	PG#	LN#	HEADS OF HOUSEHOLD LAST NAME	FIRST NAME	FREE WHITE MALES under 10	10 to 16	16 to 26	26 to 45	45 and over	FREE WHITE FEMALES under 10	10 to 16	16 to 26	26 to 45	45 and over	TOTAL ALL OTHER	TOTAL SLAVES	TOTALS	DISTRICT/TOWNSHIP	NOTES
Chesterfield	21	26	Cole	Barnabas	3	2		1		3		2	1				12		
Chesterfield	21	27	Sampson	Sylvanus	1			1		1	1		1				5		
Chesterfield	21	28	Bartlett	Jabez	2		1	1		2		1	1				8		
Chesterfield	21	29	Hayden	John	2	1	2		1			2	1				9		
Chesterfield	21	30	Litchfield	Ensign	1		1					1					3		
Chesterfield	21	31	Green	Eleanor	1						1	1	1				4		
Chesterfield	21	32	Pierce	Ezekiel			1			1			1				3		
Chesterfield	21	33	Thayer	Stephen	1			1		1		1	1				5		
Chesterfield	21	34	Butts	Richard				1		3			1	1			6		
Chesterfield	21	35	Stone	John 2d	1	2	1		1	2		2	1				10		
Chesterfield	21	36	Cowing	Gatheliu			1		1		1	1		1			5		
Chesterfield	21	37	Bryant	Patrick	5			1		1			1				8		
Chesterfield	22	1	Whiton	Abijah		1		1		3	1	2	1				9		
Chesterfield	22	2	Keen	William	2	1		1		2	2		1				9		
Chesterfield	22	3	Cowing	David	1			1		3			1				6		
Chesterfield	22	4	Cowing	Luther	3			1				1					5		
Chesterfield	22	5	Lee	Charles	4			1					1				6		
Chesterfield	22	6	Culver	Ephraim	2			1					1				4		
Chesterfield	22	7	Goodenough	John	1	1	2		1	1	1	2	1				10		
Chesterfield	22	8	Brown	Oliver	2	1		1			1	1	1				7		
Chesterfield	22	9	Livermore	Solomon			1			4		1	1	1			8		
Chesterfield	22	10	Bisbee	Gideon	2	2		1		1	1	2	1				10		
Chesterfield	22	11	Buck	Isaac		2	1		1	2	1	1	1				9		
Chesterfield	22	12	Reed	Samuel	2	1	1	1		2		1	1				9		
Chesterfield	22	13	Macomber	David	4	2	2		1		2		1				12		
Chesterfield	22	14	Littlefield	Daniel			1		1					1			3		
Chesterfield	22	15	Packard	Jared	1		1			2		1					5		
Chesterfield	22	16	Russell	Joanna		1				1	1	1					5		
Chesterfield	22	17	Stone	John	1	1		1		2			1				6		
Chesterfield	22	18	Phillips	Ezra		1	1		1		2		1	1			7		
Chesterfield	22	19	Ballard	James				1									1		
Chesterfield	22	20	Bonney	Walter	2	1	1	1		2	1		1				9		
Chesterfield	22	21	Damon	James	2			1		2	3		1				9		
Chesterfield	22	22	Peirce	James			1	1					1	1			4		
Chesterfield	22	23	Davis	William	1	1		1		3	2		1				9		
Chesterfield	22	24	Davis	Samuel	1			1					1				3		
Chesterfield	22	25	Coleman	Nathaniel	3	1	2	1		1	2		1				11		
Chesterfield	22	26	Townsend	Moses	1	2		1		1	1	1	1				8		
Chesterfield	22	27	Hamilton	Robert Jr	2	1		1		3			1				8		
Chesterfield	22	28	Torey	Joseph	1	2	2	1		3	1	1	1				12		
Chesterfield	22	29	Damon	David			1	1		1			1				4		
Chesterfield	22	30	Starkweather	Robert				1						1			2		
Chesterfield	22	31	Spring	John	1	1		1		1	2	5	1				12		
Chesterfield	22	32	Torrey	Stephen			1			1				1			3		
Chesterfield	22	33	Taylor	Seth Junr	2		1	1		1			1				6		
Chesterfield	22	34	Taylor	Seth		1		1			1	1	1				5		
Chesterfield	22	35	Kingsley	Asahel	1			1		1	1	1					5		
Chesterfield	22	36	Kingsley	Ebenezer	3			1		2			1				7		
Chesterfield	22	37	Littlefield	Jacob		2					2	1	1				7		
Chesterfield	22	38	Keith	William				1						1			2		
Chesterfield	22	39	Carr	Martin	2		1	1		3	1		1				9		
Chesterfield	23	1	Banister	William	3	2	1	1		1	1	1	1				11		
Chesterfield	23	2	Bryant	Eli	2	1		1		1			1				6		
Chesterfield	23	3	Bryant	Asahel	1			1		1			1				4		
Chesterfield	23	4	Kingsley	Moses		1			1		1	3		1			7		
Chesterfield	23	5	Warner	Elijah	2	2			1	2		3		1			11		
Chesterfield	23	6	Rogers	Thomas		1		1						2			4		
Chesterfield	23	7	King	Eleazer	1			1		1		1					4		
Chesterfield	23	8	Bonney	Benjamin		1	1		1	1		1	1	1			7		
Chesterfield	23	9	Watson	Isaiah	1	1	1				1	1					5		
Chesterfield	23	10	Anderson	David	1			1		2	1		1				6		
Chesterfield	23	11	Anderson	Jonathan				1					1				2		
Chesterfield	23	12	Nichols	Joseph		1		1						2			4		
Chesterfield	23	13	White	Noah	2	3		1		2	1		1				10		
Chesterfield	23	14	Kingsley	Moses Jun	2			1		1			1				5		
Chesterfield	23	15	Strong	Peter	1	1	2		1			2		1			8		
Chesterfield	23	16	Witherell	John	3	1		1		2	1		2				10		
Chesterfield	23	17	Bonney	David	2			1		2			1				6		
Chesterfield	23	18	Vinton	Abiather	4	3		1		1			1				10		
Chesterfield	23	19	Shaw	Zachariah				1									1		
Chesterfield	23	20	Dunlap	George		1		1			1		1				4		
Chesterfield	23	21	Torrey	David	1	2			1	1	1		1				7		
Chesterfield	23	22	Witherell	Elisha Jr	1			1				1					4		
Chesterfield	23	23	Witherell	Elihu			2		1			3		1			7		
Chesterfield	23	24	Studley	David		2			1				1				5		
Chesterfield	23	25	Jewell	Marvel	2	1		1		2			1				7		
Chesterfield	23	26	Perry	Josiah		2			1		1		1	1			6		
Chesterfield	23	27	Damon	Ichabod					1				2	1			4		
Chesterfield	23	28	Damon	Ichabod Jr	1		2	1		1			1				6		

TOWN	PG#	LN#	LAST NAME	FIRST NAME	FREE WHITE MALES					FREE WHITE FEMALES					TOTAL ALL OTHER	TOTAL SLAVES	TOTALS	DISTRICT/ TOWNSHIP	NOTES
					under 10	10 to 16	16 to 26	26 to 45	45 and over	under 10	10 to 16	16 to 26	26 to 45	45 and over					
Chesterfield	23	29	Pynchon	Elizabeth								1	2	1			4		
Chesterfield	23	30	Thomas	Samuel	2				1	1	1	1	1	1			8		
Chesterfield	23	31	Stephens	John				1						1			2		
Chesterfield	23	32	Stephens	John Jr	2	1		1		3	1		1				9		
Chesterfield	23	33	Pynchon	John		1	1		1					1			4		
Chesterfield	23	34	Bates	Elibeus	1			1		1			1				4		
Chesterfield	23	35	Stevenson	Nathl				1		2			1				4		
Chesterfield	23	36	Damon	Calid 2d	1	1		1		2		1	1				7		
Chesterfield	23	37	Peirce	Penelope							1	1					2		
Chesterfield	24	1	Watkins	Willard	3			1					1				5		
Chesterfield	24	2	Curtis	Beriah	2	1			1	3				1			8		
Chesterfield	24	3	James	Thomas	1			1		3	1			1			7		
Chesterfield	24	4	House	John		1	1		1		1	2		1			7		
Chesterfield	24	5	House	John Jun			1					1					2		
Chesterfield	24	6	Ludden	Bezer	2			1		2			1	1			7		
Chesterfield	24	7	Utley	Samuel	3	2		1		1		1	1				9		
Chesterfield	24	8	Burnell	John Jr	2	2	2	1		1	1	1	1				11		
Chesterfield	24	9	Russell	John				1		1	2			1			5		
Chesterfield	24	10	Turner	Asa	1		1			1		1					4		
Chesterfield	24	11	Russell	Solomon	3			1		2	1		1	1			9		
Chesterfield	24	12	Kittridge	John	4		1	1		1			1				8		
Chesterfield	24	13	Ludden	Elisha			1			1		1					3		
Chesterfield	24	14	Burnell	Joseph Jr	3	2		1	1	2		1	1				11		
Chesterfield	24	15	Polly	Thomas	1			1					1	3			6		
Chesterfield	24	16	Bates	Nehemiah			2		1					1			4		
Chesterfield	24	17	Pearl	James	1			1		1			1				4		
Chesterfield	24	18	Healy	Ebenezer		2	2	1		1			1		1		8		
Chesterfield	24	19	Darling	Simeon	1	1		1		3	1		1				8		
Chesterfield	24	20	Sheldon	Caleb	2			1		1	1		1				6		
Chesterfield	24	21	Wilder	Lot	3		1	1		2	2		1				10		
Chesterfield	24	22	Wilder	Zachariah	1	3	2	1		3			1				11		
Chesterfield	24	23	Stulson	Abiel			1		1		1	1	1				5		
Chesterfield	24	24	Stebbins	Levi	1	1	1	1					1				5		
Chesterfield	24	25	Parsons	Elias	3	1	1	1				2	1				9		
Chesterfield	24	26	Ingram	Timothy	3			1				2	1				7		
Chesterfield	24	27	Haden	Noah			1	1			2		1				5		
Chesterfield	24	28	Damon	Isaiah	1	2		1					1	1			6		
Chesterfield	24	29	Damon	Isaac	2	2	3	1			1	1	1				11		
Chesterfield	24	30	Damon	Caleb				2			2			2			6		
Chesterfield	24	31	Damon	Caleb 3d			1			1		1					3		
Chesterfield	24	32	Peirce	Benjamin			1	1		3			1				6		
Chesterfield	24	33	Peirce	Benja Jun	2		1					1					4		
Chesterfield	24	34	Anderson	Alanson				1		3			1				5		
Chesterfield	24	35	Sylvester	Seth			2	1				2		2			7		
Chesterfield	24	36	Rogers	Joshua			1	1			2	2	1				7		
Chesterfield	24	37	Rogers	James				1									1		
Chesterfield	24	38	Curtis	Luther		1	1	1		1	1	2		1			8		
Chesterfield	25	1	Hamilton	Robert		1		1	1	2	1	1	1	1			9		
Chesterfield	25	2	King	Silas			1		1	2		1		1			6		
Chesterfield	25	3	Kidd	Charles		1	2	1		1		3		1			9		
Chesterfield	25	4	Thompson	Thomas				1					1				2		

TOWN	PG#	LN#	LAST NAME	FIRST NAME	M under 10	M 10 to 16	M 16 to 26	M 26 to 45	M 45 and over	F under 10	F 10 to 16	F 16 to 26	F 26 to 45	F 45 and over	TOTAL ALL OTHER	TOTAL SLAVES	TOTALS	DISTRICT/ TOWNSHIP	NOTES
Colrain	184	1	Clark	John Jr	2		1	1					1				5		
Colrain	184	2	Clark	Ichabod	2			1		2			1				6		
Colrain	184	3	Call	John				1						3			4		
Colrain	184	4	Call	John Jr	4	2				1	2		1				11		
Colrain	184	5	Clark	Daniel	2	2		2	1		1	2	1	1			12		
Colrain	184	6	Canady	John	1	1		1		3	1		1				8		
Colrain	184	7	Chandler	Clark	1		1	1		3		2	1				9		
Colrain	184	8	Cushing	S Asaph	1			1		2			1				5		
Colrain	184	9	Clark	Noah	1	1	1		1	1	1	1	1	1			9		
Colrain	184	10	Clark	William		2	1	1				1	1	1			7		
Colrain	184	11	Carlton	Benjamin		2			1	3	1		1				8		
Colrain	184	12	Caldwell	William	2	1	3	1					1				8		
Colrain	184	13	Cary	Aaron		1	1		1	1	1	1		1			7		
Colrain	184	14	Clark	Dolleway				2									2		
Colrain	184	15	Coolidge	Josiah		2	1		1	1	1		1	1			8		
Colrain	184	16	Clark	David	2			1					1				4		
Colrain	184	17	Crandal	Paul		2		1				2		1			6		
Colrain	184	18	Culbeth	Benoni	2	1			1	2			1				7		
Colrain	185	1	Champlin	William	3		2	1		2	2	5	1		1		17		
Colrain	185	2	Carryl	Nathanael				1						2			3		
Colrain	185	3	Dalrymple	David Jun	2	1		1		2			1				7		
Colrain	185	4	Donelon	Lydia	1					2			1				4		
Colrain	185	5	Dean	Christopher	2	2	1		1	1		2	1				10		
Colrain	185	6	Denison	Nathan		1	2	1		2			1				8		
Colrain	185	7	Donelson	Matthew	2		2	3			2	1	1				11		
Colrain	185	8	Dalrymple	Hark	2		1	1		1		1	1	1			8		
Colrain	185	9	Davenport	Edward	1	1	2		1		1	1		1			8		
Colrain	185	10	Dalrymple	David	1		2	2	1	3		1	1	1			12		
Colrain	185	11	Donelson	Moses			2	1		1		2	1	1			8		
Colrain	185	12	Donelson	Reuben	4	1		1				1	1				8		
Colrain	185	13	Dalrymple	Winslow			1			3			1				5		
Colrain	185	14	Davenport	Paul	4	1		1		1	1		1				9		
Colrain	185	15	Dunham	Abiel	1	1		1		2	1		1				7		
Colrain	185	16	Davis	John				1						1			2		
Colrain	185	17	Dalrymple	Edward	4			1		1	1		1				8		
Colrain	185	18	Eddy	Ephraim	1	2		1			1		1				6		
Colrain	185	19	Eddy	Samuel		1		1		1	1	1					5		
Colrain	185	20	Eddy	Leonard	2			1		1			1				5		
Colrain	185	21	Eddy	Ichabod	1	1	1	1		1	1		1				7		
Colrain	185	22	Eddy	Ebenezar		1		1	1	1	1		1	1			6		
Colrain	185	23	Fulton	James Jun	1		1					1					3		
Colrain	185	24	Fox	Thomas	3			1				2	1				7		
Colrain	185	25	Farley	Benjamin	2	1		1		2	2		1				9		
Colrain	185	26	Fulton	James	3	2		1		1	1	1					9		
Colrain	185	27	Freeman	Rufus	2	1	1		1	3		1	1				10		
Colrain	185	28	Falkner	Joseph Jun	1	1		1		3	2		1				9		
Colrain	185	29	Falkner	William	1	2		1				4	1				9		
Colrain	185	30	Fairbanks	Moses		1		1		3			1	1			7		
Colrain	185	31	Fairbanks	Daniel	2		1	1		1		1	1				7		
Colrain	185	32	Farnsworth	Joseph				1		3			1				5		
Colrain	185	33	Fosket	Samuel	4			1		1			1				7		
Colrain	185	34	Foster	Nathan	2			1		1			1				5		
Colrain	185	35	Falkner	Joseph	1	1			2	2			1	1			8		
Colrain	185	36	Fowler	Thomas	3					1			1				5		
Colrain	185	37	Falkner	William Jun	1		1					1					3		
Colrain	185	38	Gragg	Jacob				1						1			2		
Colrain	186	1	Gragg	Robert	2	2	1	2	1	2	2		1				13		
Colrain	186	2	Gould	Henry	2		2		1	1	3			1			10		
Colrain	186	3	Gray	Jemima	1		2						2	1			6		
Colrain	186	4	Gay	Jonathan	1			1		4	1		1				8		
Colrain	186	5	Goodale	Joel	2	2		1		2	1		1				9		
Colrain	186	6	Handy	Charles	2	1	1	1		3	1		2	1			12		
Colrain	186	7	Houghton	Nathl		2	2	1		3			1				9		
Colrain	186	8	Holland	Oliver			1		1	3	1	2	1				9		
Colrain	186	9	Harroun	John	4		1	1		1			2				9		
Colrain	186	10	Haynes	Vinall	1		1		1		1	1		1			6		
Colrain	186	11	Harroun	David	3	1		1			1	2		1			9		
Colrain	186	12	Hulburt	James	2			1	1	2		1	1	1			9		
Colrain	186	13	Hulburt	John Jun	2			1		1			1				5		
Colrain	186	14	Houghton	Reuben		1		1	1	1		1	1	1			7		
Colrain	186	15	Holbrook	Seth	1	1	2		1	1	1		1				8		
Colrain	186	16	Harrington	Timothy		1	1		1	4	1	2	1				11		
Colrain	186	17	Holms	William	1	1		1		2	1		1				7		
Colrain	186	18	Holms	John	3	2		1		1		2		1			10		
Colrain	186	19	Hutson	Charles	2		1		1		1		1				6		
Colrain	186	20	Hall	Stephen	2			1		2			1				6		
Colrain	186	21	Jacobs	Elnathan	4	1	3		1	1	1		1				12		
Colrain	186	22	Jones	Israel	1			1					1	1			4		
Colrain	186	23	Joyner	John	1	3				2							8		

TOWN	PG#	LN#	LAST NAME	FIRST NAME	FREE WHITE MALES under 10	10 to 16	16 to 26	26 to 45	45 and over	FREE WHITE FEMALES under 10	10 to 16	16 to 26	26 to 45	45 and over	TOTAL ALL OTHER	TOTAL SLAVES	TOTALS	DISTRICT/ TOWNSHIP	NOTES
Colrain	186	24	Johnson	Isaac	3			1				1					5		
Colrain	186	25	Johnson	Moses	2	1	2		2	1	2	1	1				12		
Colrain	186	26	Johnson	Thomas	2			1		1	1		1				6		
Colrain	186	27	King	Zadock	3	1		1		2	1		1				9		
Colrain	186	28	Littlefield	Edmond	2	1		1	3	3	1		1				12		
Colrain	186	29	Littlefield	Jedediah		1		1		2	1	1	1				7		
Colrain	186	30	Littlefield	Elisha	1			1		1			1				4		
Colrain	186	31	Lane	Amos	1			1		2	1		1				6		
Colrain	186	32	Lamond	John	4			1	1	1	2		1	1			11		
Colrain	186	33	Lindsay	Stephen	2	1		1		1			1				6		
Colrain	186	34	Lyons	David			3		1		1	3		1			9		
Colrain	186	35	Lyons	Terre	3			1		1			1				6		
Colrain	186	36	Lyons	Jesse	2	1	1	1		2	1	1					9		
Colrain	186	37	Linn	John	2	1			1	2		1	1				8		
Colrain	186	38	Lock	B. Joshua	2			1		2			1				6		
Colrain	186	39	Lock	John	2			1		2			1				6		
Colrain	186	40	Leshore	Williard	2			1		1			1				5		
Colrain	187	1	Lake	Gideon	3			1		1	1			1			7		
Colrain	187	2	McGee	Jonathan	1	1	4	1	1	1	1	2	1	3			16		
Colrain	187	3	McCallen	Hugh		1	2		1		3	1	1				9		
Colrain	187	4	McCallen	Robert				1		2			1				4		
Colrain	187	5	McCallen	James	2	1		1		1	1	1					7		
Colrain	187	6	Morgan	Jabez	3			1		1			1				6		
Colrain	187	7	Morison	David	5				1	2	1	1	1		1		13		
Colrain	187	8	McGee	Jonas	3	1		1		1			2				8		
Colrain	187	9	McKowen	Lydia	1	1	1	1			1	1	1	1			8		
Colrain	187	10	Miller	Robert		1	2	2	1	1	1	2					10		
Colrain	187	11	Moseman	Jesse		1		1		2	1		1				6		
Colrain	187	12	Maning	Ephraim	1			1		1			1				4		
Colrain	187	13	McKneel	Robert	1			1					1	1			4		
Colrain	187	14	Meecham	John				1		1	1		1				4		
Colrain	187	15	Merrifield	Robery	1	1	1		1					1			5		
Colrain	187	16	Miller	William	3	1	1	1			1	1		1			9		
Colrain	187	17	McColloch	James	2	1		1		2	3		1				10		
Colrain	187	18	Martin	Enos	1	1	2		2	1		2	2	2	2		15		
Colrain	187	19	Meecham	Rebeckah	1		1			1	1	1		1			6		
Colrain	187	20	Meecham	Kingman	2			1	1	1			2	1			8		
Colrain	187	21	Maynard	William		1		1		1	3	2		1			9		
Colrain	187	22	Maynard	Thaddeus				1		2		1					4		
Colrain	187	23	Martin	Samuel	4			1					1				6		
Colrain	187	24	Morton	David	1	1	1		1		1	1		1			7		
Colrain	187	25	McCloud	Charles	3	1		1		2	1		1				9		
Colrain	187	26	Mixer	Joseph	1			1		3			1				6		
Colrain	187	27	Mixer	Timothy	1	1			1	2	1	2		1			9		
Colrain	187	28	Morton	Zacheus	1		1			1		1					4		
Colrain	187	29	Miller	Martha	2					2		2	1				7		
Colrain	187	30	McCoy	Joseph	2			1		3			1				7		
Colrain	187	31	Marsh	Elisha		2			1	2		1		1			7		
Colrain	187	32	Malester	Benjamin	1					3			1				5		
Colrain	187	33	Muxham	Zebede	1			1					1				4		
Colrain	187	34	Muxham	Abigal						1		1	1				3		
Colrain	187	35	Martin	Timothy	1	2		1		1		1					6		
Colrain	187	36	Newton	Cyprian	2			1		3			1				7		
Colrain	187	37	Newell	Solomon	2	1		1	1	2	1		1				9		
Colrain	188	1	Newhouse	William		1			1				1				3		
Colrain	188	2	Nelson	William		2		1		2	1		1				7		
Colrain	188	3	Otis	John	3			1	1		2		1	1			9		
Colrain	188	4	Otis	Christopher	1			1					1				3		
Colrain	188	5	Owen	Elisha			1	1		4	2		1				9		
Colrain	188	6	Osburn	William	1	1			1		1			1			5		
Colrain	188	7	Pattison	Sarah		1				2			1	1			5		
Colrain	188	8	Puffer	Ezra		1		1		4		1					7		
Colrain	188	9	Pattison	Josiah	1			1		5			1	1			9		
Colrain	188	10	Pierce	Zebulon	3	1	1	1		1	1	1	1				10		
Colrain	188	11	Pierce	Judah	3	1		1		2	1		1				9		
Colrain	188	12	Perril	Abraham	1	1	2		1		2	1		1			9		
Colrain	188	13	Peterson	Jonathan		2			2	1		3		1			9		
Colrain	188	14	Purington	Joseph	2		3		1	2	2	2		1			13		
Colrain	188	15	Perril	John	3	1		1	1		1		1				8		
Colrain	188	16	Purrington	Seth				1		3			2				6		
Colrain	188	17	Purrington	Joshua	2			2	1				1	1			7		
Colrain	188	18	Peck	Abraham	5		1	1		1	1		1	1			11		
Colrain	188	19	Pattison	Adam	1	2		1	1	2	1	3	1	1			13		
Colrain	188	20	Pierce	Samuel	3	1		1		2	1		1				9		
Colrain	188	21	Pierce	Eliphalet		1			1					1			3		
Colrain	188	22	Pierce	Samuel 2d		1	1				1			1			4		
Colrain	188	23	Riddle	Gawn	1	2		1	1	3	1	2	1				12		
Colrain	188	24	Rainger	Moseds			3		1		1	1		2			8		
Colrain	188	25	Ross	Samuel	3		1			1	3						11		

43

Census table — FREE WHITE MALES and FREE WHITE FEMALES age brackets (under 10 / 10 to 16 / 16 to 26 / 26 to 45 / 45 and over)

TOWN	PG#	LN#	LAST NAME	FIRST NAME	M <10	M 10-16	M 16-26	M 26-45	M 45+	F <10	F 10-16	F 16-26	F 26-45	F 45+	TOTAL ALL OTHER	TOTAL SLAVES	TOTALS	DISTRICT/ TOWNSHIP	NOTES
Colrain	188	26	Riddle	Hugh		1	1		1					1			4		
Colrain	188	27	Randal	Jacob	1	2	1	1		2	1		1				9		
Colrain	188	28	Ransom	Job			1	1		1			2				5		
Colrain	188	29	Rogers	Henry	2	2			1	1	1			1			8		
Colrain	188	30	Stewart	William					1			1		1			3		
Colrain	188	31	Stewart	David	2	1		1		3			1				8		
Colrain	188	32	Stewart	Enos	3		1	1		1	1		1		1		9		
Colrain	188	33	Stewart	John	2		1		1			2		1			7		
Colrain	188	34	Shearer	Hornaw	2		1	1		1	2		1				9		
Colrain	188	35	Savage	Mary			1			1				1			3		
Colrain	188	36	Skinner	Aaron	2			1		1			1				5		
Colrain	188	37	Skinner	Asa			1			2		1					4		
Colrain	188	38	Stewart	Hugh	3	1		1	1	1	2		1	1			11		
Colrain	188	39	Smith	David	1	1	3	1		2	2	1	1	1			13		
Colrain	188	40	Smith	Jonathan	3			1		2			1	1			8		
Colrain	189	1	Smith	Rominer	2		2	1		3	1	1	1				11		
Colrain	189	2	Shippy	Israel	2	1		2		2	2		1				10		
Colrain	189	3	Stone	Elias	3	2		1	1	2		1	1	1			12		
Colrain	189	4	Shearer	William	2	1			1			3		1			8		
Colrain	189	5	Shattuck	Abel	2		2	1		1		1	1				8		
Colrain	189	6	Stafford	Studely	2	1	2	1		2			1				9		
Colrain	189	7	Shippy	Peter				1		4			1				6		
Colrain	189	8	Shermon	Nathan	1			1		3	1	1	1				8		
Colrain	189	9	Spur	Samuel		2			1				1				6		
Colrain	189	10	Smith	Oren	2	1	1		1	2	1	2	1		2		13		
Colrain	189	11	Smith	Nathanael	2	1	1	1	1	1	1		1				9		
Colrain	189	12	Shermon	John		1	1		1	2	2	1	1				11		
Colrain	189	13	Smith	Calvin	2	1	1		1	3	2	1	1				12		
Colrain	189	14	Sheperdson	Alford				1		2		1					4		
Colrain	189	15	Sprague	Susanah	1	2				1	1		1				6		
Colrain	189	16	Truesdal	Darius	1		1						1				3		
Colrain	189	17	Thomson	David		1		1		1		2					5		
Colrain	189	18	Tolman	Stodard		1	1	1		2	2			1			8		
Colrain	189	19	Tolman	Joshua	1	1		1	1		1	1		1			7		
Colrain	189	20	Tolman	Joshua Jun	2			1				1		1			5		
Colrain	189	21	Thomson	Hugh	4	2	2	1	1	1	1	1	1	1			15		
Colrain	189	22	Taggart	James	4			1		2	2		1				10		
Colrain	189	23	Thomson	Joseph Jun	3			1		2	2		1				9		
Colrain	189	24	Thomas	Willard	2	1		1		1	1	1	1				8		
Colrain	189	25	Taggart	Samuel	2		3		1	3	2		1	1			13		
Colrain	189	26	Tinney	Stephen	1		1						1				3		
Colrain	189	27	Tanner	Oliver	1			1		3			1				6		
Colrain	189	28	Tisdale	Abraham			1			1			1				3		
Colrain	189	29	Tolman	Thomas	2			1		2	1		1				7		
Colrain	189	30	Wallace	Seth	3			1		2		1	1				8		
Colrain	189	31	Watson	John	2			1		1		1					5		
Colrain	189	32	Willson	James	2	2		1		2	1	1	1	1			11		
Colrain	189	33	Walkup	George	2			1		2			1				6		
Colrain	189	34	Wood	Moses	2	1			1		1	1	1	1			8		
Colrain	189	35	Workman	Daniel	1	1		1	1	2			2	1			9		
Colrain	189	36	Willson	Jonathan		2	3		1	1	1	1		1			10		
Colrain	189	37	White	James	4	2		1		1	1		1				10		
Colrain	189	38	Willis	Daniel	1	1		2		1		3					8		
Colrain	189	39	Wheeler	Hezekiah	2					1			1				5		
Colrain	189	40	Willson	John	2		1	1				2					6		
Colrain	189	41	Willson	David 2d	4			1		1		1	1	1			9		
Colrain	190	1	Wallace	James			1	1		1		1	2	1			7		
Colrain	190	2	Willson	Jonathan 2d		2		1		3			1				7		
Colrain	190	3	Willson	David		2	3		2		1	2		1			11		
Colrain	190	4	Watson	Robert	2		1	1						1			5		
Colrain	190	5	White	Leonard	3			1		1			1				6		
Colrain	190	6	Wilcox	Daniel	2	2	3	1			1	1		1			11		
Colrain	190	7	Weson	Oliver	1		1				1	2	1				6		
Colrain	190	8	Willis	Ezra	1	2		1		2	1		1				8		
Colrain	190	9	Wood	Edmond			2		1		1	1					6		
Colrain	190	10	Worden	John	2	2		1		2	1		1				9		
Colrain	190	11	Worden	Thomas	1	1	1	1		3	1		1				9		
Colrain	190	12	Washburn	Eliab		1			1			1		1			4		
Colrain	190	13	Willis	Josiah	1		1			1	1		1				5		
Colrain	190	14	Wilson	Robert Jun			1					1					2		
Colrain	190	15	Washbrn	Experience	2		1			1			1				5		
Colrain	190	16	Willcox	Hiel		2						1					3		
Colrain	190	17	Yaw	John	1		2					1					4		
Colrain	190	18	Procter	Mingo											8		8		
Colrain	190	19	Green	Peter											9		9		
Colrain	190	20	Jackson	John											2		2		
Colrain	190	21	James	Peter											4		4		

TOWN	PG#	LN#	LAST NAME	FIRST NAME	FREE WHITE MALES					FREE WHITE FEMALES					TOTAL ALL OTHER	TOTAL SLAVES	TOTALS	DISTRICT/ TOWNSHIP	NOTES
					under 10	10 to 16	16 to 26	26 to 45	45 and over	under 10	10 to 16	16 to 26	26 to 45	45 and over					
Conway	56	1	Allen	Caleb	2	1			1	1	2			1			8		
Conway	56	2	Amsden	Isaac			3	1				1		1			6		
Conway	56	3	Amsden	Elisha		1	1		1	1				1			5		
Conway	56	4	Abbot	Joshua					1			3		2			6		
Conway	56	5	Arms	Mercy	1	1	2	1			1	3	1	1			11		
Conway	56	6	Arms	Henry			1			1		1					3		
Conway	56	7	Andrews	James	1	1	3		1	1	1			1			9		
Conway	56	8	Andrews	James Jun	1		1						1				3		
Conway	56	9	Allis	Solomon	2	1		1	1	1	1	1					8		
Conway	56	10	Allis	Abel		1	1		1					1			4		
Conway	56	11	Allis	Joel	2		1	2	1	2		1	1	1			11		
Conway	56	12	Allis	Samuel	2			1		2	1		1				7		
Conway	56	13	Allen	Amos				1	1	1	1			2			5		
Conway	56	14	Avery	John	1	2		1		3	1			1			9		
Conway	56	15	Adams	Joel	1	1	1		1	1		1	2	1			9		
Conway	56	16	Allen	John	1			1		2	2		1				7		
Conway	56	17	Amsden	Sarah						2	1		1				4		
Conway	56	18	Burgiss	Bathsheba	3						1		1	1			6		
Conway	56	19	Bennitt	Enoch			1				1	1					3		
Conway	56	20	Bigelow	Jonathan	1			1		1		1					4		
Conway	56	21	Baker	Joel		1			1		1	1		1			5		
Conway	56	22	Baker	Isaac	1	1	1	1		1		1	1				7		
Conway	56	23	Billings	William	1		4		2	1	1	1		1			11		
Conway	56	24	Broderick	John	1	1			1	1	1	2		1			8		
Conway	56	25	Bartlet	Adoniran	1	1			1	1		1		1			5		
Conway	56	26	Bartlet	Amos	4	1		1		2			2				10		
Conway	56	27	Billings	Stephen	2			1		1			1				5		
Conway	56	28	Bigelow	John	2	1			1	2	2	1	1				10		
Conway	56	29	Bachelor	John	1			1	2	1	1	1	2				9		
Conway	56	30	Booth	Isaiah	1	1				1	1	3		1			8		
Conway	56	31	Brooks	Abner	1		2		1		1	1		1			7		
Conway	56	32	Bacon	Nathan		2		1		4	1		1				9		
Conway	56	33	Bacon	Joel	2			1	1	2			1	1			8		
Conway	56	34	Banister	John			1		1		1	1		1			5		
Conway	56	35	Bottwood	Samuel					1					1			2		
Conway	56	36	Bartlet	Calvin		1				1							2		
Conway	56	37	Bardwell	Reuben	2			1		2			1				6		
Conway	56	38	Bathrick	Gilley	1		1		1		1	1		1			6		
Conway	56	39	Bartlet	Samuel		1						1					2		
Conway	56	40	Baker	Nathaniel		1	1			2	1		1				6		
Conway	56	41	Bardwell	Eldad	2		1	1	1	1	1	1	1	1			10		
Conway	56	42	Bouker	Ithamar	3				1	1	1		1				7		
Conway	56	43	Billings	Elisha		1	1						1				4		
Conway	56	44	Belding	Noah					1				1	1			3		
Conway	56	45	Belding	Selah	1	1	1	1		2	1	1					9		
Conway	56	46	Bradford	Shubal	1			1		3			1				6		
Conway	57	1	Bradford	Edward	2			1				1					4		
Conway	57	2	Boyden	Joseph	3			1		1			1		1		7		
Conway	57	3	Boyden	Joseph Junr	2		1	1		2			1				6		
Conway	57	4	Boyden	James	2		1			2			1				6		
Conway	57	5	Boyden	John	2	2			1			2		2			9		
Conway	57	6	Boyden	John Junr	3	2		1		1		2	1				10		
Conway	57	7	Beals	Lydia		1	1						3	1			6		
Conway	57	8	Beals	Caleb	2	1			1	1	2		1				8		
Conway	57	9	Bond	Benjamin	2	1	1		1	1	1	1		1			9		
Conway	57	10	Billings	Ethan		1	1		1	1	2			1	1		8		
Conway	57	11	Bond	John Junr	1		1	1		1		1	1				6		
Conway	57	12	Bond	Jonas	2				1	1			1				5		
Conway	57	13	Bond	Consider	1		1	1	1	2			2	1			9		
Conway	57	14	Bartlet	Zeduthan	1			1		2		1					5		
Conway	57	15	Billings	Lemuel				1		5	2		1				9		
Conway	57	16	Boyden	Josiah				1			1			1			3		
Conway	57	17	Banister	Lemuel		2		1	1	3				1			7		
Conway	57	18	Burgis	Benjamin	2	1	1			1		1					7		
Conway	57	19	Bond	Adonijah		2		1		1	1	2		1			8		
Conway	57	20	Brown	Abijah	1			1					1				3		
Conway	57	21	Bond	Ezra	1			1		2			1				5		
Conway	57	22	Boyden	Daniel		1						1					2		
Conway	57	23	Beals	Rachel										2			2		
Conway	57	24	Clark	Joseph		1				1		1					3		
Conway	57	25	Cobb	Sylvanus	2	1	1		1			1	2	1			9		
Conway	57	26	Cobb	Daniel	1			1		1	1	1					5		
Conway	57	27	Clary	Elijah			2		1	1	1		1	1			8		
Conway	57	28	Clary	Joseph	1	1	1	1		1	1	1	1				8		
Conway	57	29	Cooper	Lamberton		2	1		1				1	1			6		
Conway	57	30	Clapp	Cephas	1		1	1		1	1	1	1				7		
Conway	57	31	Cole	Marcus	1			1		1	1	1					5		
Conway	57	32	Cook	Jesse	5				1		1			1			8		
Conway	57	33	Carrier	David	1	2	1	1		1	1	1	1				9		

TOWN	PG#	LN#	LAST NAME	FIRST NAME	FREE WHITE MALES					FREE WHITE FEMALES					TOTAL ALL OTHER	TOTAL SLAVES	TOTALS	DISTRICT/ TOWNSHIP	NOTES
					under 10	10 to 16	16 to 26	26 to 45	45 and over	under 10	10 to 16	16 to 26	26 to 45	45 and over					
Conway	57	34	Clary	Abel	2	1		1		1	1		1				7		
Conway	57	35	Cobb	George			1			1	2	1		1			6		
Conway	57	36	Clark	Elizabeth		1	2					2		1			6		
Conway	57	37	Childs	David		1	3	1			2		1				10		
Conway	57	38	Crittenden	Samuel	1	3	1	1		1				1			8		
Conway	57	39	Crittenden	John	4	1		1		1	1		1				9		
Conway	57	40	Crittenden	Ebenz		1	2	1			1		1				6		
Conway	57	41	Crittenden	Medad	1	2		1		1	1		1				7		
Conway	57	42	Collins	Richard	3		3		1	1				1			9		
Conway	57	43	Collins	Richard Junr	1			1		4			1				7		
Conway	57	44	Clark	Elisha		1		1	1	1	1		1				6		
Conway	57	45	Clark	Judah	3	1		1			1		1				7		
Conway	57	46	Clark	Elisha Junr		1		1		1			1				4		
Conway	57	47	Childs	Libbeus		1	1		1	2	2	1		1			9		
Conway	57	48	Cathcart	Tristram	1	1	1				1	1	1				6		
Conway	57	49	Cooley	Gideon		1	3		1	1	1			1			8		
Conway	57	50	Dwight	Seth			1			2				1			4		
Conway	57	51	DeWolf	John	1		1	1		2	1	1					7		
Conway	57	52	Dunham	Cornelius	1	1	1		1	1		1		2			8		
Conway	58	1	Dunham	Jonathan	2	2	1		2	3	1		2				13		
Conway	58	2	Dunham	Samuel		1		1		1		2					5		
Conway	58	3	Dinsmore	Abel	1	1		1		2	1		1				7		
Conway	58	4	Dinsmore	Asa	3			1		1			1				6		
Conway	58	5	Dickinson	Reuben	1	1		1		2	1		1				7		
Conway	58	6	Dickinson	James			1	1	1	2			1	1			7		
Conway	58	7	Davis	Samuel			1			1		1					3		
Conway	58	8	Davis	James		1	2		2	2	1	1		2			11		
Conway	58	9	Ellis	Barzilla	1	2		1		1			1				6		
Conway	58	10	Emerson	John		1	3		1			3		1			9		
Conway	58	11	Evans	Ebenezer			1			1		1		1			4		
Conway	58	12	Frink	Samuel	1			1		1			1				4		
Conway	58	13	Field	Solomon	2	2	4		1	1		1	1	1			13		
Conway	58	14	Farnham	Asa	2		1		1	1	2	1		1			9		
Conway	58	15	Flagg	Eleazer	2	1	1	1		2			1				8		
Conway	58	16	Frost	Joseph	2		2	1		1	1		1				8		
Conway	58	17	Field	Samuel			1		1		1	1		1			5		
Conway	58	18	Field	Nathaniel				1						1			2		
Conway	58	19	Field	Daniel	2	1		1		3			2	1			10		
Conway	58	20	Field	John	2	1		1		3			1				8		
Conway	58	21	Faxan	Thomas	2			1		1	1	1	1				7		
Conway	58	22	Field	Ebenezer			2		1		2	1		1			7		
Conway	58	23	Fisk	John		1		1		2	1	1	2				8		
Conway	58	24	Godfrey	Seth	3	1			1	3	2	1		1			12		
Conway	58	25	Guild	Israel	3			1		1			1				6		
Conway	58	26	Graham	Samuel	2	2		1		2			1				8		
Conway	58	27	Goddard	Nathaniel			1		1		1			1			4		
Conway	58	28	Goddard	Elisha	4			1		1			1				7		
Conway	58	29	Gates	Peter	3	1		1		1	2	1	1				10		
Conway	58	30	Gifford	Christopher	2			1	1	1			1	1			7		
Conway	58	31	Gifford	Paul	3			1		2	1		1				8		
Conway	58	32	Gates	Israel		1		1	1	1		1		2			7		
Conway	58	33	Gates	William	3			1	1	2		1		1			9		
Conway	58	34	Glover	Alexander	3	1	1	1		1	2		1	1			11		
Conway	58	35	Goodale	Solomon		1	1		1	1	1	2					8		
Conway	58	36	Graves	Simeon				1						1			2		
Conway	58	37	Graves	Levi	2	1	2		1	2	1		1				10		
Conway	58	38	Glover	Thomas		1				1		1					3		
Conway	58	39	Hale	Aaron	3	1	2	1		1			1				9		
Conway	58	40	Hamilton	Robert	2	1	1	1		1		2	2	1			11		
Conway	58	41	Howland	John	4	1		1		1	1			1			9		
Conway	58	42	Howland	Job	2	1		1		1			1				6		
Conway	58	43	Henry	Josiah		1	2		1	2			1	1			8		
Conway	58	44	Hamilton	William	2			2					2				6		
Conway	58	45	Harrington	Aaron			1		1	1	1	3		1			8		
Conway	58	46	Hayden	Moses		2	1			2	2	1					8		
Conway	58	47	Haywood	Samuel	1		1	1	1	2			1	1			8		
Conway	58	48	Hickox	Eliphalet	1			1		2		1					5		
Conway	59	1	Huxford	Henry	1		2		1	1	2						8		
Conway	59	2	Holloway	William	1			1				1					5		
Conway	59	3	Hobart	Israel			1					1					4		
Conway	59	4	Howard	Caleb	1			1		2			1				5		
Conway	59	5	Herrick	Elijah	2		1	1		1			1				6		
Conway	59	6	Hopkins	Seth	1	1			1			2		1			6		
Conway	59	7	Hartwell	Solomon		1			1	1		1					4		
Conway	59	8	Hartwell	Solomon Junr	4			1		1	1		1				8		
Conway	59	9	Hartwell	Francis	2	1		1		4			1				9		
Conway	59	10	Hartwell	Samuel	1		1			1		1					4		
Conway	59	11	Hall	William		1			1	2				1			5		
Conway	59	12	Hall	William Jur	2					2							7		

TOWN	PG#	LN#	HEADS OF HOUSEHOLD		FREE WHITE MALES					FREE WHITE FEMALES					TOTAL ALL OTHER	TOTAL SLAVES	TOTALS	DISTRICT/ TOWNSHIP	NOTES
			LAST NAME	FIRST NAME	under 10	10 to 16	16 to 26	26 to 45	45 and over	under 10	10 to 16	16 to 26	26 to 45	45 and over					
Conway	59	13	Hendrick	Reuben		2		1					2	2			7		
Conway	59	14	Hitchcock	Heman	2	2		1		2	2		1				10		
Conway	59	15	Hall	Elizer	2	1		1				1		1			6		
Conway	59	16	Hemmenway	Daniel	1			1		3		1					6		
Conway	59	17	Hemmenway	Jason			1		1			1		1			4		
Conway	59	18	Hillman	Lot	3	2		1		2		1	1	1			11		
Conway	59	19	Kelsey	Hiel				1									1		
Conway	59	20	Keyes	Calvin	2	1		1		3	2		1				10		
Conway	59	21	Lee	Eben	1	1	1		1		1	1		1			7		
Conway	59	22	Leonard	Roger		1		1					1	1			4		
Conway	59	23	Leonard	Augustus	3			1		1			1				6		
Conway	59	24	Leonard	Elijah	3			1		1			1				6		
Conway	59	25	Loomis	Russell	1			1		2			1				5		
Conway	59	26	Lawrence	Eleazer	2			1		2			1				6		
Conway	59	27	Lee	Sherebiah		2		1				2		1			6		
Conway	59	28	Look	James		2		1						1			4		
Conway	59	29	Look	John		1		1			1		1	1			5		
Conway	59	30	Look	Cheney	1	2		1		2		1	1				8		
Conway	59	31	Look	Peter		1		1			1	2		1			6		
Conway	59	32	Lee	Joseph	2			1		4	1		1				9		
Conway	59	33	Lee	Benjamin			1			1		1					3		
Conway	59	34	Lee	Joseph	1		2	1				1					6		
Conway	59	35	Lawrence	William		1	1		1		1			1			5		
Conway	59	36	Marsh	Abner		1		1		4			1				7		
Conway	59	37	Maynard	Timothy	1			1		2			1				5		
Conway	59	38	McClentick	John	1	1			1		1			1			5		
Conway	59	39	Merritt	Simeon	1	1		1		2			1				6		
Conway	59	40	Maynard	Pierces		2	2						1	1			6		
Conway	59	41	Moore	John	1	1	1	1		4	1		1				10		
Conway	59	42	Merritt	Asa Junr	3			1	1	1			1	1			8		
Conway	59	43	Maynard	Theodore		1					1		1				3		
Conway	59	44	Maynard	Elijah	1	2			1	2		1	1				8		
Conway	59	45	Marble	Nathaniel	3	1		1		1			1				7		
Conway	59	46	Maynard	Malachi	1	1	1			2	2			1			9		
Conway	59	47	Maynard	Moses	1			1		1		1					4		
Conway	59	48	Manter	Catherine						2	1	1		2			6		
Conway	59	49	Marble	Abijah	3	1		1		1	1		1				8		
Conway	59	50	Maynard	Calvin				1		3	1		1				6		
Conway	59	51	Nelson	William	1		1					1					3		
Conway	59	52	Newhall	Daniel		2		1			1		1				5		
Conway	59	53	Newhall	Daniel Jur		2		1		3			1	1			8		
Conway	59	54	Newhall	Jabez		1	2		1		1	2		1			8		
Conway	59	55	Newhall	Samuel		1	3	1	1				2	1			9		
Conway	59	56	Nims	Amasa		1	1				1			1			4		
Conway	59	57	Nims	Polly	2					1			1				4		
Conway	60	1	Nash	Elijah	1			1		2		1	1				6		
Conway	60	2	Northam	David	4			1			1		2	1			9		
Conway	60	3	Nims	Grace	4	1	1		1	2		2		1			12		
Conway	60	4	Oliver	Peggy										1			1		
Conway	60	5	Peck	Darius	3	1		1		3	1		1				10		
Conway	60	6	Pulcipher	Benjamin	2			1	1	3	2		1	1			11		
Conway	60	7	Pulcipher	Joseph	1	2		1		3			1				8		
Conway	60	8	Page	Theophilus		2	3	1		1				1			8		
Conway	60	9	Persons	Joel		2		1		3	1	1		1			10		
Conway	60	10	Pratt	Joseph	1	1		1		1		1	1	1			7		
Conway	60	11	Pease	John		1				1		1					3		
Conway	60	12	Packard	Elizabeth						3	1	1	1				6		
Conway	60	13	Quinn	Hugh		1		1		1				1			4		
Conway	60	14	Rider	Daniel	3			1		3	2			1			11		
Conway	60	15	Rice	Israel	2		1	1				1	1				6		
Conway	60	16	Rice	Caleb		1		1			1	2		1			6		
Conway	60	17	Rice	Timothy		2	1	1		1		3		1			9		
Conway	60	18	Rice	Israel		1		1		1		1					4		
Conway	60	19	Rice	Daniel	1		1		1				1				5		
Conway	60	20	Root	Oliver		1	2	1	2	1		2		2			11		
Conway	60	21	Russell	Elihu	3	1	1	1		2		2					10		
Conway	60	22	Rood	Levi			1										1		
Conway	60	23	Rice	Cyrus		1	2				2			1			7		
Conway	60	24	Rice	Stephen	1			1					1				3		
Conway	60	25	Redfield	Ebenezer	1	2	3		1	1	1			1			10		
Conway	60	26	Rice	Jonas				2	1					1			4		
Conway	60	27	Rice	Joel		2	2		1		1			1			7		
Conway	60	28	Rice	Joseph		1	1		1	1	1			1			6		
Conway	60	29	Rice	Benjamin	1	2	1		1								6		
Conway	60	30	Rogers	Benjamin				1		4	2		1				8		
Conway	60	31	Rockwood	Abagail	2					1			1				4		
Conway	60	32	Rice	Henry			1				1						2		
Conway	60	33	Stow	Daniel		1	1	1	1	1	1	1		1			8		
Conway	60	34	Sanderson	Cyrus	2												4		

TOWN	PG#	LN#	LAST NAME	FIRST NAME	FREE WHITE MALES					FREE WHITE FEMALES					TOTAL ALL OTHER	TOTAL SLAVES	TOTALS	DISTRICT/ TOWNSHIP	NOTES
					under 10	10 to 16	16 to 26	26 to 45	45 and over	under 10	10 to 16	16 to 26	26 to 45	45 and over					
Conway	60	35	Smith	Jonathan 2d	2			1		1		1					5		
Conway	60	36	Smith	Jonathan		1		1		6		1					9		
Conway	60	37	Stow	Joseph	1		1	1		2	1	1					7		
Conway	60	38	Smith	Joseph	1		1		1					1			4		
Conway	60	39	Stebbins	Simeon	1	2		1			1	1		1			7		
Conway	60	40	Smith	Aaron		1	1	1				1		1			5		
Conway	60	41	Stebbins	Sylvester	5		1	1			1	1	1				10		
Conway	60	42	Stebbins	Moses				1				1	1				3		
Conway	60	43	Stearns	George			2	1		1		1		1			6		
Conway	60	44	Stearns	Darius	1	1		1		1		1	1				6		
Conway	60	45	Sherman	Caleb	3	2		1		2			1				9		
Conway	60	46	Sheldon	Abner	3	2	1		1	1	1	1	1				11		
Conway	60	47	Seaver	W. Josiah		1		1	1	1	2			1			6		
Conway	60	48	Strong	Simeon	1			1					1				3		
Conway	60	49	Stacey	Caleb	3			1		2	1		1				8		
Conway	60	50	Salisbury	William	1	1		1	1	3	1		1	1			10		
Conway	61	1	Salisbury	Seth		1		1					1	1			4		
Conway	61	2	Salisbury	Stephen	2			1		2	1		1	1			8		
Conway	61	3	Sanderson	James			1		1	2	1		2				7		
Conway	61	4	Stebbins	John	3	1		1	1	1	1		1	1			10		
Conway	61	5	Stebbins	David Jur	1		1					1					3		
Conway	61	6	Severance	Jesse		1	2		1	1	2	1		1			9		
Conway	61	7	Stearns	Joel	1	1	1	1		1	1		1				7		
Conway	61	8	Toby	Prince		1	4	1	1		2	1	3	1			14		
Conway	61	9	Toby	Timothy		2	4	1	1	1	1			1			10		
Conway	61	10	Thayer	Edward	1		1			3	2	1					8		
Conway	61	11	Thayer	Daniel			1				1	1					3		
Conway	61	12	Thwing	Timothy		1	2		1		1			2			7		
Conway	61	13	Toby	Amaziah			1	1	1	1	1		1	1			7		
Conway	61	14	Thayer	Eliha			1			1		1					3		
Conway	61	15	Thayer	Adonijah	1			1		1			1	1			5		
Conway	61	16	Tayler	David Jr	2			1		2			1				6		
Conway	61	17	Tinney	Josiah	4			1		2	3		1				11		
Conway	61	18	Thatcher	Ebenezer	1			1		1			1				4		
Conway	61	19	Turner	Stephen			1		1	1		1		1			5		
Conway	61	20	Veber	David	3			1		1			1				6		
Conway	61	21	Warner	William	1		2		1		1	1		1			7		
Conway	61	22	Wells	Benjamin	2	3	1	1		2		2					11		
Conway	61	23	Warren	James	4	2			1			1	1				9		
Conway	61	24	Wilder	Samuel	3	1	1		1	2	1	2	1				12		
Conway	61	25	Woodward	Ebenezer				1				1	1				3		
Conway	61	26	Wing	Isaiah		2		1		3			1				7		
Conway	61	27	Whitney	David	1		1	1	1	3		2	1	1			11		
Conway	61	28	Woodward	Isaac	4	1	1	1		2		2					11		
Conway	61	29	Ware	Jonathan	1	1	1		1	1	2	2	1				10		
Conway	61	30	Wells	Richard		1	2			1		2	1				7		
Conway	61	31	Ware	George	1			1				1					3		
Conway	61	32	Wood	Ceaser											3		3		
Conway	61	33	Willcox	John			2	1			3	1	1				8		
Conway	61	34	Willcox	Silas		1		1		1			1				4		
Conway	61	35	Wing	John	1	2	1		1	2	1		1				9		
Conway	61	36	Ware	Samuel		1	1		1	1	1	2		2			9		
Conway	61	37	Wells	Elijah			1					1					2		
Conway	61	38	Wheat	Benjamin	1		1		1		1			1			5		
Conway	61	39	Whitney	Ira	4			1	1	2	1		1	1			11		
Conway	61	40	Wheeler	Joseph	1		1			3			2	1			8		
Conway	61	41	Williams	John		1	2	1					1				5		
Conway	61	42	Williams	Statham				1				1			2		4		
Conway	61	43	Willcox	Amos	2	1	1		1	3		2	1				11		
Conway	61	44	Wait	Reuben			1			1		1					3		
Conway	61	45	Webster	Jacob	2			1		2			1				6		
Conway	61	46	Wells	Ruth			1			1		1		1			4		
Conway	61	47	Wait	Elijah			2										2		
Conway	61	48	Wilks	John	1			1		1			1				4		

TOWN	PG#	LN#	LAST NAME	FIRST NAME	FWM under 10	FWM 10 to 16	FWM 16 to 26	FWM 26 to 45	FWM 45 and over	FWF under 10	FWF 10 to 16	FWF 16 to 26	FWF 26 to 45	FWF 45 and over	TOTAL ALL OTHER	TOTAL SLAVES	TOTALS	DISTRICT/ TOWNSHIP	NOTES
Cummington	302	1	Anderson	Joseph	2	2	2	1		2	2		1				12		
Cummington	302	2	Baker	Josiah					1		1	1	1				4		
Cummington	302	3	Baker	Daniel		1		1				1	1				4		
Cummington	302	4	Bates	Abraham			2		1	1	1	1		1			7		
Cummington	302	5	Bates	Zabbius	1			1		1	1	1	1				6		
Cummington	302	6	Bates	Abenr		1	1		1	1				2			6		
Cummington	302	7	Bates	Moses	2	2		1		2	1		1				9		
Cummington	302	8	Bates	William	3			1		2	1	3					10		
Cummington	302	9	Bates	Joel				1		1			1				3		
Cummington	302	10	Bates	Asa	1			1		1			1				4		
Cummington	302	11	Bates	Levi	1			1		1			1				4		
Cummington	302	12	Bartlett	Edward	5	1	1		1		1	1	1	1			12		
Cummington	302	13	Barrows	Abiel	2	1		1		1	1		1				7		
Cummington	302	14	Bigelow	John			2		1	2	1	1	1				8		
Cummington	302	15	Bisbee	Luther	3			1	1		1	1	1	1			9		
Cummington	302	16	Beal	Comfort	3	1		1		1			2				8		
Cummington	302	17	Beal	Daniel	3			1		3		1	1	1			10		
Cummington	302	18	Bradish	James	2	1	1	2	1	4	1	3		1			16		
Cummington	302	19	Brown	Abner					1			2		1			4		
Cummington	302	20	Burnal	Epraim	1	3		1		1	1		1				8		
Cummington	302	21	Bradley	George	1	1	1	1	1	3		1	2	1			12		
Cummington	302	22	Bates	Nehemiah Jr	1	2		1		1			1				6		
Cummington	302	23	Clemons	John	2	2	1		1		1			1			8		
Cummington	302	24	Cobb	Amos		1		1	1	2		1		1			7		
Cummington	303	1	Cushman	Jotham	1			1		1			1	2			6		
Cummington	303	2	Damon	William	2	2		1					1				6		
Cummington	303	3	Damon	Jonathan	2			1		2			1				6		
Cummington	303	4	Dawes	Daniel				1									1		
Cummington	303	5	Dawes	Robert	2		1	1		1		1	1	1			8		
Cummington	303	6	Farr	Jacob		1			1			1	2	1			6		
Cummington	303	7	Farr	Ansel	1			1					1	1			4		
Cummington	303	8	Ford	Heschiah					1				1	2			4		
Cummington	303	9	Ford	Luke			2	1					1	1			5		
Cummington	303	10	Ford	Hesk Jun	1	3		1			1		1				7		
Cummington	303	11	French	Stephen	1	1		1		2			1				6		
Cummington	303	12	Wilber	David	2			1			1		1				5		
Cummington	303	13	Shaw	Sylvanus	4			1					1	1			7		
Cummington	303	14	Bailey	Joseph	3	1	1		1		1			1			8		
Cummington	303	15	Gilbert	Thaddeus	1				1			2	1	1			6		
Cummington	303	16	Floyd	John	1	1			1			1	2	1			7		
Cummington	303	17	Gurney	Benjamin		1		1					2				4		
Cummington	303	18	Gurney	Asa	2	2		1		3	1	1	1				11		
Cummington	303	19	Harden	William		1		1		1				1			4		
Cummington	303	20	Hamlin	Isaac	1	2		1				2		1			7		
Cummington	303	21	Hill	Daniel				1						1	1		3		
Cummington	303	22	Hill	Joel		2	1	1		3			1				8		
Cummington	303	23	Hill	Daniel Jun		1		1				1		1			4		
Cummington	303	24	Hursey	John	2	1		1		2	2		1				9		
Cummington	303	25	Holebrook	Nathl	1		2	1		1			1				8		
Cummington	303	26	Howard	Stephen	3	1	1	1	1	2	2	1	1	1			14		
Cummington	303	27	Joy	Nehemiah	1	1	1	1					1				5		
Cummington	303	28	Reed	Noah	1	1			1	3	1		1				8		
Cummington	303	29	Reed	John	2	1		1		1		3	1	2			11		
Cummington	303	30	Richardson	Winslow	1		1	1	1	1			2	1			8		
Cummington	303	31	Robbins	William	1	1		1				1	1	1			6		
Cummington	303	32	Richards	Joseph	1	1		1		4	1		1				9		
Cummington	303	33	Robbins	Amariah			1			1			1				3		
Cummington	303	34	Richards	Nehemiah	3	1	1	1		1	2		1	1			11		
Cummington	303	35	Richards	David				1		2		1					4		
Cummington	303	36	Robinson	Robert		1		1				1	1	1			5		
Cummington	303	37	Ramsdell	Thomas	2		2	1		2	1	1	1				10		
Cummington	303	38	Robinson	Clerk	1	1		1		1			1	2			7		
Cummington	303	39	Remington	Joshua	1		1					1	1	1			6		
Cummington	303	40	Remington	Benjamin	2	1		1		2			1				7		
Cummington	304	1	Randall	Zeb*			1			5			1				7		
Cummington	304	2	Richards	Ezra	2			1		1		1	1				6		
Cummington	304	3	Snell	Ebenezer		1			1			1		1			4		
Cummington	304	4	Snell	Ebenezer Jun		1	1	1		1	1	1			1		7		
Cummington	304	5	Southworth	Ichabod	2	1		1		1	1		1				8		
Cummington	304	6	Snow	James	4			1		1			1				7		
Cummington	304	7	Snow	Nathan Jun			1			2			1				4		
Cummington	304	8	Stevenson	Obadiah	2			1					1				4		
Cummington	304	9	Shaw	Stephen					1					1			2		
Cummington	304	10	Shaw	Phillip		1	2						1	1			7		
Cummington	304	11	Shaw	Obed		1		1					1	1			4		
Cummington	304	12	Shaw	Ebenezer	1				1	1	1		1				5		
Cummington	304	13	Shaw	Beriah	1			1			1	1					4		
Cummington	304	14	Thomas	Noah	1			2	1	1		1	3	1			10		
Cummington	304	15	Thayer	Jacob	1	2				2			1				8		

TOWN	PG#	LN#	LAST NAME	FIRST NAME	FREE WHITE MALES					FREE WHITE FEMALES					TOTAL ALL OTHER	TOTAL SLAVES	TOTALS	DISTRICT/ TOWNSHIP	NOTES
					under 10	10 to 16	16 to 26	26 to 45	45 and over	under 10	10 to 16	16 to 26	26 to 45	45 and over					
Cummington	304	16	Thayer	Luke	2	2		1		2	2		1				10		
Cummington	304	17	Tower	Asa	1	1		1	1	2	2		1	1			10		
Cummington	304	18	Tower	Stephen	1	1	4		1	2	2	2		2			15		
Cummington	304	19	Tower	Matthew	3			1		2		1	1	1			9		
Cummington	304	20	Tower	Nathaniel		1	3		1	2			1	1			9		
Cummington	304	21	Terril	Thomas	2	1	2		1	2			1				9		
Cummington	304	22	Torry	Jona	2			1		1			1				5		
Cummington	304	23	Tower	Peter	2	1			1				1	1			6		
Cummington	304	24	Torry	Luther				1	1				1	1			4		
Cummington	304	25	Ward	Trowbridge			2			1		1		1			5		
Cummington	304	26	Warner	Joseph		1	2		1		1	1		1			7		
Cummington	304	27	Warner	Moses	1			1		2	1	1	1	1			8		
Cummington	304	28	Warner	Stephen			2		1		2	1		2			8		
Cummington	304	29	Wildair	Seth	1	1		1	1	4	1		1	1			11		
Cummington	304	30	Wildair	Abel	1			1		1		1					4		
Cummington	304	31	Whitman	Tama	1		1		1					1			4		
Cummington	304	32	Beal	John	1			1		2			1				5		
Cummington	304	33	Wheelar	Samuel	1	1		1	1	2			1				7		
Cummington	304	34	Whiton*	Jacob	2	1	1	1		2	3		1				11		
Cummington	304	35	Tinker	Josiah	1			1		2			1				5		
Cummington	304	36	Olds	Levi	1	3	2		1		1	1	1				10		
Cummington	304	37	Wood	Mary							1		1				2		
Cummington	304	38	Bryant	Peter	3			1					1				5		
Cummington	304	39	Briggs	James		1	1		1		2		2		1		8		
Cummington	304	40	Stovel	Warren	1			1					1				3		
Cummington	304	41	Keith	Luke	1	2	1		1	1				1			7		
Cummington	304	42	Knapp	Jona	1	1	2		1		2		1				8		
Cummington	304	43	Lovel	Edmond	2	1			2	1	3	2	1	1			13		
Cummington	304	44	Lovel	Joshua	2	1			1				1				5		
Cummington	304	45	Lampson	John	1				1	2	1		1				6		
Cummington	304	46	Loud	James	4			1		1	2		1				9		
Cummington	304	47	Melvin	Reuben	3	1		1	1	2			1	1			10		
Cummington	304	48	Mitchel	Willm	1	2	2		1	3	1	1	1				12		
Cummington	305	1	Mason	Joseph	1			1		2	1		1				6		
Cummington	305	2	Nash	Daniel	2	1			1		2	1		1			8		
Cummington	305	3	Nash	Jacob			1		1	1	1			1			5		
Cummington	305	4	Norton	Bela	1			1		2			1				5		
Cummington	305	5	Noyce	Cyrus				1		1		1		1			4		
Cummington	305	6	Orcott	Nathan	1	2		1		1	2		1	1			9		
Cummington	305	7	Ottis	William		1	1	1		2	1		1				7		
Cummington	305	8	Packard	Abel Jun	1	1	1		1	1	1	1	1				8		
Cummington	305	9	Packard	Adam	2	1		1	1	2			3	1			11		
Cummington	305	10	Packard	Barnabus		1	1		1			1		1			5		
Cummington	305	11	Foster	Adam		1	1		1	1	1		1				6		
Cummington	305	12	Foster	Asa	2			1			1		1				5		
Cummington	305	13	Parker	Ezra			1	1	1	3		1		1			8		
Cummington	305	14	Pettingill	Jon		1			1	2	1	1	1				7		
Cummington	305	15	Pratt	Benoni	1	1		1		2		1					6		
Cummington	305	16	Pratt	Josiah	2			1		1			1				5		
Cummington	305	17	Prentice	Elisha				1		3			1				5		
Cummington	305	18	Reed	David		1	2		1			1		1			6		
Cummington	305	19	Reed	Seth			1		1					1			3		
Cummington	305	20	Howard	Simeon	1			1				2	1				5		
Cummington	305	21	Cushing	Bela	1			1		1	2			1			6		
Cummington	305	22	Cole	Noah	1			1				1		1			4		
Cummington	305	23	Ensign	Zerah				1		2		1	1				5		
Cummington	305	24	Pierce	Bristo Negro											3		3		
Cummington	305	25	Marrs	Daniel			1					1					2		
Cummington	305	26	Whitman	Daniel			1			2		1					4		
Cummington	305	27	Bates	Calvin			1			3			1				5		
Cummington	305	28	Nash	Daniel Jun			1					1	1				3		
Cummington	305	29	Shaw	Solomon	2	1	1	1		1	1	2	1				10		
Cummington	305	30	Genins	Ephraim	2			1					1				4		
Cummington	305	31	Bates	Samuel	1			1		1			1				4		
Cummington	305	32	Shaw	James	1			1			1	1					4		
Cummington	305	33	Gurney	Amos	1			1		2			1				5		
Cummington	305	34	Dawes	Howland		1		2		2			1	1			7		
Cummington	305	35	Sipple	Jeter	2			1		2			1				6		
Cummington	305	36	Odell	Ichabod Negro											5		5		

TOWN	PG#	LN#	LAST NAME	FIRST NAME	FREE WHITE MALES					FREE WHITE FEMALES					TOTAL ALL OTHER	TOTAL SLAVES	TOTALS	DISTRICT/ TOWNSHIP	NOTES
					under 10	10 to 16	16 to 26	26 to 45	45 and over	under 10	10 to 16	16 to 26	26 to 45	45 and over					
Deerfield	51	1	Arms	Jonathan		1	3		1			2	1	1	1		10		
Deerfield	51	2	Arms	Aaron	1	1	2		1	2	1	1		2			11		
Deerfield	51	3	Arms	Thomas					1			1	1	1			4		
Deerfield	51	4	Arms	Eliphas	2	2		1		2		2	1				10		
Deerfield	51	5	Arms	Thomas Jr	1			1		1		1					4		
Deerfield	51	6	Arms	Seth	2	1		1		2	1	1	1				9		
Deerfield	51	7	Arms	Eliaken	2		1	1	1	2		2	2	1			12		
Deerfield	51	8	Arms	Elijah	1	1	1	1	1	3	1		1	1			11		
Deerfield	51	9	Allis	Eben		1		1						1			3		
Deerfield	51	10	Anderson	William		1		1						1			3		
Deerfield	51	11	Anderson	Solomon	1	2		1		1			1				6		
Deerfield	51	12	Anderson	John	1			1		1			1				4		
Deerfield	51	13	Ashley	Elihu		1	2		1		1			1	2		8		
Deerfield	51	14	Ashley	Solomon				1					1				2		
Deerfield	51	15	Anderson	Abner	3			1		2				1			7		
Deerfield	51	16	Anderson	John	1			1		1	1	2		1			7		
Deerfield	51	17	Allen	Caleb		1	3		1		1	1		1			8		
Deerfield	51	18	Alexander	Amos		1			1	1	1	1		2			7		
Deerfield	51	19	Arnold	William	1				1	1			1				4		
Deerfield	51	20	Adams	David	1			1				1					3		
Deerfield	51	21	Arms	Lemuel	3			1				1	1				6		
Deerfield	51	22	Arms	Elizabeth										2			2		
Deerfield	51	23	Barnard	Joseph	1	1	1		1	2	1	2	1				10		
Deerfield	51	24	Barnard	Ebenezer		1	2		2	1			1	2			9		
Deerfield	51	25	Barnard	Ebenezer 2d	2	1	1	2		1		1	1				9		
Deerfield	51	26	Barnard	Erastus		2	4	2		1		2					11		
Deerfield	51	27	Barnard	Elizabeth		1	1			1	2	2		1			8		
Deerfield	51	28	Bardwell	John		1	3	1				2					7		
Deerfield	51	29	Blodget	Timothy	2	1		1		1		3		1			10		
Deerfield	51	30	Blodget	Thaddeus	2			1		1	1		1				6		
Deerfield	51	31	Blodget	Samuel	2		2			2			1				7		
Deerfield	51	32	Burt	Ebenezer				1			1			1			3		
Deerfield	51	33	Berry	John	2		1	1		3	1		1	1			10		
Deerfield	51	34	Billings	Jesse	1			1		2	1						5		
Deerfield	51	35	Billings	Timothy	1		3	1		1		2					8		
Deerfield	51	36	Ball	John	1	1	2		1	3	1	1	1	1			12		
Deerfield	51	37	Blackler	John	1			1		2	2			1			7		
Deerfield	51	38	Bradley	Joseph			1	1		1	1			1			5		
Deerfield	51	39	Boyden	Frederick			1			3			1				5		
Deerfield	51	40	Burt	Stephen	1	1		1		2	1	1	1				9		
Deerfield	51	41	Birge	John				1						1			2		
Deerfield	51	42	Cook	George	3			1		1	1		1				7		
Deerfield	51	43	Catlin	Richard	1		1	1			1	1	1				6		
Deerfield	51	44	Catlin	John	1	1		1		1	2		1	1			8		
Deerfield	51	45	Chesson	Joseph		1	1	1		1		1					5		
Deerfield	52	1	Cobb	Jonathan		2	1					1			1		5		
Deerfield	52	2	Cobb	Joseph		1				3		1					5		
Deerfield	52	3	Cooley	Azariah	1	2	1	1		3	3			1			12		
Deerfield	52	4	Cooley	Eli	3	1		1		2	1	1	1				10		
Deerfield	52	5	Cooley	Abner		1	1		1	1		3		1			8		
Deerfield	52	6	Child	Noah Wright	2			1		2			1				6		
Deerfield	52	7	Child	Samuel	1	2	1	1	1		1	3		2			12		
Deerfield	52	8	Child	Samuel 2d	1	1	2	1	1	1	2	1		1			10		
Deerfield	52	9	Child	Amzi	1	1	4	1	1	1	1	1		1			12		
Deerfield	52	10	Clark	Jedediah	1	1			1		2	2		1			9		
Deerfield	52	11	Clark	William	1			1		1				1			4		
Deerfield	52	12	Clapp	John Junr	5	2		1		2	1		1				12		
Deerfield	52	13	Clapp	Erastus	2	1		1			1		1				6		
Deerfield	52	14	Clapp	John				1	1			2		1			5		
Deerfield	52	15	Clapp	Elisha	1	1	1	1		3			1				8		
Deerfield	52	16	Chapman	Jonathan		1	2		1	1	1	2		1			9		
Deerfield	52	17	Chapman	William	1			1		1							3		
Deerfield	52	18	Clary	Elijah	1			1		2	1		1				6		
Deerfield	52	19	Clary	Elihu	1			1			1		1				4		
Deerfield	52	20	Carey	Charity				1				1	1				3		
Deerfield	52	21	Chamberlain	Samuel	1	1			2	1				1			6		
Deerfield	52	22	Cooley	Rebeccah		2				1	1			1			5		
Deerfield	52	23	Chandler	Moses				1						1			2		
Deerfield	52	24	Cheney	Jedediah		1				1			1				4		
Deerfield	52	25	Clark	Merian								2		2			4		
Deerfield	52	26	Cary	Nathan	1			1					1				3		
Deerfield	52	27	Cary	Robert	1			1				1					3		
Deerfield	52	28	DeWolf	Simon			1					1					2		
Deerfield	52	29	Dodge	Caleb	3	1		1	1				1	1			8		
Deerfield	52	30	Dickinson	David					2		1	1		1			5		
Deerfield	52	31	Dickinson	Eliphalet	2	1	4		2			2	1	2			14		
Deerfield	52	32	Dickinson	J*roh Wells	2	1	4		1	1		2	1				12		
Deerfield	52	33	Dickinson	Consider		2	1	1			3		1				8		
Deerfield	52	34	Dickinson	Gideon		2	3		1				1				8		

TOWN	PG#	LN#	HEADS OF HOUSEHOLD LAST NAME	FIRST NAME	FREE WHITE MALES under 10	10 to 16	16 to 26	26 to 45	45 and over	FREE WHITE FEMALES under 10	10 to 16	16 to 26	26 to 45	45 and over	TOTAL ALL OTHER	TOTAL SLAVES	TOTALS	DISTRICT/ TOWNSHIP	NOTES
Deerfield	52	35	Dickinson	Calvin			1			1			1				3		
Deerfield	52	36	Dwelly	Samuel			1	1	1					1			4		
Deerfield	52	37	DeWolf	Elisha		1				1		1		1			4		
Deerfield	52	38	Davison	Barnabas					1			1		1			3		
Deerfield	52	39	Dodge	William		1			1	1	1		1				5		
Deerfield	52	40	Eames	Nathan	1			1	1	2			1				6		
Deerfield	52	41	Eames	Ebenezer	1			1		2			1				5		
Deerfield	52	42	Eddy	Moses	1	1		1				1	1				5		
Deerfield	52	43	Eddy	Jacob	2			1		3			1				7		
Deerfield	52	44	Frary	Nathan			2		1		1			1			5		
Deerfield	52	45	Fisk	Daniel		2			1	1				1			5		
Deerfield	52	46	Frink	Miner			1		1			1		1			4		
Deerfield	52	47	Faxon	Calvin	2			1		1			1				5		
Deerfield	53	1	Fowle	Susannah			1						1	1			3		
Deerfield	53	2	Frary	Eleanor	1			1				1					4		
Deerfield	53	3	Grandy	Remembrance	1			1		1	1		1				5		
Deerfield	53	4	Graves	Zebediah	1	1	1		1		1		1				6		
Deerfield	53	5	Gilbert	David	1			1		2			1				5		
Deerfield	53	6	Gifford	Noah	2		1		1	2			1				7		
Deerfield	53	7	Griffin	David	2		1	1		1			1				6		
Deerfield	53	8	Goff	Paul											4		4		
Deerfield	53	9	Hawks	William		1		1	1	1			1	1			6		
Deerfield	53	10	Hawks	Waitstill	2		2	1	1	1	1	2		1			11		
Deerfield	53	11	Hawks	Samuel	2	1		1		2	1		1				8		
Deerfield	53	12	Hawks	Seth Junr	2			1		2	2		1				8		
Deerfield	53	13	Hawks	Hilkiah	1	1	1	1		1	1	1	1				8		
Deerfield	53	14	Hawks	Zadok		1		1	1	1	1	1		1			7		
Deerfield	53	15	Hawks	Zun		1	1	1		2		1	1				8		
Deerfield	53	16	Hawks	Obed			1		1		1	1		2			8		
Deerfield	53	17	Hawks	Asa				1						1			2		
Deerfield	53	18	Hawks	Asa Junr	2	1		1	1	1			2				8		
Deerfield	53	19	Hawks	Paul		2	1		1			1	3	1			9		
Deerfield	53	20	Hawks	Zeeb	2	1		1		2	2		1				9		
Deerfield	53	21	Hamilton	Eben	3		2	2		2	1	1	1	1			13		
Deerfield	53	22	Hoit	Jonathan		2		1						1			4		
Deerfield	53	23	Hoit	Cephas			1			1		1					3		
Deerfield	53	24	Hoit	David				1						1			2		
Deerfield	53	25	Hoit	David Junr		2		1		1	1	2	2				9		
Deerfield	53	26	Hoit	Elihu			1			1	1		1				4		
Deerfield	53	27	Hoit	Jonathan 2d		2	2							1			5		
Deerfield	53	28	Hoit	Ebenezer			1			2			1				4		
Deerfield	53	29	Hoit	Eprephras	1			1		2		1	1				6		
Deerfield	53	30	Hitchcock	Justin	1	1	1		1			1	1	1			7		
Deerfield	53	31	Hardin	Abijah		1	1	1		4		1		1			9		
Deerfield	53	32	Hinkley	Elijah	2			1		1	1	1	1				7		
Deerfield	53	33	Harris	John				1			1	1		1			4		
Deerfield	53	34	Hofins	James		1		2		1	1		1				6		
Deerfield	53	35	Hart	Samuel	3	1		1		3			3				11		
Deerfield	53	36	Hale	James	1			1		1	1		1				5		
Deerfield	53	37	Hastings	Oliver	1	1		1		1			1				5		
Deerfield	53	38	Jewett	Enoch			1		1	1		2		1			6		
Deerfield	53	39	Jewett	Reuben	1			1		4			1				7		
Deerfield	53	40	Jones	Jehiel	2	2	2		1	1		1		1			10		
Deerfield	53	41	Jones	Jehiel Jun	3	1		1		1	1		1				8		
Deerfield	53	42	Johnson	Asa		1		1		3			1				6		
Deerfield	53	43	Jordet	Selah	1			1		2			1				5		
Deerfield	54	1	Keet	Joel	1	3		1		1	2	2	1				11		
Deerfield	54	2	Kendall	Luke	3			1		1	3		1				9		
Deerfield	54	3	Lotrick	James	1				1	1			1				4		
Deerfield	54	4	Loveland	Jonathan	1			1		1			1	1			5		
Deerfield	54	5	Lanfair	Leonard	1	1	1	1		1			1				6		
Deerfield	54	6	Lanfair	Roswell	2	1		1					1				5		
Deerfield	54	7	Lyman	Augustus		1	2	1		2	2	3			1		12		
Deerfield	54	8	Lock	Jonas		1			1			1	1				4		
Deerfield	54	9	Loveridge	Amasa	3		1		3				1				8		
Deerfield	54	10	Logan	James			1						1				2		
Deerfield	54	11	Loveridge	William	3	2	2	1		1	1		1				11		
Deerfield	54	12	Mendall	Church	1	1			1				1				4		
Deerfield	54	13	McCall	Elihu				1		1	1	1	1				5		
Deerfield	54	14	Munn	Francis				1						1			2		
Deerfield	54	15	Munn	Phinehas		1		1						1			3		
Deerfield	54	16	Merrill	Samuel	2			1				1					4		
Deerfield	54	17	Morton	Justin	1	1		1	1	3	1	1	1				11		
Deerfield	54	18	Masters	Daniel	2			2		2	1		1				8		
Deerfield	54	19	Marsh	Amos	1	2			1	4				1			9		
Deerfield	54	20	Mather	Henry	2			1		1			1				5		
Deerfield	54	21	Mack	Elihat	2			1		1			1				5		
Deerfield	54	22	Miller	Silas	2			1		2		1					6		
Deerfield	54	23	Newton	Jeremiah			1	1		1			1				4		

			HEADS OF HOUSEHOLD		FREE WHITE MALES					FREE WHITE FEMALES									
TOWN	PG#	LN#	LAST NAME	FIRST NAME	under 10	10 to 16	16 to 26	26 to 45	45 and over	under 10	10 to 16	16 to 26	26 to 45	45 and over	TOTAL ALL OTHER	TOTAL SLAVES	TOTALS	DISTRICT/ TOWNSHIP	NOTES
Deerfield	54	24	Newton	Levi			1	1	1			1		1			5		
Deerfield	54	25	Nims	Seth	2	4	5	1		1	2	1	1	1			18		
Deerfield	54	26	Nims	Elisha		1	1		1		2	1		1			7		
Deerfield	54	27	Nims	Moses					1	1	1		1				4		
Deerfield	54	28	Nims	Ariel	1	2	1		1	1		2		1			9		
Deerfield	54	29	Newcomb	Ebenezer	1	1	1		1	2	1	1	1				9		
Deerfield	54	30	Pratt	William			1	1	1			1		1			5		
Deerfield	54	31	Paine	Charles											7		7		
Deerfield	54	32	Prismis	Ezra											7		7		
Deerfield	54	33	Russell	William	2	2	1	1		1		1					8		
Deerfield	54	34	Russell	Elijah				3				1		1			5		
Deerfield	54	35	Ross	Samuel			1		1		1			1			4		
Deerfield	54	36	Robbins	Nathan		1			1	2	2		1				7		
Deerfield	54	37	Robbins	John	1	1	2		1		1			1			7		
Deerfield	54	38	Rice	John	1			1		1			1				4		
Deerfield	54	39	Rand	Aaron	1			1		2	1		1				6		
Deerfield	54	40	Ross	Thomas				1		1	1		1				4		
Deerfield	54	41	Russell	Roswell				2		1		1					4		
Deerfield	54	42	Stebbins	Joseph	1	1	2	2	1	3	3	1		1			15		
Deerfield	54	43	Stebbins	Asa	3	1	3	1		3		1	1				13		
Deerfield	55	1	Stebbins	Ebenezer	4	1	1	1		1		1	1				10		
Deerfield	55	2	Stebbins	Moses	1			1		3	1		1				7		
Deerfield	55	3	Smith	Amasa			4		1	1	1	2		1			10		
Deerfield	55	4	Smith	Samuel		1	2		1	1	1	1	1	1			9		
Deerfield	55	5	Smith	Rufus		1		2		1		2	1				7		
Deerfield	55	6	Smith	Abner	1	1	1		1	1		1		1			7		
Deerfield	55	7	Smith	Philip	6			1		2			2				11		
Deerfield	55	8	Swan	Joseph	2		2	1					1				6		
Deerfield	55	9	Sheldon	John		1	1	2	1	1	1	1		1			9		
Deerfield	55	10	Saunderson	John		3		1	1			1		1			7		
Deerfield	55	11	Sweet	Joshua	2			1		3	1		1				8		
Deerfield	55	12	Sindler	John	1			1			1		1				4		
Deerfield	55	13	Sweet	Joseph			1	1				2		1			5		
Deerfield	55	14	Sexton	David		1		1				2		1			5		
Deerfield	55	15	Sexton	Ebenezer			3	1					1	1			6		
Deerfield	55	16	Sexton	Rufus	1			1		3		2					7		
Deerfield	55	17	Sexton	Joel				1					1				2		
Deerfield	55	18	Stanhope	Samuel		1	1	1			1	1	1				6		
Deerfield	55	19	Saunderson	Joseph		1	2		1	1	1	2		1			9		
Deerfield	55	20	Smith	Chester	1			1		1		1					4		
Deerfield	55	21	Spur	Lemuel	2	1			1	3	1		1				9		
Deerfield	55	22	Taylor	John	4		2	1		2	1	1	1		1		13		
Deerfield	55	23	Tryan	William	3	2	1	1		3	1	1	1				13		
Deerfield	55	24	Tayler	Obed		1		1		1		1					4		
Deerfield	55	25	Tuttle	Ebenezer			1		1	1				1			4		
Deerfield	55	26	Tracy	George	3			1					1	1			6		
Deerfield	55	27	Thompson	Samuel	2	3		1						1			7		
Deerfield	55	28	Tryan	William Junr	1	1	1					1					4		
Deerfield	55	29	Vaughan	Joseph	1			1					1				3		
Deerfield	55	30	Wells	David			1	1		2		2		1			7		
Deerfield	55	31	Wells	Thomas	1		1	1		2			1				6		
Deerfield	55	32	Wells	Quarters	1		1	1		3			2				8		
Deerfield	55	33	Wells	Samuel	3			1					1				5		
Deerfield	55	34	Wells	Levi	1			1		4			1				7		
Deerfield	55	35	Wright	Moses	3			2		1			1				7		
Deerfield	55	36	Wright	Asahel Jun	1	1		1	2	2	1		1	2			11		
Deerfield	55	37	Wright	Judah	2			1	1	1			1	1			7		
Deerfield	55	38	Wright	Carnie	1	2	2		1	2	1		1				10		
Deerfield	55	39	Wright	Westwood Cooke	2	2	1	2	1	1				1			11		
Deerfield	55	40	Wise	Joseph	1		1		1		1			1			5		
Deerfield	55	41	Williams	Wm Stodard	2	3		3		1		1	1				11		
Deerfield	55	42	Williams	Solomon	2	2	1	2				1	1	2			11		
Deerfield	55	43	Williams	John		1	1	1					1				4		
Deerfield	55	44	Williams	Stephen	1		1			1	1	1	1	1			7		
Deerfield	55	45	Williams	Eben H.	1			1		2		3	1				8		
Deerfield	55	46	Warren	Neverson	2			1						1			4		
Deerfield	55	47	Willson	Samuel		2	1	1	1				1	2			8		
Deerfield	55	48	Whitney	Stephen	1			1		2	2	1	2		1		10		
Deerfield	55	49	Willis	Ebenezer	3	1			1		1		1				7		
Deerfield	55	50	Wilkinson	Ebenezer		1		1					1				3		
Deerfield	55	51	Wright	James				1					1				2		

TOWN	PG#	LN#	LAST NAME	FIRST NAME	FREE WHITE MALES under 10	10 to 16	16 to 26	26 to 45	45 and over	FREE WHITE FEMALES under 10	10 to 16	16 to 26	26 to 45	45 and over	TOTAL ALL OTHER	TOTAL SLAVES	TOTALS	DISTRICT/ TOWNSHIP	NOTES
Easthampton	134	1	Baley	Submit				1		3			1				5		
Easthampton	134	2	Sprague	Oliver	1	1	2	1		2	1		1	1			10		
Easthampton	134	3	Wright	Stephen Junr	1	1		1					1				4		
Easthampton	134	4	Brewer	Benaijah				1					1				2		
Easthampton	134	5	Brewer	Bildad	2		1		1	1		1	1	1			8		
Easthampton	134	6	Strong	Benjamin	2			1					1				4		
Easthampton	134	7	Robbins	Joel	1			1					1				3		
Easthampton	134	8	Hendrick	James	4	2		1		1	1	1	1				11		
Easthampton	134	9	Gladden	Azariah	1				1		1		1				4		
Easthampton	134	10	Gladden	Azariah Junr			1						1				2		
Easthampton	134	11	Sandford	John	1			1		2				1			5		
Easthampton	134	12	Clap	Aaron Junr			1			1			1				3		
Easthampton	134	13	White	Nathl	1		2		1		1	1		1			7		
Easthampton	134	14	Luddon	Ezra		1		1				1		1			4		
Easthampton	134	15	Chapman	Moses	3	1		1		1	1	1	1				9		
Easthampton	134	16	Williston	Pason	2			1		2			2				7		
Easthampton	134	17	Clap	Aaron	2	2	1		1	2	1	1		1			11		
Easthampton	134	18	Clap	Levi	1		2	1		3	2		1				10		
Easthampton	134	19	Clap	Benjamin	2	1	1		1	1	1	2		1			10		
Easthampton	134	20	Graves	John	1			1		2			1				5		
Easthampton	134	21	Clap	Adolphus	1		1			1		1					4		
Easthampton	134	22	Searl	Elisha			1			2			1				4		
Easthampton	134	23	Wright	Stephen			1	3	1			1		1			7		
Easthampton	134	24	Wright	Luther	1			1		1		1					4		
Easthampton	134	25	Lyman	Benjamin	3	1		1		2	1		1				9		
Easthampton	134	26	Kentfield	Noah				1			1		1				3		
Easthampton	134	27	Franey	Obediah	1		1					1					3		
Easthampton	134	28	Lyman	Solomon	1			1	1	2	2		1				8		
Easthampton	134	29	Clap	Joseph	2			1		3	1		1		1		9		
Easthampton	134	30	Gladden	Wm						3			1				4		
Easthampton	134	31	Clap	Hophni			1			1			1				3		
Easthampton	134	32	Clap	Thadeus	3		1	1		2		1	1				9		
Easthampton	134	33	Danks	Zadok	1			1		1			1				4		
Easthampton	135	1	Parsons	Joel Junr			1	1		2		2					6		
Easthampton	135	2	James	Jonathan Junr	2			1		2			1				6		
Easthampton	135	3	Clark	Eliakim	3			1		3			1				8		
Easthampton	135	4	Clark	Elizer	2	1	2	1		2			2				10		
Easthampton	135	5	Clark	Asahel	1		2		1	1		1	1	1			8		
Easthampton	135	6	Clark	Job	1	1	1		1		1	1		1			7		
Easthampton	135	7	James	Jonathan			1		1	1			1	2			6		
Easthampton	135	8	Brown	Rufus			1		1				1				3		
Easthampton	135	9	Clark	Elam	2	1		1	3	2		1					10		
Easthampton	135	10	Wood	Stephen	1	1							1				4		
Easthampton	135	11	Janes	Ebenezer	3			1		3			1				8		
Easthampton	135	12	Clark	Obediah		1		1					1				3		
Easthampton	135	13	Clark	Thadeus	2			1					1				4		
Easthampton	135	14	Janes	Noah	3	2	1		1		1	1	1				10		
Easthampton	135	15	Janes	Enos	1			1	1	2			1				7		
Easthampton	135	16	Janes	Hannah Wid			1							1			2		
Easthampton	135	17	Janes	Seth			1			1			1				3		
Easthampton	135	18	Alvord	Elisha	2		1		1		2			2			8		
Easthampton	135	19	Brown	Silas				1						1			2		
Easthampton	135	20	Brown	Silas Junr	1	1		1		3	1		1				8		
Easthampton	135	21	Brown	John	2	1		1		3	1	1	1				10		
Easthampton	135	22	Clark	Philip				1					1				2		
Easthampton	135	23	Clark	Uriel	1	2		1		2			1				7		
Easthampton	135	24	Parsons	Joel		1		1	1			1		1			5		
Easthampton	135	25	Brown	Benjamin	1			1					1				3		
Easthampton	135	26	Janes	Obediah				1						1			2		
Easthampton	135	27	Parsons	Thadeus			1	1				1					3		
Easthampton	135	28	Starr	Thomas		1		1		1				1			4		
Easthampton	135	29	Starr	Thomas Junr	1		1			1			1				4		
Easthampton	135	30	Ferry	Solomon Junr	1			1					1				3		
Easthampton	135	31	Ferry	Solomon			2		1			1		1			5		
Easthampton	135	32	Clark	Phineas	1	1		1		4	2	1	1				11		
Easthampton	136	1	Bartlet	Jonathan	1	1	1	1		1		1	1				7		
Easthampton	136	2	Packard	Luke				1			1		1				3		
Easthampton	136	3	Phelps	John	2			1					1				4		
Easthampton	136	4	Clark	Oliver		2	3	1		4	1		1				12		
Easthampton	136	5	Hannum	Joel		2		1		2	2	2					9		
Easthampton	136	6	Danks	Ephraim	1			1		1			1				4		
Easthampton	136	7	Lyman	Leml Junr	2		1	1				1	1				6		
Easthampton	136	8	Lyman	Justus	1	1		1				1	1				5		
Easthampton	136	9	Janes	Obediah	1		1						1				3		
Easthampton	136	10	Clap	Isaac			1						1				2		
Easthampton	136	11	Clap	Luther		1	1	1		1		1	1	1			7		
Easthampton	136	12	Chapman	David	2		1	1		2	2		1				9		
Easthampton	136	13	Clap	Jona	1	1	1		1		1	1		1			7		
Easthampton	136	14	Clap	Devan				1		2			1				4		

TOWN	PG#	LN#	LAST NAME	FIRST NAME	FREE WHITE MALES					FREE WHITE FEMALES					TOTAL ALL OTHER	TOTAL SLAVES	TOTALS	DISTRICT/ TOWNSHIP	NOTES
					under 10	10 to 16	16 to 26	26 to 45	45 and over	under 10	10 to 16	16 to 26	26 to 45	45 and over					
Easthampton	136	15	Phelps	Wm			1		1	1	1	1	1				6		
Easthampton	136	16	Phelps	Elijah	2			1					1				4		
Easthampton	136	17	Alvord	Zebediah		1		1	1				2	1			6		
Easthampton	136	18	Alvord	Phineas	2			1		2	2	1	1				9		
Easthampton	136	19	Phelps	John 2d	2			1				1					4		
Easthampton	136	20	Lyman	Leml Junr	1		2	2	1	1			1	1			9		
Easthampton	136	21	Wright	Elijah	1	1	3	2	1			1		2			11		
Easthampton	136	22	Gains	Calvin	1			1		3			1				6		
Easthampton	136	23	Wright	Elijah Junr	1		1	1					1				5		
Easthampton	136	24	Lymon	David	1				1	2		2	1	1			8		
Easthampton	136	25	Hannum	Eleazer Junr	1		1	1	1	1			1	1			7		
Easthampton	136	26	Pomroy	Solomon	1	1	1	1	2			2		1			9		
Easthampton	136	27	Clap	John	2	1	1		1		1	1		1			8		
Easthampton	136	28	Pomroy	Enos			3		1	1	1			1			7		
Easthampton	136	29	Brown	Zenas	3			1					1				5		
Easthampton	136	30	Clap	Oliver	1			1		3			1				6		
Easthampton	136	31	Pomroy	Justus	1			1		2			1				5		
Easthampton	137	1	Eliot	John	3	1			1		1		1				7		
Easthampton	137	2	Pomroy	Enos Jr	1	1	1	1				1					5		

TOWN	PG#	LN#	LAST NAME	FIRST NAME	FREE WHITE MALES					FREE WHITE FEMALES					TOTAL ALL OTHER	TOTAL SLAVES	TOTALS	DISTRICT/ TOWNSHIP	NOTES
					under 10	10 to 16	16 to 26	26 to 45	45 and over	under 10	10 to 16	16 to 26	26 to 45	45 and over					
Gill	85	1	Brown	David	2			1		1	1			1			6		
Gill	85	2	Burnett	Nathaniel	1			1		2			1				5		
Gill	85	3	Burnett	John				1					2				3		
Gill	85	4	Carter	Benjamin			2	1		4	2		1				10		
Gill	85	5	Casey	Francis				1									1		
Gill	85	6	Coombs	Joshua			1	1			1		1				4		
Gill	85	7	Coombs	Joshua Jun	4	1		1		1	1		1				9		
Gill	85	8	Chase	Pierce			1					1		1			3		
Gill	85	9	Carrier	Benjamin	2	1		1		3			1				8		
Gill	85	10	Darby	Eleazer		1		1				1					3		
Gill	85	11	Darling	Jedediah	2	2		1		2			2				9		
Gill	85	12	Darling	John	1			1		6			1				9		
Gill	85	13	Evers	John	1		2		1	2	3		1				10		
Gill	85	14	Evers	Henry	1	1	1		2	2	1	1		2			11		
Gill	85	15	Evers	James	1	1						1					3		
Gill	85	16	Field	Ebenezer		1	2		2	2		1		1			9		
Gill	86	1	Field	Rodolphus			1			1		1					3		
Gill	86	2	Gain	Jehiel	2			1		1			1				5		
Gill	86	3	Gain	George			1			1		1					3		
Gill	86	4	Gain	Davis			1	1		1		1	1				5		
Gill	86	5	Goodrich	George	1	4	1		1	3			2				12		
Gill	86	6	Green	Benjamin	1	2	1		1	1	1	1		1			9		
Gill	86	7	Goodlow	Francis		2		1		2	1		1				7		
Gill	86	8	Goodale	Job				1		1		1	1				4		
Gill	86	9	Hathaway	Samuel		1		1					1				3		
Gill	86	10	Horsley	Benjamin				1						1			2		
Gill	86	11	Horsley	Jonathan	3		2			2			1				8		
Gill	86	12	Howland	John			1				1		1				3		
Gill	86	13	Howland	Salmon	1		1			2	1	1					6		
Gill	86	14	Holton	Nathaniel	1		2	1		4	1	1					10		
Gill	86	15	Horsley	Benjamin 2d	1	1		1		1	1	1					6		
Gill	86	16	Holister	Elisha	3		2						2				7		
Gill	86	17	Horsley	Isaiah	3		1	1					1				6		
Gill	86	18	Gilman	Shubal	2			1		2			1				6		
Gill	86	19	Howland	Seth		1	1	1				1		1			5		
Gill	86	20	Hodge	Seth		1		1	1	3	2		1	1			10		
Gill	86	21	Horsley	Rufus	1		1			1		1					4		
Gill	86	22	Horsley	Benjamin 3d	1			1		1		1					4		
Gill	86	23	Howland	George		2	1	1					1				5		
Gill	86	24	Janes	Samuel		1		1		4		1	1				8		
Gill	86	25	Jackson	John	1		2	1			1		1				6		
Gill	86	26	Henry	Jemima	1		2	1			1	1		1			7		
Gill	86	27	Luce	Joseph		1				1		1					3		
Gill	86	28	Loveland	Frederick	1			1		3	1	1					7		
Gill	86	29	Leonard	Samuel		1		1		1	1			1			5		
Gill	86	30	Lyon	Samuel		1		1						1			3		
Gill	86	31	Lawson	William	1			1		3			1				6		
Gill	86	32	Luce	Samuel	2	1	3		1	2			1				10		
Gill	86	33	Mallard	Solomon	1		1			1		1					4		
Gill	86	34	Munn	Seth	2	2		1		3	1		1				10		
Gill	87	1	Munn	Noah	1		1	1	1		2	1		1			8		
Gill	87	2	Munn	John		3		1		1	1		1				7		
Gill	87	3	Munn	Elisha		2	1	1		3	1		2				10		
Gill	87	4	Morley	Demick	2	1	1	1		2	1	1	1				10		
Gill	87	5	Morley	John	1	1		1		1	2		1				7		
Gill	87	6	Mayhew	Wilmore	2	1		1		1			1				6		
Gill	87	7	Mange	Peter	2			1					1				4		
Gill	87	8	Potter	Ichabod	1	1		1		3			1				7		
Gill	87	9	Parmenter	Josiah		1		1		4	1		1				8		
Gill	87	10	Phillips	Willis	1			1				1					3		
Gill	87	11	Parmenter	Asahel				1		2			2				5		
Gill	87	12	Rice	Enos	1			1		2		1	1				6		
Gill	87	13	Richards	Edward		1	1		1		1			1			5		
Gill	87	14	Roberts	Amaziah		1		1	1					1			4		
Gill	87	15	Roberts	Ebenezer	3		1	2		1	1	1	1	1			11		
Gill	87	16	Richards	Moses	2			1		2			1				6		
Gill	87	17	Richards	Charles				1		1			1				3		
Gill	87	18	Richards	Perin	1			1		3			1				6		
Gill	87	19	Ripley	Laban	1			1		2			1				5		
Gill	87	20	Rice	Benjamin		1	1	1		2	1	1	1				8		
Gill	87	21	Rice	Samuel		2	1	1			1		1		1		7		
Gill	87	22	Rice	Levi	1		1						1				3		
Gill	87	23	Ripley	Eli	2			1			1						4		
Gill	87	24	Severence	Abner	1	1		1			1		1				6		
Gill	87	25	Sprague	Jonathan				1			1		1				3		
Gill	87	26	Shattock	Rueben		1		1	1		1		1				5		
Gill	87	27	Starkweather	Elisha	2		1	1		1	1		1				7		
Gill	87	28	Stacy	Gilbert	1	1		1		1			1				5		
Gill	87	29	Stebbins	Elisha		1	2		1		1		1				6		

TOWN	PG#	LN#	LAST NAME	FIRST NAME	FREE WHITE MALES					FREE WHITE FEMALES					TOTAL ALL OTHER	TOTAL SLAVES	TOTALS	DISTRICT/ TOWNSHIP	NOTES
					under 10	10 to 16	16 to 26	26 to 45	45 and over	under 10	10 to 16	16 to 26	26 to 45	45 and over					
Gill	87	30	Stanhope	Jonas	3			1		3		1					8		
Gill	87	31	Stangton	Samuel	1	1	2		1	1		2		1			9		
Gill	88	1	Squires	David	2	3		1		2			1	1			10		
Gill	88	2	Slate	Ebenezer	1		1		1			1	1				5		
Gill	88	3	Scott	Moses	2	3		1		1	1		1				9		
Gill	88	4	Spooner	Levi	2			1					1				4		
Gill	88	5	Sprague	Joseph				1		1			1				3		
Gill	88	6	Selick	Frederick				1									1		
Gill	88	7	Thomson	John		1	1		1		2			1			6		
Gill	88	8	Wrisley	Jonathan	1			1		3		1	1				7		
Gill	88	9	Wrisley	Elijah	2	1	1		1	1	1	2		1			10		
Gill	88	10	Wrisley	David		1	1		1				1	2			6		
Gill	88	11	Wrisley	Asahel		1	1		1	2	1			1			7		
Gill	88	12	Wrisley	David Jun				1		3			1				5		
Gill	88	13	Wrisley	Joseph	2	1		1		2			1				7		
Gill	88	14	Wrisley	Caleb	2		1			1		1					5		
Gill	88	15	Wrisley	Eleazer		1		1				1		1			4		
Gill	88	16	Wrisley	Obed	1		1			1		1					4		
Gill	88	17	Wrisley	Sylvannus			1					1					2		
Gill	88	18	Wrisley	Eleazer Jnr				1		1							2		
Gill	88	19	Walmer	William	2		1	1		1	1		1	1			8		
Gill	88	20	White	Robert	4	1		1		1			1				8		
Gill	88	21	Webster	William	2			1		1			1				5		
Gill	88	22	Woodward	Job		1		1		4	1		1				8		
Gill	88	23	Webster	Hannah			3				1	1	1	1			7		

TOWN	PG#	LN#	HEADS OF HOUSEHOLD		FREE WHITE MALES					FREE WHITE FEMALES					TOTAL ALL OTHER	TOTAL SLAVES	TOTALS	DISTRICT/ TOWNSHIP	NOTES
			LAST NAME	FIRST NAME	under 10	10 to 16	16 to 26	26 to 45	45 and over	under 10	10 to 16	16 to 26	26 to 45	45 and over					
Goshen	309	1	Abel	Joshua		2		1				1		1			5		
Goshen	309	2	Abel	Joshua Jun	2	1		1		3			1				8		
Goshen	309	3	Abel	Benjm	1	3	1	1		3	1	1	1				12		
Goshen	309	4	Abel	Natha	1	1		1		3	1		1				8		
Goshen	309	5	Anderson	Ebenezer			1	1			2	1	1				6		
Goshen	309	6	Bryant	Caleb		1		1				1					3		
Goshen	309	7	Brown	Daniel				1			1	1	1				4		
Goshen	309	8	Brown	Thomas			2		1	1	1		1				6		
Goshen	309	9	Beal	Adam	2	1	2		1	1		1	2	1			11		
Goshen	309	10	Beal	Enoch	3	2	1	1			1	1	1	2			12		
Goshen	309	11	Burges	Benjm		2		1		1	1	3		1			9		
Goshen	309	12	Basset	Joseph	1	3			1	3	1		1				10		
Goshen	309	13	Blake	Joseph			1		1				1				3		
Goshen	309	14	Baker	Abner	4	2			1	1	1	1					10		
Goshen	309	15	Butler	Solomon	2			1				1	1				5		
Goshen	309	16	Brown	Greenwood	1	1		1		3	1		1				8		
Goshen	309	17	Buckingham	Jeddl				1		1		2		1			5		
Goshen	309	18	Billington	Nathl			3		1	1			1				6		
Goshen	309	19	Corban	Ezekiel				1					1				2		
Goshen	309	20	Cushman	Caleb	1		2		1	2	2		1				9		
Goshen	310	1	Caryell	John		1		1		1			1				4		
Goshen	310	2	Gatheart	Gershom	1	1		1		2		1	1				7		
Goshen	310	3	Draper	Reuben		3	4		1	1	1	1		1			12		
Goshen	310	4	Damon	Abner	4			1		1	1		1				8		
Goshen	310	5	Fuller	Nathan	1	3	1		1				2				8		
Goshen	310	6	Boyd	Jacob G	1	1	1	1		3			1				8		
Goshen	310	7	Grimes	Charles		1				1	3		1				6		
Goshen	310	8	Grant	Asa		1					1		1				4		
Goshen	310	9	Gustin	Molly Wid.	1	1	1			1		1		1			7		
Goshen	310	10	Halloch	William		1		1			1		1				4		
Goshen	310	11	Allen	Phillip Negro											3		3		
Goshen	310	12	James	John		1		1		1			1				4		
Goshen	310	13	James	Malachi	2	1	1	1		2	1	1	1				10		
Goshen	310	14	James	Moses	2	3		1		3	1		1				11		
Goshen	310	15	Tipson	John	2	2	1		1	2	1		1				10		
Goshen	310	16	Tipson	Joseph	1	2	1	1		3		1	1				10		
Goshen	310	17	Tipson	Samuel	3			1		1			1				6		
Goshen	310	18	Hunt	John		1					1	1	1				4		
Goshen	310	19	King	John	1	2		1	1	1			1				8		
Goshen	310	20	Kellogg	Stephen	1	1	1	1		2	2		1				9		
Goshen	310	21	Kingman	Isaac		1	2		2	1	1		2				9		
Goshen	310	22	Maning	Phineas	2			1		4			1				8		
Goshen	310	23	Lyon	Lemuel		1	1	1		1	2		1				7		
Goshen	310	24	Lyon	Cyrus	2	1	2		1	1	1		1				9		
Goshen	310	25	Lyman	Timothy			4		1	1	1		1				8		
Goshen	310	26	Montague	Luke	3		1						1				5		
Goshen	310	27	Maynard	Joseph	1	2	1		1	2		1		2			10		
Goshen	310	28	White	Seth		1					2						3		
Goshen	311	1	Maynard	Nehemiah	1		2		1	1	1	1					7		
Goshen	311	2	Howe	Reuben				1			1		1				3		
Goshen	311	3	Morse	Shepard		1		1		2	1	1					6		
Goshen	311	4	Mott	Samuel		1		1		1			1				4		
Goshen	311	5	Hammond	Joseph	1			1		3	2		1				8		
Goshen	311	6	Hammond	Alpheus	3			1		1			1				6		
Goshen	311	7	Hammond	Thaddeus	2			1		2	1		1				7		
Goshen	311	8	Orcott	Anigen	1	1		1	1	1			2	1			8		
Goshen	311	9	Orcott	Thomas			1			1			1				3		
Goshen	311	10	Orcott	James	3			1		1			1				6		
Goshen	311	11	Olds	Samuel	2	1		1		1		3		1			9		
Goshen	311	12	Orr	James	1	1		1		2			1				6		
Goshen	311	13	Putney	Ebenezer	2	2	2	1	1		2		2				12		
Goshen	311	14	Parsons	Eben		3	1			1	1	1					7		
Goshen	311	15	Parsons	Justus	4		1	1		1	1		1				9		
Goshen	311	16	Parsons	Silas	2	2		1		3	2		1				11		
Goshen	311	17	Parsons	Solomon	1		1	1		2	1		1				7		
Goshen	311	18	Packard	Joshua Jun	1			1	1	2			1	1			7		
Goshen	311	19	Powers	John	4	3		1		2		1	1				12		
Goshen	311	20	Parsons	Elisha		1			1	1	1		1				5		
Goshen	311	21	Partridge	Isaac	1			1		2			1				5		
Goshen	311	22	Putney	Aron	1			1		2	1						5		
Goshen	311	23	Prispt	John											7		7		
Goshen	311	24	Rogers	John	1	1		1		2			1				6		
Goshen	311	25	Stearns	John	3			1		1		1	1				7		
Goshen	311	26	Salmon	John			1			1		1					3		
Goshen	311	27	Smith	John		1	1		1		3		1				7		
Goshen	311	28	Stone	Ambrose	2	2		1		2			1				8		
Goshen	312	1	Stearns	Cyrus	3	2		1		1		1					8		
Goshen	312	2	Show	John		2					2		1				5		
Goshen	312	3	Stone	Sylvanus	3	2		1		1		1	1				9		

TOWN	PG#	LN#	LAST NAME	FIRST NAME	under 10	10 to 16	16 to 26	26 to 45	45 and over	under 10	10 to 16	16 to 26	26 to 45	45 and over	TOTAL ALL OTHER	TOTAL SLAVES	TOTALS	DISTRICT/ TOWNSHIP	NOTES
Goshen	312	4	Taylor	Oliver	1		2		1	1			1				6		
Goshen	312	5	Tower	Richard	1				1			2		1			5		
Goshen	312	6	Tower	Isaac		2	1		1	3			1				8		
Goshen	312	7	Taft	Cheny	3		1	1		1		2					8		
Goshen	312	8	Tilton	Salatiel	2	1	1	1		1	1	1	1				9		
Goshen	312	9	Thayer	Oliver	1		1	1				1					4		
Goshen	312	10	White	William		2	2		1			1		1			7		
Goshen	312	11	White	Louis	1	1	1			1	1			1			6		
Goshen	312	12	White	Ebenezer	1	2		1		2			1				7		
Goshen	312	13	White	Josiah				1			1			1			3		
Goshen	312	14	White	Ezekiel	1	1	1		1		1			1			6		
Goshen	312	15	Williams	John	2	1	2	1		3	1	2	1				13		
Goshen	312	16	Williams	Jonah	5		1	1					1				8		
Goshen	312	17	Wing	Edward	1	2	3		1	2	1	1		1			12		
Goshen	312	18	Williams	John 2d	1			1				1					3		
Goshen	312	19	Willcott	Zebulon	4	1	1	1			1	1	1				10		
Goshen	312	20	Will	Jesse	3	1	1		1	3	1	2	1				13		
Goshen	312	21	Vinton	Levi		1		1		3	2	1	1				9		
Goshen	312	22	Salmon	George	1		1	1		2			1				6		
Goshen	312	23	Putney	Joseph	1		1					1					3		
Goshen	312	24	Wheelar	James	1	1			1	2		1	1				7		
Goshen	312	25	Whitman	Saml	2	2	2		1	3	2	1					13		
Goshen	312	26	Weeks	Thomas					1					1			2		
Goshen	312	27	Keith	Matthew			1					1					2		

TOWN	PG#	LN#	HEADS OF HOUSEHOLD		FREE WHITE MALES					FREE WHITE FEMALES					TOTAL ALL OTHER	TOTAL SLAVES	TOTALS	DISTRICT/ TOWNSHIP	NOTES
			LAST NAME	FIRST NAME	under 10	10 to 16	16 to 26	26 to 45	45 and over	under 10	10 to 16	16 to 26	26 to 45	45 and over					
Granby	252	1	Nash	Eleazer	1			1		1			1				4		
Granby	252	2	Nash	Phebe Wd				1						2			3		
Granby	252	3	Burnett	Jonathan		1	1	1			1			1			5		
Granby	252	4	Hunter	Thomas				1		1			1				3		
Granby	252	5	Dickinson	Joseph		1	1	1						2			5		
Granby	252	6	Smith	Nathan Dr				1					1	1			3		
Granby	252	7	Smith	James	4			1	1				1	1			8		
Granby	252	8	Smith	Samuel		1	1			1		1					4		
Granby	252	9	Montague	Jonah			1	1	1	1			1	1			6		
Granby	252	10	Preston	Joel	4		1	1		1			1				8		
Granby	252	11	Gridley	Elijah Revd	2			1		2			1				6		
Granby	252	12	Moody	Enos	3	1		1		1		1	1				8		
Granby	252	13	Smith	Jared	4		1				1		1				7		
Granby	252	14	Nash	David	2					2			1				5		
Granby	252	15	Lombard	Ariel			1			1			1				3		
Granby	252	16	Smith	Levi	4		1		1	1			1				8		
Granby	252	17	Smith	David Maj	2	1		1		2			1	1			8		
Granby	252	18	Smith	Phinehas	1	2	2	1	1				1	1			9		
Granby	252	19	Preston	John			1	1				2	3	1			8		
Granby	252	20	Moody	reuben		1	1	1		1		1					5		
Granby	252	21	Marshall	John				1									1		
Granby	252	22	Preston	Jabez		1		1		2		1	1	1			7		
Granby	252	23	Preston	Moses	1	1		1		2		2		1			8		
Granby	252	24	Preston	James		1		1						1			3		
Granby	252	25	Preston	John Jun	4		1			1			1				7		
Granby	252	26	Mandeville	John	5	1	1		1	1		2	1				12		
Granby	252	27	Patrick	John	1		1						1				3		
Granby	252	28	Stebbins	Luther	1		1					1					3		
Granby	252	29	Caswell	Abiel				1	1	1	2			1			6		
Granby	252	30	Smith	Asahel Lt				1					1	1			3		
Granby	252	31	Smith	John	1			1		3	1						6		
Granby	252	32	Clark	Noah	1	1		1		1	1		1				6		
Granby	252	33	Butterfield	Jeremiah				1									1		
Granby	252	34	Tuttle	Nathan	1		1	1		2			1				6		
Granby	252	35	Clark	Joshua		1		1		1			1	1			5		
Granby	252	36	Coye	Abraham				1						1			2		
Granby	252	37	Coye	Aaron	3	1		1		1			1	1			8		
Granby	252	38	Davis	Isaac			1						1				2		
Granby	252	39	Richard	Abigail Wd			1							1			2		
Granby	252	40	Fairfield	Thaddeus	1		1						1				3		
Granby	252	41	McNelly	Henry	3			1		3			1				8		
Granby	252	42	Totman	Samuel				1			1	1		2			5		
Granby	252	43	Corey	Isaac	1		1			1		1					4		
Granby	252	44	Able	Sarah Wd	2		2			1	1		1				7		
Granby	253	1	Able	David	1		1						1				3		
Granby	253	2	Ayres	Aaron	1	2	1	1		2		2	1				10		
Granby	253	3	Ayres	Eleazer	1	1		1		1							4		
Granby	253	4	Clark	Jotham	1			1		1		1	1				5		
Granby	253	5	Clark	Israel	2	1	1				1	1	1	1			8		
Granby	253	6	Smith	Seth	1	2	1		1	1	1			1			8		
Granby	253	7	Smith	Benjamin	1			1					1				3		
Granby	253	8	Giddings	Daniel	2			1		4			2				9		
Granby	253	9	Giddings	James		1	2	1		1		1		1			7		
Granby	253	10	Kent	Samuel			1	1	1	1		1	1				6		
Granby	253	11	Moss	Amos	1			1				2					4		
Granby	253	12	Moss	Luther				1		1		1	1				4		
Granby	253	13	Clark	Samuel Capt	1	2		2		2				1			8		
Granby	253	14	Fisher	Jacob		1				1	1						3		
Granby	253	15	Witt	John	1		1										2		
Granby	253	16	Witt	Joseph	2	1	1		1	1	1		1				8		
Granby	253	17	Rice	Joel	1	1		1		1			1				5		
Granby	253	18	Town	Israel				1						2			3		
Granby	253	19	Vinton	Abraham				1						1			2		
Granby	253	20	Hunter	Aaron	2			1		1			1				5		
Granby	253	21	Goldthwait	Elijah	2			1		2			1				6		
Granby	253	22	Moody	John Lt		1	1	1					1	1			5		
Granby	253	23	Taylor	Ebenezer				1						1			2		
Granby	253	24	Smith	Nathan Junr		2	1	1		3	1	1	1				10		
Granby	253	25	Warner	Rachel Wid										2			2		
Granby	253	26	Dickinson	Aaron Capt		1		1					1	1			4		
Granby	253	27	Parsons	Oliver	3		2	1		1			1				8		
Granby	253	28	Cook	Perez	1	1		1		1	1	1	1				7		
Granby	253	29	Smith	Hannah Wid			2	2				1	1	1			7		
Granby	253	30	Chamberlain	Stephen		1	1	1		1			1	1			6		
Granby	253	31	Hatfield	Joseph		1		1						1			3		
Granby	253	32	Copland	Robert	3			1			1		1				6		
Granby	253	33	Little	John	1			1		1		1					4		
Granby	253	34	Bartlett	Aaron	2	2		1		1	1	1	1				9		
Granby	253	35	Warner	Eleazer Capt			1		1	1			1				4		

60

TOWN	PG#	LN#	LAST NAME	FIRST NAME	under 10	10 to 16	16 to 26	26 to 45	45 and over	under 10	10 to 16	16 to 26	26 to 45	45 and over	TOTAL ALL OTHER	TOTAL SLAVES	TOTALS	DISTRICT/ TOWNSHIP	NOTES
					FREE WHITE MALES					FREE WHITE FEMALES									
Granby	253	36	Montague	John	2	1		1		1			1	1			7		
Granby	253	37	Gleason	Simon	1				1		2			1			5		
Granby	253	38	Damon	Peter			3	1				2		1			7		
Granby	253	39	Pease	William	3			1		1			1				6		
Granby	253	40	Tyler	John			2			2			1	1			6		
Granby	253	41	Carver	Aaron	1			1				1					3		
Granby	253	42	Tyler	Gurdon	3			1		1			1				6		
Granby	253	43	Chapin	Elijah				1			1	1					3		
Granby	253	44	Olds	Jesse	1		1			4		2					8		
Granby	253	45	Chapins	Pliny	1		1	1		2		1	1	1			8		
Granby	254	1	Tarbox	Adriel	2			1				1					4		
Granby	254	2	Smith	Enos Dr.			1			1	1						3		
Granby	254	3	Ferre	Noah	3	2	1		1	1			1				9		
Granby	254	4	Darvin	Ebenezer				1					1				2		
Granby	254	5	Ferre	Charles				1									1		
Granby	254	6	Ferre	Charles Jr	3	1	1	1		1			1				8		
Granby	254	7	Ferre	Luther	1		1	1		1			1				5		
Granby	254	8	Sexton	Daniel				1		1			1				3		
Granby	254	9	Moody	Gideon Ens	2		1	1		1		1					6		
Granby	254	10	Stebbins	Asaph				1			2		2				5		
Granby	254	11	Stebbins	Jona	3		1			1		1					6		
Granby	254	12	Stebbins	Herman	2		1				1						4		
Granby	254	13	Taylor	Shubael			1					1					2		
Granby	254	14	Chapin	Philander	1		1					1					3		
Granby	254	15	Taylor	Jacob				1					1				2		
Granby	254	16	Taylor	Ithamar	3		2	1		1	1		1				9		
Granby	254	17	Taylor	Silas	3		1			2		1	1				8		
Granby	254	18	Tilley	Sudderick	1	1	1			2	1		1				7		
Granby	254	19	Taylor	Samuel Dr	2		1			3		1	1				8		
Granby	254	20	Taylor	David	2		1			2	1	1					7		
Granby	254	21	Barton	Daniel	2		1			2	1		1				7		
Granby	254	22	Hathaway	Abner			1			1			1				3		
Granby	254	23	Barton	Ezekiel	1	1	1			3	1		1				8		
Granby	254	24	Barton	Simeon	1		2				1	1					5		
Granby	254	25	Barton	Titus Dr	1		1			4		1	1				8		
Granby	254	26	Bartlett	David Capt		1		1						2			4		
Granby	254	27	Barton	Samuel	1		2					1					4		
Granby	254	28	Abbe	Abner	2	2	1	1		2	1		1	1			11		
Granby	254	29	Bartlett	Asahel	3	2					1		2	1			10		
Granby	254	30	Bartlett	Oliver	1	1	1	1			2	1	1				8		
Granby	254	31	Bartlett	Alpheus		1						1					2		
Granby	254	32	Dickinson	Samuel		1		1				1		1			4		
Granby	254	33	Dickinson	Eli Dr	2		3	1		2	2	1	2				13		
Granby	254	34	Smith	Ebenezer		2	1	1		1	1	2		1			9		
Granby	254	35	Alvard	Gad	1	1	1	1		1	1	1	1				8		
Granby	254	36	Robinson	Joel	1		1					1					3		
Granby	254	37	Warner	Elijah	1					3			1				5		
Granby	254	38	Birchard	Israel	4			1				1	1				7		
Granby	254	39	Birchard	Jabez	3		2	1		1		1	1				9		
Granby	254	40	Eastman	William	3	1		1				1	1	1			8		
Granby	254	41	Eastman	Joseph	3	1			1	2		1		1			9		
Granby	254	42	Dickinson	Job	1	1		1		2			1				6		
Granby	254	43	Dickinson	Waitstill			1		1			1		1			4		
Granby	254	44	Cowls	Cheester Dr.	2			1				1					4		
Granby	255	1	Smith	Experience Ens		1		1	2					1			5		
Granby	255	2	Moody	Simeon	1	2	1		1		1	2		1			9		
Granby	255	3	Moody	Aaron	2		1	1	1		2			1			8		
Granby	255	4	Eastman	Eunice Wd	1	2	1							1			5		
Granby	255	5	Church	David Dr		2	1		1	1				1			6		
Granby	255	6	Murry	John				1				1					2		

TOWN	PG#	LN#	LAST NAME	FIRST NAME	FREE WHITE MALES under 10	10 to 16	16 to 26	26 to 45	45 and over	FREE WHITE FEMALES under 10	10 to 16	16 to 26	26 to 45	45 and over	TOTAL ALL OTHER	TOTAL SLAVES	TOTALS	DISTRICT/TOWNSHIP	NOTES
Granville East Society	527	1	Parsons	Israel	1	1		1		2	1		1				7		
Granville East Society	527	2	Spelman	Timothy	1	2		1		3		2	1				10		
Granville East Society	527	3	Spelman	Israel					1		1	1	1				4		
Granville East Society	527	4	Spelman	Aaron & Elisha	1			1	1			2					5		
Granville East Society	527	5	Collins	Claudius L			1	1		4			1				7		
Granville East Society	527	6	Winchell	Martin	1			1	1			2					5		
Granville East Society	527	7	Spelman	Stephen	2	1	1		1	1	1	2		2			11		
Granville East Society	527	8	Mons	Martin	2	2		1		2			1	1			9		
Granville East Society	527	9	Kelly	Martin	1		1	1		1	1		1				6		
Granville East Society	527	10	Seymour	Asa	3	1	1	1		1	1	1	1				10		
Granville East Society	527	11	Spelman	Charles	1			1		1	1		1				5		
Granville East Society	527	12	Clark	David	1			1		4	2	1	1				10		
Granville East Society	527	13	Tinker	Martin	1					2			1	3			8		
Granville East Society	527	14	Gibbons	Bildad	3	2	1	1		1	1	2					11		
Granville East Society	527	15	Cooley	Daniel	1	2	3		1	2			2				11		
Granville East Society	527	16	Spelman	Jesse			1	1				1					3		
Granville East Society	527	17	Mons	Ashbel	2	2		1		4			1				10		
Granville East Society	527	18	Miner	Christopher	1				1		1			1			4		
Granville East Society	527	19	Bissel	Dan			1				1		1	1			4		
Granville East Society	527	20	Di*men	Richard		1		1	1		1			1			5		
Granville East Society	527	21	Bigelow	Aaron	1			1		1		1					4		
Granville East Society	527	22	Cooley	George	1	1	1		1	1	1		1				7		
Granville East Society	527	23	Fox	Elisha	3	1		1		3			1				9		
Granville East Society	527	24	Gibbons	Jeddiah	1			1		3			1				6		
Granville East Society	527	25	Gibbons	Elisha	1			1	1	5			1	1			10		
Granville East Society	527	26	Buttolph	Abijah	1			1		3	3		1				9		
Granville East Society	527	27	Watrous	Benjamin	2			1		2			1	1			7		
Granville East Society	527	28	Clark	Hannah	2	1		1	1	2			1				8		
Granville East Society	529	1	Root	Stephen	1	1			1								3		
Granville East Society	529	2	Bancroft	Comfort		1	2			1	2	1	1	1			9		
Granville East Society	529	3	Bancroft	Lemuel	1		1					1					3		
Granville East Society	529	4	Moore	Elias	1			1		4	3		1				10		
Granville East Society	529	5	Cooley	Zadock	2			1		3	1		1				8		
Granville East Society	529	6	Rowley	Roswell	1	1		1		3	1		1				8		
Granville East Society	529	7	Woolworth	Phinehas	2	2	2		1	3			1				11		
Granville East Society	529	8	Moore	Joseph	3	1		1		2	1		1				9		
Granville East Society	529	9	Graves	Enoch	2			1		3			1				7		
Granville East Society	529	10	Graves	Asher	3			1		1	1		1				7		
Granville East Society	529	11	Clark	Nathaniel	1			1				1	2				5		
Granville East Society	529	12	Graves	Roswell	3			1					1	1			6		
Granville East Society	529	13	Rose	Timothy	2	1		1	1	2	2		1	1			11		
Granville East Society	529	14	Clark	Joel	1			1		3	1						6		
Granville East Society	529	15	Peters	William	1	1			1	1	2		3				9		
Granville East Society	529	16	Coe	James	2			1				1		1			5		
Granville East Society	529	17	Coe	Rachel			1					2					3		
Granville East Society	529	18	Rose	Levi		1	2		1	3	2		1				10		
Granville East Society	529	19	Howe	Ephraim		1			1		1			1			4		
Granville East Society	529	20	Rose	Justus	3	1		1		2	1		1	1			10		
Granville East Society	529	21	Thrall	Samuel	4	2		1		2			1				10		
Granville East Society	529	22	Winchell	Dan				1		2	1		1				5		
Granville East Society	529	23	Riley	Joseph			1				1			1			4		
Granville East Society	529	24	Clark	Amos	1	1	1		1	2	1		1	1			9		
Granville East Society	529	25	Graves	Reuben	1	1	2		1		1	2		1			10		
Granville East Society	529	26	Gitchel	William	2			1		1		1	1				6		
Granville East Society	529	27	Stow	Elisha		2		1		1		1	1				6		
Granville East Society	529	28	Miller	Eliphas	2		2		1	2		1	1	1			10		
Granville East Society	529	29	Rose	Lemuel	1	1		1		3	1		1				8		
Granville East Society	529	30	Rose	Levi	1			1		2			1				5		
Granville East Society	529	31	Rose	Hiram	1			1		3			1				6		
Granville East Society	529	32	S*	John			1		1			2		1			5		
Granville East Society	529	33	Forbs	Jonathan			2		1					1			4		
Granville East Society	529	34	Gains	Samuel		2			1	1		1	1	1			7		
Granville East Society	529	35	Church	Abijah		1			2			2		2			7		
Granville East Society	529	36	Church	Isaac	1			1				1	1				4		
Granville East Society	529	37	Jones	David		2		1		2	1	1	1				9		
Granville East Society	529	38	Cooley	Clark		2	1		1	1		2		1			8		
Granville East Society	529	39	Clark	Ichabod				1		2		1					4		
Granville East Society	531	1	Gibbons	Timothy	1	2	1	1		3	1		1				10		
Granville East Society	531	2	Ellis	William					1			1					3		
Granville East Society	531	3	Clark	Samuel	3	1	3		1	2	1		1				12		
Granville East Society	531	4	Whitney	Uriah		2		1						1			4		
Granville East Society	531	5	Pratt	Phinehas		2		1				1		1			5		
Granville East Society	531	6	Pratt	Alderton	1			1		2		1		1			6		
Granville East Society	531	7	Kirby	Joseph	1	1		1		2			1	1			7		
Granville East Society	531	8	Jones	Daniel	2			1		2			1				6		
Granville East Society	531	9	Rose	Gamaliel	4			1		1			1				7		
Granville East Society	531	10	Clark	Samuel	2		1	1		3			1				8		
Granville East Society	531	11	Burbank	Thomas				2		1		1	1	1	1		7		
Granville East Society	531	12	Root	Amos	2	2		1	2		1	1		1			11		

TOWN	PG#	LN#	LAST NAME	FIRST NAME	FREE WHITE MALES					FREE WHITE FEMALES					TOTAL ALL OTHER	TOTAL SLAVES	TOTALS	DISTRICT/ TOWNSHIP	NOTES
					under 10	10 to 16	16 to 26	26 to 45	45 and over	under 10	10 to 16	16 to 26	26 to 45	45 and over					
Granville East Society	531	13	Sanders	Nathan		1		1				2	1				5		
Granville East Society	531	14	Tinker	Charity								3		1			4		
Granville East Society	531	15	Tinker	John	3			1		2			1				7		
Granville East Society	531	16	Tinker	Sylvester	1		2	1		1		1					6		
Granville East Society	531	17	Marvin	Ezra		1	1		1					1			4		
Granville East Society	531	18	Holcomb	Alvin	2			1		1			1				5		
Granville East Society	531	19	Tillotson	Jena		1	1	1				1	1	1			6		
Granville East Society	531	20	Strickland	Jona		1	1		1	1	1	1		1			7		
Granville East Society	531	21	Rising	Abel	1	1	1		1		2	1		1			8		
Granville East Society	531	22	Williams	Samuel					1					1			2		
Granville East Society	531	23	Gillet	Thomas	1		1	3	1	1	4	1		2			14		
Granville East Society	531	24	Bancroft	Nathaniel	2			1		1			1				5		
Granville East Society	531	25	*	Joel			3		1					1			5		
Granville East Society	531	26	Strong	Eleazer	4			1		2	1		1				9		
Granville East Society	531	27	Loveland	Elizabeth		1		2						1			4		
Granville East Society	531	28	Strong	Joel	1	1		1	1	1		1	1	1			8		
Granville East Society	531	29	S*ina	Benjamin	2		1		1	2	2	1		1			10		
Granville East Society	531	30	Rose	Noadiah	3			1		1		1	1				7		
Granville East Society	531	31	Lamson	James	1			2		1		1					5		
Granville East Society	531	32	Bancroft	Azariah	2	1		1		2		1	1				8		
Granville East Society	531	33	Bancroft	Samuel		1	2		1		2			1			7		
Granville East Society	531	34	Wilcox	Eleazer		1		1				1		1			4		
Granville East Society	531	35	Strickland	Joseph			1	1						1			3		
Granville East Society	531	36	Strickland	Jona Jr		2		1		2			1				6		
Granville East Society	531	37	Bancroft	Enoch	1	2	1		1	4	1	1	1	3			15		
Granville East Society	531	38	Cooley	William Junr	2	1		1		4		1	1				10		
Granville East Society	531	39	Cooley	William	1	2	1		1	1		3	1	1			11		
Granville East Society	531	40	Brainard	Amos	3			1		2			1				7		
Granville East Society	531	41	Bradley	John	2	1	1		1	1	1		1				8		
Granville East Society	531	42	Jones	Bethiel	4			1					1				6		
Granville East Society	533	1	Clark	Lot	4			1		1			1	1			8		
Granville East Society	533	2	Osborn	Luke		1				1		1					3		
Granville East Society	533	3	Drake	Enoch	1			1				1					3		
Granville East Society	533	4	Gullich	Zadock			3	1		1		1	1				7		
Granville East Society	533	5	Rose	Shaun			1	3	1	1		2		1			9		
Granville East Society	533	6	Rose	Elisha			1		1			1		1			4		
Granville East Society	533	7	West	Joseph	1			1		1			1				4		
Granville East Society	533	8	Barlow	Jonathan				1					1				2		
Granville East Society	533	9	Barlow	Edmund	2	1		1	1	1	2	1	1	1			11		
Granville East Society	533	10	Pratt	Jerard				1	1	3	1		2	1			9		
Granville East Society	533	11	Smith	John	2	1	2		1			1	1	1			9		
Granville East Society	533	12	Smith	John 2nd	3		1	1					1				6		
Granville East Society	533	13	Steen	Benjamin		1	2			2	1	2		1			9		
Granville East Society	533	14	Dickinson	Olliver	2	2		1		2	1		1				9		
Granville East Society	533	15	Taylor	George			1		1			1		1			4		
Granville East Society	533	16	Bates	Nathaniel		1	1		1		1	2		1			7		
Granville East Society	533	17	Cooley	Timothy M. Reverand	3			1					1				5		
Granville East Society	533	18	Strickland	Elijah	1			1		1			1				4		
Granville East Society	533	19	Wilcox	Stillman		1	1	1		2			1				6		

TOWN	PG#	LN#	HEADS OF HOUSEHOLD		FREE WHITE MALES					FREE WHITE FEMALES					TOTAL ALL OTHER	TOTAL SLAVES	TOTALS	DISTRICT/ TOWNSHIP	NOTES
			LAST NAME	FIRST NAME	under 10	10 to 16	16 to 26	26 to 45	45 and over	under 10	10 to 16	16 to 26	26 to 45	45 and over					
Granville Middle Society	165	1	Pomeroy	Elihu	2	2	1		1	1	1	1	1				10		
Granville Middle Society	165	2	Booge	Aaron J		1			1	1	1	1	1				6		
Granville Middle Society	165	3	Durham	David				1		1		1					3		
Granville Middle Society	165	4	Bates	John		1			1		1	1		1			5		
Granville Middle Society	165	5	Bates	John Jun	1			1		1			1				4		
Granville Middle Society	165	6	Merry	Cornelius			1		1				1	1			4		
Granville Middle Society	165	7	Spelman	Oliver					1		1			1			3		
Granville Middle Society	165	8	Spelman	Reuben				1					2		1		4		
Granville Middle Society	165	9	Woodruff	Joseph	1	2	1		1	1		1		1			8		
Granville Middle Society	165	10	Bales	David		1				2	1		1				5		
Granville Middle Society	165	11	Bates	Abigail	3	1		1		2	2		1				10		
Granville Middle Society	165	12	Parons	Abner		1		1	1				2	1			6		
Granville Middle Society	165	13	Parons	Abner Junr	2			1			2			1			6		
Granville Middle Society	165	14	Cornwell	Ozias	3	1		1		2			1				8		
Granville Middle Society	165	15	Bates	Jacob		1	2		1			1		2			7		
Granville Middle Society	165	16	Shehnan	John			2		1		1			1			5		
Granville Middle Society	165	17	Harvey	Josiah		1			1			1	1				4		
Granville Middle Society	165	18	Robinson	Timothy			1	1	1			1		1			5		
Granville Middle Society	165	19	Scovil	Bela		2		1					1				4		
Granville Middle Society	165	20	Keep	Sylvanus	1			1		1		1					4		
Granville Middle Society	165	21	Tibbats	John	2				1				1				4		
Granville Middle Society	165	22	Clark	Ruth									1				1		
Granville Middle Society	165	23	Stow	Joseph	1	1			1			1	1	1			6		
Granville Middle Society	165	24	Knapp	Abijah	3			1		2			1				7		
Granville Middle Society	165	25	Parsons	Seth	1	1	2	1			1	1	1				8		
Granville Middle Society	165	26	Learnard	John		1	1	1			1	1	1				3		
Granville Middle Society	165	27	Rose	Seth	3		1	1			1	1	1				8		
Granville Middle Society	165	28	Higley	Levi	2			1		2		2	1				6		
Granville Middle Society	165	29	Hale	Ezekiel			1		1			2	1	1			6		
Granville Middle Society	165	30	Miller	Recompense		1	1		1		1	1		1			6		
Granville Middle Society	165	31	Barnes	Benjamin		1	1		1	1		1	1	2			8		
Granville Middle Society	166	1	Babcock	Perry	2	1		1		1			1	1			7		
Granville Middle Society	166	2	Bates	Linus		1			1				1	1			4		
Granville Middle Society	166	3	Curtis	Linus	1		1			2		1					5		
Granville Middle Society	166	4	Curtis	David		2		2						2			6		
Granville Middle Society	166	5	Curtis	Charles	1		1	1		2	1	1	1				8		
Granville Middle Society	166	6	Hunt	John		1	2		1			1		1			6		
Granville Middle Society	166	7	Howard	Henry	3	1	2		1		1	1	1				10		
Granville Middle Society	166	8	Robinson	Charles	1	2		1		2			1				7		
Granville Middle Society	166	9	Tibbats	Moses	2			1		1			1				5		
Granville Middle Society	166	10	Robinson	John		1		1		4	1		1				8		
Granville Middle Society	166	11	Robinson	Dan Junr	2		1	1		1	2		1				8		
Granville Middle Society	166	12	Frost	David	2	1	4		1	3	1			1			13		
Granville Middle Society	166	13	Adkins	Jabez	3				1	2			1				7		
Granville Middle Society	166	14	Bonney	Asa	1				1	2	2	3		1			10		
Granville Middle Society	166	15	Feebles	Harvey			1			2		1					4		
Granville Middle Society	166	16	Feebles	John Junr	3	1		1					1				6		
Granville Middle Society	166	17	Feebles	Francis	1	1				1			1				4		
Granville Middle Society	166	18	Feebles	John				1	1	1		2		1			5		
Granville Middle Society	166	19	Ely	Thomas	2		1					1	1				5		
Granville Middle Society	166	20	Bancroft	John	1	1	2		1	1	1			1			8		
Granville Middle Society	166	21	Barnes	Jeremiah	1	1	1		1	1	1			2			8		
Granville Middle Society	166	22	Bancroft	Joel			1		1		1			1			4		
Granville Middle Society	166	23	Case	Joel			1										1		
Granville Middle Society	166	24	Coe	Israel	2	1	1		1	1	1		1	1			9		
Granville Middle Society	166	25	Baldwin	Stephen	2	2		1		2		1	1				9		
Granville Middle Society	166	26	Baldwin	John	2			1					1				4		
Granville Middle Society	166	27	Baldwin	Curtiss	2			1		2			1				6		
Granville Middle Society	166	28	Baldwin	Amos		1	2		1			1	1	1			7		
Granville Middle Society	166	29	Robinson	Joel		1	1		1			1		1			5		
Granville Middle Society	166	30	Robinson	Dan	1		1		1	1		1	1	1			7		
Granville Middle Society	167	1	Coe	Anon	3			1		3			1				9		
Granville Middle Society	167	2	Coe	Joseph		1		1					2	1			5		
Granville Middle Society	167	3	Baldwin	Ebenezer			1		1			1	1	1			6		
Granville Middle Society	167	4	Coe	Ephraim	2			1		2			1	1			7		
Granville Middle Society	167	5	L*child	An*	1			1		3	3	2	1				11		
Granville Middle Society	167	6	Coe	Seth	3			1		2	2		1				9		
Granville Middle Society	167	7	Coe	David	3	1		1		2			1				8		
Granville Middle Society	167	8	Stewart	Peter	2	1	1	1		4	2		1				12		
Granville Middle Society	167	9	Cornwell	Jesse			1	1		4			1				7		
Granville Middle Society	167	10	Miller	Nathaniel	3			1					1				5		
Granville Middle Society	167	11	Putman	John	2	2		1		1			1				7		
Granville Middle Society	167	12	Rose	David	2	2	2		1	1	1	1		1			11		
Granville Middle Society	167	13	Ward	Samuel	1		1	1		1	1	1	1				7		
Granville Middle Society	167	14	Cornwell	John			1	1						1			3		
Granville Middle Society	167	15	Coe	John	1			1		1		1	1				5		
Granville Middle Society	167	16	Parsons	David	1			1	1	3			1	1			8		
Granville Middle Society	167	17	Robinson	Hannah			1					1		1			3		
Granville Middle Society	167	18	Robinson	Hezekiah		1	2						1				4		

TOWN	PG#	LN#	LAST NAME	FIRST NAME	FREE WHITE MALES					FREE WHITE FEMALES					TOTAL ALL OTHER	TOTAL SLAVES	TOTALS	DISTRICT/ TOWNSHIP	NOTES
					under 10	10 to 16	16 to 26	26 to 45	45 and over	under 10	10 to 16	16 to 26	26 to 45	45 and over					
Granville Middle Society	167	19	Parsons	Nathaniel		1		1					1				3		
Granville Middle Society	167	20	Parsons	Sarah		1						1	1	1			4		
Granville Middle Society	167	21	Parsons	Samuel	1	1		1		3		1	1				8		
Granville Middle Society	167	22	Baker	Joel Reverend		1		1			1		1				4		
Granville Middle Society	167	23	Canfield	Elizabeth										1			1		
Granville Middle Society	167	24	Phelps	John	2		2	1		2	1	1	1				10		
Granville Middle Society	167	25	Curtiss	Aaron		1			1			1		1			4		
Granville Middle Society	167	26	Curtiss	Levi	2		4	1		1		1		1			10		
Granville Middle Society	167	27	Stow	Stephen			3	1		1		1					6		
Granville Middle Society	167	28	Snow	Isaac	3			1		2		1	1				8		
Granville Middle Society	167	29	Coe	Mary										1			1		
Granville Middle Society	167	30	Coe	Benjamin		1			1	1	1			1			5		
Granville Middle Society	167	31	Barnes	Elihu	1		2	1		2		2					8		
Granville Middle Society	167	32	Leonard	Comfort								3		2			5		
Granville Middle Society	167	33	Johnson	Jabez	3		1	1	1	2			1				9		
Granville Middle Society	167	34	Baldwin	Ezra	1	1		1	1				2	1			7		
Granville Middle Society	167	35	Baldwin	Lyman	3			1		1	1		1				7		
Granville Middle Society	167	36	Rose	Abner					1			1		1			3		
Granville Middle Society	167	37	Stebbins	Francis	1			1				1					3		
Granville Middle Society	167	38	Wilcox	Billy		1	1		1	1				1			5		
Granville Middle Society	167	39	Harvey	Rufus			1			3		1	1				6		
Granville Middle Society	167	40	Wilcox	Samuel D.	1	1	1	1		2	2			1			9		
Granville Middle Society	167	41	Harger	David	2			1		1			1				5		
Granville Middle Society	167	42	Hayes	Luther	2		3					2					8		
Granville Middle Society	167	43	Lloyd	William	1			1		2			1				5		
Granville Middle Society	167	44	Adkins	Elihu		1	1	1	1				1	1			6		
Granville Middle Society	167	45	Parsons	Moses		1		1				1	1	1			5		

TOWN	PG#	LN#	LAST NAME	FIRST NAME	FREE WHITE MALES					FREE WHITE FEMALES					TOTAL ALL OTHER	TOTAL SLAVES	TOTALS	DISTRICT/ TOWNSHIP	NOTES
					under 10	10 to 16	16 to 26	26 to 45	45 and over	under 10	10 to 16	16 to 26	26 to 45	45 and over					
Granville West Society	168	1	Latham	David	2	1		1		1			1				6		
Granville West Society	168	2	Gavit	William	3	2		1		2			1				9		
Granville West Society	168	3	Mills	Stone					1					1			2		
Granville West Society	168	4	Mills	Jedediah	3			1		1			1				6		
Granville West Society	168	5	Miller	Isaac	1		1	1		1	1		1				6		
Granville West Society	168	6	Miller	Timothy	1		1		1		2	1		1	1		8		
Granville West Society	168	7	Miller	Timothy Jun		1				1		1					3		
Granville West Society	168	8	Reed	Titus	1	1		1		2			1				6		
Granville West Society	168	9	Steadman	Joseph	2			1		1			1				5		
Granville West Society	168	10	Murphy	Martin	1	1		1		3		2	1				9		
Granville West Society	168	11	Granger	Abraham	2				1	1	1	1	1				7		
Granville West Society	168	12	Stetson	Jonathan	2				1	3	1		1				8		
Granville West Society	168	13	Chappel	William	2			1		1			1				5		
Granville West Society	168	14	Baker	Joseph			1			1		1					3		
Granville West Society	168	15	Moore	Samuel	1	1		1		3	1		1				8		
Granville West Society	168	16	Slocum	David				1				1		1			3		
Granville West Society	168	17	Hull	Gideon	1			1		1				2			5		
Granville West Society	168	18	Slocum	Eleazer	1			1		1	1		1				5		
Granville West Society	168	19	Eldridge	Daniel	2			1		2	1	1	1				8		
Granville West Society	168	20	Couch	Timothy	3	1			1	1		2		1			9		
Granville West Society	168	21	Bliss	Benedict	2	1		1	1	1			2	1			9		
Granville West Society	168	22	Knight	Silas				1		2		1		1			5		
Granville West Society	168	23	Fletcher	Thaddeus				1		1			1				3		
Granville West Society	168	24	Moody	Oliver	2			1		1		1		2			7		
Granville West Society	168	25	Fox	David	3	1	1		1	1	1		1				9		
Granville West Society	168	26	Williams	Isaac	2	1		1		2	1		1				8		
Granville West Society	168	27	Leavensworth	Lydia		1					2			1			4		
Granville West Society	168	28	Fox	Thomas	1			1		1			1				3		
Granville West Society	168	29	Marshall	Perez	2		2	1		1	1		2	2			11		
Granville West Society	168	30	Tuttle	Stephen		1		1	1	1	1		1				5		
Granville West Society	168	31	Twining	Eleazer	1			1		2			1				5		
Granville West Society	168	32	Marshall	Gains		1							1				2		
Granville West Society	168	33	Burt	Caleb	2	1		1		2			1				7		
Granville West Society	168	34	Dorman	Stephen		1		1						1			3		
Granville West Society	168	35	Goff	David	2			1		3	2		1				9		
Granville West Society	168	36	Crosman	Phinias		1		1						1			3		
Granville West Society	168	37	Fowler	Oliver		1		1		1	1	2	1				7		
Granville West Society	168	38	Fowler	Daniel			1			1	1						3		
Granville West Society	168	39	Gleason	Joel	4			1		1			1				7		
Granville West Society	168	40	Gibbs	Benjamin	1			1		3			1	1			7		
Granville West Society	169	1	Wright	David		2	1	1						1			5		
Granville West Society	169	2	Rogers	Jabez		2		2		1	1	1		1			8		
Granville West Society	169	3	Brather	Araiah	2			1	1	2	1	1	1				8		
Granville West Society	169	4	Rogers	Sarah		2		2		1		1	1				7		
Granville West Society	169	5	Twining	Thomas	2		1	1	1	3		2		1			11		
Granville West Society	169	6	Sennet	Joseph	1	2	2		1	1	1			1			9		
Granville West Society	169	7	Twining	Elijah			3	1		1	1			1			7		
Granville West Society	169	8	Hardin	Ebenezer		1	1	1				1		1			5		
Granville West Society	169	9	Freeman	William	3	1		1		1	1		1				8		
Granville West Society	169	10	Crosman	Tulley	2			1					1				4		
Granville West Society	169	11	Higgins	Solomon	2	1		1		3		1	1				9		
Granville West Society	169	12	Clark	Jonathan	2			1		3	2	2	1				11		
Granville West Society	169	13	Pratt	Justin	1	2	1		1	1			1				7		
Granville West Society	169	14	Snow	Ephraim	3	1		1		1	2	2	1				11		
Granville West Society	169	15	Wright	Jabez	1		1						1				3		
Granville West Society	169	16	Kingsley	Stephen	2			1	1	1			1	1			7		
Granville West Society	169	17	Marshall	Perez				1			1		1				3		
Granville West Society	169	18	Gleason	John	2	2	2	1		1	2		1	1			12		
Granville West Society	169	19	Mills	Cephas	3	1	1	1		2	2	3	1				14		
Granville West Society	169	20	Smith	Elezer		1		1					2	1			5		
Granville West Society	169	21	Akins	William	2			1		1		1					5		
Granville West Society	169	22	Gillbard	Noah	1			1		2			1				5		
Granville West Society	169	23	Moore	William	1	1		1		2	2	1					8		
Granville West Society	169	24	Moore	Asher			1						1				2		
Granville West Society	169	25	Hardin	Isaac	1	1		1		1	1		1				6		
Granville West Society	169	26	Stewart	Archibald				1		1		3		1			6		
Granville West Society	169	27	Moore	Marvin	2			1	1			1	2	1			8		
Granville West Society	169	28	Hall	Nathan		1	1	1				2	1				6		
Granville West Society	169	29	Harrison	Roger Revd			1						1				2		
Granville West Society	169	30	Cowles	William	2			1		2			1				7		
Granville West Society	169	31	Fowler	Titus			1	1	1	2	2	1	1	1			10		
Granville West Society	169	32	Allen	Nathan	1	1		1				1	1	1			6		
Granville West Society	169	33	Wright	Jonathan	2			1		1			1				7		
Granville West Society	169	34	Slocum	Cornelus	1			1		1	1	1					5		
Granville West Society	169	35	Fowler	John		2		1		3			1				7		
Granville West Society	169	36	Bidwell	George		1		1						1			3		
Granville West Society	169	37	Hawley	Jesse	1			1					1				3		
Granville West Society	169	38	Hamilton	Gad	2	1		1		2		1	1				8		
Granville West Society	169	39	Parsons	Philip	1	1		1		3	2		1				9		

TOWN	PG#	LN#	LAST NAME	FIRST NAME	FREE WHITE MALES					FREE WHITE FEMALES					TOTAL ALL OTHER	TOTAL SLAVES	TOTALS	DISTRICT/ TOWNSHIP	NOTES
					under 10	10 to 16	16 to 26	26 to 45	45 and over	under 10	10 to 16	16 to 26	26 to 45	45 and over					
Granville West Society	170	1	Warren	Elisha	1	1	1			3	2		1				9		
Granville West Society	170	2	Dodge	Stephen		2			1			2		2			7		
Granville West Society	170	3	Bumpuss	Latathiel	1			1		1			1				4		
Granville West Society	170	4	Andrews	Jonah	1	2	1	1					1				6		
Granville West Society	170	5	Burrill	Israel			1			2			1				4		
Granville West Society	170	6	Goth	Moses		1	1		1			1		1			5		
Granville West Society	170	7	Hamilton	James	1	1	1		1	2	1	1		1			9		
Granville West Society	170	8	Hamilton	Robert		1			1			2		1			5		
Granville West Society	170	9	Hamilton	Henry		1			1			2		1			5		
Granville West Society	170	10	Hamilton	Thomas	1		1		1		1	1		1			6		
Granville West Society	170	11	Manchester	John	2	1		1		1	2	1	1				9		
Granville West Society	170	12	Remington	Holden	1	1		1		3	1		1				8		
Granville West Society	170	13	Eldridge	Daniel	2			1		2	1		1				7		
Granville West Society	170	14	Brown	Andrew Jun			1					1					2		
Granville West Society	170	15	Hull	John	1			1		3			1				6		
Granville West Society	170	16	Steadman	Phebe	1						1		1				3		
Granville West Society	170	17	Hull	Robert	3	1		1		1			1				7		
Granville West Society	170	18	Steadman	Samuel	1			1	1			1	2				6		
Granville West Society	170	19	Slocum	Hull	2	1		1		2			1				7		
Granville West Society	170	20	Steadman	Thomas			1	1		3		2	1	1			9		
Granville West Society	170	21	Cooley	Gaius		1		1		2	1		1				6		
Granville West Society	170	22	Brown	Andrew	2	2		1		2	1		1				9		
Granville West Society	170	23	Babcock	John	1			1		3			1				6		
Granville West Society	170	24	Hubbard	Titus	1	1		1		1			1				5		
Granville West Society	170	25	Remington	Anthony	2	1		1		4	1	1	1				11		
Granville West Society	170	26	Cannon	Ezekiel	1			1					1				3		
Granville West Society	170	27	Butter	Selah	1	1		1		3			1				7		
Granville West Society	170	28	Sweatman	Reuben	1	1	1		1	1	1		1				7		
Granville West Society	170	29	Kellogg	Phinehas	1			1		2	1		1				6		
Granville West Society	170	30	Ba*	William	3			1		2							6		
Granville West Society	170	31	Barnes	Phinas		1	2		1			2		1			7		
Granville West Society	170	32	Hall	Samuel	2		1	1	1	1	1	1	1	1			10		
Granville West Society	170	33	Hall	Jesse	1	1		1		1			1				5		
Granville West Society	170	34	Hubbard	Ebenezer				1						2			3		
Granville West Society	170	35	Barnes	Ebenezer	1	2	1			2			2				9		
Granville West Society	170	36	Stewart	Alexander	2			1		2	2		1				8		
Granville West Society	170	37	Twining	William	3	1		1		1	1		1				8		

TOWN	PG#	LN#	LAST NAME	FIRST NAME	FREE WHITE MALES					FREE WHITE FEMALES					TOTAL ALL OTHER	TOTAL SLAVES	TOTALS	DISTRICT/ TOWNSHIP	NOTES
					under 10	10 to 16	16 to 26	26 to 45	45 and over	under 10	10 to 16	16 to 26	26 to 45	45 and over					
Greenfield	71	1	Ames	Ambrose			2	1		5			1		1		10		
Greenfield	71	2	Arms	Solomon		1		1		2	1		2	1			8		
Greenfield	71	3	Allen	Ebenezer	3	1		1	1	1	1		2	1			11		
Greenfield	71	4	Arms	Moses		1	1		1	1	1	1	1				7		
Greenfield	71	5	Allen	Quintus	2			1		3			2	2			10		
Greenfield	71	6	Allen	Amos	3			1		3			1				8		
Greenfield	71	7	Arms	Ebenezer	1	1	1	1		2	2		1				9		
Greenfield	71	8	Allen	Joel	3	2		1		1	1	1	1				10		
Greenfield	71	9	Atherton	Jonathan				1					1				2		
Greenfield	71	10	Allen	Ebenezer Jnr	1	2	3		1	1	1	1	1				11		
Greenfield	71	11	Allen	Elijah	1	1		1		3	1		1				8		
Greenfield	71	12	Allen	Job	1				1	1				1			4		
Greenfield	71	13	Atherton	Oliver				1				2		1			4		
Greenfield	71	14	Alvord	Elijah	1		4	1		2			1				9		
Greenfield	72	1	Allen	Elihu		1		1		1			1				4		
Greenfield	72	2	Atherton	Joseph	2		1	1		1	1	1	1				8		
Greenfield	72	3	Alexander	John	1			1		3			2	1			8		
Greenfield	72	4	Atherton	Joseph Jr	1			1		3			1				6		
Greenfield	72	5	Brown	Wanton	1								1				3		
Greenfield	72	6	Bascom	Ezekiel			1	1	1		1			1			5		
Greenfield	72	7	Billings	Ebenezer	2			1	1	2	1	1		1			9		
Greenfield	72	8	Billings	Thomas			1		1	1				1			4		
Greenfield	72	9	Billings	Edward	1	1			1				1	2			6		
Greenfield	72	10	Boynton	John		2			1	4	1	1		1			10		
Greenfield	72	11	Bell	John	2			1		3			1	1			8		
Greenfield	72	12	Bush	John	1	1			1	2	2		1				8		
Greenfield	72	13	Bascom	Joseph	1	1			1	1	1			1			6		
Greenfield	72	14	Brooks	David	1	1			1	2	1		1				7		
Greenfield	72	15	Brooks	Silas			1						1				2		
Greenfield	72	16	Battis	Joseph	2		1						1				4		
Greenfield	72	17	Corse	Asher	1	1	1	1	1	2	2	2		1			12		
Greenfield	72	18	Cone	Robert	2	2		1		3			1				9		
Greenfield	72	19	Cushman	Consider	2			1		4			1				8		
Greenfield	72	20	Clay	Daniel	3	1		1			1		1				7		
Greenfield	72	21	Chapman	Thoma	1	1			1	1	1		1				6		
Greenfield	72	22	Clap	Caleb			1	1		3			2				7		
Greenfield	72	23	Coleman	Elijah			1	1	1			1		1			5		
Greenfield	72	24	Cornwell	Amos	3	1	1	1		3			1				10		
Greenfield	72	25	Clark	John				1						1			2		
Greenfield	72	26	Clark	Enoch	1			1		1			1				4		
Greenfield	72	27	Clark	William	2	1	1	1		1	2	1	1				10		
Greenfield	72	28	Castilo	Peter					1	1	1		1				4		
Greenfield	72	29	Daggot	Gideon	2	1		1		1			1	1			7		
Greenfield	72	30	Denio	Enos	1			1		1		1	1	2			7		
Greenfield	72	31	Dickman	Thomas			2	1		3			1	1			8		
Greenfield	72	32	Foster	Isaac	4			1		1		1	1				8		
Greenfield	73	1	Forbes	Daniel	2		1	1		2			1				7		
Greenfield	73	2	Frazier	Jabez				1		1			1				3		
Greenfield	73	3	Graves	Eli	1					1		1					4		
Greenfield	73	4	Grinell	George		1	1		1		1	2	1	1			8		
Greenfield	73	5	Grinell	Wise	1	2	2		1	2		1	1				10		
Greenfield	73	6	Grinell	William	2				1	2	2			1			8		
Greenfield	73	7	Graves	Rufus	3			1		2			1				7		
Greenfield	73	8	Graves	Ebenezer			1	1						1			3		
Greenfield	73	9	Graves	Job	2	2	1	1		2	1		1				10		
Greenfield	73	10	Goodman	Elihu		1	1		1	3	1			1			8		
Greenfield	73	11	Griswould	Theophilus	2	3		1		4	1	1	1				13		
Greenfield	73	12	Gilligan	Thoma	2			1		3			1				7		
Greenfield	73	13	Graves	John		1	1		2				1	1			6		
Greenfield	73	14	Gilbert	Eliel	2		1	1		2			1	1			8		
Greenfield	73	15	Graves	Ebenezer Junr	1		1	1					1				4		
Greenfield	73	16	Gates	Stephen	2			1		2				1			6		
Greenfield	73	17	Hastings	Benjamin Jr	2		1	1		3	1		1				9		
Greenfield	73	18	Hastings	Joseph		1	1	1				1		1			6		
Greenfield	73	19	Hawkins	Jourden	1			1					1				3		
Greenfield	73	20	Hastings	Selah	2	1		1		3	1		1				9		
Greenfield	73	21	Hindsdale	Ariel			1		1	4	1	4		1			12		
Greenfield	73	22	Hindsdale	Samuel			1		1		1	2		1			6		
Greenfield	73	23	Hall	John C.				1		1			1				4		
Greenfield	73	24	Hubbard	Ephraim	1		1	1		1	2	1	1				8		
Greenfield	73	25	Hastings	Ephraim		1	1	1				1		1			5		
Greenfield	73	26	Hall	Timothy		3	4		1	1			1	1			11		
Greenfield	73	27	Hastings	Lemuel	1	1	2		1			1		1			7		
Greenfield	73	28	Hastings	Oliver	3	1	1	1				1		1			7		
Greenfield	73	29	Hitchcock	Merrick	2	1			1	1		1					7		
Greenfield	73	30	Hitchcock	Charles			1	1		1			1				4		
Greenfield	73	31	Hastings	Benjamin					1				1	1			3		
Greenfield	73	32	Johnson	Richard					1					1			2		
Greenfield	73	33	Johnson	Elias	3		2	1		2		2	1				11		

TOWN	PG#	LN#	LAST NAME	FIRST NAME	FREE WHITE MALES					FREE WHITE FEMALES					TOTAL ALL OTHER	TOTAL SLAVES	TOTALS	DISTRICT/ TOWNSHIP	NOTES
					under 10	10 to 16	16 to 26	26 to 45	45 and over	under 10	10 to 16	16 to 26	26 to 45	45 and over					
Greenfield	73	34	Jones	Phineus		1	1		1		1	1	1				6		
Greenfield	73	35	Johnson	Calvin			1					1					2		
Greenfield	73	36	Lyman	Elihu		3	1		1		1		1	1	1		9		
Greenfield	73	37	Leavitt	Jonathan				1		3		1	1				6		
Greenfield	74	1	Leavitt	Hart		1	1	1			1		1				5		
Greenfield	74	2	Lyon	John	2	1		1		4	1		1				10		
Greenfield	74	3	Lyon	Caleb				1					1		2		4		
Greenfield	74	4	Lamb	Elijah	4		1	1		1			1				8		
Greenfield	74	5	Loveland	Epaphroditus	2	1		1		2		1	1				8		
Greenfield	74	6	Logan	James					1	1			1	2			5		
Greenfield	74	7	Morse	Calvin			1			1		1					3		
Greenfield	74	8	Munn	Calvin	3	1	5	5		2	1	1	2				20		
Greenfield	74	9	Martindale	Uriah	4	2	1	1		1	2		1				12		
Greenfield	74	10	McHard	William	2	1		1		3	1		1				9		
Greenfield	74	11	Martindale	Christian								1		1			2		
Greenfield	74	12	Mach	Abner	2			1	1	1		1		1			7		
Greenfield	74	13	Munn	David	1			1		1			1				4		
Greenfield	74	14	Mitchell	Elijah	1			1	1	3		2	3	1			12		
Greenfield	74	15	Mitchell	William	1		1						1				3		
Greenfield	74	16	Munn	Simeon	3	1		1		2			1				8		
Greenfield	74	17	Newton	Roger			2		1			1	1	1			6		
Greenfield	74	18	Newton	Ozias			1			1		1					3		
Greenfield	74	19	Nickerson	David	2		1	1		1	1		1				7		
Greenfield	74	20	Nickerson	Enoch	2			1		3			1				7		
Greenfield	74	21	Nash	Sylvanus		1	2		1	2	1	1		2			10		
Greenfield	74	22	Nash	Daniel					1		2	1		1			5		
Greenfield	74	23	Nims	Hull	3		2	1		3	1	1	1	1			13		
Greenfield	74	24	Newton	John Junr	2		5		1	2	2		1				13		
Greenfield	74	25	Newton	John			1		1				1				3		
Greenfield	74	26	Newton	Samuel	2	1		1		1	1		1				7		
Greenfield	74	27	Newton	Isaac	1		1		1		1			1			5		
Greenfield	74	28	Newton	Asher	2	2		1		2	1	2	1				11		
Greenfield	74	29	Newcomb	Richard C.	2	1		1		1		1	2				8		
Greenfield	74	30	Nash	Jubal	2	1	2	1		3	2	1	1				13		
Greenfield	74	31	Nutting	Joseph	4	1		1		1			1	1			9		
Greenfield	74	32	Nash	Eber			1			1		1					3		
Greenfield	74	33	Parsons	Amos	1	1		1		1	1	1	1				7		
Greenfield	74	34	Pratt	Stephen	1	2			1			4		1			9		
Greenfield	74	35	Pickett	Samuel	1	1		1	1	2	2		1	1			10		
Greenfield	74	36	Pickett	Daniel	2		2		1	1	1	2		1			10		
Greenfield	75	1	Peirce	Samuel	1		2	1		3			1				8		
Greenfield	75	2	Pitt	John	4	2			1	1		1	3	1			13		
Greenfield	75	3	Phillips	Israel	3			1					1				5		
Greenfield	75	4	Post	Cornelius					1					1			2		
Greenfield	75	5	Roggers	Samuel	2			1						1			4		
Greenfield	75	6	Ripley	Jerom		2	1	2		4	2		1				12		
Greenfield	75	7	Russell	John	2		1	1		1			1	1			7		
Greenfield	75	8	Rugg	Joshua			1			3			1				5		
Greenfield	75	9	Sawtwell	John	1		1			1			1				4		
Greenfield	75	10	Smead	David	1		2	2	2	1	2		1				12		
Greenfield	75	11	Smead	David Jun	1			1		2			1				5		
Greenfield	75	12	Skinner	Benajah	1			1		2			1				5		
Greenfield	75	13	Smead	Thomas	1		1	1		2		1					6		
Greenfield	75	14	Severence	Jonathan			2	1					2	1			6		
Greenfield	75	15	Severence	Joseph	3		3			3	3		1				12		
Greenfield	75	16	Smead	Daniel		1	1		1			1	2	1			7		
Greenfield	75	17	Smead	Lemuel	1	1	2		2	1				1			8		
Greenfield	75	18	Stebbens	Samuel	1	1	1	1		3	1	1		1			10		
Greenfield	75	19	Smith	Elijah	3	1		1		1	1		1				7		
Greenfield	75	20	Smead	Hannah		2	3			1		1		1			8		
Greenfield	75	21	Smead	Jonathan		1	1	1	1		1	2	1	1			9		
Greenfield	75	22	Strickland	John				1					1	1			3		
Greenfield	75	23	Strickland	David	1	2		1		2			1				7		
Greenfield	75	24	Strickland	John	2		2		1	1	2		1				9		
Greenfield	75	25	Stone	John	2			1		1		1	1		1		7		
Greenfield	75	26	Stevens	Abiel	3			1		1			1	1			7		
Greenfield	75	27	Smith	Clement			1	1		1	2		1				6		
Greenfield	75	28	Smead	Julia	1	1		1			1	1					5		
Greenfield	75	29	Starr	William	1	2	1			2		1	1				9		
Greenfield	75	30	Stiles	Levi	3			1		1			1				6		
Greenfield	75	31	Swan	Benjamin		1	1	1		3		1	2				9		
Greenfield	75	32	Stevens	John	1			1		1			1				4		
Greenfield	75	33	Starks	Silas	1			1		2		1					5		
Greenfield	75	34	Smith	Joel	2			1		1			1				6		
Greenfield	75	35	Whipple	Daniel	1			1		1			1	1			5		
Greenfield	75	36	Wells	Joel	2	1		1		1			1				6		
Greenfield	75	37	Willard	Renel	1	3		1		2	1	1					10		
Greenfield	76	1	Wait	William	2		1	1		3	1		1				9		
Greenfield	76	2	Wells	Samuel Junr	5	1									1		10		

TOWN	PG#	LN#	LAST NAME	FIRST NAME	FREE WHITE MALES					FREE WHITE FEMALES					TOTAL ALL OTHER	TOTAL SLAVES	TOTALS	DISTRICT/ TOWNSHIP	NOTES
					under 10	10 to 16	16 to 26	26 to 45	45 and over	under 10	10 to 16	16 to 26	26 to 45	45 and over					
Greenfield	76	3	Wells	Agrippa	4		1	1	1		1		2	1			11		
Greenfield	76	4	Wells	Elisha	3	1		1	1	1	2	1	1				11		
Greenfield	76	5	Wells	Eleazer		1	1	1	1			1		1			6		
Greenfield	76	6	Wells	Joseph	3	1	1	2	1	2	1	1	1				13		
Greenfield	76	7	Willard	Benah	1	1	1		1	1	2	1	2				10		
Greenfield	76	8	Wells	Abner		1	1		1					1			4		
Greenfield	76	9	Wells	Daniel	2	1	1	1		2	2		1				10		
Greenfield	76	10	Wells	Silas		1	1	1						1			4		
Greenfield	76	11	Wells	Obed	3	1	1	1		1	3		1				11		
Greenfield	76	12	Witmore	Thomas			1		1	1				1			4		
Greenfield	76	13	Woodward	John					1	1	3			1			6		
Greenfield	76	14	Wells	Samuel					1			1		1			3		
Greenfield	76	15	Wardwell	Jotham	4			1		1			1				7		
Greenfield	76	16	Wells	Ephraim	1		1	1		2		2		1			8		

TOWN	PG#	LN#	LAST NAME	FIRST NAME	FREE WHITE MALES					FREE WHITE FEMALES					TOTAL ALL OTHER	TOTAL SLAVES	TOTALS	DISTRICT/ TOWNSHIP	NOTES
					under 10	10 to 16	16 to 26	26 to 45	45 and over	under 10	10 to 16	16 to 26	26 to 45	45 and over					
Greenwich	218	1	Rich	John Capt	1	1	1		1			1		1			6		
Greenwich	218	2	Crosby	Joshua Revd	2		3	1		3		1	1				11		
Greenwich	218	3	Alden	Ezra				1			1	2		1			5		
Greenwich	218	4	Alden	Ezra Junr	4			1		1		1	1				8		
Greenwich	218	5	Alden	Jonathan				1						1			2		
Greenwich	218	6	Alden	Oliver	1	1	1		1		2	1		1			8		
Greenwich	218	7	Alhimon	John			1	1		1			1				4		
Greenwich	218	8	Skinner	Benj	3			1		2	3			1			10		
Greenwich	218	9	Brewer	James				1						1			2		
Greenwich	218	10	Besse	James	2			1		2	1		1				7		
Greenwich	218	11	Babbit	Elijah			1	1		1	2	1	1				7		
Greenwich	218	12	Babbit	Jonathan	1			1		4			1				7		
Greenwich	218	13	Burr	Rufus	1	2		1		2	1		1				8		
Greenwich	218	14	Brown	Moses	2		2	1		2	2	2	1				12		
Greenwich	218	15	Burt	Ebenz	1			1		3		3	1				9		
Greenwich	218	16	Barns	Moses			2	1	1	1		1		1			7		
Greenwich	218	17	Briggs	Ephm				1		4	3	3	1				12		
Greenwich	218	18	Butterfield	Henry	1	1	1		1	1			1	1			7		
Greenwich	218	19	Blackman	Rolland		1	1		1	1	1	1	1				7		
Greenwich	218	20	Blackman	Amos			1	1									2		
Greenwich	219	1	Blackman	Moses	1		1					1					3		
Greenwich	219	2	Blackman	Peter Jr		1		1	1	2			1	1			7		
Greenwich	219	3	Bartlett	Sylvanus	2			1		2			1				6		
Greenwich	219	4	Blodgett	Joseph Revd		1	1	1		2		1		1			7		
Greenwich	219	5	Covel	Thomas	2		1			1		1					5		
Greenwich	219	6	Clark	Rolland Deac	3	1	1		1	2	1		1				10		
Greenwich	219	7	Cutlar	Dudley & Ebenz	2	1		1	1		1		1	1			8		
Greenwich	219	8	Cannon	Cornelius	3	1			2	1	1	3	1				12		
Greenwich	219	9	Caswell	George Junr				2		2		2					6		
Greenwich	219	10	Colburn	Jabez	1			1	1	1			1				5		
Greenwich	219	11	Cooley	Azareah	2	1			1	2	2		1				9		
Greenwich	219	12	Collins	Treat	1	2			1	1	1			1			7		
Greenwich	219	13	Cooley	Reuben	4	2	1		1		1	2	1				12		
Greenwich	219	14	Caswell	George Junr				1		1		3	1				6		
Greenwich	219	15	Cotton	Reuben Lt	1		1	1		1	2	1	1				8		
Greenwich	219	16	Cary	Thomas			1			1		1					3		
Greenwich	219	17	Drake	Ephraim	2			1		1	1		1				6		
Greenwich	219	18	Bailey	John		1	1	1				1		1			5		
Greenwich	219	19	Alden	John A.	2	1		1		2	1		1				8		
Greenwich	219	20	Dewing	Andrew		1			1			1		1			4		
Greenwich	219	21	Doubledee	Joseph	3	1		1			1		1				7		
Greenwich	219	22	Ayres	John			3	1	1	1	3	2		1			12		
Greenwich	219	23	Burt	Isaac	1			1		1		1	1				5		
Greenwich	219	24	Eaton	Nathl		1			1					1			3		
Greenwich	219	25	Eaton	Calvin	1	1	2	1		2		1	1				9		
Greenwich	219	26	Brooks	Caleb	3	3			1			1	1				9		
Greenwich	219	27	Eddy	Abner	4	2			1	1	1	2	1				12		
Greenwich	219	28	Emerson	Robt	1			1		1			1	1			5		
Greenwich	219	29	Fobes	Joseph				1									1		
Greenwich	219	30	Baker	James	2	2			1	1		1					7		
Greenwich	219	31	Fobes	Jesse	2	1		1		3			1	1			9		
Greenwich	219	32	Fisher	Ebenz	2	2		1		3			1				9		
Greenwich	219	33	Fisher	Leml				1		3			1				5		
Greenwich	219	34	Fimace	David	3			1	2	1			1				8		
Greenwich	219	35	Field	Benja				1				1		1			3		
Greenwich	219	36	Field	Robt Esq			3		1		1	2	1	1			9		
Greenwich	219	37	Canady	Peleg Capt	1		1	1		1	1	1					6		
Greenwich	219	38	Foster	Tilly	2	1			1	2			1				7		
Greenwich	219	39	Fobes	Joseph P.				1		2			1				4		
Greenwich	220	1	Gleason	Isaac			1					1					2		
Greenwich	220	2	Gleason	Simeon			1	1		1		1	1	1			6		
Greenwich	220	3	Grun	Benja	1		1		1		1			1			5		
Greenwich	220	4	Gibbs	John			1	1		2		2	1	1			8		
Greenwich	220	5	Gibbs	Jesse	1		1	1				1		1			5		
Greenwich	220	6	Gibbs	Jesse Junr			1			2			1				4		
Greenwich	220	7	Gibbs	Emerson	2			1		2		1	1	1			8		
Greenwich	220	8	Gardner	John	1	2			1			1	1				6		
Greenwich	220	9	Gross	Micah		1	1		2	2	1		1	2			10		
Greenwich	220	10	Howard	James	2			1					1				4		
Greenwich	220	11	Hinds	Timothy Capt		1	3		1		1	2		1			9		
Greenwich	220	12	Hindrick	Joseph Lt	3		1		1	1		1	1	1			9		
Greenwich	220	13	Haskell	David	2	1		1		1			1				6		
Greenwich	220	14	Foster	Daniel	3			1					1				5		
Greenwich	220	15	Harris	Oliver	1	1		1		2	1	1	1				8		
Greenwich	220	16	Haskell	Elias Lt.	2	2	1		1			1	1		1		9		
Greenwich	220	17	Howe	Solomon	3	2	1		1			3	1				11		
Greenwich	220	18	Hack	Esther Wd	3								1				4		
Greenwich	220	19	Gibbs	Benja	2		1	1			1		1				6		
Greenwich	220	20	Higgins	Henry						1		1	2	1	1		8		

TOWN	PG#	LN#	LAST NAME	FIRST NAME	FREE WHITE MALES					FREE WHITE FEMALES					TOTAL ALL OTHER	TOTAL SLAVES	TOTALS	DISTRICT/ TOWNSHIP	NOTES
					under 10	10 to 16	16 to 26	26 to 45	45 and over	under 10	10 to 16	16 to 26	26 to 45	45 and over					
Greenwich	220	21	Hunter	Isaac	3		1	1	1	1		1		1			9		
Greenwich	220	22	Hooker	Benja	3	3	1	1	1	2		1	1	1			14		
Greenwich	220	23	Hooker	Joseph Jr		1		1			1		1				4		
Greenwich	220	24	Harwood	Benja	3			1		1	1		1				7		
Greenwich	220	25	Hooker	Josepg Capt.		1			1		1			1			4		
Greenwich	220	26	Barton	Jedediah	1	1		1		1			1				5		
Greenwich	220	27	Hail	Samuel		2		1	1	1				1			6		
Greenwich	220	28	Herrington	Lemuel		1		1	1	1		1	1				6		
Greenwich	220	29	Kimball	Hezekiah	4	1			1	1	1			1			9		
Greenwich	220	30	Train	Isaac	2	1			1	2	1	1					8		
Greenwich	220	31	Hendrick	James	1		1					1					3		
Greenwich	220	32	Johnson	Stephen	1	3	1		1	1		1		1			9		
Greenwich	220	33	Johnson	Aaron	2	2		1		1		1		1			8		
Greenwich	220	34	Johnson	John			1			1	1	1					4		
Greenwich	220	35	Harwood	Jacob	3			1		2	2	1					9		
Greenwich	220	36	Lindsey	Norris	4	1		1		2	1		1				10		
Greenwich	220	37	Latham	Winslow	1			1	1	3	3		1	1			11		
Greenwich	221	1	Lampson	Daniel				1	1	1	1	1		1			6		
Greenwich	221	2	Lane	Nathanl		1			1	3	1		1				7		
Greenwich	221	3	Lathrop	Alden	1		1	1		2			1				6		
Greenwich	221	4	Lyscomb	Saml				1		4			1				6		
Greenwich	221	5	Lathrop	Seth		1	1		1			1		1			5		
Greenwich	221	6	McKee	John	1				1	1				1			4		
Greenwich	221	7	Messenger	James	2	1		1		1	1						6		
Greenwich	221	8	Morton	Wm			2		1			1		2			6		
Greenwich	221	9	Mitchel	Thomas	1	1		1		1	1	1					6		
Greenwich	221	10	Mills	James	4	2	2	1						1			10		
Greenwich	221	11	Kingsley	Calvin		1			1	2				1			5		
Greenwich	221	12	Newcomb	Elisha	2			1		4			1				8		
Greenwich	221	13	Newcomb	Nehemh	1	2		1		2		1	1				8		
Greenwich	221	14	Newcomb	David			1		1		1			1			4		
Greenwich	221	15	Newcomb	Bradford		1			1	2	1	1	1				7		
Greenwich	221	16	Powers	Aaron			1		1	1				1			4		
Greenwich	221	17	Osborn	Zebudee	1	2			1		1	4		1			10		
Greenwich	221	18	Powers	Isaac Esq	1				1	1			1				4		
Greenwich	221	19	Powers	Jeremiah				1	6								7		
Greenwich	221	20	Powers	Polly Wd	1							1					2		
Greenwich	221	21	Powers	Nathan		3		1	1	1		2		1			9		
Greenwich	221	22	Powers	Clark	1			1	1	1			1	1			6		
Greenwich	221	23	Powers	Abijah Capt	3	1		1			1		1	1			8		
Greenwich	221	24	Powers	Thos Maj	1	2	3	2	1		2	3		1			15		
Greenwich	221	25	Patterson	David	1		2		1		1			1			6		
Greenwich	221	26	Patterson	William		1			1		1			1			4		
Greenwich	221	27	Patterson	Robt				1	1			1		1			4		
Greenwich	221	28	Pepper	John		1		1		1			1				4		
Greenwich	221	29	Paine	Paul				1		3	1		1				6		
Greenwich	221	30	Patten	Daniel	1	1			1	1			1				5		
Greenwich	221	31	Pope	Joseph	1	1		1	1			1	1	1			7		
Greenwich	221	32	Taylor	Samuel	2				1	1			1				5		
Greenwich	221	33	Woodward	Solomon				1				1					2		
Greenwich	221	34	Stone	James Lt.			1	1		3	2		1				8		
Greenwich	221	35	Hickson	Ezra		1			1			1	1				4		
Greenwich	221	36	Rich	Ebenz Deac			2		1	1		1	1				6		
Greenwich	221	37	Richards	James	2		2	1				1					6		
Greenwich	221	38	Russell	Daniel			1	1	1		1		1				5		
Greenwich	221	39	Rider	Benjamin	2	1		1	1	2		1	1				9		
Greenwich	222	1	Rich	Barnabas	3	1		1			1		1	1			8		
Greenwich	222	2	Rogers	John	2	1		1	1	4	1		1	1			12		
Greenwich	222	3	Ruggles	Joseph			3		1	1	1		1	1			8		
Greenwich	222	4	Rich	Ebenz Jr Lt	2	1			1	1	1			1			7		
Greenwich	222	5	Randell	Ichabod		1			1	1		2		1			6		
Greenwich	222	6	Randell	Titus	1			1		1		1					4		
Greenwich	222	7	Rice	John	1			1		3			1				6		
Greenwich	222	8	Rogers	David		2		1					1				4		
Greenwich	222	9	Randell	Jabez					1					1			2		
Greenwich	222	10	Russell	Peter	1	1			1	1		2		1			7		
Greenwich	222	11	Richardson	Benja		1			1					1			3		
Greenwich	222	12	Mason	Wd	1					1			1				3		
Greenwich	222	13	Rogers	Stephen	1				1	2			1				5		
Greenwich	222	14	Sears	Rolland	1	1		1		3	1		1				8		
Greenwich	222	15	Calhoon	Samuel	2			1		2			1				6		
Greenwich	222	16	Stevers	Robt	3		1			1		1					6		
Greenwich	222	17	Stone	Luke	1		2					2					5		
Greenwich	222	18	Stone	Simeon Deacn		1	1		1	1	1			1			6		
Greenwich	222	19	Spring	Issac B	2	1		1		1	1	1	1				8		
Greenwich	222	20	Shearer	Reuben	4	2	1	1		1		1	1				11		
Greenwich	222	21	Sweatland	David		1		1	1	3		2		1			9		
Greenwich	222	22	Steveman	Isaac		1	2	1	1		1	2	1	1			10		
Greenwich	222	23	Sears	Barnabas	1	1		1		3			1	2			9		

| TOWN | PG# | LN# | HEADS OF HOUSEHOLD | | FREE WHITE MALES | | | | | FREE WHITE FEMALES | | | | | TOTAL ALL OTHER | TOTAL SLAVES | TOTALS | DISTRICT/ TOWNSHIP | NOTES |
			LAST NAME	FIRST NAME	under 10	10 to 16	16 to 26	26 to 45	45 and over	under 10	10 to 16	16 to 26	26 to 45	45 and over					
Greenwich	222	24	Stone	William Doct		1	1	1		1	1	1	1				7		
Greenwich	222	25	Stone	John	2		2		1	1		1	1				8		
Greenwich	222	26	Sloan	Daniel	3			1		1	1		1				7		
Greenwich	222	27	Snow	Reuben		1	1		1	1	2	2		1			9		
Greenwich	222	28	Snow	Stephen	2			1			1		1				5		
Greenwich	222	29	Spooner	Thomas	3	1		1		1	1		1				8		
Greenwich	222	30	Savage	Abraham		1		1						1			3		
Greenwich	222	31	Stowell	Oliver	3	1	1		1	1	2	1		1			11		
Greenwich	222	32	Stone	Samuel	1	2			1	1				1			6		
Greenwich	222	33	Stevens	John	2	1			1	1	2		1	1			9		
Greenwich	222	34	Spear	Silas	1		1	1		2		1		1			7		
Greenwich	222	35	Brice	Abijah	1				1	1	2			1			6		
Greenwich	223	1	Town	John			1		1					1			3		
Greenwich	223	2	Tucker	Ephraim		1	1		1					1			4		
Greenwich	223	3	Town	Reuben				1									1		
Greenwich	223	4	Town	Elijah				1									1		
Greenwich	223	5	Trask	Israel Doct		2	1		1	2		2	1				9		
Greenwich	223	6	Thomas	Israel	1				1	1			1				4		
Greenwich	223	7	Tillson	Stephen		1	3		2		1	1	1	1			10		
Greenwich	223	8	Titus	Simeone	2	1	3	1	1	1	2	2		1			14		
Greenwich	223	9	Thomas	William	3			1		1	2		1				8		
Greenwich	223	10	Town	Levi	3			2		3			2				10		
Greenwich	223	11	Torry	Samuel	2	2		1		2			1				8		
Greenwich	223	12	Thayer	John Jun	2			1	1	2	2		1				9		
Greenwich	223	13	Train	Jonathan	4	1		1	1		1		1				9		
Greenwich	223	14	Toplouf	Gurdon	2			1		1		1					5		
Greenwich	223	15	Toplouf	Luther				1									1		
Greenwich	223	16	Underwood	Kingsley	2		1	1		1			1				6		
Greenwich	223	17	Whalen	Amos	1		1		1		1	2	1				7		
Greenwich	223	18	Town	John Jr	3			1		2		1	1				8		
Greenwich	223	19	Wheeler	Samuel	3		1		1		2	1	1				9		
Greenwich	223	20	Walker	James	1	1		1		1	1		1				6		
Greenwich	223	21	Whitcomb	Nathaniel	1			1		4			1				7		
Greenwich	223	22	Whitcomb	James	1			1		2			1				5		
Greenwich	223	23	Wood	Aaron	3	1		1		2			1				8		
Greenwich	223	24	Woodward	Seth		2	2		1	3	1		1				10		
Greenwich	223	25	Whitcomb	Ebenezr	2	1	1		1	1	2	1	1				10		
Greenwich	223	26	Weeks	Amiel	1		1		1	1	1	1		1			7		
Greenwich	223	27	Wood	Benjamin		1	1		1	2		2		1			8		
Greenwich	223	28	Walkins	Thomas	1	2	1	1				2	1				8		
Greenwich	223	29	Wyot	Stephen				1						1			2		
Greenwich	223	30	Washburn	Cornelius	2		1		1	1		1					6		
Greenwich	223	31	West	Roger Lt.	2	1			2		1		2	1			9		
Greenwich	223	32	Town	Jonathan	1			1		1		1					4		
Greenwich	223	33	Tompkin	Thomas					1			1		1			3		
Greenwich	224	1	Tompkin	Thomas Jr	1			1		1			1				4		
Greenwich	224	2	Hind	Joseph		1			1	1							3		
Greenwich	224	3	Sprout	Ebenz	2	1		1		2		1					8		
Greenwich	224	4	Randell	Isaiah	2	1		1				1	1				6		
Greenwich	224	5	Wood	William				1		1		1		1			4		
Greenwich	224	6	Sloan	James				1						1			2		
Greenwich	224	7	Besse	Abram	1			1		2		1					5		
Greenwich	224	8	Wight	David		1	1	2			1		1				6		
Greenwich	224	9	Sears	Freeman	3		1	1	1	2	1		1	1	2		13		
Greenwich	224	10	Pharoah	Jepthah Blak Man											3		3		
Greenwich	224	11	Pope	Freeman	1	1	1	1		2			1				7		
Greenwich	224	12	Snow	Eli		1	1					1		1			4		
Greenwich	224	13	Daggett	Ebenz	3			1		2			1				7		
Greenwich	224	14	Barton	Jedediah	2			1		1			1				5		
Greenwich	224	15	Green	Ebenz			1			1		1					3		
Greenwich	224	16	Blackman	Barnabas		1	2		1	1			1	1			7		
Greenwich	224	17	Windslow	John	1				1	1	1	1	1				6		
Greenwich	224	18	Marten	Aaron		2			1	1	1		1				6		
Greenwich	224	19	Wight	John			1	2				1		1			5		
Greenwich	224	20	Stone	Daniel			1			1		1					3		

TOWN	PG#	LN#	LAST NAME	FIRST NAME	FREE WHITE MALES					FREE WHITE FEMALES					TOTAL ALL OTHER	TOTAL SLAVES	TOTALS	DISTRICT/ TOWNSHIP	NOTES
					under 10	10 to 16	16 to 26	26 to 45	45 and over	under 10	10 to 16	16 to 26	26 to 45	45 and over					
Hadley	285	1	Montague	William	2			1		1	2		1				7		
Hadley	285	2	Russell	John	2	1	1	1		2	1		1				9		
Hadley	285	3	Russell	Daniel	1	1	2	1	1			2	1	1			10		
Hadley	285	4	Stockbridge	David	3	1	3	2	2	1	2	3	2				19		
Hadley	285	5	Clark	Seth				1					1				2		
Hadley	285	6	Wright	Paul			1					1					2		
Hadley	285	7	Hobard	John	3		1	1		1			1				7		
Hadley	285	8	Hobard	George Jun	1		1			1		1					4		
Hadley	285	9	Washburn	Salmon			1			1			1				3		
Hadley	285	10	Bartlet	Daniel	4	2	3	1		2	1		1				14		
Hadley	285	11	Smith	Caleb	1	2	1	1		3	1		1				10		
Hadley	285	12	Smith	Simeon	3		1			1			1				6		
Hadley	285	13	Whitney	Ebenezer	1		1	1		1	1						5		
Hadley	285	14	Washburn	Luther	1			1		3			1				6		
Hadley	285	15	Smith	Erstus	1			1		4			1				7		
Hadley	285	16	Smith	Benjamin Jun	1		1	1		1			1	1			6		
Hadley	285	17	Belding	Stephen			1	1		3		1	1				7		
Hadley	285	18	Smith	Elihu	2	1	1		1	1	1	1					8		
Hadley	285	19	Sturtevant	Francis		1	1			1	1						4		
Hadley	285	20	Frary	Elisha	1			2		4	1	1	1				10		
Hadley	285	21	Congdon	Jarius	1	1		1			1	1	1				6		
Hadley	285	22	Hobard	George	1	1			1	2	3		1				9		
Hadley	285	23	Osburn	Richard	3		1	1		1	1	1					8		
Hadley	285	24	Andries	George				1					1				2		
Hadley	285	25	Dickinson	Levi	4	3		1		1			1				10		
Hadley	285	26	Gale	Levi	2	1		1		1	1		1				7		
Hadley	285	27	Trayner	Francis		1		1		1	1	2	1				8		
Hadley	285	28	Powel	William	1			1						1	2		5		
Hadley	285	29	Boston	Joshua											4		4		
Hadley	285	30	Montague	John		1	1	1		1	1	1		1			7		
Hadley	285	31	Smith	Elisha				1						2			3		
Hadley	285	32	Cook	Solomon	3	1		1		2			1				8		
Hadley	285	33	Cook	Elihu		2		1		2		1	1				7		
Hadley	285	34	Shipman	William	1	1		1		2	1	1		1			8		
Hadley	285	35	Brown	Samuel	1			1					1				3		
Hadley	286	1	Smith	Josiah				1					1				2		
Hadley	286	2	Grover	Hosea	2			1					1	1			5		
Hadley	286	3	Smith	Jedediah		1	1	1		1	1		1				6		
Hadley	286	4	Kellogg	Gardner & Josiah	3		2	1		5			3	2			16		
Hadley	286	5	Kellogg	Moses Jun		2	1				1						4		
Hadley	286	6	Kellogg	Benjamin	1			1		2	1		1				6		
Hadley	286	7	Kellogg	Moses			1	1	1			1	1	1			6		
Hadley	286	8	White	Daniel		1		1	1		1	3	1				8		
Hadley	286	9	Rider	Stephen	3		1						1				5		
Hadley	286	10	Pierce	Josiah	1	1	2	1	1				1	2			9		
Hadley	286	11	Pierce	William		1		1					1	1			4		
Hadley	286	12	White	Elijah	1		1	1					1				4		
Hadley	286	13	Brooks	John				1		1		1	2	3			8		
Hadley	286	14	Way	Ralph											6		6		
Hadley	286	15	Cook	Seth				1				1		1			3		
Hadley	286	16	Kneeland	Edward	2			1		3			1				7		
Hadley	286	17	Gates	Josiah		1		1						2			4		
Hadley	286	18	Wallace	Daniel		1		1					1				3		
Hadley	286	19	Carrier	Isaiah		1		1				1	1	2			6		
Hadley	286	20	White	Moses	1	1		1		1			1	2			7		
Hadley	286	21	Dickinson	John		1	3	1		1	1		1				8		
Hadley	286	22	Smith	Enos		2	3	1		1	1	1	1				10		
Hadley	286	23	Smith	John 2nd	1	1	1	1		2	1	1	1				9		
Hadley	286	24	Cook	James	1	1	1			1			1	1			6		
Hadley	286	25	Cook	Joseph				1					2	1			4		
Hadley	286	26	Cook	Coleman				1				2		1			4		
Hadley	286	27	Smith	Perez	1	1		1		1	1		1	1			7		
Hadley	286	28	White	Nathaniel				1		1		1	1				4		
Hadley	286	29	Smith	John			1	1		5		2	1	1			11		
Hadley	286	30	Marsh	Eliphalet	1		2	1					1				5		
Hadley	286	31	Fox	Abraham		2		1		1				1			5		
Hadley	286	32	Goodale	Levi	1			1		2			1				5		
Hadley	286	33	Cook	Waitstill	3	2		2		1			1				10		
Hadley	286	34	Warner	Noadiah			1	1		2				1			5		
Hadley	286	35	Warner	Lemuel		1	1	1		1	1	1		2			9		
Hadley	286	36	Sheldon	Samll				1						1			2		
Hadley	287	1	Cook	Gad	1		2	1		1	1		1				7		
Hadley	287	2	Smith	Thomas	1	2		1		2	1						8		
Hadley	287	3	Peck	Joseph				1						1			2		
Hadley	287	4	Cook	Jonathan				1						1			2		
Hadley	287	5	Marsh	Marcy	1					1		1	1				4		
Hadley	287	6	Lott	Elisha			1					2		1			4		
Hadley	287	7	Warner	Jonathan	1		1			1			1	1			5		
Hadley	287	8	White	Ebenezer	1		1	1		3			1	1			9		

TOWN	PG#	LN#	LAST NAME	FIRST NAME	under 10	10 to 16	16 to 26	26 to 45	45 and over	under 10	10 to 16	16 to 26	26 to 45	45 and over	TOTAL ALL OTHER	TOTAL SLAVES	TOTALS	DISTRICT/ TOWNSHIP	NOTES
			HEADS OF HOUSEHOLD		FREE WHITE MALES					FREE WHITE FEMALES									
Hadley	287	9	Marsh	Daniel		2			2	2	1		1				8		
Hadley	287	10	Marsh	Abigail							1		1	1			3		
Hadley	287	11	Porter	Jonathan E.	2		1	1		1		1	1				7		
Hadley	287	12	Porter	William	2	1	3	1		2		2	1				10		
Hadley	287	13	Cook	Elisha		1	2		1	1	2	1		2			10		
Hadley	287	14	Cook	William W.		1		1		3			1				6		
Hadley	287	15	Cook	Job	1		1						1				3		
Hadley	287	16	Gaylord	Samuel		1	2	1				2		1	1		8		
Hadley	287	17	Hopkins	Samuel Revd	1		1	1	1	1			1		1		7		
Hadley	287	18	Porter	Pierpont		1				2		1	1				5		
Hadley	287	19	Hubbard	Elisha	1	1		2		2		2		1			9		
Hadley	287	20	Porter	Samuel	1	1	1	2		4	2		2				13		
Hadley	287	21	Porter	Moses	2			1		2			1	1	2		9		
Hadley	287	22	Smith	Eliakim	1			2		2	1	1					8		
Hadley	287	23	Montague	Jedediah	2	1		1		3		1	1	1			10		
Hadley	287	24	Montague	Stephen		1	3		1	2		1					8		
Hadley	287	25	Nash	John	1		1					1					3		
Hadley	287	26	Hubbard	Hezekiah	3		1					1	2	1			8		
Hadley	287	27	Smith	Chileab		1	2		1		1	1					7		
Hadley	287	28	Smith	Warhum		2		1	1	2		2	1				9		
Hadley	287	29	Newton	Elizabeth	1			2		1		1		1			6		
Hadley	287	30	Smith	Windsor	3	1		2		2	1	1	1				11		
Hadley	287	31	Granger	Holeum	2			1		2			1				6		
Hadley	287	32	Cook	Andrew	1			1					1	1	1		5		
Hadley	287	33	Hodge	John	1	1		1		3			1				7		
Hadley	287	34	Hodge	William	2	2	1	1	1	1	1	1	1	1			12		
Hadley	287	35	Cook	William			1		2			3		1			7		
Hadley	287	36	Dickinson	Amariah	1			1	1	1	1		1				6		
Hadley	287	37	Porter	Eleazer	3	1	1		1	1	2	1	1		1		12		
Hadley	287	38	Dickinson	Daniel	2	2	2	1		1	1	1	1				11		
Hadley	287	39	Stockwell	Timothy		1		1		1		1	1				5		
Hadley	288	1	Symons	Nathan	1	1		1		1		2		1			7		
Hadley	288	2	Cook	John		1	3	1		1		2		1			9		
Hadley	288	3	Cook	Dan	2			1	1	2		1	2				9		
Hadley	288	4	Smith	Joseph	2	1	2	1	1			1	1				9		
Hadley	288	5	Abbott	Amos	3			1				1					5		
Hadley	288	6	Evelth	John	1	2		1		4			1				9		
Hadley	288	7	Gaylord	Nehemiah	3	1	1		1		2	1		1			10		
Hadley	288	8	Nash	Josiah		1			1	3	1	1		1			8		
Hadley	288	9	Abbott	Daniel	3			1	1	3			2				10		
Hadley	288	10	Hawley	Chester	2		1	1		2		2					8		
Hadley	288	11	Potter	Robert			1		1		1	1		1			5		
Hadley	288	12	Cooley	Samuel	2			1		1			1				5		
Hadley	288	13	Kellogg	Daniel	1			1	1			2	1	1			7		
Hadley	288	14	Darling	Alpheus	2			1				1					4		
Hadley	288	15	Pomeroy	Ebenezer	1	1		1	1	2			1	1			8		
Hadley	288	16	Lyman	Caleb		1		1	2	1	1		1				7		
Hadley	288	17	Lyman	Israel	2	1	2		1	3				2			11		
Hadley	288	18	Lyman	Zadock	1		1	1		1	1		2				7		
Hadley	288	19	Johnson	Stephen	2	1		1		2	1	1	1				9		
Hadley	288	20	Bartlett	John		2		2				1		2			7		
Hadley	288	21	Warner	Oringe		1	1		1	1		1		1			6		
Hadley	288	22	Cook	Stephen		1	2					2			2		7		
Hadley	288	23	Warner	Elihu	3			1		2	2		1				9		
Hadley	288	24	Dickinson	Cotton		1		1		1	2	2	1				8		
Hadley	288	25	Smith	Seth	3	2			1	1		1	1		1		10		
Hadley	288	26	Dickinson	William	1			1		1		1		1			5		
Hadley	288	27	Smith	Jacob		1		1		2			1	1			6		
Hadley	288	28	Dickinson	Elisha	1	1		1		1	1	1	1				8		
Hadley	288	29	Eastman	Timothy	1	2			1	2	1	1		1			9		
Hadley	288	30	Hopkins	Timothy	1	1	1	1	1	1			1				7		
Hadley	288	31	Woodward	Samuel		1				1		1					3		
Hadley	288	32	Smith	Elihu 2nd	2			1		3		1	1				8		
Hadley	288	33	Smith	Oliver	1	1	1	1	2	1	1	2	1	1			12		
Hadley	288	34	Goodman	Stephen			3		1			1		1			6		
Hadley	288	35	Avery	Uriah	1	1		1		2	2		1				8		
Hadley	288	36	Bigalow	Amos	3	1		1		1			1				7		
Hadley	288	37	Chadwell	Mathew	3			1					1				5		
Hadley	288	38	Phelps	Charles		1	2		2	1		1		1	1		9		
Hadley	289	1	McGeorge	Horatio T.	2	2			1	4	1		1				11		
Hadley	289	2	Dickinson	Oliver		1	2	1				1	1				6		
Hadley	289	3	Hastings	Waitstil	1		1					1					3		
Hadley	289	4	Dickinson	John	3			1					1				5		
Hadley	289	5	Belon	Amariah	2			1		1		1					5		
Hadley	289	6	Robbins	Willard			1	1			1	1	1				5		
Hadley	289	7	Roth	Widow								2		1			3		
Hadley	289	8	Smith	Elias	2	1			1	3			1				8		

TOWN	PG#	LN#	LAST NAME	FIRST NAME	FWM under 10	10 to 16	16 to 26	26 to 45	45 and over	FWF under 10	10 to 16	16 to 26	26 to 45	45 and over	TOTAL ALL OTHER	TOTAL SLAVES	TOTALS	DISTRICT/ TOWNSHIP	NOTES
Hatfield	11	1	Hastings	Perez	2		1		1	1	1	1	1				8		
Hatfield	11	2	Bardwell	Hannah	3	1	2						1	1			8		
Hatfield	11	3	Dickinson	Daniel			2		1	1	1		1				6		
Hatfield	11	4	Rosevelt	Jacob					1				1				2		
Hatfield	11	5	West	David			1	1	1	2	3		1				9		
Hatfield	11	6	Bliss	Abijah	2	1		1					1	1			6		
Hatfield	11	7	Dickinson	Roger				1		5	2		1				9		
Hatfield	11	8	Morton	Seth			1		1				1				3		
Hatfield	11	9	Dickinson	Joseph		1	1		1		2		1				6		
Hatfield	11	10	Bardwell	Elijah		1						1					2		
Hatfield	11	11	Dickinson	Elihu		1	2		1	2	1		1				8		
Hatfield	11	12	Smith	Mary				1						1			2		
Hatfield	11	13	Morton	Ebenezer	1	1		1		1	1	1	1				7		
Hatfield	11	14	Hastings	John Jun	2	1		1		2	1		1				8		
Hatfield	11	15	Wait	Lucius	1	2		1		4			1				9		
Hatfield	11	16	Scott	James		1						1					2		
Hatfield	11	17	Wait	Benjamin	1	3		1		3			1	1			10		
Hatfield	11	18	Allis	Silas	1		1			1			1	1			5		
Hatfield	12	1	Morton	Benj			1	1		1	1		1				5		
Hatfield	12	2	Morton	William	2	2		1		4		1	1	1			12		
Hatfield	12	3	Morton	Lois									2				2		
Hatfield	12	4	Smith	Rufus		1		1					1				3		
Hatfield	12	5	White	Cotton			5	1				2					8		
Hatfield	12	6	Smith	Benjamin			1			1	1		1				4		
Hatfield	12	7	Lyman	Joseph		1	1	1	1		1	1		1			7		
Hatfield	12	8	Smith	Elijah	1	1	1	1			1	1	1				7		
Hatfield	12	9	Wells	Amasa	3	1		1		1			2	1			9		
Hatfield	12	10	Partridge	Cotton	1	1	1	1		2		1	1		1		9		
Hatfield	12	11	Partridge	Samuel		1	1		1		1		1	1	1		7		
Hatfield	12	12	Dicksinson	Lemuel	2		2		1		2		1				8		
Hatfield	12	13	Billings	Silas		4		1		1	2		2		2		12		
Hatfield	12	14	Billings	David		1		1	1	1	2		1				7		
Hatfield	12	15	Parsons	Israel	3		1	1		2	1		1				9		
Hatfield	12	16	Billings	Jesse	4		2		1				2				9		
Hatfield	12	17	Gearey	Nathan	1	2		1		2	1	1	1				9		
Hatfield	12	18	Day	Joel	4	2		1			1		1				9		
Hatfield	12	19	Maltby	Isaac	2		1	1	2	2	1		1	1			11		
Hatfield	12	20	Field	Medad			1	1	1	1	1		1				6		
Hatfield	12	21	Warner	Moses	1	1	1		1	2		2					8		
Hatfield	12	22	Partridge	Samuel 2d		1	1		1	2	1			2			8		
Hatfield	12	23	Hubbard	John	3		1	1		1	1		2	1	1		11		
Hatfield	12	24	Dickinson	Elijah	1	1	2	1	1	1	1	1	1				10		
Hatfield	12	25	Smith	Amasa	1		1			1		1					4		
Hatfield	12	26	Hammond	Nathaniel	1			1		1			1				4		
Hatfield	12	27	Nash	Elijah	2	1		1		5			2				11		
Hatfield	12	28	Morton	Elihu	1		1		1	1	2	3		1			10		
Hatfield	12	29	Meckins	Levi					2				1				3		
Hatfield	12	30	Porter	Jonathan	2	1	1		1	1	1	2	1				10		
Hatfield	12	31	White	Ebenezer			1			2	1	1	1				6		
Hatfield	12	32	Graves	Perez		1	1		1			1		1			5		
Hatfield	12	33	Graves	Solomon	2			1		1			1				5		
Hatfield	12	34	Graves	Seth		1	1	1				1	1				5		
Hatfield	12	35	White	Elihu	1			1	1	2			1				6		
Hatfield	12	36	Graves	Silas		2		1			1	1	1				6		
Hatfield	12	37	Fitch	Ebenezer		1	1		1			1		1			5		
Hatfield	12	38	Graves	Levi			1					1					2		
Hatfield	12	39	Dickinson	Jonathan	2			1	1	2			1				7		
Hatfield	13	1	Cole	Elizabeth		1	2					2		1			6		
Hatfield	13	2	Dickinson	John	1			1			1		1				4		
Hatfield	13	3	Hastings	John		1	2		1		2	2	1				9		
Hatfield	13	4	Smith	Joseph	3			1		2		1	1				8		
Hatfield	13	5	White	Daniel		1		1				1	1				5		
Hatfield	13	6	McNeal	Daniel	2			1		1			1				5		
Hatfield	13	7	Ballard	John			1		1	1	2		1				6		
Hatfield	13	8	Morton	Perez	1	2		1	1	2			1				8		
Hatfield	13	9	Chapin	Frederic	1	1	1	1		2			1	1			8		
Hatfield	13	10	Wells	Moses			1			2		1					4		
Hatfield	13	11	Robbins	Elihu			1			2		1			1		5		
Hatfield	13	12	Graves	Phineas			1			1			1				3		
Hatfield	13	13	Porter	Silas	3		2	1		1	2	1	1				11		
Hatfield	13	14	Wells	Patience									2				2		
Hatfield	13	15	Remington	Jason											6		6		
Hatfield	13	16	Smith	Joseph 2d	2	1		1		1			1				6		
Hatfield	13	17	Gilbert	Enon	2			1		1		1					5		
Hatfield	13	18	Smith	Sylvanus		1				1		1					3		
Hatfield	13	19	Graves	Israel	3			1		2		1	1				8		
Hatfield	13	20	Wells	Samuel					1								1		
Hatfield	13	21	Nash	Enos	1		1					1					3		
Hatfield	13	22	Allis	John	1	1		1				2	1		2		8		

TOWN	PG#	LN#	LAST NAME	FIRST NAME	FREE WHITE MALES					FREE WHITE FEMALES					TOTAL ALL OTHER	TOTAL SLAVES	TOTALS	DISTRICT/ TOWNSHIP	NOTES
					under 10	10 to 16	16 to 26	26 to 45	45 and over	under 10	10 to 16	16 to 26	26 to 45	45 and over					
Hatfield	13	23	Allis	William	1	2		1		3	1		1		1		10		
Hatfield	13	24	Wilke	Henry	4	1	1		1		2			1			10		
Hatfield	13	25	Gloyd	James	1		1	1	1	2	3	1		1			11		
Hatfield	13	26	Smith	Adna	2	1	1	1			1	1	1				8		
Hatfield	13	27	Easton	Princes											4		4		
Hatfield	13	28	Colkins	William	1			1		2			1				5		
Hatfield	13	29	Wait	Nehemiah		1	1	1				1	1				5		
Hatfield	13	30	Billings	Abraham		1			1	2	2		1				7		
Hatfield	13	31	Dickinson	Samuel	2				1			1	1				5		
Hatfield	13	32	Dickinson	Abina	1			1		1			1				4		
Hatfield	13	33	Wells	Benjamin			1	1					1				3		
Hatfield	13	34	Morton	Elijah	3			1		2	1		1				8		
Hatfield	13	35	Dickinson	Alpheus	2			1				1					4		
Hatfield	13	36	Belden	Jabez				1						2			3		
Hatfield	14	1	Morton	Jonah	1	1		1		2			1	1	1		8		
Hatfield	14	2	White	Elijah	2			1		3		1					7		
Hatfield	14	3	Clarke	John				1		1		2		2			6		
Hatfield	14	4	Smith	Samuel	1			1		1		3		1			7		
Hatfield	14	5	Bissell	Moses	1	2		1		1	1	2		1			9		
Hatfield	14	6	Wait	Elisha			1	1					1				3		
Hatfield	14	7	Wait	Elisha Jun	2			1				1					4		
Hatfield	14	8	Morton	Gideon	3		2			1			1				7		
Hatfield	14	9	Field	Zachariah				1				1	1				3		
Hatfield	14	10	Field	Seth	2			1		2			1				6		
Hatfield	14	11	Morton	Solomon	1			1		2	2		1				7		
Hatfield	14	12	Belding	Joseph		1	1		1	2	1			1			7		
Hatfield	14	13	Coleman	Samuel	2		1			1		1					5		
Hatfield	14	14	Coleman	Niles	1	1							1				3		
Hatfield	14	15	Sewall	Hezekiah											3		3		
Hatfield	14	16	Pease	Solomon	1		2		1		1	2		1			8		
Hatfield	14	17	Guild	Joseph		1		1	1			1	1				5		
Hatfield	14	18	Scott	Ebenezer	1	1		1			1		1				5		
Hatfield	14	19	Frazier	Henry											6		6		
Hatfield	14	20	Snow	Solomon	2			1		1	1	1	1				7		
Hatfield	14	21	Carlisle	Samuel				1		1	1	1	1	1			5		
Hatfield	14	22	Belding	Samuel	2		2						1				6		
Hatfield	14	23	Pierce	Jonathan		1		1	1			1		1			5		
Hatfield	14	24	Dickinson	Aaron	1	2	1		1	2	1	1	1				10		
Hatfield	14	25	Harding	Abiel	3	1		1		1	1		1				8		
Hatfield	14	26	Banks	Thomas				1					1				2		
Hatfield	14	27	Frary	Nathaniel				2				1	1				4		
Hatfield	14	28	Wait	Gad	2			1		1			1				5		
Hatfield	14	29	Dwight	Ebenezer	1	1			3	1	2	1	1	1			11		
Hatfield	14	30	Davis	Ebenezer	2	1		1		1	2	1		1			10		
Hatfield	14	31	Morse	Avander	1	1	1		1	1	2	1	1				9		
Hatfield	14	32	Gillet	Josiah	2	1		1		1		1		1			7		
Hatfield	14	33	Hannum	Silas	1		1			1		1	1				5		
Hatfield	14	34	Warren	Bevil			1			2		1					4		
Hatfield	14	35	Green	Stephen			2		1				1	1			5		

TOWN	PG#	LN#	LAST NAME	FIRST NAME	FREE WHITE MALES under 10	10 to 16	16 to 26	26 to 45	45 and over	FREE WHITE FEMALES under 10	10 to 16	16 to 26	26 to 45	45 and over	TOTAL ALL OTHER	TOTAL SLAVES	TOTALS	DISTRICT/ TOWNSHIP	NOTES
Hawley	331	1	Amsden	Elisha	1			1		1			1				4		
Hawley	331	2	Allis	Lucius	1		1	1		1			1	1			6		
Hawley	331	3	Butrick	Joseph			1			1		1					3		
Hawley	331	4	Baker	Timothy	1	1			1	1	2	1		1			8		
Hawley	331	5	Baxter	Edward			1			2		1		1			5		
Hawley	331	6	Bangs	Joseph	2		1	1		2	3	1	1				11		
Hawley	331	7	Bangs	Zenas	4	1		1		1	1		1				9		
Hawley	332	1	Baker	Elkhanah			1	1		4		1	1				8		
Hawley	332	2	Baker	Rufus	1		1			1		1					4		
Hawley	332	3	Burt	Aaron	2		1	1		2			1	1			8		
Hawley	332	4	Brown	Jonah		1	1		1	3	1	1		1			9		
Hawley	332	5	Beals	John															
Hawley	332	6	Burroughs	David	1	1		2		2	1		2	1			10		
Hawley	332	7	Barlow	Ebenz	2	1			1	2			1				7		
Hawley	332	8	Bartlet	Joel			1			1			1				3		
Hawley	332	9	Blood	Asa	3	1	1	1			1		1				8		
Hawley	332	10	Barnard	Joseph			1					1					2		
Hawley	332	11	Baker	Hollister		1						1					2		
Hawley	332	12	Canada	Micah	2			1		2			1	1			7		
Hawley	332	13	Curtis	Hosea		1	1		1			2		1			6		
Hawley	332	14	Crittenden	Amos		1	2		1	1	2			2			9		
Hawley	332	15	Campbell	John	3	1		1		1		1		1			8		
Hawley	332	16	Campbell	Joseph	2		1						1				4		
Hawley	332	17	Curtis	Beldad	1		1	1				1	1				5		
Hawley	332	18	Clark	Phinehas	3			1					1				5		
Hawley	332	19	Crittenden	Simeon	2		1			2		1	1				7		
Hawley	332	20	Clark	Jotham	1			1				1	1				4		
Hawley	332	21	Clark	Moses	1		1			3	1	1					7		
Hawley	332	22	Cooley	Noah		2	1	1				1		1			6		
Hawley	332	23	Cooley	Reuben		1		1				2		1			5		
Hawley	332	24	Crosby	Ebenz		1	3	1	1	2	2	2		1			13		
Hawley	332	25	Colburn	Nathan	2		1			2			1	1			7		
Hawley	332	26	Cobb	Jonathan	3	2	1	1		1	2		1				11		
Hawley	332	27	Crowel	Ebenz	2		1			2	1	1					7		
Hawley	332	28	Coney	John	3	3		1		2			1				10		
Hawley	332	29	Colson	Christopher		1		1		2			1				5		
Hawley	332	30	Chamberlain	Aaron			1			2			1				4		
Hawley	332	31	Cleveland	John	4		1				1		1				7		
Hawley	332	32	Curtis	Vincent	3		1				1		1				6		
Hawley	332	33	Combs	Ezra	2		1						1				4		
Hawley	332	34	Damon	Stephen	3		1			1	2		1				8		
Hawley	332	35	Dodge	Silas	1		1			2			1	1			6		
Hawley	333	1	Darby	Edward	3	1	1					1					6		
Hawley	333	2	Dickinson	Ebenz	2			1		2	3		1				9		
Hawley	333	3	Daniels	Abiram	1		1					1					3		
Hawley	333	4	Dinsmore	Abel		1	1			2		1					5		
Hawley	333	5	Easton	Joseph	3	1	1			1	1		1	1			9		
Hawley	333	6	Edgeston	Joseph		1	2	1	1			1		1			7		
Hawley	333	7	Edgeston	Oliver								1	1				3		
Hawley	333	8	Eldred	Saml		1	2		1					1			5		
Hawley	333	9	Easton	Justus	2	1		1		2			1				7		
Hawley	333	10	Fuller	Jonathan	4	1		1		1	1		1				9		
Hawley	333	11	Forbes	David	1	1	1						1				4		
Hawley	333	12	Ferguson	Saml	3	2		1		1	1		1				9		
Hawley	333	13	Field	Elijah	1	1	1		1	2	1	1	1				9		
Hawley	333	14	Farnsworth	Willm		1		1				1		1			4		
Hawley	333	15	Fuller	Jason	2		1			3	1		1	1			9		
Hawley	333	16	Farnsworth	Willm Jr	4		1	1		2			1				9		
Hawley	333	17	Fletcher	David		2		1		2		1	1				7		
Hawley	333	18	Glover	Edward L.	3		1				1	1	1				7		
Hawley	333	19	Grant	Jonathan Rev.	1		1	1		3		1	1				8		
Hawley	333	20	Graves	Jonah	1	1		1		1	1		1				6		
Hawley	333	21	Goodspeed	Nathl		1		1						1			3		
Hawley	333	22	Hadlock	John			1			1		1					3		
Hawley	333	23	Hammond	John			1			1		1					3		
Hawley	333	24	Hunt	John															
Hawley	333	25	Hawks	Ichabod	2	2		1			1		1				7		
Hawley	333	26	Hawes	Edmund	2		1	1		1				1			6		
Hawley	333	27	Hall	Seth		1		1	1	1	1		1				6		
Hawley	333	28	Hall	Ebenz	1	1	1	1		2	3	1					10		
Hawley	334	1	Hitchcock	Saml	1	2		1	1	2	1	1	1	1			11		
Hawley	334	2	Hitchcock	Saml Jr		1				1			1				3		
Hawley	334	3	Hitchcock	Arthur	1	1		1		3	1	1	1				9		
Hawley	334	4	Hawks	Zadoch	3	1		1				1	1				7		
Hawley	334	5	Hosford	Stephen	2	1		1		3			1				8		
Hawley	334	6	Harmon	Elijah	2	1	1		1		2		1				8		
Hawley	334	7	Howard	Joseph		1						1					2		
Hawley	334	8	Jenkins	Stephen	1			1		2			1				5		
Hawley	334	9	King	Thomas			2	1		1				1			6		

TOWN	PG#	LN#	LAST NAME	FIRST NAME	FREE WHITE MALES					FREE WHITE FEMALES					TOTAL ALL OTHER	TOTAL SLAVES	TOTALS	DISTRICT/ TOWNSHIP	NOTES
					under 10	10 to 16	16 to 26	26 to 45	45 and over	under 10	10 to 16	16 to 26	26 to 45	45 and over					
Hawley	334	10	King	Amos		1			1	4	1		1				8		
Hawley	334	11	Kelsey	Eliab	1			1				1					3		
Hawley	334	12	King	Jonas	1			1			1		1				4		
Hawley	334	13	Lilly	Silas Jun				1		3			1				5		
Hawley	334	14	Longley	Edmund Esq		2	2		1		1	1		1			8		
Hawley	334	15	Longley	Joseph		1			1	1	1	1		2			7		
Hawley	334	16	Longley	Joseph Jr	1			1		2			1				5		
Hawley	334	17	Look	Noah	2	1		1			1		1				6		
Hawley	334	18	Lathrop	Zephl	3	1		1		1	2		1				9		
Hawley	334	19	Lamoin	Benjm	3	1		1		2			1				8		
Hawley	334	20	Lilly	Zenas				1					1				2		
Hawley	334	21	Longley	Zimos	1			1		1		1					4		
Hawley	334	22	Maynard	Daniel	4	1		1			1		1				8		
Hawley	334	23	Munson	Salmon	1			1		2		1					5		
Hawley	334	24	Marsh	Joseph				1						1			2		
Hawley	334	25	Marsh	Joseph Jr	2			1		1			1				5		
Hawley	334	26	Mantor	James			1			1	1	1					4		
Hawley	334	27	Parker	Willm	1		1	1		1		1		1			6		
Hawley	334	28	Packard	Ichabod	3	2		1		1			1	1			9		
Hawley	334	29	Porter	Edward			1	1		1				1			4		
Hawley	334	30	Parsivil	James				1			1			1			3		
Hawley	334	31	Pomroy	Ebenz	1		1	1		1			1				5		
Hawley	334	32	Parker	Nathl	1	1	1		1			2		1			7		
Hawley	334	33	Parsavil	Oren			1			1		1					3		
Hawley	334	34	Rogers	Abisha															
Hawley	334	35	Rogers	Moses			1										1		
Hawley	334	36	Rice	Jonas	2	2			1	2		1	1				9		
Hawley	334	37	Russell	Saml		1		1		3		1					6		
Hawley	334	38	Stoddard	Saml															
Hawley	334	39	Shaw	Hosea	1		1					1					3		
Hawley	335	1	Smith	Allen	2			1		2			1				6		
Hawley	335	2	Smith	Stephen	2				1		1			2			6		
Hawley	335	3	Scott	Phinehas	3	2	1	1		2	1	1		1			12		
Hawley	335	4	Scott	Isaac	3			1		1		1	1				7		
Hawley	335	5	Sears	Rufus	2			1		2			1				6		
Hawley	335	6	Sears	Roland		1	3	1	1			2		1			9		
Hawley	335	7	Shelly	Joshua			1		1			1		1			4		
Hawley	335	8	Smith	Sylvenus	2	1	1		1	3	2			1			11		
Hawley	335	9	Sanford	Willm			1	1					1				3		
Hawley	335	10	Sprague	Benjm				1		3	1	2					7		
Hawley	335	11	Smith	Daniel		1			1			1	1	1			5		
Hawley	335	12	Spafford	Jonathan			1		1					1			3		
Hawley	335	13	Sprague	Preserved		1	2					1					4		
Hawley	335	14	Thayer	Asa	1	1	1		1		1	1		1			7		
Hawley	335	15	Taylor	John		1	1		1			3	1				7		
Hawley	335	16	Thorp	Bishop			1			2		1					4		
Hawley	335	17	Thorp	Thomas				1		2		1					4		
Hawley	335	18	Wells	Lemuel		1	1		2		1			2			7		
Hawley	335	19	Wood	Zebedee				1				1	1				3		
Hawley	335	20	Wood	Andrews	3	1		1		2			1				8		
Hawley	335	21	West	Nathan		1		1	1		1			1			5		
Hawley	335	22	Wilcox	Josiah			1	1		1			1				4		
Hawley	335	23	White	Eliphalet			2	1		1			1				5		
Hawley	335	24	Warrich	Hezekiah		1		1		2	1	1					6		
Hawley	335	25	Worthington	Timothy	?	1		1	1	?		1	1				9		
Hawley	335	26	West	Asa	1			1				1					5		
Hawley	335	27	Wells	Elisha	1	1	1		1		2	2					8		
Hawley	335	28	Williams	Caleb	1			1		2			1				5		
Hawley	335	29	West	Billy			1			1			1				3		

TOWN	PG#	LN#	LAST NAME	FIRST NAME	FREE WHITE MALES					FREE WHITE FEMALES					TOTAL ALL OTHER	TOTAL SLAVES	TOTALS	DISTRICT/ TOWNSHIP	NOTES
					under 10	10 to 16	16 to 26	26 to 45	45 and over	under 10	10 to 16	16 to 26	26 to 45	45 and over					
Heath	195	1	Barker	Joseph	1			1				1					3		
Heath	195	2	Cheney	Hezekiah	2			1				1					4		
Heath	195	3	Cowls	Seth	1			1		2			1				5		
Heath	195	4	Christee	William	1		1		1		3	1		1			8		
Heath	195	5	Cowles	Agustus			1	1		2		1					5		
Heath	195	6	Chapin	Zebinah	3			1				1	1				6		
Heath	195	7	Colman	Job		2	1		1			1		1			6		
Heath	195	8	Chapin	Jacob	1	1		1		4	1		1				9		
Heath	195	9	Chapin	Isaac	1	1		1		2	1	1					8		
Heath	195	10	Davison	Josiah				1						1			2		
Heath	195	11	Dalrymple	Thos	1			1					1				3		
Heath	195	12	Davison	Levi	1		1			1		1					4		
Heath	195	13	Eddy	David			1	1				1	1				4		
Heath	196	1	Farnsworth	Benjm	4		1						1				6		
Heath	196	2	Graves	Joel			1			4	1		1				7		
Heath	196	3	Gleason	Daniel	1	1		1		2		1					6		
Heath	196	4	Gleason	Solomon	2	1		1		4	1		1				10		
Heath	196	5	Gleason	Varnum			1	1				1					4		
Heath	196	6	Gould	Isaac	1	1		1		4	1	2		1			11		
Heath	196	7	Henry	David	1			1		1		1	1				5		
Heath	196	8	Hunt	Peter			1	1		1			1				4		
Heath	196	9	Hunt	William	2		1	1		1	1		1				7		
Heath	196	10	Harris	Valentine	1	1	1		1			1		1			6		
Heath	196	11	Heywood	Moses		1	1		1	1		1		1			6		
Heath	196	12	Hunt	Parley	2	2		1		2			1				8		
Heath	196	13	Heywood	Solomon	1			1		2			1				5		
Heath	196	14	Herington	Thomas	1	1	1	1		2	1	1	1				9		
Heath	196	15	Harris	Daniel	1					1	1	1					5		
Heath	196	16	Hunt	Samuel					1			1	1				3		
Heath	196	17	Harris	Silas	1			1		2		1					5		
Heath	196	18	Jaquigh	Benjamin	4			1					1				6		
Heath	196	19	Pattison	Jonathan	1		1	1		2		1					6		
Heath	196	20	Kinsman	Samuel			1			2	1						4		
Heath	196	21	Kindrick	John	2	1	2		1	1	1		1				10		
Heath	196	22	Leavit	Jonathan			3		1		1	1	1	1			8		
Heath	196	23	Leavit	Roger	1		1	1		1		1					5		
Heath	196	24	Maxwell	Benjamin		2	2	1					1				6		
Heath	196	25	Maxwell	Hugh	3			1		1			2	1			8		
Heath	196	26	Maxwell	Benjm Jun			1	1									2		
Heath	196	27	Nash	Revere	1			1		1		1					4		
Heath	197	1	Nims	Jonathan	2	1		1		1	1	1					7		
Heath	197	2	Nims	Calvin	1			1		1		1					4		
Heath	197	3	Rugg	Reuben	1	2	1		1	1		2					8		
Heath	197	4	Smith	Samuel	2	2		1		1	1	1					8		
Heath	197	5	Spaulding	Samson				1		2		1					4		
Heath	197	6	Smith	Phineas		1	1		1					1			4		
Heath	197	7	Snow	Joseph				1						1			2		
Heath	197	8	Smith	Aaron	1		1	1		1		1					6		
Heath	197	9	Spaulding	Joseph			1	1			1			1			4		
Heath	197	10	Strong	Joseph	3	1		1		2		1					8		
Heath	197	11	Severance	Selah	1	1		1				1					4		
Heath	197	12	Stone	Thomas				1	1		1	1					4		
Heath	197	13	Spaulding	Samson Jr			1			2		1					4		
Heath	197	14	Thair	Silas	2	1		1		2		1					7		
Heath	197	15	Temple	Salman			1	1				1					3		
Heath	197	16	Temple	Seth	3	1		1		2	1	1	1	1			11		
Heath	197	17	Temple	Solomon		1	3	1		2			1				8		
Heath	197	18	Thair	Asil			1	1				2	1				5		
Heath	197	19	Thair	Asil Jun		1		1	1	1		1	1				6		
Heath	197	20	Trask	William	1	3		1		2		1					8		
Heath	197	21	Thair	Caleb Jun	1		1		1	1		1		1			6		
Heath	197	22	Thomson	Stephen	1	1	1	1		3	2	1					10		
Heath	197	23	Thair	Jonathan		1	1	1		4			2	1			10		
Heath	197	24	Thair	Jonah		1		1		1		1	1				5		
Heath	197	25	Thair	Artemas	2			1					1				4		
Heath	197	26	Town	Thomas	1		1		2	1							5		
Heath	197	27	Tilden	Benjamin	1	3	1		1	3	1		1				11		
Heath	197	28	Tucker	Ebenezer	2		2	1		2			1		1		9		
Heath	197	29	Vincen	Joshua	4			1					1				7		
Heath	197	30	White	Benjamin	3	2	2		1		1	1		1			11		
Heath	197	31	Williams	John	1	2	1		1		1	2		1			9		
Heath	197	32	Walker	Thomas	4			1				1					6		
Heath	197	33	Warfield	Joshua	2	1	1	1		1	1	1	1				9		
Heath	198	1	Wilson	Caleb	2	1		1		1		1					6		
Heath	198	2	Wilder	Willis	1		2	1		2	1	2		1			10		
Heath	198	3	White	James		2			1			4	1	1			9		
Heath	198	4	White	Luke	4	1		1		1	1	1	1				10		
Heath	198	5	White	Asaph		1	3		1		1			1			7		
Heath	198	6	White	David				1		1		1					3		

TOWN	PG#	LN#	LAST NAME	FIRST NAME	FREE WHITE MALES					FREE WHITE FEMALES					TOTAL ALL OTHER	TOTAL SLAVES	TOTALS	DISTRICT/ TOWNSHIP	NOTES
					under 10	10 to 16	16 to 26	26 to 45	45 and over	under 10	10 to 16	16 to 26	26 to 45	45 and over					
Heath	198	7	Wait	Abel	1		1					2					4		
Heath	198	8	Warfield	Job				1					1				2		
Heath	198	9	Young	Henry		2		1		2				1			6		

TOWN	PG#	LN#	LAST NAME	FIRST NAME	FREE WHITE MALES under 10	10 to 16	16 to 26	26 to 45	45 and over	FREE WHITE FEMALES under 10	10 to 16	16 to 26	26 to 45	45 and over	TOTAL ALL OTHER	TOTAL SLAVES	TOTALS	DISTRICT/ TOWNSHIP	NOTES
Holland	278	1	May	Rufus	1	1		1		2	2	1	1				9		
Holland	278	2	Dorrell	Thomas	2	1			1			1		1			6		
Holland	278	3	Webber	Ezra		1	1	2				1					5		
Holland	278	4	Wallis	David	3	2		1		1		1	1				9		
Holland	278	5	Wallis	Thomas Doct.	2		1		1		2			1			7		
Holland	278	6	Rosebrook	Gershom	1		2		1			2		1			7		
Holland	278	7	Weatherby	Ebenezer	1			1		2			1				5		
Holland	278	8	Polley	John	1	1	1						1	1			6		
Holland	278	9	Lyon	Alfred Col.	1	1	1		1	2	3	2	1				12		
Holland	278	10	Ballard	Sherebiah				1					1				2		
Holland	278	11	Webber	Sewal		1	1	1		1			1	1			6		
Holland	278	12	Wallis	Alfred	2			1		1			1				5		
Holland	278	13	Bruce	Joseph			1	1			1		1				4		
Holland	278	14	Perrin	S. Hollowell		1	3	1		3		1	1				10		
Holland	278	15	Partridge	Isaac		1		1		4		1					7		
Holland	278	16	Smith	Seth Doct.			2	1				1	1				5		
Holland	278	17	Perrin	Lyrell	2	1		1	1	2			1	1			9		
Holland	278	18	Goodell	Ichabod Lt.		1	1		1				1	1			5		
Holland	278	19	Lyon	Ebenezer		2	2		1				1				7		
Holland	278	20	Glazier	Calvin	1	2		1		4			1				9		
Holland	278	21	Stacy	Mark		1	1		1		1	1		1			6		
Holland	278	22	Allen	Reuben	2			1		2			1				6		
Holland	279	1	Kimball	Asa	1			1		3			1				6		
Holland	279	2	Ballard	Jonathan	3			1					1				5		
Holland	279	3	Negro	Mundy											2		2		
Holland	279	4	Webber	Andrew				1		1	1	1		1			5		
Holland	279	5	Allen	Abel Lt.	1		2	1		1	1		1				7		
Holland	279	6	Belknap	William	1		1	2					1	1			6		
Holland	279	7	Paddock	John	1	1		1		1	1		1				6		
Holland	279	8	Paddock	James				1					1				2		
Holland	279	9	Janes	Eliphalet				2					2				4		
Holland	279	10	Frizzel	James		1		1	1			1	1	1			6		
Holland	279	11	Webber	Saml Jr Deacn	3		2	1				1		1			8		
Holland	279	12	Webber	Rinaldo Capt.	1	1		1		1		1	1				6		
Holland	279	13	Fuller	James	2	1	1	1		1	1	1	1				9		
Holland	279	14	Anderson	David		1	1		1			1		1			5		
Holland	279	15	Sherman	Jeremiah				2		2	2	1		1			8		
Holland	279	16	Thompson	Jacob			1	1				1		1			4		
Holland	279	17	Marcy	Wd	1	2	2			1			1	2			9		
Holland	279	18	Fay	David	1	1	1	1	1	2	1	1	1				10		
Holland	279	19	Williams	John	1			1		2			1				5		
Holland	279	20	Marcy	James	1			1				1	1				4		
Holland	279	21	Webber	Samuel		1		1					1	1			4		
Holland	279	22	Webber	Prenance		1		1			1		1				4		
Holland	279	23	Webber	Henry				1					2				3		
Holland	279	24	Reeves	Ezra Rev.				1					1				2		
Holland	279	25	Webber	S. Edward		1	2	1		2	1		1				8		
Holland	279	26	Barrett	Joshua		1	1			1			1				4		
Holland	279	27	Bond	Ephraim		1	2		1		1	1		2			8		
Holland	279	28	Morris	Ebenz		1		1		2			1				5		
Holland	279	29	May	Nehemiah	2	1		1					1	1			6		
Holland	279	30	May	Uriel	1			1		1			1				4		
Holland	279	31	Upham	Jona	2			1		1		1	1				6		
Holland	279	32	Wallis	Alanson	1	1		1		1		1	1				6		
Holland	279	33	Rosebrook	Jona	4			1					1				6		
Holland	279	34	Wallis	Renaldo	1			1		2			1				5		
Holland	279	35	Beals	Levi	1			1				1					3		
Holland	279	36	Beals	Benjamin				1					1				2		
Holland	279	37	Webber	Bradley	1			1		1			1	1			5		
Holland	279	38	Kind	Darius	1	1		1					2				5		
Holland	279	39	Henry	Robert		1	2		1	3	2		1				10		
Holland	279	40	Smalledge	Jona	1	1		2				3	1				8		
Holland	279	41	Munger	Simeon			1			5			1				7		
Holland	279	42	Reeves	Benja	1	1	1	1			1	1	1				7		
Holland	280	1	Morse	Eben	2	1	1		1	1				1			7		
Holland	280	2	Thompson	Asa	1			1		1	1	1	1				6		
Holland	280	3	Doalph	Amasa				1				1					2		
Holland	280	4	Clark	Moses	3			1		1	3		1				9		
Holland	280	5	Bradford	Perez	1	1		1	2				1	1			7		
Holland	280	6	Anderson	Timothy	2		1	1		1			1	1			7		
Holland	280	7	Webber	Reuben	2	2	2	1		2			1	1			11		
Holland	280	8	Halladay	Eunice									1				1		
Holland	280	9	Graham	Moses	1			1		1			1	1			5		
Holland	280	10	Anderson	David 2d	1			1		1			2				5		
Holland	280	11	Webber	Benja				1					1				2		
Holland	280	12	Hind	Loviah									1				1		

TOWN	PG#	LN#	LAST NAME	FIRST NAME	FREE WHITE MALES					FREE WHITE FEMALES					TOTAL ALL OTHER	TOTAL SLAVES	TOTALS	DISTRICT/ TOWNSHIP	NOTES
					under 10	10 to 16	16 to 26	26 to 45	45 and over	under 10	10 to 16	16 to 26	26 to 45	45 and over					
Leverett	113	1	Ashley	Stephen		1	1		1				1				5		
Leverett	113	2	Adams	Erastus		1	3		1		1	2		1			9		
Leverett	113	3	Ayres	Jesse	2	1		1		2	2	1					9		
Leverett	113	4	Ainsworth	Willm	1		2		1			1	1				6		
Leverett	113	5	Ashley	Warden	1	1						1					3		
Leverett	113	6	Adams	a negro											1		1		
Leverett	113	7	Bartlet	Samuel	1			1		1		1					4		
Leverett	113	8	Broad	Enos	3	1		1				1		1			7		
Leverett	113	9	Butterfield	Abel		2			1		1			1			5		
Leverett	113	10	Ball	Silas		1	2		1	2				1			7		
Leverett	113	11	Bartlet	Henry			1			2			1				4		
Leverett	113	12	Bates	James	2			1		3	1			1			8		
Leverett	113	13	Bater	Obediah				1			1			1			3		
Leverett	113	14	Boutwell	Ebenz	2	1		1		1				1			6		
Leverett	113	15	Cowle	Josiah			2	1		1		2		1			7		
Leverett	113	16	Corking	Caleb		2		1		2	1		1				7		
Leverett	113	17	Cowle	Isaac				1				1		1			3		
Leverett	114	1	Cowle	Burden	1			1		1				1			4		
Leverett	114	2	Clary	Phinehas	1	1		1				2		1			6		
Leverett	114	3	Clary	Elisha				1				2		1			4		
Leverett	114	4	Curtis	James		1		1						1			3		
Leverett	114	5	Cutter	Jairus	2			1		2				1			6		
Leverett	114	6	Clark	Luther	1			1		1				1			4		
Leverett	114	7	Curtis	Ebenz				1		1				1			3		
Leverett	114	8	Cutter	Abraham		1		1						1			3		
Leverett	114	9	Cadwell	Isaac	1			1						1			3		
Leverett	114	10	Cowle	Seth			1						1				2		
Leverett	114	11	Camp	Martha										1			1		
Leverett	114	12	Clary	David			1			1			1				3		
Leverett	114	13	Doty	James	2	1		1		1	1		1				7		
Leverett	114	14	Dike	Aden	1	1		1		1			1				5		
Leverett	114	15	Davis	Abraham	4	1		1					1				7		
Leverett	114	16	Eames	Charles			1			1			1				3		
Leverett	114	17	Elliot	Ebenz					1				1				2		
Leverett	114	18	Field	Seth		1	3	1				1	1	1			8		
Leverett	114	19	Field	Rufus			1										1		
Leverett	114	20	Field	Jonathan		2	1	1					2	1			7		
Leverett	114	21	Field	William	1	1	1	1		1	2	1					8		
Leverett	114	22	Field	Luther	1			1		1			1				4		
Leverett	114	23	Field	Moses	3	1		1		1	1	1	1				9		
Leverett	114	24	Field	Erastus			1						1				2		
Leverett	114	25	Field	Jonathan 2d		1	3	1				1	1	1			8		
Leverett	114	26	Field	Paras	3			1		2			1				7		
Leverett	114	27	Field	Roswell			1	1				1	1				4		
Leverett	114	28	Felt	Jonathan	1	2						2	1				6		
Leverett	114	29	Glazier	Jonathan	3			1		1		2		1			8		
Leverett	114	30	Gould	Samuel			1			1			1				3		
Leverett	114	31	Gould	Solomon		2	1	1		1	1			2			9		
Leverett	114	32	Glazier	John	1		1						1				3		
Leverett	114	33	Graves	Moses		1	2	1			1			1			6		
Leverett	114	34	Graves	Enos	2	1		1		2	1		1				8		
Leverett	115	1	Gardner	Andrew	1	2	1		1	1	1	2					9		
Leverett	115	2	Gill	John			1							1			3		
Leverett	115	3	Gould	Noah				2						1			3		
Leverett	115	4	Glazier	Benja	2	1		1		3	2	1					10		
Leverett	115	5	Graves	Daniel		2		1		1			2				6		
Leverett	115	6	Graves	Joseph	1	1		1		2	1		1				7		
Leverett	115	7	Gilbert	Lewis	1	2	2	1		3		1	1				11		
Leverett	115	8	Graves	Rufus	1			1					1				3		
Leverett	115	9	Graves	Silas				1						1			2		
Leverett	115	10	Hobert	Joshua	3	1		1		2	1		1				9		
Leverett	115	11	Fair	Robert	4	1		1		1			1				8		
Leverett	115	12	Hubbard	William	1	1		1		4		2	1				10		
Leverett	115	13	Hubbard	Gideon	1	2	1			2	1			1			9		
Leverett	115	14	Hemenway	Josiah				1			1			1			3		
Leverett	115	15	Hemenway	Willm	1			1				1					3		
Leverett	115	16	Howard	Hezekh	1		1	1	1	1			1	2			8		
Leverett	115	17	Holden	Isaac		2							1				3		
Leverett	115	18	Hemenway	Elipht			1						1				2		
Leverett	115	19	Jackson	Jeremiah	1			1				2		1			5		
Leverett	115	20	Jones	Samuel		1	1	1		2	1			2			8		
Leverett	115	21	Keet	Jonathan		1		1		3	2	2					9		
Leverett	115	22	Kitley	John				1						1			2		
Leverett	115	23	Keep	Chileas		1	1					3					5		
Leverett	115	24	Kitley	Willm		1		1		2	2		1				7		
Leverett	115	25	Keet	Reuben	1			1		1		1					4		
Leverett	115	26	Leasure	Saml	1	1		1		2	2		1				8		
Leverett	115	27	Lee	Gideon		1	1		1		1	2		1			7		
Leverett	115	28	Matthews	Silas		1	1	2	1		1	1					7		

TOWN	PG#	LN#	LAST NAME	FIRST NAME	FREE WHITE MALES					FREE WHITE FEMALES					TOTAL ALL OTHER	TOTAL SLAVES	TOTALS	DISTRICT/ TOWNSHIP	NOTES
					under 10	10 to 16	16 to 26	26 to 45	45 and over	under 10	10 to 16	16 to 26	26 to 45	45 and over					
Leverett	115	29	Moore	Asa	3	3			1				1				8		
Leverett	115	30	Morton	Enos	2			1					1				4		
Leverett	115	31	Montague	Elijah	1			1		3			2				7		
Leverett	115	32	Moore	Alvin	1			1		2			1				5		
Leverett	115	33	Morse	Amasa	1			1		2			1				5		
Leverett	115	34	Newton	Paul		1	1		1	1	2	1	1				8		
Leverett	115	35	Nurse	Reuben		1		1		1		1	1				5		
Leverett	116	1	Pearce	Alden	2			1		1		2	1				7		
Leverett	116	2	Pratt	Ephraim	3			1		1			1				6		
Leverett	116	3	Porter	Jacob	1	1		1		1	1		2				7		
Leverett	116	4	Richardson	Francis	1			1		3			1				6		
Leverett	116	5	Richardson	Jereh				1				1		1			3		
Leverett	116	6	Richardson	John	2			1		1			1				5		
Leverett	116	7	Rice	Josiah	2			1		2			1				6		
Leverett	116	8	Richardson	Amasa	2		1				1	1					5		
Leverett	116	9	Rice	Abel	2	1		1		2	2		1				9		
Leverett	116	10	Smith	Joel	2	1			2	2	1	1	1	1			11		
Leverett	116	11	Smith	Joel Junr	1			1		4	1		1				8		
Leverett	116	12	Smith	Joseph	1			1		2	1	1		1			7		
Leverett	116	13	Smith	Moses				1				1		1			3		
Leverett	116	14	Stockwell	John	2	1		1				1	2				7		
Leverett	116	15	Shumway	Elijah	1			1		2	1		1				6		
Leverett	116	16	Smith	Jonathan	2	2		1		2			1				8		
Leverett	116	17	Sanders	Hannah						1			1				2		
Leverett	116	18	Thayer	Calvin	2	1		1					1				5		
Leverett	116	19	Torrey	Jacob		1			1		1			1			4		
Leverett	116	20	Thayer	Joshua	1	1	1	1		2	1	1	1				9		
Leverett	116	21	Turner	Mich	2	1	1		1	3	1			1			10		
Leverett	116	22	Temple	Silas		1			1				1	1			4		
Leverett	116	23	Woodbury	John	2	1	1		1	1	2	3		1			12		
Leverett	116	24	Wildes	Samuel	2			1		2			1				6		
Leverett	116	25	Wildes	Dolling				1		3			1				5		
Leverett	116	26	Woodbury	Seth	3	3		1		1			1	1			10		
Leverett	116	27	Woodbury	Knowlton	3			1		2			1				7		
Leverett	116	28	Winchester	Willm				1					1				2		
Leverett	116	29	Wedge	Thomas	2			1		1			1				5		
Leverett	116	30	Watson	Samuel	1			1		2			1				5		
Leverett	116	31	Willis	Samuel	2			1		4	2		1				10		
Leverett	116	32	Wheelock	John	4	2						1	1	1			10		
Leverett	116	33	Williams	Henry		1	2		1	1	2		1	1			9		
Leverett	116	34	Willard	Josiah	1		1	1		1	1		1				6		
Leverett	117	1	White	Matthew	2	2		1		2			1				8		
Leverett	117	2	Wedge	Abijah	3			1		1			1				6		

TOWN	PG#	LN#	HEADS OF HOUSEHOLD		FREE WHITE MALES					FREE WHITE FEMALES					TOTAL ALL OTHER	TOTAL SLAVES	TOTALS	DISTRICT/ TOWNSHIP	NOTES
			LAST NAME	FIRST NAME	under 10	10 to 16	16 to 26	26 to 45	45 and over	under 10	10 to 16	16 to 26	26 to 45	45 and over					
Leyden	80	1	Avery	Nathaniel	2	2			1	2	1		1	1			10		
Leyden	80	2	Avery	Nathan			1		1			2	1	1			6		
Leyden	80	3	Allen	Simon	1	1	2		1		1	1		1			8		
Leyden	80	4	Adams	Elijah	2	1	1		1		1			1			7		
Leyden	80	5	Babcock	Derius				1	1	1		1					3		
Leyden	80	6	Bush	Uriah	1	1		1		2			1				6		
Leyden	80	7	Budington	Jonathan	1		1		1			1	1				5		
Leyden	80	8	Babcock	Ezra	4	1		1		1		1	1				9		
Leyden	80	9	Bulfinch	Bedgood	3	2			1	1	1			2			10		
Leyden	80	10	Ball	Benjamin					1		1		1				3		
Leyden	80	11	Bliss	Peter	3			1		2			1	1			8		
Leyden	80	12	Brown	Nathaniel	3			1					1				5		
Leyden	80	13	Bardwell	Comider	2			2		1			1				6		
Leyden	80	14	Babcock	Oliver	1		3		2		2		1	2			11		
Leyden	80	15	Bullock	Israel	1	2			2	1	1	1		1			9		
Leyden	81	1	Bardwell	Henry	3	1		1					1		4		10		
Leyden	81	2	Babcock	Peleg	1	1	1		1	1				1	1		7		
Leyden	81	3	Baker	Benjamin	1	1	1		1	2	1			1			8		
Leyden	81	4	Baker	Elijah	1		1		1	1			1				5		
Leyden	81	5	Brown	Amos	2			1		2	2		1	1			9		
Leyden	81	6	Babcock	Joseph	3			1		1		1	3	1			10		
Leyden	81	7	Brown	Elisha	1	1	1		1	1		1	1	1			8		
Leyden	81	8	Brown	Jarad	2	1			1	2		1	1				8		
Leyden	81	9	Brown	Thomas				1		1			1				3		
Leyden	81	10	Brown	Elisha Junr	1			1					1				3		
Leyden	81	11	Burrows	Amos	1			1					1				3		
Leyden	81	12	Briggs	Enoch	3	1		2	1	3			3	1			14		
Leyden	81	13	Babcock	Paul	4	1		1		1	1		1				9		
Leyden	81	14	Barstow	Alpheus		1	1		1		1	1		1	1		7		
Leyden	81	15	Chapen	Julias		1		1				1	2				5		
Leyden	81	16	Chapen	Consider				1		3	3		1				8		
Leyden	81	17	Carpenter	Nathaniel			3		1		1		2	1			8		
Leyden	81	18	Clark	David				1					1				2		
Leyden	81	19	Clark	Alexander	1			1		1			1				4		
Leyden	81	20	Crumb	Phinius	2	1	3		1		2	1		1			11		
Leyden	81	21	Crandell	Jarad			2		1	1	1	1		1	2		9		
Leyden	81	22	Clark	Davis	1	1		1			1		1				5		
Leyden	81	23	Clark	Alpheus	1	1	1					1					4		
Leyden	81	24	Chapen	Selah	2		3		1		1	1		1			10		
Leyden	81	25	Chapen	Daniel		1	2		1			1	2	1			8		
Leyden	81	26	Clark	Matthew	2	2		1				1	1				7		
Leyden	81	27	Crawford	Joseph	1			1		2	1		1				6		
Leyden	81	28	Clark	Elisha	1		2		1		1	1	1				7		
Leyden	81	29	Cooledge	Daniel		1	1		1			1		1			5		
Leyden	81	30	Corse	John	2			1					1				4		
Leyden	81	31	Cambell	John Junr	2	2		1	1		1	1	2	1			11		
Leyden	81	32	Cambell	Samuel	2			1		2	3		1				9		
Leyden	81	33	Clark	William		1	1			1	2	2		1			9		
Leyden	81	34	Crouch	William	2			1	1	3	1		1				8		
Leyden	81	35	Champlin	Joseph	2			1		1	1		1				6		
Leyden	81	36	Downing	John	3	2	3		1		1			1			11		
Leyden	82	1	Denison	David	1	1		1		2	2	1		1			9		
Leyden	82	2	Denison	Edward	1	1	1	1		3		1	1				9		
Leyden	82	3	Dorrell	William	1	2		1			1	2	1	1			9		
Leyden	82	4	Demick	Solomon	4			1		2			1				8		
Leyden	82	5	Davenport	Oliver				1		4			1				6		
Leyden	82	6	Davis	Joseph		1		1		4	2		1				9		
Leyden	82	7	Dean	Samuel		2			1	3			1				7		
Leyden	82	8	Eddy	Benjamin	1	1		1		4			1				8		
Leyden	82	9	Glen	John	2	1	3		1	2	1		1				11		
Leyden	82	10	Edwards	Abel	1			1		1		1					4		
Leyden	82	11	Evans	John				1	1	1				1			4		
Leyden	82	12	Glen	Richard	1	2	1		1			3		2			12		
Leyden	82	13	Glen	Richard Junr				1					1				2		
Leyden	82	14	Euda	John	2	1		1		3	2		1				10		
Leyden	82	15	Eliott	Lemuel	2			1		3			1				7		
Leyden	82	16	Edwards	Ebenezer	2			1		2			1				6		
Leyden	82	17	Frizzell	Michael		1			1			1		1			4		
Leyden	82	18	Frizzell	Reuben			1		1			1	1				4		
Leyden	82	19	Fairbanks	Nathan	3	1		1		3	1	2					11		
Leyden	82	20	Foster	Ezekiel	2	2	2		1	2	1		1				11		
Leyden	82	21	Field	John	2		2	1		1	2	1	1				10		
Leyden	82	22	Frizzell	Zenus	3			1		1			1				6		
Leyden	82	23	Foster	Lemuel	2	1		1		3			1				8		
Leyden	82	24	Fitch	Ezra		1		1		1			1				4		
Leyden	82	25	Frizzell	Reuben Jr	2			1		2	1		1				7		
Leyden	82	26	Greenell	Benjamin		1		1		2	1		1				6		
Leyden	82	27	Greenell	Richard	1	1			1	1	2	2		1			9		
Leyden	82	28	Greenell	Paul	4				1								7		

85

TOWN	PG#	LN#	HEADS OF HOUSEHOLD		FREE WHITE MALES					FREE WHITE FEMALES					TOTAL ALL OTHER	TOTAL SLAVES	TOTALS	DISTRICT/ TOWNSHIP	NOTES
			LAST NAME	FIRST NAME	under 10	10 to 16	16 to 26	26 to 45	45 and over	under 10	10 to 16	16 to 26	26 to 45	45 and over					
Leyden	82	29	Gates	Peter			1		1	2	3	1		1			9		
Leyden	82	30	Greenell	Benjamin				1		1			2				4		
Leyden	82	31	Greenell	Joseph		1		1		1	1	1		1			6		
Leyden	82	32	Hibbard	Asa	1	1		1		2	3	1		1			10		
Leyden	82	33	How	Antipas	1	1	2	1		1			2				8		
Leyden	82	34	Henry	Andrew	2	1		1		4		1	1	1			11		
Leyden	83	1	Hawkins	Amaziah	2		1	1		2	2	1	1				10		
Leyden	83	2	Hunt	Charles	3	1		1			1	1	1				8		
Leyden	83	3	Hastings	Nathan				1		4							5		
Leyden	83	4	Hunt	John			1	1		1				1			4		
Leyden	83	5	Ingell	Benoni	3		1			2			1				7		
Leyden	83	6	Kent	Zenus	1	1		1		2	2		1				8		
Leyden	83	7	Kenyon	Paul	3			1		1			1				6		
Leyden	83	8	Kentley	John	1	1	2		1	2	1	1		1			10		
Leyden	83	9	Kelton	Benjamin		1	1	1		3	1			1			8		
Leyden	83	10	Love	Susanna								3	1				4		
Leyden	83	11	Lampkin	Simeon	1		1					1					3		
Leyden	83	12	Lincoln	Levi	1	2	1	1		2			1				8		
Leyden	83	13	Lyman	Seth				1		3			1				5		
Leyden	83	14	Lord	William	1		1					1					3		
Leyden	83	15	Martin	William	3			2					1				6		
Leyden	83	16	Macumber	William	3			1			1		1				6		
Leyden	83	17	Miller	John	1			1		1			1				4		
Leyden	83	18	Moore	John Jr		3		1		3	1		1				9		
Leyden	83	19	Morgan	Benjamin	2	2		1		3	1		1				10		
Leyden	83	20	Morton	Michael	1			1		1			1				4		
Leyden	83	21	Moore	John			1		1	1			1				4		
Leyden	83	22	Marshall	Joseph		2		1		3	1	2	1				10		
Leyden	83	23	Macumber	Lemuel				1		3			1				5		
Leyden	83	24	Nelson	Edward				1		4			1				6		
Leyden	83	25	Noyes	Oliver	3	2	1	1		1			1				9		
Leyden	83	26	Newton	Asahel		1	2		1		2	1		2			9		
Leyden	83	27	Newcomb	Hezekiah Jun	3		1	1		3			1				9		
Leyden	83	28	Newcomb	Daniel			1					1		1			3		
Leyden	83	29	Newell	Jesse		1		1		4	1		1				8		
Leyden	83	30	Olmstead	Jonathan		1	2	1	1			1		1			7		
Leyden	83	31	Orvis	William		1		1		4	2		1				9		
Leyden	83	32	Peckam	Isaac			2			3			1				6		
Leyden	83	33	Perry	Abel	2	1		1				1		1			6		
Leyden	83	34	Potter	David	1	2	1		1	2	1	2		1			11		
Leyden	84	1	Pichard	Charles		1	1		1	2				1			6		
Leyden	84	2	Parmenter	Reuben	2	2		1		2	1		1				9		
Leyden	84	3	Phillips	James	2	1			1	3	1	1		1			10		
Leyden	84	4	Phillips	Peter	1	1		1		1	1		1	1			7		
Leyden	84	5	Rounds	Hezekiah	1			1		1	2		1				6		
Leyden	84	6	Rice	Samuel	1			1		1			1				4		
Leyden	84	7	Richardson	Jonathan	1		1	1	1	4		1	1	1			11		
Leyden	84	8	Stearns	Eleaner									1				1		
Leyden	84	9	Stedmon	Philemon	2			1		2			1				8		
Leyden	84	10	Smith	Israel	3	3		1		1		1	1				10		
Leyden	84	11	Sworence	Matthew	4	1	4	2	1		3		2	1			18		
Leyden	84	12	Shelden	Reuben	2	1	2		1	1			1				8		
Leyden	84	13	Sheperson	Joseph	2	1		1		3			1		1		9		
Leyden	84	14	Stearns	Charles	2	2		1		2	1	1	1				10		
Leyden	84	15	Shattoch	Ezra	3	3	2	1				2	1				12		
Leyden	84	16	Sabens	Jedediah	2		1						1				4		
Leyden	84	17	Thorn	Henry	1	1		1		3	1		1				8		
Leyden	84	18	Tylor	Peter	3	1		1		1	1		1				8		
Leyden	84	19	Vining	John		1		1		1			1				6		
Leyden	84	20	Wells	Thomas		1	1	1		1	3	1	1				9		
Leyden	84	21	Wild	John	3			1		3	1		1				9		
Leyden	84	22	Wells	Simeon	1			1		3	1		1				7		
Leyden	84	23	Wadsworth	Amos				1					1				2		
Leyden	84	24	Wilbur	Uriah		1	1	1				3		1			7		
Leyden	84	25	Wilbur	John	1			1		3	1	2					8		
Leyden	84	26	Wells	Asa	2	2	1	1				2		1			9		
Leyden	84	27	Wells	Nev		2	2	1	1			2	1	1			10		
Leyden	84	28	Wells	Joshua	1	1		1		4		1					8		
Leyden	84	29	Wagner	Elizabeth	1					1				1			3		
Leyden	84	30	Wagner	Francis			1			1		1					3		
Leyden	84	31	Waterhouse	Nathan			1				2		1				4		
Leyden	84	32	Washburn	Nehemiah	4	1		1		1		1					8		

TOWN	PG#	LN#	HEADS OF HOUSEHOLD LAST NAME	FIRST NAME	FREE WHITE MALES under 10	10 to 16	16 to 26	26 to 45	45 and over	FREE WHITE FEMALES under 10	10 to 16	16 to 26	26 to 45	45 and over	TOTAL ALL OTHER	TOTAL SLAVES	TOTALS	DISTRICT/ TOWNSHIP	NOTES
Longmeadow	91	1	Taylor	Nathaniel	2			1			1		1				5		
Longmeadow	91	2	Pratt	Jacob		2	1		1	1		1		1			7		
Longmeadow	91	3	Cosby	Whiting	4		1			1	1		1	1			9		
Longmeadow	91	4	Ashley	Stephen			1	1		1			1				4		
Longmeadow	91	5	Ashley	Noah			1			1		1					3		
Longmeadow	91	6	Brown	Jere			1				1		1				3		
Longmeadow	91	7	Gowdy	William	1	1		1		3	1		1				8		
Longmeadow	91	8	Taylor	Err	2	1		1		1			2				7		
Longmeadow	91	9	Frost	Isaac			1		2			1		1			5		
Longmeadow	91	10	Webber	Edward		1	1	1		1	1		1				6		
Longmeadow	91	11	Ashley	Justin		1		1		2			1				5		
Longmeadow	91	12	Mills	Sarah Wid		2				1			1				4		
Longmeadow	91	13	Billings	Thaddeus	3	1	1	1		2	1		1				10		
Longmeadow	91	14	Swetland	Theophilus	2		1		1	2	1						7		
Longmeadow	91	15	Hills	Moses	1	2	2		1			2	1	1			10		
Longmeadow	91	16	Field	Alexr Capt.	1		2	1				1	2	1			8		
Longmeadow	91	17	Field	Moses Capt.				2					1				3		
Longmeadow	91	18	Field	Moses Junr	1		1	1		1			1				5		
Longmeadow	91	19	Hale	Thomas	1		1	1		1	2			2			8		
Longmeadow	91	20	Cooley	Eli				1									1		
Longmeadow	91	21	Cooley	John 2d			1			3							4		
Longmeadow	92	1	Cooley	Stephen	3	1		1					1				6		
Longmeadow	92	2	Cooley	Calvin	2		2	1		2			1	1			9		
Longmeadow	92	3	Woolworth	Richard Jr	1	1	1	1		1			1				6		
Longmeadow	92	4	Cooley	Josiah	1	1	1	1		1	2		1				8		
Longmeadow	92	5	White	Lewis Dr		1		1		2			1				5		
Longmeadow	92	6	Dwight	Oliver	1		1	1		1	1	1					6		
Longmeadow	92	7	Dwight	Elihu	1			1	2	1			1	1			7		
Longmeadow	92	8	Chapin	Jabez	2					2			1				6		
Longmeadow	92	9	Cooley	Gideon			1			1			1				3		
Longmeadow	92	10	Chapman	Nathl Captn	2		1		1	2	1		1				8		
Longmeadow	92	11	Chandler	Stephen Jun	2	1			1	1			1				6		
Longmeadow	92	12	Colton	George				1						1			2		
Longmeadow	92	13	Colton	Demas	3			1		2	1		1				8		
Longmeadow	92	14	Steel	Seth	3			1		1			2				7		
Longmeadow	92	15	Stebbins	Medad	2			1				1		3			7		
Longmeadow	92	16	Cooley	John			1	1					1	1			4		
Longmeadow	92	17	Stebbins	Ezra		1		1					1	1			4		
Longmeadow	92	18	Stebbins	Zadek	1	1		1			1		1				5		
Longmeadow	92	19	Colton	Solomon 2d	2			1					1				4		
Longmeadow	92	20	Woolworth	Richard		1		2	1				1	1			6		
Longmeadow	92	21	Simonds	Catherine Wd	1					2	1		1				5		
Longmeadow	92	22	Colton	Zadock	2			1				2					5		
Longmeadow	92	23	Stephenson	Calvin	3	1	1	1		3			1				10		
Longmeadow	92	24	Kibbe	Samuel		2	1	1				1	1				6		
Longmeadow	92	25	Simonds	Grace Wd		2	1							1			4		
Longmeadow	92	26	Hulbert	Asa	2			1		2			1				6		
Longmeadow	92	27	Brown	Jesse			1			1	1						3		
Longmeadow	92	28	Fern	Charles	2	2			1	3			1				9		
Longmeadow	92	29	Root	Daniel Junr			1						1				2		
Longmeadow	92	30	Root	Daniel	1	2	1		2	2	1		1	1			11		
Longmeadow	92	31	Harris	Phebe	1	1		1			1		2				6		
Longmeadow	92	32	Richardson	Stephen	1	2	1		1	1		1		1			8		
Longmeadow	92	33	Chapman	Abiel	1			1					1				3		
Longmeadow	92	34	Thompson	Charles Jr	1			1				1					3		
Longmeadow	92	35	Brown	Joseph				1					1				2		
Longmeadow	92	36	Brown	Samuel	1	1		1		2			1				6		
Longmeadow	92	37	Hancock	Abiel		3	1	1					1				6		
Longmeadow	92	38	Wood	Submit										1			1		
Longmeadow	92	39	Wood	Edward		1				1		1					3		
Longmeadow	92	40	Lyon	Kimbal	1	1		1		1			1				5		
Longmeadow	92	41	Britton	Joseph	2	1		1		1							5		
Longmeadow	93	1	Fairman	Ithamar	1			1		1	2		1				6		
Longmeadow	93	2	Talcott	Aaron		1		1				1	1				4		
Longmeadow	93	3	Russell	Emery		1	1		1		1			1			5		
Longmeadow	93	4	Colburn	John	1			1		1		1					4		
Longmeadow	93	5	Ewings	Joshua				1					1				2		
Longmeadow	93	6	Wolcott	Benjamin					1								1		
Longmeadow	93	7	Russell	Wolcott	2			1		2			1				6		
Longmeadow	93	8	Russell	Oliver			1			1		1					3		
Longmeadow	93	9	Russell	Ellis			1	1				1		1			4		
Longmeadow	93	10	Cooley	Hanan			1	1					1				3		
Longmeadow	93	11	Cotton	Solomon					1					1			2		
Longmeadow	93	12	Ely	Ethan	1	2	1	1		3	1		2				11		
Longmeadow	93	13	Ely	Nathaniel	1	1			1	3	1		1	1	2		11		
Longmeadow	93	14	Raynolds	Samuel	2			1		3	1	1	1				9		
Longmeadow	93	15	Colton	Alpheus	1	1	5	1		2	1		1				12		
Longmeadow	93	16	Woodworth	Azariah	1	1	5	1		2	1		1				12		
Longmeadow	93	17	Storrs	Richard Rev	4			1					1				7		

TOWN	PG#	LN#	LAST NAME	FIRST NAME	M under 10	M 10 to 16	M 16 to 26	M 26 to 45	M 45 and over	F under 10	F 10 to 16	F 16 to 26	F 26 to 45	F 45 and over	TOTAL ALL OTHER	TOTAL SLAVES	TOTALS	DISTRICT/ TOWNSHIP	NOTES
Longmeadow	93	18	Bliss	Ebenezer		1		1	1				1	1			5		
Longmeadow	93	19	Bliss	Noah	2	1	1	1			1		2				8		
Longmeadow	93	20	Silcock	Robert	2	1	1	1		3	1	1	1	1			12		
Longmeadow	93	21	Burt	Nathaniel			1		1		1	1	1	1			6		
Longmeadow	93	22	Williams	Samuel		1	2		1		1	1	2	1			9		
Longmeadow	93	23	White	David		2	1		1	1		1		1			7		
Longmeadow	93	24	Grosvenor	Charles	1		1			1		1					4		
Longmeadow	93	25	Bliss	Nathaniel	1				1	1		1	1				5		
Longmeadow	93	26	Colton	Elihu	2	1	1	1		1		1		1			8		
Longmeadow	93	27	Keep	Mathew				1						1			2		
Longmeadow	93	28	Colton	Chandler	2			1		1		1					5		
Longmeadow	93	29	Rumrill	Nehemiah				1						1			2		
Longmeadow	93	30	Rumrill	Levi	3			1		1			1				6		
Longmeadow	93	31	Field	Oliver				1						1			2		
Longmeadow	93	32	Bliss	Zadock	2	1		1									4		
Longmeadow	93	33	Chandler	Abner	2			2		2		1	1				8		
Longmeadow	93	34	Chandler	Stephen				1				1	1				3		
Longmeadow	93	35	Chase	Berry		1	1				1		1	1			5		
Longmeadow	93	36	Chase	Berry Junr	5			1					1				7		
Longmeadow	93	37	Welman	Jacob	4	1		1		1			1				8		
Longmeadow	93	38	Colton	Luther Majr	3	1	1	1		3	1	1	1	1			13		
Longmeadow	93	39	Colton	Asa	1		1	1		3			1	2			9		
Longmeadow	93	40	Coomes	Walter	2			1		2			1				6		
Longmeadow	93	41	Hale	Sarah								1	1	1			3		
Longmeadow	94	1	Coomes	John	3			1		1	2		1	1	1		10		
Longmeadow	94	2	Coomes	Samuel				1		1			1				3		
Longmeadow	94	3	Colton	Jacob				1		1		1					3		
Longmeadow	94	4	Colton	Erstus	1			1				1					3		
Longmeadow	94	5	Burt	Calvin Capt	2	2		1		2	1		2				10		
Longmeadow	94	6	Burt	David Capt		2		1		1	2						6		
Longmeadow	94	7	Wilson	David	1			1					1				3		
Longmeadow	94	8	Booth	Peter	1			1					1				3		
Longmeadow	94	9	Stebbins	William	3			1		2			1				7		
Longmeadow	94	10	White	Walter	2		1	1		1			1				6		
Longmeadow	94	11	Hale	Jonathan Esq		1	1		1					2			5		
Longmeadow	94	12	Goldthwait	Erstus	2			1					1				4		
Longmeadow	94	13	Frost	Joshua Dr	1			1		1	1		1				5		
Longmeadow	94	14	Blanchard	Oliver				1					1				2		
Longmeadow	94	15	Cooley	Lewis			1						1				2		
Longmeadow	94	16	Booth	David	1			1		1			1				4		
Longmeadow	94	17	Hale	Hezekiah Lt		1	1	2				1	1				6		
Longmeadow	94	18	Colton	Gideon Junr			1	1		1	1	1	1				6		
Longmeadow	94	19	Colton	Samuel		1	2			1		1					5		
Longmeadow	94	20	Bliss	Aaron		1	1	1					1	1			5		
Longmeadow	94	21	Colton	Thomas	2			1					1	1			5		
Longmeadow	94	22	Keep	Moses				2					1	2			5		
Longmeadow	94	23	Keep	Stephen	2		1			1			1				5		
Longmeadow	94	24	Colton	Thomas Jr	2		1			2	1	1	1				8		
Longmeadow	94	25	Taylor	Eliab	1			1		1			1				4		
Longmeadow	94	26	Colton	Asahel	1			1		2			1				5		
Longmeadow	94	27	Thompson	Rufus	2			1		1	2		1				7		
Longmeadow	94	28	Crandall	Levi	2			1		1			1				5		
Longmeadow	94	29	Collins	Stephen			1	1						1			3		
Longmeadow	94	30	Bliss	Gaius	2	1	2		1	4		1	1				12		
Longmeadow	94	31	Keep	Samuel	1	1	1	1	1	2	1	1	2				11		
Longmeadow	94	32	Keep	Samuel Junr			1					1					2		
Longmeadow	94	33	Colton	Israel		2	1		1	1	1		1	1			8		
Longmeadow	94	34	Burt	Gideon Col	1	4	1		1		1		1	1			10		
Longmeadow	94	35	Colton	Wm Deacn	1	1	1		1		1	1		1			7		
Longmeadow	94	36	Colton	Levi			1			2		1					4		
Longmeadow	94	37	Colton	Simeone Ens		1			1	2	1		1				6		
Longmeadow	94	38	Colton	Henry Dr	1		1	1		1		1	1				6		
Longmeadow	94	39	Colton	Mary Wd								1		1			2		
Longmeadow	94	40	Colton	Jabez		2		2		1			1				6		
Longmeadow	94	41	Rumrill	Ebenezer				1		1			1				3		
Longmeadow	95	1	Colton	Martin	2			1		2	1	1	1	1			9		
Longmeadow	95	2	Pease	Peter						2		1					3		
Longmeadow	95	3	Hitchcock	Lydia										1			1		
Longmeadow	95	4	Hale	Abner		1		2			1	1					7		
Longmeadow	95	5	Hale	John	1	1		1		2			1				6		
Longmeadow	95	6	Hale	Elam			1				1	1					3		
Longmeadow	95	7	Pease	Simeon	3	1		1		1			1				7		
Longmeadow	95	8	Burt	Elijah	1	1	2	1	1		1	1	2	1			11		
Longmeadow	95	9	Burt	Luther			1						1				2		
Longmeadow	95	10	Pease	Abiel		1	2						1				4		
Longmeadow	95	11	Thompson	William		2		1				1		1			5		
Longmeadow	95	12	Thompson	Charles	1	2		1			1	1		1			7		
Longmeadow	95	13	Hills	Jacob	2	1		1		2			1				7		
Longmeadow	95	14	McGregory	Ebenezer			2		1	2		1	1				8		

TOWN	PG#	LN#	HEADS OF HOUSEHOLD		FREE WHITE MALES					FREE WHITE FEMALES					TOTAL ALL OTHER	TOTAL SLAVES	TOTALS	DISTRICT/ TOWNSHIP	NOTES
			LAST NAME	FIRST NAME	under 10	10 to 16	16 to 26	26 to 45	45 and over	under 10	10 to 16	16 to 26	26 to 45	45 and over					
Longmeadow	95	15	Brown	Timothy					1					1			2		
Longmeadow	95	16	Kibbe	Gideon			2		1			1		1			5		
Longmeadow	95	17	Hunn	Ephraim	1	1		1		3		1					7		
Longmeadow	95	18	Markhand	Israel	1			1		2			1				5		
Longmeadow	95	19	Spencer	Israel			1		1	1		1		1			5		
Longmeadow	95	20	Waters	Nathaniel	2			1		1	1	1					6		
Longmeadow	95	21	Booth	John	1			1		3	1	1					7		
Longmeadow	95	22	Hatch	Abner		4			1	1				1			7		
Longmeadow	95	23	Pease	Heman	2	1		1	1	1	2		1	1			10		
Longmeadow	95	24	Parsons	Daniel					1			2		1			4		
Longmeadow	95	25	Huntington	Thomas Dr	1	1			1			3		1			7		
Longmeadow	95	26	Thompson	Samuel		1	1	1						1			4		
Longmeadow	95	27	Brumley	Stephen	1			1		2		1					5		

TOWN	PG#	LN#	HEADS OF HOUSEHOLD LAST NAME	FIRST NAME	FREE WHITE MALES under 10	10 to 16	16 to 26	26 to 45	45 and over	FREE WHITE FEMALES under 10	10 to 16	16 to 26	26 to 45	45 and over	TOTAL ALL OTHER	TOTAL SLAVES	TOTALS	DISTRICT/ TOWNSHIP	NOTES
Ludlow	255	1	Frost	Noah		1		1		3	2		1				8		
Ludlow	255	2	Nash	Timothy	2			1					1	1			5		
Ludlow	255	3	Nash	Joel				1					1				2		
Ludlow	255	4	Frost	Samuel		1	2	1		2	1		1				8		
Ludlow	255	5	Dodge	Asa	2			1		1			1				5		
Ludlow	255	6	Simmons	Paul Geer	3			1		1			1				6		
Ludlow	255	7	Kimball	Nathaniel	1		1					1					3		
Ludlow	255	8	Colton	Aaron	1	2	2	1		2	1	1	1				11		
Ludlow	255	9	Keyes	Lemuel	2			1		4			2	1			10		
Ludlow	255	10	Temple	Silas		1				1		1					3		
Ludlow	255	11	Temple	Thomas	2		2	1		1		1		1			8		
Ludlow	255	12	Willey	Gates			1			1		1					3		
Ludlow	255	13	Wright	Elam	1		1					1					3		
Ludlow	255	14	Keyes	Timo Deacn				1					1				2		
Ludlow	255	15	Bishop	Hooper		1		1		2			1				5		
Ludlow	255	16	Pratt	Cyrus	3			1		2			1	1			8		
Ludlow	255	17	Putnam	Eli	1		1	1		1	1		1				5		
Ludlow	255	18	Putnam	Abner		3		1		1			1				6		
Ludlow	255	19	Moffett	Mathew	2		1	1		2			1				7		
Ludlow	255	20	Strickland	Nehemiah	1	1	1	1		1			1				6		
Ludlow	255	21	Galkins	Rufus		1		1						1			3		
Ludlow	255	22	Dick	Richard											8		8		
Ludlow	256	1	Nelson	Aaron		3	2	1		1	1	1					9		
Ludlow	256	2	Chesire	Mary Wid									1	3			4		
Ludlow	256	3	Chasun	Henry M.	1	1		1		2	1		1	1			8		
Ludlow	256	4	Miller	George	2		1	1		3			1				8		
Ludlow	256	5	Wood	Moses	3	1		1		1			1				7		
Ludlow	256	6	Miller	Joseph				1				1	1				3		
Ludlow	256	7	Miller	Joseph Jr	1	1	2	1		3		1	2		1		12		
Ludlow	256	8	Wilder	Moses Lt				1					1				2		
Ludlow	256	9	Wright	Benjamin	2	1	1			1		1	1				8		
Ludlow	256	10	Wright	Thaddeus	1		1			2			1				5		
Ludlow	256	11	Burt	Reuben	3			1		1	2		1	1			9		
Ludlow	256	12	Wright	Abel				1		1			1				3		
Ludlow	256	13	Lamb	Joseph								1					1		
Ludlow	256	14	Wright	Abel Jr			1			2			1				4		
Ludlow	256	15	Wright	Timothy		1		1					1				3		
Ludlow	256	16	Wright	Goss	2			1					1				44		
Ludlow	256	17	Daniels	Asa	1	1	1	1		2			1				7		
Ludlow	256	18	Daniels	David		1		1	1		1	1		1			6		
Ludlow	256	19	Seranton	John		1			1		1			1			4		
Ludlow	256	20	Daniels	Peter			1					1					2		
Ludlow	256	21	Olds	Samuel	2			1		1	1		1				7		
Ludlow	256	22	Hills	Asa	2			1		1	1	1					6		
Ludlow	256	23	Snow	Jeremiah	1			1		1			1				4		
Ludlow	256	24	Paine	David			2		1			1					4		
Ludlow	256	25	Brewer	Chauney		1	3			1	1						6		
Ludlow	256	26	Miller	Leonard	1		1	1		1		3	2				10		
Ludlow	256	27	Wackoff	Peter											3		3		
Ludlow	256	28	Snow	Natha Capt				1					1		1		3		
Ludlow	256	29	Gilligan	John			1			2			1	1			5		
Ludlow	256	30	Miller	Aaron John	1	1		1		1		1	1				6		
Ludlow	256	31	Huntley	Richard		1	1	1				1		1			5		
Ludlow	256	32	Tarbox	Solomon			1	1				1		1			4		
Ludlow	256	33	Carver	David				1					1				2		
Ludlow	256	34	Carver	Jona	2			1		1			2				6		
Ludlow	256	35	Carver	Warren	1			1									2		
Ludlow	256	36	Cook	David	2		1	1					1				5		
Ludlow	256	37	Munger	Joseph	1	2	2	1		2			1	1			10		
Ludlow	256	38	Wachburn	Elijah		1	1			2	1	1					6		
Ludlow	256	39	Burr	Timothy	2	1		1		2			1				7		
Ludlow	256	40	Beebe	Sherwood			1			2			1				4		
Ludlow	256	41	Rude	Zephaniah		2		1						1			4		
Ludlow	256	42	Rude	Moses		1						1					2		
Ludlow	256	43	Chapin	Job	1	1		1		1			1				5		
Ludlow	256	44	Barber	Lewis	1	1		1					1				3		
Ludlow	256	45	Barber	Ebenezer				1				1		1			3		
Ludlow	256	46	Barber	Ebenezer Jr	3	1						1	1				7		
Ludlow	256	47	Chapin	Berazeel	2					2			1				5		
Ludlow	257	1	Chapin	Olivia				1				2		1			4		
Ludlow	257	2	Burt	Jepthah	3	1	1	1						1			7		
Ludlow	257	3	Root	Timothy		2		1		4	1			1			9		
Ludlow	257	4	Lyon	Stephen		1					1	1		1			4		
Ludlow	257	5	Sheldon	James Jr			1			1			1				3		
Ludlow	257	6	Lyon	David Deacn			1	1		1			1	2			6		
Ludlow	257	7	Lyon	Gad	3			1					1				5		
Ludlow	257	8	Sikes	John Lt		2	2	1		1	1	2		1			10		
Ludlow	257	9	Sheldon	James		1		1		1			2	1			6		
Ludlow	257	10	Wood	Obadiah Doct			1							1			3		

TOWN	PG#	LN#	LAST NAME	FIRST NAME	FREE WHITE MALES					FREE WHITE FEMALES					TOTAL ALL OTHER	TOTAL SLAVES	TOTALS	DISTRICT/ TOWNSHIP	NOTES
					under 10	10 to 16	16 to 26	26 to 45	45 and over	under 10	10 to 16	16 to 26	26 to 45	45 and over					
Ludlow	257	11	Moor	Timothy	1		1						1				3		
Ludlow	257	12	Fuller	Elisha	3	1	2		1	1	1	1					10		
Ludlow	257	13	Pinney	Joseph				1						1			2		
Ludlow	257	14	Jones	Stephen	1	1	2	1			2	1	1				9		
Ludlow	257	15	Fuller	Joshua			1					1					2		
Ludlow	257	16	Sikes	Benjamin				1					1	1			3		
Ludlow	257	17	Sikes	Benjamin Jr	2			1		3	1		1				8		
Ludlow	257	18	Sikes	Increase			1	1			1		1				4		
Ludlow	257	19	Sikes	Pleny	2			1		2			1				6		
Ludlow	257	20	Lumbard	Jonathan			1	1	1					1			4		
Ludlow	257	21	Sikes	Mercy Wid									2	1			3		
Ludlow	257	22	Lumbard	David			1			1		1					3		
Ludlow	257	23	Alden	Josiah	4			1		1		1					7		
Ludlow	257	24	Lumbard	Jonathan Jr		1	1			2	1	1					6		
Ludlow	257	25	Willson	John	2	1		1				1	1				6		
Ludlow	257	26	Hannum	Daniel	3	1	1			1		1					7		
Ludlow	257	27	Burr	Jona Jr	1		1					1					3		
Ludlow	257	28	Burr	Preeman	1		1					1					3		
Ludlow	257	29	Burr	Jonathan				1			1	2		1	1		6		
Ludlow	257	30	Sikes	Jonathan	3	2	1			1		1					8		
Ludlow	257	31	Lumbard	Abiel	3		1			1		1					6		
Ludlow	257	32	Hitchcock	Ambrose	1		1			1		1	1				5		
Ludlow	257	33	Fuller	Ezekiel	3		1	1		1	2	1	1				10		
Ludlow	257	34	Pease	Job		1	1		1	1	1	1		1			7		
Ludlow	257	35	Peak	Asa	1		1			1		1					4		
Ludlow	257	36	Kendall	James	1	1			1	1		1	1				6		
Ludlow	257	37	Kendall	Chapman		1						1					2		
Ludlow	257	38	Pearson	Ezra		2	1		1				1				5		
Ludlow	257	39	Pearson	Adin	2		1			1	1						5		
Ludlow	257	40	Nash	Sylvester Doctr		1					1						2		
Ludlow	257	41	Jennings	John		3	1			2		1	2	1			10		
Ludlow	257	42	Kendall	Ruel	3		1			1				1			6		
Ludlow	257	43	Kendall	James Jr	2		1					1	1				5		
Ludlow	258	1	Hubbard	Eliha		1	1	1			1		1				5		
Ludlow	258	2	Hubbard	Felix	2		1					1					4		
Ludlow	258	3	Clough	Jonathan			1						1				2		
Ludlow	258	4	Clough	Dan	1		1				1						3		
Ludlow	258	5	Goodell	Jabez	2	1	1	1	1	2	1		1				10		
Ludlow	258	6	Talmage	Nathaniel	2	1		1		1	1			1			7		
Ludlow	258	7	Clough	Timothy		1		1		3				1			6		
Ludlow	258	8	Little	Charlotte Wid.	1						2	1	1				5		

| | | | HEADS OF HOUSEHOLD | | FREE WHITE MALES | | | | | FREE WHITE FEMALES | | | | | | | | | |
TOWN	PG#	LN#	LAST NAME	FIRST NAME	under 10	10 to 16	16 to 26	26 to 45	45 and over	under 10	10 to 16	16 to 26	26 to 45	45 and over	TOTAL ALL OTHER	TOTAL SLAVES	TOTALS	DISTRICT/TOWNSHIP	NOTES
Middlefield	155	1	Dickson	John	2	1	2	1			1		1				8		
Middlefield	155	2	Dickson	Nabby Widw	2					1			1				4		
Middlefield	155	3	Spencer	John Junr			1										1		
Middlefield	155	4	Wood	Artemas	2			1		1			1				5		
Middlefield	155	5	Allen	Timothy	2	1		1					1				5		
Middlefield	155	6	Skinner	William	1	1	1		1	1		2		1			8		
Middlefield	155	7	McElwain	Timothy Capt	1	1	3		1	2	2	1		1			12		
Middlefield	155	8	McElwain	Timothy Junr		1		1		1		2					5		
Middlefield	155	9	Smith	Matthew Capt	2	3			1	1		1	1				9		
Middlefield	155	10	Pelton	Ithamer		1	1	1					1	1			5		
Middlefield	155	11	Robbins	Job Deac		1	2		1		1	2		2			9		
Middlefield	155	12	Woodard	Jonathan			1						1				2		
Middlefield	155	13	Skinner	Molly Widw									1				1		
Middlefield	155	14	Russ	Hezekiah			1							1			2		
Middlefield	155	15	Bissell	Israel	2	1			1	2	1		1				8		
Middlefield	155	16	Pelton	Ithamer Junr			1			1		1					3		
Middlefield	155	17	Coleman	William Doct	2	1	1	1		1			1				7		
Middlefield	155	18	Blossom	Thomas	3	1	2		1			1	1				9		
Middlefield	155	19	Taylor	Samuel	2			1		2			1	1			7		
Middlefield	155	20	Blish	Oliver		1		1		1			2				5		
Middlefield	155	21	Emmons	Ebenezer Ensn	1		1	2		2		1					7		
Middlefield	156	1	Mack	David Colo		1	5		1	3	3	2	1				16		
Middlefield	156	2	Kibbey	Bildad				1					1				2		
Middlefield	156	3	Taylor	Lewis	1	2			1				1	1			6		
Middlefield	156	4	Nash	Jonathan Revd	3	1		1					1	1			7		
Middlefield	156	5	Russel	Alpheus	1			1		2			1				5		
Middlefield	156	6	Dickson	James Lieut	2		2	1				3		1			9		
Middlefield	156	7	Church	Uriah		2				1		1	1				6		
Middlefield	156	8	Russel	Abel	3			1	1			2	1				9		
Middlefield	156	9	Meacham	John			1	1						1			3		
Middlefield	156	10	Meacham	Ambros			1						1				2		
Middlefield	156	11	Stewart	Benjamin	1			1						1			3		
Middlefield	156	12	Newton	John	3	2		1		1			1				8		
Middlefield	156	13	Coates	John		1	1	1	1			2	1	1			8		
Middlefield	156	14	Clark	Samuel		2	2		1	1	1	1		1			9		
Middlefield	156	15	Meacham	Philip	2	1		1					1				5		
Middlefield	156	16	Meacham	James	1	1		1		2			1				6		
Middlefield	156	17	Fellows	Parker				1		3			1				5		
Middlefield	156	18	Starr	Martin	1			1					1				4		
Middlefield	156	19	Clark	Silas				1		1	1		1				4		
Middlefield	156	20	Babcock	Daniel	2			1		4	1		1				9		
Middlefield	156	21	May	William	3			1		2			1				7		
Middlefield	156	22	Durant	Thomas	2		2		1	2		2		1			10		
Middlefield	156	23	Phelps	David	1		1			1		1					4		
Middlefield	156	24	Russel	Gideon	3	3		1		1			1				9		
Middlefield	156	25	Wares	Elias	2	3			1	1			1				8		
Middlefield	156	26	Gleason	Isaac	2	2	1		1	3	1	2	1				13		
Middlefield	156	27	Pease	Gad	1			1	1	3							7		
Middlefield	156	28	Denmon	John		1		1				1		1			5		
Middlefield	156	29	Blush	Benjamin	1		1		1	2	2	1		1			9		
Middlefield	156	30	Benjamin	Asa	2				1	1	1		1				6		
Middlefield	156	31	Booth	Simeon				1						1			2		
Middlefield	156	32	Booth	Elan			1			2		1					4		
Middlefield	156	33	Vaderkin	Henry	2	1		1		1	1		1				7		
Middlefield	156	34	Wright	Jude	1	1		1				1	2				6		
Middlefield	156	35	Smith	Rufus	1			1				1	1				4		
Middlefield	156	36	Streeter	Isaac H.	2	1		1		1	1	2	1				9		
Middlefield	156	37	Jones	Arba		1				1			1				3		
Middlefield	156	38	Pelton	Ezra			2	1		3	1	2					9		
Middlefield	156	39	Jones	Ezra	2			1				1		1			5		
Middlefield	156	40	Jones	John	1		1			1				1			4		
Middlefield	156	41	Wardwell	Eliakim				1						1			2		
Middlefield	156	42	Wardwell	Dennis	2		1						1				4		
Middlefield	157	1	Gillet	Russel	1		1			2			1				5		
Middlefield	157	2	Clap	Abner		1		1		2	2			1			7		
Middlefield	157	3	Clap	Abner Junr		1				1		1					3		
Middlefield	157	4	White	Elijah	2		2		1	3	2		1				11		
Middlefield	157	5	Hamilton	Samuel	3	1		1		1	2		1				9		
Middlefield	157	6	Garnwell	James	1			1		2			1				5		
Middlefield	157	7	Little	Edward			2		1		1			1			5		
Middlefield	157	8	Hollon	James			1	1						1			3		
Middlefield	157	9	Hollon	George	1			1		1		1					4		
Middlefield	157	10	Wright	Nathan Capt.	2	1	1			1	1	2					10		
Middlefield	157	11	Gilbert	Charles	1			1		2			1				5		
Middlefield	157	12	Wheeler	John	2			1					1				4		
Middlefield	157	13	Graves	Erastus			1						1				2		
Middlefield	157	14	Ward	Thomas			1			3			1				5		
Middlefield	157	15	Pease	Israel	4	1		1		1		1	1	1			10		
Middlefield	157	16	Ingham	Erastus			2		1	1	1	1					7		

TOWN	PG#	LN#	LAST NAME	FIRST NAME	under 10	10 to 16	16 to 26	26 to 45	45 and over	under 10	10 to 16	16 to 26	26 to 45	45 and over	TOTAL ALL OTHER	TOTAL SLAVES	TOTALS	DISTRICT/ TOWNSHIP	NOTES
			HEADS OF HOUSEHOLD		FREE WHITE MALES					FREE WHITE FEMALES									
Middlefield	157	17	Wood	Thomas				1				1		1			3		
Middlefield	157	18	Smith	Calvin	4	1	1	1		1	2		1				11		
Middlefield	157	19	Clap	Orriss	2			1		2		1					6		
Middlefield	157	20	Meker	John				1					1				2		
Middlefield	157	21	Pease	Dan				1									1		
Middlefield	157	22	Grainger	Luther	2	1			1	4	1	1	1				11		
Middlefield	157	23	Hamilton	William	2			1		2	1		1				7		
Middlefield	157	24	Loveland	Malachi	1			1					1				3		
Middlefield	157	25	Alderman	Daniel	1			1		1		1					4		
Middlefield	157	26	Phelps	Benjamin					1					1			2		
Middlefield	157	27	Bush	Edward	1			1		1		1	1				5		
Middlefield	157	28	Collins	Ebenezer	3				1	1	1			1			7		
Middlefield	157	29	Phelps	Obediah				1		1		1	1				4		
Middlefield	157	30	Churchill	Elijah	2	1		1		1	1		1				7		
Middlefield	157	31	Metcalf	John	2		1	1		1		1	1				7		
Middlefield	157	32	Meacham	Andrew	1		1	1		2			2	2			9		
Middlefield	157	33	Wood	Stephen				1		1			1				3		
Middlefield	157	34	Jones	Benajah Lieut	2			1		2	3		1				9		
Middlefield	157	35	Pinney	John Junr	1			1		2		1					5		
Middlefield	157	36	Mack	Elisha Capt	1	1	1	1		2	1	2	1				10		
Middlefield	157	37	Little	Bezaleel		1	4		1	2	1		1				10		
Middlefield	157	38	Ward	John	1			1		3			1				6		
Middlefield	157	39	Pinney	John			1		1				2	1			5		
Middlefield	157	40	Root	Solomon	4			1		1			1				7		
Middlefield	158	1	Root	Daniel	3			1		2			1				7		
Middlefield	158	2	Root	Thomas				1						1			2		
Middlefield	158	3	Clark	James		2	1	1				1		1			6		
Middlefield	158	4	Reed	Christopher			1						1				2		
Middlefield	158	5	Selden	Ebenezer				1						1			2		
Middlefield	158	6	Loveland	Andrew	2			1		2		1					6		
Middlefield	158	7	Meach	Elijah	2	1		1		2	1		1				8		
Middlefield	158	8	Loveland	Paine	1	1		1		1	1	1		1			7		
Middlefield	158	9	Merifield	Ozem			2			1		1					4		
Middlefield	158	10	Ingrahm	Solomon	1	1	1	1		2		1	1				8		
Middlefield	158	11	Graves	Amasa		1	1			1			2	1			6		
Middlefield	158	12	Crowell	Enoch			2	1	1		1	3					8		
Middlefield	158	13	Church	William		1	1	1	1			2		1			7		
Middlefield	158	14	Goudy	Samuel	2	1		1			1	1	1				7		
Middlefield	158	15	Church	Ambross		1				1		1					3		
Middlefield	158	16	Church	Green			1			2							3		
Middlefield	158	17	Perkins	Phineas Capt.	1	1			1	2		2		1			8		
Middlefield	158	18	Moore	Joseph				1			1	2		1			5		
Middlefield	158	19	Bissell	Justus	2	2	1	1		2		1	1				10		
Middlefield	158	20	Graham	William				1			2	1	1				5		
Middlefield	158	21	Vining	Elkanah			1					1					2		
Middlefield	158	22	Vining	Elan			1			1		1					3		
Middlefield	158	23	Taylor	William	3	1			1	3			1				9		
Middlefield	158	24	Bissell	Robert	2			1		1			2				6		
Middlefield	158	25	Crowell	Eli	1			1					1				3		
Middlefield	158	26	William	Prince											5		5		
Middlefield	158	27	Norcutt	Silvenus			3		1	1		2		1			8		
Middlefield	158	28	Smith	Joseph Lieut	1			1		1			1				4		
Middlefield	158	29	Smith	John	2	1		1		1			1				6		
Middlefield	158	30	Cone	Cyrus		1		1		1	1	1	1				6		
Middlefield	158	31	Gray	Samuel				1		1				1			3		
Middlefield	158	32	Blush	Amasa		1	1							1			3		
Middlefield	158	33	Wood	Simeon	1			1				2					4		
Middlefield	158	34	Bartlet	Isaac		2	1	1				1		1			6		
Middlefield	158	35	Spencer	John		2	1	1		1		2		1			8		
Middlefield	158	36	Egelston	Benjamin		1	2	1		2	1	1					9		
Middlefield	158	37	Bush	Silas	1			1		2		1					5		
Middlefield	158	38	Lealand	Ebenezer		1		1			2			1			5		
Middlefield	158	39	Lealand	Luther			1										1		
Middlefield	158	40	Lealand	Lemuel	1			1		1			1				4		
Middlefield	159	1	Ely	Jonathan	1	2		1				1		1			6		
Middlefield	159	2	Coates	Theodore			1			2		1					4		
Middlefield	159	3	Convass	Benjamin				1						1			2		
Middlefield	159	4	West	Russel			1							1			2		
Middlefield	159	5	Chapain	Abner	2			1		2		1					6		
Middlefield	159	6	Sandford	Elias	1	2	3		1	1		1		1			10		

TOWN	PG#	LN#	HEADS OF HOUSEHOLD		FREE WHITE MALES					FREE WHITE FEMALES					TOTAL ALL OTHER	TOTAL SLAVES	TOTALS	DISTRICT/ TOWNSHIP	NOTES
			LAST NAME	FIRST NAME	under 10	10 to 16	16 to 26	26 to 45	45 and over	under 10	10 to 16	16 to 26	26 to 45	45 and over					
Monson	262	1	White	Sanford					1	1	2	2		1			7		
Monson	262	2	White	John	2	2		1		3		1	1				10		
Monson	262	3	Henley	Isaac	1		1						1				3		
Monson	262	4	Ives	Jesse Revd		1		1				2	1				6		
Monson	262	5	Keep	Simeon		2	1	1	1			2	1	1			9		
Monson	262	6	King	Samuel	1		1		1			2		1			6		
Monson	262	7	Gates	Asa	2	1	1	1		2		1	1				9		
Monson	262	8	Fields	Theodore	1			1		3			1				6		
Monson	262	9	Dexter	John					1				1	1			3		
Monson	262	10	Dexter	Leonard	1			1		1			1				4		
Monson	262	11	Norcross	Joel	1		1						1	1			4		
Monson	262	12	Goodale	Abel Esq		2		1		1	1			2			7		
Monson	262	13	Upham	Samuel	1			1		2		1	1	2			8		
Monson	262	14	Upham	Benjamin		1		1				1					3		
Monson	262	15	Webber	Samuel Jr	1			1		3			1				6		
Monson	262	16	Keep	Love Wd		1	2			1	2			3			9		
Monson	262	17	Ballow	Peter				1				1		1			3		
Monson	262	18	Ballow	Seth	1		1						1				3		
Monson	262	19	Ferre	Jona		1		1						2			5		
Monson	262	20	Webber	Samuel	1			1		1	2	2		1			8		
Monson	262	21	Webber	Kimbal		1							1				2		
Monson	262	22	Merrick	Royal	2	1	1	1		2	1	1	1				10		
Monson	263	1	Hyde	David Capt			1	1		1				2			5		
Monson	263	2	Hyde	William B.	1			1		4			1				7		
Monson	263	3	Smith	Nathan	3	1	2	2				1	1				10		
Monson	263	4	Chapin	Justin	1	1		1		3			1				7		
Monson	263	5	McDowell	William	1	1		1		2				1			6		
Monson	263	6	Chandler	Elijah		1	2	1		1		2		1			8		
Monson	263	7	Ward	Uriah	2		1	1		2			1	1			8		
Monson	263	8	Ward	William			1	1						1			3		
Monson	263	9	Stebbins	Bethuel								3		1			4		
Monson	263	10	Stebbins	Bethuel 2d	3	1		1						1			6		
Monson	263	11	Moor	Alexander				1		1	1	2					5		
Monson	263	12	Moor	Alexn Junr				1		3			1				5		
Monson	263	13	Pomhey	Cato											9		9		
Monson	263	14	Storey	Jethro											7		7		
Monson	263	15	Merrick	Noah	1			1		1	1	1					5		
Monson	263	16	Taylor	John				2			1			2			5		
Monson	263	17	Davis	Stephen	1								1				3		
Monson	263	18	Minard	Amos	1		1	1					1				4		
Monson	263	19	Shaw	John			1			1			1				3		
Monson	263	20	Cooley	Abner	1	1		1		1			1	1			6		
Monson	263	21	Shaw	James	2	1		1		2			1				7		
Monson	263	22	Hatch	Stephen			1	1		1		1					4		
Monson	263	23	Dutton	Oliver	1			1		2		1	1				6		
Monson	263	24	Hatch	Elijah	1			1		1		1	2	1			7		
Monson	263	25	Hatch	Baker	1			1		2			1				5		
Monson	263	26	Trumbull	Elijah	3			1		2			1	1			8		
Monson	263	27	Trumbull	John	2	2		1		2			1				8		
Monson	263	28	Savor	John				1				1					2		
Monson	263	29	Stebbins	Asahel				1						1			2		
Monson	263	30	Moor	Gideon	1			1		1			1				4		
Monson	263	31	Stebbins	Jesse		1	1	1		1	1	2	1	1			9		
Monson	263	32	Stebbins	Luther	2			1					1				4		
Monson	263	33	Squire	David	2			1		2			1				6		
Monson	263	34	Shields	David S.	1	1	1	1		1	2	2	1				10		
Monson	263	35	Merrick	Jona				1		1	1	1	1				5		
Monson	263	36	Merrick	Miner		1	1					1					3		
Monson	263	37	Hitchcock	Anna										2			2		
Monson	263	38	Fay	Jude	2	1			2	1	1	3	1				11		
Monson	263	39	Utley	Azel	1	1	1	2		1			2				8		
Monson	263	40	Norcross	William	1	1	4	1		1	1	2	3				14		
Monson	263	41	Sherman	Joseph	2	2		1			1	1					8		
Monson	263	42	Merrick	Phinehas			1	1		1			1	1			5		
Monson	263	43	Warriner	Stephen	1			1		3				1			6		
Monson	263	44	Merrick	Lewis	3	1		1		1	1		1				8		
Monson	263	45	Hyde	Ephraim	3	2	2		1	1	1	2	1				13		
Monson	264	1	Walker	Luther				1		2			1				4		
Monson	264	2	Shumway	Levins		1		1		1		1					4		
Monson	264	3	Davison	Ebenezer				1			1		1				3		
Monson	264	4	March	Seth	3			1		1	1		1				7		
Monson	264	5	Sabin	Darius				1		2			1				4		
Monson	264	6	Dewolfe	Elisha			1			1		1					3		
Monson	264	7	Avery	Asa	2		2	1		1	1	1					8		
Monson	264	8	Merrick	Roswell				1					1				2		
Monson	264	9	Fuller	Benjamin	2	1		2		3			1	1			10		
Monson	264	10	Fuller	Joshua				1						1			2		
Monson	264	11	Hoar	Nathan				1						1			2		
Monson	264	12	Hoar	Nathan Jr	1	1		1		4	1		1				9		

94

TOWN	PG#	LN#	LAST NAME	FIRST NAME	under 10	10 to 16	16 to 26	26 to 45	45 and over	under 10	10 to 16	16 to 26	26 to 45	45 and over	TOTAL ALL OTHER	TOTAL SLAVES	TOTALS	DISTRICT/ TOWNSHIP	NOTES
			HEADS OF HOUSEHOLD		FREE WHITE MALES					FREE WHITE FEMALES									
Monson	264	13	Gardner	Sherman	4			1		2	1		1				9		
Monson	264	14	Allard	John	3		1	1		3		1	1	1			11		
Monson	264	15	Fuller	Abraham	4			1		2	2		1				10		
Monson	264	16	Cotton	George	1		1		1				1	1			5		
Monson	264	17	Cotton	Simon	1			1					1				3		
Monson	264	18	Cotton	Gad Capt	1	1	1		1	3	1	3		1			12		
Monson	264	19	Bliss	Jacob		1	1		1			1		1			5		
Monson	264	20	Wright	Jacob		1		1			1			1			4		
Monson	264	21	Delamater	Elijah	1			1		2	1		1				6		
Monson	264	22	Lincoln	John	1			1		3	1		1				7		
Monson	264	23	Wolfe	Levi	2			1					1				4		
Monson	264	24	Curtiss	Ebenezer				1					1				2		
Monson	264	25	Cummings	Simeon				1		2	2		1				6		
Monson	264	26	Warner	Nathan	2	1		1		2	1	1	1				9		
Monson	264	27	Coye	Uriah				1						1			2		
Monson	264	28	Butler	Daniel				1						1			2		
Monson	264	29	Butler	Benjamin	1			1		1			1				4		
Monson	264	30	Butler	Nathaniel				1		3			1				5		
Monson	264	31	Cross	Stephen	2	1	1			2		1	1				8		
Monson	264	32	Hawes	Jacob	1			1		2			1				5		
Monson	264	33	Knowlton	Ezra	2			1		2	1		1				7		
Monson	264	34	Hayes	Shadrach	3	1		1		2	2	1	1				11		
Monson	264	35	Knowlton	Amasa	1			1		2			1				5		
Monson	264	36	Roberts	Sally				1						2			3		
Monson	264	37	Goodwill	William			1						1				2		
Monson	264	38	Bliss	Reuben	1	1	2		1	1	2		1				9		
Monson	264	39	Gardner	Caleb															Enumeration left blank
Monson	264	40	Bliss	Aaron	3			1		1		1					6		
Monson	264	41	Bliss	Josiah				1					1				2		
Monson	264	42	Harvey	Amasa	1	1	3		1	1	1		1				9		
Monson	264	43	Burdick	Shephard			1					1					2		
Monson	264	44	Gardner	Caleb	1		1				1	1					4		
Monson	264	45	Lanphear	Aaron				1						1			2		
Monson	264	46	Lanphear	Aaron Jr	4			1					1				6		
Monson	265	1	Lanphear	Uriel	1			1		2			1				5		
Monson	265	2	Lanphear	Jeheel				1					1				2		
Monson	265	3	Bates	Ford	3	2		1					1	1			8		
Monson	265	4	Burnham	Abigail Widow	1	1					2		1				5		
Monson	265	5	Stacy	Simon	1			1		2	1	1		1			7		
Monson	265	6	Stacy	William	2	1	1	1		1	1			1			8		
Monson	265	7	Gardner	Simeon	2		1						1				4		
Monson	265	8	Avery	Gardner	1			1		2		1		1			6		
Monson	265	9	Wood	Ebenezer				1						1			2		
Monson	265	10	Burdick	Pardon			1						1				2		
Monson	265	11	Wood	Stephen	1			1		1	1		1				5		
Monson	265	12	Wood	Jonathan	1	1		1					1				4		
Monson	265	13	Puffer	Tisdale	1			1		2		1					5		
Monson	265	14	Brown	Abner Colo	1	1		1		4	1	2	1				11		
Monson	265	15	Newell	Stephen	2					2	2	1	1				8		
Monson	265	16	Lamb	Charles	2					2			1				5		
Monson	265	17	Shaw	John Dr	2		3		1	1	1		1				9		
Monson	265	18	Pease	Amos		1	1			1			1				4		
Monson	265	19	Pease	Gideon	1	1	2	1		1	2	1					10		
Monson	265	20	Firmin	Salmon	1			1					1				3		
Monson	265	21	Meacham	Isaac	1	1		1		3	2		1	1			10		
Monson	265	22	Butler	Anna Wd			1							1			2		
Monson	265	23	Butler	Azariah	2			1		3		1	1				8		
Monson	265	24	Butler	Samuel	1		1					1					3		
Monson	265	25	Fuller	Joshua Lt				1				1	1				3		
Monson	265	26	Fuller	Joshua Jr	2	1	1	1		1			1				7		
Monson	265	27	Davis	Jesse				1		1	1	1		1			5		
Monson	265	28	Brumley	Nathan		1		1		1			1				4		
Monson	265	29	Edgerton	Dan			1			3			1				5		
Monson	265	30	Edgerton	John				1					1	1			3		
Monson	265	31	Steed	Jonathan		1	1			1			1				4		
Monson	265	32	Rider	Benjamin		1	1		1		1			1			5		
Monson	265	33	Burgess	Levi	1			1		1			1				4		
Monson	265	34	Trusdale	Pearly	1		1	1		1	1	1					6		
Monson	265	35	Bumstead	Joseph	1		2						1				4		
Monson	265	36	White	Asa	1	1	2		1	1	1	1		2			10		
Monson	265	37	Labin	Oliver		2		1		1			1	1			6		
Monson	265	38	Prior	John	3			1			2		1				7		
Monson	265	39	Newell	Abijah				1				1		1			3		
Monson	265	40	Newell	Abijah Jr	1	1		1		4			1				8		
Monson	265	41	Chapin	Jonathan			2		1		1	1		1			6		
Monson	265	42	Vinton	Calvin	1		1	1		1	1	1	1				7		
Monson	265	43	Blodget	Paul	3			1		1	1		1				7		
Monson	265	44	Vinton	Caleb	4			1		1		1	1				8		
Monson	265	45	Shaw	Absolome	1	1				3			1				7		
Monson	266	1	Ward	Comfort				1					1	1			3		

95

TOWN	PG#	LN#	LAST NAME	FIRST NAME	FREE WHITE MALES under 10	10 to 16	16 to 26	26 to 45	45 and over	FREE WHITE FEMALES under 10	10 to 16	16 to 26	26 to 45	45 and over	TOTAL ALL OTHER	TOTAL SLAVES	TOTALS	DISTRICT/ TOWNSHIP	NOTES
Monson	266	2	Shaw	Luther		1	1					1					3		
Monson	266	3	Fuller	John	1			1		1			1				4		
Monson	266	4	Bennett	Israel	2	3	1	1		2		1	1				11		
Monson	266	5	White	John					1		1		1				3		
Monson	266	6	Mixter	Daniel	3	1			1	1	2		1				9		
Monson	266	7	Hakes	Jonathan	2	1	1		1	1	2			1			9		
Monson	266	8	Hide	Enoch		2			1	1	1	1		1			7		
Monson	266	9	Short	Manassah	2			1		2			1				6		
Monson	266	10	Fuller	Eleazer	3	2	1		1			3		1			11		
Monson	266	11	Torrey	Jonathan		1		1		2			1	1			6		
Monson	266	12	Torrey	Joseph				1		3			1				5		
Monson	266	13	Ross	Micah	2		2		1	2	1	1					9		
Monson	266	14	Sull	Richard		1	1		1	1				1			5		
Monson	266	15	Ross	Zephaniah	2		1					1					4		
Monson	266	16	Dousett	Philemon	2			1		1			1	1			6		
Monson	266	17	Hubbard	Russel	1	2		1		2	1		1				8		
Monson	266	18	Osburn	Daniel	1			1		1		1	1				5		
Monson	266	19	Stinson	Joseph	1	1	2		1	2		1		1			8		
Monson	266	20	Cady	Henry G.	1		1	2		1		1					6		
Monson	266	21	Bush	Stephen	1	1		1		1	3		1				8		
Monson	266	22	Loomis	Justus		1		1		1	2		1				6		
Monson	266	23	Fuller	Sylvanus		2	1		1	1	2	1	1				9		
Monson	266	24	Davis	Samuel		1		1		3	1		1				7		
Monson	266	25	May	William	2				1		1	1		1			6		
Monson	266	26	Williams	Ambrose	3		1	1		1	2			2			10		
Monson	266	27	Hoar	Jona	2			1		2	1		1				7		
Monson	266	28	Hoar	Reuben		2		1			1	2	1				7		
Monson	266	29	Bush	Erastus		1		1					1				3		
Monson	266	30	Bradway	Daniel					1				1				2		
Monson	266	31	Bradway	Daniel Jr			2					1					3		
Monson	266	32	Labin	Noah	1	2			1			1		1			6		
Monson	266	33	Munn	Jason		1	1			1			1				4		
Monson	266	34	Stebbins	James		1	1		1	1	1		1				6		
Monson	266	35	Newton	Stephen	5			1			1		1				8		
Monson	266	36	Wittaker	Eddy Doct			1			1		1					3		
Monson	266	37	Hitchcock	Gad	1	1		1		2	1	1	1				8		
Monson	266	38	Rust	Elisha	2			1		1		1					5		
Monson	266	39	Rust	Ebenezer				1						1			2		
Monson	266	40	Munn	Benjamin					1		1	1	1				4		
Monson	266	41	Munn	Marsena	2			1		1		1	1				6		
Monson	266	42	Ellinwood	Tertius	1			1		2			1				5		
Monson	266	43	Riddle	Thomas		1		1			1		1				4		
Monson	266	44	Gordin	William	2			1		2			1				6		
Monson	266	45	Goodell	Eliphalet				1					1				2		
Monson	267	1	Skinner	Thomas	2			1		3			1				7		
Monson	267	2	Baker	Joseph				1				1	1				3		
Monson	267	3	Haynes	Daniel	2	1	1	1		2	2		1				10		
Monson	267	4	Webber	Francis	1	1	2		1	1	1			1			8		
Monson	267	5	Dormound	James	2		1		1	2	2		1				9		
Monson	267	6	Gage	Aaron Dr	1	2		1		1			1				6		
Monson	267	7	Bugbee	Moses	1	1		1		3	1		1				8		
Monson	267	8	Underwood	Nehemiah	1		1						1				3		
Monson	267	9	Knight	Benjamin				1						1			2		
Monson	267	10	Walker	Enos	2		1						1				4		
Monson	267	11	Knight	Asher	3	1	1	1		1	2		1				10		
Monson	267	12	Chaffee	Chadwick	3		1	1		1		1					7		
Monson	267	13	Hoar	Edmund	1			1		1	1		1				5		
Monson	267	14	Ellis	Benjamin					1	1				1			3		
Monson	267	15	Jennings	Abel		1		1					1	1			4		
Monson	267	16	Gardner	Richard	1	1	1	1		3	1		1	1			10		
Monson	267	17	Burnett	Daniel		1		1			1			1	1		5		
Monson	267	18	Bugbee	Stephen		1		1				2		1			5		
Monson	267	19	Chld	Erastus	1			1					1				3		
Monson	267	20	Fay	Mary Wd		1	1							1			3		
Monson	267	21	Allard	Daniel				1		1	1			1			4		
Monson	267	22	Coburn	David	1			1			2	1	1				6		
Monson	267	23	Walbridge	William	1			1		1		1		1			5		
Monson	267	24	Williams	Stephen		1						1	1				3		
Monson	267	25	Trask	Daniel		1			1	1	2		1				6		
Monson	267	26	Underwood	Reuben	1	1		1		1			1				5		
Monson	267	27	Trask	Peter		1	1		1	1	1	2		1			8		
Monson	267	28	Bugbee	Parker				1				1					2		
Monson	267	29	Chaffee	Chas Doct				1		4			1				6		
Monson	267	30	Moulton	Freeborn				1				3		1			6		
Monson	267	31	Tupper	Thomas				1									1		
Monson	267	32	Tupper	William		1		1					1	1			4		
Monson	267	33	Tupper	Ezra	3	1		1		1	1		1				8		
Monson	267	34	Tupper	Ichabod		1	1		1	2		1		1			7		
Monson	267	35	Moulton	Freeborn Jr		1						1					3		

TOWN	PG#	LN#	HEADS OF HOUSEHOLD		FREE WHITE MALES					FREE WHITE FEMALES					TOTAL ALL OTHER	TOTAL SLAVES	TOTALS	DISTRICT/ TOWNSHIP	NOTES
			LAST NAME	FIRST NAME	under 10	10 to 16	16 to 26	26 to 45	45 and over	under 10	10 to 16	16 to 26	26 to 45	45 and over					
Monson	267	36	Bradway	William	1	1		1	1		1			1			6		
Monson	267	37	Bradway	Abel	2			1		1			1				5		
Monson	267	38	Moulton	Daniel	1	2	1	1		4	2		1	1			13		
Monson	267	39	Moulton	Joseph	3	1			1	1	1	1		1			9		
Monson	267	40	Moulton	Ariel	1			1		1		1					4		
Monson	267	41	Moulton	Jeremiah	2		1					1					4		
Monson	267	42	Munger	Joseph		1	1		1	2	1		1				7		
Monson	267	43	Moulton	Abner	1	1	1		1	1	1		1				7		
Monson	267	44	Moulton	Jesse	1		1			1		1					4		
Monson	268	1	Needham	Anthony	1			1				1					3		
Monson	268	2	Squire	John				1						1			2		
Monson	268	3	Squire	Solomon	5	3		1		1			1				11		
Monson	268	4	Pitts	John			1	1					1				3		
Monson	268	5	Pitts	Jeremiah			1			1	1	1					5		
Monson	268	6	Greenstill	John	4			1		1			1				7		
Monson	268	7	Pevey	Elijah Capt	1		1		1	2	3	1	1				10		
Monson	268	8	Williams	David	2	1		1		2	2		1				9		
Monson	268	9	Shaw	John 4th			1	1	1				1				4		
Monson	268	10	Shaw	Sylvanus	2		1					1					5		
Monson	268	11	Stebbins	Hazadiah	1	1		1		2	2	1	1				9		
Monson	268	12	Stebbins	Hazadiah Jr			1					1					2		
Monson	268	13	Green	Solomon	2	2		1		1			1				7		
Monson	268	14	Green	Reuben	1	1		1		2	1		1				7		
Monson	268	15	Stebbins	Thaddeus	2			1		3			1	1			8		
Monson	268	16	Munn	Reuben Col		1	1					1		1			4		
Monson	268	17	Munn	Elijah	1			1		1		1					4		
Monson	268	18	Hovey	Elijah	3			1		3		1	1				9		
Monson	268	19	Smith	Benjamin	1	1			1	1		1	1				6		
Monson	268	20	Munn	Jeremy Capt	2	1	1		1	2	1	1	1				11		
Monson	268	21	Blanchard	Jona		1			1		2	1	1				6		
Monson	268	22	Blanchard	Chester	2			1		1			1				5		
Monson	268	23	Blanchard	Jonathan Jr	1			1		1			1				4		
Monson	268	24	Groves	Nicholas				1									1		
Monson	268	25	Groves	Samuel	2		1	1		2		2	1				9		
Monson	268	26	White	Calvin	1	1		1		2			1				6		
Monson	268	27	Fuller	Abraham				1						1			2		
Monson	268	28	Fuller	Stephen			1			1		1					3		
Monson	268	29	Carpenter	Daniel		2		1		1	1		1				6		
Monson	268	30	King	Samuel		1	1	1				2	1				6		
Monson	268	31	Chamberlain	Pliny	2			1		3			1				7		
Monson	268	32	Grout	Joseph Doct	1	1	1		1	1	1		1				7		
Monson	268	33	Pepper	Timothy	1	1	1		1	1		1	1				7		
Monson	268	34	Anderson	Thomas Doct				1				1	1	1			4		
Monson	268	35	Holmes	Isaac	1		2					1					4		
Monson	268	36	Rogers	Jasper			1			4		1					6		
Monson	268	37	Montgomery	Peter											2		2		

97

TOWN	PG#	LN#	LAST NAME	FIRST NAME	M <10	M 10-16	M 16-26	M 26-45	M 45+	F <10	F 10-16	F 16-26	F 26-45	F 45+	TOTAL ALL OTHER	TOTAL SLAVES	TOTALS	DISTRICT/TOWNSHIP	NOTES
Montague	44	1	Alvord	Caleb		2	3	2	1	2	1	1		1			13		
Montague	44	2	Arms	David		1			1					1			3		
Montague	44	3	Anderson	Ezra	1			2		2		1		1			7		
Montague	44	4	Anderson	Mathew				1									1		
Montague	44	5	Austin	James			2	1	2			1		1			7		
Montague	44	6	Anderson	Elizabeth				1						1			2		
Montague	44	7	Armstrong	Timothy	1	1		1	1	2			1				7		
Montague	44	8	Andrews	Moses	1		1	1		1	2		1				7		
Montague	44	9	Alexander	Joseph	1			1					1				3		
Montague	44	10	Alexander	Ebenezer	1	1		1		2	1		1				7		
Montague	44	11	Brown	Peter	1	1	1		1	1	2	1	1				9		
Montague	44	12	Bissel	William	2	1			1	2	1		2				9		
Montague	44	13	Bissel	Jonathan Marsh	2	1		1				1		1			6		
Montague	44	14	Beebe	Roswell				1		1		1		1			4		
Montague	44	15	Blye	Joseph			1			1			1				3		
Montague	44	16	Burnham	Daniel			1				1						2		
Montague	44	17	Bardwell	Moses	3	2		3		2		2	1				13		
Montague	44	18	Bardwell	Enoch				1						1			2		
Montague	44	19	Bardwell	Thomas	2			1		4			1				8		
Montague	44	20	Brooks	Benjamin	2			1				1					4		
Montague	44	21	Burnham	Josiah		1		1						1			3		
Montague	45	1	Burnham	Moses	3		1			1	2		1	1			9		
Montague	45	2	Bartlett	Daniel	1			1		2	1		1				6		
Montague	45	3	Bartlett	Darius	2	1		1		2			1				7		
Montague	45	4	Benjamin	Levi	2	1		1						1			5		
Montague	45	5	Bardwell	Samuel		1	2	1	1	2	1	1					10		
Montague	45	6	Bangs	Mark	1			1		2			1	1			6		
Montague	45	7	Bartlett	Ebenezer	2	1			1	3	2		1				10		
Montague	45	8	Benjamin	Caleb			1	1					1				3		
Montague	45	9	Benjamin	Joel	4		1			1	1		1				8		
Montague	45	10	Benjamin	Abel				1									1		
Montague	45	11	Ballard	Luther	1	1		1		4			1				8		
Montague	45	12	Bancraft	Kendall		1	1		1			2		1			6		
Montague	45	13	Bartlett	Elisha	3	2			1	1		2		1			10		
Montague	45	14	Burnham	Silas	3			1		2			1				7		
Montague	45	15	Bangs	John		1		1		5			1				8		
Montague	45	16	Beebe	John	1		1					1					3		
Montague	45	17	Brooks	Moses		1			1	4	3		1				10		
Montague	45	18	Chapman	James	2			1		3		1	1				8		
Montague	45	19	Chadwick	George	2		1		1	3	3		1				11		
Montague	45	20	Clark	Hezekiah		2		1		1		1		1			6		
Montague	45	21	Cushman	Azel	1			1		1	2		1				6		
Montague	45	22	Clapp	Elihu	2		1	1		1			1				6		
Montague	45	23	Clapp	Joseph	2		3	1			1	1	1				10		
Montague	45	24	Clapp	Daniel		1	1		1	2	1	2		1	1		10		
Montague	45	25	Cummins	Elijah				1					1				2		
Montague	45	26	Cummins	Reuben			1			3			1				5		
Montague	45	27	Coon	William			1			1		1					3		
Montague	45	28	Clark	Barnham	1			1		1			1				4		
Montague	45	29	Clapp	Solomon		2			1			1		1			5		
Montague	45	30	Canada	Isaac		1		1				2		1			5		
Montague	45	31	Clark	Lemuel	3	1		1		1			1				7		
Montague	45	32	Death	Benjamin	2	1	1		1	2	1	1		1			10		
Montague	45	33	Death	Jotham				1	1	3			1	1			7		
Montague	45	34	Death	Aaron		1	1	1		3	1	1	1				9		
Montague	45	35	Darling	Stephen	1			1					1				3		
Montague	45	36	Evers	Henry	1	1	1		1	1		1		1			7		
Montague	45	37	Fuller	Asa				1						1			2		
Montague	45	38	Fuller	Isaiah				1						1			2		
Montague	45	39	Fuller	John	2	1		1		2	1		1				8		
Montague	45	40	Frizzle	Earl	3			1		1		1					6		
Montague	45	41	Gunn	Chester	1			1		1			1				4		
Montague	45	42	Gunn	Asahel	2		1	1		2	3	1	1				11		
Montague	45	43	Gunn	Rufus			1										1		
Montague	46	1	Gunn	Eleanor	1					1				1			3		
Montague	46	2	Gunn	Nathaniel Jr	1	2			1	2	1	2		1			10		
Montague	46	3	Gunn	Nathaniel				1						1			2		
Montague	46	4	Gunn	Hannah		1					1	1	1				4		
Montague	46	5	Gunn	Martin	1	1		1		2			1				7		
Montague	46	6	Gunn	Moses		1	1	1			1	1	1				6		
Montague	46	7	Gunn	Salmon	1			1		2	1		1				6		
Montague	46	8	Gunn	Joseph		1							1				2		
Montague	46	9	Gunn	Elijah			2				1	1	1				6		
Montague	46	10	Gunn	William	2			1		1			1				5		
Montague	46	11	Gunn	Israel		2			1			1		1			5		
Montague	46	12	Gunn	Eli			1						1				2		
Montague	46	13	Gunn	Abel	1	1		1		3		1	1				8		
Montague	46	14	Godard	Ebenezer	1	1	2	1	1	1				1			8		
Montague	46	15	Grover	Ebenezer			2	1	1				1				6		

TOWN	PG#	LN#	HEADS OF HOUSEHOLD LAST NAME	FIRST NAME	FREE WHITE MALES under 10	10 to 16	16 to 26	26 to 45	45 and over	FREE WHITE FEMALES under 10	10 to 16	16 to 26	26 to 45	45 and over	TOTAL ALL OTHER	TOTAL SLAVES	TOTALS	DISTRICT/ TOWNSHIP	NOTES
Montague	46	16	Gunn	Elisha	3			1		3			1				8		
Montague	46	17	Graves	Noah	1				1					1			3		
Montague	46	18	Graves	Asa	1	1		1		1			1				5		
Montague	46	19	Grover	Martin	1			1		2			1				5		
Montague	46	20	Houghton	Jonathan	2	1		1		2			1	1			8		
Montague	46	21	Hunt	Ephraim				1					1				2		
Montague	46	22	Hunter	David	1	2			1	1	1			1			7		
Montague	46	23	Hunt	Peter	1		1		1		1	1		1			6		
Montague	46	24	Hill	John					1		1		1				3		
Montague	46	25	Hoar	William	1			1		1		1					4		
Montague	46	26	Heeb	Reuben		1	2					1					4		
Montague	46	27	Kinsley	Caleb		1	1		1	3	1		1				8		
Montague	46	28	Lawrence	Samuel	1				1	2	1		1				6		
Montague	46	29	Loveland	George		2		1		2			1				6		
Montague	46	30	Marsh	Jonathan		2	1	1		1		1	1				7		
Montague	46	31	Merchant	Mathew		1		1		2			1				5		
Montague	46	32	Merchant	Joseph	1	3		1		3		2	1				11		
Montague	46	33	Montague	Medad	2	2		1		2		2	1				10		
Montague	46	34	Monroe	Benjamin					1	1			2				4		
Montague	46	35	Marsh	Joshua	2			1	1				1	1			7		
Montague	46	36	Marsh	Samuel	4	1		1	1				1				8		
Montague	46	37	Marsh	Enos Junr	1	1		1		2	2		1				8		
Montague	46	38	Morley	Thomas	1	1		1		2	1	1	1				8		
Montague	46	39	Marsh	Ebenezer Jr		1	2		1	1			1	1			7		
Montague	46	40	Marsh	Ephraim Junr	2	1			1					2			6		
Montague	46	41	Mack	Elisha			12	10	1		1	1	1				26		
Montague	46	42	Mayo	Joseph			1										1		
Montague	47	1	Marsh	Ebenezer	1		1	1				1					4		
Montague	47	2	Mack	Daniel Gates				1			1	1					3		
Montague	47	3	Mack	Samuel			1			1		1					3		
Montague	47	4	Nash	Judah Revd				1					1				2		
Montague	47	5	Nash	Judah Jr	2			1		1	1	1	1		1		8		
Montague	47	6	Newton	Moses			1					1					2		
Montague	47	7	Osgood	Joseph	1			1		1			1				4		
Montague	47	8	Osgood	Samuel	2			1		1			1				5		
Montague	47	9	Prescott	Josiah	1	1	2		1	1	1	2		1			10		
Montague	47	10	Payne	Edward	2	2	4		1		1	1		1			12		
Montague	47	11	Prescott	Benjamin	2	4	16	40	4	2			2				70		at the Locks & Canal
Montague	47	12	Perry	Silas	3			1		2			1				7		
Montague	47	13	Payne	James			1			1		1					3		
Montague	47	14	Potter	Edward			1		1				1				3		
Montague	47	15	Plumb	Joel			1			2		1	1				5		
Montague	47	16	Root	Joseph		2	1		1			2	1				7		
Montague	47	17	Root	Elisha		1	3		1		1		1	1			8		
Montague	47	18	Rice	Samuel			1			1		1					3		
Montague	47	19	Rice	Gershom			1			1		1					3		
Montague	47	20	Rice	Jedutham	3	2		1		1	1		1				9		
Montague	47	21	Rice	Josiah		2			1			2		1			6		
Montague	47	22	Root	Moses		1	3		1			1	1	1			8		
Montague	47	23	Root	Jonathan	1	1	1		1		1	1		1			7		
Montague	47	24	Root	Phillip	1		2	2	1	2			1	1			10		
Montague	47	25	Root	Martin	2		1		1	2	3			1			10		
Montague	47	26	Rowe	Daniel	1		2		1		2	1		1			8		
Montague	47	27	Rawson	Edmund		2	1		1	1		3		1			9		
Montague	47	28	Rawson	Samuel	3	1		1		2	1		1				9		
Montague	47	29	Rawson	Joseph	3	1		1		1			1				7		
Montague	47	30	Rice	Ephraim			2	1	1		1			1			6		
Montague	47	31	Ruggles	Edward	1	1	5	2		4	1	1	1				16		
Montague	47	32	Scott	Rufus			1			2		1					4		
Montague	47	33	Searl	Joshua			1		1					1			3		
Montague	47	34	Smith	Samuel		1		1	1	2	2		2	1			10		
Montague	47	35	Scott	Eleazer	2			1	1	1	1			1			6		
Montague	47	36	Scott	Ira	1	2	1	1		2	1	1	1				10		
Montague	47	37	Scott	Reuben Jr	2			1	1				1				5		
Montague	47	38	Sperry	Obed	2			1		1			1				5		
Montague	47	39	Stewart	James	1	2	1		1	3			1				9		
Montague	47	40	Stewart	Lucy			1					1		1			3		
Montague	47	41	Smith	Benjm Parsons	1			1		1	2	1	1				7		
Montague	47	42	Smith	Joseph			1					1					2		
Montague	48	1	Scranton	Gershom	1			1					1				3		
Montague	48	2	Severance	Moses		2		1			1	1		1			6		
Montague	48	3	Taylor	David	1	1	1	1		2			1	1			8		
Montague	48	4	Tuttle	Nathan					1					1			2		
Montague	48	5	Thompson	Peter	1			1		3			1				6		
Montague	48	6	Taylor	Joseph	2			1	1	2		2	2	1			11		
Montague	48	7	Taylor	Aaron		1		1	1	3	1		1	1			9		
Montague	48	8	Thayer	Caleb	4	1		1		2	2	1	1				12		
Montague	48	9	Tolls	Jared	2	1	1		1	2			1				9		
Montague	48	10	Tolls	Jared Junr			1			1		1					3		
Montague	48	11	Taft	Lyman	4	2	1	1		1			1	1			11		

TOWN	PG#	LN#	LAST NAME	FIRST NAME	FREE WHITE MALES					FREE WHITE FEMALES					TOTAL ALL OTHER	TOTAL SLAVES	TOTALS	DISTRICT/ TOWNSHIP	NOTES
					under 10	10 to 16	16 to 26	26 to 45	45 and over	under 10	10 to 16	16 to 26	26 to 45	45 and over					
Montague	48	12	Tilden	Elisha	3	2			1		1		1				8		
Montague	48	13	Tuttle	Nathan Junr	2			1		2			1				6		
Montague	48	14	Taylor	Daniel		1		1		2			1				5		
Montague	48	15	Taylor	Samuel	1	1			1		1			1			5		
Montague	48	16	Taylor	Patten	2			1		4	2		1				10		
Montague	48	17	Wells	Henry		1	1		1		1	3		2			9		
Montague	48	18	Wells	Cornelius			1	1					1				3		
Montague	48	19	Wrisley	Samuel		1		1		2	2	1	1	1			9		
Montague	48	20	Whitney	Zachariah					1				1	1			3		
Montague	48	21	Whitney	Ebenezer	3	2		1		1			1				8		
Montague	48	22	Wright	Abner	1		1		1	1	1	2		1			8		
Montague	48	23	Wright	Elisha	1	2	1		2	1		1		2			10		
Montague	48	24	Wise	William	1	1		1		3			1				7		
Montague	48	25	Winslow	Nathaniel	1			1									3		
Montague	48	26	Woods	Firman			1		1		1	1	1				5		
Montague	48	27	West	Jonathan		1											1		
Montague	48	28	Winslow	Seth	2			1		3			1				7		
Montague	48	29	Whitmore	Asa	2		1						1				4		
Montague	48	30	Winslow	James	1	2	1		1	1	2	1		1			10		
Montague	48	31	William	Williams	4	1	1		1	3	1			1			12		
Montague	48	32	Williams	Joseph	2			1		2			1				6		
Montague	48	33	William	John	1		1			1		1					4		
Montague	48	34	Whitcomb	Jonathan	1			1		4	2		1				9		
Montague	48	35	Winslow	Josiah				1									1		

TOWN	PG#	LN#	HEADS OF HOUSEHOLD LAST NAME	FIRST NAME	FREE WHITE MALES under 10	10 to 16	16 to 26	26 to 45	45 and over	FREE WHITE FEMALES under 10	10 to 16	16 to 26	26 to 45	45 and over	TOTAL ALL OTHER	TOTAL SLAVES	TOTALS	DISTRICT/ TOWNSHIP	NOTES
Montgomery	159	1	Adams	Levi Lieut	2	1		1		2			1				7		
Montgomery	159	2	Maynard	Moses	2	3		1		3			1				10		
Montgomery	159	3	Herrick	Jonathan	4		1	1		1			1				8		
Montgomery	159	4	Gorham	Joseph		1	1		1	1				1			5		
Montgomery	159	5	Shirtliff	Jonathan		1	1		1			1	1				5		
Montgomery	159	6	Shirtliff	Elisha		1				2		1					4		
Montgomery	159	7	Hopkins	Benjamin	1			1		2		1					5		
Montgomery	159	8	Gorham	George	4			1			1	1	1				8		
Montgomery	159	9	Hollyday	Zacheus	3				1	1			1				6		
Montgomery	159	10	Shirtliff	Asa	2			1		2			1				6		
Montgomery	159	11	Clap	Phineas				1						1			2		
Montgomery	159	12	Clap	Phineas Junr	2			1		1			1				5		
Montgomery	159	13	Clap	Robertson		1						1					2		
Montgomery	159	14	Clap	Abigail Wid			1	1		2	1	1	1				7		
Montgomery	159	15	Clap	Cyrus		1						1					2		
Montgomery	159	16	Author	Richard	2		1					1					4		
Montgomery	159	17	Chapman	Abner	2			1				1					4		
Montgomery	159	18	Avery	Ephraim	2	2		1		1	1	1					8		
Montgomery	159	19	Wheeler	Fradrick	1		1			1		1					4		
Montgomery	159	20	Bozworth	Zadock				1					1				2		
Montgomery	160	1	Bozworth	Raymon			1			3		1					5		
Montgomery	160	2	Wheeler	James		2		1		3		2	1				9		
Montgomery	160	3	King	Gamaliel	1			1		3		1					6		
Montgomery	160	4	Hatch	Moses	4		1	1			1		1				8		
Montgomery	160	5	Searl	Jesse Doct			1			1	1	1					4		
Montgomery	160	6	Moor	Joel 2d		1	2		1	1	1		1				7		
Montgomery	160	7	Shirtliff	Noah	2	1		1		1		1					6		
Montgomery	160	8	Moor	Oliver	1			1		2		1					6		
Montgomery	160	9	Stockwell	Enos			1	1					2				4		
Montgomery	160	10	Moor	Orrin	1			1				1					3		
Montgomery	160	11	Carter	Elias			1			1		1					3		
Montgomery	160	12	Maynard	Amos				1			1	1					3		
Montgomery	160	13	Crow	David		1		1	1	1		1					5		
Montgomery	160	14	Crow	David Junr	1		2				1						4		
Montgomery	160	15	Beach	Moses	2			1		1		1					5		
Montgomery	160	16	Morse	Chester	1	1			1	3	2	1					9		
Montgomery	160	17	Taylor	Edward Esq		1	1	1				2	1		1		7		
Montgomery	160	18	Mallery	Truman	1		1	1		2	1	1					7		
Montgomery	160	19	Barnes	Aziel			1			3		1					5		
Montgomery	160	20	Hunter	John		1	3	1			1		1				7		
Montgomery	160	21	Brant	John	1	1	1	1		4	1	1					10		
Montgomery	160	22	Parks	Aaron Lieut	2	1	1	1	1	1	1	1		1			10		
Montgomery	160	23	Clark	Elizabeth Widw		1							1				2		
Montgomery	160	24	Cooley	Lydia Widw		1							1				2		
Montgomery	160	25	Crow	Thomas		1		1	2	2		1					7		
Montgomery	160	26	Moore	Joel	1			1			1		1				4		
Montgomery	160	27	Maynard	Reuben		1	2	1		2	2		1				9		
Montgomery	160	28	Tiffany	Elizabeth Widw	1	1	2			1	1		1				7		
Montgomery	160	29	Meachum	Margaret	1					1			1				3		
Montgomery	160	30	Moore	Guy	2			1				1					5		
Montgomery	160	31	Gorham	John		1						1					2		
Montgomery	160	32	Clark	Daniel	3	1		1		2		1	1				9		
Montgomery	160	33	Munk	Elias					1				1				0		
Montgomery	160	34	Grinman	Sampson					1				1				2		
Montgomery	160	35	Martin	Asa	1	1		1		4		1					8		
Montgomery	160	36	Avery	William	1	1	1	1		2	3	1					10		
Montgomery	160	37	Wright	Samuel		1		2				1	1				5		
Montgomery	160	38	Wright	James	4			1				1					6		
Montgomery	160	39	Wright	Samuel Junr	1	1		1		2		1					6		
Montgomery	160	40	Grant	John			1		1	3	1	1					7		
Montgomery	160	41	Wright	Charles	1	1		1		1		1					5		
Montgomery	161	1	Frisby	Nathan		1		1					1				3		
Montgomery	161	2	Frisby	Amos	2		1				1						4		
Montgomery	161	3	Phelps	Sylvester		1		1				1					3		
Montgomery	161	4	Hall	John	1	1		1					1				4		
Montgomery	161	5	Wheeler	Thomas				1		3			1				5		
Montgomery	161	6	Chapman	Isaac			3	1				1	1				6		
Montgomery	161	7	Avery	Bansford	2			1		1	2	2	1				9		
Montgomery	161	8	Avery	Samuel	2		1	1		3		1	1				9		
Montgomery	161	9	Squire	Sylvester Capt	1	2	1	1		1		1					7		
Montgomery	161	10	Greenslit	Joseph		1		1		2		1	1				6		
Montgomery	161	11	Bozworth	Joshua	3			1		1		1					6		
Montgomery	161	12	Squire	Abial				1					1				2		
Montgomery	161	13	Hegwin	John	1			1				1					3		
Montgomery	161	14	Bozworth	Zadock Capt	2			1		2	1	1					7		
Montgomery	161	15	Higley	David	1			1				1					3		
Montgomery	161	16	Chapman	Isaac	2			1		2		1					6		
Montgomery	161	17	Knap	Reuben	1	2	1	1				1	1				7		
Montgomery	161	18	Pettip	Abial	3	1		1		1		1	1				9		

TOWN	PG#	LN#	LAST NAME	FIRST NAME	FREE WHITE MALES					FREE WHITE FEMALES					TOTAL ALL OTHER	TOTAL SLAVES	TOTALS	DISTRICT/ TOWNSHIP	NOTES
					under 10	10 to 16	16 to 26	26 to 45	45 and over	under 10	10 to 16	16 to 26	26 to 45	45 and over					
Montgomery	161	19	Herrick	Stephen	2			1		1	3		1				8		
Montgomery	161	20	Herrick	Jonathan			2		1					1			4		
Montgomery	161	21	Root	Martin	2	1	2		1	1	1	1	1				10		
Montgomery	161	22	Chandler	Samuel	3	1		1			2		1				8		
Montgomery	161	23	Hitchcock	Chauncry				1									1		
Montgomery	161	24	Capron	David			1										1		
Montgomery	161	25	Chauncy	Russel			1										1		
Montgomery	161	26	Falley	Richard Lieut		1	3	1	1			2		1			9		
Montgomery	161	27	Allen	Samuel	1		1					1					3		
Montgomery	161	28	Flowers	Joseph			1										1		
Montgomery	161	29	Knowles	Seth			1										1		
Montgomery	161	30	Sanderson	Elnathan			1										1		
Montgomery	161	31	Killburn	Samuel			1		1								2		
Montgomery	161	32	Cushing	Joseph			1										1		
Montgomery	161	33	Falley	Russel				1		2			1				4		
Montgomery	161	34	Wright	David				1									1		
Montgomery	161	35	Broad	Aaron			1										1		
Montgomery	161	36	Ensign	Reuben			1										1		
Montgomery	161	37	Ensign	Datis			1										1		
Montgomery	161	38	Hegwin	John 2d					1		1	2		1			5		
Montgomery	161	39	Carter	William			1										1		
Montgomery	161	40	Carter	Charles			1										1		
Montgomery	161	41	Killburn	Thomas			1										1		
Montgomery	161	42	Hutchinson	Elisha		1	1		1					1			4		
Montgomery	161	43	Hutchinson	Israel			1						1				2		
Montgomery	162	1	Andrus	Jacob					1					1			2		
Montgomery	162	2	Andrus	Jacob Junr	1			1		2		1					5		
Montgomery	162	3	Moore	Joel	2			1		2			1				6		
Montgomery	162	4	Hegwin	Thomas			1						1				2		
Montgomery	162	5	Hegwin	Amos	1			1		1		1					4		
Montgomery	162	6	Barret	Daniel Ensn	3	2			1	1	2	1	1	2			13		
Montgomery	162	7	Allen	David	3			1		1			1		1		7		
Montgomery	162	8	Finch	Preserved	2			1		2			1				6		

TOWN	PG#	LN#	LAST NAME	FIRST NAME	FREE WHITE MALES under 10	10 to 16	16 to 26	26 to 45	45 and over	FREE WHITE FEMALES under 10	10 to 16	16 to 26	26 to 45	45 and over	TOTAL ALL OTHER	TOTAL SLAVES	TOTALS	DISTRICT/ TOWNSHIP	NOTES
New Salem	96	1	Allen	Ezra	1		3	1		1		1					7		
New Salem	96	2	Aldrich	Jesse			1		1				2	1			5		
New Salem	96	3	Aldrich	Peleg	1		1			1		1					4		
New Salem	96	4	Akers	Peter	1			1					1				3		
New Salem	96	5	Andrews	Thomas			2		1	1			1				5		
New Salem	96	6	Adams	Thomas		1	1		1	1	2			1			7		
New Salem	96	7	Adams	Amos	1			1		5			1				8		
New Salem	96	8	Adams	Joel	1			1		2	1		1				6		
New Salem	96	9	Andrews	Daniel			1			1		1					3		
New Salem	96	10	Adams	John		1	1		1					1			4		
New Salem	96	11	Briggs	Ebenezer				1						1			2		
New Salem	96	12	Ballard	Jeremiah			1	1					1	1			4		
New Salem	96	13	Boyce	Jacob	2			3		2	1		1	2			11		
New Salem	96	14	Berry	William	3	1	1		1		1		1				8		
New Salem	96	15	Berry	James	1			1	1	2		3		1			9		
New Salem	96	16	Briggs	Richard		1	1		1	1	1	2		1			8		
New Salem	96	17	Bridge	Thomas				1	1	1	1			1			4		
New Salem	96	18	Bridge	Josiah			1			3			1				5		
New Salem	96	19	Benson	Samuel	2	2		1		2			1				8		
New Salem	96	20	Bangs	Nathaniel	2			1		3			1				7		
New Salem	96	21	Benson	Comiden	2			1		1	1		1				6		
New Salem	97	1	Briggs	Jacob	1			1					1				3		
New Salem	97	2	Barron	Stephen			1										1		
New Salem	97	3	Bates	Jacob	1		1		1	1		1		1			6		
New Salem	97	4	Boyden	Amos	1			1	1				1	1			5		
New Salem	97	5	Barnard	Francis		1	1							1			3		
New Salem	97	6	Ballard	James	3	1		1		3	1		1				10		
New Salem	97	7	Barton	Edward		2		1		1			1				5		
New Salem	97	8	Bullard	Benjamin			1	1		1		1					4		
New Salem	97	9	Barrows	Eleazer				1				1		1			3		
New Salem	97	10	Banister	Andrew	1			1		3	1		1				7		
New Salem	97	11	Childs	David				1	1	3	2		1	1			9		
New Salem	97	12	Cowles	Rufus	1	1		1				1	1				5		
New Salem	97	13	Chamberlin	John	1	1	3		1	1			2		1		10		
New Salem	97	14	Chamberlin	John 2d		1	1		1	2	1	2		1			9		
New Salem	97	15	Cary	John	2	1			1			1	2	1			8		
New Salem	97	16	Cook	Samuel	2				1	2	1	1	1				8		
New Salem	97	17	Cook	Samuel 2d		1		1					1				3		
New Salem	97	18	Crossett	Samuel		2		1				1	1				5		
New Salem	97	19	Childs	Joseph	1		1		1	2	2	2	1				10		
New Salem	97	20	Cannon	Simeon	1	1	2		1	1			1				7		
New Salem	97	21	Cook	Henry	3			1		1				1			6		
New Salem	97	22	Chamberlin	Nathl		1	1		1			1		1			5		
New Salem	97	23	Chamberlin	Zach	1			1		1		1					4		
New Salem	97	24	Curtis	Daniel		1		1			1	2		1			6		
New Salem	97	25	Curtis	Moses		1	2		1	1	1			1			7		
New Salem	97	26	Curtis	Daniel Jr	3	1		1		1	1		1				8		
New Salem	97	27	Clark	Perez	1			1	1					2			6		
New Salem	97	28	Curtis	James	2			1		2	1	1	1	1			9		
New Salem	97	29	Clark	John	1		2		1		1	1		1			7		
New Salem	97	30	Clark	John 2d		1		1						1			3		
New Salem	97	31	Clark	Samuel				1									1		
New Salem	97	32	Chase	Simon	2		3		1	1	1		1				9		
New Salem	97	33	Chase	David	1			1		2			1				5		
New Salem	97	34	Clark	Nathaniel	1			1		3			1				6		
New Salem	97	35	Curtis	Asa		1		1		1	1	1		1			6		
New Salem	97	36	Cannon	John		1	1		1		1			1			5		
New Salem	97	37	Clark	Thomas	2			1		2	1		1				7		
New Salem	98	1	Cahoon	Sampson				1		1		1		1			4		
New Salem	98	2	Clark	Perez Junr	1			1		1			1				4		
New Salem	98	3	Clark	Elisha	1		1						1				3		
New Salem	98	4	Clark	Alden	2			1		2			1				6		
New Salem	98	5	Cary	Willm H			1										1		
New Salem	98	6	Crossett	Richd G.	4	2		1			1			1			9		
New Salem	98	7	Cary	Widow						1		1		1			3		
New Salem	98	8	Derby	Roger			1			2	1		1				5		
New Salem	98	9	Davis	Sarah	1	1				2	1	1	1				7		
New Salem	98	10	Day	Peletiah	2	1					1	1					6		
New Salem	98	11	Day	James	2			1			1	3					7		
New Salem	98	12	Day	Samuel	2			1		3			1				7		
New Salem	98	13	Dunn	Samuel				1		1			1				3		
New Salem	98	14	Dean	Gilbert	1	1		1		3			1				7		
New Salem	98	15	Dunton	Ebenezer	2			1		1			1				5		
New Salem	98	16	Davis	Joseph			1										1		
New Salem	98	17	Elliot	Samuel			1							1			2		
New Salem	98	18	Ellis	Gregory	2			1				1					4		
New Salem	98	19	Eddy	Rufus			1							1			2		
New Salem	98	20	Eddy	John				1						1			2		
New Salem	98	21	Ellis	John	2		1	1				1					5		

TOWN	PG#	LN#	HEADS OF HOUSEHOLD LAST NAME	FIRST NAME	FREE WHITE MALES under 10	10 to 16	16 to 26	26 to 45	45 and over	FREE WHITE FEMALES under 10	10 to 16	16 to 26	26 to 45	45 and over	TOTAL ALL OTHER	TOTAL SLAVES	TOTALS	DISTRICT/ TOWNSHIP	NOTES
New Salem	98	22	Ellis	Paul	3	2		1					1				7		
New Salem	98	23	Fish	Abel				1					1	1			3		
New Salem	98	24	Felton	Joseph	1			1		1	1		1				5		
New Salem	98	25	Felton	James	1		1	1	1	1		2		1			8		
New Salem	98	26	Felton	Ebenezer 2d	1			1	1	1			1				5		
New Salem	98	27	Felton	Nathl			1	1	1	1		1	1	1			7		
New Salem	98	28	Felton	Stephen	3	2	1	1	1	1		2	1	1			13		
New Salem	98	29	Foster	Daniel	2	1	1	1	1	2		1	1	1			11		
New Salem	98	30	Foster	Amos			1		2			3	1				7		
New Salem	98	31	Foster	Joel		2			1			2	1		1		7		
New Salem	98	32	Furniss	William				1					1				2		
New Salem	98	33	Fisk	Nathaniel	1	1		1		2	2		1				8		
New Salem	98	34	Foster	Samuel				1		2		1					4		
New Salem	98	35	Foster	Jonathan			2		1				1				4		
New Salem	98	36	Foster	Samuel 2d	1			1		2	1		3	1			9		
New Salem	98	37	Ford	Josiah		2	1		1			2		1			7		
New Salem	98	38	Felton	Martin	1			1		1			1				4		
New Salem	98	39	Furbush	Aaron		2	2		1	1	1	1		1			9		
New Salem	99	1	Fry	Levi	2	2		1		1			1				7		
New Salem	99	2	French	Jonathan			1		1	2	1						5		
New Salem	99	3	Fry	John 2d			1			1		1					3		
New Salem	99	4	Felton	Daniel				1					1	1			3		
New Salem	99	5	Gage	Nathaniel	4			1					1				6		
New Salem	99	6	Giles	William	1	1	1		1	1		1		1			7		
New Salem	99	7	Gibbs	Solomon			2		1	2		2		1			8		
New Salem	99	8	Gibbs	Solomon Junr	2			1		1		1					5		
New Salem	99	9	Goodale	Ebenezer				1					1				2		
New Salem	99	10	Ganson	Joseph		1				2	2		1				7		
New Salem	99	11	Goodale	Jonathan	1			1						1			3		
New Salem	99	12	Goodale	James		1		1		1			1				4		
New Salem	99	13	Giles	John		2	1		1			1	1		1		7		
New Salem	99	14	Giles	Daniel	2			1		2			1				6		
New Salem	99	15	Goldthwait	Robert	1			1	1	3			1				7		
New Salem	99	16	Gay	Ebenezer		1		1	1	2		1		1			7		
New Salem	99	17	Goldthwait	Joseph	1			1		1			1				4		
New Salem	99	18	Gay	Eliphalet	3			1					1				5		
New Salem	99	19	Ganson	Nathan		1		1	1	1			1				5		
New Salem	99	20	Giles	John Junr	3			1		1	1		1				7		
New Salem	99	21	Giles	Joseph			1						1				2		
New Salem	99	22	Goodenow	Almer	3			1		1	1		1				7		
New Salem	99	23	Grout	George		1											1		
New Salem	99	24	Haskins	Joseph	1		1	1	1	1		2		1			8		
New Salem	99	25	Hastings	Consider			1	1		1		1	1				5		
New Salem	99	26	Hart	John	3	1		1				2		1			8		
New Salem	99	27	Hemenway	Joseph	2			1	1	1		1	1	1			8		
New Salem	99	28	Hunt	David	1	1		1	1	1		1	2	1			9		
New Salem	99	29	Hoar	Shadrach	1	2	2	1	1				2	1			10		
New Salem	99	30	Hoar	Robert	1	1	2		1	2				1			8		
New Salem	99	31	Hoar	John	1			1					1				7		
New Salem	99	32	Haskins	William			1	1		3	1		1	1			8		
New Salem	99	33	Haskins	Silas		1	1			1		1					4		
New Salem	99	34	Haskins	Shadrach 2d		1	1	1		1	1		1				6		
New Salem	99	35	Haskins	Paul	3	2	1		1	2	1	1		1			12		
New Salem	99	36	Haskins	Luke	1			1	1	3			1				7		
New Salem	99	37	Haskins	Seth		2			1	4		2	1				10		
New Salem	99	38	Haskins	George		1	1					1	1				4		
New Salem	100	1	Houlton	Joseph	1	1	1	1		2	1	1	1				9		
New Salem	100	2	Hemenway	Samuel				1				2		2			5		
New Salem	100	3	Hascall	John			1		1				1				4		
New Salem	100	4	Hascall	Benjamin	3	2	2	1	1			1	1		1		12		
New Salem	100	5	Hascall	Jacob			1		1	1		2					5		
New Salem	100	6	Haven	William				1			1	1					3		
New Salem	100	7	Haven	Philip		2		1		1	1			1			6		
New Salem	100	8	Harris	Ezra		2	1		1	1		1	1	1			8		
New Salem	100	9	Hodgkin	Joseph	1			1		3			1				6		
New Salem	100	10	Hammond	Barnabas	1		1					1					3		
New Salem	100	11	Hemenway	Joshua Jr		1	1	1				2	1				6		
New Salem	100	12	Herrington	John			1	1					1				3		
New Salem	100	13	Hagur	Aaron	1			1		4	1		1				10		
New Salem	100	14	Holt	William		1	1	1	1		2			1			7		
New Salem	100	15	Holt	Jonathan		2			1		1		1				5		
New Salem	100	16	Huntington	John				1		1		1					3		
New Salem	100	17	Hascall	Saml Junr	2			1		2			1				6		
New Salem	100	18	Hodgkin	Samuel	2	2		1		1	1		1				8		
New Salem	100	19	Hinds	Francis	2		1						1				4		
New Salem	100	20	Hussey	James											9		9		
New Salem	100	21	Hall	James											5		5		
New Salem	100	22	Johnson	Solomon	2	1			1	2			1				7		
New Salem	100	23	Kellogg	Ezekiel Jr	3		3		2	1		2	3	1			15		

TOWN	PG#	LN#	LAST NAME	FIRST NAME	FREE WHITE MALES under 10	10 to 16	16 to 26	26 to 45	45 and over	FREE WHITE FEMALES under 10	10 to 16	16 to 26	26 to 45	45 and over	TOTAL ALL OTHER	TOTAL SLAVES	TOTALS	DISTRICT/TOWNSHIP	NOTES
New Salem	100	24	Kellogg	Samuel		1	1		1	1		1		1			6		
New Salem	100	25	Kendall	Samuel	2	1	2	2	1		1	1	1				11		
New Salem	100	26	Knights	William	2	1		1		2	2		1				9		
New Salem	100	27	King	Samuel				1		1		2		1			5		
New Salem	100	28	King	John		2		1				1		1			5		
New Salem	100	29	King	John Junr	3			1		1			1				6		
New Salem	100	30	King	William	1	1		1					1				4		
New Salem	100	31	King	Jonathan	2			1		1			1				5		
New Salem	100	32	Kimball	Phinehas	1		1	1	1	1			1	1			7		
New Salem	100	33	King	Stephen	1			1					1				3		
New Salem	100	34	King	Samuel 2d	3	2	1	1		1	2		1				11		
New Salem	100	35	Lindsey	David	1			1				3		1			6		
New Salem	100	36	Lindsey	Hab	2	1	1		1			1	1				7		
New Salem	100	37	Lawson	David		1		1		2			1				5		
New Salem	100	38	Learned	Moses		1		1		1	1	1	1				6		
New Salem	101	1	Lawson	Jonathan	1	2		1		2	1		1				8		
New Salem	101	2	Learned	William				1					1				2		
New Salem	101	3	Learned	Nehemiah		1		1		1	1		1				5		
New Salem	101	4	Luce	William		1		1					3	1			6		
New Salem	101	5	Lawson	David Junr	2			1				1					4		
New Salem	101	6	Luce	William Jr	1		1					1					3		
New Salem	101	7	Lyon	Eleazer	3			1		1			1				6		
New Salem	101	8	Lyon	Daniel	1	1		1			1		1				5		
New Salem	101	9	Merriam	Mary			1			2	2	2		1			8		
New Salem	101	10	Moulton	Daniel			2		1			1		1			5		
New Salem	101	11	Moulton	Samuel	2			1					1				4		
New Salem	101	12	Moulton	Daniel Jr	2		1					1					4		
New Salem	101	13	Marval	Stephen	1			1		2			1				5		
New Salem	101	14	Meacham	Jonathan		2			1	3	1	2	1				10		
New Salem	101	15	Martin	Matthew	3	1	1	1			1		1				8		
New Salem	101	16	Manning	Samuel		1		1					1				3		
New Salem	101	17	Merriam	Jesse		2	1		1			2		1			7		
New Salem	101	18	Merriam	William	1			1		1				1			4		
New Salem	101	19	Moody	Ezra	1		1	1		1			1				5		
New Salem	101	20	Morgan	Widow								1	1				2		
New Salem	101	21	Newell	Phebe	1					2			1				4		
New Salem	101	22	Newton	Sylvanus			1			3			1				5		
New Salem	101	23	Nye	Nathaniel				1						1			2		
New Salem	101	24	Orcutt	Josiah		1		1					1				3		
New Salem	101	25	Oakes	John	2			1		1			1				5		
New Salem	101	26	Oakes	Stephen	1			1		1			1	1			5		
New Salem	101	27	Oakes	Elijah	2			1					1				4		
New Salem	101	28	Orcutt	Samuel			1	1		3			1				6		
New Salem	101	29	Orcutt	Bels	1	1	1		1			2		1			7		
New Salem	101	30	Pearce	Jesse	3	2		1			2		1				9		
New Salem	101	31	Pearce	Samuel					1			4	1				6		
New Salem	101	32	Page	Timothy		1	2		1				1	2			7		
New Salem	101	33	Putnam	John	1			2	1	4		2	1	1			13		
New Salem	101	34	Putnam	Joshua Jr	3		1	1					3				8		
New Salem	101	35	Putnam	Aaron	1	1		1			1	2	2	1	1		10		
New Salem	101	36	Putnam	Jacob		1		1		2			1				5		
New Salem	101	37	Putnam	Joseph	1	1		1		1		2		1			7		
New Salem	101	38	Pearce	Jonathan				1					1				2		
New Salem	101	39	Pearce	John	2			1		1	1		1				6		
New Salem	101	40	Pearce	Daniel		2		1		2	1		1				7		
New Salem	102	1	Pearce	Varney	1	2			1	2	1	1		2			10		
New Salem	102	2	Pearce	Josiah	1		2		1	2	1		1	1			9		
New Salem	102	3	Perkins	John F			2										2		
New Salem	102	4	Powars	Stephen	1	1		1		1	1		1				6		
New Salem	102	5	Powers	Asa	3	1		1		2			1				8		
New Salem	102	6	Pebbles	Willm H	2			1		2			1				6		
New Salem	102	7	Page	William				1					1	1			3		
New Salem	102	8	Page	Samuel	3	1	1	1		2	1		1				11		
New Salem	102	9	Page	Isaac	2			1		2			1				6		
New Salem	102	10	Page	John	1		1	1					1				4		
New Salem	102	11	Peabody	Phinehas	3	1			1				1				6		
New Salem	102	12	Pearce	Abraham		1	1	1				2		1			6		
New Salem	102	13	Pearce	Samuel 2d		2	1		1	1	1	1					7		
New Salem	102	14	Pearce	Samuel 3d		1			1	1	1		1				5		
New Salem	102	15	Pearce	Stephen	1	3	1		1	1		1		1			9		
New Salem	102	16	Pearce	Amos	1			1					1				3		
New Salem	102	17	Putnam	Daniel	1	1		1		1			1				5		
New Salem	102	18	Putnam	Samuel	2			1					1				4		
New Salem	102	19	Perry	Joseph	2	1	2		1	2	1		1				10		
New Salem	102	20	Pheney	Noah	2	2	2		1	2			1				10		
New Salem	102	21	Polly	Pliny		1				1		1					3		
New Salem	102	22	Perkins	Nathl			1			1		1					3		
New Salem	102	23	Pearce	Caleb	1	1		1				1					4		
New Salem	102	24	Perry	Eli	2			1		1							6		

TOWN	PG#	LN#	LAST NAME	FIRST NAME	FREE WHITE MALES					FREE WHITE FEMALES					TOTAL ALL OTHER	TOTAL SLAVES	TOTALS	DISTRICT/ TOWNSHIP	NOTES
					under 10	10 to 16	16 to 26	26 to 45	45 and over	under 10	10 to 16	16 to 26	26 to 45	45 and over					
New Salem	102	25	Packard	Timothy		1	1		2	1	1	1		2			9		
New Salem	102	26	Pearce	John 2d	1	2		1		2	1		1				8		
New Salem	102	27	Rockwood	Joseph				1						1			2		
New Salem	102	28	Rice	Jonathan				1				1	1				3		
New Salem	102	29	Reynolds	Enos			2	1				1	1	1			6		
New Salem	102	30	Reynolds	Enos Jr	2		1			2			1				6		
New Salem	102	31	Reed	Amos	2		1	1		2	2	1	1				10		
New Salem	102	32	Russell	Eli		1	2	1		1				1			6		
New Salem	102	33	Russell	Jonathan			2	1			1			1			5		
New Salem	102	34	Richmond	Sylvanus	1			1		1		1					4		
New Salem	102	35	Rawson	Lemuel	4			1		1			1				7		
New Salem	102	36	Reed	Isaac	2	1		1		2	1		1				8		
New Salem	102	37	Rawson	Secretary			1										1		
New Salem	102	38	Shaw	Daniel	2	1		1			1		1				6		
New Salem	102	39	Stratton	Shubael C.		2	2	1		2		1					8		
New Salem	102	40	Smith	Timothy	2	1		1		1			1				6		
New Salem	103	1	Smith	John	2		1	1		1	1		1				7		
New Salem	103	2	Sexton	Judah	1			1				1					3		
New Salem	103	3	Sampson	Peter			1		1	4	2	3	1				12		
New Salem	103	4	Stacey	Nymphas	2	1	1	1		3	2		1				11		
New Salem	103	5	Stacey	Rufus Jr	3			1		2			1	1			8		
New Salem	103	6	Southick	Jonathan				1						1			2		
New Salem	103	7	Southick	William			1			1		1					3		
New Salem	103	8	Southick	Simeon	1	1		1		2	1		1				7		
New Salem	103	9	Sampson	Jacob	2	2	1		1			1	2	2			11		
New Salem	103	10	Sampson	George	2			1		3			1				7		
New Salem	103	11	Sloan	James W.				1		5			1				7		
New Salem	103	12	Stimpson	Elias	2		2					2		1			8		
New Salem	103	13	Stiles	Foster	1	1		1					2				5		
New Salem	103	14	Stone	Seth		1		1						1			3		
New Salem	103	15	Smith	David			1			2			1				4		
New Salem	103	16	Steel	John	1			1				2		1			5		
New Salem	103	17	Steel	Samuel	1			1		2			1				5		
New Salem	103	18	Smith	Braddyl	3			1		2			1				7		
New Salem	103	19	Stone	Samuel	3	1		1		2	1		1				9		
New Salem	103	20	Sibley	Solomon				1						1			2		
New Salem	103	21	Smith	Edward	2	1		1		2	1		1				8		
New Salem	103	22	Sanders	Nathan					1	1	2	1		1			6		
New Salem	103	23	Stacey	Benjamin		1		1		2	1	2		1			8		
New Salem	103	24	Southick	Benjamin	2	1		1		2			1	1			8		
New Salem	103	25	Stratton	Zebulon		1		1		2	1			1			6		
New Salem	103	26	Stacey	Rufus				1						1			2		
New Salem	103	27	Shaw	James	2	1		1		2			2				8		
New Salem	103	28	Shaw	Amos				1		3		1					5		
New Salem	103	29	Shelly	Job		1	2	1		1		1	1				7		
New Salem	103	30	Sanders	Oliver	1		1					1					3		
New Salem	103	31	Sexton	David	1	1	1	1		1		1	1				7		
New Salem	103	32	Trask	John	1		1	1		1		1	1				6		
New Salem	103	33	Thomas	Amos	3	1	1	1	1	2	1	2		1			13		
New Salem	103	34	Twitchell	Benoni	2			1					1				4		
New Salem	103	35	Thompson	Caleb	2	2		1		1			1	1			8		
New Salem	103	36	Twitchell	Enos			3	1					1				5		
New Salem	103	37	Twitchell	John	1	2			1	3	3		1	1			12		
New Salem	103	38	Thompson	James	2	1	1	1		2		1	1				9		
New Salem	103	39	Trask	John 2d	1	1			2	2	1	3	1				11		
New Salem	104	1	Townsend	Jonathan	2	1		1		2	1		1				8		
New Salem	104	2	Town	Eliphalet		1	1	1		2	2		1				8		
New Salem	104	3	Town	Joel				1			1	1	1				4		
New Salem	104	4	Torry	Ebenezer	1			1				1	1	1			5		
New Salem	104	5	Tyrell	Jacob		1		1		2		1	1	1			7		
New Salem	104	6	Turner	Zadok	2			1		4			1	1			9		
New Salem	104	7	Turner	Micah		1		1						1			3		
New Salem	104	8	Taylor	Mary		1							1	1			3		
New Salem	104	9	Thayer	Ahar		1	1	1		2			1	1			7		
New Salem	104	10	Twitchell	David		1							1				2		
New Salem	104	11	Upham	Edward	1	2		1		2	2		1				9		
New Salem	104	12	Upton	Timothy	1		3	1				2		2			9		
New Salem	104	13	Upton	Stephen			1					1					2		
New Salem	104	14	Vaughan	Nathan	1	3	3	1		3			1	1			13		
New Salem	104	15	Vorce	Asa		1		1				2		1			5		
New Salem	104	16	Wyart	Joshua	1			1	1	2			1	1			7		
New Salem	104	17	Walker	Abiathar		2	1	1		1		3					8		
New Salem	104	18	Watson	William		2		1				1					4		
New Salem	104	19	Weste	John	2			1		1			1				5		
New Salem	104	20	Wheeler	Benjamin	1	1	2		1	1	2			1			9		
New Salem	104	21	Wheeler	Joshua	2	1	2		1	4	1	1		1			13		
New Salem	104	22	Waite	Phinehas	1	1			1	2	1			1			7		
New Salem	104	23	Wilder	Elijah	1			1				1					3		
New Salem	104	24	Winship	Benjamin	2			1		2			1				6		
New Salem	104	25	Wheeler	James				1		3			1				5		

TOWN	PG#	LN#	LAST NAME	FIRST NAME	FREE WHITE MALES					FREE WHITE FEMALES					TOTAL ALL OTHER	TOTAL SLAVES	TOTALS	DISTRICT/ TOWNSHIP	NOTES
					under 10	10 to 16	16 to 26	26 to 45	45 and over	under 10	10 to 16	16 to 26	26 to 45	45 and over					
New Salem	104	26	Walker	Jesse	2			1		3	1		1				8		
New Salem	104	27	Wood	John	2			1		2			1				6		
New Salem	104	28	Wilber	Jacob			1		1			1		1			4		
New Salem	104	29	Wheeler	Joel					1					1			2		
New Salem	104	30	Weste	Daniel	1				1	1		1		1			5		

TOWN	PG#	LN#	HEADS OF HOUSEHOLD LAST NAME	FIRST NAME	FREE WHITE MALES under 10	10 to 16	16 to 26	26 to 45	45 and over	FREE WHITE FEMALES under 10	10 to 16	16 to 26	26 to 45	45 and over	TOTAL ALL OTHER	TOTAL SLAVES	TOTALS	DISTRICT/ TOWNSHIP	NOTES
Northampton	2	1	Bartlett	Benja				1					1				2		
Northampton	2	2	Bartlett	Preserved	1			1		1		1					4		
Northampton	2	3	Lyman	Levi	1	1	1	1		3	1		1				9		
Northampton	2	4	Kingsley	Harpies				1					1	1			3		
Northampton	2	5	Starkweather	Charles		2	1	1		3	1	1	1				10		
Northampton	2	6	Wright	Sarah	1								1	1			3		
Northampton	2	7	Parsons	Joseph				2						2			4		
Northampton	2	8	Parsons	Oliver	3	1		1		2			1				8		
Northampton	2	9	Parsons	Joseph Junr	1			1				2	1				5		
Northampton	2	10	Clap	George				1		3			1				5		
Northampton	2	11	Parsons	Timothy		1		1					1		1		4		
Northampton	2	12	Bliss	William		2				1	1	1					5		
Northampton	2	13	Rogers	George		2	1										3		
Northampton	2	14	Judd	David			1	1		1			1				4		
Northampton	2	15	Parsons	Noah		1	1	1					1	3			7		
Northampton	2	16	Parsons	Hannah	1					1		1	1				4		
Northampton	2	17	Allen	Solomon		1		1		1		2	1	1			7		
Northampton	2	18	Strong	John	1		1	1				2		1			6		
Northampton	2	19	Strong	John Jun				1		2		1					4		
Northampton	2	20	Strong	Nathan	1	3		1	1	1	2		1				10		
Northampton	2	21	Strong	Timothy				1					1				2		
Northampton	3	1	Kingsley	Enos	1		2	1				1	3	1			9		
Northampton	3	2	Pomeroy	Quantus			3	1		1		1	2	1			9		
Northampton	3	3	Mann	Elias		1	1	1		1	1	1	1				7		
Northampton	3	4	Strong	Eleazer	1	1	1	1		2	2		1				9		
Northampton	3	5	Baral	Lewis			1	1					1	1			4		
Northampton	3	6	Pratt	Amasa			1					1	1				3		
Northampton	3	7	Clark	Joel			2	1					1	2			6		
Northampton	3	8	Summer	David	1		1			1			1				4		
Northampton	3	9	Clap	Asahel		2	2	1			1			1			7		
Northampton	3	10	Allen	Phineas		1				1			1				3		
Northampton	3	11	Clark	David				1					1				2		
Northampton	3	12	Clark	David Jun	2			1		2			1				6		
Northampton	3	13	Edwards	Gideon		1							1				2		
Northampton	3	14	Edwards	Medad				1						1			2		
Northampton	3	15	Edwards	Medad Jr			1			1			1				3		
Northampton	3	16	Clap	Azariah	3			1		1		1	1				7		
Northampton	3	17	Barnard	Israel	1	1	2			1	1	1	1				10		
Northampton	3	18	Lyman	Sylvester	1	1	2			2		1					7		
Northampton	3	19	Clark	Jonah				1					1				2		
Northampton	3	20	Clark	Lemuel	4		1	1		1			1				8		
Northampton	3	21	Clap	Seth				1		1	2			1			5		
Northampton	3	22	Clap	Seth Junr	1			1		1		1					4		
Northampton	3	23	Davis	Patience	1					1		1	1				4		
Northampton	3	24	Clap	John	1	1	1	3		1	1	1	1				10		
Northampton	3	25	Clap	Ebenezer	1	1	1						1				4		
Northampton	3	26	Phelps	Nathaniel	2	2	1	1	1	1	1	2	1				12		
Northampton	3	27	Porter	Hezekiah				1					1	1	1		4		
Northampton	3	28	Edwards	Nathaniel 2d			1			1			1				3		
Northampton	3	29	Phelps	Eliphalet		1		1				1	1	1			5		
Northampton	3	30	Phelps	Rufus		1		1		3			1				6		
Northampton	3	31	Phelps	Andrew	2	1	1	2		3		1		1			11		
Northampton	3	32	Strong	Jonathan Junr	1			1					1				3		
Northampton	3	33	Strong	Jonathan			2	1				1		1			5		
Northampton	3	34	Strong	Ebenezer				1				1		1			3		
Northampton	3	35	Buckman	Andrew		1	1							1			3		
Northampton	3	36	Clark	Stephen		1	1	1		1		1		2			7		
Northampton	3	37	Edwards	Benjamin		1	2	1		1			1				6		
Northampton	3	38	Prust	Israel			2	1				1		1			5		
Northampton	3	39	*	Jeremiah	1		2	1				1	1				6		
Northampton	4	1	Prust	Chester			1	1					1				3		
Northampton	4	2	Prust	Seth	2		1	1						1			5		
Northampton	4	3	Clark	Nathaniel		2	2	1		1							6		
Northampton	4	4	Ellis	John	2			1		1			1				5		
Northampton	4	5	Scott	Elijah			1					1	1				3		
Northampton	4	6	Clap	Simeon				1		1				1			3		
Northampton	4	7	Clap	Simeon Jun	1			1		1		1	1				5		
Northampton	4	8	Clap	Warham	1			1		2			1				5		
Northampton	4	9	Strong	Belah	2	1	1	1	1	2		1	1	1			11		
Northampton	4	10	Kellogg	Eli	2	1	1	1				1	1				7		
Northampton	4	11	Copeland	Smith	2		1	1		2			1				7		
Northampton	4	12	Hunt	David	1			1		2		1	2				7		
Northampton	4	13	Brick	John			1	1		1			1				4		
Northampton	4	14	Hunt	Ebenezer			4		1			2		1	1		9		
Northampton	4	15	Strong	Ithamer		1			2			1	1	1	1		7		
Northampton	4	16	Strong	David	2	1	1	1		1			1				7		
Northampton	4	17	Lyman	Erastus			1	2					1	1	3		8		
Northampton	4	18	Pomeroy	Asahel	1	1	4	4	2	1		2	5	1	1		22		
Northampton	4	19	Lyman	Joseph Jun	2					2		1	1	1			13		

TOWN	PG#	LN#	LAST NAME	FIRST NAME	FREE WHITE MALES					FREE WHITE FEMALES					TOTAL ALL OTHER	TOTAL SLAVES	TOTALS	DISTRICT/ TOWNSHIP	NOTES
					under 10	10 to 16	16 to 26	26 to 45	45 and over	under 10	10 to 16	16 to 26	26 to 45	45 and over					
Northampton	4	20	King	Samuel	1			2	1	1			3	1			9		
Northampton	4	21	Ingalls	James	3	2		1		2		1					9		
Northampton	4	22	Butler	William		1	10	3		2		1	1	1	1		20		
Northampton	4	23	Wright	Daniel		1	2	1		3	1		1				9		
Northampton	4	24	Mather	Warham	1			1	1	1	1		1				6		
Northampton	4	25	Roberts	Reuben	1			1		1			1				4		
Northampton	4	26	Strong	Oliver						1		1	2				4		
Northampton	4	27	Gere	Isaac	1		1	1			1	1					5		
Northampton	4	28	Pomeroy	Oliver	1	1	1	1		1			1				6		
Northampton	4	29	Parsons	Samuel			1	1					1				3		
Northampton	4	30	Murray	Hannah		1							1				2		
Northampton	4	31	Ramsdell	Jesse		2				1		1					4		
Northampton	4	32	Butler	Simeon	2		1	1		1	1	1					7		
Northampton	4	33	Tappan	Benjamin		2			1		1	2		1			7		
Northampton	4	34	Fowell	Nathaniel		1	4		1	1	2	1		1			11		
Northampton	4	35	Warner	Daniel Junr	5	1	1		1	1	2	1	1				13		
Northampton	4	36	Clarke	Samuel Jr	2	4	1	1				1	1				10		
Northampton	5	1	Pre*	Benjamin			1			3	1	1	1				7		
Northampton	5	2	Starrs	Nathan			4	2			1		1	1	1		10		
Northampton	5	3	Lyman	Joseph					1				2	1			4		
Northampton	5	4	Clarke	Samuel		1	2	1		2	2	1	1				10		
Northampton	5	5	Stoddard	Solomon		1	1		1				1	1			5		
Northampton	5	6	Stoddard	John				1		2	1						4		
Northampton	5	7	Brick	Joseph H	1			2		2	1	1					8		
Northampton	5	8	Wright	Aaron			1	1					1				3		
Northampton	5	9	Wright	Aaron Jun	2		1	1		1			1				6		
Northampton	5	10	Brick	Rachel		1	2						1	1			5		
Northampton	5	11	Prentice	Aaron	3			1					1				5		
Northampton	5	12	Goddard	Solomon Jr			1	1					1		1		4		
Northampton	5	13	Hawley	Mercy			1	1		1			1	1			5		
Northampton	5	14	Delano	Thomas			1	1					1				3		
Northampton	5	15	Edwards	Benja Hurd	2	2	1	1		2		1	1				10		
Northampton	5	16	Allen	Merab	1	1				1		1	1				5		
Northampton	5	17	Dwight	Cecil	2		1						1				4		
Northampton	5	18	Parsons	Seth	3	1	1	1		1			1				8		
Northampton	5	19	Parsons	Moses				1					1				2		
Northampton	5	20	King	Elizabeth			1	1	1				1	1			5		
Northampton	5	21	Pomeroy	Simeon	1	1	2			1		1		1			7		
Northampton	5	22	Brick	Eunice	2			1				1	1				5		
Northampton	5	23	Beals	William		1	1	1		1	2		1	1			8		
Northampton	5	24	King	Joseph	1			1		1	1		1				5		
Northampton	5	25	Strong	Oliver	1		1			2			1	1			6		
Northampton	5	26	King	John		3		1			1	2	1				8		
Northampton	5	27	Parsons	Elisha			1	1				2		1			5		
Northampton	5	28	Root	Eliazer				1						1			2		
Northampton	5	29	Smith	David			1			1			1				3		
Northampton	5	30	Wright	Timothy				1						1			2		
Northampton	5	31	Ware	John			1			1			1				4		
Northampton	5	32	Strong	Silas	3			1				1	1				6		
Northampton	5	33	Hgower	Webb	1		1					1					3		
Northampton	5	34	King	John Jun	1		1					1	1				4		
Northampton	5	35	Rust	Elisha	3			1		1			1				6		
Northampton	5	36	Root	Joseph				1					1				2		
Northampton	5	37	Root	Joseph Jun				1		2			1		1		5		
Northampton	5	38	Williams	Solomon	1	2	1		1	3	1	1	1				11		
Northampton	5	39	Parsons	Moses Jr	1			3		2			1				7		
Northampton	6	1	Goodrick	Amel	1			2		1			1				5		
Northampton	6	2	Hinckley	Samuel	2		1	1		2	1	1	1				9		
Northampton	6	3	Sheperd	Levi	1	1	7		2	2	2			2			17		
Northampton	6	4	Dickinson	Josiah	1	2	9	1	3	2	2			1	1		22		
Northampton	6	5	Lyman	Abigail		2	1	1				3	1				8		
Northampton	6	6	Wallcut	Lot	1		1			1		1					4		
Northampton	6	7	Coy	Asahel			1						1				3		
Northampton	6	8	Wilds	Jesse		1							1				3		
Northampton	6	9	Butler	Daniel	1	1		1		2	1	1	1				8		
Northampton	6	10	Sage	Lewis S	2		1	1		3			1				8		
Northampton	6	11	Mather	Elisha		2	1		1				1	1			6		
Northampton	6	12	Cook	Joseph	2			1		1	1	1	1	1			8		
Northampton	6	13	Rupell	Hezekiah			1	1	1				1	1			5		
Northampton	6	14	Rupell	Hezekiah Jr	2		2	2					1	1			8		
Northampton	6	15	Cook	Justin		1		1		1			1				4		
Northampton	6	16	White	Job	1	3	1	11	3	1	1	2		1	1		58		
Northampton	6	17	Legg	Moses	3	1		1		1	1	1	1				9		
Northampton	6	18	Burt	Edward	1		1						1				3		
Northampton	6	19	Bates	James	1		1			2			1				5		
Northampton	6	20	Hunt	David	1		1			1			1				4		
Northampton	6	21	Clarke	Joseph	2			1		1	1	1	1				7		
Northampton	6	22	Helton	John	1			1						2			4		
Northampton	6	23	Strong	Simeon		2				1	1	1					7		

TOWN	PG#	LN#	LAST NAME	FIRST NAME	FREE WHITE MALES					FREE WHITE FEMALES					TOTAL ALL OTHER	TOTAL SLAVES	TOTALS	DISTRICT/ TOWNSHIP	NOTES
					under 10	10 to 16	16 to 26	26 to 45	45 and over	under 10	10 to 16	16 to 26	26 to 45	45 and over					
Northampton	6	24	Collson	William						1		1	1				3		
Northampton	6	25	Bridgman	Elizabeth	2					1		1	1				5		
Northampton	6	26	Tanner	Nathan	2			1		3			1				7		
Northampton	6	27	Coates	Stephen					1				1				3		
Northampton	6	28	Barnard	Julius	1		3	1		1	1		1				8		
Northampton	6	29	Parsons	Simeon			1		1			2	2				6		
Northampton	6	30	Parsons	Simeon Jun	1	1		1		2	1		1				7		
Northampton	6	31	Hutchens	Joseph		1		1	1	1		1		1			5		
Northampton	6	32	Hutchens	Hezekiah	3			1			3		1				8		
Northampton	6	33	Graves	Elisha	3		1	1		1	2			1			9		
Northampton	6	34	Wicker	Jacob	2		2	1			1		1				7		
Northampton	6	35	Clark	Pharez		2	1	1	1	3			1				9		
Northampton	6	36	Wright	Ornace		1		1			1	1	1	2			7		
Northampton	6	37	Wright	Jonah	3			1				1	1				6		
Northampton	6	38	Wright	Asahel		1		2					1				4		
Northampton	7	1	Strong	Caleb	2	2	2		1	1	1	1	1	2			13		
Northampton	7	2	Waterman	Roger	2			1		1			1				5		
Northampton	7	3	Chapman	Charles	1	2	1	1		2		3	1				11		
Northampton	7	4	Clap	Bohan	2		1	2		2			2				9		
Northampton	7	5	Lyman	Abner	1		1	2	1			2		2			9		
Northampton	7	6	Parsons	Warham		2		1	1	1	2		1				8		
Northampton	7	7	Parsons	Nathaniel			2	1				2	1				6		
Northampton	7	8	Russell	Seth	1	1		1		2		1			1		7		
Northampton	7	9	Lyman	Luke	2		2		1	2	1	1	1	1			11		
Northampton	7	10	Wright	Asahel	2	1		1	1	1			1	1			8		
Northampton	7	11	Wright	Israel	1			1				1					3		
Northampton	7	12	Wilder	Shubal	1		1	1		3	2		1				9		
Northampton	7	13	Wright	Ursula		1	1	1				2		1			7		
Northampton	7	14	Wright	Samuel	1	1	1			2		1	1				8		
Northampton	7	15	Wright	Solomon				1		1				1			3		
Northampton	7	16	Parsons	Josiah	1	2	1	1		3	1		1	1			11		
Northampton	7	17	Wright	Elijah				1					1	1			3		
Northampton	7	18	Clark	Lyman	2	1		1	1	1		2	1				9		
Northampton	7	19	Wright	Enos	2		2		1	1	2		1				9		
Northampton	7	20	Wright	Ebenezer				1									1		
Northampton	7	21	Alvard	Elizabeth										2			2		
Northampton	7	22	Hunt	Luther	2			1		1		1					5		
Northampton	7	23	Wright	Moses		1		1	1	1	1		1	1			6		
Northampton	7	24	Parsons	Beulah								1		2			3		
Northampton	7	25	Russell	Thaddeus	2		1	1				1					5		
Northampton	7	26	Edwards	Vester	2			1		2			1				6		
Northampton	7	27	Lyman	John				1				2	2				5		
Northampton	7	28	Clark	Israel	3			1		1			1				6		
Northampton	7	29	Clap	Sarah	1	1				1	1		1	1			6		
Northampton	7	30	Lane	Ebenezer	1	1	2		1	1	2	3		1	1		13		
Northampton	7	31	Clark	Job	1		1	1		3	2		1				9		
Northampton	7	32	Clark	Jonas		2			1	1	1			1			6		
Northampton	7	33	Clark	Martha										2			2		
Northampton	7	34	Reed	William				1		1	1	1					4		
Northampton	7	35	Tower	Elkanah				1				1					2		
Northampton	7	36	Strong	Daniel	1		1		1	1	1	2					8		
Northampton	7	37	Sheldon	Benjamin		1		1	1	1	1	1	1				7		
Northampton	7	38	Bottom	John	1			1		3			1	1			7		
Northampton	8	1	Strong	Elijah	2	2	1		1			1		1			8		
Northampton	8	2	Day	Simeon	1			1		1	2		1	1			7		
Northampton	8	3	Birge	Hannah									1				1		
Northampton	8	4	Phelps	Seaward	1			1					1				3		
Northampton	8	5	Phelps	Eben	2		2	2	1	1		2	1	1			12		
Northampton	8	6	Shaller	John	1					1		2		1			5		
Northampton	8	7	Bolten	William			1	1		1	1		1				5		
Northampton	8	8	McGeorge	Catharine									1	1			2		
Northampton	8	9	Blackman	George			1			5			1				7		
Northampton	8	10	Day	Nathaniel				1			1	1		1			4		
Northampton	8	11	Day	Nathaniel Jun	2			1		1			1				5		
Northampton	8	12	Pomeroy	William	3	2		1				1	1				8		
Northampton	8	13	Marshall	Ethan	1				1	1			1				4		
Northampton	8	14	Clark	Silas			1	1			3	1	1				7		
Northampton	8	15	Cook	Aaron			1	1					1				3		
Northampton	8	16	Cook	Aaron Jun	2		1					1	1				5		
Northampton	8	17	Hunt	Daniel	1	1	1		1		1		1	1			7		
Northampton	8	18	Parsons	Phinehas	1	1	1		1		1	1		2			8		
Northampton	8	19	Clark	Isaac	3	2		1			1	1	1				9		
Northampton	8	20	Rust	Mary									2				2		
Northampton	8	21	Pomeroy	Daniel				1			1			1	1		4		
Northampton	8	22	Clark	Erastus		3	3	1	2	1		2					12		
Northampton	8	23	Clark	Luther	2	1	1	1			1	2					8		
Northampton	8	24	Clark	Eli	4		1	1	1		1	1					9		
Northampton	8	25	Clark	Benjamin	1			1		2	1		1				6		
Northampton	8	26	Judd	William		2	1	1			3	2	1				10		

TOWN	PG#	LN#	LAST NAME	FIRST NAME	FREE WHITE MALES under 10	10 to 16	16 to 26	26 to 45	45 and over	FREE WHITE FEMALES under 10	10 to 16	16 to 26	26 to 45	45 and over	TOTAL ALL OTHER	TOTAL SLAVES	TOTALS	DISTRICT/ TOWNSHIP	NOTES
Northampton	8	27	Bridgman	Noah	2			1	1			1		1			6		
Northampton	8	28	Bridgman	Erastus	2	2		1		1	2		1				9		
Northampton	8	29	Hunt	Elijah		1	1		1		1	1	1				6		
Northampton	8	30	Cook	Elijah	1		1	1			1	1					5		
Northampton	8	31	Pomeroy	Gaius	1	1	1	1		1		1	1				7		
Northampton	8	32	Hitchcock	Elias			1			3			1				5		
Northampton	8	33	Lyman	William	1			1		2	2	1	1		1		9		
Northampton	8	34	Baker	John		1			2				1				4		
Northampton	8	35	Smith	Justin				2		1		1		1			5		
Northampton	8	36	Clark	Solomon		2	1		1	1	1	2	1	1			10		
Northampton	8	37	Clark	Daniel					1				1				2		
Northampton	8	38	Wallis	Mary	2	1							1	1			5		
Northampton	8	39	Clark	Medad				1	1	1			1				3		
Northampton	8	40	Clark	Jared				1					3	1			5		
Northampton	9	1	Clark	William Jr	2	1	1	1	1	2	1		3				12		
Northampton	9	2	Jewett	Timothy	2	1		1		2			1				7		
Northampton	9	3	Phelps	Jonathan				2				2	1				5		
Northampton	9	4	Steel	Moses			1			3	1		1				6		
Northampton	9	5	Lee	Samuel	1					2		1					6		
Northampton	9	6	Edwards	William	2		10	1			1	1	1		2		18		
Northampton	9	7	Gershom	Samuel		2			1	4	1	2		2	3		15		
Northampton	9	8	Hunt	Abner	1	1	1	1		2	1	1	1	1			10		
Northampton	9	9	Alvord	Elisha	1		1		1	1			1				5		
Northampton	9	10	Smith	Ira			1			1		1					3		
Northampton	9	11	Phelps	Samuel			2		1			1		2			6		
Northampton	9	12	Burt	Gaius	1		1	1		2			1				6		
Northampton	9	13	Burt	Esther						1			2	1			4		
Northampton	9	14	Edwards	Simeon		1			1	3	2		1				8		
Northampton	9	15	Bartlett	Moses	1				1		2		1				5		
Northampton	9	16	Hulburt	James			2		1			1		1			5		
Northampton	9	17	Strong	Noah	1			1		1		1					4		
Northampton	9	18	Taylor	Rachel						5	1		1				7		
Northampton	9	19	Hulbert	Seth	1			1		3			1				6		
Northampton	9	20	Parsons	Asahel		2	1	1		1	2		2				9		
Northampton	9	21	Parsons	Jonathan		1		1		1			1				4		
Northampton	9	22	Lyman	Gaius	1		1	1		1			1				5		
Northampton	9	23	Lyman	Elias	1	1	2		1			2		1			8		
Northampton	9	24	Lee	Walter	3			1		1			1				6		
Northampton	9	25	Smith	Lewis	4	1		1	1	1	1		2				11		
Northampton	9	26	Wait	Abijah		1	4	2	1		1	2		1			12		
Northampton	9	27	Lyman	Joel		1			1		1	2		1			6		
Northampton	9	28	Day	Eli		1		1		3	2		1				8		
Northampton	9	29	Hatheway	Guilford	3			1		1	2		1				8		
Northampton	9	30	Wait	Josiah	2			1		1	2	2		1			9		
Northampton	9	31	French	Josiah	2			1		1			1				5		
Northampton	9	32	Alvord	John	1	1			1	2		1	1		2		9		
Northampton	9	33	Stebbins	John	1			1		2	1		1				6		
Northampton	9	34	Brunson	Abraham			1		1			1		2			5		
Northampton	9	35	Henman	Luke C	1			1				1					3		
Northampton	9	36	Pomeroy	Sylvanus	1			1		2	2						6		
Northampton	9	37	Thorpe	Timothy		1		1					1				3		
Northampton	9	38	Morgan	Judah		2		1			1		2	1			7		
Northampton	9	39	Morgan	Festus		1					1						2		
Northampton	10	1	Pomeroy	Pheobus	3			1		1			1				6		
Northampton	10	2	Pomeroy	Medad			1	1			1		1				4		
Northampton	10	3	Seegur	Charles L	3	1		3		5			2				14		
Northampton	10	4	Farnum	Clement	2			1		1	1		1				6		
Northampton	10	5	French	Sampson		1		1		1	1			1			5		
Northampton	10	6	Lee	Nathl	1			1		4			1				7		
Northampton	10	7	Babcock	Elisha	2			1		2		1					6		
Northampton	10	8	Warner	Joseph	4	1	2		2		2	1	1	2			15		
Northampton	10	9	Day	Luke	1			1		3			1				6		
Northampton	10	10	Smith	James	2	1	1		1			2		1			8		
Northampton	10	11	Birge	Simeon		1			1	1			1	1			5		
Northampton	10	12	Curtiss	Molly			1			2		1	1				5		
Northampton	10	13	Clark	Calvin	2		1	1		1			1				6		
Northampton	10	14	Washburn	Nehemiah				1			1	1	1				4		
Northampton	10	15	Holmes	James	2		2		1	4	2		1				12		
Northampton	10	16	Saxe	John									1				2		
Northampton	10	17	Curtiss	John	3			1				1					6		
Northampton	10	18	Wilds	Thomas	3	2		1		1	1		1				9		
Northampton	10	19	Wilds	Elkanah			1					1					2		
Northampton	10	20	Root	Simeon			1	1			1		1				4		
Northampton	10	21	Edwards	Nathaniel	1		5		1	2	1	2		2			14		
Northampton	10	22	Knapp	Lemuel	3			1		1			1				6		
Northampton	10	23	Allen	Elijah	1		1	1		2	2	1	1				9		
Northampton	10	24	Kingsbury	Samuel	1	1			1	1				1			5		
Northampton	10	25	Slack	Christopher			1		1					1			3		
Northampton	10	26	Cole	Ebenezer					1					1			2		
Northampton	10	27	Cole	Thomas	1			1		2		1					5		

TOWN	PG#	LN#	LAST NAME	FIRST NAME	FREE WHITE MALES					FREE WHITE FEMALES					TOTAL ALL OTHER	TOTAL SLAVES	TOTALS	DISTRICT/ TOWNSHIP	NOTES
					under 10	10 to 16	16 to 26	26 to 45	45 and over	under 10	10 to 16	16 to 26	26 to 45	45 and over					
Northampton	10	28	Pelton	Reuben	1	1	1		1		2	1		1			8		
Northampton	10	29	Stockwell	William		1			1	1	1	2		1			7		
Northampton	10	30	Stockwell	Walter	2			1		2			1				6		
Northampton	10	31	Stockwell	William Jr	1			1		1		1					4		
Northampton	10	32	Bartlett	Elijah	1		1	1		1	2	1	1				8		
Northampton	10	33	Bartlett	Enos	1			1		1		1					4		
Northampton	10	34	Nichols	Joshua	1			1		4	2		1				9		
Northampton	10	35	Bartlett	Moses Jr	2			1		2		1					6		
Northampton	10	36	Davis	Jonathn			2	1		1	2		1	1			8		
Northampton	10	37	Munyon	Jonathn				1		2		1					4		
Northampton	10	38	Miller	John					1				1	1			3		
Northampton	10	39	Miller	Jacob	2			1	1	1			1				6		
Northampton	11	1	Miller	Jonathan	1	2		1		3	1		1				9		
Northampton	11	2	Culver	Lemuel					1		1			1			3		
Northampton	11	3	Kniep	Christensen	3		1	1			3		1				9		
Northampton	11	4	Slack	David				1					1				2		
Northampton	11	5	Slack	Willard	2			1		1			1				5		
Northampton	11	6	Bosworth	Oliver		1		1				1		1			5		
Northampton	11	7	Pelton	David		1	2		1	1	1			1			7		
Northampton	11	8	Alvord	Timothy					1		2			1			4		
Northampton	11	9	Strong	Medad	2	1		1		1	1		1				7		
Northampton	11	10	Strong	Huit	1		1			2			1				5		
Northampton	11	11	Judd	Samuel	1	1		1		2	1		1				7		
Northampton	11	12	Strong	Joel				1				1		1			3		
Northampton	11	13	Clark	Aaron	2	1	1	1		1	1		1				8		
Northampton	11	14	Labrin	Andrew				1		1	1	1		2			6		
Northampton	11	15	Searle	Elisha				1		2	1		1				5		
Northampton	11	16	Mather	Elisha 2d				1				1					2		

TOWN	PG#	LN#	LAST NAME	FIRST NAME	FREE WHITE MALES under 10	10 to 16	16 to 26	26 to 45	45 and over	FREE WHITE FEMALES under 10	10 to 16	16 to 26	26 to 45	45 and over	TOTAL ALL OTHER	TOTAL SLAVES	TOTALS	DISTRICT/ TOWNSHIP	NOTES
Northfield	27	1	Allen	Samuel C.	4			1		1	1	1		1			9		
Northfield	27	2	Alexander	Elisha	1		2		2		1	1		1			8		
Northfield	27	3	Alexander	Simeon Jr		2		1		2	2	1	1				9		
Northfield	27	4	Alexander	Thomas				1	1					1			3		
Northfield	27	5	Alexander	Medad	2	1		2		1			1				7		
Northfield	27	6	Askey	William		1			1		1	2		1			6		
Northfield	27	7	Boyden	Simeon1			1		2		1		1				5		
Northfield	27	8	Barber	David		2	4	1		3	2	1	1	1			15		
Northfield	27	9	Barret	John			1	1		6		1	2				11		
Northfield	27	10	Belding	Jonathan		1	2		1			1	2	1			8		
Northfield	27	11	Belcher	William	2	1	3		1	3	1	1	1				13		
Northfield	27	12	Billings	Barnabas	1			1		2	1		2				7		
Northfield	27	13	Burton	Benjamin	1	1			1		1	1	1	2			8		
Northfield	27	14	Belding	Joseph				1									1		
Northfield	27	15	Bogle	John	2	2			1	1	1		1				8		
Northfield	27	16	Bishop	Nathaniel	1			1					1				3		
Northfield	27	17	Butler	Nathaniel	1			1		2			1				5		
Northfield	27	18	Corse	Gad			2		1	1	1	1	1	1			8		
Northfield	27	19	Carrier	Phillip				1			1			1			3		
Northfield	28	1	Champion	Tho				1				1		1			3		
Northfield	28	2	Caldwell	John	2	1	1	1		2			1				8		
Northfield	28	3	Collar	Hezekiah	3			1		2			1				7		
Northfield	28	4	Collar	Uriah		1			1	1	2		1				6		
Northfield	28	5	Callender	Benjamin			1			2	1		1				5		
Northfield	28	6	Dyke	Aaron	3			1		1	1		1				7		
Northfield	28	7	Dickinson	Obadiah	3		1	1		4	1	1	2				13		
Northfield	28	8	Dickinson	Benoni	2	2	1		1		1	1		1			9		
Northfield	28	9	Dickinson	Titus		1		1			1		1				4		
Northfield	28	10	Doolittle	Lucius			1	1		1	1		2	1			7		
Northfield	28	11	Dutton	Timothy		1	2	1			1			1	1		7		
Northfield	28	12	Dickinson	Moses Junr	1		1			2			1	1			6		
Northfield	28	13	Ellis	William	3		2			1		1					7		
Northfield	28	14	Earl	Robert	1		1					1					3		
Northfield	28	15	Elgar	Thomas				1		1			1				3		
Northfield	28	16	Field	Medad		1		1		1	1		1				5		
Northfield	28	17	Field	Phinehas	2	1		1	1	2	1		1				9		
Northfield	28	18	Fan	John				1					1				2		
Northfield	28	19	Farrar	Adam	1		1			1			1				4		
Northfield	28	20	Field	Ebenezer				1					1				2		
Northfield	28	21	Field	Abner	3	2			1	2	1	2	1				12		
Northfield	28	22	Field	George	2	1	1		1				1	1			7		
Northfield	28	23	Field	Rufus	1		2		1		2	1	2	1			10		
Northfield	28	24	Field	Sylvester			1			2		1					4		
Northfield	28	25	Field	John		1	2		1	1	1	2					9		
Northfield	28	26	Field	Walter	1	2	1	1		3	2	2	1				13		
Northfield	28	27	Field	Samuel	2		3	1		3		2	1	2			14		
Northfield	28	28	Field	Zachariah	1	1	1	1		3		1	1				9		
Northfield	28	29	Freeman	Dan	1	1				1				1			5		
Northfield	28	30	Field	William		1		1			1			2			6		
Northfield	28	31	Frizzle	Martha		1						1		1			3		
Northfield	28	32	Field	Keziah	1									1			2		
Northfield	28	33	Field	Henry	2	2		2		1	1	1	1				10		
Northfield	28	34	Freelove	Wilber	1		1			2	1			1			6		
Northfield	28	35	Gilbert	Cornelius	1		1						1				3		
Northfield	28	36	Griggs	Joseph		1		1			1		2				5		
Northfield	28	37	Goodenough		1		1	1				1					4		First name blank
Northfield	28	38	Hunt	Elsworth	1	1	1					1					4		
Northfield	28	39	Havens	Simon			1		1		1	1	1				5		
Northfield	28	40	Holton	Luther		2					1		1				4		
Northfield	29	1	Holton	John	2	3	2		1	2	1		1				12		
Northfield	29	2	Houghton	Edward		2	3	1		1	2	4	2				15		
Northfield	29	3	Holton	Elijah		3			1	1		3					9		
Northfield	29	4	Holton	Elisha	2	1	1	1			2		1				8		
Northfield	29	5	Hunt	Elisha		1	1	2	1	1	2		1	1			10		
Northfield	29	6	Hurlbut	Isaac				1			1		1				3		
Northfield	29	7	Hurlbut	Gabriel	1	2		1		4	1		1				10		
Northfield	29	8	Holton	Samuel		2	1	1	1	2		3		1			11		
Northfield	29	9	Holden	James	4			1		1		1	1				8		
Northfield	29	10	Janes	Jonathan	1	1	2	1		1	1		1				8		
Northfield	29	11	Janes	Ebenezer	1		3		1				1	1			7		
Northfield	29	12	Janes	Xenophon			1			3		1					5		
Northfield	29	13	Kendrick	Oliver	2		1		1	1	1	1	2	1			10		
Northfield	29	14	Lyman	James		4			1	1	1		1				8		
Northfield	29	15	Lyman	Caleb	1	2	1	1	1	2	1	1	1				11		
Northfield	29	16	Lamb	Isaac			1			1	1	1					4		
Northfield	29	17	Lincoln	Zadock		1				1			1				3		
Northfield	29	18	Lyman	Seth		3		1				2	1	1			8		
Northfield	29	19	Lyman	Simeon		1		2	1		1	1	1				7		
Northfield	29	20	Lyman	William Swan	1		1					1					3		
Northfield	29	21	Miriam	James	1		1	1		4			1				8		

TOWN	PG#	LN#	LAST NAME	FIRST NAME	FREE WHITE MALES					FREE WHITE FEMALES					TOTAL ALL OTHER	TOTAL SLAVES	TOTALS	DISTRICT/ TOWNSHIP	NOTES
					under 10	10 to 16	16 to 26	26 to 45	45 and over	under 10	10 to 16	16 to 26	26 to 45	45 and over					
Northfield	29	22	Mallery	Simeon	1	1		1		2	2		1				8		
Northfield	29	23	Miller	Daniel	3			1	1				1				6		
Northfield	29	24	Morgan	Frederick	1			1		1		1					4		
Northfield	29	25	Mattoon	Phillip	1		2		1		2		1				7		
Northfield	29	26	McCarter	Dennis		1			1	1	1		1				5		
Northfield	29	27	Mattoon	Samuel		2			1		3	1	1				8		
Northfield	29	28	Mattoon	Elijah	1		1		1		1	2	1				7		
Northfield	29	29	Mattoon	Isaac	2			2		1			1				6		
Northfield	29	30	Mattoon	Samuel Jr	1			1		3			1				6		
Northfield	29	31	Maynard	Asa	2			1		1			1				5		
Northfield	29	32	Merriman	Samuel					1			2	1				4		
Northfield	29	33	Merriman	Levi	1			1		3	1		1				7		
Northfield	29	34	Merriman	Elijah	1			1					1				3		
Northfield	29	35	Miner	Clement	5			1					1				7		
Northfield	29	36	Moody	Isaiah			1	1				1					3		
Northfield	29	37	Morgan	Noah	2	3	1		1		1			1			9		
Northfield	29	38	Morgan	Noah Junr	1			1				1					3		
Northfield	29	39	Morgan	reuben					1			1		1			3		
Northfield	29	40	Morgan	Alpheus	2			1		2			2				7		
Northfield	29	41	McCoy	Lemuel	4			1		2	1		1				9		
Northfield	30	1	Nettleton	Edward	3			1		1	1		1				7		
Northfield	30	2	Norton	Selah	2		1	1		4		1	1	1			11		
Northfield	30	3	Page	Lewis	3		3	1		2		1	2				12		
Northfield	30	4	Page	Thomas					1				1				2		
Northfield	30	5	Pomeroy	Medad		2	2		1	1		1	1	1			9		
Northfield	30	6	Pomeroy	Shammah		1	1	1	1	1		1		1			7		
Northfield	30	7	Prentice	Samuel	1	1		1		1			1				5		
Northfield	30	8	Prindle	Nathan		2	1		1	1		1	1				7		
Northfield	30	9	Perry	Noah	2	1	3		1	1	1			1			10		
Northfield	30	10	Priest	Calvin				1					1				2		
Northfield	30	11	Phillips	Oliver			1			1		1					3		
Northfield	30	12	Peabody	Amos	2	1			1	2	2		1				9		
Northfield	30	13	Pehlps	Elihu	3		1	1			1		1				7		
Northfield	30	14	Patterson	Theron				1					1				2		
Northfield	30	15	Preston	Lemuel	2	2	1	1		2			1				9		
Northfield	30	16	Robbins	Asa	2			1		2	1		1				7		
Northfield	30	17	Rockwood	Thomas	2	1	1	1		2		1	1				9		
Northfield	30	18	Richards	Daniel	2	1		1		1	2		1				8		
Northfield	30	19	Rice	Silas	1	1			1					1			6		
Northfield	30	20	Rowley	Israel				1					1				2		
Northfield	30	21	Sawyer	Thomas	2		2	1		2	1		1				9		
Northfield	30	22	Sawyer	Abner	1			1		1		1	1				5		
Northfield	30	23	Smith	Reuben	1		2	2	1		1	2		2			11		
Northfield	30	24	Sloter	Adam	1			1		5			1				8		
Northfield	30	25	Stratton	Calvin	1	1	1	1	1			1	1				7		
Northfield	30	26	Stebbins	Asahel	1		1	1		1			3		1		8		
Northfield	30	27	Stratton	Elijah		2			1	1		2		1			7		
Northfield	30	28	Stratton	Rufus	4	1		1	1	1		1	2	1			12		
Northfield	30	29	Stratton	Hezekiah	3		1		1		1	1	1	1			11		
Northfield	30	30	Stratton	Asa	3	2	1		1		1	1	1				10		
Northfield	30	31	Stratton	Caleb			1		1				1				3		
Northfield	30	32	Strowbridge	James	1				1			2		1			5		
Northfield	30	33	Shepardson	Amos	1	2	1		1	1			1				7		
Northfield	30	34	Trip	Robert	2				1	1			1				5		
Northfield	31	1	Tiffany	Edward	3	1	2	1	1	1		1	1	1			12		
Northfield	31	2	Vose	Solomon	1		1	1		1		1	1				6		
Northfield	31	3	Webster	Ezekiel	1	3	1	1		2	1	1	1				11		
Northfield	31	4	Wright	Eldad	1	1		1		2	1		1				7		
Northfield	31	5	Wright	Donaldus				1					1				2		
Northfield	31	6	Wright	Eliphaz			1		1	1		1		1			5		
Northfield	31	7	Wright	Reuben		1		1	1		1		1	1			6		
Northfield	31	8	Wright	Oliver		1	1		1		1	1		1			6		
Northfield	31	9	Wood	Barzillai	1				1	3		1	1				7		
Northfield	31	10	Wood	Samuel	1			1		2		2					6		
Northfield	31	11	White	Ebenezer	1	2			1	1			1	1			7		
Northfield	31	12	Watrip	Oliver		1	2		1			1		1			6		
Northfield	31	13	Williams	Charles	2			1				1					4		
Northfield	31	14	Woodward	John	3			1			1		1				6		
Northfield	31	15	Whiting	Jabez		1	2	1		2	2	1	1				10		
Northfield	31	16	Wright	David		2	1		1	1			1	1			7		
Northfield	31	17	Walton	John	2			1		2					1		6		
Northfield	31	18	Wilson	Ebenezer	1		1			2		1					5		
Northfield	31	19	Weeks	Uriah		1		1					1				3		
Northfield	31	20	Winchester	Amasa			1					1	1				3		
Northfield	31	21	Wells	Solomon	2					1		1					4		
Northfield	31	22	White	John					1				1				2		

114

TOWN	PG#	LN#	HEADS OF HOUSEHOLD		FREE WHITE MALES					FREE WHITE FEMALES					TOTAL ALL OTHER	TOTAL SLAVES	TOTALS	DISTRICT/TOWNSHIP	NOTES
			LAST NAME	FIRST NAME	under 10	10 to 16	16 to 26	26 to 45	45 and over	under 10	10 to 16	16 to 26	26 to 45	45 and over					
Norwich	151	1	Angel	Stephen	2			1				1		1			5		
Norwich	151	2	Porter	Samuel	2		1					1					4		
Norwich	151	3	Sampson	Knellum	2	1		1		2		1					7		
Norwich	151	4	Briant	Nathaniel	2		1			1		1					5		
Norwich	151	5	Weeks	Hezekiah			2		1	1	1			1			6		
Norwich	151	6	Weeks	Lemuel		1						1					2		
Norwich	151	7	Weeks	Samuel	4		1			1		1					7		
Norwich	151	8	Weeks	William	1		1			1		1					4		
Norwich	151	9	Rude	John			1		1		1	1		1			5		
Norwich	151	10	Rude	John Junr	2		1			2			1				6		
Norwich	151	11	Knight	Samuel	2		1						1				4		
Norwich	151	12	Sampson	Silvenus	2		1			1	1		1				6		
Norwich	151	13	Williams	Isaac	1				1			1	1	1			5		
Norwich	151	14	Knight	Phineas	3	1		1		1	1		1				8		
Norwich	151	15	Burton	Samuel			1			1		1					3		
Norwich	151	16	Burton	Hannah Wid	2	1	1				1	1		1			7		
Norwich	151	17	Peck	Caleb				1		2			1	1			5		
Norwich	151	18	Taylor	Stephen			1										1		
Norwich	151	19	Bazwick	E*	1	1	1			1		1					5		
Norwich	151	20	Ewell	James	2	4	2	1		3			1				13		
Norwich	151	21	Dimock	Joseph Junr	2		1			2	1		1				7		
Norwich	151	22	Dimock	Joseph	1		2		1			1	1				6		
Norwich	151	23	Dimock	Aaron	1	1		1		1		1					5		
Norwich	151	24	Dimock	Thomas			1			1		1					3		
Norwich	151	25	Sandford	Holsa	3		1						1				5		
Norwich	151	26	Sandford	Ruth Wid			1						1	2			4		
Norwich	151	27	Darrow	Zacheus	3					1	3	1					8		
Norwich	151	28	Darrow	Amaziah	1	1		1		1	1	1					6		
Norwich	151	29	Bancroft	Jonathan	1		2		2			2	1	1			9		
Norwich	151	30	Averett	Nathaniel			2		1	1	1			1			6		
Norwich	151	31	Edwards	Benjamin			1			3		1					5		
Norwich	151	32	Knight	Elizabeth Wid										1			1		
Norwich	151	33	Knight	Sylvester		1		1		1		2					5		
Norwich	151	34	Hall	Aaron	1	1		1		2	2		1				8		
Norwich	151	35	Graves	Obediah		1		1		1		1					4		
Norwich	151	36	Lovewell	Jonathan				1		2	1		1				5		
Norwich	151	37	Darrow	Amaziah Junr			1					1					2		
Norwich	151	38	Brown	Levi	1		1			1		1					4		
Norwich	151	39	King	Micah			1	1				2	1				5		
Norwich	151	40	Lyman	Rufus			1					1					2		
Norwich	151	41	Lyman	Asahel			1					1					2		
Norwich	152	1	Warner	Moses		1		1				1	1	1			5		
Norwich	152	2	Williams	Daniel Jr				1			1	1	1				4		
Norwich	152	3	Dewey	Levi Lieut	3		1	1		2	1		1				9		
Norwich	152	4	Sackel	Zavan Lieut	3	2	2	1		1	1		1				11		
Norwich	152	5	Stebbens	Gad Doct	1			1		1				1			4		
Norwich	152	6	Benjamin	Rozwell			1	1				1	1	1			5		
Norwich	152	7	Scott	David Lieut			1				1	1		1			5		
Norwich	152	8	Crow	John				1		2		1	1	1			6		
Norwich	152	9	Smith	Martin Lieut				1		2	1		1				5		
Norwich	152	10	Hollon	James Doct	1		1					1					3		
Norwich	152	11	Fobes	Walter Capt	3	1	1	1	1	1	1	1	1		1		12		
Norwich	152	12	Mixer	Phineas	1	2			1	2	2	1					9		
Norwich	152	13	Lamb	Eliphalet		1		1			2	1					5		
Norwich	152	14	Herrish	Moses			1	1		4		1					7		
Norwich	152	15	Henry	Joseph Lieut	1			1		3	1		1				7		
Norwich	152	16	Johnson	Elisha	1	1	3		1	4	1		1				12		
Norwich	152	17	Weller	Moses	4		2	1	1	2	1	2	1	1			15		
Norwich	152	18	Stanton	Daniel	1			1		2		1					5		
Norwich	152	19	Liffingwell	Elisha	1	2	1		1	2		2	1				10		
Norwich	152	20	Davis	Clarissa	1					1		1					3		
Norwich	152	21	Phelps	Mary Wid			1							1			2		
Norwich	152	22	Eno	James		1				1	2		1	1			6		
Norwich	152	23	Fobes	Samuel	1	1		1		2	1		1				7		
Norwich	152	24	Geer	Margaret Wid		1	1	1				1		1			5		
Norwich	152	25	Prier	Simeon	2	1	1		1	2	1	1	1				10		
Norwich	152	26	Geer	Nathan	2			1		4	2		1				10		
Norwich	152	27	White	Joseph		1						1	1				5		
Norwich	152	28	White	Joseph Junr	1		1	1		2			1	1			7		
Norwich	152	29	White	Eleazer				1		3		1					5		
Norwich	152	30	White	Thomas		2	2		1	3	1	1		1			11		
Norwich	152	31	White	Samuel		1		1						1			3		
Norwich	152	32	White	Jabez	2		1						1				4		
Norwich	152	33	Ormsbury	Nathan	1			1				1	1				4		
Norwich	152	34	Searles	Hinney	1		1					1					3		
Norwich	152	35	Carpenter	Israel		1		1		3		1					6		
Norwich	152	36	Cook	Amos		1				1		1					3		
Norwich	152	37	Harriss	Lemuel		1	1			2	1	1					6		
Norwich	152	38	Stanton	Abel	1	2	2		1	2			1				10		

TOWN	PG#	LN#	HEADS OF HOUSEHOLD		FREE WHITE MALES					FREE WHITE FEMALES					TOTAL ALL OTHER	TOTAL SLAVES	TOTALS	DISTRICT/ TOWNSHIP	NOTES
			LAST NAME	FIRST NAME	under 10	10 to 16	16 to 26	26 to 45	45 and over	under 10	10 to 16	16 to 26	26 to 45	45 and over					
Norwich	152	39	Thomas	Salmon	1	1		1		2			1				6		
Norwich	152	40	Shoals	Joseph	1	2	1		1	1		2		2			10		
Norwich	152	41	Meachum	Ebinezer	3		2		1	1	2	2	1				12		
Norwich	152	42	Meachum	Enoch	3			1		2			1				7		
Norwich	152	43	Elliss	John	2			1		2	1		1				7		
Norwich	153	1	Tinker	Elisha	1	1	1	1		1	1		1				7		
Norwich	153	2	Rust	Gershom			1			3			1				5		
Norwich	153	3	Briant	Rodolphus			1			3	1	1	1				7		
Norwich	153	4	Stanton	Elisha		1	1		1	5	1	2	1				12		
Norwich	153	5	Morton	James		1	1	1					1				4		
Norwich	153	6	Morton	Josiah		1		1		3			1				6		
Norwich	153	7	Burton	Barnard	2			1		1	1			2			7		
Norwich	153	8	Tanner	John	1			1		3			1				6		
Norwich	153	9	Cort	Isaac	1	3	1		1	3	1	1	1				12		
Norwich	153	10	Williams	Charles	2	1	2		1	1		1	1				9		
Norwich	153	11	Pitcher	Jonathan	4	2		1		1	1	1	1				11		
Norwich	153	12	Miller	William Deac		1	2	1						1			5		
Norwich	153	13	Stanton	Abel Junr			1			1			1				3		
Norwich	153	14	Meachum	Stephen	1		1			2			1				5		
Norwich	153	15	Leonard	Daniel	1	1	1		1			2	1				7		
Norwich	153	16	Cowing	Tela			1			1		1					3		
Norwich	153	17	Stockwell	Levi			1					1					2		
Norwich	153	18	Weatherby	Thomas	3			1		1			1				6		
Norwich	153	19	Mitchel	Reuben		1		1		1		1					4		
Norwich	153	20	Phillips	Ezra	1			1		3			1				6		
Norwich	153	21	Taggart	James			1										1		
Norwich	153	22	Lyman	Giles		1	2	1			1		1				6		
Norwich	153	23	Rust	Zebulon	2	1		1		1	1		1				7		
Norwich	153	24	Lyman	Seth					1			1	1				3		
Norwich	153	25	Pomoroy	Titus Deac	4		1	1		1			1				8		
Norwich	153	26	Parks	Levi		1		1				2					4		
Norwich	153	27	Bancroft	Edmon Doct		1			1	1	2	1					6		
Norwich	153	28	Parks	Joseph	1	1						3	1				7		
Norwich	153	29	Parks	Uriah	4			1		1		1	1				8		
Norwich	153	30	Danks	Sylvester			1				1						2		
Norwich	153	31	Parks	Joseph Junr			1			3		1					5		
Norwich	153	32	Parks	Miner			1			1		1					3		
Norwich	153	33	Searl	Joel		1				1		1					3		
Norwich	153	34	Searl	Asahel	1	1	1				2	1	1				7		
Norwich	153	35	Kirkland	Samuel Capt			1			2		2					5		
Norwich	153	36	Kirkland	John Esq			1	1			2		1				5		
Norwich	153	37	Dunlap	John	1			1		1			1				4		
Norwich	153	38	Higgins	Ebenezer	3	2	1	1				2	1				10		
Norwich	153	39	Wilson	Elijah	3	2			1			2		1			9		
Norwich	153	40	Washborn	Jonathan				1				3	1				5		
Norwich	153	41	Washborn	Josiah		1							1				2		
Norwich	153	42	Woodbridge	John		1	1						1	1			4		
Norwich	153	43	Pilcher	Nathan	3			1		1		1		1			7		
Norwich	154	1	Willard	Humphrey		1		1		3			1				7		
Norwich	154	2	Talcutt	Eleazer	1			1		5		1	1	1			10		
Norwich	154	3	Shelden	Hinney		2	1		1	3	1	2	1				11		
Norwich	154	4	Burt	Noah	1	1		1		2	1		1				7		
Norwich	154	5	Joy	Jess Capt		2			1			2		1			6		
Norwich	154	6	Adams	Moses		1	1		1	2		1	1	1			8		
Norwich	154	7	Adams	Thadeus	2	1		1		2	2	1	1				10		
Norwich	154	8	Montegue	Moses Lt.			1			1	2		1				5		
Norwich	154	9	Warner	Samuel Lieut		1	1		1			1	1				5		
Norwich	154	10	Kirkland	Daniel		1											1		
Norwich	154	11	Howard	Wid										1			1		
Norwich	154	12	Whitney	Peter	1	3		1		2	1		1				9		
Norwich	154	13	Wright	Gideon	2	1	1	1		1			1				7		
Norwich	154	14	Sylvester	Eliakim Doct			1						1				2		
Norwich	154	15	Williams	Daniel 2d	1	1		1		3	1	1	1				9		
Norwich	154	16	Williams	Isaac	2	1		1			1		1				6		
Norwich	154	17	Fairman	Samuel Lieut	1	1		1		2		2		1			8		
Norwich	154	18	Chapin	Ezra	3	2	1	1			1	1	1				10		
Norwich	154	19	Fobes	William Dea	1	1	1	2			1		1				7		
Norwich	154	20	Tracy	Stephen Rev	1		3	1	1	1	2	1	1				11		
Norwich	154	21	Griswould	John				1			1		1				3		
Norwich	154	22	Griswould	John Junr	4			1					1				6		
Norwich	154	23	Griswould	Ashur	1		1	1		2			1				6		
Norwich	154	24	Hollyday	Job	2	1		1		2	2	1	1	1			11		
Norwich	154	25	Kenny	Cesar											6		6		
Norwich	154	26	Spicewood	Sylvester											2		2		
Norwich	154	27	Perkins	York											3		3		
Norwich	154	28	Rhoads	Rhoda											5		5		
Norwich	154	29	Starkweather	Prince										1	6		7		
Norwich	154	30	Fuller	Zeblon											5		5		
Norwich	154	31	Everet	Isaac			1								5		6		

TOWN	PG#	LN#	HEADS OF HOUSEHOLD		FREE WHITE MALES					FREE WHITE FEMALES					TOTAL ALL OTHER	TOTAL SLAVES	TOTALS	DISTRICT/ TOWNSHIP	NOTES
			LAST NAME	FIRST NAME	under 10	10 to 16	16 to 26	26 to 45	45 and over	under 10	10 to 16	16 to 26	26 to 45	45 and over					
Norwich	154	32	Brewster	Charles											2		2		
Norwich	154	33	Wickum	Prince											1		1		

TOWN	PG#	LN#	LAST NAME	FIRST NAME	FREE WHITE MALES					FREE WHITE FEMALES					TOTAL ALL OTHER	TOTAL SLAVES	TOTALS	DISTRICT/ TOWNSHIP	NOTES
					under 10	10 to 16	16 to 26	26 to 45	45 and over	under 10	10 to 16	16 to 26	26 to 45	45 and over					
Orange	41	1	Allen	James	1		1		1	1	2	1	1				8		
Orange	41	2	Atwood	Ebenezer				2			1		1				4		
Orange	41	3	Albee	Asa		1		1	1	1	1	2		1			8		
Orange	41	4	Aldrich	Asa		1			1	1				1			4		
Orange	41	5	Battle	John			1		1		1	1		1			5		
Orange	41	6	Battle	Sherman				1				1					2		
Orange	41	7	Ball	Elijah	1	2	1		1	1	1	1	1				9		
Orange	41	8	Baker	Sherebiah	1	1	2		1	2		2		1			10		
Orange	41	9	Baker	Lewis	3			1		1	1		1				7		
Orange	41	10	Battle	Phinehas	1			1					1				3		
Orange	41	11	Briggs	Samuel		4	1	1		1	2		1	1			11		
Orange	41	12	Briggs	Micah	2	1		1		1			1				6		
Orange	41	13	Bulloch	Welcome		1		1		1	1	1	1				6		
Orange	41	14	Bachelor	Joel	1	1		1				1					4		
Orange	41	15	Briggs	Adam	3			1		2	2		1				9		
Orange	41	16	Babbit	Ira			1			1							2		
Orange	41	17	Bulloch	Cromwell		1				2		1					4		
Orange	41	18	Cheney	Nathaniel	2	1		1		1			1				6		
Orange	41	19	Cheney	Levi	2	2			1	1		2		1			9		
Orange	41	20	Chapin	Oliver		2	2	2			2	1	1				10		
Orange	41	21	Cheney	Moses	3			1		3	1		1				9		
Orange	41	22	Cheney	David	2	1		1		2			1				7		
Orange	41	23	Collar	Samuel	1	1	1	1		2	1		1				8		
Orange	41	24	Cheney	Ebenezer	3	1	1		1	1	1	1	1				10		
Orange	41	25	Collar	Artemas	2			1		1		1					5		
Orange	41	26	Cheney	Nathan	2			1		3			1				7		
Orange	41	27	Cobb	Isiah	2	1	4		1	1	1			1			11		
Orange	41	28	Cuttin	John				1		4				1			6		
Orange	41	29	Cady	Justin			1			1		1		1			4		
Orange	41	30	Cleveland	David			1			1		1					3		
Orange	41	31	Chase	Aaron	2			1		2	1						6		
Orange	41	32	Doan	Joseph	1		1	1	1		1	2		1			8		
Orange	41	33	Dexter	Benjamin			1		1		1	3		1			7		
Orange	41	34	Dunbar	David			1		1	1	1			1			5		
Orange	41	35	Dewey	Silas	1			1		1			1				4		
Orange	41	36	Dexter	Wheeler	1		1					1					3		
Orange	41	37	Esty	Oliver	1	1		1		1		1	1				6		
Orange	41	38	Ellis	Seth		3		1				1	1				6		
Orange	41	39	Ellis	Moses	3			1		1		1	1				7		
Orange	41	40	Ellis	John				1					1				2		
Orange	41	41	Ellis	Nathan		2		1					1				4		
Orange	41	42	Forrester	John	2	2		1		1		1	1				8		
Orange	41	43	Godard	Nathan	1	1		1				3		1			7		
Orange	42	1	Foster	James			1						1				2		
Orange	42	2	Foskett	Ebenezer	1	2	2		1			1	1				8		
Orange	42	3	Goddard	Jonathan	1	2	1	1			1		1				7		
Orange	42	4	Godard	Hezekiah	1	2		1		3			1				8		
Orange	42	5	Godard	John	2			1		2			1				6		
Orange	42	6	Gilles	Alpheus		1		1	1	2			1				6		
Orange	42	7	Gould	William	3	1		1		4	2		1				12		
Orange	42	8	Goodale	Zina	1	1		1		4	1		1				9		
Orange	42	9	Godard	Ebenezer	2	1	3		1	1	2			1			11		
Orange	42	10	Godard	Asa	1	3		1	1	2	1		1	1			11		
Orange	42	11	Gates	Solomon				1					1				2		
Orange	42	12	Gilbert	Joseph			1				1	1					3		
Orange	42	13	Harrington	Daniel	3	1		1		1	1		1				8		
Orange	42	14	Harrington	Jason	1	1			1		2		1				6		
Orange	42	15	Hayward	Lemuel			1		1				1				3		
Orange	42	16	Hill	Joshua	1	1	1		1				1				5		
Orange	42	17	Holden	Jeduthan				1					1				2		
Orange	42	18	Hemenway	Ezra	1		2			2		1					6		
Orange	42	19	Hill	David		2	1		2	1	1	1		2			10		
Orange	42	20	Jones	Jonathan Junr	2	1		1		1			1				6		
Orange	42	21	Jennings	Peleg	1			1			2			1			5		
Orange	42	22	Johnson	Elisha	3		3			2	2		1	1			12		
Orange	42	23	Jones	Jonathan				1					1				2		
Orange	42	24	Johnson	Jonathan	1		1			1		1					4		
Orange	42	25	Johnson	Solomon		1	1					1		1			5		
Orange	42	26	Kinsley	Abiel	1	2		1		1		2	1				8		
Orange	42	27	Knowles	Samuel	1	1		1		3			1				7		
Orange	42	28	Knapp	Jonah	2			1		1			1				5		
Orange	42	29	Lord	William Junr	1	1		1		3	1		1				8		
Orange	42	30	Lord	Preston	2			1	1	4	1	2		1			12		
Orange	42	31	Lord	Asa		1		1			1	1	1				5		
Orange	42	32	Lord	Joseph		2		1				1	1				5		
Orange	42	33	Lord	Ichabod			1	1									2		
Orange	42	34	Legg	Hepsibah	1		1					2	1				5		
Orange	42	35	Legg	David		1			1	4		1	1				8		
Orange	42	36	Metcalf	Saville				1				1					3		

TOWN	PG#	LN#	LAST NAME	FIRST NAME	under 10	10 to 16	16 to 26	26 to 45	45 and over	under 10	10 to 16	16 to 26	26 to 45	45 and over	TOTAL ALL OTHER	TOTAL SLAVES	TOTALS	DISTRICT/ TOWNSHIP	NOTES
Orange	42	37	Metcalf	Silas	2			1		2	1		1				7		
Orange	42	38	Marble	Silas			3	1	1	1	1		1	1			9		
Orange	42	39	Maycumber	Samuel				1		1	2	1		1			6		
Orange	42	40	Mayo	Calvin	1		1					1					3		
Orange	42	41	Mayo	Dorothy	1		1			2	2	1	1				8		
Orange	42	42	Mills	James	1		1		1			1		1			5		
Orange	42	43	Metcalf	Joseph		1	3		1		2	1		1			9		
Orange	43	1	Mills	James Junr	1		1			1		1					4		
Orange	43	2	Mathews	Jeremiah				1		1	1						3		
Orange	43	3	Manly	Obed	2			1		2		1					6		
Orange	43	4	Pitts	Samuel Bishop	1	1	2	1	1		1	2		1			10		
Orange	43	5	Porter	Benjamin	1			1		3	1		1				7		
Orange	43	6	Robbins	Phinehas				1					1				2		
Orange	43	7	Ruggles	Samuel		1	1	1		1	1	1					6		
Orange	43	8	Richmond	Perez	1		1		1	2		1		1			7		
Orange	43	9	Smith	Jonathan	3			1				1	1	2			8		
Orange	43	10	Sumner	Salem	2			1		2			1				6		
Orange	43	11	Stearns	William	2	1	1		1	3	1	1	1				11		
Orange	43	12	Streeter	Adam		1		1		3			1				6		
Orange	43	13	Snow	Jesse				1		1		1					3		
Orange	43	14	Smith	Amasa				1		3			1				5		
Orange	43	15	Stearns	Nathaniel	1	1		1		3			1				7		
Orange	43	16	Stanford	Lyman	2			1		1		2					6		
Orange	43	17	Sadler	Abiel		2			1	4	1		1				9		
Orange	43	18	Sawyer	William			1					1					2		
Orange	43	19	Temple	Hananiah			2		1	1		3		1			8		
Orange	43	20	Tucker	Joshua	1		1			1		1					4		
Orange	43	21	Thayer	Joel	1			1		3	1		1				7		
Orange	43	22	Woods	Benjamin		2	1		1			4		1			9		
Orange	43	23	Ward	Edward	4		1		1		2		1				9		
Orange	43	24	Woodard	Amos	2	2		1		3	1		1				10		
Orange	43	25	Wheelock	John			1										1		
Orange	43	26	Wheelock	Alexander	1	2	2		1	2	1		1				10		
Orange	43	27	Woodcock	Nathaniel				1				1		1			3		
Orange	43	28	Ward	Sylvanus	1		2	1		1	1		1	1			8		
Orange	43	29	Ward	Ashbel	1		1					1					3		
Orange	43	30	Whitney	Jabez	2			1		3			1				7		
Orange	43	31	Ward	Nemiah		1			1			2		1			5		
Orange	43	32	Wheelock	Noah			1					1					2		
Orange	43	33	Ward	Amos			1			2			1				4		
Orange	43	34	Ward	Daniel		2				1			1				4		
Orange	43	35	Willmoth	Nathaniel	2			1		2			1				6		
Orange	43	36	Willmoth	Jotham	1			1		4	2	1	1				10		
Orange	43	37	Witherbee	Paul			1					1					2		
Orange	43	38	Woodard	Jonathan				1		1				1			3		

TOWN	PG#	LN#	LAST NAME	FIRST NAME	FREE WHITE MALES					FREE WHITE FEMALES					TOTAL ALL OTHER	TOTAL SLAVES	TOTALS	DISTRICT/ TOWNSHIP	NOTES
					under 10	10 to 16	16 to 26	26 to 45	45 and over	under 10	10 to 16	16 to 26	26 to 45	45 and over					
Palmer	258	1	McMaster	Hugh Jr		2			1		1		1				5		
Palmer	258	2	Farrell	Josiah	1	1		1		1			1				5		
Palmer	258	3	Backus	Samuel	1			1		2	1		1				6		
Palmer	258	4	Goodman	William	2			1		1			1				5		
Palmer	258	5	Eddy	Charles			1		1	2	2		1				7		
Palmer	258	6	Shearer	Jonathan Dr	3		1	1		2	1	1	1				10		
Palmer	258	7	Fowler	John				1					1	1			3		
Palmer	258	8	Weaver	Benjamin	1	2		1		2	1		1				8		
Palmer	258	9	Moore	David	3			1		1	1		1				7		
Palmer	258	10	Corey	William				1									1		
Palmer	258	11	Graves	Horace				1		2			1				4		
Palmer	258	12	Graves	Aaron Majr				1	1								2		
Palmer	258	13	Potter	Wm	2			1		2			1		1		7		
Palmer	258	14	Scott	Calvin Doct	2	1		1		1	1		1		2		9		
Palmer	258	15	Bates	Asa		1	2	1	1			1	1	1	2		10		
Palmer	258	16	King	James				1				1	1				3		
Palmer	258	17	Rider	Enos	2			1		3	2		1				9		
Palmer	258	18	Shearer	John	1		1	1		1			1				5		
Palmer	258	19	Moore	Hugh		1	1	1		2							5		
Palmer	258	20	Moore	Hugh Jur	1			1		2		1					5		
Palmer	258	21	Cleaveland	Hopestill				1					1				2		
Palmer	258	22	Richardson	James		1				1		1					3		
Palmer	258	23	Graves	Gideon	1			1		5			1				8		
Palmer	259	1	Shearer	Noah	2			1		1			1		1		6		
Palmer	259	2	Shearer	David	2	1	1	1	1	2			1				9		
Palmer	259	3	Graves	Simeon				1					1				2		
Palmer	259	4	Roberts	Nathaniel	3			1		2			1				7		
Palmer	259	5	Graves	Daniel				1					1				2		
Palmer	259	6	Morgan	Martin			1			1		1					3		
Palmer	259	7	Hill	Elijah	3			1		1			1				6		
Palmer	259	8	King	John	1	1	1					1					4		
Palmer	259	9	Cleaveland	Samuel	1			1				1					3		
Palmer	259	10	Gordon	Cosmo			1										1		
Palmer	259	11	Cushman	Consider		1		1		1			1				4		
Palmer	259	12	Moore	David				1		1			2				4		
Palmer	259	13	Moore	Aaron	1			1		3			1				6		
Palmer	259	14	Farrell	Isaac	1	2		1			1		1				6		
Palmer	259	15	Knight	Theophilus	2	1	1						1				5		
Palmer	259	16	McElwain	John A	4		1	1			1	1	2	2			12		
Palmer	259	17	McElwain	Roger	2			1		3			1				7		
Palmer	259	18	Cooley	Zadok	2	1		1		1	1		1				7		
Palmer	259	19	Olds	Enoch	3			1		1			1				6		
Palmer	259	20	Borden	Ezekiel	2	1	1						2				6		
Palmer	259	21	Darling	Sarah Wd							1	1	1				3		
Palmer	259	22	Farrington	Amos			1					1					2		
Palmer	259	23	Moore	Jonathan		1	1	1				1		1			5		
Palmer	259	24	Pool	Thomas		1		1						1			3		
Palmer	259	25	Farrell	Timothy	1		3	1				2	1				8		
Palmer	259	26	Tangill	Benja Capt.		2	2	1			1	2	1				9		
Palmer	259	27	Cutler	James	1			1		1			2				5		
Palmer	259	28	McMaster	Clark	2			1		3			1				7		
Palmer	259	29	McMaster	John	2	1		1		1		1	1				7		
Palmer	259	30	Hamilton	Asa	3			1					1				5		
Palmer	259	31	Coye	Nehemiah	2		1	1		1	1	1	1				8		
Palmer	259	32	Farrell	William	2	1		1		1	1		1				7		
Palmer	259	33	Jones	Ebenezer		1	1		1	2	1		1				7		
Palmer	259	34	Pool	Thomas Junr	1		1					1					3		
Palmer	259	35	Davis	Nathan 2d	1	1		1					1				4		
Palmer	259	36	Spear	Luther				1		3	1		1				6		
Palmer	259	37	Spear	William		1		1		2	1		2	1			8		
Palmer	259	38	Hastings	Roswell	3	1		1			1	1		1			8		
Palmer	259	39	Thompson	Nathan	2	1		1					1				5		
Palmer	259	40	Thompson	Rufus		1	1	1					2	1			6		
Palmer	259	41	Durant	Nathaniel				1		1			1				3		
Palmer	259	42	Walton	Patrick Capt.		1		1		1	1	4	1				9		
Palmer	259	43	Mendon	Wm			1						1				2		
Palmer	259	44	Parkhurst	Wm	1			1		4	1		1				8		
Palmer	259	45	McMaster	Hugh		1	1		1		1		1				5		
Palmer	260	1	Burrill	Ebenezer	2			1					1				4		
Palmer	260	2	McMitchell	Benjamin	2			1		1			1				5		
Palmer	260	3	McMitchell	Robert		1	1		1	2	2		1				8		
Palmer	260	4	Smith	Joseph	2	2		1	1	2		1	1				10		
Palmer	260	5	McClanathan	Thomas			3		1	2	1	1	1				9		
Palmer	260	6	Shaw	James		1	1	1		1		2					6		
Palmer	260	7	Sedgwick	Gordon	1	1	1	1	1	3	1	3	1				13		
Palmer	260	8	Foster	Bryant				1						2			3		
Palmer	260	9	Foster	Willson	1		1	1		1			1				5		
Palmer	260	10	Smith	Robert	1	1	1	2	1	2	1	1	1	1			12		
Palmer	260	11	Smith	James Lt		1	2	3		1	1	2		1			11		

TOWN	PG#	LN#	LAST NAME	FIRST NAME	FREE WHITE MALES					FREE WHITE FEMALES					TOTAL ALL OTHER	TOTAL SLAVES	TOTALS	DISTRICT/ TOWNSHIP	NOTES
					under 10	10 to 16	16 to 26	26 to 45	45 and over	under 10	10 to 16	16 to 26	26 to 45	45 and over					
Palmer	260	12	Smith	John A	1		1		2	1	1	2		2			10		
Palmer	260	13	Foster	William			1	1		3			1				6		
Palmer	260	14	Lamb	Jabez Dr	2	1			1		1	2	1				8		
Palmer	260	15	McMaster	John 2d	2			1	1	2		1	1				8		
Palmer	260	16	Shaw	Noah	2	2		1			1		1				7		
Palmer	260	17	Gates	Micah	1	1		1		1	1		1	1			7		
Palmer	260	18	McClanathan	Saml Deacn			4		1		2	1	1	1			10		
Palmer	260	19	Dunbar	John			3		1				1	1			6		
Palmer	260	20	Brown	Solomon			1			1			1	1			4		
Palmer	260	21	Brown	Seth	2		1			2			1				6		
Palmer	260	22	Stephens	Henry		1		1		1		1		1			5		
Palmer	260	23	Stephens	Levi	1			1		2				1			5		
Palmer	260	24	Bacon	Benjamin			1					1		1			3		
Palmer	260	25	Bacon	Simeon	2	1		1		2			1				7		
Palmer	260	26	McMaster	Joshua			1	1				1		1			4		
Palmer	260	27	Merrill	Wm	2	1		1		3	1		1				9		
Palmer	260	28	Grover	Stephen	1	1			1	2	1		1				7		
Palmer	260	29	Grover	Robert			1			1			1				3		
Palmer	260	30	Blackmore	Margaret Widow										1			1		
Palmer	260	31	Hitchcock	Winchester	1			1				2					4		
Palmer	260	32	Allen	Anna										1			1		
Palmer	260	33	Hobb	Nathaniel			1			2			1				4		
Palmer	260	34	Trim	Benjamin	3	3			1	2	1		1				11		
Palmer	260	35	Strickland	James	3			1		2			1				7		
Palmer	260	36	Shaw	Erwin	2	1	1		1	2	2	1	1				11		
Palmer	260	37	Ward	Abijah Lt		2		1	1	1	1		2		2		10		
Palmer	260	38	Davis	Nathan	1	1		1					1				4		
Palmer	260	39	Hamilton	John Lt		1	1		1				1	1			5		
Palmer	260	40	Parsons	Joshua	1		2		1			1	1	1			7		
Palmer	260	41	Hitchcock	Luke	4	2	1		1		1	1	1				11		
Palmer	260	42	McMaster	Robert				1					1				2		
Palmer	260	43	McMaster	Reuben			1			1		2					4		
Palmer	260	44	Pugnant	John											5		5		
Palmer	261	1	Ward	Asa		1	1	1		2		1	1				7		
Palmer	261	2	May	Ebenezer											2		2		
Palmer	261	3	Cumings	Benjamin	1		1					1					3		
Palmer	261	4	Allen	Abner	3			1		1			1				6		
Palmer	261	5	Allen	Ephraim				1				1		1			3		
Palmer	261	6	Cummings	Isaac		1		1	1	1		2		1			7		
Palmer	261	7	Warren	Isaac	2		1	1		1	1	1	1				8		
Palmer	261	8	King	William			2	1	1			2		1			7		
Palmer	261	9	King	John			2	1	1			2		1			7		
Palmer	261	10	Durant	John			1	1									2		
Palmer	261	11	Shaw	Moses	1			1				1	1				4		
Palmer	261	12	Warriner	William		2		1		1		2		1			7		
Palmer	261	13	Mann	David	2			1	1	3		1	1	1			10		
Palmer	261	14	Brekenridge	Obadiah			1					1	1	1			4		
Palmer	261	15	Robinson	Moses	2			1		3	1	1	1				9		
Palmer	261	16	Fleming	David	1		1		1				1	2			6		
Palmer	261	17	Fleming	Joseph	3			1		2			1				7		
Palmer	261	18	Shaw	Joshua Dr				1		1		1		1			4		
Palmer	261	19	Shaw	Solomon	1	1		1		1			1				5		
Palmer	261	20	Adams	John	2			1		3		1	1				8		
Palmer	261	21	Davis	Nathan	2	1	1	1		1			1				7		
Palmer	261	22	Adams	Andrew 2d		1				2			1				5		
Palmer	261	23	Keith	Peter	1			1		2	3		1				8		
Palmer	261	24	Webber	Ebenezer Col.	3	1			1	1	1	1		1			9		
Palmer	261	25	Hamilton	James				1				1		1			3		
Palmer	261	26	Hamilton	John 2d	1	1		1		1			1				5		
Palmer	261	27	Withington	Joseph		1		1					1	1			4		
Palmer	261	28	Wadsworth	Ebenezer				1		2			1				4		
Palmer	261	29	Converse	Jacob	1		1	1		1		1					5		
Palmer	261	30	King	Jesse	2		2	1		4	1	1	1				12		
Palmer	261	31	Rogers	John	3	1		1		1		2	1	1			11		
Palmer	261	32	Ferre	Judah	1	3	2		1	1		3		1			12		
Palmer	261	33	Brainerd	Timothy	1		1		1	3	2	1	1				10		
Palmer	261	34	Barrett	Moses		1	2		1	1	2			1			8		
Palmer	261	35	Brainerd	Asa	3			1		1			1				6		
Palmer	261	36	Walkins	Abner	3							1					4		
Palmer	261	37	Hendrick	Samuel	3			1		1	1	2	1	1			10		
Palmer	261	38	Converse	Alpheus		1	3	1				1	1				7		
Palmer	261	39	Adams	Andrew		2	1	1	1	1				1			7		
Palmer	261	40	Walker	Silvanus		1	1	1		1			1	1			6		
Palmer	261	41	Abbot	Gideon		1	1	1		1			1				4		
Palmer	261	42	Tupper	William	2		1	1		1			1				6		
Palmer	261	43	Mason	William	4		1	1		2			1				9		
Palmer	261	44	Blodget	Admatha	2			1		2		1					6		
Palmer	262	1	Merrick	Aaron			1	1	1		1	1		1			6		
Palmer	262	2	Cooley	Jonathan		2	1	1		1		1	1				8		

TOWN	PG#	LN#	LAST NAME	FIRST NAME	under 10	10 to 16	16 to 26	26 to 45	45 and over	under 10	10 to 16	16 to 26	26 to 45	45 and over	TOTAL ALL OTHER	TOTAL SLAVES	TOTALS	DISTRICT/ TOWNSHIP	NOTES
			HEADS OF HOUSEHOLD		FREE WHITE MALES					FREE WHITE FEMALES									
Palmer	262	3	Baldwin	Moses Revd		1			1	1		2		1			6		
Palmer	262	4	Haynes	David	1			1		3	1		1				7		
Palmer	262	5	King	Thomas Deacn					1				1	2			4		
Palmer	262	6	King	Daniel	5	2	2		1				1				11		
Palmer	262	7	King	David Lt.		1			1					1			3		
Palmer	262	8	King	Jno Capt.		1			1					1			3		
Palmer	262	9	Watson	John				1				1					2		
Palmer	262	10	Shaw	John				1		3			1				5		
Palmer	262	11	Badlwin	William	3			1			1		1				6		
Palmer	262	12	King	Gideon	2	1	2	1		1	1	1	1				10		
Palmer	262	13	King	Benjamin	3	2		1		3			1	1			11		
Palmer	262	14	Spear	David	1	1	1		1		1	1	1				7		

TOWN	PG#	LN#	LAST NAME	FIRST NAME	FREE WHITE MALES					FREE WHITE FEMALES					TOTAL ALL OTHER	TOTAL SLAVES	TOTALS	DISTRICT/ TOWNSHIP	NOTES
					under 10	10 to 16	16 to 26	26 to 45	45 and over	under 10	10 to 16	16 to 26	26 to 45	45 and over					
Pelham	213	1	Abercrombie	Samuel				1									1		
Pelham	213	2	Abercrombie	James	1	2			1	2	1	2		1			10		
Pelham	213	3	Akins	Joseph	2			1		2			1				6		
Pelham	213	4	Ayers	Buenos	1			1		2			1				5		
Pelham	213	5	Abercrombie	Isaac Esq	2		1	1					1				5		
Pelham	213	6	Bartlett	Benja	3	1		1		2			1				8		
Pelham	213	7	Bartlett	Solomon				1		3		1					5		
Pelham	213	8	Barber	John	3	1		1	1	2	1		1				10		
Pelham	213	9	Baker	Isaac	3			1	1	1			2	1			9		
Pelham	213	10	Berry	Alman	2		2		1	1		1	2	2			11		
Pelham	213	11	Bryant	Seth	2			1	1	2		1	1	1			9		
Pelham	213	12	Baldwin	Wm			1		1			1		1			4		
Pelham	213	13	Brown	Matthew			1		1	1				1			4		
Pelham	213	14	Babbett	Samuel	1	1		1	1	2	1		1	1			9		
Pelham	213	15	Boynton	Ebenz				1		1			1				3		
Pelham	213	16	Baker	Ezekiel	4	1		1		1			1				8		
Pelham	213	17	Crozier	Asabah H & Mary Florin	1	1				2	1		3				8		
Pelham	213	18	Bartlett	Aaron	5		1		1		2	1	1				11		
Pelham	213	19	Chapin	Luther	2	1	1	1	1	1			2	1			10		
Pelham	213	20	Clarkshun	Adam		1	1				1	1		1			5		
Pelham	213	21	Crawford	Levi	2	1		1	1				1	1			7		
Pelham	213	22	Conkey	Thomas	1	2		1		1	1		1				7		
Pelham	213	23	Cowen	James	3	2		1		2		2	1				11		
Pelham	213	24	Cowen	George		1		1				1	1				4		
Pelham	213	25	Conkey	Isaac				1		1	1	1					4		
Pelham	213	26	Conkey	Elisha	1	1	1		1	1		1		1			7		
Pelham	213	27	Conkey	Alexr		2	1			2		1	1				7		
Pelham	213	28	Conkey	David	1	1		1		1	1		1				7		
Pelham	213	29	Steel	Saml			1		1					1			3		
Pelham	213	30	Conkey	John Maj		1	4		1	3	1	2		1			13		
Pelham	213	31	Conkey	Isaac				1		1			1				3		
Pelham	213	32	Conkey	Wm	1	1	1		1	1	1		1	2			9		
Pelham	213	33	Conkey	Alexr					1					1			2		
Pelham	213	34	Crozett	Robt		3			1	2		1		1			8		
Pelham	213	35	Dunlap	James		1	1	1	1		1			2			7		
Pelham	213	36	Darimon	Phinehas	1	1	1		1		2	2		1			9		
Pelham	213	37	Dunlap	William	1				1					2			4		
Pelham	214	1	Edson	Seth	3	1		1	1	1		1	1	1			9		
Pelham	214	2	Fay	Artemas			1	1		1							3		
Pelham	214	3	Griffin	Jonathan		1				2		1					4		
Pelham	214	4	Gray	Adam C.			4		1	1		1		1			8		
Pelham	214	5	Gates	Ebenezar		1				1		1					3		
Pelham	214	6	Gray	Justus	3			1		1			1				6		
Pelham	214	7	Gray	Ebenz Decon	1	1	4	1	1	2	1	1	2	1			15		
Pelham	214	8	Gray	John 2d	3			1	1	1	1	1	1	1			10		
Pelham	214	9	Goodale	Andrew	5			1		1		1					8		
Pelham	214	10	Gray	Matthew		1	1		1		1			1			5		
Pelham	214	11	Gray	Jona & Eliot	1		1	1	1	4	1	1	2	1			13		
Pelham	214	12	Gray	John	2	1		1		2		1		1			8		
Pelham	214	13	Gray	Jeremiah	1			1		3		1					6		
Pelham	214	14	Gray	Danl Decon					1			1		1			3		
Pelham	214	15	Gray	Patrick			1			3			1				5		
Pelham	214	16	Gray	Moses	2			1	2	1		1	1	1			9		
Pelham	214	17	Gray	Thomas		1		1	1		1		1				5		
Pelham	214	18	Gray	Jacob	1	1	1		1		1			1			6		
Pelham	214	19	Montgomery	Thomas	1	1			1	3	3			1			10		
Pelham	214	20	Goodale	John	3			1		1			1				6		
Pelham	214	21	Grout	Joel	1	1		1		2			1				6		
Pelham	214	22	Hood	Jona	1				1			1	1	1			5		
Pelham	214	23	Howard	Silas	1		1		1	2	1	1					8		
Pelham	214	24	Hyde	James	3	1		1		2	1		1				9		
Pelham	214	25	Hackett	Giddeon Jr	1			1	1	1			1	1			6		
Pelham	214	26	Harkins	Daniel	1	1		1		3	2		1				9		
Pelham	214	27	Hamilton	Jos Doct	1	3			1	1		1		1			8		
Pelham	214	28	Hinch	John	1	1		1		1	1			1			6		
Pelham	214	29	Harkins	John	1	1	1		1		2	1	1				8		
Pelham	214	30	Harkins	David	1	1		1			2	1		1			7		
Pelham	214	31	Hubbard	Elijah	2			1		1		1	1				6		
Pelham	214	32	Houston	David	4			1		1	1	1	1	1			10		
Pelham	214	33	Hinds	Nehemiah Doct	1	1	4	1	1	2	2	2		2			16		
Pelham	214	34	Hyde	Samuel	2			1	1	2	1		2				9		
Pelham	214	35	Harkins	Jno Capt	3	2	1	1		2	1	1					11		
Pelham	215	1	Hayden	Thomas	1	1			1	2	1						7		
Pelham	215	2	Hunter	James	1		1	2	2			1		1			8		
Pelham	215	3	Conkey	Andrew	1	1			1	2	1		1				7		
Pelham	215	4	Kingman	Henry Capt	2		1	1			1		1				6		
Pelham	215	5	Brigham	Lycomb	3			1		1		1					6		
Pelham	215	6	Houstin	Robt	3	2	1	1		1		1	1	1			11		
Pelham	215	7	Abercrombie	Robt				1		1			1				3		

TOWN	PG#	LN#	LAST NAME	FIRST NAME	FREE WHITE MALES under 10	10 to 16	16 to 26	26 to 45	45 and over	FREE WHITE FEMALES under 10	10 to 16	16 to 26	26 to 45	45 and over	TOTAL ALL OTHER	TOTAL SLAVES	TOTALS	DISTRICT/ TOWNSHIP	NOTES
Pelham	215	8	Johnson	Adam				1									1		
Pelham	215	9	Jones	Jacob				1						1			2		
Pelham	215	10	Johnson	Hugh	2	1		1				1	2	1			8		
Pelham	215	11	Jewett	Benja	2	1		2		3			1	1			10		
Pelham	215	12	Johnson	Wm	2	1	1	1	1			1	1	1			9		
Pelham	215	13	Johnson	Samuel				1				1	1				3		
Pelham	215	14	Johnson	John	1			1				1					3		
Pelham	215	15	King	Robt	1			1		2			1				5		
Pelham	215	16	King	Peter	1	2		1		3			2				9		
Pelham	215	17	King	James	4	2	1		1			4	1	1			14		
Pelham	215	18	Cook	Abram			1		1	2			1	1			6		
Pelham	215	19	Pelham	Thos	1				1	1			1				4		
Pelham	215	20	Lewis	Wm			1		1			2		2			6		
Pelham	215	21	Lathrop	Isaac	1	2		1			1		1				6		
Pelham	215	22	Leach	Jonathan	2		1	1	1	1		1	1	2			10		
Pelham	215	23	Lothridge	Robt		2				1		1	2	1			7		
Pelham	215	24	Lyscomb	Ebenz				1						1			2		
Pelham	215	25	Lindsey	James	1			1		2		1		1			6		
Pelham	215	26	Lyon	Asaph			1	1					1				3		
Pelham	215	27	Latham	James				1		2	1						4		
Pelham	215	28	McMillen	James		2	3		1	1	1	1		1			10		
Pelham	215	29	McComber	George	1			2		1			1				5		
Pelham	215	30	May	John				1					1				2		
Pelham	215	31	McMillen	Wm	1	3	1	1		3			1				10		
Pelham	215	32	McMillen	John	1	2		1		2		2	1				9		
Pelham	215	33	McMillen	Jeremh	1			1		2		1	1				6		
Pelham	215	34	McMillen	Jona	2	1		1		2	1	1	1	1			10		
Pelham	215	35	McLam	John	3	1	1	1					1				7		
Pelham	215	36	McCullough	Robt Jr			1	1		1			1				4		
Pelham	215	37	McCullock	Henry	2			1		2			1				6		
Pelham	215	38	Munsell	Elisha	1			1	1				2	1			6		
Pelham	216	1	Mills	William				1						1			2		
Pelham	216	2	McCullock	John	2	1		1					1				5		
Pelham	216	3	Pettingale	Margaret						1				1			2		
Pelham	216	4	Newhall	Levi				1		1			1				3		
Pelham	216	5	Winter	David	2			1		1			1				5		
Pelham	216	6	Ormston	Robt				1									1		
Pelham	216	7	Oliver	Andrew Revd	2			1		3	3		1				10		
Pelham	216	8	Oliver	George	1			1		2	1			1			6		
Pelham	216	9	Pebbles	John		1	2		1			1	1	1			7		
Pelham	216	10	Pattern	Christopher	1			1		2	2		1	1			8		
Pelham	216	11	Park	Stewart J			1	1		1	1	1					5		
Pelham	216	12	Packard	Jacob	1	2		1	1	2	1		1	1			10		
Pelham	216	13	Packard	Jona	5			2		2	1		2				12		
Pelham	216	14	Packard	Eliab		1		1						1			3		
Pelham	216	15	Packard	Eliab Jr				1		2			1				4		
Pelham	216	16	Packard	Salmon	2			1					1				4		
Pelham	216	17	Rhoades	Solomon	3	2	1		1	2	1	1					11		
Pelham	216	18	Rankin	John Lt	2	1	2		1		1			1			8		
Pelham	216	19	Rankin	James	1	1		1		5		1	1				10		
Pelham	216	20	Reniff	Abisha	1			1		2			1	1			6		
Pelham	216	21	Sears	Joseph	1		1							1			3		
Pelham	216	22	Smith	Oliver	3	2		1		2	1		1				10		
Pelham	216	23	Southworth	Abia Doct	2			1		1	1		1				6		
Pelham	216	24	Stevenson	Saml	1		1	1				1		1			5		
Pelham	216	25	Sloan	Saml		1	3		1	2	1			1			9		
Pelham	216	26	Sloan	David		2	2		1					2			7		
Pelham	216	27	Shaw	Ezra	1			1				1					3		
Pelham	216	28	Selfridge	Rebekhah										1			1		
Pelham	216	29	Sampson	Nathl Deacn	2		1		1	1	1		1	2			9		
Pelham	216	30	Shaw	Jacob	2			1		1		1					5		
Pelham	216	31	Turner	Levi	2			1		3	2		1				9		
Pelham	216	32	Tower	Isaac	3	2			1	1	1	1	1				10		
Pelham	216	33	Tinkham	Joseph			1	1				1		1			4		
Pelham	216	34	Thompson	Jno Capt				1						1			2		
Pelham	216	35	Thompson	James	1	1	1		1	1		3	1	1			11		
Pelham	216	36	Thompson	Thomas	3	2	2	1				1	1				10		
Pelham	216	37	Tyler	Daniel	2	1	1		1	2		1	1				9		
Pelham	216	38	Thurton	Eliza		1	2					1	2	1			7		
Pelham	217	1	Wood	Levi	1	2		1		2	1		1				8		
Pelham	217	2	Wait	David Ens		1		1			1	1	1				5		
Pelham	217	3	Wright	Ebenz		1		1		1		2		1			6		
Pelham	217	4	Andrews	Stephen	1	2		1		1			2				7		
Pelham	217	5	William	Silas	3	1		1		3	2		1				11		
Pelham	217	6	Wilson	William			2		1	2	2			1			8		
Pelham	217	7	Allen	Samuel	1		1	1					1	1			5		
Pelham	217	8	Walker	Abel Jr	2			1			1						4		
Pelham	217	9	Parmore	Martin	1		1				1						3		
Pelham	217	10	Felton	Benja	1			1		1			1				5		

TOWN	PG#	LN#	LAST NAME	FIRST NAME	FREE WHITE MALES					FREE WHITE FEMALES					TOTAL ALL OTHER	TOTAL SLAVES	TOTALS	DISTRICT/ TOWNSHIP	NOTES
					under 10	10 to 16	16 to 26	26 to 45	45 and over	under 10	10 to 16	16 to 26	26 to 45	45 and over					
Pelham	217	11	Turner	Ellis	2			1		3			1				7		
Pelham	217	12	Taylor	John				1		1		2	1	1			6		
Pelham	217	13	Snow	Barnabas			1					1					2		
Pelham	217	14	Burr	Huldah	1						1	2	2				6		
Pelham	217	15	Darling	John	1	1		1			1	1	1				6		
Pelham	217	16	Chase	Abial	3	1			1	1	1			1			8		
Pelham	217	17	Cranfield	Thomas	1				1	2	1		1				6		
Pelham	217	18	Washburn	Abram	3				1	1	1		1	1			8		
Pelham	217	19	Hannum	David	3		1	1					1				6		
Pelham	217	20	King	Robt	2			1	1	2			1	1			8		
Pelham	217	21	Newhall	David	1			1				1					3		
Pelham	217	22	Abercrombie	Robt	1				1					1			3		
Pelham	217	23	Clarkshun	Mathew	2	1	1	1	1	1	1	4		1			13		

TOWN	PG#	LN#	LAST NAME	FIRST NAME	FREE WHITE MALES					FREE WHITE FEMALES					TOTAL ALL OTHER	TOTAL SLAVES	TOTALS	DISTRICT/ TOWNSHIP	NOTES
					under 10	10 to 16	16 to 26	26 to 45	45 and over	under 10	10 to 16	16 to 26	26 to 45	45 and over					
Plainfield	306	1	Allen	Jacob	2			1		1	3		1				8		
Plainfield	306	2	Burroughs	Simon	3		3		1	1	2	2	1				13		
Plainfield	306	3	Gardner	Benjamin		1	1		1		2	1		1			7		
Plainfield	306	4	Gardner	Jacob	2	2		1		2			1				8		
Plainfield	306	5	Bisbee	Ebenezer	1	1	3		1	2	1	1	1				11		
Plainfield	306	6	Bisbee	Elisha	3	1		1		2	1		1				9		
Plainfield	306	7	Beal	Joseph		2		1		1	2		1				7		
Plainfield	306	8	Beal	Samuel	1		1					1	1				4		
Plainfield	306	9	Burton	David	1	1		1		3			1				7		
Plainfield	306	10	Burton	Nathan					1		2		1	1			5		
Plainfield	306	11	Beal	Amariah		1	2		1	1	1			1			7		
Plainfield	306	12	Bates	Ephrm	2	1		1		1			1				6		
Plainfield	306	13	Beal	Peter	2	1	2	1	1	1			1	1			10		
Plainfield	306	14	Beal	Caleb	3	2	2	1			1		2	1			12		
Plainfield	306	15	Cuningham	John	1	1	1		1					1			5		
Plainfield	306	16	Cuningham	James			1				1						2		
Plainfield	306	17	Clark	Abm	3	1			1	1	1	2	1				10		
Plainfield	306	18	Clark	Jacob	1	1		1		2	2	2	1				10		
Plainfield	306	19	Cook	Andrew			1		1			2		1			5		
Plainfield	306	20	Cook	John			1				2		2				5		
Plainfield	306	21	Colson	Ebenz Jr	3	1	1	1		2	1	1	1				11		
Plainfield	306	22	Colson	Ebenezer				1					1				2		
Plainfield	306	23	Clark	Joseph	2			1		1	2	1	1				8		
Plainfield	306	24	Colson	John	1			1		2			1				5		
Plainfield	306	25	Colson	Mary		1					1			1			3		
Plainfield	306	26	Daniels	John	1			1		2		1	1	1			7		
Plainfield	306	27	Eldridge	Ezekiel		3			1	2				1			7		
Plainfield	307	1	Ford	Andrew	1	1	2		1	4	1		1				11		
Plainfield	307	2	Ford	Solomon			1	1		3			1				6		
Plainfield	307	3	Ford	Elijah		1			1	4	1		1				8		
Plainfield	307	4	Ford	Seth			1	1					1				3		
Plainfield	307	5	Blanchard	Simeon	2			1		2			1				6		
Plainfield	307	6	Fay	Elijah	1			1		2	1			1			6		
Plainfield	307	7	Ford	Thomas					1					1			2		
Plainfield	307	8	Eldridge	Samuel	1			1		1		1	1				5		
Plainfield	307	9	Gloyd	Jacob				1	1	1	1			1			4		
Plainfield	307	10	Gloyd	Asa	1			1	1	4	2		1				10		
Plainfield	307	11	Gloyd	Ephrm	2	1		1		2	1		1				8		
Plainfield	307	12	Gloyd	Joseph	1	1		1		2			1				6		
Plainfield	307	13	Gloyd	Benjm	1			1		2			1				5		
Plainfield	307	14	Hamlin	John	2	1		1		2	1		1				8		
Plainfield	307	15	Howard	James	2	2		1		1			1				7		
Plainfield	307	16	Hollice	Stephen	1	1		1		1	1		1				6		
Plainfield	307	17	Eldridge	Moses	3			1		1			1				6		
Plainfield	307	18	Hawes	Elihah D	1		1					1					3		
Plainfield	307	19	Joy	Isaac		1		1				1	1				4		
Plainfield	307	20	Joy	Caleb		1	2		1			1		1			6		
Plainfield	307	21	Job	Asa	2	1			1	3	3	1					11		
Plainfield	307	22	Joy	Isaac Jun		2		1		1							4		
Plainfield	307	23	Joy	Joseph	2			1		2	1		1				7		
Plainfield	307	24	Joy	Jacob		1		1			1						3		
Plainfield	307	25	Joy	Jacob Jun	2	1		1		2	1		1				8		
Plainfield	307	26	Jones	Ruth			1				1			1			3		
Plainfield	307	27	Karr	Benjm		2	1		2	2	2			1			10		
Plainfield	307	28	Ford	Daniel	3	2	2		1	1	1	1		1			12		
Plainfield	307	29	Josleyn	William	1			1		2			1				5		
Plainfield	307	30	Noyce	Jonathan	2			1		2			1				6		
Plainfield	307	31	Nash	Ebenezer	1			1	1	2			1	1			7		
Plainfield	307	32	Nash	Elijah	2	1		1	1	1	1	1	1	1			10		
Plainfield	307	33	Nash	Jacob	1			1		3	1		2	1			9		
Plainfield	307	34	Nash	Noah	3			1		1		1	1				7		
Plainfield	307	35	Packard	John		1		1			1	1		1			5		
Plainfield	307	36	Packard	Phillip		1		1					1				4		
Plainfield	307	37	Packard	Noah	2	1			2	1	3	1		2			12		
Plainfield	307	38	Packard	Barna	1			1		3	1		1				7		
Plainfield	307	39	Packard	Luther	2	1				1	1		1				6		
Plainfield	307	40	Packard	Perez	1		1	1		1			1	1			6		
Plainfield	307	41	Packard	Timothy	2	1				2			1				7		
Plainfield	307	42	Pool	Abijah	1	1			1	1		1		1			5		
Plainfield	307	43	Pool	Jeptha Jun	1			1		2			1				5		
Plainfield	307	44	Pool	Jeptha	3	1	1	1		2	1			1			10		
Plainfield	308	1	Pool	Jacob				1		3	1		1				6		
Plainfield	308	2	Peirce	Alpheus	2			1		4			1				8		
Plainfield	308	3	Pratt	Solomon	1	1	2		1	2			2				9		
Plainfield	308	4	Pratt	Whitcom	2	1		1		4			1				9		
Plainfield	308	5	Pratt	Daniel	2			1					1				4		
Plainfield	308	6	Perkins	George	2			1		1			1				5		
Plainfield	308	7	Perkins	Jona			1	1		2		1		1			6		
Plainfield	308	8	Orcott	David	1			1		1			1				4		

TOWN	PG#	LN#	LAST NAME	FIRST NAME	under 10	10 to 16	16 to 26	26 to 45	45 and over	under 10	10 to 16	16 to 26	26 to 45	45 and over	TOTAL ALL OTHER	TOTAL SLAVES	TOTALS	DISTRICT/ TOWNSHIP	NOTES
					FREE WHITE MALES					FREE WHITE FEMALES									
Plainfield	308	9	Reed	Cylence		1	1			1	1	1		1			6		
Plainfield	308	10	Robinson	Jeremiah	2	1			1	1	2	2		1			10		
Plainfield	308	11	Richards	James	3	1	1	1			1	1	1				9		
Plainfield	308	12	Robinson	Oliver	2			1		1			1				5		
Plainfield	308	13	Thomson	Luther				1			1		1				3		
Plainfield	308	14	Shaw	Solomon	4		1		1	1		1		1			9		
Plainfield	308	15	Shaw	Thomas	1			1		2			1				5		
Plainfield	308	16	Shaw	Joshua Jun	1			1	1	2			1	1			7		
Plainfield	308	17	Shaw	Joshua		1			1		1	1		1			5		
Plainfield	308	18	Shaw	John	1	1		1		1		1	1				6		
Plainfield	308	19	Shaw	Josiah	1	2		1		1	1		1				7		
Plainfield	308	20	Shaw	Mary		1	1					1	1				4		
Plainfield	308	21	Curtice	Edward			2					1					3		
Plainfield	308	22	Stockwell	Jeremiah		2		1		2		1	1				7		
Plainfield	308	23	Snow	Abijah	3		1		1	1	2	1	1				10		
Plainfield	308	24	Snow	Calvin	1			1		1	1		1				5		
Plainfield	308	25	Streeter	Samuel	3	2	1		1		2	1	1				11		
Plainfield	308	26	Streeter	Asa	1	1	1	1			2		1				7		
Plainfield	308	27	Turril	Amos	1	1		1		1	1		1				6		
Plainfield	308	28	Turril	Oliver			1			2		1					4		
Plainfield	308	29	Torry	Abner			1		1			1	1				4		
Plainfield	308	30	Torry	Jona	2	1	2	1		1	2		1				10		
Plainfield	308	31	Torry	Barnee	1			1		1		1					4		
Plainfield	308	32	Torry	Josiah	1	1	1	1		2	1	1		1			9		
Plainfield	308	33	Towne	Benjm	1	1	1		1		1	2		1			8		
Plainfield	308	34	Vining	George	2	2	2		1	2	1		1				11		
Plainfield	308	35	Whitten	Peter	2	2			1	3		1		1			10		
Plainfield	308	36	Whitten	David	1			1		2		1	1				6		
Plainfield	308	37	White	Caleb	2		1		1			1		2			7		
Plainfield	308	38	White	Zibee		1		1		1			1				4		
Plainfield	308	39	Warner	Abel	3	2		1		2		1	1				10		
Plainfield	308	40	Warner	Elijah	1	1	1	1		2		1	1				8		
Plainfield	308	41	Whitmarsh	Noah				1		3			1				5		
Plainfield	308	42	Stowel	David	2					1			1	1			6		
Plainfield	308	43	Hallock	Moses	3	1	2	1		1			1				9		
Plainfield	308	44	Bates	Abner Jun	1		1					1	1				4		
Plainfield	308	45	Brown	Samuel		1	1		1					1			4		
Plainfield	308	46	Snow	Nathan					1		1			1			3		
Plainfield	309	1	Reed	Ezekiel					1			1		1			3		
Plainfield	309	2	Thayer	Nathll	1	1		1				1		1			5		

TOWN	PG#	LN#	LAST NAME	FIRST NAME	FREE WHITE MALES					FREE WHITE FEMALES					TOTAL ALL OTHER	TOTAL SLAVES	TOTALS	DISTRICT/ TOWNSHIP	NOTES
					under 10	10 to 16	16 to 26	26 to 45	45 and over	under 10	10 to 16	16 to 26	26 to 45	45 and over					
Rowe	198	1	Adams	John			1	1	1			2		1			6		
Rowe	198	2	Allen	Ebenezer	2			1		2			1				6		
Rowe	198	3	Bailey	Israel				1					1				2		
Rowe	198	4	Bullard	Moses	1			1		1		1					4		
Rowe	198	5	Brown	Noah	1	2	2		1		1	2		1			10		
Rowe	198	6	Burton	Asa	1	2			1	2	2	2			1		11		
Rowe	198	7	Benton	Zebulon	3	2	1		1	2	1		1				11		
Rowe	198	8	Brown	John	2			1					1				4		
Rowe	198	9	Blacksbe	Caleb	3	3		1			1		1				9		
Rowe	198	10	Barr	Cornelius	4			1		1			1				7		
Rowe	198	11	Brown	Stephen	3			1		1			1				6		
Rowe	198	12	Barr	Simeon	3			1		1	1		1				7		
Rowe	198	13	Barr	Abijah	2			1	1	2			1	1			8		
Rowe	198	14	Barret	Lemuel			2		1			1		2			6		
Rowe	198	15	Brown	Consider				1	1	1				2			4		
Rowe	198	16	Brown	James				1					1	1			3		
Rowe	198	17	Basset	Charles	1			1			1		1				4		
Rowe	198	18	Bradley	Ebenezer	1	1		1		2			1				6		
Rowe	199	1	Bliss	Jacob		2				3			1				7		
Rowe	199	2	Chapin	Gideon		2	2		1			1		1			7		
Rowe	199	3	Chapin	Gideon Jnr				1				1					2		
Rowe	199	4	Cheney	John	1			1		1		1					4		
Rowe	199	5	Coburn	Jedediah				1		3			1				5		
Rowe	199	6	Carpenter	Timothy	1			1		3			1				6		
Rowe	199	7	Clark	Reuben		1		1		1	1		1				5		
Rowe	199	8	Cheney	Thomas	2			1				1					4		
Rowe	199	9	Colton	Lois	1					1		1					3		
Rowe	199	10	Colton	Silas	1			1		2		1	1				6		
Rowe	199	11	Chapin	Abner		1			1			1		1			6		
Rowe	199	12	Cooper	Issac	1	2		1		2	1	1	1				9		
Rowe	199	13	Cutting	Eliphalet	1			1	1	3	1	1	1				9		
Rowe	199	14	Cross	Jude	2			1		1			1				5		
Rowe	199	15	Corbet	Nathanael			2		1					1			4		
Rowe	199	16	Carpenter	Josiah	1			1		1		1	1				5		
Rowe	199	17	Carey	Stephen				1					1				2		
Rowe	199	18	Chapin	Abner Jnr				1					1				2		
Rowe	199	19	Chapin	Shadrach			2		1	1				1			5		
Rowe	199	20	Chandler	Lewis	1			1		1	1		1				5		
Rowe	199	21	Chapin	Alpheus				1				1					2		
Rowe	199	22	Dodge	Joshua	2		1	1	1	1		2	1				9		
Rowe	199	23	Foster	Asa 2d	1	1	2	1		1			1				7		
Rowe	199	24	Fisher	John		1	1		1	1		2	1				7		
Rowe	199	25	Foster	Nathan	1	1	1		1	2	1	2		1			10		
Rowe	199	26	Foster	Asa	2				1	2	3		1				9		
Rowe	199	27	Foster	Standish			2		1			1		1			5		
Rowe	199	28	Gleason	Stephen	2			1		2	1		1				7		
Rowe	199	29	Gleason	Jonah			4		1	1		1		1			8		
Rowe	199	30	Goodnow	Thomas		1		1		1			1	1			6		
Rowe	199	31	Goodspead	Judah	1	1			1	1				2			7		
Rowe	199	32	Gleason	Aaron	1	2	1	1	1	1		2		1			10		
Rowe	200	1	Haynes	Pardon	2			1		2		1	1				7		
Rowe	200	2	Hibard	John			2		1			1		1			5		
Rowe	200	3	Hill	Ephraim	1		1		1	1		2		1			6		
Rowe	200	4	Hall	Joel	2			1		2			1				6		
Rowe	200	5	Hines	Joel	1		1			1		1					4		
Rowe	200	6	Knolton	Timothy Jr	2	1		1		3			1				8		
Rowe	200	7	Knolton	Timothy			1		1	1		3		1			7		
Rowe	200	8	Kenfield	Herman		1		1		1			1				4		
Rowe	200	9	Langdon	Isaac			2	2	1	1				1			7		
Rowe	200	10	Langdon	Sloman	2			1		1			1	1			6		
Rowe	200	11	Marsh	Jonathan Jr	1			1	1	1		1	1	1			7		
Rowe	200	12	Merril	Theddeus	1		1	1		3	2	1	1				10		
Rowe	200	13	Middleditch	William				1		3	1			1			6		
Rowe	200	14	Mason	Selah	1		1						1				3		
Rowe	200	15	Nims	Ebenezar		1			1		1	1		1			5		
Rowe	200	16	Nims	Samuel		1						1					2		
Rowe	200	17	Nolton	Nathan	3	1		1		1			1	1			8		
Rowe	200	18	Newall	Daniel	1		1			2		1					5		
Rowe	200	19	Nash	Silvester				1						1			2		
Rowe	200	20	Potter	Ambrose	1			1	1	1				1			5		
Rowe	200	21	Potter	Baldwin	4	1		1		1	1		1				9		
Rowe	200	22	Pierpoint	Hezekiah			1	1		1				1			4		
Rowe	200	23	Paine	Asa	1		1						1				3		
Rowe	200	24	Richardson	Amos	1		1						1				3		
Rowe	200	25	Shaw	Gideon	1			2		2			1				6		
Rowe	200	26	Streeter	Moses		1	3		2			1		2			9		
Rowe	200	27	Stone	Benjamin		2		1	1	2	1		1	1			9		
Rowe	200	28	Shumway	Benjan	1	2	2		1	1	1	1		1			10		
Rowe	200	29	Stafford	Job				1		3	2		1				7		

TOWN	PG#	LN#	LAST NAME	FIRST NAME	FREE WHITE MALES					FREE WHITE FEMALES					TOTAL ALL OTHER	TOTAL SLAVES	TOTALS	DISTRICT/ TOWNSHIP	NOTES
					under 10	10 to 16	16 to 26	26 to 45	45 and over	under 10	10 to 16	16 to 26	26 to 45	45 and over					
Rowe	200	30	Slater	Isaac	2	2	1	1		2			1				9		
Rowe	200	31	Smith	Preserved	1	1		1					1				4		
Rowe	200	32	Thomas	Ebenezer		1	1			2			1				5		
Rowe	200	33	Thomas	Archabald			1	1	1	1		2		2			8		
Rowe	200	34	Taylor	Humphrey		1	1		1	1	2	1		1			8		
Rowe	201	1	Taylor	William	1	1	1		1				1				5		
Rowe	201	2	Tuttle	David	3			1		2			1				7		
Rowe	201	3	Tod	Titus	1			1		2			1				5		
Rowe	201	4	Thurber	Ores				1		3			1				5		
Rowe	201	5	Tuttle	Ezra	2			1		1			1				5		
Rowe	201	6	Willson	Henry	1			1	1	1			1	1			6		
Rowe	201	7	White	Nahum	1			1		1		1					4		
Rowe	201	8	Willson	Henry Jnr	4			1		1		1					7		
Rowe	201	9	Wares	Abijah	3		1	1		1	1		1				8		
Rowe	201	10	Willson	Warren	1			1		1		1					4		
Rowe	201	11	Wells	John		2	1		1	1		2	1	1			9		
Rowe	201	12	Warner	Nodiah		1		1						1			3		
Rowe	201	13	Warner	Daniel		1						1					2		

TOWN	PG#	LN#	LAST NAME	FIRST NAME	FREE WHITE MALES					FREE WHITE FEMALES					TOTAL ALL OTHER	TOTAL SLAVES	TOTALS	DISTRICT/ TOWNSHIP	NOTES
					under 10	10 to 16	16 to 26	26 to 45	45 and over	under 10	10 to 16	16 to 26	26 to 45	45 and over					
Russell	137	1	Palmer	Isaac	1	2	1	1	1	2	1	1	1				11		
Russell	137	2	Ward	John	1	1			1	2				1			6		
Russell	137	3	Tran	John				1		2				1			4		
Russell	137	4	Starling	Danl		1		1					1				3		
Russell	137	5	Mallory	Jonah			1		1		1	1		1			5		
Russell	137	6	Mallory	John A	1			1		2	1		1				6		
Russell	137	7	Cohrin	Abner	2		1		1	2	1		1				8		
Russell	137	8	Parks	Henry		1	1	1	1	1	1		1	1			8		
Russell	137	9	Parks	Nathan	3					3	1						8		
Russell	137	10	Trimon	Josiah			1						1				2		
Russell	137	11	Mallory	Jacob				1					1				2		
Russell	137	12	Mallory	Andrews	2			1		4	1		1				10		
Russell	137	13	Phelps	John	2		1		1	2	1	1		1			9		
Russell	137	14	Stebbins	John			1			1			1				3		
Russell	137	15	Stebbins	Danl				1					1				2		
Russell	138	1	Stebbins	Saml			1			2			1				4		
Russell	138	2	Thomas	Lovwell		1	1					1		1			5		
Russell	138	3	Andrews	Richard	1			1		3		1					6		
Russell	138	4	Doolittle	Titus	1		1			1		2	1				7		
Russell	138	5	Doolittle	Titus Jnr	1	1	1	1		2	1	1					8		
Russell	138	6	Rowley	Martin		1		1				1	1				4		
Russell	138	7	Parks	Reuben	2		3	1		2	3	1	1	1			14		
Russell	138	8	Hollady	Josiah		1		1		1			1				4		
Russell	138	9	Hollady	Josiah Jr	5		1	1					1				8		
Russell	138	10	Field	Thomas	4			1		2		1					8		
Russell	138	11	Dewsey	Israel	1			1		1		1					4		
Russell	138	12	Stoncliff	Wm	2	2		1	1	2	1	1	1				11		
Russell	138	13	Smith	Roswell			1			1			1				3		
Russell	138	14	Bishop	Amos				1						1			2		
Russell	138	15	Kirkland	Danl				1		2		1		1			5		
Russell	138	16	Stewart	Andrew	2			1		3	3	1	1				11		
Russell	138	17	Fowler	Josiah	1		1					1					3		
Russell	138	18	Gould	Wm	1			2				1					4		
Russell	138	19	Parks	Elias	1			1			1		1				4		
Russell	138	20	Haise	Jospeh	3			1					1	1			6		
Russell	138	21	Haise	Eli	2					1			1				4		
Russell	138	22	Bradley	Abraham	3	2		1		1	1		1				9		
Russell	138	23	Stiles	Enoch	1		1	1		1		1					5		
Russell	138	24	Webster	Elezor				1					1				2		
Russell	138	25	Hamlin	Harris	2			1		4			1				8		
Russell	138	26	Ward	Amos	1			1		3			1				6		
Russell	138	27	Bishop	Levi	1			1		1		1					4		
Russell	138	28	Hazard	James	3			1		2		1	1		1		9		
Russell	138	29	Hazard	robert	1				1				1	1	1		4		
Russell	138	30	Newton	Elias			1			1		1					3		
Russell	138	31	Langton	Gad	1			1		1			1				4		
Russell	139	1	Chapman	Levi	2			1		2			1				6		
Russell	139	2	Chapman	Saml				1		1			1				3		
Russell	139	3	Loomis	Jacob	2	1	3		1			2		1			10		
Russell	139	4	Carter	Chandler	2			1		1			1				5		
Russell	139	5	Chapman	Benja	2			1		1			1				5		
Russell	139	6	Carter	Nehemiah		3		1				1		1			6		
Russell	139	7	Hewes	Stephen	1			1					1				4		
Russell	139	8	Hewes	Grace Wid.								1		1			2		
Russell	139	9	Moore	David			1			1		1					3		
Russell	139	10	Hewes	Henery			1			1		1					3		
Russell	139	11	Todd	Benjamin	1	3			1	3			1				9		
Russell	139	12	H*ter	Benjamin				1		3	1		1				6		
Russell	139	13	Noble	Silas	3	1		1		2		1	1				9		
Russell	139	14	Tuttle	Abel	1	1	2	1					1	1			7		
Russell	139	15	Bishop	Newman	1	1		1		2	2	1	1				9		
Russell	139	16	Bishop	James			1	1		1			1	1			5		
Russell	139	17	Russel	Richard	2	1	1			1	1	1	1				9		
Russell	139	18	Phelps	Moses	2			1		2	1		1				7		
Russell	139	19	Goudy	Alexander		1		1		3	2		1				8		
Russell	139	20	Granger	Benjamin			1	1		2		1	1	1			7		
Russell	139	21	Newton	Jesse		1	2	1		2		1					8		
Russell	139	22	Williams	Saml	1	1	3		1	1	2	1	1				12		
Russell	139	23	Clark	Thomas	2			1		2		1					6		
Russell	139	24	Blakley	Baley	1	1		1		1			1				6		
Russell	139	25	Sparrey	Isaac				1									1		
Russell	139	26	Clark	Ephraim				1			1	3		1			6		
Russell	139	27	McKein	Abel	2			1		1			1				5		

TOWN	PG#	LN#	LAST NAME	FIRST NAME	FREE WHITE MALES					FREE WHITE FEMALES					TOTAL ALL OTHER	TOTAL SLAVES	TOTALS	DISTRICT/ TOWNSHIP	NOTES
					under 10	10 to 16	16 to 26	26 to 45	45 and over	under 10	10 to 16	16 to 26	26 to 45	45 and over					
Shelburne	319	1	Anderson	John				1	1								2		
Shelburne	319	2	Atherton	Adonijah	1	1	1		2	2	2	1		1			11		
Shelburne	319	3	Allen	Sylvanus	1	1	1		1	2	2	2		1			11		
Shelburne	319	4	Alword	Zevah	2					2			1				6		
Shelburne	319	5	Anderson	David	2	2	1	1		2			1				9		
Shelburne	319	6	Anderson	James	4	1	1	1		1	1		1				10		
Shelburne	319	7	Allis	Ebenz		1			2		1	2		2			8		
Shelburne	319	8	Briggs	Jabez	1	1		1		2	1		1				7		
Shelburne	319	9	Bordwell	Enoch			3										3		
Shelburne	319	10	Blazedel	Willm				1		2				1			4		
Shelburne	319	11	Bliss	Daniel			2		1	2				1			6		
Shelburne	319	12	Bordwell	Abigail		2	2						2	1			7		
Shelburne	319	13	Bull	Willm	3	2	1	1	1		1		2				11		
Shelburne	319	14	Boyd	John	2			1	1		1	1	1	1			8		
Shelburne	319	15	Boyd	Saml	1	1	1		1	1	2	1	1				9		
Shelburne	319	16	Boyd	John Junr	2			1			1		1				5		
Shelburne	320	1	Barnard	Theodore		1	1		1		2		2				7		
Shelburne	320	2	Barnard	David	4	2		1			1		1				9		
Shelburne	320	3	Barnard	Elisha		1		1		2			1				5		
Shelburne	320	4	Bordwell	Gideon	1	1	1		1	1		1	1				7		
Shelburne	320	5	Bordwell	Reuben	2				1	2	1	2		1			9		
Shelburne	320	6	Briggs	Sarah										1			1		
Shelburne	320	7	Bordwell	Philena			2			1	1		1				5		
Shelburne	320	8	Bordwell	Zenas			1			1		1					3		
Shelburne	320	9	Bordwell	Polly	1					1	1		1				4		
Shelburne	320	10	Chapman	John	2	1			1	3	1	1	1				10		
Shelburne	320	11	Clark	Oliver	2	1		1		1			1				6		
Shelburne	320	12	Clark	Alexander	1		1	1	1				2	1			7		
Shelburne	320	13	Crosman	Elkanah					1			1		1			3		
Shelburne	320	14	Crosman	Josiah		1		1		1			1				4		
Shelburne	320	15	Crosman	Barnabas	1			1				1					3		
Shelburne	320	16	Crosman	Zeph		1				1		1					3		
Shelburne	320	17	Child	Ebenz	1	2	1	1			1	2	1				9		
Shelburne	320	18	Child	Asa		1	1	1		1				2			6		
Shelburne	320	19	Chandler	Moses			1	1		4	1		1				8		
Shelburne	320	20	Cook	Rufus				1		1	1		1				4		
Shelburne	320	21	Comstock	Charles		1		1		2			1				5		
Shelburne	320	22	Cummins	Jabez	1			1		1	1		1				5		
Shelburne	320	23	Child	Reuben	3	1		1			1		1				7		
Shelburne	320	24	Cady	Ephraim	1			1		2			1				5		
Shelburne	320	25	Dole	Parker	1		1		1	1	3			1			8		
Shelburne	320	26	Dole	Parker Junr			1			3			1				5		
Shelburne	320	27	Dole	Josiah	3		1			1			1				6		
Shelburne	320	28	Drury	Thomas			1		1		1	1		1			5		
Shelburne	320	29	Dodge	Saml		1	1	1		1				1			5		
Shelburne	320	30	Dodge	Nathl			2	1		1	1			1			6		
Shelburne	320	31	Dodge	Azariah	1			1		1			1				4		
Shelburne	321	1	Dodge	Rebecca	1	2						3		1			7		
Shelburne	321	2	Dole	Isaac	2			1		2			1				6		
Shelburne	321	3	Dole	Moses	1			1		1		1					4		
Shelburne	321	4	Dickinson	James	1	1		1					1				4		
Shelburne	321	5	Dole	Dinsmore	3			1		1		1	1				7		
Shelburne	321	6	Farrah	Nathl		1		1		1	1	2					6		
Shelburne	321	7	Fellows	Joseph			1		1				1	1			4		
Shelburne	321	8	Fitch	Uriah					1			1		1			3		
Shelburne	321	9	Fellows	Saml Jr	3			1					1				5		
Shelburne	321	10	Fellows	John Capt.	2		1		1	2	3			1			10		
Shelburne	321	11	Fellows	Wiilis	3	3	1			2	3	1	1				14		
Shelburne	321	12	Foster	Jeremiah	1		2		1			2	1	1			8		
Shelburne	321	13	Fisk	Levi		1	1		1					2			5		
Shelburne	321	14	Farnsworth	Levi	1			1		1			1				4		
Shelburne	321	15	Fisk	Saml	3		1	1		1	1	1	1		1		10		
Shelburne	321	16	Fisk	Daniel	1	1	1	1	1	2		1	1	1			10		
Shelburne	321	17	Fisk	Simeon	2	3		2	2			3	2	2			16		
Shelburne	321	18	Fellows	Solomon	1	1		1		2		1	1				7		
Shelburne	321	19	Fisk	Ebenz	2	2	1		1	1	1	1		1			10		
Shelburne	321	20	Foster	Nathl					1	2	1			1			5		
Shelburne	321	21	Goodnow	Abner	3			1		1	1	1	1				8		
Shelburne	321	22	Haskel	Roger	2	1			1			3		1			8		
Shelburne	321	23	Holloway	Peter	2	1	2		1	2	1		1				10		
Shelburne	321	24	Hawk	Moses	1	3		1		1	2	1	1				10		
Shelburne	321	25	Hawk	Solomon	1		2	1		3	2	1		1			11		
Shelburne	321	26	Hart	Ebenz	1			1		1			1				4		
Shelburne	322	1	Joyner	Edward					1			2		1			4		
Shelburne	322	2	Joyner	Willm	2			1		1			1				5		
Shelburne	322	3	Jennings	Ephraim	2			1		1			1				5		
Shelburne	322	4	Kemp	Lawrence	1		1	1	1			1	1		1		7		
Shelburne	322	5	Kemp	Willm															
Shelburne	322	6	Kellogg	Julia	3		1	1		2	2		1	1			11		

TOWN	PG#	LN#	LAST NAME	FIRST NAME	FREE WHITE MALES under 10	10 to 16	16 to 26	26 to 45	45 and over	FREE WHITE FEMALES under 10	10 to 16	16 to 26	26 to 45	45 and over	TOTAL ALL OTHER	TOTAL SLAVES	TOTALS	DISTRICT/ TOWNSHIP	NOTES
Shelburne	322	7	Keyes	Joseph	3				1	3	1		1				9		
Shelburne	322	8	Kemp	Daniel		2	1					2		1			6		
Shelburne	322	9	Lasheur	Abner	1		1	1		1		1	1				6		
Shelburne	322	10	Long	Stephen	1	1	1		1	5	1	2	1				13		
Shelburne	322	11	Lawson	John	2		1	1	1	3	1	2		2			13		
Shelburne	322	12	Long	John 2d				1		2			1				4		
Shelburne	322	13	Long	Willm	2	1	3	1		2	1	1	1		3		15		
Shelburne	322	14	Long	David	2	2	1		1	2	2	2		1			13		
Shelburne	322	15	Long	Aaron	1	1		1		3	1	1	1	1			10		
Shelburne	322	16	Long	John Esq		1	2		1	2	1			1			8		
Shelburne	322	17	Loveridge	John				1		1			1				3		
Shelburne	322	18	Liester	Francis				1		3				1			5		
Shelburne	322	19	Loveridge	Edward		1			1	1			1				4		
Shelburne	322	20	Larabbe	Asa	2			1		2			1				6		
Shelburne	322	21	Maynard	William	2			1		2			1				6		
Shelburne	322	22	Merrill	John	3	1		1		1	1		1				8		
Shelburne	322	23	Merrill	Nathl	2		3	1	1	2	1		1	1			12		
Shelburne	322	24	Morton	Joshua	1			1		2		1					5		
Shelburne	322	25	McLatton	Robert L.	1			1		1	1		1				5		
Shelburne	322	26	Martin	Isaac				1						1			2		
Shelburne	322	27	McKee	Willm	2		2		1	1	2	1		1			10		
Shelburne	323	1	Newcomb	Willm	1			1		2			2				6		
Shelburne	323	2	Nims	Elijah				1				1					2		
Shelburne	323	3	Nims	Daniel					1					1			2		
Shelburne	323	4	Nims	Daniel Jr	1			1		3			1				6		
Shelburne	323	5	Nims	Reuben	1		2		1		2	1	1	1			9		
Shelburne	323	6	Nash	Lydia		1		1				1		1			4		
Shelburne	323	7	Nims	Asa	1	1	1	1	1	1	2		1	1			10		
Shelburne	323	8	Packard	Neo. Theophilus		1	1					1	1				4		
Shelburne	323	9	Phinney	David	3	1	2	1		3	2		1				13		
Shelburne	323	10	Peck	Abner	2			1		3			1				7		
Shelburne	323	11	Pebble	Patrick	2			1		1		1					5		
Shelburne	323	12	Riddle	Robert	3			1		2	3		1				10		
Shelburne	323	13	Randall	Benjm	1	1	1		1			1	1				6		
Shelburne	323	14	Randall	Avery	1			1		3	3		1				9		
Shelburne	323	15	Randall	Russell				1					1				2		
Shelburne	323	16	Rice	Jonas			1		1					2			4		
Shelburne	323	17	Ransom	Jabez		1	1		1		1	3		2			9		
Shelburne	323	18	Ransom	Calvin	2	1			1	2	1		1				8		
Shelburne	323	19	Ransom	Joshua				1						1			2		
Shelburne	323	20	Sherman	Christopher	1			1		1			1				4		
Shelburne	323	21	Severance	Joseph	1		1	1		1		2	1				7		
Shelburne	323	22	Smead	Elihu	2	1	1	1		3			1	1			10		
Shelburne	323	23	Senver	Elijah	1	1	1	2	1		1	1		1			9		
Shelburne	323	24	Stratton	Eliphalet			2	2		4		1	1	1			11		
Shelburne	323	25	Skinner	Aaron			2	1	1				1	1			6		
Shelburne	323	26	Severance	Solomon	2	2		1		3		1	1				10		
Shelburne	324	1	Severance	Jonathan	1	1			1	2			1				6		
Shelburne	324	2	Sanders	Aaron			1			2		2		1			6		
Shelburne	324	3	Smith	Saml			1					1	1				3		
Shelburne	324	4	Smead	Saml	2	1	1		1			1		1			7		
Shelburne	324	5	Severance	Saml	2			1		2	2		1				8		
Shelburne	324	6	Smith	Sarah								1		1			2		
Shelburne	324	7	Severance	Martin Jr	2	1	1		2	4	2	2	3	1			18		
Shelburne	324	8	Smith	Edward		1	1		1	2	1	2		1			9		
Shelburne	324	9	Steel	Levi	1		3		1			2		1			8		
Shelburne	324	10	Stewart	John	1		1	1	1	2		1	1	2			10		
Shelburne	324	11	Sibley	David		1			1	1				1			4		
Shelburne	324	12	Seaver	Elijah Jr				1				1					2		
Shelburne	324	13	Stewart	Robert		1			1			1		1			4		
Shelburne	324	14	Sweet	Henry		1	1	1		1		2		1			7		
Shelburne	324	15	Taylor	John		2			1	1	1		1				6		
Shelburne	324	16	Taylor	Stephen		1		1				1	1				4		
Shelburne	324	17	Tennant	Saml	1	2		1	1	2	2		1	1			11		
Shelburne	324	18	Tinney	Saml	3			1					1				5		
Shelburne	324	19	Whitney	Joseph	1				1	2	2	1		1			8		
Shelburne	324	20	White	Aaron			1		1		1	1		1			5		
Shelburne	324	21	Winter	Isaac	1	2	1	1			1	1	1	1			9		
Shelburne	324	22	Wilson	David			2					1					3		
Shelburne	324	23	Wells	David Esq	2	1	1	3	1	1			2	1			12		
Shelburne	324	24	Wells	David Junr		2			1	1	1		1	1			7		
Shelburne	324	25	Wilson	Robert				1					1	1			3		
Shelburne	324	26	Wilson	James	2	1	1		1	2		1	2	1			11		
Shelburne	324	27	Wilson	Thomas	3	1		1				1		1			7		
Shelburne	324	28	Willis	Josiah	2	2			1	1			1				7		
Shelburne	324	29	Waters	John	1		1						1				3		
Shelburne	325	1	Watson	James	1	1	1	1		1		1					6		
Shelburne	325	2	Wright	Saml	1		1					1					3		
Shelburne	325	3	Whitney	Moses	1		1	1		1		1					5		

TOWN	PG#	LN#	HEADS OF HOUSEHOLD		FREE WHITE MALES					FREE WHITE FEMALES					TOTAL ALL OTHER	TOTAL SLAVES	TOTALS	DISTRICT/ TOWNSHIP	NOTES
			LAST NAME	FIRST NAME	under 10	10 to 16	16 to 26	26 to 45	45 and over	under 10	10 to 16	16 to 26	26 to 45	45 and over					
Shelburne	325	4	Warren	Isaac	4			1		1	1		1				8		
Shelburne	325	5	Williams	Dudley	2			1		2			1				6		
Shelburne	325	6	White	Reuben											4		4		

TOWN	PG#	LN#	LAST NAME	FIRST NAME	FREE WHITE MALES under 10	10 to 16	16 to 26	26 to 45	45 and over	FREE WHITE FEMALES under 10	10 to 16	16 to 26	26 to 45	45 and over	TOTAL ALL OTHER	TOTAL SLAVES	TOTALS	DISTRICT/TOWNSHIP	NOTES
Shutesbury	108	1	Adams	Isaiah				1									1		
Shutesbury	108	2	Adams	Asa	1	2		1				1		1			6		
Shutesbury	108	3	Allen	Robert	2	1		1		1	1		1				7		
Shutesbury	108	4	Ashley	James		3	1		1				1				6		
Shutesbury	108	5	Briggs	Ebenezer		1			1		2		1				5		
Shutesbury	108	6	Briggs	Liss	1		1				1						3		
Shutesbury	108	7	Briggs	Wiram	3			1					1				5		
Shutesbury	108	8	Briggs	Josiah L.	2			1		2			1				6		
Shutesbury	108	9	Briggs	John		2	1		1			2	1	1			8		
Shutesbury	108	10	Briggs	Nathaniel	2			1		1		1	1				6		
Shutesbury	108	11	Briggs	Job	2	2		1		3	1		1				10		
Shutesbury	108	12	Burnham	Thomas		1		1				3		1			6		
Shutesbury	108	13	Blanchard	Lemuel	1	1		1	1	1		1	1	1			8		
Shutesbury	108	14	Bearse	Foard	1	1	2		1		1			1			7		
Shutesbury	108	15	Ball	Joseph	2			1	1	1		1					6		
Shutesbury	108	16	Bruce	Ephraim			1		1			1		1			4		
Shutesbury	108	17	Bruce	William	2			1			1		1	1			6		
Shutesbury	108	18	Bridge	Joseph		1			2	1	2		1				7		
Shutesbury	109	1	Butterfield	Abraham	2		1		1	1	1		1				7		
Shutesbury	109	2	Bayley	James	4			1		1	2		1				9		
Shutesbury	109	3	Belcher	Silence	1	1					1		1				4		
Shutesbury	109	4	Carter	Benjamin			1					1					2		
Shutesbury	109	5	Cady	Samuel	3	2		1		2			1				9		
Shutesbury	109	6	Cady	Jeremiah	1	1	1		1	1	2		1				8		
Shutesbury	109	7	Crossett	Edward	3	1	1		1		1	2		1			10		
Shutesbury	109	8	Crocker	Oliver	2			1		1	1		1				6		
Shutesbury	109	9	Crocker	Hesph Jr	2	1		1		1	1		1				7		
Shutesbury	109	10	Conkley	John			1					1					2		
Shutesbury	109	11	Clark	Nathaniel		3	1		1		1			1			7		
Shutesbury	109	12	Caswell	Elijah	1			1		2	1		1				6		
Shutesbury	109	13	Chamberlin	Peter	1			1		4		1	1				8		
Shutesbury	109	14	Carver	John	2			1		1			1				5		
Shutesbury	109	15	Crosman	Asa	3			1					1				5		
Shutesbury	109	16	Crosbee	Levi				1			1						2		
Shutesbury	109	17	Cummings	Benja	1			1		2			1				5		
Shutesbury	109	18	Cummings	David	3			1		1			1				6		
Shutesbury	109	19	Carter	John	1			1		2			1				5		
Shutesbury	109	20	Cunningham	John	1		1	1						1			4		
Shutesbury	109	21	Dillingham	Paul	1	2		1		2	2		1				9		
Shutesbury	109	22	Dane	Benjamin	2			1		1	1		1				6		
Shutesbury	109	23	Eager	Noah	2			1		1	1		1				6		
Shutesbury	109	24	Edson	Elijah	1			1		2			1				5		
Shutesbury	109	25	Felton	Benjamin		1	2		1		1		1				6		
Shutesbury	109	26	Felton	Amos		1	1		1		2		1				6		
Shutesbury	109	27	Fish	Ezra	2	1		1		1	2	1	1				9		
Shutesbury	109	28	Gold	Sewall		1					1						2		
Shutesbury	109	29	Giles	James	1			1			1						3		
Shutesbury	109	30	Grout	John				1					1				2		
Shutesbury	109	31	Goodman	William				1		1			1				3		
Shutesbury	109	32	Green	Samuel		1					2						3		
Shutesbury	109	33	Hill	Noah		1	2		1	1			1				6		
Shutesbury	109	34	Hamilton	Andrew		1	1		1		1		1				5		
Shutesbury	109	35	Hamilton	Patrick	2	1			1	1		1	1				7		
Shutesbury	109	36	Haskins	Joseph	3	1			1	2		2	1	2			12		
Shutesbury	110	1	Haskins	Job	1		1						1				3		
Shutesbury	110	2	Haskell	John	1	1		1			1		1				5		
Shutesbury	110	3	Haskell	Levi			1			2	1						4		
Shutesbury	110	4	Henry	Luther		1		1		3			1				6		
Shutesbury	110	5	Hoar	Luther		1		1		3			1				6		
Shutesbury	110	6	Hoar	Warren	1			1					1				3		
Shutesbury	110	7	Hodge	Asa	1	1	1		1				1				5		
Shutesbury	110	8	Hunt	Gardner	2			1		2			1				6		
Shutesbury	110	9	Hunt	William	2			1		1			1				5		
Shutesbury	110	10	Hunt	William 2d	1			1		2			1				5		
Shutesbury	110	11	Jones	Levi				1					1				2		
Shutesbury	110	12	Jones	Josiah	1	1		1		2	1		1				7		
Shutesbury	110	13	Johnson	John	1	2	3		1	1	1		1				10		
Shutesbury	110	14	Johnson	Hugh M.	2			1		2			1				6		
Shutesbury	110	15	Juckets	Daniel				1		1				1			3		
Shutesbury	110	16	Juckets	Daniel Jr	2	1		1		1			1				6		
Shutesbury	110	17	Jackson	Peter											5		5		
Shutesbury	110	18	Kimball	Ebenezer	2			1					1				4		
Shutesbury	110	19	Kimball	Boyce					1					1			2		
Shutesbury	110	20	Kimball	Boyce Jr	4	2	1		1		1	1		1			11		
Shutesbury	110	21	King	Ebenezer	1			1		1			1				4		
Shutesbury	110	22	Kibbey	Thomas	1			1					1				3		
Shutesbury	110	23	Kellogg	Samuel	3			1		2			1				7		
Shutesbury	110	24	Leonard	Archelous		1		2		1		1	1				6		
Shutesbury	110	25	Leonard	Archs Jr	2							1					4		

TOWN	PG#	LN#	LAST NAME	FIRST NAME	FWM under 10	FWM 10 to 16	FWM 16 to 26	FWM 26 to 45	FWM 45 and over	FWF under 10	FWF 10 to 16	FWF 16 to 26	FWF 26 to 45	FWF 45 and over	TOTAL ALL OTHER	TOTAL SLAVES	TOTALS	DISTRICT/ TOWNSHIP	NOTES
Shutesbury	110	26	Leonard	Simeon	2	2		1		2			1				8		
Shutesbury	110	27	Leonard	Ezra	2			1			1		1	2			7		
Shutesbury	110	28	Lock	Increase			1					1					2		
Shutesbury	110	29	Livermore	Elijah	3			1		1			1				6		
Shutesbury	110	30	Lewis	Joseph	1			1					1				5		
Shutesbury	110	31	Lumbard	Benja	1				1		2	1		1			6		
Shutesbury	110	32	Macomber	Cyrus			1						1				2		
Shutesbury	110	33	Mayo	Moses	1	1		1	1		2	2	1				9		
Shutesbury	110	34	Macomber	George		2	2	1				2	1				8		
Shutesbury	111	1	Macomber	John				1		2			1				4		
Shutesbury	111	2	Morse	Amasa		1	1	1						1			4		
Shutesbury	111	3	Morse	Abel		1				1			1				3		
Shutesbury	111	4	Maynard	Oliver	1		1			1			1				4		
Shutesbury	111	5	Marvell	Parkell	1		1					1					3		
Shutesbury	111	6	Ney	Jonathan		1	1	1		1	1	1	1				7		
Shutesbury	111	7	Newton	John	1		1			3			1				6		
Shutesbury	111	8	Peirce	Jonathan		3		1			2		1				7		
Shutesbury	111	9	Peirce	John				1					1				2		
Shutesbury	111	10	Peirce	Nathan		1		1		4	1	1	1				9		
Shutesbury	111	11	Pike	Aaron	1			1		2			1				5		
Shutesbury	111	12	Powers	John				1		2			1				4		
Shutesbury	111	13	Powers	Asa		1	1	1						1			4		
Shutesbury	111	14	Powers	Stephen	1	1	2	1		3	1	1		1			11		
Shutesbury	111	15	Pratt	Micah				1						1			2		
Shutesbury	111	16	Pratt	Artemas	2	1		1		1			1				7		
Shutesbury	111	17	Pratt	Abraham	4			1		1			2				8		
Shutesbury	111	18	Pratt	David		2		1		3	1	1		1			9		
Shutesbury	111	19	Pierpont	William	1			1		3			1				6		
Shutesbury	111	20	Peckens	David	2			1		2	1		1				7		
Shutesbury	111	21	Peirce	Peleg	1		1					1					3		
Shutesbury	111	22	Pratt	Micah Jr	1		1	1						1			4		
Shutesbury	111	23	Pratt	Phinehas			1			3			1				5		
Shutesbury	111	24	Richardson	Joseph	1	1	1	1			1			1			6		
Shutesbury	111	25	Richardson	Zacheus			1				1						2		
Shutesbury	111	26	Richards	Calvin	1	1		1		3		1	1	1			9		
Shutesbury	111	27	Richards	Samuel	3			1		1	1		1				7		
Shutesbury	111	28	Ray	Benjamin	3	1		1		2			1	1			9		
Shutesbury	111	29	Reed	Benjamin		2	1	1					1	1			6		
Shutesbury	111	30	Reed	Benja Jr	3			1		2			1				7		
Shutesbury	111	31	Reed	John	1		1						1				3		
Shutesbury	111	32	Raymond	Thaddeus	2			1		1			1				5		
Shutesbury	111	33	Reynolds	Ebenezer	1			1		1			1				4		
Shutesbury	111	34	Reynolds	Jairus	2			1		2			1				6		
Shutesbury	111	35	Reynolds	James		2		1				1	1	1			6		
Shutesbury	112	1	Richardson	Samuel			2						1				3		
Shutesbury	112	2	Raymond	Asa	4			1		1			1	1			8		
Shutesbury	112	3	Reynolds	Ezra	1			1		2			1				5		
Shutesbury	112	4	Rogers	Abijah	1			1				1					3		
Shutesbury	112	5	Reynolds	Josiah	3			1		1			1	1			7		
Shutesbury	112	6	Smith	Job	3	2			1		1	2		1			10		
Shutesbury	112	7	Smith	Nathl			1	1		2		1		2			7		
Shutesbury	112	8	Spear	Moses	1			1	1	1			3	1			8		
Shutesbury	112	9	Spear	Eli	2	2	2	1		2			1				10		
Shutesbury	112	10	Spear	Luther	5	4		1				2	1				13		
Shutesbury	112	11	Spear	Moses Jr	1	3		1		2	1		1				9		
Shutesbury	112	12	Spear	Stephen	?		1			2	3		1				9		
Shutesbury	112	13	Stirtevant	James		1		1		2			1				5		
Shutesbury	112	14	Stirtevant	Archl				1		1			1				3		
Shutesbury	112	15	Sampson	Peter	3			1		2			1				7		
Shutesbury	112	16	Stratton	Nathl	2			1		1			1				5		
Shutesbury	112	17	Shaw	Darling	2	1	1	1		3	2		1				11		
Shutesbury	112	18	Sumner	John D.		1		1				2	2	1			7		
Shutesbury	112	19	Smalledge	Joseph			1	1				2					4		
Shutesbury	112	20	Sanders	Nathan	2			1					1				4		
Shutesbury	112	21	Smith	Samuel		1						1					2		
Shutesbury	112	22	Stockwell	Elisha	2			1					1				4		
Shutesbury	112	23	Sinclair	Francis	1	1			1	1	1		1				6		
Shutesbury	112	24	Thayer	Jesse	1				1				1	1			4		
Shutesbury	112	25	Thayer	Stephen			1			1	1						3		
Shutesbury	112	26	Upton	Benjamin		1			1	3	1			1			7		
Shutesbury	112	27	Vaughan	Thomas		1		1				1		1			4		
Shutesbury	112	28	Vaughan	Ebenezer	1	1		1		2	2		1				8		
Shutesbury	112	29	Winter	Jesse	1	1		1		2				1			6		
Shutesbury	112	30	Winter	Benja	1	1		1		3	1			1			8		
Shutesbury	112	31	Ward	William			2					1					3		
Shutesbury	112	32	Wilber	John	1	1		1				1		1			5		
Shutesbury	112	33	Wheeler	Ephraim	2	2	1	1		1		2	1	1			11		
Shutesbury	112	34	Wood	Samuel	2	2			1			2		1			8		
Shutesbury	113	1	Works	Daniel				1		3			1				5		

TOWN	PG#	LN#	HEADS OF HOUSEHOLD		FREE WHITE MALES					FREE WHITE FEMALES					TOTAL ALL OTHER	TOTAL SLAVES	TOTALS	DISTRICT/ TOWNSHIP	NOTES
			LAST NAME	FIRST NAME	under 10	10 to 16	16 to 26	26 to 45	45 and over	under 10	10 to 16	16 to 26	26 to 45	45 and over					
Shutesbury	113	2	White	John	3	1		1		2	1	1	1				10		
Shutesbury	113	3	Wilber	John Jr			1			1		1					3		
Shutesbury	113	4	Winch	John	1			1					1				3		
Shutesbury	113	5	Wier	William					1			1		1			3		
Shutesbury	113	6	Wilber	Elias			1					1					2		
Shutesbury	113	7	Young	Mercy									1				1		

| TOWN | PG# | LN# | HEADS OF HOUSEHOLD | | FREE WHITE MALES | | | | | FREE WHITE FEMALES | | | | | TOTAL ALL OTHER | TOTAL SLAVES | TOTALS | DISTRICT/ TOWNSHIP | NOTES |
			LAST NAME	FIRST NAME	under 10	10 to 16	16 to 26	26 to 45	45 and over	under 10	10 to 16	16 to 26	26 to 45	45 and over					
South Brimfield	275	1	Walker	Marshal	3	1	1	1		1		1	1				9		
South Brimfield	275	2	Needham	Catherine Wid	1		1					1	1				4		
South Brimfield	275	3	Nelson	Timothy	1			1		3	3		1	1			10		
South Brimfield	275	4	Smith	James		1	1		1				1				5		
South Brimfield	275	5	Converse	Josiah	2			1		2			1				6		
South Brimfield	275	6	Howard	Josiah	2			1		3			1	1			8		
South Brimfield	275	7	Coddington	Elijah Rev.					1			1		1			3		
South Brimfield	275	8	Robinson	Amariah	3			1					1				5		
South Brimfield	275	9	Fisk	Hezh Capt.	3	2	1	1			1	2	1				11		
South Brimfield	275	10	Wight	Polly Wid	2							1	1	1			5		
South Brimfield	275	11	Munger	Darius Esq	1		1		1	1		1	1	1			7		
South Brimfield	275	12	Weatherly	Wm		2		1						1			4		
South Brimfield	275	13	Fisk	David		1							1				2		
South Brimfield	275	14	Wheeler	James		2		1		2	2	1	1				9		
South Brimfield	275	15	Snow	Amos				1					1				2		
South Brimfield	275	16	Rogers	Abijah	1			1		2			1				5		
South Brimfield	275	17	Storrs	Chester	1			1					1	1			4		
South Brimfield	275	18	Moulton	Ebenezer		1			1			2	1				5		
South Brimfield	275	19	Wales	Royal				1		1			1				3		
South Brimfield	275	20	Babcock	Jeremiah			1		1				1				3		
South Brimfield	275	21	Davis	Abijah		1		1		2			1				5		
South Brimfield	276	1	Munger	John Deac	1	1	1	1	1			1		2			8		
South Brimfield	276	2	Andruss	Robert		2	1	1		2		1	1				8		
South Brimfield	276	3	Simpson	Edward	1			1		2			1				5		
South Brimfield	276	4	Moulton	Calvin	1	1		1		2		2	1				8		
South Brimfield	276	5	Nichols	Malachi	1	1	1		1	3	1	1	1				10		
South Brimfield	276	6	Rogers	Nathaniel		1		1			1	1		2			6		
South Brimfield	276	7	Ames	Rebecca	1								1				2		
South Brimfield	276	8	Fenton	Timothy		1		1					1				3		
South Brimfield	276	9	Fenton	Wm					1					1			2		
South Brimfield	276	10	Alden	Josiah	1		1		1	1				1			5		
South Brimfield	276	11	Snow	James	2			1		2	1		1				7		
South Brimfield	276	12	Robinson	Nathan	2			1		1			1				5		
South Brimfield	276	13	Nelson	Eli	1			1					1	1			4		
South Brimfield	276	14	Walker	James		1		1						1			3		
South Brimfield	276	15	Walker	Benja				1				1	1				3		
South Brimfield	276	16	Walker	Benja Jr	1			1				1					3		
South Brimfield	276	17	Richmond	Jonathan C	1			1			1		1				4		
South Brimfield	276	18	Pease	Jno		1		1						1			3		
South Brimfield	276	19	Walker	Joseph	3			1					1				5		
South Brimfield	276	20	Vineka	Andrew	2	1		1		1		1		1			7		
South Brimfield	276	21	Edson	Caleb	2	1	1	1		4	1		1				11		
South Brimfield	276	22	Case	Stephen	3			1		1			1				6		
South Brimfield	276	23	Pratt	Ebenezer		2	1	1		3	1	1	1				10		
South Brimfield	276	24	Shaw	John	3		1	1				1	1				7		
South Brimfield	276	25	Fenton	Eunice						1			1				2		
South Brimfield	276	26	Grinell	Samuel		1		1		1				1			4		
South Brimfield	276	27	Needham	Jeremiah			1	1		1		1		1			5		
South Brimfield	276	28	Green	Daniel		2		1				2		1			6		
South Brimfield	276	29	McIn*	Abraham	1			1		1		1	1				5		
South Brimfield	276	30	Needham	Jasper				1						1			2		
South Brimfield	276	31	Johnson	Stephen	1			1				1					3		
South Brimfield	276	32	Shaw	Samuel	2	2		1					1				6		
South Brimfield	276	33	Fisk	Asa Capt.	2	1	1	1					1	1			7		
South Brimfield	276	34	Gage	Thaddeus	2	1		1				1	1	1			7		
South Brimfield	276	35	Hodges	Eliphalet	1		1	1		3	?		1	1			10		
South Brimfield	276	36	Fuller	Phinehas		1		1		3			1				6		
South Brimfield	276	37	Shaw	Julius	1			1		1			1				4		
South Brimfield	276	38	Dennison	Twiss	1			1				1					3		
South Brimfield	276	39	Winchester	Ruth Wid										1			1		
South Brimfield	276	40	Tiffany	James	1	1	2	1		2	1	1	1				10		
South Brimfield	276	41	Needham	Wid Hannah		1	2					1		1			5		
South Brimfield	276	42	Welles	Ezekiel	1		1		1	2	2						7		
South Brimfield	277	1	Needham	Humphrey	1		2	1		3		1					8		
South Brimfield	277	2	Needham	Stephen	2	1		1		2		1					7		
South Brimfield	277	3	Perry	Abner	2	1			1	1	1	2	1				9		
South Brimfield	277	4	Willard	Samuel		1		1		3			1				6		
South Brimfield	277	5	Perry	Joseph	1		1		1			1		1			7		
South Brimfield	277	6	Perry	Micah	1			1		2		2		1			6		
South Brimfield	277	7	Perry	Isaac	2	1		1		2			1				7		
South Brimfield	277	8	Rogers	Stephen	1			1		1	1	1	1				6		
South Brimfield	277	9	Hodges	David				1		1			1	2			5		
South Brimfield	277	10	Sherman	Timothy	1	1			1			2	1	1			7		
South Brimfield	277	11	Blood	Isaiah					1					1			2		
South Brimfield	277	12	Blood	Simeon	1			1		2	1			1			6		
South Brimfield	277	13	Blood	Patty Wid	1							1		1			3		
South Brimfield	277	14	Nelson	George	3			1				1		1			6		
South Brimfield	277	15	Green	Robert				1		3				1			5		
South Brimfield	277	16	Munger	Solomon	1	1	1		1			2		1			7		

TOWN	PG#	LN#	HEADS OF HOUSEHOLD		FREE WHITE MALES					FREE WHITE FEMALES					TOTAL ALL OTHER	TOTAL SLAVES	TOTALS	DISTRICT/ TOWNSHIP	NOTES
			LAST NAME	FIRST NAME	under 10	10 to 16	16 to 26	26 to 45	45 and over	under 10	10 to 16	16 to 26	26 to 45	45 and over					
South Brimfield	277	17	Alden	Elijah	2	1		1			1	1	1				7		
South Brimfield	277	18	Moulton	Robert	3	1			1		1			1			7		
South Brimfield	277	19	Winchester	Benjamin	4				1	1	1		1				8		
South Brimfield	277	20	Ward	Benjamin		1			1			2		1			5		
South Brimfield	277	21	Darby	Alpheus	2	1		1		1	1	1	1				8		
South Brimfield	277	22	Gardner	S. Charles			1		1				1				3		
South Brimfield	277	23	Ames	Ebenezer					1				1				2		
South Brimfield	277	24	Gardner	William			1	1	1				1				4		
South Brimfield	277	25	Gardner	Humphrey	3			1		2	1		1				8		
South Brimfield	277	26	Gardner	Steward	2			1		3	1		1				8		
South Brimfield	277	27	Ames	Ebenezer Jr	2			1		1			1				5		
South Brimfield	277	28	Green	Sarah Wid										3			3		
South Brimfield	277	29	Green	Joel	1	1			1		1	2		1			7		
South Brimfield	277	30	Gardner	S. Josiah	1	2	1	1		1		1	1				8		
South Brimfield	277	31	Nutting	David	2		2		2	1	1	1	1	2			12		
South Brimfield	277	32	Nutting	Eben	1		1					1					3		
South Brimfield	277	33	Hassett	James		2			1	3	1		1				8		
South Brimfield	277	34	Nellson	Solomon	1	1			1	1				1			4		
South Brimfield	277	35	Badger	Nathan	2			1		1			1	1			6		
South Brimfield	277	36	Potter	Abijah	2	2		1		2	1		1				9		
South Brimfield	277	37	Wheeler	James		2			1	2	2			1			8		
South Brimfield	277	38	Holten	Asa	2				1	2		1	1				7		
South Brimfield	277	39	Dimmuck	Gideon			1		1	1	1		1				5		
South Brimfield	277	40	Nelson	Samuel			1		1	2			1				5		
South Brimfield	277	41	Nellson	Hezh	1			1		1		1					4		
South Brimfield	277	42	Washburn	Ebenz	3	2		1		1	1		1				9		
South Brimfield	278	1	Snell	Isaiah		1		1		3	1		1				7		
South Brimfield	278	2	Snell	Wid									2	1			3		
South Brimfield	278	3	Rogers	Joel Dr.				1					1				2		
South Brimfield	278	4	Rogers	Darius	2	1		1					1				5		
South Brimfield	278	5	Rogers	John				1			1	1					3		
South Brimfield	278	6	Fisk	Asa Jun			1			2			1				4		

TOWN	PG#	LN#	LAST NAME	FIRST NAME	FREE WHITE MALES					FREE WHITE FEMALES					TOTAL ALL OTHER	TOTAL SLAVES	TOTALS	DISTRICT/TOWNSHIP	NOTES
					under 10	10 to 16	16 to 26	26 to 45	45 and over	under 10	10 to 16	16 to 26	26 to 45	45 and over					
South Hadley	248	1	Lamb	Daniel Jr		1		2		1		1					5		
South Hadley	248	2	Smith	Jonathan	3	1	2		1					2			9		
South Hadley	248	3	Lamb	Daniel	2		1		1	2			2				8		
South Hadley	248	4	Taylor	Oliver					1			1		1			3		
South Hadley	248	5	Taylor	Moses	3			1		2			1				7		
South Hadley	248	6	Richardson	Robert	1				1				1	1			4		
South Hadley	248	7	Parsons	Ebenezer		1			1		2	2		1			7		
South Hadley	248	8	Pomeroy	Simeon		2	1	1			1	1	1	1			8		
South Hadley	248	9	Smith	Luther	2			1	1	2	1		1				8		
South Hadley	248	10	Hix	Jona		1	4	1		3	2		1				12		
South Hadley	248	11	Bennett	John	1	1	4	1		3	1	1	1				13		
South Hadley	248	12	Day	Justin		1						1					2		
South Hadley	248	13	Loomer	Frederick	1	1		1					1				4		
South Hadley	248	14	Taylor	Elihu			1						1				2		
South Hadley	248	15	Robinson	Jacob	1			2		1			1				5		
South Hadley	248	16	Taylor	William				1					1				2		
South Hadley	248	17	Taylor	Wm Junr			2	1					2				5		
South Hadley	248	18	White	Enoch Dr		2	1	1	1	1	1	1		2			10		
South Hadley	248	19	Lamb	Ezekiel	1	1	1	2		1			2				8		
South Hadley	248	20	Judd	Levi	2	1		1		2	1		1				8		
South Hadley	248	21	Judd	Allen	2			1	1			1					5		
South Hadley	248	22	Taylor	Dorothy Wd			4					2		1			7		
South Hadley	249	1	Bridges	John		1			1	1	1		1				5		
South Hadley	249	2	Judd	Thomas Jr		1			1	3	1	1	1				8		
South Hadley	249	3	Smith	Darus	1	1	2		1	3	2		1				11		
South Hadley	249	4	Smith	Perez	3	2	2		1			1		1			10		
South Hadley	249	5	Smith	Ephraim		1	1		1	1	1		1				6		
South Hadley	249	6	Smith	Silas Dr	2		3		1	2	1		1				10		
South Hadley	249	7	White	Simeon	1	1	1	1		1	1		1				7		
South Hadley	249	8	Gaylord	Oliver		1		1		1	2	1		1			7		
South Hadley	249	9	Church	Zenas			1			1		1		1			4		
South Hadley	249	10	Fuller	Asabel				1					1				2		
South Hadley	249	11	Goodman	Calvin	1		1					1					3		
South Hadley	249	12	Goodman	Huldah Wd			1						1				2		
South Hadley	249	13	Lamb	Pendleton	1		1					1					3		
South Hadley	249	14	Taylor	Comfort Wd									1				1		
South Hadley	249	15	Lamb	Rowell	2		1			2			1				6		
South Hadley	249	16	McMaster	Wd	1								1				2		
South Hadley	249	17	Bellows	Elihu	3			1		1		1					6		
South Hadley	249	18	Alvard	Samuel	1	2	2	1		3	1		1				11		
South Hadley	249	19	Brewster	Jesse	1		1	1		1	1	1	1				7		
South Hadley	249	20	Barns	William		1			1	1	2		1				6		
South Hadley	249	21	Day	Ezra		1	3		1	1	1		1	1			9		
South Hadley	249	22	Alvard	Azariah Capt.	1		1		1		1			1			5		
South Hadley	249	23	White	Aaron	1	1			1			1		1			5		
South Hadley	249	24	Day	Asa	1			1		4			1				7		
South Hadley	249	25	Alvard	Gideon		1	1		1				1	1			5		
South Hadley	249	26	Thorington	Joseph	1			1		1	1		1				5		
South Hadley	249	27	Negro	Freeman											6		6		
South Hadley	249	28	Bills	Sheribiah	1		1	1		2	1		1				7		
South Hadley	249	29	Collins	James		1	2	1		1				1			6		
South Hadley	249	30	Graves	Aaron	3		2		1	1		1					8		
South Hadley	249	31	Preston	St Gardner	1				1	2			1				5		
South Hadley	249	32	Preston	Job	?			1					1	1			5		
South Hadley	249	33	Mitchell	Philip											3		3		
South Hadley	249	34	Kellogg	Amos	1	1			1	2			1				6		
South Hadley	249	35	Kellogg	Ebenezer				1					1				2		
South Hadley	249	36	Kellogg	Joseph		1		1		1		1	1				5		
South Hadley	249	37	Kellogg	Eliakim	3			1		2	1		1				8		
South Hadley	249	38	Smith	Eli				1				1					2		
South Hadley	249	39	Hilyard	Anna Miss								1	2				3		
South Hadley	249	40	Hilyard	Timothy			1		1			1	1				4		
South Hadley	249	41	Church	Josiah	1	1				3	1			1			8		
South Hadley	249	42	Burr	Benjamin	1			1				1					4		
South Hadley	249	43	Ingraham	Nathaniel	1	2	1		1		1	2					9		
South Hadley	249	44	Ingraham	Ebenr			1			1		1					3		
South Hadley	250	1	Church	John				1					1				2		
South Hadley	250	2	Church	Pliny		1				1	1		1				4		
South Hadley	250	3	Snow	Ebenezer		1			1				1				3		
South Hadley	250	4	Bailey	Noah		1		1	1	2	1						6		
South Hadley	250	5	Morgan	Nathaniel	2		2	1		1				1			7		
South Hadley	250	6	Bartlett	Aaron	1		2	1			1		1	3			9		
South Hadley	250	7	Preston	Samuel	2	2		2		1	2	2	2	1			14		
South Hadley	250	8	Preston	Benoni				1					1				2		
South Hadley	250	9	White	Ebenezer	2			1		2			1	1			7		
South Hadley	250	10	Wait	Martin Jr	1			1		1			1				4		
South Hadley	250	11	Wait	Martin		1			1			2		1			5		
South Hadley	250	12	Ely	Caleb				1						1			2		
South Hadley	250	13	Haight	Justus			1			1		2					4		

TOWN	PG#	LN#	LAST NAME	FIRST NAME	FREE WHITE MALES					FREE WHITE FEMALES					TOTAL ALL OTHER	TOTAL SLAVES	TOTALS	DISTRICT/ TOWNSHIP	NOTES
					under 10	10 to 16	16 to 26	26 to 45	45 and over	under 10	10 to 16	16 to 26	26 to 45	45 and over					
South Hadley	250	14	Williams	Eleazer	1					5			1				7		
South Hadley	250	15	Alvard	Justin	1			1		1			1				4		
South Hadley	250	16	Goodman	Ithamar	1	1		1		3			1				7		
South Hadley	250	17	Smith	Mary									1				1		
South Hadley	250	18	White	Samuel			1	1			1	2		1			6		
South Hadley	250	19	Nash	Elihu				1						1			2		
South Hadley	250	20	White	Joel	1			1		1			1				4		
South Hadley	250	21	Alvard	Bezaleel	2	1	2	1		1			1	1			9		
South Hadley	250	22	Ayman	Solomon	1								1	1			3		
South Hadley	250	23	Bissell	Elihu Dr		1		1				1	1				4		
South Hadley	250	24	Snow	Josiah				1						1			2		
South Hadley	250	25	Judd	Elijah	1			1		2			1				5		
South Hadley	250	26	Stebbins	Daniel Dr		1		1				1	1				4		
South Hadley	250	27	Hayes	Joel Revd		2			1	2	1	1	1				8		
South Hadley	250	28	Goodman	Petey	3	2	1	1		1			1				9		
South Hadley	250	29	White	Joseph	2		1	2		1	1	1	1				9		
South Hadley	250	30	Doane	James	1		1	1		3		1	1				8		
South Hadley	250	31	Judd	Reuben Lt		1			1			2	1	1			6		
South Hadley	250	32	Moody	Joseph Jr	2	1		1		1		1	1				7		
South Hadley	250	33	Henry	Ammah										1			1		
South Hadley	250	34	Pendergrass	Peter				1			1			1			3		
South Hadley	250	35	Crowfoot	Daniel				1						1			2		
South Hadley	250	36	Woodworth	James	2	1		1		4	1		1				10		
South Hadley	250	37	Taylor	Oliver Jun	2			1		2		1	1				7		
South Hadley	250	38	White	Thomas				1									1		
South Hadley	250	39	Stickney	John		2		1						1			4		
South Hadley	250	40	Taylor	Noah	2			1		1			1				5		
South Hadley	250	41	Taylor	Reuben		1	1	1					2	1			6		
South Hadley	250	42	Taylor	Reuben Jr	3		1						1				5		
South Hadley	250	43	Pike	David	2			1		2			1				6		
South Hadley	250	44	Woodbridge	Jahleel		1	1		2		1		1				6		
South Hadley	250	45	Woodbridge	Ruggles Esq		2	2	1				1		1			7		
South Hadley	250	46	White	Abigail Wd								2	1				3		
South Hadley	251	1	White	Reuben		1		1		1	1		1				5		
South Hadley	251	2	Mitchell	Mary Wd		1							1	1			3		
South Hadley	251	3	White	Josiah Jr		1	1	1		3	3		1				10		
South Hadley	251	4	Clark	Asa	2		1	1					1	2			7		
South Hadley	251	5	Montague	Timothy				1		1		2		1			5		
South Hadley	251	6	Rumsill	Asa				1		3	1	1					6		
South Hadley	251	7	Goodman	Nathan			1						1				2		
South Hadley	251	8	White	Josiah Maj		1		1				1	1	1			5		
South Hadley	251	9	White	Eldad	4	1		1		1			1				8		
South Hadley	251	10	Moody	Noah	2	1			1	2	1		1	1			9		
South Hadley	251	11	Kirkland	Samuel		1		1				2		1			5		
South Hadley	251	12	Montague	Elijah	2	1	1	1		1	1	1	1	1			10		
South Hadley	251	13	Wheldon	Jonathan	1			1		2	2		1				7		
South Hadley	251	14	Smith	Hezekiah		1	1		1			1		1			5		
South Hadley	251	15	Moody	Josiah			2		1					1			5		
South Hadley	251	16	Moody	Sylvester	2		1	1					1				5		
South Hadley	251	17	Moody	Ebenezer	1	1	2		1			1		1			7		
South Hadley	251	18	Moody	Daniel Capt.	3	1	1	1					2				8		
South Hadley	251	19	Moody	Eliphaz	2		1	1		3			1	1			9		
South Hadley	251	20	Moody	Seth	3		1		3	2	2	2	1				14		
South Hadley	251	21	Patrick	Agnes Wd		1						2		1			4		
South Hadley	251	22	Snow	Josiah Jr				1		2		1	1				5		
South Hadley	251	23	Smith	Pelah	1	1		1		2			1	1			7		
South Hadley	251	24	Nash	Asa	1	1	1	1	1	2			1	1			9		
South Hadley	251	25	Vinton	Samuel Doct				1						1			2		
South Hadley	251	26	Vinton	Abiather	3	1	2	1		1		1	1				10		

TOWN	PG#	LN#	HEADS OF HOUSEHOLD		FREE WHITE MALES					FREE WHITE FEMALES					TOTAL ALL OTHER	TOTAL SLAVES	TOTALS	DISTRICT/ TOWNSHIP	NOTES
			LAST NAME	FIRST NAME	under 10	10 to 16	16 to 26	26 to 45	45 and over	under 10	10 to 16	16 to 26	26 to 45	45 and over					
Southampton	128	1	Maynard	Stephen	2	1		1		2	1		1	1			9		
Southampton	128	2	Strong	Joseph			1				1						2		
Southampton	128	3	Williams	Philip			2			1		1					4		
Southampton	128	4	Williams	Amos		1					1						2		
Southampton	128	5	Bates	Aaron	1	1		1		1	1		1				6		
Southampton	128	6	Bates	Stephen					1					1			2		
Southampton	128	7	Bates	Stephen Junr	2	1		1		1		1					6		
Southampton	128	8	Sheldon	Abner		1	3		1				1				7		
Southampton	128	9	Sheldon	Silas			1		1	1		1		1			5		
Southampton	128	10	Searl	Zopher			2		1	1	1			1			6		
Southampton	128	11	Burt	Hannah Wd			1					1		1			3		
Southampton	128	12	Searl	Clark			1					1					2		
Southampton	128	13	Clark	Noah	2	2		1		1	1		1				8		
Southampton	128	14	Burt	Saml	2	3	1	1		3		3	1				14		
Southampton	128	15	Loomis	Allexander				1				3		1			5		
Southampton	128	16	Loomis	Amos	2			1		1			1				5		
Southampton	129	1	Hatch	Eliphlet			1		1	1	2		1				6		
Southampton	129	2	Searl	Israel	1	1		1		1		1					5		
Southampton	129	3	Burt	Martin Junr			1					1					2		
Southampton	129	4	Dooly	Asahel			1							1			2		
Southampton	129	5	Dooly	Noah	1		1			1		1					4		
Southampton	129	6	Dooly	Wm			1					1					2		
Southampton	129	7	Bunday	Ephraim			1			4			1				6		
Southampton	129	8	Bunday	Elijah	4		1						1				6		
Southampton	129	9	Brockway	Isaiah		2			1	1		2	1	1			8		
Southampton	129	10	Root	Aaron	2			1		1			1				5		
Southampton	129	11	Burt	Martin	2	1			1	2	1	2		1			10		
Southampton	129	12	Parsons	Isaac	1		2		1	1	1	2		2			10		
Southampton	129	13	Southworth	Joseph	2	1				3			1				8		
Southampton	129	14	Lyman	Thomas		3		1		2	2		1				9		
Southampton	129	15	Bunday	Moses			1			2		1					4		
Southampton	129	16	King	Phineas	1	1		1		2	1		1				7		
Southampton	129	17	Lyman	Elias	5		1	2	1			1	1				11		
Southampton	129	18	Williams	Saxton			1			1			1				3		
Southampton	129	19	Lyman	Elias Junr		1	3	1		2		2	1				10		
Southampton	129	20	Pomroy	Joel			1	1	1	2			1				6		
Southampton	129	21	Hannum	Asahel	1				1	1	1	1	1				6		
Southampton	129	22	Pomroy	Ichabod	3			1		2	3		1				10		
Southampton	129	23	Pomroy	Gad	1	1	1	1		1	1		1				7		
Southampton	129	24	Kinsley	Danl			1		1			1		2			5		
Southampton	129	25	Edwards	Luther	1	1	2	1		1	1	1					8		
Southampton	129	26	Strong	Elihu	4	1		1					1				7		
Southampton	129	27	Edwards	Elisha	2		1	1		2			1	1			8		
Southampton	129	28	Rust	Ebenezer	2	1		1		2	1		1				8		
Southampton	129	29	Judd	Jona Revd			1		2			1	1	1			6		
Southampton	129	30	Judd	Frederick	1	2		1		2			1				7		
Southampton	129	31	Birge	Asahel				1					1	1			3		
Southampton	129	32	Birge	Asahel Junr			2			2			1				5		
Southampton	130	1	King	Douglas		1			1					1			3		
Southampton	130	2	King	Belah	1			1		1			1				4		
Southampton	130	3	Clap	Peres	1	1	1		1	4	1	1	1				11		
Southampton	130	4	Clark	Timothy			1	1		2			1	1			6		
Southampton	130	5	Chapman	Asahel	2	1	1	1		2			1				8		
Southampton	130	6	Clark	Timothy Junr	1		1		1		1	1					6		
Southampton	130	7	Sheldon	Kemima Wd			1			1	1	2		1			6		
Southampton	130	8	Wait	Elisha		1	1			1	1		1				5		
Southampton	130	9	Searl	Zepher Junr	2	1	1	1		2	1		1				9		
Southampton	130	10	Sheldon	Israel	3	1			1	1	1			1			8		
Southampton	130	11	Searl	Job	3		1	1		1	2		1				9		
Southampton	130	12	Wait	John		1	1		1				1	1			5		
Southampton	130	13	Clark	Justes	2		1	1		2	1	1	1				9		
Southampton	130	14	Miller	Roger		1	1		1	1			4				8		
Southampton	130	15	Searl	Bildad			2		1				1	1			5		
Southampton	130	16	Herrlburt	Stephen		1			1				1	1			4		
Southampton	130	17	Sheldon	Noah	2			1		1			1				5		
Southampton	130	18	Wellar	Ebenezer	1		1		2				1				5		
Southampton	130	19	Sheldon	Ebenezer					1			1		1			3		
Southampton	130	20	Sheldon	Ebenezer Junr	1	1		1		2	1		1				7		
Southampton	130	21	Sheldon	Joseph			1			1		1					3		
Southampton	130	22	Sheldon	Stephen		2			1		1			1			5		
Southampton	130	23	Sheldon	Aretas	2			1		1	1		1				6		
Southampton	130	24	Strong	John		1		1	1	2		2		1			8		
Southampton	130	25	Strong	John Junr			1						2				3		
Southampton	130	26	Loomis	Shim	1	2			1	1	3		1	1			10		
Southampton	130	27	Colman	Saml		1	1		1	1		1	1				6		
Southampton	130	28	Bascum	Elisha	2			1		1	1		1				6		
Southampton	130	29	Bascum	King	1		2	1		2			1	1			8		
Southampton	130	30	Woodbridge	Sylvster	1		1		1				1	1			5		
Southampton	130	31	Danks	Moses			1			1			1	2			5		

TOWN	PG#	LN#	LAST NAME	FIRST NAME	FREE WHITE MALES under 10	10 to 16	16 to 26	26 to 45	45 and over	FREE WHITE FEMALES under 10	10 to 16	16 to 26	26 to 45	45 and over	TOTAL ALL OTHER	TOTAL SLAVES	TOTALS	DISTRICT/ TOWNSHIP	NOTES
Southampton	131	1	Danks	Robert				1	1			1		1			4		
Southampton	131	2	Danks	Elijah					1	1			1				3		
Southampton	131	3	Lyman	Gaius	1		1	1		1		3					7		
Southampton	131	4	Parks	Phiny	2			1		1			1				5		
Southampton	131	5	Barns	Nathan	1	1		1		1	1		1				6		
Southampton	131	6	Clap	Silas	3	1		1		1	1		1				8		
Southampton	131	7	Clap	Timothy	1	1		1		1	1		2	1			8		
Southampton	131	8	Searl	Justus		1	1	1				1		2			6		
Southampton	131	9	Hurlburt	Douglas	2			1		1			1				5		
Southampton	131	10	Searl	Aaron				1									1		
Southampton	131	11	Searl	Ira	1			1		3			1				6		
Southampton	131	12	Searl	Moses	1	2		1		1				1			6		
Southampton	131	13	Clap	Elijah Junr		2		1		2			1				6		
Southampton	131	14	Clap	Samll		1	1	1						1			4		
Southampton	131	15	Clap	Samll Jun	1			1		1			1				4		
Southampton	131	16	Clap	Elisha	3	1		1					1				6		
Southampton	131	17	Clap	Elizabeth Wd		1								1			2		
Southampton	131	18	Loomis	Nathaniel		1						1					2		
Southampton	131	19	Clap	Elijah		1		1					1	1			4		
Southampton	131	20	Clap	Chester			1					1					2		
Southampton	131	21	Clap	Luther	1			1		3			1				6		
Southampton	131	22	Clap	Moses			3	1		1	1		1				7		
Southampton	131	23	Searl	Nathan		3		1		1	1			1			7		
Southampton	131	24	Strong	Aaron	1			2		1			1				5		
Southampton	131	25	Strong	Elias	2			1					1				4		
Southampton	131	26	Barns	Wm				1	1		1		1	1			5		
Southampton	131	27	Barns	Wm Junr	2	1		1					1				5		
Southampton	131	28	Strong	Job		2	1	1		2			1				7		
Southampton	131	29	Barns	Benjamin		1		1		1	1	1	1				6		
Southampton	131	30	Clap	Eli	2	1		1		1	1	1	1				8		
Southampton	131	31	Danks	Saml				1						1			2		
Southampton	131	32	Danks	Saml Junr	1	1	2	1		3		1	1				10		
Southampton	131	33	Luckore	Lemuel		1	1	1		1			1				5		
Southampton	131	34	Searl	Elizabeth Wd								2	1				3		
Southampton	131	35	Searl	Nathaniel			1	3				1	1				6		
Southampton	132	1	Searl	Abijah	1		2	1		1	3						8		
Southampton	132	2	Searl	Gideon	2			1		1		1	1				6		
Southampton	132	3	Searl	Gaius	1		1					1					3		
Southampton	132	4	Searl	Levi				1				1	1				3		
Southampton	132	5	Searl	Nathaniel Junr			1	1				1					3		
Southampton	132	6	Searl	Gideon Junr	1	1		1		1	1		1				6		
Southampton	132	7	Eliot	Francis				1					1				2		
Southampton	132	8	Strong	Bohan	1			1					1				3		
Southampton	132	9	Strong	Stephen			1					1					2		
Southampton	132	10	Chapman	Paul			1	1					1				3		
Southampton	132	11	Rust	Lemuel		1		1		1			1	1			5		
Southampton	132	12	Lymon	John	1		2	1		1			2	1			8		
Southampton	132	13	Clark	Elisha	1			1		1		1	1				5		
Southampton	132	14	Hannum	Timothy				1				2	1				4		
Southampton	132	15	Clark	Selah Junr				1		1			1	1			4		
Southampton	132	16	Thorp	David			2	1	1				1				5		
Southampton	132	17	Clap	Joel	1	1	1	1		1	3		1				9		
Southampton	132	18	Clap	Joel Junr			1						1				2		
Southampton	132	19	Pomroy	Aaron Junr				1		2			1				4		
Southampton	132	20	Pomroy	Aaron					1					1			2		
Southampton	132	21	Miller	John			1	1		4	2		1				9		
Southampton	132	22	Strong	Waitstill	1	2		1		1		3		1			9		
Southampton	132	23	Clark	Selah Junr				1						2			3		
Southampton	132	24	Clark	Amasa	4			1		1			1				7		
Southampton	132	25	Clark	Oliver				1			1	2		2			6		
Southampton	132	26	Clark	Oliver Junr	2			1		2			1				6		
Southampton	132	27	Porter	Jehiel		1		1				4		1			7		
Southampton	132	28	Pomroy	Ira	2			1		2	1		1	1			8		
Southampton	132	29	Strong	Roswel	1	1		2		3	1		1				9		
Southampton	132	30	Pomroy	Leml			2	1					1	1			6		
Southampton	132	31	Pomroy	Calib	1		1	1				1		1			5		
Southampton	132	32	Pomroy	Jacob			2	1		1	1	1		1			7		
Southampton	132	33	Pomroy	Ebenezer		1	1	1						1			4		
Southampton	133	1	Strong	Asahel		2		1					1	1			5		
Southampton	133	2	Baldwin	Wm		1		1			1	1		1			5		
Southampton	133	3	Pomroy	Elihue	1			1			1	1		1			5		
Southampton	133	4	Pomroy	Anne Wd	1	1	1					1	1				5		
Southampton	133	5	Pomroy	Asahel	2			1	1	2	1		1	2			10		
Southampton	133	6	Pomroy	Gideon	2	2		1		2			1				8		
Southampton	133	7	Rogers	John	1		1		1	2	2	2					9		
Southampton	133	8	Rogers	Elisha	2	1		1		2				2			8		
Southampton	133	9	Pomroy	Isaac	2	2	1	1		1			1				8		
Southampton	133	10	Hannum	Phebe Wd	1	2				1	1	1	1				7		
Southampton	133	11	Clap	Roger	2	1			1			1		1			8		

142

TOWN	PG#	LN#	LAST NAME	FIRST NAME	FREE WHITE MALES					FREE WHITE FEMALES					TOTAL ALL OTHER	TOTAL SLAVES	TOTALS	DISTRICT/ TOWNSHIP	NOTES
					under 10	10 to 16	16 to 26	26 to 45	45 and over	under 10	10 to 16	16 to 26	26 to 45	45 and over					
Southampton	133	12	Colman	Lemuel	2	1	4		1	1	1	1	1	1			13		
Southampton	133	13	Torrey	Calvin	1	2		1		1	1		1	1			8		
Southampton	133	14	Lyman	John Junr	1			1			1	1					4		
Southampton	133	15	Frary	Nathaniel	1		1	1	1	1	1	1	1				8		
Southampton	133	16	Braimin	Danl				1						1			2		
Southampton	133	17	Braimin	Uziel		1				2		1					4		
Southampton	133	18	Pomroy	Lemuel		3		1		1	3	1	1				10		
Southampton	133	19	Bartlet	Moses	1			1			1		1				4		
Southampton	133	20	Bartlet	Joseph	1	1		1		3	1		1				8		
Southampton	133	21	Clap	Thadeus	1							1					2		
Southampton	133	22	Loomis	Artiman	1			1		3			1				6		

TOWN	PG#	LN#	LAST NAME	FIRST NAME	FREE WHITE MALES					FREE WHITE FEMALES					TOTAL ALL OTHER	TOTAL SLAVES	TOTALS	DISTRICT/ TOWNSHIP	NOTES
					under 10	10 to 16	16 to 26	26 to 45	45 and over	under 10	10 to 16	16 to 26	26 to 45	45 and over					
Southwick	358	1	Adams	Rufus	1	2	1	1	1	1		1		1			9		
Southwick	358	2	Andruss	Lemuel			1			1		1					3		
Southwick	358	3	Bigelow	Titus	1				1					1			3		
Southwick	358	4	Bill	Erastus	1	2		1		1	1	1					7		
Southwick	358	5	Bill	Jonathan	2	1			1	1		1		1			7		
Southwick	358	6	Bartlett	Sylvanus	3	1	1		1	2		1	1				10		
Southwick	358	7	Byington	Samuel	3	1	2		1		1	1		1			10		
Southwick	358	8	Byington	Joel			1		1			1		1			4		
Southwick	358	9	Booth	Ephraim		1	1		1	1	1	1		1			7		
Southwick	358	10	Brown	Brigham		1		1		2	1		1				6		
Southwick	358	11	Carter	Solomon	2			1		1			1				5		
Southwick	358	12	Clark	Reuben		1	2		1			2	1				7		
Southwick	358	13	Campbell	Abigail	1									1			2		
Southwick	358	14	Carter	Isaac	2	1	1	1		2			1				8		
Southwick	358	15	Chamberlain	Ephraim		2	1		1	1		2		1			8		
Southwick	358	16	Cardell	John	2	1		1			1	1	1				7		
Southwick	358	17	Cannon	Ziba		1		1		2	1		2				7		
Southwick	358	18	Campbell	Thomas	2	1	2		1	3	1		2	1			13		
Southwick	358	19	Carter	Jonathan		1	2		1		1			1			6		
Southwick	358	20	Carter	Asa			1			1		1					3		
Southwick	358	21	Dunham	Jabez		2		1					1	1			5		
Southwick	358	22	Dewey	Gad		2		1	1			2		1			7		
Southwick	358	23	Dickinson	Richard		1		1					1				3		
Southwick	358	24	Ducey	Elijah	2		1						1				4		
Southwick	358	25	Edwards	Warham	1				1					1			3		
Southwick	358	26	Ensign	Datis	3	2	3		1	1				1			11		
Southwick	358	27	Easton	James	1	2	1	1	1	2	1		1	2			12		
Southwick	358	28	Easton	Ashbel	3	2		1			1		1				8		
Southwick	358	29	Forward	Joseph	1	1	2		1	2	1	1					10		
Southwick	358	30	Foot	Enos			1	1		1	1	1					5		
Southwick	358	31	French	Aaron	1	2		1		1			1	1			7		
Southwick	358	32	Fowler	David	1	1	1		1	1	2	1					8		
Southwick	358	33	Frazier	Jared		1		2				1					4		
Southwick	358	34	Fowler	Noble	3	1		1					1				6		
Southwick	358	35	Fowler	Bildad		1		1		1	1			1			5		
Southwick	358	36	Fowler	Daniel		1		1		1				1			4		
Southwick	358	37	Fowler	Saul	2		1	1		1	1	1					7		
Southwick	358	38	Fowler	Isaac		1	1				1		1				5		
Southwick	358	39	Fowler	Silas			2	1	1	1			1				6		
Southwick	358	40	French	Daniel	2			1		3			1				7		
Southwick	358	41	Gillet	Isaac	5	1			1	1	1		1				10		
Southwick	358	42	Granger	Asahel	1		1	1		3			1				7		
Southwick	358	43	Gilbert	Mercy								1		1			2		
Southwick	358	44	Granger	Holcomb	4	1		1		2			1				9		
Southwick	358	45	Granger	Ithamar	2			1		2	1		1				7		
Southwick	358	46	Granger	George		1	2		1		1			1			6		
Southwick	358	47	Gross	Jonah	2	1	1	1		1	2			1			9		
Southwick	358	48	Hays	Jonathan				1						1			2		
Southwick	358	49	Hanchet	Thomas	4		1	1					1	1	1		9		
Southwick	358	50	Hays	Moses	1	1	2		1	3	1	1		1			11		
Southwick	358	51	Hall	Elisha	1			1				1					3		
Southwick	358	52	Hough	Thomas			4		1		1			1			7		
Southwick	358	53	Holcomb	Martin	1		1		1			1		1			5		
Southwick	358	54	Holcomb	Samuel	1			1		1		1					4		
Southwick	358	55	Holcomb	Roger	3			1		2			1				7		
Southwick	359	1	Hall	Medad	1				1					1			3		
Southwick	359	2	Ingraham	Gamaliel		1		1		3			1				6		
Southwick	359	3	Johnson	Samuel				1						1			2		
Southwick	359	4	Johnson	Samuel Jr				1			1		1				3		
Southwick	359	5	Johnson	Abner	1			1		3			1				6		
Southwick	359	6	Johnson	Amos	1	1			1	1	1	1		1			7		
Southwick	359	7	Jacobs	William	1			1		3			1				6		
Southwick	359	8	Ives	David		2	2	1	1			2		1			9		
Southwick	359	9	Kent	David		1	1		1			1					4		
Southwick	359	10	Kent	Ezra				1						1			2		
Southwick	359	11	Kent	Ezra Junr	1	1		1		4			1				8		
Southwick	359	12	Kent	Josiah	1	1		1		1	1	2	1				8		
Southwick	359	13	Kellogg	Samuel				1						1			3		
Southwick	359	14	Kellogg	Anna	3	2				1		1	1				8		
Southwick	359	15	Lawnsbury	David	2	1	1			3			1				8		
Southwick	359	16	Langdon	Roswell	1		1	2		1			1				6		
Southwick	359	17	Langdon	Job	1	1		1		1			1				5		
Southwick	359	18	Loomis	Noah Junr	1	1	1		2	1		1					7		
Southwick	359	19	Loomis	Nehemiah	2	1	1		1	1	1	1	1	1			10		
Southwick	359	20	Laflin	Heman	1		1		1			1					4		
Southwick	359	21	Laflin	Matthew				1			1			1	2		5		
Southwick	359	22	Laflin	Matthew Jr	2	2		1		2		1	1				9		
Southwick	359	23	Loomis	Noah Junr				1						1			2		
Southwick	359	24	Latham	Edward	1	1	1					1					4		

TOWN	PG#	LN#	LAST NAME	FIRST NAME	FREE WHITE MALES					FREE WHITE FEMALES					TOTAL ALL OTHER	TOTAL SLAVES	TOTALS	DISTRICT/ TOWNSHIP	NOTES
					under 10	10 to 16	16 to 26	26 to 45	45 and over	under 10	10 to 16	16 to 26	26 to 45	45 and over					
Southwick	359	25	Loomis	Ham	4	2	1	1		1	1		1				11		
Southwick	359	26	Loomis	Elizur	1	1	1			1			1				5		
Southwick	359	27	Lee	Campbell	3			1		2			1				7		
Southwick	359	28	Loomis	Shem	1	1	1	1		4	1		1				10		
Southwick	359	29	Miller	William					1	1				1			3		
Southwick	359	30	Miller	Elias			1				1		1				3		
Southwick	359	31	Messenger	Horace			1				1			1			3		
Southwick	359	32	Miller	William Jr	2			1				1					4		
Southwick	359	33	Miller	Asa	1			1		1	1						5		
Southwick	359	34	Mather	William		1		1	1		2	1		1			7		
Southwick	359	35	Meacham	Paul	2	1		1		2	2	1	1				10		
Southwick	359	36	Marlow	Daniel				1					1				2		
Southwick	359	37	Messenger	Jehiel	1			1		1		1					4		
Southwick	359	38	Noble	Tehan		1			2				1				4		
Southwick	359	39	Norton	Robert	1		1		1	1	1	1		1			7		
Southwick	359	40	Norton	Eldad	3	1			1				1				6		
Southwick	359	41	Noble	Amos		1		1				1	1				4		
Southwick	359	42	Noble	Timothy		1		1	1	1	1	1	1				7		
Southwick	359	43	Nelson	Luther	1			1	1	1			1	1			6		
Southwick	359	44	Nelson	James Y.	2			1		1	2		1				7		
Southwick	359	45	Norton	Hannah										2			2		
Southwick	359	46	Noble	Reuben	1			1		2			1				5		
Southwick	359	47	Owen	Samuel					1					1			2		
Southwick	359	48	Owen	Samuel Junr			1			2			1				4		
Southwick	359	49	Hosmer	William	2		1		1	1		1	1				7		
Southwick	359	50	Olds	Samuel	3	1		1	1	2		3		1			12		
Southwick	359	51	Olds	Justice		1						1					2		
Southwick	359	52	Olds	Moses	2					3	2		1				9		
Southwick	359	53	Olds	Levi			2			1		1					4		
Southwick	359	54	Perkins	Israel	2	1	1	1		2			1	2			10		
Southwick	359	55	Parker	Eliha	2			1	1	2			1				7		
Southwick	359	56	Palmer	William	1	1		1		3	1		1				8		
Southwick	359	57	Palmer	Levi	4			1					1	1			7		
Southwick	359	58	Benton	Bristor											4		4		
Southwick	360	1	Root	Talmon		1		1		1			1				4		
Southwick	360	2	Rising	Benjamin Jr		1							1				2		
Southwick	360	3	Rising	Heman	2			1					1				4		
Southwick	360	4	Rising	Asahel	1		1			1		1					4		
Southwick	360	5	Rockwell	John		1	1		1		2			1			6		
Southwick	360	6	Rising	Abraham		1	1	1		1			1				5		
Southwick	360	7	Rising	Amos		1		1	1	2	1	2		1			9		
Southwick	360	8	Root	Zur	1	1	2		1		1			1			7		
Southwick	360	9	Root	Noah			1				1						2		
Southwick	360	10	Rexford	Danison		1	3	1		2	1	1					9		
Southwick	360	11	Root	Gideon				1			1		1				3		
Southwick	360	12	Root	Gideon Junr	1	1		1		2			1				6		
Southwick	360	13	Rising	Ranah	1	1			2	1	1	1					7		
Southwick	360	14	Rising	Alexander	1			1		1			1				4		
Southwick	360	15	Reed	George					1					1			2		
Southwick	360	16	Southwell	Phineas				1	1					1			3		
Southwick	360	17	Stiles	Gideon		1	1		1			2	1	1			7		
Southwick	360	18	Stiles	Shubael	2	1		1		3	1	2	1				11		
Southwick	360	19	Sexton	Stephen	1		1		1		2			2			7		
Southwick	360	20	Smith	Abiel		1	?	1		1			1	1			6		
Southwick	360	21	Stiles	Doras		2		1		1			1	1			6		
Southwick	360	22	Stevens	Titus		1		?		1			1				5		
Southwick	360	23	Stephans	Solomon Jr	1	1	1	1		1	1	1	1				8		
Southwick	360	24	Smith	Oliver	2			1			1		1				5		
Southwick	360	25	Stevens	Soloman					1					1			2		
Southwick	360	26	Sacket	Pliny		2			1		1	2		1			7		
Southwick	361	1	Smith	Isaac			1	2					1				4		
Southwick	361	2	Taylor	James		1		1					1				3		
Southwick	361	3	Talmadge	John		1	1	1		3		1		1			8		
Southwick	361	4	Utley	Oliver		1	1			4			2				9		
Southwick	361	5	Wilcox	David			1	1				1		1			4		
Southwick	361	6	Warner	Daniel		1			1				1				3		
Southwick	361	7	Whiting	Jonathan					1				1				2		
Southwick	361	8	Woodworth	Chester		1		1				1					3		

145

TOWN	PG#	LN#	LAST NAME	FIRST NAME	FREE WHITE MALES under 10	10 to 16	16 to 26	26 to 45	45 and over	FREE WHITE FEMALES under 10	10 to 16	16 to 26	26 to 45	45 and over	TOTAL ALL OTHER	TOTAL SLAVES	TOTALS	DISTRICT/ TOWNSHIP	NOTES
Springfield	239	1	Colton	Dimond	2			1		2	1	1	1				8		
Springfield	239	2	Lumbard	Daniel			2	3		6		2	1				14		
Springfield	239	3	Sheldon	Charles	1	1			1	2	1		1				7		
Springfield	239	4	Sheldon	William		2	1	1				1	2	1			8		
Springfield	239	5	Marble	Joel				1					1				2		
Springfield	239	6	Williams	Eleazer			1	1					2	1			5		
Springfield	239	7	Parsons	Zenas				1		1			1	1	1		4		
Springfield	239	8	Bliss	Daniel	1	1		1		2	1	1					7		
Springfield	239	9	Gardner	Jonathan	3	1		1		3			1				9		
Springfield	239	10	Tucker	Ebenezer	2			1			1		1				5		
Springfield	239	11	Church	Moses			1		1	1			1	1			5		
Springfield	239	12	Harris	Nancy Wd		1		1				1		1			4		
Springfield	239	13	Rumrill	Alexander			2	1		1	1	1					6		
Springfield	239	14	Lombard	Jemima Wd								1		1			2		
Springfield	239	15	Pynchon	William Esq			3	1	1	1			1				7		
Springfield	239	16	Pynchon	John				1			1						2		
Springfield	239	17	Parsons	Sarah Wd				1		1	1	1		1			5		
Springfield	239	18	Lumbard	Justin			1	1	1	3		2					8		
Springfield	239	19	Smith	William Col.	2	1	1		1	1			1				8		
Springfield	239	20	Worthington	Mary Wd	2		2						2	1			7		
Springfield	239	21	Pynchon	Rebecca Wd						1			2				3		
Springfield	239	22	Pynchon	Abigail Wd			1						1				2		
Springfield	239	23	Hooker	John Esq	3			1		3	1	1	1	2			12		
Springfield	239	24	Sanderson	Jeduthon	2	1		1		2			1				7		
Springfield	239	25	Lyman	Samuel Esq	1		1	1					2	2			7		
Springfield	239	26	Brooks	Rufus	1			1		2			1				5		
Springfield	239	27	Harris	William						2			1				3		
Springfield	239	28	Brewer	Chauncey Esq	2		2	1	1	2	2	1	1				12		
Springfield	239	29	Ball	Benja G.	2	2		1		1		1	1				8		
Springfield	239	30	Williston	Thomas				1		1	1	1	1				5		
Springfield	239	31	Boylstone	Edward		1		1		1			2				5		
Springfield	239	32	Bales	Eli	2			1					1				4		
Springfield	239	33	Stebbins	Zebina	4	1	1	2		1		1	1				11		
Springfield	239	34	Howard	Bezaleel Revd	3			1		1	1	1					8		
Springfield	239	35	Wright	David				1				1	1				3		
Springfield	239	36	Wilner	Hendrick	3			1		1			1				6		
Springfield	239	37	Nash	Rebecca Wd	2							1		1			4		
Springfield	239	38	Addleton	Beulah Wd		1						1		1			3		
Springfield	239	39	Spendler	John Saml			1					1	1				3		
Springfield	239	40	Ferre	John				1					1				2		
Springfield	239	41	Day	Abner	1		1		1	1	1		1				6		
Springfield	239	42	Hammond	Lettice			1					1					2		
Springfield	239	43	Munroe	John	1			1				1					3		
Springfield	240	1	Mills	William			2					1	1				4		
Springfield	240	2	Bond	Forbush	2			1		1	1		1				6		
Springfield	240	3	Bisbee	Benjamin	2			1					1				4		
Springfield	240	4	Smith	Michael	2			1					1				4		
Springfield	240	5	Warner	Zacha			1		1				1				3		
Springfield	240	6	Snow	Jeremiah					1				1				2		
Springfield	240	7	Edwards	John L.	1			1		1		1					4		
Springfield	240	8	Day	Mary Wd		1				1		1	1				4		
Springfield	240	9	Miller	Clark			1					1					2		
Springfield	240	10	Kellogg	Joseph	1			1		1			1	1			5		
Springfield	240	11	Lincoln	Walker			1			1		1					3		
Springfield	240	12	Look	Benjamin	1			1		2			1				5		
Springfield	240	13	White	Zenas			3					1					4		
Springfield	240	14	Coye	Fitch				1		2			1				4		
Springfield	240	15	Lewis	Joseph	5			1		1			1				8		
Springfield	240	16	Nash	Ebenezer	2			1		1			1				5		
Springfield	240	17	Buell	Abel	2		5	3		2		1					13		
Springfield	240	18	Green	Benjamin		1	3	8	1	3	1		1				18		
Springfield	240	19	Prince	Daniel		1		1		2			1				5		
Springfield	240	20	Packard	Ephraim	3			1		1			1				6		
Springfield	240	21	Stebbins	Ithamar			1			1			1				3		
Springfield	240	22	Hatfield	Joseph	3			1		2			1				7		
Springfield	240	23	Bliss	Pelatiah			2	1		1			1				5		
Springfield	240	24	Miller	Joseph		1		1				1		2			5		
Springfield	240	25	Stebbins	Moses		1		1		2			1				5		
Springfield	240	26	Stebbins	Festus	2			1		1		1					5		
Springfield	240	27	Stebbins	Rachel Wd									1				1		
Springfield	240	28	Stebbins	Calvin	1	1		1		3			1				7		
Springfield	240	29	Rude	Elias	1			1		2			1				5		
Springfield	240	30	Ball	Wm	2		1	1		1			1				6		
Springfield	240	31	Stebbins	Thos Capt					1		1		1				3		
Springfield	240	32	Stebbins	Walter	1			1					1				3		
Springfield	240	33	Stebbins	Joseph	2	1	1	1	1			2	1	2			11		
Springfield	240	34	Wright	George				1					1				2		
Springfield	240	35	Wright	Darius			1			1			1				3		
Springfield	240	36	Carew	Joseph			3	2				1					7		

146

TOWN	PG#	LN#	LAST NAME	FIRST NAME	FREE WHITE MALES					FREE WHITE FEMALES					TOTAL ALL OTHER	TOTAL SLAVES	TOTALS	DISTRICT/ TOWNSHIP	NOTES
					under 10	10 to 16	16 to 26	26 to 45	45 and over	under 10	10 to 16	16 to 26	26 to 45	45 and over					
Springfield	240	37	Warriner	Isaac		1			1	1		1		1			5		
Springfield	240	38	Chapin	Israel Capt	3	1	1		1	1	1	1	1	1			11		
Springfield	240	39	Chapin	Judah		2		1	1	2	1		1				8		
Springfield	240	40	Munn	Samuel				1						4			5		
Springfield	240	41	Stebbins	Samuel		1			1				1	1			4		
Springfield	240	42	Stebbins	Ithamar	2		1			1		1					5		
Springfield	240	43	Hitchcock	Josiah Lt		1	1	1					1				4		
Springfield	240	44	Hitchcock	Heber	3			1		1			1				6		
Springfield	241	1	Hitchcock	Luther Capt		1	1		1	4		2		1			10		
Springfield	241	2	Hitchcock	Josiah Jr	3			1		1			1				6		
Springfield	241	3	Hitchcock	Ruth Wd		1				1		2		2			6		
Springfield	241	4	Stebbins	Edward		1		1				1	1	1			5		
Springfield	241	5	Stebbins	Elam	2			1		2			1				6		
Springfield	241	6	Burt	Rex	1			1		2		1					5		
Springfield	241	7	Chapin	Paul	3	2			1	1	1		1				9		
Springfield	241	8	Stedman	Phinehas		1	2		1	1		1		1			7		
Springfield	241	9	Burgess	Joseph Capt	1		1		1					1			4		
Springfield	241	10	Wright	Stephen		1	1		1	1	3			1			9		
Springfield	241	11	Howard	Asa			1			1		1					3		
Springfield	241	12	Morgan	Ebenezer		1		1		1			1				4		
Springfield	241	13	Loomis	Hezekiah	2			1		1		1					5		
Springfield	241	14	Alworth	Stephen	2		2	1		1	1	1					8		
Springfield	241	15	Horton	Gad		2	1		1	1	2	1		1			9		
Springfield	241	16	Horton	Ruel	1			1		1		1					4		
Springfield	241	17	Horton	Stephen				1						1			2		
Springfield	241	18	Horton	Peggy										2			2		
Springfield	241	19	Paulk	John		1		1			1		1				4		
Springfield	241	20	Butts	Nathaniel	2	1		1		1	1	2		1			9		
Springfield	241	21	Butts	Jabez	1	1						1					3		
Springfield	241	22	Butts	Mason	1	1						1					3		
Springfield	241	23	Hitchcock	Levi	4	1						1	1				7		
Springfield	241	24	Williston	Godfrey			1			2			1				4		
Springfield	241	25	Slafter	Anthony		1	1		1			1		1			5		
Springfield	241	26	Slafter	Samuel	1			1		3			2				7		
Springfield	241	27	Frost	Henry		1	1	1						1			5		
Springfield	241	28	Frost	Asa			1			2			1				4		
Springfield	241	29	Washburn	Hezekiah			1			1			1				3		
Springfield	241	30	Bliss	Reuben				1						1			2		
Springfield	241	31	Bliss	Calvin		1		1		1			1				4		
Springfield	241	32	Fern	Luther			1			1			1				3		
Springfield	241	33	Wright	Calvin 2d			1			1		1					3		
Springfield	241	34	Bliss	Elizabeth Wd							1			4			5		
Springfield	241	35	Bliss	Charles	1		1		1	1			2				5		
Springfield	241	36	Bliss	Alexander	3	1	4		1	2		1	2				14		
Springfield	241	37	Bliss	Ebenezer	2	1	3		1	3		1	1				12		
Springfield	241	38	Bliss	Zenas	3	2		1		1	1		1				9		
Springfield	241	39	Theving	Samuel	1			1		3			1				6		
Springfield	241	40	Warner	John				1									1		
Springfield	241	41	Warner	John Jun	2	1		1			1		1				6		
Springfield	241	42	Warner	Gerald				1		1				1			3		
Springfield	241	43	Warner	Luther	2			1		1	1		1				6		
Springfield	241	44	Bliss	Nathan			1	1									2		
Springfield	242	1	Bliss	Gaius			1			1			1				3		
Springfield	242	2	Bliss	Justin	1		1	2		3		1	1				9		
Springfield	242	3	Bliss	Festus	2		2	1					1				6		
Springfield	242	4	Bliss	Pitt	2		1	1		1			1				6		
Springfield	242	5	Dwight	Thomas Esq	3		1	1		1	2		1				9		
Springfield	242	6	Munn	John	1		1	1		1		1					5		
Springfield	242	7	Clapp	Parson	1	1		1		1		2					7		
Springfield	242	8	Colton	William		1		1	1	1	1	1	1				7		
Springfield	242	9	Hunt	William	1	1		1		1			1				5		
Springfield	242	10	Bliss	Moses Esq		1	1	1	1	2		2	1	1			10		
Springfield	242	11	Bliss	George Esq	1			1		2	1	1	1				7		
Springfield	242	12	Collins	Ariel			1	1		1		2	1				6		
Springfield	242	13	Nevers	Hannah Widw			2						1	1			4		
Springfield	242	14	Collins	Oliver	2		1	1		2			1				7		
Springfield	242	15	Bailes	Thomas	1	2	1	1	2		1	2		2			12		
Springfield	242	16	Ashley	Moses			2										2		
Springfield	242	17	Dwight	Jonathan Esq	2		3		1			1	1	2			10		
Springfield	242	18	Dwight	Jona Jr	1	1		1		1		1	1				6		
Springfield	242	19	Dwight	James L.	1		3	1		3	1	3					12		
Springfield	242	20	Bliss	Luke	1				2	1	1			1			6		
Springfield	242	21	Church	Jonathan	2			1		1	1		1				6		
Springfield	242	22	Williams	Joseph Esq		1		1		1	1	1					6		
Springfield	242	23	Lloyd	William			2			1			1				4		
Springfield	242	24	Sargeant	Thomas	2	1	2	1					2				8		
Springfield	242	25	Clark	Asahel	1	1		1		1			1	1			6		
Springfield	242	26	Fern	Uriah	1		1	1		2			1				6		
Springfield	242	27	Stebbins	John			5	7		3							17		

TOWN	PG#	LN#	LAST NAME	FIRST NAME	FREE WHITE MALES					FREE WHITE FEMALES					TOTAL ALL OTHER	TOTAL SLAVES	TOTALS	DISTRICT/ TOWNSHIP	NOTES
					under 10	10 to 16	16 to 26	26 to 45	45 and over	under 10	10 to 16	16 to 26	26 to 45	45 and over					
Springfield	242	28	White	Martin	2			1		1			1				5		
Springfield	242	29	Orr	Robert B.	1		1	1		1		2					6		
Springfield	242	30	White	Preserved Jr		1			2		1	1		1			6		
Springfield	242	31	White	Luther	1		1						1				3		
Springfield	242	32	Collins	John			1			1		1					3		
Springfield	242	33	Harding	Daniel	2				1	2			1				6		
Springfield	242	34	Bliss	Gad					1		2			3			6		
Springfield	242	35	Byers	James	1		1		1	1	2			2			8		
Springfield	242	36	Byers	James Jr		1		1		1	1						4		
Springfield	242	37	Parsons	Jacklan			1			1			1				3		
Springfield	242	38	Grout	Micah					1					1			2		
Springfield	242	39	Simond	Abner			1										1		
Springfield	242	40	Bryant	Jno Capt	3				1	1	2	1	1				9		
Springfield	242	41	Colton	Andrew					1					1			2		
Springfield	242	42	Hopkins	Joseph			1			1			1				3		
Springfield	242	43	Colton	Charles Capt					2		1	1	2				6		
Springfield	242	44	Bates	George		2		1						1			4		
Springfield	243	1	Popkins	Benjamin				1		1		1					3		
Springfield	243	2	Warner	John		1	2		1	1							5		
Springfield	243	3	Clough	Joseph		2		1						1			4		
Springfield	243	4	Bates	Lewis	1			1		2			1				5		
Springfield	243	5	Ferre	Solomon	1	2			1	1				1			6		
Springfield	243	6	Ferre	Mary Wd										3			3		
Springfield	243	7	Brewer	George			1		1	2	1			1			6		
Springfield	243	8	Burgess	Reuben Lt	2			1		2	1		1	1			8		
Springfield	243	9	Ferre	Thaddeus				1		3	1		1				6		
Springfield	243	10	Burgess	Joseph	1			1		1			1				4		
Springfield	243	11	Butler	William	3			1		1	1		1				7		
Springfield	243	12	Benton	Jonathan	2	1	1		1					1			6		
Springfield	243	13	Bliss	Nathan Jr	2		1	1		2	1		1				8		
Springfield	243	14	Faulk	Festus	1		1						1				3		
Springfield	243	15	Russell	Ebenezer		1	1		1	1	2		1				7		
Springfield	243	16	Russell	Abigail Wd								1					1		
Springfield	243	17	Parker	Enos			1	1		2		1	1				8		
Springfield	243	18	Parker	Russell	1			1		1			1				4		
Springfield	243	19	Parsons	Lemuel	1	2		1		2			1				7		
Springfield	243	20	Keyes	Jonas	2	1		1		2			1				7		
Springfield	243	21	Marsh	Philander		1						1					2		
Springfield	243	22	Bennett	James	1				1	3	1	1		1			9		
Springfield	243	23	Webster	Joel	4	1		1		1		1					8		
Springfield	243	24	Webster	Joseph		1	1	1		1				1			5		
Springfield	243	25	Murphy	Timothy	1	1	2		1	3	1	1	1				11		
Springfield	243	26	Kingsbury	Luther			1					1					2		
Springfield	243	27	Fosgate	Joshua	1			1		1			1	1			5		
Springfield	243	28	Ames	David	2			2		3	2	1	1	1			12		
Springfield	243	29	Orr	Robert		1		1						1			3		
Springfield	243	30	Baker	Asa	1		2	2		1		2	1				9		
Springfield	243	31	Caswell	Solomon		6		1						1			8		
Springfield	243	32	Bartlett	Frederick			1						1				2		
Springfield	243	33	Crook	John			1			1			1				3		
Springfield	243	34	Dale	John															Enumeration left blank
Springfield	243	35	Moore	Justus		2	1		1	3			1	1			9		
Springfield	243	36	Ely	Horace	1		1	1		1	1	1					6		
Springfield	243	37	Bannister	Joseph	1			1			1			1			4		
Springfield	243	38	Bannister	Freeman	1		2	1		2			1				7		
Springfield	243	39	Sparks	Lemuel	3			1					1				5		
Springfield	243	40	Hawkins	George		1	1		1		1	1		1			6		
Springfield	243	41	Stebbins	Aaron		1		1		1	1	1					5		
Springfield	243	42	Harris	Samuel		3	3	1		4	1	1	1				14		
Springfield	243	43	Hancock	Thomas	3	2		1		1			1	1			9		
Springfield	244	1	Cooley	Clark	1			1		2			1				5		
Springfield	244	2	Swetland	Daniel		1		1		1	1	1	1				6		
Springfield	244	3	Davis	Aaron Jun				1		2		1					4		
Springfield	244	4	Swetland	Jacob	1			1		2			1				5		
Springfield	244	5	Russell	Abner	3	1	1	1		1			1				8		
Springfield	244	6	Richardson	John	3			1		1			1				6		
Springfield	244	7	Eaton	Silvanus		1	1		1		1	2	1				7		
Springfield	244	8	Dale	Thomas															Enumeration left blank
Springfield	244	9	Atwell	Jno				1		2		1					4		
Springfield	244	10	Barns	Samuel	1			1		1			1				4		
Springfield	244	11	Gay	Levi		1		1						1			3		
Springfield	244	12	Lumbard	Obed	1	1	1	1		3	1		1	1			10		
Springfield	244	13	Wardwell	Benjamin			3		1	1				1			6		
Springfield	244	14	Wardwell	Samuel			1						1				2		
Springfield	244	15	Newton	Oliver				1						1			2		
Springfield	244	16	Newton	Oliver Jr	1		1			1		1					4		
Springfield	244	17	Stephenson	Abiather Jr			1			1			1				3		
Springfield	244	18	McClenche	Robert		1	1							1			3		
Springfield	244	19	Worthington	Stephen	2			1		1			1				5		
Springfield	244	20	Smith	George	1			1					1				3		
Springfield	244	21	Stephenson	Abiather	1			1		1	1	1		1			6		

TOWN	PG#	LN#	LAST NAME	FIRST NAME	FREE WHITE MALES					FREE WHITE FEMALES					TOTAL ALL OTHER	TOTAL SLAVES	TOTALS	DISTRICT/ TOWNSHIP	NOTES
					under 10	10 to 16	16 to 26	26 to 45	45 and over	under 10	10 to 16	16 to 26	26 to 45	45 and over					
Springfield	244	22	Stephenson	Benajah				1				1		1			3		
Springfield	244	23	Burt	Frederick				1		1				1			3		
Springfield	244	24	Murphy	Daniel		1		1				1		1			4		
Springfield	244	25	Burt	Moses				1						1			2		
Springfield	244	26	Burt	Moses Junr	1			2		1	1	2					7		
Springfield	244	27	Burt	Martin	1		1					1					3		
Springfield	244	28	Lumbard	Joseph	2	1		1		3			1				8		
Springfield	244	29	Bartlett	Asher	1	1		1					1				4		
Springfield	244	30	Bonney	David				1			1			1			3		
Springfield	244	31	Bartlett	Pliny			1					1					2		
Springfield	244	32	Warriner	Ebenezer				1									1		
Springfield	244	33	Warriner	Ebenezer Jr	1	2	1	1				1	1	1			8		
Springfield	244	34	Biss	Jacob	4	1	2	1		2	1	1	1				13		
Springfield	244	35	Blake	George	1	1	2	1		2	1		1				9		
Springfield	244	36	Cooley	George	1			1					1				3		
Springfield	244	37	Warriner	Daniel	1			1		2			1				5		
Springfield	244	38	Warriner	Martin	1			1		2			1				5		
Springfield	244	39	Wright	Daniel	1			1		1		1		1			5		
Springfield	244	40	Cooley	Samuel	2					1		1		1			6		
Springfield	244	41	Morton	Thomas			1	1		1				1			5		
Springfield	244	42	Robertson	Joseph	1			1				1					3		
Springfield	244	43	Ashley	Vashti Wd										1			1		
Springfield	244	44	Ashley	Daniel	2	1		1		1	1		1				7		
Springfield	245	1	Ashley	John	1	1			1	2	1			1			7		
Springfield	245	2	Ashley	Phebe Wd			1							1			2		
Springfield	245	3	Cooley	William		1	3		1	1	1			1			8		
Springfield	245	4	Sikes	Rufus	2	1	1	1		3		1	1	1			11		
Springfield	245	5	Cooley	Jacob				1									1		
Springfield	245	6	Cooley	Earl	2	1		1		2	1			1			8		
Springfield	245	7	Fletcher	Ira	1										8		9		
Springfield	245	8	Burt	Jno Lt	1	1	2		1			1	3	1			10		
Springfield	245	9	Bonner	David Jr	2			1		1	1		1				6		
Springfield	245	10	Morgan	Samuel		1		1		1	1			1			5		
Springfield	245	11	Bliss	Paul	1			1		1			1				4		
Springfield	245	12	Ferry	Joseph Capt		1		1		1			1	1			5		
Springfield	245	13	Ferry	Caleb			1			1			1				3		
Springfield	245	14	Ferry	Joseph Junr		1		1		1			1				4		
Springfield	245	15	Wolcott	Apaphras				1					1				2		
Springfield	245	16	Wolcott	James	2	1		1		1			1				6		
Springfield	245	17	Pendleton	Caleb Jr	1			1		2			1				5		
Springfield	245	18	Pendleton	Nathan	2		1	1		1			1	1			7		
Springfield	245	19	Pendleton	Jesse	1		1										2		
Springfield	245	20	Pendleton	Henry		1				1		1					3		
Springfield	245	21	Fairfield	Levi	1			1									2		
Springfield	245	22	Frink	John	1		1		1	2	2		1				8		
Springfield	245	23	Frink	Gillis	1	2	2	1		2		2	1				11		
Springfield	245	24	Frink	Thomas	4	2		1		1	1		1				10		
Springfield	245	25	Wright	Eleazer	3	2		1		1	1		1				9		
Springfield	245	26	Griswould	Joseph Lt	1	1	1	1		2	1	2	1				10		
Springfield	245	27	Chapin	Timothy	2	1		1		1			1				7		
Springfield	245	28	Allen	Joseph	3	1		1					1				6		
Springfield	245	29	Eaton	James	1	1	1	1		2			1	1			8		
Springfield	245	30	Chapin	Jehiel	1	1		1		2	1		1				7		
Springfield	245	31	Chapin	Ezekiel	3	?		1		1			1	£			10		
Springfield	245	32	Chapin	John	1		2		1	1			1				6		
Springfield	245	33	Smith	Philip		1			1	4	2	1	1				10		
Springfield	245	34	McKinstry	John Revd			3	1				1	2	1			8		
Springfield	245	35	Bement	Lois Wd										1			1		
Springfield	245	36	Chapin	Ephm Capt			2	1						1			4		
Springfield	245	37	Chapin	Frederick	1		2			1	1	1					6		
Springfield	245	38	Chapin	Moses	2	1	1	1		1	1		1				8		
Springfield	245	39	Chapin	Ashbel	2		1	1		2			1				7		
Springfield	245	40	Morgan	Aaron		1		1				2		1			5		
Springfield	245	41	Chapin	George	1			1		3			1				6		
Springfield	245	42	Chapin	Abel Col	3	2	1	1				1	1	1	1		11		
Springfield	245	43	Chapin	Mary Wd		1		1				1	1				4		
Springfield	245	44	Chapin	Lucy Wd		1							1	1			3		
Springfield	246	1	Chapin	Roswell	3			1		1			1				6		
Springfield	246	2	Chapin	Eunice Wd				1						1			2		
Springfield	246	3	Chapin	Silas Col	3	1	1	1		1	3	1	1				12		
Springfield	246	4	Chapin	Phins Capt	1	1	1		2	2	1		1				9		
Springfield	246	5	Chapin	Benjamin				1		1	1		1				4		
Springfield	246	6	Chapin	Ephraim Jr	1	2	1	1		2	1		1				9		
Springfield	246	7	Chapin	William		1			1			1		1			4		
Springfield	246	8	Chapin	Seth				1						1			2		
Springfield	246	9	Chapin	Zenas	1	1		1		2			1				6		
Springfield	246	10	Chapin	Seth Junr		2		1					1				4		
Springfield	246	11	Chapin	Zerah	2		2	1		3		1	1				10		
Springfield	246	12	Bliss	Moses 2d	2	1	1		1	1		2		1			9		
Springfield	246	13	Chapin	Solomon	1	1	1		1			1		1			6		

TOWN	PG#	LN#	HEADS OF HOUSEHOLD LAST NAME	FIRST NAME	FREE WHITE MALES under 10	10 to 16	16 to 26	26 to 45	45 and over	FREE WHITE FEMALES under 10	10 to 16	16 to 26	26 to 45	45 and over	TOTAL ALL OTHER	TOTAL SLAVES	TOTALS	DISTRICT/ TOWNSHIP	NOTES
Springfield	246	14	Chapin	William 2d	1	1	2	1			1	1	1				8		
Springfield	246	15	Chapin	Japhel	5	1	1	1			1	1	1				11		
Springfield	246	16	Chapin	Henry	2			1		1				1			5		
Springfield	246	17	Chapin	Joseph				1						1			2		
Springfield	246	18	Burt	Samuel			1			4			1				6		
Springfield	246	19	Chapin	Thomas	2		1			2			1	1			7		
Springfield	246	20	Frost	Noah				1			1			1			3		
Springfield	246	21	Chapin	Jabez	2	1		1		2	2		1				9		
Springfield	246	22	Vanhorn	Azariah				1			1		1				3		
Springfield	246	23	Vanhorn	Gad			1			3			1	1			6		
Springfield	246	24	Ferry	Peter	1			1		3			1				6		
Springfield	246	25	Wright	Calvin	4		1			1			1	2			9		
Springfield	246	26	Wright	Robert			1			1		1					3		
Springfield	246	27	Pease	Joseph			2						1				3		
Springfield	246	28	Vanhorn	Ruel	1			1		2		1					5		
Springfield	246	29	Vanhorn	Calvin		1		1		2	1		1				6		
Springfield	246	30	Dutton	Jeremiah				1						1			2		
Springfield	246	31	Bullard	Benjamin	1	1		1		2			1				6		
Springfield	246	32	Holkens	Joseph	3		1			1			1				6		
Springfield	246	33	Chapin	Daniel	1			1		2			1				5		
Springfield	246	34	Brown	Collins		1		1				1		1			4		
Springfield	246	35	Brown	Collins Jr	1			1		2			1				5		
Springfield	246	36	Chapin	Ithamar	3	1		1		2	1		1				9		
Springfield	246	37	Chapin	Levi	2	1	1		1	1	2	2	1				11		
Springfield	246	38	Frost	Reuben	1			1		4	2		1				9		
Springfield	246	39	Frost	Joel				1		3		1					5		
Springfield	246	40	Edson	Benjamin	3	1		1		1	2		1				9		
Springfield	246	41	Edson	Jacob		1		1				2		2			6		
Springfield	246	42	Cooley	Ariel	3		3	1		2			1				10		
Springfield	246	43	Shaw	Thomas	1	2		1		3			1				8		
Springfield	247	1	Redway	Comfort				1		2	2		1				6		
Springfield	247	2	Charles	George			3	1					1				5		
Springfield	247	3	Rockwood	Isaac	1			1		1			1				4		
Springfield	247	4	Gould	Joseph	1		5		2	2	1	1		1			13		
Springfield	247	5	Snell	Josiah	1		2	1	1	1	2						8		
Springfield	247	6	Shelly	Joshua	1		1			1		1					4		
Springfield	247	7	Sampson	Philemon			1			4			1				6		
Springfield	247	8	McQuivey	Solomon	1		1			4			1				7		
Springfield	247	9	Popkins	Stephen	3	1		1		3		1		1			10		
Springfield	247	10	Dale	Thomas		2	6	5				1	1				15		
Springfield	247	11	Caswell	Samuel	1	1	2	1		1		1		1			8		
Springfield	247	12	Bagley	Amy Wd			4	1					1				6		
Springfield	247	13	Thayer	Ambrose			4	1		1			1				7		
Springfield	247	14	Broad	Aaron		1	2	1		2		1		1			8		
Springfield	247	15	Crane	Abner	1		1					1					3		
Springfield	247	16	Lyman	Com Capt & his Comp			24	17					2				43		
Springfield	247	17	Burbank	Ebenezer	2	1				1	1		1				7		
Springfield	247	18	Talcott	White			2						1				3		
Springfield	247	19	Vanhorn	Abraham				1						1			2		
Springfield	247	20	Chapin	Phebe Wd		1								1			2		
Springfield	247	21	Cotton	Stephen				1					1	1			3		
Springfield	247	22	Lanphear	Arnold	2			1		1		1					5		
Springfield	247	23	Barber	Abner	2		1	1					1				5		
Springfield	247	24	Chapin	Ascenath Wd		1				1			1				3		
Springfield	247	25	White	Wm				1						2			3		
Springfield	247	26	Pooler	Penuel	1	1		1		1	1	1		1			7		
Springfield	247	27	Hills	Asahel	2		1			1		1					5		
Springfield	247	28	Hix	Nathan			1					1					2		
Springfield	247	29	Briggs	John	1		1			1			1				4		
Springfield	247	30	Fairfield	Thomas				1				1	1	1			4		
Springfield	247	31	Lyon	Asa	1		1					1					3		
Springfield	247	32	Bennett	Sarah Wd								2	1				3		
Springfield	247	33	Johnson	Charles	3		1			1		1					6		
Springfield	247	34	Paulk	Samuel	1			1		1				2			5		
Springfield	247	35	Burr	Ansel		1				1	1						3		
Springfield	247	36	Burgess	Robert			1			2		1					4		
Springfield	247	37	Avery	Abel	3		2	2	1	1	1	1	1				12		
Springfield	247	38	Bisbee	Benjamin	1			1		1			1				4		
Springfield	247	39	Fowler	Benja											2		2		
Springfield	247	40	Lawrence	William			1			1			1				3		
Springfield	247	41	Newell	John				1						1			2		
Springfield	247	42	Vanhorn	Gaius	1			1		2			1				5		
Springfield	247	43	Hancock	Abel	2			1		2			2	1			8		
Springfield	247	44	Dart	Levi	1	1		1					1				4		
Springfield	248	1	Mercy	Benjamin	1			1					1				3		
Springfield	248	2	Crocker	Nathan				1		2	1	1					5		
Springfield	248	3	Wright	Charles	2			1		1			1				5		
Springfield	248	4	Phillips	John				1							1		2		
Springfield	248	5	Kingsbury	Samuel		1		1				1		1			4		
Springfield	248	6	Shaw	Daniel	1	2		1					1				5		
Springfield	248	7	Sanger	Jedidiah	2			1			1		1				5		
Springfield	248	8	Russell	Elijah		1	1					1					3		
Springfield	248	9	Jones	Pelatiah				1									1		
Springfield	248	10	Russell	Luther		1						1					2		
Springfield	248	11	Foster	John			1						1				2		
Springfield	248	12	Hawkins	Samuel	2			1		1			1				5		

TOWN	PG#	LN#	HEADS OF HOUSEHOLD LAST NAME	FIRST NAME	FREE WHITE MALES under 10	10 to 16	16 to 26	26 to 45	45 and over	FREE WHITE FEMALES under 10	10 to 16	16 to 26	26 to 45	45 and over	TOTAL ALL OTHER	TOTAL SLAVES	TOTALS	DISTRICT/ TOWNSHIP	NOTES
Sunderland	282	1	Hubbard	Elisha	1			1		1			1				4		
Sunderland	282	2	Packard	Samuel			1		1					1			3		
Sunderland	282	3	Cattin	Timothy		1			1			1		1			4		
Sunderland	282	4	Russell	Israel			1	1				1	1	1			5		
Sunderland	282	5	Graves	Elias	4	1		1			1	1	1				9		
Sunderland	282	6	Montague	David	1	2	1	1		2		1	1				9		
Sunderland	282	7	Cooley	Simon		1		1	1	2	1	1		1			8		
Sunderland	282	8	Hunt	Melzar		2	1	1		2	1	1	1				9		
Sunderland	282	9	Farnum	Heman	1			1		1	2		1				6		
Sunderland	282	10	Graves	Benjamin	2			1		1	1		1				6		
Sunderland	282	11	Graves	David	3	1	2	1		1	1		1				10		
Sunderland	282	12	Hubbard	Phinehas	2	1	2	1				1					7		
Sunderland	282	13	Montague	Daniel		1		1	1	1			1	1			6		
Sunderland	282	14	Delano	William	1	1		1		1		1	2				8		
Sunderland	282	15	Rowe	John Junr	1	2	2		1	2		1	1				10		
Sunderland	282	16	Cooley	Gideon	2	1	1	1		1	1	1		1			9		
Sunderland	282	17	Smith	Elisha		1	2	1		2	1	1		1			9		
Sunderland	282	18	Montague	John	1		1		1	1	1	2		1			8		
Sunderland	282	19	Clark	Thomas			1	1		1		1	1	1			6		
Sunderland	282	20	Graves	Maria							1		1	1			3		
Sunderland	283	1	Graves	Cotton	2		2			1	1						6		
Sunderland	283	2	Alexander	Miles	2		1		1	1		1	1	1			8		
Sunderland	283	3	Church	Samuel				1		2			1				4		
Sunderland	283	4	Weaver	Samuel	4			1		2			1	1			9		
Sunderland	283	5	Sanderson	William	3			1					1				5		
Sunderland	283	6	Graves	Phinehas		1		1		2			1	1			6		
Sunderland	283	7	Russell	Phillip	2	1	1		1	1		1	1				8		
Sunderland	283	8	Daniels	Amos	1			1	1	1				1			6		
Sunderland	283	9	Ashly	Gideon			1		1		1	4		1			8		
Sunderland	283	10	Clark	Lemuel	3	1	1		1		1	1	1				9		
Sunderland	283	11	Saunders	Abraham		2	3	1						1			7		
Sunderland	283	12	Field	Thomas			1				1		2				4		
Sunderland	283	13	Graham	Lucius			1	1		1		1	1	1			5		
Sunderland	283	14	Rice	Nathaniel	3		2			2			1	1			9		
Sunderland	283	15	Rowe	John				1				2	1				4		
Sunderland	283	16	Rowe	Elijah	3			1					1				5		
Sunderland	283	17	Smith	Nathaniel		2	5	1		1			1				10		
Sunderland	283	18	Tuttle	John	3	1		1		3			1	1			10		
Sunderland	283	19	Wright	Abner			1			1		1					3		
Sunderland	283	20	Rice	Nahum	2			1		1			1				5		
Sunderland	283	21	Sprague	David			1	1				1		1			4		
Sunderland	283	22	Wiley	Ebenezor	3	1	1	1		1	1		1				9		
Sunderland	283	23	Cooley	Anna	1	1	2			1	1		2	1			9		
Sunderland	283	24	Crocker	Zacheus		1	2	1	1	1				1			7		
Sunderland	283	25	Hubbard	Giles			2		1	2	1			1			7		
Sunderland	283	26	Russell	Zebina			1										1		
Sunderland	283	27	Clark	Sylvanus	1	1		1			1		1				5		
Sunderland	283	28	Clark	Justus	3			1					1				5		
Sunderland	283	29	Whitemore	Daniel	1		2		1		1	1		1			7		
Sunderland	283	30	Parker	Asa	2		1		1	1	2			1			8		

151

TOWN	PG#	LN#	LAST NAME	FIRST NAME	FREE WHITE MALES					FREE WHITE FEMALES					TOTAL ALL OTHER	TOTAL SLAVES	TOTALS	DISTRICT/ TOWNSHIP	NOTES
					under 10	10 to 16	16 to 26	26 to 45	45 and over	under 10	10 to 16	16 to 26	26 to 45	45 and over					
Ware	225	1	Anderson	William			3	2	1	1	2			1			10		
Ware	225	2	Andrews	Lemuel	1			1		3	1		1				7		
Ware	225	3	Andrews	Aaron			1	1		1			1				4		
Ware	225	4	Andrews	Prince			1					1					2		
Ware	225	5	Andrews	John	1			1				1					3		
Ware	225	6	Blair	Samuel	1	1		1		1	1		1	1			7		
Ware	225	7	Blair	John	1			2		1			1				5		
Ware	225	8	Bush	Solomon			1	1									2		
Ware	225	9	Bacon	Penuel	1			1				1					3		
Ware	225	10	Bacon	Thomas	1	1		1		3			1				7		
Ware	225	11	Barney	Charles	2		2		1	2			1				8		
Ware	225	12	Bodwine	William	2	3		1		1		1	1	1			10		
Ware	225	13	Breckinridge	Wm Capt			1		1			1		1			4		
Ware	225	14	Breckinridge	Wm Jr		1	1		1	2	1			1			7		
Ware	225	15	Breckinridge	James	2	1	1		1	2	1		1	1			10		
Ware	225	16	Breckinridge	George	3	2		1		1			1				8		
Ware	225	17	Breckinridge	Francis Capt		1		1					1				3		
Ware	225	18	Brown	David Lt	1	1	2		1				1				6		
Ware	225	19	Brown	Moses		1	1	1		2	2	1	1				9		
Ware	225	20	Brown	Samuel		1	1		1	2			1				6		
Ware	225	21	Brown	Samuel Jun		1			1				1				3		
Ware	225	22	Bascom	Nathan	1			1		1			1				4		
Ware	225	23	Barr	Joseph	2			1					1				4		
Ware	225	24	Cross	Nathan			1			1		1					3		
Ware	225	25	Cutter	William		1	1			1		1					4		
Ware	225	26	Cummings	Abraham Lt		1	1	1		1			2	1			7		
Ware	225	27	Cummings	Simeon		1			1	2	1	3		1			9		
Ware	225	28	Convey	William		1			1	2			1				5		
Ware	225	29	Cummings	Job	3	1	1		2	1	1	1	1	1			12		
Ware	225	30	Cross	John	1	1			1			1		1			5		
Ware	225	31	Converse	Phinehas	2				1	2	2			1			8		
Ware	225	32	Crain	Amaziah	1	1	2		1	5	2		1	1			15		
Ware	225	33	Cutler	Solomon	1	1	1	1		2	1	1					9		
Ware	225	34	Cutler	Solomon	1	1	1	1		2	1	1					9		
Ware	225	35	Cutler	Elijah		2	1		1	1		2	1				8		
Ware	225	36	Cross	Ezra	2			1		2			1				6		
Ware	225	37	Done	Wm Capt			5	1					1				7		
Ware	225	38	Darling	Willard	1			1					1				3		
Ware	225	39	Davis	Elihu	2			1		1		1					5		
Ware	226	1	Davis	Enos	1			2		1			1	1			6		
Ware	226	2	Densmore	Samuel		1	1	1	1	2				2			8		
Ware	226	3	Densmore	Thomas	2	1	1		2		1	2		2			11		
Ware	226	4	Densmore	Abraham	3	1	2	1		1	1		1				10		
Ware	226	5	Densmore	Thomas Junr			1					1					2		
Ware	226	6	Ellis	Seth	2	3		1		1			1				8		
Ware	226	7	Eaton	Darius	2			1		2			1				6		
Ware	226	8	Foster	Jona	2	1		1	1			1	1	1			8		
Ware	226	9	Furbush	James	1	1	1		1	3			1				8		
Ware	226	10	Fitzgerald	William	2	1			1		2	1	1				8		
Ware	226	11	Gould	Danl Deac	1	2	1		1	1		3		1			10		
Ware	226	12	Gould	David		2	3		1	2		1	1	2			12		
Ware	226	13	Gaines	James	4	2			1				1				8		
Ware	226	14	Godfray	Samuel	1		1					1					3		
Ware	226	15	Gardner	John 2d			1			1		1					3		
Ware	226	16	Gould	Ebenz		1	1		1	3	1		1				8		
Ware	226	17	Gardner	John	2			1		1			1				5		
Ware	226	18	Gray	Joseph			2	1				3		1			7		
Ware	226	19	Gilmore	James	1	1	2		1	1	1	2	1	1			11		
Ware	226	20	Gilmore	John			2		1			2		1			6		
Ware	226	21	Herrington	John				1		4			1				6		
Ware	226	22	Hudson	Eli		1			1	1	2			1			6		
Ware	226	23	Harwood	Andrew	1		2		1	2	2			1			9		
Ware	226	24	Harwood	John	1			1				1					3		
Ware	226	25	Hyde	Othiniel	1	1			1		1	1		1			6		
Ware	226	26	Hutchinson	Samuel	2	1			1	3	4	1	1				13		
Ware	226	27	Harwood	Benjamin	1	1			1		1	3	1				8		
Ware	226	28	Haywood	Cary	2	2			1	2			1				8		
Ware	226	29	Hamilton	John Lt.			1	1			1	1	1	1			5		
Ware	226	30	Jenkins	John		1		1		2	1		1				6		
Ware	226	31	Joslin	Abraham		1	2		1	2	2	1		1			10		
Ware	226	32	Long	Rufus Doct	2		1	1		2		1	1				8		
Ware	226	33	Lamberton	James Ens	3	1			1		1		1	1			8		
Ware	226	34	Lemberton	Seth	1	1		1	2	2			1	1			9		
Ware	226	35	Lemberton	David	1			1		1			1				4		
Ware	226	36	Leonard	Dan		2	2		1		1	1		1			8		
Ware	226	37	Lasell	Jacob	4	3			1				1				9		
Ware	227	1	Lewis	Jesse	3			1		2			1				7		
Ware	227	2	Lammon	James				1					1				2		
Ware	227	3	Lammon	James Jr	1	1	1			1		1	1	1			9		

TOWN	PG#	LN#	LAST NAME	FIRST NAME	FREE WHITE MALES					FREE WHITE FEMALES					TOTAL ALL OTHER	TOTAL SLAVES	TOTALS	DISTRICT/ TOWNSHIP	NOTES
					under 10	10 to 16	16 to 26	26 to 45	45 and over	under 10	10 to 16	16 to 26	26 to 45	45 and over					
Ware	227	4	Lammon	David	1			1		2	1		1				6		
Ware	227	5	Lammon	Wm Jr	2			1		1		1	1				6		
Ware	227	6	Magoon	Isaac	1	1	2	2			1		1		1		9		
Ware	227	7	Magoon	Alexr	1	1	2	2	1		1		3		1		13		
Ware	227	8	Morse	Phillo	1	1	1		1	1	1	1	1	1			9		
Ware	227	9	Hyde	John	1		1		1	2	1		1				7		
Ware	227	10	Merritt	Ichabod	2	2		1			2		1				8		
Ware	227	11	Merritt	Ezekiel L.	3			1		1			1				6		
Ware	227	12	Morton	Thomas	3			1					1				6		
Ware	227	13	McClintock	Thomas	2	1			1	1			1				6		
Ware	227	14	Morse	Reuben Revd	2			1		1		1					5		
Ware	227	15	Marsh	Thomas	1	1	3		1	1	2	2		1			12		
Ware	227	16	Marsh	Jona		1	5	1		1	1			1			10		
Ware	227	17	Marsh	Judah Jr Lt	1	1	1	1	1	1		1					7		
Ware	227	18	McKoy	Nell	3	4			1	2		1	1				12		
Ware	227	19	Marsh	Ephraim	1			1		1			1				4		
Ware	227	20	Wheeler	Jesse	1	2		1		3	2		1				10		
Ware	227	21	Nye	Samuel	3					1					1		5		
Ware	227	22	Osborn	John			1	1			1	1	1	1			6		
Ware	227	23	Page	Wm Deacn	1		2	1	1	2	2	1					10		
Ware	227	24	Patrick	Wm		1	1		1		1		1				5		
Ware	227	25	Patrick	Thomas	3		1	1		1	3		1				10		
Ware	227	26	Pepper	Isaac		2		1		3	2	1	1				10		
Ware	227	27	Pepper	Stephen	2			1		3	1	1	2				10		
Ware	227	28	Pepper	Joseph	2	1		1		1		1	1				7		
Ware	227	29	Pepper	Thomas			1						1				2		
Ware	227	30	Patrick	Isaac	1			1		1		1					4		
Ware	227	31	Quinton	Thomas	1	1			1		2		3				8		
Ware	227	32	Quinton	Robt	1			1		1		2					5		
Ware	227	33	Rich	Elkanah	1			1			1	1					4		
Ware	227	34	Road	Jonas			1										1		
Ware	227	35	Rich	Apollas		1			1		1	3		1			7		
Ware	227	36	Rockwell	Seth	2	1		1					1				5		
Ware	227	37	Randell	Titus			1			1		1					3		
Ware	228	1	Rogers	Daniel				1					1				2		
Ware	228	2	Shaw	John		1	1	1					2				5		
Ware	228	3	Shaw	John 2d Lt	2	1	2	1				2	1	1			10		
Ware	228	4	Shaw	David		1	1	1				1					4		
Ware	228	5	Snell	Lewis	1			1		1			1				4		
Ware	228	6	Snell	Thomas	1			1		5			1	1			9		
Ware	228	7	Simonds	Jonathan		1		1					1				3		
Ware	228	8	Simonds	Judah	2	2			1			2		1			8		
Ware	228	9	Studufant	James	2			1		1			1				5		
Ware	228	10	Sherman	Reuben	2	1		1	1	2	2		2				11		
Ware	228	11	Sherman	Ebenz	2	1		1	1	3			1				9		
Ware	228	12	Scott	Ephraim	4		1	1				1	1				8		
Ware	228	13	Swift	Lemuel	1		1	1		2	1		1				7		
Ware	228	14	Smith	Lemuel Jr	1			1		2			1				5		
Ware	228	15	Stacy	Joel	2			1					1				4		
Ware	228	16	Steel	John D.	1			1		2	1		1				6		
Ware	228	17	Thomas	Nehemiah		1			1	3		2		1			8		
Ware	228	18	Smith	Reuben		1	1					1	1				4		
Ware	228	19	Stacy	Lemuel		1						1					2		
Ware	228	20	Thompson	Benja Jr		?			1	1	1		1				6		
Ware	228	21	Tinney	Daniel		1			1	2	1		1				6		
Ware	228	22	Tisdale	John Junr	2			1	1			1	3				8		
Ware	228	23	Thayer	Jedediah	3			1		1	2		1				8		
Ware	228	24	Thayer	Enoch	3	1			1		1		1				7		
Ware	228	25	Thrasher	George		2		1			2	1		1			7		
Ware	228	26	Titus	Ebenezer	1			1		2			1				5		
Ware	228	27	Haynes	Benjamin	2			1		2			1				6		
Ware	228	28	Wilder	John	1	1	2		1		2			1			8		
Ware	228	29	Wheeler	John	2	1		1		1			1				6		
Ware	228	30	Ward	Reuben	2			1		3	1		1				8		
Ware	228	31	Wood	Jonathan	2	2		1		3	1		1				10		
Ware	228	32	Windslow	Thomas		1		1	1	1	1		1	1			7		
Ware	228	33	Babbett	Samuel	3	1			1	2			1				8		
Ware	228	34	Bond	Jacob	3			1		1			1				6		
Ware	228	35	Lazell	William					1					1			2		
Ware	228	36	Peterson	Charles									3				3		
Ware	228	37	Thayer	Silas	1	1			1	2	1		1				7		

TOWN	PG#	LN#	LAST NAME	FIRST NAME	FREE WHITE MALES					FREE WHITE FEMALES					TOTAL ALL OTHER	TOTAL SLAVES	TOTALS	DISTRICT/TOWNSHIP	NOTES
					under 10	10 to 16	16 to 26	26 to 45	45 and over	under 10	10 to 16	16 to 26	26 to 45	45 and over					
Warwick	36	1	Atwood	Joshua	2	3	1	1		1			1	1			10		
Warwick	36	2	Atwood	Phillip	1	1	1	1			1		1				6		
Warwick	36	3	Atwood	Isaac	1	1		1		4	2		1				10		
Warwick	36	4	Abbot	Abraham	1	1			1	2	2		1				8		
Warwick	36	5	Aldridge	Benajah	1	2		1		3			1				8		
Warwick	36	6	Bancraft	Jacob	1			1		1	1		1				5		
Warwick	36	7	Ball	Stephen			1					1		1			3		
Warwick	36	8	Bass	Obadiah					1		1			2			4		
Warwick	36	9	Burnett	Joshua	2			1		1		1					5		
Warwick	36	10	Burnett	William Junr	1		1			1			1				4		
Warwick	36	11	Ball	Samuel	2			1				2					5		
Warwick	36	12	Bancraft	Daniel				1		2			1				4		
Warwick	36	13	Brown	George	2			1					1				6		
Warwick	36	14	Bowen	John	2		1		1	1	1	1					7		
Warwick	36	15	Bowen	James		2	1	1		1	1		2				8		
Warwick	36	16	Barras	Nathan		2			1	2			1				6		
Warwick	36	17	Barnes	Abraham Junr	1			1				1					3		
Warwick	36	18	Ball	Jonas	1		1			1	2	4		1			11		
Warwick	36	19	Ball	Samuel	2			1		2		1					7		
Warwick	36	20	Brown	Elisha		1		1				1					3		
Warwick	36	21	Bancraft	William	1	2	1	1	1	2	2			1			11		
Warwick	36	22	Bancraft	Ebenezer	1	2	1		1	2		1		1			9		
Warwick	36	23	Bowman	Samuel	1	1	1		1	2		2		1			9		
Warwick	36	24	Barnes	Abraham					1			1		1			3		
Warwick	36	25	Barnes	Samuel	1	1		1		2	1		1				7		
Warwick	36	26	Ball	James	4	1		1		3	3		1	1			14		
Warwick	36	27	Burnett	Andrew	1	1	3		1	1	2	1		1			11		
Warwick	36	28	Barnes	Willard	1	1		1		2	1		1				7		
Warwick	36	29	Barber	Joseph	1		2		1			2		2			8		
Warwick	36	30	Blake	Jonathan	1		2		1		2	2		1			9		
Warwick	36	31	Blake	James			1					1					2		
Warwick	36	32	Burnett	William					1		1			1			3		
Warwick	36	33	Barber	Zachariah	1		2		1	1	1	1		1			8		
Warwick	36	34	Ball	John	1			1		1	1		1				5		
Warwick	36	35	Burnett	Henry		1			1			1		1			4		
Warwick	36	36	Bangs	Josiah	1	1		1		1	1		1				6		
Warwick	36	37	Ball	Jono Clark	1			1		2			1				5		
Warwick	36	38	Clark	Jonas	1	1	1		1	2	1		1				8		
Warwick	36	39	Chase	John	1			1				1					3		
Warwick	36	40	Cook	Daniel			1		1		1	1		2			6		
Warwick	36	41	Conant	Asa		2	1	1		1	1	1		1			8		
Warwick	36	42	Conant	Benjamin		2		1		4	2		1				10		
Warwick	37	1	Cook	Nathan		1		1		1	1		1				5		
Warwick	37	2	Cobb	William Junr	1		1	1		1		2					6		
Warwick	37	3	Cobb	William		1			1				1				3		
Warwick	37	4	Conant	Josiah	3			1		1	1		1				7		
Warwick	37	5	Champney	Humphrey A.	1		1	1		2	2		1				8		
Warwick	37	6	Cobb	Richard	2	1			1	2	1	1		1			9		
Warwick	37	7	Chase	Thomas	1		1		1		1	1	1	2			8		
Warwick	37	8	Conant	Benjamin Dr.			1		1		1	1		1			5		
Warwick	37	9	Delve	Peter			1					1	1				3		
Warwick	37	10	Delve	Jonathan	2		1			2			1				6		
Warwick	37	11	Davis	Jonathan				1			2		1				4		
Warwick	37	12	Dyke	William	1	1			1	1		1		1			6		
Warwick	37	13	Eddy	Abel	1	1	2		1			2		1			8		
Warwick	37	14	Esty	Jacob		1		1			1			2			5		
Warwick	37	15	Eaton	Robert				1					1				2		
Warwick	37	16	Eddy	Ebenezer	1			1				1					3		
Warwick	37	17	Eager	James	1			1		2			1				5		
Warwick	37	18	Fair	Thomas	3			1		1	2		1				8		
Warwick	37	19	Fay	Moses				1					1				2		
Warwick	37	20	Fay	Samuel			1	1		3		1					6		
Warwick	37	21	Fisher	Israel	2			1	1	2	1		1	1			9		
Warwick	37	22	Fuller	Isaiah	2	1	1		1		1			1			7		
Warwick	37	23	Fisher	Abijah	1		1	1		2			1				6		
Warwick	37	24	Fisher	George				1				1					2		
Warwick	37	25	Gold	Asa	3			1		2			1				7		
Warwick	37	26	Goldsbury	John					1			1		1			3		
Warwick	37	27	Goldsbury	James	3	2		1				1	1	1			9		
Warwick	37	28	Gale	Josiah	1		1	2	1	1	3		1				10		
Warwick	37	29	Gale	Jonathan		1	2		1	2	1			1			8		
Warwick	37	30	Gale	John	4			1		1			1	1			8		
Warwick	37	31	Gale	Emery			2						1				3		
Warwick	37	32	Goodale	Ephraim	1			1									2		
Warwick	37	33	Gold	Thomas Junior	2		1					1					4		
Warwick	37	34	Gold	Thomas				1				1		1			3		
Warwick	37	35	Gale	David				1						1			2		
Warwick	37	36	Gale	Alpheus	2			1		2	1		1				7		
Warwick	37	37	Gale	Jesse				1				1					2		

TOWN	PG#	LN#	LAST NAME	FIRST NAME	M under 10	M 10 to 16	M 16 to 26	M 26 to 45	M 45 and over	F under 10	F 10 to 16	F 16 to 26	F 26 to 45	F 45 and over	TOTAL ALL OTHER	TOTAL SLAVES	TOTALS	DISTRICT/TOWNSHIP	NOTES
Warwick	37	38	Goodale	John	1		2		1		1		1	1			7		
Warwick	37	39	Goodale	Joseph					1					1			2		
Warwick	37	40	Gaffield	Daniel	1	1		1					1				4		
Warwick	37	41	Gale	David Junr	3			1		2			1				7		
Warwick	37	42	Gurney	John				1					1				2		
Warwick	37	43	Hazeltine	Benjamin	2	2	3	1		1	1		1				11		
Warwick	38	1	Hastings	Nathan			1		1	3		1					6		
Warwick	38	2	Hastings	Jonas			1			1				1			3		
Warwick	38	3	How	Abraham			1										1		
Warwick	38	4	Hurd	Thomas		2		1		3	2	1	1				10		
Warwick	38	5	Howard	Calvin		1				1		1					3		
Warwick	38	6	Hastings	Isaac	2		2		1	3		1		1			10		
Warwick	38	7	Holmes	James		1				2		1					4		
Warwick	38	8	Hemenway	Asa			1				1		1				3		
Warwick	38	9	Jennings	Joel		1	1			2	2		1	2			9		
Warwick	38	10	Johnson	Mason	2		1						1				4		
Warwick	38	11	Kelton	Nathan		1		1				3		1			6		
Warwick	38	12	Kelton	Thomas		1		1			1	3		1			7		
Warwick	38	13	Kelton	Aaron	2		1			1	1	1					6		
Warwick	38	14	Kelton	Enoch				1						1			2		
Warwick	38	15	Kelton	James		1		1			1			1			4		
Warwick	38	16	Kelton	Rufus	3		1			1		1					6		
Warwick	38	17	Kelton	George	1		1					1					3		
Warwick	38	18	Leonard	Moses				1				1		1			3		
Warwick	38	19	Leonard	Nathan	1			1		1			1				4		
Warwick	38	20	Leonard	Jonas		1	1		1	1	2	2		1			9		
Warwick	38	21	Leonard	Francis		1			1	1	1	2		1			7		
Warwick	38	22	Laroc	John Charles	3			1						1			5		
Warwick	38	23	Leonard	Abraham	1			1		1		1					4		
Warwick	38	24	Lawrence	Eleazer				1		1				1			3		
Warwick	38	25	Moses	Samuel		1		1		1	1	1		2			7		
Warwick	38	26	Mellen	Gilbert	3		1	1				1	1				7		
Warwick	38	27	Mallard	John				1				1		1			3		
Warwick	38	28	Moore	John		2	1		1	2	1	1		1			9		
Warwick	38	29	Moore	Jonathan		1	1		1		1	2		2			8		
Warwick	38	30	Moore	Mark	2	2	2		1	2		2	1				12		
Warwick	38	31	Morse	Aaron			1		1			1		1			4		
Warwick	38	32	Mayo	Caleb	1		3		1	4	3	1	1				14		
Warwick	38	33	Moore	Samuel	1	2			1	3	1		1				9		
Warwick	38	34	Merrick	Bezaleel	3	1	1	1		1	1	1	1				10		
Warwick	38	35	Morse	Samuel	1			1		1				1			4		
Warwick	38	36	Melady	Samuel			1	1		1			1				4		
Warwick	38	37	Mellen	Samuel			1	1					1	1			4		
Warwick	38	38	Mallard	Thomas	2	1		1			1		1				6		
Warwick	38	39	Mayo	Joseph	2	2						1	1				7		
Warwick	38	40	Moore	Jonathan Jr			1						1				2		
Warwick	38	41	Marsh	Amos	1			1		2			1				5		
Warwick	38	42	Miller	Christian				1						1			2		
Warwick	39	1	Nurse	William	2	1		1		1	2	2	1				10		
Warwick	39	2	Ormsbury	John			1		1		1	1		1			6		
Warwick	39	3	Petty	Ebenezer	1					1		1	1				4		
Warwick	39	4	Pond	Joseph	1		1			3		1					6		
Warwick	39	5	Pierce	Ebenezer	2	2		1				1	1				7		
Warwick	39	6	Perry	David		1	2		1			1		1	1		7		
Warwick	39	7	Pickering	William	2			1		1		1	1				6		
Warwick	39	8	Pratt	John			1		1				1	2			5		
Warwick	39	9	Proctor	Peter		1	1		1		2	1	2				8		
Warwick	39	10	Pomeroy	Josiah			1		1		1	1		1			5		
Warwick	39	11	Pomeroy	Josiah Junr	2	1		1		1			1				6		
Warwick	39	12	Proctor	Peter Junr	1			1					1				3		
Warwick	39	13	Packard	Jacob	2	1			1			1		1			6		
Warwick	39	14	Perry	Asa			1		1	1	1	1					5		
Warwick	39	15	Pennyman	Bunyan	1		1	1		2		1					6		
Warwick	39	16	Rawson	Josiah Junr		1	4		2			1	1	1			10		
Warwick	39	17	Robbins	Ephraim			1	2	1			1	1	1			7		
Warwick	39	18	Rich	Jacob	2	2	2		1	1		2		1			11		
Warwick	39	19	Russel	Justus			1	1				1					3		
Warwick	39	20	Ripley	Peter		1	1		1		1	1		1			6		
Warwick	39	21	Robbins	Isaac	1			1				1	1				4		
Warwick	39	22	Reed	Samuel	2	1			1		2		1				7		
Warwick	39	23	Rich	Caleb	1	1	1		1	3	2	2	1				12		
Warwick	39	24	Smith	Joseph	3	1			1			1	1	1			8		
Warwick	39	25	Stearns	Simeon			1						1	1			3		
Warwick	39	26	Stearns	Nathaniel		1	2		1		1	1	1				7		
Warwick	39	27	Symonds	Benjamin			1		1	3	2	1					9		
Warwick	39	28	Stevens	Wilder	2	1	1		1	1	3	2	1	1			13		
Warwick	39	29	Stevens	Abraham	3			1		3			1				8		
Warwick	39	30	Stockwell	James		3	1		1	2	1			1			9		
Warwick	39	31	Smith	Jonathan	1		2	2		1		1	3	2			13		

TOWN	PG#	LN#	LAST NAME	FIRST NAME	under 10	10 to 16	16 to 26	26 to 45	45 and over	under 10	10 to 16	16 to 26	26 to 45	45 and over	TOTAL ALL OTHER	TOTAL SLAVES	TOTALS	DISTRICT/ TOWNSHIP	NOTES
Warwick	39	32	Smith	Zachariah	1	1			1			1	1				5		
Warwick	39	33	Smith	Moses		1		1		2		1					5		
Warwick	39	34	Symonds	William	1			1		2			1				5		
Warwick	39	35	Stearns	Ebenezer			1		1			2		1			5		
Warwick	39	36	Stow	Thomas	1		2	1		2		1	1				8		
Warwick	39	37	Smith	Josiah	2	1		1		2	2	1	1				10		
Warwick	39	38	Smith	Abner		1	2		1		1	2		1			8		
Warwick	39	39	Shepardson	Jonathan	1			1		1	1		1				5		
Warwick	39	40	Stevens	Nathaniel Gove	1	1	1		1			2		1			7		
Warwick	39	41	Smith	Samuel V Junr	3			1	1			2		1			8		
Warwick	39	42	Stearns	Ebenezer Jr		1											1		
Warwick	39	43	Severy	Jonathan	2	1			1	1				1			6		
Warwick	39	44	Solter	William				1	1	1				1			3		
Warwick	40	1	Westcoat	Richard Jr		1		1		3			1	1			7		
Warwick	40	2	Westcoat	Richard				1						1			2		
Warwick	40	3	Weeks	Richard				1						1			2		
Warwick	40	4	Williams	Ebenezer	3	1		1		3	1	1					10		
Warwick	40	5	Willson	John Junr		1	1	1		1		1					5		
Warwick	40	6	Williams	Nathaniel W	2	1	1					1					5		
Warwick	40	7	Watts	Nicholas		1	1		1		1	1		1			6		
Warwick	40	8	Whitney	John		1			1		1	3		1			7		
Warwick	40	9	Whitney	Daniel		1	2		1			2		1			7		
Warwick	40	10	Witherell	Elijah		1	1					1					3		
Warwick	40	11	Williams	Tryphena		1					2	1		1			5		
Warwick	40	12	Williams	Dudley		1				1			1				3		
Warwick	40	13	White	Jacob	3	1		1		2	1	1					9		
Warwick	40	14	Wheelock	Eleazer	1			1		3	1	1	1				8		
Warwick	40	15	Warwick	Jesse	1		1		1	2	2	2		1			10		
Warwick	40	16	Willson	Jonathan		2	1	1		1			1				6		
Warwick	40	17	Weeks	Caleb	1		1			1		1					4		
Warwick	40	18	Whitney	Palmer	1		1		1			2		1			6		
Warwick	40	19	Willson	John				1						1			2		
Warwick	40	20	Williams	Joseph	3	1		1		1			1				7		
Warwick	40	21	Wheelock	Jonathan			1					1					2		
Warwick	40	22	Whiting	John		2		1	1	1	2			1			8		
Warwick	40	23	Weeks	John			1			2			1				4		
Warwick	40	24	Whitney	Joseph		1			1			1		1			4		
Warwick	40	25	Young	Robert		1	1		1	1		2		2			8		
Warwick	40	26	Thayer	Asa	1		2	1		1	1	1	1				8		
Warwick	40	27	Town	Ephraim		1			1	2	1	2	1				8		
Warwick	40	28	Tuel	Benjamin		1	4	1	1	1	1			1			10		
Warwick	40	29	Tuel	Thomas			1										1		
Warwick	40	30	Town	Tabitha		1						1		3			5		
Warwick	40	31	Tuel	Benjamin Junr			1										1		
Warwick	40	32	Thompson	Ebenezer			1			3			1				5		
Warwick	40	33	Timpson	Robert	2	1			1	1				1			6		

TOWN	PG#	LN#	LAST NAME	FIRST NAME	FREE WHITE MALES under 10	10 to 16	16 to 26	26 to 45	45 and over	FREE WHITE FEMALES under 10	10 to 16	16 to 26	26 to 45	45 and over	TOTAL ALL OTHER	TOTAL SLAVES	TOTALS	DISTRICT/ TOWNSHIP	NOTES
Wendell	105	1	Atherton	Thomas	1		2		1		1			1			6		
Wendell	105	2	Austin	Josiah	3	1			1	1		1	1	1			9		
Wendell	105	3	Allen	Abner	1	1		1		2			1				6		
Wendell	105	4	Allen	Stephen	1	1	1		2	3		1	1	1			11		
Wendell	105	5	Ballard	Josiah	3			1	1	1		1	2	1			10		
Wendell	105	6	Ballard	Sylvanus	1				1				1				3		
Wendell	105	7	Brewer	Nathan	2	2	2		1	1		2		1			11		
Wendell	105	8	Beaman	Lemuel			2		1					1			4		
Wendell	105	9	Bent	Joel	1			1		1			1				4		
Wendell	105	10	Boynton	David			2		1			1		1			5		
Wendell	105	11	Bullard	Silas	2			1				1					4		
Wendell	105	12	Butler	Calvin	1			1		2			1				5		
Wendell	105	13	Bartlet	Perley	1	1		1		2			1				6		
Wendell	105	14	Crosbee	Jonathan	1		1		1		1	2		2			8		
Wendell	105	15	Clark	Elijah	1		1	1		2	1		1				7		
Wendell	105	16	Cutler	Jacob	1			1			1	1	1				5		
Wendell	105	17	Chase	John	1			1		1		1					4		
Wendell	105	18	Champney	William	1	1		1					1				4		
Wendell	105	19	Caswell	Simon	2								1				4		
Wendell	105	20	Dresser	Oliver				1	1			1		2			5		
Wendell	105	21	Dresser	Oliver Jr	1			1					1				3		
Wendell	105	22	Drury	Zechariah	3	1	2		1	1	1		1				10		
Wendell	105	23	Death	John	1			1					1				3		
Wendell	105	24	Emerson	Jesse		1	2		1			1		1			6		
Wendell	105	25	Evers	Elihu		1	1			1			1				4		
Wendell	105	26	Evans	Henry		1			1	1	2			2			7		
Wendell	105	27	Fisher	Aaron	1	1	1	1		3			1				8		
Wendell	105	28	Fisher	Jesse	3			1		2			1				7		
Wendell	105	29	Fisk	Zedekiah	2		1	1		1	1	1					8		
Wendell	105	30	Fisk	Daniel	3			1				1					5		
Wendell	105	31	Fisk	Daniel 2d			1	1		1		1					4		
Wendell	105	32	Fisk	Jonathan Junr		1		1		1		1		1			5		
Wendell	105	33	Fisk	Jonas	3			1		1			1				6		
Wendell	105	34	Fosket	Joel	4			1		2			1	1			9		
Wendell	105	35	Fay	Enoch	1			1				1					3		
Wendell	105	36	Green	Joshua	2			1				1	1				5		
Wendell	105	37	Greenwood	Samuel				1				1					2		
Wendell	106	1	Goss	Reuben	2		1		1			1	1				6		
Wendell	106	2	Gates	Silas	2			1		2			1				6		
Wendell	106	3	Harris	Samuel	4	2	1		1		1	1		1			11		
Wendell	106	4	How	Cyprian		1		1						2			4		
Wendell	106	5	How	Abel	1	1		1		1	1	2		1			8		
Wendell	106	6	How	Ephraim	2	2			1	1			1				7		
Wendell	106	7	How	Asa		1		1		2			1				5		
Wendell	106	8	Haskell	Nathan		1		1				1	1				4		
Wendell	106	9	Hammond	Jeremh	2			1				1	1				5		
Wendell	106	10	Hunt	Alden			1			1		1					3		
Wendell	106	11	Jones	John			1	1		1	1	1					5		
Wendell	106	12	Jones	Silas					1		1	2		1			5		
Wendell	106	13	Jones	Silas Junr			1			1		1					3		
Wendell	106	14	Johnson	Joseph		1	2		1			1		1			6		
Wendell	106	15	Johnson	Ebenezer	1	2	1		1	1	2	1		1			10		
Wendell	106	16	Johnson	Nathl	1	2			1	2	1		1	1			9		
Wendell	106	17	Kilburn	Joseph	1		1	2		3	2		1				10		
Wendell	106	18	Kilburn	Joshua	1		1	1		2	1		1				7		
Wendell	106	19	Kidder	Jonathan	1			1					1				3		
Wendell	106	20	Leach	Lemuel		2	4		1				1	1			9		
Wendell	106	21	Leach	Peter	1		1	1		1			1				5		
Wendell	106	22	Lock	Bazaleel		1	1	1				1					4		
Wendell	106	23	Lock	Ephraim			1			2	1		1				5		
Wendell	106	24	Lock	Moses	1				1	2			1				5		
Wendell	106	25	Lawrence	William	1	1	2		1		1	2		1			9		
Wendell	106	26	Moore	Richard		1			1			1					4		
Wendell	106	27	Moore	Benjamin			1			2			1				4		
Wendell	106	28	Moore	Amos	1		1			1		1					4		
Wendell	106	29	Moore	Cornelius	1			1		1		1					4		
Wendell	106	30	Metcalf	John		1		1		1			1				4		
Wendell	106	31	Macomber	Job	1			1		1			1				4		
Wendell	106	32	Needham	Joshua	1			1		3	1		1				7		
Wendell	106	33	Osgood	Jonathan		1		1	1			2		1			6		
Wendell	106	34	Osgood	Josiah					1		1	1		1			4		
Wendell	106	35	Osgood	Luke		2	1		1		1	1		1			7		
Wendell	106	36	Osgood	Elihu	1	1	1	2			1		2				8		
Wendell	106	37	Osgood	Samuel	1	1		1		1			2				6		
Wendell	106	38	Osgood	Josiah Junr	1	1		1		3			1				7		
Wendell	107	1	Osgood	David	1			1		1	1		1				5		
Wendell	107	2	Osgood	John			1			1		1					3		
Wendell	107	3	Orcutt	John				1				1					2		
Wendell	107	4	Prentice	John	1	2	1		1					1			7		

TOWN	PG#	LN#	LAST NAME	FIRST NAME	FREE WHITE MALES					FREE WHITE FEMALES					TOTAL ALL OTHER	TOTAL SLAVES	TOTALS	DISTRICT/ TOWNSHIP	NOTES
					under 10	10 to 16	16 to 26	26 to 45	45 and over	under 10	10 to 16	16 to 26	26 to 45	45 and over					
Wendell	107	5	Porter	Daniel	1		1	1		1	1		1				7		
Wendell	107	6	Porter	Job	1			1		2			1				5		
Wendell	107	7	Porter	Noah	1			1					1				3		
Wendell	107	8	Phillips	Jason	2			1		1		1					5		
Wendell	107	9	Porter	Mercy						1			1	1			3		
Wendell	107	10	Parks	Samuel	2			1					1				4		
Wendell	107	11	Pratt	Ephraim					1					1			2		
Wendell	107	12	Paul	James			1			3			1				5		
Wendell	107	13	Rand	Aaron					1					1			2		
Wendell	107	14	Rand	Hananiah			2	1					1	1			5		
Wendell	107	15	Rand	Daniel	5	1		1					1				8		
Wendell	107	16	Reed	Samuel		1		1		3	1		1				7		
Wendell	107	17	Rice	Samuel R.	1			1		3			1	1			7		
Wendell	107	18	Ross	John			3		1			1		1			6		
Wendell	107	19	Ross	Ephraim	2	1		1		1			1				6		
Wendell	107	20	Rogers	Isaac	3		1	1		1	1	1					8		
Wendell	107	21	Robbins	James	1			1				1	1	1			5		
Wendell	107	22	Rockwood	Nehemiah					1	1				1			3		
Wendell	107	23	Russell	Jonathan	1	1			1		2			1			6		
Wendell	107	24	Russell	Joseph	1			1		2			1				5		
Wendell	107	25	Sweetser	Henry		1		1	1				1	1			5		
Wendell	107	26	Stone	Abraham					1				1	1			3		
Wendell	107	27	Stone	Abraham Jr			1			2			1				4		
Wendell	107	28	Stone	Matthew	2			1		2		3					8		
Wendell	107	29	Stone	Levi	1			1						1			3		
Wendell	107	30	Stone	Clark	1			1		2			1				5		
Wendell	107	31	Stiles	Edmund					1			1		1			3		
Wendell	107	32	Stiles	Phinehas					1	2			1				4		
Wendell	107	33	Stiles	Benjamin		1	2		1	1		2		1			8		
Wendell	107	34	Sawyer	Joseph	3			2		1			1				7		
Wendell	107	35	Sawyer	Jabez	1	1		1					1				4		
Wendell	107	36	Sawyer	Ephraim		2			1	1	1		1				6		
Wendell	107	37	Sylvester	James	1		3			1			1				6		
Wendell	107	38	Thomas	Foxwell			2		1			1		1			5		
Wendell	107	39	Whitacker	David	4	2			1			1	2	1			11		
Wendell	107	40	Wilder	Nathaniel	2	1	2		1				1	1			8		
Wendell	108	1	Wilder	Nathl 2d	1	2			1		1			1			6		
Wendell	108	2	Wilder	Bazeleel	1	2			1		1			1			6		
Wendell	108	3	Wilder	Silas	1			1					1				3		
Wendell	108	4	Washburn	Elisha	1		1		1				1	1			5		
Wendell	108	5	Washburn	Elisha Jr			1			1			1				3		
Wendell	108	6	Washburn	William	4	1		1		1			1				8		
Wendell	108	7	Washburn	Libee	1			1					1				3		
Wendell	108	8	Watkins	Stephen	2	1		1		2		2					8		
Wendell	108	9	Watkins	Francis	2	1		1		1	1	1		1			8		
Wendell	108	10	Wright	Silas	1			1					1				3		
Wendell	108	11	Whitcomb	Dills	2	1		1		2		1	1				8		
Wendell	108	12	Woodward	Jonas	2			1		1			1				5		
Wendell	108	13	Wood	Thomas			1	1		2			1				5		
Wendell	108	14	Wood	Eli	2			1		1		1					5		
Wendell	108	15	Wyeth	Gad	3			1	1	1			1	1			8		
Wendell	108	16	Winslow	Josiah	1		1						1				3		

158

TOWN	PG#	LN#	HEADS OF HOUSEHOLD		FREE WHITE MALES					FREE WHITE FEMALES					TOTAL ALL OTHER	TOTAL SLAVES	TOTALS	DISTRICT/ TOWNSHIP	NOTES
			LAST NAME	FIRST NAME	under 10	10 to 16	16 to 26	26 to 45	45 and over	under 10	10 to 16	16 to 26	26 to 45	45 and over					
West Springfield	349	1	Ashley	John				1						1			2		
West Springfield	349	2	Ashley	Solomon			1			2			1				4		
West Springfield	349	3	Ashley	David		2	2	1				2		1			8		
West Springfield	349	4	Ashley	David Junr			1	1			1		1				4		
West Springfield	349	5	Ashley	Joseph		1			1	1			1	1			5		
West Springfield	349	6	Ashley	Joseph Junr	3				1	1	1		1				7		
West Springfield	349	7	Ashley	Ebenezer			1	1		1			1				4		
West Springfield	349	8	Atkins	Josiah	3	2		1		1			3	1			11		
West Springfield	349	9	Ashley	Benjamin		1	2	1				1	1	1			7		
West Springfield	349	10	Ashley	Moses	1			2		1			2				6		
West Springfield	349	11	Alford	Benjamin	1		1	1					1				4		
West Springfield	349	12	Andrew	Asahel											6		6		
West Springfield	349	13	Alvord	Samuel	1	1		1		1	1		1				6		
West Springfield	349	14	Barker	Grave	3			1		2			1				7		
West Springfield	349	15	Bliss	Caleb		1	1		1	1	1			1			6		
West Springfield	349	16	Bagg	Orpha	1		2	1			1	2		1			8		
West Springfield	349	17	Bagg	Frederick	1	1			1	1	1	1		1			7		
West Springfield	349	18	Brooks	Levi	2		1	1		2	1		1	1			9		
West Springfield	349	19	Bagg	Walter	1			2			1		1				5		
West Springfield	349	20	Barker	Samuel	1	1	1	1		1				1			6		
West Springfield	349	21	Bliss	Hosea	1		2			1		1					5		
West Springfield	349	22	Bagg	Oliver		1		1		2	1			1			6		
West Springfield	349	23	Bagg	Judah		2		1		1		2	1				7		
West Springfield	349	24	Bagg	John	1	1			1		1	2					6		
West Springfield	349	25	Bond	Benjamin			1			1		1					3		
West Springfield	349	26	Bagg	Aaron		1	1			1	2	1					6		
West Springfield	349	27	Brooks	Simon	5		1			1	1	1					9		
West Springfield	349	28	Brooks	Thomas	1		2	1		2	2	1	1				10		
West Springfield	349	29	Barker	Mary								1	1		1		3		
West Springfield	349	30	Breck	George				1				1					2		
West Springfield	349	31	Bliss	Pelatiah		5	1	1			1	2		1			11		
West Springfield	349	32	Bagg	Washam		1		1		1	3		1				7		
West Springfield	349	33	Black	Samuel		1		1		3	1		1				7		
West Springfield	350	1	Bagg	Ezekiel	1	2		1		2	1		1				8		
West Springfield	350	2	Cooley	Roger Jr	2	1	1	1		1			1				7		
West Springfield	350	3	Chapin	Reuben			1	1			1		1				4		
West Springfield	350	4	Chapin	Reuben Jr	2		1						1				4		
West Springfield	350	5	Cooley	Walter	1	1	1		2	3			1				9		
West Springfield	350	6	Cooley	Jonathan	2	1	1		1	1	1	2		1			10		
West Springfield	350	7	Carew	Joseph	1		1	1			1	1	1				6		
West Springfield	350	8	Cooley	John	1		1	1	1		1	1	1				7		
West Springfield	350	9	Champion	Medes	1			1		2		1	1				6		
West Springfield	350	10	Cooper	Samuel	2			1					1				4		
West Springfield	350	11	Chapin	Moses A.	4		1	1		1		1					8		
West Springfield	350	12	Cooley	Alexander	1	2		1	1	1			1				7		
West Springfield	350	13	Champion	Reuben	4	1	2	1		1	1		1				11		
West Springfield	350	14	Colburn	Nathaniel		1	1	1			1		1				5		
West Springfield	350	15	Cook	Elizer		1	2					1					4		
West Springfield	350	16	Cooley	David	1			1						2			4		
West Springfield	350	17	Doan	Bethuel				1		2		1					4		
West Springfield	350	18	Day	Henry	1	1	2	1		3		1					9		
West Springfield	350	19	Day	Daniel	1		1		1	2	1	1	1				8		
West Springfield	350	20	Day	Thomas	3		1	1				1	1				7		
West Springfield	350	21	Day	Thomas Jr			1			1		1					3		
West Springfield	350	22	Doan	James			1	1		1		1					4		
West Springfield	350	23	Day	Edmund	1			1		3		1	2				8		
West Springfield	350	24	Day	Ezekiel		1		1			2	1	1				6		
West Springfield	350	25	Day	Ezekiel Jr	2	1		1				1					5		
West Springfield	350	26	Day	Ebenezer				1				1					2		
West Springfield	350	27	Day	Jacob	3		1	1		1	1		2				9		
West Springfield	350	28	Day	Heman	1		2	1		3	1	1	1				10		
West Springfield	350	29	Day	Moses			1			3		1					5		
West Springfield	350	30	Day	Benjamin	2	1		1				2	1				8		
West Springfield	350	31	Day	Aaron			2	1				1	1				5		
West Springfield	350	32	Eldridge	Mulford	1	1		1		2	1		1				7		
West Springfield	350	33	Ely	Justin		2	2	2			1	1		1			9		
West Springfield	350	34	Ely	John	3	4		1	1			1		1			11		
West Springfield	350	35	Ely	Darius	3			1		1	2		2	1	1		11		
West Springfield	350	36	Ely	Levi	2			1					1				4		
West Springfield	350	37	Ely	Silence			1							2			3		
West Springfield	350	38	Ely	William				1					1				2		
West Springfield	350	39	Ely	Daniel	2	1		1		1	1		1				7		
West Springfield	350	40	Ely	George	2	1		1		2	1		1				8		
West Springfield	350	41	Ely	Elihu 2d	1		1					1					3		
West Springfield	350	42	Ely	Martin	2		3		1	2	1	3		1			13		
West Springfield	350	43	Ely	Nathaniel				1				1	1				3		
West Springfield	350	44	Ely	Cotton	2	1		1		1			1				6		
West Springfield	350	45	Ely	Abigail								1		1			2		
West Springfield	350	46	Ely	Solomon			2			1		1					4		

TOWN	PG#	LN#	LAST NAME	FIRST NAME	FREE WHITE MALES					FREE WHITE FEMALES					TOTAL ALL OTHER	TOTAL SLAVES	TOTALS	DISTRICT/ TOWNSHIP	NOTES
					under 10	10 to 16	16 to 26	26 to 45	45 and over	under 10	10 to 16	16 to 26	26 to 45	45 and over					
West Springfield	350	47	Farnam	Elijah	2			1		2			1				6		
West Springfield	350	48	Farnam	Jesse	1		1			1		1					4		
West Springfield	350	49	Felt	Mary	1					2	1		1	1			6		
West Springfield	350	50	Farnam	John					1			1		1			3		
West Springfield	350	51	Gaylord	John		1	1					1					3		
West Springfield	350	52	Goff	Silas	2			1		2			1				6		
West Springfield	350	53	Gaylord	Nathaniel		1	1		1				1	1			5		
West Springfield	350	54	Gaylord	Ebenezer			1			1		1					3		
West Springfield	350	55	Griffin	Watson	2				1	1	1	1	1				7		
West Springfield	350	56	Green	Jeptha	3	1			1			1	1				7		
West Springfield	351	1	Goodrich	Elijah		1	1	1		2			1				6		
West Springfield	351	2	Goff	Lois			1				1			1			3		
West Springfield	351	3	How	John	2			1		2			1				6		
West Springfield	351	4	Hazy	John					1					1			2		
West Springfield	351	5	Hutchins	Thomas					1			1		3			5		
West Springfield	351	6	Ives	Rebekah		2					1			1			4		
West Springfield	351	7	Kent	Ruggles	1	1	1	1		1			2				7		
West Springfield	351	8	Kent	James		1	2	1		1		2					7		
West Springfield	351	9	Lathrop	Samuel				2		1		1			2		6		
West Springfield	351	10	Lathrop	Seth	1	2	1	1			1	2	1				9		
West Springfield	351	11	Leonard	Catherine			1				1			2			4		
West Springfield	351	12	Loomis	Noadiah		1	1		1	1		1	1	1			7		
West Springfield	351	13	Leonard	Gideon	1			1		1		1	2	1			8		
West Springfield	351	14	Loomis	Clarke				1		2		1					4		
West Springfield	351	15	Loomis	Josiah	3			1		1			1				6		
West Springfield	351	16	Leonard	Seth	2			1		2			2	1			8		
West Springfield	351	17	Lathrop	Joseph			1		1		1			1			4		
West Springfield	351	18	Miller	Asa	2	1	2		1	2	1	2		1			12		
West Springfield	351	19	Miller	Israel		1		1		1			1				4		
West Springfield	351	20	Morgan	Ezekiel				1						1			2		
West Springfield	351	21	Moffat	Daniel		1	3	1		2	1		1	1			10		
West Springfield	351	22	Morgan	Abner	1	1		2		2			1	1			8		
West Springfield	351	23	Morgan	Ebenezer		1			1			1		1			4		
West Springfield	351	24	Morgan	Joel	1			1		1		1					4		
West Springfield	351	25	Morgan	Willliam			1	1			2	1	1				6		
West Springfield	351	26	Miller	Stephen			1					1					2		
West Springfield	351	27	Morgan	Samuel				1					2				3		
West Springfield	351	28	Knowlton	Jonathan	2			1		1			1				5		
West Springfield	351	29	Merrick	Tilley	1	2	1		1	1		2		2			10		
West Springfield	351	30	Miller	Calvin	1			1					1				3		
West Springfield	351	31	Morgan	James				1					1				2		
West Springfield	351	32	Nelson	Ruth						3	2		2	1			8		
West Springfield	351	33	Orcutt	Joseph		1		1		2		1					5		
West Springfield	351	34	Perkins	Elisha	2	1			1	2			1				7		
West Springfield	351	35	Pepper	Gaius	1			1		2			1				5		
West Springfield	351	36	Parsons	Jonathan	2			1	1	1	1	1		1			8		
West Springfield	351	37	Perkins	Israel	1			1					1				3		
West Springfield	351	38	Palmer	Edmund	3	3				2			1				10		
West Springfield	351	39	Price	James					1		2	3		1			7		
West Springfield	351	40	Rockwell	John				1		1		1		1			4		
West Springfield	351	41	Rogers	Sarah								1		1			2		
West Springfield	351	42	Rogers	Henry	2	1		1		1			2				7		
West Springfield	351	43	Rogers	Abner	3		2	3			1		1	1			11		
West Springfield	351	44	Rogers	David	1			1	1			2	1				6		
West Springfield	351	45	Rogers	Elijah			2			1	1		1				5		
West Springfield	351	46	Rogers	Jesse			1	1					2				4		
West Springfield	351	47	Stebbins	Solomon	1	1	2	1	2	1	1	1	2				12		
West Springfield	351	48	Scovel	John				1				1					3		
West Springfield	351	49	Smith	Daniel		1	1	1	1			1	2	1			8		
West Springfield	351	50	Smith	Simeon	1	1	1		1	2	2	1	1				10		
West Springfield	351	51	Stebbins	Jere	2	1		1			1	2	1		3		11		
West Springfield	351	52	Smith	Jared		1		1		1			1				4		
West Springfield	351	53	Smith	Jonathan	1			2	1				2				6		
West Springfield	351	54	Strong	Selah	1			1					2				4		
West Springfield	351	55	Smith	Samuel	2	1	2	1					1				7		
West Springfield	351	56	Smith	Solomon		1			1		1	1	1				5		
West Springfield	351	57	Smith	David			2	1				1	1				5		
West Springfield	352	1	Smith	Noadiah	5			1				1					7		
West Springfield	352	2	Smith	Margaret			1				1	1	1				4		
West Springfield	352	3	Smith	Elizabeth			1					3	1				5		
West Springfield	352	4	Thornton	Medad				1		1			1				3		
West Springfield	352	5	Thornton	Elisha			1			2			1				4		
West Springfield	352	6	Todd	Solomon	1				1			1		1			4		
West Springfield	352	7	Taylor	Freeman	2			1		3			1				7		
West Springfield	352	8	Turner	Gurdan		2			1		1	3		1			8		
West Springfield	352	9	Taylor	Thomas	2			1		1		1	1	1			7		
West Springfield	352	10	Taylor	Dan	1	1	1	1		2	1	1	1				9		
West Springfield	352	11	Taylor	Paul			1					1					2		
West Springfield	352	12	Taylor	John				1		1			1				4		

160

TOWN	PG#	LN#	LAST NAME	FIRST NAME	FREE WHITE MALES					FREE WHITE FEMALES					TOTAL ALL OTHER	TOTAL SLAVES	TOTALS	DISTRICT/ TOWNSHIP	NOTES
					under 10	10 to 16	16 to 26	26 to 45	45 and over	under 10	10 to 16	16 to 26	26 to 45	45 and over					
West Springfield	352	13	Taylor	Chauncy	1	1			1	1	1	2		1			8		
West Springfield	352	14	Taylor	Stephen	1	1		1		2	1		1				7		
West Springfield	352	15	Taylor	Nathaniel				1						1			2		
West Springfield	352	16	Vanhorne	John				2			1			2			5		
West Springfield	352	17	Ward	Samuel			1	1						1			3		
West Springfield	352	18	White	Daniel				1					1				2		
West Springfield	352	19	White	Pliny	1			1					1				3		
West Springfield	352	20	White	Aaron	3	1			2	1	1		1	1			10		
West Springfield	352	21	White	Joseph		1	1		1			1		1			5		
West Springfield	352	22	Wilson	John		1			1					1			3		
West Springfield	352	23	Williston	Israel	1	1			1			2		1			6		
West Springfield	352	24	Williston	Nathaniel	3		2		1			1					7		
West Springfield	352	25	Williston	John	2	1			1			4		1			9		
West Springfield	352	26	White	Horace		1	2		1		1	1		1	1		8		
West Springfield	352	27	Watrus	Smith	1			1		2			1				5		
West Springfield	352	28	Worthy	Valentine		1	1		1	1	1	1		1			7		
West Springfield	352	29	Ward	Josiah	1			1					1				3		
West Springfield	352	30	Ward	Samuel Jr				1		2		1					4		
West Springfield	352	31	Allen	Jonathan			2		1					1			4		
West Springfield	352	32	Allen	Gideon	2	1		1		1	1		1				7		
West Springfield	352	33	Adams	Seth	1	1			1	1			1				5		
West Springfield	352	34	Adams	Levi	1	1	2			1			1				6		
West Springfield	352	35	Allen	William	2	2	1		1		1			1			8		
West Springfield	352	36	Bow	Thaddeus		1		1		1	1	1	1				6		
West Springfield	352	37	Bolles	Benjamin				1		1			1				3		
West Springfield	352	38	Bedortha	Stephen	1	2	1		1	2		1		1			9		
West Springfield	352	39	Bates	Eleazer	3	1			1	1	1	3	1				11		
West Springfield	352	40	Bedortha	Jonathan			1			2		1					4		
West Springfield	352	41	Bliss	Jedidiah	1			1		1			1				6		
West Springfield	352	42	Burbank	Abraham			2	1	1	1	1	1		2	1		10		
West Springfield	352	43	Barber	John				1					1	1			3		
West Springfield	352	44	Barber	Joel	1	2		1		1			1				6		
West Springfield	352	45	Beech	Samuel	3	1	1			2			1				8		
West Springfield	352	46	Bliss	Stephen	1			1		2			1				5		
West Springfield	352	47	Bedortha	Samuel		1		1					2	1			5		
West Springfield	352	48	Bedortha	Eli	1			1					1				3		
West Springfield	352	49	Bedortha	Joseph		1	1	1	1			1	2	1			8		
West Springfield	352	50	Bedortha	Luther	2			1		1		1					5		
West Springfield	352	51	Bow	Isaac		2	1	1				2		1			7		
West Springfield	352	52	Baldwin	Elnathan	1		1	1				1					4		
West Springfield	352	53	Bishop	Daniel		1		1		2		1					5		
West Springfield	352	54	Ball	Eli	2	2		1	1	3		1	1				11		
West Springfield	352	55	Bement	Edmund	1			1				1					3		
West Springfield	352	56	Barber	Sarah								1	1				2		
West Springfield	352	57	Button	Asa		1			1			3		1			6		
West Springfield	353	1	Button	Joseph	1			1			1	1					4		
West Springfield	353	2	Bowker	Catherine		1		1		1		1	1				5		
West Springfield	353	3	Copley	Matthus	1			1				3					5		
West Springfield	353	4	Cooley	Isaac	1	1		1		2			1				7		
West Springfield	353	5	Cruttenton	Amos				1		1	1		1				4		
West Springfield	353	6	Cooper	Enoch			2	1				2	1	1			7		
West Springfield	353	7	Cooper	Enoch Jr	2		1	1		2	1		1				8		
West Springfield	353	8	Dennis	John	1			1		2	2		1				7		
West Springfield	353	9	Dunham	Jabez					1				1	1			3		
West Springfield	353	10	Eaton	Nathaniel		1	1	1		2	1		2				8		
West Springfield	353	11	Elsworth	Gustavus					1		1	1		1			4		
West Springfield	353	12	Egleston	John	1	1			1	2	1	1	1				8		
West Springfield	353	13	Feland	Joseph				1						1			2		
West Springfield	353	14	Feland	Isaac			1			1		1					3		
West Springfield	353	15	Flower	Samuel		1	2		1	1		2		1	1		9		
West Springfield	353	16	Fourman	Jared		1					1		1				3		
West Springfield	353	17	Fowler	John			1		1		1			1			4		
West Springfield	353	18	Fletcher	Ozias											13		13		
West Springfield	353	19	Fletcher	Archelaus											9		9		
West Springfield	353	20	Fowler	Walter	1		1					1			1		4		
West Springfield	353	21	Flower	Oxas	2				1			1		1			5		
West Springfield	353	22	Flower	Horace			1			1			1				3		
West Springfield	353	23	Flower	Timothy	1	2			1			2	1	1			8		
West Springfield	353	24	Ferry	Moses		1	1		1	2	2		2				9		
West Springfield	353	25	Fowler	Roger	1			1		1		1					4		
West Springfield	353	26	Feland	Henry	2		1					1					4		
West Springfield	353	27	Ferry	William	1			1		4			1				7		
West Springfield	353	28	Granger	Justin	1				1	1	2	1	2	1			9		
West Springfield	353	29	Goss	Andrew	1				1				1	1			4		
West Springfield	353	30	Grace	Joseph		2	1					2	1				7		
West Springfield	353	31	Griswold	Sylvanus				1				3		1			5		
West Springfield	353	32	Goss	Gideon	1			1					1				3		
West Springfield	353	33	Holt	Uriah	2	1	1		1		1	2		1			9		
West Springfield	353	34	Hale	Jonathan		1	1			1	1		1				5		

161

TOWN	PG#	LN#	LAST NAME	FIRST NAME	FREE WHITE MALES under 10	10 to 16	16 to 26	26 to 45	45 and over	FREE WHITE FEMALES under 10	10 to 16	16 to 26	26 to 45	45 and over	TOTAL ALL OTHER	TOTAL SLAVES	TOTALS	DISTRICT/ TOWNSHIP	NOTES
West Springfield	353	35	Horton	Timothy	1	1	1	1	1			1	1				7		
West Springfield	353	36	Hamlin	Ichiel	2		2		1		1	2	1				9		
West Springfield	353	37	Hazen	Frederick	3			1		2			1	2			9		
West Springfield	353	38	Kingsbury	Leonard	1		1			1		1					4		
West Springfield	353	39	Feller	John	1		1					1					3		
West Springfield	353	40	King	James			1	1	1				1				4		
West Springfield	353	41	King	James Junr	2	1		1		1			1				6		
West Springfield	353	42	Kent	Ezekiel	3			2		2		1	1				9		
West Springfield	353	43	Jackson	Samuel											2		2		
West Springfield	353	44	Leonard	Pliny		1	1		1		2		1	1			7		
West Springfield	353	45	Leonard	Eliphalet				1					1				2		
West Springfield	353	46	Leonard	Henry	1	1	1			2	1	1					7		
West Springfield	353	47	Leonard	Oliver				2	3			1	1				7		
West Springfield	353	48	Leonard	Preserved				1									1		
West Springfield	353	49	Loomis	Uriah	3	2		1		2	1		1				10		
West Springfield	353	50	Loomis	Justice	1		2		1	2	1		1				8		
West Springfield	353	51	Leonard	Abel				2				2	1				5		
West Springfield	353	52	Leonard	Justin	1	1	1	1		1		1	1	1			8		
West Springfield	354	1	Leonard	Asaph			1			1	1	1					5		
West Springfield	354	2	Lothrop	Elijah		1	2		1	2		2	1				9		
West Springfield	354	3	Leonard	Juba	1	2	3		1		1	1		1			10		
West Springfield	354	4	Leonard	Thaddeus		1	1	1	1		1		1				6		
West Springfield	354	5	Leonard	Roswell	2	1	1	1		3	1		1				10		
West Springfield	354	6	Leonard	Noah	2		1	1	1	1	1		1				9		
West Springfield	354	7	Leonard	Reuben Jr		1	1		1		1		1				5		
West Springfield	354	8	Leonard	Gribert	2	1	1	1		1	1	1	2				10		
West Springfield	354	9	Leonard	George		1		1	1		1	1	3				8		
West Springfield	354	10	Leonard	Austin			3	1			1		1				6		
West Springfield	354	11	Leonard	William	1			1		2	2	2					9		
West Springfield	354	12	Leonard	Daniel	1		4		1	2		2	1	1			12		
West Springfield	354	13	Leonard	John	1		1		1	1	1	1	1				8		
West Springfield	354	14	Leonard	Russell		1	1	2	1				1				6		
West Springfield	354	15	Leonard	Rufus			1			2		1					4		
West Springfield	354	16	Leonard	Preserved Jr	1	1	1			1	1						5		
West Springfield	354	17	Leonard	Selden			3				1						4		
West Springfield	354	18	Leonard	Mary			1				1	2	1				5		
West Springfield	354	19	Leonard	Moses	3			1		2	1	2	1	1			11		
West Springfield	354	20	Lancktan	Israel		1	1		1	2	1		1				7		
West Springfield	354	21	Leonard	Phineas	4	2	1		1	2	1	1					12		
West Springfield	354	22	Leonard	Editha									2				2		
West Springfield	354	23	Lancktan	Seth	1	3		1		3	1		1				10		
West Springfield	354	24	Leonard	Ezekiel	4	1		1		1	1	1					9		
West Springfield	354	25	Leonard	Charles		1		1	1		1	2					6		
West Springfield	354	26	McIntier	William	2		1		1	2	1	2	1				10		
West Springfield	354	27	Morley	Gideon		1	1		1		1		1	1			6		
West Springfield	354	28	Morley	Walter	2			1		1		1					5		
West Springfield	354	29	McIntier	Jesse			1	2		2		1					6		
West Springfield	354	30	McIntier	Jesse Jr	1			2		1		1					5		
West Springfield	354	31	Morley	David	2	2	1	1		4		1					11		
West Springfield	354	32	McIntier	Samuel		1		1			1	1							
West Springfield	354	33	Morley	Isaac				1					1				2		
West Springfield	354	34	Morley	Isaac Junr	1	1		1		2	1		1				7		
West Springfield	354	35	Marchand	William				1					1				2		
West Springfield	354	36	Morley	Asahel	1			1			1		1				7		
West Springfield	354	37	Miller	Apollos				1					1				2		
West Springfield	354	38	Munger	Daniel	1	2	1		2	1	1		1				9		
West Springfield	354	39	Mersick	Daniel	3	1		1		2	1		1				9		
West Springfield	354	40	Mason	David	1	1			1		3		1				7		
West Springfield	354	41	Norton	Philo	1			1		2			1				5		
West Springfield	354	42	Nuell	Ebenezer	2	1			1	1			1				6		
West Springfield	354	43	Norman	John	2	1	1	1		1	1	1	1				9		
West Springfield	354	44	Onkamer	Chloe											2		2		
West Springfield	354	45	Petty	Thomas				1			1		1				3		
West Springfield	354	46	Phillips	Thompson	2	1	1		1	1	1		1				8		
West Springfield	354	47	Parker	Jacob				1					1				2		
West Springfield	354	48	Phillips	Simeon	1			1			1		1				4		
West Springfield	354	49	Phillips	Gideon				1	2		1						4		
West Springfield	354	50	Palmer	Samuel	3			1		1	1		1				7		
West Springfield	354	51	Purchase	Jonathan	1		2		1	1			1				6		
West Springfield	354	52	Purchase	Charles	2			1			2		1				6		
West Springfield	354	53	Perkins	Joseph		1		1		1			1				4		
West Springfield	354	54	Palmer	Frederick	1			1					1				3		
West Springfield	354	55	Porter	John				1			2		1				4		
West Springfield	354	56	Phelps	Lucy		1	1		1		1	1					5		
West Springfield	354	57	Porter	Elijah	1			1		2		1	1				6		
West Springfield	354	58	Peters	Andrew											3		3		
West Springfield	354	59	Rowley	Nathan				1					1				2		
West Springfield	354	60	Russell	Elias			1					1					2		
West Springfield	355	1	Remington	Seneca	1								1				2		
West Springfield	355	2	Roe	Seth		1			1		1						4		

162

TOWN	PG#	LN#	HEADS OF HOUSEHOLD		FREE WHITE MALES					FREE WHITE FEMALES					TOTAL ALL OTHER	TOTAL SLAVES	TOTALS	DISTRICT/ TOWNSHIP	NOTES
			LAST NAME	FIRST NAME	under 10	10 to 16	16 to 26	26 to 45	45 and over	under 10	10 to 16	16 to 26	26 to 45	45 and over					
West Springfield	355	3	Ripley	Abraham	2			1					1				4		
West Springfield	355	4	Stockwell	Samuel			1	2						3			6		
West Springfield	355	5	Stevenson	Erastus	2			1					1				4		
West Springfield	355	6	Smith	Joseph		2		2			1		1				6		
West Springfield	355	7	Selden	Joseph				1						1			2		
West Springfield	355	8	Smith	Thomas				1	1				1	1			4		
West Springfield	355	9	Smith	Alexander	2			1		2		1	1				7		
West Springfield	355	10	Stiles	Dinah	1						1	2	1				5		
West Springfield	355	11	Stannard	Joseph				1			2		1				4		
West Springfield	355	12	Stannard	Seth	1			1		2			1				5		
West Springfield	355	13	Stannard	Oliver		1				1	1	1					4		
West Springfield	355	14	Spear	Joshua				1		2			1				4		
West Springfield	355	15	Sargeant	Ebenezer	1		1	1		2	1		1				7		
West Springfield	355	16	Sargeant	James		1				2		1					4		
West Springfield	355	17	Stephenson	John			1						1				2		
West Springfield	355	18	Stiles	Horace	1			1		1			1				3		
West Springfield	355	19	Starkweather	Cyrus			1			2	1		1				5		
West Springfield	355	20	Smith	Samuel	1	1		1		1	1	3		1			9		
West Springfield	355	21	Tucker	Morris	2		1	1					1				5		
West Springfield	355	22	Todd	Jesse				1		1				1			3		
West Springfield	355	23	Upham	Leonard	1	1		1				1		1			5		
West Springfield	355	24	Viets	Simeon	1		2						1	1			5		
West Springfield	355	25	Upham	James		1		1		1			1	1			5		
West Springfield	355	26	White	Daniel Junr		1		2		2	1		1	1			8		
West Springfield	355	27	Winchell	John				1		1	2	2		1			7		
West Springfield	355	28	Winchell	David	3			1		1			1				6		
West Springfield	355	29	Wade	James	3	1		1		2	1	1					9		
West Springfield	355	30	Warriner	Lewis	2	1	1	1		1		1	1				8		
West Springfield	355	31	Worthington	Jonathan	1		2	1		1	2		1				8		
West Springfield	355	32	Worthington	Amos	1	1							1				3		
West Springfield	355	33	Winchell	Jacob	1	1	1	1				1		1			6		
West Springfield	355	34	Wightman	Jesse	4			1					1				6		
West Springfield	355	35	Warriner	Gad		1		1		4	1		2	1			10		
West Springfield	355	36	Worthington	John	2			1		2			1				6		
West Springfield	355	37	Wedger	Ebenezer	1			1		2			1				5		
West Springfield	355	38	Worthington	Heman		1		1		2			1				5		
West Springfield	355	39	Worthington	David	2		4	1		1			1				9		
West Springfield	355	40	Allen	Amos		1		2				1		1			5		
West Springfield	355	41	Allen	Enos	1					2			1				5		
West Springfield	355	42	Allen	Bishop	2	1	2	1		2	1		2				11		
West Springfield	355	43	Ashley	Elisha	1		1	1		3			2	1			9		
West Springfield	355	44	Bradley	Nathaniel	1	1	1	1		1	1	1					7		
West Springfield	355	45	Black	Alexander	1			1		1			1				4		
West Springfield	355	46	Ball	Charles	2	1		1		1	1	1	2				9		
West Springfield	355	47	Bracket	Ruth						1		1	1				3		
West Springfield	355	48	Baird	Isaac				1						1			2		
West Springfield	355	49	Black	Mary	1								1	1			3		
West Springfield	355	50	Boyd	Elizabeth						1			1				2		
West Springfield	355	51	Barker	Ephraim	2		2			1		1	2	1			9		
West Springfield	355	52	Bassett	Benjamin	1	1	1	1		3	1		1				9		
West Springfield	355	53	Boyd	William	2	1		1		2		1		1			8		
West Springfield	355	54	Brooks	Nathan	3			1		1			1				6		
West Springfield	355	55	Chapin	Asahel		3	1	1		1		1	1				8		
West Springfield	355	56	Chapin	Martin		1		1		2			1				5		
West Springfield	356	1	Chapin	Eunice		1	1						2	1			5		
West Springfield	356	2	Chapin	Miriam										2			2		
West Springfield	356	3	Clough	Uriah	2	3		1	1	2			1	1			11		
West Springfield	356	4	Cushman	Jesse	1			1		4			1				7		
West Springfield	356	5	Cooper	Jacob	4			1					1	1			7		
West Springfield	356	6	Carrier	Joseph	2	1		1		1			1				6		
West Springfield	356	7	Carrier	Jeremiah				1				1	1				3		
West Springfield	356	8	Carrier	Jeremiah Jr	2			1		1			1				5		
West Springfield	356	9	Curtis	Lysander				1				1	1				3		
West Springfield	356	10	Chapin	Bathsheba		1					1	1		1			4		
West Springfield	356	11	Day	John				1			1	2	2				6		
West Springfield	356	12	Day	Jedidiah	1		1	1		1	1	1					6		
West Springfield	356	13	Day	Brigham	3		1						1				5		
West Springfield	356	14	Day	Eleazer	1		2	1		1			1	1			8		
West Springfield	356	15	Day	Joel		1	1	1		1			1	1			6		
West Springfield	356	16	Day	Joel Jr	1	2	1			3	2		1				11		
West Springfield	356	17	Day	James	2			1		2			2				7		
West Springfield	356	18	Day	Joseph			1	1	1			2		1			6		
West Springfield	356	19	Danks	Caleb	1			1		3			2	1			8		
West Springfield	356	20	Danks	Eliakim	1			1		3	2		1				8		
West Springfield	356	21	Ely	Joseph			1	1				1	3				6		
West Springfield	356	22	Ely	Benjamin		1		2	1			1		1			6		
West Springfield	356	23	Ely	Robert	2			1		1			1				5		
West Springfield	356	24	Ely	Moses	3	2		1	1	1	1		1	1			11		
West Springfield	356	25	Ey	Russell				1				1		1			3		
West Springfield	356	26	Ely	Enoch	3			1		1	1	1	1				7		
West Springfield	356	27	Ely	Elihu	1	1		2		3		1	1				9		
West Springfield	356	28	Ely	Erasmus		1		1		3			1				6		
West Springfield	356	29	Ely	C*	1			1		3	1	1	1				8		
West Springfield	356	30	*ell	Le*	4	1	1	1		2	1		1				11		
West Springfield	356	31	Ferry	Charles	2			1		1			1				5		
West Springfield	356	32	Frink	Luther			1	1		4		1		1			8		
West Springfield	356	33	Fuller	Bushman											6		6		
West Springfield	356	34	Goodyear	Austin	3			1		1			1				6		
West Springfield	356	35	Gill	Samuel	1		1	1		1	1		1				6		

163

TOWN	PG#	LN#	LAST NAME	FIRST NAME	FREE WHITE MALES					FREE WHITE FEMALES					TOTAL ALL OTHER	TOTAL SLAVES	TOTALS	DISTRICT/ TOWNSHIP	NOTES
					under 10	10 to 16	16 to 26	26 to 45	45 and over	under 10	10 to 16	16 to 26	26 to 45	45 and over					
West Springfield	356	36	Hitchcock	Perez	2	1	1	1					1	2			8		
West Springfield	356	37	Humaston	James				1						1			2		
West Springfield	356	38	Humaston	James 2d	3	2	2	1		1	1	2	1				13		
West Springfield	356	39	Humaston	Caleb	1	1	4	1		1	2	2	1				13		
West Springfield	356	40	Howard	Joseph	1	1		1		1	1		1				6		
West Springfield	356	41	Howard	Andrew			1	1		1			2				5		
West Springfield	356	42	Howard	Thomas Jr	1			1				1					3		
West Springfield	356	43	Howard	Thomas				1					1				2		
West Springfield	356	44	Howe	Ichabod		1		1		2	1			1			6		
West Springfield	356	45	Hart	Charles	3			1		1	1		1				6		
West Springfield	356	46	Howard	Pember	2			1		1			1				5		
West Springfield	356	47	Jones	Ebenezer 2d	1	1			2	1			1				6		
West Springfield	356	48	Jones	Ebenezer 3d			1			1			1				3		
West Springfield	356	49	Jones	Gideon 2d		1		1		1	1		1				5		
West Springfield	356	50	Jones	Hezekiah	1			1						1			3		
West Springfield	356	51	Ives	Jeremiah			1	1		3	1	1					7		
West Springfield	356	52	Ives	Abraham	1		1			1			1				4		
West Springfield	356	53	Jones	Ithamar	5	1		1		1			1				9		
West Springfield	356	54	Kendall	David	1			1				1					3		
West Springfield	356	55	Ludington	John	1	1	2		1	1		2		1			9		
West Springfield	356	56	Ludington	Daniel	2	2		1				2		1			8		
West Springfield	357	1	Ludington	Jude	1	1		1	1	1	1		2				8		
West Springfield	357	2	Morgan	Jesse		1		1				1	1				4		
West Springfield	357	3	Morgan	Joseph		1	1		1			1	2	1			7		
West Springfield	357	4	Morgan	Titus			1	1				1		1			4		
West Springfield	357	5	Morgan	Julius	1		1	1				1					4		
West Springfield	357	6	Miller	John	2	1		1		1	1	1					8		
West Springfield	357	7	Miller	Abner	1		1	1		2		1	1				7		
West Springfield	357	8	McWethy	Nathaniel		1	1	1					2				5		
West Springfield	357	9	Morgan	Erastus	2			1		1	1		1				6		
West Springfield	357	10	Morgan	Lucas	1	1	1	1	1	2		2	1				10		
West Springfield	357	11	Nelson	Lemuel	1		1			3	2	1	1				9		
West Springfield	357	12	rcutt	David		1		1				1		1			4		
West Springfield	357	13	Ornes	Michael	2		1		1	1	2			1			8		
West Springfield	357	14	Perkins	William	3			1		1			1				6		
West Springfield	357	15	Pearson	Samuel		2		1		1	1			1			6		
West Springfield	357	16	Parsons	Luke	2	1		1		4			1	1			10		
West Springfield	357	17	Roberts	Eli	3			1					1				5		
West Springfield	357	18	Richardson	Isaac	2	1	1		1	1	1	1	1				9		
West Springfield	357	19	Roberts	William		2		1				1					4		
West Springfield	357	20	Rogers	Josiah			1	1	1	1	1			1			6		
West Springfield	357	21	Rogers	Josiah 2d	1		1	2		1	1		1				7		
West Springfield	357	22	Rogers	Eli		1			1	1				1			4		
West Springfield	357	23	Street	Joshua			2	1			1	1	1				6		
West Springfield	357	24	Searls	Simeon	3			1		2			1				7		
West Springfield	357	25	Searls	Lemuel	1			1		1			1				4		
West Springfield	357	26	Stickman	Frederick				1		1			1	1			4		
West Springfield	357	27	Street	Glover	2	1		1		2			1				7		
West Springfield	357	28	Street	Caleb M.	3			1					1				5		
West Springfield	357	29	Stevens	Nathan		1		1			1						3		
West Springfield	357	30	Stevens	Nathan Junr			1			1			1				3		
West Springfield	357	31	Tuttle	Electa	1					1			1				3		
West Springfield	357	32	Tuttle	Tilly		1	1		1		1			1			5		
West Springfield	357	33	Thorp	Eli	1			1		3	1		1				7		
West Springfield	357	34	Thorp	Moses	2	1		1				1					5		
West Springfield	357	35	Tuttle	Michael			1			1		1					3		
West Springfield	357	36	Wolcott	Jesse	2	1	1		1	2			1				8		
West Springfield	357	37	Wolcott	David	4			1			1	1	1				8		
West Springfield	357	38	Wolcott	Solomon	1			1		1			1				4		
West Springfield	357	39	Wolcott	Noah	1		1	1		3	1		1				8		
West Springfield	357	40	Wade	Nathan L.	2			1		2			1				6		
West Springfield	357	41	Williams	David			1						1	1			3		
West Springfield	357	42	Williams	Roger	1		1			1	1						4		
West Springfield	357	43	Warner	Noah	2	2		1		1		1	1				8		
West Springfield	357	44	Williams	Elijah		2			1	3			1				7		

TOWN	PG#	LN#	HEADS OF HOUSEHOLD		FREE WHITE MALES					FREE WHITE FEMALES					TOTAL ALL OTHER	TOTAL SLAVES	TOTALS	DISTRICT/TOWNSHIP	NOTES
			LAST NAME	FIRST NAME	under 10	10 to 16	16 to 26	26 to 45	45 and over	under 10	10 to 16	16 to 26	26 to 45	45 and over					
Westfield	118	1	*	James		3					1	1					5		Last name faded
Westfield	118	2	Root	Silas	2		1	1	1	1		1	2	1			10		
Westfield	118	3	Ashley	Wm	1	1	1		1		1	1		1			7		
Westfield	118	4	Bush	Aaron	3	2	1	1	1	1		1		1			11		
Westfield	118	5	Fowler	Blackleach	1	1	1		1	2	1	1	1				9		
Westfield	118	6	Fowler	Amos	1	1	1	1			1		1	1			7		
Westfield	118	7	Mosley	Noah	2			1		1		1					5		
Westfield	118	8	Dewey	David		1			1				1				3		
Westfield	118	9	Dewey	Amos	3		2	1			1		1				8		
Westfield	118	10	Dewey	Timothy	2	3	1		1	1		2	1	1			12		
Westfield	118	11	Fowler	Luther		1	1		1			1					4		
Westfield	118	12	Fowler	Jared	2			1		2			1				6		
Westfield	118	13	Fowler	John		1			1	1	2	1	1				7		
Westfield	118	14	Sears	John				1			1	1	1				4		
Westfield	118	15	Noble	Asa	1	1			1	1	1			1			6		
Westfield	118	16	Loomis	Curtis			1			4		1					6		
Westfield	118	17	Taylor	Samuel	2	3			1	1				1			8		
Westfield	118	18	Noble	Mathew			2		1			1		1			5		
Westfield	118	19	Noble	Jared	2		1	1		1	1			1			7		
Westfield	118	20	Taylor	Jedidiah	2	1	1		1	1	2		1	1			10		
Westfield	119	1	Lord	David	1				1	3			1				6		
Westfield	119	2	Hanchet	Moses			1	1									2		
Westfield	119	3	Fowler	Daniel	1	1	2	1	1	2		1	2	1			12		
Westfield	119	4	Holcomb	Enoch Jun		2		1		1	2	3		1			10		
Westfield	119	5	Noble	Wm	1		1						1				3		
Westfield	119	6	Noble	Jacob	2	1		1		1			1				6		
Westfield	119	7	Noble	Benjamin		1		1		1			1				4		
Westfield	119	8	Mosley	Azariah	1	1		1			1		2	1			7		
Westfield	119	9	Sacket	Royal	2			1		1	1		1				6		
Westfield	119	10	Sacket	Wm		1	2		1	1	1		1	1			8		
Westfield	119	11	Bush	Amos	1	1	1		1	1		1	1				7		
Westfield	119	12	Root	Joseph		1	1		1	1	1	2		1			8		
Westfield	119	13	Holcomb	Enoch		1	1	1					1	1			6		
Westfield	119	14	Williams	Thomas		1		1					1				3		
Westfield	119	15	Phelps	Mary Wd			1					1		1			3		
Westfield	119	16	Phelps	David	1			1		2		1					5		
Westfield	119	17	Stiles	Simeon			1	1					1				3		
Westfield	119	18	Stiles	John		1		1		3			1				6		
Westfield	119	19	Ashley	Noah			1				1		1				3		
Westfield	119	20	Shepard	Simeon	1			1		1			1				4		
Westfield	119	21	Fowler	Ebenezer			1		1				1				3		
Westfield	119	22	Fowler	Justus	2	1		1			1		1				6		
Westfield	119	23	Smith	Simon	3	1		1			2		1				8		
Westfield	119	24	Root	Saml	2		1		1	3	1	1	1				10		
Westfield	119	25	Dewey	Eliab	2	2	1		1	1		1	1	1			10		
Westfield	119	26	Stiles	Simeon Junr	1	2		1		2		1	1				8		
Westfield	119	27	Dewey	Eliab Junr	3	1		1					1				6		
Westfield	119	28	Combs	Tamzin Wd	3						1	1	1	1			7		
Westfield	119	29	Mein	Armer	1			1		2	1		1				6		
Westfield	119	30	Weller	Jared	1		1	1		4			1				8		
Westfield	119	31	Weller	Sarah Wd	1	1	1	1				1		1			6		
Westfield	119	32	Weller	Oliver	1	2	2	1	1			2		1			10		
Westfield	119	33	Ashley	Stephen	3		1	1		1		1	1				8		
Westfield	119	34	Smith	John				1		1		1					3		
Westfield	119	35	Ingersoll	John		1		1		1	1	1			1		6		
Westfield	119	36	Wright	Rodrick	1	1	2	1		3	1		1				10		
Westfield	120	1	Phelps	Solomon	3			1		1		1					6		
Westfield	120	2	Bates	Elijah				1				1			1		3		
Westfield	120	3	Mosley	Israel			3		1	5			2		1		12		
Westfield	120	4	Whitney	Abel	3		3	2		2	2	4	1				17		
Westfield	120	5	Phelps	John	1	1	3		1		1	3		2			12		
Westfield	120	6	Mosley	Pliny	1	1	1		1	3		1	1				9		
Westfield	120	7	King	Aaron	1	1		1				2					5		
Westfield	120	8	King	Silas Capt.	2	1	1	1		1	1		1				8		
Westfield	120	9	Mather	John	1	1	1	2		1	1	1	1				9		
Westfield	120	10	Mosley	Jeremiah	1	1	1				2	3	1	1	1		11		
Westfield	120	11	Snell	Nahum P			1			3		1	1				6		
Westfield	120	12	Clap	Ezra Capt	4	1				1	1	1	1				9		
Westfield	120	13	Ballantine	John	1				1			1		1			4		
Westfield	120	14	Mather	Saml Esq	1		2		1	2	1			1			8		
Westfield	120	15	Ashley	Israel		2			1		1	2		1			7		
Westfield	120	16	Douglas	Stephen	2	1		1		1		2					7		
Westfield	120	17	Davis	Wm				1					1				2		
Westfield	120	18	Williams	Reuben		1	1		2		1			1			6		
Westfield	120	19	Ingersoll	Charles		1	1			2	1		1	1			7		
Westfield	120	20	Grant	Alexander			1	1									2		
Westfield	120	21	Wheaton	Marshal	3		1	1		1	1		1				8		
Westfield	120	22	Mosley	Hannah Wd	1			1		2	1	2	2	1			10		
Westfield	120	23	Whitney	Charlotte Wd		2	4			1			1				8		
Westfield	120	24	Mason	Benjamin	1		1		1	2			1				6		

Town	PG#	LN#	Last Name	First Name	Males under 10	Males 10 to 16	Males 16 to 26	Males 26 to 45	Males 45 and over	Females under 10	Females 10 to 16	Females 16 to 26	Females 26 to 45	Females 45 and over	Total All Other	Total Slaves	Totals	District/Township	Notes
Westfield	120	25	Bush	Zachariah	1		3		1	1		1		1			8		
Westfield	120	26	Atwater	Noah Revd		3	1		1		3		1				11		
Westfield	120	27	Morse	Jacob	2	2	2		1	1	1	4	1				14		
Westfield	120	28	Palmer	Gad				1		1	2	1	1				6		
Westfield	120	29	Bush	Zadok	1	2	1		1	2	1	1	1	1	2		13		
Westfield	120	30	King	Bohan	4	1	5	1	1				2	1	1		16		
Westfield	120	31	Sacket	Adnah	1		3		1			1		2			8		
Westfield	121	1	Fowler	Samll Esq	2				1	3	1		2				9		
Westfield	121	2	Hasting	Benjamin				1		2	1	1					5		
Westfield	121	3	Farnum	Joel	3		1	1		2	1		1				9		
Westfield	121	4	Kellogg	Samll Esq	1	1		1				1	1				5		
Westfield	121	5	Dewey	Noah		1		1	2	1	2	2	1				10		
Westfield	121	6	Harrison	Stephen	1			1	1	2			1	1			7		
Westfield	121	7	Harrison	Reuben	1	1		1		3	1		1				6		
Westfield	121	8	Verts	Seth		1	1		1	1	1		1				6		
Westfield	121	9	Noble	Noah			1					1					2		
Westfield	121	10	Shepard	Silence	2			1				1	1	1			6		
Westfield	121	11	Allen	Moses	2			1		3			1	1			8		
Westfield	121	12	Sacket	Asher	1	1			1	1		1		1			6		
Westfield	121	13	Sacket	John	2			1		1			1				5		
Westfield	121	14	Cadwell	Timothy	2			1		3	1		1				8		
Westfield	121	15	Bosworth	Saml	1	2	1			2	1		1				8		
Westfield	121	16	Bosworth	Caleb	2	1			1	1	1		1				7		
Westfield	121	17	Mumford	Wm	2		1	1		2			1				7		
Westfield	121	18	Farnum	John		2		1		2	1			1			7		
Westfield	121	19	Dean	Samll	4	1		1	1	1	2		1	1			12		
Westfield	121	20	Egleston	Jehiel	1				1	2	1		1				6		
Westfield	121	21	Sacket	Manarola	3			1		1			1				6		
Westfield	121	22	Atwater	John		1			1	1	1		1				6		
Westfield	121	23	Root	Gad	3	1	1		1		2	1	1				10		
Westfield	121	24	Wellar	John	1				1	1		1		1			5		
Westfield	121	25	Wellar	Aaron			1	1				2		1			5		
Westfield	121	26	Parks	Warham Esq	3	1	3		2	2	3	1	2		1		18		
Westfield	121	27	Mosley	Wm	4	2		1		1	1		1				10		
Westfield	121	28	Sacket	Moses	2	1	1		1	1	1	1		1			9		
Westfield	121	29	Kellogg	Gad				1					1				2		
Westfield	121	30	Sacket	Ozern	1	1	2	1	1		1	1	1	1			10		
Westfield	121	31	Carlile	Jonathan	3			1		3	1		1				9		
Westfield	122	1	Fowler	Frederick	2	1	2	2		1	1		1				10		
Westfield	122	2	Gibbons	John	2	2		1	1	4	1	2	1				14		
Westfield	122	3	Sacket	Wm Junr	2	2		1		3			1				9		
Westfield	122	4	Shepard	Wm Esq		1	1		2		1	3		1	1		10		
Westfield	122	5	Lee	Stephen	3				1				1				5		
Westfield	122	6	Graves	John					1	2			1				4		
Westfield	122	7	Sumner	Joshua			1	1			2		1				5		
Westfield	122	8	Noble	Thomas					1			2	2				5		
Westfield	122	9	Whipple	Joshua					1				1				2		
Westfield	122	10	Nimox	Richard	2				1	1	1	2		1			8		
Westfield	122	11	Bush	Walter				1		3	1						5		
Westfield	122	12	Noble	Calvin	1	1		1		1	1		1				6		
Westfield	122	13	Sacket	Noble	1			1				2					4		
Westfield	122	14	Lee	Zadok	1		1	1	1	2	1	1		2			10		
Westfield	122	15	Brass	Henery	2			1		2	1		1				7		
Westfield	122	16	Nimox	Noble			1			2		1					4		
Westfield	122	17	Williams	Naboth	1		1			3	1		1				7		
Westfield	122	18	Sacket	Jona				1		3	2		1				7		
Westfield	122	19	Harmon	Elinor	1					2			1				4		
Westfield	122	20	Shepard	Ezekiel			1			1		1					3		
Westfield	122	21	Sacket	Eliakim	1		1			2			2				6		
Westfield	122	22	Noble	Heman	1		1			1		1					4		
Westfield	122	23	Tucker	Dick Negro											3		3		
Westfield	122	24	Sacket	Gad	1	1	1		1	2			1				7		
Westfield	122	25	Williams	Ephraim	3			1		2			1				7		
Westfield	122	26	Streeter	Levi	2		1			1		1					5		
Westfield	122	27	Trask	Elizabeth	1	2					1		1				5		
Westfield	122	28	Larabee	Tiler	1		1		1	3		1		1			8		
Westfield	122	29	Sacket	Joel		1		1		1	1	1					5		
Westfield	122	30	Shepard	Jared	2			1		3			1				7		
Westfield	122	31	Noble	Saml	3	3			1	3			1	1			13		
Westfield	123	1	Ingersoll	Oliver		1	1	2			1	1	1	1			8		
Westfield	123	2	Carew	Asahel	4			1		3	1						9		
Westfield	123	3	Beebe	Artimas	2			1		2			1				6		
Westfield	123	4	Davids	Daniel	2	1			1	2	1	1	1				9		
Westfield	123	5	Sexton	Elizabeth Wd		1	1			1				1			4		
Westfield	123	6	Pease	Titus			2			2		1					5		
Westfield	123	7	Noble	Bartholomew	1			1		1		1	1	1			6		
Westfield	123	8	Ashley	Eli	1		2		1				1	2			7		
Westfield	123	9	Parks	Roland	1	1		1		1			1				5		
Westfield	123	10	Loomis	Abigal Wd	1									2			3		

166

TOWN	PG#	LN#	LAST NAME	FIRST NAME	FWM under 10	FWM 10 to 16	FWM 16 to 26	FWM 26 to 45	FWM 45 and over	FWF under 10	FWF 10 to 16	FWF 16 to 26	FWF 26 to 45	FWF 45 and over	TOTAL ALL OTHER	TOTAL SLAVES	TOTALS	DISTRICT/ TOWNSHIP	NOTES
Westfield	123	11	Negro	Flora											5		5		
Westfield	123	12	Dewey	Israel	2	2			1	1			1	1			8		
Westfield	123	13	Dewey	Moses Capt	1	1	1	1	1	2		1	1	1			10		
Westfield	123	14	Porter	Isaac	1	1	1		1	1	1	1	1				8		
Westfield	123	15	Porter	Elijah	1	1			1	2	1	1					7		
Westfield	123	16	Liswell	Thomas	2	1		1		1	2		1				8		
Westfield	123	17	Vanhorn	Derrick	1	1			1	5	1	1	1				11		
Westfield	123	18	Loomis	Enoch	1	1	1		1	1	2	2		1			10		
Westfield	123	19	Fowler	Isaac		1	1	1		1	1		1				6		
Westfield	123	20	Dewey	John	2	2	1		1	1		1	1				9		
Westfield	123	21	Rose	Thomas	1			1	1	2			1	1			7		
Westfield	123	22	Dewey	Solomon	1			1		3	1		1	1			8		
Westfield	123	23	Ensign	Isaac	2	3	1	1		3			1	1			12		
Westfield	123	24	Martindale	Joel	1			1		2		1	1				6		
Westfield	123	25	Martindale	Saml				1		1			1				3		
Westfield	123	26	Loomis	Pliny	1	1	1	1			1		1				6		
Westfield	123	27	Dewey	Josiah	1	1	2		1	1	1	1		1			9		
Westfield	123	28	Rice	Joseph	1	1			1	2			1	1			7		
Westfield	123	29	Copley	Benjamin	1					1	1		1	1			6		
Westfield	123	30	Smith	John			1	1	1	2		1	1	1			8		
Westfield	123	31	Dewey	Roswell	3		1	1		1			1				7		
Westfield	124	1	Hambleton	Adam				1		1	1		1				4		
Westfield	124	2	Noble	Seth Mr	1			1		2	1		1				6		
Westfield	124	3	Veits	Seth Junr	1		1					1					3		
Westfield	124	4	Copley	Noah				1					1				2		
Westfield	124	5	Dewey	Josiah Junr	2	1	1	1		1	1		1				8		
Westfield	124	6	Smith	Darias	1			1		2			1				5		
Westfield	124	7	Day	Luke				1						1			2		
Westfield	124	8	Veits	John	1		1			2			1				5		
Westfield	124	9	Day	Ambrose	5		1					1	1				8		
Westfield	124	10	Day	Gideon		1		1				1	1	1			5		
Westfield	124	11	Phelps	Oliver	1	1		1		3	2		1				9		
Westfield	124	12	Noble	Daniel		1		1				2		1			5		
Westfield	124	13	Noble	Harris			1						1				2		
Westfield	124	14	Yeoman	Elijah	2	1	2	1		1	1	1	1				10		
Westfield	124	15	Tiffany	Wm	2			1			1	1	1				6		
Westfield	124	16	Owen	Abijah	2	1	1		1	3	2		1	1			12		
Westfield	124	17	Owen	Asahel	2	1	1		1	1	1	1	1				9		
Westfield	124	18	Owen	Carnie	2	1	1	1		3			1	1			10		
Westfield	124	19	Tuttle	Ichabod	1		1			1		1					4		
Westfield	124	20	Gaylord	John	2	1		1		1		1					6		
Westfield	124	21	Mowat	James			1				1		1				3		
Westfield	124	22	Prentis	Nathaniel		2	1		1		1			1			6		
Westfield	124	23	Bancroft	John	3	1	2		1	3	1	2		2	4		19		
Westfield	124	24	Rowe	Joseph		1		1		5		1	1				9		
Westfield	124	25	Root	Noadiah	2		1		1	2			1				7		
Westfield	124	26	Smith	Silvanus	1		1		1	1	1		1				6		
Westfield	124	27	Williams	Roswell	3		1				1						5		
Westfield	124	28	Kellogg	Cotton	2		1			2			1				6		
Westfield	124	29	Babcock	Irena						1				1			2		
Westfield	124	30	Gaylord	Wm				1						1			2		
Westfield	124	31	Gaylord	Robert	2			1		1	3		1				8		
Westfield	124	32	Searl	Biddad	1			1		3			1				6		
Westfield	124	33	Searl	Stephen	1	3		1		2			1				8		
Westfield	125	1	Pitcher	Elijah				1		1			1				3		
Westfield	125	2	Pitcher	Danll	4	1		1		3	1		1				11		
Westfield	125	3	Pitcher	Reuben	3	1	2	1		1	2		1				11		
Westfield	125	4	Herrick	Aaron			1					1					2		
Westfield	125	5	Stoddard	Georg A				1		1		1	1				4		
Westfield	125	6	Southwell	David			2					1					3		
Westfield	125	7	Fowler	Eli	2		1			2			1				6		
Westfield	125	8	Clap	Pliny	1	1			1	2	1		1				7		
Westfield	125	9	Luchore	Lemuel	2		1					1					4		
Westfield	125	10	Egleston	Eber		2	1		1	3		1	1				9		
Westfield	125	11	Egleston	Simeon	2	2		1		2			1	1			9		
Westfield	125	12	Lee	Elisha	2	1		1		2			1				9		
Westfield	125	13	Lee	Ichabod		1		1		1				1			4		
Westfield	125	14	Root	Enoch			1			1	1						3		
Westfield	125	15	Bewel	Saml		1	2		1					1			5		
Westfield	125	16	Clark	Roswel	2	1		1		1		1		1			7		
Westfield	125	17	Stoddard	Ralph		2		1		1	1		1				6		
Westfield	125	18	Arther	Hannah Wd		1	2					3		1			7		
Westfield	125	19	Arther	Bradford			1			1	1						3		
Westfield	125	20	Stephens	Ira			1			2	1						4		
Westfield	125	21	Root	Stephen	1	1	3		1	3	1		1	2			13		
Westfield	125	22	Rogers	Jonathan				1						1			2		
Westfield	125	23	Rogers	Eli	5		1					1					7		
Westfield	125	24	Dewey	Aaron	1	1	1	1	1	1	1	1	1	1			10		
Westfield	125	25	Stoddard	Avery			1	1		2			1				7		

TOWN	PG#	LN#	LAST NAME	FIRST NAME	FREE WHITE MALES					FREE WHITE FEMALES					TOTAL ALL OTHER	TOTAL SLAVES	TOTALS	DISTRICT/ TOWNSHIP	NOTES
					under 10	10 to 16	16 to 26	26 to 45	45 and over	under 10	10 to 16	16 to 26	26 to 45	45 and over					
Westfield	125	26	Stephens	Rufus			1		1		1			1			4		
Westfield	125	27	Moor	Lucretia Wd	1		1			1	1		2	1			7		
Westfield	125	28	Allen	Ransford			1						1	1			3		
Westfield	125	29	Otis	James	3	1	1			1	1		1				9		
Westfield	125	30	Bogue	Amos			1			1			1				3		
Westfield	125	31	Moor	Abigal Wd		1	2		1		1	3		2			10		
Westfield	125	32	Williams	Ebenezer	1			1									2		
Westfield	125	33	Whipple	Joshua Jun	1		1			1			1				4		
Westfield	125	34	Otis	Jabez	1			1		2			1				5		
Westfield	126	1	Topliff	John	1	3			2	4			1	1			12		
Westfield	126	2	Bush	Elijah	1			1					1				3		
Westfield	126	3	Chapman	Calib	2	2			1	1	2		1				9		
Westfield	126	4	Avery	Abel	4		1	1			2		1				9		
Westfield	126	5	Bush	Silas		1	2	1	1		2			1			8		
Westfield	126	6	Lewis	Gould	2	1		1		1	1		1				7		
Westfield	126	7	Lewis	James				1					1				2		
Westfield	126	8	Atkins	Luther	2	1		1		2	1	2	1				10		
Westfield	126	9	Upson	Simeone	3			1		2			1				7		
Westfield	126	10	Baldwin	Jabez		2	1	1			2	1		1			9		
Westfield	126	11	Atkins	Chancey	3	1	1	1		1	2	1	1				11		
Westfield	126	12	Furrow	Peter			1		1		2			1			5		
Westfield	126	13	Brown	Uriah		2	1		1					1			5		
Westfield	126	14	Grainger	Eli	1					1			1				3		
Westfield	126	15	Tinker	Martin Capt	5	1	2		1			1	1	1			12		
Westfield	126	16	Fowler	Ebenezer Jun	2		1	1		2	1	1	1				9		
Westfield	126	17	Dewey	Benjamin		1	1		1		1	2		1	1		8		
Westfield	126	18	Dewey	James	1			1		1			1				4		
Westfield	126	19	Dewey	Joseph			2		1				2	1			6		
Westfield	126	20	Hiscock	Wm			1		1			2		1			5		
Westfield	126	21	French	Thomas	1			1		3			1				6		
Westfield	126	22	Drake	Moses				1			1		2	1			5		
Westfield	126	23	Shepard	Solomon	1	1	2		1			1		1			7		
Westfield	126	24	Brown	Roswel	1	2		1		3		1					9		
Westfield	126	25	Fowler	Ashbel	1	1		1		4			1				8		
Westfield	126	26	Tiffeny	Saml	1			1		2			1				5		
Westfield	126	27	Fox	Jonathan D.	1			1		3		1					6		
Westfield	126	28	Stiles	Darreas							1			1			2		
Westfield	126	29	Stiles	Martin				1						1			2		
Westfield	126	30	Stiles	Martin Junr	1	2	4		1	1	1	1					12		
Westfield	126	31	Weatherby	Charles	1		1						1				3		
Westfield	126	32	Newton	Roswel	3	1			1	1	1		1				8		
Westfield	127	1	Kellogg	Josiah	2	1		1		2	1		1				8		
Westfield	127	2	Bush	Jared		1	2		1		1			1			6		
Westfield	127	3	Gillet	Nathaniel			2					1					3		
Westfield	127	4	Gates	Matthias	4		1			1	1		1	1			9		
Westfield	127	5	Drake	Moses Junr	3		1			1			1				6		
Westfield	127	6	Noble	Eager	1		1			1	2	2	1				8		
Westfield	127	7	Mix	Timothy		1		1				2		1			5		
Westfield	127	8	Nelson	Aaron	1	1	2	1			1	1		1			8		
Westfield	127	9	Loomis	Joshua		1	2		1	3	2	1		1			11		
Westfield	127	10	Loomis	John			2			1		1		1			5		
Westfield	127	11	Loomis	Justus	3	1		1		2	2		1				10		
Westfield	127	12	Stockin	Amasa	2	1		1		2	1		1				8		
Westfield	127	13	Blake	John E	1		1			1			1				4		
Westfield	127	14	Blake	Thomas	1			1		1			1				4		
Westfield	127	15	Carter	Wm	2	1		1		4			1				9		
Westfield	127	16	Sacket	Moses 2d	3			1		1			1				6		
Westfield	127	17	Noble	Mark	1		1	1	1	2			1	1			8		
Westfield	127	18	Sacket	Ezra	1	1	1		1	3	2	1		1			11		
Westfield	127	19	Grainger	Elijah	2		1			2		1					6		
Westfield	127	20	Sacket	Stephen Junr	1	2					1						4		
Westfield	127	21	Sacket	Stephen	1		1			1	2		1				7		
Westfield	127	22	Killam	Thomas	2	1	1		1	1		1		1			8		
Westfield	127	23	Williams	Philip			1			2			1				4		
Westfield	127	24	Greenwood	Homes	2		1						1				4		
Westfield	127	25	Gibson	Saml				1		1				1			3		
Westfield	127	26	Steward	Lemuel				1		1			1				3		
Westfield	127	27	Munson	Stephen	1	1		1		1			1				5		
Westfield	127	28	Phelps	Ezra	2	2		1		3	1		1				10		
Westfield	127	29	Mills	Joshua	3			1					1				5		
Westfield	127	30	Phelps	Noah		1	1		1	1	1	1		1			7		
Westfield	127	31	Phelps	Moses		1	1						1	1			5		
Westfield	127	32	Perkins	Wm	2			1		3			1				7		
Westfield	128	1	Lee	Solomon	1	1			1	1	1	1		1			7		
Westfield	128	2	Trimon	Simeon	2			1	1	2			1	1			8		
Westfield	128	3	Dewey	Russel			2		1		2		1				6		
Westfield	128	4	Shepard	Noah	2			1		2			1				6		
Westfield	128	5	Douglass	Sparra	3			1		1			1				6		
Westfield	128	6	Stiles	Ephraim	1	1		1		4	1		1				9		
Westfield	128	7	Smith	Matthew	1		1		1	2			1				6		

TOWN	PG#	LN#	HEADS OF HOUSEHOLD		FREE WHITE MALES					FREE WHITE FEMALES					TOTAL ALL OTHER	TOTAL SLAVES	TOTALS	DISTRICT/ TOWNSHIP	NOTES
			LAST NAME	FIRST NAME	under 10	10 to 16	16 to 26	26 to 45	45 and over	under 10	10 to 16	16 to 26	26 to 45	45 and over					
Westfield	128	8	Parks	Amos	1	1	1		1		1			1			6		
Westfield	128	9	Negro	Aeoro											4		4		
Westfield	128	10	Negro	Brister											3		3		

TOWN	PG#	LN#	LAST NAME	FIRST NAME	FREE WHITE MALES					FREE WHITE FEMALES					TOTAL ALL OTHER	TOTAL SLAVES	TOTALS	DISTRICT/ TOWNSHIP	NOTES
					under 10	10 to 16	16 to 26	26 to 45	45 and over	under 10	10 to 16	16 to 26	26 to 45	45 and over					
Westhampton	15	1	Wright	Ephraim	1	2	1		1	1		2		1			9		
Westhampton	15	2	Elwell	Thomas			1		1	1	2	1		1			7		
Westhampton	15	3	French	Joshua B.	2			1					1				4		
Westhampton	15	4	Pomeroy	Stephen	2			1		2			1				6		
Westhampton	15	5	Clark	Martin	1	1	1		1	1	1	2		1			9		
Westhampton	15	6	Norton	Elijah		1			1					1			3		
Westhampton	15	7	Norton	Joseph			1			1	1	1					4		
Westhampton	15	8	Judd	Sylvetser	1	2	2		1	2	1	1		1			11		
Westhampton	15	9	Gee	Ebenezer		2			1		1	1	1		2		8		
Westhampton	15	10	Norton	Elijah Junr	3			1			1		1				6		
Westhampton	15	11	Clark	Jacob	2	1	1	1		1		1					7		
Westhampton	15	12	Chapman	David		1	1		1	1			2	1			7		
Westhampton	15	13	Lyman	Azariah		1	1		1				2	1			6		
Westhampton	15	14	Wright	Oliver			1		1			1		1			4		
Westhampton	15	15	Kingsley	Noah	1	1	1			1		1					5		
Westhampton	15	16	Edwards	Samuel		2		1				1		1			5		
Westhampton	15	17	Judd	Solomon	1	1	3	1			2	1	1				10		
Westhampton	16	1	Kingsley	Ezra			1			1		2					4		
Westhampton	16	2	Bartlett	Joel				1				1		1			3		
Westhampton	16	3	Bartlett	Noah	3			1						1			5		
Westhampton	16	4	French	Ebenezer Jr	1	1	1	1		1	2	1	1				9		
Westhampton	16	5	French	Ebenezer				1						1			2		
Westhampton	16	6	French	Nathan	1	1		1		1		1					5		
Westhampton	16	7	Bartlett	Cornelius	1	2		1		3		1	1				9		
Westhampton	16	8	Bartlett	William	1			1	1	1	2	2	1		1		10		
Westhampton	16	9	Bartlett	Phineas	1			1		2		1	1				6		
Westhampton	16	10	Bartlett	Elihu	2				1	1		1					5		
Westhampton	16	11	Lyman	Rufus	2	2	2		1			1	3		1		12		
Westhampton	16	12	Strong	Noah		1	1		1				3	1			7		
Westhampton	16	13	Soal	David	3			1					1				5		
Westhampton	16	14	Strong	Benajah	2				1	1				1			5		
Westhampton	16	15	Everett	Mary								1		1			2		
Westhampton	16	16	Fisher	Aaron			2	1		1			1	1			6		
Westhampton	16	17	Post	Levi		1		1						1			3		
Westhampton	16	18	Post	Levi Junr			1					2					3		
Westhampton	16	19	Parsons	Justin	1		1	1		2	1		1				7		
Westhampton	16	20	Clark	Reuben	2	1		1		1		1	1				7		
Westhampton	16	21	Post	Oliver	1	2	1		1	1		1		1			8		
Westhampton	16	22	Clark	Giles	2			1		2			1				7		
Westhampton	16	23	Strong	Amasa		1	2		1	1	1	2		1			9		
Westhampton	16	24	Montague	Peter	1	1				1	1		1				6		
Westhampton	16	25	Butterfield	Solomon	1			1		2			1				5		
Westhampton	16	26	Strong	John			1		1				1	1			4		
Westhampton	16	27	Whitney	John	2			1		1		1	1				6		
Westhampton	16	28	Smith	Levi		2	1		1	2				1			7		
Westhampton	16	29	Kingsley	Joseph	1	2	2		1			2		1			9		
Westhampton	16	30	Kingsley	Joseph Jr	1		2	1		1		1					6		
Westhampton	16	31	Kingsley	Samuel		1	1	1				2		1			6		
Westhampton	16	32	Clark	Paul	2	2			1	2	1			1			9		
Westhampton	16	33	Hale	Enoch	1	2			1	2	2	1		1			10		
Westhampton	16	34	Burt	Joel	2	1		1			1		1				6		
Westhampton	16	35	Clark	Abner				1		1				1			3		
Westhampton	16	36	French	Samuel				1				2		1			4		
Westhampton	16	37	French	Jared	1			1		1		1					4		
Westhampton	17	1	French	Martha										2			2		
Westhampton	17	2	Coats	Reuben	1	2			1	1		1		1			7		
Westhampton	17	3	Clark	Jonathan				1						1			2		
Westhampton	17	4	Clark	Jonathan Jr	3			1				1					5		
Westhampton	17	5	Baker	John		1	2					1	1	1			7		
Westhampton	17	6	Loud	Caleb	1			1				1					3		
Westhampton	17	7	Hitchcock	Jonathan	1		1	1		1			1				5		
Westhampton	17	8	Clap	Elisha B			2							1			3		
Westhampton	17	9	Hooker	William	2	3	1	1		1		1		1			10		
Westhampton	17	10	Hunt	Jared	1	1	1	1		2	2	1					9		
Westhampton	17	11	Clark	Seth	1		1	1		3	2	2	1				11		
Westhampton	17	12	Clark	Gideon				1				2	1				4		
Westhampton	17	13	Clark	Henaz	2			1		3			1				7		
Westhampton	17	14	Clark	Gideon Jun		1	1		1			1	4		1		9		
Westhampton	17	15	Wales	Jonathan	3	1	1	1		1	1	1	1	1			11		
Westhampton	17	16	Clap	Diademi	3								1	1			5		
Westhampton	17	17	Parsons	Medad	1			1		2			1				5		
Westhampton	17	18	Bullard	John				1				1		1			3		
Westhampton	17	19	Boyden	Elisha	2			1		1				1			5		
Westhampton	17	20	Bullard	Isaac	2	1		1		1				1			6		
Westhampton	17	21	Baker	Simeon	1			1		3			1				6		
Westhampton	17	22	Rust	Joel		1		1		3			1				6		
Westhampton	17	23	Parsons	Bela		1			1					1			3		
Westhampton	17	24	Clap	Oliver	1	1			1		1		1				5		
Westhampton	17	25	Clap	Sylvanus	2								1				4		

TOWN	PG#	LN#	LAST NAME	FIRST NAME	under 10	10 to 16	16 to 26	26 to 45	45 and over	under 10	10 to 16	16 to 26	26 to 45	45 and over	TOTAL ALL OTHER	TOTAL SLAVES	TOTALS	DISTRICT/ TOWNSHIP	NOTES
Westhampton	17	26	Payne	Ebenezer			2		1					1			4		
Westhampton	17	27	Southworth	Benjamin					1		1			1			3		
Westhampton	17	28	Alvord	Jonathan					1				4	1			6		
Westhampton	17	29	Chilson	Joseph Jun			1			1		1					3		
Westhampton	17	30	Pratt	Thomas	2	1	1	1		2			1				8		
Westhampton	17	31	Alvord	Ahiela			2		1		1		1				5		
Westhampton	17	32	Pitsinger	John	1	3			1				1				6		
Westhampton	17	33	Chilson	Joseph	3		1		1		1	1		1			8		
Westhampton	17	34	French	Jonatha	1			1		2			1				5		
Westhampton	17	35	Bartlett	Benjamin			1			3	1						5		
Westhampton	17	36	French	Abiather		1			2	2				1			6		
Westhampton	17	37	Stearns	Ebenezer	1				1					2			4		
Westhampton	18	1	Parsons	Israel		1	1		1			3		1			7		
Westhampton	18	2	Clark	Titus			2	1				2					5		
Westhampton	18	3	Clark	Nathan		3	2		1			1		1			8		
Westhampton	18	4	Thayer	Asa			2		1		1	1		1			6		
Westhampton	18	5	Phelps	Timothy	1		2		1		1	1		1			7		
Westhampton	18	6	Thayer	Elias	3	1	1		1	1	2		1				10		
Westhampton	18	7	Wright	Phineas			2		1			1		1			5		
Westhampton	18	8	Prentice	Peleg	2			1		1			1				5		
Westhampton	18	9	Alvord	Eliab			2			3			1				6		
Westhampton	18	10	Parsons	Noah	1	3	1	1		2			1				9		
Westhampton	18	11	Clark	Matthew	2	2			1	1			1				7		
Westhampton	18	12	Kingsley	Thaddeus	1	2			1	1			1				6		
Westhampton	18	13	Edwards	Justin	1	1	1		1	1	1	1		1			8		
Westhampton	18	14	Wood	David	1		1	1		3	1		1	1			9		
Westhampton	18	15	Pomeroy	Pliny			1		1	1	1	1	1	1			7		
Westhampton	18	16	Parsons	David	2		1		1	1	1			1			7		
Westhampton	18	17	Bridges	Nathaniel	2			1					1				4		
Westhampton	18	18	Cook	Caleb	1			1				1					3		
Westhampton	18	19	Smith	Willard	1	1	1	1		2	1		1				8		
Westhampton	18	20	Brewster	Nathan					1		1	2		1			5		
Westhampton	18	21	Brewster	Jonah			1					1					2		
Westhampton	18	22	Edwards	Timothy		1	1		1	1		2		1			7		
Westhampton	18	23	Bridgman	Elisha				1		1			1				3		
Westhampton	18	24	Bridgman	Ismail	1			1		3			1				6		
Westhampton	18	25	Kingsley	Medad	2	2		1					2	1			8		
Westhampton	18	26	Cook	Noah	2	2		1		1	1		1				8		
Westhampton	18	27	Rust	Elijah	1	1		1		1	1	1	1				7		
Westhampton	18	28	Edwards	Daniel			2	1		2		1	2				8		
Westhampton	18	29	Wright	Samuel	2			1		2	1	1	1				8		
Westhampton	18	30	Rhoades	Samuel			1	1				1					3		
Westhampton	18	31	Damon	Nathan	3			1		1	1		2				8		
Westhampton	18	32	Wright	Reuben	1	1			1	1	1		1				6		
Westhampton	18	33	Claflin	Levi	3			1		1			1				6		
Westhampton	18	34	Sheldon	Isaac				1		1		1	2	1			6		

171

TOWN	PG#	LN#	LAST NAME	FIRST NAME	FREE WHITE MALES					FREE WHITE FEMALES					TOTAL ALL OTHER	TOTAL SLAVES	TOTALS	DISTRICT/TOWNSHIP	NOTES
					under 10	10 to 16	16 to 26	26 to 45	45 and over	under 10	10 to 16	16 to 26	26 to 45	45 and over					
Whately	65	1	Allis	Daniel	2	2		1		3			1				9		
Whately	65	2	Adkins	Elijah	1			1				2					4		
Whately	65	3	Adkins	Solomon	1	1	1	1	1	1			1	1			8		
Whately	65	4	Brown	Edward		1			1					2			4		
Whately	65	5	Burroughs	Stephen	1				1		1		1				4		
Whately	66	6	Bacon	Jonathan	1	1		1		3		1					7		
Whately	66	7	Bardwell	Noah		2	1		1			3		1			8		
Whately	66	8	Brown	Isaiah			2		1		1			1			5		
Whately	66	9	Brown	John	2	1	3		1	1			1				9		
Whately	66	10	Beldin	Joshua Jun		1	1			5	1	1					9		
Whately	66	11	Bardwell	Asa	1			1	1	3			1	1			8		
Whately	66	12	Beldin	Elisha	1		1	1	1				2	1			7		
Whately	66	13	Bacon	Philo			1	1			2	1	1	1			7		
Whately	66	14	Beldin	Joshua	1		4	1	1	1	1	1		1			11		
Whately	66	15	Bardwell	Asa Jr	2			1		1	1		1				6		
Whately	66	16	Bardwell	Chester		1				1		2					4		
Whately	66	17	Bardwell	Charles		2						1					3		
Whately	66	18	Bird	Enoch	2	1	1		1	2	1		1				9		
Whately	66	19	Crafts	Seth	1			1	1	1			1	1			6		
Whately	66	20	Crafts	Graves	4	2		1		2	1		1				11		
Whately	66	21	Cartwell	Thomas	1			1		3	3		1				9		
Whately	66	22	Cary	Richard	2			1		1	1	2	1				8		
Whately	66	23	Crafts	Reuben	1	1		2	1	2	1		1				9		
Whately	66	24	Crafts	Moses	1	1		1					1	1			5		
Whately	66	25	Crafts	John	1		1		1	1	1			1			6		
Whately	66	26	Cooley	Benjamin			1			1			1				3		
Whately	66	27	Coleman	Nathaniel				1		2			1				4		
Whately	66	28	Crafts	Joseph	4			1		1	1	1					8		
Whately	66	29	Clark	Peter	1			1		4			1				7		
Whately	66	30	Dickinson	Charles	1		1					1					3		
Whately	66	31	Dickinson	Samuel			3		1					1			5		
Whately	66	32	Dickinson	Abner			1					1	1		1		4		
Whately	66	33	Dickinson	Zeher	2	2		1		2	1		1				9		
Whately	66	34	Dickinson	Benjm	1		1		1	1				1			5		
Whately	66	35	Frary	Seth	1	1	2	1		2	1		1				9		
Whately	66	36	Frary	Eleazer	1			1		3			1				6		
Whately	66	37	Frary	Isaac	1	1		1		3	1		1				8		
Whately	66	38	Frary	Phinehas		1	3		1		1		2				8		
Whately	66	39	Field	Zenas	4				1	2	1	1	2	1			12		
Whately	66	40	Grimes	Samuel			1			1		1					3		
Whately	66	41	Graves	Reuben	2	1		1		1		1					6		
Whately	66	42	Graves	Joel	1	2		1		2			2	1			9		
Whately	66	43	Graves	Martin	1	1	3		1			1		1			8		
Whately	66	44	Graves	Oliver			1					1		1			3		
Whately	66	45	Graves	Oliver Jr	4			1		1			1				7		
Whately	66	46	Graves	Selah	3	3			1	1		1	1				10		
Whately	67	1	Graves	Solomon	2		2	1		2			2				9		
Whately	67	2	Graves	John		1			1	1	1	1	1				6		
Whately	67	3	Graves	David			1	1				1		1			4		
Whately	67	4	Graves	Moses	3			1		1		1					6		
Whately	67	5	Gilbert	Josiah			1	1		1			1				4		
Whately	67	6	Granger	John	2			1					1				4		
Whately	67	7	Harwood	Francis	4			1					1				6		
Whately	67	8	Hill	Joseph	1	1	2		1			3		1			9		
Whately	67	9	Morton	Daniel	1			1		2			1				5		
Whately	67	10	Mather	William	1		4	1	1	4			1	1			13		
Whately	67	11	Morton	Asa	1	1	1		1	2		1	1	1			9		
Whately	67	12	Morton	Consider	2	1		1		2			1	1			8		
Whately	67	13	Morton	Samuel		1		1			1	1	1				5		
Whately	67	14	Morton	Levi	4	2			1	1	1	1		1			11		
Whately	67	15	Munson	Moses	1		1		1			1		1			5		
Whately	67	16	Munson	Moses Jun	4		2	2			1	1	2				12		
Whately	67	17	Morton	Simeon		1	1	1		1	1						6		
Whately	67	18	Munson	Reuben	2		4					2	2	1			11		
Whately	67	19	Morton	Oliver		1	3			1		1		1			7		
Whately	67	20	Nash	Joseph	1	2	1		1	2		1		1			9		
Whately	67	21	Orcutt	Stephen	2		2			1	1						6		
Whately	67	22	Parker	Benjamin	1	1	1	1		3	2	1					10		
Whately	67	23	Rogers	George			1		1	1				1			4		
Whately	67	24	Roberts	George				1		2				1			4		
Whately	67	25	Stacy	Rufus	4	1		1		1			2	1			10		
Whately	67	26	Sanderson	Thomas	2	1	6		1		1	1		1			13		
Whately	67	27	Smith	Calvin		1						1					2		
Whately	67	28	Scott	Benjamin	1			1	1	1		1		2			7		
Whately	67	29	Smith	Isaac	3			1		1		1		1			7		
Whately	67	30	Scott	Abraham	1			1		1		1					4		
Whately	67	31	Smith	William	2			1				1					4		
Whately	67	32	Smith	Asa	2		2	1		1			1				7		
Whately	67	33	Smith	Gad	2	1	1	1	1	1	1	1	1	1			11		

TOWN	PG#	LN#	LAST NAME	FIRST NAME	FREE WHITE MALES under 10	10 to 16	16 to 26	26 to 45	45 and over	FREE WHITE FEMALES under 10	10 to 16	16 to 26	26 to 45	45 and over	TOTAL ALL OTHER	TOTAL SLAVES	TOTALS	DISTRICT/ TOWNSHIP	NOTES
Whately	67	34	Smith	Elijah	2			1	1		1		1				6		
Whately	67	35	Hales	Henry		1			1					1			3		
Whately	68	1	Smith	John		1		1	1			2		1			6		
Whately	68	2	Scott	Abel	1	1			2	1	2	1	2	1			11		
Whately	68	3	Scott	Selah	2				1	3	1	1		1			9		
Whately	68	4	Smith	Jonathan		1	1	1	1		1	1		2			8		
Whately	68	5	Sanderson	Isaac	4	1	1	1		1	2		1				11		
Whately	68	6	Sanderson	Asa	3	1	1	1		3		1	1				11		
Whately	68	7	Scott	Mary	1	1	1			1			1	1			6		
Whately	68	8	Stockbridge	David			1			1		1					3		
Whately	68	9	Smith	Phillip	3	1		1	1	2		1	1	1			11		
Whately	68	10	Smith	Martin		1						1					2		
Whately	68	11	Sanderson	David	1		2	1		2			1				7		
Whately	68	12	Smith	Jonathan Jr	1			1		1		1	1				5		
Whately	68	13	Train	Oliver	4	1		1		1			1				8		
Whately	68	14	Todd	Asa	1	2		1		2	1	1	1	1			10		
Whately	68	15	White	Salman Jun	2	1	1	1		1	2	1	1				10		
Whately	68	16	Wells	Rufus	1	1	2		1	1	1	1		1			9		
Whately	68	17	Wait	Elihu	2	2	1	1		1	3	1	1				12		
Whately	68	18	White	Salman					1		1		2	1			5		
Whately	68	19	White	John	1			1		1	1		1				5		
Whately	68	20	Wait	Consider	5			1		1	2		1				10		
Whately	68	21	Wait	Joel Junr	2	2	1		1	1	2			3			12		
Whately	68	22	Wait	Lemuel	1		3		1	1	1	4		1			12		
Whately	68	23	Wells	Perez	1	1	1	1					1				5		
Whately	68	24	Wait	Joel		1			1		1			1			4		
Whately	68	25	Wait	Jeremiah		1				1		1					3		
Whately	68	26	Wait	Nathan	1			1		2			1				5		
Whately	68	27	Wait	Nehemiah		1				1		1					3		
Whately	68	28	Wait	Jeremiah				1					1				2		
Whately	68	29	Wait	Jonathan		1				2	1	1					5		
Whately	68	30	Wait	Benjamin	1			1		2			1				5		

TOWN	PG#	LN#	LAST NAME	FIRST NAME	FWM under 10	FWM 10 to 16	FWM 16 to 26	FWM 26 to 45	FWM 45 and over	FWF under 10	FWF 10 to 16	FWF 16 to 26	FWF 26 to 45	FWF 45 and over	TOTAL ALL OTHER	TOTAL SLAVES	TOTALS	DISTRICT/ TOWNSHIP	NOTES
Wilbraham	232	1	Whitney	Joseph		1	1		1		1	1		1			6		
Wilbraham	232	2	Peterson	Nathaniel			1					1					2		
Wilbraham	232	3	Hamlin	John	1	2		1		1		1		1			7		
Wilbraham	232	4	Miner	Samuel	2	1	1	1			1	1					7		
Wilbraham	232	5	Griswould	Solomon	1		1		1	1	1	1		1			7		
Wilbraham	232	6	Abbe	Joseph		2		1				2	1				6		
Wilbraham	232	7	Torrey	Samuel	4	1			1		1	1	1				9		
Wilbraham	232	8	Hunn	Gideon	2			1				1					4		
Wilbraham	232	9	Ward	Jacob	1	3			1			1		1			7		
Wilbraham	232	10	Kibbe	Asa	1	2		1					1				5		
Wilbraham	232	11	Coye	Abraham		1						1					2		
Wilbraham	232	12	Clarke	Joseph		1			1			1		1			4		
Wilbraham	232	13	Shepard	Isaac	1			1					1	1			4		
Wilbraham	232	14	Davis	Sarah Wd	1								2				3		
Wilbraham	232	15	Battin	John	3	1			1		1	1		1			8		
Wilbraham	232	16	Walker	Asa				1		3		1		1			6		
Wilbraham	232	17	Langdon	Paul Capt.			1	1	1					1			4		
Wilbraham	232	18	Langdon	John		1	1					1		1			4		
Wilbraham	232	19	Leach	Benanuel	1	1	2		1	1		1		2			9		
Wilbraham	232	20	Langdon	Paul Junr	2	2		1				1	1				7		
Wilbraham	232	21	Chapin	Abner		1	1		1	1	1			1			6		
Wilbraham	232	22	Chapin	Samuel	2		1	2		2		2	1				10		
Wilbraham	232	23	Stebbins	Eldad		2	1	1				1		1			6		
Wilbraham	232	24	Stebbins	David	2			1		3			1				7		
Wilbraham	232	25	Rogers	Elisha	1			1		1			1				4		
Wilbraham	232	26	McCray	John	2		1	1		1			1				6		
Wilbraham	232	27	Stebbins	Chloe Wd	2		2				1			1			6		
Wilbraham	232	28	Stebbins	Mary Wd				1			2	1	3				7		
Wilbraham	232	29	Isham	Daniel	1			2		1		1		1			6		
Wilbraham	232	30	Newton	Jotham	1		1	1		2			1				6		
Wilbraham	232	31	Stebbins	Sarah Wd	2	1	3				2	1		1			10		
Wilbraham	232	32	Theving	John	3	2		1	1	2	2		1	1			13		
Wilbraham	232	33	Beebe	Jemima Wd									1				1		
Wilbraham	232	34	Sessions	Robert	3	1	2		1	3	2	1	1	1			15		
Wilbraham	232	35	Warriner	Samuel			1		1					1			3		
Wilbraham	232	36	Hitchcock	Othneel				1						1			2		
Wilbraham	232	37	Hitchcock	Simon	2			1		1			1				5		
Wilbraham	232	38	Hitchcock	Reuben			1		1	1	1			1			5		
Wilbraham	232	39	Hitchcock	John Deacn				1									1		
Wilbraham	232	40	Lathrop	Joseph Captn	4		1	1			1		1				8		
Wilbraham	232	41	Stebbins	James	1			1		1	1	1					5		
Wilbraham	232	42	Stedman	Abigail Wd		1	1			2	1	1					6		
Wilbraham	232	43	Works	John	4	1	1	1		1		1	1				10		
Wilbraham	233	1	Cobb	William		1		1		4	1						8		
Wilbraham	233	2	Wright	Henry		1		1	2	2		1	1				8		
Wilbraham	233	3	Warriner	Ethan			1	2		2			2				7		
Wilbraham	233	4	Babcock	Horace	2			1			1	1					5		
Wilbraham	233	5	Stebbins	Gilbert			1			1		1					3		
Wilbraham	233	6	Armstrong	Samuel	1			1		2			1				5		
Wilbraham	233	7	Woodward	Elisha	1		1					1					3		
Wilbraham	233	8	Loomis	Louisa Wd						3		1	1				5		
Wilbraham	233	9	Lyon	Philip	1			1		3				1			6		
Wilbraham	233	10	Lyon	Jacob			1						1				2		
Wilbraham	233	11	Hitchcock	Aaron		1	1	1		1	1		1				6		
Wilbraham	233	12	Warner	Daniel	1			1		1			1				4		
Wilbraham	233	13	Warner	Jesse	3	1		1		1	1		1				8		
Wilbraham	233	14	Copeland	Asahel				1		3			1				5		
Wilbraham	233	15	Ward	Nehemiah	2			1		3			1				7		
Wilbraham	233	16	Warriner	Moses				1				1					2		
Wilbraham	233	17	King	Asaph		1			1	3	1	2	1				9		
Wilbraham	233	18	Adams	John Jr	1	2		1		2			1				7		
Wilbraham	233	19	Adams	John				1						1			2		
Wilbraham	233	20	Adams	John				1						1			2		
Wilbraham	233	21	Bliss	Thomas	1		2		1	2	2			1			9		
Wilbraham	233	22	Burt	Moses	2		1	1					1	1	1		7		
Wilbraham	233	23	Warriner	Solomon	2	1	2		1	1		2		1			10		
Wilbraham	233	24	Hammond	James				1			1		1				3		
Wilbraham	233	25	Warner	Azriel	1			1		2		1	1				6		
Wilbraham	233	26	Warriner	Abner	3	1	1	1	1	1		2		1			11		
Wilbraham	233	27	Merrick	Samuel Fisk	2	1	1		1	2	2	1		2			12		
Wilbraham	233	28	Ainsworth	Nathaniel	1	1	1	1					1				5		
Wilbraham	233	29	Warriner	Mary Wd						1	3	1		1			6		
Wilbraham	233	30	Sisson	Augustus	3		2		1	1			1				8		
Wilbraham	233	31	Witten	Ezra Revd	2		1	1		1	1	1	1				8		
Wilbraham	233	32	Burt	Gideon Dr		1	2		1		1	2		3			10		
Wilbraham	233	33	Morgan	Philip		1				1	1		1				4		
Wilbraham	233	34	Sexton	Joseph	2	1	1	1		1			1				7		
Wilbraham	233	35	Chapin	Jason	1	1	1	2		1		1		1			8		
Wilbraham	233	36	Merrick	Jona	1								1		1		9		

TOWN	PG#	LN#	HEADS OF HOUSEHOLD		FREE WHITE MALES					FREE WHITE FEMALES					TOTAL ALL OTHER	TOTAL SLAVES	TOTALS	DISTRICT/ TOWNSHIP	NOTES
			LAST NAME	FIRST NAME	under 10	10 to 16	16 to 26	26 to 45	45 and over	under 10	10 to 16	16 to 26	26 to 45	45 and over					
Wilbraham	233	37	Merrick	Cheleab B	1	1	1		1	1	1	1		1			8		
Wilbraham	233	38	Utley	Stephen	2		1	1					1				5		
Wilbraham	233	39	Cadwell	Pliny	2		1	1		1			1				6		
Wilbraham	233	40	Bliss	David		2	2		1	1	1	2		1			10		
Wilbraham	233	41	Bliss	Jonathan		1	1	1			1	2		1			7		
Wilbraham	233	42	Stebbins	Noah		1			1			3		1			6		
Wilbraham	233	43	Stebbins	Noah Jun				1		4		1	1				7		
Wilbraham	234	1	Ufford	John	2	1		2		1	1	1					8		
Wilbraham	234	2	Brewer	William			4		1		2			1	2		10		
Wilbraham	234	3	Brewer	Gaius	2	1	1		1	1	1	4	1				12		
Wilbraham	234	4	Brewer	Charles	2	1	2		1	1		2		1			10		
Wilbraham	234	5	Rusell	John		1			1	1			1				4		
Wilbraham	234	6	Warriner	David			2		2		1	1		2			8		
Wilbraham	234	7	Buell	William	3	1		1		2	1		1				9		
Wilbraham	234	8	Shepard	Elisha		1		1		1			1				4		
Wilbraham	234	9	Bliss	Abel	1		1		1	1	2		1		1		8		
Wilbraham	234	10	Jones	Thomas				1		2	2	1	1				7		
Wilbraham	234	11	Jones	Rufus	1			1				1					3		
Wilbraham	234	12	Erving	James		1		1					1				3		
Wilbraham	234	13	Charles	Solomon				1					1				2		
Wilbraham	234	14	Bliss	Levi		1		1		1	1	2		1			7		
Wilbraham	234	15	Howard	Thomas	1	1		1		1		1					5		
Wilbraham	234	16	Howard	Harvey	2	1	1	1		1		1					7		
Wilbraham	234	17	Marble	Joseph	1	2		1		3		1	1	1			10		
Wilbraham	234	18	Tinkham	Peter	2	1		1		3	1		1				9		
Wilbraham	234	19	Lord	John	3	1		1		1	2	1	1				10		
Wilbraham	234	20	Beebe	Amos	3	2	1		1	1	1		1				10		
Wilbraham	234	21	Walden	Elisha	3	1	1	1		2			1				9		
Wilbraham	234	22	Walden	Jonathan			2		1			1	1				5		
Wilbraham	234	23	Goss	Ezra	2			1		2			1				6		
Wilbraham	234	24	Warner	Samuel				1		1		1	1				4		
Wilbraham	234	25	Warner	Samuel Jr	1	1	1	1		2		1					7		
Wilbraham	234	26	Bartlett	Lydia Wd										2			2		
Wilbraham	234	27	Allen	Benjamin	3			1		3			1				8		
Wilbraham	234	28	Jones	Asa	1	3	1		1					2			8		
Wilbraham	234	29	Phelps	Elijah	3	2	1		1	3		1	1				12		
Wilbraham	234	30	Atchinson	Benoni			3		1			1	1				6		
Wilbraham	234	31	Barker	Ezra				1					1				2		
Wilbraham	234	32	Barker	Ezra Junr	2			1		1	1		1				6		
Wilbraham	234	33	Johnson	William	3			1				1	1				6		
Wilbraham	234	34	Fuller	Ephraim	4	2	2		1	2	1	1	1				14		
Wilbraham	234	35	Frost	Timothy	2	1		1					1				5		
Wilbraham	234	36	Bailey	Robert	1	1		1		2	1	1	1		1		9		
Wilbraham	234	37	Bailey	Constant	1		1					1					3		
Wilbraham	234	38	Knowlton	Nathl Capt	1			1		2		1					5		
Wilbraham	234	39	Cadwell	Stephen			2		1		1			1			5		
Wilbraham	234	40	Ely	Jonathan				1						1			2		
Wilbraham	234	41	Ely	Judah	1	2			1	2	1	2	1				10		
Wilbraham	234	42	Bartlett	Moses K.		1		1				1	1	2			6		
Wilbraham	234	43	Ely	Jonathan Junr		1	1		1	1	3		1				8		
Wilbraham	234	44	Shaw	James		1	1		1				1	1	1		5		
Wilbraham	235	1	Bliss	Aaron				1					1	1	1		3		
Wilbraham	235	2	Mixter	Phinehas			1				1	2	1				5		
Wilbraham	235	3	Bliss	Obed	2		1	1		2		1	3		1		12		
Wilbraham	235	4	Bliss	Silas		2			1			2		1			6		
Wilbraham	235	5	Bliss	Oliver		1	2	2	1			1		1	1		9		
Wilbraham	235	6	Butler	Phebe								1		1			2		
Wilbraham	235	7	Shepard	Elisha Junr	1			1		3	1	1					7		
Wilbraham	235	8	Fosgate	Zenas			1					1					2		
Wilbraham	235	9	Glower	John	2	1	3		1	1	3		1				12		
Wilbraham	235	10	Grosvenor	Moses	1	1	2	1		1		2					8		
Wilbraham	235	11	Bliss	Jesse	2			1		1		1	1				6		
Wilbraham	235	12	Kilbourn	Samuel			1	1		2		1	1				6		
Wilbraham	235	13	Kilbourn	Luther	4			1		1	1	1					8		
Wilbraham	235	14	Kilbourn	Jona	2	1	1					2					6		
Wilbraham	235	15	Bliss	Stephen				1					1				2		
Wilbraham	235	16	Newell	Daniel	1	1		1		1			1				5		
Wilbraham	235	17	Calkins	Asa	1	1		1		3	2		1				9		
Wilbraham	235	18	Clark	Seth Junr	3		2			1	1		1				8		
Wilbraham	235	19	Willey	Charles	1							1	1				3		
Wilbraham	235	20	Walbridge	Joshua	1							1	1				3		
Wilbraham	235	21	Clark	Eli			1			4		1					6		
Wilbraham	235	22	Clark	Seth				1									1		
Wilbraham	235	23	Cleaveland	Elisha	2	1		1		3	1	1	1				10		
Wilbraham	235	24	Larnard	Samuel		1	2		1		1	1		1			7		
Wilbraham	235	25	Burr	Timothy	3	1	2	1		2		1	2				12		
Wilbraham	235	26	Wright	Zebulon				1			2	2	1				6		
Wilbraham	235	27	Wright	Ezekiel	3		2		1			1	2	1			10		
Wilbraham	235	28	Heaton	Philemon		1						1	1				5		

175

TOWN	PG#	LN#	HEADS OF HOUSEHOLD		FREE WHITE MALES					FREE WHITE FEMALES					TOTAL ALL OTHER	TOTAL SLAVES	TOTALS	DISTRICT/ TOWNSHIP	NOTES
			LAST NAME	FIRST NAME	under 10	10 to 16	16 to 26	26 to 45	45 and over	under 10	10 to 16	16 to 26	26 to 45	45 and over					
Wilbraham	235	29	Plumley	John			1		1		2			1			5		
Wilbraham	235	30	Plumley	John Jr			1			3			1				5		
Wilbraham	235	31	Eddy	James			1					1					2		
Wilbraham	235	32	Bliss	Gideon	4			1		1			1				7		
Wilbraham	235	33	Morgan	John	2		1		1	2		1	1				8		
Wilbraham	235	34	Hill	Collins	4			1		1			1				7		
Wilbraham	235	35	Crane	Joseph		2	1						1	1			5		
Wilbraham	235	36	Ringe	William	3	2			1	1	2	1	1				11		
Wilbraham	235	37	Pinney	Fuller			1	1		1			1				4		
Wilbraham	235	38	Cadwell	Daniel	3			1				1		1			6		
Wilbraham	235	39	Cadwell	Ebenezer	1				1		1	1	1	1			6		
Wilbraham	235	40	Cadwell	John	4			1		1	1		1				8		
Wilbraham	235	41	Stebbins	Frederick	1			1		2			1				5		
Wilbraham	235	42	Hitchcock	David				1					1				2		
Wilbraham	235	43	Cadwell	David	2			1					1				4		
Wilbraham	236	1	Bishop	Eleazer	2			1		1			1				5		
Wilbraham	236	2	Stebbins	Justin			1		1		1	1		1			5		
Wilbraham	236	3	Stebbins	Walter					1	1			1				3		
Wilbraham	236	4	Partridge	Deuty	3	1			1	2		1	1				9		
Wilbraham	236	5	Calkins	David	2	1		1		2			1				7		
Wilbraham	236	6	Daniels	James	3		1			1	1	1					7		
Wilbraham	236	7	Mack	Nathan	1		1	1		1		1		1			6		
Wilbraham	236	8	Bliss	Ithamer			1			1		1					3		
Wilbraham	236	9	Bordin	Selden	3			1		1	2		1				8		
Wilbraham	236	10	Calkins	Ezekiel	1	1		1		2			2				7		
Wilbraham	236	11	Day	Alven	2			1		3			1				7		
Wilbraham	236	12	Woodward	Thankful Wd			1							1			2		
Wilbraham	236	13	Tillotson	Eleazer	1		1	1		2	2	1	1				10		
Wilbraham	236	14	Chapin	Zebulon	1	1			1	2	2						8		
Wilbraham	236	15	Phillips	Benjamin	1			1		3	2			1			8		
Wilbraham	236	16	Webster	Elijah	3			1					1				5		
Wilbraham	236	17	Chapin	Isaac			1			1							2		
Wilbraham	236	18	Calkins	James	1	1	2		1	4		1		1			11		
Wilbraham	236	19	Hancock	Moses	1	2		1		3		1	1				9		
Wilbraham	236	20	Wallridge	Peter	2			1		1			1				5		
Wilbraham	236	21	Stebbins	Phinehas Jr	2	1		1		1			1				6		
Wilbraham	236	22	Stebbins	Augustus	4			1		1			1				7		
Wilbraham	236	23	Carpenter	John		1	1		1			2		1			6		
Wilbraham	236	24	Chappel	Gordon				1					1				3		
Wilbraham	236	25	Stewart	John	1	1		1		3	1		1				8		
Wilbraham	236	26	Chapin	Ephraim	1	1		1	1	1	1			1			7		
Wilbraham	236	27	King	Parmenas				1						1			2		
Wilbraham	236	28	King	Parmenas Jr			1	1		2			1				5		
Wilbraham	236	29	King	David				1			1		1				3		
Wilbraham	236	30	Crocker	Rowland				1						2			3		
Wilbraham	236	31	Crocker	Enoch	1		1	1		1			1				5		
Wilbraham	236	32	Cone	Newell			1						1				2		
Wilbraham	236	33	Cone	Mathew					1	1				1			3		
Wilbraham	236	34	Cone	Ichabod				1			1		1				3		
Wilbraham	236	35	Saunders	Reuben	1			1		1			1				4		
Wilbraham	236	36	Wright	Solomon		1	1		1	1	1			1			6		
Wilbraham	236	37	Hancock	Gideon				1		4			2				7		
Wilbraham	236	38	Beebe	Steward Capt.	1		1		1	2		2		1			8		
Wilbraham	236	39	Dunham	Salathiel	2	1		1		2			1				7		
Wilbraham	236	40	Tillotson	Eleazer Junr	2	1		1		3			1				8		
Wilbraham	236	41	Chaffee	Joel Jr		1		1					1				3		
Wilbraham	236	42	Hendrick	Reuben	3			1		1			1				6		
Wilbraham	236	43	Hendrick	Jabez					1				1	1			3		
Wilbraham	237	1	Hendrick	Abijah	2			1					1				4		
Wilbraham	237	2	Chaffee	Comfort Jr	2			1	1	1			1	1			7		
Wilbraham	237	3	Maxson	Mathew		1	1		1	2	1	1		1			8		
Wilbraham	237	4	Button	Elizabeth Wd			2							1			3		
Wilbraham	237	5	West	Stephen	2	1		1		2			1				7		
Wilbraham	237	6	Shepard	Jonah	1			1		2			1				5		
Wilbraham	237	7	Day	Eriel	2			1		1			1				5		
Wilbraham	237	8	Russell	Robert		1			1			2		1			5		
Wilbraham	237	9	Russell	Ezekiel					1					1			2		
Wilbraham	237	10	Russell	Benjamin		1	1					1		1			4		
Wilbraham	237	11	Cone	Zenas	1			1		1	1		1				5		
Wilbraham	237	12	Cone	Mathew Jr	1			1		1			1				4		
Wilbraham	237	13	Tilden	William	1				1	3	2			1			8		
Wilbraham	237	14	Ammidown	Titus	1	1		1	4	1			1				9		
Wilbraham	237	15	Newell	Asa	3			1		1			1				6		
Wilbraham	237	16	Chaffee	Joel				1						1			2		
Wilbraham	237	17	Sisson	Nathan		1	2		1			2		1			7		
Wilbraham	237	18	Dunham	Eli				1						2			3		
Wilbraham	237	19	Firmin	John Jr				1					1				2		
Wilbraham	237	20	Green	Eliphalat	1	2			1	1		2	1				8		
Wilbraham	237	21	Stebbins	Phinihas Esq			1	1		1			1				6		

TOWN	PG#	LN#	HEADS OF HOUSEHOLD		FREE WHITE MALES					FREE WHITE FEMALES					TOTAL ALL OTHER	TOTAL SLAVES	TOTALS	DISTRICT/ TOWNSHIP	NOTES
			LAST NAME	FIRST NAME	under 10	10 to 16	16 to 26	26 to 45	45 and over	under 10	10 to 16	16 to 26	26 to 45	45 and over					
Wilbraham	237	22	Stebbins	Moses Junr	2	2			1		1	2		1			9		
Wilbraham	237	23	Stebbins	Moses			1	1					1				3		
Wilbraham	237	24	Chaffee	Simeon		1	1		1		1	1		2			7		
Wilbraham	237	25	Chaffee	Asa Jr		1	1	1		1		2	1				7		
Wilbraham	237	26	Ainsworth	Amasa	2			1		1			1	1			6		
Wilbraham	237	27	Button	Elijah	2		1		1	2	1	1	1				9		
Wilbraham	237	28	Dean	Joel		1			1								2		
Wilbraham	237	29	Burt	Enoch	3				1					1			5		
Wilbraham	237	30	Burt	Walter				1			1		1				3		
Wilbraham	237	31	Burt	David		1	2		1	1	1		1	1			8		
Wilbraham	237	32	Burt	Samuel			1				1						2		
Wilbraham	237	33	Morris	Rebecca Wd			1			1	3	2	1				8		
Wilbraham	237	34	Morris	Isaac	1	1			1	2	1	2	1				9		
Wilbraham	237	35	Bumstead	Joseph			1		1	1		1					4		
Wilbraham	237	36	Chaffee	Asa				1			1	1		1			4		
Wilbraham	237	37	Chaffee	Ephraim	2	1		1		2	2		1				9		
Wilbraham	237	38	Chaffee	Calvin	2	1		1		1			1				6		
Wilbraham	237	39	Brumley	Asa			1	1			1		1				4		
Wilbraham	237	40	Pease	Nathan			1		1		1		1				4		
Wilbraham	237	41	Pease	Nathan Jun	1			1				1					3		
Wilbraham	237	42	Goodwill	John		1		1		1		1	1	1			6		
Wilbraham	237	43	Firmin	John			2		1	1			1				5		
Wilbraham	238	1	Wood	William		1	1		1			1		1			5		
Wilbraham	238	2	Wood	Jacob				1		2			1				4		
Wilbraham	238	3	Warren	Seth		1	1	1					1				4		
Wilbraham	238	4	Stebbins	Timothy	3			1		1			1				6		
Wilbraham	238	5	Murphy	Daniel	1			1					1				3		
Wilbraham	238	6	Dean	Weston				1		1			1				3		
Wilbraham	238	7	Goodwill	Justin	2			1		1			1				5		
Wilbraham	238	8	Stebbins	Calvin	1	1			1	3	2		1				9		
Wilbraham	238	9	Warren	Moses Revd	2	1		1		1			1				6		
Wilbraham	238	10	Flynt	Jonathan		1	4		1	1	2	3		1			13		
Wilbraham	238	11	Pinney	Joel				1				2					3		
Wilbraham	238	12	Harrington	Benja	1					2			1				4		
Wilbraham	238	13	Clark	Enos			1	2									3		
Wilbraham	238	14	Jones	Isaac	2	1		1		3	1			1			9		
Wilbraham	238	15	Stebbins	Zadock			1		1				1	1			4		
Wilbraham	238	16	Stebbins	Zadock Jr	2			1			1	1					5		
Wilbraham	238	17	Stebbins	John			1	1		1		1					3		
Wilbraham	238	18	Chaffee	Comfort				1									1		
Wilbraham	238	19	Chaffee	Nathl Bliss	3			1		1		2					7		
Wilbraham	238	20	Bliss	John Esq				1						1			2		
Wilbraham	238	21	Morris	Edward	1	2	2	1		4		1	1				12		
Wilbraham	238	22	Chaffee	Asa Jr		1	1	1		1		2	1				7		
Wilbraham	238	23	Stacy	Ebenezer	1	2	1		1	1	1	1	1	2			11		
Wilbraham	238	24	Sexton	Samuel				1						1			2		
Wilbraham	238	25	Sexton	Noah	2		1				1						4		
Wilbraham	238	26	Sexton	Oliver	2	2	1			2			1				8		
Wilbraham	238	27	Parsons	Stephen				1						1			2		
Wilbraham	238	28	Parsons	Stephen Jr	3	1		1					1				6		
Wilbraham	238	29	Parsons	Oliver	1			1		1		1					4		
Wilbraham	238	30	Burdick	Adam	2	1		2		3	2		1				11		
Wilbraham	238	31	Cadwell	Moses	1						1		1				3		

TOWN	PG#	LN#	LAST NAME	FIRST NAME	FREE WHITE MALES					FREE WHITE FEMALES					TOTAL ALL OTHER	TOTAL SLAVES	TOTALS	DISTRICT/ TOWNSHIP	NOTES
					under 10	10 to 16	16 to 26	26 to 45	45 and over	under 10	10 to 16	16 to 26	26 to 45	45 and over					
Williamsburg	441	1	Wait	John	1	2	2		1		1	1		1			9		
Williamsburg	441	2	Williams	John					1					1			2		
Williamsburg	441	3	Williams	Grace			1			2		2					5		
Williamsburg	441	4	Warner	Paul				1		2			1				4		
Williamsburg	441	5	Williams	Joseph	3			1					1				5		
Williamsburg	441	6	Washburn	Stephen			1	1		1			1				4		
Williamsburg	441	7	White	Asa	2	1		1		2		1	1	1			9		
Williamsburg	441	8	Wade	Amasa	1			1		1		1					4		
Williamsburg	441	9	Wait	Salmon		1	1	1		1		1					6		
Williamsburg	441	10	Williams	Abner	2	1		1		2	1		1				8		
Williamsburg	441	11	Warner	Nathan	2	1		1					1				5		
Williamsburg	442	1	Thayer	Eliphalet	1		1						1				3		
Williamsburg	442	2	Truesdall	Daniel				1				1		1			3		
Williamsburg	442	3	Titus	Samuel	1		1						1				3		
Williamsburg	442	4	Thomspn	Edward	2			1		2			1				6		
Williamsburg	442	5	Thayer	Oliver Junr	1		1						1				3		
Williamsburg	442	6	Warner	Jonathan		1	1	1	1		2						6		
Williamsburg	442	7	Wallcott	Samuel	2	1		1		2			1				7		
Williamsburg	442	8	Wales	William				1				1	1				3		
Williamsburg	442	9	Wait	Joseph		1		1		1	1	1					6		
Williamsburg	442	10	Wait	Elijah			3	1					1				5		
Williamsburg	442	11	Warner	Joshua	2		2	1			1		1				7		
Williamsburg	442	12	Warren	Mather				1			2		1				4		
Williamsburg	442	13	White	Ezekiel		1		1		3			1				6		
Williamsburg	442	14	Warren	Orange H.	3			1		2			1				7		
Williamsburg	442	15	Warren	Cotton M.	1			1		2			1				5		
Williamsburg	442	16	Williams	Jacob		2		1		2			1				6		
Williamsburg	442	17	Wild	Jesse			1	2	1	1			2	1			7		
Williamsburg	442	18	Warner	Mark	2			1		3			1				7		
Williamsburg	442	19	Whitcomb	James	1	1		1		5			1				9		
Williamsburg	442	20	Warner	Aaron				1		1			1				3		
Williamsburg	442	21	Warner	Seth	1			1				1					3		
Williamsburg	442	22	Wells	John	1		1	1		2			1				6		
Williamsburg	442	23	Wells	Elisha	2	1		1		1	1		1				7		
Williamsburg	442	24	Walcott	Elijah	2	1		1		3			1				8		
Williamsburg	443	1	Perry	Abiel	3		3	1		1	3	1	1				13		
Williamsburg	443	2	Phinney	Isaac Junr	1			1		3	2		1				8		
Williamsburg	443	3	Pomeroy	Josiah	1		1						1				3		
Williamsburg	443	4	Parker	Josiah	1	1			1	1	1	1	1				7		
Williamsburg	443	5	Root	Elias	1			1		1	1		1				5		
Williamsburg	443	6	Rich	Joel	2			1		2			1				6		
Williamsburg	443	7	Strong	Joseph	1		1	1		1		1		1			6		
Williamsburg	443	8	Strong	Gelston	1		1	1		2	2		1				8		
Williamsburg	443	9	Strong	Ezra				1			1			1			3		
Williamsburg	443	10	Strong	Solomon			1			2			1				4		
Williamsburg	443	11	Smith	James				1			1	1	1				4		
Williamsburg	443	12	Scott	David	3	1		1	1	4	1	2		1			14		
Williamsburg	443	13	Shiff	Obadiah		1		1		3	2		1				8		
Williamsburg	443	14	Starks	John	3	1	1					2	1				9		
Williamsburg	443	15	Starks	Nathan		2	1	1		4	1	1	1				11		
Williamsburg	443	16	Stewart	John	1	2		1	1	2	1			1			9		
Williamsburg	443	17	Smith	Obadiah	2		1	1		1			1				6		
Williamsburg	443	18	Stacey	Mark	2	1		1		2			1				7		
Williamsburg	443	19	Thayer	Elkanah	3		2		1	1	2	1	1				12		
Williamsburg	443	20	Taylor	Edmond	1			1		1			1				4		
Williamsburg	443	21	Tileston	Cornelius	2	2		1		1	1		1				8		
Williamsburg	443	22	Thayer	Abel		1	2	1	1	1		1	2	1			10		
Williamsburg	443	23	Thayer	Joshua	1			1					1				3		
Williamsburg	443	24	Thayer	Oliver	2		2	1		2	1	1	1				10		
Williamsburg	444	1	Miller	Cyrus	2	1	1	1		2	2	2	1		1		13		
Williamsburg	444	2	Mayhew	Arnold	1			1		1		1	1				5		
Williamsburg	444	3	Miller	Alexander		2		1		2	1		1				8		
Williamsburg	444	4	Miller	Samuel		1	1					1					3		
Williamsburg	444	5	Mayhew	Zachariah		3	1	1		1			1				7		
Williamsburg	444	6	Meekins	Joseph	2			1		2			1				6		
Williamsburg	444	7	Mayhew	Thomas				1		2			1				4		
Williamsburg	444	8	Newport	Peter											5		5		
Williamsburg	444	9	Nash	Moses				1		4			1				6		
Williamsburg	444	10	Nash	Samuel	2			1		1		1					5		
Williamsburg	444	11	Nash	Thomas	2			1					1				4		
Williamsburg	444	12	Nash	John	2	2		1		2		1	1				9		
Williamsburg	444	13	Nash	Elisha			2		1		1	1		1			6		
Williamsburg	444	14	Norton	Freeman		1	3		1	1	1	2		1			10		
Williamsburg	444	15	Norton	Phebe			1						2	1			4		
Williamsburg	444	16	Porter	David	4	2	1	1		2	1	1	1				13		
Williamsburg	444	17	Paine	Elijah				1				1		1			3		
Williamsburg	444	18	Paine	John			1			1		1					3		
Williamsburg	444	19	Paine	Seth			1			2			1				4		
Williamsburg	444	20	Phinney	Nathan	1		1	1		2			1				7		

TOWN	PG#	LN#	HEADS OF HOUSEHOLD		FREE WHITE MALES					FREE WHITE FEMALES					TOTAL ALL OTHER	TOTAL SLAVES	TOTALS	DISTRICT/ TOWNSHIP	NOTES
			LAST NAME	FIRST NAME	under 10	10 to 16	16 to 26	26 to 45	45 and over	under 10	10 to 16	16 to 26	26 to 45	45 and over					
Williamsburg	444	21	Paine	Ebenezer	3	2		1		2			1				9		
Williamsburg	444	22	Phinney	Zenas	1			1		3		1					6		
Williamsburg	444	23	Phinney	Isaac			1	1				1		1			4		
Williamsburg	444	24	Pomeroy	Benjamin		1		1			1	2		1			6		
Williamsburg	445	1	Johnson	Caleb	1	3		1		1		1		1			8		
Williamsburg	445	2	Jones	Benjamin	2	2	2		1	2	1	2		1			13		
Williamsburg	445	3	Jones	James			1						1				2		
Williamsburg	445	4	Kingsley	Seth		1		1		3	1		1				7		
Williamsburg	445	5	Kingsley	Supply			1			2			2	1			6		
Williamsburg	445	6	Kingsley	Timothy			1			2			1				4		
Williamsburg	445	7	King	William			1		1		3			1			6		
Williamsburg	445	8	Kelton	Elijah	1	2		1		2			1				7		
Williamsburg	445	9	Leonard	Nehemiah	1	1	1		1	2	1	1		1			9		
Williamsburg	445	10	Ludden	Benjamin		1	1	1		3	2		1				9		
Williamsburg	445	11	Ludden	James				1	1			2		1			5		
Williamsburg	445	12	Little	Isaac	2	2		1					1				6		
Williamsburg	445	13	Luce	Elijah	1		1	1		1		1					5		
Williamsburg	445	14	Ludden	Asa		1			1	2	2			1			7		
Williamsburg	445	15	Luce	Zachariah			3		1			2		1			7		
Williamsburg	445	16	Little	Robert	1	1		1		1		1	1				6		
Williamsburg	445	17	Lyon	Lemuel				1					1				2		
Williamsburg	445	18	Mayhew	Lathrop	1			1		2			1				5		
Williamsburg	445	19	Meekins	Thomas				1					1				2		
Williamsburg	445	20	Manter	Francis	3			1		3			2				9		
Williamsburg	445	21	Miller	Stephen	2	3			1	3	1		1				11		
Williamsburg	445	22	Morton	Elisha	2			1		2	1		1				7		
Williamsburg	445	23	Miller	John	1	1		1					1	1			5		
Williamsburg	445	24	Meekins	Stephen	2			1		2	1		1				7		
Williamsburg	446	1	Graves	Lemuel	2				1			2	1				6		
Williamsburg	446	2	Graves	Elnathan				1		3			1				5		
Williamsburg	446	3	Graves	Perez	2	3		1		2			1				9		
Williamsburg	446	4	Graves	Lucius	2		2	1		2	1		1				9		
Williamsburg	446	5	Graves	Elihu	1	1	1		1	1			1				6		
Williamsburg	446	6	Guilford	Timothy		1				1	1	1		1			5		
Williamsburg	446	7	Guilford	William			1	1	1					1			4		
Williamsburg	446	8	Geer	Reuben				1									1		
Williamsburg	446	9	Graves	Stephen	1		1			1		1					4		
Williamsburg	446	10	Guilford	Simeon	1			1		2	1		1				6		
Williamsburg	446	11	Hill	Ephraim	3			1		3			1				8		
Williamsburg	446	12	Hunt	Abijah	1		2		1	1	1	1	1				9		
Williamsburg	446	13	Hemmenway	Ichabod		2	2		1		1			2			8		
Williamsburg	446	14	Hunt	Elisha	3	1		1	1				1	1			8		
Williamsburg	446	15	Hyde	Rufus			4	1	1			1		2			9		
Williamsburg	446	16	Hadlock	Josiah	2	2	1		1			1		1			8		
Williamsburg	446	17	Hickox	Benjamin	3	2		1		2	1		1				10		
Williamsburg	446	18	Hayden	Cotton	4			1		3			1				9		
Williamsburg	446	19	Hayden	Josiah				1			1	1			1		4		
Williamsburg	446	20	Hannan	Josiah	1			1		1	1						4		
Williamsburg	446	21	Hubbard	Elisha	1	2		1		3		1	1				9		
Williamsburg	446	22	Hemmenway	Jason	1			1		2			1				5		
Williamsburg	446	23	Hunt	Abijah Junr	2		1			1		1					5		
Williamsburg	446	24	Hunt	Anthony	3			1		2	1		1				8		
Williamsburg	446	25	Hamer	George	1			1		1		1					4		
Williamsburg	446	26	Hill	Sampson				1		1	1		1				4		
Williamsburg	446	27	Harris	Job	2			1		1		1					5		
Williamsburg	447	1	Clark	Ezra	1			1		1			1				4		
Williamsburg	447	2	Clayhorn	James	3	1			1	3	2	1	1				12		
Williamsburg	447	3	Cary	Joseph Junr	1	2	1	1		3	1	1	1				11		
Williamsburg	447	4	Cole	Samuel	2	1	1	1		3			1				9		
Williamsburg	447	5	Cathcart	Thomas	5			1					1				7		
Williamsburg	447	6	Cary	Joseph				1					1				2		
Williamsburg	447	7	Cary	Abner	2			1		1			1				5		
Williamsburg	447	8	Curtiss	John Day	3	2			1	3			1				10		
Williamsburg	447	9	Coffin	Matthew		1		1				1					3		
Williamsburg	447	10	Curtiss	Isaac	1				1	3	1	1	1				8		
Williamsburg	447	11	Crawford	Andrew	1	1		1		1	1		1				6		
Williamsburg	447	12	Colwell	Redford											7		7		
Williamsburg	447	13	Dunham	Hezekiah		1	1	1	1		1	1		1			7		
Williamsburg	447	14	Dwight	Dorus		1	2					1		1			6		
Williamsburg	447	15	Dwight	Josiah	1					1			1				4		
Williamsburg	447	16	Davidson	John	1	2		1		2		1	1				8		
Williamsburg	447	17	Davenport	George	2			1		1	1		1				6		
Williamsburg	447	18	Davis	Paul			1	1		3			1	1			7		
Williamsburg	447	19	Frost	Josiah	4			1		1	1		1	1			9		
Williamsburg	447	20	Fairfield	Samuel		1	1		1			1		1			5		
Williamsburg	447	21	Fairfield	Ira Northerly	2	1		1					1				5		
Williamsburg	447	22	French	John Owen	2	1		1		3		1	1	1			10		
Williamsburg	447	23	French	Asa	3	2		1		2	1		1				10		
Williamsburg	447	24	French	Jacob	2	3		1	1	4			1	1			13		

TOWN	PG#	LN#	LAST NAME	FIRST NAME	FREE WHITE MALES					FREE WHITE FEMALES					TOTAL ALL OTHER	TOTAL SLAVES	TOTALS	DISTRICT/ TOWNSHIP	NOTES
					under 10	10 to 16	16 to 26	26 to 45	45 and over	under 10	10 to 16	16 to 26	26 to 45	45 and over					
Williamsburg	447	25	Fisher	Ephraim			3		1	1	2	2		1			10		
Williamsburg	447	26	Fisk	David	2			1					1				4		
Williamsburg	448	1	Appleby	Michael	1		1		1	1	3		1				8		
Williamsburg	448	2	Arnold	Prince											1		1		
Williamsburg	448	3	Bassett	Silas		1			1		1	2					5		
Williamsburg	448	4	Brown	Abner	2			1					1				4		
Williamsburg	448	5	Bangs	James									2				2		
Williamsburg	448	6	Bartlet	Simeon Jun	1	1		1		3			1				7		
Williamsburg	448	7	Bodman	Samuel			1	1			1	1		1			6		
Williamsburg	448	8	Bird	Ebenezer	1				1			1		1			4		
Williamsburg	448	9	Bagley	John		1			1	1	1			1			5		
Williamsburg	448	10	Butler	Athearn			1	1		2	1		1				6		
Williamsburg	448	11	Bodman	Joseph	1		1		1	1		1	1	1			7		
Williamsburg	448	12	Burroughs	Ebenezer	2		1		1	2			1				7		
Williamsburg	448	13	Bradford	Samuel			1		1			1		1			4		
Williamsburg	448	14	Bulcard	Adam	3	1		1			1		1				7		
Williamsburg	448	15	Bodman	William	1	1	4		1	1	1	2		1			12		
Williamsburg	448	16	Bodman	Joseph Junr	2		1	1		1		1					6		
Williamsburg	448	17	Bartlet	Thaddeus	1			1	1	1			2	1			7		
Williamsburg	448	18	Bartlet	Ebenezer	1		2			1		1					5		
Williamsburg	448	19	Bagley	Eliakim			1			1		1					3		
Williamsburg	448	20	Bodman	Noah			1					1					2		
Williamsburg	448	21	Barnard	Benjamin	1			1		1		1	1				5		
Williamsburg	448	22	Cleaveland	Roswell	1			1		3	2		1				8		
Williamsburg	448	23	Cleaveland	Amasa	1	1	1	1	1	2		1	1				9		
Williamsburg	448	24	Cleaveland	Nehemiah	1	1			1	5	3	1	1	1			14		

TOWN	PG#	LN#	LAST NAME	FIRST NAME	FREE WHITE MALES					FREE WHITE FEMALES					TOTAL ALL OTHER	TOTAL SLAVES	TOTALS	DISTRICT/ TOWNSHIP	NOTES
					under 10	10 to 16	16 to 26	26 to 45	45 and over	under 10	10 to 16	16 to 26	26 to 45	45 and over					
Worthington	297	1	Eager	Nahum		1	1		1		1		1	1			6		
Worthington	297	2	Gove	William			1	1				2	1				5		
Worthington	297	3	Gove	William Jun		1	1	1		1		1					5		
Worthington	297	4	Niles	Stephen	1	1		1		3			1				7		
Worthington	297	5	Brewster	Moses	1		1	1		2		1					6		
Worthington	297	6	Starkweather	Ezra				1				1	1		1		4		
Worthington	297	7	Ramsdell	Matthew		2		1			1	1	1				6		
Worthington	297	8	Ramsdell	James				1					1				2		
Worthington	297	9	Clapp	Charles	1	1			1	1			1				5		
Worthington	297	10	Kingman	Isaiah		1	1					3					5		
Worthington	297	11	Fuller	Lemuel	1			1		1		1					4		
Worthington	297	12	Daniels	Dan	1	2	1	1		1	2		1				9		
Worthington	297	13	Burr	Israel	1	1	1		1	3	1	1	1				10		
Worthington	297	14	Austin	John		2		1						1			4		
Worthington	297	15	Leonard	Levi	3			1		3			1				7		
Worthington	297	16	Much	Cyprain		1	1	1		2	1		1				7		
Worthington	297	17	Much	Timothy		1	1	2	1	2	1		1				10		
Worthington	297	18	Fitch	Walter			1	1				1	1				4		
Worthington	297	19	Woodbridge	Jonathan	1		1	1		3	1						8		
Worthington	297	20	Adams	Eliashel			1	1	1			1	1	1			6		
Worthington	298	1	Bigelow	Asa			1			1		1					3		
Worthington	298	2	Buffington	Samuel		2	1			1		1	1				6		
Worthington	298	3	Hasen	Nathan	2		1	2		1	1		1				8		
Worthington	298	4	Herrick	Ebenezer		2	2		1	1	1	2		1			10		
Worthington	298	5	Collins	Daniel	2	1		1		2		1	1				8		
Worthington	298	6	Wiles	Oliver	2			1					1				4		
Worthington	298	7	Saffard	Elias			4										4		
Worthington	298	8	Tinker	John	1			1		1	1						4		
Worthington	298	9	Follit	Samuel	1		1	1						1			4		
Worthington	298	10	Huntington	Simon		3	1				4	1					9		
Worthington	298	11	Ward	David		2	1			4	1	1					9		
Worthington	298	12	Cotterill	Nicholas	3				1	1	1	1					7		
Worthington	298	13	Gardner	Mary									1				1		
Worthington	298	14	Hitchcock	Reuben			1	1		2		1	1				6		
Worthington	298	15	Eager	William			1										1		
Worthington	298	16	Newell	John			1			1		1					3		
Worthington	298	17	Hanchet	Zaccheus	1	1	1		1			1	1				6		
Worthington	298	18	Hanchet	Zaccheus Jun	2			1					1				4		
Worthington	298	19	Huntington	Obed	1			1		3	1						6		
Worthington	298	20	Sexton	Noah	1			1		2			1				5		
Worthington	298	21	Kingman	Samuel		1	1			1	1		1				5		
Worthington	298	22	Pomroy	Jonathan		1		1		1	1		1				5		
Worthington	298	23	Haun	Eleazer	1			1				1		1			4		
Worthington	298	24	Benjamin	Roger	2	2	1	1		3			1	1			11		
Worthington	298	25	Randall	Gershom		1	2		1	2		2		1			9		
Worthington	298	26	Leonard	Ebenezer		1	1		1		2	1	1	1			8		
Worthington	298	27	Marsh	Rufus	1		1	1		1	2	1	1	1			9		
Worthington	298	28	Morse	Josiah	2			1					1	1			6		
Worthington	298	29	Cleavland	Newcom	1		2	1		1		1	1	1			8		
Worthington	298	30	Hathaway	Jonathan			1			2		1					4		
Worthington	298	31	Buck	Thomas	1	1	1		1	2	1			1			8		
Worthington	298	32	Buck	Thomas Jun	1		1					1					3		
Worthington	298	33	Wilson	Simeon		1		1		4		1					7		
Worthington	298	34	Cole	Elijah	3			1		1	4	1					10		
Worthington	298	35	Niles	Ebenezer		1	1		1	1		1		1			6		
Worthington	298	36	Convers	Saml D.					1			1	1				3		
Worthington	298	37	Convers	Elisha	1		1					1					3		
Worthington	298	38	Blackman	James		2			1		1			1			5		
Worthington	298	39	Metcalf	Eli	1	1	1	1		1		3		1			9		
Worthington	298	40	Metcalf	Jubal	1			1		2			1				5		
Worthington	299	1	Higgins	Elijah															Name crossed off
Worthington	299	2	Wilson	Benjn	1			1				1		1			4		
Worthington	299	3	Gardner	Reuben		2	1			1	1	1	1				7		
Worthington	299	4	Gardner	Townsend	3			1		3	2		1				10		
Worthington	299	5	Phillips	Jeremiah	1		1	1		1	1		1				6		
Worthington	299	6	Dunbar	Hosea			1						1				2		
Worthington	299	7	Watt	John	1		1		1	1	1	2		1			8		
Worthington	299	8	Tower	Samuel Jun	2	1		1		1			1				6		
Worthington	299	9	Cushing	Ezekiel	3			1				1		1			7		
Worthington	299	10	Sprague	Daniel	2			1		3	1		1				8		
Worthington	299	11	Tower	Samuel	1		1	1	1			1		1			6		
Worthington	299	12	Crosby	David	1			1					3				5		
Worthington	299	13	Scott	Hector	1			1		2		1					5		
Worthington	299	14	Ross	Amasa		1	1		1			1	1				5		
Worthington	299	15	Spalding	Asa	1	2	2		1	2			1				9		
Worthington	299	16	Ludden	Daniel	2			1					1				4		
Worthington	299	17	Herrick	Asa	3	1			1	2	1	1	1				10		
Worthington	299	18	Phelps	Travis			1					1	1				3		
Worthington	299	19	Thresher	Simeon	3		1	1		1			1		4		11		
Worthington	299	20	Beech	Cyrus	2		1					1					4		

TOWN	PG#	LN#	LAST NAME	FIRST NAME	FREE WHITE MALES under 10	10 to 16	16 to 26	26 to 45	45 and over	FREE WHITE FEMALES under 10	10 to 16	16 to 26	26 to 45	45 and over	TOTAL ALL OTHER	TOTAL SLAVES	TOTALS	DISTRICT/ TOWNSHIP	NOTES
Worthington	299	21	Leonard	Simeon	1	1		1	1	2	1		1	1			9		
Worthington	299	22	Brainard	Timothy			1	1				1					3		
Worthington	299	23	Harden	Jonathan	1		1	1		2			1				6		
Worthington	299	24	Webster	Constant	2	2			1	3		1	1	1			11		
Worthington	299	25	Parsons	Sylvanus	3			1		1	4		1				10		
Worthington	299	26	Kinne	John	1	1		1	1	1	1		1	1			8		
Worthington	299	27	Tower	Joseph		1		1			1	1	1				5		
Worthington	299	28	Tower	Abner	1			1		2			1				5		
Worthington	299	29	Spencer	Ashbel	2			1		1			1				5		
Worthington	299	30	Spencer	Fredrick	1	1							1				3		
Worthington	299	31	Spencer	Daniel	2			1		2	1		1				7		
Worthington	299	32	Tash	Moses Negro											6		6		
Worthington	299	33	Thorum	Negro											4		4		
Worthington	299	34	Burton	Sexton	1			1		2			1				5		
Worthington	299	35	Stanton	Peter	3				1				1				5		
Worthington	299	36	Branch	Nathan		2	1		1	1		2	1				8		
Worthington	300	1	Cotterill	Asa	3	1	1		1			2		1			9		
Worthington	300	2	Alvord	Daniel	3			1		1	1		1				7		
Worthington	300	3	Ross	James			1			1			1				3		
Worthington	300	4	Ross	Shelah	4			1		1			1				7		
Worthington	300	5	Hall	Thomas Jun	2			1		1			1				5		
Worthington	300	6	Burton	Asa		1		1		3	2		1				8		
Worthington	300	7	Drury	Jonathan		2	1	1		2		2		1			9		
Worthington	300	8	Parish	Oliver	4	3		1		2			1				11		
Worthington	300	9	Keyes	Jotham	2			1					1				4		
Worthington	300	10	Tuttle	David		1				1		1					3		
Worthington	300	11	Mann	Nathan	2	1	1	1		2	1		1				9		
Worthington	300	12	Parker	Eli	2		1		1	1		1	1	1			8		
Worthington	300	13	Benjamin	Salah	2			1		2			1				6		
Worthington	300	14	Hall	Thomas	1	1		1		2	1	1		1			8		
Worthington	300	15	Childs	Ebenezer	1		4	1		2		1		1			10		
Worthington	300	16	Randall	Joel	2			1		1			1				5		
Worthington	300	17	Randall	Ephraim		1		1		2	2	1					7		
Worthington	300	18	Wadsworth	William			1			1		2					4		
Worthington	300	19	Bailey	John	2	1		1		3	2		1				10		
Worthington	300	20	Sherman	Asa	3			1		1			1				6		
Worthington	300	21	Hunt	David	1			1		1		1					4		
Worthington	300	22	Kingman	Adam	1	1		1						1			4		
Worthington	300	23	Knowles	Rufus	2		1	1		2			1				7		
Worthington	300	24	Dunham	George	1	2		1		2			1				7		
Worthington	300	25	Parish	John		1		1						1			3		
Worthington	300	26	Trink	Amos		1		1				2		1			5		
Worthington	300	27	Leonard	Amos			1	1				1		1			4		
Worthington	300	28	Leonard	Joshua	1			1					1				3		
Worthington	300	29	Kent	Amos	1			1		4	1	2	1				10		
Worthington	300	30	Leonard	Ezra	1	1	1	1		1		1		2			8		
Worthington	300	31	Webber	Ebenezer		1	1					1					3		
Worthington	300	32	Moore	William	1	2			1	3		1	1				9		
Worthington	300	33	Brewster	Jonah	2		1	1		1			1				6		
Worthington	300	34	Marsh	Joseph	1	1	1	1		1	1	1	1				8		
Worthington	300	35	Leonard	Jonas	2	2		1		2		1	1				9		
Worthington	300	36	Leonard	Nathan Jun		1	1		1			2		1			6		
Worthington	300	37	Wheelar	William	1			1		3			1	1			7		
Worthington	301	1	Brewster	Elisha		1	1		1	3	1		1				8		
Worthington	301	2	Morse	Elijah	3	1		1		1		1	1				8		
Worthington	301	3	Morse	Samuel		1	2	1	1	1			1				7		
Worthington	301	4	Parish	Ephm	1	1	1		1	4		2	1				11		
Worthington	301	5	Brewster	Jona	3	1		1		1	2	1	1				10		
Worthington	301	6	Curtis	Elijah	1		1	1		1		1	1				6		
Worthington	301	7	Williams	Ebenezer	1	2		1		1	1	1	1				8		
Worthington	301	8	Woodward	Daniel		1		1					1				3		
Worthington	301	9	Prentice	Phineas		1	1			3			2				7		
Worthington	301	10	Peters	Prince Negro											2		2		
Worthington	301	11	Niles	Peter		1						1					2		
Worthington	301	12	Follit	Isaac		1		1	1	1	2	2	1				9		
Worthington	301	13	Tower	Shubel	1			1		2	1		1				6		
Worthington	301	14	Bates	Amasa	1	1		1		1	1	1					6		
Worthington	301	15	Hubbard	Daniel			3										3		
Worthington	301	16	Wibourn	James		1		1		1				3			6		
Worthington	301	17	Patridge	John		1		1			1		1				4		
Worthington	301	18	Patridge	John Jun		1						1					2		
Worthington	301	19	Patridge	Ebenezer	2			1				1					4		
Worthington	301	20	Collins	Nathaniel				1		1			1				3		
Worthington	301	21	Kinne	Daniel	2		2	1				3	1				9		
Worthington	301	22	Penington	Amos			2		1	3	2	1					9		
Worthington	301	23	Durkin	Joseph		1		1		1	1	1					5		
Worthington	301	24	Herrick	Isaac	3	3	1		1	1			1				10		
Worthington	301	25	Prentice	Jona		1	1		1			2		2			7		
Worthington	301	26	Benjamin	James	3	2		1		2	2		1				11		

TOWN	PG#	LN#	LAST NAME	FIRST NAME	under 10	10 to 16	16 to 26	26 to 45	45 and over	under 10	10 to 16	16 to 26	26 to 45	45 and over	TOTAL ALL OTHER	TOTAL SLAVES	TOTALS	DISTRICT/ TOWNSHIP	NOTES
			HEADS OF HOUSEHOLD		FREE WHITE MALES					FREE WHITE FEMALES									
Worthington	301	27	Prentice	Isaac	2	1	1	1			1	1		2			9		
Worthington	301	28	Higgins	Barre	1		1	1		1		1					5		
Worthington	301	29	Leonard	John		1			1		1		1				4		
Worthington	301	30	Leonard	Asa	1			1		1	1						4		
Worthington	301	31	Leonard	Elisha	1	1	3		1	1				1			8		
Worthington	301	32	Dayley	John	1		1		1	1	1			1			6		
Worthington	301	33	Turner	Thion		2	2	1	1	2	1		1	1			11		
Worthington	301	34	Willys	Mace		2	1	1			2		1				7		
Worthington	301	35	Kelly	John		1			1			4		2			8		
Worthington	301	36	Woods	David		1			1				1	1			4		
Worthington	301	37	Fitch	Adrian	1			1					1				3		
Worthington	301	38	Webber	John				1		3			1				5		
Worthington	301	39	Cook	Samuel	2		1		1	2			1	1			8		
Worthington	301	40	Warner	Matthew		1	2		1			2		2			8		
Worthington	301	41	Parish	Cyprain	1	1	1		1	2	1		1				8		
Worthington	301	42	Tinker	Elihu	1	1	1		1				1	1			6		
Worthington	301	43	Gardner	Elijah		1		1						1			3		
Worthington	301	44	Forward	Reuben		1		1		2	1		1				6		
Worthington	301	45	King	Eleazer	1	3			1	3			1				9		
Worthington	301	46	King	Jona	1				1	2	1		1				6		
Worthington	301	47	Patch	Barzilla	3	1		1		2			1				8		
Worthington	302	1	Tanner	George	3	1		1		2			1				8		
Worthington	302	2	Parsons	Azariah	1	1	1	1			2	1	1				8		
Worthington	302	3	Hatch	Thomas	3			1	1	2			1				8		
Worthington	302	4	Hatch	Zephaniah		1	1	1			1			1			5		
Worthington	302	5	Bemiss	Samuel	2	1		1			1	4	1	1			11		
Worthington	302	6	Bass	Hezekiah				1						1			2		
Worthington	302	7	Sampson	Issachar	1		1	1		1		1					5		
Worthington	302	8	Starkweather	Charles	1	2		1		3		1	1				9		
Worthington	302	9	Wilber	Jeddediah		1			1			1		1			4		
Worthington	302	10	Bates	Isaiah	1		1		1	1	2	1	1				8		
Worthington	302	11	Porter	Jacob		1	1		1	1	2		1				7		
Worthington	302	12	Holdredge	Asher			1		1	1		1	1	1			6		
Worthington	302	13	Tubs	Wido		1								1			2		
Worthington	302	14	Tinker	Nehemiah	1			1		1		1					4		
Worthington	302	15	Ducy	Joseph	1			1	1	2	1	1	1	1			9		
Worthington	302	16	Vinton	Mrs								2		1			3		

Table header: HEADS OF HOUSEHOLD — FREE WHITE MALES (under 10, 10 to 16, 16 to 26, 26 to 45, 45 and over) — FREE WHITE FEMALES (under 10, 10 to 16, 16 to 26, 26 to 45, 45 and over)

TOWN	PG#	LN#	LAST NAME	FIRST NAME	M <10	M 10-16	M 16-26	M 26-45	M 45+	F <10	F 10-16	F 16-26	F 26-45	F 45+	TOTAL ALL OTHER	TOTAL SLAVES	TOTALS	DISTRICT/TOWNSHIP	NOTES
Westfield	118	1	*	James		3					1	1					5		Last name faded
Northampton	3	39	*	Jeremiah	1		2		1	1	1						6		
Granville East Soc	531	25	*	Joel			3	1						1			5		
West Springfield	356	30	*ell	Le*	4	1	1	1		2	1		1				11		
Granby	254	28	Abbe	Abner	2	2	1		1	2	1		1	1			11		
Wilbraham	232	6	Abbe	Joseph		2		1				2		1			6		
Chester	148	2	Abbot	Abial	2	1	1	1		2	2		1				10		
Warwick	36	4	Abbot	Abraham	1	1		1		2	2		1				8		
Chester	147	37	Abbot	Ebenezer	2		1	1		1	3	1	1				10		
Palmer	261	41	Abbot	Gideon			1	1		1			1				4		
Chester	148	1	Abbot	Joseph			1	1			1	2		1			6		
Conway	56	4	Abbot	Joshua				1				3		2			6		
Chester	147	35	Abbot	Lois Wd		2	1			3	1	1	1				10		
Brimfield	272	37	Abbot	Zebadiah	2	1		1		2	2			2			10		
Hadley	288	5	Abbott	Amos	3		1				1						5		
Hadley	288	9	Abbott	Daniel	3		1	1		3			2				10		
Belchertown	208	7	Abbott	James	2		2	1		2	1		1				9		
Amherst	294	25	Abby	Mason	2	1	1			1	1		1				7		
Buckland	325	4	Abby	Reuben	2		1						1				4		
Goshen	309	3	Abel	Benjm	1	3	1	1		3	1	1	1				12		
Goshen	309	1	Abel	Joshua		2		1			1			1			5		
Goshen	309	2	Abel	Joshua Jun	2	1		1		3			1				8		
Goshen	309	4	Abel	Natha	1	1		1		3	1		1				8		
Pelham	213	5	Abercrombie	Isaac Esq	2		1	1					1				5		
Pelham	213	2	Abercrombie	James	1	2		1		2	1	2		1			10		
Pelham	215	7	Abercrombie	Robt				1		1			1				3		
Pelham	217	22	Abercrombie	Robt	1			1						1			3		
Pelham	213	1	Abercrombie	Samuel			1										1		
Granby	253	1	Able	David	1		1						1				3		
Granby	252	44	Able	Sarah Wd	2		2			1	1		1				7		
Leverett	113	6	Adams	a negro											1		1		
New Salem	96	7	Adams	Amos	1		1			5		1					8		
Palmer	261	39	Adams	Andrew		2	1	1	1	1			1				7		
Palmer	261	22	Adams	Andrew 2d		1		1		2			1				5		
Shutesbury	108	2	Adams	Asa	1	2		1				1		1			6		
Deerfield	51	20	Adams	David	1		1					1					3		
Worthington	297	20	Adams	Eliashel		1	1	1			1	1	1				6		
Leyden	80	4	Adams	Elijah	2	1	1					1	1	1			7		
Amherst	291	29	Adams	Eliphalet	1			1		1	1	1					5		
Leverett	113	2	Adams	Erastus		1	3	1			1	2	1				9		
Shutesbury	108	1	Adams	Isaiah				1									1		
Conway	56	15	Adams	Joel	1	1	1	1		1	1	2		1			9		
New Salem	96	8	Adams	Joel	1		1			2		1	1				6		
New Salem	96	10	Adams	John		1	1	1						1			4		
Palmer	261	20	Adams	John	2			1		3		1	1				8		
Rowe	198	1	Adams	John		1	1	1				2		1			6		
Wilbraham	233	19	Adams	John				1						1			2		
Wilbraham	233	20	Adams	John				1						1			2		
Wilbraham	233	18	Adams	John Jr	1	2		1		2			1				7		
West Springfield	352	34	Adams	Levi	1	1	2			1		1					6		
Montgomery	159	1	Adams	Levi Lieut	2	1		1		2			1				7		
Norwich	154	6	Adams	Moses		1	1		1		1	1	1				8		
Brimfield	274	2	Adams	Nathl	1	1		1		1	2		1				7		
Southwick	358	1	Adams	Rufus	1	2	1	1		1		1		1			9		
West Springfield	352	33	Adams	Seth	1	1		1		1			1				5		
Norwich	154	7	Adams	Thadeus	2		1	1		2	2	1					10		
New Salem	96	6	Adams	Thomas		1	1	1		1	2		1				7		
Belchertown	204	10	Adams	Wm	1	1	1					1	1				5		
Springfield	239	38	Addleton	Beulah Wd		1						1		1			3		
Blanford	181	28	Adkins	David		1	1		1	1	3			1			8		
Granville Mid Soc.	167	44	Adkins	Elihu		1	1	1	1				1	1			6		
Whately	65	2	Adkins	Elijah	1			1			2						4		
Granville Mid Soc.	166	13	Adkins	Jabez	3			1		2			1				7		
Whately	65	3	Adkins	Solomon	1	1	1	1	1	1			1	1			8		
Brimfield	274	28	Aikins	John				1		1			1				3		
Wilbraham	237	26	Ainsworth	Amasa	2			1		1			1	1			6		
Wilbraham	233	28	Ainsworth	Nathaniel	1	1	1						1	1			5		
Leverett	113	4	Ainsworth	Willm	1		2					1	1				6		
New Salem	96	4	Akers	Peter	1		1							1			3		
Pelham	213	3	Akins	Joseph	2		1			2			1				6		
Granville West Soc	169	21	Akins	William	2		1			1		1					5		
Orange	41	3	Albee	Asa		1	1	1		1	2			1			8		
Ashfield	337	1	Alden	Barnabas		1	2	1		4	1	1	2	1			13		
Ashfield	337	2	Alden	David Junr	1	1		1		3	2		1				9		
Ashfield	337	9	Alden	Ebenz				1				1							
South Brimfield	277	17	Alden	Elijah	2	1		1			1	1	1				7		
Greenwich	218	3	Alden	Ezra				1			1	2		1			5		
Greenwich	218	4	Alden	Ezra Junr	4			1		1		1	1				8		
Ashfield	337	10	Alden	Henry	1			1		2			1				5		
Ashfield	337	8	Alden	John	2		1	1		4	1	1	1				13		

TOWN	PG#	LN#	LAST NAME	FIRST NAME	FREE WHITE MALES					FREE WHITE FEMALES					TOTAL ALL OTHER	TOTAL SLAVES	TOTALS	DISTRICT/ TOWNSHIP	NOTES
					under 10	10 to 16	16 to 26	26 to 45	45 and over	under 10	10 to 16	16 to 26	26 to 45	45 and over					
Greenwich	219	19	Alden	John A.	2	1		1		2	1		1				8		
Greenwich	218	5	Alden	Jonathan					1					1			2		
Ludlow	257	23	Alden	Josiah	4			1		1			1				7		
South Brimfield	276	10	Alden	Josiah	1		1		1	1				1			5		
Greenwich	218	6	Alden	Oliver	1	1	1		1			2	1	1			8		
Middlefield	157	25	Alderman	Daniel	1			1		1		1					4		
Orange	41	4	Aldrich	Asa		1		1		1			1				4		
Ashfield	337	4	Aldrich	Benjm	3	1		1		1			1				7		
New Salem	96	2	Aldrich	Jesse		1		1				2	1				5		
New Salem	96	3	Aldrich	Peleg	1		1			1			1				4		
Ashfield	337	3	Aldrich	Solomon	3	2		1		1	1		1				9		
Warwick	36	5	Aldridge	Benajah	1	2		1		3			1				8		
Barnardston	76	6	Aldridge	Joseph	2			1		1			1	1			6		
Deerfield	51	18	Alexander	Amos		1		1		1	1	1		2			7		
Montague	44	10	Alexander	Ebenezer	1	1		1		2	1		1				7		
Northfield	27	2	Alexander	Elisha	1		2		2	1	1		1				8		
Barnardston	76	5	Alexander	George		1				1	1						3		
Greenfield	72	3	Alexander	John	1		1			3			2	1			8		
Montague	44	9	Alexander	Joseph	1		1						1				3		
Northfield	27	5	Alexander	Medad	2	1		2		1			1				7		
Sunderland	283	2	Alexander	Miles	2		1	1		1		1	1	1			8		
Chester	145	35	Alexander	Nathaniel Capt	1	1		1		1	2	2		1			9		
Northfield	27	3	Alexander	Simeon Jr	2		1			2	2	1	1				9		
Northfield	27	4	Alexander	Thomas			1	1					1				3		
West Springfield	349	11	Alford	Benjamin	1		1	1					1				4		
Barnardston	76	3	Alger	Simon		1	1		1	1		1	1				6		
Greenwich	218	7	Alhimon	John		1	1		1				1				4		
Monson	267	21	Allard	Daniel			1	1		1			1				4		
Monson	264	14	Allard	John	3		1	1		3		1	1	1			11		
Holland	279	5	Allen	Abel Lt.	1		2	1		1	1			1			7		
Palmer	261	4	Allen	Abner	3			1		1			1				6		
Wendell	105	3	Allen	Abner	1	1		1		2			1				6		
Brimfield	273	19	Allen	Alfred	2	1		1		1			1				6		
Conway	56	13	Allen	Amos				1		1	1			2			5		
Greenfield	71	6	Allen	Amos	3			1		3			1				8		
West Springfield	355	40	Allen	Amos		1		2			1		1				5		
Barnardston	76	1	Allen	Anna							1		1				2		
Palmer	260	32	Allen	Anna									1				1		
Wilbraham	234	27	Allen	Benjamin	3			1		3			1				8		
West Springfield	355	42	Allen	Bishop	2	1	2	1		2	1	2					11		
Conway	56	1	Allen	Caleb	2	1			1	1	2			1			8		
Deerfield	51	17	Allen	Caleb		1	3		1		1	1		1			8		
Montgomery	162	7	Allen	David	3			1		1			1		1		7		
Greenfield	71	3	Allen	Ebenezer	3	1		1	1	1	1		2	1			11		
Rowe	198	2	Allen	Ebenezer	2			1		2			1				6		
Greenfield	71	10	Allen	Ebenezer Jnr	1	2	3		1	1	1	1	1				11		
Belchertown	208	6	Allen	Edmond Capt	1	2	2		1	4	3		1				14		
Greenfield	72	1	Allen	Elihu		1		1		1			1				4		
Brimfield	273	3	Allen	Elijah	2		1	1		3			1				8		
Greenfield	71	11	Allen	Elijah	1	1		1		3	1		1				8		
Northampton	10	23	Allen	Elijah	1		1	1		2	2	1	1				9		
West Springfield	355	41	Allen	Enos	1			1		2			1				5		
Palmer	261	5	Allen	Ephraim				1				1		1			3		
New Salem	96	1	Allen	Ezra	1		3	1		1		1					7		
West Springfield	352	32	Allen	Gideon	2	1		1		1	1		1				7		
Plainfield	306	1	Allen	Jacob	2			1		1	3	1					8		
Orange	41	1	Allen	James	1		1		1	2	1	1		1			8		
Greenfield	71	12	Allen	Job	1			1		1				1			4		
Greenfield	71	8	Allen	Joel	3	2		1		1	1	1	1				10		
Conway	56	16	Allen	John	1			1		2	2		1				7		
Barnardston	76	2	Allen	Jonathan	4	1				1			1				7		
West Springfield	352	31	Allen	Jonathan		2		1						1			4		
Barnardston	76	7	Allen	Joseph	1	1		1		2	1		1				7		
Buckland	325	1	Allen	Joseph		1		1		1		2					5		
Springfield	245	28	Allen	Joseph	3	1		1					1				6		
Northampton	5	16	Allen	Merab	1	1				1		1	1				5		
Westfield	121	11	Allen	Moses	2			1		3			1	1			8		
Belchertown	212	6	Allen	Nathan	4			1		1			1				7		
Granville West Soc	169	32	Allen	Nathan	1	1			1	1		1	1				6		
Goshen	310	11	Allen	Phillip Negro											3		3		
Northampton	3	10	Allen	Phineas		1		1		1			1				3		
Greenfield	71	5	Allen	Quintus	2		1			3		2	2				10		
Westfield	125	28	Allen	Ransford		1						1		1			3		
Holland	278	22	Allen	Reuben	2			1		2			1				6		
Shutesbury	108	3	Allen	Robert	2	1		1		1	1		1				7		
Montgomery	161	27	Allen	Samuel	1		1						1				3		
Pelham	217	7	Allen	Samuel	1		1					1	1				5		
Northfield	27	1	Allen	Samuel C.	4			1		1	1	1		1			9		
Leyden	80	3	Allen	Simon	1	1	2		1		1	1		1			8		
Northampton	2	17	Allen	Solomon		1			1	1		2	1	1			7		

185

TOWN	PG#	LN#	LAST NAME	FIRST NAME	\<10	10–16	16–26	26–45	45+	\<10	10–16	16–26	26–45	45+	TOTAL ALL OTHER	TOTAL SLAVES	TOTALS	DISTRICT/ TOWNSHIP	NOTES
			HEADS OF HOUSEHOLD		FREE WHITE MALES					FREE WHITE FEMALES									
Wendell	105	4	Allen	Stephen	1	1	1		2	3		1	1	1			11		
Shelburne	319	3	Allen	Sylvanus	1	1	1		1	2	2	2		1			11		
Chesterfield	21	6	Allen	Timothy				1					1				2		
Middlefield	155	5	Allen	Timothy	2	1	1					1					5		
West Springfield	352	35	Allen	William	2	2	1		1		1			1			8		
Ashfield	337	14	Allis	Abel			1	1			2		1				5		
Conway	56	10	Allis	Abel		1	1		1				1				4		
Whately	65	1	Allis	Daniel	2	2	1			3		1					9		
Deerfield	51	9	Allis	Eben		1	1						1				3		
Shelburne	319	7	Allis	Ebenz		1			2		1	2		2			8		
Conway	56	11	Allis	Joel	2		1	2	1	2		1	1	1			11		
Hatfield	13	22	Allis	John	1	1		1				2	1		2		8		
Ashfield	337	6	Allis	Lemuel		1	2		1		2	1					8		
Hawley	331	2	Allis	Lucius	1		1	1		1			1	1			6		
Conway	56	12	Allis	Samuel	2			1		2	1		1				7		
Hatfield	11	18	Allis	Silas	1		1			1		1		1			5		
Conway	56	9	Allis	Solomon	2	1		1	1	1	1						8		
Buckland	325	3	Allis	Stephen	2	1	2	1			2	1					9		
Barnardston	76	4	Allis	Thomas				1					1				2		
Hatfield	13	23	Allis	William	1	2		1		3	1		1		1		10		
Brimfield	273	6	Alllen	Caleb	2			1		1		1	1				6		
Blanford	178	28	Almy	Job		1		1			1	1					4		
South Hadley	249	22	Alvard	Azariah Capt.	1		1		1		1		1				5		
South Hadley	250	21	Alvard	Bezaleel	2	1	2	1		1		1	1				9		
Northampton	7	21	Alvard	Elizabeth									2				2		
Granby	254	35	Alvard	Gad	1	1	1	1		1	1	1	1				8		
South Hadley	249	25	Alvard	Gideon		1	1		1			1	1				5		
South Hadley	250	15	Alvard	Justin	1		1			1			1				4		
South Hadley	249	18	Alvard	Samuel	1	2	2		1	3	1		1				11		
Westhampton	17	31	Alvord	Ahiela		2		1		1		1					5		
Montague	44	1	Alvord	Caleb	2	3	2	1		2	1	1		1			13		
Worthington	300	2	Alvord	Daniel	3			1		1	1		1				7		
Westhampton	18	9	Alvord	Eliab			2			3		1					6		
Greenfield	71	14	Alvord	Elijah	1		4	1		2			1				9		
Easthampton	135	18	Alvord	Elisha	2		1		1		2			2			8		
Northampton	9	9	Alvord	Elisha	1		1		1	1		1					5		
Northampton	9	32	Alvord	John	1	1		1		2	1	1		2			9		
Westhampton	17	28	Alvord	Jonathan				1			4		1				6		
Easthampton	136	18	Alvord	Phineas	2			1		2	2	1	1				9		
West Springfield	349	13	Alvord	Samuel	1	1		1		1	1		1				6		
Northampton	11	8	Alvord	Timothy				1		2			1				4		
Easthampton	136	17	Alvord	Zebediah		1		1	1			2	1				6		
Shelburne	319	4	Alword	Zevah	2			1		2			1				6		
Springfield	241	14	Alworth	Stephen	2		2	1		1	1		1				8		
Greenfield	71	1	Ames	Ambrose		2	1			5			1		1		10		
Springfield	243	28	Ames	David	2		2			3	2	1	1	1			12		
South Brimfield	277	23	Ames	Ebenezer				1					1				2		
South Brimfield	277	27	Ames	Ebenezer Jr	2			1		1		1					5		
Buckland	325	2	Ames	John	1		4	1		3		1	1				11		
South Brimfield	276	7	Ames	Rebecca	1							1					2		
Belchertown	212	4	Ames	Robert		1			1			1	1				4		
Ashfield	337	12	Amible	Barnabas	2			1		2		1					6		
Ashfield	337	11	Amiden	Mary			1					1		1			3		
Wilbraham	237	14	Ammidown	Titus	1	1		1	4	1			1				9		
Conway	56	3	Amsden	Elisha		1	1		1	1			1				5		
Hawley	331	1	Amsden	Elisha	1			1		1		1					4		
Conway	56	2	Amsden	Isaac			3		1			1		1			6		
Conway	56	17	Amsden	Sarah						2	1		1				4		
Deerfield	51	15	Anderson	Abner	3			1		2			1				7		
Chesterfield	24	34	Anderson	Alanson				1		3			1				5		
Brimfield	274	24	Anderson	Amasa	2			1				1					4		
Chesterfield	23	10	Anderson	David	1			1		2	1		1				6		
Holland	279	14	Anderson	David		1	1		1		1		1				5		
Shelburne	319	5	Anderson	David	2	2	1	1		2			1				9		
Holland	280	10	Anderson	David 2d	1			1		1			2				5		
Goshen	309	5	Anderson	Ebenezer			1	1			2	1	1				6		
Montague	44	6	Anderson	Elizabeth				1					1				2		
Montague	44	3	Anderson	Ezra	1			2		2		1	1				7		
Blanford	175	3	Anderson	James	3	1		1		1		1	1				8		
Shelburne	319	6	Anderson	James	4	1	1	1		1	1		1				10		
Deerfield	51	12	Anderson	John	1			1		1			1				4		
Deerfield	51	16	Anderson	John	1			1		1		1	2				7		
Shelburne	319	1	Anderson	John			1	1									2		
Chesterfield	23	11	Anderson	Jonathan				1					1				2		
Cummington	302	1	Anderson	Joseph	2	2	2	1		2	2		1				12		
Brimfield	274	22	Anderson	Margaret Wd		1							1				2		
Montague	44	4	Anderson	Mathew			1										1		
Deerfield	51	11	Anderson	Solomon	1	2		1		1			1				6		
Monson	268	34	Anderson	Thomas Doct				1			1	1	1				4		
Holland	280	6	Anderson	Timothy	2		1	1		1			1	1			7		

TOWN	PG#	LN#	LAST NAME	FIRST NAME	FREE WHITE MALES					FREE WHITE FEMALES					TOTAL ALL OTHER	TOTAL SLAVES	TOTALS	DISTRICT/ TOWNSHIP	NOTES
					under 10	10 to 16	16 to 26	26 to 45	45 and over	under 10	10 to 16	16 to 26	26 to 45	45 and over					
Deerfield	51	10	Anderson	William		1		1						1			3		
Ware	225	1	Anderson	William		3	2	1		1	2			1			10		
West Springfield	349	12	Andrew	Asahel											6		6		
Ware	225	3	Andrews	Aaron			1	1		1			1				4		
New Salem	96	9	Andrews	Daniel		1				1		1					3		
Ashfield	337	13	Andrews	James	3		2		1	1	2		1				10		
Conway	56	7	Andrews	James	1	1	3		1	1	1			1			9		
Conway	56	8	Andrews	James Jun	1		1						1				3		
Ware	225	5	Andrews	John	1			1				1					3		
Granville West Soc	170	4	Andrews	Jonah	1	2	1		1				1				6		
Ware	225	2	Andrews	Lemuel	1			1		3	1		1				7		
Montague	44	8	Andrews	Moses	1		1	1		1	2		1				7		
Ashfield	337	7	Andrews	Otis	2			1		2			1				6		
Ware	225	4	Andrews	Prince			1					1					2		
Russell	138	3	Andrews	Richard	1			1		3			1				6		
Pelham	217	4	Andrews	Stephen	1	2		1		1			2				7		
New Salem	96	5	Andrews	Thomas		2		1		1			1				5		
Hadley	285	24	Andries	George				1						1			2		
Montgomery	162	1	Andrus	Jacob				1						1			2		
Montgomery	162	2	Andrus	Jacob Junr	1			1		2		1					5		
Southwick	358	2	Andruss	Lemuel			1			1		1					3		
South Brimfield	276	2	Andruss	Robert		2	1	1		2		1	1				8		
Norwich	151	1	Angel	Stephen	2			1				1	1				5		
Buckland	325	5	Annible	Edward	1			1		2	2	1	1				8		
Ashfield	337	5	Annible	Saml Jr			1			1		1					3		
Brimfield	270	37	Annis	Molley Wd						2	1		1				4		
Williamsburg	448	1	Appleby	Michael	1		1		1	1	3		1				8		
Deerfield	51	2	Arms	Aaron	1	2		1		2	1	2	1	1			11		
Montague	44	2	Arms	David		1		1						1			3		
Greenfield	71	7	Arms	Ebenezer	1	1	1	1		2	2		1				9		
Deerfield	51	7	Arms	Eliaken	2		1	1	1	2		2	2	1			12		
Deerfield	51	8	Arms	Elijah	1	1	1	1	1	3	1		1	1			11		
Deerfield	51	4	Arms	Eliphas	2	2		1		2		2	1				10		
Deerfield	51	22	Arms	Elizabeth										2			2		
Conway	56	6	Arms	Henry			1			1		1					3		
Deerfield	51	1	Arms	Jonathan		1	3		1			2	1	1	1		10		
Deerfield	51	21	Arms	Lemuel	3			1					1	1			6		
Conway	56	5	Arms	Mercy	1	1	2	1			1	3	1	1			11		
Greenfield	71	4	Arms	Moses		1	1		1	1	1	1	1				7		
Brimfield	272	5	Arms	Polly Wd	1					1			1				3		
Deerfield	51	6	Arms	Seth	2	1		1		2	1	1	1				9		
Greenfield	71	2	Arms	Solomon		1		1		2	1		2	1			8		
Deerfield	51	3	Arms	Thomas				1			1	1	1				4		
Deerfield	51	5	Arms	Thomas Jr	1			1		1	1						4		
Wilbraham	233	6	Armstrong	Samuel	1			1		2			1				5		
Montague	44	7	Armstrong	Timothy	1	1		1	1	2			1				7		
Williamsburg	448	2	Arnold	Prince											1		1		
Deerfield	51	19	Arnold	William	1			1		1			1				4		
Chester	144	35	Arnsworth	Edward	1			1		2			1				5		
Westfield	125	19	Arther	Bradford		1				1		1					3		
Westfield	125	18	Arther	Hannah Wd		1	2				3			1			7		
West Springfield	349	9	Ashley	Benjamin		1	2		1			1	1	1			7		
Springfield	244	44	Ashley	Daniel	2	1		1		1	1		1				7		
West Springfield	349	3	Ashley	David		2	2		1			2		1			8		
West Springfield	349	4	Ashley	David Junr			1	1			1		1				4		
West Springfield	349	7	Ashley	Ebenezer			1	1			1		1				4		
Westfield	123	8	Ashley	Eli	1			1					1	2			7		
Deerfield	51	13	Ashley	Elihu		1	2				1		1		2		8		
West Springfield	355	43	Ashley	Elisha	1		1	1		3			2	1			9		
Westfield	120	15	Ashley	Israel		2			1		1	2		1			7		
Shutesbury	108	4	Ashley	James		3	1		1					1			6		
Springfield	245	1	Ashley	John	1	1			1	2		1		1			7		
West Springfield	349	1	Ashley	John				1						1			2		
West Springfield	349	5	Ashley	Joseph		1			1	1			1	1			5		
West Springfield	349	6	Ashley	Joseph Junr	3			1		1	1		1				7		
Longmeadow	91	11	Ashley	Justin		1		1		2			1				5		
Springfield	242	16	Ashley	Moses		2											2		
West Springfield	349	10	Ashley	Moses	1		2			1			2				6		
Longmeadow	91	5	Ashley	Noah		1				1		1					3		
Westfield	119	19	Ashley	Noah		1				1		1					3		
Springfield	245	2	Ashley	Phebe Wd		1							1				2		
Belchertown	209	32	Ashley	Saml		1		1		1			1				4		
Deerfield	51	14	Ashley	Solomon				1						1			2		
West Springfield	349	2	Ashley	Solomon			1			2			1				4		
Leverett	113	1	Ashley	Stephen		1	1		1	1			1				5		
Longmeadow	91	4	Ashley	Stephen		1		1				1		1			4		
Westfield	119	33	Ashley	Stephen	3		1	1		1		1	1				8		
Springfield	244	43	Ashley	Vashti Wd										1			1		
Leverett	113	5	Ashley	Warden	1		1						1				3		
Westfield	118	3	Ashley	Wm	1	1	1		1		1	1		1			7		

TOWN	PG#	LN#	LAST NAME	FIRST NAME	FREE WHITE MALES under 10	10 to 16	16 to 26	26 to 45	45 and over	FREE WHITE FEMALES under 10	10 to 16	16 to 26	26 to 45	45 and over	TOTAL ALL OTHER	TOTAL SLAVES	TOTALS	DISTRICT/TOWNSHIP	NOTES
Sunderland	283	9	Ashly	Gideon		1		1			1	4		1			8		
Blanford	181	21	Ashman	Eli P	1		1	1				2					5		
Northfield	27	6	Askey	William		1					1	2		1			6		
Brimfield	269	4	Aspinwall	Prince	1	1	1	1	1		1	2	1				9		
Wilbraham	234	30	Atchinson	Benoni		3		1					1	1			6		
Shelburne	319	2	Atherton	Adonijah	1	1	1		2	2	2	1		1			11		
Greenfield	71	9	Atherton	Jonathan				1						1			2		
Greenfield	72	2	Atherton	Joseph	2		1	1		1	1	1	1				8		
Greenfield	72	4	Atherton	Joseph Jr	1			1		3			1				6		
Greenfield	71	13	Atherton	Oliver				1			2		1				4		
Wendell	105	1	Atherton	Thomas	1		2		1		1			1			6		
Westfield	126	11	Atkins	Chancey	3	1	1	1		1	2	1	1				11		
West Springfield	349	8	Atkins	Josiah	3	2			1	1		3		1			11		
Westfield	126	8	Atkins	Luther	2	1	1			2	1	2	1				10		
Westfield	121	22	Atwater	John		1			1	2	1		1				6		
Westfield	120	26	Atwater	Noah Revd		3	1		1		3			1			11		
Blanford	181	23	Atwater	Russel	5		2	1	1				1	1			11		
Springfield	244	9	Atwell	Jno				1		2		1					4		
Orange	41	2	Atwood	Ebenezer			2			1		1					4		
Warwick	36	3	Atwood	Isaac	1	1		1		4	2		1				10		
Belchertown	208	5	Atwood	John	2			1		1		1					5		
Warwick	36	1	Atwood	Joshua	2	3	1	1		1			1	1			10		
Warwick	36		Atwood	Phillip	1	1	1	1			1		1				6		
Montague	44	5	Austin	James			2	1	2		1		1				7		
Worthington	297	14	Austin	John			2		1				1				4		
Wendell	105	2	Austin	Josiah	3	1		1	1		1	1	1				9		
Montgomery	159	16	Author	Richard	2		1					1					4		
Norwich	151	30	Averett	Nathaniel		2		1	1	1		1					6		
Springfield	247	37	Avery	Abel	3		2	2	1	1	1	1	1				12		
Westfield	126	4	Avery	Abel	4		1	1			2		1				9		
Monson	264	7	Avery	Asa	2		2	1			1	1					8		
Montgomery	161	7	Avery	Bansford	2			1	1	2	2	1					9		
Montgomery	159	18	Avery	Ephraim	2	2		1		1	1		1				8		
Monson	265	8	Avery	Gardner	1			1		2		1		1			6		
Conway	56	14	Avery	John	1	2		1		3	1			1			9		
Leyden	80	2	Avery	Nathan		1		1			2	1	1				6		
Leyden	80	1	Avery	Nathaniel	2	2		1		2	1		1	1			10		
Montgomery	161	8	Avery	Samuel	2		1	1		3			1	1			9		
Hadley	288	35	Avery	Uriah	1	1		1		2	2		1				8		
Montgomery	160	36	Avery	William	1	1	1	1		2	3		1				10		
Amherst	291	25	Ayer	Amos	1			1	1	1	1	1					6		
Pelham	213	4	Ayers	Buenos	1			1		2		1					5		
South Hadley	250	22	Ayman	Solomon	1								1	1			3		
Granby	253	2	Ayres	Aaron	1	2	1		2	2		2		1			10		
Chester	145	1	Ayres	Asa	1			1		2	1		1				6		
Granby	253	3	Ayres	Eleazer	1	1			1		1						4		
Leverett	113	3	Ayres	Jesse	2	1		1			2	2	1				9		
Greenwich	219	22	Ayres	John		3	1	1	1	3	2		1				12		
Brimfield	271	10	Ayres	Thomas	4			1		1	1		1				8		
Granville West Soc	170	30	Ba*	William	3			1		2							6		
Pelham	213	14	Babbett	Samuel	1	1		1	1	2	1		1	1			9		
Ware	228	33	Babbett	Samuel	3	1		1		2			1				8		
Greenwich	218	11	Babbit	Elijah			1	1		1	2	1	1				7		
Orange	41	16	Babbit	Ira			1			1							2		
Greenwich	218	12	Babbit	Jonathan	1		1		4			1					7		
Middlefield	156	20	Babcock	Daniel	2		1		4	1		1					9		
Leyden	80	5	Babcock	Derius			1	1	1								3		
Northampton	10	7	Babcock	Elisha	2		1		2		1						6		
Leyden	80	8	Babcock	Ezra	4	1		1	1		1	1					9		
Wilbraham	233	4	Babcock	Horace	2		1			1	1						5		
Westfield	124	29	Babcock	Irena					1			1					2		
Blanford	176	25	Babcock	James	2		1		2		1						6		
South Brimfield	275	20	Babcock	Jeremiah		1		1			1						3		
Blanford	182	12	Babcock	John	1		2	1		1			1				6		
Granville West Soc	170	23	Babcock	John	1			1	3		1						6		
Leyden	81	6	Babcock	Joseph	3		1		1	1	3	1					10		
Leyden	80	14	Babcock	Oliver	1	3		2		2	1	2					11		
Leyden	81	13	Babcock	Paul	4	1		1		1	1		1				9		
Leyden	81	2	Babcock	Peleg	1	1	1		1	1				1	1		7		
Granville Mid Soc.	166	1	Babcock	Perry	2		1		1		1		1	1			7		
Orange	41	14	Bachelor	Joel	1	1		1			1						4		
Conway	56	29	Bachelor	John	1			1	2	1	1	1		2			9		
Buckland	326	3	Bachelor	Nathan	1			1			1	1					4		
Ashfield	338	2	Bachelor	Saml	1		1		1		1		1				5		
Blanford	180	16	Backett	John	1	2	1		3		1		1				10		
Palmer	258	3	Backus	Samuel	1			1		2	1		1				6		
Brimfield	270	35	Bacon	Amasa	1		1					1					3		
Palmer	260	24	Bacon	Benjamin			1				1		1				3		
Brimfield	270	34	Bacon	James				1	1		2		1				5		
Conway	56	33	Bacon	Joel	2		1	1		2			1	1			8		

TOWN	PG#	LN#	HEADS OF HOUSEHOLD		FREE WHITE MALES					FREE WHITE FEMALES					TOTAL ALL OTHER	TOTAL SLAVES	TOTALS	DISTRICT/ TOWNSHIP	NOTES
			LAST NAME	FIRST NAME	under 10	10 to 16	16 to 26	26 to 45	45 and over	under 10	10 to 16	16 to 26	26 to 45	45 and over					
Whately	66	6	Bacon	Jonathan	1	1		1		3		1					7		
Conway	56	32	Bacon	Nathan		2		1		4	1		1				9		
Ware	225	9	Bacon	Penuel	1			1				1					3		
Whately	66	13	Bacon	Philo			1	1		2	1	1	1				7		
Palmer	260	25	Bacon	Simeon	2	1		1		2			1				7		
Ware	225	10	Bacon	Thomas	1	1		1		3			1				7		
Chester	145	34	Bacon	Timothy		1			1	1	2		1				6		
Blanford	180	10	Badger	Joseph Revd	1	2		1		2	1		1				8		
South Brimfield	277	35	Badger	Nathan	2			1		1			1	1			6		
Palmer	262	11	Badlwin	William	3			1			1		1				6		
West Springfield	349	26	Bagg	Aaron			1	1			1	2	1				6		
West Springfield	350	1	Bagg	Ezekiel	1	2		1		2	1		1				8		
West Springfield	349	17	Bagg	Frederick	1	1			1	1	1	1		1			7		
West Springfield	349	24	Bagg	John	1	1			1		1	2					6		
West Springfield	349	23	Bagg	Judah		2		1		1		2	1				7		
West Springfield	349	22	Bagg	Oliver			1		1	2	1			1			6		
West Springfield	349	16	Bagg	Orpha	1		2	1			1	2		1			8		
West Springfield	349	28	Bagg	Thomas	1		2		1	2	2	1	1				10		
West Springfield	349	19	Bagg	Walter	1				2		1		1				5		
West Springfield	349	32	Bagg	Washam		1			1		1	3		1			7		
Belchertown	208	20	Baggs	Noble		1	1		1			4		1			8		
Springfield	247	12	Bagley	Amy Wd			4	1					1				6		
Williamsburg	448	19	Bagley	Eliakim		1			1	1		1					3		
Williamsburg	448	9	Bagley	John	1			1	1	1				1			5		
Brimfield	271	35	Bailes	Lemuel	1	2		1		3	2	3	1				13		
Springfield	242	15	Bailes	Thomas	1	2	1	1	2		1	2		2			12		
Wilbraham	234	37	Bailey	Constant	1		1			1							3		
Rowe	198	3	Bailey	Israel				1				1					2		
Belchertown	204	24	Bailey	John		1		1		1			1				4		
Greenwich	219	18	Bailey	John		1	1	1				1		1			5		
Worthington	300	19	Bailey	John	2	1		1		3	2		1				10		
Cummington	303	14	Bailey	Joseph	3	1	1		1		1			1			8		
Chesterfield	20	18	Bailey	Joseph S.				1				1					2		
South Hadley	250	4	Bailey	Noah		1		1	1		2	1					6		
Wilbraham	234	36	Bailey	Robert	1	1		1		2	1	1	1		1		9		
West Springfield	355	48	Baird	Isaac				1					1				2		
Goshen	309	14	Baker	Abner	4	2		1		1	1	1					10		
Ashfield	338	22	Baker	Allen			3										3		
Springfield	243	30	Baker	Asa	1		2	2		1		2	1				9		
Leyden	81	3	Baker	Benjamin	1	1	1		1	2	1		1				8		
Cummington	302	3	Baker	Daniel		1		1				1	1				4		
Amherst	292	18	Baker	Elijah				1					1				2		
Leyden	81	4	Baker	Elijah	1		1		1	1			1				5		
Chesterfield	19	10	Baker	Elisha	1			1		2	1		1				6		
Hawley	332	1	Baker	Elkhanah		1	1			4		1	1				8		
Amherst	292	17	Baker	Enos	2	1	1			2			1				7		
Pelham	213	16	Baker	Ezekiel	4	1		1		1			1				8		
Hawley	332	11	Baker	Hollister		1							1				2		
Amherst	289	14	Baker	Isaac		1	1						1				3		
Conway	56	22	Baker	Isaac	1	1	1	1		1		1	1				7		
Pelham	213	9	Baker	Isaac	3			1	1	1			2	1			9		
Greenwich	219	30	Baker	James	2	2		1		1			1				7		
Conway	56	21	Baker	Joel			1		1		1	1		1			5		
Granville Mid Soc.	167	22	Baker	Joel Reverend		1		1			1		1				4		
Blanford	101	15	Baker	John	2		1					1					4		
Northampton	8	34	Baker	John		1			2			1					4		
Westhampton	17	5	Baker	John		1	2		1			1	1	1			7		
Brimfield	273	31	Baker	Joseph		1		1		4			1				7		
Granville West Soc	168	14	Baker	Joseph			1			1		1					3		
Monson	267	2	Baker	Joseph				1					1	1			3		
Cummington	302	2	Baker	Josiah				1			1	1	1				4		
Chesterfield	20	15	Baker	Lemuel		1							1				2		
Orange	41	9	Baker	Lewis	3		1			1	1		1				7		
Amherst	292	19	Baker	Martin	1			1		1			1				4		
Conway	56	40	Baker	Nathaniel		1	1			2	1		1				6		
Hawley	332	2	Baker	Rufus	1			1		1		1					4		
Chesterfield	20	11	Baker	Seth	2			1		1		1					5		
Orange	41	8	Baker	Sherebiah	1	1	2		1	2		2		1			10		
Westhampton	17	21	Baker	Simeon	1			1		3			1				6		
Chesterfield	20	13	Baker	Stephen				1					1	1			3		
Chesterfield	20	12	Baker	Thaddeus		1		1		2			1				5		
Chesterfield	20	14	Baker	Thomas				1				1					2		
Hawley	331	4	Baker	Timothy	1	1		1		1	2	1	1				8		
Belchertown	207	6	Baker	William Jr	1	3		1		1			1				7		
Ashfield	338	10	Balding	Ebenz		1		1	1	1			1	1			6		
Granville Mid Soc.	166	28	Balding	Amos		1	2		1			1	1	1			7		
Granville Mid Soc.	166	27	Baldwin	Curtiss	2			1		1			1	1			6		
Ashfield	338	17	Baldwin	David		1		1			2		1				5		
Ashfield	338	18	Baldwin	David Jr	1		1			2			1				5		
Granville Mid Soc.	167	3	Baldwin	Ebenezer			1	1		1		1	1	1			6		

TOWN	PG#	LN#	LAST NAME	FIRST NAME	FWM under 10	FWM 10 to 16	FWM 16 to 26	FWM 26 to 45	FWM 45 and over	FWF under 10	FWF 10 to 16	FWF 16 to 26	FWF 26 to 45	FWF 45 and over	TOTAL ALL OTHER	TOTAL SLAVES	TOTALS	DISTRICT/ TOWNSHIP	NOTES
West Springfield	352	52	Baldwin	Elnathan	1		1	1					1				4		
Granville Mid Soc.	167	34	Baldwin	Ezra	1	1		1	1				2	1			7		
Westfield	126	10	Baldwin	Jabez		2	1	1	1		2	1		1			9		
Ashfield	338	20	Baldwin	John	1			1		2			1				5		
Granville Mid Soc.	166	26	Baldwin	John	2			1					1				4		
Ashfield	338	19	Baldwin	Jonathan	3			1					1				5		
Granville Mid Soc.	167	35	Baldwin	Lyman	3			1		1	1		1				7		
Palmer	262	3	Baldwin	Moses Revd		1			1	1		2		1			6		
Granville Mid Soc.	166	25	Baldwin	Stephen	2	2		1		2			1	1			9		
Pelham	213	12	Baldwin	Wm			1		1			1		1			4		
Southampton	133	2	Baldwin	Wm		1			1		1	1		1			5		
Granville Mid Soc.	165	10	Bales	David			1			2	1		1				5		
Springfield	239	32	Bales	Eli	2			1					1				4		
Easthampton	134	1	Baley	Submit			1			3			1				5		
Springfield	239	29	Ball	Benja G.	2	2		1		1		1		1			8		
Leyden	80	10	Ball	Benjamin			1			1		1					3		
West Springfield	355	46	Ball	Charles	2	1		1		1	1	1	2				9		
West Springfield	352	54	Ball	Eli	2	2		1	1	3		1	1				11		
Orange	41	7	Ball	Elijah	1	2	1		1	1	1	1	1				9		
Warwick	36	26	Ball	James	4	1		1		3	3		1	1			14		
Deerfield	51	36	Ball	John	1	1	2		1	3	1	1	1	1			12		
Warwick	36	34	Ball	John	1			1		1	1		1				5		
Warwick	36	18	Ball	Jonas	1		1		1	1	2	4		1			11		
Warwick	36	37	Ball	Jono Clark	1			1		2			1				5		
Shutesbury	108	15	Ball	Joseph	2			1	1	1			1				6		
Warwick	36	11	Ball	Samuel	2			1				2					5		
Warwick	36	19	Ball	Samuel	2			1		2	1		1				7		
Leverett	113	10	Ball	Silas		1	2		1	2				1			7		
Warwick	36	7	Ball	Stephen		1					1		1				3		
Springfield	240	30	Ball	Wm	2		1	1		1		1					6		
Westfield	120	13	Ballantine	John	1			1				1		1			4		
Buckland	325	11	Ballard	Benjm			1			2			1				5		
Chesterfield	22	19	Ballard	James			1										1		
New Salem	97	6	Ballard	James	3	1		1		3	1		1				10		
New Salem	96	12	Ballard	Jeremiah			1	1				1	1				4		
Hatfield	13	7	Ballard	John		1		1		1	2		1				6		
Holland	279	2	Ballard	Jonathan	3			1					1				5		
Buckland	325	10	Ballard	Joseph	1	1		1				2					5		
Wendell	105	5	Ballard	Josiah	3		1	1		1		1	2	1			10		
Montague	45	11	Ballard	Luther	1	1		1		4			1				8		
Holland	278	10	Ballard	Sherebiah			1						1				2		
Wendell	105	6	Ballard	Sylvanus	1			1				1					3		
Brimfield	271	2	Ballow	Peter		1				1		1		2			5		
Monson	262	17	Ballow	Peter			1				1		1				3		
Monson	262	18	Ballow	Seth	1		1				1						3		
Warwick	36	12	Bancraft	Daniel			1			2		1					4		
Warwick	36	15	Bancraft	Ebenezer	1	2	1			2		1		1			9		
Warwick	36	6	Bancraft	Jacob	1			1		1	1		1				5		
Montague	45	12	Bancraft	Kendall		1	1		1			2		1			6		
Warwick	36	21	Bancraft	William	1	2	1	1	1	2	2			1			11		
Granville East Soc	531	32	Bancroft	Azariah	2	1		1		2		1	1				8		
Granville East Soc	529	2	Bancroft	Comfort		1	2			1	2	1	1	1			9		
Norwich	153	27	Bancroft	Edmon Doct		1				1	1	2	1				6		
Granville East Soc	531	37	Bancroft	Enoch	1	2	1		1	4	1	1	1	3			15		
Granville Mid Soc.	166	22	Bancroft	Joel		1		1				1		1			4		
Granville Mid Soc.	166	20	Bancroft	John	1	1	2		1	1	1			1			8		
Westfield	124	23	Bancroft	John	3	1	2		1	3	1	2		2	4		19		
Norwich	151	29	Bancroft	Jonathan	1		2		2		2	1		1			9		
Granville East Soc	529	3	Bancroft	Lemuel	1	1						1					3		
Granville East Soc	531	24	Bancroft	Nathaniel	2			1		1			1				5		
Granville East Soc	531	33	Bancroft	Samuel		1	2		1		2			1			7		
Williamsburg	448	5	Bangs	James									2				2		
Montague	45	15	Bangs	John		1		1		5			1				8		
Hawley	331	6	Bangs	Joseph	2		1	1		2	3	1	1				11		
Warwick	36	36	Bangs	Josiah	1	1		1		1	1		1				6		
Montague	45	6	Bangs	Mark	1			1		2			1	1			6		
New Salem	96	20	Bangs	Nathaniel	2			1		3			1				7		
Hawley	331	1	Bangs	Zenas	4	1		1		1	1		1				9		
Belchertown	211	25	Banister	Abner C.	1		1			1		2					5		
New Salem	97	10	Banister	Andrew	1			1		3	1		1				7		
Conway	56	34	Banister	John			1		1		1	1		1			5		
Conway	57	17	Banister	Lemuel		2	1		1	3				1			8		
Chesterfield	23	1	Banister	William	3	2	1		1	1	1	1	1				11		
Hatfield	14	26	Banks	Thomas				1					1				2		
Springfield	243	38	Bannister	Freeman	1		2	1		2			1				7		
Springfield	243	37	Bannister	Joseph	1			1			1			1			4		
Northampton	3	5	Baral	Lewis			1	1			1	1					4		
Springfield	247	23	Barber	Abner	2		1	1					1				5		
Northfield	27	8	Barber	David		2	4	1		3	2	1	1	1			15		
Ludlow	256	45	Barber	Ebenezer					1			1		1			3		

Town	PG#	LN#	LAST NAME	FIRST NAME	FREE WHITE MALES					FREE WHITE FEMALES					TOTAL ALL OTHER	TOTAL SLAVES	TOTALS	DISTRICT/ TOWNSHIP	NOTES
					under 10	10 to 16	16 to 26	26 to 45	45 and over	under 10	10 to 16	16 to 26	26 to 45	45 and over					
Ludlow	256	46	Barber	Ebenezer Jr	3	1		1			1		1				7		
Ashfield	338	16	Barber	Elisha															Enumeration left blank
West Springfield	352	44	Barber	Joel	1	2		1		1		1					6		
Pelham	213	8	Barber	John	3	1		1	1	2	1	1					10		
West Springfield	352	43	Barber	John				1				1	1				3		
Warwick	36	29	Barber	Joseph	1		2		1		2		2				8		
Ludlow	256	44	Barber	Lewis	1	1		1			1						3		
West Springfield	352	56	Barber	Sarah							1		1				2		
Warwick	36	33	Barber	Zachariah	1		2		1	1	1	1		1			8		
Whately	66	11	Bardwell	Asa	1			1	1	3		1	1				8		
Whately	66	15	Bardwell	Asa Jr	2			1		1	1	1					6		
Whately	66	17	Bardwell	Charles		2					1						3		
Whately	66	16	Bardwell	Chester		1				1	2						4		
Leyden	80	13	Bardwell	Comider	2			2		1		1					6		
Conway	56	41	Bardwell	Eldad	2		1	1	1	1	1	1	1	1			10		
Hatfield	11	10	Bardwell	Elijah		1					1						2		
Belchertown	208	12	Bardwell	Elijah Capt	2	1	1	1		2		3	1				11		
Montague	44	18	Bardwell	Enoch				1				1					2		
Hatfield	11	2	Bardwell	Hannah	3	1	2				1	1					8		
Leyden	81	1	Bardwell	Henry	3	1		1				1			4		10		
Deerfield	51	28	Bardwell	John		1	3	1			2						7		
Belchertown	204	15	Bardwell	Jona Jewett		2		1	4		2	1					10		
Belchertown	210	32	Bardwell	Joseph	1	1	1		1	1	1	2		1			9		
Belchertown	208	19	Bardwell	Martin		1		1	2	2		1					7		
Belchertown	204	6	Bardwell	Martin Jr	1			1			1						3		
Montague	44	17	Bardwell	Moses	3	2		3		2		2	1				13		
Whately	66	7	Bardwell	Noah		2	1		1		3		1				8		
Conway	56	37	Bardwell	Reuben	2			1		2		1					6		
Ashfield	338	23	Bardwell	Saml			1				1						2		
Montague	45	5	Bardwell	Samuel		1	2	1	1	2	1	1	1				10		
Belchertown	208	13	Bardwell	Simeon	3	1	1		1	2		1					9		
Montague	44	19	Bardwell	Thomas	2			1	4		1						8		
Belchertown	208	17	Baret	Smith	2	1		1	1	1	1						7		
Chester	145	32	Barker	Abijah	1	1		1	1	1	2		1				8		
West Springfield	355	51	Barker	Ephraim	2			2		1		1	2	1			9		
Wilbraham	234	31	Barker	Ezra				1					1				2		
Wilbraham	234	32	Barker	Ezra Junr	2			1		1	1	1					6		
West Springfield	349	14	Barker	Grave	3			1		2		1					7		
Heath	195	1	Barker	Joseph	1			1			1						3		
West Springfield	349	29	Barker	Mary							1		1	1			3		
Belchertown	208	10	Barker	Nathl		2		1		1	1	1					6		
West Springfield	349	20	Barker	Samuel	1	1	1	1		1		1					6		
Hawley	332	7	Barlow	Ebenz	2	1			1	2		1					7		
Granville East Soc	533	9	Barlow	Edmund	2	1		1	1	1	2	1	1	1			11		
Granville East Soc	533	8	Barlow	Jonathan				1				1					2		
Belchertown	208	11	Barnabas	Nathan	3			1		1	1		1				7		
Williamsburg	448	21	Barnard	Benjamin	1			1		1		1	1				5		
Shelburne	320	2	Barnard	David	4	2		1			1		1				9		
Deerfield	51	24	Barnard	Ebenezer		1	2		2	1		1	2				9		
Deerfield	51	25	Barnard	Ebenezer 2d	2	1	1	2		1		1	1				9		
Shelburne	320	3	Barnard	Elisha		1		1		2		1					5		
Deerfield	51	27	Barnard	Elizabeth		1	1		1	2	2		1				8		
Deerfield	51	26	Barnard	Erastus		?	4	?	1		2						11		
New Salem	97	5	Barnard	Francis		1		1				1					3		
Northampton	3	17	Barnard	Israel	1	1	2	2	1	1	1	1					10		
Deerfield	51	23	Barnard	Joseph	1	1	1		1	2	1	2	1				10		
Hawley	332	10	Barnard	Joseph				1			1						2		
Northampton	6	28	Barnard	Julius	1		3	1		1	1	1					8		
Shelburne	320	1	Barnard	Theodore		1	1		1	2		2					7		
Warwick	36	24	Barnes	Abraham				1			1		1				3		
Warwick	36	17	Barnes	Abraham Junr	1			1			1						3		
Montgomery	160	19	Barnes	Aziel				1		3		1					5		
Granville Mid Soc.	165	31	Barnes	Benjamin		1	1		1		1	1	2				8		
Granville West Soc	170	35	Barnes	Ebenezer	1	2	1	1		2		2					9		
Granville Mid Soc.	167	31	Barnes	Elihu	1		2	1		2		2					8		
Granville Mid Soc.	166	21	Barnes	Jeremiah	1	1	1		1	1	1		2				8		
Granville West Soc	170	31	Barnes	Phinas		1	2				2		1				7		
Warwick	36	25	Barnes	Samuel	1	1		1		2	1		1				7		
Warwick	36	28	Barnes	Willard	1	1		1		2	1		1				7		
Ware	225	11	Barney	Charles	2		2		1	2			1				8		
Southampton	131	29	Barns	Benjamin		1		1		1	1	1	1				6		
Greenwich	218	16	Barns	Moses		2	1	1	1		1		1				7		
Southampton	131	5	Barns	Nathan	1	1		1	1	1	1						6		
Springfield	244	10	Barns	Samuel	1		1		1		1						4		
South Hadley	249	20	Barns	William		1		1		1	2		1				6		
Southampton	131	26	Barns	Wm			1	1		1		1	1				5		
Southampton	131	27	Barns	Wm Junr	2	1	1				1						5		
Rowe	198	13	Barr	Abijah	2			1	2			2	1				8		
Rowe	198	10	Barr	Cornelius	4		1		1			1					7		
Ware	225	23	Barr	Joseph	2			1			1						4		

TOWN	PG#	LN#	LAST NAME	FIRST NAME	FREE WHITE MALES under 10	10 to 16	16 to 26	26 to 45	45 and over	FREE WHITE FEMALES under 10	10 to 16	16 to 26	26 to 45	45 and over	TOTAL ALL OTHER	TOTAL SLAVES	TOTALS	DISTRICT/TOWNSHIP	NOTES
Rowe	198	12	Barr	Simeon	3			1		1	1		1				7		
Warwick	36	16	Barras	Nathan		2		1		2			1				6		
Montgomery	162	6	Barret	Daniel Ensn	3	2		1		1	2	1	1	2			13		
Northfield	27	9	Barret	John			1	1		6		1	2				11		
Rowe	198	14	Barret	Lemuel		2		1				1		2			6		
Holland	279	26	Barrett	Joshua			1	1		1			1				4		
Palmer	261	34	Barrett	Moses		1	2		1	1	2			1			8		
New Salem	97	2	Barron	Stephen		1											1		
Cummington	302	13	Barrows	Abiel	2	1		1		1	1		1				7		
New Salem	97	9	Barrows	Eleazer				1				1		1			3		
Brimfield	269	10	Barrows	Gershom Capt.		1		1						1			3		
Brimfield	273	41	Barrows	Joel	4			1					1				6		
Leyden	81	14	Barstow	Alpheus		1	1		1		1	1		1	1		7		
Conway	56	25	Bartlet	Adoniran	1	1		1		1			1				5		
Conway	56	26	Bartlet	Amos	4	1	1			2		2					10		
Conway	56	36	Bartlet	Calvin		1				1							2		
Hadley	285	10	Bartlet	Daniel	4	2	3	1		2	1		1				14		
Williamsburg	448	18	Bartlet	Ebenezer	1	2				1	1						5		
Leverett	113	11	Bartlet	Henry			1			2		1					4		
Middlefield	158	34	Bartlet	Isaac		2	1	1			1		1				6		
Hawley	332	8	Bartlet	Joel			1			1			1				3		
Easthampton	136	1	Bartlet	Jonathan	1	1	1	1		1		1	1				7		
Southampton	133	20	Bartlet	Joseph	1	1		1		3	1		1				8		
Southampton	133	19	Bartlet	Moses	1			1				1		1			4		
Wendell	105	13	Bartlet	Perley	1	1		1		2			1				6		
Conway	56	39	Bartlet	Samuel		1						1					2		
Leverett	113	7	Bartlet	Samuel	1			1		1	1						4		
Williamsburg	448	6	Bartlet	Simeon Jun	1	1		1		3		1					7		
Williamsburg	448	17	Bartlet	Thaddeus	1		1	1		1			2	1			7		
Conway	57	14	Bartlet	Zeduthan	1		1			2		1					5		
Granby	253	34	Bartlett	Aaron	2	2		1		1	1	1	1				9		
Pelham	213	18	Bartlett	Aaron	5		1	1		2	1	1					11		
South Hadley	250	6	Bartlett	Aaron	1		2	1		1		1	3				9		
Granby	254	31	Bartlett	Alpheus			1				1						2		
Granby	254	29	Bartlett	Asahel	3	2		1			1		2	1			10		
Springfield	244	29	Bartlett	Asher	1	1		1					1				4		
Northampton	2	1	Bartlett	Benja				1					1				2		
Pelham	213	6	Bartlett	Benja	3	1		1		2			1				8		
Westhampton	17	35	Bartlett	Benjamin			1			3		1					5		
Westhampton	16	7	Bartlett	Cornelius	1	2		1		3		1	1				9		
Montague	45	2	Bartlett	Daniel	1			1		2	1		1				6		
Montague	45	3	Bartlett	Darius	2	1		1		2			1				7		
Belchertown	204	11	Bartlett	David			1		1			1		2			5		
Blanford	176	4	Bartlett	Ebenezer		2	1	1		2			1				7		
Montague	45	7	Bartlett	Ebenezer	2	1		1		3	2		1				10		
Cummington	302	12	Bartlett	Edward	5	1	1		1		1	1	1	1			12		
Westhampton	16	10	Bartlett	Elihu	2			1		1			1				5		
Northampton	10	32	Bartlett	Elijah	1		1	1		1	2	1	1				8		
Montague	45	13	Bartlett	Elisha	3	2		1		1		2		1			10		
Northampton	10	33	Bartlett	Enos	1		1			1		1					4		
Springfield	243	32	Bartlett	Frederick			1					1					2		
Belchertown	208	14	Bartlett	Isaac	2		1				1	1	1				6		
Chesterfield	21	28	Bartlett	Jabez	2	1	1			2		1	1				8		
Westhampton	16	2	Bartlett	Joel				1				1		1			3		
Hadley	288	20	Bartlett	John		2		2				1		2			7		
Wilbraham	234	26	Bartlett	Lydia Wd										2			2		
Northampton	9	15	Bartlett	Moses	1			1		2		1					5		
Northampton	10	35	Bartlett	Moses Jr	2			1		2		1					6		
Wilbraham	234	42	Bartlett	Moses K.		1		1				1	1	2			6		
Westhampton	16	3	Bartlett	Noah	3			1					1				5		
Granby	254	30	Bartlett	Oliver	1	1	1	1			2	1	1				8		
Belchertown	204	18	Bartlett	Phillip			1										1		
Westhampton	16	9	Bartlett	Phineas	1			1		2		1	1				6		
Springfield	244	31	Bartlett	Pliny		1						1					2		
Northampton	2	2	Bartlett	Preserved	1			1		1		1					4		
Ashfield	337	15	Bartlett	Sarah	1		1					1		1			4		
Belchertown	208	7	Bartlett	Solomon	1			1	1	1	1		1				6		
Pelham	213	7	Bartlett	Solomon				1		3	1						5		
Greenwich	219	3	Bartlett	Sylvanus	2			1		2			1				6		
Southwick	358	6	Bartlett	Sylvanus	3	1	1		1	2			1	1			10		
Granby	254	25	Bartlett	Titus Dr	1			1		4		1	1				8		
Westhampton	16	8	Bartlett	William	1					1	2	2	1		1		10		
Granby	254	21	Barton	Daniel	2			1		2	1		1				7		
Granby	254	26	Barton	David Capt		1		1						2			4		
New Salem	97	7	Barton	Edward		2		1		1			1				5		
Granby	254	23	Barton	Ezekiel	1	1		1		3	1		1				8		
Greenwich	220	26	Barton	Jedediah	1	1		1		1			1				5		
Greenwich	224	14	Barton	Jedediah	2			1		1			1				5		
Belchertown	208	15	Barton	Reuben				1						1			2		
Belchertown	203	10	Barton	Reuben Jr	1			1		2			1				5		

TOWN	PG#	LN#	LAST NAME	FIRST NAME	FREE WHITE MALES under 10	10 to 16	16 to 26	26 to 45	45 and over	FREE WHITE FEMALES under 10	10 to 16	16 to 26	26 to 45	45 and over	TOTAL ALL OTHER	TOTAL SLAVES	TOTALS	DISTRICT/ TOWNSHIP	NOTES
Granby	254	27	Barton	Samuel	1		2						1				4		
Granby	254	24	Barton	Simeon	1			2			1	1					5		
Chester	144	12	Bascom	Aaron Revd	1	1	1		1		2	1	1				8		
Greenfield	72	6	Bascom	Ezekiel		1	1	1			1			1			5		
Chester	149	13	Bascom	James	4	1		1			1		1				8		
Greenfield	72	13	Bascom	Joseph	1	1			1	1	1			1			6		
Ware	225	22	Bascom	Nathan	1			1		1			1				4		
Southampton	130	28	Bascum	Elisha	2			1		1	1		1				6		
Southampton	130	29	Bascum	King	1		2	1		2			1	1			8		
Worthington	302	6	Bass	Hezekiah				1						1			2		
Warwick	36	8	Bass	Obadiah				1			1			2			4		
Rowe	198	17	Basset	Charles	1			1			1	1					4		
Goshen	309	12	Basset	Joseph	1	3			1	3	1		1				10		
West Springfield	355	52	Bassett	Benjamin	1	1	1		1	3	1		1				9		
Ashfield	338	14	Bassett	Elisha		2	1		1			1		1			6		
Ashfield	338	15	Bassett	Lot	3	1	1		1		2	2		1			11		
Williamsburg	448	3	Bassett	Silas		1			1		1	2					5		
Leverett	113	13	Bater	Obediah				1			1		1				3		
Southampton	128	5	Bates	Aaron	1		1		1	1		1	1				6		
Cummington	302	6	Bates	Abenr		1	1		1			1		2			6		
Granville Mid Soc.	165	11	Bates	Abigail	3	1			1		2	2		1			10		
Chesterfield	19	3	Bates	Abner				1			2		1				4		
Chesterfield	19	4	Bates	Abner Jun	2			1		1		1					5		
Plainfield	308	44	Bates	Abner Jun	1		1					1	1				4		
Cummington	302	4	Bates	Abraham			2		1	1	1	1		1			7		
Worthington	301	14	Bates	Amasa	1	1		1		1	1	1					6		
Cummington	302	10	Bates	Asa	1			1		1			1				4		
Palmer	258	15	Bates	Asa		1	2	1	1			1	1	1	2		10		
Chesterfield	20	9	Bates	Benjamin		1			1	1			1				4		
Chesterfield	20	10	Bates	Benjamin Jr	2			1		1		1					5		
Chesterfield	20	16	Bates	Caleb	1	1		1		2	2		1				8		
Cummington	305	27	Bates	Calvin				1		3			1				5		
West Springfield	352	39	Bates	Eleazer	3	1			1	1	3	1					11		
Chesterfield	23	34	Bates	Elibeus	1			1		1			1				4		
Westfield	120	2	Bates	Elijah				1				1			1		3		
Brimfield	272	42	Bates	Elisha				1		2			1				4		
Plainfield	306	12	Bates	Ephrm	2		1	1		1			1				6		
Monson	265	3	Bates	Ford	3	2		1				1	1				8		
Springfield	242	44	Bates	George		2		1						1			4		
Worthington	302	10	Bates	Isaiah	1		1		1	1	2	1	1				8		
Granville Mid Soc.	165	15	Bates	Jacob		1	2		1			1		2			7		
New Salem	97	3	Bates	Jacob	1		1		1	1		1		1			6		
Leverett	113	12	Bates	James	2			1		3	1		1				8		
Northampton	6	19	Bates	James	1			1		2			1				5		
Cummington	302	9	Bates	Joel				1		1			1				3		
Chesterfield	19	5	Bates	John				1		1		1					3		
Granville Mid Soc.	165	4	Bates	John		1			1		1	1		1			5		
Granville Mid Soc.	165	5	Bates	John Jun	1			1		1			1				4		
Blanford	177	9	Bates	Lemuel	1	2		1		2		1	1				8		
Cummington	302	11	Bates	Levi	1			1		1			1				4		
Springfield	243	4	Bates	Lewis	1			1		2			1				5		
Granville Mid Soc.	166	2	Bates	Linus		1			1			1		1			4		
Brimfield	273	8	Bates	Moses	2			1		1			1	1			6		
Cummington	302	7	Bates	Moses	2	2		1		2	1	1					9		
Granville East Soc	533	16	Bates	Nathaniel		1	1		1		1	2		1			7		
Chesterfield	24	16	Bates	Nehemiah		2		1						1			4		
Cummington	302	22	Bates	Nehemiah Jr	1	2		1		1			1				6		
Chester	148	14	Bates	Reuben	3			1		1		1	1				7		
Brimfield	273	1	Bates	Rufus	2			1		1		1	1				6		
Cummington	305	31	Bates	Samuel	1			1		1			1				4		
Brimfield	273	10	Bates	Samuel Junr				1		1			1				3		
Brimfield	273	9	Bates	Samuel Lt				1					1	1			4		
Brimfield	274	13	Bates	Simeon		1	1		1			3		1			7		
Southampton	128	6	Bates	Stephen				1						1			2		
Southampton	128	7	Bates	Stephen Junr	2	1		1		1		1					6		
Cummington	302	8	Bates	William	3			1		2	1	3					10		
Cummington	302	5	Bates	Zabbius	1			1		1	1	1					6		
Conway	56	38	Bathrick	Gilley	1		1		1		1	1		1			6		
Wilbraham	232	15	Battin	John	3	1			1		1	1		1			8		
Greenfield	72	16	Battis	Joseph	2		1					1					4		
Orange	41	5	Battle	John			1		1		1	1					5		
Orange	41	10	Battle	Phinehas	1			1					1				3		
Orange	41	6	Battle	Sherman			1					1					2		
Hawley	331	5	Baxter	Edward				1		2		1		1			5		
Brimfield	273	33	Baxter	John				1		1			1				3		
Shutesbury	109	2	Bayley	James	4			1		1	2		1				9		
Norwich	151	19	Bazwick	E*	1	1	1			1		1					5		
Montgomery	160	15	Beach	Moses	2			1		1			1				5		
Goshen	309	9	Beal	Adam	2	1	2		1	1	1	2		1			11		
Plainfield	306	11	Beal	Amariah		1	2		1	1	1			1			7		

193

TOWN	PG#	LN#	LAST NAME	FIRST NAME	FWM under 10	FWM 10 to 16	FWM 16 to 26	FWM 26 to 45	FWM 45 and over	FWF under 10	FWF 10 to 16	FWF 16 to 26	FWF 26 to 45	FWF 45 and over	TOTAL ALL OTHER	TOTAL SLAVES	TOTALS	DISTRICT/TOWNSHIP	NOTES
Plainfield	306	14	Beal	Caleb	3	2	2	1			1		2	1			12		
Cummington	302	16	Beal	Comfort	3	1		1		1			2				8		
Cummington	302	17	Beal	Daniel	3			1		3		1	1	1			10		
Goshen	309	10	Beal	Enoch	3	2	1	1			1	1	1	2			12		
Cummington	304	32	Beal	John	1			1		2			1				5		
Plainfield	306	7	Beal	Joseph			2		1	1	2		1				7		
Plainfield	306	13	Beal	Peter	2	1	2	1	1	1			1	1			10		
Plainfield	306	8	Beal	Samuel	1								1	1			4		
Holland	279	36	Beals	Benjamin				1					1				2		
Conway	57	8	Beals	Caleb	2	1				1	1	2	1				8		
Hawley	332	5	Beals	John															
Holland	279	35	Beals	Levi	1			1			1						3		
Conway	57	7	Beals	Lydia		1	1					3		1			6		
Conway	57	23	Beals	Rachel										2			2		
Northampton	5	23	Beals	William		1	1	1		1	2		1	1			8		
Wendell	105	8	Beaman	Lemuel		2		1					1				4		
Chester	145	13	Beamiss	Nathaniel	3			1				1					5		
Chester	145	12	Beamiss	Sylvester	1	1	2			3	1		1				10		
Blanford	175	1	Beard	James		1		1	1	1	1		1	1			7		
Blanford	179	32	Beard	John		1		1	1	1			1	1			6		
Blanford	178	36	Beard	Joseph		1		1		1	2		1				6		
Shutesbury	108	14	Bearse	Foard	1	1	2	1		1			1				7		
West Springfield	352	48	Bedortha	Eli	1			1			1						3		
West Springfield	352	40	Bedortha	Jonathan		1				2		1					4		
West Springfield	352	49	Bedortha	Joseph		1	1	1	1			1	2	1			8		
West Springfield	352	50	Bedortha	Luther	2			1		1		1					5		
West Springfield	352	47	Bedortha	Samuel		1			1				2	1			5		
West Springfield	352	38	Bedortha	Stephen	1	2	1		1	2		1		1			9		
Wilbraham	234	20	Beebe	Amos	3	2	1		1	1	1		1				10		
Westfield	123	3	Beebe	Artimas	2			1		2			1				6		
Wilbraham	232	33	Beebe	Jemima Wd									1				1		
Montague	45	16	Beebe	John	1			1				1					3		
Montague	44	14	Beebe	Roswell				1		1		1		1			4		
Ludlow	256	40	Beebe	Sherwood			1			2		1					4		
Wilbraham	236	38	Beebe	Steward Capt.	1		1			1	2	2		1			8		
Worthington	299	20	Beech	Cyrus	2		1						1				4		
West Springfield	352	45	Beech	Samuel	3	1	1			2			1				8		
Amherst	291	17	Beffel	Apahel			1	1		1	1						4		
Shutesbury	109	3	Belcher	Silence	1	1				1		1					4		
Northfield	27	11	Belcher	William	2	1	3		1	3	1	1	1				13		
Hatfield	13	36	Belden	Jabez				1						2			3		
Whately	66	12	Beldin	Elisha	1		1	1		1			2	1			7		
Whately	66	14	Beldin	Joshua	1	4	1	1		1	1	1					11		
Whately	66	10	Beldin	Joshua Jun		1	1			5	1	1					9		
Chester	146	15	Belding	Amos	1	1						1					3		
Ashfield	338	1	Belding	Daniel	6	1	2		1	1	2	3					16		
Amherst	291	14	Belding	Hezekiah		1	1	1		1			1				5		
Ashfield	338	3	Belding	John	3		1	1		2	2	1					10		
Northfield	27	10	Belding	Jonathan		1	2		1		1	2	1				8		
Hatfield	14	12	Belding	Joseph		1	1		1	2	1			1			7		
Northfield	27	14	Belding	Joseph			1										1		
Conway	56	44	Belding	Noah					1				1	1			3		
Chester	146	14	Belding	Othniel	1	1			1	2	1	1	1				8		
Buckland	325	8	Belding	Saml	2			2		1			1				6		
Ashfield	337	21	Belding	Saml Jr		1		1		1				1			4		
Hatfield	14	22	Belding	Samuel	2		2			1			1				6		
Conway	56	45	Belding	Selah	1	1	1			2	1	1	1				9		
Hadley	285	17	Belding	Stephen			1	1		3	1	1					7		
Chesterfield	20	27	Beldon	Jonathan		1		1		3	1			1			7		
Holland	279	6	Belknap	William	1			1				2	1	1			6		
Chester	148	3	Bell	Aaron		2	1							1			4		
Chester	143	11	Bell	Aaron Junr	1		1			1		2					5		
Chester	143	6	Bell	Abraham	3			1		2	1						7		
Chester	147	33	Bell	James	1	1	1	1		2	1	1					8		
Greenfield	72	11	Bell	John	2		1			3			1	1			8		
Chester	148	6	Bell	Justus		1				3	1	1					6		
Chester	149	17	Bell	Samuel	1	1		1		1	2			2			9		
Chester	148	5	Bell	William	1	1		1		1			1	1			6		
South Hadley	249	17	Bellows	Elihu	3			1		1		1					6		
Hadley	289	5	Belon	Amariah	2			1		1		1					5		
West Springfield	352	55	Bement	Edmund	1					1		1					3		
Brimfield	272	21	Bement	Jesse				1		1			1				3		
Brimfield	272	20	Bement	John		1				1			1				3		
Springfield	245	35	Bement	Lois Wd									1				1		
Worthington	302	5	Bemiss	Samuel	2	1		1		1	4	1	1				11		
Ashfield	337	16	Bemont	John		1					3		1				6		
Ashfield	337	18	Bemont	John Junr	3	1				1			1				7		
Ashfield	337	17	Bemont	Phinehas	3			1			2	1					7		
Ashfield	337	20	Bemont	Reuben	3	1		1			1		1				7		
Ashfield	338	25	Bemont	Sama	3			1		1			1				6		
Montague	45	10	Benjamin	Abel				1									1		

TOWN	PG#	LN#	LAST NAME	FIRST NAME	FREE WHITE MALES					FREE WHITE FEMALES					TOTAL ALL OTHER	TOTAL SLAVES	TOTALS	DISTRICT/ TOWNSHIP	NOTES
					under 10	10 to 16	16 to 26	26 to 45	45 and over	under 10	10 to 16	16 to 26	26 to 45	45 and over					
Middlefield	156	30	Benjamin	Asa	2				1	1	1		1				6		
Montague	45	8	Benjamin	Caleb			1	1					1				3		
Worthington	301	26	Benjamin	James	3	2		1		2	2	1					11		
Montague	45	9	Benjamin	Joel	4		1			1	1	1					8		
Montague	45	4	Benjamin	Levi	2	1	1						1				5		
Worthington	298	24	Benjamin	Roger	2	2	1	1		3		1	1				11		
Norwich	152	6	Benjamin	Rozwell		1	1					1	1	1			5		
Worthington	300	13	Benjamin	Salah	2		1			2			1				6		
Buckland	326	19	Benjm	Carter	2		1			3			1				7		
Blanford	181	22	Bennet	Judah		1		1					1				3		
Monson	266	4	Bennett	Israel	2	3	1	1		2		1	1				11		
Springfield	243	22	Bennett	James	1	1		1		3	1	1		1			9		
South Hadley	248	11	Bennett	John	1	1	4	1		3	1	1	1				13		
Brimfield	273	45	Bennett	Jonathan	1		1			1			1				4		
Springfield	247	32	Bennett	Sarah Wd								2	1				3		
Conway	56	19	Bennitt	Enoch		1				1		1					3		
New Salem	96	21	Benson	Comiden	2		1			1	1		1				6		
New Salem	96	19	Benson	Samuel	2	2	1			2			1				8		
Wendell	105	9	Bent	Joel	1		1			1			1				4		
Ashfield	337	19	Benton	Bezer	1	1		1			1		1				5		
Southwick	359	58	Benton	Bristor											4		4		
Springfield	243	12	Benton	Jonathan	2	1	1						1				6		
Rowe	198	7	Benton	Zebulon	3	2	1			2	1		1				11		
Brimfield	273	2	Berly	Lynel	2		1			3		1	1				8		
Pelham	213	10	Berry	Alman	2		2		1	1		1	2	2			11		
New Salem	96	15	Berry	James	1		1	1		2		3		1			9		
Deerfield	51	33	Berry	John	2		1			3	1		1	1			10		
New Salem	96	14	Berry	William	3	1	1			1		1					8		
Greenwich	224	7	Besse	Abram	1		1			2		1					5		
Greenwich	218	10	Besse	James	2		1			2	1		1				7		
Chesterfield	19	6	Beswick	Charles				1			1	1	1				4		
Chesterfield	19	7	Beswick	Charles Jr	2		1			3			1				7		
Westfield	125	15	Bewel	Samll		1	2	1					1				5		
Belchertown	208	18	Bibbee	James		1	1	1					1				4		
Belchertown	203	2	Bicknal	Timo	1		1			1			1				4		
Belchertown	208	21	Bicknal	Wm		1		1			1		1				4		
Chester	149	12	Bidlake	Jonathan	1	1							1				3		
Granville West Soc	169	36	Bidwell	George		1		1					1				3		
Hadley	288	36	Bigalow	Amos	3	1		1		1			1				7		
Chester	147	2	Bigalow	Daniel	1			1		2		1	1				6		
Chester	146	36	Bigalow	James		1		1		3	2		1				8		
Chester	143	2	Bigalow	John	4			1		2	1		1				9		
Granville East Soc	527	21	Bigelow	Aaron	1			1		1		1					4		
Worthington	298	1	Bigelow	Asa				1		1		1					3		
Conway	56	28	Bigelow	John	2	1			1	2	2		1	1			10		
Cummington	302	14	Bigelow	John			2		1	2	1	1	1				8		
Conway	56	20	Bigelow	Jonathan	1			1		1		1					4		
Southwick	358	3	Bigelow	Titus	1			1					1				3		
Belchertown	209	1	Biglow	Samuel				1					1				2		
Southwick	358	4	Bill	Erastus	1	2		1		1	1		1				7		
Southwick	358	5	Bill	Jonathan	2	1		1		1		1	1				7		
Amherst	291	36	Billings	Aaron	3		2	1		2	1		1				10		
Hatfield	13	30	Billings	Abraham		1		1			2	2		1			7		
Northfield	27	12	Billings	Barnabas	1			1		2	1		2				7		
Belchertown	204	14	Billings	Benja		2	1	2			2	1		2			10		
Hatfield	12	14	Billings	David		1		1	1		1	2		1			7		
Greenfield	72	7	Billings	Ebenezer	2		1		1	2	1	1					9		
Greenfield	72	9	Billings	Edward	1	1		1			1	2					6		
Conway	56	43	Billings	Elisha		1	1	1					1				4		
Conway	57	10	Billings	Ethan		1	1		1	1	2		1	1			8		
Deerfield	51	34	Billings	Jesse	1			1		2	1						5		
Hatfield	12	16	Billings	Jesse	4		2		1				2				9		
Amherst	289	8	Billings	Joel		1	3			1		1		1			7		
Amherst	296	2	Billings	John	3			1	1	6		1	3	1			16		
Belchertown	204	16	Billings	Joseph Jr	2	2		1	1	2		1	2	1			12		
Conway	57	15	Billings	Lemuel			1			5	2		1				9		
Chesterfield	19	11	Billings	Levett				1		1	1	1		1			5		
Hatfield	12	13	Billings	Silas			4			1	2		2	2	2		12		
Belchertown	209	2	Billings	Stephen	1		1						1				3		
Conway	56	27	Billings	Stephen	2		1			1			1				5		
Longmeadow	91	13	Billings	Thaddeus	3	1	1	1		2	1		1				10		
Greenfield	72	8	Billings	Thomas		1		1		1			1				4		
Deerfield	51	35	Billings	Timothy	1	3	1			1		2					8		
Conway	56	23	Billings	William	1	4		2		1	1	1		1			11		
Goshen	309	18	Billington	Nathl		3		1		1				1			6		
South Hadley	249	28	Bills	Sheribiah	1		1	1		2	1		1				7		
Granby	254	38	Birchard	Israel	4		1				1		1				7		
Granby	254	39	Birchard	Jabez	3		2			1		1	1				9		
Williamsburg	448	8	Bird	Ebenezer	1			1			1		1				4		
Whately	66	18	Bird	Enoch	2	1	1		1	2	1		1				9		

195

TOWN	PG#	LN#	LAST NAME	FIRST NAME	M u10	M 10-16	M 16-26	M 26-45	M 45+	F u10	F 10-16	F 16-26	F 26-45	F 45+	TOTAL ALL OTHER	TOTAL SLAVES	TOTALS	DISTRICT/ TOWNSHIP	NOTES
Southampton	129	31	Birge	Asahel				1					1	1			3		
Southampton	129	32	Birge	Asahel Junr			2			2			1				5		
Northampton	8	3	Birge	Hannah										1			1		
Deerfield	51	41	Birge	John				1						1			2		
Northampton	10	11	Birge	Simeon		1		1		1		1		1			5		
Springfield	240	3	Bisbee	Benjamin	2		1						1				4		
Springfield	247	38	Bisbee	Benjamin	1		1			1			1				4		
Plainfield	306	5	Bisbee	Ebenezer	1	1	3		1	2	1	1	1				11		
Plainfield	306	6	Bisbee	Elisha	3	1		1		2	1		1				9		
Chesterfield	22	10	Bisbee	Gideon	2	2		1		1	1	2	1				10		
Cummington	302	15	Bisbee	Luther	3			1	1	1		1	1	1			9		
Russell	138	14	Bishop	Amos				1						1			2		
West Springfield	352	53	Bishop	Daniel		1		1		2		1					5		
Wilbraham	236	1	Bishop	Eleazer	2			1		1			1				5		
Ludlow	255	15	Bishop	Hooper		1		1		2			1				5		
Russell	139	16	Bishop	James			1	1		1			1	1			5		
Blanford	182	1	Bishop	Jesse	1			1		4		1		2			9		
Ashfield	338	4	Bishop	Joseph				1			1		1				3		
Blanford	180	18	Bishop	Joseph	1			1		4		1	1				8		
Russell	138	27	Bishop	Levi	1			1		1		1					4		
Northfield	27	16	Bishop	Nathaniel	1			1						1			3		
Russell	139	15	Bishop	Newman	1	1		1		2	2	1					9		
Brimfield	269	30	Bishop	Richard		2	1	1		2	1			2			9		
Springfield	244	34	Biss	Jacob	4	1	2	1		2	1	1	1				13		
Granville East Soc	527	19	Bissel	Dan		1		1				1		1			4		
Montague	44	13	Bissel	Jonathan Marsh	2	1		1			1		1				6		
Montague	44	12	Bissel	William	2	1		1		2	1	2					9		
Belchertown	204	17	Bissell	Ebenz	2			1		1			1				5		
South Hadley	250	23	Bissell	Elihu Dr		1		1			1		1				4		
Middlefield	155	15	Bissell	Israel	2	1		1		2	1		1				8		
Middlefield	158	19	Bissell	Justus	2	2	1			1			1	1			10		
Hatfield	14	5	Bissell	Moses	1	2		1		1	1	2		1			9		
Chesterfield	21	4	Bissell	Noah		1	2	1		3	2	1					10		
Middlefield	158	24	Bissell	Robert	2			1		1			2				6		
Amherst	289	10	Bixbee	Rufus			1	1				1					3		
West Springfield	355	45	Black	Alexander	1			1					1				4		
West Springfield	355	49	Black	Mary	1								1	1			3		
West Springfield	349	33	Black	Samuel		1		1		3	1		1				7		
Deerfield	51	37	Blackler	John	1			1		2	2			1			7		
Greenwich	218	20	Blackman	Amos			1	1									2		
Greenwich	224	16	Blackman	Barnabas		1	2	1				1	1	1			7		
Chester	147	8	Blackman	Elijah Maj	1		2	1				1		1			6		
Northampton	8	9	Blackman	George			1	5				1					7		
Worthington	298	38	Blackman	James	2			1		1				1			5		
Belchertown	203	7	Blackman	Jona Jewett											1		1		
Greenwich	219	1	Blackman	Moses	1		1						1				3		
Greenwich	219	2	Blackman	Peter Jr		1	1	1		2			1	1			7		
Greenwich	218	19	Blackman	Rolland		1	1	1		1	1	1	1				7		
Belchertown	212	3	Blackmar	David	1	1		1		3			1				7		
Buckland	325	12	Blackmer	John H.	1	2		1		2	1		1				8		
Buckland	325	6	Blackmer	Rowland				1		1				1			3		
Palmer	260	30	Blackmore	Margaret Widow										1			1		
Brimfield	269	36	Blackmore	Willard			1			1		1					3		
Rowe	198	9	Blacksbe	Caleb	3	3	1				1		1				9		
Blanford	176	10	Blair	Adam	2	1		1		1	2			1			8		
Blanford	176	1	Blair	Alexr			1		1			1	1	1			5		
Blanford	176	21	Blair	Asa	2	1	2			1	1		1	1			9		
Blanford	176	20	Blair	David		1	2	1					1	1			6		
Blanford	178	16	Blair	Enoch	3			1				1		1			6		
Blanford	175	25	Blair	George	3	1		1		3	1		1				10		
Blanford	175	26	Blair	George Jun	2		1						1				4		
Blanford	176	36	Blair	Isaac		2	2		1	1			2	1			9		
Blanford	181	5	Blair	Jacob			1	2		1			1	1			6		
Blanford	182	21	Blair	Jacob			1						1				2		
Blanford	175	35	Blair	John	2	1	2		1		1	1					10		
Blanford	178	17	Blair	John	3	1		1				1	2				8		
Ware	225	7	Blair	John	1		2			1			1				5		
Amherst	292	4	Blair	Joseph	1	1							1				3		
Belchertown	204	2	Blair	Joseph	2			1		2	2		1				8		
Brimfield	269	33	Blair	Oliver	1	1	1			2		1					6		
Blanford	181	29	Blair	Reuben	2		1	1		1	1		1				7		
Blanford	181	24	Blair	Robert Jun	1	1			1	2		3	1	1			10		
Blanford	176	17	Blair	Rufus	2	1	2	1		1			1	1			10		
Ware	225	6	Blair	Samuel	1	1		1		1			1	1			7		
Blanford	175	10	Blair	Timothy		1		1					1				3		
Springfield	244	35	Blake	George	1	1	2	1		2	1		1				9		
Warwick	36	31	Blake	James			1					1					2		
Westfield	127	13	Blake	John E	1		1			1			1				4		
Warwick	36	30	Blake	Jonathan	1		2		1		2	2		1			9		
Goshen	309	13	Blake	Joseph		1		1						1			3		
Ashfield	338	21	Blake	Silas	2			1		1			1				5		
Westfield	127	14	Blake	Thomas	1			1		1			1				4		

196

TOWN	PG#	LN#	LAST NAME	FIRST NAME	FREE WHITE MALES					FREE WHITE FEMALES					TOTAL ALL OTHER	TOTAL SLAVES	TOTALS	DISTRICT/ TOWNSHIP	NOTES
					under 10	10 to 16	16 to 26	26 to 45	45 and over	under 10	10 to 16	16 to 26	26 to 45	45 and over					
Russell	139	24	Blakley	Baley	1	1			1	1		1		1			6		
Monson	268	22	Blanchard	Chester	2			1		1			1				5		
Monson	268	21	Blanchard	Jona		1			1			2	1	1			6		
Monson	268	23	Blanchard	Jonathan Jr	1			1		1			1				4		
Shutesbury	108	13	Blanchard	Lemuel	1	1		1	1	1	1		1	1			8		
Longmeadow	94	14	Blanchard	Oliver			1						1				2		
Plainfield	307	5	Blanchard	Simeon	2			1		2			1				6		
Brimfield	272	31	Blashfield	Alfred		1	1			2			1	1			6		
Brimfield	272	38	Blashfield	Betty									1				1		
Brimfield	270	39	Blashfield	Jno Jr			1		1				1				3		
Brimfield	271	15	Blashfield	John				1					1				2		
Brimfield	271	17	Blashfield	Luke				1	1				1				3		
Brimfield	273	13	Blashfield	Ozeon Capt	1	1	1		1	3	1	1	2				11		
Shelburne	319	10	Blazedel	Willm				1		2			1				4		
Middlefield	155	20	Blish	Oliver		1		1		1			2				5		
Brimfield	269	21	Bliss	Aaron	1		1	2				1	1				6		
Longmeadow	94	20	Bliss	Aaron		1	1	1				1	1				5		
Monson	264	40	Bliss	Aaron	3			1		1		1					6		
Wilbraham	235	1	Bliss	Aaron				1						1	1		3		
Wilbraham	234	9	Bliss	Abel	1		1		1		1	2		1	1		8		
Hatfield	11	6	Bliss	Abijah	2	1		1					1	1			6		
Springfield	241	36	Bliss	Alexander	3	1	4		1	2		1	2				14		
Granville West Soc	168	21	Bliss	Benedict	2	1		1	1	1			2	1			9		
West Springfield	349	15	Bliss	Caleb		1	1		1	1	1		1				6		
Springfield	241	31	Bliss	Calvin		1			1	1			1				4		
Springfield	241	35	Bliss	Charles	1		1		1				2				5		
Shelburne	319	11	Bliss	Daniel		2		1		2				1			6		
Springfield	239	8	Bliss	Daniel	1	1			1		2	1	1				7		
Wilbraham	233	40	Bliss	David		2	2		1	1	1	2		1			10		
Longmeadow	93	18	Bliss	Ebenezer		1		1	1				1	1			5		
Springfield	241	37	Bliss	Ebenezer	2	1	3		1	3		1	1				12		
Belchertown	204	22	Bliss	Ebenz		2	1	1		1	1		1				7		
Springfield	241	34	Bliss	Elizabeth Wd								1		4			5		
Springfield	242	3	Bliss	Festus	2		2	1					1				6		
Springfield	242	34	Bliss	Gad				1			2		3				6		
Longmeadow	94	30	Bliss	Gaius	2	1	2	1		4		1	1				12		
Springfield	242	1	Bliss	Gaius			1			1			1				3		
Springfield	242	11	Bliss	George Esq	1			1		2	1	1	1				7		
Wilbraham	235	32	Bliss	Gideon	4			1		1			1				7		
West Springfield	349	21	Bliss	Hosea	1		2			1		1					5		
Brimfield	271	39	Bliss	Ichabod			1			3	1	2	1				8		
Wilbraham	236	8	Bliss	Ithamer		1				1		1					3		
Monson	264	19	Bliss	Jacob		1	1		1			1		1			5		
Rowe	199	1	Bliss	Jacob		2		1		3		1					7		
West Springfield	352	41	Bliss	Jedidiah	1	1		1	1	1		1					6		
Wilbraham	235	11	Bliss	Jesse	2			1		1		1	1				6		
Wilbraham	238	20	Bliss	John Esq				1						1			2		
Wilbraham	233	41	Bliss	Jonathan		1	1	1		1	2		1				7		
Monson	264	41	Bliss	Josiah				1					1				2		
Springfield	242	2	Bliss	Justin	1		1	2		3		1	1				9		
Wilbraham	234	14	Bliss	Levi		1		1		1	1	2		1			7		
Springfield	242	20	Bliss	Luke	1			2		1	1		1				6		
Springfield	246	12	Bliss	Moses 2d	2	1	1		1	1		2		1			9		
Springfield	242	10	Bliss	Moses Esq		1	1	1	1	2		2	1	1			10		
Springfield	241	44	Bliss	Nathan			1	1									?		
Springfield	243	13	Bliss	Nathan Jr	2		1	1		2	1		1				8		
Longmeadow	93	25	Bliss	Nathaniel	1			1		1		1	1				5		
Longmeadow	93	19	Bliss	Noah	2	1	1	1			1		2				8		
Wilbraham	235	3	Bliss	Obed	2			1		2		1	3		1		12		
Wilbraham	235	5	Bliss	Oliver		1	2	2	1			1		1	1		9		
Springfield	245	11	Bliss	Paul	1			1		1			1				4		
Springfield	240	23	Bliss	Pelatiah		2	1			1			1				5		
West Springfield	349	31	Bliss	Pelatiah		5	1	1			1	2		1			11		
Leyden	80	11	Bliss	Peter	3			1		2			1	1			8		
Springfield	242	4	Bliss	Pitt	2		1	1				1		1			6		
Monson	264	38	Bliss	Reuben	1	1	2		1	1		2		1			9		
Springfield	241	30	Bliss	Reuben				1					1				2		
Wilbraham	235	4	Bliss	Silas		2			1			2		1			6		
West Springfield	352	46	Bliss	Stephen	1			1		2			1				5		
Wilbraham	235	15	Bliss	Stephen				1					1				2		
Brimfield	269	19	Bliss	Thomas	1	2	4		1	1		1	3		1		14		
Wilbraham	233	21	Bliss	Thomas	1		2		1	2	2			1			9		
Northampton	2	12	Bliss	William		2				1	1	1					5		
Longmeadow	93	32	Bliss	Zadock	2	1		1									4		
Springfield	241	38	Bliss	Zenas	3	2		1		1	1		1				9		
Palmer	261	44	Blodget	Admatha	2			1		2			1				6		
Amherst	291	26	Blodget	Asahel	2		1	1				1		1			6		
Amherst	291	30	Blodget	David	3			1		2	3	1	1				11		
Monson	265	43	Blodget	Paul	3					1			1				7		

TOWN	PG#	LN#	LAST NAME	FIRST NAME	FREE WHITE MALES					FREE WHITE FEMALES					TOTAL ALL OTHER	TOTAL SLAVES	TOTALS	DISTRICT/ TOWNSHIP	NOTES
					under 10	10 to 16	16 to 26	26 to 45	45 and over	under 10	10 to 16	16 to 26	26 to 45	45 and over					
Deerfield	51	31	Blodget	Samuel	2		2			2			1				7		
Deerfield	51	30	Blodget	Thaddeus	2			1		1	1		1				6		
Deerfield	51	29	Blodget	Timothy	2	1	1		1	1		3		1			10		
Brimfield	270	44	Blodgett	Daniel	1			1				1					3		
Brimfield	270	5	Blodgett	Jonas Dr	1		3		1	1	2		1				9		
Greenwich	219	4	Blodgett	Joseph Revd	1		1	1		2		1		1			7		
Hawley	332	9	Blood	Asa	3	1	1	1			1		1				8		
South Brimfield	277	11	Blood	Isaiah			1						1				2		
South Brimfield	277	13	Blood	Patty Wid	1						1			1			3		
South Brimfield	277	12	Blood	Simeon	1			1		2	1		1				6		
Middlefield	155	18	Blossom	Thomas	3	1	2		1			1	1				9		
Ashfield	338	26	Blotchet	Aaron		1				2		1					4		
Middlefield	158	32	Blush	Amasa		1	1						1				3		
Middlefield	156	29	Blush	Benjamin	1		1		1	2	2	1		1			9		
Montague	44	15	Blye	Joseph			1			1			1				3		
Williamsburg	448	11	Bodman	Joseph	1		1		1	1		1	1	1			7		
Williamsburg	448	16	Bodman	Joseph Junr	2		1	1		1		1					6		
Williamsburg	448	20	Bodman	Noah			1					1					2		
Williamsburg	448	7	Bodman	Samuel		1	1	1		1	1		1				6		
Williamsburg	448	15	Bodman	William	1	1	4		1	1	1	2		1			12		
Ware	225	12	Bodwine	William	2	3		1		1		1	1	1			10		
Barnardston	76	10	Bogg	Israel	3		1		1	1	3	1	1				11		
Northfield	27	15	Bogle	John	2	2		1	1	1	1		1				8		
Westfield	125	30	Bogue	Amos			1			1		1					3		
Blanford	176	18	Boies	David	2	1	3		1		1	1		1			10		
Blanford	178	35	Boies	Elias			1					1					2		
Blanford	175	28	Boies	Gardner			1					1					2		
Blanford	175	31	Boies	Joel	3	2		1			1	1					8		
Blanford	178	8	Boies	John		2		1				1					4		
Blanford	182	8	Boies	Levi	1		1	3			1	1					7		
Blanford	176	14	Boies	Reuben		2		1		1	2		2		1		9		
Blanford	175	27	Boies	Rufus		1		1		1		1					3		
Blanford	176	29	Boies	Saml	2	1		1	2	4	1	2	1	1			15		
Blanford	176	8	Boies	Samuel	1	3	2		1	2	1		1				11		
Blanford	176	34	Boies	Samuel	2	1		1	1	4			1	1			11		
Blanford	176	23	Boies	William	2	1		1	1		1		1				7		
Blanford	178	41	Bois	Margaret		1				1	2		1				5		
West Springfield	352	37	Bolles	Benjamin			1			1			1				3		
Northampton	8	7	Bolten	William		1	1			1		1					5		
Amherst	289	9	Boman	William	1	1	1		1		1	2		1			8		
Conway	57	19	Bond	Adonijah		2		1		1	1	2		1			8		
Brimfield	273	23	Bond	Bailey		1	1					1					3		
Conway	57	9	Bond	Benjamin	2	1		1		1	1	1		1			9		
West Springfield	349	25	Bond	Benjamin			1			1		1					3		
Conway	57	13	Bond	Consider	1		1	1	1	2			2	1			9		
Holland	279	27	Bond	Ephraim		1	2		1		1	1		2			8		
Conway	57	21	Bond	Ezra	1			1		2			1				5		
Springfield	240	2	Bond	Forbush	2			1		1	1		1				6		
Ware	228	34	Bond	Jacob	3			1		1			1				6		
Brimfield	271	11	Bond	John		1		1			1	1	1				5		
Conway	57	11	Bond	John Junr	1		1	1			1	1					6		
Conway	57	12	Bond	Jonas	2			1			1	1					5		
Brimfield	271	21	Bond	Mark				2					1				3		
Brimfield	274	20	Bond	Nathan	2	1						1					4		
Brimfield	271	22	Bond	Rowlandson	1		1			1		1					4		
Amherst	290	11	Bond	Solomon	1		1			1		1					4		
Springfield	245	9	Bonner	David Jr	2		1			1	1	1					6		
Granville Mid Soc.	166	14	Bonney	Asa	1			1	2	2	3		1				10		
Chesterfield	23	8	Bonney	Benjamin		1	1	1		1		1	1	1			7		
Chesterfield	23	17	Bonney	David	2			1		2		1					6		
Springfield	244	30	Bonney	David				1		1		1		1			3		
Chesterfield	20	35	Bonney	Luke		3	1	1		1		1		1			8		
Chesterfield	22	20	Bonney	Walter	2	1	1			2	1	1					8		
Granville Mid Soc.	165	2	Booge	Aaron J		1		1		1	1	1	1				6		
Longmeadow	94	16	Booth	David	1			1		1			1				4		
Middlefield	156	32	Booth	Elan			1			2		1					4		
Southwick	358	9	Booth	Ephraim		1	1		1	1	1	1		1			7		
Conway	56	30	Booth	Isaiah	1	1				1	1	3		1			8		
Longmeadow	95	21	Booth	John	1			1		3	1	1					7		
Longmeadow	94	8	Booth	Peter	1			1				1					3		
Middlefield	156	31	Booth	Simeon				1					1				2		
Palmer	259	20	Borden	Ezekiel	2		1	1					2				6		
Wilbraham	236	9	Bordin	Selden	3			1		2		1					8		
Shelburne	319	12	Bordwell	Abigail		2	2						2	1			7		
Shelburne	319	9	Bordwell	Enoch			3										3		
Shelburne	320	4	Bordwell	Gideon	1	1	1		1	1		1	1				7		
Shelburne	320	7	Bordwell	Philena		2					1	1		1			5		
Shelburne	320	6	Bordwell	Polly	1					1		1		1			4		
Shelburne	320	5	Bordwell	Reuben	2			1		2	1	2		1			9		
Shelburne	320	8	Bordwell	Zenas		1				1		1					3		
Ashfield	338	24	Borthwick	Peter		1				1		1					3		

TOWN	PG#	LN#	LAST NAME	FIRST NAME	FREE WHITE MALES					FREE WHITE FEMALES					TOTAL ALL OTHER	TOTAL SLAVES	TOTALS	DISTRICT/ TOWNSHIP	NOTES
					under 10	10 to 16	16 to 26	26 to 45	45 and over	under 10	10 to 16	16 to 26	26 to 45	45 and over					
Hadley	285	29	Boston	Joshua											4		4		
Westfield	121	16	Bosworth	Caleb	2	1			1	1	1		1				7		
Northampton	11	6	Bosworth	Oliver		1		1			1		1	1			5		
Westfield	121	15	Bosworth	Saml	1	2	1			2	1		1				8		
Amherst	289	1	Bothwood	Solomon		1	2	2		1			3	2			11		
Northampton	7	38	Bottom	John	1			1		3			1	1			7		
Conway	56	35	Bottwood	Samuel				1					1				2		
Amherst	296	1	Bottwood	Wlliam		1	1	1		3	1		1	1			9		
Conway	56	42	Bouker	Ithamar	3			1		1	1		1				7		
Leverett	113	14	Boutwell	Ebenz	2	1		1		1			1				6		
West Springfield	352	51	Bow	Isaac		2	1		1			2		1			7		
West Springfield	352	36	Bow	Thaddeus		1		1		1	1	1	1				6		
Belchertown	211	20	Bowden	Benja		1		1		1	1		1				5		
Warwick	36	15	Bowen	James		2	1	1		1	1		2				8		
Warwick	36	14	Bowen	John	2		1		1	1	1	1					7		
Blanford	177	11	Bowers	Benjamin	2		1	1	1				3	1			9		
West Springfield	353	2	Bowker	Catherine		1		1		1			1	1			5		
Warwick	36	23	Bowman	Samuel	1	1	1		1	2			2	1			9		
New Salem	96	13	Boyce	Jacob	2			3		2	1		1	2			11		
West Springfield	355	50	Boyd	Elizabeth						1			1				2		
Goshen	310	6	Boyd	Jacob G	1	1	1	1		3			1				8		
Shelburne	319	14	Boyd	John	2			1	1	1	1	1	1				8		
Shelburne	319	16	Boyd	John Junr	2			1		1		1					5		
Shelburne	319	15	Boyd	Saml	1	1	1		1	1	2	1	1				9		
West Springfield	355	53	Boyd	William	2	1			1	2		1		1			8		
New Salem	97	4	Boyden	Amos	1			1	1				1	1			5		
Conway	57	22	Boyden	Daniel		1							1				2		
Buckland	326	7	Boyden	Elijah		1		1		1	1	1					5		
Westhampton	17	19	Boyden	Elisha	2			1		1			1				5		
Deerfield	51	39	Boyden	Frederick				1		3			1				5		
Conway	57	4	Boyden	James	2			1		2			1				6		
Conway	57	5	Boyden	John	2	2		1				2		2			9		
Conway	57	6	Boyden	John Junr	3	2		1		1		2	1				10		
Conway	57	2	Boyden	Joseph	3			1		1			1		1		7		
Conway	57	3	Boyden	Joseph Junr	2	1		1		2	1		1				8		
Conway	57	16	Boyden	Josiah				1		1				1			3		
Northfield	27	7	Boyden	Simeon1		1		2		1		1					5		
Springfield	239	31	Boylstone	Edward		1		1		1			2				5		
Wendell	105	10	Boynton	David		2		1			1		1				5		
Pelham	213	15	Boynton	Ebenz			1			1		1					3		
Greenfield	72	10	Boynton	John		2		1		4	1	1		1			10		
Montgomery	161	11	Bozworth	Joshua	3			1		1			1				6		
Montgomery	160	1	Bozworth	Raymon		1				3		1					5		
Montgomery	159	20	Bozworth	Zadock				1					1				2		
Montgomery	161	14	Bozworth	Zadock Capt	2			1		2	1		1				7		
Ashfield	338	13	Bracket	Benjm	3	1		1		2	1		1				9		
Buckland	326	5	Bracket	James	2			1					1				4		
West Springfield	355	47	Bracket	Ruth						1		1	1				3		
Blanford	182	3	Brackett	John	1	2	1	1		3			1	1			10		
Buckland	325	9	Brackey	Saml		1		1		2			1				5		
Conway	57	1	Bradford	Edward	2			1					1				4		
Holland	280	5	Bradford	Perez	1	1			1	2			1	1			7		
Williamsburg	448	13	Bradford	Samuel		1		1			1			1			4		
Conway	56	46	Bradford	Shubal	1			1		3			1				6		
Cummington	302	18	Bradish	James	2	1	1	2	1	4	1	3		1			16		
Russell	138	22	Bradley	Abraham	3	2		1		1	1		1				9		
Rowe	198	18	Bradley	Ebenezer	1		1		1	2			1				6		
Cummington	302	21	Bradley	George	1	1	1	1	1	3		1	2	1			12		
Granville East Soc	531	41	Bradley	John	2	1	1		1	1	1		1				8		
Deerfield	51	38	Bradley	Joseph			1	1		1	1			1			5		
West Springfield	355	44	Bradley	Nathaniel	1	1	1		1	1	1	1					7		
Monson	267	37	Bradway	Abel	2		1			1			1				5		
Monson	266	30	Bradway	Daniel				1						1			2		
Monson	266	31	Bradway	Daniel Jr		2						1					3		
Monson	267	36	Bradway	William	1	1		1	1	1				1			6		
Southampton	133	16	Braimin	Danl				1						1			2		
Southampton	133	17	Braimin	Uziel		1				2		1					4		
Granville East Soc	531	40	Brainard	Amos	3			1		2			1				7		
Worthington	299	22	Brainard	Timothy		1	1					1					3		
Palmer	261	35	Brainerd	Asa	3			1		1			1				6		
Palmer	261	33	Brainerd	Timothy	1		1		1	3	2	1	1				10		
Worthington	299	36	Branch	Nathan		2	1		1	1		2	1				8		
Montgomery	160	21	Brant	John	1	1	1	1		4	1		1				10		
Ashfield	338	11	Brant	Zebulon		1		1		1	1			1			5		
Chester	148	9	Brass	Garret	3			1		1			1				6		
Westfield	122	15	Brass	Henery	2			1		2	1		1				7		
Granville West Soc	169	3	Brather	Araiah	2			1		2	1		1	1			8		
West Springfield	349	30	Breck	George				1				1					2		
Ware	225	17	Breckinridge	Francis Capt		1		1					1				3		
Ware	225	16	Breckinridge	George	3	2				1			1				8		

TOWN	PG#	LN#	LAST NAME	FIRST NAME	FREE WHITE MALES under 10	10 to 16	16 to 26	26 to 45	45 and over	FREE WHITE FEMALES under 10	10 to 16	16 to 26	26 to 45	45 and over	TOTAL ALL OTHER	TOTAL SLAVES	TOTALS	DISTRICT/ TOWNSHIP	NOTES
Ware	225	15	Breckinridge	James	2	1	1		1	2	1		1	1			10		
Ware	225	13	Breckinridge	Wm Capt		1		1					1	1			4		
Ware	225	14	Breckinridge	Wm Jr		1	1		1		2	1		1			7		
Palmer	261	14	Brekenridge	Obadiah				1				1	1	1			4		
Easthampton	134	4	Brewer	Benaijah			1						1				2		
Easthampton	134	5	Brewer	Bildad	2		1		1	1		1	1	1			8		
Wilbraham	234	4	Brewer	Charles	2	1	2		1	1		2		1			10		
Springfield	239	28	Brewer	Chauncey Esq	2		2	1	1		2	2	1	1			12		
Ludlow	256	25	Brewer	Chauney		1	3					1	1				6		
Wilbraham	234	3	Brewer	Gaius	2	1	1		1	1		1	4	1			12		
Springfield	243	7	Brewer	George		1		1		2	1			1			6		
Greenwich	218	9	Brewer	James				1						1			2		
Wendell	105	7	Brewer	Nathan	2	2		1		1		2		1			11		
Wilbraham	234	2	Brewer	William		4		1			2			1	2		10		
Norwich	154	32	Brewster	Charles											2		2		
Worthington	301	1	Brewster	Elisha		1	1		1	3	1		1				8		
South Hadley	249	19	Brewster	Jesse	1		1		1	1	1	1	1				7		
Worthington	301	5	Brewster	Jona	3	1		1		1		2	1	1			10		
Westhampton	18	21	Brewster	Jonah		1							1				2		
Worthington	300	33	Brewster	Jonah	2		1	1		1		1	1				7		
Worthington	297	5	Brewster	Moses	1		1	1		2		1					6		
Westhampton	18	20	Brewster	Nathan				1			1	2		1			5		
Blanford	175	13	Brewster	Vial											3		3		
Norwich	151	4	Briant	Nathaniel	2			1				1		1			5		
Norwich	153	3	Briant	Rodolphus			1			3	1	1	1				7		
Greenwich	222	35	Brice	Abijah	1			1		1	2		1				6		
Northampton	5	22	Brick	Eunice	2							1	1				5		
Northampton	4	13	Brick	John			1	1				1	1				4		
Northampton	5	7	Brick	Joseph H	1			2		2	1	1	1				8		
Northampton	5	10	Brick	Rachel		1	2					1		1			5		
Shutesbury	108	18	Bridge	Joseph		1		2			1	2		1			7		
New Salem	96	18	Bridge	Josiah			1			3			1				5		
New Salem	96	17	Bridge	Thomas				1	1				1	1			4		
Belchertown	204	13	Bridgeman	Joseph	1		3		1	1	2	2		1			11		
Belchertown	204	12	Bridgeman	Oliver		1	2		1		2		1				7		
Belchertown	204	23	Bridgeman	Wright	1		2	1				1					5		
Blanford	181	14	Bridgen	Thomas				1		3			1				5		
South Hadley	249	1	Bridges	John		1		1			1	1		1			5		
Westhampton	18	17	Bridges	Nathaniel	2			1					1				4		
Westhampton	18	23	Bridgman	Elisha			1		1				1				3		
Northampton	6	25	Bridgman	Elizabeth	2					1		1	1				5		
Northampton	8	28	Bridgman	Erastus	2	2		1		1	2			1			9		
Westhampton	18	24	Bridgman	Ismail	1		1			3			1				6		
Northampton	8	27	Bridgman	Noah	2		1	1				1		1			6		
Orange	41	15	Briggs	Adam	3		1			2	2		1				9		
New Salem	96	11	Briggs	Ebenezer				1						1			2		
Shutesbury	108	5	Briggs	Ebenezer		1				1		2		1			5		
Leyden	81	12	Briggs	Enoch	3	1		2	1	3			3	1			14		
Greenwich	218	17	Briggs	Ephm				1		4	3	3	1				12		
Shelburne	319	8	Briggs	Jabez	1	1		1		2	1		1				7		
New Salem	97	1	Briggs	Jacob	1			1						1			3		
Cummington	304	39	Briggs	James		1	1		1		2		2		1		8		
Ashfield	338	12	Briggs	Jasper	2		1					1					4		
Shutesbury	108	11	Briggs	Job	2	2		1		3	1		1				10		
Shutesbury	108	9	Briggs	John	2	1		1			2	1	1				8		
Springfield	247	29	Briggs	John	1			1		1			1				4		
Shutesbury	108	8	Briggs	Josiah L.	2			1		2				1			6		
Shutesbury	108	6	Briggs	Liss	1		1					1					3		
Orange	41	12	Briggs	Micah	2	1		1		1			1				6		
Shutesbury	108	10	Briggs	Nathaniel	2			1		1		1	1				6		
New Salem	96	16	Briggs	Richard		1	1		1	1	1	2		1			8		
Orange	41	11	Briggs	Samuel		4		1	1	1		2	1	1			11		
Shelburne	320	6	Briggs	Sarah									1				1		
Shutesbury	108	7	Briggs	Wiram	3		1						1				5		
Barnardston	76	9	Briggs	Zadoch	3	1		1		1	2	2	1				11		
Pelham	215	5	Brigham	Lycomb	3		1			1	1						6		
Chesterfield	19	12	Britt	Ebenz			1			1		1					3		
Longmeadow	92	41	Britton	Joseph	2	1		1		1							5		
Montgomery	161	35	Broad	Aaron		1											1		
Springfield	247	14	Broad	Aaron		1	2		1	2			1	1			8		
Leverett	113	8	Broad	Enos	3	1		1			1			1			7		
Southampton	129	9	Brockway	Isaiah		2		1		1		2	1	1			8		
Conway	56	24	Broderick	John	1	1		1		1	1	2		1			8		
Ashfield	338	6	Bronson	Roger	1			1		1		1					4		
Conway	56	31	Brooks	Abner	1		2				1	1					8		
Buckland	326	2	Brooks	Alpheus		2	1			5			1				9		
Montague	44	20	Brooks	Benjamin	2		1					1					4		
Greenwich	219	26	Brooks	Caleb	3	3			1			1	1				9		
Greenfield	72	14	Brooks	David	1	1		1		2	1		1				7		
Buckland	326	1	Brooks	Jabez		1					1						4		

TOWN	PG#	LN#	LAST NAME	FIRST NAME	FREE WHITE MALES under 10	10 to 16	16 to 26	26 to 45	45 and over	FREE WHITE FEMALES under 10	10 to 16	16 to 26	26 to 45	45 and over	TOTAL ALL OTHER	TOTAL SLAVES	TOTALS	DISTRICT/ TOWNSHIP	NOTES
Barnardston	77	12	Brooks	John		1			1				1	1			4		
Hadley	286	13	Brooks	John					1	1	1	2		3			8		
West Springfield	349	18	Brooks	Levi	2		1	1		2	1		1	1			9		
Montague	45	17	Brooks	Moses		1			1	4	3		1				10		
West Springfield	355	54	Brooks	Nathan	3			1		1			1				6		
Springfield	239	26	Brooks	Rufus	1			1		2			1				5		
Greenfield	72	15	Brooks	Silas		1							1				2		
West Springfield	349	27	Brooks	Simon	5			1		1	1		1				9		
Brimfield	270	4	Brooks	Sylvanus				1		3	1		1				7		
Conway	57	20	Brown	Abijah	1			1					1				3		
Cummington	302	19	Brown	Abner				1				2		1			4		
Williamsburg	448	4	Brown	Abner	2			1					1				4		
Monson	265	14	Brown	Abner Colo	1	1		1		4	1	2	1				11		
Leyden	81	5	Brown	Amos	2			1		2	2		1	1			9		
Granville West Soc	170	22	Brown	Andrew	2	2		1		2	1		1				9		
Granville West Soc	170	14	Brown	Andrew Jun			1						1				2		
Brimfield	272	6	Brown	Archelaus	2		1		1	1	2	1	1				9		
Brimfield	269	18	Brown	Bartholomew	1	1	2	1	1		1	1	1	1			10		
Easthampton	135	25	Brown	Benjamin	1			1					1				3		
Southwick	358	10	Brown	Brigham		1		1		2	1		1				6		
Belchertown	204	21	Brown	Charles Lieut	2			1		2			1				6		
Brimfield	272	15	Brown	Clark Revd	1	1		1			1	1		1			6		
Springfield	246	34	Brown	Collins			1		1			1		1			4		
Springfield	246	35	Brown	Collins Jr	1			1		2			1				5		
Rowe	198	15	Brown	Consider					1	1				2			4		
Goshen	309	7	Brown	Daniel					1			1	1	1			4		
Gill	85	1	Brown	David	2				1	1	1			1			6		
Ware	225	18	Brown	David Lt	1	1	2						1				6		
Whately	65	4	Brown	Edward		1		1						2			4		
Leyden	81	7	Brown	Elisha	1	1	1		1	1			1	1	1		8		
Warwick	36	20	Brown	Elisha		1		1					1				3		
Leyden	81	10	Brown	Elisha Junr	1			1					1				3		
Warwick	36	13	Brown	George	2			1					1				6		
Goshen	309	16	Brown	Greenwood	1	1		1		3	1			1			8		
Brimfield	271	25	Brown	Isachar Deacn	1	1	1		1			1		1			6		
Brimfield	271	26	Brown	Isachar Jr			1			2		1					4		
Whately	66	8	Brown	Isaiah		2		1			1			1			5		
Blanford	178	14	Brown	James				1		2			1				4		
Rowe	198	16	Brown	James				1					1	1			3		
Blanford	179	14	Brown	Jane						1			1	1			3		
Leyden	81	8	Brown	Jarad	2	1		1		2			1	1			8		
Longmeadow	91	6	Brown	Jere				1					1	1			3		
Longmeadow	92	27	Brown	Jesse			1			1			1				3		
Easthampton	135	21	Brown	John	2	1		1		3	1	1	1				10		
Rowe	198	8	Brown	John	2			1					1				4		
Whately	66	9	Brown	John	2	1	3		1	1			1				9		
Hawley	332	4	Brown	Jonah		1	1		1	3	1	1		1			9		
Brimfield	269	8	Brown	Jonathan		1	2		1		1	2		1			8		
Longmeadow	92	35	Brown	Joseph				1						1			2		
Ashfield	338	9	Brown	Leml	3	1		1		2			1				8		
Norwich	151	38	Brown	Levi	1			1		1		1					4		
Pelham	213	13	Brown	Matthew		1		1	1				1				4		
Greenwich	218	14	Brown	Moses	2	2	1			2	2	2	1				12		
Ware	225	19	Brown	Moses		1	1	1		2	2	1	1				9		
Belchertown	204	19	Brown	Nathan Capt	3	1		1		1	1		1		1		9		
Leyden	80	12	Brown	Nathaniel	3			1					1				5		
Rowe	198	5	Brown	Noah	1	2	2		1	1		2		1			10		
Chesterfield	22	8	Brown	Oliver	2	1		1			1	1	1				7		
Montague	44	11	Brown	Peter	1	1	1		1	1	2	1	1				9		
Belchertown	204	20	Brown	Robt	1	1		1		3	1	1	1				9		
Westfield	126	24	Brown	Roswel	1	2		1		3	1		1				9		
Easthampton	135	8	Brown	Rufus			1		1					1			3		
Hadley	285	35	Brown	Samuel	1			1				1					3		
Longmeadow	92	36	Brown	Samuel	1	1		1		2			1				6		
Plainfield	308	45	Brown	Samuel		1	1	1						1			4		
Ware	225	20	Brown	Samuel		1	1	1		2				1			6		
Ware	225	21	Brown	Samuel Jun		1		1					1				3		
Palmer	260	21	Brown	Seth	2			1		2			1				6		
Easthampton	135	19	Brown	Silas				1						1			2		
Easthampton	135	20	Brown	Silas Junr	1	1		1		3	1		1				8		
Palmer	260	20	Brown	Solomon				1		1			1	1			4		
Rowe	198	11	Brown	Stephen	3			1		1			1				6		
Belchertown	208	16	Brown	Thomas	1		1	1					2	1			6		
Goshen	309	8	Brown	Thomas			2		1		1	1		1			6		
Leyden	81	9	Brown	Thomas				1		1			1				3		
Belchertown	203	5	Brown	Thomas 2d				1					1	1			3		
Longmeadow	95	15	Brown	Timothy					1					1			2		
Westfield	126	13	Brown	Uriah		2	1		1					1			5		
Greenfield	72	5	Brown	Wanton	1			1				1					3		
Blanford	178	25	Brown	William		1	1		1					1			3		

TOWN	PG#	LN#	LAST NAME	FIRST NAME	FREE WHITE MALES					FREE WHITE FEMALES					TOTAL ALL OTHER	TOTAL SLAVES	TOTALS	DISTRICT/ TOWNSHIP	NOTES
					under 10	10 to 16	16 to 26	26 to 45	45 and over	under 10	10 to 16	16 to 26	26 to 45	45 and over					
Blanford	178	21	Brown	William 2nd	1			1		4	1		1				8		
Easthampton	136	29	Brown	Zenas	3			1					1				5		
Brimfield	274	21	Browning	Davis	1	1		1		2	1		1				7		
Brimfield	274	16	Browning	James			1					1					2		
Brimfield	274	19	Browning	Joseph Esq				1				1		1	1		4		
Shutesbury	108	16	Bruce	Ephraim		1		1					1	1			4		
Blanford	175	2	Bruce	Jesse	3	1		1				1	1	1			8		
Holland	278	13	Bruce	Joseph		1		1					1	1			4		
Shutesbury	108	17	Bruce	William	2			1				1	1	1			6		
Wilbraham	237	39	Brumley	Asa			1	1					1	1			4		
Monson	265	28	Brumley	Nathan		1		1		1			1				4		
Longmeadow	95	27	Brumley	Stephen	1			1		2			1				5		
Northampton	9	34	Brunson	Abraham		1		1					1	2			5		
Chesterfield	23	3	Bryant	Asahel	1			1		1			1				4		
Goshen	309	6	Bryant	Caleb		1		1					1				3		
Chesterfield	23	2	Bryant	Eli	2	1		1		1			1				6		
Springfield	242	40	Bryant	Jno Capt	3			1		1	2	1	1				9		
Chesterfield	21	10	Bryant	Nathaniel		1		1					1	2			5		
Chesterfield	21	37	Bryant	Patrick	5			1		1			1				8		
Cummington	304	38	Bryant	Peter	3			1					1				5		
Pelham	213	11	Bryant	Seth	2		1	1		2		1	1	1			9		
Chesterfield	21	11	Buck	Daniel	4	3		1		2	1	1	1				13		
Chesterfield	22	11	Buck	Isaac		2	1	1		2	1	1	1				9		
Chesterfield	21	7	Buck	Mathew				1						1			2		
Worthington	298	31	Buck	Thomas	1	1	1			2	1			1			8		
Worthington	298	32	Buck	Thomas Jun	1		1						1				3		
Goshen	309	17	Buckingham	Jeddl				1		1		2		1			5		
Northampton	3	35	Buckman	Andrew		1	1										3		
Leyden	80	7	Budington	Jonathan	1			1				1	1				5		
Springfield	240	17	Buell	Abel	2	5	3			2	1						13		
Wilbraham	234	7	Buell	William	3	1		1		2	1		1				9		
Worthington	298	2	Buffington	Samuel		2	1			1			1	1			6		
Brimfield	270	31	Bugbee	Calvin	3			1					1	1			6		
Brimfield	272	35	Bugbee	David		1		1		2	1			2			7		
Brimfield	269	35	Bugbee	Ebenezer			1						1				2		
Monson	267	7	Bugbee	Moses	1	1		1		3	1		1				8		
Monson	267	28	Bugbee	Parker			1						1				2		
Monson	267	18	Bugbee	Stephen		1		1					2	1			5		
Williamsburg	448	14	Bulcard	Adam	3	1		1					1	1			7		
Leyden	80	9	Bulfinch	Bedgood	3	2		1		1	1			2			10		
Shelburne	319	13	Bull	Willm	3	2	1	1	1		1		2				11		
New Salem	97	8	Bullard	Benjamin		1	1			1			1				4		
Springfield	246	31	Bullard	Benjamin	1	1		1		2			1				6		
Brimfield	273	11	Bullard	David	1	2		1					1	1			6		
Westhampton	17	20	Bullard	Isaac	2	1		1		1			1				6		
Buckland	326	8	Bullard	John				1					1				2		
Westhampton	17	18	Bullard	John				1					1	1			3		
Buckland	326	4	Bullard	John Jr	1								1				3		
Rowe	198	4	Bullard	Moses	1		1			1			1				4		
Wendell	105	11	Bullard	Silas	2		1						1				4		
Orange	41	17	Bulloch	Cromwell			1			2			1				4		
Orange	41	13	Bulloch	Welcome			1	1			1	1	1	1			6		
Leyden	80	8	Bullock	Israel	1	2		2		1	1			1			9		
Granville West Soc	170	3	Bumpuss	Latathiel	1		1			1			1				4		
Monson	265	35	Bumstead	Joseph	1	2							1				4		
Wilbraham	237	35	Bumstead	Joseph		1		1			1		1				4		
Southampton	129	8	Bunday	Elijah	4			1					1				6		
Southampton	129	7	Bunday	Ephraim			1			4			1				6		
Southampton	129	15	Bunday	Moses		1				2		1					4		
Blanford	177	12	Bunnel	Jonathan	1		1	1		1			1				5		
West Springfield	352	42	Burbank	Abraham		2	1	1		1	1	1		2	1		10		
Springfield	247	17	Burbank	Ebenezer	2	1		1		1	1		1				7		
Belchertown	203	1	Burbank	John	1					1		1	1				5		
Granville East Soc	531	11	Burbank	Thomas			2					1	1	1	1		7		
Wilbraham	238	30	Burdick	Adam	2	1		2		3	2		1				11		
Monson	265	10	Burdick	Pardon			1						1				2		
Monson	264	43	Burdick	Shephard			1						1				2		
Goshen	309	11	Burges	Benjm		2		1		1	1	3		1			9		
Springfield	243	10	Burgess	Joseph	1		1			1			1				4		
Springfield	241	9	Burgess	Joseph Capt	1	1	1							1			4		
Monson	265	33	Burgess	Levi	1		1			1		1					4		
Springfield	243	8	Burgess	Reuben Lt	2			1		2		1					8		
Springfield	247	36	Burgess	Robert			1			2			1				4		
Conway	57	18	Burgis	Benjamin	2	1	1	1				1		1			7		
Conway	56	18	Burgiss	Bathsheba	3							1	1	1			6		
Barnardston	77	13	Burk	Lovina	1	2	1		1			1	1	2			9		
Cummington	302	20	Burnal	Epraim	1	3		1		1	1		1				8		
Chesterfield	24	8	Burnell	John Jr	2	2	2	1		1		1	1	1			11		
Chesterfield	24	14	Burnell	Joseph Jr	3	2		1	1	2		1	1				11		
Ashfield	338	5	Burnet	Archibald	1	1	1		1	2	2			1			9		

TOWN	PG#	LN#	LAST NAME	FIRST NAME	FREE WHITE MALES under 10	10 to 16	16 to 26	26 to 45	45 and over	FREE WHITE FEMALES under 10	10 to 16	16 to 26	26 to 45	45 and over	TOTAL ALL OTHER	TOTAL SLAVES	TOTALS	DISTRICT/TOWNSHIP	NOTES
Warwick	36	27	Burnett	Andrew	1	1	3		1	1	2	1		1			11		
Monson	267	17	Burnett	Daniel		1			1		1		1	1	1		5		
Warwick	36	35	Burnett	Henry		1			1				1	1			4		
Gill	85	3	Burnett	John					1				2				3		
Granby	252	3	Burnett	Jonathan		1	1		1		1			1			5		
Barnardston	76	8	Burnett	Joseph		1			1		1	3		1			7		
Warwick	36	9	Burnett	Joshua	2			1		1		1					5		
Gill	85	2	Burnett	Nathaniel	1			1		2			1				5		
Warwick	36	32	Burnett	William				1		1		1					3		
Warwick	36	10	Burnett	William Junr	1		1			1		1					4		
Monson	265	4	Burnham	Abigail Widow	1	1				2			1				5		
Montague	44	16	Burnham	Daniel			1					1					2		
Barnardston	77	11	Burnham	Elisha			1	1			2		1				5		
Amherst	292	40	Burnham	James	2	1		1		1	2		1				8		
Montague	44	21	Burnham	Josiah			1	1					1				3		
Montague	45	1	Burnham	Moses	3			1		1	2		1	1			9		
Belchertown	211	31	Burnham	Reuben	1			1		2			1				5		
Montague	45	14	Burnham	Silas	3			1		2			1				7		
Shutesbury	108	12	Burnham	Thomas		1			1			3		1			6		
Springfield	247	35	Burr	Ansel			1			1		1					3		
South Hadley	249	42	Burr	Benjamin	1			1			1		1				4		
Pelham	217	14	Burr	Huldah	1						1	2	2				6		
Worthington	297	13	Burr	Israel	1	1	1		1	3	1	1	1				10		
Ludlow	257	27	Burr	Jona Jr	1			1					1				3		
Ludlow	257	29	Burr	Jonathan				1		1	2		1	1	1		6		
Ludlow	257	28	Burr	Preeman	1			1					1				3		
Greenwich	218	13	Burr	Rufus	1	2		1		2	1		1				8		
Ludlow	256	39	Burr	Timothy	2	1		1		2			1				7		
Wilbraham	235	25	Burr	Timothy	3	1	2		1	2			1	2			12		
Palmer	260	1	Burrill	Ebenezer	2			1					1				4		
Granville West Soc	170	5	Burrill	Israel			1			2			1				4		
Hawley	332	6	Burroughs	David	1	1		2		2	1		2	1			10		
Williamsburg	448	12	Burroughs	Ebenezer	2		1		1	2			1				7		
Plainfield	306	2	Burroughs	Simon	3		3		1	1	2	2	1				13		
Whately	65	5	Burroughs	Stephen	1			1			1		1				4		
Leyden	81	11	Burrows	Amos	1			1					1				3		
Blanford	176	31	Burster	Joseph B	1			1		3	2		1				8		
Hawley	332	3	Burt	Aaron	2			1	1	2			1	1			8		
Granville West Soc	168	33	Burt	Caleb	2	1		1		2			1				7		
Longmeadow	94	5	Burt	Calvin Capt	2	2		1		2	1		2				10		
Brimfield	273	14	Burt	Daniel		1	2		1	2			1	1			8		
Wilbraham	237	31	Burt	David		1	2		1	1	1		1	1			8		
Longmeadow	94	6	Burt	David Capt			2					1	2				6		
Deerfield	51	32	Burt	Ebenezer					1		1		1				3		
Greenwich	218	15	Burt	Ebenz	1			1		3		3	1				9		
Northampton	6	18	Burt	Edward	1			1				1					3		
Longmeadow	95	8	Burt	Elijah	1	1	2	1	1	1	1	2	1				11		
Wilbraham	237	29	Burt	Enoch	3			1						1			5		
Northampton	9	13	Burt	Esther						1			2	1			4		
Springfield	244	23	Burt	Frederick				1		1			1				3		
Northampton	9	12	Burt	Gaius	1		1	1		2			1				6		
Longmeadow	94	34	Burt	Gideon Col	1	4	1		1	1			1	1			10		
Wilbraham	233	32	Burt	Gideon Dr		1	2	1		1	2	3					10		
Southampton	128	11	Burt	Hannah Wd			1					1		1			3		
Greenwich	219	23	Burt	Isaac	1			1		1		1	1				5		
Ludlow	257	2	Burt	Jepthah	3	1	1		1				1				7		
Springfield	245	8	Burt	Jno Lt	1	1	2		1	1	3		1				10		
Westhampton	16	34	Burt	Joel	2	1		1			1		1				6		
Longmeadow	95	9	Burt	Luther				1					1				2		
Springfield	244	27	Burt	Martin	1		1						1				3		
Southampton	129	11	Burt	Martin	2	1		1		2	1	2		1			10		
Southampton	129	3	Burt	Martin Junr			1						1				2		
Springfield	244	25	Burt	Moses				1						1			2		
Wilbraham	233	22	Burt	Moses	2		1	1					1	1	1		7		
Springfield	244	26	Burt	Moses Junr	1		2			1	1	2					7		
Longmeadow	93	21	Burt	Nathaniel		1		1			1	1	1	1			6		
Ludlow	256	11	Burt	Reuben	3			1		1	2		1	1			9		
Springfield	241	6	Burt	Rex	1			1		2		1					5		
Southampton	128	14	Burt	Saml	2	3	1	1		3		3	1				14		
Springfield	246	18	Burt	Samuel			1			4			1				6		
Wilbraham	237	32	Burt	Samuel			1						1				2		
Deerfield	51	40	Burt	Stephen	1	1	1		1	2	1	1	1				9		
Wilbraham	237	30	Burt	Walter			1				1		1				3		
Norwich	154	4	Burt	Noah	1	1		1		2		1					7		
Rowe	198	6	Burton	Asa	1	2			1	2	2	2			1		11		
Worthington	300	6	Burton	Asa			1		1	3	2		1				8		
Norwich	153	7	Burton	Barnard	2			1		1	1			2			7		
Northfield	27	13	Burton	Benjamin	1	1		1		1	1	1	2				8		
Plainfield	306	9	Burton	David	1	1		1		3				1			7		
Norwich	151	16	Burton	Hannah Wid	2	1	1			1	1		1				7		

TOWN	PG#	LN#	HEADS OF HOUSEHOLD		FREE WHITE MALES					FREE WHITE FEMALES					TOTAL ALL OTHER	TOTAL SLAVES	TOTALS	DISTRICT/ TOWNSHIP	NOTES
			LAST NAME	FIRST NAME	under 10	10 to 16	16 to 26	26 to 45	45 and over	under 10	10 to 16	16 to 26	26 to 45	45 and over					
Plainfield	306	10	Burton	Nathan				1			2		1	1			5		
Ashfield	338	7	Burton	Saml				1						1			2		
Norwich	151	15	Burton	Samuel			1			1		1					3		
Worthington	299	34	Burton	Sexton	1			1		2			1				5		
Westfield	118	4	Bush	Aaron	3	2	1	1	1	1		1		1			11		
Westfield	119	11	Bush	Amos	1	1	1		1	1		1	1				7		
Middlefield	157	27	Bush	Edward	1			1		1		1	1				5		
Westfield	126	2	Bush	Elijah	1			1				1					3		
Chester	145	22	Bush	Enoch Lieut	1			1		2		1		1			6		
Monson	266	29	Bush	Erastus		1		1					1				3		
Chester	146	38	Bush	Gerthom		1			1					1			3		
Belchertown	205	34	Bush	Hezekiah Esq			1					1		1			3		
Westfield	127	2	Bush	Jared		1	2		1	1			1				6		
Greenfield	72	12	Bush	John	1	1			1	2	2	1					8		
Chester	145	30	Bush	Oliver		1		1		1		1					4		
Middlefield	158	37	Bush	Silas	1		1			2		1					5		
Westfield	126	5	Bush	Silas	1	2	1	1		2			1				8		
Ware	225	8	Bush	Solomon		1	1										2		
Monson	266	21	Bush	Stephen	1	1		1		1	3	1					8		
Leyden	80	6	Bush	Uriah	1	1		1		2		1					6		
Westfield	122	11	Bush	Walter			1			3		1					5		
Westfield	120	25	Bush	Zachariah	1		3		1	1		1		1			8		
Westfield	120	29	Bush	Zadok	1	2	1		1	2	1	1	1	1	2		13		
Monson	265	22	Butler	Anna Wd			1							1			2		
Williamsburg	448	10	Butler	Athearn		1	1			2	1	1					6		
Monson	265	23	Butler	Azariah	2			1		3		1	1				8		
Monson	264	29	Butler	Benjamin	1			1		1		1					4		
Wendell	105	12	Butler	Calvin	1			1		2		1					5		
Monson	264	28	Butler	Daniel				1						1			2		
Northampton	6	9	Butler	Daniel	1	1		1		2	1	1					8		
Blanford	181	1	Butler	David	2			1		1	1	1					6		
Ashfield	338	8	Butler	Davis	1		1		1	1		1		1			6		
Buckland	325	7	Butler	James		1	2			4	2	1	1				12		
Monson	264	30	Butler	Nathaniel			1			3		1					5		
Northfield	27	17	Butler	Nathaniel	1			1		2		1					5		
Buckland	326	6	Butler	Peter	2			1		2		1					6		
Wilbraham	235	6	Butler	Phebe								1	1				2		
Monson	265	24	Butler	Samuel	1	1						1					3		
Northampton	4	32	Butler	Simeon	2		1	1		1	1	1					7		
Goshen	309	15	Butler	Solomon	2			1					1	1			5		
Belchertown	203	8	Butler	Stephen			1			1		1	1				4		
Northampton	4	22	Butler	William		1	10	3		2		1	1	1	1		20		
Springfield	243	11	Butler	William	3			1		1	1		1				7		
Hawley	331	3	Butrick	Joseph		1				1		1					3		
Granville West Soc	170	27	Butter	Selah	1	1		1		3		1					7		
Leverett	113	9	Butterfield	Abel		2		1		1				1			5		
Shutesbury	109	1	Butterfield	Abraham	2	1		1		1	1	1					7		
Greenwich	218	18	Butterfield	Henry	1	1	1		1	1			1	1			7		
Granby	252	33	Butterfield	Jeremiah				1									1		
Westhampton	16	25	Butterfield	Solomon	1			1		2		1					5		
Brimfield	272	32	Butterworth	William	1			1		3	1	1					7		
Granville East Soc	527	26	Buttolph	Abijah	1			1		3	3	1					9		
Blanford	179	31	Buttolph	Star		1		1		3		1					6		
West Springfield	352	57	Button	Asa		1			1			3		1			6		
Belchertown	208	9	Button	Elias	1	1	2		1	2	1		1				9		
Wilbraham	237	27	Button	Elijah	2		1		1	2	1	1	1				9		
Wilbraham	237	4	Button	Elizabeth Wd		2								1			3		
West Springfield	353	1	Button	Joseph	1			1		1	1						4		
Blanford	180	7	Button	Perry	3	1		1				1					6		
Springfield	241	21	Butts	Jabez	1		1					1					3		
Springfield	241	22	Butts	Mason	1		1					1					3		
Springfield	241	20	Butts	Nathaniel	2		1		1	1	1	2		1			9		
Chesterfield	21	34	Butts	Richard			1			3		1	1				6		
Belchertown	204	9	Buxton	Wm		1		1		3				1			6		
Springfield	242	35	Byers	James	1		1		1	1	2			2			8		
Springfield	242	36	Byers	James Jr		1	1			1	1						4		
Southwick	358	6	Byington	Joel		1		1		1		1		1			4		
Southwick	358	7	Byington	Samuel	3	1	2		1	1	1		1				10		
Wilbraham	235	38	Cadwell	Daniel	3			1			1		1				6		
Wilbraham	235	43	Cadwell	David	2			1				1					4		
Wilbraham	235	39	Cadwell	Ebenezer	1			1		1	1	1	1				6		
Leverett	114	9	Cadwell	Isaac	1		1					1					3		
Wilbraham	235	40	Cadwell	John	4		1			1	1	1					8		
Wilbraham	238	31	Cadwell	Moses	1					1	1						3		
Wilbraham	233	39	Cadwell	Pliny	2		1	1		1		1					6		
Wilbraham	234	57	Cadwell	Stephen		2		1		1			1				5		
Westfield	121	14	Cadwell	Timothy	2			1		3	1	1					8		
Chester	147	5	Cady	Asa Lieut.		1	1		1	1	1	1					6		
Shelburne	320	24	Cady	Ephraim	1			1		2		1					5		
Monson	266	20	Cady	Henry G.	1		1	2		1		1					6		

TOWN	PG#	LN#	LAST NAME	FIRST NAME	FREE WHITE MALES					FREE WHITE FEMALES					TOTAL ALL OTHER	TOTAL SLAVES	TOTALS	DISTRICT/ TOWNSHIP	NOTES
					under 10	10 to 16	16 to 26	26 to 45	45 and over	under 10	10 to 16	16 to 26	26 to 45	45 and over					
Shutesbury	109	6	Cady	Jeremiah	1	1	1		1	1	2		1				8		
Orange	41	29	Cady	Justin			1		1		1		1				4		
Shutesbury	109	5	Cady	Samuel	3	2		1		2			1				9		
New Salem	98	1	Cahoon	Sampson				1		1		1		1			4		
Northfield	28	2	Caldwell	John	2	1	1	1		2			1				8		
Colrain	184	12	Caldwell	William	2	1	3		1				1				8		
Greenwich	222	15	Calhoon	Samuel	2			1		2			1				6		
Wilbraham	235	17	Calkins	Asa	1	1			1	3	2		1				9		
Wilbraham	236	5	Calkins	David	2	1		1		2			1				7		
Wilbraham	236	10	Calkins	Ezekiel	1	1		1		2			2				7		
Wilbraham	236	18	Calkins	James	1	1	2		1	4		1		1			11		
Colrain	184	3	Call	John				1						3			4		
Colrain	184	4	Call	John Jr	4	2		1		1	2		1				11		
Northfield	28	5	Callender	Benjamin		1				2	1	1					5		
Leyden	81	31	Cambell	John Junr	2	2		1	1		1	1	2	1			11		
Leyden	81	32	Cambell	Samuel	2			1		2	3		1				9		
Leverett	114	11	Camp	Martha									1				1		
Southwick	358	13	Campbell	Abigail	1								1				2		
Chester	144	29	Campbell	James	1	2	1		1	2		1		1			9		
Hawley	332	15	Campbell	John	3	1		1	1	1		1		1			8		
Hawley	332	16	Campbell	Joseph	2		1						1				4		
Chester	144	24	Campbell	Matthew	1	1	1			1		1			1		6		
Southwick	358	18	Campbell	Thomas	2	1	2		1	3	1		2	1			13		
Blanford	179	25	Canada	David	3	2	2		1	1	1		1				11		
Montague	45	30	Canada	Isaac		1		1		2			1				5		
Blanford	180	13	Canada	John	4		1	1	1	1	2		1				11		
Blanford	180	8	Canada	John Jr	4		1	2	1	1	1	1					11		
Hawley	332	12	Canada	Micah	2			1		2			1	1			7		
Blanford	181	11	Canada	William		1	2		1		1		1				6		
Colrain	184	6	Canady	John	1	1		1		3	1		1				8		
Greenwich	219	37	Canady	Peleg Capt	1		1	1		1	1	1					6		
Granville Mid Soc.	167	23	Canfield	Elizabeth									1				1		
Greenwich	219	8	Cannon	Cornelius	3	1		2		1	1	3	1				12		
Blanford	175	20	Cannon	Elisha			1			1		1					3		
Granville West Soc	170	26	Cannon	Ezekiel	1			1					1				3		
Blanford	178	15	Cannon	Isaac	1			1		2	1	2					7		
New Salem	97	36	Cannon	John		1	1	1			1		1				5		
Blanford	177	2	Cannon	Martin	1			1		3	2		1				8		
Blanford	181	7	Cannon	Nathan	1	2	1		1	3	1		1	1			11		
Blanford	179	13	Cannon	Samuel		1		1		1	1		1				5		
New Salem	97	20	Cannon	Simeon	1	1	2		1	1			1				7		
Blanford	176	26	Cannon	William I.	1	1		1		3	2		1				9		
Southwick	358	17	Cannon	Ziba		1		1		2	1		2				7		
Belchertown	208	34	Capen	Purchase	2	2	3		1	1	1		1				11		
Montgomery	161	24	Capron	David			1										1		
Blanford	177	24	Card	Daniel			1						1				2		
Southwick	358	16	Cardell	John	2	1		1			1	1	1				7		
Westfield	123	2	Carew	Asahel	4			1		3		1					9		
Springfield	240	36	Carew	Joseph			3	2			1		1				7		
West Springfield	350	7	Carew	Joseph	1		1		1		1	1	1				6		
Deerfield	52	20	Carey	Charity			1					1	1				3		
Rowe	199	17	Carey	Stephen			1						1				2		
Westfield	121	31	Carlile	Jonathan	3			1		3	1		1				9		
Chester	147	24	Carlisle	John			1	1		1	1	1		1			6		
Hatfield	14	21	Carlisle	Samuel				1	1	1		1	1				5		
Chester	150	9	Carlisle	William	1			1		3				1			6		
Colrain	184	11	Carlton	Benjamin		2		1		3	1		1				8		
Chester	149	16	Carpenter	Benjamin	3			1		1			1				6		
Monson	268	29	Carpenter	Daniel			2	1		1	1		1				6		
Chester	144	5	Carpenter	Ebenezer			1										1		
Norwich	152	35	Carpenter	Israel		1		1		3		1					6		
Wilbraham	236	23	Carpenter	John		1	1		1			2		1			6		
Rowe	199	16	Carpenter	Josiah	1			1		1		1	1				5		
Leyden	81	17	Carpenter	Nathaniel		3		1			1	2	1				8		
Amherst	290	15	Carpenter	Richard	1		1	1		2		1		1			7		
Rowe	199	6	Carpenter	Timothy	1		1			3			1				6		
Ashfield	339	9	Carr	Amos	2	2	1					1					6		
Chesterfield	22	39	Carr	Martin	2		1	1		3	1		1				9		
Gill	85	9	Carrier	Benjamin	2	1		1		3			1				8		
Conway	57	33	Carrier	David	1	2	1	1		1	1	1	1				9		
Hadley	286	19	Carrier	Isaiah		1		1			1	1		2			6		
West Springfield	356	7	Carrier	Jeremiah									1	1					
West Springfield	356	8	Carrier	Jeremiah Jr	2		1				1		1				5		
West Springfield	356	6	Carrier	Joseph	2	1		1			1		1				6		
Northfield	27	19	Carrier	Phillip				1			1		1				3		
Colrain	185	2	Carryl	Nathanael				1						2			3		
Southwick	358	20	Carter	Asa			1				1		1				3		
Gill	85	4	Carter	Benjamin		2		1		4	2		1				10		
Shutesbury	109	4	Carter	Benjamin		1						1					2		
Russell	139	4	Carter	Chandler	2		1			1			1				5		
Montgomery	161	40	Carter	Charles			1										1		

TOWN	PG#	LN#	LAST NAME	FIRST NAME	FREE WHITE MALES under 10	10 to 16	16 to 26	26 to 45	45 and over	FREE WHITE FEMALES under 10	10 to 16	16 to 26	26 to 45	45 and over	TOTAL ALL OTHER	TOTAL SLAVES	TOTALS	DISTRICT/ TOWNSHIP	NOTES
Blanford	178	43	Carter	Elias		1		1			1	1		1			5		
Buckland	326	16	Carter	Elias	1		2	2	1			1	2	1			10		
Montgomery	160	11	Carter	Elias			1					1		1			3		
Buckland	326	23	Carter	Elias Jr	3		1			3		1					8		
Buckland	326	24	Carter	Elijah			1					2		1			4		
Buckland	326	20	Carter	Elisha		1	1		1	2	1		1				7		
Southwick	358	14	Carter	Isaac	2	1	1	1		2			1				8		
Blanford	178	42	Carter	John	2	1		1			1	2		1			8		
Chester	150	2	Carter	John	1	1		1		1	1		1				6		
Shutesbury	109	19	Carter	John	1			1		2			1				5		
Southwick	358	19	Carter	Jonathan		1	2		1		1			1			6		
Russell	139	6	Carter	Nehemiah		3		1				1		1			6		
Buckland	326	18	Carter	Sama		1				1	1	1		1			5		
Southwick	358	11	Carter	Solomon	2			1		1			1				5		
Montgomery	161	39	Carter	William		1											1		
Westfield	127	15	Carter	Wm	2	1		1		4			1				9		
Whately	66	21	Cartwell	Thomas	1			1		3	3		1				9		
Granby	253	41	Carver	Aaron	1			1				1					3		
Ludlow	256	33	Carver	David				1						1			2		
Shutesbury	109	14	Carver	John	2			1		1			1				5		
Ludlow	256	34	Carver	Jona	2			1		1			2				6		
Ludlow	256	35	Carver	Warren	1			1									2		
Colrain	184	13	Cary	Aaron		1	1		1	1	1	1		1			7		
Williamsburg	447	7	Cary	Abner	2			1		1			1				5		
New Salem	97	15	Cary	John	2	1		1			1	2		1			8		
Williamsburg	447	6	Cary	Joseph				1						1			2		
Williamsburg	447	3	Cary	Joseph Junr	1	2	1	1		3	1	1	1				11		
Deerfield	52	26	Cary	Nathan	1			1					1				3		
Whately	66	22	Cary	Richard	2			1		1	1	2		1			8		
Deerfield	52	27	Cary	Robert	1			1					1				3		
Greenwich	219	16	Cary	Thomas				1		1			1				3		
New Salem	98	7	Cary	Widow						1		1		1			3		
New Salem	98	5	Cary	Willm H			1										1		
Goshen	310	1	Caryell	John		1		1		1			1				4		
Ashfield	339	8	Case	James	2			1		2		1		1			7		
Granville Mid Soc.	166	23	Case	Joel			1										1		
South Brimfield	276	22	Case	Stephen	3			1		1			1				6		
Gill	85	5	Casey	Francis				1									1		
Greenfield	72	28	Castilo	Peter				1		1	1		1				4		
Granby	252	29	Caswell	Abiel	1			1		1	2			1			6		
Shutesbury	109	12	Caswell	Elijah	1			1		2	1		1				6		
Greenwich	219	9	Caswell	George Junr				2		2		2					6		
Greenwich	219	14	Caswell	George Junr				1		1		3		1			6		
Springfield	247	11	Caswell	Samuel	1	1	2	1		1		1		1			8		
Wendell	105	19	Caswell	Simon	2			1					1				4		
Springfield	243	31	Caswell	Solomon			6	1						1			8		
Williamsburg	447	5	Cathcart	Thomas	5			1					1				7		
Conway	57	48	Cathcart	Tristram	1	1	1					1	1	1			6		
Deerfield	51	44	Catlin	John	1	1		1		1	2		1	1			8		
Deerfield	51	43	Catlin	Richard	1		1	1				1	1	1			6		
Sunderland	282	3	Cattin	Timothy		1		1				1		1			4		
Hadley	288	37	Chadwell	Mathew	3			1					1				5		
Montague	45	19	Chadwick	George	2		1		1	3	3		1				11		
Wilbraham	237	36	Chaffee	Asa				1		1	1		1				4		
Wilbraham	237	25	Chaffee	Asa Jr		1	1	1		1		2	1				7		
Wilbraham	238	22	Chaffee	Asa Jr		1	1	1		1		2	1				7		
Wilbraham	237	38	Chaffee	Calvin	2	1		1		1			1				6		
Monson	267	12	Chaffee	Chadwick	3		1	1		1		1					7		
Monson	267	29	Chaffee	Chas Doct			1			4			1				6		
Wilbraham	238	18	Chaffee	Comfort				1									1		
Wilbraham	237	2	Chaffee	Comfort Jr	2		1	1		1			1	1			7		
Wilbraham	237	37	Chaffee	Ephraim	2	1		1		2	2		1				9		
Wilbraham	237	16	Chaffee	Joel				1						1			2		
Wilbraham	236	41	Chaffee	Joel Jr		1		1					1				3		
Wilbraham	238	19	Chaffee	Nathl Bliss	3			1		1		2					7		
Wilbraham	237	24	Chaffee	Simeon		1	1		1	1	1			2			7		
Hawley	332	30	Chamberlain	Aaron				1			2			1			4		
Southwick	358	15	Chamberlain	Ephraim		2	1		1	1		2		1			8		
Monson	268	31	Chamberlain	Pliny	2			1		3			1				7		
Deerfield	52	21	Chamberlain	Samuel	1	1			2	1				1			6		
Granby	253	30	Chamberlain	Stephen		1	1		1	1	1			1			6		
New Salem	97	13	Chamberlin	John	1	1	3		1	1		2		1			10		
New Salem	97	14	Chamberlin	John 2d		1	1		1	2	1	2		1			9		
New Salem	97	22	Chamberlin	Nathl		1	1		1			1		1			5		
Shutesbury	109	13	Chamberlin	Peter	1			1		4		1	1				8		
New Salem	97	23	Chamberlin	Zach	1			1		1		1					4		
Charlemont	191	4	Chambers	John				1		3			1				5		
West Springfield	350	9	Champion	Medes	1			1		2		1	1				6		
West Springfield	350	13	Champion	Reuben	4	1	2	1		1	1		1				11		
Northfield	28	1	Champion	Tho				1			1			1			3		

TOWN	PG#	LN#	LAST NAME	FIRST NAME	FREE WHITE MALES					FREE WHITE FEMALES					TOTAL ALL OTHER	TOTAL SLAVES	TOTALS	DISTRICT/ TOWNSHIP	NOTES
					under 10	10 to 16	16 to 26	26 to 45	45 and over	under 10	10 to 16	16 to 26	26 to 45	45 and over					
Leyden	81	35	Champlin	Joseph	2			1		1	1		1				6		
Colrain	185	1	Champlin	William	3		2	1		2	2	5	1		1		17		
Warwick	37	5	Champney	Humphrey A.	1		1	1		2	2		1				8		
Wendell	105	18	Champney	William	1	1		1					1				4		
Longmeadow	93	33	Chandler	Abner	2			2		2		1	1				8		
Colrain	184	7	Chandler	Clark	1		1	1		3		2	1				9		
Monson	263	6	Chandler	Elijah		1	2		1		1	2		1			8		
Rowe	199	20	Chandler	Lewis	1			1		1	1		1				5		
Deerfield	52	23	Chandler	Moses				1						1			2		
Shelburne	320	19	Chandler	Moses			1	1		4	1		1				8		
Montgomery	161	22	Chandler	Samuel	3	1		1				2	1				8		
Longmeadow	93	34	Chandler	Stephen				1				1	1				3		
Longmeadow	92	11	Chandler	Stephen Jun	2	1		1			1		1				6		
Middlefield	159	5	Chapain	Abner	2			1		2		1					6		
Barnardston	77	16	Chapen	Caleb Junr	5	1		1					1				8		
Leyden	81	16	Chapen	Consider				1		3	3		1				8		
Leyden	81	25	Chapen	Daniel		1	2		1			1	2	1			8		
Barnardston	77	19	Chapen	Hezekiah			1		1		1	1		1			5		
Barnardston	77	20	Chapen	Israel	2	1		1			1		1				6		
Barnardston	77	18	Chapen	Joel				1						1			2		
Barnardston	77	24	Chapen	Joel Junr	2			1					1				4		
Leyden	81	15	Chapen	Julias		1		1				1	2				5		
Leyden	81	24	Chapen	Selah	2		3		1	1	1	1		1			10		
Barnardston	77	15	Chapen	Zalmuna	3		1	1		1			1				8		
Springfield	245	42	Chapin	Abel Col	3	2	1	1				1	1	1	1		11		
Rowe	199	11	Chapin	Abner		1			1	2		1		1			6		
Wilbraham	232	21	Chapin	Abner		1	1		1	1	1		1				6		
Rowe	199	18	Chapin	Abner Jnr			1					1					2		
Rowe	199	21	Chapin	Alpheus			1				1						2		
West Springfield	355	55	Chapin	Asahel		3	1		1	1		1		1			8		
Springfield	247	24	Chapin	Ascenath Wd		1				1			1				3		
Springfield	245	39	Chapin	Ashbel	2		1	1		2			1				7		
West Springfield	356	10	Chapin	Bathsheba			1				1	1		1			4		
Springfield	246	5	Chapin	Benjamin			1			1	1		1				4		
Ludlow	256	47	Chapin	Berazeel	2					2			1				5		
Springfield	246	33	Chapin	Daniel	1			1		2			1				5		
Granby	253	43	Chapin	Elijah				1			1	1					3		
Springfield	245	36	Chapin	Ephm Capt			2	1						1			4		
Wilbraham	236	26	Chapin	Ephraim	1	1		1	1	1	1			1			7		
Springfield	246	6	Chapin	Ephraim Jr	1	2	1	1		2	1		1				9		
West Springfield	356	1	Chapin	Eunice		1	1					2		1			5		
Springfield	246	2	Chapin	Eunice Wd			1							1			2		
Springfield	245	31	Chapin	Ezekiel	3	2		1		1			1	2			10		
Norwich	154	18	Chapin	Ezra	3	2	1	1			1	1	1				10		
Hatfield	13	9	Chapin	Frederic	1	1	1	1		2			1	1			8		
Springfield	245	37	Chapin	Frederick	1		2			1	1	1					6		
Springfield	245	41	Chapin	George	1			1		3			1				6		
Rowe	199	2	Chapin	Gideon		2	2		1			1		1			7		
Rowe	199	3	Chapin	Gideon Jnr			1					1					2		
Springfield	246	16	Chapin	Henry	2			1		1				1			5		
Heath	195	9	Chapin	Isaac	1		1		1	2		1	1	1			8		
Wilbraham	236	17	Chapin	Isaac			1				1						2		
Springfield	240	38	Chapin	Israel Capt	3	1	1		1	1	1	1	1	1			11		
Springfield	246	36	Chapin	Ithamar	3	1		1		2	1		1				9		
Longmeadow	92	8	Chapin	Jabez	2			1		2			1				6		
Springfield	246	31	Chapin	Jabez	2		1	1		2	2		1				9		
Heath	195	8	Chapin	Jacob	1	1	1			4		1	1				9		
Springfield	246	15	Chapin	Japhel	5	1	1	1			1	1	1				11		
Buckland	326	9	Chapin	Japhet	2	2		1	1	3		1	1				11		
Wilbraham	233	35	Chapin	Jason	1	1	1	2		1	1		1				8		
Springfield	245	30	Chapin	Jehiel	1	1		1		2	1		1				7		
Ludlow	256	43	Chapin	Job	1	1		1		1			1				5		
Springfield	245	32	Chapin	John	1		2		1	1			1				6		
Monson	265	41	Chapin	Jonathan			2		1		1	1		1			6		
Springfield	246	17	Chapin	Joseph				1						1			2		
Springfield	240	39	Chapin	Judah		2		1	1	2	1		1				8		
Monson	263	4	Chapin	Justin	1	1		1		3			1				7		
Springfield	246	37	Chapin	Levi	2	1	1		1	1	2	2	1				11		
Springfield	245	44	Chapin	Lucy Wd		1					1		1				3		
Pelham	213	19	Chapin	Luther	2	1	1	1	1	1			2	1			10		
West Springfield	355	56	Chapin	Martin		1		1		2		1					5		
Springfield	245	43	Chapin	Mary Wd		1	1						1	1			4		
West Springfield	356	2	Chapin	Miriam										2			2		
Springfield	245	38	Chapin	Moses	2	1	1			1	1		1				8		
West Springfield	350	11	Chapin	Moses A.	4		1	1			1		1				8		
Orange	41	20	Chapin	Oliver		2	2	2			2	1	1				10		
Ludlow	257	1	Chapin	Olivia				1			2		1				4		
Springfield	241	7	Chapin	Paul	3	2			1	1	1		1				9		
Springfield	247	20	Chapin	Phebe Wd		1								1			2		
Granby	254	14	Chapin	Philander	1			1					1				3		
Springfield	246	4	Chapin	Phins Capt	1	1	1		2	2	1		1				9		

TOWN	PG#	LN#	LAST NAME	FIRST NAME	FREE WHITE MALES under 10	10 to 16	16 to 26	26 to 45	45 and over	FREE WHITE FEMALES under 10	10 to 16	16 to 26	26 to 45	45 and over	TOTAL ALL OTHER	TOTAL SLAVES	TOTALS	DISTRICT/ TOWNSHIP	NOTES
West Springfield	350	3	Chapin	Reuben			1	1					1	1			4		
West Springfield	350	4	Chapin	Reuben Jr	2		1						1				4		
Springfield	246	1	Chapin	Roswell	3			1		1			1				6		
Brimfield	274	8	Chapin	Rufus	2	1	1						1				5		
Wilbraham	232	22	Chapin	Samuel	2	1	2			2		2	1				10		
Springfield	246	8	Chapin	Seth				1						1			2		
Springfield	246	10	Chapin	Seth Junr		2		1					1				4		
Rowe	199	19	Chapin	Shadrach		2		1		1				1			5		
Springfield	246	3	Chapin	Silas Col	3	1	1	1		1	3	1	1				12		
Springfield	246	13	Chapin	Solomon	1	1	1	1				1		1			6		
Springfield	246	19	Chapin	Thomas	2	1				2			1	1			7		
Springfield	245	27	Chapin	Timothy	2	1		1		1			1	1			7		
Springfield	246	7	Chapin	William		1		1				1		1			4		
Springfield	246	14	Chapin	William 2d	1	1	2	1				1	1	1			8		
Heath	195	6	Chapin	Zebinah	3			1					1	1			6		
Wilbraham	236	14	Chapin	Zebulon	1	1			1	2	2			1			8		
Springfield	246	9	Chapin	Zenas	1	1				2			1	1			6		
Springfield	246	11	Chapin	Zerah	2		2	1		3		1		1			10		
Granby	253	45	Chapins	Pliny	1	1	1			2		1	1	1			8		
Longmeadow	92	33	Chapman	Abiel	1		1						1				3		
Montgomery	159	17	Chapman	Abner	2		1					1					4		
Southampton	130	5	Chapman	Asahel	2	1	1	1		2			1				8		
Russell	139	15	Chapman	Benja	2		1					1	1				5		
Westfield	126	3	Chapman	Calib	2	2		1		1	2		1				9		
Northampton	7	3	Chapman	Charles	1	2	1	1		2		3	1				11		
Easthampton	136	12	Chapman	David	2		1	1		2	2		1				9		
Westhampton	15	12	Chapman	David		1	1		1	1			2	1			7		
Montgomery	161	6	Chapman	Isaac		3		1				1		1			6		
Montgomery	161	16	Chapman	Isaac	2		1			2		1					6		
Montague	45	18	Chapman	James	2		1			3		1	1				8		
Shelburne	320	10	Chapman	John	2	1			1	3	1	1	1				10		
Deerfield	52	16	Chapman	Jonathan		1	2		1	1	1	2		1			9		
Russell	139	1	Chapman	Levi	2			1		2			1				6		
Easthampton	134	15	Chapman	Moses	3	1		1		1	1	1					9		
Longmeadow	92	10	Chapman	Nathl Captn	2		1	1		2	1		1				8		
Southampton	132	10	Chapman	Paul		1	1					1					3		
Russell	139	2	Chapman	Saml			1			1			1				3		
Greenfield	72	21	Chapman	Thoma	1	1				1		1	1				6		
Deerfield	52	17	Chapman	William	1		1					1					3		
Belchertown	204	25	Chapman	Wm Lt	2	2	1	1					1				7		
Wilbraham	236	24	Chappel	Gordon			1			1			1				3		
Granville West Soc	168	13	Chappel	William	2		1			1			1				5		
Brimfield	271	19	Charles	Aaron Capt	1		1	1				1		1			5		
Brimfield	274	29	Charles	Aaron Jr		1	1	1				1		1			5		
Brimfield	273	21	Charles	Abraham		1	1	1				1					4		
Brimfield	271	20	Charles	Arunah			1				1		1				3		
Springfield	247	2	Charles	George		3	1						1				5		
Brimfield	271	18	Charles	Levi		1	1						1				3		
Brimfield	273	29	Charles	Nathanl	1	1		1		2			1				6		
Brimfield	272	28	Charles	Nehemiah		1	1			1	1	1					6		
Brimfield	271	40	Charles	Simeon	1		1	1			2	1					7		
Wilbraham	234	13	Charles	Solomon				1					1				2		
Brimfield	269	2	Charles	Thomas		1				1	1	1					5		
Orange	41	31	Chase	Aaron	2		1			2	1						6		
Pelham	217	16	Chase	Abial	3	1		1		1	1			1			8		
Longmeadow	93	35	Chase	Berry		1	1	1			1			1			5		
Longmeadow	93	36	Chase	Berry Junr	5			1					1				7		
Chester	147	22	Chase	Christopher	3		1				1		1				6		
New Salem	97	33	Chase	David	1		1			2			1				5		
Warwick	36	39	Chase	John	1		1						1				3		
Wendell	105	17	Chase	John	1			1		1	1						4		
Gill	85	8	Chase	Pierce		1						1		1			3		
Amherst	294	32	Chase	Ral*			1			1		1			1		4		
New Salem	97	32	Chase	Simon	2	3		1		1	1	1					9		
Warwick	37	7	Chase	Thomas	1		1	1			1	1	1	2			8		
Belchertown	204	29	Chase	Timothy	2	1		1		3	1		1				9		
Ludlow	256	3	Chasun	Henry M.	1	1		1		2	1		1	1			8		
Montgomery	161	25	Chauncy	Russel		1											1		
Orange	41	22	Cheney	David	2	1	1			1			1				7		
Orange	41	24	Cheney	Ebenezer	3	1	1	1		1	1	1	1				10		
Heath	195	2	Cheney	Hezekiah	2		1					1					4		
Deerfield	52	24	Cheney	Jedediah		1	1					1					4		
Rowe	199	6	Cheney	John	1		1			1		1					4		
Orange	41	19	Cheney	Levi	2	2		1		1		2		1			9		
Orange	41	21	Cheney	Moses	3		1			3	1		1				9		
Orange	41	26	Cheney	Nathan	2		1			3			1				7		
Orange	41	18	Cheney	Nathaniel	2	1	1			1			1				6		
Rowe	199	8	Cheney	Thomas	2		1					1					4		
Ludlow	256	2	Chesire	Mary Wid									1	3			4		
Deerfield	51	45	Chesson	Joseph		1	1	1			1		1				5		

TOWN	PG#	LN#	HEADS OF HOUSEHOLD		FREE WHITE MALES					FREE WHITE FEMALES					TOTAL ALL OTHER	TOTAL SLAVES	TOTALS	DISTRICT/ TOWNSHIP	NOTES
			LAST NAME	FIRST NAME	under 10	10 to 16	16 to 26	26 to 45	45 and over	under 10	10 to 16	16 to 26	26 to 45	45 and over					
Deerfield	52	9	Child	Amzi	1	1	4	1	1	1	1	1		1			12		
Shelburne	320	18	Child	Asa		1	1		1	1				2			6		
Shelburne	320	17	Child	Ebenz	1	2	1	1			1	2	1				9		
Deerfield	52	6	Child	Noah Wright	2			1			2		1				6		
Shelburne	320	23	Child	Reuben	3	1		1			1		1				7		
Deerfield	52	7	Child	Samuel	1	2	1	1	1		1	3		2			12		
Deerfield	52	8	Child	Samuel 2d	1	1	2		1	1	2	1		1			10		
Conway	57	37	Childs	David	2	1	3	1			2		1				10		
New Salem	97	11	Childs	David			1	1		3	2		1	1			9		
Worthington	300	15	Childs	Ebenezer	1		4		1	2		1		1			10		
New Salem	97	19	Childs	Joseph	1		1		1	2	2	2	1				10		
Conway	57	47	Childs	Libbeus		1	1		1	2	2	1		1			9		
Buckland	326	10	Chilson	Joseph				1	1	1				1			4		
Westhampton	17	33	Chilson	Joseph	3		1		1	1	1		1				8		
Westhampton	17	29	Chilson	Joseph Jun			1			1		1					3		
Monson	267	19	Chld	Erastus	1			1					1				3		
Heath	195	4	Christee	William	1		1		1	3	1		1				8		
Granville East Soc	529	35	Church	Abijah		1			2			2		2			7		
Middlefield	158	15	Church	Ambross		1				1		1					3		
Ashfield	339	1	Church	Caleb	1	1		1				1		1			5		
Ashfield	339	12	Church	Caleb Jr			1					1					2		
Granby	255	5	Church	David Dr		2	1	1		1				1			6		
Amherst	292	39	Church	Giles	3		2	1		1	1	1	1				10		
Middlefield	158	16	Church	Green			1			2							3		
Granville East Soc	529	36	Church	Isaac	1		1			1			1				4		
Belchertown	204	3	Church	John	2		1			2			1				6		
South Hadley	250	1	Church	John			1						1				2		
Springfield	242	21	Church	Jonathan	2		1			1	1		1				6		
Amherst	292	13	Church	Joseph			1						1				2		
Amherst	292	12	Church	Joseph Junr	3	2		1		1	1		1	1			10		
South Hadley	249	41	Church	Josiah	1	1			1	3	1			1			8		
Springfield	239	11	Church	Moses			1		1			1	1	1			5		
South Hadley	250	2	Church	Pliny			1				1	1		1			4		
Chester	146	7	Church	Richard	3		1			3			1				8		
Sunderland	283	3	Church	Samuel				1		2			1				4		
Ashfield	339	14	Church	Seth		1						1					2		
Middlefield	156	7	Church	Uriah		2		1		1		1	1				6		
Middlefield	158	13	Church	William	1	1	1	1				2		1			7		
South Hadley	249	9	Church	Zenas			1			1		1		1			4		
Middlefield	157	30	Churchill	Elijah	2	1		1		1	1		1				7		
Westhampton	18	33	Claflin	Levi	3		1			1			1				6		
Easthampton	134	17	Clap	Aaron	2	2	1		1	2	1	1		1			11		
Easthampton	134	12	Clap	Aaron Junr			1			1			1				3		
Montgomery	159	14	Clap	Abigail Wid			1	1			2	1	1	1			7		
Middlefield	157	2	Clap	Abner			1		1	2	2		1				7		
Middlefield	157	3	Clap	Abner Junr			1			1			1				3		
Easthampton	134	21	Clap	Adolphus	1		1			1			1				4		
Chesterfield	20	3	Clap	Amasa	1	2	2		1			1		2			9		
Northampton	3	9	Clap	Asahel		2	2		1	1			1				7		
Northampton	3	16	Clap	Azariah	3			1		1		1	1				7		
Easthampton	134	19	Clap	Benjamin	2	1	1		1	1	1	2		1			10		
Northampton	7	4	Clap	Bohan	2		1	2		2			2				9		
Greenfield	72	22	Clap	Caleb			1	1		3			2				7		
Southampton	131	20	Clap	Chester			1					1					2		
Montgomery	159	15	Clap	Cyrus		1					1						2		
Easthampton	136	14	Clap	Devan			1			2			1				4		
Westhampton	17	16	Clap	Diademi	3					1		1					5		
Northampton	3	25	Clap	Ebenezer	1	1	1						1				4		
Southampton	131	30	Clap	Eli	2	1			1	1	1	1	1				8		
Southampton	131	19	Clap	Elijah		1		1					1	1			4		
Southampton	131	13	Clap	Elijah Junr		2		1		2			1				6		
Southampton	131	16	Clap	Elisha	3	1							1				6		
Westhampton	17	8	Clap	Elisha B			2							1			3		
Southampton	131	17	Clap	Elizabeth Wd			1							1			2		
Westfield	120	12	Clap	Ezra Capt	4	1				1	1	1	1				9		
Northampton	2	10	Clap	George				1		3			1				5		
Easthampton	134	31	Clap	Hophni				1		1							3		
Easthampton	136	10	Clap	Isaac			1					1					2		
Southampton	132	17	Clap	Joel	1	1	1		1		1	3		1			9		
Southampton	132	18	Clap	Joel Junr			1					1					2		
Easthampton	136	27	Clap	John	2	1	1		1	1	1		1				8		
Northampton	3	24	Clap	John	1	1	1	3		1	1	1	1				10		
Easthampton	136	13	Clap	Jona	1	1	1		1	1	1		1				7		
Easthampton	134	29	Clap	Joseph	2			1		3	1		1		1		9		
Easthampton	134	18	Clap	Levi	1		2	1		3	2		1				10		
Easthampton	136	11	Clap	Luther		1	1	1		1		1	1	1			7		
Southampton	131	21	Clap	Luther	1			1		3			1				6		
Southampton	131	22	Clap	Moses			3	1		1	1		1				7		
Easthampton	136	30	Clap	Oliver	1			1		3			1				6		
Westhampton	17	24	Clap	Oliver	1	1			1		1		1				5		

TOWN	PG#	LN#	LAST NAME	FIRST NAME	FREE WHITE MALES <10	10-16	16-26	26-45	45+	FREE WHITE FEMALES <10	10-16	16-26	26-45	45+	TOTAL ALL OTHER	TOTAL SLAVES	TOTALS	DISTRICT/ TOWNSHIP	NOTES
Middlefield	157	19	Clap	Orriss	2			1		2		1					6		
Chesterfield	20	4	Clap	Paul		1				2	1	1					5		
Southampton	130	3	Clap	Peres	1	1	1		1	4	1	1	1				11		
Montgomery	159	11	Clap	Phineas				1						1			2		
Montgomery	159	12	Clap	Phineas Junr	2			1		1			1				5		
Westfield	125	8	Clap	Pliny	1	1			1	2	1			1			7		
Montgomery	159	13	Clap	Robertson			1				1						2		
Southampton	133	11	Clap	Roger	2	1		1		2	1		1				8		
Southampton	131	14	Clap	Samll			1	1						1			4		
Southampton	131	15	Clap	Samll Jun	1			1		1			1				4		
Northampton	7	29	Clap	Sarah	1	1				1	1		1	1			6		
Northampton	3	21	Clap	Seth				1		1	2		1				5		
Northampton	3	22	Clap	Seth Junr	1			1		1		1					4		
Southampton	131	6	Clap	Silas	3	1		1		1	1		1				8		
Northampton	4	6	Clap	Simeon				1		1			1				3		
Northampton	4	7	Clap	Simeon Jun	1			1		1		1	1				5		
Westhampton	17	25	Clap	Sylvanus	2			1					1				4		
Easthampton	134	32	Clap	Thadeus	3		1	1		2		1	1				9		
Southampton	133	21	Clap	Thadeus	1							1					2		
Southampton	131	7	Clap	Timothy	1	1				1	1		2	1			8		
Northampton	4	8	Clap	Warham	1			1		2			1				5		
Conway	57	30	Clapp	Cephas	1		1	1		1	1	1	1				7		
Worthington	297	9	Clapp	Charles	1	1		1		1			1				5		
Montague	45	24	Clapp	Daniel		1	1		1	2	1	2		1	1		10		
Montague	45	22	Clapp	Elihu	2		1	1		1			1				6		
Deerfield	52	15	Clapp	Elisha	1	1	1	1		3			1				8		
Deerfield	52	13	Clapp	Erastus	2	1		1			1		1				6		
Deerfield	52	14	Clapp	John				1					1				2		
Deerfield	52	12	Clapp	John Junr	5	2		1		2	1		1				12		
Montague	45	23	Clapp	Joseph	2		3	1		1		1	1	1			10		
Amherst	292	2	Clapp	Oliver		1		1	1					1			4		
Springfield	242	7	Clapp	Parson	1	1	1	1		1		2					7		
Montague	45	21	Clapp	Solomon		2		1				1	1				5		
Chester	146	19	Claps	Eliakim Ens	2			1		2	1		1		1		8		
Northampton	11	13	Clark	Aaron	2	1	1		1	1	1		1				8		
Plainfield	306	17	Clark	Abm	3	1		1		1	1	2	1				10		
Westhampton	16	35	Clark	Abner				1			1		1				3		
New Salem	98	4	Clark	Alden	2			1		2			1				6		
Leyden	81	19	Clark	Alexander	1			1		1			1				4		
Shelburne	320	12	Clark	Alexander	1		1	1	1				2	1			7		
Leyden	81	23	Clark	Alpheus	1	1	1				1						4		
Ashfield	339	7	Clark	Alvin	2	1							1				5		
Southampton	132	24	Clark	Amasa	4			1		1			1				7		
Granville East Soc	529	24	Clark	Amos	1	1	1		1	2	1		1	1			9		
South Hadley	251	4	Clark	Asa	2		1	1					1	2			7		
Easthampton	135	5	Clark	Asahel	1		2		1	1		1	1	1			8		
Springfield	242	25	Clark	Asahel	1	1		1		1			1	1			6		
Montague	45	28	Clark	Barnham	1			1		1			1				4		
Northampton	8	25	Clark	Benjamin	1			1		2	1		1				6		
Belchertown	204	31	Clark	Caleb			1							3			4		
Northampton	10	13	Clark	Calvin	2		1	1		1			1				6		
Colrain	184	5	Clark	Daniel	2	2		2	1		1	2	1	1			12		
Montgomery	160	32	Clark	Daniel	3	1		1		2		1	1				9		
Northampton	8	37	Clark	Daniel				1						1			2		
Colrain	184	16	Clark	David	2			1					1				4		
Granville East Soc	527	12	Clark	David	1			1		4	2	1	1				10		
Leyden	81	18	Clark	David				1					1				2		
Northampton	3	11	Clark	David				1					1				2		
Northampton	3	12	Clark	David Jun	2			1		2			1				6		
Leyden	81	22	Clark	Davis	1	1		1			1		1				5		
Colrain	184	14	Clark	Dolleway				2									2		
Easthampton	135	9	Clark	Elam	2		1	1	3	2		1					10		
Belchertown	204	30	Clark	Eleazr Capt	1	2	2				1	1	1				9		
Northampton	8	24	Clark	Eli	4		1	1	1			1	1				9		
Wilbraham	235	21	Clark	Eli			1			4	1						6		
Easthampton	135	3	Clark	Eliakim	3			1		3			1				8		
Wendell	105	15	Clark	Elijah	1		1	1		2	1		1				7		
Brimfield	272	41	Clark	Eliphalet	2	2		1		2			1				8		
Amherst	290	23	Clark	Elisha			1			2			1				4		
Conway	57	44	Clark	Elisha		1		1	1		1	1		1			6		
Leyden	81	28	Clark	Elisha	1		2	1		1	1	1					7		
New Salem	98	3	Clark	Elisha	1			1					1				3		
Southampton	132	15	Clark	Elisha	1			1		1	1		1				5		
Conway	57	46	Clark	Elisha Junr		1		1		1			1				4		
Conway	57	36	Clark	Elizabeth		1	2					2		1			6		
Montgomery	160	23	Clark	Elizabeth Widw			1							1			2		
Easthampton	135	4	Clark	Elizer	2	1	2	1		2			2				10		
Greenfield	72	26	Clark	Enoch	1			1					1				4		
Belchertown	208	24	Clark	Enos		2	1	1	1	1		1		1			8		
Wilbraham	238	13	Clark	Enos		1	2										3		

TOWN	PG#	LN#	LAST NAME	FIRST NAME	FREE WHITE MALES under 10	10 to 16	16 to 26	26 to 45	45 and over	FREE WHITE FEMALES under 10	10 to 16	16 to 26	26 to 45	45 and over	TOTAL ALL OTHER	TOTAL SLAVES	TOTALS	DISTRICT/ TOWNSHIP	NOTES
Russell	139	26	Clark	Ephraim					1			1	3	1			6		
Northampton	8	22	Clark	Erastus		3	3	1	2	1		2					12		
Williamsburg	447	1	Clark	Ezra	1			1		1				1			4		
Westhampton	17	12	Clark	Gideon				1					2	1			4		
Westhampton	17	14	Clark	Gideon Jun		1	1	1				1	4	1			9		
Westhampton	16	22	Clark	Giles	2			1		2			1	1			7		
Granville East Soc	527	28	Clark	Hannah	2	1		1	1	2			1				8		
Westhampton	17	13	Clark	Henaz	2			1					3	1			7		
Montague	45	20	Clark	Hezekiah			2		1	1			1	1			6		
Colrain	184	2	Clark	Ichabod	2			1		2			1				6		
Granville East Soc	529	39	Clark	Ichabod				1		2			1				4		
Amherst	294	29	Clark	Irena	3					1		1		1			6		
Northampton	8	19	Clark	Isaac	3	2		1				1	1	1			9		
Granby	253	5	Clark	Israel	2	1	1	1				1	1	1			8		
Northampton	7	28	Clark	Israel	3			1		1				1			6		
Plainfield	306	18	Clark	Jacob	1	1		1		2	2	2	1				10		
Westhampton	15	11	Clark	Jacob	2	1	1			1			1				7		
Buckland	326	22	Clark	James	1			1				3		1			6		
Middlefield	158	3	Clark	James		2	1						1	1			6		
Northampton	8	40	Clark	Jared				1					3	1			5		
Deerfield	52	10	Clark	Jedediah	1	1		1				2	2	1			8		
Easthampton	135	6	Clark	Job	1	1	1	1				1	1	1			7		
Northampton	7	31	Clark	Job	1		1	1				3	2	1			9		
Granville East Soc	529	14	Clark	Joel	1			1				3	1				6		
Northampton	3	7	Clark	Joel			2	1					1	2			6		
Buckland	326	17	Clark	John			1										1		
Greenfield	72	25	Clark	John			1							1			2		
New Salem	97	29	Clark	John	1		2					1	1	1			7		
New Salem	97	30	Clark	John 2d		1		1						1			3		
Colrain	184	1	Clark	John Jr	2		1	1						1			5		
Chester	147	21	Clark	John Scott	2			1		1		1		1			6		
Northampton	3	19	Clark	Jonah				1					1				2		
Northampton	7	32	Clark	Jonas		2		1		1	1			1			6		
Warwick	36	38	Clark	Jonas	1	1	1			1		2	1				8		
Granville West Soc	169	12	Clark	Jonathan	2			1		3		2	2	1			11		
Westhampton	17	3	Clark	Jonathan				1						1			2		
Westhampton	17	4	Clark	Jonathan Jr	3			1					1				5		
Conway	57	24	Clark	Joseph		1				1			1				3		
Plainfield	306	23	Clark	Joseph	2			1		1		2	1				8		
Granby	252	35	Clark	Joshua		1		1		1			1	1			5		
Granby	253	4	Clark	Jotham	1			1		1	1			1			5		
Hawley	332	20	Clark	Jotham	1			1					1	1			4		
Amherst	289	3	Clark	Judah			1						1	1			3		
Conway	57	45	Clark	Judah	3	1		1				1		1			7		
Southampton	130	13	Clark	Justes	2		1	1		2		1	1				9		
Sunderland	283	28	Clark	Justus	3			1						1			5		
Montague	45	31	Clark	Lemuel	3	1		1		1				1			7		
Northampton	3	20	Clark	Lemuel	4		1	1		1				1			8		
Sunderland	283	10	Clark	Lemuel	3	1		1				1	1	1			9		
Granville East Soc	533	1	Clark	Lot	4			1		1			1	1			8		
Leverett	114	6	Clark	Luther	1			1		1			1				4		
Northampton	8	23	Clark	Luther	2	1	1	1				1	2				8		
Northampton	7	18	Clark	Lyman	1	1		1	1	1			2	1			9		
Northampton	7	33	Clark	Martha									2				2		
Westhampton	15	5	Clark	Martin	1	1	1		1	1		2		1			9		
Leyden	81	26	Clark	Matthew	2	2	1					1	1				7		
Westhampton	18	11	Clark	Matthew	2	2	1			1			1				7		
Northampton	8	39	Clark	Medad				1		1			1				3		
Deerfield	52	25	Clark	Merian									2	2			4		
Hawley	332	21	Clark	Moses	1			1		3	1	1					7		
Holland	280	4	Clark	Moses	3			1		1	3	1					9		
Amherst	290	34	Clark	Nathan	2			1					1				4		
Westhampton	18	3	Clark	Nathan		3	2	1					1	1			8		
Granville East Soc	529	11	Clark	Nathaniel	1			1		2			1				5		
New Salem	97	34	Clark	Nathaniel	1			1		3			1				6		
Northampton	4	3	Clark	Nathaniel		2	2	1				1					6		
Shutesbury	109	11	Clark	Nathaniel		3	1	1				1		1			7		
Colrain	184	9	Clark	Noah	1	1	1		1	1	1	1	1	1			9		
Granby	252	32	Clark	Noah	1	1		1		1		1		1			6		
Southampton	128	13	Clark	Noah	2	2		1		1			1				8		
Easthampton	135	12	Clark	Obediah		1		1						1			3		
Easthampton	136	4	Clark	Oliver		2	3	1		4		1	1				12		
Shelburne	320	11	Clark	Oliver	2	1		1		1				1			6		
Southampton	132	25	Clark	Oliver				1				1	2	2			6		
Southampton	132	26	Clark	Oliver Junr	2			1		2			1				6		
Chester	145	39	Clark	Orrin	2			1					1				4		
Westhampton	16	32	Clark	Paul	2	2			1	2		1	1				9		
New Salem	97	27	Clark	Perez	1		1	1					1	2			6		
New Salem	98	2	Clark	Perez Junr	1			1				1	1				4		

TOWN	PG#	LN#	LAST NAME	FIRST NAME	FREE WHITE MALES					FREE WHITE FEMALES					TOTAL ALL OTHER	TOTAL SLAVES	TOTALS	DISTRICT/ TOWNSHIP	NOTES
					under 10	10 to 16	16 to 26	26 to 45	45 and over	under 10	10 to 16	16 to 26	26 to 45	45 and over					
Whately	66	29	Clark	Peter	1			1	4				1				7		
Northampton	6	35	Clark	Pharez		2	1	1	1	3			1				9		
Easthampton	135	22	Clark	Philip				1						1			2		
Easthampton	135	32	Clark	Phineas	1	1			4	2	1	1					11		
Hawley	332	18	Clark	Phinehas	3			1					1				5		
Belchertown	208	27	Clark	Phinehas B.				1		1	1			1			4		
Rowe	199	7	Clark	Reuben		1		1		1	1		1				5		
Southwick	358	12	Clark	Reuben		1	2		1			2	1				7		
Westhampton	16	20	Clark	Reuben	2	1		1		1		1	1				7		
Buckland	326	21	Clark	Robert		1		1				1		1			4		
Buckland	326	25	Clark	Robert Jr	2	1						1					4		
Greenwich	219	6	Clark	Rolland Deac	3	1	1		1	2	1		1				10		
Westfield	125	16	Clark	Roswel	2	1		1		1		1		1			7		
Granville Mid Soc.	165	22	Clark	Ruth									1				1		
Granville East Soc	531	3	Clark	Samuel	3	1	3	1		2	1		1				12		
Granville East Soc	531	10	Clark	Samuel	2		1	1		3			1				8		
Middlefield	156	14	Clark	Samuel		2	2		1	1	1	1		1			9		
New Salem	97	31	Clark	Samuel				1									1		
Granby	253	13	Clark	Samuel Capt	1		2		2		2			1			8		
Southampton	132	15	Clark	Selah Junr				1		1			1	1			4		
Southampton	132	23	Clark	Selah Junr				1						2			3		
Hadley	285	5	Clark	Seth				1						1			2		
Westhampton	17	11	Clark	Seth	1		1	1		3	2	2	1				11		
Wilbraham	235	22	Clark	Seth				1									1		
Ashfield	338	28	Clark	Silas	1		3	1		2		1	1				9		
Middlefield	156	19	Clark	Silas			1			1	1		1				4		
Northampton	8	14	Clark	Silas				1	1		3	1	1				7		
Amherst	289	2	Clark	Simeon	1	1		1	1	1			3	1			9		
Amherst	294	28	Clark	Simeon Jun		1		1		1	2			1			6		
Chester	150	12	Clark	Simon		1		1				1					3		
Northampton	8	36	Clark	Solomon		2	1		1	1	1	2	1	1			10		
Northampton	3	36	Clark	Stephen		1	1		1	1		1		2			7		
Sunderland	283	27	Clark	Sylvanus	1	1		1			1		1				5		
Easthampton	135	13	Clark	Thadeus	2		1						1				4		
New Salem	97	37	Clark	Thomas	2		1			2	1	1					7		
Russell	139	23	Clark	Thomas	2		1			2		1					6		
Sunderland	282	19	Clark	Thomas			1	1		1		1	1	1			6		
Southampton	130	4	Clark	Timothy			1	1		2			1	1			6		
Southampton	130	6	Clark	Timothy Junr	1		1		1		1	1		1			6		
Westhampton	18	2	Clark	Titus			2	1				2					5		
Easthampton	135	23	Clark	Uriel	1	2		1		2			1				7		
Colrain	184	10	Clark	William		2	1	1		1		1	1				7		
Deerfield	52	11	Clark	William	1			1		1				1			4		
Greenfield	72	27	Clark	William	2	1	1	1		1	2	1	1				10		
Leyden	81	33	Clark	William		1	1		1	1	2	2		1			9		
Northampton	9	1	Clark	William Jr	2	1	1	1	1	2	1		3				12		
Belchertown	208	23	Clark	Wm				1			1			1			3		
Wilbraham	235		Clark	Seth Junr	3		2			1	1		1				8		
Hatfield	14	3	Clarke	John				1		1		2		2			6		
Northampton	6	21	Clarke	Joseph	2			1		1	1	1	1				7		
Wilbraham	232	12	Clarke	Joseph		1		1				1		1			4		
Northampton	5	4	Clarke	Samuel			1	2	1		2	2	1	1			10		
Northampton	4	36	Clarke	Samuel Jr	2	4	1	1				1	1				10		
Pelham	213	20	Clarkshun	Adam		1	1			1	1		1				5		
Pelham	217	23	Clarkshun	Mathew	2	1	1	1	1	1	1	4		1			13		
Conway	57	34	Clary	Abel	2	1		1		1	1		1				7		
Leverett	114	12	Clary	David			1			1			1				3		
Deerfield	52	19	Clary	Elihu	1							1	1				4		
Conway	57	27	Clary	Elijah			2		1	1	1		1				6		
Deerfield	52	18	Clary	Elijah	1			1		2	1		1				6		
Leverett	114	3	Clary	Elisha				1			2			1			4		
Conway	57	28	Clary	Joseph	1	1	1			1	1	1					8		
Leverett	114	2	Clary	Phinehas	1	1		1			2		1				6		
Greenfield	72	20	Clay	Daniel	3	1		1			1		1				7		
Williamsburg	447	2	Clayhorn	James	3	1			1	3	2	1	1				12		
Williamsburg	448	23	Cleaveland	Amasa	1	1	1	1	1	2		1	1				9		
Wilbraham	235	23	Cleaveland	Elisha	2	1		1		3	1	1	1				10		
Belchertown	208	25	Cleaveland	Freeman	2		1			1	1	1					6		
Palmer	258	21	Cleaveland	Hopestill			1						1				2		
Belchertown	208	28	Cleaveland	Jesse		1	1					1					3		
Williamsburg	448	24	Cleaveland	Nehemiah	1	1		1		5	3	1	1	1			14		
Williamsburg	448	22	Cleaveland	Roswell	1			1		3		2	1				8		
Chesterfield	21	8	Cleaveland	Samuel	3			1		2		2	1				9		
Palmer	259	9	Cleaveland	Samuel	1		1					1					3		
Worthington	298	29	Cleavland	Newcom	1		2	1			1		1	1			8		
Cummington	302	23	Clemons	John	2	2	1		1		1			1			8		
Orange	41	30	Cleveland	David		1				1	1						3		
Hawley	332	31	Cleveland	John	4		1			1		1					7		
Belchertown	211	7	Clifford	Samuel	1	1		1		3	2		1				9		
Belchertown	204	27	Clough	Amasa	3	1	1	1	1	1	1	2	1	1			13		

TOWN	PG#	LN#	LAST NAME	FIRST NAME	FREE WHITE MALES					FREE WHITE FEMALES					TOTAL ALL OTHER	TOTAL SLAVES	TOTALS	DISTRICT/ TOWNSHIP	NOTES
					under 10	10 to 16	16 to 26	26 to 45	45 and over	under 10	10 to 16	16 to 26	26 to 45	45 and over					
Belchertown	204	28	Clough	Benja		2		1			2		1				6		
Ashfield	339	13	Clough	Calvin	2	1	1	1		1		1	1				8		
Ludlow	258	4	Clough	Dan	1		1					1					3		
Ludlow	258	3	Clough	Jonathan				1					1				2		
Springfield	243	3	Clough	Joseph		2		1					1				4		
Ludlow	258	7	Clough	Timothy		1		1		3			1				6		
West Springfield	356	3	Clough	Uriah	2	3		1	1	2		1	1				11		
Middlefield	156	13	Coates	John		1	1	1	1			2	1	1			8		
Northampton	6	27	Coates	Stephen				1	1				1				3		
Middlefield	159	2	Coates	Theodore				1		2		1					4		
Westhampton	17	2	Coats	Reuben	1	2			1	1		1		1			7		
Cummington	302	24	Cobb	Amos		1		1	1	2		1	1				7		
Conway	57	26	Cobb	Daniel	1			1		1	1	1					5		
Charlemont	191	1	Cobb	Elisha			1		1		1			1			4		
Conway	57	35	Cobb	George			1			1	2	1		1			6		
Orange	41	27	Cobb	Isiah	2	1	4		1	1	1			1			11		
Chester	143	20	Cobb	John			1			1			1				3		
Deerfield	52	1	Cobb	Jonathan			2	1					1		1		5		
Hawley	332	26	Cobb	Jonathan	3	2	1		1	1	2		1				11		
Deerfield	52	2	Cobb	Joseph				1		3			1				5		
Buckland	326	27	Cobb	Josiah Junr	2			1		2		1					6		
Charlemont	191	2	Cobb	Nathanael			1			1		1					3		
Ashfield	339	15	Cobb	Priscilla		1	1				1			1			4		
Warwick	37	6	Cobb	Richard	2	1			1	2	1	1		1			9		
Conway	57	25	Cobb	Sylvanus	2	1	1		1		1	2		1			9		
Warwick	37	3	Cobb	William		1			1					1			3		
Wilbraham	233	1	Cobb	William		1			1	4	1		1				8		
Warwick	37	2	Cobb	William Junr	1		1	1		1		2					6		
Monson	267	22	Coburn	David	1			1			2	1	1				6		
Rowe	199	5	Coburn	Jedediah			1			3			1				5		
Blanford	179	2	Cochran	Cornelus		1		1						1			3		
Blanford	176	37	Cochran	John	1		2		1	2	2	4		1			13		
South Brimfield	275	7	Coddington	Elijah Rev.				1			1		1				3		
Granville Mid Soc.	167	1	Coe	Anon	3	1		1		3		1					9		
Granville Mid Soc.	167	30	Coe	Benjamin		1		1	1	1	1		1				5		
Granville Mid Soc.	167	7	Coe	David	3	1		1		2			1				8		
Granville Mid Soc.	167	4	Coe	Ephraim	2			1		2		1	1				7		
Blanford	181	9	Coe	Gad	3	1		1		1			1				7		
Granville Mid Soc.	166	24	Coe	Israel	2	1	1		1	1	1		1	1			9		
Granville East Soc	529	16	Coe	James	2			1				1		1			5		
Granville Mid Soc.	167	15	Coe	John	1			1		1		1	1				5		
Granville Mid Soc.	167	2	Coe	Joseph		1		1				2		1			5		
Granville Mid Soc.	167	29	Coe	Mary									1				1		
Granville East Soc	529	17	Coe	Rachel		1						2					3		
Granville Mid Soc.	167	6	Coe	Seth	3			1		2	2		1				9		
Williamsburg	447	9	Coffin	Matthew		1		1				1					3		
Chesterfield	19	9	Cogswell	Ezra				1			2		1				4		
Chesterfield	19	8	Cogswell	Hezekiah	2			1		2			1				6		
Russell	137	7	Cohrin	Abner	2		1		1	2	1		1				8		
Greenwich	219	10	Colburn	Jabez	1			1	1	1			1				5		
Longmeadow	93	4	Colburn	John	1			1		1		1					4		
Hawley	332	25	Colburn	Nathan	2			1		2			1	1			7		
West Springfield	350	14	Colburn	Nathaniel		1	1		1			1		1			5		
Chesterfield	21	24	Cole	Amariah		1	3	1	1	3	2	1	1				13		
Chesterfield	21	26	Cole	Barnabas	3	2		1		3		2	1				12		
Chesterfield	21	25	Cole	Consider	2	2		1		1		1	1				8		
Northampton	10	26	Cole	Ebenezer				1						1			2		
Worthington	298	34	Cole	Elijah	3			1		1	4		1				10		
Hatfield	13	1	Cole	Elizabeth		1	2					2		1			6		
Conway	57	31	Cole	Marcus	1			1		1	1	1					5		
Cummington	305	22	Cole	Noah	1			1				1	1				4		
Williamsburg	447	4	Cole	Samuel	2	1	1	1		3			1				9		
Northampton	10	27	Cole	Thomas	1			1		2		1					5		
Greenfield	72	23	Coleman	Elijah		1	1	1				1		1			5		
Chesterfield	22	25	Coleman	Nathaniel	3	1	2	1		1	2		1				11		
Whately	66	27	Coleman	Nathaniel				1		1	2		1				4		
Hatfield	14	14	Coleman	Niles	1	1		1					1				3		
Hatfield	14	13	Coleman	Samuel	2		1			1		1					5		
Amherst	289	7	Coleman	Seth		2		1		1	1		1		1		7		
Amherst	293	7	Coleman	Seth Junr	1			1		1		1					4		
Middlefield	155	17	Coleman	William Doct	2	1	1	1					1				7		
Hatfield	13	28	Colkins	William	1			1		2			1				5		
Orange	41	25	Collar	Artemas	2			1		1		1					5		
Northfield	28	3	Collar	Hezekiah	3			1		2			1				7		
Orange	41	23	Collar	Samuel	1	1	1	1		2	1		1				8		
Northfield	28	4	Collar	Uriah		1			1	1			1				6		
Springfield	242	12	Collins	Ariel				1		1		2	1	1			6		
Chester	145	20	Collins	Calvin	4	1		1				1					7		
Granville East Soc	527	5	Collins	Claudius L		1	1			4			1				7		
Brimfield	271	1	Collins	Daniel	3	1		1		1			1				7		

TOWN	PG#	LN#	LAST NAME	FIRST NAME	FREE WHITE MALES					FREE WHITE FEMALES					TOTAL ALL OTHER	TOTAL SLAVES	TOTALS	DISTRICT/ TOWNSHIP	NOTES
					under 10	10 to 16	16 to 26	26 to 45	45 and over	under 10	10 to 16	16 to 26	26 to 45	45 and over					
Worthington	298	5	Collins	Daniel	2	1		1		2		1	1				8		
Middlefield	157	28	Collins	Ebenezer	3			1		1	1			1			7		
South Hadley	249	29	Collins	James		1	2	1		1				1			6		
Springfield	242	32	Collins	John		1				1		1					3		
Ashfield	339	3	Collins	Joseph	1		2	1				1					5		
Brimfield	269	3	Collins	Lewis		1		1					1	1			4		
Chester	149	24	Collins	Nathaniel	2	1		1		3			1				8		
Worthington	301	20	Collins	Nathaniel				1			1			1			3		
Springfield	242	14	Collins	Oliver	2		1	1		2			1				7		
Conway	57	42	Collins	Richard	3		3	1		1				1			9		
Conway	57	43	Collins	Richard Junr	1			1		4			1				7		
Longmeadow	94	29	Collins	Stephen			1	1						1			3		
Greenwich	219	12	Collins	Treat	1	2		1		1	1			1			7		
Chester	145	5	Collins	William	1	1	1	1		2		1	1				8		
Blanford	175	12	Collister	John	1	1		1		2	1	1	1				8		
Northampton	6	24	Collson	William						1		1	1				3		
Buckland	326	11	Colman	Gershom		1	1	1						1			4		
Heath	195	7	Colman	Job		2	1	1				1					6		
Southampton	133	12	Colman	Lemuel	2	1	4	1		1	1	1	1	1			13		
Buckland	326	12	Colman	Nathl		1		1			1		2				5		
Southampton	130	27	Colman	Saml		1	1	1		1		1	1				6		
Hawley	332	29	Colson	Christopher		1		1		2			1				5		
Plainfield	306	22	Colson	Ebenezer				1						1			2		
Plainfield	306	21	Colson	Ebenz Jr	3	1	1	1		2	1	1	1				11		
Plainfield	306	24	Colson	John	1			1		2			1				5		
Plainfield	306	25	Colson	Mary		1						1		1			3		
Ludlow	255	8	Colton	Aaron	1	2	2	1		2		1	1	1			11		
Longmeadow	93	15	Colton	Alpheus	1	1	5	1		2		1	1				12		
Springfield	242	41	Colton	Andrew				1						1			2		
Longmeadow	93	39	Colton	Asa	1		1	1		3			1	2			9		
Longmeadow	94	26	Colton	Asahel	1			1		2			1				5		
Longmeadow	93	28	Colton	Chandler	2			1		1			1				5		
Springfield	242	43	Colton	Charles Capt				2				1	1	2			6		
Chester	143	19	Colton	Chauncy	1		1			1		1					4		
Longmeadow	92	13	Colton	Demas	3			1		2	1		1				8		
Springfield	239	1	Colton	Dimond	2			1		2	1	1	1				8		
Longmeadow	93	26	Colton	Elihu	2	1	1	1		1	1		1				8		
Longmeadow	94	4	Colton	Erstus	1			1				1					3		
Longmeadow	92	12	Colton	George				1					1				2		
Longmeadow	94	18	Colton	Gideon Junr			1	1		1	1	1	1				6		
Longmeadow	94	38	Colton	Henry Dr	1		1	1		1		1	1				6		
Longmeadow	94	33	Colton	Israel		2	1	1		1	1	1		1			8		
Longmeadow	94	40	Colton	Jabez		2		2		1				1			6		
Longmeadow	94	3	Colton	Jacob				1		1		1					3		
Longmeadow	94	36	Colton	Levi				1		2		1					4		
Rowe	199	9	Colton	Lois	1					1		1					3		
Longmeadow	93	38	Colton	Luther Majr	3	1	1	1		3	1	1	1	1			13		
Longmeadow	95	1	Colton	Martin	2			1		2	1	1	1	1			9		
Longmeadow	94	39	Colton	Mary Wd								1		1			2		
Longmeadow	94	19	Colton	Samuel		1	2			1		1					5		
Rowe	199	10	Colton	Silas	1			1		2		1	1				6		
Longmeadow	94	37	Colton	Simeone Ens		1		1		2	1		1				6		
Longmeadow	92	19	Colton	Solomon 2d	2			1					1				4		
Longmeadow	94	21	Colton	Thomas	2			1					1	1			5		
Longmeadow	94	24	Colton	Thomas Jr	2			1		2	1	1					8		
Springfield	242	8	Colton	William		1		1	1		1	1	1	1			7		
Longmeadow	94	35	Colton	Wm Deacn	1	1	1	1			1	1		1			7		
Longmeadow	92	22	Colton	Zadock	2			1					2				5		
Williamsburg	447	12	Colwell	Redford											7		7		
Hawley	332	33	Combs	Ezra	2			1				1					4		
Chester	149	25	Combs	Nathaniel	1			1		2			1				5		
Westfield	119	28	Combs	Tamzin Wd	3						1	1	1	1			7		
Shelburne	320	21	Comstock	Charles		1		1		2			1				5		
Belchertown	208	26	Comstock	Jacob Jr		1	1				1		1				5		
Warwick	36	41	Conant	Asa		2	1	1		1	1	1		1			8		
Warwick	36	42	Conant	Benjamin		2		1		4	2		1				10		
Warwick	37	8	Conant	Benjamin Dr.		1		1			1	1		1			5		
Warwick	37	4	Conant	Josiah	3			1		1	1		1				7		
Middlefield	158	30	Cone	Cyrus		1		1		1	1	1					6		
Wilbraham	236	34	Cone	Ichabod				1			1		1				3		
Wilbraham	236	33	Cone	Mathew				1			1			1			3		
Wilbraham	237	12	Cone	Mathew Jr	1			1		1			1				4		
Wilbraham	236	32	Cone	Newell				1					1				2		
Greenfield	72	18	Cone	Robert	2	2		1		3			1				9		
Wilbraham	237	11	Cone	Zenas	1			1		1	1		1				5		
Hawley	332	28	Coney	John	3	3		1		2			1				10		
Hadley	285	21	Congdon	Jarius	1	1		1			1	1	1				6		
Pelham	213	27	Conkey	Alexr			2	1		2	1	1					7		
Pelham	213	33	Conkey	Alexr				1						1			2		
Pelham	215	3	Conkey	Andrew	1	1		1		2	1		1				7		

TOWN	PG#	LN#	LAST NAME	FIRST NAME	FREE WHITE MALES under 10	10 to 16	16 to 26	26 to 45	45 and over	FREE WHITE FEMALES under 10	10 to 16	16 to 26	26 to 45	45 and over	TOTAL ALL OTHER	TOTAL SLAVES	TOTALS	DISTRICT/ TOWNSHIP	NOTES
Pelham	213	28	Conkey	David	1	1	1		1	1		1		1			7		
Pelham	213	26	Conkey	Elisha	1	1	1		1	1		1		1			7		
Pelham	213	25	Conkey	Isaac				1		1	1	1					4		
Pelham	213	31	Conkey	Isaac			1						1				3		
Pelham	213	30	Conkey	John Maj		1	4		1	3	1	2		1			13		
Pelham	213	22	Conkey	Thomas	1	2		1		1	1		1				7		
Pelham	213	32	Conkey	Wm	1	1	1		1	1	1		1	2			9		
Shutesbury	109	10	Conkley	John		1							1				2		
Barnardston	77	23	Connabell	John		2		1		2	3	1		3			12		
Barnardston	77	17	Connabell	Jonathan			2					1	1				4		
Blanford	176	32	Conoughey	David	1			1		1	2	1		1			7		
Middlefield	159	3	Convass	Benjamin				1						1			2		
Worthington	298	37	Convers	Elisha	1		1					1					3		
Worthington	298	36	Convers	Saml D.				1				1		1			3		
Palmer	261	38	Converse	Alpheus		1	3	1				1	1				7		
Palmer	261	29	Converse	Jacob	1		1	1		1		1					5		
Belchertown	204	32	Converse	James		2	2	1		1				1			7		
South Brimfield	275	5	Converse	Josiah	2		1			2			1				6		
Ware	225	31	Converse	Phinehas	2			1			2	2		1			8		
Ware	225	28	Convey	William		1		1		2			1				5		
Northampton	8	15	Cook	Aaron			1	1						1			3		
Northampton	8	16	Cook	Aaron Jun	2			1		1		1					5		
Buckland	326	26	Cook	Abel		1	2		1	3			1				8		
Pelham	215	18	Cook	Abram		1		1		2		1	1				6		
Barnardston	77	22	Cook	Amasa		2		1		1		1		1			6		
Norwich	152	36	Cook	Amos		1				1		1					3		
Hadley	287	32	Cook	Andrew	1			1				1	1		1		5		
Plainfield	306	19	Cook	Andrew		1		1				2	1				5		
Westhampton	18	18	Cook	Caleb	1			1				1					3		
Hadley	286	26	Cook	Coleman				1				2	1				4		
Hadley	288	3	Cook	Dan	2			1	1	2		1	2				9		
Warwick	36	40	Cook	Daniel		1		1		1	1		2				6		
Ludlow	256	36	Cook	David	2		1	1				1					5		
Hadley	285	33	Cook	Elihu		2		1		2		1	1				7		
Northampton	8	30	Cook	Elijah	1		1	1			1	1					5		
Hadley	287	13	Cook	Elisha		1	2		1	1	2	1		2			10		
West Springfield	350	15	Cook	Elizer		1	2					1					4		
Hadley	287	1	Cook	Gad	1		2	1		1	1		1				7		
Deerfield	51	42	Cook	George	3			1		1	1		1				7		
New Salem	97	21	Cook	Henry	3		1			1				1			6		
Hadley	286	24	Cook	James	1	1	1			1		1		1			6		
Hadley	287	15	Cook	Job	1		1					1					3		
Hadley	288	2	Cook	John		1	3	1		1		2	1				9		
Plainfield	306	20	Cook	John		1				2		2					5		
Hadley	287	4	Cook	Jonathan				1						1			2		
Hadley	286	25	Cook	Joseph				1					2	1			4		
Northampton	6	12	Cook	Joseph	2		1			1	1	1	1	1			8		
Buckland	326	15	Cook	Josiah Junr	1	2		2		1		1	1	1			9		
Northampton	6	15	Cook	Justin		1	1				1	1					4		
Ashfield	339	2	Cook	Levi	3	2		2	1	1	1	1	1	1			13		
Amherst	289	17	Cook	Martin	1	1		1			1		1				5		
Buckland	326	13	Cook	Nathan			1	1		3	1	1		1			8		
Warwick	37	1	Cook	Nathan		1		1		1	1	1					5		
Westhampton	18	26	Cook	Noah	2	2		1		1	1	1					8		
Granby	253	28	Cook	Perez	1	1		1		1	1	1		1			7		
Chester	148	30	Cook	Perley		1		1		3		2					7		
Shelburne	320	20	Cook	Rufus			1			1	1		1				4		
New Salem	97	16	Cook	Samuel	2			1		2	1	1	1				8		
Worthington	301	39	Cook	Samuel	2		1		1	2			1	1			8		
New Salem	97	17	Cook	Samuel 2d		1		1				1					3		
Hadley	286	15	Cook	Seth				1				1		1			3		
Hadley	285	32	Cook	Solomon	3	1		1		2		1					8		
Hadley	288	22	Cook	Stephen		1		2					2		2		7		
Hadley	286	33	Cook	Waitstill	3	2		2		1	1		1				10		
Hadley	287	35	Cook	William		1		2				3		1			7		
Hadley	287	14	Cook	William W.		1		1		3			1				6		
Conway	57	32	Cook	Jesse	5			1		1				1			8		
Leyden	81	29	Cooledge	Daniel		1	1	1				1		1			5		
Deerfield	52	5	Cooley	Abner		1	1	1		1	3			1			8		
Monson	263	20	Cooley	Abner	1	1		1		1			1	1			6		
West Springfield	350	12	Cooley	Alexander	1	2	1	1			1		1				7		
Sunderland	283	23	Cooley	Anna	1	1	2			1	1	2	1				9		
Springfield	246	42	Cooley	Ariel	3		3	1				2	1				10		
Greenwich	219	11	Cooley	Azareah	2	1		1		2	2	1					9		
Deerfield	52	3	Cooley	Azariah	1	2	1	1		3	3			1			12		
Whately	66	26	Cooley	Benjamin			1			1		1					3		
Longmeadow	92	2	Cooley	Calvin	2		2	1		2		1	1				9		
Granville East Soc	529	38	Cooley	Clark		2	1			1		2		1			8		
Springfield	244	1	Cooley	Clark	1		1			2			1				5		
Amherst	292	41	Cooley	Daniel	1	1	1		1	1			1				6		

			HEADS OF HOUSEHOLD		FREE WHITE MALES					FREE WHITE FEMALES					TOTAL ALL OTHER	TOTAL SLAVES	TOTALS	DISTRICT/ TOWNSHIP	NOTES
TOWN	PG#	LN#	LAST NAME	FIRST NAME	under 10	10 to 16	16 to 26	26 to 45	45 and over	under 10	10 to 16	16 to 26	26 to 45	45 and over					
Granville East Soc	527	15	Cooley	Daniel	1	2	3		1	2			2				11		
West Springfield	350	16	Cooley	David	1			1						2			4		
Springfield	245	6	Cooley	Earl	2	1		1		2	1		1				8		
Deerfield	52	4	Cooley	Eli	3	1		1		2	1	1	1				10		
Longmeadow	91	20	Cooley	Eli				1									1		
Granville West Soc	170	21	Cooley	Gaius		1		1		2	1		1				6		
Granville East Soc	527	22	Cooley	George	1	1	1		1		1	1		1			7		
Springfield	244	36	Cooley	George	1			1					1				3		
Conway	57	49	Cooley	Gideon		1	3		1	1	1		1				8		
Longmeadow	92	9	Cooley	Gideon			1			1		1					3		
Sunderland	282	16	Cooley	Gideon	2	1	1	1		1	1	1		1			9		
Longmeadow	93	10	Cooley	Hanan			1	1				1					3		
West Springfield	353	4	Cooley	Isaac	1	1	1		1	2			1				7		
Springfield	245	5	Cooley	Jacob				1									1		
West Springfield	350	8	Cooley	John	1		1	1	1			1	1	1			7		
Longmeadow	92	16	Cooley	John		1	1						1	1			4		
Longmeadow	91	21	Cooley	John 2d			1			3							4		
Palmer	262	2	Cooley	Jonathan		2		1		1	1			1			8		
West Springfield	350	6	Cooley	Jonathan	2	1	1		1	1	1	2		1			10		
Longmeadow	92	4	Cooley	Josiah	1	1	1		1	1	2		1				8		
Longmeadow	94	15	Cooley	Lewis			1						1				2		
Montgomery	160	24	Cooley	Lydia Widw			1							1			2		
Hawley	332	22	Cooley	Noah	2	1		1			1		1				6		
Barnardston	77	25	Cooley	Oliver			1			2			1				4		
Deerfield	52	22	Cooley	Rebeccah		2				1	1			1			5		
Hawley	332	23	Cooley	Reuben		1		1				2		1			5		
Greenwich	219	13	Cooley	Reuben	4	2	1		1		1	2	1				12		
West Springfield	350	2	Cooley	Roger Jr	2	1	1		1	1			1				7		
Hadley	288	12	Cooley	Samuel	2		1			1			1				5		
Springfield	244	40	Cooley	Samuel	2		1			1		1		1			6		
Chester	150	11	Cooley	Seneca			1			1		1					3		
Sunderland	282	7	Cooley	Simon		1		1	1	2	1	1		1			8		
Longmeadow	92	1	Cooley	Stephen	3	1		1					1				6		
Brimfield	272	9	Cooley	Thomas			1						1				2		
Chester	150	10	Cooley	Timothy	2	1		1		2	2			1			9		
Granville East Soc	533	17	Cooley	Timothy M. Reverand	3		1						1				5		
West Springfield	350	5	Cooley	Walter	1	1	1		2	3			1				9		
Granville East Soc	531	39	Cooley	William	1	2	1		1	1		3	1	1			11		
Springfield	245	3	Cooley	William		1	3		1	1	1			1			8		
Granville East Soc	531	38	Cooley	William Junr	2	1		1		4			1	1			10		
Granville East Soc	529	5	Cooley	Zadock	2			1		3	1			1			8		
Palmer	259	18	Cooley	Zadok	2	1		1		1	1			1			7		
Colrain	184	15	Coolidge	Josiah	2	1		1		1	1		1	1			8		
Gill	85	6	Coombs	Joshua			1	1				1		1			4		
Gill	85	7	Coombs	Joshua Jun	4	1		1		1	1			1			9		
Longmeadow	94	1	Coomes	John	3			1		1	2		1	1	1		10		
Longmeadow	94	2	Coomes	Samuel			1			1			1				3		
Longmeadow	93	40	Coomes	Walter	2		1			2			1				6		
Montague	45	27	Coon	William			1			1		1					3		
West Springfield	353	6	Cooper	Enoch		2		1				2	1	1			7		
West Springfield	353	7	Cooper	Enoch Jr	2		1	1		2	1			1			8		
Rowe	199	12	Cooper	Issac	1	2		1		2	1	1		1			9		
West Springfield	356	5	Cooper	Jacob	4			1					1	1			7		
Conway	57	29	Cooper	Lamberton		2	1		1				1	1			6		
West Springfield	350	10	Cooper	Samuel	2			1					1				4		
Wilbraham	233	14	Copeland	Asahel			1			3			1				5		
Northampton	4	11	Copeland	Smith	2		1	1		2			1				7		
Granby	253	32	Copland	Robert	3			1			1			1			6		
Westfield	123	29	Copley	Benjamin	1		1	1		1			1	1			6		
West Springfield	353	3	Copley	Matthus	1			1				3					5		
Westfield	124	4	Copley	Noah				1						1			2		
Goshen	309	19	Corban	Ezekiel				1						1			2		
Rowe	199	15	Corbet	Nathanael		2		1						1			4		
Granby	252	43	Corey	Isaac	1			1		1		1					4		
Palmer	258	10	Corey	William			1										1		
Leverett	113	16	Corking	Caleb		2		1		2	1			1			7		
Greenfield	72	24	Cornwell	Amos	3	1	1	1		3				1			10		
Granville Mid Soc.	167	9	Cornwell	Jesse		1	1			4				1			7		
Granville Mid Soc.	167	14	Cornwell	John		1		1						1			3		
Granville Mid Soc.	165	14	Cornwell	Ozias	3	1		1		2			1				8		
Greenfield	72	17	Corse	Asher	1	1	1	1	1	2	2	2		1			12		
Northfield	27	18	Corse	Gad		2		1		1	1	1	1				8		
Leyden	81	30	Corse	John	2		1							1			4		
Norwich	153	9	Cort	Isaac	1		3		1	3	1	1		1			12		
Chester	144	9	Corvel	Lemuel		1		1				3		1			6		
Longmeadow	91	3	Cosby	Whiting	4			1		1	1		1	1			9		
Worthington	300	1	Cotterill	Asa	3	1	1		1			2		1			9		
Worthington	298	12	Cotterill	Nicholas	3			1		1	1			1			7		
Monson	264	18	Cotton	Gad Capt	1		1	1		3	1	3		1			12		
Monson	264	16	Cotton	George	1		1		1				1	1			5		

TOWN	PG#	LN#	LAST NAME	FIRST NAME	FREE WHITE MALES under 10	10 to 16	16 to 26	26 to 45	45 and over	FREE WHITE FEMALES under 10	10 to 16	16 to 26	26 to 45	45 and over	TOTAL ALL OTHER	TOTAL SLAVES	TOTALS	DISTRICT/ TOWNSHIP	NOTES
Greenwich	219	15	Cotton	Reuben Lt	1		1	1		1	2	1					8		
Monson	264	17	Cotton	Simon	1		1					1					3		
Longmeadow	93	11	Cotton	Solomon				1						1			2		
Springfield	247	21	Cotton	Stephen				1					1	1			3		
Granville West Soc	168	20	Couch	Timothy	3	1		1	1	1		2		1			9		
Greenwich	219	5	Covel	Thomas	2		1			1		1					5		
Pelham	213	24	Cowen	George		1		1				1	1				4		
Pelham	213	23	Cowen	James	3	2		1		2		2	1				11		
Chesterfield	22	3	Cowing	David	1			1		3			1				6		
Chesterfield	21	36	Cowing	Gatheliu			1		1		1	1		1			5		
Chesterfield	21	15	Cowing	John	1	2		1		5			1	1			11		
Chesterfield	22	4	Cowing	Luther	3			1					1				5		
Chesterfield	21	16	Cowing	Reuben	3			1		1	1	1					7		
Norwich	153	16	Cowing	Tela			1			1		1					3		
Belchertown	208	37	Cowl	John Capt	2	2	2	1	1	1	1		1	1			12		
Belchertown	208	36	Cowl	Joshua	1			1				1					3		
Belchertown	208	38	Cowl	Josiah	2	1		1		1			1	1			7		
Belchertown	208	22	Cowl	Amasa		1		1		1			1				4		
Leverett	114	1	Cowle	Burden	1			1		1			1				4		
Leverett	113	17	Cowle	Isaac				1				1		1			3		
Leverett	113	15	Cowle	Josiah			2		1		1	2		1			7		
Leverett	114	10	Cowle	Seth			1					1					2		
Heath	195	5	Cowles	Agustus			1	1		2		1					5		
Amherst	290	16	Cowles	David			3	1	1			1		1			7		
Amherst	293	2	Cowles	Enos		1			1	2	1		2				7		
Amherst	290	17	Cowles	Hannah			1					1	2	1			5		
Amherst	290	1	Cowles	Levi				1		1		1	1				4		
Amherst	290	2	Cowles	Oliver	1			1		1			1				4		
Amherst	294	27	Cowles	Reuben	2	1			1	1	1	1	1				8		
New Salem	97	12	Cowles	Rufus	1	1		1				1	1				5		
Amherst	290	3	Cowles	Simeon	3	1	1		1	1		1	2	1			11		
Granville West Soc	169	30	Cowles	William	2			1		2	1		1				7		
Granby	254	44	Cowls	Cheester Dr.	2			1				1					4		
Heath	195	3	Cowls	Seth	1			1		2			1				5		
Belchertown	208	35	Cowls	John Lt	1	2	1	1		1		1	1				8		
Chester	146	22	Cox	James				1					1				2		
Chester	146	23	Cox	Polly Carpus	2			1		2			1				6		
Northampton	6	7	Coy	Asahel				1		1			1				3		
Granby	252	37	Coye	Aaron	3		1		1	1		1	1				8		
Granby	252	36	Coye	Abraham				1						1			2		
Wilbraham	232	11	Coye	Abraham			1					1					2		
Springfield	240	14	Coye	Fitch				1		2			1				4		
Palmer	259	31	Coye	Nehemiah	2		1		1	1	1	1	1				8		
Monson	264	27	Coye	Uriah				1					1				2		
Amherst	293	19	Coye	Wyllis				1		3			1				5		
Whately	66	20	Crafts	Graves	4	2		1		2	1		1				11		
Whately	66	25	Crafts	John	1		1		1	1	1			1			6		
Whately	66	28	Crafts	Joseph	4			1		1	1	1					8		
Whately	66	24	Crafts	Moses	1	1		1		1				1			5		
Whately	66	23	Crafts	Reuben	1	1		2	1	2	1		1				9		
Whately	66	19	Crafts	Seth	1			1	1	1			1	1			6		
Ware	225	32	Crain	Amaziah	1	1	2		1	5	2		1	1			15		
Colrain	184	17	Crandal	Paul		2	1				2		1				6		
Longmeadow	94	28	Crandall	Levi	2			1		1			1				5		
Leyden	81	21	Crandell	Jarad			2		1	1	1		1	1	2		9		
Springfield	247	15	Crane	Abner	1		1					1					3		
Wilbraham	235	35	Crane	Joseph		2	1						1	1			5		
Pelham	217	17	Cranfield	Thomas	1			1		2	1		1				6		
Ashfield	338	31	Cranston	Abner	2			1		2	1		1				7		
Ashfield	338	30	Cranston	Asa	2	2		1		1		1	1				8		
Ashfield	339	11	Cranston	David	1	1		1	1	1			1				5		
Ashfield	338	27	Cranston	Elisha Jr	1	1	4	1		3	1		1				12		
Ashfield	339	10	Cranston	Jonathan	3	1		1	1	2	2	1		1			12		
Williamsburg	447	11	Crawford	Andrew	1	1		1		1	1		1				6		
Leyden	81	27	Crawford	Joseph	1			1		2	1		1				6		
Pelham	213	21	Crawford	Levi	2	1		1	1				1	1			7		
Hawley	332	14	Crittenden	Amos		1	2		1		1	2		2			9		
Conway	57	40	Crittenden	Ebenz		1	2	1				1	1				6		
Conway	57	39	Crittenden	John	4	1		1		1	1		1				9		
Conway	57	41	Crittenden	Medad	1	2		1		1	1		1				7		
Conway	57	38	Crittenden	Samuel	1	3	1	1		1				1			8		
Hawley	332	19	Crittenden	Simeon	2			1		2			1	1			7		
Wilbraham	236	31	Crocker	Enoch	1		1	1		1			1				5		
Shutesbury	109	9	Crocker	Hesph Jr	2	1		1		1	1		1				7		
Springfield	248	2	Crocker	Nathan				1		2		1	1				5		
Shutesbury	109	8	Crocker	Oliver	2			1		1	1		1				6		
Wilbraham	236	30	Crocker	Rowland					1					2			3		
Sunderland	283	24	Crocker	Zacheus		1	2	1	1	1				1			7		
Springfield	243	33	Crook	John				1		1		1					3		
Blanford	179	23	Crooks	James	2	1		1		2			1				7		
Blanford	179	12	Crooks	John	2	2		1			1			1			7		

			HEADS OF HOUSEHOLD		FREE WHITE MALES					FREE WHITE FEMALES					TOTAL ALL OTHER	TOTAL SLAVES	TOTALS	DISTRICT/ TOWNSHIP	NOTES
TOWN	PG#	LN#	LAST NAME	FIRST NAME	under 10	10 to 16	16 to 26	26 to 45	45 and over	under 10	10 to 16	16 to 26	26 to 45	45 and over					
Blanford	180	14	Crooks	William		1		1	1			1		1			5		
Wendell	105	14	Crosbee	Jonathan	1		1		1		1	2		2			8		
Shutesbury	109	16	Crosbee	Levi			1					1					2		
Worthington	299	12	Crosby	David	1		1					3					5		
Hawley	332	24	Crosby	Ebenz		1	3	1	1	2	2		1				13		
Charlemont	191	3	Crosby	Jonathan	3	1		1		2			1				8		
Greenwich	218	2	Crosby	Joshua Revd	2	3	1			3		1	1				11		
Shutesbury	109	15	Crosman	Asa	3		1						1				5		
Shelburne	320	15	Crosman	Barnabas	1		1						1				3		
Shelburne	320	13	Crosman	Elkanah				1				1		1			3		
Shelburne	320	14	Crosman	Josiah		1		1		1			1				4		
Granville West Soc	168	36	Crosman	Phinias		1		1						1			3		
Granville West Soc	169	10	Crosman	Tulley	2		1						1				4		
Shelburne	320	16	Crosman	Zeph			1			1		1					3		
Ashfield	339	6	Cross	Cephas	1		1	2		4	1		1				10		
Chester	144	25	Cross	David	2	1		1		2	1		2				9		
Ware	225	36	Cross	Ezra	2			1		2			1				6		
Buckland	326	14	Cross	Jeduthan	1			1		3			1	1			7		
Ashfield	339	5	Cross	John	1	1		1		1	1	2		2			9		
Ware	225	30	Cross	John	1	1			1				1	1			5		
Rowe	199	14	Cross	Jude	2			1		1			1				5		
Ware	225	24	Cross	Nathan				1		1		1					3		
Ashfield	338	29	Cross	Stephen	1	1	1		1	3	1		1				9		
Monson	264	31	Cross	Stephen	2	1	1			2			1	1			8		
Shutesbury	109	7	Crossett	Edward	3	1	1		1		1	2		1			10		
New Salem	98	6	Crossett	Richd G.	4	2		1				1		1			9		
New Salem	97	18	Crossett	Samuel	2			1			1	1					5		
Brimfield	271	30	Crouch	Ephraim	2			1		1			1				5		
Leyden	81	34	Crouch	William	2			1		3	1			1			8		
Montgomery	160	13	Crow	David		1		1	1		1			1			5		
Montgomery	160	14	Crow	David Junr	1		2						1				4		
Norwich	152	8	Crow	John					1	2		1	1	1			6		
Montgomery	160	25	Crow	Thomas		1		1	2	2				1			7		
Hawley	332	27	Crowel	Ebenz	2			1		2	1	1					7		
Middlefield	158	25	Crowell	Eli	1			1					1				3		
Middlefield	158	12	Crowell	Enoch			2	1	1	1	3						8		
South Hadley	250	35	Crowfoot	Daniel				1						1			2		
Pelham	213	34	Crozett	Robt		3		1		2		1		1			8		
Pelham	213	17	Crozier	Asabah H & Mary Florin	1	1				2	1	3					8		
Ashfield	339	4	Crudenton	Isaac		1		1					1	1			4		
Leyden	81	20	Crumb	Phinius	2	1	3	1		2	1			1			11		
West Springfield	353	5	Cruttenton	Amos				1		1	1		1				4		
Colrain	184	18	Culbeth	Benoni	2	1		1		2			1				7		
Blanford	179	17	Culver	Asa	2	2	1	1			1	1	1	1			10		
Chester	150	5	Culver	Asahel		1	1					1	1				4		
Chester	148	26	Culver	Charles	1	1	2	1				2		1			8		
Chesterfield	22	6	Culver	Ephraim	2		1						1				4		
Northampton	11	2	Culver	Lemuel				1				1		1			3		
Palmer	261	3	Cumings	Benjamin	1	1							1				3		
Ware	225	26	Cummings	Abraham Lt		1	1	1		1			2	1			7		
Shutesbury	109	17	Cummings	Benja	1			1		2				1			5		
Shutesbury	109	18	Cummings	David	3			1		1				1			6		
Palmer	261	6	Cummings	Isaac		1		1	1	1		2		1			7		
Ware	225	29	Cummings	Job	3	1	1		2	1	1	1	1	1			12		
Monson	264	25	Cummings	Simeon			1			2	2	1					6		
Ware	225	27	Cummings	Simeon		1		1		2	1	3		1			9		
Montague	45	25	Cummins	Elijah				1					1				2		
Shelburne	320	22	Cummins	Jabez	1			1		1	1			1			5		
Montague	45	26	Cummins	Reuben				1		3			1				5		
Plainfield	306	16	Cuningham	James				1					1				2		
Plainfield	306	15	Cuningham	John	1	1	1	1						1			5		
Shutesbury	109	20	Cunningham	John	1			1					1	1			4		
Belchertown	204	26	Currier	Samuel	2			1		1			1				5		
Plainfield	308	21	Curtice	Edward			2						1				3		
New Salem	97	35	Curtis	Asa		1		1		1	1	1		1			6		
Hawley	332	17	Curtis	Beldad	1			1	1				1	1			5		
Chesterfield	24	2	Curtis	Beriah	2	1				3		1	1				8		
Granville Mid Soc.	166	5	Curtis	Charles	1		1	1		2	1	1	1				8		
New Salem	97	24	Curtis	Daniel		1		1			1	2		1			6		
New Salem	97	26	Curtis	Daniel Jr	3	1		1		1	1		1				8		
Granville Mid Soc.	166	4	Curtis	David			2			2				2			6		
Leverett	114	7	Curtis	Ebenz				1				1		1			3		
Worthington	301	6	Curtis	Elijah	1		1	1		1			1	1			6		
Hawley	332	13	Curtis	Hosea		1	1		1			2		1			6		
Leverett	114	4	Curtis	James		1		1						1			3		
New Salem	97	28	Curtis	James	2			1		2	1	1	1	1			9		
Blanford	177	4	Curtis	Jeremiah	2			1		2			1				6		
Granville Mid Soc.	166	3	Curtis	Linus	1		1			2			1				5		
Chesterfield	24	38	Curtis	Luther		1	1	1		1	1	2		1			8		
West Springfield	356	9	Curtis	Lysander		1					1	1					3		

218

TOWN	PG#	LN#	LAST NAME	FIRST NAME	FREE WHITE MALES					FREE WHITE FEMALES					TOTAL ALL OTHER	TOTAL SLAVES	TOTALS	DISTRICT/ TOWNSHIP	NOTES
					under 10	10 to 16	16 to 26	26 to 45	45 and over	under 10	10 to 16	16 to 26	26 to 45	45 and over					
New Salem	97	25	Curtis	Moses		1	2		1	1	1			1			7		
Hawley	332	32	Curtis	Vincent	3			1			1		1				6		
Granville Mid Soc.	167	25	Curtiss	Aaron		1		1			1			1			4		
Monson	264	24	Curtiss	Ebenezer			1					1					2		
Williamsburg	447	10	Curtiss	Isaac	1			1		3	1	1	1				8		
Northampton	10	17	Curtiss	John	3			1			1		1				6		
Williamsburg	447	8	Curtiss	John Day	3	2		1		3			1				10		
Granville Mid Soc.	167	26	Curtiss	Levi	2		4	1		1		1		1			10		
Northampton	10	12	Curtiss	Molly		1				2		1	1				5		
Chesterfield	19	19	Cushing	Abel	1	1		1		3			1				7		
Cummington	305	21	Cushing	Bela	1			1		1	2			1			6		
Worthington	299	9	Cushing	Ezekiel	3	1		1			1		1				7		
Montgomery	161	32	Cushing	Joseph		1											1		
Colrain	184	8	Cushing	S Asaph	1			1		2			1				5		
Barnardston	77	21	Cushman	Artimas		1		1		4	1	2		1			10		
Montague	45	21	Cushman	Azel	1			1		1	2		1				6		
Goshen	309	20	Cushman	Caleb	1		2		1	2	2		1				9		
Greenfield	72	19	Cushman	Consider	2			1		4			1				8		
Palmer	259	11	Cushman	Consider		1		1			1			1			4		
Amherst	290	26	Cushman	Epraim	1			1		3	2	1	1				9		
West Springfield	356	4	Cushman	Jesse	1			1		4			1				7		
Cummington	303	1	Cushman	Jotham	1			1		1			1	2			6		
Barnardston	77	14	Cushman	Rachael	1	1	3			2				1			8		
Greenwich	219	7	Cutlar	Dudley & Ebenz	2	1		1	1	1		1	1	1			8		
Ware	225	35	Cutler	Elijah		2	1		1	1		2	1				8		
Wendell	105	16	Cutler	Jacob	1			1		1	1	1					5		
Palmer	259	27	Cutler	James	1			1		1			2				5		
Ware	225	33	Cutler	Solomon	1	1	1	1		2	1	1	1				9		
Ware	225	34	Cutler	Solomon	1	1	1	1		2	1	1	1				9		
Leverett	114	8	Cutter	Abraham		1		1						1			3		
Leverett	114	5	Cutter	Jairus	2			1		2			1				6		
Amherst	289	4	Cutter	Robert			4		1		1	2		2			10		
Ware	225	25	Cutter	William		1	1			1		1					4		
Orange	41	28	Cuttin	John				1		4				1			6		
Rowe	199	13	Cutting	Eliphalet	1			1	1	3	1	1	1				9		
Belchertown	208	30	Dagget	Samuel		1		1					1	1			4		
Greenwich	224	13	Daggett	Ebenz	3			1		2			1				7		
Greenfield	72	29	Daggot	Gideon	2	1		1		1		1	1				7		
Springfield	243	34	Dale	John															Enumeration left blank
Belchertown	209	7	Dale	Joshua		1	2		1		1			1			6		
Springfield	244	8	Dale	Thomas															Enumeration left blank
Springfield	247	10	Dale	Thomas		2	6	5				1	1				15		
Colrain	185	10	Dalrymple	David	1		2	2	1	3		1	1	1			12		
Colrain	185	3	Dalrymple	David Jun	2	1		1		2			1				7		
Colrain	185	17	Dalrymple	Edward	4			1		1	1			1			8		
Colrain	185	8	Dalrymple	Hark	2			1	1	1		1	1	1			8		
Heath	195	11	Dalrymple	Thos	1			1					1				3		
Colrain	185	13	Dalrymple	Winslow		1				3			1				5		
Goshen	310	4	Damon	Abner	4			1		1	1		1				8		
Chesterfield	24	30	Damon	Caleb				2			2			2			6		
Chesterfield	24	31	Damon	Caleb 3d		1				1		1					3		
Chesterfield	23	36	Damon	Calid 2d	1	1		1		2		1	1				7		
Chesterfield	22	13	Damon	David			1	1		1			1				4		
Ashfield	339	20	Damon	Edward	1			1		3	2		1				8		
Chesterfield	22	27	Damon	Ichabod				1					2	1			4		
Chesterfield	23	28	Damon	Ichabod Jr	1	2		1		1			1				6		
Chesterfield	24	29	Damon	Isaac	2	2	3	1			1	1	1				11		
Chesterfield	24	28	Damon	Isaiah	1	2		1					1	1			6		
Chesterfield	22	21	Damon	James	2			1		2	3		1				9		
Cummington	303	3	Damon	Jonathan	2			1		2			1				6		
Westhampton	18	31	Damon	Nathan	3			1		1	1		2				8		
Granby	253	38	Damon	Peter			3		1			2		1			7		
Hawley	332	34	Damon	Stephen	3			1		1	2		1				8		
Cummington	303	2	Damon	William	2	2		1					1				6		
Amherst	294	16	Dana	Amariah	1	2			1	2	1	1		1			9		
Shutesbury	109	22	Dane	Benjamin	2			1		1	1		1				6		
Hawley	333	3	Daniels	Abiram	1			1					1				3		
Sunderland	283	8	Daniels	Amos	1			1	1	1		1		1			6		
Ludlow	256	17	Daniels	Asa	1	1	1	1		2			1				7		
Worthington	297	12	Daniels	Dan	1	2	1	1		1	2		1				9		
Ludlow	256	18	Daniels	David		1		1	1		1	1		1			6		
Wilbraham	236	6	Daniels	James	3		1					1	1	1			7		
Plainfield	306	26	Daniels	John	1			1		2		1	1	1			7		
Ludlow	256	20	Daniels	Peter		1							1				2		
Brimfield	271	32	Danielson	Benja				1					1				2		
Brimfield	274	15	Danielson	Luther	3	1		1		1		1	1				8		
West Springfield	356	19	Danks	Caleb	1			1		3			2	1			8		
West Springfield	356	20	Danks	Eliakim	1			1		3	2		1				8		
Southampton	131	2	Danks	Elijah				1		1			1				3		
Easthampton	136	6	Danks	Ephraim	1			1		1			1				4		

TOWN	PG#	LN#	LAST NAME	FIRST NAME	FREE WHITE MALES					FREE WHITE FEMALES					TOTAL ALL OTHER	TOTAL SLAVES	TOTALS	DISTRICT/ TOWNSHIP	NOTES
					under 10	10 to 16	16 to 26	26 to 45	45 and over	under 10	10 to 16	16 to 26	26 to 45	45 and over					
Southampton	130	31	Danks	Moses		1		1				1		2			5		
Southampton	131	1	Danks	Robert			1	1				1		1			4		
Southampton	131	31	Danks	Saml				1						1			2		
Southampton	131	32	Danks	Saml Junr	1	1	2		1	3			1	1			10		
Norwich	153	30	Danks	Sylvester			1					1					2		
Easthampton	134	33	Danks	Zadok	1			1	1	1			1				4		
South Brimfield	277	21	Darby	Alpheus	2	1		1		1	1	1	1				8		
Hawley	333	1	Darby	Edward	3	1		1					1				6		
Gill	85	10	Darby	Eleazer		1		1					1				3		
Ashfield	339	24	Darby	Saml	1		1						1				3		
Pelham	213	36	Darimon	Phinehas	1	1	1		1		2	2		1			9		
Hadley	288	14	Darling	Alpheus	2			1				1					4		
Brimfield	270	29	Darling	Asa	1							1		1			3		
Barnardston	77	27	Darling	Elind		1		1		3			1				6		
Gill	85	11	Darling	Jedediah	2	2		1		2			2				9		
Gill	85	12	Darling	John	1			1		6			1				9		
Pelham	217	15	Darling	John	1	1		1			1	1	1				6		
Palmer	259	21	Darling	Sarah Wd							1	1		1			3		
Chesterfield	24	19	Darling	Simeon	1	1		1		3	1		1				8		
Montague	45	35	Darling	Stephen	1			1					1				3		
Ware	225	38	Darling	Willard	1		1						1				3		
Norwich	151	28	Darrow	Amaziah	1		1	1		1	1		1				6		
Norwich	151	37	Darrow	Amaziah Junr			1					1					2		
Norwich	151	27	Darrow	Zacheus	3					1	3		1				8		
Springfield	247	44	Dart	Levi	1	1		1					1				4		
Granby	254	4	Darvin	Ebenezer				1						1			2		
Colrain	185	9	Davenport	Edward	1	1	2		1		1	1		1			8		
Williamsburg	447	17	Davenport	George	2			1		1	1			1			6		
Leyden	82	5	Davenport	Oliver				1		4			1				6		
Colrain	185	14	Davenport	Paul	4	1		1		1	1		1				9		
Westfield	123	4	Davids	Daniel	2	1				2	1	1	1				9		
Williamsburg	447	16	Davidson	John	1	2		1		2		1	1				8		
Brimfield	271	31	Davidson	Nthl Majr				1						1			2		
Belchertown	209	4	Davis	Aaron	3			1		2			1				7		
Springfield	244	3	Davis	Aaron Jun			1			2		1					4		
South Brimfield	275	21	Davis	Abijah		1		1		2			1				5		
Leverett	114	15	Davis	Abraham	4	1		1					1				7		
Norwich	152	20	Davis	Clarissa	1						1		1				3		
Hatfield	14	30	Davis	Ebenezer	2	1	1		1	2	1	1		1			10		
Ware	225	39	Davis	Elihu	2		1			1		1					5		
Ware	226	1	Davis	Enos	1		2			1			1	1			6		
Granby	252	38	Davis	Isaac		1						1					2		
Conway	58	8	Davis	James		1	2	2		2	1	1		2			11		
Monson	265	27	Davis	Jesse				1		1	1	1		1			5		
Colrain	185	16	Davis	John				1						1			2		
Warwick	37	11	Davis	Jonathan				1			2		1				4		
Northampton	10	36	Davis	Jonathn			2	1		1	2		1	1			8		
Leyden	82	6	Davis	Joseph		1		1		4	2		1				9		
New Salem	98	16	Davis	Joseph		1											1		
Buckland	327	2	Davis	Josiah	2	2		1		4	1		1				44		
Belchertown	209	5	Davis	Moses	2	1		1		2			1				7		
Palmer	260	38	Davis	Nathan	1	1	1						1				4		
Palmer	261	21	Davis	Nathan	2	1	1	1		1			1				7		
Palmer	259	35	Davis	Nathan 2d	1	1	1						1				4		
Northampton	3	23	Davis	Patience	1					1		1		1			4		
Williamsburg	447	18	Davis	Paul			1	1		3			1	1			7		
Belchertown	209	6	Davis	Samuel		2		1		1			1				5		
Chesterfield	22	24	Davis	Samuel	1			1					1				3		
Conway	58	7	Davis	Samuel			1			1		1					3		
Monson	266	24	Davis	Samuel		1		1		3	1		1				7		
New Salem	98	9	Davis	Sarah	1	1				2	1	1	1				7		
Wilbraham	232	14	Davis	Sarah Wd	1									2			3		
Monson	263	17	Davis	Stephen	1			1					1				3		
Ashfield	339	23	Davis	Sylvester	1			1				1					3		
Chesterfield	22	23	Davis	William	1	1		1		3	2		1				9		
Westfield	120	17	Davis	Wm				1					1				2		
Deerfield	52	38	Davison	Barnabas				1					1	1			3		
Monson	264	3	Davison	Ebenezer				1				1	1				3		
Heath	195	10	Davison	Josiah				1						1			2		
Heath	195	12	Davison	Levi	1		1			1		1					4		
Cummington	303	4	Dawes	Daniel			1										1		
Cummington	305	34	Dawes	Howland		1	2					2	1	1			7		
Cummington	303	5	Dawes	Robert	2	1	1			1		1	1	1			8		
Brimfield	275	21	Dawson	Diminicus	2	1	2	1		1	1	2		1			11	South Brimfield	
West Springfield	350	31	Day	Aaron		2	1				1	1		1			5		
Springfield	239	41	Day	Abner	1		1			1	1		1				6		
Chester	146	10	Day	Abraham	2		1			1		1					5		
Wilbraham	236	11	Day	Alven	2		1			3			1				7		
Westfield	124	9	Day	Ambrose	5		1					1	1				8		
South Hadley	249	24	Day	Asa	1		1			4			1				7		

TOWN	PG#	LN#	LAST NAME	FIRST NAME	FREE WHITE MALES					FREE WHITE FEMALES					TOTAL ALL OTHER	TOTAL SLAVES	TOTALS	DISTRICT/ TOWNSHIP	NOTES
					under 10	10 to 16	16 to 26	26 to 45	45 and over	under 10	10 to 16	16 to 26	26 to 45	45 and over					
West Springfield	350	30	Day	Benjamin	2	1	1		1				2	1			8		
West Springfield	356	13	Day	Brigham	3			1					1				5		
West Springfield	350	19	Day	Daniel	1		1		1	2	1	1	1				8		
West Springfield	350	26	Day	Ebenezer				1					1				2		
West Springfield	350	23	Day	Edmund	1			1		3			1	2			8		
West Springfield	356	14	Day	Eleazer	1		2		1	1		1	1	1			8		
Northampton	9	28	Day	Eli		1		1		3	2		1				8		
Wilbraham	237	7	Day	Eriel	2			1		1			1				5		
West Springfield	350	24	Day	Ezekiel			1		1			2	1	1			6		
West Springfield	350	25	Day	Ezekiel Jr	2	1		1					1				5		
South Hadley	249	21	Day	Ezra		1	3		1	1	1		1	1			9		
Westfield	124	10	Day	Gideon		1		1			1	1	1				5		
West Springfield	350	28	Day	Heman	1		2		1	3	1	1	1				10		
West Springfield	350	18	Day	Henry	1	1	2	1		3		1					9		
Chester	146	11	day	Irena Wd		1	1	1						1			4		
West Springfield	350	27	Day	Jacob	3		1		1	1	1			2			9		
New Salem	98	11	Day	James	2			1			1	3					7		
West Springfield	356	17	Day	James	2		1			2			2				7		
West Springfield	356	12	Day	Jedidiah	1		1		1		1	1	1				6		
Hatfield	12	18	Day	Joel	4	2		1			1		1				9		
West Springfield	356	15	Day	Joel		1	1	1		1		1	1				6		
West Springfield	356	16	Day	Joel Jr	1	2	1		1	3	2		1				11		
West Springfield	356	11	Day	John				1			1	2	2				6		
West Springfield	356	18	Day	Joseph		1	1	1			2		1				6		
South Hadley	248	12	Day	Justin		1					1						2		
Northampton	10	9	Day	Luke	1			1		3			1				6		
Westfield	124	7	Day	Luke				1					1				2		
Springfield	240	8	Day	Mary Wd		1				1		1		1			4		
West Springfield	350	29	Day	Moses			1			3		1					5		
Northampton	8	10	Day	Nathaniel				1			1	1	1				4		
Northampton	8	11	Day	Nathaniel Jun	2			1		1			1				5		
New Salem	98	10	Day	Peletiah	2	1		1			1	1					6		
New Salem	98	12	Day	Samuel	2		1		3			1					7		
Northampton	8	2	Day	Simeon	1			1		1	2		1	1			7		
West Springfield	350	20	Day	Thomas	3		1		1				1	1			7		
West Springfield	350	21	Day	Thomas Jr			1		1		1						3		
Worthington	301	32	Dayley	John	1		1		1	1	1		1				6		
Blanford	180	22	Dayton	Giles	1	1	1		1			2		1			7		
Blanford	180	19	Dayton	Giles Jr		1	1		1			2		1			6		
Colrain	185	5	Dean	Christopher	2	2	1		1	1		2	1				10		
Barnardston	77	30	Dean	David	2			1		1			1				5		
New Salem	98	14	Dean	Gilbert	1	1		1		3			1				7		
Wilbraham	237	28	Dean	Joel		1					1						2		
Westfield	121	19	Dean	Samll	4	1		1	1	1	2		1	1			12		
Leyden	82	7	Dean	Samuel	2			1		3				1			7		
Wilbraham	238	6	Dean	Weston			1			1			1				3		
Belchertown	203	3	Dearing	Theodore				1				1					2		
Montague	45	34	Death	Aaron		1	1	1		3	1	1	1				9		
Montague	45	32	Death	Benjamin	2	1	1		1	2	1	1		1			10		
Wendell	105	23	Death	John	1			1				1					3		
Montague	45	33	Death	Jotham			1	1		3			1	1			7		
Monson	264	21	Delamater	Elijah	1			1		2	1		1				6		
Northampton	5	14	Delano	Thomas		1	1						1				3		
Sunderland	282	14	Delano	William	1	1		1		1		1	2	1			8		
Warwick	37	10	Delve	Jonathan	2		1			2			1				6		
Warwick	37	9	Delve	Peter			1					1	1				3		
Leyden	82	4	Demick	Solomon	4		1			2			1				8		
Greenfield	72	30	Denio	Enos	1			1		1		1	1	2			7		
Barnardston	77	26	Denio	Joseph		1		1	1	1			1	2			7		
Leyden	82	1	Denison	David	1	1		1		2	2	1		1			9		
Leyden	82	2	Denison	Edward	1	1	1	1		3		1	1				9		
Colrain	185	6	Denison	Nathan		1	2	1		2		1	1				8		
Middlefield	156	28	Denmon	John		1		1		1		1		1			5		
West Springfield	353	8	Dennis	John	1			1		2	2		1				7		
Brimfield	274	17	Dennison	George				1					1				2		
South Brimfield	276	38	Dennison	Twiss	1			1			1						3		
Ware	226	4	Densmore	Abraham	3	1	2	1		1	1		1				10		
Ware	226	2	Densmore	Samuel		1	1	1	1	2				2			8		
Ware	226	3	Densmore	Thomas	2		1		2			1	2	2			11		
Ware	226	5	Densmore	Thomas Junr		1						1					2		
New Salem	98	8	Derby	Roger			1			2	1		1				5		
Westfield	125	24	Dewey	Aaron	1	1	1	1	1	1	1	1	1	1			10		
Westfield	118	9	Dewey	Amos	3		2	1			1		1				8		
Westfield	126	17	Dewey	Benjamin		1	1		1		1	2			1		8		
Westfield	118	8	Dewey	David		1		1					1				3		
Westfield	119	25	Dewey	Eliab	2	2	1		1	1		1	1	1			10		
Westfield	119	27	Dewey	Eliab Junr	3	1		1					1				6		
Southwick	358	22	Dewey	Gad		2		1	1			2		1			7		
Westfield	123	12	Dewey	Israel	2	2		1		1			1	1			8		
Westfield	126	18	Dewey	James	1			1		1		1					4		
Chester	145	28	Dewey	John	2			1		1		1					5		

TOWN	PG#	LN#	LAST NAME	FIRST NAME	M under 10	M 10 to 16	M 16 to 26	M 26 to 45	M 45 and over	F under 10	F 10 to 16	F 16 to 26	F 26 to 45	F 45 and over	TOTAL ALL OTHER	TOTAL SLAVES	TOTALS	DISTRICT/ TOWNSHIP	NOTES
Westfield	123	20	Dewey	John	2	2	1		1	1	1		1				9		
Westfield	126	19	Dewey	Joseph		2		1				2	1				6		
Westfield	123	27	Dewey	Josiah	1	1	2		1	1	1	1		1			9		
Westfield	124	5	Dewey	Josiah Junr	2	1	1	1		1	1		1				8		
Norwich	152	3	Dewey	Levi Lieut	3		1	1		2	1		1				9		
Westfield	123	13	Dewey	Moses Capt	1	1	1	1	1	2		1	1	1			10		
Westfield	121	5	Dewey	Noah		1		1	2	1	2	2	1				10		
Westfield	123	31	Dewey	Roswell	3		1	1		1			1				7		
Westfield	128	3	Dewey	Russel		2		1		2			1				6		
Orange	41	35	Dewey	Silas	1			1		1			1				4		
Westfield	123	22	Dewey	Solomon	1			1		3	1		1	1			8		
Chester	145	31	Dewey	Stephen	2			1		2			1				6		
Barnardston	77	29	Dewey	Thomas	1		1			1		1					4		
Westfield	118	10	Dewey	Timothy	2	3	1		1	1		2	1	1			12		
Greenwich	219	20	Dewing	Andrew		1		1			1		1				4		
Deerfield	52	37	DeWolf	Elisha		1					1		1	1			4		
Conway	57	51	DeWolf	John	1		1	1		2	1	1					7		
Deerfield	52	28	DeWolf	Simon		1					1						2		
Monson	264	6	Dewolfe	Elisha		1				1		1					3		
Russell	138	11	Dewsey	Israel	1			1		1		1					4		
Orange	41	33	Dexter	Benjamin		1		1		1	3		1				7		
Monson	262	9	Dexter	John				1				1	1				3		
Monson	262	10	Dexter	Leonard	1			1		1		1					4		
Orange	41	36	Dexter	Wheeler	1		1					1					3		
Granville East Soc	527	20	Di*men	Richard		1		1	1		1		1				5		
Ludlow	255	22	Dick	Richard											8		8		
Barnardston	77	28	Dickenson	Arias	3	1	1		1	1		1					8		
Hatfield	14	24	Dickinson	Aaron	1	2	1		1	2	1	1	1				10		
Granby	253	26	Dickinson	Aaron Capt		1		1				1	1				4		
Hatfield	13	32	Dickinson	Abina	1		1			1		1					4		
Whately	66	32	Dickinson	Abner			1				1	1			1		4		
Hatfield	13	35	Dickinson	Alpheus	2		1				1						4		
Hadley	287	36	Dickinson	Amariah	1		1	1		1	1		1				6		
Amherst	291	15	Dickinson	Asa	2	2		1	1	1		4		1			12		
Amherst	290	27	Dickinson	Azariah	3	1		1		1			1	1			8		
Whately	66	34	Dickinson	Benjm	1		1		1		1		1				5		
Northfield	28	8	Dickinson	Benoni	2	2	1		1	1	1		1				9		
Deerfield	52	35	Dickinson	Calvin		1				1		1					3		
Whately	66	30	Dickinson	Charles	1							1					3		
Deerfield	52	33	Dickinson	Consider		2	1	1		3		1					8		
Hadley	288	24	Dickinson	Cotton		1		1		1	2		2	1			8		
Hadley	287	38	Dickinson	Daniel	2	2	2	1		1		1	1	1			11		
Hatfield	11	3	Dickinson	Daniel		2		1		1	1		1				6		
Ashfield	339	16	Dickinson	David		2	1			1		1					5		
Deerfield	52	30	Dickinson	David				2		1	1		1				5		
Amherst	292	14	Dickinson	Ebenezer		1		2		6			2	1			12		
Hawley	333	2	Dickinson	Ebenz	2			1		2	3		1				9		
Amherst	290	39	Dickinson	Eli			1			1			1				3		
Granby	254	33	Dickinson	Eli Dr	2		3			2	2	1	2				13		
Amherst	291	16	Dickinson	Elihu	2			1		1				1			5		
Hatfield	11	11	Dickinson	Elihu		1	2		1		2	1		1			8		
Amherst	296	3	Dickinson	Elijah		1	1	1	1	1		1	1	1			8		
Hatfield	12	24	Dickinson	Elijah	1	1	2	1	1	1	1	1	1				10		
Deerfield	52	31	Dickinson	Eliphalet	2	1	4		2		2	1	2				14		
Amherst	292	9	Dickinson	Elisha	2	1	1		1	1	2	1		2			11		
Hadley	288	28	Dickinson	Elisha	1	1		1		1	1	1	1				8		
Amherst	291	37	Dickinson	Gad		1		1					1				3		
Deerfield	52	34	Dickinson	Gideon		2	3		1		1		1				8		
Deerfield	52	32	Dickinson	J*roh Wells	2	1	4		1	1		2	1				12		
Conway	58	6	Dickinson	James		1	1	1		2		1	1				7		
Shelburne	321	4	Dickinson	James	1	1		1					1				4		
Granby	254	42	Dickinson	Job	1			1		2			1				6		
Amherst	290	24	Dickinson	John			4		1	2			1				8		
Hadley	286	21	Dickinson	John		1	3			1	1		1				8		
Hadley	289	4	Dickinson	John	3		1						1				5		
Hatfield	13	2	Dickinson	John	1			1			1		1				4		
Amherst	293	4	Dickinson	Jonathan	1	2	1		1	1	1		1				8		
Hatfield	12	39	Dickinson	Jonathan	2			1	1	2		1					7		
Amherst	292	10	Dickinson	Joseph		1	1	1		1		2		1			7		
Granby	252	5	Dickinson	Joseph		1	1			1			2				5		
Hatfield	11	9	Dickinson	Joseph		1	1		1	2			1				6		
Northampton	6	4	Dickinson	Josiah	1	2	9	1	3	2	2		1		1		22		
Amherst	293	21	Dickinson	Judah	2		1	1		1		1	1				8		
Hadley	285	25	Dickinson	Levi	4	3		1		1		1					10		
Amherst	291	31	Dickinson	Medard	2	1		1	1	1	3		1				10		
Northfield	28	12	Dickinson	Moses Junr	1			1		2			1	1			6		
Amherst	292	30	Dickinson	Nahan	1		2	1	1		2		1				8		
Amherst	290	4	Dickinson	Nathaniel		1		2		1			1	2			6		
Amherst	291		Dickinson	Noah	1			1					1				3		
Northfield	28	7	Dickinson	Obadiah	3		1	1		4	1	1	2				13		

222

TOWN	PG#	LN#	LAST NAME	FIRST NAME	under 10	10 to 16	16 to 26	26 to 45	45 and over	under 10	10 to 16	16 to 26	26 to 45	45 and over	TOTAL ALL OTHER	TOTAL SLAVES	TOTALS	DISTRICT/ TOWNSHIP	NOTES
					FREE WHITE MALES					FREE WHITE FEMALES									
Hadley	289	2	Dickinson	Oliver		1	2	1					1	1			6		
Granville East Soc	533	14	Dickinson	Olliver	2	2		1		2	1		1				9		
Amherst	293	22	Dickinson	Perez			1	1		2	2	1					7		
Conway	58	5	Dickinson	Reuben	1	1			1	2	1		1				7		
Southwick	358	23	Dickinson	Richard		1		1					1				3		
Hatfield	11	7	Dickinson	Roger				1		5	2		1				9		
Amherst	290	22	Dickinson	Ruth	1		2					1		1			5		
Amherst	293	25	Dickinson	Salomon	3	2		1		3	1		1				11		
Granby	254	32	Dickinson	Samuel		1			1			1		1			4		
Hatfield	13	31	Dickinson	Samuel	2				1			1	1				5		
Whately	66	31	Dickinson	Samuel			3		1				1				5		
Amherst	291	23	Dickinson	Seth	2			1		3	1		1				8		
Amherst	292	26	Dickinson	Silas	1			1		2	1	1					6		
Amherst	291	39	Dickinson	Simeon			1	1	1				1	2			6		
Amherst	292	7	Dickinson	Simeon Jun				1				1					2		
Amherst	292	38	Dickinson	Stephen	2			1		1			1				5		
Northfield	28	9	Dickinson	Titus		1		1				1		1			4		
Granby	254	43	Dickinson	Waitstill		1		1				1		1			4		
Amherst	291	3	Dickinson	William	3	1	1			1	1		1				8		
Hadley	288	26	Dickinson	William	1			1		1		1		1			5		
Whately	66	33	Dickinson	Zeher	2	2		1		2	1		1				9		
Amherst	291	34	Dickinson	Zimri			1			1			1				3		
Greenfield	72	31	Dickman	Thomas		2	1			3		1	1				8		
Hatfield	12	12	Dicksinson	Lemuel	2		2		1		2			1			8		
Middlefield	156	6	Dickson	James Lieut	2			2	1			3		1			9		
Middlefield	155	1	Dickson	John	2	1	2	1			1		1				8		
Middlefield	155	2	Dickson	Nabby Widw	2						1		1				4		
Leverett	114	14	Dike	Aden	1	1		1		1			1				5		
Shutesbury	109	21	Dillingham	Paul	1	2		1		2	2		1				9		
South Brimfield	277	39	Dimmuck	Gideon		1		1			1	1		1			5		
Norwich	151	23	Dimock	Aaron	1	1		1		1			1				5		
Norwich	151	22	Dimock	Joseph	1		2		1			1		1			6		
Norwich	151	21	Dimock	Joseph Junr	2			1		2	1		1				7		
Norwich	151	24	Dimock	Thomas				1		1	1		1				3		
Conway	58	3	Dinsmore	Abel	1	1		1		2	1		1				7		
Hawley	333	4	Dinsmore	Abel		1		1		2		1					5		
Conway	58	4	Dinsmore	Asa	3			1		1			1				6		
Blanford	177	23	Diver	Daniel	1	2		1	1	3	1	2		1			12		
Ashfield	339	17	Divol	Josiah	2		1	1		2			1				7		
Holland	280	3	Doalph	Amasa				1				1					2		
West Springfield	350	17	Doan	Bethuel			1			2		1					4		
West Springfield	350	22	Doan	James		1		1		1		1					4		
Orange	41	32	Doan	Joseph	1		1	1	1		1	2		1			8		
South Hadley	250	30	Doane	James	1		1	1		3	1	1					8		
Ludlow	255	5	Dodge	Asa	2			1		1			1				5		
Shelburne	320	31	Dodge	Azariah	1				1	1			1				4		
Belchertown	205	2	Dodge	Caleb					1					1			2		
Deerfield	52	29	Dodge	Caleb	3	1							1	1			8		
Rowe	199	22	Dodge	Joshua	2		1	1	1	1		2	1				9		
Shelburne	320	30	Dodge	Nathl			2		1		1	1		1			6		
Shelburne	321	1	Dodge	Rebecca	1	2						3		1			7		
Shelburne	320	29	Dodge	Saml		1	1		1	1				1			5		
Hawley	332	35	Dodge	Silas	1			1		2			1	1			6		
Granville West Soc	170	2	Dodge	Stephen		2		1				2		2			7		
Deerfield	52	39	Dodge	William		1		1	1	1	1		1				5		
Belchertown	205	3	Dodge	Zebulon	2	1	1	1		4	1	1	1				12		
Shelburne	321	5	Dole	Dinsmore	3			1		1		1	1				7		
Shelburne	321	2	Dole	Isaac	2			1		2			1				6		
Shelburne	320	27	Dole	Josiah	3			1		1			1				6		
Shelburne	321	3	Dole	Moses	1			1		1			1				4		
Shelburne	320	25	Dole	Parker	1		1		1		1	3		1			8		
Shelburne	320	26	Dole	Parker Junr			1			3			1				5		
Ware	225	37	Done	Wm Capt			5	1					1				7		
Colrain	185	4	Donelon	Lydia	1					2			1				4		
Colrain	185	7	Donelson	Matthew	2		2	3			2	1	1				11		
Colrain	185	11	Donelson	Moses			2	1		1		2	1	1			8		
Colrain	185	12	Donelson	Reuben	4	1		1				1	1				8		
Northfield	28	10	Doolittle	Lucius			1	1		1	1		2	1			7		
Russell	138	4	Doolittle	Titus	1		1		1	1	1		2				7		
Russell	138	5	Doolittle	Titus Jnr	1	1	1	1		2	1	1					8		
Southampton	129	4	Dooly	Asahel			1							1			2		
Southampton	129	5	Dooly	Noah	1		1			1			1				4		
Southampton	129	6	Dooly	Wm			1					1					2		
Granville West Soc	168	34	Dorman	Stephen		1		1						1			3		
Monson	267	5	Dormound	James	2		1		1	2	2		1				9		
Holland	278	2	Dorrell	Thomas	2	1		1				1		1			6		
Leyden	82	3	Dorrell	William	1	2		1		1		2	1	1			9		
Leverett	114	13	Doty	James	2	1		1		1	1		1				7		
Greenwich	219	21	Doubledee	Joseph	3	1		1			1		1				7		
Westfield	120	16	Douglas	Stephen	2	1		1		1		2					7		

223

TOWN	PG#	LN#	LAST NAME	FIRST NAME	FREE WHITE MALES					FREE WHITE FEMALES					TOTAL ALL OTHER	TOTAL SLAVES	TOTALS	DISTRICT/ TOWNSHIP	NOTES
					under 10	10 to 16	16 to 26	26 to 45	45 and over	under 10	10 to 16	16 to 26	26 to 45	45 and over					
Westfield	128	5	Douglass	Sparra	3			1		1			1				6		
Monson	266	16	Dousett	Philemon	2			1		1			1	1			6		
Leyden	81	36	Downing	John	3	2	3		1		1		1				11		
Chester	144	36	Drake	Abraham	3	1		1		2			1				8		
Granville East Soc	533	3	Drake	Enoch	1			1				1					3		
Greenwich	219	17	Drake	Ephraim	2			1		1	1		1				6		
Chesterfield	20	33	Drake	James	2			1					2				5		
Buckland	327	3	Drake	Jehiel	2		1			2		1					6		
Belchertown	205	14	Drake	Jonah	1			1				1		1			4		
Ashfield	339	21	Drake	Josiah	1		1	1					1				4		
Buckland	327	1	Drake	Josiah				1						1			5		
Westfield	126	22	Drake	Moses					1		1		2	1			5		
Westfield	127	5	Drake	Moses Junr	3		1			1			1				6		
Chesterfield	21	2	Drake	Noah	2		1	1		3	2	1	1	1			12		
Brimfield	273	12	Draper	George		1								1			2		
Amherst	292	23	Draper	Ichabod Revnd		1		1		1		1					4		
Brimfield	273	25	Draper	Isaac		1		1		1	1	2		1			7		
Brimfield	273	30	Draper	John				1						2			3		
Goshen	310	3	Draper	Reuben		3	4	1		1	1	1		1			12		
Belchertown	204	36	Draper	Seth		2	1						1				4		
Wendell	105	20	Dresser	Oliver			1	1					1	2			5		
Wendell	105	21	Dresser	Oliver Jr	1			1					1				3		
Worthington	300	7	Drury	Jonathan			2	1	1	2		2		1			9		
Shelburne	320	28	Drury	Thomas			1		1		1	1		1			5		
Wendell	105	22	Drury	Zechariah	3	1	2		1	1	1		1				10		
Southwick	358	24	Ducey	Elijah	2		1						1				4		
Worthington	302	15	Ducy	Joseph	1			1	1	2	1	1	1	1			9		
Brimfield	272	3	Dudley	Joseph				1									1		
Amherst	293	15	Duglass	Joseph	2			1		2			1				6		
Belchertown	204	33	Dunbar	Azel Lt	1		1	1		1	1		2				7		
Orange	41	34	Dunbar	David		1		1		1	1			1			5		
Worthington	299	6	Dunbar	Hosea			1							1			2		
Ashfield	339	22	Dunbar	Jerimiah	1	1	1			3			1				8		
Palmer	260	19	Dunbar	John			3		1				1	1			6		
Belchertown	204	34	Dunbar	Robert			1		1			1		1			4		
Chesterfield	19	2	Duncan	William	1	1	1		1	3	2		1				10		
Colrain	185	15	Dunham	Abiel	1	1		1		2	1		1				7		
Brimfield	270	12	Dunham	Benjamin	1			1		3			1				6		
Conway	57	52	Dunham	Cornelius	1	1	1	1		1		1		2			8		
Wilbraham	237	18	Dunham	Eli				1						2			3		
Worthington	300	24	Dunham	George	1	2		1		2			1				7		
Williamsburg	447	13	Dunham	Hezekiah		1	1	1	1			1	1				7		
Southwick	358	21	Dunham	Jabez	2		1						1	1			5		
West Springfield	353	9	Dunham	Jabez				1					1	1			3		
Conway	58	1	Dunham	Jonathan	2	2	1		2	3	1		2				13		
Brimfield	270	13	Dunham	Joseph			1	1		1			1				4		
Brimfield	270	14	Dunham	Joseph Jr	1	1		1		2	1	1					7		
Wilbraham	236	39	Dunham	Salathiel	2	1		1		2		1					7		
Conway	58	2	Dunham	Samuel		1		1		1		2					5		
Chesterfield	23	20	Dunlap	George		1		1		1		1					4		
Pelham	213	35	Dunlap	James	1	1	1	1		1			2				7		
Norwich	153	37	Dunlap	John	1			1		1			1				4		
Pelham	213	37	Dunlap	William	1			1					2				4		
New Salem	98	13	Dunn	Samuel				1		1			1				3		
New Salem	98	15	Dunton	Ebenezer	2			1		1			1				5		
Palmer	261	10	Durant	John			1		1								2		
Palmer	259	41	Durant	Nathaniel				1		1			1				3		
Middlefield	156	22	Durant	Thomas	2		2		1		2	2		1			10		
Granville Mid Soc.	165	3	Durham	David			1			1		1					3		
Worthington	301	23	Durkin	Joseph		1		1		1	1	1					5		
Springfield	246	30	Dutton	Jeremiah				1						1			2		
Monson	263	23	Dutton	Oliver	1			1		2		1	1				6		
Northfield	28	11	Dutton	Timothy			1	2	1		1			1	1		7		
Deerfield	52	36	Dwelly	Samuel			1	1	1				1				4		
Northampton	5	17	Dwight	Cecil	2		1					1					4		
Williamsburg	447	14	Dwight	Dorus			1	2		1			1	1			6		
Hatfield	14	29	Dwight	Ebenezer	1	1			3	1	2	1	1	1			11		
Longmeadow	92	7	Dwight	Elihu	1			1	2	1			1	1			7		
Belchertown	205	1	Dwight	Henry	3		3		1	1	1		1				10		
Springfield	242	19	Dwight	James L.	1		3	1		3	1	3					12		
Springfield	242	18	Dwight	Jona Jr	1	1		1		1			1	1			6		
Belchertown	211	29	Dwight	Jonathan			1	1									2		
Springfield	242	17	Dwight	Jonathan Esq	2		3		1		1	1		2			10		
Williamsburg	447	15	Dwight	Josiah	1			1		1			1				4		
Belchertown	204	35	Dwight	Justus	1	1		1	1		1	1		1			7		
Longmeadow	92	6	Dwight	Oliver	1		1	1		1	1	1					6		
Belchertown	209	3	Dwight	Samuel	2			1		2	3		1	1			10		
Conway	57	50	Dwight	Seth			1			2				1			4		
Springfield	242	5	Dwight	Thomas Esq	3		1	1		1	2	1					9		
Ashfield	339	18	Dyer	Benjm	2			1		1			1				5		

224

TOWN	PG#	LN#	LAST NAME	FIRST NAME	M under 10	M 10 to 16	M 16 to 26	M 26 to 45	M 45 and over	F under 10	F 10 to 16	F 16 to 26	F 26 to 45	F 45 and over	TOTAL ALL OTHER	TOTAL SLAVES	TOTALS	DISTRICT/ TOWNSHIP	NOTES
Charlemont	191	5	Dyer	James					1	1	1			1			4		
Ashfield	339	19	Dyer	Jesse	1			1					1				3		
Northfield	28	6	Dyke	Aaron	3			1		1	1		1				7		
Warwick	37	12	Dyke	William	1	1		1		1		1		1			6		
Warwick	37	17	Eager	James	1			1		2			1				5		
Worthington	297	1	Eager	Nahum		1	1		1		1		1	1			6		
Shutesbury	109	23	Eager	Noah	2			1		1	1	1					6		
Worthington	298	15	Eager	William			1										1		
Ashfield	340	6	Eages	Stephen	1			1		1		1					4		
Leverett	114	16	Eames	Charles				1		1			1				3		
Deerfield	52	41	Eames	Ebenezer	1			1		2			1				5		
Deerfield	52	40	Eames	Nathan	1			1	1	2			1				5		
Northfield	28	14	Earl	Robert	1			1					1				3		
Chester	146	8	Eastman	Benjamin		1	1						1	1			5		
Amherst	290	18	Eastman	Ebenezer	1	1	3	1	1		2	1		1			11		
Granby	255	4	Eastman	Eunice Wd	1	2	1							1			5		
Amherst	292	15	Eastman	John	1	2	1		1	2	1	2	1				11		
Amherst	290	21	Eastman	Joseph		1	2		1		1			1			6		
Granby	254	41	Eastman	Joseph	3	1		1		2		1		1			9		
Hadley	288	29	Eastman	Timothy	1	2		1		2	1	1		1			9		
Granby	254	40	Eastman	William	3	1	1					1	1	1			8		
Southwick	358	28	Easton	Ashbel	3	2		1				1		1			8		
Southwick	358	27	Easton	James	1	2	1	1	1	2		1		2			12		
Hawley	333	5	Easton	Joseph	3	1		1		1	1		1	1			9		
Hawley	333	9	Easton	Justus	2	1		1		2			1				7		
Hatfield	13	27	Easton	Princes											4		4		
Greenwich	219	25	Eaton	Calvin	1	1	2	1		2		1	1				9		
Ware	226	7	Eaton	Darius	2			1		2			1				6		
Springfield	245	29	Eaton	James	1	1	1	1		2			1	1			8		
Belchertown	205	5	Eaton	Marion	2	1	2	1		2		1					9		
West Springfield	353	10	Eaton	Nathaniel		1	1	1		2	1		2				8		
Greenwich	219	24	Eaton	Nathl		1			1				1				3		
Warwick	37	15	Eaton	Robert					1				1				2		
Springfield	244	7	Eaton	Silvanus		1	1		1		1	2	1				7		
Belchertown	205	4	Eaton	Walter	1			1					1				3		
Brimfield	271	34	Eaton	William Capt		2	2			3	1	1	1				10		
Warwick	37	13	Eddy	Abel	1	1	2		1			2		1			8		
Greenwich	219	27	Eddy	Abner	4	2			1	1	1	2	1				12		
Leyden	82	8	Eddy	Benjamin	1	1		1		4			1				8		
Palmer	258	5	Eddy	Charles			1		1	2	2		1				7		
Heath	195	13	Eddy	David			1	1				1	1				4		
Colrain	185	22	Eddy	Ebenezar		1		1		1	1		1	1			6		
Warwick	37	16	Eddy	Ebenezer	1			1				1					3		
Colrain	185	18	Eddy	Ephraim	1	2		1			1			1			6		
Belchertown	211	27	Eddy	Hezekiah			1	1					1				3		
Colrain	185	21	Eddy	Ichabod	1	1	1	1		1	1		1				7		
Deerfield	52	43	Eddy	Jacob	2			1		3			1				7		
Wilbraham	235	31	Eddy	James		1						1					2		
New Salem	98	20	Eddy	John				1						1			2		
Colrain	185	20	Eddy	Leonard	2			1		1			1				5		
Deerfield	52	42	Eddy	Moses	1	1		1			1		1				5		
Buckland	327	5	Eddy	Peletiah		1	1	1					1				4		
New Salem	98	19	Eddy	Rufus				1						1			2		
Colrain	185	19	Eddy	Samuel		1			1		1	1	1				5		
Monson	265	29	Edgerton	Dan			1			3		1					5		
Monson	265	30	Edgerton	John			1					1		1			3		
Hawley	333	6	Edgeston	Joseph		1	2	1				1		1			7		
Hawley	333	7	Edgeston	Oliver			1					1	1				3		
Springfield	246	40	Edson	Benjamin	3	1		1		1	2		1				9		
South Brimfield	276	21	Edson	Caleb	2	1	1		1	4	1		1				11		
Shutesbury	109	24	Edson	Elijah	1					2			1				5		
Springfield	246	41	Edson	Jacob			1		1			2		2			6		
Buckland	327	4	Edson	Jesse			2		1		1		1	1			6		
Pelham	214	1	Edson	Seth	3	1		1	1		1		1	1			9		
Leyden	82	10	Edwards	Abel	1			1		1		1					4		
Northampton	5	15	Edwards	Benja Hurd	2	2	1	1		2		1	1				10		
Northampton	3	37	Edwards	Benjamin		1	2		1		1		1				6		
Norwich	151	31	Edwards	Benjamin				1		3		1					5		
Westhampton	18	28	Edwards	Daniel			2	1		2		1	2				8		
Leyden	82	16	Edwards	Ebenezer	2			1		2			1				6		
Southampton	129	27	Edwards	Elisha	2		1	1		1			1	1			8		
Northampton	3	13	Edwards	Gideon			1						1				2		
Springfield	240	7	Edwards	John L.	1			1		1			1				4		
Westhampton	18	13	Edwards	Justin	1	1	1		1	1	1	1	1				8		
Southampton	129	25	Edwards	Luther	1	1	2	1		1	1	1					8		
Northampton	3	14	Edwards	Medad				1						1			2		
Northampton	3	15	Edwards	Medad Jr			1			1			1				3		
Amherst	292	24	Edwards	Nathaniel			1	1					2	1			5		
Northampton	10	21	Edwards	Nathaniel	1		5		1	2	1	2		2			14		
Chesterfield	19	18	Edwards	Oliver	2		1	1		2	2		1				9		

TOWN	PG#	LN#	LAST NAME	FIRST NAME	FREE WHITE MALES					FREE WHITE FEMALES					TOTAL ALL OTHER	TOTAL SLAVES	TOTALS	DISTRICT/ TOWNSHIP	NOTES
					under 10	10 to 16	16 to 26	26 to 45	45 and over	under 10	10 to 16	16 to 26	26 to 45	45 and over					
Amherst	292	22	Edwards	Phillip	1	2	1			1			1				6		
Westhampton	15	16	Edwards	Samuel		2		1				1		1			5		
Northampton	9	14	Edwards	Simeon		1			1	3	2	1					8		
Barnardston	77	31	Edwards	Thomas	2	1		1				3	1				8		
Westhampton	18	22	Edwards	Timothy		1	1		1	1		2		1			7		
Northampton	7	26	Edwards	Vester	2			1		2		1					6		
Southwick	358	25	Edwards	Warham	1			1					1				3		
Northampton	9	6	Edwards	William	2		10	1			1	1	1		2		18		
Northampton	3	28	Edwards	Nathaniel 2d				1		1		1					3		
Middlefield	158	36	Egelston	Benjamin		1	2		1	2	1	1	1				9		
Chester	144	34	Egelston	Jerusha Wd							1	1	1				3		
Chester	149	23	Egelston	Oliver	3			1		1			1				6		
Westfield	125	10	Egleston	Eber		2	1		1	3		1	1				9		
Westfield	121	20	Egleston	Jehiel	1			1		2	1		1				6		
West Springfield	353	12	Egleston	John	1	1		1		2	1	1	1				8		
Westfield	125	11	Egleston	Simeon	2	2		1		2			1	1			9		
Chester	144	23	Eldar	John Deac	1		1	1					1				4		
Chester	144	38	Eldar	Thomas	2	1	1	1			2						7		
Chester	144	39	Eldar	Thomas Junr	1			1			1						3		
Chester	143	14	Eldar	William	1	3		1		3	1		1	2			12		
Hawley	333	8	Eldred	Saml		1	2	1					1				5		
Granville West Soc	168	19	Eldridge	Daniel	2			1		2	1	1	1				8		
Granville West Soc	170	13	Eldridge	Daniel	2			1		2	1		1				7		
Ashfield	339	26	Eldridge	Eli	1		1	1			2		1	1			7		
Plainfield	306	27	Eldridge	Ezekiel		3		1		2			1				7		
Ashfield	339	25	Eldridge	Levi	1	1	3		1	2	2		2				12		
Plainfield	307	17	Eldridge	Moses	3			1		1			1				6		
West Springfield	350	32	Eldridge	Mulford	1	1		1		1		2		1			7		
Ashfield	340	4	Eldridge	Saml	3			1		2			2				8		
Plainfield	307	8	Eldridge	Samuel	1			1		1		1	1				5		
Northfield	28	15	Elgar	Thomas				1		1			1				3		
Southampton	132	7	Eliot	Francis			1						1				2		
Easthampton	137	1	Eliot	John	3	1		1			1		1				7		
Leyden	82	15	Eliott	Lemuel	2			1		3			1				7		
Monson	266	42	Ellinwood	Tertius	1			1		2			1				5		
Brimfield	271	14	Ellinwood	Thomas			1	1				1	1				4		
Leverett	114	17	Elliot	Ebenz				1					1				2		
New Salem	98	17	Elliot	Samuel		1							1				2		
Conway	58	9	Ellis	Barzilla	1	2	1			1			1				6		
Monson	267	14	Ellis	Benjamin			1	1					1				3		
Buckland	327	7	Ellis	Benjm	1	2	1		1	1		2		1			9		
Ashfield	339	28	Ellis	David	1	1		1		1	2		1	2			9		
New Salem	98	18	Ellis	Gregory	2		1					1					4		
Ashfield	339	27	Ellis	John		1		1				1	1	1			5		
Buckland	327	6	Ellis	John	1		1	1		3	2	2		1			11		
New Salem	98	21	Ellis	John	2		1	1					1				5		
Northampton	4	4	Ellis	John	2			1				1	1				5		
Orange	41	40	Ellis	John				1					1				2		
Ashfield	340	5	Ellis	Jonathan		1		1				1	1				6		
Orange	41	39	Ellis	Moses	3			1		1		1	1				7		
Orange	41	41	Ellis	Nathan		2		1					1				4		
New Salem	98	22	Ellis	Paul	3	2		1					1				7		
Orange	41	38	Ellis	Seth		3		1				1	1				6		
Ware	226	6	Ellis	Seth	2	3		1		1			1				8		
Buckland	327	8	Ellis	Stephen			1			1		1					3		
Granville East Soc	531	2	Ellis	William				1			1		1				3		
Northfield	28	13	Ellis	William	3		2			1	1						7		
Norwich	152	43	Elliss	John	2			1		2	1		1				7		
Chester	146	29	Elliss	Noah		1		1					1	1			4		
Chester	146	33	Elliss	Samuel		1	1	1					1				4		
Amherst	290	14	Elmer	Elijah	1	1		1		1	2		1				7		
Ashfield	340	1	Elmore	Gad	3		1	1		1	1	1	1				9		
Ashfield	339	29	Elmore	Saml	2	1		1			1		1				6		
Ashfield	340	2	Elmore	Saml Junr	2	1		1		1			1				6		
Ashfield	340	3	Elmore	Zenas	2			1		1			1				5		
Amherst	294	6	Eloner	Simeon		2		1		1		3		1			8		
West Springfield	353	11	Elsworth	Gustavus				1			1	1		1			4		
Chester	149	3	Elsworth	Jonathan		1				1	1	1					4		
Westhampton	15	2	Elwell	Thomas		1		1		1	2	1		1			7		
West Springfield	350	45	Ely	Abigail									1	1			2		
West Springfield	356	22	Ely	Benjamin		1	2	1					1	1			6		
West Springfield	356	29	Ely	C*	1			1		3	1	1	1				8		
South Hadley	250	12	Ely	Caleb			1						1				2		
West Springfield	350	44	Ely	Cotton	2	1		1		1		1					6		
West Springfield	350	39	Ely	Daniel	2	1		1		1	1		1				7		
West Springfield	350	35	Ely	Darius	3			1		1	2		2	1	1		11		
West Springfield	356	27	Ely	Elihu	1	1		2		3		1	1				9		
West Springfield	350	41	Ely	Elihu 2d	1		1						1				3		
West Springfield	356	26	Ely	Enoch	3			1		1	1		1				7		
West Springfield	356	28	Ely	Erasmus		1		1		3			1				6		
Longmeadow	93	12	Ely	Ethan	1	2	1	1		3	1		2				11		

TOWN	PG#	LN#	HEADS OF HOUSEHOLD		FREE WHITE MALES					FREE WHITE FEMALES					TOTAL ALL OTHER	TOTAL SLAVES	TOTALS	DISTRICT/ TOWNSHIP	NOTES
			LAST NAME	FIRST NAME	under 10	10 to 16	16 to 26	26 to 45	45 and over	under 10	10 to 16	16 to 26	26 to 45	45 and over					
West Springfield	350	40	Ely	George	2	1		1		2	1		1				8		
Springfield	243	36	Ely	Horace	1		1	1		1	1	1					6		
West Springfield	350	34	Ely	John	3		4		1	1		1		1			11		
Middlefield	159	1	Ely	Jonathan	1	2			1		1		1				6		
Wilbraham	234	40	Ely	Jonathan					1					1			2		
Wilbraham	234	43	Ely	Jonathan Junr		1	1		1	1	3		1				8		
West Springfield	356	21	Ely	Joseph			1	1					1	3			6		
Wilbraham	234	41	Ely	Judah	1	2			1	2	1	2	1				10		
West Springfield	350	33	Ely	Justin			2	2	2	1	1		1				9		
West Springfield	350	36	Ely	Levi	2			1					1				4		
West Springfield	350	42	Ely	Martin	2		3		1	2	1	3		1			13		
West Springfield	356	24	Ely	Moses	3	2		1	1	1	1		1	1			11		
Longmeadow	93	13	Ely	Nathaniel	1	1			1	3	1		1	1	2		11		
West Springfield	350	43	Ely	Nathaniel					1			1	1				3		
West Springfield	356	23	Ely	Robert	2			1		1			1				5		
West Springfield	350	37	Ely	Silence		1							2				3		
West Springfield	350	46	Ely	Solomon		2				1		1					4		
Granville Mid Soc.	166	19	Ely	Thomas	2			1			1	1					5		
West Springfield	350	38	Ely	William				1					1				2		
Wendell	105	24	Emerson	Jesse		1	2		1		1		1				6		
Conway	58	10	Emerson	John		1	3		1		3		1				9		
Greenwich	219	28	Emerson	Robt	1			1		1		1	1				5		
Chester	144	13	Eminom	Sylvester	1			1			1						3		
Middlefield	155	21	Emmons	Ebenezer Ensn	1		1	2		2		1					7		
Norwich	152	22	Eno	James		1			1	1	2		1				6		
Montgomery	161	37	Ensign	Datis			1										1		
Southwick	358	26	Ensign	Datis	3	2	3		1	1			1				11		
Westfield	123	23	Ensign	Isaac	2	3	1	1		3			1	1			12		
Montgomery	161	36	Ensign	Reuben			1										1		
Chester	148	28	Ensign	Seamour			1										1		
Cummington	305	23	Ensign	Zerah				1		2		1	1				5		
Wilbraham	234	12	Erving	James		1		1					1				3		
Warwick	37	14	Esty	Jacob			1		1		1			2			5		
Orange	41	37	Esty	Oliver	1	1		1		1		1	1				6		
Leyden	82	14	Euda	John	2	1		1		3	2		1				10		
Conway	58	11	Evans	Ebenezer		1		1			1		1				4		
Wendell	105	26	Evans	Henry		1				1	2		2				7		
Leyden	82	11	Evans	John			1	1	1				1				4		
Hadley	288	6	Evelth	John	1	2		1		4			1				9		
Norwich	154	31	Everet	Isaac			1								5		6		
Westhampton	16	15	Everett	Mary								1		1			2		
Wendell	105	25	Evers	Elihu		1	1			1			1				4		
Gill	85	14	Evers	Henry	1	1	1		2	2	1	1		2			11		
Montague	45	36	Evers	Henry	1	1	1		1	1		1		1			7		
Gill	85	15	Evers	James	1	1					1						3		
Gill	85	13	Evers	John	1		2		1	2	3		1				10		
Norwich	151	20	Ewell	James	2	4	2	1		3			1				13		
Chesterfield	20	5	Ewell	John			2	1	1		1	1	1				7		
Chesterfield	20	6	Ewell	Malachi			1			1		1					3		
Longmeadow	93	5	Ewings	Joshua			1					1					2		
West Springfield	356	25	Ey	Russell			1				1		1				3		
Leverett	115	11	Fair	Robert	4	1		1		1		1					8		
Warwick	37	18	Fair	Thomas	3		1			1	2	1					8		
Colrain	185	31	Fairbanks	Daniel	2		1	1		1		1	1				7		
Brimfield	273	37	Fairbanks	Ebenz Deacn		2	1	1			1		1				6		
Brimfield	273	38	Fairbanks	Henry	1			1		1		1					4		
Brimfield	273	39	Fairbanks	Joseph	2			1		1		1					5		
Colrain	185	30	Fairbanks	Moses		1		1		3			1	1			7		
Leyden	82	19	Fairbanks	Nathan	3	1		1		3	1	2					11		
Williamsburg	447	21	Fairfield	Ira Northerly	2	1		1					1				5		
Springfield	245	21	Fairfield	Levi	1			1									2		
Williamsburg	447	20	Fairfield	Samuel		1	1		1		1		1				5		
Belchertown	209	8	Fairfield	Thaddeus			4	1	1		3		1				10		
Granby	252	40	Fairfield	Thaddeus	1			1			1						3		
Springfield	247	30	Fairfield	Thomas				1			1	1	1				4		
Longmeadow	93	1	Fairman	Ithamar	1			1		1	2		1				6		
Norwich	154	17	Fairman	Samuel Lieut	1	1		1		2		2		1			8		
Charlemont	191	8	Fales	James	3	1		1		1		2	1	1			10		
Charlemont	191	9	Fales	Jeremiah			1			1		1					3		
Colrain	185	35	Falkner	Joseph	1	1			2	2			1	1			8		
Colrain	185	28	Falkner	Joseph Jun	1	1		1		3		2		1			9		
Colrain	185	29	Falkner	William	1	2		1			4	1					9		
Colrain	185	37	Falkner	William Jun	1		1				1						3		
Blanford	179	19	Falley	Daniel	3		2	1				1					7		
Chester	148	24	Falley	Richard	1	1		1			2			1			6		
Montgomery	161	26	Falley	Richard Lieut		1	3	1	1			2		1			9		
Montgomery	161	33	Falley	Russel			1			2		1					4		
Northfield	28	18	Fan	John					1				1				2		
Chester	145	9	Faning	Elisha	1	2		1		2	1	1	1				9		
Colrain	185	25	Farley	Benjamin	2	1		1		2	1		1				9		

TOWN	PG#	LN#	LAST NAME	FIRST NAME	FREE WHITE MALES under 10	10 to 16	16 to 26	26 to 45	45 and over	FREE WHITE FEMALES under 10	10 to 16	16 to 26	26 to 45	45 and over	TOTAL ALL OTHER	TOTAL SLAVES	TOTALS	DISTRICT/ TOWNSHIP	NOTES
West Springfield	350	47	Farnam	Elijah	2		1			2			1				6		
West Springfield	350	48	Farnam	Jesse	1		1			1		1					4		
West Springfield	350	50	Farnam	John				1				1		1			3		
Conway	58	14	Farnham	Asa	2		1		1	1	2	1		1			9		
Blanford	181	18	Farnham	Elisha	1	1		1		2	2	1					8		
Blanford	177	7	Farnham	Reuben	1	2	1		2		2	1		2			11		
Heath	196	1	Farnsworth	Benjm	4			1				1					6		
Colrain	185	32	Farnsworth	Joseph			1			3		1					5		
Shelburne	321	14	Farnsworth	Levi	1		1			1		1					4		
Hawley	333	14	Farnsworth	Willm		1		1			1			1			4		
Hawley	333	16	Farnsworth	Willm Jr	4		1	1		2		1					9		
Northampton	10	4	Farnum	Clement	2		1			1	1	1					6		
Sunderland	282	9	Farnum	Heman	1		1			1	2	1					6		
Westfield	121	3	Farnum	Joel	3		1	1		2	1	1					9		
Westfield	121	18	Farnum	John		2		1		2	1			1			7		
Cummington	303	7	Farr	Ansel	1		1						1	1			4		
Cummington	303	6	Farr	Jacob		1		1		1	2			1			6		
Shelburne	321	6	Farrah	Nathl		1		1		1	1	2					6		
Northfield	28	19	Farrar	Adam	1		1			1		1					4		
Brimfield	269	37	Farrel	Josiah		1	1		1		1			1			5		
Palmer	259	14	Farrell	Isaac	1	2	1			1		1					6		
Palmer	258	2	Farrell	Josiah	1	1	1			1		1					5		
Palmer	259	25	Farrell	Timothy	1		3	1			2		1				8		
Palmer	259	32	Farrell	William	2	1		1		1	1	1					7		
Palmer	259	22	Farrington	Amos			1					1					2		
Springfield	243	14	Faulk	Festus	1		1					1					3		
Conway	58	21	Faxan	Thomas	2		1			1	1	1		1			7		
Deerfield	52	47	Faxon	Calvin	2		1			1	1						5		
Pelham	214	2	Fay	Artemas			1	1		1							3		
Belchertown	209	13	Fay	Benajah	1		1			1		1					4		
Holland	279	18	Fay	David	1	1	1	1	1	2	1	1	1				10		
Plainfield	307	6	Fay	Elijah	1		1			2	1			1			6		
Wendell	105	35	Fay	Enoch	1		1						1				3		
Monson	263	38	Fay	Jude	2	1		2		1	1	3	1				11		
Brimfield	273	40	Fay	Levi	2		1	1		1	2	1					8		
Monson	267	20	Fay	Mary Wd		1	1							1			3		
Warwick	37	19	Fay	Moses				1					1				2		
Buckland	327	17	Fay	Nathan	1		1	1		3	3			1			10		
Chester	145	27	Fay	Sarah Wd	2	1	1			1		1	2				8		
Warwick	37	20	Fay	Samuel		1	1			3	1						6		
Brimfield	273	42	Faye	Jonathan		1	2	1		1	2			1			8		
Brimfield	270	42	Faye	Thomas	2	1	1			2	1			1			9		
Brimfield	270	43	Faye	Uriah		1		1						1			3		
Granville Mid Soc.	166	17	Feebles	Francis	1	1	1					1					4		
Granville Mid Soc.	166	15	Feebles	Harvey		1				2		1					4		
Granville Mid Soc.	166	18	Feebles	John			1	1		1		2					5		
Granville Mid Soc.	166	16	Feebles	John Junr	3	1	1						1				6		
West Springfield	353	26	Feland	Henry	2		1						1				4		
West Springfield	353	14	Feland	Isaac			1			1		1					3		
West Springfield	353	13	Feland	Joseph				1						1			2		
West Springfield	353	39	Feller	John	1		1						1				3		
Chester	145	11	Fellows	Jacob			1				1			1			3		
Shelburne	321	10	Fellows	John Capt.	2		1	1		2	3			1			10		
Shelburne	321	7	Fellows	Joseph		1		1					1	1			4		
Middlefield	156	17	Fellows	Parker			1			3		1					5		
Shelburne	321	9	Fellows	Saml Jr	3		1						1				5		
Shelburne	321	18	Fellows	Solomon	1	1		1		2	1	1					7		
Shelburne	321	11	Fellows	Wiilis	3		3	1		2	3	1		1			14		
Leverett	114	28	Felt	Jonathan	1	2				2	1						6		
West Springfield	350	49	Felt	Mary	1					2	1		1	1			6		
Shutesbury	109	26	Felton	Amos		1	1	1			2			1			6		
Pelham	217	10	Felton	Benja	1	1		1		1		1					5		
Shutesbury	109	25	Felton	Benjamin		1	2			1	1			1			6		
New Salem	99	4	Felton	Daniel			1						1	1			3		
New Salem	98	26	Felton	Ebenezer 2d	1		1	1		1		1					5		
New Salem	98	25	Felton	James	1	1	1	1		1		2		1			8		
New Salem	98	24	Felton	Joseph	1		1			1	1	1					5		
New Salem	98	38	Felton	Martin	1		1			1		1					4		
New Salem	98	27	Felton	Nathl		1	1	1		1		1	1	1			7		
Blanford	178	38	Felton	Seth	2		1			2		1					6		
New Salem	98	28	Felton	Stephen	3	2	1	1		1		2	1	1			13		
South Brimfield	276	26	Fenton	Eunice									1	1			2		
Brimfield	270	33	Fenton	John	1	1	3	1		3		1		1			11		
South Brimfield	276	8	Fenton	Timothy		1		1					1				3		
South Brimfield	276	9	Fenton	Wm				1						1			2		
Blanford	181	4	Ferguson	Dorothy	1		2							1			4		
Blanford	178	34	Ferguson	John	1	2		1		1	1	1		1			9		
Hawley	333	12	Ferguson	Saml	3	2	1			1	1	1					9		
Blanford	176	28	Ferguson	Samuel	1	1		1	1			2	1				7		
Blanford	179	27	Ferguson	Solomon				1									3		

TOWN	PG#	LN#	LAST NAME	FIRST NAME	FREE WHITE MALES					FREE WHITE FEMALES					TOTAL ALL OTHER	TOTAL SLAVES	TOTALS	DISTRICT/ TOWNSHIP	NOTES
					under 10	10 to 16	16 to 26	26 to 45	45 and over	under 10	10 to 16	16 to 26	26 to 45	45 and over					
Longmeadow	92	28	Fern	Charles	2	2			1	3			1				9		
Springfield	241	32	Fern	Luther			1			1			1				3		
Springfield	242	26	Fern	Uriah	1		1	1		2			1				6		
Granby	254	5	Ferre	Charles				1									1		
Granby	254	6	Ferre	Charles Jr	3	1	1	1		1			1				8		
Springfield	239	40	Ferre	John				1						1			2		
Monson	262	19	Ferre	Jona		1	1	1						2			5		
Palmer	261	32	Ferre	Judah	1	3	2		1	1		3		1			12		
Granby	254	7	Ferre	Luther	1		1	1		1			1				5		
Springfield	243	6	Ferre	Mary Wd										3			3		
Granby	254	3	Ferre	Noah	3	2	1		1	1			1				9		
Springfield	243	5	Ferre	Solomon	1	2			1	1				1			6		
Springfield	243	9	Ferre	Thaddeus				1		3	1		1				6		
Springfield	245	13	Ferry	Caleb				1		1			1				3		
West Springfield	356	31	Ferry	Charles	2			1		1			1				5		
Springfield	245	12	Ferry	Joseph Capt		1			1	1			1	1			5		
Springfield	245	14	Ferry	Joseph Junr		1		1		1			1				4		
West Springfield	353	24	Ferry	Moses		1	1			2	2		2				9		
Springfield	246	24	Ferry	Peter	1			1		3			1				6		
Easthampton	135	31	Ferry	Solomon		2		1				1		1			5		
Easthampton	135	30	Ferry	Solomon Junr	1			1					1				3		
West Springfield	353	27	Ferry	William	1			1		4			1				7		
Buckland	327	12	Fessenden	Wyman	1			1				1					3		
Northfield	28	21	Field	Abner	3	2		1		2	1	2	1				12		
Longmeadow	91	16	Field	Alexr Capt.	1		2	1				1	2	1			8		
Greenwich	219	35	Field	Benja				1				1		1			3		
Conway	58	19	Field	Daniel	2	1		1		3			2	1			10		
Conway	58	22	Field	Ebenezer			2		1		2	1		1			7		
Gill	85	16	Field	Ebenezer		1	2		2	2		1		1			9		
Northfield	28	20	Field	Ebenezer				1						1			2		
Hawley	333	13	Field	Elijah	1	1	1		1	2	1	1	1				9		
Leverett	114	24	Field	Erastus				1					1				2		
Northfield	28	22	Field	George	2	1	1		1				1	1			7		
Northfield	28	33	Field	Henry	2	2		2		1	1	1	1				10		
Barnardston	77	34	Field	Jesse	1		1		1	2	2	3	1	2			13		
Conway	58	20	Field	John	2	1		1		3			1				8		
Leyden	82	21	Field	John	2		2	1		1	2	1	1				10		
Northfield	28	25	Field	John		1	2		1	1	1	2		1			9		
Leverett	114	20	Field	Jonathan		2	1		1				2	1			7		
Leverett	114	25	Field	Jonathan 2d		1	3		1		1	1		1			8		
Charlemont	191	7	Field	Joseph	1			1				1	1				4		
Northfield	28	32	Field	Keziah	1									1			2		
Belchertown	205	6	Field	Lemuel	2	1			1	2	2		1				9		
Leverett	114	22	Field	Luther	1			1		1			1				4		
Hatfield	12	20	Field	Medad		1	1		1	1	1			1			6		
Northfield	28	16	Field	Medad		1			1	1	1		1				5		
Leverett	114	23	Field	Moses	3	1			1	1	1	1	1				9		
Longmeadow	91	17	Field	Moses Capt.					2					1			3		
Longmeadow	91	18	Field	Moses Junr	1		1		1			1		1			5		
Conway	58	18	Field	Nathaniel				1						1			2		
Longmeadow	93	31	Field	Oliver				1						1			2		
Leverett	114	26	Field	Paras	3			1		2			1				7		
Northfield	28	17	Field	Phinehas	£	1		1	1	?	1		1				9		
Greenwich	219	36	Field	Robt Esq			3		1		1	2	1	1			9		
Gill	86	1	Field	Rodolphus			1			1		1					3		
Leverett	114	27	Field	Roswell		1	1			1		1					4		
Leverett	114	19	Field	Rufus		1											1		
Northfield	28	23	Field	Rufus	1		2		1	2	1	2	1				10		
Conway	58	17	Field	Samuel			1		1	1	1		1				5		
Northfield	28	27	Field	Samuel	2	3	1		3		2	1	2				14		
Hatfield	14	10	Field	Seth	2			1		2			1				6		
Leverett	114	18	Field	Seth		1	3		1		1	1		1			8		
Conway	58	13	Field	Solomon	2	2	4		1	1		1	1	1			13		
Northfield	28	24	Field	Sylvester				1		2			1				4		
Russell	138	10	Field	Thomas	4			1		2			1				8		
Sunderland	283	12	Field	Thomas		1					1		2				4		
Northfield	28	26	Field	Walter	1	2	1	1		3	2	2	1				13		
Leverett	114	21	Field	William	1	1	1		1	1		2	1				8		
Northfield	28	30	Field	William		1	1		1		1			2			6		
Ashfield	340	10	Field	Zachariah	4	1		3		1	1		1				11		
Hatfield	14	9	Field	Zachariah				1					1	1			3		
Northfield	28	28	Field	Zachariah	1	1	1		1	3			1	1			9		
Whately	66	39	Field	Zenas	4	1			1	2	1	1	2				12		
Monson	262	8	Fields	Theodore	1			1		3			1				6		
Amherst	289	13	Fillmore	William	2		1						1				4		
Greenwich	219	34	Fimace	David	3			1	2	1			1				8		
Montgomery	162	8	Finch	Preserved	2			1		2			1				6		
Wilbraham	237	43	Firmin	John			2		1		1			1			5		
Wilbraham	237	19	Firmin	John Jr			1					1					2		
Monson	265	20	Firmin	Salmon	1			1					1				3		

TOWN	PG#	LN#	LAST NAME	FIRST NAME	FREE WHITE MALES					FREE WHITE FEMALES					TOTAL ALL OTHER	TOTAL SLAVES	TOTALS	DISTRICT/ TOWNSHIP	NOTES
					under 10	10 to 16	16 to 26	26 to 45	45 and over	under 10	10 to 16	16 to 26	26 to 45	45 and over					
New Salem	98	23	Fish	Abel				1					1	1			3		
Shutesbury	109	27	Fish	Ezra	2	1		1			1	2	1	1			9		
Amherst	294	13	Fish	Stephen	2	2	3		1	2		1		1			12		
Wendell	105	27	Fisher	Aaron	1	1	1	1		3			1				8		
Westhampton	16	16	Fisher	Aaron			2	1			1		1	1			6		
Warwick	37	23	Fisher	Abijah	1		1	1		2			1				6		
Greenwich	219	32	Fisher	Ebenz	2	2		1		3			1				9		
Williamsburg	447	25	Fisher	Ephraim		3		1	1	1	2	2		1			10		
Warwick	37	24	Fisher	George				1				1					2		
Warwick	37	21	Fisher	Israel	2			1	1	2		1		1	1		9		
Granby	253	14	Fisher	Jacob			1			1		1					3		
Wendell	105	28	Fisher	Jesse	3			1		2			1				7		
Rowe	199	24	Fisher	John		1	1		1	1		2	1				7		
Belchertown	207	37	Fisher	Joseph	1	3		1		2			1	1			9		
Greenwich	219	33	Fisher	Leml			1			3			1				5		
South Brimfield	276	33	Fisk	Asa Capt.	2	1	1		1				1	1			7		
South Brimfield	278	6	Fisk	Asa Jun			1			2			1				4		
Deerfield	52	45	Fisk	Daniel		2			1	1				1			5		
Shelburne	321	16	Fisk	Daniel	1	1	1	1		2		1	1	1			10		
Wendell	105	30	Fisk	Daniel	3			1					1				5		
Wendell	105	31	Fisk	Daniel 2d			1	1	1			1					4		
South Brimfield	275	13	Fisk	David		1						1					2		
Williamsburg	447	26	Fisk	David	2			1				1					4		
Shelburne	321	19	Fisk	Ebenz	2	2	1		1	1	1	1		1			10		
South Brimfield	275	9	Fisk	Hezh Capt.	3	2	1	1			1	2	1				11		
Conway	58	23	Fisk	John		1		1		2	1	1	2				8		
Wendell	105	33	Fisk	Jonas	3			1		1		1					6		
Wendell	105	32	Fisk	Jonathan Junr		1		1		1			1				5		
Shelburne	321	13	Fisk	Levi		1	1		1					2			5		
New Salem	98	33	Fisk	Nathaniel	1	1		1		2	2		1				8		
Shelburne	321	15	Fisk	Saml	3		1	1		1	1	1	1		1		10		
Shelburne	321	17	Fisk	Simeon	2	3		2	2			3	2	2			16		
Wendell	105	29	Fisk	Zedekiah	2		1	1		1	1	1	1				8		
Chesterfield	20	34	Fiske	Josiah			1		1		1	1		1			5		
Worthington	301	37	Fitch	Adrian	1			1					1				3		
Hatfield	12	37	Fitch	Ebenezer		1	1		1			1		1			5		
Leyden	82	24	Fitch	Ezra		1		1		1			1				4		
Shelburne	321	8	Fitch	Uriah				1			1		1				3		
Worthington	297	18	Fitch	Walter			1	1			1		1				4		
Ware	226	10	Fitzgerald	William	2	1			1		2	1	1				8		
Charlemont	191	10	Flagg	Benoni	2	1		1	1	1	1	1	1	1			10		
Conway	58	15	Flagg	Eleazer	2	1	1	1		2			1				8		
Barnardston	77	35	Flagg	Samuel	1		1	1		2	1		1				7		
Palmer	261	16	Fleming	David	1		1	1					1	2			6		
Chester	145	21	Fleming	James	1			1			1	1					4		
Palmer	261	17	Fleming	Joseph	3			1		2			1				7		
Amherst	293	30	Flemming	James	1		2	1		3		2	1	2			12		
Brimfield	275	8	Fletcher	Amos	2			1		2			1				6	South Brimfield	
West Springfield	353	19	Fletcher	Archelaus											9		9		
Hawley	333	17	Fletcher	David		2			1	2		1		1			7		
Springfield	245	7	Fletcher	Ira	1										8		9		
West Springfield	353	18	Fletcher	Ozias											13		13		
Granville West Soc	168	23	Fletcher	Thaddeus			1			1		1					3		
Ashfield	340	18	Flower	George	2			1		1			1				5		
West Springfield	353	22	Flower	Horace				1		1			1				3		
Buckland	327	13	Flower	Joseph						3	2	1	1				7		
Ashfield	340	8	Flower	Lamrock	2	1	1	1	1	1	2		1	1			11		
West Springfield	353	21	Flower	Oxas	2			1			1		1				5		
West Springfield	353	15	Flower	Samuel		1	2		1	1		2		1	1		9		
West Springfield	353	23	Flower	Timothy	1	2		1			2	1	1				8		
Ashfield	340	9	Flower	Willm	1	2				3	2	1					9		
Ashfield	340	19	Flower	Willm Junr	3			1			1						5		
Montgomery	161	28	Flowers	Joseph				1									1		
Cummington	303	16	Floyd	John	1	1		1			1	2	1				7		
Wilbraham	238	10	Flynt	Jonathan		1	4		1	1	2	3		1			13		
Belchertown	205	7	Fobes	Abner	1			1		2	1	1	1	1			8		
Greenwich	219	31	Fobes	Jesse	2	1		1		3		1	1				9		
Greenwich	219	29	Fobes	Joseph				1									1		
Greenwich	219	39	Fobes	Joseph P.			1			2			1				4		
Chester	146	17	Fobes	Nathan	3	2	1	1		1	1		1				10		
Norwich	152	23	Fobes	Samuel	1	1			1	2	1		1				7		
Norwich	152	19	Fobes	Walter Capt	3	1	1	1		1	1	1	1		1		12		
Norwich	154	19	Fobes	William Dea	1	1	1		2			1		1			7		
Worthington	301	12	Follit	Isaac		1		1	1	1	2	2	1				9		
Worthington	298	9	Follit	Samuel	1			1	1					1			4		
Southwick	358	30	Foot	Enos		1	1		1	1	1						5		
Chester	144	8	Foot	William	2	2		1		1		1		1			8		
Chester	144	19	Forbes	Agnes			2							1			3		
Greenfield	73	1	Forbes	Daniel	2		1	1		2			1				7		
Hawley	333	11	Forbes	David	1	1		1				1					4		

230

TOWN	PG#	LN#	LAST NAME	FIRST NAME	FREE WHITE MALES					FREE WHITE FEMALES					TOTAL ALL OTHER	TOTAL SLAVES	TOTALS	DISTRICT/ TOWNSHIP	NOTES
					under 10	10 to 16	16 to 26	26 to 45	45 and over	under 10	10 to 16	16 to 26	26 to 45	45 and over					
Buckland	327	14	Forbes	Edward	1	1		1		1			1				5		
Buckland	327	15	Forbes	Jotham	3			1		1			1	1			7		
Granville East Soc	529	33	Forbs	Jonathan			2	1						1			4		
Ashfield	340	17	Forbush	Ebenz		1		1		3			1				6		
Ashfield	340	20	Forbush	Thomas				1			3			1			5		
Plainfield	307	1	Ford	Andrew	1	1	2		1	4	1		1				11		
Plainfield	307	28	Ford	Daniel	3	2	2		1	1	1	1		1			12		
Plainfield	307	3	Ford	Elijah		1		1		4	1		1				8		
Cummington	303	8	Ford	Heschiah				1					1	2			4		
Cummington	303	10	Ford	Hesk Jun	1	3		1			1		1				7		
Ashfield	340	11	Ford	John	2			1				1					4		
New Salem	98	37	Ford	Josiah		2	1		1		2		1				7		
Cummington	303	9	Ford	Luke			2		1		1		1				5		
Charlemont	191	11	Ford	Samuel	4	2		1			1		1				9		
Plainfield	307	4	Ford	Seth		1	1						1				3		
Plainfield	307	2	Ford	Solomon		1	1			3			1				6		
Plainfield	307	7	Ford	Thomas				1						1			2		
Brimfield	270	30	Forgate	Daniel		1	1	1		1	1		1				6		
Orange	41	42	Forrester	John	2	2		1		1		1	1				8		
Southwick	358	29	Forward	Joseph	1	1	2	1		2	1	1	1				10		
Belchertown	209	9	Forward	Justus Revd	2		1	1	2	1	3		1				11		
Worthington	301	44	Forward	Reuben		1		1		2	1		1				6		
Springfield	243	27	Fosgate	Joshua	1			1		1			1	1			5		
Wilbraham	235	8	Fosgate	Zenas				1				1					2		
Wendell	105	34	Fosket	Joel	4			1		2			1	1			9		
Colrain	185	33	Fosket	Samuel	4			1		1			1				7		
Orange	42	2	Foskett	Ebenezer	1	2	2		1			1	1				8		
Cummington	305	11	Foster	Adam		1	1		1	1	1		1				6		
Charlemont	191	12	Foster	Amos	1	1		1		2			1				6		
New Salem	98	30	Foster	Amos		1		2			3		1				7		
Cummington	305	12	Foster	Asa	2			1			1		1				5		
Rowe	199	26	Foster	Asa	2			1		2	3		1				9		
Rowe	199	23	Foster	Asa 2d	1	1	2		1	1			1				7		
Palmer	260	8	Foster	Bryant				1						2			3		
Greenwich	220	14	Foster	Daniel	3			1					1				5		
New Salem	98	29	Foster	Daniel	2	1	1	1	1	2		1	1	1			11		
Barnardston	77	37	Foster	Ezekiel				1			1		1				3		
Leyden	82	20	Foster	Ezekiel	2	2	2	1		2	1		1				11		
Greenfield	72	32	Foster	Isaac	4			1		1		1	1				8		
Orange	42	1	Foster	James				1						1			2		
Shelburne	321	12	Foster	Jeremiah	1		2		1		2	1	1				8		
New Salem	98	31	Foster	Joel		2			1		2	1			1		7		
Springfield	248	11	Foster	John				1				1					2		
Ware	226	8	Foster	Jona	2	1		1	1		1	1	1				8		
New Salem	98	35	Foster	Jonathan		2		1					1				4		
Leyden	82	23	Foster	Lemuel	2	1		1		3			1				8		
Ashfield	340	16	Foster	Lewis		1	1				1		1				4		
Colrain	185	34	Foster	Nathan	2			1		1			1				5		
Rowe	199	25	Foster	Nathan	1	1	1		1	2	1	2		1			10		
Shelburne	321	20	Foster	Nathl				1		2	1		1				5		
New Salem	98	34	Foster	Samuel				1		2		1					4		
New Salem	98	36	Foster	Samuel 2d	1			1		2	1		3	1			9		
Rowe	199	27	Foster	Standish		2		1				1		1			5		
Greenwich	219	38	Foster	Tilly	2	1		1		2			1				7		
Palmer	260	13	Foster	William		1	1			3			1				6		
Ashfield	340	15	Foster	Willm			1	1		1	1		1				5		
Palmer	260	9	Foster	Willson	1		1	1		1			1				5		
West Springfield	353	16	Fourman	Jared		1				1			1				3		
Northampton	4	34	Fowell	Nathaniel		1	4		1	1	2	1		1			11		
Deerfield	53	1	Fowle	Susannah		1							1	1			3		
Westfield	118	6	Fowler	Amos	1	1	1				1		1	1			7		
Westfield	126	25	Fowler	Ashbel	1	1		1		4			1				8		
Springfield	247	39	Fowler	Benja											2		2		
Southwick	358	35	Fowler	Bildad		1		1		1	1		1				5		
Westfield	118	5	Fowler	Blackleach	1	1	1		1	2	1	1	1				9		
Granville West Soc	168	38	Fowler	Daniel			1			1		1					3		
Southwick	358	36	Fowler	Daniel		1		1		1			1				4		
Westfield	119	3	Fowler	Daniel	1	1	2	1	1	2		1	2	1			12		
Southwick	358	32	Fowler	David	1	1	1		1	1	2	1					8		
Westfield	119	21	Fowler	Ebenezer		1		1					1				3		
Westfield	126	16	Fowler	Ebenezer Jun	2			1		2	1	1	1				9		
Westfield	125	7	Fowler	Eli	2			1		2			1				6		
Westfield	122	1	Fowler	Frederick	2	1	2	2		1	1		1				10		
Southwick	358	38	Fowler	Isaac		1	1		1			1		1			5		
Westfield	123	19	Fowler	Isaac		1	1	1		1	1		1				6		
Westfield	118	12	Fowler	Jared	2			1		2			1				6		
Granville West Soc	169	35	Fowler	John		2		1		3			1				7		
Palmer	258	7	Fowler	John				1				1		1			3		
West Springfield	353	17	Fowler	John		1		1			1			1			4		
Westfield	118	13	Fowler	John		1			1	1		2	1	1			7		

TOWN	PG#	LN#	LAST NAME	FIRST NAME	FREE WHITE MALES					FREE WHITE FEMALES					TOTAL ALL OTHER	TOTAL SLAVES	TOTALS	DISTRICT/ TOWNSHIP	NOTES
					under 10	10 to 16	16 to 26	26 to 45	45 and over	under 10	10 to 16	16 to 26	26 to 45	45 and over					
Russell	138	17	Fowler	Josiah	1		1						1				3		
Westfield	119	22	Fowler	Justus	2	1		1			1		1				6		
Westfield	118	11	Fowler	Luther		1	1		1		1						4		
Blanford	180	21	Fowler	Medad	2	1	1		1	2	1		1				9		
Southwick	358	34	Fowler	Noble	3	1		1				1					6		
Granville West Soc	168	37	Fowler	Oliver		1			1	1	1	2		1			7		
West Springfield	353	25	Fowler	Roger	1			1		1		1					4		
Westfield	121	1	Fowler	Samll Esq	2			1		3	1		2				9		
Southwick	358	37	Fowler	Saul	2		1	1		1	1		1				7		
Southwick	358	39	Fowler	Silas		2	1	1		1			1				6		
Colrain	185	36	Fowler	Thomas	3					1			1				5		
Granville West Soc	169	31	Fowler	Titus		1	1	1		2	2	1	1	1			10		
West Springfield	353	20	Fowler	Walter	1		1					1			1		4		
Hadley	286	31	Fox	Abraham		2		1		1			1				5		
Granville West Soc	168	25	Fox	David	3	1	1		1	1	1		1				9		
Granville East Soc	527	23	Fox	Elisha	3	1		1		3			1				9		
Belchertown	208	4	Fox	Isaac				1					1				2		
Westfield	126	27	Fox	Jonathan D.	1			1		3		1					6		
Blanford	180	17	Fox	Joseph	1	1		1		3		1					7		
Blanford	182	2	Fox	Joseph	1	1		1		2	1	1	1				8		
Barnardston	77	33	Fox	Noah	3	1	1	1		3	1	2	1				13		
Colrain	185	24	Fox	Thomas	3			1			2	1					7		
Granville West Soc	168	28	Fox	Thomas	1			1					1				3		
Barnardston	77	36	Fox	William	3	2	1		1	4	1	1		1			14		
Easthampton	134	27	Franey	Obediah	1		1			1							3		
Amherst	293	23	Franklin	Nathan	1			1		1		2	1	1			7		
Deerfield	53	2	Frary	Eleanor	1			1				1		1			4		
Whately	66	36	Frary	Eleazer	1				1	3			1				6		
Hadley	285	20	Frary	Elisha	1			2		4	1	1	1				10		
Whately	66	37	Frary	Isaac	1	1		1		3	1		1				8		
Blanford	177	6	Frary	Jonathan			2	1				3		1			8		
Ashfield	340	7	Frary	Moses	1	3	1		1	3	1	3	1				14		
Deerfield	52	44	Frary	Nathan		2		1		1			1				5		
Hatfield	14	27	Frary	Nathaniel				2			1	1					4		
Southampton	133	15	Frary	Nathaniel	1		1	1	1	1	1	1					8		
Whately	66	38	Frary	Phinehas		1	3				1		2				8		
Whately	66	35	Frary	Seth	1	1	2	1		2	1		1				9		
Hatfield	14	19	Frazier	Henry											6		6		
Greenfield	73	2	Frazier	Jabez			1			1			1				3		
Southwick	358	33	Frazier	Jared		1		2				1					4		
Blanford	179	28	Freeland	Joseph	2			1		2	2	2	1				10		
Blanford	179	29	Freeland	William				1		3		1					5		
Northfield	28	34	Freelove	Wilber	1			1		2	1		1				6		
Chester	146	26	Freeman	Brewster	3			1		1	1		1				7		
Northfield	28	29	Freeman	Dan	1	1			1	1				1			5		
Blanford	177	1	Freeman	James	2	1		1			1		1	1			7		
Belchertown	208	32	Freeman	John black man											6		6		
Colrain	185	27	Freeman	Rufus	2	1	1		1	3		1	1				10		
Chester	146	27	Freeman	Silas						1			1		1		3		
Chester	146	28	Freeman	Silas Junr	1			1		4			1				7		
Granville West Soc	169	9	Freeman	William	3	1		1		1	1		1				8		
Southwick	358	31	French	Aaron	1	2		1		1			1	1			7		
Westhampton	17	36	French	Abiather		1			2	2			1				6		
Williamsburg	447	23	French	Asa	3	2		1		2	1		1				10		
Chester	146	21	French	Asahel			1					1					2		
Southwick	358	40	French	Daniel	2			1		3			1				7		
Westhampton	16	5	French	Ebenezer				1					1				2		
Westhampton	16	4	French	Ebenezer Jr	1	1	1	1		1	2	1	1				9		
Williamsburg	447	24	French	Jacob	2	3		1	1	4	1		1				13		
Westhampton	16	37	French	Jared	1			1		1		1					4		
Williamsburg	447	22	French	John Owen	2		1		1	3		1	1	1			10		
Westhampton	17	34	French	Jonatha	1			1		2			1				5		
New Salem	99	2	French	Jonathan		1		1		2	1						5		
Westhampton	15	3	French	Joshua B.	2			1					1				4		
Northampton	9	31	French	Josiah	2			1		1			1				5		
Westhampton	17	1	French	Martha									2				2		
Westhampton	16	6	French	Nathan	1	1		1		1			1				5		
Chester	146	24	French	Ozias Capt	1	1	1	1		3	1		1				9		
Northampton	10	5	French	Sampson		1			1	1	1		1				5		
Chester	146	20	French	Samuel				1		1			1				3		
Westhampton	16	36	French	Samuel				1				2	1				4		
Cummington	303	11	French	Stephen	1	1		1		2			1				6		
Westfield	126	21	French	Thomas	1			1		3			1				6		
Springfield	245	23	Frink	Gillis	1	2	2	1		2		2	1				11		
Springfield	245	22	Frink	John	1		1		1	2	2		1				8		
West Springfield	356	32	Frink	Luther			1	1		4		1		1			8		
Deerfield	52	46	Frink	Miner		1		1				1		1			4		
Conway	58	12	Frink	Samuel	1			1		1			1				4		
Springfield	245	24	Frink	Thomas	4	2		1		1	1		1				10		
Montgomery	161	2	Frisby	Amos	2		1					1					4		

TOWN	PG#	LN#	LAST NAME	FIRST NAME	FREE WHITE MALES					FREE WHITE FEMALES					TOTAL ALL OTHER	TOTAL SLAVES	TOTALS	DISTRICT/ TOWNSHIP	NOTES
					under 10	10 to 16	16 to 26	26 to 45	45 and over	under 10	10 to 16	16 to 26	26 to 45	45 and over					
Montgomery	161	1	Frisby	Nathan		1		1						1			3		
Blanford	175	9	Frisley	Chandler		1							1				2		
Barnardston	77	32	Frizell	Michael	1		1			3		1					6		
Holland	279	10	Frizzel	James		1	1	1			1	1	1				6		
Leyden	82	17	Frizzell	Michael		1		1				1	1				4		
Leyden	82	18	Frizzell	Reuben		1		1				1	1				4		
Leyden	82	25	Frizzell	Reuben Jr	2			1		2	1		1				7		
Leyden	82	22	Frizzell	Zenus	3			1		1			1				6		
Montague	45	40	Frizzle	Earl	3			1		1		1					6		
Northfield	28	31	Frizzle	Martha		1						1		1			3		
Springfield	241	28	Frost	Asa				1		2			1				4		
Brimfield	270	11	Frost	Daniel		1	4					2		1			8		
Granville Mid Soc.	166	12	Frost	David	2	1	4		1	3	1		1				13		
Springfield	241	27	Frost	Henry	1	1	1	1					1				5		
Longmeadow	91	9	Frost	Isaac		1		2				1	1				5		
Springfield	246	39	Frost	Joel			1			3		1					5		
Blanford	178	13	Frost	John	2	2		1		1		1	1				8		
Conway	58	16	Frost	Joseph	2		2	1		1	1		1				8		
Longmeadow	94	13	Frost	Joshua Dr	1			1		1		1	1				5		
Williamsburg	447	19	Frost	Josiah	4			1		1		1	1	1			9		
Ludlow	255	1	Frost	Noah		1		1		3	2		1				8		
Springfield	246	20	Frost	Noah				1					1	1			3		
Springfield	246	38	Frost	Reuben	1			1		4	2		1				9		
Ludlow	255	4	Frost	Samuel		1	2		1	2	1		1				8		
Wilbraham	234	35	Frost	Timothy	2	1		1					1				5		
New Salem	99	3	Fry	John 2d			1				1	1					3		
New Salem	99	1	Fry	Levi	2	2		1		1			1				7		
Monson	264	15	Fuller	Abraham	4			1		2	2		1				10		
Monson	268	27	Fuller	Abraham				1						1			2		
Montague	45	37	Fuller	Asa				1						1			2		
South Hadley	249	10	Fuller	Asabel				1				1					2		
Monson	264	9	Fuller	Benjamin	2	1		2		3		1	1				10		
West Springfield	356	33	Fuller	Bushman											6		6		
Monson	266	10	Fuller	Eleazer	3	2	1		1			3	1				11		
Buckland	327	10	Fuller	Eli	1		1	1		3		1	1				8		
Ludlow	257	15	Fuller	Elisha	3	1	2			1	1	1	1				10		
Wilbraham	234	34	Fuller	Ephraim	4	2	2		1	2	1	1	1				14		
Ludlow	257	33	Fuller	Ezekiel	3		1	1		1	2	1	1				10		
Buckland	327	9	Fuller	George	1		2			1		1					5		
Montague	45	38	Fuller	Isaiah				1						1			2		
Warwick	37	22	Fuller	Isaiah	2	1	1		1	1				1			7		
Holland	279	13	Fuller	James	2	1	1	1		1	1	1	1				9		
Hawley	333	15	Fuller	Jason	2			1		3	1		1	1			9		
Charlemont	191	6	Fuller	John		1	1			2			1				5		
Monson	266	3	Fuller	John	1			1		1			1				4		
Montague	45	39	Fuller	John	2	1		1		2	1		1				8		
Hawley	333	10	Fuller	Jonathan	4	1		1		1	1		1				9		
Ludlow	257	15	Fuller	Joshua		1						1					2		
Monson	264	10	Fuller	Joshua				1						1			2		
Monson	265	26	Fuller	Joshua Jr	2	1	1	1		1			1				7		
Monson	265	25	Fuller	Joshua Lt				1					1	1			3		
Ashfield	340	12	Fuller	Josiah	2	2		1		3	1		1				10		
Worthington	297	11	Fuller	Lemuel	1			1		1		1					4		
Ashfield	340	14	Fuller	Luke			1					1					2		
Goshen	310	5	Fuller	Nathan	1	3	1	1					2				8		
South Brimfield	276	36	Fuller	Phinehas		1		1		3			1				6		
Ashfield	340	13	Fuller	Solomon	1	1	1	2		1	1	1	1				9		
Monson	268	28	Fuller	Stephen				1				1	1				3		
Monson	266	23	Fuller	Sylvanus		2	1		1	1	2	1	1				9		
Buckland	327	16	Fuller	Thankful		1							1				2		
Norwich	154	30	Fuller	Zeblon											5		5		
Colrain	185	26	Fulton	James	3	2		1		1		1	1				9		
Colrain	185	23	Fulton	James Jun	1		1					1					3		
New Salem	98	39	Furbush	Aaron		2	2		1	1	1	1		1			9		
Ware	226	9	Furbush	James	1	1	1	1		3			1				8		
Buckland	327	11	Furbush	Thomas				1			1	1		1			4		
New Salem	98	32	Furniss	William			1						1				2		
Westfield	126	12	Furrow	Peter			1	1		2			1				5		
Warwick	37	40	Gaffield	Daniel	1	1	1						1				4		
Monson	267	6	Gage	Aaron Dr	1	2		1		1			1				6		
New Salem	99	5	Gage	Nathaniel	4			1				1					6		
South Brimfield	276	34	Gage	Thaddeus	2	1		1			1		1	1			7		
Gill	86	4	Gain	Davis			1		1		1		1	1			5		
Gill	86	3	Gain	George				1		1		1					3		
Gill	86	2	Gain	Jehiel	2			1		1			1				5		
Ware	226	13	Gaines	James	4	2		1					1				8		
Easthampton	136	22	Gains	Calvin	1			1		3			1				6		
Granville East Soc	529	34	Gains	Samuel		2		1		1	1	1		1			7		
Warwick	37	36	Gale	Alpheus	2			1		2	1			1			7		
Warwick	37	35	Gale	David				1					1				2		

TOWN	PG#	LN#	LAST NAME	FIRST NAME	FREE WHITE MALES					FREE WHITE FEMALES					TOTAL ALL OTHER	TOTAL SLAVES	TOTALS	DISTRICT/ TOWNSHIP	NOTES
					under 10	10 to 16	16 to 26	26 to 45	45 and over	under 10	10 to 16	16 to 26	26 to 45	45 and over					
Warwick	37	41	Gale	David Junr	3			1		2			1				7		
Warwick	37	31	Gale	Emery		2							1				3		
Warwick	37	37	Gale	Jesse			1						1				2		
Warwick	37	30	Gale	John	4		1			1		1	1				8		
Warwick	37	29	Gale	Jonathan		1	2		1	2	1		1				8		
Warwick	37	28	Gale	Josiah	1		1	2	1	1	3		1				10		
Hadley	285	26	Gale	Levi	2	1		1		1	1		1				7		
Ludlow	255	21	Galkins	Rufus		1		1						1			3		
Chester	148	11	Gamwell	John	2	2	2		1	1	1		1				11		
Chester	143	5	Gamwell	John Jr	2			1					1				4		
Chester	149	20	Gamwell	Samuel				1					1				2		
New Salem	99	10	Ganson	Joseph		1		1		2	2	1					7		
New Salem	99	19	Ganson	Nathan		1	1	1		1		1					5		
Leverett	115	1	Gardner	Andrew	1	2	1		1	1	1	2					9		
Plainfield	306	3	Gardner	Benjamin		1	1		1	2	1		1				7		
Monson	264	39	Gardner	Caleb															Enumeration left blank
Monson	264	44	Gardner	Caleb	1		1			1	1						4		
Worthington	301	43	Gardner	Elijah		1		1					1				3		
South Brimfield	277	25	Gardner	Humphrey	3			1		2	1	1					8		
Plainfield	306	4	Gardner	Jacob	2	2		1		2			1				8		
Brimfield	270	40	Gardner	Jno Jr	3	1		1			2			1			8		
Greenwich	220	8	Gardner	John	1	2			1			1	1				6		
Ware	226	17	Gardner	John	2			1		1			1				5		
Ware	226	15	Gardner	John 2d			1			1		1					3		
Springfield	239	9	Gardner	Jonathan	3	1		1		3			1				9		
Worthington	298	13	Gardner	Mary									1				1		
Worthington	299	3	Gardner	Reuben			2	1		1	1	1	1				7		
Monson	267	16	Gardner	Richard	1	1	1	1		3		1	1				10		
South Brimfield	277	22	Gardner	S. Charles			1		1				1				3		
South Brimfield	277	30	Gardner	S. Josiah	1	2	1	1		1		1	1				8		
Monson	264	13	Gardner	Sherman	4			1		2	1		1				9		
Monson	265	7	Gardner	Simeon	2	1						1					4		
South Brimfield	277	26	Gardner	Steward	2			1		3	1		1				8		
Worthington	299	4	Gardner	Townsend	3			1		3	2		1				10		
South Brimfield	277	24	Gardner	William			1	1	1				1				4		
Middlefield	157	6	Garnwell	James	1			1		2			1				5		
Amherst	291	28	Garnwell	Samuel	1			1					1				3		
Monson	262	7	Gates	Asa	2	1	1			2		1	1				9		
Pelham	214	5	Gates	Ebenezar			1			1		1					3		
Conway	58	32	Gates	Israel		1		1	1	1		1		2			7		
Belchertown	203	6	Gates	John	3			1		1			1				6		
Hadley	286	17	Gates	Josiah		1		1						2			4		
Westfield	127	4	Gates	Matthias	4			1		1	1		1	1			9		
Palmer	260	17	Gates	Micah	1	1		1		1	1		1	1			7		
Conway	58	29	Gates	Peter	3	1	1		1	2	1	1					10		
Leyden	82	29	Gates	Peter		1		1		2	3	1		1			9		
Wendell	106	2	Gates	Silas	2			1		2			1				6		
Orange	42	11	Gates	Solomon			1						1				2		
Greenfield	73	16	Gates	Stephen	2			1		2			1				6		
Belchertown	205	10	Gates	Thos Asa Lt.		2	1	1		3	1	2	1				11		
Conway	58	33	Gates	William	3			1	1	2		1		1			9		
Goshen	310	2	Gatheart	Gershom	1	1		1		2		1	1				7		
Granville West Soc	168	7	Gavit	William	3	2		1		2			1				9		
New Salem	99	16	Gay	Ebenezer		1		1	1	2		1	1				7		
New Salem	99	18	Gay	Eliphalet	3			1				1					5		
Colrain	186	4	Gay	Jonathan	1			1		4	1		1				8		
Springfield	244	11	Gay	Levi		1			1				1				3		
West Springfield	350	54	Gaylord	Ebenezer			1			1		1					3		
West Springfield	350	51	Gaylord	John	1	1							1				3		
Westfield	124	20	Gaylord	John	2	1		1			1		1				6		
West Springfield	350	53	Gaylord	Nathaniel		1	1		1				1	1			5		
Hadley	288	7	Gaylord	Nehemiah	3	1	1		1	2	1		1				10		
South Hadley	249	8	Gaylord	Oliver		1		1	1	1	2	1					7		
Westfield	124	31	Gaylord	Robert	2			1		1	3		1				8		
Hadley	287	16	Gaylord	Samuel		1	2		1			2		1	1		8		
Westfield	124	30	Gaylord	Wm			1						1				2		
Hatfield	12	17	Gearey	Nathan	1	2		1		2	1	1	1				9		
Westhampton	15	9	Gee	Ebenezer		2			1		1	1	1		2		8		
Chesterfield	20	32	Geer	Joseph	2	1	1	1			1	1	1				8		
Chester	148	22	Geer	Lylsby	4			1			1		1				7		
Norwich	152	24	Geer	Margaret Wid		1	1		1		1			1			5		
Norwich	152	26	Geer	Nathan	2			1		4	2		1				10		
Williamsburg	446	8	Geer	Reuben				1									1		
Cummington	305	30	Genins	Ephraim	2			1					1				4		
Northampton	4	27	Gere	Isaac	1		1	1			1	1					5		
Northampton	9	7	Gere	Samuel		2			1	4	1	2		2	3		15		
Granville East Soc	527	14	Gibbons	Bildad	3	2	1	1		1	1	2					11		
Granville East Soc	527	25	Gibbons	Elisha	1			1	1	5		1	1				10		
Granville East Soc	527	24	Gibbons	Jeddiah	1			1		3		1					6		
Westfield	122	2	Gibbons	John	2	2		1	1	4	1	2	1				14		

TOWN	PG#	LN#	LAST NAME	FIRST NAME	FREE WHITE MALES under 10	10 to 16	16 to 26	26 to 45	45 and over	FREE WHITE FEMALES under 10	10 to 16	16 to 26	26 to 45	45 and over	TOTAL ALL OTHER	TOTAL SLAVES	TOTALS	DISTRICT/ TOWNSHIP	NOTES
Granville East Soc	531	1	Gibbons	Timothy	1	2	1	1		3	1		1				10		
Greenwich	220	19	Gibbs	Benja	2		1	1			1		1				6		
Granville West Soc	168	40	Gibbs	Benjamin	1			1		3			1	1			7		
Blanford	175	34	Gibbs	Elijah	2	1		2		1	1		1				8		
Greenwich	220	7	Gibbs	Emerson	2		1			2		1	1	1			8		
Blanford	175	8	Gibbs	Ephraim	2	2		1	1	3	1	1	1	1			13		
Blanford	178	26	Gibbs	Isaac	1	1	1		1			1		1			6		
Blanford	178	20	Gibbs	Israel			2		1				1	1			5		
Greenwich	220	5	Gibbs	Jesse	1			1	1			1		1			5		
Greenwich	220	6	Gibbs	Jesse Junr				1		2			1				4		
Greenwich	220	4	Gibbs	John				1	1	2		2	1	1			8		
Blanford	178	37	Gibbs	Levi	1	1	1			1		1					5		
Blanford	178	39	Gibbs	Nathaniel	2			1		2			1				6		
Blanford	175	7	Gibbs	Samuel	2	1		1		2			1	1			8		
Blanford	178	19	Gibbs	Silas	1			1		1			1				4		
New Salem	99	7	Gibbs	Solomon			2		1	2		2		1			8		
New Salem	99	8	Gibbs	Solomon Junr	2			1		1		1					5		
Chester	148	21	Gibson	Roger	2				1		1	1		1			6		
Westfield	127	25	Gibson	Samll				1		1				1			3		
Granby	253	8	Giddings	Daniel	2			1		4			2				9		
Granby	253	9	Giddings	James		1	2		1	1		1		1			7		
Conway	58	30	Gifford	Christopher	2			1	1	1			1	1			7		
Deerfield	53	6	Gifford	Noah	2		1		1	2			1				7		
Conway	58	31	Gifford	Paul	3			1		2	1		1				8		
Middlefield	157	11	Gilbert	Charles	1			1		2			1				5		
Northfield	28	35	Gilbert	Cornelius	1			1					1				3		
Deerfield	53	5	Gilbert	David	1			1		2			1				5		
Blanford	179	30	Gilbert	Edmund	4	1		1				1	1				8		
Greenfield	73	14	Gilbert	Eliel	2		1		1	2		1	1				8		
Hatfield	13	17	Gilbert	Enon	2			1		1		1					5		
Orange	42	12	Gilbert	Joseph			1					1	1				3		
Barnardston	77	41	Gilbert	Joshua				1		2			1				4		
Whately	67	5	Gilbert	Josiah			1	1		1			1				4		
Leverett	115	7	Gilbert	Lewis	1	2	2	1		3		1	1				11		
Southwick	358	43	Gilbert	Mercy								1		1			2		
Cummington	303	15	Gilbert	Thaddeus	1			1		2	1		1				6		
Barnardston	77	43	Gilbert	Thoma	2	2		1		1			1				7		
Belchertown	205	12	Gilbert	Timothy	2			1		1	1		1	1			7		
Belchertown	205	13	Gilbert	John Maj	2	1	2		1	3	1		1				11		
New Salem	99	14	Giles	Daniel	2			1		2			1				6		
Charlemont	191	16	Giles	Edward			1	1		2			1	1			6		
Charlemont	191	17	Giles	Edward Jun	1			1		4			1				7		
Shutesbury	109	29	Giles	James	1			1					1				3		
New Salem	99	13	Giles	John		2	1			1	1		1	1			7		
New Salem	99	20	Giles	John Junr	3			1		1	1		1				7		
New Salem	99	21	Giles	Joseph			1					1					2		
Belchertown	205	9	Giles	Thomas Wid		1							1				2		
New Salem	99	6	Giles	William	1	1	1		1	1		1		1			7		
Leverett	115	2	Gill	John				1						1			2		
West Springfield	356	35	Gill	Samuel	1		1	1		1	1		1				6		
Granville West Soc	169	22	Gillbard	Noah	1			1		2			1				5		
Orange	42	6	Gilles	Alpheus		1		1	1	2			1				6		
Southwick	358	41	Gillet	Isaac	5	1			1	1	1		1				10		
Hatfield	14	32	Gillet	Josiah	2	1			1	1		1		1			7		
Westfield	127	3	Gillet	Nathaniel			2					1					3		
Middlefield	157	1	Gillet	Russel	1			1		2			1				5		
Granville East Soc	531	23	Gillet	Thomas	1		1	3	1	1	4	1		2			14		
Ludlow	256	29	Gilligan	John				1		2			1	1			5		
Greenfield	73	12	Gilligan	Thoma	2			1		3			1				7		
Chester	147	18	Gillmon	William	2	3	1	1		2			1				10		
Chester	148	27	Gillmore	James	1	3	1		1	2		1	1				10		
Blanford	181	26	Gillmore	Thomas	1			1		1	1						4		
Gill	86	18	Gilman	Shubal	2			1		2			1				6		
Ware	226	19	Gilmore	James	1	1	2		1	1	2	1	1				11		
Ware	226	20	Gilmore	John			2	1		2			2	1			6		
Blanford	179	8	Girder	Samuel				1						1			2		
Granville East Soc	529	26	Gitchel	William	2			1		1		1	1				6		
Easthampton	134	9	Gladden	Azariah	1			1		1			1				4		
Easthampton	134	10	Gladden	Azariah Junr			1						1				2		
Easthampton	134	30	Gladden	Wm						3			1				4		
Leverett	115	4	Glazier	Benja	2	1			1	3	2		1				10		
Holland	278	20	Glazier	Calvin	1	2		1		4				1			9		
Leverett	114	32	Glazier	John	1		1					1					3		
Leverett	114	29	Glazier	Jonathan	3				1	1	2			1			8		
Rowe	199	32	Gleason	Aaron	1	2	1	1	1	1		2		1			10		
Heath	196	3	Gleason	Daniel	1	1			1	2		1					6		
Greenwich	220	1	Gleason	Isaac			1					1					2		
Middlefield	156	26	Gleason	Isaac	2	2	1			3	1	2	1				13		
Brimfield	274	5	Gleason	Jason	2	1	1			1			1	1			7		
Granville West Soc	168	39	Gleason	Joel	4			1		1			1				7		
Granville West Soc	169	18	Gleason	John	2	2	2	1		1	2		1	1			12		

TOWN	PG#	LN#	LAST NAME	FIRST NAME	FREE WHITE MALES					FREE WHITE FEMALES					TOTAL ALL OTHER	TOTAL SLAVES	TOTALS	DISTRICT/ TOWNSHIP	NOTES
					under 10	10 to 16	16 to 26	26 to 45	45 and over	under 10	10 to 16	16 to 26	26 to 45	45 and over					
Rowe	199	29	Gleason	Jonah		4			1	1		1		1			8		
Greenwich	220	2	Gleason	Simeon			1	1	1		1	1	1				6		
Granby	253	37	Gleason	Simon	1			1			2			1			5		
Heath	196	4	Gleason	Solomon	2	1		1		4	1		1				10		
Rowe	199	28	Gleason	Stephen	2			1		2	1		1				7		
Heath	196	5	Gleason	Varnum			1	1					1	1			4		
Blanford	179	16	Gleason	William				1		1		1	1				4		
Leyden	82	9	Glen	John	2	1	3	1		2		1	1				11		
Leyden	82	12	Glen	Richard	1	2	1		1	2		3		2			12		
Leyden	82	13	Glen	Richard Junr			1						1				2		
Conway	58	34	Glover	Alexander	3	1	1	1		1	2		1	1			11		
Hawley	333	18	Glover	Edward L.	3			1			1	1	1				7		
Conway	58	38	Glover	Thomas			1			1		1					3		
Wilbraham	235	9	Glower	John	2	1	3		1	1	3		1				12		
Plainfield	307	10	Gloyd	Asa	1		1	1		4	2		1				10		
Plainfield	307	13	Gloyd	Benjm	1		1			2			1				5		
Plainfield	307	11	Gloyd	Ephrm	2		1			2	1		1				8		
Plainfield	307	9	Gloyd	Jacob				1	1		1			1			4		
Hatfield	13	25	Gloyd	James	1		1	1	1	2	3	1					11		
Plainfield	307	12	Gloyd	Joseph	1	1		1		2			1				6		
Orange	42	10	Godard	Asa	1	3		1	1	2	1		1	1			11		
Montague	46	14	Godard	Ebenezer	1	1	2	1	1	1				1			8		
Orange	42	9	Godard	Ebenezer	2	1	3		1	1	2			1			11		
Orange	42	4	Godard	Hezekiah	1	2		1		3			1				8		
Orange	42	5	Godard	John	2			1		2			1				6		
Orange	41	43	Godard	Nathan	1	1		1			3		1				7		
Conway	58	28	Goddard	Elisha	4			1		1			1				7		
Orange	42	3	Goddard	Jonathan	1	2	1			1			1				7		
Conway	58	27	Goddard	Nathaniel			1	1		1			1				4		
Northampton	5	12	Goddard	Solomon Jr			1	1				1			1		4		
Ware	226	14	Godfray	Samuel	1		1				1						3		
Conway	58	24	Godfrey	Seth	3	1		1		3	2	1		1			12		
Granville West Soc	168	35	Goff	David	2			1		3	2		1				9		
West Springfield	351	2	Goff	Lois			1			1			1				3		
Deerfield	53	8	Goff	Paul											4		4		
West Springfield	350	52	Goff	Silas	2		1			2			1				6		
Warwick	37	25	Gold	Asa	3		1			2			1				7		
Shutesbury	109	28	Gold	Sewall		1						1					2		
Warwick	37	34	Gold	Thomas				1			1		1				3		
Warwick	37	33	Gold	Thomas Junior	2	1						1					4		
Warwick	37	27	Goldsbury	James	3	2		1			1	1	1				9		
Warwick	37	26	Goldsbury	John				1			1		1				3		
Granby	253	21	Goldthwait	Elijah	2			1		2			1				6		
Longmeadow	94	12	Goldthwait	Erstus	2			1					1				4		
New Salem	99	17	Goldthwait	Joseph	1			1		1			1				4		
New Salem	99	15	Goldthwait	Robert	1			1	1	3			1				7		
Monson	262	12	Goodale	Abel Esq		2		1			1	1		2			7		
Pelham	214	9	Goodale	Andrew	5			1			1	1					8		
Amherst	293	24	Goodale	David	2		1		1			1		2			7		
New Salem	99	9	Goodale	Ebenezer				1						1			2		
Belchertown	204	8	Goodale	Elisha				1						1			2		
Warwick	37	32	Goodale	Ephraim	1		1										2		
Amherst	289	11	Goodale	Isaac		1		1				1		1			4		
New Salem	99	12	Goodale	James		1	1			1		1					4		
Gill	86	8	Goodale	Job			1	1		1		1	1				4		
Colrain	186	5	Goodale	Joel	2	2		1		2	1		1				9		
Pelham	214	20	Goodale	John	3			1		1			1				6		
Warwick	37	38	Goodale	John	1		2		1			1	1	1			7		
New Salem	99	11	Goodale	Jonathan	1			1						1			3		
Warwick	37	39	Goodale	Joseph				1						1			2		
Hadley	286	32	Goodale	Levi	1			1		2			1				5		
Belchertown	205	16	Goodale	Nathanl	1			1			1	1	1	1			6		
Conway	58	35	Goodale	Solomon		1	1			1	1	2	1				8		
Amherst	289	12	Goodale	Thomas		1	1			1	1	1					5		
Orange	42	8	Goodale	Zina	1	1		1		4	1		1				9		
Monson	266	45	Goodell	Eliphalet				1						1			2		
Holland	278	18	Goodell	Ichabod Lt.		1	1	1			1		1	1			5		
Ludlow	258	5	Goodell	Jabez	2	1	1	1		2		1	1				10		
Chesterfield	22	7	Goodenough	John	1	1	2		1	1	1	2		1			10		
Northfield	28	37	Goodenough		1		1	1				1					4		First name blank
New Salem	99	22	Goodenow	Almer	3			1		1	1		1				7		
Gill	86	7	Goodlow	Francis		2		1		2	1			1			7		
South Hadley	249	11	Goodman	Calvin	1		1						1				3		
Greenfield	73	10	Goodman	Elihu		1	1			3	1			1			8		
South Hadley	249	12	Goodman	Huldah Wd		1								1			2		
South Hadley	250	16	Goodman	Ithamar	1	1		1		3			1				7		
South Hadley	251	7	Goodman	Nathan			1					1					2		
South Hadley	250	28	Goodman	Petey	3	2	1	1		1			1				9		
Hadley	288	34	Goodman	Stephen			3		1			1	1				6		
Palmer	258	4	Goodman	William	2		1			1			1				5		

TOWN	PG#	LN#	LAST NAME	FIRST NAME	FREE WHITE MALES under 10	10 to 16	16 to 26	26 to 45	45 and over	FREE WHITE FEMALES under 10	10 to 16	16 to 26	26 to 45	45 and over	TOTAL ALL OTHER	TOTAL SLAVES	TOTALS	DISTRICT/ TOWNSHIP	NOTES
Shutesbury	109	31	Goodman	William				1		1				1			3		
Shelburne	321	21	Goodnow	Abner	3			1		1	1	1	1				8		
Rowe	199	30	Goodnow	Thomas		1		1	1	1			1	1			6		
West Springfield	351	1	Goodrich	Elijah		1	1	1		2			1				6		
Gill	86	5	Goodrich	George	1	4	1		1	3			2				12		
Northampton	6	1	Goodrick	Amel	1			2		1		1					5		
Rowe	199	31	Goodspead	Judah	1	1			1	2				2			7		
Hawley	333	21	Goodspead	Nathl		1		1						1			3		
Wilbraham	237	42	Goodwill	John		1		1		1		1	1	1			6		
Wilbraham	238	7	Goodwill	Justin	2		1			1			1				5		
Chester	147	32	Goodwill	Nathaniel	2	1	1			2		2					8		
Monson	264	37	Goodwill	William		1						1					2		
Ashfield	341	2	Goodwin	Eldad F.	2		1	1		3	2	1					11		
Blanford	175	19	Goodwin	Thomas	2	1		1		1	1	2		1			9		
Ashfield	341	4	Goodwin	Uriah		1		1						1			3		
West Springfield	356	34	Goodyear	Austin	3		1			1			1				6		
Monson	266	44	Gordin	William	2		1			1			1				6		
Palmer	259	10	Gordon	Cosmo			1										1		
Montgomery	159	8	Gorham	George	4		1				1	1	1				8		
Blanford	179	5	Gorham	Glass	4		1			1			1				7		
Blanford	182	10	Gorham	John		1	1	1						1			4		
Montgomery	160	31	Gorham	John		1						1					2		
Montgomery	159	4	Gorham	Joseph		1	1		1	1				1			5		
West Springfield	353	29	Goss	Andrew	1			1					1	1			4		
Wilbraham	234	23	Goss	Ezra	2		1			2			1				6		
West Springfield	353	32	Goss	Gideon	1		1						1				3		
Brimfield	269	17	Goss	John A			1			1			1				3		
Wendell	106	1	Goss	Reuben	2		1					1	1				6		
Granville West Soc	170	6	Goth	Moses		1	1			1			1	1			5		
Russell	139	19	Goudy	Alexander		1		1		3	2		1				8		
Middlefield	158	14	Goudy	Samuel	2	1		1			1	1	1				7		
Charlemont	191	15	Gould	Aaron	1	2	2	1		3	1		1	1			12		
Charlemont	192	5	Gould	Benjamin	1			1		4		1					7		
Ware	226	11	Gould	Danl Deac	1	2	1		1	1		3		1			10		
Ware	226	12	Gould	David		2	3		1	2		1	1	2			12		
Ware	226	16	Gould	Ebenz		1	1		1	3	1		1				8		
Barnardston	77	40	Gould	Gideon		1		1		2	2		1				7		
Colrain	186	2	Gould	Henry	2		2		1	1	3			1			10		
Heath	196	6	Gould	Isaac	1	1		1		4	1	2	1				11		
Charlemont	191	14	Gould	Jeremiah				1						1			2		
Springfield	247	4	Gould	Joseph	1	5		2		2	1	1		1			13		
Charlemont	192	1	Gould	Nathan		1		1						1			3		
Leverett	115	3	Gould	Noah				2						1			3		
Barnardston	77	42	Gould	Oliver	2	1	1	1		1		1	1				8		
Leverett	114	30	Gould	Samuel				1		1			1				3		
Leverett	114	31	Gould	Solomon			2	1	1	1	1	1		2			9		
Orange	42	7	Gould	William	3	1		1		4	2		1				12		
Russell	138	18	Gould	Wm	1			2				1					4		
Worthington	297	2	Gove	William			1		1			2		1			5		
Worthington	297	3	Gove	William Jun		1	1	1		1		1					5		
Longmeadow	91	7	Gowdy	William	1	1		1		3	1		1				8		
West Springfield	353	30	Grace	Joseph		2	1		1			2	1				7		
Colrain	185	38	Gragg	Jacob				1						1			2		
Colrain	186	1	Gragg	Robert	2	2	1	2	1	2	2		1				10		
Sunderland	283	13	Graham	Lucius			1	1			1	1	1				5		
Holland	280	9	Graham	Moses	1			1		1			1	1			5		
Conway	58	26	Graham	Samuel	2	2		1		2			1				8		
Middlefield	158	20	Graham	William				1				2	1	1			5		
Buckland	327	19	Graham	Zenas		2	1			1		1					5		
Westfield	126	14	Grainger	Eli	1					1			1				3		
Westfield	127	19	Grainger	Elijah	2		1			1			1				6		
Middlefield	157	22	Grainger	Luther	2	1		1		4	1	1	1				11		
Deerfield	53	3	Grandy	Remembrance	1			1		1	1			1			5		
Granville West Soc	168	11	Granger	Abraham	2			1		1	1	1	1				7		
Southwick	358	42	Granger	Asahel	1		1	1		3			1				7		
Russell	139	20	Granger	Benjamin		1	1			2		1	1				7		
Southwick	358	46	Granger	George		1	2		1		1			1			6		
Southwick	358	44	Granger	Holcomb	4	1		1		2			1				9		
Hadley	287	31	Granger	Holeum	2			1		2			1				6		
Southwick	358	45	Granger	Ithamar	2			1		2	1		1				7		
Whately	67	6	Granger	John	2			1						1			4		
Blanford	176	8	Granger	John M.	4	2	1		1		1		1				10		
West Springfield	353	28	Granger	Justin	1			1		1	2	1	2	1			9		
Westfield	120	20	Grant	Alexander				1	1								2		
Goshen	310	8	Grant	Asa		1		1				1	1				4		
Buckland	327	18	Grant	John				1		1	1	1	1				5		
Montgomery	160	40	Grant	John		1		1		3	1		1				7		
Hawley	333	19	Grant	Jonathan Rev.	1		1	1		3		1	1				8		
South Hadley	249	30	Graves	Aaron	3		2		1			1	1				8		
Palmer	258	12	Graves	Aaron Majr			1	1									2		

TOWN	PG#	LN#	LAST NAME	FIRST NAME	FREE WHITE MALES					FREE WHITE FEMALES					TOTAL ALL OTHER	TOTAL SLAVES	TOTALS	DISTRICT/ TOWNSHIP	NOTES
					under 10	10 to 16	16 to 26	26 to 45	45 and over	under 10	10 to 16	16 to 26	26 to 45	45 and over					
Middlefield	158	11	Graves	Amasa		1	1		1			2		1			6		
Montague	46	18	Graves	Asa	1	1		1		1		1					5		
Granville East Soc	529	10	Graves	Asher	3			1		1	1		1				7		
Sunderland	282	10	Graves	Benjamin	2			1		1	1		1				6		
Sunderland	283	1	Graves	Cotton	2			2			1	1					6		
Leverett	115	5	Graves	Daniel		2		1		1		2					6		
Palmer	259	5	Graves	Daniel					1				1				2		
Sunderland	282	11	Graves	David	3	1	2	1		1	1		1				10		
Whately	67	3	Graves	David				1	1		1		1				4		
Ashfield	341	3	Graves	Dorus	1		2						1				4		
Belchertown	205	11	Graves	Dwight	1	1	1	1			1	1		1			7		
Charlemont	192	4	Graves	Ebenezer	1	1		1		1		1					5		
Greenfield	73	8	Graves	Ebenezer				1	1				1				3		
Greenfield	73	15	Graves	Ebenezer Junr	1		1	1				1					4		
Greenfield	73	3	Graves	Eli	1			1		1		1					4		
Sunderland	282	5	Graves	Elias	4	1		1			1	1	1				9		
Williamsburg	446	5	Graves	Elihu	1	1	1		1	1			1				6		
Northampton	6	33	Graves	Elisha	3		1	1		1	2		1				9		
Williamsburg	446	2	Graves	Elnathan				1		3			1				5		
Granville East Soc	529	9	Graves	Enoch	2			1		3			1				7		
Leverett	114	34	Graves	Enos	2	1		1		2	1		1				8		
Middlefield	157	13	Graves	Erastus				1					1				2		
Palmer	258	23	Graves	Gideon	1			1		5			1				8		
Palmer	258	11	Graves	Horace				1		2			1				4		
Hatfield	13	19	Graves	Israel	3			1		2		1	1				8		
Charlemont	191	18	Graves	Jesse		1	2		1		1			1			6		
Greenfield	73	9	Graves	Job	2	2	1	1		2	1		1				10		
Heath	196	2	Graves	Joel				1		4	1		1				7		
Whately	66	42	Graves	Joel	1	2		1		2		2	1				9		
Easthampton	134	20	Graves	John	1			1		2			1				5		
Greenfield	73	13	Graves	John		1	1		2				1	1			6		
Westfield	122	6	Graves	John					1	2			1				4		
Whately	67	2	Graves	John				1	1	1	1	1	1				6		
Hawley	333	20	Graves	Jonah	1		1	1		1		1					6		
Brimfield	271	12	Graves	Joseph	1	1		1					1				4		
Leverett	115	6	Graves	Joseph	1	1		1		2	1		1				7		
Williamsburg	446	1	Graves	Lemuel	2			1			2	1					6		
Conway	58	37	Graves	Levi	2	1	2	1		2	1		1				10		
Hatfield	12	38	Graves	Levi				1				1					2		
Williamsburg	446	4	Graves	Lucius	2		2	1		2	1		1				9		
Sunderland	282	20	Graves	Maria							1		1	1			3		
Whately	66	43	Graves	Martin	1	1	3	1				1		1			8		
Leverett	114	33	Graves	Moses		1	2	1		1			1				6		
Whately	67	4	Graves	Moses	3			1		1		1					6		
Montague	46	17	Graves	Noah	1			1						1			3		
Norwich	151	35	Graves	Obediah		1		1		1		1					4		
Whately	66	44	Graves	Oliver				1				1		1			3		
Whately	66	45	Graves	Oliver Jr	4			1		1		1					7		
Hatfield	12	32	Graves	Perez		1	1	1				1		1			5		
Williamsburg	446	3	Graves	Perez	2	3		1		2			1				9		
Belchertown	205	8	Graves	Perez Lt		1	1	1		1	1		1				6		
Brimfield	271	13	Graves	Peter		2	1	1		1			1				6		
Hatfield	13	12	Graves	Phineas				1		1			1				3		
Sunderland	283	6	Graves	Phinehas		1		1		2		1	1				6		
Ashfield	341	1	Graves	Randal	3	2		1		1	1		1				9		
Granville East Soc	529	25	Graves	Reuben	1	1	2	1	1		1	2		1			10		
Whately	66	41	Graves	Reuben	2	1		1			1		1				6		
Granville East Soc	529	12	Graves	Roswell	3			1					1	1			6		
Greenfield	73	7	Graves	Rufus	3			1		2			1				7		
Leverett	115	8	Graves	Rufus	1			1					1				3		
Whately	66	46	Graves	Selah	3	3		1		1		1	1				10		
Hatfield	12	34	Graves	Seth			1	1	1			1		1			5		
Hatfield	12	36	Graves	Silas			2		1			1	1	1			6		
Leverett	115	9	Graves	Silas				1						1			2		
Conway	58	36	Graves	Simeon				1						1			2		
Palmer	259	3	Graves	Simeon				1						1			2		
Hatfield	12	33	Graves	Solomon	2			1		1			1				5		
Whately	67	1	Graves	Solomon	2		2	1		2			2				9		
Williamsburg	446	9	Graves	Stephen	1		1			1		1					4		
Deerfield	53	4	Graves	Zebediah	1	1	1		1	1			1				6		
Pelham	214	4	Gray	Adam C.			4		1	1		1		1			8		
Pelham	214	14	Gray	Danl Decon				1				1		1			3		
Pelham	214	7	Gray	Ebenz Decon	1	1	4	1		2	1	1	2	1			15		
Belchertown	209	33	Gray	Eliphalet	2			1		2	1		1				7		
Pelham	214	18	Gray	Jacob	1	1	1		1		1			1			6		
Charlemont	192	2	Gray	James		1		1		3	1		1				7		
Colrain	186	3	Gray	Jemima	1		2						2	1			6		
Pelham	214	13	Gray	Jeremiah	1			1		3			1				6		
Pelham	214	12	Gray	John	2	1		1		2		1		1			8		
Pelham	214	8	Gray	John 2d	3		1	1		1	1	1	1	1			10		

TOWN	PG#	LN#	LAST NAME	FIRST NAME	FREE WHITE MALES under 10	10 to 16	16 to 26	26 to 45	45 and over	FREE WHITE FEMALES under 10	10 to 16	16 to 26	26 to 45	45 and over	TOTAL ALL OTHER	TOTAL SLAVES	TOTALS	DISTRICT/ TOWNSHIP	NOTES
Pelham	214	11	Gray	Jona & Eliot	1		1	1	1	4	1	1	2	1			13		
Ashfield	340	22	Gray	Jonathan	1	1			1	3	1		1				8		
Ware	226	18	Gray	Joseph			2	1				3		1			7		
Pelham	214	6	Gray	Justus	3		1			1			1				6		
Pelham	214	10	Gray	Matthew		1	1		1		1			1			5		
Pelham	214	16	Gray	Moses	2			1	2	1		1	1	1			9		
Pelham	214	15	Gray	Patrick				1		3			1				5		
Ashfield	340	21	Gray	Robert		1	1		1	1	1	1	1				7		
Middlefield	158	31	Gray	Samuel			1			1				1			3		
Pelham	214	17	Gray	Thomas		1		1	1		1		1				5		
Chester	146	37	Grayham	David			2			1		1					4		
Gill	86	6	Green	Benjamin	1	2	1		1	1	1	1		1			9		
Springfield	240	18	Green	Benjamin		1	3	8	1	3	1		1				18		
Amherst	294	5	Green	Clark		1				1		1					4		
South Brimfield	276	28	Green	Daniel		2		1				2		1			6		
Charlemont	192	3	Green	Ebenezer	2		1			1			1				5		
Greenwich	224	15	Green	Ebenz		1				1		1					3		
Belchertown	209	10	Green	Ebenz Sargt			1			2			1	1			5		
Chesterfield	21	31	Green	Eleanor	1						1	1	1				4		
Wilbraham	237	20	Green	Eliphalat	1	2			1	1		2	1				8		
West Springfield	350	56	Green	Jeptha	3	1			1			1	1				7		
South Brimfield	277	29	Green	Joel	1	1			1		1	2		1			7		
Belchertown	205	15	Green	Joel Capt			1		1	1	4		1				8		
Wendell	105	36	Green	Joshua	2			1				1	1				5		
Amherst	291	9	Green	Larkin		1				1			1				3		
Colrain	190	19	Green	Peter											9		9		
Monson	268	14	Green	Reuben	1	1		1		2	1		1				7		
South Brimfield	277	15	Green	Robert			1			3			1				5		
Barnardston	77	38	Green	Samuel	2	1		1		3	3		1				11		
Shutesbury	109	32	Green	Samuel		1						2					3		
Charlemont	191	13	Green	Sarah	2	1				2	1	2	1				9		
South Brimfield	277	28	Green	Sarah Wid										3			3		
Hatfield	14	35	Green	Stephen			2		1			1	1				5		
Amherst	290	12	Green	Timothy				1									1		
Amherst	294	17	Green	Timothy	1	1			1	3	1	2		1			10		
Barnardston	77	39	Green	Woodbridge		1		1			1		1	1			5		
Amherst	294	9	Green	Zara	1			1					1				3		
Brimfield	275	14	Green	Amos		1	1		1			2					5	South Brimfield	
Monson	268	13	Green	Solomon	2	2		1		1			1				7		
Leyden	82	26	Greenell	Benjamin		1		1		2	1		1				6		
Leyden	82	30	Greenell	Benjamin		1		1		1		2					4		
Leyden	82	31	Greenell	Joseph		1		1		1	1	1		1			6		
Leyden	82	28	Greenell	Paul	4		1	1					1				7		
Leyden	82	27	Greenell	Richard	1	1			1	1	2	2		1			9		
Brimfield	272	1	Greenhill	Joel	2	2			1	2	2	1	1				11		
Montgomery	161	10	Greenslit	Joseph		1		1		2		1	1				6		
Monson	268	6	Greenstill	John	4			1		1			1				7		
Westfield	127	24	Greenwood	Homes	2		1						1				4		
Wendell	105	37	Greenwood	Samuel			1					1					2		
Granby	252	11	Gridley	Elijah Revd	2			1		2			1				6		
Chester	149	32	Griffen	Silas	4			1		1			1				7		
Deerfield	53	7	Griffin	David	2		1	1		1			1				6		
Pelham	214	3	Griffin	Jonathan			1			2		1					4		
West Springfield	350	55	Griffin	Watson	2			1		1	1	1					7		
Northfield	20	36	Griggs	Joseph		1		1				1		2			5		
Goshen	310	7	Grimes	Charles		1					1	3		1			6		
Whately	66	40	Grimes	Samuel			1				1	1					3		
Greenfield	73	4	Grinell	George		1	1		1	1	2	1	1				8		
South Brimfield	276	26	Grinell	Samuel		1		1	1				1				4		
Greenfield	73	6	Grinell	William	2			1		2	2		1				8		
Greenfield	73	5	Grinell	Wise	1	2	2		1	2		1	1				10		
Montgomery	160	34	Grinman	Sampson				1					1				2		
West Springfield	353	31	Griswold	Sylvanus				1				3	1				5		
Norwich	154	23	Griswould	Ashur	1		1	1				1					6		
Norwich	154	21	Griswould	John				1			1		1				3		
Norwich	154	22	Griswould	John Junr	4		1						1				6		
Springfield	245	26	Griswould	Joseph Lt	1	1	1	1		2	1	2	1				10		
Wilbraham	232	5	Griswould	Solomon	1		1			1	1	1	1	1			7		
Greenfield	73	11	Griswould	Theophilus	2	3		1		4	1	1	1				13		
Southwick	358	47	Gross	Jonah	2	1	1	1		1	2			1			9		
Greenwich	220	9	Gross	Micah		1	1		2	2	1		1	2			10		
Longmeadow	93	24	Grosvenor	Charles	1		1			1		1					4		
Wilbraham	235	10	Grosvenor	Moses	1	1	2	1		1		2					8		
New Salem	99	23	Grout	George			1										1		
Pelham	214	21	Grout	Joel	1	1		1		2			1				6		
Shutesbury	109	30	Grout	John				1						1			2		
Belchertown	209	20	Grout	Jona Esq				1									1		
Monson	268	32	Grout	Joseph Doct	1		1	1		1	1						7		
Springfield	242	38	Grout	Micah				1						1			2		
Montague	46	15	Grover	Ebenezer		2	1	1			1		1				6		

TOWN	PG#	LN#	LAST NAME	FIRST NAME	FREE WHITE MALES under 10	10 to 16	16 to 26	26 to 45	45 and over	FREE WHITE FEMALES under 10	10 to 16	16 to 26	26 to 45	45 and over	TOTAL ALL OTHER	TOTAL SLAVES	TOTALS	DISTRICT/TOWNSHIP	NOTES
Hadley	286	2	Grover	Hosea	2			1					1	1			5		
Palmer	260	29	Grover	Robert				1		1		1					3		
Palmer	260	28	Grover	Stephen	1	1		1		2	1		1				7		
Montague	46	19	Grover	Martin	1			1		2			1				5		
Monson	268	24	Groves	Nicholas				1									1		
Monson	268	25	Groves	Samuel	2		1	1		2		2	1				9		
Greenwich	220	3	Grun	Benja	1		1	1		1			1				5		
Blanford	175	33	Guil	Martin				1			1		1				3		
Conway	58	25	Guild	Israel	3			1		1			1				6		
Hatfield	14	17	Guild	Joseph		1		1	1				1	1			5		
Blanford	177	20	Guile	Levi	2	1		1		3			1				8		
Ashfield	340	23	Guilford	Saml	1		2	1		2	3		1				10		
Williamsburg	446	10	Guilford	Simeon	1			1		2	1		1				6		
Williamsburg	446	6	Guilford	Timothy		1		1		1	1		1				5		
Williamsburg	446	7	Guilford	William		1	1	1						1			4		
Granville East Soc	533	4	Gullich	Zadock		3	1			1		1	1				7		
Montague	46	13	Gunn	Abel	1	1		1		3		1	1				8		
Montague	45	42	Gunn	Asahel	2		1	1		2	3	1	1				11		
Montague	45	41	Gunn	Chester	1			1		1			1				4		
Montague	46	1	Gunn	Eleanor	1					1				1			3		
Montague	46	12	Gunn	Eli			1						1				2		
Montague	46	9	Gunn	Elijah		2						1	1	1			6		
Montague	46	16	Gunn	Elisha	3			1		3			1				8		
Montague	46	4	Gunn	Hannah		1					1	1	1				4		
Montague	46	11	Gunn	Israel		2			1			1		1			5		
Montague	46	8	Gunn	Joseph		1						1					2		
Montague	46	5	Gunn	Martin	1		1	1		2			1	1			7		
Montague	46	6	Gunn	Moses		1	1	1			1	1	1				6		
Montague	46	3	Gunn	Nathaniel				1						1			2		
Montague	46	2	Gunn	Nathaniel Jr	1	2			1	2	1	2		1			10		
Montague	45	43	Gunn	Rufus		1											1		
Montague	46	7	Gunn	Salmon	1			1		2		1	1				6		
Montague	46	10	Gunn	William	2			1		1			1				5		
Cummington	305	33	Gurney	Amos	1			1		2			1				5		
Cummington	303	18	Gurney	Asa	2	2		1		3	1	1	1				11		
Cummington	303	17	Gurney	Benjamin		1	1						2				4		
Warwick	37	42	Gurney	John			1						1				2		
Goshen	310	9	Gustin	Molly Wid.	1	1	1			1	1	1		1			7		
Brimfield	272	10	Guthrie	Saml Doct	2		1	1		1			1				6		
Belchertown	209	11	Guy	Amasa	2			2		2	2	1	1				10		
Russell	139	12	H*ter	Benjamin			1	3	1			1					6		
Greenwich	220	18	Hack	Esther Wd	3								1				4		
Pelham	214	25	Hackett	Giddeon Jr	1			1	1				1	1			6		
Chesterfield	24	27	Haden	Noah		1		1		2		1					5		
Hawley	333	22	Hadlock	John			1			1		1					3		
Williamsburg	446	16	Hadlock	Josiah	2	2	1		1			1		1			8		
New Salem	100	13	Hagur	Aaron	1	2				4	1	1					10		
South Hadley	250	13	Haight	Justus		1				1		2					4		
Greenwich	220	27	Hail	Samuel		2		1	1	1				1			6		
Russell	138	21	Haise	Eli	2					1			1				4		
Russell	138	20	Haise	Jospeh	3			1					1	1			6		
Monson	266	7	Hakes	Jonathan	2	1	1	1		1	2			1			9		
Conway	58	39	Hale	Aaron	3	1	2	1		1			1				9		
Longmeadow	95	4	Hale	Abner		1	1		2		1	1		1			7		
Barnardston	78	9	Hale	Chilab			1	1		1				1			4		
Barnardston	78	13	Hale	Daniel	1			1					1				3		
Longmeadow	95	6	Hale	Elam				1				1	1				3		
Barnardston	78	11	Hale	Elijah	2	2		1		1	1		1				8		
Barnardston	78	6	Hale	Elizer	2			1		2			1				6		
Westhampton	16	33	Hale	Enoch	1	2			1	2	2	1		1			10		
Granville Mid Soc.	165	29	Hale	Ezekiel		1		1			2	1	1				6		
Longmeadow	94	17	Hale	Hezekiah Lt		1	1	2				1	1				6		
Barnardston	78	4	Hale	Israel	2	2		1		1			2				8		
Deerfield	53	36	Hale	James	1			1		1	1		1				5		
Barnardston	78	3	Hale	John	2	1	1			1	1		1				7		
Longmeadow	95	5	Hale	John	1	1		1		2			1				6		
West Springfield	353	34	Hale	Jonathan		1	1				1	1		1			5		
Longmeadow	94	11	Hale	Jonathan Esq		1	1	1						2			5		
Barnardston	78	7	Hale	Samuel		1		1		3	1		1				7		
Longmeadow	93	41	Hale	Sarah							1	1	1				3		
Longmeadow	91	19	Hale	Thomas	1			1			1	2		2			8		
Whately	67	5	Hales	Henry		1		1					1				3		
Norwich	151	34	Hall	Aaron	1	1		1		2	2		1				8		
Blanford	177	16	Hall	David		3	1	1			1		1				7		
Hawley	333	28	Hall	Ebenz	1	1		1		2	3	1	1				10		
Southwick	358	51	Hall	Elisha	1			1					1				3		
Conway	59	15	Hall	Elizer	2	1		1					1	1			6		
New Salem	100	21	Hall	James											5		5		
Granville West Soc	170	33	Hall	Jesse	1	1		1		1			1				5		
Rowe	200	4	Hall	Joel	2			1		2			1				6		

240

TOWN	PG#	LN#	LAST NAME	FIRST NAME	FREE WHITE MALES					FREE WHITE FEMALES					TOTAL ALL OTHER	TOTAL SLAVES	TOTALS	DISTRICT/ TOWNSHIP	NOTES
					under 10	10 to 16	16 to 26	26 to 45	45 and over	under 10	10 to 16	16 to 26	26 to 45	45 and over					
Blanford	182	16	Hall	John	1	1		1		2		3	1				9		
Charlemont	192	19	Hall	John	1	1	2		1	2	2	1		1			11		
Montgomery	161	4	Hall	John	1	1			1				1				4		
Greenfield	73	23	Hall	John C.				1			1	1		1			4		
Blanford	177	17	Hall	Jonathan		1	2	1		1			1	1			7		
Ashfield	341	11	Hall	Joseph	5	1	1	1				2					10		
Southwick	359	1	Hall	Medad	1					1			1				3		
Granville West Soc	169	28	Hall	Nathan		1	1		1			2	1				6		
Ashfield	341	10	Hall	Nathaniel	2	1			1	2			1				7		
Ashfield	341	12	Hall	Reuben	2	1	1		1		1	2		1			9		
Ashfield	341	9	Hall	Saml	1	1	1		1	1		3		1			9		
Granville West Soc	170	32	Hall	Samuel	2		1	1	1	1	1	1	1	1			10		
Hawley	333	27	Hall	Seth		1	1		1	1	1			1			6		
Colrain	186	20	Hall	Stephen	2			1		2			1				6		
Worthington	300	14	Hall	Thomas	1	1			1	2	1	1		1			8		
Worthington	300	5	Hall	Thomas Jun	2			1		1			1				5		
Greenfield	73	26	Hall	Timothy		3	4		1	1		1		1			11		
Conway	59	11	Hall	William		1			1	2				1			5		
Conway	59	12	Hall	William Jur	2		1	1		2			1				7		
Holland	280	8	Halladay	Eunice									1				1		
Goshen	310	10	Halloch	William		1			1			1		1			4		
Plainfield	308	43	Hallock	Moses	3	1	2	1		1			1				9		
Belchertown	212	1	Hallow	Richard P.	3	2	3		1	1	1		1				12		
Chester	144	26	Hambelton	Nathan Capt		1			1	1		2		1			6		
Westfield	124	1	Hambleton	Adam				1	1	1		1		1			4		
Chester	143	1	Hamelton	David	1	1		1		2	1		1				7		
Chester	143	4	Hamelton	John	3			1		1	2		1				8		
Williamsburg	446	25	Hamer	George	1			1		1		1					4		
Shutesbury	109	34	Hamilton	Andrew		1	1		1			1		1			5		
Palmer	259	30	Hamilton	Asa	3			1					1				5		
Blanford	181	3	Hamilton	David		2			1	3	1	2		1			10		
Deerfield	53	21	Hamilton	Eben	3		2	2		2	1	1	1	1			13		
Blanford	177	29	Hamilton	Ephraim				1	1	1			2	1			6		
Blanford	178	2	Hamilton	Francis	1			1					1				3		
Granville West Soc	169	38	Hamilton	Gad	2	1		1		2		1	1				8		
Granville West Soc	170	9	Hamilton	Henry		1			1			2	1				5		
Blanford	175	23	Hamilton	Hugh	2	1		1		1		1					6		
Blanford	178	1	Hamilton	James				1		2		1					4		
Granville West Soc	170	7	Hamilton	James	1	1	1		1	2	1	1		1			9		
Palmer	261	25	Hamilton	James				1			1		1				3		
Chester	143	8	Hamilton	James Deac				1			1		1				3		
Barnardston	78	5	Hamilton	John	2		1	1		1			1				6		
Blanford	176	35	Hamilton	John	1	1	1		1		1	1	1				7		
Palmer	261	26	Hamilton	John 2d	1	1		1		1			1				5		
Chester	149	18	Hamilton	John Lieut	3	1	1			2	1	1	1				10		
Palmer	260	39	Hamilton	John Lt		1	1		1			1	1				5		
Ware	226	29	Hamilton	John Lt.			1	1		1	1	1					5		
Pelham	214	27	Hamilton	Jos Doct	1	3		1		1		1		1			8		
Chester	143	9	Hamilton	Lemuel	1		1					1					3		
Shutesbury	109	35	Hamilton	Patrick	2	1			1	1		1		1			7		
Chesterfield	25	1	Hamilton	Robert		1		1	1	2	1	1	1	1			9		
Conway	58	40	Hamilton	Robert	2	1	1	1		1		2	2	1			11		
Granville West Soc	170	8	Hamilton	Robert		1			1			2		1			5		
Chesterfield	22	27	Hamilton	Robert Jr	2	1		1		3			1				8		
Middlefield	157	5	Hamilton	Samuel	3	1		1		1	2		1				9		
Granville West Soc	170	10	Hamilton	Thomas	1		1		1	1	1		1				6		
Conway	58	44	Hamilton	William	2			2					2				6		
Middlefield	157	23	Hamilton	William	2			1		2	1		1				7		
Russell	138	25	Hamlin	Harris	2			1		4			1				8		
West Springfield	353	36	Hamlin	Ichiel	2		2		1	1	2	1					9		
Cummington	303	20	Hamlin	Isaac	1	2			1			2		1			7		
Plainfield	307	14	Hamlin	John	2	1		1		2	1		1				8		
Wilbraham	232	3	Hamlin	John	1	2		1		1	1		1				7		
Goshen	311	6	Hammond	Alpheus	3			1					1				6		
New Salem	100	10	Hammond	Barnabas	1		1					1					3		
Wilbraham	233	24	Hammond	James				1		1			1				3		
Wendell	106	9	Hammond	Jeremh	2			1				1	1				5		
Hawley	333	23	Hammond	John				1		1			1				3		
Goshen	311	5	Hammond	Joseph	1			1		3	2		1				8		
Springfield	239	42	Hammond	Lettice			1					1					2		
Hatfield	12	26	Hammond	Nathaniel	1			1		1			1				4		
Goshen	311	7	Hammond	Thaddeus	2			1		2	1		1				7		
Ashfield	341	24	Hammond	Timothy					1		1	1					4		
Westfield	119	2	Hanchet	Moses			1	1									2		
Southwick	358	49	Hanchet	Thomas	4		1	1					1	1	1		9		
Worthington	298	17	Hanchet	Zaccheus	1	1	1		1			1		1			6		
Worthington	298	18	Hanchet	Zaccheus Jun	2			1					1				4		
Springfield	247	43	Hancock	Abel	2			1		2			2	1			8		
Longmeadow	92	37	Hancock	Abiel		3	1	1					1				6		
Wilbraham	236	37	Hancock	Gideon			1			4			2				7		
Chester	149	28	Hancock	Lewis	1			1		3	3						9		

TOWN	PG#	LN#	LAST NAME	FIRST NAME	FREE WHITE MALES					FREE WHITE FEMALES					TOTAL ALL OTHER	TOTAL SLAVES	TOTALS	DISTRICT/ TOWNSHIP	NOTES
					under 10	10 to 16	16 to 26	26 to 45	45 and over	under 10	10 to 16	16 to 26	26 to 45	45 and over					
Wilbraham	236	19	Hancock	Moses	1	2		1		3		1	1				9		
Springfield	243	43	Hancock	Thomas	3	2		1		1			1	1			9		
Colrain	186	6	Handy	Charles	2	1	1	1		3	1		2	1			12		
Belchertown	205	29	Hanks	Ebenz	3	1		1		1		1	1				8		
Belchertown	205	28	Hanks	James	2	1		1	1	4		1	1	1			12		
Williamsburg	446	20	Hannan	Josiah	1			1		1		1					4		
Belchertown	206	2	Hannemon	Caleb	1				1	1			1				4		
Belchertown	205	17	Hannemon	Elijah	1					2			1				5		
Belchertown	205	33	Hannemon	Moses Jr			1	2	1			1	1				6		
Belchertown	206	1	Hannemon	Phinehas		2	2			1	1			1			7		
Belchertown	205	18	Hannemon	Rachel Wd					1		1						2		
Belchertown	208	33	Hannemon	Solomon		1		1		1				1			4		
Belchertown	205	20	Hannemon	Wm	2					1			1				5		
Blanford	181	31	Hanning	David				1	1	2	2		1				7		
Southampton	129	21	Hannum	Asahel	1				1	1	1	1	1				6		
Ludlow	257	26	Hannum	Daniel	3	1		1		1			1				7		
Pelham	217	19	Hannum	David	3		1	1					1				6		
Easthampton	136	25	Hannum	Eleazer Junr	1		1	1	1	1			1	1			7		
Easthampton	136	5	Hannum	Joel			2	1		2	2	2					9		
Southampton	133	10	Hannum	Phebe Wd	1	2				1	1	1	1				7		
Hatfield	14	33	Hannum	Silas	1			1		1		1	1				5		
Southampton	132	14	Hannum	Timothy					1	2	1		1				5		
Blanford	177	27	Harden	Joel	1	1	1	1		2			1	1			8		
Worthington	299	23	Harden	Jonathan	1		1	1		2			1				6		
Cummington	303	19	Harden	William		1		1		1				1			4		
Deerfield	53	31	Hardin	Abijah		1	1	1		4	1		1				9		
Granville West Soc	169	8	Hardin	Ebenezer		1	1	1				1		1			5		
Granville West Soc	169	25	Hardin	Isaac	1			1		1	1		1				6		
Hatfield	14	25	Harding	Abiel	3	1		1		1	1		1				8		
Springfield	242	33	Harding	Daniel	2			1		2			1				6		
Blanford	181	17	Harfield	Elizabeth		1	2			2	1	1	1				8		
Granville Mid Soc.	167	41	Harger	David	2			1		1			1				5		
Pelham	214	26	Harkins	Daniel	1	1		1		3	2		1				9		
Pelham	214	30	Harkins	David	1	1		1			2	1		1			7		
Pelham	214	35	Harkins	Jno Capt	3	2	1	1		2	1	1					11		
Pelham	214	29	Harkins	John	1	1	1		1	2	1	1					8		
Hawley	334	6	Harmon	Elijah	2	1	1		1	2		1					8		
Westfield	122	19	Harmon	Elinor	1					2			1				4		
Conway	58	45	Harrington	Aaron			1		1	1	1	3		1			8		
Wilbraham	238	12	Harrington	Benja	1					2			1				4		
Orange	42	13	Harrington	Daniel	3		1	1		1	1		1				8		
Orange	42	14	Harrington	Jason	1	1		1				2		1			6		
Colrain	186	16	Harrington	Timothy		1	1			4	1	2	1				11		
Heath	196	15	Harris	Daniel	1					1	1		1	1			5		
New Salem	100	8	Harris	Ezra		2	1		1	1		1	1	1			8		
Williamsburg	446	27	Harris	Job	2			1		1			1				5		
Deerfield	53	53	Harris	John					1	1	1		1				4		
Springfield	239	12	Harris	Nancy Wd		1		1				1		1			4		
Greenwich	220	15	Harris	Oliver	1	1			1	2	1	1	1				8		
Longmeadow	92	31	Harris	Phebe	1	1		1			1		2				6		
Springfield	243	42	Harris	Samuel		3	3	1		4	1	1	1				14		
Wendell	106	3	Harris	Samuel	4	2	1		1		1	1		1			11		
Buckland	328	3	Harris	Sarah										1			1		
Heath	196	17	Harris	Silas	1			1		2		1					5		
Heath	196	10	Harris	Valentine	1	1	1		1			1		1			6		
Springfield	239	27	Harris	William						2			1				3		
Westfield	121	7	Harrison	Reuben	1	1		1		3	1		1				8		
Granville West Soc	169	29	Harrison	Roger Revd				1					1				2		
Westfield	121	6	Harrison	Stephen	1			1	1	2			1	1			7		
Norwich	152	37	Harriss	Lemuel		1	1			2	1	1					6		
Colrain	186	11	Harroun	David	3			1				1	2	1			9		
Colrain	186	9	Harroun	John	4		1	1		1			2				9		
Blanford	182	17	Harskill	Philip	1	1			1	1	1	2		1			8		
West Springfield	356	45	Hart	Charles	3			1		1		1					6		
Shelburne	321	26	Hart	Ebenz	1			1		1		1					4		
New Salem	99	26	Hart	John	3	1		1			2		1				8		
Deerfield	53	35	Hart	Samuel	3	1		1		3			3				11		
Brimfield	269	15	Hartley	Edward		1			1	1				1			4		
Conway	59	9	Hartwell	Francis	2	1		1		4			1				9		
Charlemont	192	11	Hartwell	Jonathan				1		2	2		1				6		
Conway	59	10	Hartwell	Samuel	1		1			1		1					4		
Conway	59	7	Hartwell	Solomon		1		1		1		1		1			4		
Conway	59	8	Hartwell	Solomon Junr	4		1			1	1		1				8		
Charlemont	192	17	Hartwell	William		1		1				2		1			5		
Monson	264	42	Harvey	Amasa	1	1	3		1	1	1		1				9		
Buckland	328	1	Harvey	Jonathan	2			1		2	2			2			9		
Granville Mid Soc.	165	17	Harvey	Josiah		1			1			1		1			4		
Barnardston	78	2	Harvey	Peter			1		1				1	1			4		
Granville Mid Soc.	167	39	Harvey	Rufus				1		3		1	1				6		
Ware	226	23	Harwood	Andrew	1			2		1	2			1			9		

TOWN	PG#	LN#	LAST NAME	FIRST NAME	FREE WHITE MALES under 10	10 to 16	16 to 26	26 to 45	45 and over	FREE WHITE FEMALES under 10	10 to 16	16 to 26	26 to 45	45 and over	TOTAL ALL OTHER	TOTAL SLAVES	TOTALS	DISTRICT/ TOWNSHIP	NOTES
Greenwich	220	24	Harwood	Benja	3			1		1	1		1				7		
Ware	226	27	Harwood	Benjamin	1	1			1	1	3	1					8		
Whately	67	7	Harwood	Francis	4		1						1				6		
Greenwich	220	35	Harwood	Jacob	3			1		2	2		1				9		
Ware	226	24	Harwood	John	1			1					1				3		
New Salem	100	4	Hascall	Benjamin	3	2	2	1	1		1	1		1			12		
New Salem	100	5	Hascall	Jacob			1		1	1		2					5		
New Salem	100	3	Hascall	John			1		1			1		1			4		
New Salem	100	17	Hascall	Saml Junr	2			1		2			1				6		
Worthington	298	3	Hasen	Nathan	2		1	2		1	1		1				8		
Shelburne	321	22	Haskel	Roger	2	1			1		3			1			8		
Greenwich	220	13	Haskell	David	2	1		1		1			1				6		
Greenwich	220	16	Haskell	Elias Lt.	2	2	1		1			1	1		1		9		
Belchertown	205	23	Haskell	Jeremiah			1		1	2	1		1				6		
Shutesbury	110	2	Haskell	John	1	1			1			1		1			5		
Shutesbury	110	3	Haskell	Levi			1			2			1				4		
Wendell	106	8	Haskell	Nathan		1		1				1	1				4		
New Salem	99	38	Haskins	George			1	1				1	1				4		
Shutesbury	110	1	Haskins	Job	1		1					1					3		
New Salem	99	24	Haskins	Joseph	1		1	1	1	1			2	1			8		
Shutesbury	109	36	Haskins	Joseph	3	1		1		2		2	1	2			12		
New Salem	99	36	Haskins	Luke	1		1	1	3				1				7		
New Salem	99	35	Haskins	Paul	3	2	1		1	2	1	1		1			12		
New Salem	99	37	Haskins	Seth		2				1	4		2	1			10		
New Salem	99	34	Haskins	Shadrach 2d		1	1	1		1	1		1				6		
New Salem	99	33	Haskins	Silas		1	1			1		1					4		
New Salem	99	32	Haskins	William			1	1	3	1		1	1				8		
South Brimfield	277	33	Hassett	James		2		1	3	1		1					8		
Westfield	121	2	Hasting	Benjamin			1			2	1	1					5		
Greenfield	73	31	Hastings	Benjamin				1					1	1			3		
Greenfield	73	17	Hastings	Benjamin Jr	2		1	1		3	1		1				9		
New Salem	99	25	Hastings	Consider			1	1		1			1	1			5		
Amherst	289	15	Hastings	Elijah	1		1		1	2	1	2					8		
Greenfield	73	25	Hastings	Ephraim		1	1	1					1	1			5		
Warwick	38	6	Hastings	Isaac	2		2		1	3		1		1			10		
Hatfield	13	3	Hastings	John		1	2		1			2	2	1			9		
Hatfield	11	14	Hastings	John Jun	2	1		1		2	1		1				8		
Warwick	38	2	Hastings	Jonas			1			1				1			3		
Charlemont	192	6	Hastings	Jonathan			2	1	2	2				1			8		
Greenfield	73	18	Hastings	Joseph		1	1	1	1				1	1			6		
Greenfield	73	27	Hastings	Lemuel	1	1	2		1	1				1			7		
Amherst	292	25	Hastings	Moses	3	1	1	1		2	3	1	1				13		
Leyden	83	3	Hastings	Nathan				1		4							5		
Warwick	38	1	Hastings	Nathan		1		1		3	1						6		
Deerfield	53	37	Hastings	Oliver	1	1		1					1				5		
Greenfield	73	28	Hastings	Oliver	3	1	1	1		1				1			8		
Hatfield	11	1	Hastings	Perez	2		1		1	1	1	1	1				8		
Palmer	259	38	Hastings	Roswell	3		1				1	1					8		
Amherst	292	34	Hastings	Samuel		1	1		1	2				1			6		
Barnardston	78	8	Hastings	Samuel			2		1			1	2	1			7		
Greenfield	73	20	Hastings	Selah	2	1		1		3	1		1				9		
Buckland	327	21	Hastings	Solomon	3	1		1		2			1				8		
Amherst	292	33	Hastings	Thomas	1		2		1	2		1	1	1			9		
Hadley	289	3	Hastings	Waitstil	1		1					1					3		
Longmeadow	95	22	Hatch	Abner		4		1		1				1			7		
Monson	263	25	Hatch	Baker	1		1			2			1				5		
Monson	263	24	Hatch	Elijah	1			1		1		1	2	1			7		
Southampton	129	1	Hatch	Eliphlet		1		1		1	2		1				6		
Montgomery	160	4	Hatch	Moses	4	1	1			1		1					8		
Monson	263	22	Hatch	Stephen		1		1		1		1					4		
Worthington	302	3	Hatch	Thomas	3			1	1	2			1				8		
Blanford	181	25	Hatch	Timothy	2	1	3	1		1		1	1				10		
Worthington	302	4	Hatch	Zephaniah		1	1			1			1				5		
Granby	253	31	Hatfield	Joseph			1		1					1			3		
Springfield	240	22	Hatfield	Joseph	3			1		2			1				7		
Granby	254	22	Hathaway	Abner			1			1			1				3		
Worthington	298	30	Hathaway	Jonathan			1			2		1					4		
Gill	86	9	Hathaway	Samuel		1		1					1				3		
Belchertown	205	24	Hathaway	Thomas	1	2	1						1				5		
Northampton	9	29	Hatheway	Guilford	3			1	1	1	2		1				8		
Buckland	328	2	Hathway	Josiah	2		2		1	3		1	1				10		
Worthington	298	23	Haun	Eleazer	1			1					1	1			4		
New Salem	100	7	Haven	Philip		2		1		1	1			1			6		
New Salem	100	6	Haven	William				1			1		1				3		
Northfield	28	39	Havens	Simon			1	1				1	1	1			5		
Hawley	333	26	Hawes	Edmund	2		1	1		1				1			6		
Plainfield	307	18	Hawes	Elihah D	1		1						1				3		
Monson	264	32	Hawes	Jacob	1			1		2			1				5		
Shelburne	321	24	Hawk	Moses	1	3		1		1	2	1	1				10		
Shelburne	321	25	Hawk	Solomon	1		2	1		3	2	1		1			11		

TOWN	PG#	LN#	HEADS OF HOUSEHOLD		FREE WHITE MALES					FREE WHITE FEMALES					TOTAL ALL OTHER	TOTAL SLAVES	TOTALS	DISTRICT/ TOWNSHIP	NOTES
			LAST NAME	FIRST NAME	under 10	10 to 16	16 to 26	26 to 45	45 and over	under 10	10 to 16	16 to 26	26 to 45	45 and over					
Leyden	83	1	Hawkins	Amaziah	2		1	1		2	2	1	1				10		
Springfield	243	40	Hawkins	George		1	1		1		1	1		1			6		
Greenfield	73	19	Hawkins	Jourden	1			1				1					3		
Springfield	248	12	Hawkins	Samuel	2			1	1			1					5		
Deerfield	53	17	Hawks	Asa				1						1			2		
Deerfield	53	18	Hawks	Asa Junr	2	1		1	1	1			2				8		
Charlemont	192	14	Hawks	Elihu	3		1		1		1	1	1				8		
Charlemont	192	13	Hawks	Ephraim	3	1	1		1	1	2	1		1			11		
Charlemont	192	8	Hawks	Gershom		1		1				2		1			5		
Deerfield	53	13	Hawks	Hilkiah	1	1	1	1		1		1	1	1			8		
Hawley	333	25	Hawks	Ichabod	2	2		1			1		1				7		
Charlemont	192	16	Hawks	Israel	4	1		1					1				7		
Charlemont	192	10	Hawks	Jared	3	2	3		1	1		2		1			13		
Charlemont	192	20	Hawks	Jared Jur		1					2	1					4		
Charlemont	192	15	Hawks	Jonathan	2	1	1		1	2	1	2	1				11		
Charlemont	192	9	Hawks	Joshua		2		1		2	1	1		1			8		
Deerfield	53	16	Hawks	Obed		1	2		1		1	1		2			8		
Deerfield	53	19	Hawks	Paul		2	1		1		1	3		1			9		
Charlemont	192	12	Hawks	Rufus	2	1		1			2	1		1			8		
Deerfield	53	11	Hawks	Samuel	2			1		2		1		1			8		
Deerfield	53	12	Hawks	Seth Junr	2			1		2	2	1					8		
Deerfield	53	10	Hawks	Waitstill	2		2	1	1	1	1	2					11		
Deerfield	53	9	Hawks	William		1		1	1	1			1	1			6		
Hawley	334	4	Hawks	Zadoch	3	1		1		1			1				7		
Deerfield	53	14	Hawks	Zadok		1		1	1	1	1		1	1			7		
Deerfield	53	20	Hawks	Zeeb	2	1		1		2	2		1				9		
Deerfield	53	15	Hawks	Zun		1	1	1		2	2		1				8		
Hadley	288	10	Hawley	Chester	2		1	1		2			2				8		
Granville West Soc	169	37	Hawley	Jesse	1			1					1				3		
Northampton	5	13	Hawley	Mercy			1	1		1			1	1			5		
Amherst	290	36	Hawley	Moses				1				3					4		
Amherst	291	8	Hawley	Zachariah	3	1	1	1	1		2	1		1			11		
Amherst	291	10	Hawley	Zachariah Jun	1		1					1					3		
Williamsburg	446	18	Hayden	Cotton	4			1		3			1				9		
Chesterfield	21	29	Hayden	John	2	1	2		1			2	1				9		
Williamsburg	446	19	Hayden	Josiah				1			1	1			1		4		
Belchertown	212	5	Hayden	Moses							1		1				2		
Conway	58	46	Hayden	Moses		2	1		1	2	1	1					8		
Pelham	215	1	Hayden	Thomas	1	1			1	2	1		1				7		
Belchertown	211	32	Haydin	Moses	2			1		2		1					6		
South Hadley	250	27	Hayes	Joel Revd		2			1	2	1	1	1				8		
Granville Mid Soc.	167	42	Hayes	Luther	2		3	1				2					8		
Monson	264	34	Hayes	Shadrach	3	1		1		2	2	1	1				11		
Ware	228	27	Haynes	Benjamin	2			1		2			1				6		
Brimfield	274	12	Haynes	Daniel		1	1	2	2	1		2		1			10		
Monson	267	3	Haynes	Daniel	2	1	1	1		2	2		1				10		
Palmer	262	4	Haynes	David	1			1		3	1		1				7		
Brimfield	274	27	Haynes	Jonas		1		1	1				3	1			7		
Brimfield	274	33	Haynes	Joseph	3		1		1	3	3		1				12		
Rowe	200	1	Haynes	Pardon	2			1		2		1	1				7		
Brimfield	274	9	Haynes	Samuel			1										1		
Colrain	186	10	Haynes	Vinall	1		1		1		1	1		1			6		
Southwick	358	48	Hays	Jonathan				1					1				2		
Southwick	358	50	Hays	Moses	1	1	2		1	3	1	1		1			11		
Blanford	180	11	Hayse	Jacob		1	1		1	1			1				5		
Orange	42	15	Hayward	Lemuel		1		1						1			3		
Ware	226	28	Haywood	Cary	2	2		1		2			1				8		
Conway	58	47	Haywood	Samuel	1		1	1	1	2			1	1			8		
Russell	138	28	Hazard	James	3		1			2		1	1		1		9		
Russell	138	29	Hazard	robert	1			1					1		1		4		
Warwick	37	43	Hazeltine	Benjamin	2	2	3	1		1	1		1				11		
West Springfield	353	37	Hazen	Frederick	3			1		2			1	2			9		
West Springfield	351	4	Hazy	John				1					1				2		
Chesterfield	24	18	Healy	Ebenezer		2	2	1		1			1		1		8		
Wilbraham	235	28	Heaton	Philemon		1		1		1		1	1				5		
Montague	46	26	Heeb	Reuben		1	2						1				4		
Montgomery	162	5	Hegwin	Amos	1			1		1		1					4		
Montgomery	161	13	Hegwin	John	1			1				1					3		
Montgomery	161	38	Hegwin	John 2d				1			1	2		1			5		
Montgomery	162	4	Hegwin	Thomas			1					1					2		
Northampton	6	22	Helton	John	1			1						2			4		
Warwick	38	8	Hemenway	Asa			1			1		1					3		
Leverett	115	18	Hemenway	Elipht		1						1					2		
Orange	42	18	Hemenway	Ezra	1	2				2		1					6		
New Salem	99	27	Hemenway	Joseph	2		1	1		1		1	1	1			8		
New Salem	100	11	Hemenway	Joshua Jr		1	1	1			2		1				6		
Leverett	115	14	Hemenway	Josiah				1			1		1				3		
New Salem	100	2	Hemenway	Samuel			1			2			2				5		
Leverett	115	15	Hemenway	Willam	1		1				1						3		
Conway	59	16	Hemmenway	Daniel	1		1			3		1					6		

244

TOWN	PG#	LN#	LAST NAME	FIRST NAME	FWM under 10	FWM 10 to 16	FWM 16 to 26	FWM 26 to 45	FWM 45 and over	FWF under 10	FWF 10 to 16	FWF 16 to 26	FWF 26 to 45	FWF 45 and over	TOTAL ALL OTHER	TOTAL SLAVES	TOTALS	DISTRICT/ TOWNSHIP	NOTES
Williamsburg	446	13	Hemmenway	Ichabod		2	2		1		1			2			8		
Conway	59	17	Hemmenway	Jason			1		1		1			1			4		
Williamsburg	446	22	Hemmenway	Jason	1			1		2			1				5		
Amherst	289	16	Henderson	Timothy	2	2	2		1	1			1	1			10		
Wilbraham	237	1	Hendrick	Abijah	2		1						1				4		
Wilbraham	236	43	Hendrick	Jabez				1					1	1			3		
Easthampton	134	8	Hendrick	James	4	2		1		1	1	1	1				11		
Greenwich	220	31	Hendrick	James	1		1						1				3		
Conway	59	13	Hendrick	Reuben		2		1					2	2			7		
Wilbraham	236	42	Hendrick	Reuben	3			1		1			1				6		
Palmer	261	37	Hendrick	Samuel	3			1		1	1	2	1	1			10		
Amherst	289	18	Hendricks	James				1				1	1				3		
Blanford	180	20	Henery	Samuel	1			1	1	1	1	1		1			7		
Monson	262	3	Henley	Isaac	1		1						1				3		
Northampton	9	35	Henman	Luke C	1			1					1				3		
South Hadley	250	33	Henry	Ammah										1			1		
Chester	149	11	Henry	Andrew	1	1	1		1		2	1	1				8		
Leyden	82	34	Henry	Andrew	2	1			1	4		1	1	1			11		
Heath	196	7	Henry	David	1			1		1		1	1				5		
Blanford	178	11	Henry	James		1							1				2		
Chester	145	25	Henry	James	1	1							1				3		
Gill	86	26	Henry	Jemima	1	2	1				1	1		1			7		
Chester	149	7	Henry	John		1							2				3		
Brimfield	271	33	Henry	Jonas											8		8		
Chester	145	24	Henry	Jonas		1	2		1	2	2	1		1			10		
Norwich	152	15	Henry	Joseph Lieut	1			1		3	1		1				7		
Conway	58	43	Henry	Josiah		1	2		1	2			1	1			8		
Shutesbury	110	4	Henry	Luther		1		1		3		1					6		
Holland	279	39	Henry	Robert		1	2		1	3	2			1			10		
Chester	144	22	Henry	Samuel Lieut	1			1		1	1		1				5		
Heath	196	14	Herington	Thomas	1	1	1	1		2	1	1	1				9		
Westfield	125	4	Herrick	Aaron				1					1				2		
Worthington	299	17	Herrick	Asa	3	1		1		2	1	1	1				10		
Worthington	298	4	Herrick	Ebenezer		2	2		1	1	1	2		1			10		
Conway	59	5	Herrick	Elijah	2		1	1		1		1					6		
Worthington	301	24	Herrick	Isaac	3	3	1		1	1			1				10		
Montgomery	159	3	Herrick	Jonathan	4		1	1		1			1				8		
Montgomery	161	20	Herrick	Jonathan			2		1					1			4		
Norwich	152	14	Herrick	Moses			1	1		4			1				7		
Montgomery	161	19	Herrick	Stephen	2			1		1	3		1				8		
Chester	149	26	Herrin	Samuel	1	1		1		2	2	1		1			9		
Chester	149	27	Herrin	Solomon			1			2		1					4		
Blanford	177	28	Herring	Benjamin	3				1		2	2	1				9		
New Salem	100	12	Herrington	John			1	1					1				3		
Ware	226	21	Herrington	John			1			4			1				6		
Greenwich	220	28	Herrington	Lemuel		1		1	1	1			1	1			6		
Southampton	130	16	Herrlburt	Stephen		1		1				1		1			4		
Russell	139	8	Hewes	Grace Wid.								1		1			2		
Russell	139	10	Hewes	Henery		1				1		1					3		
Russell	139	7	Hewes	Stephen	1			1		1			1				4		
Belchertown	205	35	Hewlet	Mason Lt				1			1			1			3		
Belchertown	205	25	Hewlet	Thomas	2		1							1			4		
Heath	196	11	Heywood	Moses		1	1		1	1		1		1			6		
Heath	196	13	Heywood	Solomon	1			1		2			1				5		
Northampton	5	33	Hgower	Webb	1		1						1				3		
Rowe	200	2	Hibard	John		2		1					1	1			5		
Brimfield	274	14	Hibbard	Alpheus			1		1		1	2					4		
Leyden	82	32	Hibbard	Asa	1	1		1		2	3	1	1				10		
Williamsburg	446	17	Hickox	Benjamin	3	2		1		2	1		1				10		
Conway	58	48	Hickox	Eliphalet	1			1		2		1					5		
Greenwich	221	35	Hickson	Ezra		1		1				1	1				4		
Monson	266	8	Hide	Enoch		2		1		1	1	1					7		
Worthington	301	28	Higgins	Barre	1		1	1		1		1					5		
Norwich	153	38	Higgins	Ebenezer	3	2	1	1				2	1				10		
Worthington	299	1	Higgins	Elijah															Name crossed off
Greenwich	220	20	Higgins	Henry		1		1		1	1	2	1	1			8		
Blanford	175	32	Higgins	Nathaniel		1	1	1		1			1				5		
Granville West Soc	169	11	Higgins	Solomon	2	1		1		3			1	1			9		
Montgomery	161	15	Higley	David	1			1					1				3		
Granville Mid Soc.	165	28	Higley	Levi	2			1		2		2	1				8		
Wilbraham	235	34	Hill	Collins	4			1		1			1				7		
Cummington	303	21	Hill	Daniel				1					1		1		3		
Cummington	303	23	Hill	Daniel Jun		1		1				1		1			4		
Orange	42	19	Hill	David		2	1		2	1	1	1		2			10		
Belchertown	206	20	Hill	Ebenz				1						1			2		
Palmer	259	7	Hill	Elijah	3			1		1			1				6		
Rowe	200	3	Hill	Ephraim	1		1	1				2		1			6		
Williamsburg	446	11	Hill	Ephraim	3			1		3			1				8		
Barnardston	78	12	Hill	Jabez	4	1		1		1			1				8		
Cummington	303	22	Hill	Joel		2	1	1		3			1				8		

TOWN	PG#	LN#	LAST NAME	FIRST NAME	FREE WHITE MALES					FREE WHITE FEMALES					TOTAL ALL OTHER	TOTAL SLAVES	TOTALS	DISTRICT/ TOWNSHIP	NOTES
					under 10	10 to 16	16 to 26	26 to 45	45 and over	under 10	10 to 16	16 to 26	26 to 45	45 and over					
Montague	46	24	Hill	John				1			1		1				3		
Blanford	175	29	Hill	Joseph		1		1		3	1		1				7		
Whately	67	8	Hill	Joseph	1	1	2		1			3		1			9		
Orange	42	16	Hill	Joshua	1	1	1		1					1			5		
Shutesbury	109	33	Hill	Noah		1	2		1	1				1			6		
Williamsburg	446	26	Hill	Sampson				1		1	1			1			4		
Charlemont	192	7	Hill	Samuel	4			1		1	1			1			8		
Ashfield	341	23	Hill	Solomon			1			2			1				4		
Conway	59	18	Hillman	Lot	3	2	1			2		1	1	1			11		
Ludlow	256	22	Hills	Asa	2		1			1	1		1				6		
Springfield	247	27	Hills	Asahel	2		1			1		1					5		
Longmeadow	95	13	Hills	Jacob	2	1	1			2			1				7		
Longmeadow	91	15	Hills	Moses	1	2	2		1			2	1	1			10		
South Hadley	249	39	Hilyard	Anna Miss									1	2			3		
South Hadley	249	40	Hilyard	Timothy		1		1					1	1			4		
Pelham	214	28	Hinch	John	1	1		1		1	1			1			6		
Northampton	6		Hinckley	Samuel	2		1	1		2	1	1	1				9		
Greenwich	224	2	Hind	Joseph		1		1		1							3		
Holland	280	12	Hind	Loviah										1			1		
Greenwich	220	12	Hindrick	Joseph Lt	3		1	1		1		1	1	1			9		
New Salem	100	19	Hinds	Francis	2		1					1					4		
Pelham	214	33	Hinds	Nehemiah Doct	1	1	4	1	1	2	2		2				16		
Greenwich	220	11	Hinds	Timothy Capt		1	3	1				1	2	1			9		
Greenfield	73	21	Hindsdale	Ariel			1		1	4	1	4		1			12		
Greenfield	73	22	Hindsdale	Samuel			1		1		1	2		1			6		
Rowe	200	5	Hines	Joel	1		1			1		1					4		
Deerfield	53	32	Hinkley	Elijah	2				1	1	1	1	1				7		
Buckland	328	4	Hinkley	Solomon	3		1			1			1				6		
Chester	146	35	Hiscock	Noah	2		1			2			1				6		
Westfield	126	20	Hiscock	Wm		1		1				2		1			5		
Wilbraham	233	11	Hitchcock	Aaron		1	1	1		1	1		1				6		
Brimfield	274	1	Hitchcock	Abijah	2			1					1				4		
Ludlow	257	32	Hitchcock	Ambrose	1			1		1			1	1			5		
Monson	263	37	Hitchcock	Anna										2			2		
Hawley	334	3	Hitchcock	Arthur	1		1		1	3	1	1	1				9		
Greenfield	73	30	Hitchcock	Charles		1	1			1		1					4		
Montgomery	161	23	Hitchcock	Chauncry			1										1		
Brimfield	274	3	Hitchcock	Danl	3	1		1		1	2		2				10		
Wilbraham	235	42	Hitchcock	David				1					1				2		
Northampton	8	32	Hitchcock	Elias			1			3			1				5		
Brimfield	274	4	Hitchcock	Elijah		2		1			1	1		1			6		
Brimfield	271	38	Hitchcock	Enos	1			1		1	1	1					5		
Brimfield	270	16	Hitchcock	Ezra	1	1	1	1			1	1	1				7		
Brimfield	272	8	Hitchcock	Gad	1			1		2			1				5		
Monson	266	37	Hitchcock	Gad	1	1		1		2	1	1	1				8		
Springfield	240	44	Hitchcock	Heber	3			1		1			1				6		
Conway	59	14	Hitchcock	Heman	2	2		1		2	2		1				10		
Brimfield	271	37	Hitchcock	Jesse	1	1	2	1		3		1	1				10		
Wilbraham	232	39	Hitchcock	John Deacn				1									1		
Westhampton	17	7	Hitchcock	Jonathan	1		1	1		1			1				5		
Brimfield	270	15	Hitchcock	Joseph Dr				1						1			2		
Springfield	241	2	Hitchcock	Josiah Jr	3					1			1				6		
Springfield	240	43	Hitchcock	Josiah Lt			1	1	1					1			4		
Deerfield	53	30	Hitchcock	Justin	1	1	1		1		1	1		1			7		
Springfield	241	23	Hitchcock	Levi	4		1					1	1				7		
Palmer	260	41	Hitchcock	Luke	4	2	1		1		1	1	1				11		
Springfield	241	1	Hitchcock	Luther Capt		1	1		1	4		2		1			10		
Longmeadow	95	3	Hitchcock	Lydia										1			1		
Brimfield	270	21	Hitchcock	Mary Wido		1	2			1		2		2			8		
Brimfield	271	24	Hitchcock	Medad Capt	1	3	1			2	2	1	1				11		
Greenfield	73	29	Hitchcock	Merrick	2	1			1	1		1		1			7		
Brimfield	270	10	Hitchcock	Nathaniel		2				2	2			1			8		
Brimfield	271	36	Hitchcock	Noah		1		1		1		1		1			5		
Wilbraham	232	36	Hitchcock	Othneel				1						1			2		
West Springfield	356	36	Hitchcock	Perez	2	1	1	1				1	2				8		
Brimfield	272	23	Hitchcock	Peter				1					1				2		
Wilbraham	232	34	Hitchcock	Reuben			1		1	1	1			1			5		
Worthington	298	14	Hitchcock	Reuben			1	1		2		1		1			6		
Springfield	241	3	Hitchcock	Ruth Wd		1				1		2		2			6		
Hawley	334	1	Hitchcock	Saml	1	2		1	1	2	1	1	1	1			11		
Hawley	334	2	Hitchcock	Saml Jr			1			1			1				3		
Brimfield	272	22	Hitchcock	Samuel	1		1						1				3		
Wilbraham	232	37	Hitchcock	Simon	2			1		1			1				5		
Palmer	260	31	Hitchcock	Winchester	1			1				2					4		
South Hadley	248	10	Hix	Jona		1	4	1		3	2		1				12		
Springfield	247	28	Hix	Nathan		1							1				2		
Brimfield	269	29	Hoar	David	1	1			1			1	1	1			9		
Monson	267	13	Hoar	Edmund	1			1		1	1		1				5		
New Salem	99	31	Hoar	John	1			1		4			1				7		
Monson	266	27	Hoar	Jona	2			1		2	1		1				7		

TOWN	PG#	LN#	LAST NAME	FIRST NAME	FREE WHITE MALES					FREE WHITE FEMALES					TOTAL ALL OTHER	TOTAL SLAVES	TOTALS	DISTRICT/ TOWNSHIP	NOTES
					under 10	10 to 16	16 to 26	26 to 45	45 and over	under 10	10 to 16	16 to 26	26 to 45	45 and over					
Brimfield	269	26	Hoar	Joseph Capt.	1	1	2		1		1	1		1			8		
Shutesbury	110	5	Hoar	Luther		1		1		3			1				6		
Monson	264	11	Hoar	Nathan				1						1			2		
Monson	264	12	Hoar	Nathan Jr	1	1		1		4	1		1				9		
Monson	266	28	Hoar	Reuben		2		1				1	2	1			7		
New Salem	99	30	Hoar	Robert	1	1	2		1	2				1			8		
New Salem	99	29	Hoar	Shadrach	1	2	2	1	1				2	1			10		
Brimfield	269	28	Hoar	Solomon	1	1		1		3		1	1				8		
Shutesbury	110	6	Hoar	Warren	1			1					1				3		
Montague	46	25	Hoar	William	1			1		1		1					4		
Hadley	285	22	Hobard	George	1	1			1	2	3			1			9		
Hadley	285	8	Hobard	George Jun	1		1			1		1					4		
Hadley	285	7	Hobard	John	3		1	1		1			1				7		
Conway	59	3	Hobart	Israel		1		1				1		1			4		
Palmer	260	33	Hobb	Nathaniel			1			2			1				4		
Leverett	115	10	Hobert	Joshua	3	1		1		2	1		1				9		
Shutesbury	110	7	Hodge	Asa	1	1	1		1				1				5		
Hadley	287	33	Hodge	John	1	1		1		3			1				7		
Barnardston	78	10	Hodge	Levi		2	2		1	3	2		1				11		
Gill	86	20	Hodge	Seth		1		1	1	3	2		1	1			10		
Hadley	287	34	Hodge	William	2	2	1	1	1	1	1	1	1	1			12		
South Brimfield	277	9	Hodges	David				1	1	1		1		2			5		
South Brimfield	276	35	Hodges	Eliphalet	1		1	1		3	2		1	1			10		
New Salem	100	9	Hodgkin	Joseph	1			1		3			1				6		
New Salem	100	18	Hodgkin	Samuel	2	2		1		1	1		1				8		
Deerfield	53	34	Hofins	James		1		2		1	1		1				6		
Deerfield	53	23	Hoit	Cephas			1				1		1				3		
Deerfield	53	24	Hoit	David				1						1			2		
Deerfield	53	25	Hoit	David Junr		2		1		1	1	2	2				9		
Deerfield	53	28	Hoit	Ebenezer			1			2			1				4		
Deerfield	53	26	Hoit	Elihu			1			1	1		1				4		
Deerfield	53	29	Hoit	Eprephras	1			1		2		1	1				6		
Deerfield	53	22	Hoit	Jonathan			2		1					1			4		
Deerfield	53	27	Hoit	Jonathan 2d			2	2						1			5		
Brimfield	275	7	Holbridge	William	1	1	1		1		2	1		1			8	South Brimfield	
Brimfield	272	12	Holbrook	Nicholas		1		1	2		1		1				6		
Colrain	186	15	Holbrook	Seth	1	1	2		1	1	1		1				8		
Brimfield	272	11	Holbrook	Zenas	3			1	1				1				6		
Ashfield	341	17	Holbut	Reuben	1	2		1	1	2			1				8		
Granville East Soc	531	18	Holcomb	Alvin	2		1			1			1				5		
Westfield	119	13	Holcomb	Enoch		1	1	1	1			1	1				6		
Westfield	119	4	Holcomb	Enoch Jun		2		1		1	2	3	1				10		
Southwick	358	53	Holcomb	Martin	1		1		1			1		1			5		
Southwick	358	55	Holcomb	Roger	3			1		2			1				7		
Southwick	358	54	Holcomb	Samuel	1			1		1			1				4		
Buckland	327	22	Holden	Elihu	2			1		2		1	1				7		
Leverett	115	17	Holden	Isaac		2						1					3		
Northfield	29	9	Holden	James	4			1		1	1		1				8		
Orange	42	17	Holden	Jeduthan				1						1			2		
Worthington	302	12	Holdredge	Asher		1		1		1		1	1	1			6		
Cummington	303	25	Holebrook	Nathl	1	2		1		1		1		2			8		
Gill	86	16	Holister	Elisha	3			2					2				7		
Springfield	246	32	Holkens	Joseph	3			1		1			1				6		
Russell	138	8	Hollady	Josiah		1		1		1			1				4		
Russell	138	9	Hollady	Josiah Jr	5		1	1				1					8		
Colrain	186	8	Holland	Oliver		1		1		3	1	2	1				9		
Belchertown	205	22	Holland	Jonas	2			1		2			1				6		
Belchertown	205	21	Holland	Park Esq				1		1	2	2					6		
Plainfield	307	16	Hollice	Stephen	1	1		1		1	1		1				6		
Middlefield	157	9	Hollon	George	1			1		1		1					4		
Middlefield	157	8	Hollon	James		1		1					1				3		
Norwich	152	10	Hollon	James Doct	1			1				1					3		
Chester	143	15	Hollon	Simon E. Capt	3		1	1		2	2		1				10		
Chester	144	10	Hollon	William Doct			1						1				2		
Shelburne	321	23	Holloway	Peter	2	1	2		1	2	1		1				10		
Conway	59	2	Holloway	William	1		1		1			1		1			5		
Norwich	154	24	Hollyday	Job	2	1			1	2	2	1	1	1			11		
Montgomery	159	9	Hollyday	Zacheus	3			1		1			1				6		
Monson	268	35	Holmes	Isaac	1		2						1				4		
Northampton	10	15	Holmes	James	2		2		1	4	2		1				12		
Warwick	38	7	Holmes	James		1				2		1					4		
Amherst	293	20	Holmes	Samuel	2			1		2			1				6		
Colrain	186	18	Holms	John	3	2		1		1		2		1			10		
Colrain	186	17	Holms	William	1	1		1		2	1		1				7		
New Salem	100	15	Holt	Jonathan		2		1			1		1				5		
West Springfield	353	33	Holt	Uriah	2	1	1		1		1	2		1			9		
New Salem	100	14	Holt	William		1	1	1	1		2		1				7		
South Brimfield	277	38	Holten	Asa	2			1		2		1	1				7		
Northfield	29	3	Holton	Elijah		3			1	1		3		1			9		
Northfield	29	4	Holton	Elisha	2	1	1	1			2		1				8		

TOWN	PG#	LN#	LAST NAME	FIRST NAME	FREE WHITE MALES					FREE WHITE FEMALES					TOTAL ALL OTHER	TOTAL SLAVES	TOTALS	DISTRICT/ TOWNSHIP	NOTES
					under 10	10 to 16	16 to 26	26 to 45	45 and over	under 10	10 to 16	16 to 26	26 to 45	45 and over					
Northfield	29	1	Holton	John	2	3	2		1	2	1		1				12		
Northfield	28	40	Holton	Luther			2				1		1				4		
Gill	86	14	Holton	Nathaniel	1		2		1	4	1		1				10		
Northfield	29	8	Holton	Samuel		2	1	1	1	2		3		1			11		
Chester	145	17	Holton	William	5		1						1				7		
Pelham	214	22	Hood	Jona	1			1			1	1	1				5		
Buckland	328	5	Hook	Willm Capt.				1			1		1				3		
Greenwich	220	22	Hooker	Benja	3	3	1	1	1	2		1	1	1			14		
Springfield	239	23	Hooker	John Esq	3			1		3	1	1	1		2		12		
Greenwich	220	25	Hooker	Josepg Capt.		1		1			1		1				4		
Greenwich	220	23	Hooker	Joseph Jr		1	1					1		1			4		
Westhampton	17	9	Hooker	William	2	3	1	1		1	1		1				10		
Montgomery	159	7	Hopkins	Benjamin	1			1		2	1						5		
Springfield	242	42	Hopkins	Joseph			1		1			1					3		
Hadley	287	17	Hopkins	Samuel Revd	1		1	1	1	1			1		1		7		
Conway	59	6	Hopkins	Seth	1	1			1			2		1			6		
Hadley	288	30	Hopkins	Timothy	1	1	1	1	1	1			1				7		
Gill	86	10	Horsley	Benjamin				1					1				2		
Gill	86	15	Horsley	Benjamin 2d	1	1		1		1	1	1					6		
Gill	86	22	Horsley	Benjamin 3d	1		1			1		1					4		
Gill	86	17	Horsley	Isaiah	3		1	1					1				6		
Gill	86	11	Horsley	Jonathan	3		2			2			1				8		
Gill	86	21	Horsley	Rufus	1		1			1		1					4		
Barnardston	78	1	Horsley	Thomas	2		1						1				4		
Springfield	241	15	Horton	Gad		2	1		1	1	2	1		1			9		
Springfield	241	18	Horton	Peggy									2				2		
Springfield	241	16	Horton	Ruel	1		1				1		1				4		
Springfield	241	17	Horton	Stephen				1					1				2		
West Springfield	353	35	Horton	Timothy	1	1	1	1			1	1	1				7		
Ashfield	341	8	Hosford	Dudley	1		1			2			1				5		
Hawley	334	5	Hosford	Stephen	2	1		1		3			1				8		
Buckland	327	20	Hosley	David		2											2		
Southwick	359	49	Hosmer	William	2		1		1	1		1	1				7		
Chester	149	22	Hotchkis	Jotham	2		1			3			2	1			9		
Southwick	358	52	Hough	Thomas		4		1			1			1			7		
Northfield	29	2	Houghton	Edward		2	3	1		1	2	4	2				15		
Montague	46	20	Houghton	Jonathan	2	1		1		2			1	1			8		
Colrain	186	7	Houghton	Nathl	2	2	1			3			1				9		
Colrain	186	14	Houghton	Reuben		1	1	1		1		1	1	1			7		
New Salem	100	1	Houlton	Joseph	1	1	1	1		2	1	1	1				9		
Chesterfield	24	4	House	John		1	1		1		1	2		1			7		
Chesterfield	24	5	House	John Jun		1						1					2		
Pelham	215	6	Houstin	Robt	3	2	1		1	1		1	1	1			11		
Pelham	214	32	Houston	David	4		1			1	1	1	1	1			10		
Monson	268	18	Hovey	Elijah	3		1			3		1	1				9		
Wendell	106	5	How	Abel	1	1		1		1	1	2		1			8		
Warwick	38	3	How	Abraham			1										1		
Leyden	82	33	How	Antipas	1	1	2			1			1	2			8		
Wendell	106	7	How	Asa		1		1		2			1				5		
Wendell	106	4	How	Cyprian		1		1					2				4		
Wendell	106	6	How	Ephraim	2	2		1		1			1				7		
West Springfield	351	3	How	John	2		1			2			1				6		
Ashfield	341	21	Howard	Abijah	1		1						1				3		
West Springfield	356	41	Howard	Andrew		1	1	1				2					5		
Brimfield	274	6	Howard	Asa	2		1			2			1				6		
Springfield	241	11	Howard	Asa			1			1			1				3		
Springfield	239	34	Howard	Bezaleel Revd	3			1		1	1	1	1				8		
Conway	59	4	Howard	Caleb	1		1			2			1				5		
Warwick	38	5	Howard	Calvin		1				1			1				3		
Wilbraham	234	16	Howard	Harvey	2	1	1	1		1			1				7		
Granville Mid Soc.	166	7	Howard	Henry	3	1	2		1		1	1	1				10		
Leverett	115	16	Howard	Hezekh	1		1	1		1		1		2			8		
Greenwich	220	10	Howard	James	2		1						1				4		
Plainfield	307	15	Howard	James	2	2		1		1			1				7		
Belchertown	205	30	Howard	Jona		1		1					1				3		
Amherst	294	1	Howard	Jonathan				1	1				4	1			7		
Hawley	334	7	Howard	Joseph		1						1					2		
West Springfield	356	40	Howard	Joseph	1	1		1		1	1		1				6		
South Brimfield	275	6	Howard	Josiah	2		1			3			1	1			8		
Chesterfield	21	5	Howard	Mark	1		1			2	2		1				7		
West Springfield	356	46	Howard	Pember	2		1			1			1				5		
Brimfield	274	18	Howard	Samuel	1		1						1				3		
Belchertown	209	12	Howard	Silas	1		1	1		3	2			1	1		10		
Pelham	214	23	Howard	Silas	1		1		1	2	1	1	1				8		
Cummington	305	20	Howard	Simeon	1			1				2	1				5		
Cummington	303	26	Howard	Stephen	3	1	1	1	1	2	2	1	1	1			14		
West Springfield	356	43	Howard	Thomas				1					1				2		
Wilbraham	234	15	Howard	Thomas	1	1		1		1			1				5		
West Springfield	356	42	Howard	Thomas Jr	1		1						1				3		
Norwich	154	11	Howard	Wid										1			1		

TOWN	PG#	LN#	LAST NAME	FIRST NAME	M under 10	M 10 to 16	M 16 to 26	M 26 to 45	M 45 and over	F under 10	F 10 to 16	F 16 to 26	F 26 to 45	F 45 and over	TOTAL ALL OTHER	TOTAL SLAVES	TOTALS	DISTRICT/TOWNSHIP	NOTES
Granville East Soc	529	19	Howe	Ephraim		1		1		1				1			4		
Belchertown	205	32	Howe	Ester Doct	2	1		1		1	2			1			8		
Belchertown	211	16	Howe	Hannah Wd									1				1		
West Springfield	356	44	Howe	Ichabod		1		1		2	1			1			6		
Goshen	311	2	Howe	Reuben				1			1			1			3		
Greenwich	220	17	Howe	Solomon	3	2	1	1				3	1				11		
Belchertown	205	31	Howe	Sylvanus Lt		1	1	1	1	1	1		1	1			8		
Ashfield	341	6	Howes	Anthony		1	1		1	1		2	1				7		
Ashfield	341	19	Howes	Barnabas	1		1					1					3		
Ashfield	341	14	Howes	Ezekiel	4			1		1			1				7		
Ashfield	341	22	Howes	Heaman	5			1		1			1				8		
Ashfield	341	16	Howes	Joseph	3			1		1		1	1				7		
Ashfield	341	7	Howes	Joshua			1	1						1			3		
Ashfield	341	18	Howes	Kimbal		1	1	1				1	3	1			8		
Ashfield	341	15	Howes	Mark	1	1	1	1		2			1				7		
Ashfield	341	5	Howes	Saml				1					1				2		
Ashfield	341	13	Howes	Zachariah	2	1	2	1		2	2		1				11		
Gill	86	23	Howland	George		2	1	1						1			5		
Conway	58	42	Howland	Job	2	1		1			1		1				6		
Conway	58	41	Howland	John	4		1	1		1	1			1			9		
Gill	86	12	Howland	John				1			1			1			3		
Gill	86	13	Howland	Salmon	1		1			2	1		1				6		
Gill	86	19	Howland	Seth		1	1	1				1		1			5		
Blanford	181	2	Hstings	John	1			1					1				3		
Worthington	301	15	Hubbard	Daniel			3										3		
Granville West Soc	170	34	Hubbard	Ebenezer			1						2				3		
Ludlow	258	1	Hubbard	Eliha		1	1	1					1	1			5		
Amherst	293	11	Hubbard	Elihu	1	3			1	2	1	1	1				10		
Pelham	214	31	Hubbard	Elijah	2			1		1		1	1				6		
Hadley	287	19	Hubbard	Elisha	1	1		2		2		2		1			9		
Sunderland	282	1	Hubbard	Elisha	1		1			1			1				4		
Williamsburg	446	21	Hubbard	Elisha	1	2		1		3		1	1				9		
Greenfield	73	24	Hubbard	Ephraim	1		1	1		1	2	1		1			8		
Ludlow	258	2	Hubbard	Felix	2		1						1				4		
Leverett	115	13	Hubbard	Gideon	1	2	1	1		2	1			1			9		
Sunderland	283	25	Hubbard	Giles		2		1		2	1			1			7		
Amherst	291	22	Hubbard	Hannah		1		1		3				1			6		
Hadley	287	26	Hubbard	Hezekiah	3		1					1	2	1			8		
Hatfield	12	23	Hubbard	John	3			1	1	1	1		2	1	1		11		
Brimfield	269	11	Hubbard	John B				1						1			2		
Brimfield	269	25	Hubbard	Jonathan	1		1	1				2		1			7		
Sunderland	282	12	Hubbard	Phinehas	2	1	2	1				1					7		
Monson	266	17	Hubbard	Russel	1	2		1		2		1					8		
Ashfield	341	20	Hubbard	Samuel	2		1						1				4		
Brimfield	269	20	Hubbard	Simeon	1		1	1	1	1	2	1	1				9		
Brimfield	269	31	Hubbard	Thomas	1		1	1		3	1		1				8		
Granville West Soc	170	24	Hubbard	Titus	1	1		1		1			1				5		
Leverett	115	12	Hubbard	William	1	1			1	4		2		1			10		
Ware	226	22	Hudson	Eli		1		1		1	2			1			6		
Longmeadow	92	26	Hulbert	Asa	2		1			2			1				6		
Northampton	9	19	Hulbert	Seth	1		1			3			1				6		
Colrain	186	12	Hulburt	James	2			1	1	2		1	1	1			9		
Northampton	9	16	Hulburt	James			2	1				1	1	1			5		
Colrain	186	13	Hulburt	John Jun	2		1			1			1				5		
Granville West Soc	168	17	Hull	Gideon	1			1		1				2			5		
Granville West Soc	170	15	Hull	John	1			1		3			1				6		
Granville West Soc	170	17	Hull	Robert	3	1		1		1			1				7		
West Springfield	356	39	Humaston	Caleb	1	1	4	1		1		2	2	1			13		
West Springfield	356	37	Humaston	James			1							1			2		
West Springfield	356	38	Humaston	James 2d	3	2	2	1		1		1	2	1			13		
Longmeadow	95	17	Hunn	Ephraim	1	1				3			1				7		
Wilbraham	232	8	Hunn	Gideon	2			1					1				4		
Williamsburg	446	12	Hunt	Abijah	1	2		1		1	1	1	1	1			9		
Williamsburg	446	23	Hunt	Abijah Junr	2	1				1		1					5		
Belchertown	210	23	Hunt	Abner	2		1			2			1				6		
Northampton	9	8	Hunt	Abner	1	1	1	1		2	1	1	1	1			10		
Wendell	106	10	Hunt	Alden		1				1		1					3		
Williamsburg	446	24	Hunt	Anthony	3		1			2	1		1				8		
Leyden	83	2	Hunt	Charles	3	1	1				1	1	1				8		
Northampton	8	17	Hunt	Daniel	1	1	1	1				1	1	1			7		
New Salem	99	28	Hunt	David	1	1		1	1	1		1	2	1			9		
Northampton	4	12	Hunt	David	1			1		1		2					7		
Northampton	6	20	Hunt	David	1		1			1			1				4		
Northampton	4	14	Hunt	Ebenezer			4	1				2		1	1		9		
Northampton	8	29	Hunt	Elijah		1	1	1				1	1	1			6		
Northfield	29	5	Hunt	Elisha		1	1	2	1	1		2	1	1			10		
Williamsburg	446	14	Hunt	Elisha	3			1	1	1			1	1			8		
Northfield	28	38	Hunt	Elsworth	1	1	1						1				4		
Montague	46	21	Hunt	Ephraim				1					1				2		
Shutesbury	110	8	Hunt	Gardner	2			1		2			1				6		
Charlemont	192	18	Hunt	Jacob	2									1			7		

			HEADS OF HOUSEHOLD		FREE WHITE MALES					FREE WHITE FEMALES									
TOWN	PG#	LN#	LAST NAME	FIRST NAME	under 10	10 to 16	16 to 26	26 to 45	45 and over	under 10	10 to 16	16 to 26	26 to 45	45 and over	TOTAL ALL OTHER	TOTAL SLAVES	TOTALS	DISTRICT/ TOWNSHIP	NOTES
Westhampton	17	10	Hunt	Jared	1	1	1	1		2	2		1				9		
Belchertown	205	19	Hunt	John	1	1			1		1			1			5		
Goshen	310	18	Hunt	John			1					1	1	1			4		
Granville Mid Soc.	166	6	Hunt	John		1	2		1			1		1			6		
Hawley	333	24	Hunt	John															
Leyden	83	4	Hunt	John			1		1			1		1			4		
Blanford	175	36	Hunt	Joseph	2	1	1	1			1	2		1			9		
Northampton	7	22	Hunt	Luther	2			1		1		1					5		
Sunderland	282	8	Hunt	Melzar		2	1	1		2	1	1	1				9		
Heath	196	12	Hunt	Parley	2	2		1		2			1				8		
Heath	196	8	Hunt	Peter			1	1		1			1				4		
Montague	46	23	Hunt	Peter	1		1		1		1	1		1			6		
Heath	196	16	Hunt	Samuel				1				1	1				3		
Heath	196	9	Hunt	William	2		1	1		1	1		1				7		
Shutesbury	110	9	Hunt	William	2			1		1			1				5		
Springfield	242	9	Hunt	William	1	1		1		1			1				5		
Shutesbury	110	10	Hunt	William 2d	1			1		2			1				5		
Worthington	300	21	Hunt	David	1			1		1		1					4		
Granby	253	20	Hunter	Aaron	2			1				1	1				5		
Montague	46	22	Hunter	David	1	2		1		1	1			1			7		
Greenwich	220	21	Hunter	Isaac	3		1	1	1	1		1		1			9		
Pelham	215	2	Hunter	James	1		1	2	2			1		1			8		
Montgomery	160	20	Hunter	John		1	3		1			1		1			7		
Blanford	176	11	Hunter	Samuel	1			1		2	1		1				6		
Brimfield	270	41	Hunter	Samuel				2					2				4		
Granby	252	4	Hunter	Thomas			1	1					1				3		
Belchertown	205	26	Hunting	Amos	2		1			2	2		1				8		
Belchertown	205	27	Hunting	Elisha	2	1	1	1					1				6		
New Salem	100	16	Huntington	John			1			1		1					3		
Worthington	298	19	Huntington	Obed	1			1		3		1					6		
Worthington	298	10	Huntington	Simon		3	1			4		1					9		
Longmeadow	95	25	Huntington	Thomas Dr	1	1		1				3	1				7		
Ludlow	256	31	Huntley	Richard		1	1	1				1	1				5		
Warwick	38	4	Hurd	Thomas		2		1		3	2	1	1				10		
Southampton	131	9	Hurlburt	Douglas	2			1		1			1				5		
Northfield	29	7	Hurlbut	Gabriel	1	2		1		4	1		1				10		
Northfield	29	6	Hurlbut	Isaac				1				1	1				3		
Cummington	303	24	Hursey	John	2	1					2	2					9		
New Salem	100	20	Hussey	James											9		9		
Northampton	6	32	Hutchens	Hezekiah	3		1			3		1					8		
Northampton	6	31	Hutchens	Joseph		1		1		1		1		1			5		
West Springfield	351	5	Hutchins	Thomas				1				1		3			5		
Brimfield	271	16	Hutchinson	Eleazer				1					1				2		
Montgomery	161	42	Hutchinson	Elisha		1	1	1					1				4		
Montgomery	161	43	Hutchinson	Israel		1						1					2		
Ware	226	26	Hutchinson	Samuel	2	1		1		3	4	1	1				13		
Colrain	186	19	Hutson	Charles	2		1	1			1		1				6		
Conway	59	1	Huxford	Henry	1		2	1		1		2		1			8		
Monson	263	1	Hyde	David Capt			1	1				1		2			5		
Monson	263	45	Hyde	Ephraim	3	2	2		1	1	1	2	1				13		
Pelham	214	24	Hyde	James	3	1		1		2	1		1				9		
Ware	227	9	Hyde	John	1		1	1		2	1	1					7		
Ware	226	25	Hyde	Othiniel	1	1		1			1	1	1				6		
Williamsburg	446	15	Hyde	Rufus		4	1	1			1		2				9		
Pelham	214	34	Hyde	Samuel	2		1	1		2	1		2				9		
Monson	263	2	Hyde	William B.	1		1			4		1					7		
Chester	148	4	Ingall	Zadoc	2	1	1	1		1		1	1				8		
Northampton	4	21	Ingalls	James	3	2		1		2		1					9		
Belchertown	206	3	Ingals	Samuel		1	3	1		1	3		1				10		
Leyden	83	5	Ingell	Benoni	3		1			2		1					7		
Westfield	120	19	Ingersoll	Charles		1	1			2	1		1	1			7		
Westfield	119	35	Ingersoll	John		1		1			1	1	1		1		6		
Westfield	123	1	Ingersoll	Oliver	1	1	2			1	1	1	1				8		
Middlefield	157	16	Ingham	Erastus		2		1		1	1	1	1				7		
Blanford	182	22	Ingraham	David	2		1			1			1				5		
South Hadley	249	44	Ingraham	Ebenr		1				1	1						3		
Southwick	359		Ingraham	Gamaliel		1		1		3			1				6		
Chester	144	28	Ingraham	Jedediah	1		1			1			1				4		
South Hadley	249	43	Ingraham	Nathaniel	1	2	1		1		1	2		1			9		
Middlefield	158	10	Ingrahm	Solomon	1	1	1		1	2		1	1				8		
Amherst	290	19	Ingram	David	1			1				1	1	2			6		
Amherst	290		Ingram	Ebenezer	3		1	1		2	1	1	1				10		
Amherst	290	10	Ingram	John	1	1	1	1		2	1	1	1				9		
Belchertown	204	4	Ingram	Joseph	2		1			1		2					6		
Amherst	290	20	Ingram	Nathan	1		1						1				3		
Amherst	290	13	Ingram	Samuel			1			1	1	1					4		
Chesterfield	24	26	Ingram	Timothy	3			1				2	1				7		
Wilbraham	232	29	Isham	Daniel	1			2		1	1		1				6		
West Springfield	356	52	Ives	Abraham	1		1			1		1					4		
Southwick	359	8	Ives	David		2	2	1	1			2		1			9		

250

TOWN	PG#	LN#	LAST NAME	FIRST NAME	FREE WHITE MALES under 10	10 to 16	16 to 26	26 to 45	45 and over	FREE WHITE FEMALES under 10	10 to 16	16 to 26	26 to 45	45 and over	TOTAL ALL OTHER	TOTAL SLAVES	TOTALS	DISTRICT/ TOWNSHIP	NOTES
West Springfield	356	51	Ives	Jeremiah				1	1			3	1	1			7		
Monson	262	4	Ives	Jesse Revd		1	1		1			2	1				6		
West Springfield	351	6	Ives	Rebekah			2					1		1			4		
Blanford	176	3	Jackson	Ezra	1	1		1		3			1				7		
Leverett	115	19	Jackson	Jeremiah	1			1				2	1				5		
Chester	149	6	Jackson	John	1			1		1			2				5		
Colrain	190	20	Jackson	John											2		2		
Gill	86	25	Jackson	John	1		2	1			1		1				6		
Shutesbury	110	17	Jackson	Peter											5		5		
West Springfield	353	43	Jackson	Samuel											2		2		
Colrain	186	21	Jacobs	Elnathan	4	1	3		1	1	1		1				12		
Southwick	359	7	Jacobs	William	1			1		3			1				6		
Goshen	310	12	James	John			1	1		1			1				4		
Chester	143	13	James	John Capt	1	2		1		2	1		1	1			9		
Easthampton	135	7	James	Jonathan		1		1	1			1	2				6		
Easthampton	135	2	James	Jonathan Junr	2		1		2			1					6		
Goshen	310	13	James	Malachi	2	1	1	1		2	1	1	1				10		
Goshen	310	14	James	Moses	2	3		1		3	1		1				11		
Colrain	190	21	James	Peter											4		4		
Chesterfield	24	3	James	Thomas	1			1		3	1			1			7		
Brimfield	273	20	Janes	Cyrus	3	1	1			1	1	1					8		
Easthampton	135	11	Janes	Ebenezer	3			1		3			1				8		
Northfield	29	11	Janes	Ebenezer	1		3	1					1	1			7		
Holland	279	9	Janes	Eliphalet				2					2				4		
Easthampton	135	15	Janes	Enos	1		1	1		2	1		1				7		
Easthampton	135	16	Janes	Hannah Wid				1						1			2		
Northfield	29	10	Janes	Jonathan	1	1	2	1		1		1	1				8		
Easthampton	135	14	Janes	Noah	3	2		1		1	1	1	1				10		
Easthampton	135	26	Janes	Obediah				1					1				2		
Easthampton	136	9	Janes	Obediah	1		1						1				3		
Brimfield	273	15	Janes	Orsamus		4	1				1	1		1			8		
Brimfield	273	17	Janes	Pheny	1	1		1		1		1	1				6		
Gill	86	24	Janes	Samuel		1		1		4		1	1				8		
Easthampton	135	17	Janes	Seth				1		1			1				3		
Brimfield	273	24	Janes	William			1							1			2		
Brimfield	273	22	Janes	William Junr		1		1		4	1	1	1				9		
Northfield	29	12	Janes	Xenophon			1			3		1					5		
Heath	196	18	Jaquigh	Benjamin	4		1						1				6		
Ware	226	30	Jenkins	John		1		1		2	1		1				6		
Hawley	334	8	Jenkins	Stephen	1			1		2			1				5		
Monson	267	15	Jennings	Abel		1		1					1	1			4		
Buckland	328	12	Jennings	Ephraim		1	2		2	1				2			8		
Shelburne	322	3	Jennings	Ephraim	2			1				1	1				5		
Warwick	38	9	Jennings	Joel			1	1		2	2		1	2			9		
Ludlow	257	41	Jennings	John		3		1		2	1	2	1				10		
Orange	42	21	Jennings	Peleg	1			1		2				1			5		
Chesterfield	23	25	Jewell	Marvel	2	1		1		2			1				7		
Pelham	215	11	Jewett	Benja	2	1	2			3		1	1				10		
Deerfield	53	38	Jewett	Enoch			1		1	1		2		1			6		
Belchertown	211	22	Jewett	Jedidiah				1						1			2		
Deerfield	53	39	Jewett	Reuben	1			1		4			1				7		
Northampton	9	2	Jewett	Timothy	2	1		1		2			1				7		
Belchertown	203	11	Jinks	David	1			1			1	1					4		
Belchertown	209	14	Jinks	Lawrence		2	2	1		1			1				7		
Belchertown	203	12	Jinks	Thomas			1		1	1		1					3		
Plainfield	307	21	Job	Asa	2	1		1		3	3	1					11		
Greenwich	220	33	Johnson	Aaron	2	2	1			1		1		1			8		
Southwick	359	5	Johnson	Abner	1			1		3			1				6		
Pelham	215	8	Johnson	Adam				1									1		
Southwick	359	6	Johnson	Amos	1	1		1		1	1	1		1			7		
Deerfield	53	42	Johnson	Asa		1		1		3			1				6		
Chester	145	37	Johnson	Benjamin		1		1					1				3		
Charlemont	192	22	Johnson	Billy				1		2	1		1				5		
Williamsburg	445	1	Johnson	Caleb	1	3		1		1			1	1			8		
Greenfield	73	35	Johnson	Calvin				1					1				2		
Springfield	247	33	Johnson	Charles	3			1		1			1				6		
Buckland	328	9	Johnson	David	2			1		1	1		1				6		
Wendell	106	15	Johnson	Ebenezer	1	2	1	1		1	2	1		1			10		
Greenfield	73	33	Johnson	Elias	3	2	1			2	2		1				11		
Norwich	152	16	Johnson	Elisha	1	1	3	1		4	1		1				12		
Orange	42	22	Johnson	Elisha	3	3				2	2		1	1			12		
Chester	144	7	Johnson	Ely	3			1					1				5		
Pelham	215	10	Johnson	Hugh	2	1		1				1	2	1			8		
Shutesbury	110	14	Johnson	Hugh M.	2			1		2			1				6		
Chester	148	13	Johnson	Isaac	1			1					1				3		
Colrain	186	24	Johnson	Isaac	3			1					1				5		
Granville Mid Soc.	167	33	Johnson	Jabez	3		1	1	1	2			1				9		
Chester	148	12	Johnson	Jesse Deacn		1		1		1	2		1				6		
Greenwich	220	34	Johnson	John		1				1	1	1					4		
Pelham	215	14	Johnson	John	1		1				1						3		

TOWN	PG#	LN#	LAST NAME	FIRST NAME	FREE WHITE MALES					FREE WHITE FEMALES					TOTAL ALL OTHER	TOTAL SLAVES	TOTALS	DISTRICT/ TOWNSHIP	NOTES
					under 10	10 to 16	16 to 26	26 to 45	45 and over	under 10	10 to 16	16 to 26	26 to 45	45 and over					
Shutesbury	110	13	Johnson	John	1	2	3		1		1	1		1			10		
Blanford	179	35	Johnson	Jonas	1			1		2			1				5		
Orange	42	24	Johnson	Jonathan	1		1			1		1					4		
Barnardston	78	14	Johnson	Joseph	2			1		1			1				5		
Wendell	106	14	Johnson	Joseph		1	2		1			1		1			6		
Buckland	328	10	Johnson	Josiah		1	3		1	5	1	1		1			13		
Warwick	38	10	Johnson	Mason	2			1					1				4		
Colrain	186	25	Johnson	Moses	2	1	2		2	1	2	1	1				12		
Wendell	106	16	Johnson	Nathl	1	2			1	2	1		1	1			9		
Greenfield	73	32	Johnson	Richard				1					1				2		
Pelham	215	13	Johnson	Samuel			1				1	1					3		
Southwick	359	3	Johnson	Samuel				1					1				2		
Southwick	359	4	Johnson	Samuel Jr				1			1		1				3		
New Salem	100	22	Johnson	Solomon	2	1		1		2			1				7		
Orange	42	25	Johnson	Solomon		1	1					1		1			5		
Greenwich	220	32	Johnson	Stephen	1	3	1		1	1		1		1			9		
Hadley	288	19	Johnson	Stephen	2		1		1	2	1	1	1				9		
South Brimfield	276	31	Johnson	Stephen	1			1					1				3		
Colrain	186	26	Johnson	Thomas	2			1		1	1		1				6		
Blanford	182	5	Johnson	William	1	1			1	3	1	1	1				9		
Wilbraham	234	33	Johnson	William	3			1			1	1					6		
Pelham	215	12	Johnson	Wm	2	1	1	1	1		1	1	1				9		
Buckland	328	11	Jones	Abraham	2	1					1	1	1				7		
Buckland	328	7	Jones	Alfred	1		1	1			1	1	1				6		
Middlefield	156	37	Jones	Arba		1				1		1					3		
Wilbraham	234	28	Jones	Asa	1	3	1		1					2			8		
Middlefield	157	34	Jones	Benajah Lieut	2			1	2	3		1					9		
Williamsburg	445	2	Jones	Benjamin	2	2	2		1	2	1	2		1			13		
Granville East Soc	531	42	Jones	Bethiel	4		1					1					6		
Buckland	328	15	Jones	Bidear	3		1					1					5		
Granville East Soc	531	8	Jones	Daniel	2		1			2		1					6		
Granville East Soc	529	37	Jones	David		2	1		1	2	1	1		1			9		
Palmer	259	33	Jones	Ebenezer		1	1		1	2			1				7		
West Springfield	356	47	Jones	Ebenezer 2d	1	1			2		1			1			6		
West Springfield	356	48	Jones	Ebenezer 3d			1			1			1				3		
Buckland	328	14	Jones	Erastus	2		1										3		
Middlefield	156	39	Jones	Ezra	2			1			1		1				5		
West Springfield	356	49	Jones	Gideon 2d		1			1	1	1		1				5		
West Springfield	356	50	Jones	Hezekiah	1		1						1				3		
Wilbraham	238	14	Jones	Isaac	2	1		1		3	1		1				9		
Colrain	186	22	Jones	Israel	1			1				1	1				4		
West Springfield	356	53	Jones	Ithamar	5	1		1		1			1				9		
Pelham	215	9	Jones	Jacob			1						1				2		
Williamsburg	445	3	Jones	James		1							1				2		
Blanford	175	16	Jones	Jason											4		4		
Deerfield	53	40	Jones	Jehiel	2	2	2		1	1		1		1			10		
Deerfield	53	41	Jones	Jehiel Jun	3	1		1		1	1		1				8		
Blanford	175	14	Jones	Jethro												5	5		
Blanford	175	15	Jones	Jethro Junr												5	5		
Middlefield	156	40	Jones	John	1		1			1			1				4		
Wendell	106	11	Jones	John		1	1			1	1	1					5		
Orange	42	23	Jones	Jonathan				1					1				2		
Orange	42	20	Jones	Jonathan Junr	2	1		1		1			1				6		
Shutesbury	110	12	Jones	Josiah	1	1		1			2	1		1			7		
Shutesbury	110	11	Jones	Levi			1					1					2		
Springfield	248	9	Jones	Pelatiah			1										1		
Greenfield	73	34	Jones	Phineus		1	1		1	1	1	1					6		
Buckland	328	13	Jones	Rufus	2		1					1					4		
Wilbraham	234	11	Jones	Rufus	1			1				1					3		
Plainfield	307	26	Jones	Ruth			1				1		1				3		
Leverett	115	20	Jones	Samuel		1	1		1	2	1		2				8		
Wendell	106	12	Jones	Silas				1			1	2		1			5		
Wendell	106	13	Jones	Silas Junr			1			1		1					4		
Ludlow	257	14	Jones	Stephen	1	1	2	1			2	1	1				9		
Wilbraham	234	10	Jones	Thomas				1		2	2	1	1				7		
Buckland	328	8	Jones	Willm	1	1	2		1	2	1		1				9		
Ashfield	342	1	Jordan	Edmund	1			1		1	1		1				5		
Deerfield	53	43	Jordet	Selah	1			1		2			1				5		
Plainfield	307	29	Josleyn	William	1			1		2			1				5		
Ware	226	31	Joslin	Abraham		1	2		1	2	2	1		1			10		
Chesterfield	21	9	Joslyn	Abraham	1		2		1		2	2		1			9		
Plainfield	307	20	Joy	Caleb		1	2					1		1			6		
Plainfield	307	19	Joy	Isaac			1						1	1			4		
Plainfield	307	22	Joy	Isaac Jun		2		1		1							4		
Plainfield	307	24	Joy	Jacob		1		1					1				3		
Plainfield	307	25	Joy	Jacob Jun	2	1		1		2	1		1				8		
Norwich	154	5	Joy	Jess Capt		2					2		1	1			6		
Plainfield	307	23	Joy	Joseph	2			1		2	1		1				7		
Cummington	303	27	Joy	Nehemiah	1	1	1	1					1				5		
Shelburne	322	1	Joyner	Edward				1			2			1			4		
Colrain	186	23	Joyner	John	1	3		1		2			1				8		

252

TOWN	PG#	LN#	LAST NAME	FIRST NAME	FWM under 10	FWM 10 to 16	FWM 16 to 26	FWM 26 to 45	FWM 45 and over	FWF under 10	FWF 10 to 16	FWF 16 to 26	FWF 26 to 45	FWF 45 and over	TOTAL ALL OTHER	TOTAL SLAVES	TOTALS	DISTRICT/ TOWNSHIP	NOTES
Shelburne	322	2	Joyner	Willm	2			1		1			1				5		
Shutesbury	110	15	Juckets	Daniel					1	1			1				3		
Shutesbury	110	16	Juckets	Daniel Jr	2	1		1		1			1				6		
South Hadley	248	21	Judd	Allen	2			1	1				1				5		
Buckland	328	6	Judd	Asahel	2			1					1	1			5		
Northampton	2	14	Judd	David			1	1		1			1				4		
South Hadley	250	25	Judd	Elijah	1			1		2			1				5		
Southampton	129	30	Judd	Frederick	1	2		1		2			1				7		
Southampton	129	29	Judd	Jona Revd			1		2			1	1	1			6		
South Hadley	248	20	Judd	Levi	2	1		1		2	1		1				8		
South Hadley	250	31	Judd	Reuben Lt		1			1	2			1	1			6		
Northampton	11	11	Judd	Samuel	1	1			1	2	1		1				7		
Chester	145	2	Judd	Selethiel	4			1		1	1		1				8		
Westhampton	15	17	Judd	Solomon	1	1	3	1		2	1	1					10		
Westhampton	15	8	Judd	Sylvetser	1	2	2		1	2	1	1		1			11		
South Hadley	249	2	Judd	Thomas Jr		1			1	3	1	1	1				8		
Northampton	8	26	Judd	William			2	1	1			3	2	1			10		
Plainfield	307	27	Karr	Benjm		2	1		2	2	2			1			10		
Chesterfield	22	2	Keen	William	2		1		1	2	2		1				9		
Leverett	115	23	Keep	Chileas		1	1						3				5		
Monson	262	16	Keep	Love Wd		1	2				1	2		3			9		
Longmeadow	93	27	Keep	Mathew					1					1			2		
Longmeadow	94	22	Keep	Moses					2				1	2			5		
Longmeadow	94	31	Keep	Samuel	1	1	1	1	1	2	1	1		2			11		
Longmeadow	94	32	Keep	Samuel Junr				1					1				2		
Monson	262	5	Keep	Simeon		2	1	1	1			2	1	1			9		
Longmeadow	94	23	Keep	Stephen	2			1		1			1				5		
Granville Mid Soc.	165	20	Keep	Sylvanus	1			1		1			1				4		
Deerfield	54	1	Keet	Joel	1	3		1		1	2	2	1				11		
Leverett	115	21	Keet	Jonathan		1		1		3	2		2				9		
Leverett	115	25	Keet	Reuben	1			1		1		1					4		
Belchertown	206	11	Keith	Joseph			1	1					1				3		
Cummington	304	41	Keith	Luke	1	2	1		1	1			1				7		
Goshen	312	27	Keith	Matthew			1					1					2		
Palmer	261	23	Keith	Peter	1			1		2	3	1					8		
Belchertown	206	7	Keith	Simeon		2	2	1	1	2				1			9		
Chesterfield	22	38	Keith	William			1						1				2		
Belchertown	206	6	Keith	Zadock	2	1	3				1	3	1				11		
Ashfield	342	6	Kelley	Abner	1		3		1	1	1		1				8		
South Hadley	249	34	Kellogg	Amos	1	1		1		2			1				6		
Southwick	359	14	Kellogg	Anna	3	2				1	1		1				8		
Hadley	286	6	Kellogg	Benjamin	1			1		2	1		1				6		
Westfield	124	28	Kellogg	Cotton	2			1		2			1				6		
Amherst	291	20	Kellogg	Daniel	3	1			2			2		2			10		
Ashfield	342	4	Kellogg	Daniel	1						1		1				3		
Hadley	288	13	Kellogg	Daniel	1			1	1	2	1	1					7		
Charlemont	192	27	Kellogg	Ebenezer					1		1						2		
South Hadley	249	35	Kellogg	Ebenezer					1					1			2		
Northampton	4	10	Kellogg	Eli	2	1	1	1			1		1				7		
South Hadley	249	37	Kellogg	Eliakim	3			1		2	1		1				8		
Amherst	290	35	Kellogg	Elijah	1	1							1				3		
Amherst	290	37	Kellogg	Ephraim	3		2	1	1	3		1	1	1			13		
New Salem	100	23	Kellogg	Ezekiel Jr	3		3	2	1			2	3	1			15		
Westfield	121	29	Kellogg	Gad					1					1			2		
Hadley	286	4	Kellogg	Gardner & Josiah	3			2	1	5			3	2			16		
Amherst	291	1	Kellogg	John	1	1		1		3	1		1				8		
Amherst	293	17	Kellogg	Jonathan	1	2		1	1			1	2				8		
Amherst	290	38	Kellogg	Joseph	1	2		1		1	2		1	1			9		
South Hadley	249	36	Kellogg	Joseph		1			1	1			1	1			5		
Springfield	240	10	Kellogg	Joseph	1				1	1				1	1		5		
Westfield	127	1	Kellogg	Josiah	2	1		1		2	1		1				8		
Shelburne	322	6	Kellogg	Julia	3		1		1	2	2		1	1			11		
Amherst	294	26	Kellogg	Martin			1		1	2	2		1				7		
Amherst	294	21	Kellogg	Martin Jun	1		1						1				3		
Hadley	286	7	Kellogg	Moses			1	1	1			1	1	1			6		
Hadley	286	5	Kellogg	Moses Jun		2		1		1							4		
Granville West Soc	170	29	Kellogg	Phinehas	1			1		2	1		1				6		
Ashfield	342	9	Kellogg	Saml			1				1	1					4		
Westfield	121	4	Kellogg	Samll Esq	1	1		1				1	1				5		
New Salem	100	24	Kellogg	Samuel		1	1		1	1		1		1			6		
Shutesbury	110	23	Kellogg	Samuel	3			1		2			1				7		
Southwick	359	13	Kellogg	Samuel		1		1						1			3		
Goshen	310	20	Kellogg	Stephen	1	1	1	1		2	2		1				9		
Worthington	301	35	Kelly	John		1			1			4		2			8		
Granville East Soc	527	9	Kelly	Martin	1		1	1		1	1		1				6		
Hawley	334	11	Kelsey	Eliab	1			1					1				3		
Conway	59	19	Kelsey	Hiel				1									1		
Chester	149	10	Kelso	James			1					1					2		
Chester	149	9	Kelso	John Capt			1		1			1	1	1			5		
Chester	148	18	Kelso	Lucretia		1							1				2		

TOWN	PG#	LN#	LAST NAME	FIRST NAME	FREE WHITE MALES					FREE WHITE FEMALES					TOTAL ALL OTHER	TOTAL SLAVES	TOTALS	DISTRICT/ TOWNSHIP	NOTES
					under 10	10 to 16	16 to 26	26 to 45	45 and over	under 10	10 to 16	16 to 26	26 to 45	45 and over					
Warwick	38	13	Kelton	Aaron	2			1		1	1		1				6		
Leyden	83	9	Kelton	Benjamin		1	1		1	3	1		1				8		
Williamsburg	445	8	Kelton	Elijah	1	2		1		2			1				7		
Warwick	38	14	Kelton	Enoch				1					1				2		
Warwick	38	17	Kelton	George	1		1						1				3		
Warwick	38	15	Kelton	James		1		1		1			1				4		
Warwick	38	11	Kelton	Nathan		1		1				3	1				6		
Warwick	38	16	Kelton	Rufus	3		1			1		1					6		
Warwick	38	12	Kelton	Thomas		1		1		1		3	1				7		
Shelburne	322	8	Kemp	Daniel		2	1					2	1				6		
Shelburne	322	4	Kemp	Lawrence	1		1	1	1	1	1		1				7		
Shelburne	322	5	Kemp	Willm															
Ludlow	257	37	Kendall	Chapman		1							1				2		
Chester	144	16	Kendall	David	2			1		1	1		1				5		
West Springfield	356	54	Kendall	David	1		1					1					3		
Ludlow	257	36	Kendall	James	1	1		1		1			1	1			6		
Ludlow	257	43	Kendall	James Jr	2		1						1	1			5		
Deerfield	54	2	Kendall	Luke	3		1		1	3		1					9		
Ludlow	257	42	Kendall	Ruel	3		1		1				1				6		
New Salem	100	25	Kendall	Samuel	2	1	2	2	1	1	1	1					11		
Northfield	29	13	Kendrick	Oliver	2		1		1	1	1	2	1				10		
Rowe	200	8	Kenfield	Herman		1		1		1		1					4		
Norwich	154	25	Kenny	Cesar											6		6		
Worthington	300	29	Kent	Amos	1			1		4	1	2	1				10		
Southwick	359	9	Kent	David		1	1			1			1				4		
West Springfield	353	42	Kent	Ezekiel	3		2			2		1	1				9		
Southwick	359	10	Kent	Ezra				1					1				2		
Southwick	359	11	Kent	Ezra Junr	1	1		1		4			1				8		
West Springfield	351	8	Kent	James		1	2	1		1		2					7		
Southwick	359	12	Kent	Josiah	1	1		1		1	1	2	1				8		
West Springfield	351	7	Kent	Ruggles	1	1	1	1		1			2				7		
Granby	253	10	Kent	Samuel			1	1	1	1	1		1				6		
Leyden	83	6	Kent	Zenus	1		1	1		2		2	1				8		
Belchertown	211	18	Kentfield	David	3	1		1		5	1	1	1				13		
Belchertown	206	10	Kentfield	David 2d	1		1			1		1					4		
Belchertown	206	5	Kentfield	Ebenz	3	1		1		3	2		1				11		
Belchertown	209	15	Kentfield	Erstus	2			1		2		1					6		
Belchertown	206	9	Kentfield	Jonathan					1	1	1	2		1			6		
Belchertown	209	16	Kentfield	Josiah	2	1	1			1	1		1	1			9		
Easthampton	134	26	Kentfield	Noah				1			1			1			3		
Belchertown	206	4	Kentfield	Shubal	1			1		2			1				5		
Leyden	83	8	Kentley	John	1	1	2		1	2	1	1		1			10		
Leyden	83	7	Kenyon	Paul	3			1		1			1				6		
Conway	59	20	Keyes	Calvin	2	1		1		3	2		1				10		
Springfield	243	20	Keyes	Jonas	2	1		1		2			1				7		
Shelburne	322	7	Keyes	Joseph	3			1		3	1		1				9		
Worthington	300	9	Keyes	Jotham	2		1						1				4		
Ludlow	255	9	Keyes	Lemuel	2			1		4			2	1			10		
Ashfield	342	8	Keyes	Stephen		1		1						1			3		
Ludlow	255	14	Keyes	Timo Deacn				1						1			2		
Wilbraham	232	10	Kibbe	Asa	1	2		1					1				5		
Longmeadow	95	16	Kibbe	Gideon			2		1			1		1			5		
Longmeadow	92	24	Kibbe	Samuel			2	1				1	1				6		
Middlefield	156	2	Kibbey	Bildad				1					1				2		
Shutesbury	110	22	Kibbey	Thomas	1			1					1				3		
Chesterfield	25	3	Kidd	Charles		1	2		1	1		3		1			9		
Wendell	106	19	Kidder	Jonathan	1			1					1				3		
Wilbraham	235	14	Kilbourn	Jona	2	1	1						2				6		
Wilbraham	235	13	Kilbourn	Luther	4			1		1	1		1				8		
Wilbraham	235	12	Kilbourn	Samuel			1	1		2			1	1			6		
Ashfield	342	5	Kilburn	Jacob	4	1	1			1	1		1	1			10		
Wendell	106	17	Kilburn	Joseph	1			1	2	3	2		1				10		
Wendell	106	18	Kilburn	Joshua	1		1	1		2	1		1				7		
Buckland	328	17	Kilburn	Saml		1		1		1	2			1			6		
Westfield	127	22	Killam	Thomas	2	1	1		1	1		1		1			8		
Montgomery	161	31	Killburn	Samuel		1	1										2		
Montgomery	161	41	Killburn	Thomas		1											1		
Amherst	291	11	Kimbal	Benjamin	3			1					1				5		
Holland	279	1	Kimball	Asa	1			1		3			1				6		
Shutesbury	110	19	Kimball	Boyce				1						1			2		
Shutesbury	110	20	Kimball	Boyce Jr	4	2	1	1				1	1	1			11		
Shutesbury	110		Kimball	Ebenezer	2			1				1					4		
Greenwich	220	29	Kimball	Hezekiah	4	1			1	1		1	1				9		
Ludlow	255	7	Kimball	Nathaniel	1	1						1					3		
New Salem	100	32	Kimball	Phinehas	1		1	1	1	1			1	1			7		
Holland	279	38	Kind	Darius	1	1		1						2			5		
Charlemont	192	21	Kindrick	John			1			3			1				5		
Heath	196	21	Kindrick	John	2	1	2		1	1	1	1		1			10		
Westfield	120	7	King	Aaron		1	1		1			2					5		
Hawley	334	10	King	Amos		1			1	4	1		1				8		

| | | | HEADS OF HOUSEHOLD | | FREE WHITE MALES | | | | | FREE WHITE FEMALES | | | | | TOTAL ALL OTHER | TOTAL SLAVES | TOTALS | DISTRICT/ TOWNSHIP | NOTES |
TOWN	PG#	LN#	LAST NAME	FIRST NAME	under 10	10 to 16	16 to 26	26 to 45	45 and over	under 10	10 to 16	16 to 26	26 to 45	45 and over					
Wilbraham	233	17	King	Asaph		1			1	3	1	2	1				9		
Southampton	130	2	King	Belah	1			1		1			1				4		
Palmer	262	13	King	Benjamin	3	2		1		3			1	1			11		
Westfield	120	30	King	Bohan	4	1	5	1	1				2	1	1		16		
Palmer	262	6	King	Daniel	5	2	2		1				1				11		
Wilbraham	236	29	King	David			1				1		1				3		
Palmer	262	7	King	David Lt.		1		1						1			3		
Southampton	130	1	King	Douglas		1		1						1			3		
Shutesbury	110	21	King	Ebenezer	1		1		1			1					4		
Chesterfield	23	7	King	Eleazer	1		1		1		1						4		
Blanford	181	10	King	Elisha	1		1					1					3		
Northampton	5	20	King	Elizabeth		1	1	1				1	1				5		
Ashfield	342	3	King	Enoch	2	2		1		2	2		1				10		
Blanford	182	18	King	Esop	1	1		1		1		1					5		
Montgomery	160	3	King	Gamaliel	1			1		3		1					6		
Palmer	262	12	King	Gideon	2	1	2	1		1	1	1	1				10		
Chesterfield	19	13	King	Isaac		1							1	1			3		
Blanford	180	15	King	James			1	1		1		1		1			5		
Palmer	258	16	King	James				1					1	1			3		
Pelham	215	17	King	James	4	2	1		1			4	1	1			14		
West Springfield	353	41	King	James Junr	2	1		1		1			1				6		
Palmer	261	30	King	Jesse	2		2	1		4	1	1	1				12		
Palmer	262	8	King	Jno Capt.		1		1						1			3		
Ashfield	342	2	King	John		1		1						1			3		
Goshen	310	19	King	John	1	2		1	1	1			1	1			8		
New Salem	100	28	King	John		2			1				1	1			5		
Northampton	5	26	King	John			3		1	1	2	1					8		
Palmer	259	8	King	John	1	1	1						1				4		
Palmer	261	9	King	John			2	1	1			2		1			7		
Northampton	5	34	King	John Jun	1		1						1	1			4		
New Salem	100	29	King	John Junr	3			1					1				6		
Worthington	301	46	King	Jona	1			1		2	1		1				6		
Hawley	334	12	King	Jonas	1		1				1		1				4		
New Salem	100	31	King	Jonathan	2			1		1			1				5		
Northampton	5	24	King	Joseph	1		1			1	1		1				5		
Norwich	151	39	King	Micah			1		1			2	1				5		
Wilbraham	236	27	King	Parmenas				1						1			2		
Wilbraham	236	28	King	Parmenas Jr			1	1		2			1				5		
Pelham	215	16	King	Peter	1	2		1		3			2				9		
Southampton	129	16	King	Phineas	1	1		1		2	1		1				7		
Pelham	217	20	King	Robt	2			1	1	2			1	1			8		
Monson	262	6	King	Samuel	1		1		1			2		1			6		
Monson	268	30	King	Samuel			1	1	1			2		1			6		
New Salem	100	27	King	Samuel				1		1		2		1			5		
New Salem	100	34	King	Samuel 2d	3	2	1	1		1	2	1					11		
Chesterfield	25	2	King	Silas			1		1	2		1		1			6		
Westfield	120	8	King	Silas Capt.	2	1	1	1		1	1		1				8		
New Salem	100	33	King	Stephen	1			1					1				3		
Hawley	334	9	King	Thomas			2		1	1		1		1			6		
Palmer	262	5	King	Thomas Deacn					1			1	2				4		
New Salem	100	30	King	William	1	1							1				4		
Palmer	261	8	King	William			2	1	1			2		1			7		
Colrain	186	27	King	Zadock	3	1		1		2	1		1				9		
Pelham	215	15	King	Robt	1			1		2			1				5		
Worthington	301	45	King	Eleazer	1	3			1	3			1				9		
West Springfield	353	40	King	James			1	1	1					1			4		
Northampton	4	20	King	Samuel	1			2	1	1			3	1			9		
Williamsburg	445	7	King	William			1		1		3			1			6		
Worthington	300	22	Kingman	Adam	1	1		1						1			4		
Pelham	215	4	Kingman	Henry Capt	2		1	1				1		1			6		
Goshen	310	21	Kingman	Isaac		1	2		2			1	1	2			9		
Worthington	297	10	Kingman	Isaiah			1	1					3				5		
Worthington	298	21	Kingman	Samuel		1	1			1	1		1				5		
West Springfield	353	38	Kingsbury	Leonard	1			1			1		1				4		
Springfield	243	26	Kingsbury	Luther				1				1					2		
Northampton	10	24	Kingsbury	Samuel	1	1		1	1	1				1			5		
Springfield	248	5	Kingsbury	Samuel		1	1					1	1				4		
Chesterfield	22	35	Kingsley	Asahel	1		1			1	1	1					5		
Greenwich	221	11	Kingsley	Calvin		1		1		2			1				5		
Chesterfield	22	36	Kingsley	Ebenezer	3			1		2			1				7		
Northampton	3	1	Kingsley	Enos	1		2	1		1	3		1				9		
Westhampton	16	1	Kingsley	Ezra			1			1		2					4		
Northampton	2	4	Kingsley	Harpies				1				1	1				3		
Westhampton	16	29	Kingsley	Joseph	1	2	2	1				2		1			9		
Westhampton	16	30	Kingsley	Joseph Jr	1		2	1		1			1				6		
Westhampton	18	25	Kingsley	Medad	2	2		1					2	1			8		
Chesterfield	23	4	Kingsley	Moses		1		1				1	3	1			7		
Chesterfield	23	14	Kingsley	Moses Jun	2			1		1			1				5		
Westhampton	15	15	Kingsley	Noah	1	1	1			1		1					5		
Westhampton	16	31	Kingsley	Samuel			1	1	1				2	1			6		

TOWN	PG#	LN#	LAST NAME	FIRST NAME	FREE WHITE MALES					FREE WHITE FEMALES					TOTAL ALL OTHER	TOTAL SLAVES	TOTALS	DISTRICT/ TOWNSHIP	NOTES
					under 10	10 to 16	16 to 26	26 to 45	45 over	under 10	10 to 16	16 to 26	26 to 45	45 and over					
Williamsburg	445	4	Kingsley	Seth		1		1		3	1		1				7		
Granville West Soc	169	16	Kingsley	Stephen	2			1	1	1			1	1			7		
Williamsburg	445	5	Kingsley	Supply				1		2			2	1			6		
Westhampton	18	12	Kingsley	Thaddeus	1	2		1		1			1				6		
Williamsburg	445	6	Kingsley	Timothy				1		2			1				4		
Worthington	301	21	Kinne	Daniel	2		2		1				3	1			9		
Worthington	299	26	Kinne	John	1	1		1	1	1	1		1	1			8		
Orange	42	26	Kinsley	Abiel	1	2			1	1			2	1			8		
Montague	46	27	Kinsley	Caleb		1	1		1	3	1		1				8		
Southampton	129	24	Kinsley	Danl			1		1			1		2			5		
Barnardston	78	15	Kinsley	Elijah				1						1			2		
Barnardston	78	16	Kinsley	Gamaliel	2			1		1			1				5		
Heath	196	20	Kinsman	Samuel			1			2			1				4		
Granville East Soc	531	7	Kirby	Joseph	1	1			1	2			1	1			7		
Norwich	154	10	Kirkland	Daniel			1										1		
Russell	138	15	Kirkland	Danl				1		2		1		1			5		
Blanford	175	4	Kirkland	Elias		1		1	1	2	1			1			6		
Norwich	153	36	Kirkland	John Esq			1	1					2	1			5		
South Hadley	251	11	Kirkland	Samuel		1		1					2	1			5		
Norwich	153	35	Kirkland	Samuel Capt			1			2			2				5		
Leverett	115	22	Kitley	John				1						1			2		
Leverett	115	24	Kitley	Willm		1		1		2	2		1				7		
Chesterfield	24	12	Kittridge	John	4		1	1		1			1				8		
Montgomery	161	17	Knap	Reuben	1	2	1		1			1		1			7		
Granville Mid Soc.	165	24	Knapp	Abijah	3			1		2			1				7		
Cummington	304	42	Knapp	Jona	1	1	2		1			2		1			8		
Orange	42	28	Knapp	Jonah	2			1		1			1				5		
Northampton	10	22	Knapp	Lemuel	3			1		1			1				6		
Hadley	286	16	Kneeland	Edward	2			1		3			1				7		
Northampton	11	3	Kniep	Christensen	3		1	1			3		1				9		
Monson	267	11	Knight	Asher	3	1	1	1		1	2		1				10		
Monson	267	9	Knight	Benjamin				1						1			2		
Norwich	151	32	Knight	Elizabeth Wid									1				1		
Chesterfield	19	14	Knight	Joshua		1	1		1			2	1	1			7		
Norwich	151	14	Knight	Phineas	3	1		1		1	1		1				8		
Norwich	151	11	Knight	Samuel	2			1					1				4		
Granville West Soc	168	22	Knight	Silas				1		2		1		1			5		
Norwich	151	33	Knight	Sylvester		1		1		1		2					5		
Palmer	259	15	Knight	Theophilus	2		1	1					1				5		
New Salem	100	26	Knights	William	2	1		1		2	2		1				9		
Rowe	200	7	Knolton	Timothy			1		1	1		3		1			7		
Rowe	200	6	Knolton	Timothy Jr	2	1		1		3			1				8		
Ashfield	342	7	Knotton	Joshua	2			1		2	1		1	1			8		
Worthington	300	23	Knowles	Rufus	2			1	1	2			1				7		
Orange	42	27	Knowles	Samuel	1	1		1		3			1				7		
Buckland	328	16	Knowles	Seth	5			1		1	1		1				9		
Montgomery	161	29	Knowles	Seth				1									1		
Monson	264	35	Knowlton	Amasa	1			1		2			1				5		
Monson	264	33	Knowlton	Ezra	2			1		2	1		1				7		
West Springfield	351	28	Knowlton	Jonathan	2			1		1			1				5		
Wilbraham	234	38	Knowlton	Nathl Capt	1			1		2	1						5		
Belchertown	206	8	Knowlton	Roswell	2	1			1	2			1				7		
Blanford	178	12	Knox	David	1			1		2	1		1				6		
Blanford	178	33	Knox	David	1		1	1		2	1		1				7		
Blanford	178	24	Knox	Eli			1						1				2		
Blanford	176	2	Knox	Elijah	2			1					1				4		
Blanford	180	12	Knox	Elijah	2	2	1	1		3	1		1				11		
Blanford	176	5	Knox	John	1	3		1		1	1	2		1			10		
Blanford	177	8	Knox	John 2nd	4	1		1		2	1		1				10		
Blanford	179	6	Knox	Levi	1			1		1	1		1				5		
Blanford	182	9	Knox	Nathan Esq	2	2		1		2	1		1				9		
Blanford	176	27	Knox	Oliver	2			1	1	1	3	2		1			11		
Blanford	178	23	Knox	Samuel			1		1		1	2		1			6		
Blanford	181	20	Knox	Seth		1	2		1	1	2	2	1	1			11		
Blanford	179	7	Knox	William	2			1		1	2			1			8		
Blanford	179	33	Knox	William		1		1	1	1			1	1			6		
Blanford	181	6	Knox	William		2	2		1	1			3	1			10		
Granville Mid Soc.	167	5	L*child	An*	1			1		3	3	2	1				11		
Monson	266	32	Labin	Noah	1	2		1					1	1			6		
Monson	265	37	Labin	Oliver		2		1		1			1	1			6		
Northampton	11	14	Labrin	Andrew				1		1	1	1		2			6		
Buckland	328	22	Lachey	James	2	1		1		1	1	1	1				8		
Chester	145	18	Ladd	John	3	1		1		2	2		1				10		
Southwick	359	20	Laflin	Heman	1		1						1				4		
Southwick	359	21	Laflin	Matthew				1			1		1	1	2		5		
Southwick	359	22	Laflin	Matthew Jr	2	2		1		2		1	1				9		
Colrain	187	1	Lake	Gideon	3		1			1	1			1			7		
Monson	265	16	Lamb	Charles	2							2	1				5		
South Hadley	248	3	Lamb	Daniel	2		1	1		2			2				8		
South Hadley	248	1	Lamb	Daniel Jr		1	2			1		1					5		
Greenfield	74	4	Lamb	Elijah	4		1	1		1			1				8		
Norwich	152	13	Lamb	Eliphalet		1			1		2		1				5		

TOWN	PG#	LN#	LAST NAME	FIRST NAME	FREE WHITE MALES under 10	10 to 16	16 to 26	26 to 45	45 and over	FREE WHITE FEMALES under 10	10 to 16	16 to 26	26 to 45	45 and over	TOTAL ALL OTHER	TOTAL SLAVES	TOTALS	DISTRICT/TOWNSHIP	NOTES
South Hadley	248	19	Lamb	Ezekiel	1	1	1	2		1			2				8		
Northfield	29	16	Lamb	Isaac			1			1	1	1					4		
Palmer	260	14	Lamb	Jabez Dr	2	1			1		1	2	1				8		
Ludlow	256	13	Lamb	Joseph								1					1		
South Hadley	249	13	Lamb	Pendleton	1		1					1					3		
South Hadley	249	15	Lamb	Rowell	2		1			2			1				6		
Ware	226	33	Lamberton	James Ens	3	1		1		1			1	1			8		
Ware	227	4	Lammon	David	1			1		2	1		1				6		
Ware	227	2	Lammon	James				1					1				2		
Ware	227	3	Lammon	James Jr	1	1	1		1	1	1	1	1	1			9		
Ware	227	5	Lammon	Wm Jr	2			1		1		1	1				6		
Hawley	334	19	Lamoin	Benjm	3	1		1		2			1				8		
Colrain	186	32	Lamond	John	4			1	1	1	2		1	1			11		
Leyden	83	11	Lampkin	Simeon	1			1				1					3		
Greenwich	221	1	Lampson	Daniel			1	1		1	1	1		1			6		
Cummington	304	45	Lampson	John	1			1		2	1		1				6		
Granville East Soc	531	31	Lamson	James	1			2		1		1					5		
West Springfield	354	20	Lancktan	Israel		1	1	1		2	1		1				7		
West Springfield	354	23	Lancktan	Seth	1	3		1		3	1		1				10		
Colrain	186	31	Lane	Amos	1			1		2	1		1				6		
Northampton	7	30	Lane	Ebenezer	1	1	2		1	1	2	3		1	1		13		
Greenwich	221	2	Lane	Nathanl		1		1		3	1		1				7		
Deerfield	54	5	Lanfair	Leonard	1	1	1	1		1			1				6		
Deerfield	54	6	Lanfair	Roswell	2		1						1				5		
Rowe	200	9	Langdon	Isaac			2	2	1		1			1			7		
Southwick	359	17	Langdon	Job	1	1		1		1			1				5		
Wilbraham	232	18	Langdon	John		1		1	1			1		1			5		
Wilbraham	232	17	Langdon	Paul Capt.			1	1	1					1			4		
Wilbraham	232	20	Langdon	Paul Junr	2	2		1			1			1			7		
Southwick	359	16	Langdon	Roswell	1		1	2		1			1				6		
Rowe	200	10	Langdon	Sloman	2			1		1			1	1			6		
Russell	138	31	Langton	Gad	1			1		1			1				4		
Monson	264	45	Lanphear	Aaron				1						1			2		
Monson	264	46	Lanphear	Aaron Jr	4			1					1				6		
Springfield	247	22	Lanphear	Arnold	2			1		1		1					5		
Monson	265	2	Lanphear	Jeheel				1					1				2		
Monson	265	1	Lanphear	Uriel	1			1		2			1				5		
Shelburne	322	20	Larabbe	Asa	2			1		2			1				6		
Westfield	122	28	Larabee	Tiler	1		1		1	3		1		1			8		
Wilbraham	235	24	Larnard	Samuel		1	2	1		1	1		1				7		
Warwick	38	22	Laroc	John Charles	3			1					1				5		
Ware	226	37	Lasell	Jacob	4	3		1					1				9		
Shelburne	322	9	Lasheur	Abner	1		1	1		1		1	1				6		
Granville West Soc	168	1	Latham	David	2	1		1		1			1				6		
Southwick	359	24	Latham	Edward	1	1	1					1					4		
Pelham	215	27	Latham	James				1		2	1						4		
Greenwich	220	37	Latham	Winslow	1			1	1	3	3		1	1			11		
Greenwich	221	3	Lathrop	Alden	1		1	1		2			1				6		
Pelham	215	21	Lathrop	Isaac	1	2		1				1	1				6		
West Springfield	351	17	Lathrop	Joseph			1		1		1		1				4		
Wilbraham	232	40	Lathrop	Joseph Captn	4		1	1			1		1				8		
West Springfield	351	9	Lathrop	Samuel			2			1		1			2		6		
Greenwich	221	5	Lathrop	Seth		1	1	1			1		1				5		
West Springfield	351	10	Lathrop	Seth	1	2	1	1			1	2	1				9		
Hawley	334	18	Lathrop	Zephl	3	1		1		1	2		1				9		
Blanford	181	19	Latimer	Aholiab	3			1		1			1				6		
Blanford	182	23	Latimer	Jacob				1		2			1				4		
Southwick	359	15	Lawnsbury	David	2	1	1			3			1				8		
Conway	59	26	Lawrence	Eleazer	2			1		2			1				6		
Warwick	38	24	Lawrence	Eleazer				1	1	1				1			3		
Chesterfield	20	30	Lawrence	Iasel	1			1		1			1				4		
Montague	46	28	Lawrence	Samuel	1				1	2	1			1			6		
Conway	59	35	Lawrence	William		1	1	1		1			1				5		
Springfield	247	40	Lawrence	William			1			1			1				3		
Wendell	106	25	Lawrence	William	1	1	2		1	1	2		1				9		
New Salem	100	37	Lawson	David			1		1		2			1			5		
New Salem	101	5	Lawson	David Junr	2			1				1					4		
Shelburne	322	11	Lawson	John	2		1	1		3	1	2		2			13		
New Salem	101	1	Lawson	Jonathan	1	2		1		2	1		1				8		
Gill	86	31	Lawson	William	1			1		3			1				6		
Buckland	328	21	Lazeel	Calvin	2	2		1		2			1				8		
Buckland	328	23	Lazeel	Robert	3			1		2	1	1	2	1			11		
Ware	228	35	Lazell	William				1						1			2		
Wilbraham	232	19	Leach	Benanuel	1	1	2		1	1				2			9		
Belchertown	209	19	Leach	Cyrel	1	1	1						1	1			5		
Pelham	215	22	Leach	Jonathan	2			1			1	1	1	2			10		
Wendell	106	20	Leach	Lemuel		2	4	1					1	1			9		
Wendell	106	21	Leach	Peter	1		1	1		1			1				5		
Middlefield	158	38	Lealand	Ebenezer		1		1		2			1				5		
Middlefield	158	40	Lealand	Lemuel	1			1		1			1				4		

TOWN	PG#	LN#	LAST NAME	FIRST NAME	FWM under 10	FWM 10 to 16	FWM 16 to 26	FWM 26 to 45	FWM 45 and over	FWF under 10	FWF 10 to 16	FWF 16 to 26	FWF 26 to 45	FWF 45 and over	TOTAL ALL OTHER	TOTAL SLAVES	TOTALS	DISTRICT/ TOWNSHIP	NOTES
Middlefield	158	39	Lealand	Luther			1										1		
Granville Mid Soc.	165	26	Learnard	John		1	1	1		1	1	1					3		
New Salem	100	38	Learned	Moses			1	1		1	1	1	1				6		
New Salem	101	3	Learned	Nehemiah			1	1		1	1			1			5		
New Salem	101	2	Learned	William				1						1			2		
Leverett	115	26	Leasure	Saml	1	1		1		2	2		1				8		
Granville West Soc	168	27	Leavensworth	Lydia		1				2				1			4		
Heath	196	22	Leavit	Jonathan			3	1		1	1	1	1				8		
Heath	196	23	Leavit	Roger	1		1	1		1		1					5		
Greenfield	74	1	Leavitt	Hart		1	1	1		1		1					5		
Greenfield	73	37	Leavitt	Jonathan			1			3		1	1				6		
Conway	59	33	Lee	Benjamin		1				1		1					3		
Southwick	359	27	Lee	Campbell	3		1			2			1				7		
Chesterfield	22	5	Lee	Charles	4		1						1				6		
Conway	59	21	Lee	Eben	1	1	1		1	1	1		1				7		
Westfield	125	12	Lee	Elisha	2	1		1		2			1				9		
Chester	147	15	Lee	Enoch	2		2	1		1	2		1				9		
Leverett	115	27	Lee	Gideon		1	1		1		1	2		1			7		
Amherst	294	7	Lee	Henry	1			1			1	3		1			7		
Westfield	125	13	Lee	Ichabod			1	1			1			1			4		
Amherst	294	14	Lee	John	1	2	1		1	1	2	1		1			10		
Conway	59	32	Lee	Joseph	2			1		4	1		1				9		
Conway	59	34	Lee	Joseph	1		2	1				1					6		
Northampton	10	6	Lee	Nathl	1					4			1				7		
Northampton	9	5	Lee	Samuel	1			1		2	1		1				6		
Conway	59	27	Lee	Sherebiah			2	1				2		1			6		
Westfield	128	1	Lee	Solomon	1	1		1		1	1	1					7		
Westfield	122	5	Lee	Stephen	3			1					1				5		
Northampton	9	24	Lee	Walter	3		1			1			1				6		
Westfield	122	14	Lee	Zadok	1		1	1	1	2	1	1		2			10		
Orange	42	35	Legg	David		1		1		4		1	1				8		
Orange	42	34	Legg	Hepsibah	1	1					2	1					5		
Northampton	6	17	Legg	Moses	3	1		1		1	1		1	1			9		
Charlemont	192	26	Legget	Robert		2					1		1				5		
Charlemont	192	25	Legget	Thomas	1		1	1		1			1				5		
Charlemont	192	24	Legget	William	2		1			1			1				5		
Ware	226	35	Lemberton	David	1			1		1			1				4		
Ware	226	34	Lemberton	Seth	1	1		1	2	2			1	1			9		
Belchertown	209	18	Lemmon	John				1									1		
Belchertown	209	17	Lemmon	Saml	4	1	2		1	2			1				11		
West Springfield	353	51	Leonard	Abel				2					2	1			5		
Warwick	38	23	Leonard	Abraham	1		1			1		1					4		
Worthington	300	27	Leonard	Amos			1	1				1		1			4		
Shutesbury	110	24	Leonard	Archelous			1	2	1		1		1	1			6		
Shutesbury	110	25	Leonard	Archs Jr	2		1						1				4		
Worthington	301	30	Leonard	Asa	1		1			1	1						4		
West Springfield	354	1	Leonard	Asaph			1			1	1	1					5		
Conway	59	23	Leonard	Augustus	3		1			1		1					6		
West Springfield	354	10	Leonard	Austin		3					1		1				6		
Buckland	328	19	Leonard	Calvin	1		1			1		1		1			5		
West Springfield	351	11	Leonard	Catherine		1					1			2			4		
West Springfield	354	25	Leonard	Charles		1		1		1		1	2				6		
Granville Mid Soc.	167	32	Leonard	Comfort								3		2			5		
Ware	226	36	Leonard	Dan		2	2		1	1	1		1				8		
Norwich	153	15	Leonard	Daniel	1	1	1		1			2	1				7		
West Springfield	354	12	Leonard	Daniel	1		4		1	2		2	1	1			12		
Worthington	298	26	Leonard	Ebenezer		1	1		1	2		1	1	1			8		
West Springfield	354	22	Leonard	Editha										2			2		
Conway	59	24	Leonard	Elijah	3			1		1			1				6		
West Springfield	353	45	Leonard	Eliphalet			1							1			2		
Worthington	301	31	Leonard	Elisha	1	1	3		1		1			1			8		
West Springfield	354	24	Leonard	Ezekiel	4	1		1			1	1	1				9		
Shutesbury	110	27	Leonard	Ezra	2			1		1			1	2			7		
Worthington	300	30	Leonard	Ezra	1	1	1	1		1			1	2			8		
Warwick	38	21	Leonard	Francis		1		1		1	1	2		1			7		
West Springfield	354	9	Leonard	George		1		1	1			1	1	3			8		
West Springfield	351	13	Leonard	Gideon	1		1		1	1		1	2	1			8		
West Springfield	354	8	Leonard	Gribert	2	1	1	1			1	1	1	2			10		
West Springfield	353	46	Leonard	Henry	1	1	1			2	1	1					7		
Buckland	328	20	Leonard	Ichabod	2			1				1	1				5		
West Springfield	354	13	Leonard	John	1		1		1	1	1	1	1				8		
Worthington	301	29	Leonard	John		1		1				1		1			4		
Charlemont	192	23	Leonard	Jonas	5		1					1					7		
Warwick	38	20	Leonard	Jonas		1	1		1	1	2	2		1			9		
Worthington	300	35	Leonard	Jonas	2	2		1		2		1	1				9		
Worthington	300	28	Leonard	Joshua	1		1					1					3		
Chester	145	23	Leonard	Josiah	2			1				1		1			5		
West Springfield	354	3	Leonard	Juba	1	2	3		1	1	1		1				10		
West Springfield	353	52	Leonard	Justin	1		1			1		1	1				8		

258

TOWN	PG#	LN#	LAST NAME	FIRST NAME	FREE WHITE MALES under 10	10 to 16	16 to 26	26 to 45	45 and over	FREE WHITE FEMALES under 10	10 to 16	16 to 26	26 to 45	45 and over	TOTAL ALL OTHER	TOTAL SLAVES	TOTALS	DISTRICT/ TOWNSHIP	NOTES
Worthington	297	15	Leonard	Levi	3			1		3			1				7		
West Springfield	354	18	Leonard	Mary		1					1	2	1				5		
Warwick	38	18	Leonard	Moses				1			1			1			3		
West Springfield	354	19	Leonard	Moses	3			1		2	1	2	1	1			11		
Warwick	38	19	Leonard	Nathan	1			1		1			1				4		
Worthington	300	36	Leonard	Nathan Jun		1	1		1			2		1			6		
Williamsburg	445	9	Leonard	Nehemiah	1	1	1		1	2	1	1		1			9		
West Springfield	354	6	Leonard	Noah	2		1	1	1	1	1		1	1			9		
West Springfield	353	47	Leonard	Oliver					2	3			1	1			7		
West Springfield	354	21	Leonard	Phineas	4	2	1		1		2	1	1				12		
West Springfield	353	44	Leonard	Pliny		1	1		1		2		1	1			7		
West Springfield	353	48	Leonard	Preserved				1									1		
West Springfield	354	16	Leonard	Preserved Jr	1	1	1				1	1					5		
West Springfield	354	7	Leonard	Reuben Jr		1	1		1		1			1			5		
Conway	59	22	Leonard	Roger		1		1					1	1			4		
West Springfield	354	5	Leonard	Roswell	2	1	1	1			3	1		1			10		
West Springfield	354	15	Leonard	Rufus			1			2		1					4		
West Springfield	354	14	Leonard	Russell		1	1	2	1					1			6		
Gill	86	29	Leonard	Samuel		1		1		1	1			1			5		
West Springfield	354	17	Leonard	Selden			3					1					4		
West Springfield	351	16	Leonard	Seth	2			1		2			2	1			8		
Shutesbury	110	26	Leonard	Simeon	2	2		1		2			1				8		
Worthington	299	21	Leonard	Simeon	1	1		1	1	2		1	1	1			9		
West Springfield	354	4	Leonard	Thaddeus		1	1	1	1		1		1				6		
West Springfield	354	11	Leonard	William	1			1		2	2	2		1			9		
Buckland	328	24	Leonard	Ziba	3	1		1		1	1		1				8		
Colrain	186	40	Leshore	Williard	2			1		1			1				5		
Amherst	291	21	Lewis	Elisha			1	1	1	2			1	1			8		
Westfield	126	6	Lewis	Gould	2	1		1		1	1		1				7		
Westfield	126	7	Lewis	James				1						1			2		
Ware	227	1	Lewis	Jesse	3			1		2			1				7		
Shutesbury	110	30	Lewis	Joseph	1			1		2			1				5		
Springfield	240	15	Lewis	Joseph	5			1		1			1				8		
Pelham	215	20	Lewis	Wm			1		1			2		2			6		
Shelburne	322	18	Liester	Francis				1		3				1			5		
Norwich	152	19	Liffingwell	Elisha	1	2	1		1	2		2	1				10		
Ashfield	342	14	Lilly	Bethniel	5	2		1			1		1				10		
Ashfield	342	15	Lilly	Eliakim	3			1		2			1				7		
Ashfield	342	16	Lilly	Foster	2			1				1					4		
Ashfield	342	13	Lilly	Jonathan		1		1				1		1			4		
Hawley	334	13	Lilly	Silas Jun			1			3			1				5		
Hawley	334	20	Lilly	Zenas			1						1				2		
Belchertown	206	19	Lincoln	Ebenz	2			1		1			1				5		
Belchertown	206	13	Lincoln	Enos		1	1			1			1				4		
Monson	264	22	Lincoln	John	1			1		3	1		1				7		
Leyden	83	12	Lincoln	Levi	1	2	1	1		2			1				8		
Springfield	240	11	Lincoln	Walker			1				1	1					3		
Northfield	29	17	Lincoln	Zadock		1				1			1				3		
Colrain	186	33	Lindsay	Stephen	2	1				1	1		1				6		
New Salem	100	35	Lindsey	David	1			1				3		1			6		
New Salem	100	36	Lindsey	Hab	2	1	1		1		1	1					7		
Pelham	215	25	Lindsey	James	1			1		2				1			6		
Greenwich	220	36	Lindsey	Norris	4	1		1		2	1		1				10		
Blanford	179	20	Lindsley	Joseph				1		3			1				5		
Blanford	179	21	Lindsley	Moses	2			1	1	2			1				7		
Blanford	179	22	Lindsley	William		2		1	1	4			1				0		
Colrain	186	37	Linn	John	2	1		1		2		1	1				8		
Westfield	123	16	Liswell	Thomas	2	1		1		1	2		1				8		
Chesterfield	21	30	Litchfield	Ensign	1		1						1				3		
Middlefield	157	37	Little	Bezaleel		1	4		1	2	1		1				10		
Ludlow	258	8	Little	Charlotte Wid.	1						2	1	1				5		
Middlefield	157	7	Little	Edward			2		1		1			1			5		
Williamsburg	445	12	Little	Isaac	2	2	1						1				6		
Granby	253	33	Little	John	1			1		1		1					4		
Williamsburg	445	16	Little	Robert	1	1		1		1		1	1				6		
Chesterfield	22	14	Littlefield	Daniel		1		1						1			3		
Colrain	186	28	Littlefield	Edmond	2	1		1	3	3	1		1				12		
Colrain	186	30	Littlefield	Elisha	1			1		1			1				4		
Chesterfield	22	37	Littlefield	Jacob		2		1		2	1	1					7		
Colrain	186	29	Littlefield	Jedediah		1		1		2	1	1					7		
Brimfield	269	27	Liveny	John				1									1		
Shutesbury	110	29	Livermore	Elijah	3			1		1			1				6		
Chesterfield	22	9	Livermore	Solomon			1			4		1	1	1			8		
Blanford	178	4	Lloyd	James	3		1		1	2	1		1				9		
Blanford	177	21	Lloyd	Robert		2		1		2		1	1	1			8		
Blanford	176	13	Lloyd	William	1			1	1				1	1			5		
Granville Mid Soc.	167	43	Lloyd	William	1			1		2			1				5		
Springfield	242	23	Lloyd	William			2					1	1				4		
Colrain	186	38	Lock	B. Joshua	2			1		2			1				6		
Wendell	106	22	Lock	Bazaleel		1	1					1					4		
Wendell	106	23	Lock	Ephraim			1	1		2	1						5		

259

TOWN	PG#	LN#	LAST NAME	FIRST NAME	FREE WHITE MALES					FREE WHITE FEMALES					TOTAL ALL OTHER	TOTAL SLAVES	TOTALS	DISTRICT/ TOWNSHIP	NOTES
					under 10	10 to 16	16 to 26	26 to 45	45 and over	under 10	10 to 16	16 to 26	26 to 45	45 and over					
Shutesbury	110	28	Lock	Increase		1							1				2		
Colrain	186	39	Lock	John	2			1		2			1				6		
Deerfield	54	8	Lock	Jonas		1		1					1	1			4		
Wendell	106	24	Lock	Moses	1			1		2			1				5		
Buckland	328	25	Locke	John	2		1			2	2		1	1			9		
Deerfield	54	10	Logan	James		1							1				2		
Greenfield	74	6	Logan	James				1		1			1	2			5		
Granby	252	15	Lombard	Ariel			1			1			1				3		
Springfield	239	14	Lombard	Jemima Wd								1		1			2		
Barnardston	78	17	Lomis	Daniel				1				1		1			3		
Shelburne	322	15	Long	Aaron	1	1		1		3	1	1	1	1			10		
Shelburne	322	14	Long	David	2	2	1	1		2	2	2		1			13		
Shelburne	322	12	Long	John 2d				1		2			1				4		
Shelburne	322	16	Long	John Esq		1	2	1		2	1		1				8		
Ware	226	32	Long	Rufus Doct	2		1	1		2			1	1			8		
Shelburne	322	10	Long	Stephen	1	1	1		1	5	1	2	1				13		
Shelburne	322	13	Long	Willm	2	1	3	1		2	1	1	1		3		15		
Hawley	334	14	Longley	Edmund Esq		2	2		1		1	1		1			8		
Hawley	334	15	Longley	Joseph		1		1		1	1	1		2			7		
Hawley	334	16	Longley	Joseph Jr	1		1			2			1				5		
Hawley	334	21	Longley	Zimos	1		1			1		1					4		
Springfield	240	12	Look	Benjamin	1		1			2			1				5		
Conway	59	30	Look	Cheney	1	2		1		2		1	1				4		
Conway	59	28	Look	James			2	1					1				4		
Conway	59	29	Look	John		1	1			1		1	1				5		
Hawley	334	17	Look	Noah	2	1	1				1	1					6		
Conway	59	31	Look	Peter		1		1		1	2		1				6		
South Hadley	248	13	Loomer	Frederick	1		1						1				4		
Westfield	123	10	Loomis	Abigal Wd	1									2			3		
Southampton	128	15	Loomis	Allexander			1				3		1				5		
Southampton	128	16	Loomis	Amos	2		1			1		1					5		
Southampton	133	22	Loomis	Artiman	1		1			3		1					6		
West Springfield	351	14	Loomis	Clarke			1			2		1					4		
Westfield	118	16	Loomis	Curtis			1			4		1					6		
Southwick	359	26	Loomis	Elizur	1	1	1			1			1				5		
Westfield	123	18	Loomis	Enoch	1	1	1		1	1	2	2		1			10		
Southwick	359	25	Loomis	Ham	4	2	1	1		1	1		1				11		
Springfield	241	13	Loomis	Hezekiah	2		1				1	1					5		
Russell	139	3	Loomis	Jacob	2	1	3	1			2		1				10		
Westfield	127	10	Loomis	John		2				1		1	1				5		
Ashfield	342	12	Loomis	Jonah	2		1			1		1					5		
Westfield	127	9	Loomis	Joshua		1	2	1		3	2	1					11		
West Springfield	351	15	Loomis	Josiah	3		1			1		1					6		
West Springfield	353	50	Loomis	Justice	1		2	1		2	1		1				8		
Monson	266	22	Loomis	Justus		1		1		1	2		1				6		
Westfield	127	11	Loomis	Justus	3	1		1		2	2		1				10		
Wilbraham	233	8	Loomis	Louisa Wd						3		1	1				5		
Southampton	131	18	Loomis	Nathaniel			1					1					2		
Southwick	359	19	Loomis	Nehemiah	2	1	1		1	1	1	1	1	1			10		
West Springfield	351	12	Loomis	Noadiah		1	1		1	1		1	1	1			7		
Southwick	359	18	Loomis	Noah Junr	1	1	1		2		1			1			7		
Southwick	359	23	Loomis	Noah Junr				1						1			2		
Westfield	123	26	Loomis	Pliny	1	1	1	1			1		1				6		
Conway	59	25	Loomis	Russell	1			1		2			1				5		
Southwick	359	28	Loomis	Shem	1	1	1	1		4	1		1				10		
Southampton	130	26	Loomis	Shim	1	2		1		1	3		1	1			10		
West Springfield	353	49	Loomis	Uriah	3	2		1		2	1		1				10		
Orange	42	31	Lord	Asa		1		1			1	1	1				5		
Westfield	119	1	Lord	David	1			1		3			1				6		
Orange	42	33	Lord	Ichabod		1	1										2		
Wilbraham	234	19	Lord	John	3		1			1	2	1	1				10		
Orange	42	32	Lord	Joseph		2		1				1	1				5		
Orange	42	30	Lord	Preston	2			1	1	4	1	2	1				12		
Leyden	83	14	Lord	William	1	1							1				3		
Orange	42	29	Lord	William Junr	1	1	1			3	1		1				8		
Pelham	215	23	Lothridge	Robt		2				1	1	2		1			7		
West Springfield	354	2	Lothrop	Elijah		1	2		1	2		2	1				9		
Deerfield	54	3	Lotrick	James	1			1		1			1				4		
Hadley	287	6	Lott	Elisha		1						2		1			4		
Westhampton	17	6	Loud	Caleb	1		1					1					3		
Cummington	304	46	Loud	James	4		1			1	2		1				9		
Leyden	83	10	Love	Susanna								3		1			4		
Cummington	304	43	Lovel	Edmond	2	1		2		3	2	1	1				13		
Cummington	304	44	Lovel	Joshua	2	1		1					1				5		
Belchertown	206	14	Lovel	Silas	1		1	1		1			1				5		
Middlefield	158	6	Loveland	Andrew	2			1		2		1					6		
Granville East Soc	531	27	Loveland	Elizabeth		1	2						1						
Greenfield	74	5	Loveland	Epaphroditus	2	1		1		2			1				8		
Gill	86	28	Loveland	Frederick	1			1		3	1		1				7		
Montague	46	29	Loveland	George		2		1		2			1				6		

260

TOWN	PG#	LN#	LAST NAME	FIRST NAME	FREE WHITE MALES under 10	10 to 16	16 to 26	26 to 45	45 and over	FREE WHITE FEMALES under 10	10 to 16	16 to 26	26 to 45	45 and over	TOTAL ALL OTHER	TOTAL SLAVES	TOTALS	DISTRICT/ TOWNSHIP	NOTES
Deerfield	54	4	Loveland	Jonathan	1			1		1			1	1			5		
Middlefield	157	24	Loveland	Malachi	1			1					1				3		
Middlefield	158	8	Loveland	Paine	1	1		1		1	1	1		1			7		
Barnardston	78	18	Loveland	Thomas					1		1			1			3		
Deerfield	54	9	Loveridge	Amasa	3		1		3			1					8		
Shelburne	322	19	Loveridge	Edward		1			1		1			1			4		
Shelburne	322	17	Loveridge	John				1		1			1				3		
Deerfield	54	11	Loveridge	William	3	2	2	1		1		1		1			11		
Norwich	151	36	Lovewell	Jonathan				1		2	1		1				5		
Blanford	178	6	Loyd	James Jun	2	1		1		1			1				6		
Blanford	177	22	Loyd	John	2		1	1				1	1				6		
Williamsburg	445	13	Luce	Elijah	1		1	1		1		1					5		
Gill	86	27	Luce	Joseph		1				1		1					3		
Gill	86	32	Luce	Samuel	2	1	3		1		2			1			10		
New Salem	101	4	Luce	William		1		1				3	1				6		
New Salem	101	6	Luce	William Jr	1		1					1					3		
Williamsburg	445	15	Luce	Zachariah		3		1			2		1				7		
Westfield	125	9	Luchore	Lemuel	2			1			1						4		
Southampton	131	33	Luckore	Lemuel		1	1		1		1			1			5		
Williamsburg	445	14	Ludden	Asa		1			1	2	2			1			7		
Williamsburg	445	10	Ludden	Benjamin		1	1	1		3	2	1					9		
Chesterfield	24	6	Ludden	Bezer	2			1		2			1	1			7		
Worthington	299	16	Ludden	Daniel	2			1					1				4		
Chesterfield	24	13	Ludden	Elisha			1		1	1		1					3		
Williamsburg	445	11	Ludden	James				1		1		2		1			5		
Easthampton	134	14	Luddon	Ezra		1		1				1		1			4		
Belchertown	206	12	Luden	Enos	1	1		1		1			1	1			6		
West Springfield	356	56	Ludington	Daniel	2	2			1			2		1			8		
West Springfield	356	55	Ludington	John	1	1	2		1	1		2		1			9		
West Springfield	357	1	Ludington	Jude	1	1		1	1	1	1		2				8		
Brimfield	273	28	Lumbard	Aaron	2	2		1		2	1	1	1				10		
Ludlow	257	31	Lumbard	Abiel	3			1		1			1				6		
Shutesbury	110	31	Lumbard	Benja	1				1	2	1		1				6		
Springfield	239	2	Lumbard	Daniel			2	3		6		2	1				14		
Brimfield	273	27	Lumbard	David	3			1		2	1	1	1				9		
Ludlow	257	22	Lumbard	David				1		1		1					3		
Brimfield	271	9	Lumbard	Gideon	2		1	1		3	1		1				9		
Ludlow	257	20	Lumbard	Jonathan		1	1	1					1				4		
Ludlow	257	24	Lumbard	Jonathan Jr		1		1		2	1		1				6		
Brimfield	273	26	Lumbard	Joseph				1					1				2		
Springfield	244	28	Lumbard	Joseph	2	1		1		3			1				8		
Brimfield	273	4	Lumbard	Joseph Jr		1	1		1		1			1			5		
Springfield	239	18	Lumbard	Justin		1	1	1		3		2					8		
Springfield	244	12	Lumbard	Obed	1	1	1	1		3	1		1	1			10		
Brimfield	271	7	Lumbard	Thomas				1					1				2		
Brimfield	271	8	Lumbard	Thomas Jun	2			1		1		1	1				6		
Chester	146	34	Lunnon	William				1					1				2		
Northampton	6	5	Lyman	Abigail		2	1	1				3		1			8		
Northampton	7	5	Lyman	Abner	1		1	2	1			2		2			9		
Belchertown	209	23	Lyman	Aron Doct		1		1		5			1				8		
Norwich	151	41	Lyman	Asahel		1						1					2		
Deerfield	54	7	Lyman	Augustus		1	2	1		2	2	3			1		12		
Westhampton	15	13	Lyman	Azariah		1	1		1		2		1				6		
Easthampton	134	25	Lyman	Benjamin	3	1		1		2	1		1				9		
Hadley	288	16	Lyman	Caleb		1		1	2	1	1		1				7		
Northfield	29	15	Lyman	Caleb	1	2	1	1		2	1	1	1				11		
Springfield	247	16	Lyman	Com Capt & his Comp			24	17					2				43		
Chester	147	28	Lyman	Crispus	3			1					1				5		
Northampton	9	23	Lyman	Elias	1	1	2		1			2		1			8		
Southampton	129	17	Lyman	Elias	5		1	2	1			1	1				11		
Southampton	129	19	Lyman	Elias Junr		1	3	1		2		2	1				10		
Greenfield	73	36	Lyman	Elihu		3	1		1		1		1	1	1		9		
Northampton	4	17	Lyman	Erastus			1	2				1		1	3		8		
Northampton	9	22	Lyman	Gaius	1		1	1		1		1					5		
Southampton	131	3	Lyman	Gaius	1		1	1		1		3					7		
Belchertown	209	21	Lyman	Giles			1	1		2			1				5		
Norwich	153	22	Lyman	Giles		1	2	1			1		1				6		
Hadley	288	17	Lyman	Israel	2	1	2		1		3			2			11		
Northfield	29	14	Lyman	James		4			1	1	1		1				8		
Northampton	9	27	Lyman	Joel		1				1	1	2		1			6		
Northampton	7	27	Lyman	John					1				2	2			5		
Southampton	133	14	Lyman	John Junr	1			1			1	1					4		
Belchertown	209	22	Lyman	Jona		1		1				2					4		
Hatfield	12	7	Lyman	Joseph		1	1	1	1		1	1		1			7		
Northampton	5	3	Lyman	Joseph					1				2	1	1		5		
Northampton	4	19	Lyman	Joseph Jun	2	1	4		1	2	1	1	1				13		
Easthampton	136	8	Lyman	Justus	1	1		1			1		1				5		
Easthampton	136	7	Lyman	Leml Junr	2		1	1			1		1				6		
Easthampton	136	20	Lyman	Leml Junr	1		2	2	1	1			1	1			9		
Northampton	2	3	Lyman	Levi	1	1	1	1		3		1					9		

TOWN	PG#	LN#	LAST NAME	FIRST NAME	FREE WHITE MALES					FREE WHITE FEMALES					TOTAL ALL OTHER	TOTAL SLAVES	TOTALS	DISTRICT/ TOWNSHIP	NOTES
					under 10	10 to 16	16 to 26	26 to 45	45 and over	under 10	10 to 16	16 to 26	26 to 45	45 and over					
Northampton	7	9	Lyman	Luke	2		2		1	2	1	1	1	1			11		
Norwich	151	40	Lyman	Rufus			1						1				2		
Westhampton	16	11	Lyman	Rufus	2	2	2		1		1	3		1			12		
Springfield	239	25	Lyman	Samuel Esq	1		1		1				2	2			7		
Leyden	83	13	Lyman	Seth			1			3			1				5		
Northfield	29	18	Lyman	Seth			3		1			2	1	1			8		
Norwich	153	24	Lyman	Seth					1				1	1			3		
Northfield	29	19	Lyman	Simeon		1		2	1			1	1	1			7		
Easthampton	134	28	Lyman	Solomon	1			1	1	2		2	1				8		
Chester	147	29	Lyman	Stephen Deacn		1	2		1			1		1			6		
Chester	147	27	Lyman	Stephen Junr		1						1					2		
Northampton	3	18	Lyman	Sylvester	1	1	2				2		1				7		
Southampton	129	14	Lyman	Thomas		3		1		2	2		1				9		
Chester	147	30	Lyman	Timothy	1	1		1		1	1		1				6		
Goshen	310	25	Lyman	Timothy		4		1		1	1		1				8		
Northampton	8	33	Lyman	William	1		1			2	2	1	1		1		9		
Northfield	29	20	Lyman	William Swan	1		1					1					3		
Hadley	288	18	Lyman	Zadock	1		1	1		1	1	2					7		
Easthampton	136	24	Lymon	David	1			1			2	2	1	1			8		
Southampton	132	12	Lymon	John	1		2	1			1		2	1			8		
Ashfield	342	10	Lyon	Aaron		1		1					1	1			4		
Buckland	328	26	Lyon	Aaron		1		1		3	2		1				8		
Holland	278	9	Lyon	Alfred Col.	1	1	1		1	2	3	2	1				12		
Springfield	247	31	Lyon	Asa	1		1					1					3		
Pelham	215	26	Lyon	Asaph		1		1					1				3		
Greenfield	74	3	Lyon	Caleb			1						1		2		4		
Goshen	310	24	Lyon	Cyrus	2	1	2		1	1	1		1				9		
New Salem	101	8	Lyon	Daniel	1	1		1			1		1				5		
Ashfield	342	11	Lyon	David	3	1		1		2	1		1				9		
Ludlow	257	6	Lyon	David Deacn			1	1			1		1	2			6		
Holland	278	19	Lyon	Ebenezer		2	2	1				1		1			7		
New Salem	101	7	Lyon	Eleazer	3			1		1			1				6		
Ludlow	257	7	Lyon	Gad	3			1					1				5		
Wilbraham	233	10	Lyon	Jacob			1						1				2		
Greenfield	74	2	Lyon	John	2	1		1		4	1		1				10		
Longmeadow	92	40	Lyon	Kimbal	1	1		1		1			1				5		
Goshen	310	23	Lyon	Lemuel			1	1	1		1	2		1			7		
Williamsburg	445	17	Lyon	Lemuel				1					1				2		
Buckland	328	18	Lyon	Nathan		1		1		1	1		1				5		
Wilbraham	233	9	Lyon	Philip	1			1		3			1				6		
Gill	86	30	Lyon	Samuel		1		1					1				3		
Ludlow	257	4	Lyon	Stephen		1					1	1	1				4		
Colrain	186	34	Lyons	David		3		1		1	3		1				9		
Colrain	186	36	Lyons	Jesse	2	1	1	1		2	1	1					9		
Colrain	186	35	Lyons	Terre	3			1		1			1				6		
Pelham	215	24	Lyscomb	Ebenz				1					1				2		
Greenwich	221	4	Lyscomb	Saml			1			4			1				6		
Greenfield	74	12	Mach	Abner	2		1	1		1		1		1			7		
Montague	47	2	Mack	Daniel Gates			1			1	1						3		
Middlefield	156	1	Mack	David Colo		1	5		1	3	3	2	1				16		
Deerfield	54	21	Mack	Elihat	2			1		1			1				5		
Montague	46	41	Mack	Elisha			12	10	1	1	1	1					26		
Middlefield	157	36	Mack	Elisha Capt	1	1	1	1		2	1	2	1				10		
Wilbraham	236	7	Mack	Nathan	1		1		1	1		1		1			6		
Montague	47	3	Mack	Samuel		1				1		1					3		
Shutesbury	110	32	Macomber	Cyrus			1					1					2		
Chesterfield	22	13	Macomber	David	4	2	2		1	2		1					12		
Shutesbury	110	34	Macomber	George		2	2	1			2	1					8		
Wendell	106	31	Macomber	Job	1			1		1			1				4		
Shutesbury	111	1	Macomber	John			1			2			1				4		
Leyden	83	23	Macumber	Lemuel			1			3			1				5		
Leyden	83	16	Macumber	William	3		1				1		1				6		
Ware	227	7	Magoon	Alexr	1	1	2	2	1		1		1	3	1		13		
Ware	227	6	Magoon	Isaac	1	1	2	2			1		1		1		9		
Colrain	187	32	Malester	Benjamin	1					3			1				5		
Warwick	38	27	Mallard	John				1			1		1				3		
Gill	86	33	Mallard	Solomon	1			1			1		1				4		
Warwick	38	38	Mallard	Thomas	2	1		1			1		1				6		
Northfield	29	22	Mallery	Simeon	1	1		1		2	2		1				8		
Montgomery	160	18	Mallery	Truman	1		1	1		2	1		1				7		
Russell	137	12	Mallory	Andrews	2			1		4	1		1				10		
Russell	137	2	Mallory	Jacob				1						1			2		
Russell	137	6	Mallory	John A	1			1		2	1		1				6		
Russell	137	5	Mallory	Jonah		1		1		1	1		1				5		
Hatfield	12	19	Maltby	Isaac	2		1	1	2	2	1		1	1			11		
Granville West Soc	170	11	Manchester	John	2	1		1		1	2	1	1				9		
Granby	252	26	Mandeville	John	5	1	1		1	1	2	1					12		
Gill	87	7	Mange	Peter	2			1					1				4		
Colrain	187	12	Maning	Ephraim	1		1			1			1				4		
Goshen	310	22	Maning	Phineas	2			1		4			1				8		

TOWN	PG#	LN#	LAST NAME	FIRST NAME	FREE WHITE MALES					FREE WHITE FEMALES					TOTAL ALL OTHER	TOTAL SLAVES	TOTALS	DISTRICT/ TOWNSHIP	NOTES
					under 10	10 to 16	16 to 26	26 to 45	45 and over	under 10	10 to 16	16 to 26	26 to 45	45 and over					
Belchertown	206	16	Manley	Reuben	2	1	1	1		2	2		1				10		
Orange	43	3	Manly	Obed	2			1		2		1					6		
Palmer	261	13	Mann	David	2			1	1	3		1	1	1			10		
Northampton	3	3	Mann	Elias		1	1		1	1	1	1	1				7		
Chester	147	31	Mann	Nathan				1		2			1	1			5		
Worthington	300	11	Mann	Nathan	2	1	1	1		2	1		1				9		
New Salem	101	16	Manning	Samuel		1			1				1				3		
Ashfield	343	3	Mansfield	Paxson	3			1					1				5		
Conway	59	48	Manter	Catherine						2	1	1		2			6		
Williamsburg	445	20	Manter	Francis	3			1		3		2					9		
Hawley	334	26	Mantor	James				1		1	1	1					4		
Ashfield	343	2	Mantor	Jeremiah		1		1			1		1				4		
Ashfield	343	1	Mantor	John L.	1	1	1			1			1	1			6		
Conway	59	49	Marble	Abijah	3	1		1		1	1		1				8		
Springfield	239	5	Marble	Joel				1			1						2		
Wilbraham	234	17	Marble	Joseph	1	2		1		3		1	1	1			10		
Conway	59	45	Marble	Nathaniel	3	1		1		1			1				7		
Orange	42	38	Marble	Silas			3	1	1	1	1		1	1			9		
Monson	264	4	March	Seth	3			1		1	1		1				7		
West Springfield	354	35	Marchand	William				1					1				2		
Holland	279	20	Marcy	James	1			1				1	1				4		
Holland	279	17	Marcy	Wd	1	2	2			1		1		2			9		
Belchertown	209	28	Mark	Nathaniel	1			1		1				1			4		
Longmeadow	95	18	Markhand	Israel	1			1		2			1				5		
Southwick	359	36	Marlow	Daniel				1					1				2		
Brimfield	270	32	Marrick	Benjamin	1		2		1	1	2	1					8		
Cummington	305	25	Marrs	Daniel				1			1						2		
Hadley	287	10	Marsh	Abigail							1		1	1			3		
Conway	59	36	Marsh	Abner		1		1		4			1				7		
Deerfield	54	19	Marsh	Amos	1	2			1	4				1			9		
Warwick	38	41	Marsh	Amos	1			1		2		1					5		
Hadley	287	9	Marsh	Daniel		2		2		2	1		1				8		
Montague	47	1	Marsh	Ebenezer	1		1	1				1					4		
Montague	46	39	Marsh	Ebenezer Jr		1	2		1	1		1		1			7		
Hadley	286	30	Marsh	Eliphalet	1			2	1			1					5		
Colrain	187	31	Marsh	Elisha		2		1		2		1	1				7		
Montague	46	37	Marsh	Enos Junr	1	1		1		2	2		1				8		
Ware	227	19	Marsh	Ephraim	1			1		1			1				4		
Montague	46	40	Marsh	Ephraim Junr	2	1			1					2			6		
Ware	227	16	Marsh	Jona		1	5	1		1	1			1			10		
Amherst	290	25	Marsh	Jonathan	2	1	2		1	1	2		1				10		
Montague	46	30	Marsh	Jonathan		2	1	1		1		1	1				7		
Rowe	200	11	Marsh	Jonathan Jr	1			1	1	1		1	1	1			7		
Hawley	334	24	Marsh	Joseph				1					1				2		
Worthington	300	34	Marsh	Joseph	1	1	1	1		1	1	1	1				8		
Hawley	334	25	Marsh	Joseph Jr	2			1		1			1				5		
Montague	46	35	Marsh	Joshua	2			1	1	1			1	1			7		
Ware	227	17	Marsh	Judah Jr Lt	1	1	1	1	1	1		1					7		
Hadley	287	5	Marsh	Marcy	1					1		1	1				4		
Springfield	243	21	Marsh	Philander		1						1					2		
Worthington	298	27	Marsh	Rufus	1		1	1		1	2	1	1	1			9		
Montague	46	36	Marsh	Samuel	4	1	1	1				1					8		
Ware	227	15	Marsh	Thomas	1	1	3		1	1	2	2		1			12		
Amherst	290	28	Marshal	Isaac		2	1	2			2		2				9		
Northampton	8	13	Marshall	Ethan	1			1		1		1					4		
Granville West Soc	168	32	Marshall	Gains			1					1					2		
Granby	252	21	Marshall	John				1									1		
Leyden	83	22	Marshall	Joseph		2	1			3	1	2	1				10		
Granville West Soc	168	29	Marshall	Perez	2			2	1	1	1		2	2			11		
Granville West Soc	169	17	Marshall	Perez			1				1		1				3		
Greenwich	224	18	Marten	Aaron		2		1		1	1		1				6		
Montgomery	160	35	Martin	Asa	1	1		1		4			1				8		
Colrain	187	18	Martin	Enos	1	1	2		2	1		2	2	2	2		15		
Shelburne	322	26	Martin	Isaac				1					1				2		
New Salem	101	15	Martin	Matthew	3	1	1	1			1		1				8		
Colrain	187	23	Martin	Samuel	4			1				1					6		
Colrain	187	35	Martin	Timothy	1	2		1		1		1					6		
Leyden	83	15	Martin	William	3		2						1				6		
Greenfield	74	11	Martindale	Christian									1	1			2		
Westfield	123	24	Martindale	Joel	1			1		2		1	1				6		
Westfield	123	25	Martindale	Samll				1		1			1				3		
Greenfield	74	9	Martindale	Uriah	4	2	1		1	2	1		1				12		
New Salem	101	13	Marval	Stephen	1			1		2			1				5		
Shutesbury	111	5	Marvell	Parkell	1		1					1					3		
Granville East Soc	531	17	Marvin	Ezra		1	1		1					1			4		
Belchertown	206	15	Mason	Amos	1	1		1		1		1	1	1			7		
Westfield	120	24	Mason	Benjamin	1		1		1	2			1				6		
West Springfield	354	40	Mason	David	1	1		1				3		1			7		
Cummington	305	1	Mason	Joseph	1			1		2	1		1				6		
Brimfield	273	5	Mason	Oliver			1		1			2		1			5		

263

TOWN	PG#	LN#	LAST NAME	FIRST NAME	FREE WHITE MALES					FREE WHITE FEMALES					TOTAL ALL OTHER	TOTAL SLAVES	TOTALS	DISTRICT/ TOWNSHIP	NOTES
					under 10	10 to 16	16 to 26	26 to 45	45 over	under 10	10 to 16	16 to 26	26 to 45	45 and over					
Belchertown	209	30	Mason	Richard		1		1						1			3		
Rowe	200	14	Mason	Selah	1	1						1					3		
Greenwich	222	12	Mason	Wd	1							1	1				3		
Palmer	261	43	Mason	William	4		1	1		2		1					9		
Deerfield	54	18	Masters	Daniel	2			2		2	1		1				8		
Northampton	6	11	Mather	Elisha		2	1		1				1	1			6		
Northampton	11	16	Mather	Elisha 2d			1						1				2		
Deerfield	54	20	Mather	Henry	2		1			1			1				5		
Westfield	120	9	Mather	John	1	1	1	2		1	1	1	1				9		
Westfield	120	14	Mather	Saml Esq	1		2		1	2	1		1				8		
Northampton	4	24	Mather	Warham	1			1	1	1	1		1				6		
Southwick	359	34	Mather	William		1		1	1			2	1	1			7		
Whately	67	10	Mather	William	1		4	1	1	4			1	1			13		
Orange	43	2	Mathews	Jeremiah			1				1	1					3		
Chester	143	22	Matthews	Edmond	2		1			2			1				6		
Chester	143	21	Matthews	Gideon		3		1					1				5		
Chester	144	1	Matthews	Gideon Deac	1		1			1			1		1		5		
Chester	144	2	Matthews	Samuel Deac			1			1			1	1			4		
Leverett	115	28	Matthews	Silas		1	1	2	1			1	1				7		
Buckland	329	1	Matthewson	Philip	1		1			1	1		1				5		
Northfield	29	28	Mattoon	Elijah	1		1		1			1	2	1			7		
Northfield	29	29	Mattoon	Isaac	2			2		1			1				6		
Northfield	29	25	Mattoon	Phillip	1		2		1			2		1			7		
Northfield	29	27	Mattoon	Samuel		2		1				3	1	1			8		
Northfield	29	30	Mattoon	Samuel Jr	1			1		3			1				6		
Amherst	292	16	Mattson	Ebenezer				1					1				2		
Amherst	292	6	Mattson	Ebenezer Jun		2		1		1		1	1		1		6		
Wilbraham	237	3	Maxson	Mathew		1	1	1	1	2	1	1		1			8		
Heath	196	24	Maxwell	Benjamin		2	2	1						1			6		
Heath	196	26	Maxwell	Benjm Jun		1	1										2		
Heath	196	25	Maxwell	Hugh	3			1		1			2	1			8		
Palmer	261	2	May	Ebenezer											2		2		
Pelham	215	30	May	John				1					1				2		
Holland	279	29	May	Nehemiah	2	1		1					1	1			6		
Buckland	329	3	May	Oliver		1		1					1				3		
Holland	278	1	May	Rufus	1	1		1		2	2	1	1				9		
Holland	279	30	May	Uriel	1			1		1			1				4		
Middlefield	156	21	May	William	3			1		2			1				7		
Monson	266	25	May	William	2			1			1	1		1			6		
Orange	42	39	Maycumber	Samuel			1			1	2	1		1			6		
Williamsburg	444	2	Mayhew	Arnold	1		1			1			1	1			5		
Charlemont	192	31	Mayhew	Freeburn		3	2		1	1	1	1	1	1			11		
Williamsburg	445	18	Mayhew	Lathrop	1		1			2			1				5		
Williamsburg	444	7	Mayhew	Thomas			1			2			1				4		
Gill	87	6	Mayhew	Wilmore	2	1		1		1			1				6		
Williamsburg	444	5	Mayhew	Zachariah		3	1	1		1			1				7		
Montgomery	160	12	Maynard	Amos				1				1		1			3		
Northfield	29	31	Maynard	Asa	2			1		1			1				5		
Conway	59	50	Maynard	Calvin				1		3	1		1				6		
Hawley	334	22	Maynard	Daniel	4	1		1			1		1				8		
Conway	59	44	Maynard	Elijah	1	2			1	2		1	1				8		
Goshen	310	27	Maynard	Joseph	1	2	1		1	2		1		2			10		
Conway	59	46	Maynard	Malachi	1	1	1			2	2		1				9		
Conway	59	47	Maynard	Moses	1		1			1		1					4		
Montgomery	159	2	Maynard	Moses	2	3	1			3			1				10		
Goshen	311	1	Maynard	Nehemiah	1	2		1			1	1	1				7		
Shutesbury	111	4	Maynard	Oliver	1		1			1			1				4		
Conway	59	40	Maynard	Pierces		2	2						1	1			6		
Montgomery	160	27	Maynard	Reuben		1	2		1	2	2		1				9		
Southampton	128	1	Maynard	Stephen	2	1		1		2	1		1	1			9		
Colrain	187	22	Maynard	Thaddeus			1			2		1					4		
Conway	59	43	Maynard	Theodore		1						1							
Conway	59	37	Maynard	Timothy	1		1			2			1				5		
Colrain	187	21	Maynard	William		1		1		1	3	2		1			9		
Shelburne	322	21	Maynard	William	2		1			2			1				6		
Warwick	38	32	Mayo	Caleb	1	3		1		4	3	1	1				14		
Orange	42	40	Mayo	Calvin	1	1							1				3		
Orange	42	41	Mayo	Dorothy	1	1					2	1	1				8		
Montague	46	42	Mayo	Joseph			1										1		
Warwick	38	39	Mayo	Joseph	2	2						1	1	1			7		
Shutesbury	110	33	Mayo	Moses	1	1		1	1			2	2	1			9		
Deerfield	54	13	McCall	Elihu				1		1	1	1					5		
Colrain	187	3	McCallen	Hugh		1	2				3	1	1				9		
Colrain	187	5	McCallen	James	2	1		1			1	1	1				7		
Colrain	187	4	McCallen	Robert			1			2			1				4		
Northfield	29	26	McCarter	Dennis		1		1			1	1		1			5		
Palmer	260	18	McClanathan	Saml Deacn		4		1		2	1	1	1				10		
Palmer	260	5	McClanathan	Thomas		3		1		2	1	1	1				9		
Springfield	244	18	McClenche	Robert		1		1						1			3		
Conway	59	38	McClentick	John	1	1		1			1			1			5		

TOWN	PG#	LN#	LAST NAME	FIRST NAME	FREE WHITE MALES under 10	10 to 16	16 to 26	26 to 45	45 and over	FREE WHITE FEMALES under 10	10 to 16	16 to 26	26 to 45	45 and over	TOTAL ALL OTHER	TOTAL SLAVES	TOTALS	DISTRICT/ TOWNSHIP	NOTES
Ware	227	13	McClintock	Thomas	2	1			1	1			1				6		
Colrain	187	25	McCloud	Charles	3	1		1		2	1		1				9		
Colrain	187	17	McColloch	James	2	1		1		2	3			1			10		
Pelham	215	29	McComber	George	1			2		1			1				5		
Blanford	175	18	McConoughey	Saml					1	3			1				5		
Colrain	187	30	McCoy	Joseph	2			1		3			1				7		
Northfield	29	41	McCoy	Lemuel	4			1		2	1		1				9		
Wilbraham	232	26	McCray	John	2		1	1		1			1				6		
Pelham	215	37	McCullock	Henry	2			1					1				6		
Pelham	216	2	McCullock	John	2	1		1					1				5		
Pelham	215	36	McCullough	Robt Jr			1	1			1		1				4		
Monson	263	5	McDowell	William	1	1		1						1			6		
Palmer	259	16	McElwain	John A	4		1		1	1	1	2	2				12		
Palmer	259	17	McElwain	Roger	2			1		3			1				7		
Middlefield	155	7	McElwain	Timothy Capt	1	1	3		1	2	2	1		1			12		
Middlefield	155	8	McElwain	Timothy Junr		1		1		1		2					5		
Charlemont	192	28	McFarling	Ephraim	1		1	1		2			1				6		
Colrain	187	8	McGee	Jonas	3	1		1		1			1				8		
Colrain	187	2	McGee	Jonathan	1	1	4	1	1	1	1	2	1	3			16		
Northampton	8	8	McGeorge	Catharine									1	1			2		
Hadley	289	1	McGeorge	Horatio T.	2	2			1	4	1		1				11		
Ashfield	342	19	McGinster	Augustus	2			1		2			1				6		
Blanford	180	3	McGomery	Wm		1	1		1					1			4		
Longmeadow	95	14	McGregory	Ebenezer			2		1	2	1	1		1			8		
Greenfield	74	10	McHard	William	2	1		1		3	1		1				9		
South Brimfield	276	29	McIn*	Abraham	1			1		1		1	1				5		
West Springfield	354	29	McIntier	Jesse			1		2			2		1			6		
West Springfield	354	30	McIntier	Jesse Jr	1			2		1			1				5		
West Springfield	354	32	McIntier	Samuel		1		1				1	1				4		
West Springfield	354	26	McIntier	William	2	1		1		2	1	2	1				10		
Belchertown	209	24	McIntosh	John		1			1		1		1				4		
Greenwich	221	6	McKee	John	1				1		1			1			4		
Shelburne	322	27	McKee	Willm	2		2		1	1	2	1		1			10		
Russell	139	27	McKein	Abel	2			1		1			1				5		
Springfield	245	34	McKinstry	John Revd			3	1			1	2	1				8		
Colrain	187	13	McKneel	Robert	1			1					1	1			4		
Colrain	187	9	McKowen	Lydia	1	1	1	1		1	1	1	1				8		
Ware	227	18	McKoy	Nell	3	4			1	2			1	1			12		
Pelham	215	35	McLam	John	3	1	1	1					1				7		
Shelburne	322	25	McLatton	Robert L.	1			1		1	1		1				5		
Palmer	259	28	McMaster	Clark	2			1		3			1				7		
Palmer	259	45	McMaster	Hugh		1	1		1			1		1			5		
Palmer	258	1	McMaster	Hugh Jr		2			1		1		1				5		
Palmer	259	29	McMaster	John	2	1			1		1		1	1			7		
Palmer	260	15	McMaster	John 2d	2			1	1	2		1	1				8		
Amherst	293	3	McMaster	Joshua	2	1	1	1					1				6		
Palmer	260	26	McMaster	Joshua			1	1			1		1				4		
Palmer	260	43	McMaster	Reuben			1			1		2					4		
Palmer	260	42	McMaster	Robert				1						1			2		
South Hadley	249	16	McmAster	Wd	1									1			2		
Pelham	215	28	McMillen	James		2	3		1	1	1	1		1			10		
Pelham	215	33	McMillen	Jeremh	1			1		2		1	1				6		
Pelham	215	32	McMillen	John	1	2		1		2		2	1				9		
Pelham	215	34	McMillen	Jona	2	1		1		2	1	1	1	1			10		
Pelham	215	31	McMillen	Wm	1	3	1	1		3			1				10		
Palmer	260	2	McMitchell	Benjamin	2			1		1			1				5		
Palmer	260	3	McMitchell	Robert		1	1		1		2	2		1			8		
Hatfield	13	6	McNeal	Daniel	2			1		1			1				5		
Granby	252	41	McNelly	Henry	3			1		3			1				8		
Springfield	247	8	McQuivey	Solomon	1			1		4			1				7		
West Springfield	357	8	McWethy	Nathaniel		1	1		1				2				5		
Middlefield	158	7	Meach	Elijah	2		1		1	2	1		1				8		
Middlefield	156	10	Meacham	Ambros				1					1				2		
Middlefield	157	32	Meacham	Andrew	1		1	1		2			2	2			9		
Monson	265	21	Meacham	Isaac	1	1		1		3	2		1	1			10		
Middlefield	156	16	Meacham	James	1	1		1		2			1				6		
Middlefield	156	9	Meacham	John			1		1					1			3		
New Salem	101	14	Meacham	Jonathan		2			1	3	1	2	1				10		
Southwick	359	35	Meacham	Paul	2	1		1		2	2	1	1				10		
Middlefield	156	15	Meacham	Philip	2	1		1					1				5		
Norwich	152	41	Meachum	Ebinezer	3		2		1	1	2	2	1				12		
Norwich	152	42	Meachum	Enoch	3			1		2			1				7		
Montgomery	160	29	Meachum	Margaret	1						1		1				3		
Norwich	153	14	Meachum	Stephen	1			1		2			1				5		
Hatfield	12	29	Meckins	Levi					2					1			3		
Chesterfield	21	18	Meech	Dennis	2	1		1		1	2		1		1		9		
Colrain	187	14	Meecham	John			1			1	1		1				4		
Colrain	187	20	Meecham	Kingman	2			1	1	1			2	1			8		
Colrain	187	19	Meecham	Rebeckah	1		1			1	1	1		1			6		
Williamsburg	444	6	Meekins	Joseph	2			1		2			1				6		

TOWN	PG#	LN#	LAST NAME	FIRST NAME	FREE WHITE MALES under 10	10 to 16	16 to 26	26 to 45	45 and over	FREE WHITE FEMALES under 10	10 to 16	16 to 26	26 to 45	45 and over	TOTAL ALL OTHER	TOTAL SLAVES	TOTALS	DISTRICT/ TOWNSHIP	NOTES
Williamsburg	445	24	Meekins	Stephen	2		1			2	1		1				7		
Williamsburg	445	19	Meekins	Thomas				1					1				2		
Chester	149	21	Mehanna	John	2		1			1			1				5		
Westfield	119	29	Mein	Armer	1		1			2	1		1				6		
Middlefield	157	20	Meker	John			1						1				2		
Warwick	38	36	Melady	Samuel		1	1			1			1				4		
Warwick	38	26	Mellen	Gilbert	3		1	1				1	1				7		
Warwick	38	37	Mellen	Samuel		1	1						1	1			4		
Chester	150	3	Melvin	James		2		1		1			1				5		
Cummington	304	47	Melvin	Reuben	3	1		1	1	2			1	1			10		
Deerfield	54	12	Mendall	Church	1	1		1					1				4		
Palmer	259	43	Mendon	Wm			1						1				2		
Montague	46	32	Merchant	Joseph	1	3		1		3		2	1				11		
Montague	46	31	Merchant	Mathew		1		1		2			1				5		
Springfield	248	1	Mercy	Benjamin	1		1					1					3		
Middlefield	158	9	Merifield	Ozem		2				1			1				4		
New Salem	101	17	Merriam	Jesse		2	1	1					2	1			7		
New Salem	101	9	Merriam	Mary			1			2	2	2					8		
New Salem	101	18	Merriam	William	1		1			1			1				4		
Palmer	262	1	Merrick	Aaron			1	1	1	1	1		1				6		
Warwick	38	34	Merrick	Bezaleel	3	1	1	1		1	1	1	1				10		
Wilbraham	233	37	Merrick	Cheleab B	1	1	1			1	1	1		1			8		
Amherst	294	18	Merrick	James			2	1		1		1		1			6		
Monson	263	35	Merrick	Jona				1		1	1	1	1				5		
Wilbraham	233	36	Merrick	Jona	1		2		1	2	1		1	1	1		9		
Chesterfield	20	20	Merrick	Joseph		1	1		2	1	1	1					7		
Monson	263	44	Merrick	Lewis	3	1		1		1	1		1				8		
Monson	263	36	Merrick	Miner		1	1				1						3		
Monson	263	15	Merrick	Noah	1					1	1	1	1				5		
Monson	263	42	Merrick	Phinehas			1	1		1		1	1				5		
Monson	264	8	Merrick	Roswell			1				1						2		
Monson	262	22	Merrick	Royal	2	1	1	1		2	1	1	1				10		
Wilbraham	233	35	Merrick	Samuel Fisk	2	1	1		1	2	2	1		2			12		
West Springfield	351	29	Merrick	Tilley	1	2	1			1	1	2		2			10		
Colrain	187	15	Merrifield	Robery	1	1	1		1				1				5		
Buckland	328	27	Merril	Jesse			1			1	1	1	1				5		
Rowe	200	12	Merril	Theddeus	1		1	1		3	2	1	1				10		
Shelburne	322	22	Merrill	John	3	1		1		1	1	1					8		
Shelburne	322	23	Merrill	Nathl	2	3	1	1		2	1		1	1			12		
Deerfield	54	16	Merrill	Samuel	2		1				1						4		
Ashfield	342	22	Merrill	Stephen	2			1				1					4		
Palmer	260	27	Merrill	Wm	2	1		1		3	1		1				9		
Amherst	296	8	Merrils	Calvin	4	3	1	1		1		2	1	1			14		
Northfield	29	34	Merriman	Elijah	1		1						1				3		
Northfield	29	33	Merriman	Levi	1		1			3	1		1				7		
Northfield	29	32	Merriman	Samuel				1				2	1				4		
Blanford	182	7	Merrit	Asa	2	2	1						1	1			7		
Conway	59	42	Merritt	Asa Junr	3		1	1		1			1	1			8		
Ware	227	11	Merritt	Ezekiel L.	3		1			1			1				6		
Ware	227	10	Merritt	Ichabod	2	2	1				2		1				8		
Conway	59	39	Merritt	Simeon	1	1	1			2			1				6		
Granville Mid Soc.	165	6	Merry	Cornelius			1		1			1		1			4		
West Springfield	354	39	Mersick	Daniel	3	1	1			2	1		1				9		
Southwick	359	31	Messenger	Horace			1					1		1			3		
Greenwich	221	7	Messenger	James	2	1		1				1	1				6		
Southwick	359	37	Messenger	Jehiel	1			1		1			1				4		
Worthington	298	39	Metcalf	Eli	1	1	1		1	1			3	1			9		
Middlefield	157	31	Metcalf	John	2		1	1		1		1	1				7		
Wendell	106	30	Metcalf	John		1		1		1			1				4		
Orange	42	43	Metcalf	Joseph		1	3		1		2	1		1			9		
Worthington	298	40	Metcalf	Jubal	1			1		2			1				5		
Chesterfield	21	1	Metcalf	Phineas	1			1		3	1						6		
Orange	42	36	Metcalf	Saville		1		1						1			3		
Orange	42	37	Metcalf	Silas	2			1		2	1		1				7		
Blanford	179	24	Michel	Moses	1	2	1		1	2	1		1				9		
Rowe	200	13	Middleditch	William				1		1	3	1		1			6		
Ashfield	342	20	Mighells	Daniel		2		1			1		1				5		
Ashfield	342	21	Mighells	John	2	2		1		1			1				7		
Ashfield	342	17	Mighells	Nathl			1			2			1				4		
Ludlow	256	30	Miller	Aaron John	1	1			1	1			1	1			6		
West Springfield	357	7	Miller	Abner	1		1	1		2		1		1			7		
Williamsburg	444	3	Miller	Alexander		2		1		1	2	1		1			8		
West Springfield	354	37	Miller	Apollos			1							1			2		
Southwick	359	33	Miller	Asa	1			1		1		1	1				5		
West Springfield	351	18	Miller	Asa	2	1	2			2		1	2	1			12		
Brimfield	269	24	Miller	Benjamin				1		1	1		1				4		
West Springfield	351	30	Miller	Calvin	1			1					1				3		
Warwick	38	42	Miller	Christian				1					1				2		
Springfield	240	9	Miller	Clark		1						1					2		
Williamsburg	444	1	Miller	Cyrus	2	1	1		2	2	2	1		1	1		13		

TOWN	PG#	LN#	LAST NAME	FIRST NAME	FREE WHITE MALES					FREE WHITE FEMALES					TOTAL ALL OTHER	TOTAL SLAVES	TOTALS	DISTRICT/ TOWNSHIP	NOTES
					under 10	10 to 16	16 to 26	26 to 45	45 and over	under 10	10 to 16	16 to 26	26 to 45	45 and over					
Northfield	29	23	Miller	Daniel	3			1	1				1				6		
Brimfield	269	22	Miller	Ebenezer				1						1			2		
Southwick	359	30	Miller	Elias			1				1	1					3		
Granville East Soc	529	28	Miller	Eliphas	2		2		1	2		1	1	1			10		
Chester	145	16	Miller	Ephraim Junr	1			1					1				3		
Chester	145	14	Miller	Ephraim Lieut		1		1			1			1			4		
Ludlow	256	4	Miller	George	2		1	1		3			1				8		
Granville West Soc	168	5	Miller	Isaac	1		1	1		1	1		1				6		
West Springfield	351	19	Miller	Israel		1		1					1				4		
Northampton	10	39	Miller	Jacob	2			1	1				1				6		
Leyden	83	17	Miller	John	1			1		1			1				4		
Northampton	10	38	Miller	John				1					1	1			3		
Southampton	132	21	Miller	John			1	1		4	2		1				9		
West Springfield	357	6	Miller	John	2	1		1		1	1	1	1				8		
Williamsburg	445	23	Miller	John	1	1	1						1	1			5		
Northampton	11	1	Miller	Jonathan	1	2		1		3	1		1				9		
Chester	147	16	Miller	Jonathan		1		1			1	1		1			5		
Chester	147	17	Miller	Jonathan Junr	1		1					1					3		
Ludlow	256	6	Miller	Joseph					1			1	1				3		
Springfield	240	24	Miller	Joseph		1		1				1		2			5		
Ludlow	256	7	Miller	Joseph Jr	1	1	2	1		3		1	2		1		12		
Ludlow	256	26	Miller	Leonard	1	1	1		1	3	2		1				10		
Colrain	187	29	Miller	Martha	2					2		2	1				7		
Granville Mid Soc.	167	10	Miller	Nathaniel	3		1						1				5		
Granville Mid Soc.	165	30	Miller	Recompense		1	1		1	1	1		1				6		
Colrain	187	10	Miller	Robert		1	2	2	1	1	1	2					10		
Southampton	130	14	Miller	Roger		1	1	1		1			4				8		
Chester	145	15	Miller	Samuel	1		1			1		1					4		
Williamsburg	444	4	Miller	Samuel		1	1					1					3		
Deerfield	54	22	Miller	Silas	2			1		2		1					6		
West Springfield	351	26	Miller	Stephen			1					1					2		
Williamsburg	445	21	Miller	Stephen	2	3		1		3	1		1				11		
Granville West Soc	168	6	Miller	Timothy	1		1		1		2	1		1	1		8		
Granville West Soc	168	7	Miller	Timothy Jun			1			1		1					3		
Colrain	187	16	Miller	William	3	1	1	1			1	1	1				9		
Southwick	359	29	Miller	William				1		1			1				3		
Norwich	153	12	Miller	William Deac		1	2	1					1				5		
Southwick	359	32	Miller	William Jr	2			1				1					4		
Granville West Soc	169	19	Miller	Cephas	3	1	1	1		2	2	3	1				14		
Greenwich	221	10	Mills	James	4	2	2	1						1			10		
Orange	42	42	Mills	James	1		1	1				1	1				5		
Orange	43	1	Mills	James Junr	1		1			1		1					4		
Granville West Soc	168	4	Mills	Jedediah	3			1		1			1				6		
Westfield	127	29	Mills	Joshua	3				1				1				5		
Longmeadow	91	12	Mills	Sarah Wid		2						1		1			4		
Granville West Soc	168	3	Mills	Stone				1						1			2		
Chesterfield	21	14	Mills	Thomas			1					1					2		
Pelham	216	1	Mills	William				1					1				2		
Springfield	240	1	Mills	William		2				1	1						4		
Monson	263	18	Minard	Amos	1		1	1				1					4		
Granville East Soc	527	18	Miner	Christopher	1			1		1			1				4		
Northfield	29	35	Miner	Clement	5			1				1					7		
Chester	146	31	Miner	Rufus	1			1		3			1				6		
Wilbraham	232	4	Miner	Samuel	2	1	1		1		1		1				7		
Northfield	29	21	Miriam	James	1		1	1		4			1				8		
Charlemont	192	29	Mitchel	Asaph	2			1		1			1				5		
Norwich	153	19	Mitchel	Reuben		1		1			1		1				4		
Greenwich	221	9	Mitchel	Thomas	1	1		1		1	1	1					6		
Blanford	179	34	Mitchel	William	2		1		1			1	1	1			7		
Cummington	304	48	Mitchel	Willm	1	2	2		1	3	1	1	1				12		
Greenfield	74	14	Mitchell	Elijah	1			1	1	3		2	3	1			12		
South Hadley	251	2	Mitchell	Mary Wd		1						1	1				3		
South Hadley	249	33	Mitchell	Philip											3		3		
Greenfield	74	15	Mitchell	William	1		1						1				3		
Westfield	127	7	Mix	Timothy		1		1				2	1				5		
Colrain	187	26	Mixer	Joseph	1			1		3			1				6		
Norwich	152	12	Mixer	Phineas		2			1	2	2	1					9		
Colrain	187	27	Mixer	Timothy	1	1		1		2	1	2	1				9		
Monson	266	6	Mixter	Daniel	3	1		1		1	2		1				9		
Wilbraham	235	2	Mixter	Phinehas				1		1	2	1					5		
Brimfield	272	14	Moffartt	Joseph Doct		1		1						1			3		
West Springfield	351	21	Moffat	Daniel		1	3	1		2	1		1	1			10		
Ludlow	255	19	Moffett	Mathew	2	1			1	2			1				7		
Montague	46	34	Monroe	Benjamin				1		1			2				4		
Granville East Soc	527	17	Mons	Ashbel	2	2		1		4			1				10		
Granville East Soc	527	8	Mons	Martin	2	2		1		2			1	1			9		
Sunderland	282	13	Montague	Daniel			1	1	1			1	1	1			6		
Sunderland	282	6	Montague	David	1	2	1	1		2		1	1				9		
Charlemont	192	30	Montague	Ebenezer	1			1		2		1	1				6		
Leverett	115	31	Montague	Elijah	1			1		3			2				7		

TOWN	PG#	LN#	LAST NAME	FIRST NAME	FREE WHITE MALES under 10	10 to 16	16 to 26	26 to 45	45 and over	FREE WHITE FEMALES under 10	10 to 16	16 to 26	26 to 45	45 and over	TOTAL ALL OTHER	TOTAL SLAVES	TOTALS	DISTRICT/ TOWNSHIP	NOTES
South Hadley	251	12	Montague	Elijah	2	1	1	1		1	1	1	1	1			10		
Hadley	287	23	Montague	Jedediah	2	1		1		3		1	1	1			10		
Granby	253	36	Montague	John	2	1		1		1		1	1				7		
Hadley	285	30	Montague	John		1	1		1	1	1	1		1			7		
Sunderland	282	18	Montague	John	1		1		1	1	1	2		1			8		
Granby	252	9	Montague	Jonah		1	1	1		1		1	1				6		
Amherst	292	1	Montague	Luke			1										1		
Goshen	310	26	Montague	Luke	3								1				5		
Montague	46	33	Montague	Medad	2	2		1		2		2		1			10		
Westhampton	16	24	Montague	Peter	1	1			1	1	1		1				6		
Hadley	287	24	Montague	Stephen		1	3		1	2		1					8		
South Hadley	251	5	Montague	Timothy			1			1		2		1			5		
Hadley	285	1	Montague	William	2			1		1		2	1				7		
Amherst	292	21	Montague	Zebina		1		1	1	1		1		1			6		
Norwich	154	8	Montegue	Moses Lt.			1			1	2		1				5		
Monson	268	37	Montgomery	Peter											2		2		
Pelham	214	19	Montgomery	Thomas	1	1			1	3	3			1			10		
Granby	255	3	Moody	Aaron	2		1	1	1		2			1			8		
South Hadley	251	18	Moody	Daniel Capt.	3	1	1		1				2				8		
South Hadley	251	17	Moody	Ebenezer	1	1	2		1			1		1			7		
Amherst	294	19	Moody	Eldad				1					1				2		
Amherst	294	8	Moody	Elihu	1	1		1		2			1				6		
South Hadley	251	19	Moody	Eliphaz	2		1			3			1	1			9		
Granby	252	12	Moody	Enos	3	1		1		1		1	1				8		
New Salem	101	19	Moody	Ezra	1		1	1		1			1				5		
Granby	254	9	Moody	Gideon Ens	2		1	1			1		1				6		
Northfield	29	36	Moody	Isaiah		1	1				1						3		
Belchertown	209	25	Moody	Jacob Jr	1					3		1					6		
Amherst	294	12	Moody	Joel		1		1	1		1	2		1			7		
Granby	253	22	Moody	John Lt		1	1		1			1		1			5		
Amherst	293	10	Moody	Jonathan		1	1		1	1		1		1			6		
South Hadley	250	32	Moody	Joseph Jr	2	1		1		1	1	1					7		
South Hadley	251	15	Moody	Josiah			2	1				1		1			5		
Amherst	294	10	Moody	Lemuel	1			2	1			1	1				6		
Amherst	294	4	Moody	Medad		1		1				1	1	1			5		
South Hadley	251	10	Moody	Noah	2	1		1		2	1		1	1			9		
Granville West Soc	168	24	Moody	Oliver	2			1		1		1		2			7		
Granby	252	20	Moody	reuben		1	1	1			1		1				5		
Amherst	293	9	Moody	Rufus	1		1	1					1				4		
Ashfield	342	18	Moody	Saml	1		1					1					3		
South Hadley	251	20	Moody	Seth	3		1		3	2	2	2	1				14		
Amherst	293	14	Moody	Silas	3			1		1			1				6		
Granby	255	2	Moody	Simeon	1	2	1		1		1	2		1			9		
South Hadley	251	16	Moody	Sylvester	2		1	1				1					5		
Amherst	293	13	Moody	Asahel		1	2		1	2			1	1			8		
Westfield	125	31	Moor	Abigal Wd		1	2		1		1	3		2			10		
Monson	263	11	Moor	Alexander				1	1	1	1	2					5		
Monson	263	12	Moor	Alexn Junr				1		1	3		1				5		
Belchertown	209	36	Moor	George			1			2		1					4		
Monson	263	30	Moor	Gideon	1			1		1			1				4		
Chester	150	4	Moor	Hiram	2	2		1		3	1		1				10		
Brimfield	272	4	Moor	James	1			1		2			1				5		
Montgomery	160	6	Moor	Joel 2d		1	2	1			1	1		1			7		
Brimfield	271	42	Moor	John	1			1			1	1	1				5		
Westfield	125	27	Moor	Lucretia Wd	1		1			1	1		2	1			7		
Montgomery	160	8	Moor	Oliver	1	1		1		2			1				6		
Montgomery	160	10	Moor	Orrin	1			1					1				3		
Chester	149	8	Moor	Samuel	1		1		1	2	1		2				8		
Ludlow	257	11	Moor	Timothy	1		1					1					3		
Chester	143	7	Moor	William Lieut		1	4	1		1			1				8		
Palmer	259	13	Moore	Aaron	1		1			3		1					6		
Leverett	115	32	Moore	Alvin	1			1		2		1					5		
Wendell	106	28	Moore	Amos	1		1			1		1					4		
Leverett	115	29	Moore	Asa	3	3		1					1				8		
Granville West Soc	169	24	Moore	Asher		1						1					2		
Wendell	106	27	Moore	Benjamin			1			2		1					4		
Wendell	106	29	Moore	Cornelius	1		1			1		1					4		
Palmer	258	9	Moore	David	3		1			1		1					7		
Palmer	259	12	Moore	David				1		1		2					4		
Russell	139	9	Moore	David		1						1	1				3		
Granville East Soc	529	4	Moore	Elias	1		1			4	3	1					10		
Montgomery	160	30	Moore	Guy	2		1			1		1					5		
Palmer	258	19	Moore	Hugh		1	1	1						1			5		
Palmer	258	20	Moore	Hugh Jur	1		1			2		1					5		
Blanford	176	12	Moore	James	1		1	1		2			1	1			7		
Montgomery	160	26	Moore	Joel	1			1				1		1			4		
Montgomery	162	3	Moore	Joel	2			1		2			1				6		
Conway	59	41	Moore	John	1	1	1	1		4	1		1				10		
Leyden	83	21	Moore	John			1	1		1			1				4		
Warwick	38	28	Moore	John		2	1		1	2	1	1		1			9		

TOWN	PG#	LN#	LAST NAME	FIRST NAME	FREE WHITE MALES					FREE WHITE FEMALES					TOTAL ALL OTHER	TOTAL SLAVES	TOTALS	DISTRICT/ TOWNSHIP	NOTES
					under 10	10 to 16	16 to 26	26 to 45	45 and over	under 10	10 to 16	16 to 26	26 to 45	45 and over					
Leyden	83	18	Moore	John Jr		3		1		3	1		1				9		
Palmer	259	23	Moore	Jonathan			1	1	1			1		1			5		
Warwick	38	29	Moore	Jonathan		1	1		1		1	2		2			8		
Warwick	38	40	Moore	Jonathan Jr			1					1					2		
Granville East Soc	529	8	Moore	Joseph	3	1		1		2	1		1				9		
Middlefield	158	18	Moore	Joseph				1			1	2		1			5		
Springfield	243	35	Moore	Justus		2	1		1	3		1	1				9		
Warwick	38	30	Moore	Mark	2	2	2		1	2		2	1				12		
Granville West Soc	169	27	Moore	Marvin	2			1	1			1	2	1			8		
Wendell	106	26	Moore	Richard		1			1			1		1			4		
Blanford	177	25	Moore	Samuel	5	1		1			1	1					9		
Granville West Soc	168	15	Moore	Samuel	1	1		1		3	1						8		
Warwick	38	33	Moore	Samuel	1	2		1		3	1	1					9		
Blanford	177	19	Moore	Thomas	1	1	1		1	2	2	2	1				11		
Granville West Soc	169	23	Moore	William	1	1		1		2	2	1					8		
Worthington	300	32	Moore	William	1	2		1		3	1		1				9		
Barnardston	78	19	Moorey	George	1		1					1					3		
Belchertown	209	29	More	Noah	1			1		1			1				4		
Springfield	245	40	Morgan	Aaron		1			1			2		1			5		
Brimfield	272	33	Morgan	Aaron Maj		1	2		1	1		1		1			7		
West Springfield	351	22	Morgan	Abner	1	1		2		2			1	1			8		
Brimfield	272	13	Morgan	Abner Esq			2		1	1	1	1					7		
Northfield	29	40	Morgan	Alpheus	2			1		2			2				7		
Leyden	83	19	Morgan	Benjamin	2	2		1		3	1		1				10		
Brimfield	272	17	Morgan	Daniel	1			1		1			1				4		
Springfield	241	12	Morgan	Ebenezer			1		1		1			1			4		
West Springfield	351	23	Morgan	Ebenezer		1			1			1		1			4		
Brimfield	272	26	Morgan	Enoch	1		1		1	2		1	1	1			8		
West Springfield	357	9	Morgan	Erastus	2			1		1	1		1				6		
West Springfield	351	20	Morgan	Ezekiel				1						1			2		
Northampton	9	39	Morgan	Festus			1					1					2		
Northfield	29	24	Morgan	Frederick	1			1		1		1					4		
Colrain	187	6	Morgan	Jabez	3			1		1			1				6		
Brimfield	272	16	Morgan	Jacob	2	1		1		3		1	1				9		
West Springfield	351	31	Morgan	James				1					1				2		
West Springfield	357	2	Morgan	Jesse		1			1			1		1			4		
West Springfield	351	24	Morgan	Joel	1			1		1		1					4		
Wilbraham	235	33	Morgan	John	2			1		1	2		1	1			8		
Brimfield	274	10	Morgan	Jona		1	1		1		1		1	1			6		
West Springfield	357	3	Morgan	Joseph		1	1		1			1	2	1			7		
Brimfield	269	7	Morgan	Joseph		1		1		1				1			4		
Brimfield	269	5	Morgan	Joseph Jr	2	2	5	1		1	1	1					13		
Northampton	9	38	Morgan	Judah			2		1		1		2	1			7		
West Springfield	357	5	Morgan	Julius	1		1	1				1					4		
Brimfield	272	34	Morgan	Justin			1					1					2		
West Springfield	357	10	Morgan	Lucas	1	1	1	1	1	2		2	1				10		
Palmer	259	6	Morgan	Martin			1			1		1					3		
South Hadley	250	5	Morgan	Nathaniel	2		2	1		1				1			7		
Northfield	29	37	Morgan	Noah	2	3	1		1			1		1			9		
Northfield	29	38	Morgan	Noah Junr	1			1		1							3		
Brimfield	272	25	Morgan	Pearly	1			1		2		1					5		
Wilbraham	233	33	Morgan	Philip			1			1	1		1				4		
Northfield	29	39	Morgan	reuben				1			1		1				3		
Springfield	245	10	Morgan	Samuel		1			1		1	1		1			5		
West Springfield	351	27	Morgan	Samuel				1					2				3		
Blanford	177	13	Morgan	Simeon	3	2	1	1		1			1				9		
Belchertown	209	26	Morgan	Titus			1					1					2		
West Springfield	357	4	Morgan	Titus			1	1				1		1			4		
New Salem	101	20	Morgan	Widow								1	1				2		
West Springfield	351	25	Morgan	Willliam			1	1				2	1	1			6		
Colrain	187	7	Morison	David	5	1		1		2	1	1	1		1		13		
West Springfield	354	36	Morley	Asahel	1			1		4			1				7		
West Springfield	354	31	Morley	David	2	2	1	1		4			1				11		
Gill	87	4	Morley	Demick	2	1	1		1	2	1	1	1				10		
West Springfield	354	27	Morley	Gideon		1	1		1			1		1	1		6		
West Springfield	354	33	Morley	Isaac				1					1				2		
West Springfield	354	34	Morley	Isaac Junr	1	1		1		2	1		1				7		
Gill	87	5	Morley	John	1	1		1		1	2		1				7		
Montague	46	38	Morley	Thomas	1	1		1		2	1	1	1				8		
West Springfield	354	28	Morley	Walter	2			1		1			1				5		
Holland	279	28	Morris	Ebenz		1		1		2			1				5		
Wilbraham	238	21	Morris	Edward	1	2	2	1		4			1	1			12		
Wilbraham	237	34	Morris	Isaac	1	1			1	2	1	2	1				9		
Wilbraham	237	35	Morris	Rebecca Wd			1			1	3	2	1				8		
Blanford	182	6	Morrison	Alexander	1	1		1		2	2			1			8		
Warwick	38	31	Morse	Aaron			1		1			1		1			4		
Shutesbury	111	3	Morse	Abel			1			1			1				3		
Leverett	115	33	Morse	Amasa	1			1		2			1				5		
Shutesbury	111	2	Morse	Amasa		1	1		1					1			4		
Belchertown	209	27	Morse	Asa	1			1	1	2		1		1			7		
Hatfield	14	31	Morse	Avander	1		1	1		1		2	1	1			9		

TOWN	PG#	LN#	LAST NAME	FIRST NAME	FREE WHITE MALES under 10	10 to 16	16 to 26	26 to 45	45 and over	FREE WHITE FEMALES under 10	10 to 16	16 to 26	26 to 45	45 and over	TOTAL ALL OTHER	TOTAL SLAVES	TOTALS	DISTRICT/TOWNSHIP	NOTES
Greenfield	74	7	Morse	Calvin			1			1		1					3		
Montgomery	160	16	Morse	Chester	1	1			1	3	2		1				9		
Holland	280	1	Morse	Eben	2	1	1		1	1				1			7		
Worthington	301	2	Morse	Elijah	3	1		1		1		1	1				8		
Westfield	120	27	Morse	Jacob	2	2	2		1	1	1	4	1				14		
Worthington	298	28	Morse	Josiah	2			1		1			1	1			6		
Ware	227	8	Morse	Phillo	1	1	1		1	1	1	1	1	1			9		
Ware	227	14	Morse	Reuben Revd	2			1		1		1					5		
Warwick	38	35	Morse	Samuel	1					1		1		1			4		
Worthington	301	3	Morse	Samuel		1	2	1	1		1			1			7		
Goshen	311	3	Morse	Shepard		1		1		2	1		1				6		
Whately	67	11	Morton	Asa	1	1	1		1	2		1	1	1			9		
Hatfield	12	1	Morton	Benj		1	1			1	1		1				5		
Whately	67		Morton	Consider	2	1		1		2			1	1			8		
Whately	67	9	Morton	Daniel	1			1		2			1				5		
Colrain	187	24	Morton	David	1	1	1		1		1	1		1			7		
Hatfield	11	13	Morton	Ebenezer	1	1		1		1	1	1	1				7		
Hatfield	12	28	Morton	Elihu	1		1		1	1	2	3		1			10		
Hatfield	13	34	Morton	Elijah	3			1		2	1		1				8		
Williamsburg	445	22	Morton	Elisha	2			1		2	1		1				7		
Leverett	115	30	Morton	Enos	2			1					1				4		
Hatfield	14	8	Morton	Gideon	3			2		1			1				7		
Norwich	153	5	Morton	James		1	1		1				1				4		
Amherst	292	31	Morton	John		2		1					1				4		
Blanford	179	1	Morton	John	2		1		1			1		1			6		
Hatfield	14	1	Morton	Jonah	1	1		1		2			1	1	1		8		
Amherst	291	12	Morton	Joseph	1	1	1		1		1			1			6		
Shelburne	322	24	Morton	Joshua	1			1		2		1					5		
Norwich	153	6	Morton	Josiah		1		1		3			1				6		
Deerfield	54	17	Morton	Justin	1	1		1	1	3	1	1	1	1			11		
Whately	67	14	Morton	Levi	4	2			1	1	1	1		1			11		
Hatfield	12	3	Morton	Lois										2			2		
Leyden	83	20	Morton	Michael	1			1		1			1				4		
Whately	67	19	Morton	Oliver			1	3		1		1		1			7		
Hatfield	13	8	Morton	Perez	1	2		1	1	2			1				8		
Whately	67	13	Morton	Samuel		1		1			1	1	1				5		
Hatfield	11	8	Morton	Seth			1		1					1			3		
Whately	67	17	Morton	Simeon		1	1		1	1	1			1			6		
Hatfield	14	11	Morton	Solomon	1			1		2	2		1				7		
Springfield	244	41	Morton	Thomas			1	1	1	1				1			5		
Ware	227	12	Morton	Thomas	3			1		1		1					6		
Hatfield	12	2	Morton	William	2	2		1		4		1	1	1			12		
Greenwich	221	8	Morton	Wm			2		1			1		2			6		
Colrain	187	28	Morton	Zacheus	1		1			1		1					4		
Colrain	187	11	Moseman	Jesse		1		1		2	1		1				6		
Warwick	38	25	Moses	Samuel		1			1	1	1	1		2			7		
Westfield	119	8	Mosley	Azariah	1	1		1			1		2	1			7		
Westfield	120	22	Mosley	Hannah Wd	1		1			2	1	2	2	1			10		
Westfield	120	3	Mosley	Israel			3		1	5			2		1		12		
Westfield	120	10	Mosley	Jeremiah	1	1	1				2	3	1	1	1		11		
Westfield	118	7	Mosley	Noah	2			1		1		1					5		
Westfield	120	6	Mosley	Pliny	1	1	1		1	3		1	1				9		
Westfield	121	27	Mosley	Wm	4	2		1		1	1		1				10		
Granby	253	11	Moss	Amos	1			1				2					4		
Granby	253	12	Moss	Luther			1			1	1		1				4		
Goshen	311	4	Mott	Samuel		1		1		1			1				4		
Monson	267	43	Moulton	Abner	1	1	1		1	1	1		1				7		
Monson	267	40	Moulton	Ariel	1			1		1		1					4		
South Brimfield	276	4	Moulton	Calvin	1	1		1		2		2	1				8		
Monson	267	38	Moulton	Daniel	1	2	1	1		4	2		1	1			13		
New Salem	101	10	Moulton	Daniel		2		1				1	1				5		
New Salem	101	12	Moulton	Daniel Jr	2		1					1					4		
Brimfield	275	20	Moulton	Ebenezer	2	1			1	3		1	1				9	South Brimfield	
South Brimfield	275	18	Moulton	Ebenezer		1		1		2		1					5		
Monson	267	30	Moulton	Freeborn		1		1				3		1			6		
Monson	267	35	Moulton	Freeborn Jr		1				1		1					3		
Monson	267	41	Moulton	Jeremiah	2	1						1					4		
Monson	267	44	Moulton	Jesse	1	1				1		1					4		
Monson	267	39	Moulton	Joseph	3	1		1		1	1	1		1			9		
South Brimfield	277	18	Moulton	Robert	3	1		1		1			1				7		
New Salem	101	11	Moulton	Samuel	2		1					1					4		
Westfield	124	21	Mowat	James			1				1		1				3		
Worthington	297	16	Much	Cyprain		1	1	1		2	1		1				7		
Worthington	297	17	Much	Timothy		1	1	2	1		2	1		1			10		
Westfield	121	17	Mumford	Wm	2		1	1		2			1				7		
Brimfield	275	15	Munger	Amasa		1	1			2	2		1				7	South Brimfield	
Brimfield	275	13	Munger	Cyrus	3	1	1		1	1	1		1				9	South Brimfield	
West Springfield	354	38	Munger	Daniel	1	2	1		2			1	1	1			9		
South Brimfield	275	11	Munger	Darius Esq	1		1			1	1	1	1				7		
Brimfield	275	16	Munger	John			1							1			2	South Brimfield	

TOWN	PG#	LN#	LAST NAME	FIRST NAME	FREE WHITE MALES					FREE WHITE FEMALES					TOTAL ALL OTHER	TOTAL SLAVES	TOTALS	DISTRICT/ TOWNSHIP	NOTES
					under 10	10 to 16	16 to 26	26 to 45	45 and over	under 10	10 to 16	16 to 26	26 to 45	45 and over					
South Brimfield	276	1	Munger	John Deac	1	1	1	1	1			1		2			8		
Ludlow	256	37	Munger	Joseph	1	2	2		1	2		1		1			10		
Monson	267	42	Munger	Joseph		1	1		1	2	1		1				7		
Brimfield	275	12	Munger	Samuel					1			2		1			4	South Brimfield	
Holland	279	41	Munger	Simeon			1			5			1				7		
South Brimfield	277	16	Munger	Solomon	1	1	1		1			2		1			7		
Montgomery	160	33	Munk	Elias					1					1			2		
Monson	266	40	Munn	Benjamin					1			1	1	1			4		
Greenfield	74	8	Munn	Calvin	3	1	5	5		2	1	1	2				20		
Greenfield	74	13	Munn	David	1			1		1			1				4		
Monson	268	17	Munn	Elijah	1			1		1		1					4		
Gill	87	3	Munn	Elisha		2	1		1	3	1			2			10		
Deerfield	54	14	Munn	Francis					1					1			2		
Monson	266	33	Munn	Jason		1	1					1		1			4		
Monson	268	20	Munn	Jeremy Capt	2	1	1		1	2	1	1	1	1			11		
Gill	87	2	Munn	John		3			1	1	1			1			7		
Springfield	242	6	Munn	John	1		1	1		1		1					5		
Monson	266	41	Munn	Marsena	2			1		1		1	1				6		
Gill	87	1	Munn	Noah	1		1	1		2	1			1			8		
Deerfield	54	15	Munn	Phinehas		1		1						1			3		
Monson	268	16	Munn	Reuben Col		1	1					1		1			4		
Springfield	240	40	Munn	Samuel					1					4			5		
Gill	86	34	Munn	Seth	2	2		1		3	1			1			10		
Greenfield	74	16	Munn	Simeon	3	1		1		2			1				8		
Springfield	239	43	Munroe	John	1			1				1					3		
Pelham	215	38	Munsell	Elisha	1			1	1			2	1				6		
Whately	67	15	Munson	Moses	1		1		1			1	1				5		
Whately	67	16	Munson	Moses Jun	4		2	2			1	1	2				12		
Whately	67	18	Munson	Reuben	2		4				2	2	1				11		
Hawley	334	23	Munson	Salmon	1			1		2			1				5		
Westfield	127	27	Munson	Stephen	1	1		1		1			1				5		
Northampton	10	37	Munyon	Jonathn				1	1	2		1					4		
Springfield	244	24	Murphy	Daniel		1		1			1		1				4		
Wilbraham	238	5	Murphy	Daniel	1		1						1				3		
Granville West Soc	168	10	Murphy	Martin	1	1		1		3		2	1				9		
Springfield	243	25	Murphy	Timothy	1		1	2		3	1	1	1				11		
Northampton	4	30	Murray	Hannah		1								1			2		
Granby	255	6	Murry	John				1					1				2		
Colrain	187	34	Muxham	Abigal						1		1	1				3		
Colrain	187	33	Muxham	Zebede	1		1			1			1				4		
South Hadley	251	24	Nash	Asa	1	1	1	1	1	2			1	1			9		
Cummington	305	2	Nash	Daniel	2	1			1	2	1			1			8		
Greenfield	74	22	Nash	Daniel					1	2	1			1			5		
Cummington	305	28	Nash	Daniel Jun			1					1	1				3		
Granby	252	14	Nash	David	2					2			1				5		
Plainfield	307	31	Nash	Ebenezer	1			1	1	2			1	1			7		
Springfield	240	16	Nash	Ebenezer	2			1		1			1				5		
Greenfield	74	32	Nash	Eber		1						1	1				3		
Granby	252	1	Nash	Eleazer	1			1	1			1					4		
South Hadley	250	19	Nash	Elihu				1						1			2		
Conway	60	1	Nash	Elijah	1			1		2		1	1				6		
Hatfield	12	27	Nash	Elijah	2	1		1		5			2				11		
Plainfield	307	32	Nash	Elijah	2	1		1	1	1	1	1	1	1			10		
Williamsburg	444	13	Nash	Elisha		2		1		1	1		1				6		
Hatfield	13	21	Nash	Enos	1			1				1					3		
Amherst	292	8	Nash	Eunie		1				2			1				4		
Cummington	305	3	Nash	Jacob		1		1		1	1			1			5		
Plainfield	307	33	Nash	Jacob	1			1		3	1		2	1			9		
Ludlow	255	3	Nash	Joel				1					1				2		
Hadley	287	25	Nash	John	1		1					1					3		
Williamsburg	444	12	Nash	John	2	2		1		2		1	1				9		
Middlefield	156	4	Nash	Jonathan Revd	3	1		1				1	1				7		
Charlemont	192	33	Nash	Joseph	1		1	1		1		1	1				6		
Whately	67	20	Nash	Joseph	1	2	1		1		1		1				9		
Hadley	288	8	Nash	Josiah		1		1		3	1	1		1			8		
Greenfield	74	30	Nash	Jubal	2	1	2	1		3	2	1	1				13		
Montague	47	5	Nash	Judah Jr	2			1		1	1	1	1		1		8		
Montague	47	4	Nash	Judah Revd				1						1			2		
Shelburne	323	6	Nash	Lydia		1		1				1		1			4		
Amherst	291	24	Nash	Moses	4		1						1				6		
Williamsburg	444	9	Nash	Moses			1			4			1				6		
Plainfield	307	34	Nash	Noah	3			1		1		1	1				7		
Granby	252	2	Nash	Phebe Wd				1						2			3		
Springfield	239	37	Nash	Rebecca Wd	2							1		1			4		
Amherst	292	37	Nash	Reuben	2	1	1		1	2	1	1	1				10		
Heath	196	27	Nash	Revere	1			1		1			1				4		
Williamsburg	444	10	Nash	Samuel	2			1		1		1					5		
Rowe	200	19	Nash	Silvester				1						1			2		
Greenfield	74	21	Nash	Sylvanus		1	2		1	2		1	1	2			10		
Ludlow	257	40	Nash	Sylvester Doctr			1					1					2		

TOWN	PG#	LN#	LAST NAME	FIRST NAME	FREE WHITE MALES under 10	10 to 16	16 to 26	26 to 45	45 and over	FREE WHITE FEMALES under 10	10 to 16	16 to 26	26 to 45	45 and over	TOTAL ALL OTHER	TOTAL SLAVES	TOTALS	DISTRICT/ TOWNSHIP	NOTES
Williamsburg	444	11	Nash	Thomas	2			1					1				4		
Ludlow	255	2	Nash	Timothy	2			1					1	1			5		
Monson	268	1	Needham	Anthony	1			1					1				3		
South Brimfield	275	2	Needham	Catherine Wid	1		1					1		1			4		
Brimfield	275	19	Needham	David Capt	2	2	1		1	3		1	1				11	South Brimfield	
South Brimfield	277	1	Needham	Humphrey	1		2		1		3		1				8		
South Brimfield	276	30	Needham	Jasper				1						1			2		
South Brimfield	276	27	Needham	Jeremiah			1	1	1	1		1					5		
Wendell	106	32	Needham	Joshua	1			1		3	1		1				7		
South Brimfield	277	2	Needham	Stephen	2	1		1			2		1				7		
South Brimfield	276	41	Needham	Wid Hannah		1	2				1			1			5		
Westfield	128	9	Negro	Aeoro											4		4		
Westfield	128	10	Negro	Brister											3		3		
Westfield	123	11	Negro	Flora											5		5		
South Hadley	249	27	Negro	Freeman											6		6		
Holland	279	3	Negro	Mundy											2		2		
South Brimfield	277	41	Nellson	Hezh	1			1		1		1					4		
South Brimfield	277	34	Nellson	Solomon	1	1		1						1			4		
Ludlow	256	1	Nelson	Aaron		3	2	1		1	1			1			9		
Westfield	127	8	Nelson	Aaron	1	1	2		1		1	1		1			8		
Amherst	294	15	Nelson	Benja		2	1		1		1			1			6		
Brimfield	274	32	Nelson	Benjamin	1	1	2	1			2	1		1			9		
Leyden	83	24	Nelson	Edward			1			4		1					6		
South Brimfield	276	13	Nelson	Eli	1			1				1		1			4		
South Brimfield	277	14	Nelson	George	3		1				1		1				6		
Southwick	359	44	Nelson	James Y.	2		1			1	2		1				7		
West Springfield	357	11	Nelson	Lemuel	1		1			3	2	1	1				9		
Southwick	359	43	Nelson	Luther	1		1	1		1		1	1				6		
West Springfield	351	32	Nelson	Ruth						3	2		2	1			8		
South Brimfield	277	40	Nelson	Samuel		1		1			2			1			5		
Buckland	329	6	Nelson	Stephen		1		1		3			1				6		
South Brimfield	275	3	Nelson	Timothy	1			1		3	3		1	1			10		
Colrain	188	2	Nelson	William		2		1		2		1	1				7		
Conway	59	51	Nelson	William	1		1						1				3		
Northfield	30	1	Nettleton	Edward	3			1		1	1		1				7		
Springfield	242	13	Nevers	Hannah Widw			2						1	1			4		
Rowe	200	18	Newall	Daniel	1		1			2			1				5		
Greenwich	221	15	Newcomb	Bradford		1		1		2	1	1	1				7		
Leyden	83	28	Newcomb	Daniel			1				1			1			3		
Greenwich	221	14	Newcomb	David			1	1		1				1			4		
Deerfield	54	29	Newcomb	Ebenezer	1	1	1		1	2	1	1	1				9		
Greenwich	221	12	Newcomb	Elisha	2		1			4		1					8		
Barnardston	78	24	Newcomb	Hezekiah	1	2	2	1			1	3		1			11		
Leyden	83	27	Newcomb	Hezekiah Jun	3		1	1		3			1				9		
Greenwich	221	13	Newcomb	Nehemh	1	2		1		2		1	1				8		
Greenfield	74	29	Newcomb	Richard C.	2	1		1		1		1	2				8		
Barnardston	78	22	Newcomb	William	1		1						1				3		
Barnardston	78	25	Newcomb	William	4	2	2		1		1			1			11		
Shelburne	323	1	Newcomb	Willm	1			1		2			2				6		
Monson	265	39	Newell	Abijah				1			1		1				3		
Monson	265	40	Newell	Abijah Jr	1	1		1		4			1				8		
Wilbraham	237	15	Newell	Asa	3			1		1			1				6		
Wilbraham	235	16	Newell	Daniel	1	1		1		1			1				5		
Leyden	83	29	Newell	Jesse		1		1		4	1		1				8		
Springfield	247	41	Newell	John				1						1			2		
Worthington	298	16	Newell	John		1				1		1					3		
New Salem	101	21	Newell	Phebe	1					2			1				4		
Colrain	187	37	Newell	Solomon	2	1		1	1	2	1		1				9		
Monson	265	15	Newell	Stephen	2					2	2	1	1				8		
Conway	59	52	Newhall	Daniel		2		1		1		1					5		
Conway	59	53	Newhall	Daniel Jur		2		1		3		1	1				8		
Pelham	217	21	Newhall	David	1			1					1				3		
Conway	59	54	Newhall	Jabez		1	2		1		1	2		1			8		
Pelham	216	4	Newhall	Levi			1	1				1					3		
Belchertown	206	17	Newhall	Nathan	1		1		1	1		1		1			6		
Conway	59	55	Newhall	Samuel		1	3	1	1			2	1				9		
Belchertown	208	29	Newhall	Theodore		1		1		1	1		1				5		
Colrain	188	1	Newhouse	William	1			1					1				3		
Williamsburg	444	8	Newport	Peter											5		5		
Ashfield	343	5	Newton	Asa	2	2		1		2			1	1			9		
Leyden	83	26	Newton	Asahel		1	2		1		2	1	2				9		
Greenfield	74	28	Newton	Asher	2	2		1		2		1	2	1			11		
Colrain	187	36	Newton	Cyprian	2			1		3			1				7		
Russell	138	30	Newton	Elias		1		1			1						3		
Hadley	287	29	Newton	Elizabeth	1		2			1		1		1			6		
Ashfield	343	6	Newton	George			1			1			1				3		
Greenfield	74	27	Newton	Isaac	1		1			1		1		1			5		
Deerfield	54	23	Newton	Jeremiah		1	1			1			1				4		
Russell	139	21	Newton	Jesse		1	2		1	2		1		1			8		
Greenfield	74	25	Newton	John			1	1						1			3		

TOWN	PG#	LN#	LAST NAME	FIRST NAME	FREE WHITE MALES under 10	10 to 16	16 to 26	26 to 45	45 and over	FREE WHITE FEMALES under 10	10 to 16	16 to 26	26 to 45	45 and over	TOTAL ALL OTHER	TOTAL SLAVES	TOTALS	DISTRICT/ TOWNSHIP	NOTES
Middlefield	156	12	Newton	John	3	2		1		1			1				8		
Shutesbury	111	7	Newton	John	1			1		3			1				6		
Greenfield	74	24	Newton	John Junr	2		5		1	2	2		1				13		
Wilbraham	232	30	Newton	Jotham	1		1	1		2			1				6		
Deerfield	54	24	Newton	Levi			1	1	1			1		1			5		
Montague	47	6	Newton	Moses				1					1				2		
Springfield	244	15	Newton	Oliver					1					1			2		
Springfield	244	16	Newton	Oliver Jr	1		1			1		1					4		
Greenfield	74	18	Newton	Ozias			1			1		1					3		
Leverett	115	34	Newton	Paul		1	1		1	1	2	1	1				8		
Greenfield	74	17	Newton	Roger		2		1				1	1	1			6		
Westfield	126	32	Newton	Roswel	3	1			1		1	1		1			8		
Greenfield	74	26	Newton	Samuel	2	1		1		1	1		1				7		
Monson	266	35	Newton	Stephen	5			1			1		1				8		
New Salem	101	22	Newton	Sylvanus			1			3			1				5		
Shutesbury	111	6	Ney	Jonathan		1	1		1	1	1	1	1				7		
Blanford	177	26	Nice	George	2	2			1	2			1				8		
Charlemont	192	36	Nichels	Asa	4			1					1				6		
Charlemont	192	35	Nichels	James	1			1		2			1				5		
Charlemont	192	34	Nichels	Thomas		1	3		1		1			1			7		
Charlemont	192	32	Nichels	Thomas Jur	2			1			1		1				5		
Brimfield	271	29	Nichols	Abner				1					1				2		
Buckland	329	5	Nichols	Asa			1			1		1	1				4		
Brimfield	270	36	Nichols	Asher		2		1		1			1				5		
Brimfield	270	18	Nichols	Daniel	5			1		1			1				8		
Belchertown	209	31	Nichols	Elijah		1	1			3			1				6		
Brimfield	270	28	Nichols	Jabez Capt		1	2		1	1	1	3		1			10		
Brimfield	270	38	Nichols	John	1	2			1	3	1			1			9		
Buckland	329	8	Nichols	Joseph	2		1			1			1				5		
Chesterfield	23	12	Nichols	Joseph		1		1						2			4		
Northampton	10	34	Nichols	Joshua	1			1		4	2		1				9		
Brimfield	270	19	Nichols	Lois Wido			1					1		1			3		
South Brimfield	276	5	Nichols	Malachi	1	1	1		1	3	1	1	1				10		
Barnardston	78	23	Nichols	Nathan	2			1		1	1		1				6		
Buckland	329	7	Nichols	Saml			1			1		1					3		
Brimfield	271	28	Nichols	Samuel Capt		1	1		1			1		2			6		
Brimfield	270	17	Nichols	Stephen				1			1			1			3		
Brimfield	271	27	Nichols	Zadok	1	1	2		1	1	1	1		1			9		
Barnardston	78	21	Nickerson	Covel				1					1				2		
Greenfield	74	19	Nickerson	David	2		1	1		1	1		1				7		
Barnardston	78	20	Nickerson	Edward	2	2		1		1			1				7		
Greenfield	74	20	Nickerson	Enoch	2			1		3			1				7		
Barnardston	78	26	Nightingale	Ebenezer	1		1		1		1	1		1			6		
Worthington	298	35	Niles	Ebenezer		1	1		1	1		1		1			6		
Worthington	301	11	Niles	Peter			1					1					2		
Worthington	297	4	Niles	Stephen	1	1		1		3			1				7		
Blanford	180	4	Nimmocks	Mary	1			1					2	1			5		
Westfield	122	16	Nimox	Noble			1			2		1					4		
Westfield	122	10	Nimox	Richard	2			1		1	1	2		1			8		
Conway	59	56	Nims	Amasa		1	1			1			1				4		
Deerfield	54	28	Nims	Ariel	1	2	1			1		2		1			9		
Shelburne	323	7	Nims	Asa	1	1	1	1	1	1	2		1	1			10		
Heath	197	2	Nims	Calvin	1			1		1		1					4		
Shelburne	323	3	Nims	Daniel				1						1			2		
Shelburne	323	4	Nims	Daniel Jr	1			1		3			1				6		
Rowe	200	15	Nims	Ebenezar		1			1	1	1		1				5		
Shelburne	323	2	Nims	Elijah			1					1					2		
Deerfield	54	26	Nims	Elisha		1	1		1	2	1		1				7		
Conway	60	3	Nims	Grace	4	1	1		1	2		2		1			12		
Greenfield	74	23	Nims	Hull	3		2	1		3	1	1	1	1			13		
Buckland	329	4	Nims	John	3		1		1	2	2	4	1				14		
Heath	197	1	Nims	Jonathan	2	1		1		1	1		1				7		
Deerfield	54	27	Nims	Moses				1		1	1		1				4		
Conway	59	57	Nims	Polly	2					1			1				4		
Shelburne	323	5	Nims	Reuben	1		2		1	2	1	1	1				9		
Rowe	200	16	Nims	Samuel		1						1					2		
Deerfield	54	25	Nims	Seth	2	4	5	1		1	2	1	1	1			18		
Buckland	329	2	Nitt	Adam M.	1	2		1		1	1		1				7		
Southwick	359	41	Noble	Amos		1		1				1	1				4		
Westfield	118	15	Noble	Asa	1	1			1	1	1			1			6		
Westfield	123	7	Noble	Bartholomew	1			1		1		1	1	1			6		
Westfield	119	7	Noble	Benjamin		1		1		1			1				4		
Westfield	122	12	Noble	Calvin	1	1		1		1	1		1				6		
Westfield	124	12	Noble	Daniel		1			1			2		1			5		
Westfield	127	6	Noble	Eager	1			1		1	2	2	1				8		
Westfield	124	13	Noble	Harris		1							1				2		
Westfield	122	22	Noble	Heman	1		1			1		1					4		
Westfield	119	6	Noble	Jacob	2		1		1	1			1				6		
Westfield	118	19	Noble	Jared	2		1	1		1	1			1			7		
Blanford	181	30	Noble	John	1	1			1					1			4		

TOWN	PG#	LN#	LAST NAME	FIRST NAME	FREE WHITE MALES under 10	10 to 16	16 to 26	26 to 45	45 and over	FREE WHITE FEMALES under 10	10 to 16	16 to 26	26 to 45	45 and over	TOTAL ALL OTHER	TOTAL SLAVES	TOTALS	DISTRICT/ TOWNSHIP	NOTES
Westfield	127	17	Noble	Mark	1		1	1	1	2			1	1			8		
Westfield	118	18	Noble	Mathew			2		1		1		1				5		
Westfield	121	9	Noble	Noah			1					1					2		
Southwick	359	46	Noble	Reuben	1			1		2			1				5		
Westfield	122	31	Noble	Saml	3	3		1		1	3		1	1			13		
Westfield	124	2	Noble	Seth Mr	1			1		2	1		1				6		
Russell	139	13	Noble	Silas	3	1		1		2	1		1				9		
Blanford	180	6	Noble	Solomon	3	1				1			1				6		
Southwick	359	38	Noble	Tehan		1		2					1				4		
Westfield	122	8	Noble	Thomas				1					2	2			5		
Southwick	359	42	Noble	Timothy		1		1	1	1	1	1	1				7		
Chester	145	38	Noble	Warham		1					1						2		
Westfield	119	5	Noble	Wm	1		1						1				3		
Blanford	182	11	Nobles	Elihu			1	4	1			1	1				8		
Rowe	200	17	Nolton	Nathan	3	1		1		1			1	1			8		
Chester	143	18	Noney	James	1	2	3		1	2	1	2		2			14		
Monson	262	11	Norcross	Joel	1		1					1		1			4		
Monson	263	40	Norcross	William	1	1	4		1	1	1	2	3				14		
Middlefield	158	27	Norcutt	Silvenus			3		1	1		2		1			8		
West Springfield	354	43	Norman	John	2	1	1	1		1	1	1	1				9		
Conway	60	2	Northam	David	4			1			1	2	1				9		
Cummington	305	4	Norton	Bela	1			1		2			1				5		
Southwick	359	40	Norton	Eldad	3	1		1					1				6		
Westhampton	15	6	Norton	Elijah		1		1					1				3		
Westhampton	15	10	Norton	Elijah Junr	3			1			1	1					6		
Williamsburg	444	14	Norton	Freeman		1	3		1	1	1	2		1			10		
Southwick	359	45	Norton	Hannah									2				2		
Westhampton	15	7	Norton	Joseph			1			1	1	1					4		
Williamsburg	444	15	Norton	Phebe			1						2	1			4		
West Springfield	354	41	Norton	Philo	1			1		2			1				5		
Southwick	359	39	Norton	Robert	1		1		1	1	1	1		1			7		
Ashfield	343	4	Norton	Selah	3		1		1	2	3			1			11		
Northfield	30	2	Norton	Selah	2		1	1		4		1	1	1			11		
Cummington	305	5	Noyce	Cyrus			1			1		1	1				4		
Plainfield	307	30	Noyce	Jonathan	2			1		2			1				6		
Leyden	83	25	Noyes	Oliver	3	2	1	1		1			1				9		
West Springfield	354	42	Nuell	Ebenezer	2	1		1		1			1				6		
Leverett	115	35	Nurse	Reuben		1		1		1		1	1				5		
Warwick	39	1	Nurse	William	2	1		1		1	2	2	1				10		
South Brimfield	277	31	Nutting	David	2		2		2	1	1	1	1	2			12		
South Brimfield	277	32	Nutting	Eben	1		1						1				3		
Brimfield	270	9	Nutting	James		1	1		1		2	2		1			8		
Brimfield	270	8	Nutting	Jonathan		1	2		1			1		1			6		
Greenfield	74	31	Nutting	Joseph	4	1		1		1			1	1			9		
New Salem	101	23	Nye	Nathaniel				1					1				2		
Ware	227	21	Nye	Samuel	3					1					1		5		
New Salem	101	27	Oakes	Elijah	2			1				1					4		
New Salem	101	25	Oakes	John	2			1		1		1					5		
New Salem	101	26	Oakes	Stephen	1			1		1			1	1			5		
Cummington	305	36	Odell	Ichabod Negro											5		5		
Belchertown	211	17	Olds	David		1							1	1			3		
Palmer	259	17	Olds	Enoch	3			1		1			1				6		
Granby	253	44	Olds	Jesse	1		1			4		2					8		
Southwick	359	51	Olds	Justice			1					1					2		
Belchertown	209	35	Olds	Justin		1	1		1	2	1	1		1			8		
Cummington	304	36	Olds	Levi	1	3	2		1		1	1	1				10		
Southwick	359	53	Olds	Levi			2			1		1					4		
Southwick	359	52	Olds	Moses	2			1		3	2	1					9		
Goshen	311	11	Olds	Samuel	2	1		1		1		3		1			9		
Ludlow	256	21	Olds	Samuel	2			1		1	1	1		1			7		
Southwick	359	50	Olds	Samuel	3	1	1	1		2		3		1			12		
Pelham	216	7	Oliver	Andrew Revd	2			1		3	3	1					10		
Pelham	216	8	Oliver	George	1			1		2	1	1					6		
Conway	60	4	Oliver	Peggy									1				1		
Leyden	83	30	Olmstead	Jonathan		1	2	1	1			1	1				7		
West Springfield	354	44	Onkamer	Chloe											2		2		
Goshen	311	8	Orcott	Anigen	1	1		1	1			2	1				8		
Plainfield	308	8	Orcott	David	1		1			1		1					4		
Goshen	311	10	Orcott	James	3			1		1		1					6		
Cummington	305	6	Orcott	Nathan	1	2		1		1	2		1	1			9		
Goshen	311	9	Orcott	Thomas				1		1		1					3		
New Salem	101	29	Orcutt	Bels	1	1	1		1			2	1				7		
Wendell	107	3	Orcutt	John				1					1				2		
West Springfield	351	33	Orcutt	Joseph		1		1		2		1					5		
New Salem	101	24	Orcutt	Josiah		1		1					1				3		
New Salem	101	28	Orcutt	Samuel		1	1			3			1				6		
Whately	67	21	Orcutt	Stephen	2		2					1	1				6		
Warwick	39	2	Ormsbury	John			1		1	1	1	1		1			6		
Norwich	152	33	Ormsbury	Nathan	1			1			1		1				4		
Pelham	216	6	Ormston	Robt			1										1		

TOWN	PG#	LN#	LAST NAME	FIRST NAME	FREE WHITE MALES					FREE WHITE FEMALES					TOTAL ALL OTHER	TOTAL SLAVES	TOTALS	DISTRICT/ TOWNSHIP	NOTES
					under 10	10 to 16	16 to 26	26 to 45	45 and over	under 10	10 to 16	16 to 26	26 to 45	45 and over					
West Springfield	357	13	Ornes	Michael	2		1		1		1	2		1			8		
Goshen	311	12	Orr	James	1	1			1		2			1			6		
Springfield	243	29	Orr	Robert			1		1					1			3		
Springfield	242	29	Orr	Robert B.	1		1	1		1		2					6		
Leyden	83	31	Orvis	William		1			1	4	2		1				9		
Blanford	176	33	Osborn	Alexander	1	1		1					1				4		
Blanford	176	38	Osborn	David	2			1					1				4		
Blanford	179	26	Osborn	John	2			1		1			1				5		
Ware	227	22	Osborn	John			1	1		1	1		1	1			6		
Blanford	175	24	Osborn	Jonathan			1			3			1				5		
Blanford	180	1	Osborn	Luke			2		1			1		1			5		
Granville East Soc	533	2	Osborn	Luke		1				1		1					3		
Greenwich	221	17	Osborn	Zebudee	1	2			1	1	4			1			10		
Monson	266	18	Osburn	Daniel	1				1	1		1	1				5		
Hadley	285	23	Osburn	Richard	3		1	1		1	1	1					8		
Colrain	188	6	Osburn	William	1	1			1		1			1			5		
Wendell	107	1	Osgood	David	1			1		1	1	1					5		
Wendell	106	36	Osgood	Elihu	1	1	1	2			1		2				8		
Wendell	107	2	Osgood	John		1				1		1					3		
Wendell	106	33	Osgood	Jonathan		1		1	1			2		1			6		
Montague	47	7	Osgood	Joseph	1			1		1			1				4		
Wendell	106	34	Osgood	Josiah				1		1	1		1				4		
Wendell	106	38	Osgood	Josiah Junr	1	1		1		3			1				7		
Wendell	106	35	Osgood	Luke		2	1		1	1	1		1				7		
Montague	47	8	Osgood	Samuel	2			1		1			1				5		
Wendell	106	37	Osgood	Samuel	1	1		1		1			2				6		
Colrain	188	4	Otis	Christopher	1			1					1				3		
Westfield	125	34	Otis	Jabez	1			1		2		1					5		
Westfield	125	29	Otis	James	3	1	1		1		1	1		1			9		
Colrain	188	3	Otis	John	3			1	1		2		1	1			9		
Chester	149	30	Otis	Samuel	1			1		1		1					4		
Cummington	305	7	Ottis	William	1		1	1		2	1		1				7		
Westfield	124	16	Owen	Abijah	2	1	1		1	3	2		1	1			12		
Westfield	124	17	Owen	Asahel	2	1	1		1	1	1	1	1				9		
Westfield	124	18	Owen	Carnie	2	1	1	1		3		1	1				10		
Colrain	188	5	Owen	Elisha		1	1			4	2		1				9		
Southwick	359	47	Owen	Samuel				1					1				2		
Southwick	359	48	Owen	Samuel Junr			1			2			1				4		
Belchertown	209	34	Owens	Eliazr	4	2		1			1		1				9		
Cummington	305	8	Packard	Abel Jun	1	1	1		1	1	1	1	1				8		
Belchertown	206	22	Packard	Abram	1	2	1		1	1				2			8		
Cummington	305	9	Packard	Adam	2	1		1	1	2			3	1			11		
Plainfield	307	38	Packard	Barna	1			1		3	1		1				7		
Cummington	305	10	Packard	Barnabus		1	1		1			1		1			5		
Ashfield	343	21	Packard	Caleb	3	1		1		1	2	1	1				10		
Pelham	216	14	Packard	Eliab		1		1					1				3		
Pelham	216	15	Packard	Eliab Jr			1			2			1				4		
Conway	60	12	Packard	Elizabeth						3	1	1	1				6		
Springfield	240	20	Packard	Ephraim	3			1		1		1					6		
Hawley	334	28	Packard	Ichabod	3	2		1		1			1	1			9		
Pelham	216	12	Packard	Jacob	1		1	1		2	1		1	1			10		
Warwick	39	13	Packard	Jacob	2	1			1		1			1			6		
Chesterfield	22	15	Packard	Jared	1		1			2		1					5		
Plainfield	307	35	Packard	John		1			1	1	1		1				5		
Pelham	216	13	Packard	Jona	5			2		2		1	2				12		
Goshen	311	18	Packard	Joshua Jun	1		1	1		2			1	1			7		
Easthampton	136	2	Packard	Luke			1			1		1					3		
Plainfield	307	39	Packard	Luther	2	1				1	1		1				6		
Shelburne	323	8	Packard	Neo. Theophilus		1	1				1	1					4		
Plainfield	307	37	Packard	Noah	2	1			2	1	3	1		2			12		
Plainfield	307	40	Packard	Perez	1			1		1			1	1			6		
Plainfield	307	36	Packard	Phillip		1		1		1			1				4		
Pelham	216	16	Packard	Salmon	2			1					1				4		
Sunderland	282	2	Packard	Samuel		1		1					1				3		
Belchertown	206	26	Packard	Solomon			1										1		
New Salem	102	25	Packard	Timothy		1	1		2	1	1	1		2			9		
Plainfield	307	41	Packard	Timothy	2	1		1		2			1				7		
Holland	279	8	Paddock	James				1					1				2		
Holland	279	7	Paddock	John	1	1		1		1	1		1				6		
New Salem	102	9	Page	Isaac	2			1		2			1				6		
New Salem	102	10	Page	John	1		1	1					1				4		
Northfield	30	3	Page	Lewis	3		3	1		2		1	2				12		
New Salem	102	8	Page	Samuel	3	1	1	1	1	2	1		1				11		
Conway	60	8	Page	Theophilus		2	3		1	1				1			8		
Northfield	30	4	Page	Thomas				1					1				2		
New Salem	101	32	Page	Timothy		1	2						1	1			7		
New Salem	102	7	Page	William				1				1	1				3		
Ware	227	23	Page	Wm Deacn	1		2	1	1	2	2	1					10		
Rowe	200	23	Paine	Asa	1		1						1				3		
Deerfield	54	31	Paine	Charles											7		7		

Town	PG#	LN#	Last Name	First Name	FWM <10	FWM 10-16	FWM 16-26	FWM 26-45	FWM 45+	FWF <10	FWF 10-16	FWF 16-26	FWF 26-45	FWF 45+	Total All Other	Total Slaves	Totals	District/Township	Notes
Ludlow	256	24	Paine	David		2		1					1				4		
Williamsburg	444	21	Paine	Ebenezer	3	2		1		2			1				9		
Ashfield	344	6	Paine	Elijah	2		1	1		1	1		1				7		
Williamsburg	444	17	Paine	Elijah				1			1		1				3		
Williamsburg	444	18	Paine	John			1			1		1					3		
Ashfield	344	10	Paine	Joseph Junr	2		1			2		1					6		
Ashfield	344	7	Paine	Joseph R.				1			1		1				3		
Greenwich	221	29	Paine	Paul			1			3	1	1					6		
Williamsburg	444	19	Paine	Seth			1			2		1					4		
West Springfield	351	38	Palmer	Edmund	3	3	1			2		1					10		
West Springfield	354	54	Palmer	Frederick	1		1					1					3		
Westfield	120	28	Palmer	Gad			1			1	2	1	1				6		
Russell	137	1	Palmer	Isaac	1	2	1	1	1	2	1	1	1				11		
Southwick	359	57	Palmer	Levi	4		1					1	1				7		
West Springfield	354	50	Palmer	Samuel	3		1			1	1	1					7		
Southwick	359	56	Palmer	William	1	1	1			3		1					8		
Worthington	301	41	Parish	Cyprain	1	1		1		2	1	1					8		
Worthington	301	4	Parish	Ephm	1	1	1		1	4		2	1				11		
Worthington	300	25	Parish	John		1		1					1				3		
Worthington	300	8	Parish	Oliver	4	3		1		2		1					11		
Pelham	216	11	Park	Stewart J		1	1			1	1	1					5		
Sunderland	283	30	Parker	Asa	2			1		1	2		1				8		
Whately	67	22	Parker	Benjamin	1	1	1	1		3	2	1					10		
Amherst	291	18	Parker	Eli	2		1		1	2	2		1	1			10		
Worthington	300	12	Parker	Eli	2		1		1	1		1	1	1			8		
Amherst	291	19	Parker	Eli Junr	2			1		2	2	1	1				9		
Southwick	359	55	Parker	Eliha	2			1	1			1					7		
Ashfield	343	22	Parker	Elisha		2	1		1	1			1				6		
Springfield	243	17	Parker	Enos			1	1		2		1	1				8		
Cummington	305	13	Parker	Ezra		1	1	1		3		1		1			8		
West Springfield	354	47	Parker	Jacob				1					1				2		
Brimfield	273	44	Parker	James	1			1		3		1					6		
Charlemont	193	1	Parker	James		1		1		2		1					5		
Williamsburg	443	4	Parker	Josiah	1	1			1	1	1	1	1				7		
Brimfield	274	23	Parker	Nathaniel	5	1	1	1				1	1				10		
Hawley	334	32	Parker	Nathl	1	1	1		1			2		1			7		
Springfield	243	18	Parker	Russell	1			1		1		1					4		
Charlemont	193	2	Parker	Samuel		1	4		1		1		1				8		
Ashfield	344	15	Parker	Sylvanus	2			1		2		1					6		
Hawley	334	27	Parker	Willm	1			1	1	1		1		1			6		
Palmer	259	44	Parkhurst	Wm	1			1		4	1	1					8		
Montgomery	160	22	Parks	Aaron Lieut	2	1	1	1	1		1	1		1			10		
Westfield	128	8	Parks	Amos	1	1	1		1		1			1			6		
Russell	138	19	Parks	Elias	1			1			1	1					4		
Russell	137	8	Parks	Henry		1	1	1		1	1		1	1			8		
Barnardston	78	31	Parks	Jonathan	2		1	1		2		1					7		
Norwich	153	28	Parks	Joseph	1	1		1				3	1				7		
Norwich	153	31	Parks	Joseph Junr			1			3		1					5		
Norwich	153	26	Parks	Levi		1	1				2						4		
Norwich	153	32	Parks	Miner			1			1		1					3		
Russell	137	9	Parks	Nathan	3					3	1	1					8		
Southampton	131	4	Parks	Phiny	2		1			1		1					5		
Barnardston	78	32	Parks	Reuben		1	2		1		1			1			6		
Russell	138	7	Parks	Reuben	2	3	1			2	3	1	1	1			14		
Blanford	179	9	Parks	Roger	1	3		1				1	1	1			8		
Westfield	123	9	Parks	Roland	1	1		1		1		1					5		
Wendell	107	10	Parks	Samuel	2		1					1					4		
Norwich	153	29	Parks	Uriah	4		1			1		1	1				8		
Westfield	121	26	Parks	Warham Esq	3	1	3		2	2	3	1	2		1		18		
Gill	87	11	Parmenter	Asahel				1		2			2				5		
Chester	147	36	Parmenter	Deacn John N.		2	1	1			2			1			7		
Barnardston	78	28	Parmenter	Elias	1	1	1		1	1	2	3		1			11		
Barnardston	78	30	Parmenter	Jason				1			1	1					3		
Gill	87	9	Parmenter	Josiah		1		1		4	1		1				8		
Leyden	84	2	Parmenter	Reuben	2	2	1			2	1	1					9		
Pelham	217	9	Parmore	Martin	1		1					1					3		
Granville Mid Soc.	165	12	Parons	Abner		1		1	1				2	1			6		
Granville Mid Soc.	165	13	Parons	Abner Junr	2			1		2		1					6		
Hawley	334	33	Parsavil	Oren		1				1		1					3		
Hawley	334	30	Parsivil	James				1		1		1					3		
Belchertown	208	8	Parson	Eldad	2	2		1	1	2	1	2					11		
Greenfield	74	33	Parsons	Amos	1	1		1		1	1	1					7		
Northampton	9	20	Parsons	Asahel			2	1	1		1	2		2			9		
Charlemont	193	5	Parsons	Azariah				1		2			1				4		
Worthington	302	2	Parsons	Azariah	1	1	1			2	1	1					8		
Westhampton	17	23	Parsons	Bela		1							1				3		
Chesterfield	20	22	Parsons	Benja		1		1			1		1				4		
Northampton	7	24	Parsons	Beulah								1		2			3		
Longmeadow	95	24	Parsons	Daniel				1			2		1				4		
Granville Mid Soc.	167	16	Parsons	David	1			1	1	3			1	1			8		

TOWN	PG#	LN#	LAST NAME	FIRST NAME	FREE WHITE MALES under 10	10 to 16	16 to 26	26 to 45	45 and over	FREE WHITE FEMALES under 10	10 to 16	16 to 26	26 to 45	45 and over	TOTAL ALL OTHER	TOTAL SLAVES	TOTALS	DISTRICT/ TOWNSHIP	NOTES
Westhampton	18	16	Parsons	David	2		1		1	1	1			1			7		
Amherst	296	5	Parsons	David Revd	2	2			1	3	2	1	1	1			13		
Goshen	311	14	Parsons	Eben			3	1			1	1	1				7		
South Hadley	248	7	Parsons	Ebenezer		1			1		2	2		1			7		
Chesterfield	24	25	Parsons	Elias	3	1	1	1				2	1				9		
Goshen	311	20	Parsons	Elisha		1			1	1	1		1				5		
Northampton	5	27	Parsons	Elisha			1	1			2		1				5		
Amherst	296	4	Parsons	Gideon	3	1		1		2	1		1				9		
Chester	147	19	Parsons	Gideon		1		1		1	1	1			1		6		
Northampton	2	16	Parsons	Hannah	1					1		1	1				4		
Southampton	129	12	Parsons	Isaac	1		2		1	1	1	2		2			10		
Granville East Soc	527	1	Parsons	Israel	1	1		1		2	1		1				7		
Hatfield	12	15	Parsons	Israel	3		1	1		2	1		1				9		
Westhampton	18	1	Parsons	Israel	1	1		1			3		1				7		
Springfield	242	37	Parsons	Jacklan				1		1			1				3		
Easthampton	135	24	Parsons	Joel		1		1	1		1		1				5		
Easthampton	135	1	Parsons	Joel Junr		1	1			2		2					6		
Northampton	9	21	Parsons	Jonathan		1		1		1		1					4		
West Springfield	351	36	Parsons	Jonathan	2			1	1	1	1	1		1			8		
Northampton	2	7	Parsons	Joseph				2					2				4		
Northampton	2	9	Parsons	Joseph Junr	1			1			2		1				5		
Palmer	260	40	Parsons	Joshua	1		2		1		1	1	1				7		
Northampton	7	16	Parsons	Josiah	1	2	1	1		3	1		1	1			11		
Westhampton	16	19	Parsons	Justin	1		1	1		2	1		1				7		
Goshen	311	15	Parsons	Justus	4		1	1		1	1		1				9		
Springfield	243	19	Parsons	Lemuel	1	2			1	2			1				7		
West Springfield	357	16	Parsons	Luke	2	1		1		4			1	1			10		
Westhampton	17	17	Parsons	Medad	1			1			2		1				5		
Granville Mid Soc.	167	45	Parsons	Moses		1		1			1	1	1				5		
Northampton	5	19	Parsons	Moses				1					1				2		
Northampton	5	39	Parsons	Moses Jr	1			3		2			1				7		
Granville Mid Soc.	167	19	Parsons	Nathaniel		1		1					1				3		
Northampton	7	7	Parsons	Nathaniel			2	1			2		1				6		
Charlemont	193	6	Parsons	Noah	1			1			1						3		
Northampton	2	15	Parsons	Noah		1	1		1		1		3				7		
Westhampton	18	10	Parsons	Noah	1	3	1	1		2			1				9		
Granby	253	27	Parsons	Oliver	3		2	1		1			1				8		
Northampton	2	8	Parsons	Oliver	3	1		1		2			1				8		
Wilbraham	238	29	Parsons	Oliver	1			1		1		1					4		
Granville West Soc	169	39	Parsons	Philip	1	1		1		3	2		1				9		
Northampton	8	18	Parsons	Phinehas	1	1	1		1		1	1		2			8		
Granville Mid Soc.	167	21	Parsons	Samuel	1	1		1		3		1	1				8		
Northampton	4	29	Parsons	Samuel			1	1			1						3		
Granville Mid Soc.	167	20	Parsons	Sarah			1				1	1	1				4		
Springfield	239	17	Parsons	Sarah Wd			1			1	1	1		1			5		
Granville Mid Soc.	165	25	Parsons	Seth	1	1	2	1			1	1	1				8		
Northampton	5	18	Parsons	Seth	3	1	1	1		1			1				8		
Goshen	311	16	Parsons	Silas	2	2		1		3			2	1			11		
Northampton	6	29	Parsons	Simeon		1		1				2	2				6		
Northampton	6	30	Parsons	Simeon Jun	1	1		1		2	1		1				7		
Goshen	311	17	Parsons	Solomon	1		1	1		2	1		1				7		
Wilbraham	238	27	Parsons	Stephen				1					1				2		
Wilbraham	238	28	Parsons	Stephen Jr	3	1		1					1				6		
Worthington	299	25	Parsons	Sylvanus	3			1		1	4		1				10		
Chester	147	20	Parsons	Thadeus			1			1		1					3		
Easthampton	135	27	Parsons	Thadeus			1	1			1						3		
Northampton	2	11	Parsons	Timothy		1		1			1		1		1		4		
Northampton	7	6	Parsons	Warham		2		1	1	2			1				8		
Springfield	239	7	Parsons	Zenas				1			1			1	1		4		
Hatfield	12	10	Partridge	Cotton	1	1	1	1		2		1	1		1		9		
Wilbraham	236	4	Partridge	Deuty	3	1		1		2		1	1				9		
Brimfield	272	29	Partridge	Frederick			1			2		1					4		
Goshen	311	21	Partridge	Isaac	1			1		2		1					5		
Holland	278	15	Partridge	Isaac		1		1		4	1						7		
Brimfield	273	32	Partridge	Joseph	2		1	1		1			1				6		
Hatfield	12	11	Partridge	Samuel		1	1		1	1		1		1	1		7		
Hatfield	12	22	Partridge	Samuel 2d		1	1		1	2	1			2			8		
Worthington	301	47	Patch	Barzilla	3	1		1		2			1				8		
Chesterfield	21	23	Patch	Ephraim				1			2		1				4		
Chesterfield	21	22	Patch	Thomas	3			1		3		1					8		
South Hadley	251	21	Patrick	Agnes Wd		1					2		1				4		
Ware	227	30	Patrick	Isaac	1			1		1		1					4		
Ashfield	343	18	Patrick	John	1					2		1					4		
Granby	252	27	Patrick	John	1			1				1					3		
Brimfield	270	7	Patrick	Reuben Capt	1	1	1	2		3	1	1	1				11		
Ashfield	343	19	Patrick	Silas	1	2	1	2		1			1	1			9		
Ware	227	25	Patrick	Thomas	3	1	1		1	3		1					10		
Ware	227	24	Patrick	Wm		1	1		1	1			1				5		
Worthington	301	19	Patridge	Ebenezer	2			1			1						4		
Worthington	301	17	Patridge	John		1			1		1		1				4		

277

TOWN	PG#	LN#	LAST NAME	FIRST NAME	FREE WHITE MALES					FREE WHITE FEMALES					TOTAL ALL OTHER	TOTAL SLAVES	TOTALS	DISTRICT/ TOWNSHIP	NOTES
					under 10	10 to 16	16 to 26	26 to 45	45 and over	under 10	10 to 16	16 to 26	26 to 45	45 and over					
Worthington	301	18	Patridge	John Jun			1						1				2		
Greenwich	221	30	Patten	Daniel	1	1		1		1		1					5		
Pelham	216	10	Pattern	Christopher	1			1		2	2		1	1			8		
Greenwich	221	25	Patterson	David	1		2				1		1				6		
Greenwich	221	27	Patterson	Robt			1	1			1		1				4		
Northfield	30	14	Patterson	Theron			1				1						2		
Greenwich	221	26	Patterson	William		1		1		1			1				4		
Colrain	188	19	Pattison	Adam	1	2		1	1	2	1	3	1	1			13		
Heath	196	19	Pattison	Jonathan	1		1	1		2			1				6		
Colrain	188	9	Pattison	Josiah	1		1			5			1	1			9		
Colrain	188	7	Pattison	Sarah		1				2			1	1			5		
Wendell	107	12	Paul	James			1			3			1				5		
Springfield	241	19	Paulk	John		1						1		1			4		
Springfield	247	34	Paulk	Samuel	1			1		1		1		2			5		
Westhampton	17	26	Payne	Ebenezer		2		1						1			4		
Montague	47	10	Payne	Edward	2	2	4	1			1	1		1			12		
Montague	47	13	Payne	James			1			1		1					3		
Northfield	30	12	Peabody	Amos	2	1		1		2	2		1				9		
New Salem	102	11	Peabody	Phinehas	3	1		1					1				6		
Ludlow	257	35	Peak	Asa	1		1			1			1				4		
New Salem	102	12	Pearce	Abraham		1	1	1				2		1			6		
Leverett	116	1	Pearce	Alden	2		1			1		2	1				7		
New Salem	102	16	Pearce	Amos	1		1						1				3		
New Salem	102	23	Pearce	Caleb	1	1	1					1					4		
New Salem	101	40	Pearce	Daniel		2		1		2	1		1				7		
New Salem	101	30	Pearce	Jesse	3	2		1			2		1				9		
New Salem	101	39	Pearce	John	2			1		1	1		1				6		
New Salem	102	26	Pearce	John 2d	1	2		1		1			1				8		
New Salem	101	38	Pearce	Jonathan				1						1			2		
New Salem	102	2	Pearce	Josiah	1		2			1	2	1		1	1		9		
New Salem	101	31	Pearce	Samuel				1					4	1			6		
New Salem	102	13	Pearce	Samuel 2d		2	1		1		1	1	1				7		
New Salem	102	14	Pearce	Samuel 3d		1			1		1	1	1				5		
New Salem	102	15	Pearce	Stephen	1	3	1			1	1			1			9		
New Salem	102	1	Pearce	Varney	1	2		1		2	1	1		2			10		
Chesterfield	24	17	Pearl	James	1			1		1			1				4		
Ludlow	257	39	Pearson	Adin	2			1			1	1					5		
Ludlow	257	38	Pearson	Ezra		2	1			1				1			5		
West Springfield	357	15	Pearson	Samuel		2		1		1	1		1				6		
Longmeadow	95	10	Pease	Abiel		1	2						1				4		
Blanford	176	16	Pease	Abner	1	1	1			1	1		1				6		
Monson	265	18	Pease	Amos		1	1			1			1				4		
Middlefield	157	21	Pease	Dan				1									1		
Middlefield	156	27	Pease	Gad	1			1	1	3			1				7		
Monson	265	19	Pease	Gideon	1	1	2		1	1	2	1		1			10		
Longmeadow	95	23	Pease	Heman	2	1		1	1	1	2		1	1			10		
Middlefield	157	15	Pease	Israel	4	1		1		1	1	1	1				10		
Chester	146	9	Pease	James	1		1			1			1				4		
South Brimfield	276	18	Pease	Jno		1		1						1			3		
Ludlow	257	34	Pease	Job		1	1		1	1	1	1		1			7		
Conway	60	11	Pease	John		1				1		1					3		
Springfield	246	27	Pease	Joseph		2							1				3		
Wilbraham	237	40	Pease	Nathan		1		1					1	1			4		
Wilbraham	237	41	Pease	Nathan Jun	1			1					1				3		
Longmeadow	95	2	Pease	Peter							2	1					3		
Longmeadow	95	7	Pease	Simeon	3	1		1		1			1				7		
Hatfield	14	16	Pease	Solomon	1		2		1	1	2		1				8		
Westfield	123	6	Pease	Titus			2			2			1				5		
Granby	253	39	Pease	William	3		1			1			1				6		
Shelburne	323	11	Pebble	Patrick	2		1			1			1				5		
Amherst	292	11	Pebbles	Francis	2		1						1				4		
Pelham	216	9	Pebbles	John		1	2		1			1	1	1			7		
New Salem	102	6	Pebbles	Willm H	2		1			2			1				6		
Shelburne	323	10	Peck	Abner	2		1			3			1				7		
Colrain	188	18	Peck	Abraham	5		1	1		1	1		1	1			11		
Norwich	151	17	Peck	Caleb				1		2			1	1			5		
Conway	60	10	Peck	Darius	3	1		1		3	1		1				10		
Hadley	287	3	Peck	Joseph				1						1			2		
Amherst	292	28	Peck	Joseph P		1						1					2		
Leyden	83	32	Peckam	Isaac			2			3			1				6		
Shutesbury	111	20	Peckens	David	2		1			2	1		1				7		
Belchertown	206	21	Peeso	John		1	1			2	1		1				6		
Northfield	30	13	Pehlps	Elihu	3		1	1			1		1				7		
Plainfield	308	2	Peirce	Alpheus	2		1			4			1				8		
Chesterfield	24	33	Peirce	Benja Jun	2	1							1				4		
Chesterfield	24	32	Peirce	Benjamin		1		1		3				1			6		
Chesterfield	22	22	Peirce	James			1	1					1	1			4		
Shutesbury	111	9	Peirce	John				1						1			2		
Shutesbury	111	8	Peirce	Jonathan		3		1				2		1			7		
Shutesbury	111	10	Peirce	Nathan		1		1		4	1	1	1				9		

278

TOWN	PG#	LN#	LAST NAME	FIRST NAME	FREE WHITE MALES under 10	10 to 16	16 to 26	26 to 45	45 and over	FREE WHITE FEMALES under 10	10 to 16	16 to 26	26 to 45	45 and over	TOTAL ALL OTHER	TOTAL SLAVES	TOTALS	DISTRICT/ TOWNSHIP	NOTES
Shutesbury	111	21	Peirce	Peleg	1		1					1					3		
Chesterfield	23	37	Peirce	Penelope							1	1					2		
Greenfield	75	1	Peirce	Samuel	1		2	1		3			1				8		
Pelham	215	19	Pelham	Thos	1			1		1			1				4		
Buckland	329	9	Pelton	Cale	3			1					1				5		
Northampton	11	7	Pelton	David		1	2		1	1	1			1			7		
Middlefield	156	38	Pelton	Ezra			2	1		3	1	2					9		
Middlefield	155	10	Pelton	Ithamer		1	1		1				1	1			5		
Middlefield	155	16	Pelton	Ithamer Junr				1		1		1					3		
Northampton	10	28	Pelton	Reuben	1	1	1		1		2	1		1			8		
Chester	143	16	Pelton	Tabor	1	1		1		4			1				8		
Blanford	182	14	Pelton	Thomas			1			6		1	1				9		
South Hadley	250	34	Pendergrass	Peter				1			1		1				3		
Springfield	245	17	Pendleton	Caleb Jr	1			1		2			1				5		
Springfield	245	20	Pendleton	Henry		1				1		1					3		
Springfield	245	19	Pendleton	Jesse	1	1											2		
Springfield	245	18	Pendleton	Nathan	2		1	1		1			1	1			7		
Worthington	301	22	Penington	Amos		2		1		3	2		1				9		
Warwick	39	15	Pennyman	Bunyan	1		1	1		2		1					6		
West Springfield	351	35	Pepper	Gaius	1			1		2			1				5		
Ware	227	26	Pepper	Isaac		2		1		3	2	1	1				10		
Greenwich	221	28	Pepper	John		1		1		1			1				4		
Ware	227	28	Pepper	Joseph	2	1			1	1		1	1				7		
Ware	227	27	Pepper	Stephen	2			1		3	1	1	2				10		
Ware	227	29	Pepper	Thomas		1						1					2		
Monson	268	33	Pepper	Timothy	1	1	1		1	1		1	1				7		
Ashfield	344	11	Perkins	Abiezer	2	3	1			1		1	1				9		
Buckland	329	10	Perkins	Edmund	3		1	1	1	2		1	1	2			12		
Ashfield	344	16	Perkins	Eliab	2	1	1		1	1		1					7		
West Springfield	351	34	Perkins	Elisha	2	1			1	2				1			7		
Plainfield	308	6	Perkins	George	2			1		1			1				5		
Southwick	359	54	Perkins	Israel	2	1	1		1	2			1	2			10		
West Springfield	351	37	Perkins	Israel	1			1					1				3		
New Salem	102	3	Perkins	John F		2											2		
Plainfield	308	7	Perkins	Jona			1	1		2		1		1			6		
West Springfield	354	53	Perkins	Joseph		1		1		1			1				4		
Amherst	291	2	Perkins	Nathan	1			1		1		1					4		
New Salem	102	22	Perkins	Nathl		1		1		1		1					3		
Middlefield	158	17	Perkins	Phineas Capt.	1	1		1		2		2	1				8		
Buckland	329	15	Perkins	Rufus	3		1	1		1	3		1				10		
Belchertown	209	40	Perkins	Samuel		1	1		1			3		1			7		
Belchertown	209	41	Perkins	Samuel Jr				1				1					2		
Ashfield	343	20	Perkins	Timothy	2	2		1		1			1				7		
West Springfield	357	14	Perkins	William	3			1		1			1				6		
Westfield	127	32	Perkins	Wm	2			1		3			1				7		
Norwich	154	27	Perkins	York											3		3		
Colrain	188	12	Perril	Abraham	1	1	2		1	2	1		1				9		
Colrain	188	15	Perril	John	3	1		1	1	1		1					8		
Holland	278	17	Perrin	Lyrell	2	1		1	1	2			1	1			9		
Holland	278	14	Perrin	S. Hollowell		1	3	1		3		1	1				10		
Leyden	83	33	Perry	Abel	2	1				1		1					6		
Williamsburg	443	1	Perry	Abiel	3		3	1		1	3	1	1				13		
South Brimfield	277	3	Perry	Abner	?	1			1	1	1	2	1				9		
Warwick	39	14	Perry	Asa		1		1		1	1		1				5		
Warwick	39	6	Perry	David	1	2		1		1			1	1			7		
New Salem	102	24	Perry	Eli	2			1		1	1		1				6		
South Brimfield	277	7	Perry	Isaac	2	1		1		2			1				7		
Ashfield	344	5	Perry	John	2			1	1	1			2				7		
Amherst	289	5	Perry	Jonathan		1	1	1		4	2		1				10		
New Salem	102	19	Perry	Joseph	2	2	1	1		2	1		1				10		
South Brimfield	277	5	Perry	Joseph	1		1	1		2			1	1			7		
Chesterfield	23	26	Perry	Josiah		2			1	2		1	1	1			6		
South Brimfield	277	6	Perry	Micah			1			2		2		1			6		
Northfield	30	9	Perry	Noah	2	1	3		1	1	1		1				10		
Montague	47	12	Perry	Silas	3			1		2			1				7		
Conway	60	9	Persons	Joel		2	1		1	3	1	1		1			10		
West Springfield	354	58	Peters	Andrew											3		3		
Worthington	301	10	Peters	Prince Negro											2		2		
Granville East Soc	529	15	Peters	William	1	1		1		1	2		3				9		
Ware	228	36	Peters	Charles											3		3		
Colrain	188	13	Peterson	Jonathan		2		2		1		3		1			9		
Wilbraham	232	2	Peterson	Nathaniel		1							1				2		
Pelham	216	3	Pettingale	Margaret									1	1			2		
Belchertown	206	24	Pettingall	Nathaniel	1	1		1		1	1		1				6		
Belchertown	206	25	Pettingall	Paul				1		3			1				5		
Belchertown	206	23	Pettingall	Stephen	1		1		1	2			1	1			7		
Cummington	305	14	Pettingill	Jon		1		1		2	1	1	1				7		
Montgomery	161	18	Pettip	Abial	3	1		1		1	1	1	1				9		
Warwick	39	3	Petty	Ebenezer	1					1			1	1			4		
West Springfield	354	45	Petty	Thomas					1								3		

279

TOWN	PG#	LN#	LAST NAME	FIRST NAME	FREE WHITE MALES under 10	10 to 16	16 to 26	26 to 45	45 and over	FREE WHITE FEMALES under 10	10 to 16	16 to 26	26 to 45	45 and over	TOTAL ALL OTHER	TOTAL SLAVES	TOTALS	DISTRICT/ TOWNSHIP	NOTES
Monson	268	7	Pevey	Elijah Capt	1		1		1	2	3	1	1				10		
Greenwich	224	10	Pharoah	Jepthah Blak Man											3		3		
Blanford	181	8	Pheland	John	2		1	1		1	1		1				7		
Northampton	3	31	Phelps	Andrew	2	1	1	2		3		1		1			11		
Belchertown	209	39	Phelps	Benjamin	1	1		1		1	1		1				6		
Middlefield	157	26	Phelps	Benjamin				1						1			2		
Hadley	288	38	Phelps	Charles		1	2		2	1		1		1	1		9		
Middlefield	156	23	Phelps	David	1		1			1		1					4		
Westfield	119	16	Phelps	David	1			1		2		1					5		
Belchertown	211	26	Phelps	Dudley	1		1				1		1				4		
Northampton	8	5	Phelps	Eben	2		2	2	1	1		2	1	1			12		
Belchertown	209	38	Phelps	Eliakim Capt	1	1	2		1	2	1		1				9		
Easthampton	136	16	Phelps	Elijah	2		1					1					4		
Wilbraham	234	29	Phelps	Elijah	3	2	1		1	3		1	1				12		
Northampton	3	29	Phelps	Eliphalet		1		1		1	1	1					5		
Westfield	127	28	Phelps	Ezra	2	2		1		3	1			1			10		
Easthampton	136	3	Phelps	John	2		1						1				4		
Granville Mid Soc.	167	24	Phelps	John	2		2	1		2		1	1	1			10		
Russell	137	13	Phelps	John	2		1		1	2	1	1		1			9		
Westfield	120	5	Phelps	John	1	1	3		1		1	3		2			12		
Easthampton	136	19	Phelps	John 2d	2		1					1					4		
Northampton	9	3	Phelps	Jonathan				2					2	1			5		
West Springfield	354	56	Phelps	Lucy		1	1			1		1		1			5		
Belchertown	209	37	Phelps	Martin Doct	1	1		1		2	1	1	1				8		
Westfield	119	15	Phelps	Mary Wd		1					1			1			3		
Norwich	152	21	Phelps	Mary Wid		1								1			2		
Russell	139	18	Phelps	Moses	2		1			2	1			1			7		
Westfield	127	31	Phelps	Moses		1	1	1				1		1			5		
Northampton	3	26	Phelps	Nathaniel	2	2	1	1	1	1		1	2	1			12		
Belchertown	210	1	Phelps	Noah		1		1				1					3		
Westfield	127	30	Phelps	Noah		1	1		1	1	1	1		1			7		
Middlefield	157	29	Phelps	Obediah			1			1		1	1				4		
Westfield	124	11	Phelps	Oliver	1	1		1		3	2		1				9		
Blanford	178	3	Phelps	Philip	2	2	2		1	4		2		1			14		
Northampton	3	30	Phelps	Rufus		1		1		3		1					6		
Northampton	9	11	Phelps	Samuel		2		1				1		2			6		
Northampton	8	4	Phelps	Seaward	1								1				3		
Chester	144	21	Phelps	Seth Lieut	1		3	1		2	1			1			9		
Westfield	120	1	Phelps	Solomon	3			1		1		1					6		
Chesterfield	21	3	Phelps	Spencer		1	1		1	1		1	1				6		
Montgomery	161	3	Phelps	Sylvester		1	1						1				3		
Westhampton	18	5	Phelps	Timothy	1		2		1		1	1		1			7		
Worthington	299	18	Phelps	Travis		1						1	1				3		
Easthampton	136	15	Phelps	Wm		1		1		1	1	1					6		
New Salem	102	20	Pheney	Noah	2	2	2		1	2			1				10		
Blanford	175	5	Phillip	Eliphalet	2	2		1	1	2	1		1				10		
Ashfield	343	24	Phillips	Abner	1	1		1	1			1	1				8		
Wilbraham	236	15	Phillips	Benjamin	1			1		3	2			1			8		
Ashfield	343	14	Phillips	Caleb	2	1		1		3	1	2	1				11		
Ashfield	344	2	Phillips	David				1			1			1			3		
Ashfield	344	13	Phillips	David	3		1					1					5		
Ashfield	343	25	Phillips	Elijah	1	2		1		3	1		1	1			10		
Chesterfield	22	18	Phillips	Ezra		1	1		1		2		1	1			7		
Norwich	153	20	Phillips	Ezra	1			1		3		1					6		
West Springfield	354	49	Phillips	Gideon				1			2	1					4		
Ashfield	344	9	Phillips	Israel			1			1		1					3		
Greenfield	75	3	Phillips	Israel	3		1					1					5		
Leyden	84	3	Phillips	James	2	1		1		3	1	1		1			10		
Wendell	107	8	Phillips	Jason	2		1			1		1					5		
Worthington	299	5	Phillips	Jeremiah	1		1	1		1	1		1				6		
Springfield	248	4	Phillips	John				1							1		2		
Northfield	30	11	Phillips	Oliver		1				1		1					3		
Leyden	84	4	Phillips	Peter	1	1		1		1	1	1	1				7		
Ashfield	343	23	Phillips	Phillip	2		1				1	2					6		
Ashfield	343	15	Phillips	Saml	2	2		1		2		1					8		
Ashfield	344	14	Phillips	Saml	1		1			2	1						5		
Ashfield	343	26	Phillips	Simeon	2		1					1					4		
West Springfield	354	48	Phillips	Simeon	1			1			1			1			4		
Ashfield	344	1	Phillips	Spencer	2			1		1	2			1			7		
Ashfield	344	8	Phillips	Thomas		1	1				1	1		1			6		
West Springfield	354	46	Phillips	Thompson	2	1	1		1	1		1					8		
Ashfield	343	27	Phillips	Vesparian	1	2	1				1	1		2			9		
Gill	87	10	Phillips	Willis	1		1					1					3		
Shelburne	323	9	Phinney	David	3	1	2	1		3	2		1				13		
Chesterfield	21	21	Phinney	Ephraim	1				1		2	1		1			6		
Williamsburg	444	23	Phinney	Isaac			1	1				1		1			4		
Williamsburg	443	2	Phinney	Isaac Junr	1		1			3	2	1					8		
Williamsburg	444	20	Phinney	Nathan	1	1	1			2		1		1			7		
Williamsburg	444	22	Phinney	Zenas	1		1			3	1						6		
Charlemont	193	7	Phips	George	2	1		1		2		1					7		
Leyden	84	1	Pichard	Charles		1	1				2		1				6		

280

TOWN	PG#	LN#	HEADS OF HOUSEHOLD		FREE WHITE MALES					FREE WHITE FEMALES					TOTAL ALL OTHER	TOTAL SLAVES	TOTALS	DISTRICT/ TOWNSHIP	NOTES
			LAST NAME	FIRST NAME	under 10	10 to 16	16 to 26	26 to 45	45 and over	under 10	10 to 16	16 to 26	26 to 45	45 and over					
Warwick	39	7	Pickering	William	2			1		1	1		1				6		
Greenfield	74	36	Pickett	Daniel	2		2	1		1	1	2	1				10		
Greenfield	74	35	Pickett	Samuel	1	1		1	1	2	2		1	1			10		
Cummington	305	24	Pierce	Bristo Negro											3		3		
Warwick	39	5	Pierce	Ebenezer	2	2		1			1		1				7		
Colrain	188	21	Pierce	Eliphalet		1		1					1				3		
Chesterfield	21	32	Pierce	Ezekiel			1			1			1				3		
Hatfield	14	23	Pierce	Jonathan		1	1	1				1	1				5		
Charlemont	193	3	Pierce	Josiah	2		2	1		2			1				8		
Hadley	286	10	Pierce	Josiah	1	1	2	1	1				1	2			9		
Colrain	188	11	Pierce	Judah	3	1		1		2	1		1				9		
Colrain	188	20	Pierce	Samuel	3	1		1		2	1		1				9		
Colrain	188	22	Pierce	Samuel 2d		1	1				1		1				4		
Brimfield	272	30	Pierce	Seth	1	1	2			1	1		1				7		
Brimfield	271	3	Pierce	Subbiness		1	1			2		1					5		
Hadley	286	11	Pierce	William		1		1			1		1				4		
Colrain	188	10	Pierce	Zebulon	3	1	1	1		1	1	1	1				10		
Rowe	200	22	Pierpoint	Hezekiah			1	1		1			1				4		
Shutesbury	111	19	Pierpont	William	1		1			3			1				6		
Shutesbury	111	11	Pike	Aaron	1		1			2			1				5		
South Hadley	250	43	Pike	David	2		1			2			1				6		
Charlemont	193	4	Pike	Elisha	1	1		1		4			1				8		
Chester	143	17	Pike	Samuel				1		4			1				6		
Norwich	153	43	Pilcher	Nathan	3		1	1				1	1				7		
Barnardston	78	27	Pinks	John	4			1	1	1			1				8		
Wilbraham	235	37	Pinney	Fuller		1	1			1			1				4		
Wilbraham	238	11	Pinney	Joel			1					2					3		
Middlefield	157	39	Pinney	John		1	1						2	1			5		
Middlefield	157	35	Pinney	John Junr	1		1			2	1						5		
Ludlow	257	13	Pinney	Joseph			1							1			2		
Westfield	125	2	Pitcher	Danll	4	1		1		3	1		1				11		
Westfield	125	1	Pitcher	Elijah				1		1			1				3		
Norwich	153	11	Pitcher	Jonathan	4	2		1		1	1	1	1				11		
Westfield	125	3	Pitcher	Reuben	3	1	2	1		1	2		1				11		
Westhampton	17	32	Pitsinger	John	1	3		1					1				6		
Greenfield	75	2	Pitt	John	4	2		1		1	1	3		1			13		
Monson	268	5	Pitts	Jeremiah				1		1	1	1	1				5		
Monson	268	4	Pitts	John			1	1					1				3		
Orange	43	4	Pitts	Samuel Bishop	1	1	2	1		1		1	2	1			10		
Chester	147	13	Plum	Charles	1	1		2		1			1				6		
Chester	147	14	Plum	Comfort	1		1						1				3		
Chester	149	15	Plum	Jacob		1				3			1				5		
Montague	47	15	Plumb	Joel			1			2		1	1				5		
Wilbraham	235	29	Plumley	John		1		1		2			1				5		
Wilbraham	235	30	Plumley	John Jr		1				3			1				5		
Holland	278	8	Polley	John	1	1	1	1					1	1			6		
New Salem	102	21	Polly	Pliny		1				1		1					3		
Chesterfield	24	15	Polly	Thomas	1		1						1	3			6		
Chester	147	34	Pomeroy	Amasa	1	1		1		1		3	1				8		
Northampton	4	18	Pomeroy	Asahel	1	1	4	4	2	1	2	5	1		1		22		
Williamsburg	444	24	Pomeroy	Benjamin		1		1			1	2	1				6		
Northampton	8	21	Pomeroy	Daniel				1		1			1		1		4		
Amherst	292	32	Pomeroy	David	1	1		1	1	3	1		1	1			10		
Hadley	288	15	Pomeroy	Ebenezer	1	1		1	1	2			1	1			8		
Granville Mid Soc.	165	1	Pomeroy	Elihu	2	2	1	1		1	1	1	1				10		
Northampton	8	31	Pomeroy	Gaius	1	1	1	1		1		1	1				7		
Chester	146	13	Pomeroy	Joseph	4	2		1		1	1		1				10		
Warwick	39	10	Pomeroy	Josiah		1		1			1	1	1				5		
Williamsburg	443	3	Pomeroy	Josiah	1		1						1				3		
Warwick	39	11	Pomeroy	Josiah Junr	2	1		1		1			1				6		
Chester	146	25	Pomeroy	Luther Capt	1			1		3	3		1				9		
Northampton	10	2	Pomeroy	Medad				1	1			1		1			4		
Northfield	30	5	Pomeroy	Medad	2	2		1		1		1	1	1			9		
Northampton	4	28	Pomeroy	Oliver	1	1	1	1		1			1				6		
Northampton	10	1	Pomeroy	Pheobus	3			1		1			1				6		
Westhampton	18	15	Pomeroy	Pliny		1		1		1	1	1	1	1			7		
Northampton	3	2	Pomeroy	Quantus			3	1		1	1	2	1				9		
Northfield	30	6	Pomeroy	Shammah		1	1	1		1		1	1	1			7		
Amherst	292	27	Pomeroy	Simeon	2	2		1		1		1	1	1			9		
Northampton	5	21	Pomeroy	Simeon	1	1	2			1		1	1				7		
South Hadley	248	8	Pomeroy	Simeon		2	1	1		1	1	1	1				8		
Westhampton	15	4	Pomeroy	Stephen	2			1		2			1				6		
Northampton	9	36	Pomeroy	Sylvanus	1			1		2	2						6		
Northampton	8	12	Pomeroy	William	3	2		1				1	1				8		
Monson	263	13	Pomhey	Cato											9		9		
Norwich	153	25	Pomeroy	Titus Deac	4		1	1		1			1				8		
Southampton	132	20	Pomroy	Aaron				1					1				2		
Southampton	132	19	Pomroy	Aaron Junr			1			2			1				4		
Southampton	133	4	Pomroy	Anne Wd	1	1				1		1	1				5		

TOWN	PG#	LN#	LAST NAME	FIRST NAME	FREE WHITE MALES					FREE WHITE FEMALES					TOTAL ALL OTHER	TOTAL SLAVES	TOTALS	DISTRICT/ TOWNSHIP	NOTES
					under 10	10 to 16	16 to 26	26 to 45	45 and over	under 10	10 to 16	16 to 26	26 to 45	45 and over					
Southampton	133	5	Pomroy	Asahel	2			1	1	2	1		1	2			10		
Southampton	132	31	Pomroy	Calib	1		1		1			1		1			5		
Southampton	132	33	Pomroy	Ebenezer		1	1		1					1			4		
Hawley	334	31	Pomroy	Ebenz	1		1	1		1			1				5		
Southampton	133	3	Pomroy	Elihue	1				1		1	1		1			5		
Buckland	329	11	Pomroy	Enos	3	1	1	1		2	1	1	1				11		
Easthampton	136	28	Pomroy	Enos			3	1		1	1		1				7		
Easthampton	137	2	Pomroy	Enos Jr	1	1	1	1				1					5		
Southampton	129	23	Pomroy	Gad	1	1	1		1	1	1		1				7		
Southampton	133	6	Pomroy	Gideon	2	2			1	2			1				8		
Southampton	129	22	Pomroy	Ichabod	3				1	2	3		1				10		
Southampton	132	28	Pomroy	Ira	2				1	2	1		1	1			8		
Southampton	133	9	Pomroy	Isaac	2	2	1		1		1		1				8		
Southampton	132	32	Pomroy	Jacob			2	1		1	1	1		1			7		
Southampton	129	20	Pomroy	Joel		1	1	1		2			1				6		
Worthington	298	22	Pomroy	Jonathan		1			1	1	1		1				5		
Easthampton	136	31	Pomroy	Justus	1				1	2			1				5		
Southampton	132	30	Pomroy	Leml			2	1			1		1	1			6		
Southampton	133	18	Pomroy	Lemuel			3		1		1	3	1	1			10		
Easthampton	136	26	Pomroy	Solomon	1	1	1	1	2			2		1			9		
Warwick	39	4	Pond	Joseph	1		1			3		1					6		
Plainfield	307	42	Pool	Abijah	1	1			1		1		1				5		
Plainfield	308	1	Pool	Jacob			1			3	1		1				6		
Plainfield	307	44	Pool	Jeptha	3	1	1	1		2	1		1				10		
Plainfield	307	43	Pool	Jeptha Jun	1			1		2			1				5		
Palmer	259	24	Pool	Thomas		1		1					1				3		
Palmer	259	34	Pool	Thomas Junr	1		1					1					3		
Springfield	247	26	Pooler	Penuel	1	1			1	1	1		1				7		
Greenwich	224	11	Pope	Freeman	1	1	1			2			1				7		
Greenwich	221	31	Pope	Joseph	1	1		1	1			1	1	1			7		
Springfield	243	1	Popkins	Benjamin			1			1		1					3		
Springfield	247	9	Popkins	Stephen	3	1			1	3		1		1			10		
Ashfield	344	3	Porter	Asa	4			1		1			1				7		
Orange	43	5	Porter	Benjamin	1			1		3	1		1				7		
Belchertown	210	2	Porter	Daniel		1			1		1		1				4		
Wendell	107	5	Porter	Daniel	1		1	1		1	1	1	1				7		
Williamsburg	444	16	Porter	David	4	2	1	1		2	1	1	1				13		
Hawley	334	29	Porter	Edward		1		1		1			1				4		
Hadley	287	37	Porter	Eleazer	3	1	1	1		1	2	1	1		1		12		
West Springfield	354	57	Porter	Elijah	1			1		2		1	1				6		
Westfield	123	15	Porter	Elijah	1	1			1	2	1	1					7		
Northampton	3	27	Porter	Hezekiah				1		1	1		1				4		
Westfield	123	14	Porter	Isaac	1	1	1		1	1	1	1	1				8		
Leverett	116	3	Porter	Jacob	1	1		1		1	1		2				7		
Worthington	302	11	Porter	Jacob		1	1		1		1	2		1			7		
Southampton	132	27	Porter	Jehiel		1			1				4	1			7		
Wendell	107	6	Porter	Job	1			1		2			1				5		
Ashfield	343	10	Porter	John	1	1	1		1		2	1		1			8		
West Springfield	354	55	Porter	John				1			2		1				4		
Ashfield	343	12	Porter	John 2d	1		1			2		1					5		
Hatfield	12	30	Porter	Jonathan	2	1	1		1	1	1	2		1			10		
Hadley	287	11	Porter	Jonathan E.	2		1	1		1		1	1				7		
Ashfield	343	11	Porter	Joseph	2	3	1		1		2	1	1				11		
Ashfield	344	4	Porter	Joshua	2			1		1			1				5		
Wendell	107	9	Porter	Mercy						1			1	1			3		
Hadley	287	21	Porter	Moses	2			1		2			1	1	2		9		
Ashfield	343	9	Porter	Nehemiah				1			1		1				3		
Wendell	107	7	Porter	Noah	1			1					1				3		
Hadley	287	18	Porter	Pierpont			1			2		1	1				5		
Ashfield	343	13	Porter	Saml	2		1		1	1	3		1				9		
Hadley	287	20	Porter	Samuel	1	1	1	2		4	2		2				13		
Norwich	151	2	Porter	Samuel	2		1						1				4		
Hatfield	13	13	Porter	Silas	3		2	1		1	2	1	1				11		
Ashfield	343	8	Porter	Simeon			1					1					2		
Hadley	287	12	Porter	William	2	1	3	1		2		2	1				10		
Greenfield	75	4	Post	Cornelius				1					1				2		
Westhampton	16	17	Post	Levi		1		1					1				3		
Westhampton	16	18	Post	Levi Junr			1				2						3		
Westhampton	16	21	Post	Oliver	1	2	1		1	1		1		1			8		
South Brimfield	277	36	Potter	Abijah	2	2			1	2	1		1				9		
Rowe	200	20	Potter	Ambrose	1		1	1		1			1				5		
Rowe	200	21	Potter	Baldwin	4	1		1		1	1		1				9		
Leyden	83	34	Potter	David	1	2	1		1	2	1	2		1			11		
Montague	47	14	Potter	Edward		1		1					1				3		
Gill	87	8	Potter	Ichabod	1		1		1	3			1				7		
Amherst	293	1	Potter	Joseph	1	2		1			1	1	1	1			8		
Buckland	329	13	Potter	Joseph	1	1			1	1		1	1				6		
Hadley	288	11	Potter	Robert			1		1		1	1		1			5		
Palmer	258	13	Potter	Wm	2			1		2			1		1		7		
New Salem	102	4	Powars	Stephen	1	1		1		1	1		1				6		
Hadley	285	28	Powel	William	1			1						1	2		5		

282

TOWN	PG#	LN#	HEADS OF HOUSEHOLD		FREE WHITE MALES					FREE WHITE FEMALES					TOTAL ALL OTHER	TOTAL SLAVES	TOTALS	DISTRICT/ TOWNSHIP	NOTES
			LAST NAME	FIRST NAME	under 10	10 to 16	16 to 26	26 to 45	45 and over	under 10	10 to 16	16 to 26	26 to 45	45 and over					
Greenwich	221	16	Powers	Aaron		1			1	1				1			4		
Greenwich	221	23	Powers	Abijah Capt	3	1		1			1		1	1			8		
New Salem	102	5	Powers	Asa	3	1		1		2			1				8		
Shutesbury	111	13	Powers	Asa		1	1		1					1			4		
Greenwich	221	22	Powers	Clark	1			1	1				1	1			6		
Brimfield	270	1	Powers	Eli			2			1		1					4		
Brimfield	269	38	Powers	Isaac		1		1						1			3		
Greenwich	221	18	Powers	Isaac Esq	1			1		1			1				4		
Greenwich	221	19	Powers	Jeremiah				1	6								7		
Goshen	311	19	Powers	John	4	3		1		2		1	1				12		
Shutesbury	111	12	Powers	John				1		2		1					4		
Greenwich	221	21	Powers	Nathan		3		1	1	1		2		1			9		
Greenwich	221	20	Powers	Polly Wd	1								1				2		
Brimfield	269	39	Powers	Stephen	1	1	1	1		1		1	1				7		
Shutesbury	111	14	Powers	Stephen	1	1	2		1	3	1	1		1			11		
Greenwich	221	24	Powers	Thos Maj	1	2	3	2	1		2	3		1			15		
Shutesbury	111	17	Pratt	Abraham	4			1		1			2				8		
Granville East Soc	531	6	Pratt	Alderton	1			1		2	1		1				6		
Northampton	3	6	Pratt	Amasa			1					1	1				3		
Shutesbury	111	16	Pratt	Artemas	2	1		1		2			1				7		
Cummington	305	15	Pratt	Benoni	1	1		1		2		1					6		
Ludlow	255	16	Pratt	Cyrus	3			1		2			1	1			8		
Plainfield	308	5	Pratt	Daniel	2			1					1				4		
Shutesbury	111	18	Pratt	David		2		1		3	1	1		1			9		
Belchertown	206	27	Pratt	David Capt	3	2	1		1	1	1	2		1			12		
Amherst	291	7	Pratt	Ebenezer	1			1		2		1					5		
South Brimfield	276	23	Pratt	Ebenezer		2	1		1	3	1	1	1				10		
Leverett	116	2	Pratt	Ephraim	3			1		1			1				6		
Wendell	107	11	Pratt	Ephraim				1						1			2		
Belchertown	206	28	Pratt	Jabez			1				1	1	1				5		
Longmeadow	91	2	Pratt	Jacob		2	1		1	1		1		1			7		
Granville East Soc	533	10	Pratt	Jerard			1	1		3	1		2	1			9		
Blanford	182	4	Pratt	John	1			1			1		1	1			5		
Warwick	39	8	Pratt	John			1		1				1	2			5		
Conway	60	10	Pratt	Joseph	1	1		1		1		1	1	1			7		
Cummington	305	16	Pratt	Josiah	2			1		1			1				5		
Granville West Soc	169	13	Pratt	Justin	1	2	1		1	1				1			7		
Amherst	291	6	Pratt	Matthew		2		1				1		1			5		
Belchertown	206	18	Pratt	Micah	1			1		1	1	2		1			7		
Shutesbury	111	15	Pratt	Micah				1						1			2		
Shutesbury	111	22	Pratt	Micah Jr	1		1	1						1			4		
Granville East Soc	531	5	Pratt	Phinehas		2		1				1		1			5		
Shutesbury	111	23	Pratt	Phinehas				1		3			1				5		
Plainfield	308	3	Pratt	Solomon	1	1	2		1	2			2				9		
Greenfield	74	34	Pratt	Stephen	1	2		1				4		1			9		
Westhampton	17	30	Pratt	Thomas	2	1	1	1		2			1				8		
Plainfield	308	4	Pratt	Whitcom	2	1		1		4			1				9		
Deerfield	54	30	Pratt	William		1	1	1				1		1			5		
Northampton	5	1	Pre*	Benjamin				1			3	1	1	1			7		
Northampton	5	11	Prentice	Aaron	3			1					1				5		
Chester	145	7	Prentice	Asahel	1			1			1		1				4		
Cummington	305	17	Prentice	Elisha				1		3			1				5		
Worthington	301	27	Prentice	Isaac	2	1	1	1			1	1		2			9		
Wendell	107	4	Prentice	John	1	?	1					1		1			7		
Worthington	301	25	Prentice	Jona		1	1					2		2			7		
Chester	145	8	Prentice	Joseph	1			1		2		1					5		
Belchertown	206	29	Prentice	Moses				1		1	3		1				6		
Westhampton	18	8	Prentice	Peleg	2			1		1			1				5		
Worthington	301	9	Prentice	Phineas			1	1		3		2					7		
Northfield	30	7	Prentice	Samuel	1	1		1				1		1			5		
Westfield	124	22	Prentis	Nathaniel		2	1		1		1			1			6		
Montague	47	11	Prescott	Benjamin	2	4	16	40	4	2			2				70		at the Locks & Canal
Montague	47	9	Prescott	Josiah	1	1	2		1	1		1	2	1			10		
South Hadley	250	8	Preston	Benoni				1						1			2		
Granby	252	22	Preston	Jabez		1		1		2		1	1	1			7		
Belchertown	210	3	Preston	Jacob Jr	1	1		1			1	2		1			7		
Granby	252	24	Preston	James		1		1						1			3		
South Hadley	249	32	Preston	Job	2			1					1	1			5		
Granby	252	10	Preston	Joel	4		1	1		1			1				8		
Granby	252	19	Preston	John				1	1		2	3		1			8		
Granby	252	25	Preston	John Jun	4			1		1			1				7		
Belchertown	204	5	Preston	Justus	1		1			1		1					4		
Northfield	30	15	Preston	Lemuel	2	2	1	1		2			1				9		
Granby	252	23	Preston	Moses	1	1		1		2		2		1			8		
South Hadley	250	7	Preston	Samuel	2	2		2		1	2	2	2	1			14		
South Hadley	249	31	Preston	St Gardner	1				1	2			1				5		
West Springfield	351	39	Price	James				1			2	3		1			7		
Norwich	152	25	Prier	Simeon	2	1	1		1	2	1	1		1			10		
Northfield	30	10	Priest	Calvin				1					1				2		
Springfield	240	19	Prince	Daniel		1		1		2			1				5		

TOWN	PG#	LN#	LAST NAME	FIRST NAME	FREE WHITE MALES under 10	10 to 16	16 to 26	26 to 45	45 and over	FREE WHITE FEMALES under 10	10 to 16	16 to 26	26 to 45	45 and over	TOTAL ALL OTHER	TOTAL SLAVES	TOTALS	DISTRICT/ TOWNSHIP	NOTES
Buckland	329	14	Prince	Saml	2	1	1	1		1	1	1	1				9		
Northfield	30	8	Prindle	Nathan		2	1		1		1		1	1			7		
Monson	265	38	Prior	John	3			1			2		1				7		
Deerfield	54	32	Prismis	Ezra											7		7		
Goshen	311	23	Prispt	John											7		7		
Chester	149	31	Procter	Josiah	3				1			1	1				6		
Colrain	190	18	Procter	Mingo											8		8		
Warwick	39	9	Proctor	Peter		1	1		1	2	1	2					8		
Warwick	39	12	Proctor	Peter Junr	1			1				1					3		
Northampton	4	1	Prust	Chester			1	1				1					3		
Northampton	3	38	Prust	Israel			2		1			1		1			5		
Northampton	4	2	Prust	Seth	2		1	1				1					5		
Colrain	188	8	Puffer	Ezra		1		1		4		1					7		
Monson	265	13	Puffer	Tisdale	1			1		2		1					5		
Palmer	260	44	Pugnant	John											5		5		
Conway	60	6	Pulcipher	Benjamin	2			1	1	3	2		1	1			11		
Conway	60	7	Pulcipher	Joseph	1	2			1	3		1					8		
West Springfield	354	52	Purchase	Charles	2			1			2		1				6		
West Springfield	354	51	Purchase	Jonathan	1		2	1		1		1					6		
Colrain	188	14	Purington	Joseph	2	3		1		2	2	2		1			13		
Colrain	188	17	Purrington	Joshua	2		2	1				1	1				7		
Colrain	188	16	Purrington	Seth			1			3		2					6		
Barnardston	78	29	Pursile	Ezra	1	1	2		1	1	1			1			8		
Granville Mid Soc.	167	11	Putman	John	2	2		1		1			1				7		
New Salem	101	35	Putnam	Aaron	1	1		1		1	2	2	1		1		10		
Ludlow	255	18	Putnam	Abner		3		1		1		1					6		
New Salem	102	17	Putnam	Daniel	1	1		1		1		1					5		
Ludlow	255	17	Putnam	Eli	1		1		1	1		1					5		
New Salem	101	36	Putnam	Jacob		1		1		2		1					5		
New Salem	101	33	Putnam	John	1	1		2	1	4		2	1	1			13		
New Salem	101	37	Putnam	Joseph	1	1		1		1		2		1			7		
New Salem	101	34	Putnam	Joshua Jr	3		1	1				3					8		
New Salem	102	18	Putnam	Samuel	2			1				1					4		
Buckland	329	12	Putnam	Willm	1	2		1		2			1				7		
Goshen	311	22	Putney	Aron	1			1		2		1					5		
Goshen	311	13	Putney	Ebenezer	2	2	2	1	1			2		2			12		
Ashfield	343	17	Putney	Ebenz	1			1		2		1					5		
Ashfield	343	16	Putney	Elisha		1		1		1	1	2		1			7		
Ashfield	343	7	Putney	Jedediah			2						1				3		
Ashfield	344	12	Putney	Jedediah			1										1		
Goshen	312	23	Putney	Joseph	1		1					1					3		
Springfield	239	22	Pynchon	Abigail Wd			1						1				2		
Chesterfield	23	29	Pynchon	Elizabeth							1	2	1				4		
Chesterfield	23	33	Pynchon	John		1	1		1				1				4		
Springfield	239	16	Pynchon	John				1			1						2		
Springfield	239	21	Pynchon	Rebecca Wd								1		2			3		
Brimfield	272	2	Pynchon	Stephen Esq			1			1		1					3		
Springfield	239	15	Pynchon	William Esq		3	1	1		1			1				7		
Chester	143	10	Quigley	Adam	1		1	1				1	1				5		
Chester	149	19	Quigley	Hugh	3	1		1		3		1	1				10		
Chester	143	12	Quigley	James	3			1		1	1		1				7		
Chester	143	3	Quigley	William	2	2	1		2			3	1				11		
Conway	60	13	Quinn	Hugh		1		1		1				1			4		
Ware	227	32	Quinton	Robt	1		1	1				2					5		
Ware	227	31	Quinton	Thomas	1	1		1				2		3			8		
Colrain	188	24	Rainger	Moseds		3		1				1	1	2			8		
Worthington	297	8	Ramsdell	James			1						1				2		
Northampton	4	31	Ramsdell	Jesse		2		1				1					4		
Worthington	297	7	Ramsdell	Matthew		2		1			1	1	1				6		
Cummington	303	37	Ramsdell	Thomas	2		2	1		2	1	1	1				10		
Deerfield	54	39	Rand	Aaron	1			1		2	1		1				6		
Wendell	107	13	Rand	Aaron				1					1				2		
Wendell	107	15	Rand	Daniel	5	1		1					1				8		
Wendell	107	14	Rand	Hananiah		2		1				1	1				5		
Colrain	188	27	Randal	Jacob	1	2	1	1		2	1		1				9		
Shelburne	323	14	Randall	Avery	1			1		3	3		1				9		
Shelburne	323	13	Randall	Benjm	1	1	1	1			1	1					6		
Worthington	300	17	Randall	Ephraim		1		1		2	2	1					7		
Worthington	298	25	Randall	Gershom		1	2		1	2		2		1			9		
Worthington	300	16	Randall	Joel	2			1		1		1					5		
Shelburne	323	15	Randall	Russell			1					1					2		
Cummington	304	1	Randall	Zeb*			1			5		1					7		
Greenwich	222	5	Randell	Ichabod		1		1		1	2		1				6		
Greenwich	224	4	Randell	Isaiah	2	1	1				1	1					6		
Belchertown	207	1	Randell	Israel	2	2	1	1	1		1			1			9		
Greenwich	222	9	Randell	Jabez			1							1			2		
Belchertown	206	35	Randell	Joseph	1	1		1	1	1		2		1			8		
Belchertown	210	9	Randell	Jotham	2		1						1				4		
Belchertown	206	36	Randell	Nehemiah	3		1	1				1					6		
Greenwich	222	6	Randell	Titus	1		1			1		1					4		

TOWN	PG#	LN#	LAST NAME	FIRST NAME	FREE WHITE MALES					FREE WHITE FEMALES					TOTAL ALL OTHER	TOTAL SLAVES	TOTALS	DISTRICT/ TOWNSHIP	NOTES
					under 10	10 to 16	16 to 26	26 to 45	45 and over	under 10	10 to 16	16 to 26	26 to 45	45 and over					
Ware	227	37	Randell	Titus				1		1		1					3		
Belchertown	204	1	Ranger	Ephraim			1			2		1					4		
Pelham	216	19	Rankin	James	1	1		1		5		1	1				10		
Pelham	216	18	Rankin	John Lt	2	1	2		1		1			1			8		
Blanford	176	6	Ranney	Abner		4	2	2	1		1	1		1			12		
Ashfield	344	19	Ranney	Francis	1	1		1	1	1		1	3	1			10		
Ashfield	344	17	Ranney	George	1	1	1		1			1	3	1			9		
Ashfield	344	25	Ranney	Saml	1			1					1				3		
Ashfield	344	18	Ranney	Thomas		1	1		1			1		1			5		
Shelburne	323	18	Ransom	Calvin	2	1			1	2	1		1				8		
Shelburne	323	17	Ransom	Jabez		1	1		1		1	3		2			9		
Colrain	188	28	Ransom	Job			1	1		1			2				5		
Shelburne	323	19	Ransom	Joshua					1					1			2		
Montague	47	27	Rawson	Edmund		2	1		1	1			3	1			9		
Montague	47	29	Rawson	Joseph	3	1		1		1			1				7		
Warwick	39	16	Rawson	Josiah Junr		1	4		2		1	1		1			10		
New Salem	102	35	Rawson	Lemuel	4			1		1			1				7		
Buckland	329	19	Rawson	Moses		1	1		1	2	1		1				7		
Montague	47	28	Rawson	Samuel	3	1		1		2	1		1				9		
New Salem	102	37	Rawson	Secretary			1										1		
Shutesbury	111	28	Ray	Benjamin	3	1		1		2			1	1			9		
Shutesbury	112	2	Raymond	Asa	4			1		1			1	1			8		
Shutesbury	111	32	Raymond	Thaddeus	2			1		1			1				5		
Longmeadow	93	14	Raynolds	Samuel	2			1		3	1	1	1				9		
West Springfield	357	12	routt	David			1		1			1		1			4		
Belchertown	206	30	Read	Joseph	2	3			1	2	1	1					10		
Conway	60	25	Redfield	Ebenezer	1	2	3		1	1	1			1			10		
Springfield	247	1	Redway	Comfort			1			2	2		1				6		
Blanford	179	15	Reed	Amos	3	2	1	1		1	2	1					11		
New Salem	102	31	Reed	Amos	2		1		1	2	2	1					10		
Shutesbury	111	30	Reed	Benja Jr	3			1		2			1				7		
Shutesbury	111	29	Reed	Benjamin		2	1		1			1		1			6		
Middlefield	158	4	Reed	Christopher			1						1				2		
Plainfield	308	9	Reed	Cylence		1	1			1	1	1		1			6		
Cummington	305	18	Reed	David		1	2		1			1		1			6		
Plainfield	309	1	Reed	Ezekiel				1			1			1			3		
Southwick	360	15	Reed	George				1						1			2		
New Salem	102	36	Reed	Isaac	2	1		1		2	1		1				8		
Cummington	303	29	Reed	John	2	1		1		1		3	1	2			11		
Shutesbury	111	31	Reed	John	1		1					1					3		
Cummington	303	28	Reed	Noah	1	1			1	3	1		1				8		
Chesterfield	22	12	Reed	Samuel	2	1	1	1		2		1	1				9		
Warwick	39	22	Reed	Samuel	2	1			1	2			1				7		
Wendell	107	16	Reed	Samuel		1		1		3	1		1				7		
Cummington	305	19	Reed	Seth			1		1					1			3		
Blanford	177	14	Reed	Thomas	1	1		1		1		1					5		
Granville West Soc	168	8	Reed	Titus	1	1		1		2			1				6		
Northampton	7	34	Reed	William			1			1	1		1				4		
Holland	279	42	Reeves	Benja	1	1	1	1			1	1	1				7		
Holland	279	24	Reeves	Ezra Rev.				1					1				2		
Granville West Soc	170	25	Remington	Anthony	2	1		1		4	1	1	1				11		
Cummington	303	40	Remington	Benjamin	2	1		1		2			1				7		
Granville West Soc	170	12	Remington	Holden	1	1		1		3	1		1				8		
Hatfield	13	15	Remington	Jason											6		6		
Cummington	303	39	Remington	Joshua	1		1		1		1	1		1			6		
West Springfield	355	1	Remington	Seneca	1								1				2		
Pelham	216	20	Reniff	Abisha	1			1		2			1	1			6		
Buckland	329	17	Reniff	George	4			1		2			1				8		
Southwick	360	10	Rexford	Danison		1	3	1		2	1		1				9		
Shutesbury	111	33	Reynolds	Ebenezer	1			1		1			1				4		
New Salem	102	29	Reynolds	Enos			2		1			1	1	1			6		
New Salem	102	30	Reynolds	Enos Jr	2			1		2			1				6		
Shutesbury	112	3	Reynolds	Ezra	1			1		2			1				6		
Shutesbury	111	34	Reynolds	Jairus	2			1		2			1				6		
Shutesbury	111	35	Reynolds	James		2		1				1	1	1			6		
Shutesbury	112	5	Reynolds	Josiah	3			1		1	1		1				7		
Belchertown	211	30	Rhoades	Aaron	1	1		1		2			1				6		
Chesterfield	19	15	Rhoades	Joseph	1	1	1	2	1		1	2	1	1			11		
Chesterfield	19	16	Rhoades	Samuel		1	1		1			1		1			5		
Westhampton	18	30	Rhoades	Samuel			1	1				1					3		
Pelham	216	17	Rhoades	Solomon	3	2	1		1	2	1	1					11		
Norwich	154	28	Rhoads	Rhoda											5		5		
Belchertown	210	12	Rhodes	Thaddeus			1	1		1		1		1			5		
Charlemont	193	20	Rice	Aaron				1				1	1				3		
Charlemont	193	14	Rice	Aaron Jur	4			1		2			1	1			10		
Leverett	116	9	Rice	Abel	2	1		1		2	2		1				9		
Chesterfield	20	2	Rice	Alvin			1	1		1			1				4		
Charlemont	193	19	Rice	Artemas	1	1	1	1		2	1		1	1			9		
Conway	60	29	Rice	Benjamin	1	2	1		1					1			6		
Gill	87	20	Rice	Benjamin		1	1	1		2	1	1					8		

285

TOWN	PG#	LN#	LAST NAME	FIRST NAME	FREE WHITE MALES					FREE WHITE FEMALES					TOTAL ALL OTHER	TOTAL SLAVES	TOTALS	DISTRICT/ TOWNSHIP	NOTES
					under 10	10 to 16	16 to 26	26 to 45	45 and over	under 10	10 to 16	16 to 26	26 to 45	45 and over					
Conway	60	16	Rice	Caleb		1			1		1	2		1			6		
Charlemont	193	13	Rice	Calvin		1		1			1		1				4		
Charlemont	193	11	Rice	Catherine			1							1			2		
Conway	60	23	Rice	Cyrus		1	2		1		2			1			7		
Conway	60	19	Rice	Daniel	1	1		1		1			1				5		
Charlemont	193	10	Rice	David			1					1					2		
Gill	87	12	Rice	Enos	1			1		2		1	1				6		
Montague	47	30	Rice	Ephraim		2	1	1		1			1				6		
Charlemont	193	12	Rice	Ezra		1								1			2		
Montague	47	19	Rice	Gershom			1			1			1				3		
Conway	60	32	Rice	Henry			1					1					2		
Conway	60	15	Rice	Israel	2			1	1				1	1			6		
Conway	60	18	Rice	Israel		1		1		1		1					4		
Montague	47	20	Rice	Jedutham	3	2		1		1	1		1				9		
Charlemont	193	8	Rice	Joel	2	1		1		2			1				7		
Conway	60	27	Rice	Joel		2	2		1		1			1			7		
Granby	253	17	Rice	Joel	1	1		1		1			1				5		
Charlemont	193	15	Rice	John		1	1		1	2	2		1				8		
Deerfield	54	38	Rice	John	1			1		1			1				4		
Greenwich	222	7	Rice	John	1			1		3			1				6		
Conway	60	26	Rice	Jonas				2	1					1			4		
Hawley	334	36	Rice	Jonas	2	2			1	2		1	1				9		
Shelburne	323	16	Rice	Jonas			1		1					2			4		
New Salem	102	28	Rice	Jonathan				1				1		1			3		
Charlemont	193	16	Rice	Joseph	1	1			1	2	1		1				7		
Conway	60	28	Rice	Joseph		1	1		1	1	1			1			6		
Westfield	123	28	Rice	Joseph	1	1			1	2			1	1			7		
Leverett	116	7	Rice	Josiah	2			1		2			1				6		
Montague	47	21	Rice	Josiah		2			1			2		1			6		
Gill	87	22	Rice	Levi	1		1						1				3		
Charlemont	193	18	Rice	Luke	1			1				1	1				4		
Charlemont	193	17	Rice	Martin	2	2	1		1	1	2	1	1				11		
Sunderland	283	20	Rice	Nahum	2			1			1		1				5		
Belchertown	210	11	Rice	Nathan		1		1					1				3		
Sunderland	283	14	Rice	Nathaniel	3			2		2			1	1			9		
Charlemont	193	23	Rice	Ruth			1				2			1			4		
Charlemont	193	22	Rice	Samuel	1	2	1		1	2	1	3	1				12		
Gill	87	21	Rice	Samuel		2	1		1	1			1		1		7		
Leyden	84	6	Rice	Samuel	1			1		1			1				4		
Montague	47	18	Rice	Samuel			1			1			1				3		
Wendell	107	17	Rice	Samuel R.	1			1		3			1	1			7		
Northfield	30	19	Rice	Silas	1	1			1	2				1			6		
Charlemont	193	28	Rice	Silvanus			3	1						1			5		
Charlemont	193	21	Rice	Silvanus Jur	2			1				1					4		
Conway	60	24	Rice	Stephen	1		1						1				3		
Belchertown	210	8	Rice	Timothy		2			1			3		1			7		
Conway	60	17	Rice	Timothy		2	1		1	1		3		1			9		
Amherst	294	20	Rice	William	3	1		1		2			1				8		
Ware	227	35	Rich	Apollas		1			1		1	3		1			7		
Greenwich	222	1	Rich	Barnabas	3			1			1		1	1			8		
Warwick	39	23	Rich	Caleb	1	1	1		1	3	2	2	1				12		
Greenwich	221	36	Rich	Ebenz Deac		2		1	1		1		1				6		
Greenwich	222	4	Rich	Ebenz Jr Lt	2	1		1		1	1			1			7		
Ware	227	33	Rich	Elkanah	1			1			1	1					4		
Warwick	39	18	Rich	Jacob	2	2	2		1	1		2		1			11		
Williamsburg	443	6	Rich	Joel	2			1		2			1				6		
Greenwich	218	1	Rich	John Capt	1	1	1		1			1		1			6		
Granby	252	39	Richard	Abigail Wd		1								1			2		
Ashfield	344	23	Richards	Calvin	3			1		2	2	1	1				10		
Gill	87	17	Richards	Charles			1				1			1			3		
Northfield	30	18	Richards	Daniel	2	1		1		1	2		1				8		
Cummington	303	35	Richards	David			1			2		1					4		
Gill	87	13	Richards	Edward		1	1		1		1			1			5		
Cummington	304	2	Richards	Ezra	2				1	1	1			1			6		
Greenwich	221	37	Richards	James	2		2	1				1					6		
Plainfield	308	11	Richards	James	3	1	1	1			1	1	1				9		
Gill	87	16	Richards	Moses	2			1		2			1				6		
Cummington	303	34	Richards	Nehemiah	3	1	1	1		1	2		1	1			11		
Gill	87	18	Richards	Perin	1			1		3			1				6		
Shutesbury	111	27	Richards	Samuel	3			1		1	1			1			7		
Shutesbury	111	26	Richards	Calvin	1	1		1		3		1	1	1			9		
Cummington	303	32	Richards	Joseph	1			1	1	4	1		1				9		
Leverett	116	8	Richardson	Amasa	2		1					1	1				5		
Rowe	200	24	Richardson	Amos	1		1						1				3		
Greenwich	222	11	Richardson	Benja		1		1						1			3		
Leverett	116	4	Richardson	Francis	1			1		3			1				6		
West Springfield	357	18	Richardson	Isaac	2	1	1		1	1	1	1	1				9		
Palmer	258	22	Richardson	James		1				1		1					3		
Leverett	116	5	Richardson	Jereh				1				1		1			3		
Leverett	116	6	Richardson	John	2			1		1			1				5		

TOWN	PG#	LN#	LAST NAME	FIRST NAME	FREE WHITE MALES					FREE WHITE FEMALES					TOTAL ALL OTHER	TOTAL SLAVES	TOTALS	DISTRICT/ TOWNSHIP	NOTES
					under 10	10 to 16	16 to 26	26 to 45	45 and over	under 10	10 to 16	16 to 26	26 to 45	45 and over					
Springfield	244	6	Richardson	John	3			1		1			1				6		
Leyden	84	7	Richardson	Jonathan	1		1	1	1	4		1	1	1			11		
Shutesbury	111	24	Richardson	Joseph	1	1	1		1		1			1			6		
South Hadley	248	6	Richardson	Robert	1				1				1	1			4		
Shutesbury	112	1	Richardson	Samuel			2						1				3		
Longmeadow	92	32	Richardson	Stephen	1	2	1		1	1		1		1			8		
Cummington	303	30	Richardson	Winslow	1		1	1	1	1		2		1			8		
Shutesbury	111	25	Richardson	Zacheus			1					1					2		
South Brimfield	276	17	Richmond	Jonathan C	1			1			1		1				4		
Orange	43	8	Richmond	Perez	1		1		1	2		1		1			7		
New Salem	102	34	Richmond	Sylvanus	1			1		1		1					4		
Ashfield	344	24	Richmond	Zephh	3			1		1			1				6		
Colrain	188	23	Riddle	Gawn	1	2		1	1	3	1	2	1				12		
Colrain	188	26	Riddle	Hugh		1	1		1					1			4		
Shelburne	323	12	Riddle	Robert	3			1		2	3		1				10		
Charlemont	193	9	Riddle	Samuel	2			1		1	1		1				6		
Monson	266	43	Riddle	Thomas			1	1				1		1			4		
Greenwich	221	39	Rider	Benjamin	2	1		1	1	2		1	1				9		
Monson	265	32	Rider	Benjamin		1	1		1		1			1			5		
Belchertown	206	34	Rider	Daniel	4			1		1			1				7		
Conway	60	14	Rider	Daniel	3		1		1	3	2			1			11		
Palmer	258	17	Rider	Enos	2			1		3	2		1				9		
Hadley	286	9	Rider	Stephen	3		1						1				5		
Granville East Soc	529	23	Riley	Joseph			1		1			1		1			4		
Chester	146	4	Riley	Julias	1	3	1		1	1		2		1			10		
Blanford	180	2	Ring	Robert		1	1		1	2	1			1			7		
Wilbraham	235	36	Ringe	William	3	2			1	1	2	1	1				11		
West Springfield	355	3	Ripley	Abraham	2		1						1				4		
Gill	87	23	Ripley	Eli	2		1						1				4		
Greenfield	75	6	Ripley	Jerom		2	1	2		4	2		1				12		
Gill	87	19	Ripley	Laban	1			1		2			1				5		
Warwick	39	20	Ripley	Peter		1	1		1		1	1		1			6		
Granville East Soc	531	21	Rising	Abel	1	1	1		1	2	1		1				8		
Southwick	360	6	Rising	Abraham		1	1	1		1			1				5		
Southwick	360	14	Rising	Alexander	1			1		1			1				4		
Southwick	360	7	Rising	Amos		1		1	1	2	1	2		1			9		
Southwick	360	4	Rising	Asahel	1		1			1			1				4		
Southwick	360	2	Rising	Benjamin Jr				1					1				2		
Southwick	360	3	Rising	Heman	2		1						1				4		
Southwick	360	13	Rising	Ranah	1	1			2	1	1	1					7		
Barnardston	78	33	Ritter	John	1	2		1		2	1	1	1				9		
Ware	227	34	Road	Jonas		1											1		
Cummington	303	33	Robbins	Amariah			1			1			1				3		
Northfield	30	16	Robbins	Asa	2			1		2	1		1				7		
Hatfield	13	11	Robbins	Elihu				1		2		1			1		5		
Warwick	39	17	Robbins	Ephraim		1	2	1		1	1		1				7		
Amherst	293	27	Robbins	Isaac	2			1		3	1	1	1	1			10		
Warwick	39	21	Robbins	Isaac	1			1			1		1				4		
Wendell	107	21	Robbins	James	1			1			1	1	1				5		
Chesterfield	20	31	Robbins	Jesse											3		3		
Middlefield	155	11	Robbins	Job Deac		1	2		1		1	2		2			9		
Easthampton	134	7	Robbins	Joel	1			1					1				3		
Deerfield	54	37	Robbins	John	1	1	2		1	1			1				7		
Amherst	293	29	Robbins	Joseph		1	1				1	1					4		
Deerfield	54	36	Robbins	Nathan		1		1		2	2		1				7		
Orange	43	6	Robbins	Phinehas			1						1				2		
Belchertown	206	32	Robbins	Samuel	1	1	1		1	1	1			1			7		
Hadley	289	6	Robbins	Willard		1	1			1	1	1					5		
Cummington	303	31	Robbins	William	1	1			1	1	1			1			6		
Gill	87	14	Roberts	Amaziah		1		1	1	1				1			4		
Gill	87	15	Roberts	Ebenezer	3		1		2	1	1	1	1	1			11		
West Springfield	357	17	Roberts	Eli	3			1					1				5		
Whately	67	24	Roberts	George				1	2				1				4		
Palmer	259	4	Roberts	Nathaniel	3			1		2			1				7		
Northampton	4	25	Roberts	Reuben	1			1		1			1				4		
Monson	264	36	Roberts	Sally				1						2			3		
West Springfield	357	19	Roberts	William		2		1				1					4		
Springfield	244	42	Robertson	Joseph	1			1				1					3		
South Brimfield	275	8	Robinson	Amariah	3			1					1				5		
Granville Mid Soc.	166	8	Robinson	Charles	1	2		1		2			1				7		
Cummington	303	38	Robinson	Clerk	1	1		1		1			1	2			7		
Granville Mid Soc.	166	30	Robinson	Dan	1		1			1			1				7		
Granville Mid Soc.	166	11	Robinson	Dan Junr	2		1	1		1	2		1				8		
Granville Mid Soc.	167	17	Robinson	Hannah		1					1		1				3		
Granville Mid Soc.	167	18	Robinson	Hezekiah	1	2						1					4		
Barnardston	79	5	Robinson	Hulda		1				2	1	1					5		
Belchertown	206	31	Robinson	Israel				1						1			2		
South Hadley	248	15	Robinson	Jacob	1			2		1			1				5		
Plainfield	308	10	Robinson	Jeremiah	2	1		1		1	2	2		1			10		
Granby	254	36	Robinson	Joel	1		1					1					3		

TOWN	PG#	LN#	LAST NAME	FIRST NAME	FREE WHITE MALES					FREE WHITE FEMALES					TOTAL ALL OTHER	TOTAL SLAVES	TOTALS	DISTRICT/ TOWNSHIP	NOTES
					under 10	10 to 16	16 to 26	26 to 45	45 and over	under 10	10 to 16	16 to 26	26 to 45	45 and over					
Granville Mid Soc.	166	29	Robinson	Joel		1	1		1		1			1			5		
Granville Mid Soc.	166	10	Robinson	John		1		1		4	1		1				8		
Belchertown	210	10	Robinson	Josiah Jr				1				1	1	1			4		
Palmer	261	15	Robinson	Moses	2			1		3	1	1		1			9		
South Brimfield	276	12	Robinson	Nathan	2			1		1			1				5		
Plainfield	308	12	Robinson	Oliver	2			1		1			1				5		
Cummington	303	36	Robinson	Robert			1		1		1	1		1			5		
Granville Mid Soc.	165	18	Robinson	Timothy			1	1	1			1		1			5		
Chesterfield	20	28	Robinson	Zebulon			2		1			1	1	1			6		
Chesterfield	21	13	Robinson	Zebulon	2			1		2		1	1				7		
Blanford	176	9	Rockwell	Amasa	2			1		1			1				5		
Brimfield	273	7	Rockwell	John				1		2			1				4		
Southwick	360	5	Rockwell	John		1	1		1		2			1			6		
West Springfield	351	40	Rockwell	John				1		1		1		1			4		
Ware	227	36	Rockwell	Seth	2	1		1						1			5		
Conway	60	31	Rockwood	Abagail	2			1						1			4		
Springfield	247	3	Rockwood	Isaac	1			1		1				1			4		
New Salem	102	27	Rockwood	Joseph					1					1			2		
Wendell	107	22	Rockwood	Nehemiah					1	1				1			3		
Northfield	30	17	Rockwood	Thomas	2	1	1	1		2		1	1				9		
West Springfield	355	2	Roe	Seth		1		1		1				1			4		
Shutesbury	112	4	Rogers	Abijah	1			1				1					3		
South Brimfield	275	16	Rogers	Abijah	1			1			2			1			5		
Hawley	334	34	Rogers	Abisha															
West Springfield	351	43	Rogers	Abner	3		2	3				1	1	1			11		
Conway	60	30	Rogers	Benjamin				1		4	2	1					8		
Ashfield	344	11	Rogers	Benjm		1		1	1			1		1			5		
Ware	228	1	Rogers	Daniel				1						1			2		
South Brimfield	278	4	Rogers	Darius	2	1		1						1			5		
Greenwich	222	8	Rogers	David		2		1						1			4		
West Springfield	351	44	Rogers	David	1			1	1			2	1				6		
West Springfield	357	22	Rogers	Eli		1		1		1				1			4		
Westfield	125	23	Rogers	Eli	5		1					1					7		
West Springfield	351	45	Rogers	Elijah			2			1	1	1					5		
Southampton	133	8	Rogers	Elisha	2	1		1			2			2			8		
Wilbraham	232	25	Rogers	Elisha	1			1		1		1					4		
Northampton	2	13	Rogers	George			2	1									3		
Whately	67	23	Rogers	George		1		1		1				1			4		
Colrain	188	29	Rogers	Henry	2	2		1		1	1			1			8		
West Springfield	351	42	Rogers	Henry	2	1		1		1			2				7		
Wendell	107	20	Rogers	Isaac	3		1	1				1	1	1			8		
Granville West Soc	169	2	Rogers	Jabez			2			2	1	1		1			8		
Chesterfield	24	37	Rogers	James				1									1		
Monson	268	36	Rogers	Jasper				1		4		1					6		
West Springfield	351	46	Rogers	Jesse			1	1						2			4		
South Brimfield	278	3	Rogers	Joel Dr.				1						1			2		
Goshen	311	24	Rogers	John	1	1		1		2			1				6		
Greenwich	222	2	Rogers	John	2	1		1	1	4	1		1	1			12		
Palmer	261	31	Rogers	John	3	1	1		1	1		2	1	1			11		
South Brimfield	278	5	Rogers	John				1				1	1				3		
Southampton	133	7	Rogers	John	1		1			2	2	2					9		
Westfield	125	22	Rogers	Jonathan				1						1			2		
Brimfield	275	4	Rogers	Joseph		1	1	1			1			1			5	South Brimfield	
Ashfield	344	21	Rogers	Joshua				1		2			1	1			5		
Chesterfield	24	36	Rogers	Joshua		1		1		2	2	1					7		
West Springfield	357	20	Rogers	Josiah		1	1	1			1	1		1			6		
West Springfield	357	21	Rogers	Josiah 2d	1		1	2			1	1		1			7		
Hawley	334	35	Rogers	Moses				1									1		
Barnardston	79	4	Rogers	Nathan	1	1						1					3		
South Brimfield	276	6	Rogers	Nathaniel		1		1			1	1		2			6		
Brimfield	275	18	Rogers	Oliver	2			1		2		1	1				7	South Brimfield	
Charlemont	193	27	Rogers	Oren	1			1		1	1						4		
Granville West Soc	169	4	Rogers	Sarah		2		2		1		1	1				7		
West Springfield	351	41	Rogers	Sarah								1		1			2		
Greenwich	222	13	Rogers	Stephen	1			1		2		1					5		
South Brimfield	277	8	Rogers	Stephen	1			1		1	1	1		1			6		
Chesterfield	23	6	Rogers	Thomas		1		1						2			4		
Greenfield	75	5	Roggers	Samuel	2			1						1			4		
Amherst	290	30	Rood	Abigal										1			1		
Conway	60	22	Rood	Levi		1											1		
Buckland	329	16	Rood	Thaddeus	4			1		2			1				8		
Southampton	129	10	Root	Aaron	2			1		1			1				5		
Granville East Soc	531	12	Root	Amos	2	2	1	1	2			1	1	1			11		
Middlefield	158	1	Root	Daniel	3			1		2			1				7		
Longmeadow	92	30	Root	Daniel	1	2		1		2	2	1	1	1			11		
Longmeadow	92	29	Root	Daniel Junr			1						1				2		
Belchertown	210	5	Root	Darius				1		1			1				3		
Williamsburg	443	5	Root	Elias	1			1		1	1		1				5		
Northampton	5	28	Root	Eliazer				1					1				2		
Belchertown	210	6	Root	Elisha				1									4		

288

TOWN	PG#	LN#	LAST NAME	FIRST NAME	FREE WHITE MALES under 10	10 to 16	16 to 26	26 to 45	45 and over	FREE WHITE FEMALES under 10	10 to 16	16 to 26	26 to 45	45 and over	TOTAL ALL OTHER	TOTAL SLAVES	TOTALS	DISTRICT/ TOWNSHIP	NOTES
Montague	47	17	Root	Elisha		1	3		1		1		1	1			8		
Westfield	125	14	Root	Enoch			1			1		1					3		
Westfield	121	23	Root	Gad	3	1	1		1		2	1	1				10		
Southwick	360	11	Root	Gideon				1			1		1				3		
Southwick	360	12	Root	Gideon Junr	1	1		1		2		1					6		
Montague	47	23	Root	Jonathan	1	1	1		1		1	1		1			7		
Montague	47	16	Root	Joseph		2	1		1			2	1				7		
Northampton	5	36	Root	Joseph				1					1				2		
Westfield	119	12	Root	Joseph		1	1		1	1	1	2		1			8		
Northampton	5	37	Root	Joseph Jun			1			2		1			1		5		
Montague	47	25	Root	Martin	2		1		1	2	3			1			10		
Montgomery	161	21	Root	Martin	2	1	2		1	1	1	1	1				10		
Montague	47	22	Root	Moses		1	3		1			1	1	1			8		
Westfield	124	25	Root	Noadiah	2		1		1		2			1			7		
Southwick	360	9	Root	Noah			1				1						2		
Conway	60	20	Root	Oliver		1	2	1	2	1		2		2			11		
Belchertown	210	4	Root	Orlando		2		1			1	1	1				6		
Montague	47	24	Root	Phillip	1		2	2	1			1		1			10		
Belchertown	210	7	Root	Remembrance	1		1				1		1				4		
Westfield	119	24	Root	Saml	2		1		1	3	1	1	1				10		
Barnardston	79	3	Root	Samuel	3	1		1	1	2			1				9		
Westfield	118	2	Root	Silas	2		1	1	1	1		1	2	1			10		
Northampton	10	20	Root	Simeon		1	1				1		1				4		
Middlefield	157	40	Root	Solomon	4		1			1			1				7		
Granville East Soc	529	1	Root	Stephen	1	1		1									3		
Westfield	125	21	Root	Stephen	1	1	3		1	3	1		1	2			13		
Southwick	360	1	Root	Talmon		1		1		1			1				4		
Middlefield	158	2	Root	Thomas				1						1			2		
Ludlow	257	3	Root	Timothy		2		1		4	1			1			9		
Southwick	360	8	Root	Zur	1	1	2		1		1			1			7		
Granville Mid Soc.	167	36	Rose	Abner				1			1			1			3		
Granville Mid Soc.	167	12	Rose	David	2	2	2		1	1	1	1		1			11		
Granville East Soc	533	6	Rose	Elisha		1		1			1		1				4		
Granville East Soc	531	9	Rose	Gamaliel	4		1		1			1					7		
Granville East Soc	529	31	Rose	Hiram	1			1		3		1					6		
Granville East Soc	529	20	Rose	Justus	3	1		1		2	1		1	1			10		
Granville East Soc	529	29	Rose	Lemuel	1	1		1		3	1		1				8		
Granville East Soc	529	18	Rose	Levi		1	2		1	3	2		1				10		
Granville East Soc	529	30	Rose	Levi	1			1		2			1				5		
Granville East Soc	531	30	Rose	Noadiah	3			1		1		1	1				7		
Granville Mid Soc.	165	27	Rose	Seth	3	1	1				1	1	1				8		
Granville East Soc	533	5	Rose	Shaun		1	3	1		1		2		1			9		
Westfield	123	21	Rose	Thomas	1		1	1		2			1	1			7		
Granville East Soc	529	13	Rose	Timothy	2	1		1	1	2	2		1	1			11		
Holland	278	6	Rosebrook	Gershom	1		2		1			2		1			7		
Holland	279	33	Rosebrook	Jona	4			1					1				6		
Hatfield	11	4	Rosevelt	Jacob				1						1			2		
Worthington	299	14	Ross	Amasa		1	1		1		1		1				5		
Wendell	107	19	Ross	Ephraim	2	1		1		1			1				6		
Worthington	300	3	Ross	James			1				1		1				3		
Wendell	107	18	Ross	John			3		1			1		1			6		
Monson	266	13	Ross	Micah	2		2		1	2	1	1					9		
Colrain	188	25	Ross	Samuel	3		1	1		1	3	1	1				11		
Deerfield	54	35	Ross	Samuel			1		1	1				1			4		
Worthington	300	4	Ross	Shelah	4			1		1			1				7		
Deerfield	54	40	Ross	Thomas			1			1	1		1				4		
Monson	266	15	Ross	Zephaniah	2	1						1					4		
Hadley	289	7	Roth	Widow								2		1			3		
Leyden	84	5	Rounds	Hezekiah	1		1		1		2		1				6		
Amherst	290	32	Rowe	Abel	1		2					2					5		
Montague	47	26	Rowe	Daniel	1		2		1	2	1		1				8		
Sunderland	283	16	Rowe	Elijah	3		1						1				5		
Sunderland	283	15	Rowe	John				1			2	1					4		
Sunderland	282	15	Rowe	John Junr	1	2	2		1	2		1	1				10		
Westfield	124	24	Rowe	Joseph		1		1		5	1		1				9		
Northfield	30	20	Rowley	Israel				1						1			2		
Russell	138	6	Rowley	Martin	1			1				1		1			4		
West Springfield	354	59	Rowley	Nathan				1						1			2		
Granville East Soc	529	6	Rowley	Roswell	1	1		1		3	1		1				8		
Charlemont	193	26	Rudd	Andrew		2		1			1		1				5		
Charlemont	193	25	Rudd	Nathanael	1		1						1				3		
Charlemont	193	24	Rudd	Zebbeus	2	2		2	1	2			1	1			11		
Buckland	329	18	Ruddock	Edward	3		1	1				1					6		
Springfield	240	29	Rudd	Elias	1		1			2		1					5		
Norwich	151	9	Rude	John		1		1		1	1		1				5		
Norwich	151	10	Rude	John Junr	2		1			2		1					6		
Ludlow	256	42	Rude	Moses		1					1						2		
Ashfield	344	20	Rude	Sebrus	1	1	1	1		2	1		1	1			9		
Ludlow	256	41	Rude	Zephaniah		2		1						1			4		
Greenfield	75	8	Rugg	Joshua			1			3			1				5		

TOWN	PG#	LN#	LAST NAME	FIRST NAME	FREE WHITE MALES					FREE WHITE FEMALES					TOTAL ALL OTHER	TOTAL SLAVES	TOTALS	DISTRICT/ TOWNSHIP	NOTES
					under 10	10 to 16	16 to 26	26 to 45	45 and over	under 10	10 to 16	16 to 26	26 to 45	45 and over					
Heath	197	3	Rugg	Reuben	1	2	1		1	1		2					8		
Montague	47	31	Ruggles	Edward	1	1	5	2		4	1	1	1				16		
Greenwich	222	3	Ruggles	Joseph			3		1	1	1		1	1			8		
Belchertown	206	33	Ruggles	Mary Wd	1	1							1				3		
Orange	43	7	Ruggles	Samuel		1	1	1			1	1	1				6		
Springfield	239	13	Rumrill	Alexander		2	1			1	1	1					6		
Longmeadow	94	41	Rumrill	Ebenezer				1			1		1				3		
Longmeadow	93	30	Rumrill	Levi	3			1		1		1					6		
Longmeadow	93	29	Rumrill	Nehemiah				1					1				2		
South Hadley	251	6	Rumsill	Asa			1			3	1	1					6		
Northampton	6	13	Rupell	Hezekiah		1	1	1			1		1				5		
Northampton	6	14	Rupell	Hezekiah Jr	2		2	2				1	1				8		
Wilbraham	234	5	Rusell	John		1		1		1		1					4		
Middlefield	155	14	Russ	Hezekiah		1							1				2		
Middlefield	156	8	Russel	Abel	3			1	1	1			2	1			9		
Middlefield	156	5	Russel	Alpheus	1			1		2			1				5		
Middlefield	156	24	Russel	Gideon	3	3		1		1			1				9		
Warwick	39	19	Russel	Justus		1	1					1					3		
Russell	139	17	Russel	Richard	2	1	1		1	1	1	1	1				9		
Brimfield	272	7	Russell	Abigail Wd						1	1		1				3		
Springfield	243	16	Russell	Abigail Wd									1				1		
Springfield	244	5	Russell	Abner	3	1	1	1		1			1				8		
Wilbraham	237	10	Russell	Benjamin	1	1					1		1				4		
Greenwich	221	38	Russell	Daniel		1	1	1		1		1					5		
Hadley	285	3	Russell	Daniel	1	1	2	1	1		2	1	1				10		
Springfield	243	15	Russell	Ebenezer		1	1		1	1	2		1				7		
New Salem	102	32	Russell	Eli		1	2		1	1			1				6		
West Springfield	354	60	Russell	Elias		1						1					2		
Conway	60	21	Russell	Elihu	3	1	1	1		2		2					10		
Deerfield	54	34	Russell	Elijah			3				1		1				5		
Springfield	248	8	Russell	Elijah		1	1				1						3		
Longmeadow	93	9	Russell	Ellis		1		1			1		1				4		
Longmeadow	93	3	Russell	Emery	1	1		1		1		1					5		
Wilbraham	237	9	Russell	Ezekiel				1					1				2		
Sunderland	282	4	Russell	Israel		1	1				1	1	1				5		
Chesterfield	22	16	Russell	Joanna		1				1	1	1		1			5		
Chesterfield	24	9	Russell	John			1			1	2		1				5		
Greenfield	75	7	Russell	John	2		1	1		1		1	1				7		
Hadley	285	2	Russell	John	2	1	1	1		2	1		1				9		
New Salem	102	33	Russell	Jonathan		2		1		1			1				5		
Wendell	107	23	Russell	Jonathan	1	1		1		2			1				6		
Wendell	107	24	Russell	Joseph	1			1		2		1					5		
Springfield	248	10	Russell	Luther		1					1						2		
Longmeadow	93	8	Russell	Oliver		1				1	1						3		
Greenwich	222	10	Russell	Peter	1	1		1		1		2	1				7		
Sunderland	283	7	Russell	Phillip	2	1	1		1	1		1	1				8		
Wilbraham	237	8	Russell	Robert		1		1			2		1				5		
Deerfield	54	41	Russell	Roswell			2			1		1					4		
Hawley	334	37	Russell	Saml		1		1		3		1					6		
Northampton	7	8	Russell	Seth	1	1		1		2		1			1		7		
Chesterfield	24	11	Russell	Solomon	3			1		2	1		1	1			9		
Northampton	7	25	Russell	Thaddeus	2		1	1				1					5		
Brimfield	273	35	Russell	Titus	1	1		1		1		1	2				7		
Deerfield	54	33	Russell	William	2	2	1	1		1		1					8		
Longmeadow	93	7	Russell	Wolcott	2			1		2			1				6		
Sunderland	283	26	Russell	Zebina		1											1		
Monson	266	39	Rust	Ebenezer				1					1				2		
Southampton	129	28	Rust	Ebenezer	2	1		1		2	1		1				8		
Westhampton	18	27	Rust	Elijah	1	1		1		1	1	1	1				7		
Monson	266	38	Rust	Elisha	2		1			1		1					5		
Northampton	5	35	Rust	Elisha	3		1			1		1					6		
Norwich	153	2	Rust	Gershom			1			3		1					5		
Westhampton	17	22	Rust	Joel		1	1			3		1					6		
Chester	147	1	Rust	Joseph Ashley		1				1	1	1					4		
Chester	148	16	Rust	Justin	2		1			1	1	1					6		
Southampton	132	11	Rust	Lemuel		1		1		1		1		1			5		
Northampton	8	20	Rust	Mary									2				2		
Norwich	153	23	Rust	Zebulon	2	1		1		1	1		1				7		
Barnardston	78	34	Ryther	David	3	1		1	1	2	1		1	1			11		
Barnardston	79	1	Ryther	David Junr	3		1	1			2		1				8		
Barnardston	79	2	Ryther	Peter		2				1	1	1					5		
Granville East Soc	529	32	S*	John		1		1			2		1				5		
Granville East Soc	531	29	S*ina	Benjamin	2		1		1	2	2	1		1			10		
Leyden	84	16	Sabens	Jedediah	2		1						1				4		
Monson	264	5	Sabin	Darius			1			2		1					4		
Norwich	152	4	Sackel	Zavan Lieut	3	2	2		1	1	1		1				11		
Westfield	120	31	Sacket	Adnah	1		3		1			1		2			8		
Westfield	121	12	Sacket	Asher	1			1	1		1			1			6		
Westfield	122	21	Sacket	Eliakim	1		1			2			2				6		
Westfield	127	18	Sacket	Ezra	1	1	1		1	3	2	1		1			11		

290

TOWN	PG#	LN#	LAST NAME	FIRST NAME	FWM under 10	FWM 10 to 16	FWM 16 to 26	FWM 26 to 45	FWM 45 and over	FWF under 10	FWF 10 to 16	FWF 16 to 26	FWF 26 to 45	FWF 45 and over	TOTAL ALL OTHER	TOTAL SLAVES	TOTALS	DISTRICT/ TOWNSHIP	NOTES
Westfield	122	24	Sacket	Gad	1	1	1		1	2			1				7		
Westfield	122	29	Sacket	Joel		1		1		1	1	1					5		
Westfield	121	13	Sacket	John	2			1		1			1				5		
Westfield	122	18	Sacket	Jona				1		3	2		1				7		
Westfield	121	21	Sacket	Manarola	3			1		1			1				6		
Westfield	121	28	Sacket	Moses	2	1	1		1	1	1	1		1			9		
Westfield	127	16	Sacket	Moses 2d	3			1		1			1				6		
Westfield	122	13	Sacket	Noble	1								2				4		
Westfield	121	30	Sacket	Ozern	1	1	2	1	1		1	1	1	1			10		
Southwick	360	26	Sacket	Pliny		2			1	1	2			1			7		
Westfield	119	9	Sacket	Royal	2			1		1	1		1				6		
Westfield	127	21	Sacket	Stephen	1		1		1	1	2		1				7		
Westfield	127	20	Sacket	Stephen Junr	1	2							1				4		
Chester	144	20	Sacket	Washam		2							1				3		
Westfield	119	10	Sacket	Wm		1	2		1	1	1		1	1			8		
Westfield	122	3	Sacket	Wm Junr	2	2		1		3			1				9		
Orange	43	17	Sadler	Abiel		2		1		4	1		1				9		
Ashfield	345	16	Sadler	John		1		1		2	1	1	1				7		
Ashfield	345	21	Sadler	Joshua	2	2		1		2	1		1				9		
Ashfield	345	27	Sadler	Noah	2	1		1		2	1		1				8		
Worthington	298	7	Saffard	Elias		4											4		
Northampton	6	10	Sage	Lewis S	2		1	1		3			1				8		
Brimfield	269	16	Salisbury	Benjamin		1		1		1		1	1				5		
Conway	61	1	Salisbury	Seth		1		1					1	1			4		
Conway	61	2	Salisbury	Stephen	2			1		2	1		1	1			8		
Conway	60	50	Salisbury	William	1	1		1	1	3	1		1	1			10		
Goshen	312	22	Salmon	George	1		1	1		2			1				6		
Goshen	311	26	Salmon	John		1				1		1					3		
New Salem	103	10	Sampson	George	2			1		3			1				7		
Worthington	302	7	Sampson	Issachar	1		1	1		1		1					5		
New Salem	103	9	Sampson	Jacob	2	2	1		1		1	2		2			11		
Norwich	151	3	Sampson	Knellum	2	1		1		1			1				7		
Pelham	216	29	Sampson	Nathl Deacn	2		1		1	1	1		1	2			9		
New Salem	103	3	Sampson	Peter		1		1		4	2	3	1				12		
Shutesbury	112	15	Sampson	Peter	3			1		2			1				7		
Springfield	247	7	Sampson	Philemon		1				4			1				6		
Norwich	151	12	Sampson	Silvenus	2			1		1	1		1				6		
Chesterfield	21	27	Sampson	Sylvanus	1			1		1	1		1				5		
Blanford	179	11	San*	David	1	1	1		1	3	1	3		1			12		
Shelburne	324	2	Sanders	Aaron			1			2		2		1			6		
Leverett	116	17	Sanders	Hannah								1	1				2		
Granville East Soc	531	13	Sanders	Nathan		1		1				2	1				5		
New Salem	103	22	Sanders	Nathan				1		1	2	1		1			6		
Shutesbury	112	20	Sanders	Nathan	2			1					1				4		
New Salem	103	30	Sanders	Oliver	1		1						1				3		
Whately	68	6	Sanderson	Asa	3	1	1	1		3			1	1			11		
Conway	60	34	Sanderson	Cyrus	2			1					1				4		
Whately	68	11	Sanderson	David	1		2	1		2			1				7		
Ashfield	345	28	Sanderson	Elnathan	2	1			1	1	1		1				7		
Chester	149	29	Sanderson	Elnathan		1								1			2		
Montgomery	161	30	Sanderson	Elnathan				1									1		
Whately	68	5	Sanderson	Isaac	4	1	1	1		1	2		1				11		
Conway	61	3	Sanderson	James		1		1		2	1		2				7		
Springfield	239	24	Sanderson	Jeduthon	2	1		1		2				1			7		
Barnardston	79	28	Sanderson	Joseph	1	2	1			1	1						6		
Ashfield	345	29	Sanderson	Morcena	1		1			1		1					4		
Chester	145	33	Sanderson	Silvanus Lt	2	2	1	1		2		2					10		
Whately	67	26	Sanderson	Thomas	2	1	6	1		1	1		1				13		
Blanford	178	18	Sanderson	Trial	2		1			2	1	1					7		
Sunderland	283	5	Sanderson	William	3		1						1				5		
Chester	147	3	Sandford	Daniel	3		1			2			1				7		
Middlefield	159	6	Sandford	Elias	1	2	3	1		1		1		1			10		
Norwich	151	25	Sandford	Holsa	3		1						1				5		
Easthampton	134	11	Sandford	John	1		1			2			1				5		
Norwich	151	26	Sandford	Ruth Wid		1							1	2			4		
Belchertown	208	1	Sanford	Ichabod	1	1	5	1			1	1					10		
Hawley	335	9	Sanford	Willm		1	1					1					3		
Springfield	248	7	Sanger	Jedidiah	2		1				1		1				5		
West Springfield	355	15	Sargeant	Ebenezer	1		1		1	2	1		1				7		
West Springfield	355	16	Sargeant	James			1			2		1					4		
Springfield	242	24	Sargeant	Thomas	2	1	2	1				2					8		
Sunderland	283	11	Saunders	Abraham		2	3	1						1			7		
Wilbraham	236	35	Saunders	Reuben	1		1			1		1					4		
Deerfield	55	10	Saunderson	John		3	1		1			1		1			7		
Deerfield	55	19	Saunderson	Joseph		1	2	1		1	1	2		1			9		
Ashfield	345	23	Savage	Abraham	3	2	1	1		1	1	1	1	1			12		
Buckland	329	27	Savage	Abraham	3	2	1	1		1	1	1	1	1			12		
Greenwich	222	30	Savage	Abraham		1		1						1			3		
Blanford	179	4	Savage	John		1		1						1			3		
Colrain	188	35	Savage	Mary			1			1				1			3		
Monson	263	28	Savor	John			1					1					2		

TOWN	PG#	LN#	LAST NAME	FIRST NAME	FREE WHITE MALES					FREE WHITE FEMALES					TOTAL ALL OTHER	TOTAL SLAVES	TOTALS	DISTRICT/ TOWNSHIP	NOTES
					under 10	10 to 16	16 to 26	26 to 45	45 and over	under 10	10 to 16	16 to 26	26 to 45	45 and over					
Greenfield	75	9	Sawtwell	John	1			1		1			1				4		
Northfield	30	22	Sawyer	Abner	1			1		1		1	1				5		
Wendell	107	36	Sawyer	Ephraim		2			1	1	1		1				6		
Wendell	107	35	Sawyer	Jabez	1	1		1				1					4		
Wendell	107	34	Sawyer	Joseph	3			2		1			1				7		
Northfield	30	21	Sawyer	Thomas	2		2	1		2	1		1				9		
Orange	43	18	Sawyer	William			1						1				2		
Northampton	10	16	Saxe	John				1					1				2		
Whately	68	2	Scott	Abel	1	1		2		1	2	1	2	1			11		
Whately	67	30	Scott	Abraham	1			1			1		1				4		
Blanford	182	15	Scott	Benjamin	2	1		1		1			1				6		
Whately	67	28	Scott	Benjamin	1			1	1	1		1		2			7		
Palmer	258	14	Scott	Calvin Doct	2	1		1		1	1		1		2		9		
Charlemont	194	1	Scott	Consider		2				1		1					4		
Williamsburg	443	12	Scott	David	3	1		1	1	4	1	2		1			14		
Norwich	152	7	Scott	David Lieut		1		1		1	1		1				5		
Hatfield	14	18	Scott	Ebenezer	1	1		1		1			1				5		
Montague	47	35	Scott	Eleazer	2			1		1	1		1				6		
Barnardston	79	13	Scott	Elihu	2	1		1		1			1	1			7		
Northampton	4	5	Scott	Elijah			1				1		1				3		
Ware	228	12	Scott	Ephraim	4		1	1				1	1				8		
Worthington	299	13	Scott	Hector	1			1		2			1				5		
Montague	47	36	Scott	Ira	1	2	1	1		2	1	1	1				10		
Hawley	335	4	Scott	Isaac	3			1		1			1	1			7		
Amherst	290	33	Scott	Israel	1		1	1		2			1				6		
Chester	148	32	Scott	James	1	1		1		1			1				5		
Hatfield	11	16	Scott	James		1							1				2		
Brimfield	273	34	Scott	John				1				1	1				3		
Whately	68	7	Scott	Mary	1	1	1			1			1	1			6		
Barnardston	79	15	Scott	Moses		1		1		2	2	1		1			8		
Gill	88	3	Scott	Moses	2	3		1		1	1		1				9		
Hawley	335	3	Scott	Phinehas	3	2	1	1		2	1	1		1			12		
Montague	47	37	Scott	Reuben Jr	2		1	1					1				5		
Barnardston	79	24	Scott	Rufus	1		1					1					3		
Montague	47	32	Scott	Rufus		1				2			1				4		
Whately	68	3	Scott	Selah	2			1		3	1	1		1			9		
Blanford	175	30	Scott	William		2	1			2	1		1	1			8		
Chester	148	31	Scott	William	1	1		1		1	1		1				6		
West Springfield	351	48	Scovel	John			1				1		1				3		
Granville Mid Soc.	165	19	Scovil	Bela		2		1					1				4		
Montague	48	1	Scranton	Gershom	1		1						1				3		
Belchertown	210	13	Scranton	Samuel	1		1	1		1	1	2		2			9		
Southampton	131	10	Searl	Aaron				1									1		
Southampton	132	1	Searl	Abijah	1		2	1		1	3						8		
Norwich	153	34	Searl	Asahel	1	1	1				2	1	1				7		
Westfield	124	32	Searl	Biddad	1			1		3	1						6		
Southampton	130	15	Searl	Bildad		2		1				1	1				5		
Southampton	128	12	Searl	Clark		1						1					2		
Amherst	293	26	Searl	Elisha				1					1				2		
Easthampton	134	22	Searl	Elisha			1			2		1					4		
Southampton	131	34	Searl	Elizabeth Wd								2	1				3		
Southampton	132	3	Searl	Gaius	1		1				1						3		
Southampton	132	2	Searl	Gideon	2			1		1		1	1				6		
Southampton	132	6	Searl	Gideon Junr	1	1		1		1	1		1				6		
Southampton	131	11	Searl	Ira	1			1		3			1				6		
Southampton	129	2	Searl	Israel	1	1		1		1			1				5		
Montgomery	160	5	Searl	Jesse Doct				1		1	1		1				4		
Southampton	130	11	Searl	Job	3		1	1		1	2		1				9		
Montague	47	33	Searl	Joshua			1	1					1				3		
Southampton	131	8	Searl	Justus		1	1	1				1		2			6		
Southampton	132	4	Searl	Levi			1				1		1				3		
Southampton	131	12	Searl	Moses	1	2		1		1			1				6		
Southampton	131	23	Searl	Nathan		3		1		1	1		1				7		
Southampton	131	35	Searl	Nathaniel			1	3					1	1			6		
Southampton	132	5	Searl	Nathaniel Junr		1		1				1					3		
Westfield	124	33	Searl	Stephen	1	3		1		2			1				8		
Southampton	130	9	Searl	Zepher Junr	2	1	1	1		2	1		1				9		
Southampton	128	10	Searl	Zopher		2		1		1	1		1				6		
Norwich	153	33	Searl	Joel		1				1		1					3		
Northampton	11	15	Searle	Elisha				1		2	1		1				5		
Norwich	152	34	Searles	Hinney	1		1				1						3		
Chester	147	9	Searles	Zenas	1	2	1	1		3			2				10		
West Springfield	357	25	Searls	Lemuel	1			1		1		1					4		
West Springfield	357	24	Searls	Simeon	3			1		2			1				7		
Greenwich	222	23	Sears	Barnabas	1	1		1		3			1	2			9		
Ashfield	344	29	Sears	Enos		2		1		1	1	2		1			8		
Greenwich	224	9	Sears	Freeman	3		1	1	1	2		1	1	1	2		13		
Westfield	118	14	Sears	John			1			1	1	1					4		
Ashfield	344	26	Sears	Jonathan		1	2	2	1	1	3	1		1			12		
Pelham	216	21	Sears	Joseph	1			1					1				3		

TOWN	PG#	LN#	LAST NAME	FIRST NAME	FREE WHITE MALES					FREE WHITE FEMALES					TOTAL ALL OTHER	TOTAL SLAVES	TOTALS	DISTRICT/ TOWNSHIP	NOTES
					under 10	10 to 16	16 to 26	26 to 45	45 and over	under 10	10 to 16	16 to 26	26 to 45	45 and over					
Ashfield	344	27	Sears	Paul	2	1			1	3	2	1	1				11		
Ashfield	345	19	Sears	Peter			1		1					1			3		
Ashfield	344	28	Sears	Roland	2	3	1		1	1		2		1			11		
Hawley	335	6	Sears	Roland		1	3	1	1			2		1			9		
Greenwich	222	14	Sears	Rolland	1	1			1	3	1		1				8		
Hawley	335	5	Sears	Rufus	2			1		2		1					6		
Ashfield	345	26	Sears	seth				1					1				2		
Shelburne	324	12	Seaver	Elijah Jr				1			1						2		
Conway	60	47	Seaver	W. Josiah			1		1	1	2			1			6		
Chester	148	33	Seaward	Joel				1					1				2		
Chester	149	2	Seaward	Joel Junr	1		2	1		2		1	1				8		
Chester	149	1	Seaward	Nathan	1			1	1	3	1		1				8		
Palmer	260	7	Sedgwick	Gordon	1	1	1	1	1	3	1	3	1				13		
Northampton	10	3	Seegur	Charles L	3	1		3		5			2				14		
Chester	144	18	Seischo	Joseph	1		1					1					3		
Ashfield	344	30	Selden	Asa		1		1		2			1				5		
Middlefield	158	5	Selden	Ebenezer				1						1			2		
West Springfield	355	7	Selden	Joseph				1						1			2		
Pelham	216	28	Selfridge	Rebekhah										1			1		
Gill	88	6	Selick	Frederick			1										1		
Granville West Soc	169	6	Sennet	Joseph	1	2	2		1	1	1			1			9		
Shelburne	323	23	Senver	Elijah	1	1	1	2	1		1	1		1			9		
Ludlow	256	19	Seranton	John		1			1	1				1			4		
Brimfield	274	7	Sesions	Alex Col		1	3		1		1	1		1			8		
Brimfield	272	36	Sesions	Saml Capt	1	1	1	1	1	1		2					8		
Wilbraham	232	34	Sessions	Robert	3	1	2		1	3	2	1	1	1			15		
Conway	61	6	Severance	Jesse		1	2		1	1	2	1		1			9		
Shelburne	324	1	Severance	Jonathan	1	1			1		2			1			6		
Shelburne	323	21	Severance	Joseph	1		1	1		1		2	1				7		
Shelburne	324	7	Severance	Martin Jr	2	1	1		2	4	2	2	3	1			18		
Montague	48	2	Severance	Moses		2		1			1	1		1			6		
Shelburne	324	5	Severance	Saml	2			1		2	2		1				8		
Heath	197	11	Severance	Selah	1	1		1				1					4		
Shelburne	323	26	Severance	Solomon	2	2		1		3		1	1				10		
Gill	87	24	Severence	Abner	1	1	1		1		1			1			6		
Barnardston	79	11	Severence	David				1		2		1	1				5		
Barnardston	79	25	Severence	John					1			1					2		
Greenfield	75	14	Severence	Jonathan			2	1					2	1			6		
Greenfield	75	15	Severence	Joseph	3		2	1		2	3		1				12		
Warwick	39	43	Severy	Jonathan	2	1				1	1			1			6		
Hatfield	14	15	Sewall	Hezekiah											3		3		
Granby	254	8	Sexton	Daniel				1			1			1			3		
Deerfield	55	14	Sexton	David		1			1			2		1			5		
New Salem	103	31	Sexton	David	1	1	1	1		1			1	1			7		
Deerfield	55	15	Sexton	Ebenezer		3	1						1	1			6		
Westfield	123	5	Sexton	Elizabeth Wd		1	1			1				1			4		
Deerfield	55	17	Sexton	Joel				1					1				2		
Wilbraham	233	34	Sexton	Joseph	2	1	1	1				1	1				7		
New Salem	103	2	Sexton	Judah	1			1				1					3		
Wilbraham	238	25	Sexton	Noah	2			1				1					4		
Worthington	298	20	Sexton	Noah	1				1	2			1				5		
Wilbraham	238	26	Sexton	Oliver	2	2		1		2			1				8		
Deerfield	55	16	Sexton	Rufus	1			1		3		2					7		
Wilbraham	238	24	Sexton	Samuel				1						1			2		
Southwick	360	19	Sexton	Stephen	1		1		1	2				2			7		
Granville East Soc	527	10	Seymour	Asa	3	1	1	1		1	1	1	1				10		
Chesterfield	20	24	Shaddock	Samuel		1	1		1			1		1			5		
Northampton	8	6	Shaller	John	1			1		2			1				5		
Leyden	84	15	Shattoch	Ezra	3	3	2		1			2		1			12		
Gill	87	26	Shattock	Rueben		1		1	1			1		1			5		
Colrain	189	5	Shattuck	Abel	2		2	1		1		1	1				8		
Monson	265	45	Shaw	Absolome	1		1		1	3			1				7		
New Salem	103	28	Shaw	Amos			1			3		1					5		
Chesterfield	19	1	Shaw	Asa		1			1			1		1			4		
Buckland	330	3	Shaw	Benjm	1	1		1	1	1	1	2	1				9		
Cummington	304	13	Shaw	Beriah	1			1				1	1				4		
Belchertown	210	26	Shaw	Daniel	2	3	1		1	4		2	1				14		
Brimfield	274	31	Shaw	Daniel	2		1	2		1			1				7		
New Salem	102	38	Shaw	Daniel	2	1		1			1		1				6		
Springfield	248	6	Shaw	Daniel	1	2		1					1				5		
Shutesbury	112	17	Shaw	Darling	2	1	1	1		3	2		1				11		
Ware	228	4	Shaw	David		1	1	1				1					4		
Cummington	304	12	Shaw	Ebenezer	1			1		1		1	1				5		
Belchertown	207	13	Shaw	Elias			1			1			1				3		
Belchertown	211	24	Shaw	Elias			1					1					2		
Palmer	260	36	Shaw	Erwin	2	1	1		1	2	2	1	1				11		
Pelham	216	27	Shaw	Ezra	1			1				1					3		
Brimfield	274	30	Shaw	George		1			1					1			3		
Rowe	200	25	Shaw	Gideon	1			2		2			1				6		
Hawley	334	39	Shaw	Hosea	1		1					1					3		

TOWN	PG#	LN#	LAST NAME	FIRST NAME	FREE WHITE MALES under 10	10 to 16	16 to 26	26 to 45	45 and over	FREE WHITE FEMALES under 10	10 to 16	16 to 26	26 to 45	45 and over	TOTAL ALL OTHER	TOTAL SLAVES	TOTALS	DISTRICT/ TOWNSHIP	NOTES
Pelham	216	30	Shaw	Jacob	2			1		1		1					5		
Cummington	305	32	Shaw	James	1			1		1	1						4		
Monson	263	21	Shaw	James	2	1		1		2		1					7		
New Salem	103	27	Shaw	James	2	1		1		2		2					8		
Palmer	260	6	Shaw	James		1	1	1		1		2					6		
Wilbraham	234	44	Shaw	James		1	1		1					1	1		5		
Monson	263	19	Shaw	John			1			1		1					3		
Palmer	262	10	Shaw	John			1			3		1					5		
Plainfield	308	18	Shaw	John	1			1			1	1	1				6		
South Brimfield	276	24	Shaw	John	3		1	1			1		1				7		
Ware	228	2	Shaw	John			1	1	1				2				5		
Ware	228	3	Shaw	John 2d Lt	2	1	2	1				2	1	1			10		
Monson	268	9	Shaw	John 4th			1	1	1				1				4		
Monson	265	27	Shaw	John Dr	2		3	1	1	1			1				9		
Brimfield	270	6	Shaw	Joshua	1		1			1		1					4		
Plainfield	308	17	Shaw	Joshua		1		1		1	1		1				5		
Palmer	261	18	Shaw	Joshua Dr			1	1			1		1				4		
Plainfield	308	16	Shaw	Joshua Jun	1		1	1		2			1	1			7		
Plainfield	308	19	Shaw	Josiah	1	2		1		1	1		1				7		
South Brimfield	276	37	Shaw	Julius	1			1		1			1				4		
Monson	266	2	Shaw	Luther		1	1					1					3		
Plainfield	308	20	Shaw	Mary		1	1					1	1				4		
Palmer	261	11	Shaw	Moses	1			1				1	1				4		
Palmer	260	16	Shaw	Noah	2	2		1				1	1				7		
Cummington	304	11	Shaw	Obed		1		1				1	1				4		
Cummington	304	10	Shaw	Phillip		1	2		1	1		1		1			7		
South Brimfield	276	32	Shaw	Samuel	2	2		1					1				6		
Brimfield	270	2	Shaw	Samuel	3		1			1	1	1					7		
Buckland	329	22	Shaw	Simeon	1		1		1	1	1		1				6		
Cummington	305	29	Shaw	Solomon	2	1	1	1		1	1	2	1				10		
Palmer	261	19	Shaw	Solomon	1	1		1		1			1				5		
Plainfield	308	14	Shaw	Solomon	4		1		1	1		1		1			9		
Cummington	304	9	Shaw	Stephen				1					1				2		
Cummington	303	13	Shaw	Sylvanus	4		1						1	1			7		
Monson	268	10	Shaw	Sylvanus	2		1			1	1						5		
Plainfield	308	15	Shaw	Thomas	1		1			2		1					5		
Springfield	246	43	Shaw	Thomas	1	2	1			3		1					8		
Belchertown	207	12	Shaw	William		3		1		1			1				6		
Chesterfield	23	19	Shaw	Zachariah				1									1		
Palmer	259	2	Shearer	David	2	1	1	1	1	2			1				9		
Colrain	188	34	Shearer	Hornaw	2		2	1		1	2		1				9		
Palmer	258	18	Shearer	John	1		1	1			1		1				5		
Palmer	258	6	Shearer	Jonathan Dr	3		1	1		2	1	1	1				10		
Palmer	259	1	Shearer	Noah	2			1		1			1		1		6		
Greenwich	222	20	Shearer	Reuben	4	2	1	1		1		1	1				11		
Colrain	189	4	Shearer	William	2	1		1				3	1				8		
Granville Mid Soc.	165	16	Shehnan	John		2		1		1			1				5		
Barnardston	79	20	Shelden	Amasa		1		1	1				2				5		
Barnardston	79	18	Shelden	Asad	3			1	1	1			1				7		
Barnardston	79	19	Shelden	Elisha	2	1		1		1	2		1		1		9		
Norwich	154	3	Shelden	Hinney		2	1	1		3	1	2	1				11		
Barnardston	79	6	Shelden	Jonathan	1		1		1	2		1		1			7		
Leyden	84	12	Shelden	Reuben	2	1	2	1		1			1				8		
Barnardston	79	10	Shelden	Timothy			1			2		1	1				5		
Conway	60	46	Shelden	Abner	3	2	1	1		1	1	1	1				11		
Southampton	128	8	Shelden	Abner		1	3		1	1		1					7		
Southampton	130	23	Shelden	Aretas	2		1			1	1	1					6		
Northampton	7	37	Shelden	Benjamin		1		1	1	1	1	1	1				7		
Chesterfield	24	20	Shelden	Caleb	2			1		1	1		1				6		
Springfield	239	3	Shelden	Charles	1	1		1		2	1		1				7		
Southampton	130	19	Shelden	Ebenezer				1			1		1				3		
Southampton	130	20	Shelden	Ebenezer Junr	1	1		1		2	1		1				7		
Westhampton	18	34	Shelden	Isaac				1			1	2	1				6		
Southampton	130	10	Shelden	Israel	3	1		1			1	1		1			8		
Ludlow	257	9	Shelden	James			1	1		1			2	1			6		
Ludlow	257	5	Shelden	James Jr			1	1		1		1					3		
Deerfield	55	9	Shelden	John		1	1	2	1	1	1	1	1				9		
Southampton	130	21	Shelden	Joseph		1					1	1					3		
Southampton	130	18	Shelden	Kemima Wd			1				1	2	1				6		
Southampton	130	17	Shelden	Noah	2			1				1	1				5		
Buckland	330	4	Shelden	Saml		1						1					2		
Hadley	286	36	Shelden	Samll				1						1			2		
Southampton	128	9	Shelden	Silas		1		1	1	1		1					5		
Southampton	130	22	Shelden	Stephen		2		1			1		1				5		
Springfield	239	4	Shelden	William		2	1	1				1	2	1			8		
New Salem	103	29	Shelly	Job		1	2	1		1		1	1				7		
Hawley	335	7	Shelly	Joshua		1		1				1	1				4		
Springfield	247	6	Shelly	Joshua	1		1			1		1					4		
Chester	145	26	Shepard	Charles	2			1		1		1			1		7		
Chester	144	14	Shepard	David		1	1	1	1	2	1		1				8		

294

TOWN	PG#	LN#	LAST NAME	FIRST NAME	FREE WHITE MALES					FREE WHITE FEMALES					TOTAL ALL OTHER	TOTAL SLAVES	TOTALS	DISTRICT/ TOWNSHIP	NOTES
					under 10	10 to 16	16 to 26	26 to 45	45 and over	under 10	10 to 16	16 to 26	26 to 45	45 and over					
Wilbraham	234	8	Shepard	Elisha		1		1			1			1			4		
Wilbraham	235	7	Shepard	Elisha Junr	1		1			3	1	1					7		
Westfield	122	20	Shepard	Ezekiel		1				1		1					3		
Wilbraham	232	13	Shepard	Isaac	1			1		1			1				4		
Westfield	122	30	Shepard	Jared	2			1		3			1				7		
Wilbraham	237	6	Shepard	Jonah	1			1		2			1				5		
Chester	144	11	Shepard	Mather		1	1			1		2					5		
Westfield	128	4	Shepard	Noah	2			1		2			1				6		
Blanford	182	19	Shepard	Oliver	3			1		1			1				6		
Blanford	180	9	Shepard	Sarah	1								1	1			3		
Westfield	121	10	Shepard	Silence	2			1				1	1	1			6		
Westfield	119	20	Shepard	Simeon	1			1		1			1				4		
Westfield	126	23	Shepard	Solomon	1	1	2			1		1		1			7		
Westfield	122	4	Shepard	Wm Esq		1	1	2		1	3		1		1		10		
Northfield	30	33	Shepardson	Amos	1	2	1			1	1		1				7		
Warwick	39	39	Shepardson	Jonathan	1			1		1	1		1				5		
Northampton	6	3	Sheperd	Levi	1	1	7		2	2	2			2			17		
Colrain	189	14	Sheperdson	Alford				1		2		1					4		
Leyden	84	13	Sheperson	Joseph	2	1				3			1		1		9		
Buckland	330	1	Shephard	Joseph		1		1		2				2			6		
Blanford	178	10	Shephed	Elijah	4	1		1		1	1	1					9		
Blanford	178	7	Shephed	Jonathan	2	2		1				1	1	2			9		
Blanford	178	5	Shephed	Marian	1						2	1	1	1			6		
Ashfield	345	17	Sheppard	Isaac	1	1	1		1	1	1			1			7		
Ashfield	345	18	Sheppard	Isaac Junr	1	1		1		1	1			1			6		
Belchertown	210	19	Sherbrook	Ephraim		1			1	1	1	2		1			7		
Worthington	300	20	Sherman	Asa	3			1		1			1				6		
Brimfield	273	43	Sherman	Barzilla	1		1	1		1			1	2			7		
Brimfield	272	27	Sherman	Belsey Wido	2		2			1	1	1		1			8		
Brimfield	272	19	Sherman	Benjamin	1			1		1			1				4		
Conway	60	45	Sherman	Caleb	3	2		1		2			1				9		
Shelburne	323	20	Sherman	Christopher	1			1		1			1				4		
Ware	228	11	Sherman	Ebenz	2	1		1	1	3			1				9		
Holland	279	15	Sherman	Jeremiah				2		2	2	1		1			8		
Brimfield	270	20	Sherman	John Jr	1			1		2			1				5		
Brimfield	272	18	Sherman	Jona Capt									1	1			2		
Monson	263	41	Sherman	Joseph	2	2		1			1	1	1				8		
Ware	228	10	Sherman	Reuben	2	1		1	1	2	2		2				11		
Brimfield	272	24	Sherman	Thomas	2	1	2	1	1			1	1	1			10		
South Brimfield	277	10	Sherman	Timothy	1	1		1		2	1			1			7		
Colrain	189	12	Sherman	John		1	1	1		2	2	2		1			11		
Colrain	189	8	Sherman	Nathan	1			1		3	1	1	1				8		
Ashfield	345	11	Sherwin	John				1						1			2		
Ashfield	345	12	Sherwin	Nathl	2	1		1	1	2	1		1	1			10		
Monson	263	34	Shields	David S.	1		1	1	1	2	2	1		1			10		
Williamsburg	443	13	Shiff	Obadiah		1			1	3	2	1					8		
Hadley	285	34	Shipman	William	1	1			1	2	1	1		1			8		
Charlemont	193	31	Shippy	Christopher	2		1		1	2	1			1			8		
Colrain	189	2	Shippy	Israel	2	1		2		2	2		1				10		
Charlemont	193	30	Shippy	Peter				2						2			4		
Colrain	189	7	Shippy	Peter				1		4			1				6		
Montgomery	159	10	Shirtliff	Asa	2			1		2			1				6		
Montgomery	159	6	Shirtliff	Elisha		1				2		1					4		
Montgomery	159	5	Shirtliff	Jonathan		1	1	1				1		1			5		
Montgomery	160	7	Shirtliff	Noah	?		1		1		1						6		
Norwich	152	40	Shoals	Joseph	1	2	1		1	1		2		2			10		
Belchertown	210	14	Shong	Phinehas Capt	1	1	2	1		2	2	1	1	1			12		
Monson	266	9	Short	Manassah	2			1		2			1				6		
Goshen	312	2	Show	John		2					2		1				5		
Belchertown	210	21	Shumway	Asa	1			1	1	1		2	1	1			8		
Rowe	200	28	Shumway	Benjan	1	2	2	1		1	1	1		1			10		
Belchertown	207	9	Shumway	Cyrel		2	1	1		2				1			7		
Belchertown	207	4	Shumway	David	2	2		1		1	1	1		1			9		
Leverett	116	15	Shumway	Elijah	1			1		2	1		1				6		
Monson	264	2	Shumway	Levins		1		1		1		1					4		
Belchertown	207	7	Shumway	Nathan	3			1	1		1	1	1				8		
Belchertown	207	8	Shumway	Penwell			1										1		
Belchertown	207	5	Shumway	Solomon		1		1	1	1	2	1		2			9		
Belchertown	208	2	Shumway	Stephen	1			1		3	2	2	1				10		
Belchertown	211	21	Shumway	Whitney	1			1		2			1				5		
Charlemont	194	6	Shurtleaf	James	3			1		1		1					6		
Charlemont	193	33	Shurtleaf	Silas				1			1	1		1			4		
Shelburne	324	11	Sibley	David		1		1			1			1			4		
New Salem	103	20	Sibley	Solomon			1							1			2		
Ludlow	257	16	Sikes	Benjamin			1					1	1				3		
Ludlow	257	17	Sikes	Benjamin Jr	2			1		3	1		1				8		
Ludlow	257	18	Sikes	Increase			1	1				1	1				4		
Ludlow	257	8	Sikes	John Lt		2	2	1		1	1	2		1			10		
Ludlow	257	30	Sikes	Jonathan	3	2		1		1			1				8		
Ludlow	257	21	Sikes	Mercy Wid									2	1			3		
Ludlow	257	19	Sikes	Pleny	2			1		2			1				6		

TOWN	PG#	LN#	LAST NAME	FIRST NAME	FREE WHITE MALES					FREE WHITE FEMALES					TOTAL ALL OTHER	TOTAL SLAVES	TOTALS	DISTRICT/ TOWNSHIP	NOTES
					under 10	10 to 16	16 to 26	26 to 45	45 and over	under 10	10 to 16	16 to 26	26 to 45	45 and over					
Springfield	245	4	Sikes	Rufus	2	1	1	1		3		1	1	1			11		
Longmeadow	93	20	Silcock	Robert	2	1	1	1		3	1	1	1	1			12		
Barnardston	79	27	Silner	Samuel Junr	4	1	2		1		1	2		1			12		
Belchertown	210	15	Simmington	Michael	2			1		2			1				6		
Ludlow	255	6	Simmons	Paul Geer	3			1		1			1				6		
Springfield	242	39	Simond	Abner				1									1		
Longmeadow	92	21	Simonds	Catherine Wd	1					2	1		1				5		
Longmeadow	92	25	Simonds	Grace Wd		2	1							1			4		
Ware	228	7	Simonds	Jonathan			1		1					1			3		
Ware	228	8	Simonds	Judah	2	2		1			2		1				8		
Blanford	181	27	Simons	Timothy		1		1				1		1			4		
South Brimfield	276	3	Simpson	Edward	1			1		2			1				5		
Shutesbury	112	23	Sinclair	Francis	1	1		1	1	1		1					6		
Deerfield	55	12	Sindler	John	1			1			1		1				4		
Blanford	178	40	Sinnet	James	4	1		1		2			1				9		
Blanford	175	22	Sinnet	John	1			1		2	1						5		
Cummington	305	35	Sipple	Jeter	2			1		2			1				6		
Wilbraham	233	30	Sisson	Augustus	3		2	1		1			1				8		
Wilbraham	237	17	Sisson	Nathan		1	2		1		2		1				7		
Blanford	181	16	Sizer	Anthony	1	1		1		3			1				7		
Chester	147	12	Sizer	John	1		1						1				3		
Chester	147	10	Sizer	William Capt	1	2	2	1	1	2	1	1	1				12		
Chester	147	11	Sizer	William Ens			1		1		1		1				4		
Colrain	188	36	Skinner	Aaron	2			1		1			1				5		
Shelburne	323	25	Skinner	Aaron		2	1	1			1		1				6		
Colrain	188	37	Skinner	Asa			1			2		1					4		
Chester	145	40	Skinner	Augustus	2	1		1		2			1				7		
Greenfield	75	12	Skinner	Benajah	1			1		2			1				5		
Greenwich	218	8	Skinner	Benj	3			1		2	3			1			10		
Middlefield	155	13	Skinner	Molly Widw								1					1		
Monson	267	1	Skinner	Thomas	2			1		3			1				7		
Middlefield	155	6	Skinner	William	1	1	1		1	1		2		1			8		
Northampton	10	25	Slack	Christopher		1		1						1			3		
Northampton	11	4	Slack	David			1					1					2		
Northampton	11	5	Slack	Willard	2		1			1		1					5		
Blanford	179	10	Slade	James				1						1			2		
Springfield	241	25	Slafter	Anthony		1	1	1				1	1				5		
Springfield	241	26	Slafter	Samuel	1			1		3			2				7		
Barnardston	79	8	Slate	Daniel				1		1			1	1			4		
Gill	88	2	Slate	Ebenezer	1		1		1				1	1			5		
Barnardston	79	16	Slate	Israel	2	1		1		3	2		1				10		
Barnardston	79	14	Slate	Jonathan		1	1		1			2		1			6		
Barnardston	79	7	Slate	Joseph		1		1		2		1		1			6		
Barnardston	79	9	Slate	Joseph Junr	1			1		2			1				5		
Barnardston	79	23	Slate	Zebediah	3	2	1		1	1		2	1				11		
Rowe	200	30	Slater	Isaac	2	2	1		1	2			1				9		
Chester	146	30	Slayton	Asa Lieut		2		1	1	2			1				7		
Chester	144	27	Slayton	Ebenezer	3	1	2	1		1	1	1	1				11		
Greenwich	222	26	Sloan	Daniel	3			1		1	1		1				7		
Pelham	216	26	Sloan	David		2	2		1					2			7		
Greenwich	224	6	Sloan	James				1						1			2		
New Salem	103	11	Sloan	James W.			1			5		1					7		
Pelham	216	25	Sloan	Saml	1	3		1		2	1		1				9		
Granville West Soc	169	34	Slocum	Cornelus	1			1		1	1	1					5		
Granville West Soc	168	16	Slocum	David				1			1		1				3		
Granville West Soc	168	18	Slocum	Eleazer	1			1		1	1	1					5		
Granville West Soc	170	19	Slocum	Hull	2	1		1		2			1				7		
Blanford	177	3	Sloper	Samuel	1	1	1		1	1		2	1	1			9		
Northfield	30	24	Sloter	Adam	1			1		5			1				8		
Holland	279	40	Smalledge	Jona	1	1			2			3		1			8		
Shutesbury	112	19	Smalledge	Joseph		1		1			2						4		
Greenfield	75	16	Smead	Daniel		1	1		1		1	2	1				7		
Greenfield	75	10	Smead	David	1		2	2	2	1	2		2				12		
Greenfield	75	11	Smead	David Jun	1			1		2			1				5		
Shelburne	323	22	Smead	Elihu	2	1	1	1		3		1	1				10		
Greenfield	75	20	Smead	Hannah		2	3			1			1	1			8		
Greenfield	75	21	Smead	Jonathan		1	1	1	1		1	2	1	1			9		
Greenfield	75	28	Smead	Julia	1	1		1			1	1					5		
Greenfield	75	17	Smead	Lemuel	1	1	2		2		1			1			8		
Shelburne	324	4	Smead	Saml	2	1	1		1			1	1				7		
Greenfield	75	13	Smead	Thomas	1		1	1		2			1				6		
Conway	60	40	Smith	Aaron		1	1		1			1		1			5		
Heath	197	8	Smith	Aaron	1			1	1	1			1	1			6		
Brimfield	270	26	Smith	Abel		1		1						1			3		
Buckland	329	28	Smith	Abel		1		1					1	1			4		
Southwick	360	20	Smith	Abiel			2		1			1	1	1			6		
Ashfield	345	25	Smith	Abner	2			2		3	2		1	1			11		
Deerfield	55	6	Smith	Abner	1	1	1		1	1		1		1			7		
Warwick	39	38	Smith	Abner		1	2		1		1	2		1			8		
Chester	144	33	Smith	Abner Lieut	1			1		2	1			3			10		

TOWN	PG#	LN#	LAST NAME	FIRST NAME	M under 10	M 10 to 16	M 16 to 26	M 26 to 45	M 45 and over	F under 10	F 10 to 16	F 16 to 26	F 26 to 45	F 45 and over	TOTAL ALL OTHER	TOTAL SLAVES	TOTALS	DISTRICT/TOWNSHIP	NOTES
Hatfield	13	26	Smith	Adna	2	1	1	1			1	1	1				8		
West Springfield	355	9	Smith	Alexander	2			1		2		1	1				7		
Hawley	335	1	Smith	Allen	2			1		2			1				6		
Deerfield	55	3	Smith	Amasa			4		1	1	1	2		1			10		
Hatfield	12	25	Smith	Amasa	1		1			1		1					4		
Orange	43	14	Smith	Amasa				1		3			1				5		
Belchertown	207	3	Smith	Amasa Maj	4			1	1	1	1		1	2			11		
Charlemont	193	32	Smith	Andrew		2		1		4	1	1	1				10		
Amherst	294	30	Smith	Arad			1						1				2		
Amherst	294	3	Smith	Asa	1	1		1		3			1				7		
Whately	67	32	Smith	Asa	2		2	1		1			1				7		
Granby	252	30	Smith	Asahel Lt				1				1	1				3		
Amherst	293	5	Smith	Benjamin		1		1	1	1	1		1	1			7		
Granby	253	7	Smith	Benjamin	1			1					1				3		
Hatfield	12	6	Smith	Benjamin				1		1	1		1				4		
Monson	268	19	Smith	Benjamin	1	1			1	1		1	1				6		
Hadley	285	16	Smith	Benjamin Jun	1			1	1	1			1	1			6		
Montague	47	41	Smith	Benjm Parsons	1			1		1	2	1	1				7		
New Salem	103	18	Smith	Braddyl	3			1		2			1				7		
Hadley	285	11	Smith	Caleb	1	2	1	1		3	1		1				10		
Colrain	189	13	Smith	Calvin	2	1	1	1		3	2	1	1				12		
Middlefield	157	18	Smith	Calvin	4	1	1	1		1	2		1				11		
Whately	67	27	Smith	Calvin		1						1					2		
Amherst	293	16	Smith	Chester	1		1						1				3		
Deerfield	55	20	Smith	Chester	1		1			1		1					4		
Hadley	287	27	Smith	Chileab		1	2		1	1	1			1			7		
Ashfield	345	4	Smith	Chipman	3		1	1		1	2		1	1			10		
Greenfield	75	27	Smith	Clement			1	1		1	2		1				6		
Hawley	335	11	Smith	Daniel		1			1			1	1	1			5		
West Springfield	351	49	Smith	Daniel		1	1	1	1			1	2	1			8		
Chester	148	20	Smith	Daniel		2	1			3	1	1	1				9		
Chester	144	15	Smith	Daniel 2d	2		1	1		1	1		1	1			8		
Belchertown	207	2	Smith	Daniel Lt		1	1	1		1			1				5		
Westfield	124	6	Smith	Darias	1		1			2			1				5		
South Hadley	249	3	Smith	Darus	1	1	2	1		3	2		1				11		
Amherst	290	8	Smith	David	1			1	1	1			1	2			7		
Ashfield	345	3	Smith	David	1	1		1		3			1				7		
Colrain	188	39	Smith	David	1	1	3	1		2	2	1	1	1			13		
New Salem	103	15	Smith	David				1		2			1				4		
Northampton	5	29	Smith	David				1		1			1				3		
West Springfield	351	57	Smith	David			2	1					1	1			5		
Granby	252	17	Smith	David Maj	2	1		1		2			1	1			8		
Granby	254	34	Smith	Ebenezer		2	1	1		1	1	2		1			9		
Ashfield	345	22	Smith	Ebenz	2			1		1		1					5		
New Salem	103	21	Smith	Edward	2	1		1		2	1		1				8		
Shelburne	324	8	Smith	Edward		1	1		1	2	1	2		1			9		
Ashfield	345	14	Smith	Ehiliab 3d	2			1		2			1				6		
Ashfield	345	13	Smith	Ehiliab Junr				1			1			1			3		
Amherst	294	23	Smith	Eleazer			1		1	1			1	1			5		
Granville West Soc	169	20	Smith	Elezer		1			1			2		1			5		
South Hadley	249	38	Smith	Eli				1				1					2		
Hadley	287	22	Smith	Eliakim	1			2		2	1	1		1			8		
Hadley	299	9	Smith	Elias	2	1			1	3			1				8		
Hadley	285	18	Smith	Elihu	2	1	1	1			1	1	1				8		
Hadley	288	32	Smith	Elihu 2nd	2			1		3		1	1				8		
Amherst	290	9	Smith	Elijah				1		2			1				4		
Ashfield	345	6	Smith	Elijah			1		1	1		1		1			5		
Greenfield	75	19	Smith	Elijah	3	1		1		1	1						7		
Hatfield	12	8	Smith	Elijah	1	1	1	1			1	1	1				7		
Whately	67	34	Smith	Elijah	2		1	1				1					6		
Amherst	293	18	Smith	Elisha	1			1			1	2		1			6		
Buckland	329	20	Smith	Elisha	1	1		1			1	1		1			6		
Hadley	285	31	Smith	Elisha				1						2			3		
Sunderland	282	17	Smith	Elisha		1		2	1	2	1	1		1			9		
West Springfield	352	3	Smith	Elizabeth		1							3	1			5		
Buckland	330	5	Smith	Enos	1	1	2		1	1			1				7		
Hadley	286	22	Smith	Enos		2	3		1	1	1	1		1			10		
Granby	254	2	Smith	Enos Dr.			1				1	1					3		
South Hadley	249	5	Smith	Ephraim		1	1		1	1	1		1				6		
Hadley	285	15	Smith	Erstus	1			1		4			1				7		
Amherst	293	28	Smith	Ethan		2		2			1		2	1			8		
Granby	255	1	Smith	Experience Ens		1		1	2					1			5		
Amherst	290	31	Smith	Friend	1		1	1		3			1	1			8		
Whately	67	33	Smith	Gad	2	1	1	1	1	1	1	1	1	1			11		
Springfield	244	20	Smith	George	1			1					1				3		
Granby	253	29	Smith	Hannah Wid			2	2				1	1	1			7		
South Hadley	251	14	Smith	Hezekiah		1	1		1		1	1		1			5		
Belchertown	207	11	Smith	Hezekiah				1				2	1				4		
Northampton	9	10	Smith	Ira			1			1		1					3		
Chester	144	6	Smith	Isaac	1		1			1			1				4		

TOWN	PG#	LN#	LAST NAME	FIRST NAME	FREE WHITE MALES					FREE WHITE FEMALES					TOTAL ALL OTHER	TOTAL SLAVES	TOTALS	DISTRICT/ TOWNSHIP	NOTES
					under 10	10 to 16	16 to 26	26 to 45	45 and over	under 10	10 to 16	16 to 26	26 to 45	45 and over					
Southwick	361	1	Smith	Isaac			1	2					1				4		
Whately	67	29	Smith	Isaac	3			1		1		1		1			7		
Leyden	84	10	Smith	Israel	3	3		1		1		1	1				10		
Amherst	294	22	Smith	Ithamar	2		1	1		2	2		1				9		
Hadley	288	27	Smith	Jacob		1		1		2			1	1			6		
Belchertown	210	18	Smith	James		1	1		1			1	1				5		
Granby	252	7	Smith	James	4			1	1				1	1			8		
Northampton	10	10	Smith	James	2	1	1		1			2		1			8		
South Brimfield	275	4	Smith	James		1	1					1		1			5		
Williamsburg	443	11	Smith	James				1				1	1	1			4		
Palmer	260	11	Smith	James Lt		2	3		1	1	1	2		1			11		
Granby	252	13	Smith	Jared	4		1					1	1				7		
West Springfield	351	52	Smith	Jared		1		1				1		1			4		
Blanford	177	18	Smith	Jeddiah		2	2		1	2	1		1				9		
Hadley	286	3	Smith	Jedediah		1	1		1	1	1		1				6		
Ashfield	345	15	Smith	Jeduthan	3	1		1	1	3			1	1			11		
Chester	146	6	Smith	Jesse		1		1		3			1				6		
Chester	144	32	Smith	Joab	3			1		1	2		1				8		
Shutesbury	112	6	Smith	Job	3	2		1			1	2		1			10		
Greenfield	75	34	Smith	Joel	2			1		2			1				6		
Leverett	116	10	Smith	Joel	2	1			2	2	1	1	1	1			11		
Leverett	116	11	Smith	Joel Junr	1			1		4	1		1				8		
Blanford	178	27	Smith	John	1	1		1		1			1				5		
Goshen	311	27	Smith	John		1	1		1			3		1			7		
Granby	252	31	Smith	John	1			1		3			1				6		
Granville East Soc	533	11	Smith	John	2	1	2		1		1	1		1			9		
Hadley	286	29	Smith	John			1	1		5		2	1	1			11		
Middlefield	158	29	Smith	John	2	1		1		1			1				6		
New Salem	103	1	Smith	John	2		1	1		1	1		1				7		
Westfield	119	34	Smith	John			1			1		1					3		
Westfield	123	30	Smith	John			1	1	1	2		1	1	1			8		
Whately	68	1	Smith	John		1		1	1			2		1			6		
Chester	147	23	Smith	John	2	1	1		1	2	1		1				9		
Chester	148	17	Smith	John 2d				1		1			1				3		
Granville East Soc	533	12	Smith	John 2nd	3		1	1					1				6		
Hadley	286	23	Smith	John 2nd	1	1	1		1	2	1	1	1				9		
Palmer	260	12	Smith	John A	1		1		2	1	1	2		2			10		
Chester	144	3	Smith	John Deac				1				1		1			3		
Chester	144	4	Smith	John Junr				1				1	1				3		
Amherst	290	6	Smith	Jonathan				1				1					2		
Belchertown	210	20	Smith	Jonathan	1		1		1	1				1			5		
Colrain	188	40	Smith	Jonathan	3					2		1	1				8		
Conway	60	36	Smith	Jonathan		1		1		6			1				9		
Leverett	116	16	Smith	Jonathan	2	2		1		2			1				8		
Orange	43	9	Smith	Jonathan	3			1				1	1	2			8		
South Hadley	248	2	Smith	Jonathan	3	1	2	1						2			9		
Warwick	39	31	Smith	Jonathan	1	2	2		1	3	2		1				13		
West Springfield	351	53	Smith	Jonathan	1		2	1						2			6		
Whately	68	4	Smith	Jonathan		1	1	1	1			1	1	2			8		
Conway	60	35	Smith	Jonathan 2d	2			1		1		1					5		
Whately	68	12	Smith	Jonathan Jr	1			1		1		1	1				5		
Ashfield	345	7	Smith	Jonathan Junr	4	1		1		1	1		1				9		
Ashfield	345	24	Smith	Joseph	1		1	1						1			4		
Barnardston	79	12	Smith	Joseph	2	1	3		1		2	1	1				11		
Conway	60	38	Smith	Joseph	1		1	1						1			4		
Hadley	288	4	Smith	Joseph	2	1	2	1					1	1			9		
Hatfield	13	4	Smith	Joseph	3			1			2		1	1			8		
Leverett	116	12	Smith	Joseph	1			1		2	1	1		1			7		
Montague	47	42	Smith	Joseph				1					1				2		
Palmer	260	4	Smith	Joseph	2	2		1	1	1	1		1	1			10		
Warwick	39	24	Smith	Joseph	3	1		1				1	1	1			8		
West Springfield	355	6	Smith	Joseph		2		2			1		1				6		
Hatfield	13	16	Smith	Joseph 2d	2	1		1		1			1				6		
Middlefield	158	28	Smith	Joseph Lieut	1			1		1			1				4		
Hadley	286	1	Smith	Josiah			1					1					2		
Warwick	39	37	Smith	Josiah	2	1		1		2	2	1	1				10		
Northampton	8	35	Smith	Justin			2		1		1		1				5		
Buckland	329	23	Smith	Lemuel			1	1			1		1				4		
Ware	228	14	Smith	Lemuel Jr	1			1		2			1				5		
Granby	252	16	Smith	Levi	4		1		1	1			1				8		
Westhampton	16	28	Smith	Levi		2	1		1	2				1			7		
Northampton	9	25	Smith	Lewis	4	1		1		1	1	1		2			11		
South Hadley	248	9	Smith	Luther	2			1	1	2	1		1				8		
West Springfield	352	2	Smith	Margaret		1						1	1	1			4		
Ashfield	345	5	Smith	Martin	1			1		2			1				5		
Whately	68	10	Smith	Martin		1							1				2		
Norwich	152	9	Smith	Martin Lieut				1				1	2	1			5		
Hatfield	11	12	Smith	Mary			1							1			2		
South Hadley	250	17	Smith	Mary									1				1		
Westfield	128	7	Smith	Matthew	1		1		1	2		1					6		

298

TOWN	PG#	LN#	LAST NAME	FIRST NAME	FREE WHITE MALES under 10	10 to 16	16 to 26	26 to 45	45 and over	FREE WHITE FEMALES under 10	10 to 16	16 to 26	26 to 45	45 and over	TOTAL ALL OTHER	TOTAL SLAVES	TOTALS	DISTRICT/ TOWNSHIP	NOTES
Middlefield	155	9	Smith	Matthew Capt	2	3		1		1		1	1				9		
Springfield	240	4	Smith	Michael	2			1					1				4		
Amherst	289	19	Smith	Moses	1			1		2			1				5		
Barnardston	79	29	Smith	Moses				1			1			1			3		
Leverett	116	13	Smith	Moses				1				1	1				3		
Warwick	39	33	Smith	Moses		1		1		2		1					5		
Amherst	293	8	Smith	Nath Alexander			1	1				1	1				4		
Monson	263	3	Smith	Nathan	3	1	2	2				1	1				10		
Granby	252	6	Smith	Nathan Dr					1			1	1				3		
Granby	253	24	Smith	Nathan Junr		2	1	1		3	1	1	1				10		
Colrain	189	11	Smith	Nathanael	2	1	1	1	1	1	1		1				9		
Sunderland	283	17	Smith	Nathaniel		2	5	1		1			1				10		
Shutesbury	112	7	Smith	Nathl			1	1	2		1		2				7		
West Springfield	352	1	Smith	Noadiah	5			1					1				7		
Amherst	290	7	Smith	Noah			1	1				3		1			6		
Williamsburg	443	17	Smith	Obadiah	2		1	1		1			1				6		
Hadley	288	33	Smith	Oliver	1	1	1	1	2	1	1	2	1	1			12		
Pelham	216	22	Smith	Oliver	3	2		1		2	1		1				10		
Southwick	360	24	Smith	Oliver	2			1			1		1				5		
Colrain	189	10	Smith	Oren	2	1	1		1	2	1	2	1		2		13		
South Hadley	251	23	Smith	Pelah	1	1		1		2		1	1				7		
Hadley	286	27	Smith	Perez	1	1			1	1	1		1	1			7		
South Hadley	249	4	Smith	Perez	3	2	2		1			1		1			10		
Deerfield	55	7	Smith	Philip	6			1		2			2				11		
Springfield	245	33	Smith	Philip		1		1		4	2	1	1				10		
Whately	68	9	Smith	Phillip	3	1		1	1	2		1	1	1			11		
Heath	197	6	Smith	Phineas		1	1		1					1			4		
Granby	252	18	Smith	Phinehas	1	2	2	1	1			1		1			9		
Rowe	200	31	Smith	Preserved	1	1				1			1				4		
Northfield	30	23	Smith	Reuben	1		2	2	1		1	2		2			11		
Ware	228	18	Smith	Reuben			1	1				1	1				4		
Blanford	178	31	Smith	Robert	3	1		1		1	1		1				8		
Chester	146	5	Smith	Robert				1					1				2		
Palmer	260	10	Smith	Robert	1	1	1	2	1	2	1	1	1	1			12		
Colrain	189	1	Smith	Rominer	2		2	1		3	1	1	1				11		
Russell	138	13	Smith	Roswell			1			1			1				3		
Brimfield	270	27	Smith	Royal		1		1						1			3		
Deerfield	55	5	Smith	Rufus		1			2	1		2	1				7		
Hatfield	12	4	Smith	Rufus		1		1					1				3		
Middlefield	156	35	Smith	Rufus	1			1				1	1				4		
Buckland	329	24	Smith	Saml	2			1		1			1				5		
Shelburne	324	3	Smith	Saml				1				1	1				3		
Amherst	294	31	Smith	Samuel	1			1		2	1	1	1				8		
Blanford	178	29	Smith	Samuel				1					1				2		
Deerfield	55	4	Smith	Samuel		1	2		1	1	1	1	1	1			9		
Granby	252	8	Smith	Samuel		1	1			1		1					4		
Hatfield	14	4	Smith	Samuel	1			1		1		3		1			7		
Heath	197	4	Smith	Samuel	2	2		1		1	1		1				8		
Montague	47	34	Smith	Samuel		1		1	1	2	2		2	1			10		
Shutesbury	112	21	Smith	Samuel			1					1					2		
West Springfield	351	55	Smith	Samuel	2	1	2	1					1				7		
West Springfield	355	20	Smith	Samuel	1	1			1	1	1	3		1			9		
Warwick	39	41	Smith	Samuel V Junr	3			1	1		2		1				8		
Amherst	294	2	Smith	Sarah	2	3	1			1		1	1				9		
Shelburne	324	6	Smith	Sarah								1		1			2		
Granby	253	6	Smith	Seth	1	2	1		1	1	1		1				8		
Hadley	288	25	Smith	Seth	3	2			1	1		1	1		1		10		
Holland	278	16	Smith	Seth Doct.		2	1					1	1				5		
South Hadley	249	6	Smith	Silas Dr	2		3		1		2	1		1			10		
Westfield	124	26	Smith	Silvanus	1		1		1	1	1		1				6		
Hadley	285	12	Smith	Simeon	3			1		1			1				6		
West Springfield	351	50	Smith	Simeon	1	1	1		1	2	1	2	1				10		
Westfield	119	23	Smith	Simon	3	1		1			2	1					8		
West Springfield	351	56	Smith	Solomon		1			1			1	1	1			5		
Amherst	292	20	Smith	Stephen			1	1	1			1		1			5		
Hawley	335	2	Smith	Stephen	2			1		1			2				6		
Hatfield	13	18	Smith	Sylvanus		1			1		1						3		
Hawley	335	8	Smith	Sylvenus	2	1	1		1	3	2		1				11		
Belchertown	208	39	Smith	Thomas	2	1		1		2	1		1				8		
Hadley	287	2	Smith	Thomas	1	2		1		2	1		1				8		
West Springfield	355	8	Smith	Thomas				1		1			1	1			4		
Amherst	293	6	Smith	Timothy	2			1		1			1	1			6		
New Salem	102	40	Smith	Timothy	2		1		1		1		1				6		
Hadley	287	28	Smith	Warhum		2		1	1	2			2	1			9		
Westhampton	18	19	Smith	Willard	1	1	1	1		2	1		1				8		
Whately	67	31	Smith	William	2			1				1					4		
Chester	147	25	Smith	William	2	1		1			1	2	1				8		
Chester	144	40	Smith	William 2d				1		3			1				5		
Springfield	239	19	Smith	William Col.	2	1	1		1	1	1		1				8		
Hadley	287	30	Smith	Windsor	3	1		2		2		1	1	1			11		

TOWN	PG#	LN#	LAST NAME	FIRST NAME	FREE WHITE MALES					FREE WHITE FEMALES					TOTAL ALL OTHER	TOTAL SLAVES	TOTALS	DISTRICT/ TOWNSHIP	NOTES
					under 10	10 to 16	16 to 26	26 to 45	45 and over	under 10	10 to 16	16 to 26	26 to 45	45 and over					
Warwick	39	32	Smith	Zachariah	1	1			1				1	1			5		
Cummington	304	3	Snell	Ebenezer		1			1			1		1			4		
Cummington	304	4	Snell	Ebenezer Jun		1	1	1		1	1	1			1		7		
South Brimfield	278	1	Snell	Isaiah		1		1		3	1		1				7		
Springfield	247	5	Snell	Josiah	1		2	1	1		1	2					8		
Ware	228	5	Snell	Lewis	1			1		1			1				4		
Westfield	120	11	Snell	Nahum P				1		3		1	1				6		
Ware	228	6	Snell	Thomas	1			1		5			1	1			9		
South Brimfield	278	2	Snell	Wid									2	1			3		
Plainfield	308	23	Snow	Abijah	3		1		1	1	2	1	1				10		
South Brimfield	275	15	Snow	Amos			1					1					2		
Pelham	217	13	Snow	Barnabas		1						1					2		
Plainfield	308	24	Snow	Calvin	1			1		1	1		1				5		
South Hadley	250	3	Snow	Ebenezer		1		1					1				3		
Greenwich	224	12	Snow	Eli		1	1				1		1				4		
Granville West Soc	169	14	Snow	Ephraim	3	1			1	2	1	2	1				11		
Granville Mid Soc.	167	28	Snow	Isaac	3			1		2		1	1				8		
Cummington	304	6	Snow	James	4			1		1			1				7		
South Brimfield	276	11	Snow	James	2			1		2	1		1				7		
Ludlow	256	23	Snow	Jeremiah	1			1		1			1				4		
Springfield	240	6	Snow	Jeremiah				1						1			2		
Orange	43	13	Snow	Jesse			1			1		1					3		
Heath	197	7	Snow	Joseph				1					1				2		
South Hadley	250	24	Snow	Josiah				1					1				2		
South Hadley	251	22	Snow	Josiah Jr			1			2		1	1				5		
Ludlow	256	28	Snow	Natha Capt				1					1	1	1		3		
Plainfield	308	46	Snow	Nathan				1			1		1				3		
Cummington	304	7	Snow	Nathan Jun			1			2			1				4		
Barnardston	79	22	Snow	Prince	1	1	1	1	1	1		1		1			8		
Greenwich	222	27	Snow	Reuben		1	1		1	1	2	2		1			9		
Hatfield	14	20	Snow	Solomon	2			1		1	1	1	1				7		
Greenwich	222	28	Snow	Stephen	2			1		1		1					5		
Westhampton	16	13	Soal	David	3		1					1					5		
Warwick	39	44	Solter	William				1	1				1				3		
Chester	148	29	Soule	Elizabeth	2						1	1	1				5		
New Salem	103	24	Southick	Benjamin	2	1		1		2			1	1			8		
New Salem	103	6	Southick	Jonathan				1						1			2		
New Salem	103	8	Southick	Simeon	1	1		1		2	1		1				7		
New Salem	103	7	Southick	William			1			1		1					3		
Westfield	125	6	Southwell	David			2				1						3		
Southwick	360	16	Southwell	Phineas			1	1					1				3		
Pelham	216	23	Southworth	Abia Doct	2			1		1	1	1					6		
Westhampton	17	27	Southworth	Benjamin				1		1		1					3		
Cummington	304	5	Southworth	Ichabod	2	1		1	1	1		1		1			8		
Southampton	129	13	Southworth	Joseph	2	1			1	3			1				8		
Hawley	335	12	Spafford	Jonathan			1	1					1				3		
Worthington	299	15	Spalding	Asa	1	2	2		1	2			1				9		
Buckland	330	2	Spalding	Josiah Rev.		1			1	2	2			1			7		
Springfield	243	39	Sparks	Lemuel	3			1					1				5		
Russell	139	25	Sparrey	Isaac				1									1		
Heath	197	9	Spaulding	Joseph		1		1			1			1			4		
Heath	197	5	Spaulding	Samson			1			2		1					4		
Heath	197	13	Spaulding	Samson Jr			1			2		1					4		
Palmer	262	14	Spear	David	1	1	1		1	1	1	1					7		
Shutesbury	112	9	Spear	Eli	2	2	2	1		2		1					10		
West Springfield	355	14	Spear	Joshua				1		2		1					4		
Palmer	259	36	Spear	Luther				1		3	1		1				6		
Shutesbury	112	10	Spear	Luther	5	4		1			2	1					13		
Shutesbury	112	8	Spear	Moses	1			1	1	1		3	1				8		
Shutesbury	112	11	Spear	Moses Jr	1	3		1		2	1		1				9		
Greenwich	222	34	Spear	Silas	1		1	1		2	1		1				7		
Shutesbury	112	12	Spear	Stephen	2			1		2	3		1				9		
Palmer	259	37	Spear	William		1		1		2	1	2	1				8		
Granville East Soc	527	4	Spelman	Aaron & Elisha	1			1	1		2						5		
Granville East Soc	527	11	Spelman	Charles	1			1		1	1		1				5		
Granville East Soc	527	3	Spelman	Israel				1			1	1	1				4		
Granville East Soc	527	16	Spelman	Jesse		1	1				1						3		
Granville Mid Soc.	165	7	Spelman	Oliver				1		1			1				3		
Granville Mid Soc.	165	8	Spelman	Reuben		1						2			1		4		
Granville East Soc	527	7	Spelman	Stephen	2	1	1		1	1	2			2			11		
Granville East Soc	527	2	Spelman	Timothy	1	2		1		3		2	1				10		
Worthington	299	29	Spencer	Ashbel	2			1		1		1					5		
Worthington	299	31	Spencer	Daniel	2			1		2	1		1				7		
Worthington	299	30	Spencer	Fredrick	1		1				1						3		
Longmeadow	95	19	Spencer	Israel		1		1		1		1	1				5		
Middlefield	158	35	Spencer	John		2	1		1	1		2	1				8		
Middlefield	155	3	Spencer	John Junr			1										1		
Springfield	239	39	Spendler	John Saml				1		1		1					3		
Blanford	182	24	Sperry	Elihu		1		1	1	2		1		2			8		
Blanford	182	20	Sperry	Elihu Jr		1	2		1	3	1		2				10		

TOWN	PG#	LN#	LAST NAME	FIRST NAME	FWM under 10	FWM 10-16	FWM 16-26	FWM 26-45	FWM 45+	FWF under 10	FWF 10-16	FWF 16-26	FWF 26-45	FWF 45+	TOTAL ALL OTHER	TOTAL SLAVES	TOTALS	DISTRICT/ TOWNSHIP	NOTES
Montague	47	38	Sperry	Obed	2			1		1			1				5		
Norwich	154	26	Spicewood	Sylvester											2		2		
Gill	88	4	Spooner	Levi	2		1						1				4		
Greenwich	222	29	Spooner	Thomas	3	1		1		1	1		1				8		
Barnardston	79	17	Sprague	Asa			2					1	1	1			5		
Buckland	329	21	Sprague	Benjm	3			1		3	1	3	1				12		
Hawley	335	10	Sprague	Benjm				1		3	1	2					7		
Worthington	299	10	Sprague	Daniel	2			1		3	1		1				8		
Sunderland	283	21	Sprague	David			1	1			1			1			4		
Brimfield	271	6	Sprague	Hosea	2	1		1		2			1				7		
Buckland	329	25	Sprague	Jonathan				1						1			2		
Gill	87	25	Sprague	Jonathan				1			1			1			3		
Buckland	329	26	Sprague	Jonathan Jr	2			1		3			1				7		
Gill	88	5	Sprague	Joseph				1		1			1				3		
Easthampton	134	2	Sprague	Oliver	1	1	2	1		2	1		1	1			10		
Hawley	335	13	Sprague	Preserved		1	2						1				4		
Colrain	189	15	Sprague	Susanah	1	2				1	1		1				6		
Greenwich	222	19	Spring	Issac B	2	1		1		1	1	1	1				8		
Chesterfield	22	31	Spring	John	1	1		1		1	2	5	1				12		
Greenwich	224	3	Sprout	Ebenz	2	1		1		2			1				8		
Deerfield	55	21	Spur	Lemuel	2	1			1	3	1		1				9		
Colrain	189	9	Spur	Samuel		2			1	2			1				6		
Montgomery	161	12	Squire	Abial				1						1			2		
Belchertown	210	17	Squire	Daniel			1	1						1			3		
Monson	263	33	Squire	David	2			1		2			1				6		
Chester	145	41	Squire	Ezekiel				1						1			2		
Chester	146	1	Squire	Ezekiel Junr	3		1	1					1				6		
Monson	268	2	Squire	John				1						1			2		
Monson	268	3	Squire	Solomon	5	3			1	1			1				11		
Montgomery	161	9	Squire	Sylvester Capt	1	2	1		1	1			1				7		
Gill	88	1	Squires	David	2	3		1		2			1	1			10		
Barnardston	79	21	Squires	Medad	2		2	1		1			1	1			8		
New Salem	103	23	Stacey	Benjamin		1		1		2	1	2	1				8		
Conway	60	49	Stacey	Caleb	3			1		2	1		1				8		
Williamsburg	443	18	Stacey	Mark	2	1		1		2			1				7		
New Salem	103	4	Stacey	Nymphas	2	1	1	1		3	2		1				11		
New Salem	103	26	Stacey	Rufus				1						1			2		
New Salem	103	5	Stacey	Rufus Jr	3			1		2			1	1			8		
Wilbraham	238	23	Stacy	Ebenezer	1	2	1		1	1	1	1	1	2			11		
Gill	87	28	Stacy	Gilbert	1	1		1		1			1				5		
Ware	228	15	Stacy	Joel	2		1						1				4		
Ware	228	19	Stacy	Lemuel		1					1						2		
Holland	278	21	Stacy	Mark		1	1		1	1	1		1				6		
Whately	67	25	Stacy	Rufus	4	1		1		1			2	1			10		
Monson	265	5	Stacy	Simon	1				1	2	1	1		1			7		
Monson	265	6	Stacy	William	2	1	1		1	1	1			1			8		
Rowe	200	29	Stafford	Job				1		3	2		1				7		
Colrain	189	6	Stafford	Studely	2	1	2	1		2			1				9		
Ashfield	345	20	Standish	Israel		1		1				1	1				4		
Amherst	291	38	Standley	Edward A	3		1	1		2			1				8		
Orange	43	16	Stanford	Lyman	2			1		1		2					6		
Charlemont	194	5	Stanford	Moses		1	1		1	1	1		1				6		
Gill	87	31	Stangton	Samuel	1	1	2		1	1		2		1			9		
Gill	87	30	Stanhope	Jonas	3			1		3			1				8		
Deerfield	55	18	Stanhope	Samuel		1	1	1			1	1	1				6		
West Springfield	355	11	Stannard	Joseph				1			2			1			4		
West Springfield	355	13	Stannard	Oliver			1			1	1						4		
West Springfield	355	12	Stannard	Seth	1		1			2			1				5		
Norwich	152	38	Stanton	Abel	1	2	2		1	2	1			1			10		
Norwich	153	13	Stanton	Abel Junr			1			1			1				3		
Norwich	152	18	Stanton	Daniel	1		1			2		1					5		
Norwich	153	4	Stanton	Elisha		1	1		1	5	1	2	1				12		
Worthington	299	35	Stanton	Peter	3							1	1				5		
Williamsburg	443	14	Starks	John	3	1	1		1			2	1				9		
Williamsburg	443	15	Starks	Nathan		2	1	1		4	1	1	1				11		
Greenfield	75	33	Starks	Silas	1			1		2			1				5		
Northampton	2	5	Starkweather	Charles		2	1	1		3	1	1	1				10		
Worthington	302	8	Starkweather	Charles	1	2		1		3	1	1					9		
West Springfield	355	19	Starkweather	Cyrus				1		2	1	1					5		
Gill	87	27	Starkweather	Elisha	2		1	1		1	1		1				7		
Worthington	297	6	Starkweather	Ezra					1		1	1			1		4		
Norwich	154	29	Starkweather	Prince										1			7		
Chesterfield	22	30	Starkweather	Robert					1					1			2		
Chesterfield	20	23	Starkweather	Robert Jr	1	1	1	1		2			1				7		
Russell	137	4	Starling	Danl		1	1						1				3		
Middlefield	156	18	Starr	Martin	1			1		1			1				4		
Easthampton	135	28	Starr	Thomas		1			1	1				1			4		
Easthampton	135	29	Starr	Thomas Junr	1		1			1			1				4		
Greenfield	75	29	Starr	William	1	2	1	1		2		1	1				9		
Northampton	5	2	Starrs	Nathan			4	2				1	1	1	1		10		

TOWN	PG#	LN#	LAST NAME	FIRST NAME	FREE WHITE MALES					FREE WHITE FEMALES					TOTAL ALL OTHER	TOTAL SLAVES	TOTALS	DISTRICT/ TOWNSHIP	NOTES
					under 10	10 to 16	16 to 26	26 to 45	45 and over	under 10	10 to 16	16 to 26	26 to 45	45 and over					
Belchertown	210	16	Stary	Caleb	1	1		1		2			1				6		
Belchertown	210	22	Stary	Isaac Capt	1	1	1		1		1		1				6		
Belchertown	210	24	Stary	Moses	2			1		2			1				6		
Granville West Soc	168	9	Steadman	Joseph	2			1		1			1				6		
Granville West Soc	170	16	Steadman	Phebe	1							1	1				3		
Granville West Soc	170	18	Steadman	Samuel	1		1	1					1	2			6		
Granville West Soc	170	20	Steadman	Thomas			1	1		3	2	1	1				9		
Leyden	84	14	Stearns	Charles	2	2		1		2	1		1	1			10		
Goshen	312	1	Stearns	Cyrus	3	2		1			1	1					8		
Conway	60	44	Stearns	Darius	1	1		1		1		1	1				6		
Warwick	39	35	Stearns	Ebenezer		1		1				2		1			5		
Westhampton	17	37	Stearns	Ebenezer	1			1						2			4		
Warwick	39	42	Stearns	Ebenezer Jr		1											1		
Leyden	84	8	Stearns	Eleaner									1				1		
Conway	60	43	Stearns	George		2		1		1		1		1			6		
Conway	61	7	Stearns	Joel	1	1	1	1		1	1		1				7		
Goshen	311	25	Stearns	John	3		1			1		1	1				7		
Charlemont	193	29	Stearns	Levi		2		1		1		1	1				7		
Orange	43	15	Stearns	Nathaniel	1	1		1		3			1				7		
Warwick	39	26	Stearns	Nathaniel		1	2	1				1	1	1			7		
Warwick	39	25	Stearns	Simeon		1						1		1			3		
Charlemont	194	3	Stearns	Timothy	1		1			1		1					4		
Orange	43	11	Stearns	William	2	1	1		1	3	1	1	1				11		
Norwich	152	5	Stebbens	Gad Doct	1			1		1			1				4		
Greenfield	75	18	Stebbens	Samuel	1	1	1	1		3	1	1		1			10		
Springfield	243	41	Stebbins	Aaron		1			1	1	1	1					5		
Brimfield	269	14	Stebbins	Abijah			1			1	1		1				4		
Brimfield	270	25	Stebbins	Abner			1	1				1	1				4		
Brimfield	270	24	Stebbins	Abner Jr	2	1		1		4	2		1				11		
Deerfield	54	43	Stebbins	Asa	3	1	3	1		3		1	1				13		
Monson	263	29	Stebbins	Asahel				1					1				2		
Northfield	30	26	Stebbins	Asahel	1		1	1		1		3			1		8		
Granby	254		Stebbins	Asaph					1			2	2				5		
Wilbraham	236	22	Stebbins	Augustus	4			1		1			1				7		
Brimfield	270	22	Stebbins	Benja Capt			2	1					1				4		
Monson	263	9	Stebbins	Bethuel								3	1				4		
Monson	263	10	Stebbins	Bethuel 2d	3	1		1					1				6		
Springfield	240	28	Stebbins	Calvin	1	1		1		3			1				7		
Wilbraham	238	8	Stebbins	Calvin	1	1			1	3	2		1				9		
Wilbraham	232	27	Stebbins	Chloe Wd	2		2			1				1			6		
South Hadley	250	26	Stebbins	Daniel Dr		1		1				1	1				4		
Russell	137	15	Stebbins	Danl				1						1			2		
Wilbraham	232	24	Stebbins	David	2			1		3			1				7		
Conway	61	5	Stebbins	David Jur	1	1							1				3		
Deerfield	55	1	Stebbins	Ebenezer	4	1	1	1		1		1	1				10		
Springfield	241	4	Stebbins	Edward		1			1	1	1	1					5		
Springfield	241	5	Stebbins	Elam	2			1		2			1				6		
Wilbraham	232	23	Stebbins	Eldad		2	1	1				1		1			6		
Gill	87	29	Stebbins	Elisha		1	2			1		1					6		
Longmeadow	92	17	Stebbins	Ezra		1		1				1	1				4		
Springfield	240	26	Stebbins	Festus	2			1		1			1				5		
Granville Mid Soc.	167	37	Stebbins	Francis	1			1					1				3		
Wilbraham	235	41	Stebbins	Frederick	1			1		2			1				5		
Belchertown	207	10	Stebbins	Giddeon Capt		1	1	2	1	1		4		1			11		
Wilbraham	233	5	Stebbins	Gilbert				1		1			1				3		
Monson	268	11	Stebbins	Hazadiah	1	1		1		2	2	1	1				9		
Monson	268	12	Stebbins	Hazadiah Jr		1							1				2		
Granby	254	12	Stebbins	Herman	2			1					1				4		
Springfield	240	21	Stebbins	Ithamar				1		1			1				3		
Springfield	240	42	Stebbins	Ithamar	2		1			1			1				5		
Monson	266	34	Stebbins	James		1	1		1	1	1			1			6		
Wilbraham	232	41	Stebbins	James	1			1		1	1	1					5		
West Springfield	351	51	Stebbins	Jere	2	1		1		1	2	1			3		11		
Monson	263	31	Stebbins	Jesse		1	1		1	1	2	1	1				9		
Conway	61	4	Stebbins	John	3	1		1	1	1			1	1			10		
Northampton	9	33	Stebbins	John	1			1		2	1		1				6		
Russell	137	14	Stebbins	John				1		1			1				3		
Springfield	242	27	Stebbins	John			5	7		3		2					17		
Wilbraham	238	17	Stebbins	John				1		1			1				3		
Granby	254	11	Stebbins	Jona	3			1		1			1				6		
Deerfield	54	42	Stebbins	Joseph	1	1	2	2	1	3	3	1		1			15		
Springfield	240	33	Stebbins	Joseph	2	1	1	1	1			2	1	2			11		
Wilbraham	236	2	Stebbins	Justin			1		1	1	1		1				5		
Brimfield	269	13	Stebbins	Levi		1		1					1	2			5		
Chesterfield	24	24	Stebbins	Levi	1	1	1	1						1			5		
Granby	252	28	Stebbins	Luther	1		1						1				3		
Monson	263	32	Stebbins	Luther	2			1					1				4		
Wilbraham	232	28	Stebbins	Mary Wd			1				2	1		3			7		
Longmeadow	92	15	Stebbins	Medad	2			1				1		3			7		
Conway	60	42	Stebbins	Moses					1				1	1			3		

TOWN	PG#	LN#	LAST NAME	FIRST NAME	FREE WHITE MALES under 10	10 to 16	16 to 26	26 to 45	45 and over	FREE WHITE FEMALES under 10	10 to 16	16 to 26	26 to 45	45 and over	TOTAL ALL OTHER	TOTAL SLAVES	TOTALS	DISTRICT/ TOWNSHIP	NOTES
Deerfield	55	2	Stebbins	Moses	1			1		3	1		1				7		
Springfield	240	25	Stebbins	Moses		1		1		2			1				5		
Wilbraham	237	23	Stebbins	Moses			1	1					1				3		
Wilbraham	237	22	Stebbins	Moses Junr	2	2		1			1	2		1			9		
Wilbraham	233	42	Stebbins	Noah		1		1				3		1			6		
Wilbraham	233	43	Stebbins	Noah Jun			1			4		1	1				7		
Wilbraham	236	21	Stebbins	Phinehas Jr	2	1		1		1			1				6		
Wilbraham	237	21	Stebbins	Phinihas Esq			1	1	1		1	1	1				6		
Springfield	240	27	Stebbins	Rachel Wd									1				1		
Russell	138	1	Stebbins	Saml			1			2			1				4		
Springfield	240	41	Stebbins	Samuel		1		1				1	1				4		
Wilbraham	232	31	Stebbins	Sarah Wd	2	1	3				2	1		1			10		
Conway	60	39	Stebbins	Simeon	1	2		1		1	1		1				7		
West Springfield	351	47	Stebbins	Solomon	1	1	2	1	2	1	1	1	2				12		
Conway	60	41	Stebbins	Sylvester	5		1	1			1	1	1				10		
Monson	268	15	Stebbins	Thaddeus	2			1		3			1	1			8		
Springfield	240	31	Stebbins	Thos Capt				1		1			1				3		
Wilbraham	238	4	Stebbins	Timothy	3			1		1			1				6		
Brimfield	270	23	Stebbins	Uriah	3			1		1			1				6		
Springfield	240	32	Stebbins	Walter	1			1					1				3		
Wilbraham	236	3	Stebbins	Walter			1			1			1				3		
Longmeadow	94	9	Stebbins	William	3			1		2			1				7		
Longmeadow	92	18	Stebbins	Zadek	1	1		1		1			1				5		
Wilbraham	238	15	Stebbins	Zadock			1		1			1	1				4		
Wilbraham	238	16	Stebbins	Zadock Jr	2			1		1		1					5		
Springfield	239	33	Stebbins	Zebina	4	1	1	2		1		1	1				11		
Brimfield	269	12	Stebbins	Zerah				1									1		
Wilbraham	232	42	Stedman	Abigail Wd		1	1			2	1		1				6		
Springfield	241	8	Stedman	Phinehas		1	2			1		1	1	1			7		
Leyden	84	9	Stedmon	Philemon	2			1		2	2		1				8		
Monson	265	31	Steed	Jonathan		1	1			1		1					4		
Charlemont	194	2	Steel	Elijah	1			1		2			1				5		
Belchertown	207	25	Steel	John		1											1		
New Salem	103	16	Steel	John	1			1				2		1			5		
Ware	228	16	Steel	John D.	1			1		2	1		1				6		
Shelburne	324	9	Steel	Levi	1		3		1			2		1			8		
Northampton	9	4	Steel	Moses			1			3	1		1				6		
Pelham	213	29	Steel	Saml		1		1					1				3		
New Salem	103	17	Steel	Samuel	1			1		2			1				5		
Longmeadow	92	14	Steel	Seth	3			1		1			2				7		
Granville East Soc	533	13	Steen	Benjamin		1	2			2	1	2		1			9		
Southwick	360	23	Stephans	Solomon Jr	1	1	1	1		1	1	1	1				8		
Palmer	260	22	Stephens	Henry		1			1	1		1		1			5		
Westfield	125	20	Stephens	Ira			1			2		1					4		
Chester	145	10	Stephens	John	1		2		1				1	1			7		
Chesterfield	23	32	Stephens	John Jr	2	1		1		3	1		1				9		
Palmer	260	23	Stephens	Levi	1			1		2				1			5		
Amherst	290	5	Stephens	Phinehas	2			1		1		1					5		
Westfield	125	26	Stephens	Rufus		1		1		1		1					4		
Chesterfield	23	31	Stephens	John				1						1			2		
Longmeadow	92	23	Stephenson	Calvin	3	1	1	1		3			1				10		
Chester	146	33	Stephenson	Eli			1			1			1				3		
Chesterfield	20	25	Stephenson	John			1							1			2		
West Springfield	355	17	Stephenson	John			1						1				2		
Chesterfield	20	26	Stephenson	John Jun	2	1		1		3	1		1				9		
Springfield	244	21	Stephenson	Abiather	1			1		1	1	1		1			6		
Springfield	244	17	Stephenson	Abiather Jr			1			1			1				3		
Springfield	244	22	Stephenson	Benajah				1			1		1				3		
Granville West Soc	168	12	Stetson	Jonathan	2			1		3	1		1				8		
Greenwich	222	22	Steveman	Isaac		1	2	1	1		1	2	1	1			10		
Greenfield	75	26	Stevens	Abiel	3			1		1			1	1			7		
Warwick	39	29	Stevens	Abraham	3			1		3			1				8		
Greenfield	75	32	Stevens	John	1			1		1			1				4		
Greenwich	222	33	Stevens	John	2	1		1		1	2		1	1			9		
West Springfield	357	30	Stevens	Nathan Junr		1				1			1				3		
Warwick	39	40	Stevens	Nathaniel Gove	1	1	1		1			2		1			7		
Southwick	360	25	Stevens	Soloman				1						1			2		
Southwick	360	22	Stevens	Titus		1		2		1			1				5		
Warwick	39	28	Stevens	Wilder	2	1	1		1	1	3	2	1	1			13		
West Springfield	357	29	Stevens	Nathan		1			1		1						3		
West Springfield	355	5	Stevenson	Erastus	2			1					1				4		
Chesterfield	23	35	Stevenson	Nathl			1			2			1				4		
Cummington	304	8	Stevenson	Obadiah	2			1					1				4		
Pelham	216	24	Stevenson	Saml	1		1	1				1		1			5		
Greenwich	222	16	Stevers	Robt	3		1			1		1					6		
Westfield	127	26	Steward	Lemuel			1			1			1				3		
Granville West Soc	170	36	Stewart	Alexander	2			1		2	2		1				8		
Russell	138	16	Stewart	Andrew	2			1		3	3	1	1				11		
Granville West Soc	169	26	Stewart	Archibald				1		1		3		1			6		
Middlefield	156	11	Stewart	Benjamin	1			1						1			3		

303

TOWN	PG#	LN#	LAST NAME	FIRST NAME	FREE WHITE MALES					FREE WHITE FEMALES					TOTAL ALL OTHER	TOTAL SLAVES	TOTALS	DISTRICT/ TOWNSHIP	NOTES
					under 10	10 to 16	16 to 26	26 to 45	45 and over	under 10	10 to 16	16 to 26	26 to 45	45 and over					
Colrain	188	31	Stewart	David	2	1		1		3			1				8		
Colrain	188	32	Stewart	Enos	3		1	1		1	1		1		1		9		
Colrain	188	38	Stewart	Hugh	3	1		1	1	1	2		1	1			11		
Brimfield	275	11	Stewart	James			1	1				1	1	1			5	South Brimfield	
Montague	47	39	Stewart	James	1	2	1		1	3			1				9		
Colrain	188	33	Stewart	John	2		1		1			2		1			7		
Shelburne	324	10	Stewart	John	1		1	1	1	2		1	1	2			10		
Wilbraham	236	25	Stewart	John	1	1		1		3	1	1					8		
Williamsburg	443	16	Stewart	John	1	2	1		1	2	1		1				9		
Montague	47	40	Stewart	Lucy			1					1		1			3		
Blanford	175	11	Stewart	Moses	2	2		1		1	1	1					8		
Blanford	179	3	Stewart	Nathan	1	2			1	1	1	1					7		
Brimfield	275	10	Stewart	Paul		2		1		3	1		1	1			9	South Brimfield	
Granville Mid Soc.	167	8	Stewart	Peter	2	1	1	1		4	2		1				12		
Shelburne	324	13	Stewart	Robert		1			1			1		1			4		
Blanford	176	24	Stewart	Solomon			1		1					1			3		
Blanford	178	32	Stewart	William	2		1		1	3		2		1			11		
Colrain	188	30	Stewart	William				1				1		1			3		
West Springfield	357	26	Stickman	Frederick			1				1		1	1			4		
South Hadley	250	39	Stickney	John		2		1						1			4		
Chester	149	5	Stiles	Ashbel				1			1	1		1			4		
Wendell	107	33	Stiles	Benjamin		1	2		1		1	2		1			8		
Westfield	126	28	Stiles	Darreas							1			1			2		
West Springfield	355	10	Stiles	Dinah	1							1	2	1			5		
Southwick	360	21	Stiles	Doras			2		1	1			1	1			6		
Wendell	107	31	Stiles	Edmund				1				1		1			3		
Russell	138	23	Stiles	Enoch	1		1	1		1		1					5		
Westfield	128	6	Stiles	Ephraim	1	1		1		4	1		1				9		
New Salem	103	13	Stiles	Foster	1	1			1				2				5		
Southwick	360	17	Stiles	Gideon		1	1		1			2	1	1			7		
West Springfield	355	18	Stiles	Horace	1		1			1			1				3		
Westfield	119	18	Stiles	John		1		1		3			1				6		
Greenfield	75	30	Stiles	Levi	3			1		1			1				6		
Westfield	126	29	Stiles	Martin				1						1			2		
Westfield	126	30	Stiles	Martin Junr	1	2	4		1	1	1	1		1			12		
Wendell	107	32	Stiles	Phinehas				1		2	1						4		
Chester	149	4	Stiles	Samuel Lieut	4	1		1		1	2		1				10		
Southwick	360	18	Stiles	Shubael	2	1		1		3	1	2	1				11		
Westfield	119	17	Stiles	Simeon		1		1						1			3		
Westfield	119	26	Stiles	Simeon Junr	1	2		1		2	1	1					8		
New Salem	103	12	Stimpson	Elias	2		2		1		2			1			8		
Monson	266	19	Stinson	Joseph	1	1	2		1		2			1			8		
Shutesbury	112	14	Stirtevant	Archl			1			1		1					3		
Shutesbury	112	13	Stirtevant	James		1			1		2			1			5		
Ashfield	345	9	Stoching	Abraham	1	1	1	1	1	1			1	1			8		
Ashfield	345	10	Stoching	Amos	1		2	1		3			1				8		
Ashfield	345	8	Stoching	Joseph				1						1			2		
Hadley	285	4	Stockbridge	David	3	1	3	2	2	1	2	3		2			19		
Whately	68	8	Stockbridge	David			1				1		1				3		
Westfield	127	12	Stockin	Amasa	2	1		1		2	1		1				8		
Shutesbury	112	22	Stockwell	Elisha	2			1					1				4		
Montgomery	160	9	Stockwell	Enos			1	1						2			4		
Warwick	39	30	Stockwell	James		3	1		1	2	1			1			9		
Plainfield	308	22	Stockwell	Jeremiah		2		1		2		1	1				7		
Leverett	116	14	Stockwell	John	2	1			1			1	2				7		
Norwich	153	17	Stockwell	Levi			1						1				2		
West Springfield	355	4	Stockwell	Samuel			1	2						3			6		
Hadley	287	39	Stockwell	Timothy			1		1	1		1	1				5		
Northampton	10	30	Stockwell	Walter	2			1		2			1				6		
Northampton	10	29	Stockwell	William		1		1		1	1	2		1			7		
Northampton	10	31	Stockwell	William Jr	1			1		1		1					4		
Westfield	125	25	Stoddard	Avery		1	1			2		2		1			7		
Westfield	125	5	Stoddard	Georg A			1				1	1					4		
Northampton	5	6	Stoddard	John			1				2	1					4		
Westfield	125	17	Stoddard	Ralph		2		1		1	1		1				6		
Hawley	334	38	Stoddard	Saml															
Northampton	5	5	Stoddard	Solomon		1	1		1				1	1			5		
Russell	138	12	Stoncliff	Wm	2	2		1	1	2	1	1	1				11		
Wendell	107	26	Stone	Abraham				1				1	1				3		
Wendell	107	27	Stone	Abraham Jr		1				2		1					4		
Goshen	311	28	Stone	Ambrose	2	2		1		2			1				8		
Rowe	200	27	Stone	Benjamin		2		1	1	2	1		1	1			9		
Wendell	107	30	Stone	Clark	1			1		2			1				5		
Greenwich	224	20	Stone	Daniel			1				1	1					3		
Colrain	189	3	Stone	Elias	3	2		1	1	2	1		1	1			12		
Greenwich	221	34	Stone	James Lt.		1	1			3	2		1				8		
Chesterfield	22	17	Stone	John	1	1			1	2			1				6		
Greenfield	75	25	Stone	John	2			1		1		1	1		1		7		
Greenwich	222	31	Stone	John	2		2		1	1		1	1				8		
Chesterfield	21	35	Stone	John 2d	1	2	1		1	2		2	1				10		
Wendell	107	29	Stone	Levi	1			1					1				3		

TOWN	PG#	LN#	LAST NAME	FIRST NAME	M under 10	M 10 to 16	M 16 to 26	M 26 to 45	M 45 and over	F under 10	F 10 to 16	F 16 to 26	F 26 to 45	F 45 and over	TOTAL ALL OTHER	TOTAL SLAVES	TOTALS	DISTRICT/ TOWNSHIP	NOTES
Greenwich	222	17	Stone	Luke	1		2						2				5		
Wendell	107	28	Stone	Matthew	2			1		2	3						8		
Greenwich	222	32	Stone	Samuel	1	2			1	1				1			6		
New Salem	103	19	Stone	Samuel	3	1		1		2	1		1				9		
New Salem	103	14	Stone	Seth		1		1					1				3		
Greenwich	222	18	Stone	Simeon Deacn		1	1		1	1	1			1			6		
Goshen	312	3	Stone	Sylvanus	3	2		1		1		1	1				9		
Brimfield	274	11	Stone	Thomas	2	1			1					1			5		
Heath	197	12	Stone	Thomas					1	1		1	1				4		
Chester	148	15	Stone	William	1		1		1	1			1				5		
Greenwich	222	24	Stone	William Doct		1	1	1		1	1	1	1				7		
Monson	263	14	Storey	Jethro											7		7		
South Brimfield	275	17	Storrs	Chester	1			1				1	1				4		
Longmeadow	93	17	Storrs	Richard Rev	4			1			1		1				7		
Cummington	304	40	Stovel	Warren	1			1					1				3		
Conway	60	33	Stow	Daniel		1	1	1	1	1	1	1		1			8		
Blanford	179	18	Stow	Ebenezer		1	1			1		2	1		1		6		
Granville East Soc	529	27	Stow	Elisha		2		1		1		1	1				6		
Conway	60	37	Stow	Joseph	1		1	1		2	1	1					7		
Granville Mid Soc.	165	23	Stow	Joseph	1	1			1			1	1	1			6		
Granville Mid Soc.	167	27	Stow	Stephen			3	1		1			1				6		
Warwick	39	36	Stow	Thomas	1		2	1		2		1	1				8		
Plainfield	308	42	Stowel	David	2			1		1			1	1			6		
Ashfield	345	1	Stowell	Caleb	1	1		1		2	2		1				8		
Ashfield	345	2	Stowell	David	2			1		1			1				5		
Greenwich	222	31	Stowell	Oliver	3	1	1		1	1	2	1		1			11		
Northfield	30	30	Stratton	Asa	3	2	1	1			1	1	1				10		
Northfield	30	31	Stratton	Caleb			1		1				1				3		
Northfield	30	25	Stratton	Calvin	1	1	1	1					1	1			7		
Northfield	30	27	Stratton	Elijah		2		1		1	2			1			7		
Shelburne	323	24	Stratton	Eliphalet			2	2		4	1	1	1				11		
Northfield	30	29	Stratton	Hezekiah	3	1	2	1			1	1	1	1			11		
Shutesbury	112	16	Stratton	Nathl	2			1		1			1				5		
Northfield	30	28	Stratton	Rufus	4	1	1		1	1		1	2	1			12		
New Salem	102	39	Stratton	Shubael C.		2	2	1		2		1					8		
New Salem	103	25	Stratton	Zebulon		1			1	2	1		1				6		
West Springfield	357	28	Street	Caleb M.	3			1					1				5		
West Springfield	357	27	Street	Glover	2	1		1		2			1				7		
West Springfield	357	23	Street	Joshua			2	1				1	1	1			6		
Orange	43	12	Streeter	Adam		1		1		3			1				6		
Plainfield	308	26	Streeter	Asa	1	1	1	1			2		1				7		
Middlefield	156	36	Streeter	Isaac H.	2	1		1		1	1	2	1				9		
Westfield	122	26	Streeter	Levi	2		1			1			1				5		
Rowe	200	26	Streeter	Moses		1	3		2			1		2			9		
Barnardston	79	26	Streeter	Pearly	2	1		1		3			1				8		
Plainfield	308	25	Streeter	Samuel	3	2	1		1		2	1	1				11		
Greenfield	75	23	Strickland	David	1	2		1		2			1				7		
Granville East Soc	533	18	Strickland	Elijah	1			1		1			1				4		
Palmer	260	35	Strickland	James	3			1		2			1				7		
Greenfield	75	22	Strickland	John				1					1	1			3		
Greenfield	75	24	Strickland	John	2		2	1			1	2	1				9		
Granville East Soc	531	20	Strickland	Jona		1	1		1	1	1	1		1			7		
Granville East Soc	531	36	Strickland	Jona Jr	2		1			2			1				6		
Granville East Soc	531	35	Strickland	Joseph			1	1						1			3		
Ludlow	255	20	Strickland	Nehemiah	1	1	1		1	1			1				6		
Southampton	131	24	Strong	Aaron	1			2		1		1					5		
Westhampton	16	23	Strong	Amasa		1	2	1		1	1	2		1			9		
Southampton	133	1	Strong	Asahel		2		1					1	1			5		
Northampton	4	9	Strong	Belah	2	1	1	1	1	2	1	1	1				11		
Westhampton	16	14	Strong	Benajah	2			1			1			1			5		
Easthampton	134	6	Strong	Benjamin	2			1					1				4		
Southampton	132	8	Strong	Bohan	1			1					1				3		
Northampton	7	1	Strong	Caleb	2	2	2		1	1	1	1	1	2			13		
Northampton	7	36	Strong	Daniel	1			1	1	1	1	2	1				8		
Northampton	4	16	Strong	David	2	1	1	1		1			1				7		
Northampton	3	34	Strong	Ebenezer				1			1			1			3		
Granville East Soc	531	26	Strong	Eleazer	4			1		2	1		1				9		
Northampton	3	4	Strong	Eleazer	1	1	1		1	2	2		1				9		
Southampton	131	25	Strong	Elias	2			1					1				4		
Southampton	129	26	Strong	Elihu	4	1		1					1				7		
Northampton	8	1	Strong	Elijah	2	2	1			1			1	1			8		
Williamsburg	443	9	Strong	Ezra				1			1			1			3		
Williamsburg	443	8	Strong	Gelston	1		1	1		2	2		1				8		
Northampton	11	10	Strong	Huit	1			1		2			1				5		
Northampton	4	15	Strong	Ithamer		1			2	1		1	1		1		7		
Southampton	131	28	Strong	Job		2	1						1				7		
Granville East Soc	531	28	Strong	Joel	1			1	1	1		1	1	1			8		
Northampton	11	12	Strong	Joel				1				1	1				3		
Northampton	2	18	Strong	John	1		1	1				2	1				6		
Southampton	130	24	Strong	John		1		1	1	2			1				8		

TOWN	PG#	LN#	LAST NAME	FIRST NAME	FREE WHITE MALES under 10	10 to 16	16 to 26	26 to 45	45 and over	FREE WHITE FEMALES under 10	10 to 16	16 to 26	26 to 45	45 and over	TOTAL ALL OTHER	TOTAL SLAVES	TOTALS	DISTRICT/TOWNSHIP	NOTES
Westhampton	16	26	Strong	John			1		1			1		1			4		
Northampton	2	19	Strong	John Jun			1			2		1					4		
Southampton	130	25	Strong	John Junr			1						2				3		
Northampton	3	33	Strong	Jonathan			2		1			1		1			5		
Northampton	3	32	Strong	Jonathan Junr	1			1				1					3		
Heath	197	10	Strong	Joseph	3	1			1	2			1				8		
Southampton	128	2	Strong	Joseph			1				1						2		
Williamsburg	443	7	Strong	Joseph	1			1		1		1		1			6		
Northampton	11	9	Strong	Medad	2	1			1	1	1		1				7		
Northampton	2	20	Strong	Nathan	1	3		1	1	1	2		1				10		
Northampton	9	17	Strong	Noah	1			1		1		1					4		
Westhampton	16	12	Strong	Noah		1	1		1			3	1				7		
Northampton	4	26	Strong	Oliver						1		1	2				4		
Northampton	5	25	Strong	Oliver	1		1			2			1	1			6		
Chesterfield	23	15	Strong	Peter	1	1	2		1			2		1			8		
Southampton	132	29	Strong	Roswel	1	1		2		3	1		1				9		
West Springfield	351	54	Strong	Selah	1			1						2			4		
Northampton	5	32	Strong	Silas	3		1					1	1				6		
Conway	60	48	Strong	Simeon	1		1					1					3		
Northampton	6	23	Strong	Simeon		2		1	1	1	1		1				7		
Amherst	289	6	Strong	Simeon Esq		1	3		1		1	1	1	1	1		9		
Williamsburg	443	10	Strong	Solomon			1			2		1					4		
Southampton	132	9	Strong	Stephen			1				1						2		
Northampton	2	21	Strong	Timothy				1				1					2		
Southampton	132	22	Strong	Waitstill	1	2		1		1		3		1			9		
Northfield	30	32	Strowbridge	James	1			1				2		1			5		
Chesterfield	23	24	Studley	David		2		1	1				1				5		
Ware	228	9	Studufant	James	2			1				1					5		
Chesterfield	24	23	Stulson	Abiel		1				1	1	1					5		
Hadley	285	19	Sturtevant	Francis		1	1			1	1						4		
Amherst	291	13	Stutson	Hgideon	1	1		1		3	2		1				9		
Monson	266	14	Sull	Richard		1	1		1		1		1				5		
Northampton	3	8	Summer	David	1			1		1			1				4		
Shutesbury	112	18	Sumner	John D.		1		1				2	2	1			7		
Westfield	122	7	Sumner	Joshua		1	1			2			1				5		
Orange	43	10	Sumner	Salem	2			1		2			1				6		
Greenfield	75	31	Swan	Benjamin		1	1	1		3		1	2				9		
Deerfield	55	8	Swan	Joseph	2		2	1					1				6		
Charlemont	194	4	Swan	Josiah		1	2		1			1		1			6		
Greenwich	222	21	Sweatland	David		1		1	1	3		2		1			9		
Granville West Soc	170	28	Sweatman	Reuben	1	1	1		1	1	1		1				7		
Shelburne	324	14	Sweet	Henry		1	1		1	1		2		1			7		
Deerfield	55	13	Sweet	Joseph			1	1				2		1			5		
Deerfield	55	11	Sweet	Joshua	2			1		3	1		1				8		
Wendell	107	25	Sweetser	Henry		1		1	1			1		1			5		
Springfield	244	2	Swetland	Daniel		1		1		1	1	1	1				6		
Springfield	244	5	Swetland	Jacob	1				1	2			1				5		
Longmeadow	91	14	Swetland	Theophilus	2		1			2	1	1					7		
Ware	228	13	Swift	Lemuel	1		1	1		2		1	1				7		
Leyden	84	11	Sworence	Matthew	4	1	4	2	1		3		2	1			18		
Norwich	154	14	Sylvester	Eliakim Doct				1					1				2		
Chesterfield	20	17	Sylvester	George H	1		1	1		1			1				5		
Chesterfield	21	20	Sylvester	Gershom	1	1		1		1			1				5		
Wendell	107	37	Sylvester	James	1		3			1			1				6		
Chesterfield	20	8	Sylvester	Luke				2						2			4		
Chesterfield	21	12	Sylvester	Nathaniel		1	3		1	2	2						9		
Chesterfield	21	19	Sylvester	Nehemiah	1		2		1	2	2	2		1			11		
Chesterfield	24	35	Sylvester	Seth			2		1				2	1			7		
Warwick	39	27	Symonds	Benjamin			1		1	3	2	1		1			9		
Warwick	39	34	Symonds	William	1			1		2		1					5		
Hadley	288	1	Symons	Nathan	1	1			1	1		2		1			7		
Goshen	312	7	Taft	Cheny	3		1	1		1		2					8		
Montague	48	11	Taft	Lyman	4	2	1	1		1		1	1				11		
Blanford	175	6	Taggard	Benjamin	1	1		1		3			1				7		
Colrain	189	22	Taggart	James	4			1		2	2		1				10		
Norwich	153	21	Taggart	James			1										1		
Colrain	189	25	Taggart	Samuel	2		3		1	3	2		1	1			13		
Longmeadow	93	2	Talcott	Aaron		1		1				1	1				4		
Springfield	247	18	Talcott	White			2				1						3		
Norwich	154	2	Talcutt	Eleazer	1			1		5		1	1	1			10		
Southwick	361	3	Talmadge	John		1	1	1		3		1		1			8		
Ludlow	258	6	Talmage	Nathaniel	2		1	1		1	1		1				7		
Palmer	259	26	Tangill	Benja Capt.		2	2		1		1	2		1			9		
Chester	146	3	Tanner	Clark	1	1		1		4			1				8		
Worthington	302	1	Tanner	George	3	1		1		2			1				8		
Norwich	153	8	Tanner	John	1			1		3			1				6		
Northampton	6		Tanner	Nathan	2			1		3			1				7		
Colrain	189	27	Tanner	Oliver	1			1		3			1				6		
Chester	148	25	Tanner	Silas	1		1						1				3		
Northampton	4	33	Tappan	Benjamin		2			1		1	2		1			7		

306

TOWN	PG#	LN#	LAST NAME	FIRST NAME	FREE WHITE MALES					FREE WHITE FEMALES					TOTAL ALL OTHER	TOTAL SLAVES	TOTALS	DISTRICT/ TOWNSHIP	NOTES
					under 10	10 to 16	16 to 26	26 to 45	45 and over	under 10	10 to 16	16 to 26	26 to 45	45 and over					
Brimfield	272	40	Tarbill	Elijah	2		1		1		1	1		1			7		
Brimfield	273	16	Tarbill	Elijah Junr		2				1		1					4		
Granby	254	1	Tarbox	Adriel	2			1				1					4		
Ludlow	256	32	Tarbox	Solomon		1		1				1		1			4		
Worthington	299	32	Tash	Moses Negro											6		6		
Conway	61	16	Tayler	David Jr	2			1		2			1				6		
Deerfield	55	24	Tayler	Obed		1		1		1			1				4		
Montague	48	7	Taylor	Aaron		1		1	1	3	1		1	1			9		
Chester	145	3	Taylor	Amos		1			1		1	2		1			6		
Buckland	330	22	Taylor	Barnabas			1		1			1	1				4		
West Springfield	352	13	Taylor	Chauncy	1	1			1	1		1	2		1		8		
South Hadley	249	14	Taylor	Comfort Wd									1				1		
West Springfield	352	10	Taylor	Dan	1	1	1	1		2	1	1	1				9		
Montague	48	14	Taylor	Daniel		1		1		2			1				5		
Granby	254	20	Taylor	David	2			1		2	1	1					7		
Montague	48	3	Taylor	David	1	1	1	1		2		1	1				8		
South Hadley	248	22	Taylor	Dorothy Wd			4					2		1			7		
Granby	253	23	Taylor	Ebenezer				1						1			2		
Ashfield	345	32	Taylor	Ebenz			1	1					2	1			5		
Williamsburg	443	20	Taylor	Edmond	1			1			1			1			4		
Chester	145	6	Taylor	Edward	3			1		2			1				7		
Montgomery	160	17	Taylor	Edward Esq		1	1		1			2		1	1		7		
Longmeadow	94	25	Taylor	Eliab	1		1			1			1				4		
South Hadley	248	14	Taylor	Elihu			1						1				2		
Buckland	330	18	Taylor	Enos	2	1		1		1		1					6		
Longmeadow	91	8	Taylor	Err	2	1		1		1			2				7		
Ashfield	345	34	Taylor	Ezekiel	2	1		1		2			1				7		
West Springfield	352	7	Taylor	Freeman	2			1		3			1				7		
Granville East Soc	533	15	Taylor	George		1		1			1		1				4		
Rowe	200	34	Taylor	Humphrey		1	1		1	1	2	1		1			8		
Ashfield	345	36	Taylor	Isaiah	2			1		2			1				6		
Granby	254	16	Taylor	Ithamar	3		2		1	1	1			1			9		
Granby	254	15	Taylor	Jacob				1						1			2		
Southwick	361	2	Taylor	James		1		1					1				3		
Westfield	118	20	Taylor	Jedidiah	2	1	1		1	1	2		1	1			10		
Ashfield	345	30	Taylor	John	1	1	1	1		2	3		1				10		
Chester	146	16	Taylor	John	1			1		1			1				4		
Deerfield	55	22	Taylor	John	4		2	1		2	1	1	1		1		13		
Hawley	335	15	Taylor	John		1	1		1			3		1			7		
Monson	263	16	Taylor	John				2			1		2				5		
Pelham	217	12	Taylor	John			1		1	1		2	1	1			6		
Shelburne	324	15	Taylor	John		2		1			1	1	1				6		
West Springfield	352	12	Taylor	John				1		1	1		1	1			4		
Montague	48	6	Taylor	Joseph	2		1	1		2		2	2	1			11		
Buckland	330	12	Taylor	Joshua Jr	2			1		2	4		1				10		
Buckland	330	15	Taylor	Leml	2		3	1		1		2	1				10		
Middlefield	156	3	Taylor	Lewis	1	2		1				1	1				6		
New Salem	104	8	Taylor	Mary		1						1	1				3		
South Hadley	248	5	Taylor	Moses	3			1		2			1				7		
Longmeadow	91	1	Taylor	Nathaniel	2			1			1		1				5		
West Springfield	352	15	Taylor	Nathaniel				1						1			2		
South Hadley	250	40	Taylor	Noah	2			1		1			1				5		
Goshen	312	4	Taylor	Oliver	1	2				1		1					6		
South Hadley	248	4	Taylor	Oliver				1					1				3		
South Hadley	250	37	Taylor	Oliver Jun	2			1		2		1	1				7		
Montague	48	16	Taylor	Patten	2			1		4	2		1				10		
West Springfield	352	11	Taylor	Paul		1						1					2		
Northampton	9	18	Taylor	Rachel						5	1		1				7		
South Hadley	250	41	Taylor	Reuben		1	1		1				2	1			6		
South Hadley	250	42	Taylor	Reuben Jr	3			1					1				5		
Charlemont	194	9	Taylor	Rufus	2			1		3			1				7		
Buckland	330	16	Taylor	Saml Esq			2	1	1		1	3		1			9		
Buckland	330	17	Taylor	Saml Junr	2	1		1		1	1						6		
Greenwich	221	32	Taylor	Samuel	2			1		1			1				5		
Middlefield	155	19	Taylor	Samuel	2			1		2			1	1			7		
Montague	48	15	Taylor	Samuel	1	1			1		1		1				5		
Westfield	118	17	Taylor	Samuel	2	3		1		1			1				8		
Granby	254	19	Taylor	Samuel Dr	2			1		3			1	1			8		
Charlemont	194	7	Taylor	Sarah							1			1			2		
Chesterfield	22	34	Taylor	Seth		1		1			1	1	1				5		
Chesterfield	22	33	Taylor	Seth Junr	2	1	1			1			1				6		
Granby	254	13	Taylor	Shubael		1							1				2		
Granby	254	17	Taylor	Silas	3			1		2		1	1				8		
Ashfield	345	35	Taylor	Stephen	3			1		1			1				6		
Norwich	151	18	Taylor	Stephen		1											1		
Shelburne	324	16	Taylor	Stephen		1	1				1	1					4		
West Springfield	352	14	Taylor	Stephen	1	1		1		2	1		1				7		
Charlemont	194	8	Taylor	Tertius	1	1	1		1			1	1	2			8		
West Springfield	352	9	Taylor	Thomas	2			1		1	1		1	1			7		
Belchertown	208	31	Taylor	Will		1			1		1			1			4		

TOWN	PG#	LN#	LAST NAME	FIRST NAME	FREE WHITE MALES					FREE WHITE FEMALES					TOTAL ALL OTHER	TOTAL SLAVES	TOTALS	DISTRICT/ TOWNSHIP	NOTES
					under 10	10 to 16	16 to 26	26 to 45	45 and over	under 10	10 to 16	16 to 26	26 to 45	45 and over					
Chester	145	4	Taylor	William	2			1						1			4		
Middlefield	158	23	Taylor	William	3	1			1	3			1				9		
Rowe	201	1	Taylor	William	1	1	1		1				1				5		
South Hadley	248	16	Taylor	William				1						1			2		
Buckland	330	13	Taylor	Willm	1	2		1		2	2		1				9		
South Hadley	248	17	Taylor	Wm Junr			2	1					2				5		
Orange	43	19	Temple	Hananiah			2		1	1		3		1			8		
Heath	197	15	Temple	Salman			1		1				1				3		
Heath	197	16	Temple	Seth	3	1			1	2	1	1	1	1			11		
Leverett	116	22	Temple	Silas		1		1					1	1			4		
Ludlow	255	10	Temple	Silas		1				1		1					3		
Heath	197	17	Temple	Solomon		1	3		1		2			1			8		
Ludlow	255	11	Temple	Thomas	2			2	1	1		1		1			8		
Shelburne	324	17	Tennant	Saml	1	2		1	1	2	2		1	1			11		
Cummington	304	21	Terril	Thomas	2	1	2	1		2			1				9		
Heath	197	25	Thair	Artemas	2			1					1				4		
Heath	197	18	Thair	Asil		1		1				2		1			5		
Heath	197	19	Thair	Asil Jun		1		1	1	1		1	1				6		
Heath	197	21	Thair	Caleb Jun	1		1		1	1		1		1			6		
Heath	197	24	Thair	Jonah		1		1		1		1		1			5		
Heath	197	23	Thair	Jonathan		1	1	1		4			2	1			10		
Heath	197	14	Thair	Silas	2	1		1		2			1				7		
Conway	61	18	Thatcher	Ebenezer	1			1		1			1				4		
Williamsburg	443	22	Thayer	Abel		1	2	1	1	1		1	2	1			10		
Conway	61	15	Thayer	Adonijah	1			1		1			1	1			5		
New Salem	104	9	Thayer	Ahar			1	1	1	2			1	1			7		
Springfield	247	13	Thayer	Ambrose			4	1		1			1				7		
Hawley	335	14	Thayer	Asa	1	1	1		1		1	1		1			7		
Warwick	40	26	Thayer	Asa	1		2	1		1	1	1	1				8		
Westhampton	18	4	Thayer	Asa			2		1		1	1		1			6		
Montague	48	8	Thayer	Caleb	4	1		1		2	2	1	1				12		
Leverett	116	18	Thayer	Calvin	2	1		1					1				5		
Conway	61	11	Thayer	Daniel		1						1	1				3		
Conway	61	10	Thayer	Edward	1		1			3	2		1				8		
Westhampton	18	6	Thayer	Elias	3	1	1		1	1	2		1				10		
Conway	61	14	Thayer	Eliha		1				1		1					3		
Belchertown	204	7	Thayer	Elijah	5	1			1			3		1			11		
Buckland	330	8	Thayer	Elijah		1		1			2		1				5		
Buckland	330	9	Thayer	Elijah Jr	1		1					1					3		
Williamsburg	442	1	Thayer	Eliphalet	1		1					1					3		
Williamsburg	443	19	Thayer	Elkanah	3		2		1	1	2	1	1	1			12		
Ware	228	24	Thayer	Enoch	3	1			1		1		1				7		
Cummington	304	15	Thayer	Jacob	1	2		1		2		1	1				8		
Ware	228	23	Thayer	Jedediah	3			1		1	2		1				8		
Shutesbury	112	24	Thayer	Jesse	1			1				1		1			4		
Chesterfield	21	17	Thayer	Joel	1	1	1	1					1				5		
Orange	43	21	Thayer	Joel	1			1		3	1		1				7		
Belchertown	207	15	Thayer	John	2	2		1		2	2		1				10		
Greenwich	223	12	Thayer	John Jun	2			1	1	2	2		1				9		
Leverett	116	20	Thayer	Joshua	1	1	1	1		2	1	1	1				9		
Williamsburg	443	23	Thayer	Joshua	1			1					1				3		
Amherst	292	29	Thayer	Josiah	2	3	2		1		1		1	1			11		
Cummington	304	16	Thayer	Luke	2	2		1		2	2		1				10		
Plainfield	309	2	Thayer	Nathll	1	1		1				1		1			5		
Goshen	312	9	Thayer	Oliver	1		1	1				1					4		
Williamsburg	443	24	Thayer	Oliver	2		2		1	2	1	1		1			10		
Williamsburg	442	5	Thayer	Oliver Junr	1		1					1					3		
Belchertown	207	16	Thayer	Reuben	2	2		1		2		1	1				9		
Ware	228	37	Thayer	Silas	1	1		1		2	1		1				7		
Chesterfield	21	33	Thayer	Stephen	1			1		1		1	1				5		
Shutesbury	112	25	Thayer	Stephen		1				1		1					3		
Wilbraham	232	32	Theving	John	3	2		1	1	2	2		1	1			13		
Springfield	241	39	Theving	Samuel	1					3			1	1			6		
New Salem	103	33	Thomas	Amos	3	1	1	1	1	2	1	2		1			13		
Rowe	200	33	Thomas	Archabald		1	1	1		1		2		2			8		
Rowe	200	32	Thomas	Ebenezer		1	1			2			1				5		
Wendell	107	38	Thomas	Foxwell		2		1			1			1			5		
Greenwich	223	6	Thomas	Israel	1			1		1			1				4		
Russell	138	2	Thomas	Lovwell		1	1					1		1			5		
Ware	228	17	Thomas	Nehemiah		1		1		3		2		1			8		
Cummington	304	14	Thomas	Noah	1		2	1		1		1	3	1			10		
Norwich	152	39	Thomas	Salmon	1	1		1		2			1				6		
Chesterfield	23	30	Thomas	Samuel	2			1		1	1	1	1	1			8		
Colrain	189	24	Thomas	Willard	2	1		1		1	1	1	1				8		
Greenwich	223	9	Thomas	William	3			1		1	2		1				8		
Holland	280	2	Thompson	Asa	1			1			1	1	1	1			6		
Ware	228	20	Thompson	Benja Jr		2		1			1	1		1			6		
New Salem	103	35	Thompson	Caleb	2	2		1		1			1	1			8		
Longmeadow	95	12	Thompson	Charles	1		2		1		1	1		1			7		
Longmeadow	92	34	Thompson	Charles Jr	1			1				1					3		

TOWN	PG#	LN#	LAST NAME	FIRST NAME	FREE WHITE MALES					FREE WHITE FEMALES					TOTAL ALL OTHER	TOTAL SLAVES	TOTALS	DISTRICT/ TOWNSHIP	NOTES
					under 10	10 to 16	16 to 26	26 to 45	45 and over	under 10	10 to 16	16 to 26	26 to 45	45 and over					
Warwick	40	32	Thompson	Ebenezer				1		3			1				5		
Holland	279	16	Thompson	Jacob				1	1			1		1			4		
Belchertown	210	29	Thompson	James	1		1	1	1		2	1		1			8		
New Salem	103	38	Thompson	James	2	1	1		1	2		1	1				9		
Pelham	216	35	Thompson	James	1	1	1		1	1	1	3	1	1			11		
Pelham	216	34	Thompson	Jno Capt				1					1				2		
Brimfield	274	25	Thompson	Jonathan Lt				1					1				2		
Palmer	259	39	Thompson	Nathan	2	1		1					1				5		
Montague	48	5	Thompson	Peter	1			1		3			1				6		
Longmeadow	94	27	Thompson	Rufus	2			1		1	2		1				7		
Palmer	259	40	Thompson	Rufus		1	1	1				2		1			6		
Buckland	330	23	Thompson	Saml				1				1		1			3		
Deerfield	55	27	Thompson	Samuel	2	3		1						1			7		
Longmeadow	95	26	Thompson	Samuel		1	1	1					1				4		
Blanford	176	39	Thompson	Sanford		1	1		1			1	1				5		
Brimfield	274	26	Thompson	Sylvanus	2	1	1		1	1	2		1				9		
Chesterfield	25	4	Thompson	Thomas				1					1				2		
Pelham	216	36	Thompson	Thomas	3	2	2		1		1	1		1			10		
Longmeadow	95	11	Thompson	William		2			1			1	1				5		
Colrain	189	17	Thomson	David		1		1		1		2					5		
Colrain	189	21	Thomson	Hugh	4	2	2	1	1	1	1	1	1	1			15		
Gill	88	7	Thomson	John		1	1		1		2			1			6		
Colrain	189	23	Thomson	Joseph Jun	3			1		2	2		1				9		
Plainfield	308	13	Thomson	Luther				1		1			1				3		
Heath	197	22	Thomson	Stephen	1	1	1	1		3	2	1					10		
Williamsburg	442	4	Thomspn	Edward	2			1		2			1				6		
South Hadley	249	26	Thorington	Joseph	1			1		1	1			1			5		
Leyden	84	17	Thorn	Henry	1	1		1		3	1			1			8		
West Springfield	352	5	Thornton	Elisha				1		1			1				4		
West Springfield	352	4	Thornton	Medad					1	1				1			3		
Hawley	335	16	Thorp	Bishop			1			2		1					4		
Southampton	132	16	Thorp	David		2	1	1						1			5		
West Springfield	357	33	Thorp	Eli	1			1		3	1		1				7		
West Springfield	357	34	Thorp	Moses	2	1		1					1				5		
Hawley	335	17	Thorp	Thomas				1		2		1					4		
Northampton	9	37	Thorpe	Timothy		1		1					1				3		
Worthington	299	33	Thorum	Negro											4		4		
Granville East Soc	529	21	Thrall	Samuel	4	2	1	1		1			1				10		
Ware	228	25	Thrasher	George		2		1		2	1		1				7		
Worthington	299	19	Thresher	Simeon	3		1	1		1			1		4		11		
Rowe	201	4	Thurber	Ores				1		3			1				5		
Pelham	216	38	Thurton	Eliza		1	2				1	2		1			7		
Conway	61	12	Thwing	Timothy		1	2		1		1			2			7		
Granville Mid Soc.	165	21	Tibbats	John	2			1					1				4		
Granville Mid Soc.	166	9	Tibbats	Moses	2			1		1			1				5		
Northfield	31	1	Tiffany	Edward	3	1	2	1	1	1		1	1	1			12		
Montgomery	160	28	Tiffany	Elizabeth Widw	1	1	2			1	1						7		
South Brimfield	276	40	Tiffany	James	1		2	1		2	1	1	1				10		
Westfield	124	15	Tiffany	Wm	2			1			1	1	1				6		
Westfield	126	26	Tiffeny	Samll	1			1		2			1				5		
Heath	197	27	Tilden	Benjamin	1	3	1		1	3	1			1			11		
Montague	48	12	Tilden	Elisha	3	2			1	1	1						8		
Wilbraham	237	13	Tilden	William	1			1		3	2			1			8		
Williamsburg	442	21	Tileston	Cornelius	2	2		1		1	1		1				8		
Brimfield	273	18	Till	James											2		?		
Granby	254	18	Tilley	Sudderick	1	1		1		2	1		1				7		
Wilbraham	236	13	Tillotson	Eleazer	1			1	1	1	2	2	1				10		
Wilbraham	236	40	Tillotson	Eleazer Junr	2	1		1		3			1				8		
Granville East Soc	531	19	Tillotson	Jena		1	1	1				1	1	1			6		
Greenwich	223	7	Tillson	Stephen		1	3		2	1	1	1	1				10		
Goshen	312	8	Tilton	Salatiel	2	1	1	1		1	1	1					9		
Warwick	40	33	Timpson	Robert	2	1								1			6		
Granville East Soc	531	14	Tinker	Charity								3		1			4		
Worthington	301	42	Tinker	Elihu	1	1	1		1				1	1			6		
Norwich	153	1	Tinker	Elisha	1	1	1	1		1	1		1				7		
Granville East Soc	531	15	Tinker	John	3			1		2			1				7		
Worthington	298	8	Tinker	John	1			1				1	1				4		
Cummington	304	35	Tinker	Josiah	1			1		2			1				5		
Granville East Soc	527	13	Tinker	Martin	1			1		2			1	3			8		
Westfield	126	15	Tinker	Martin Capt	5	1	2		1			1	1	1			12		
Worthington	302	14	Tinker	Nehemiah	1			1		1			1				4		
Chester	148	8	Tinker	Rufus	3	2		1					1				8		
Chester	148	7	Tinker	Silas	1	3	1		1			3		1			10		
Chester	148	23	Tinker	Sylvester			1					1					2		
Granville East Soc	531	16	Tinker	Sylvester	1		2	1		1			1				6		
Pelham	216	33	Tinkham	Joseph		1	1			1			1				4		
Wilbraham	234	18	Tinkham	Peter	2	1		1		3	1		1				9		
Ware	228	21	Tinney	Daniel		1		1			2	1		1			6		
Charlemont	194	10	Tinney	Josiah		1		1		2		1	1				6		
Conway	61	17	Tinney	Josiah	4			1		2	3	1					11		

TOWN	PG#	LN#	LAST NAME	FIRST NAME	FREE WHITE MALES					FREE WHITE FEMALES					TOTAL ALL OTHER	TOTAL SLAVES	TOTALS	DISTRICT/ TOWNSHIP	NOTES
					under 10	10 to 16	16 to 26	26 to 45	45 and over	under 10	10 to 16	16 to 26	26 to 45	45 and over					
Shelburne	324	18	Tinney	Saml	3			1					1				5		
Colrain	189	26	Tinney	Stephen	1		1					1					3		
Goshen	310	15	Tipson	John	2	2	1		1	2	1		1				10		
Goshen	310	16	Tipson	Joseph	1	2	1	1		3		1	1				10		
Goshen	310	17	Tipson	Samuel	3			1		1			1				6		
Colrain	189	28	Tisdale	Abraham			1			1			1				3		
Ware	228	22	Tisdale	John Junr	2			1	1				1	3			8		
Ware	228	26	Titus	Ebenezer	1			1		2			1				5		
Williamsburg	442	3	Titus	Samuel	1			1					1				3		
Greenwich	223	8	Titus	Simeone	2	1	3	1	1	1	2	2		1			14		
Conway	61	13	Toby	Amaziah		1	1	1		1	1		1	1			7		
Ashfield	345	31	Toby	Elijah	1			1					1				3		
Buckland	330	20	Toby	Isaac	1	2			1	2	1	1		1			9		
Conway	61	8	Toby	Prince		1	4	1	1		2	1	3	1			14		
Conway	61	9	Toby	Timothy		2	4		1	1	1			1			10		
Rowe	201	3	Tod	Titus	1			1		2			1				5		
Whately	68	14	Todd	Asa	1	2		1		2	1	1	1	1			10		
Russell	139	11	Todd	Benjamin	1	3			1	3			1				9		
West Springfield	355	22	Todd	Jesse				1	1	1			1				3		
West Springfield	352	6	Todd	Solomon	1			1			1		1				4		
Montague	48	9	Tolls	Jared	2	1	1		1	2	1			1			9		
Montague	48	10	Tolls	Jared Junr			1			1		1							
Colrain	189	19	Tolman	Joshua	1	1		1	1		1	1		1			7		
Colrain	189	20	Tolman	Joshua Jun	2			1			1		1				5		
Colrain	189	18	Tolman	Stodard		1	1	1		2	2			1			8		
Colrain	189	29	Tolman	Thomas	2			1		2	1		1				7		
Greenwich	223	33	Tompkin	Thomas				1			1		1				3		
Greenwich	224	1	Tompkin	Thomas Jr	1			1		1			1				4		
Chester	144	30	Toogood	William Capt			2		1					1			4		
Westfield	126	1	Topliff	John	1	3			2	4			1	1			12		
Greenwich	223	14	Toplouf	Gurdon	2			1		1		1					5		
Greenwich	223	15	Toplouf	Luther				1									1		
Chesterfield	22	28	Torey	Joseph	1	2	2	1		3	1	1	1				12		
Belchertown	211	23	Torrance	Jeduthene	1		1			1			1				4		
Belchertown	207	14	Torrance	Wm		1	1		1			1		2			6		
Southampton	133	13	Torrey	Calvin	1	2		1		1	1		1	1			8		
Chesterfield	23	21	Torrey	David	1	2			1		1	1		1			7		
Leverett	116	19	Torrey	Jacob		1			1		1			1			4		
Monson	266	11	Torrey	Jonathan		1		1		2			1	1			6		
Monson	266	12	Torrey	Joseph				1		3			1				5		
Wilbraham	232	7	Torrey	Samuel	4	1		1			1	1	1				9		
Chesterfield	22	32	Torrey	Stephen				1		1				1			3		
Plainfield	308	29	Torry	Abner			1		1			1	1				4		
Plainfield	308	31	Torry	Barnee	1			1		1		1					4		
New Salem	104	4	Torry	Ebenezer	1			1			1	1		1			5		
Belchertown	210	27	Torry	Ezra		2			1		2			1			6		
Plainfield	308	30	Torry	Jona	2	1	2		1	1	2		1				10		
Cummington	304	22	Torry	Jona	2			1		1			1				5		
Plainfield	308	32	Torry	Josiah	1	1	1	1		2	1	1		1			9		
Cummington	304	24	Torry	Luther			1	1				1	1				4		
Greenwich	223	11	Torry	Samuel	2	2		1		2			1				8		
Granby	252	42	Totman	Samuel				1		1	1		2				5		
Worthington	299	28	Tower	Abner	1			1		1			1				5		
Cummington	304	17	Tower	Asa	1	1		1	1	2	2		1	1			10		
Northampton	7	35	Tower	Elkanah			1				1						2		
Goshen	312	6	Tower	Isaac		2	1		1	3			1				8		
Pelham	216	32	Tower	Isaac	3	2			1	1	1	1	1				10		
Worthington	299	29	Tower	Joseph			1		1			1	1	1			5		
Cummington	304	19	Tower	Matthew	3			1		2		1	1	1			9		
Cummington	304	20	Tower	Nathaniel		1	3		1	2			1	1			9		
Cummington	304	23	Tower	Peter	2	1		1					1	1			6		
Goshen	312	5	Tower	Richard	1			1				2		1			5		
Worthington	299	11	Tower	Samuel	1		1	1		1			1				6		
Worthington	299	8	Tower	Samuel Jun	2	1		1		1			1				6		
Worthington	301	13	Tower	Shubel	1			1		2	1		1				6		
Cummington	304	18	Tower	Stephen	1	1	4		1	2	2	2		2			15		
Ashfield	345	33	Tower	Thomas	3	1	1		1	1	2	2		1			11		
Belchertown	210	31	Town	Amasa	2	1											4		
Greenwich	223	4	Town	Elijah			1										1		
Warwick	40	27	Town	Ephraim		1		1		2	1	2	1				8		
Granby	253	18	Town	Israel			1							2			3		
New Salem	104	3	Town	Joel				1			1	1					4		
Greenwich	223	1	Town	John		1								1			3		
Greenwich	223	18	Town	John Jr	3			1		2		1	1				8		
Belchertown	210	28	Town	Jona Capt	1	1		2				1	1				6		
Greenwich	223	32	Town	Jonathan	1			1		1		1					4		
Greenwich	223	10	Town	Levi	3			2		3			2				10		
Greenwich	223	3	Town	Reuben				1									1		
Belchertown	207	17	Town	Solomon	2	1		1		1	1		1				7		
Warwick	40	30	Town	Tabitha		1					1		3				5		

TOWN	PG#	LN#	LAST NAME	FIRST NAME	FREE WHITE MALES					FREE WHITE FEMALES					TOTAL ALL OTHER	TOTAL SLAVES	TOTALS	DISTRICT/ TOWNSHIP	NOTES
					under 10	10 to 16	16 to 26	26 to 45	45 and over	under 10	10 to 16	16 to 26	26 to 45	45 and over					
Heath	197	26	Town	Thomas	1		1		2		1						5		
New Salem	104	2	Town	Eliphalet		1	1		1	2	2		1				8		
Plainfield	308	33	Towne	Benjm	1	1	1		1		1	2		1			8		
Brimfield	273	36	Townley	Reuben			2		2		1			2			7		
New Salem	104	1	Townsend	Jonathan	2	1		1		2	1		1				8		
Chesterfield	22	26	Townsend	Moses	1	2		1		1	1	1	1				8		
Buckland	330	14	Townsley	Dan	3			1		2			1				7		
Deerfield	55	26	Tracy	George	3			1					1	1			6		
Norwich	154	20	Tracy	Stephen Rev	1	3	1	1	1	1	2	1					11		
Greenwich	220	30	Train	Isaac	2	1			1		2	1	1				8		
Greenwich	223	13	Train	Jonathan	4	1		1	1		1			1			9		
Whately	68	13	Train	Oliver	4	1		1		1			1				8		
Russell	137	3	Tran	John				1		2				1			4		
Monson	267	25	Trask	Daniel		1		1	1	1	1		1				6		
Westfield	122	27	Trask	Elizabeth	1	2					1			1			5		
Greenwich	223	5	Trask	Israel Doct		2	1		1	2		2	1				9		
New Salem	103	32	Trask	John	1			1	1	1			1	1			6		
New Salem	103	39	Trask	John 2d	1	1			2	2	1	3	1				11		
Monson	267	27	Trask	Peter		1	1		1	1		1	2	1			8		
Heath	197	20	Trask	William	1	3		1		2			1				8		
Blanford	175	21	Tray	Giles	1	2		1		1		1	1	1			8		
Hadley	285	27	Trayner	Francis			1		1	1	1	1	2	1			8		
Palmer	260	34	Trim	Benjamin	3	3		1		2	1			1			11		
Russell	137	10	Trimon	Josiah		1						1					2		
Westfield	128	2	Trimon	Simeon	2			1	1	2			1	1			8		
Worthington	300	26	Trink	Amos		1			1			2		1			5		
Northfield	30	34	Trip	Robert	2			1	1	1			1				5		
Buckland	330	21	Trow	Benjm	1			1		3			1				6		
Buckland	330	19	Trowbridge	Daniel	3	1	1	1		1	1	1	1				10		
Colrain	189	16	Truesdal	Darius	1		1						1				3		
Williamsburg	442	2	Truesdall	Daniel				1			1		1				3		
Buckland	330	7	Truesdel	Leml	1		1			1	1						4		
Buckland	330	6	Truesdel	Saml				1		1	1						3		
Monson	263	26	Trumbull	Elijah	3			1		2			1	1			8		
Monson	263	27	Trumbull	John	2	2		1		2			1				8		
Monson	265	34	Trusdale	Pearly	1		1	1		1	1	1					6		
Deerfield	55	23	Tryan	William	3	2	1	1		3	1	1	1				13		
Deerfield	55	28	Tryan	William Junr	1	1	1					1					4		
Buckland	330	10	Tryon	Josiah		1	1					1					3		
Buckland	330	11	Tryon	Timothy	1		1			1		1					4		
Worthington	302	13	Tubs	Wido		1								1			2		
Westfield	122	23	Tucker	Dick Negro											3		3		
Heath	197	28	Tucker	Ebenezer	2		2	1		2			1		1		9		
Springfield	239	10	Tucker	Ebenezer	2			1			1		1				5		
Greenwich	223	2	Tucker	Ephraim		1	1		1					1			4		
Brimfield	271	23	Tucker	Jos				1						1			2		
Orange	43	20	Tucker	Joshua	1		1			1		1					4		
West Springfield	355	21	Tucker	Morris	2			1	1				1				5		
Warwick	40	28	Tuel	Benjamin		1	4	1	1	1		1		1			10		
Warwick	40	31	Tuel	Benjamin Junr		1											1		
Warwick	40	29	Tuel	Thomas			1										1		
Monson	267	33	Tupper	Ezra	3	1		1		1	1		1				8		
Monson	267	34	Tupper	Ichabod		1	1		1	2		1		1			7		
Monson	267	31	Tupper	Thomas				1									1		
Monson	267	32	Tupper	William		1		1				1	1				4		
Palmer	261	42	Tupper	William	2		1	1		1			1				6		
Chesterfield	24	10	Turner	Asa	1		1			1		1					4		
Pelham	217	11	Turner	Ellis	2			1		3			1				7		
West Springfield	352	8	Turner	Gurdan		2			1		1	3		1			8		
Pelham	216	31	Turner	Levi	2			1		3	2		1				9		
New Salem	104	7	Turner	Micah		1		1						1			3		
Leverett	116	21	Turner	Mich	2	1	1		1	3	1			1			10		
Belchertown	210	30	Turner	Samuel			1	1		2			1	1			6		
Conway	61	19	Turner	Stephen		1		1		1		1		1			5		
Worthington	301	33	Turner	Thion		2	2	1	1	2	1		1	1			11		
New Salem	104	6	Turner	Zadok	2			1		4		1	1				9		
Plainfield	308	27	Turril	Amos	1	1		1		1	1		1				6		
Plainfield	308	28	Turril	Oliver				1		2		1					4		
Russell	139	14	Tuttle	Abel	1	1	2						1	1			7		
Rowe	201	2	Tuttle	David	3			1		2			1				7		
Worthington	300	10	Tuttle	David		1				1		1					3		
Deerfield	55	25	Tuttle	Ebenezer		1		1		1				1			4		
West Springfield	357	31	Tuttle	Electa	1						1		1				3		
Rowe	201	5	Tuttle	Ezra	2			1		1			1				5		
Westfield	124	19	Tuttle	Ichabod	1		1			1		1					4		
Sunderland	283	18	Tuttle	John	3	1		1		3			1	1			10		
West Springfield	357	35	Tuttle	Michael		1				1		1					3		
Granby	252	34	Tuttle	Nathan	1			1	1	2			1				6		
Montague	48	4	Tuttle	Nathan				1						1			2		
Montague	48	13	Tuttle	Nathan Junr	2		1			2			1				6		

TOWN	PG#	LN#	LAST NAME	FIRST NAME	FREE WHITE MALES under 10	10 to 16	16 to 26	26 to 45	45 and over	FREE WHITE FEMALES under 10	10 to 16	16 to 26	26 to 45	45 and over	TOTAL ALL OTHER	TOTAL SLAVES	TOTALS	DISTRICT/ TOWNSHIP	NOTES
Granville West Soc	168	30	Tuttle	Stephen		1		1		1	1			1			5		
West Springfield	357	32	Tuttle	Tilly		1	1		1				1	1			5		
Blanford	178	30	Twaddle	Daniel	1	1			1		1			1			5		
Granville West Soc	168	31	Twining	Eleazer	1			1		2			1				5		
Granville West Soc	169	7	Twining	Elijah			3	1		1	1			1			7		
Granville West Soc	169	5	Twining	Thomas	2		1	1	1	3		2		1			11		
Granville West Soc	170	37	Twining	William	3	1		1		1	1		1				8		
New Salem	103	34	Twitchell	Benoni	2			1					1				4		
New Salem	104	10	Twitchell	David		1							1				2		
New Salem	103	36	Twitchell	Enos			3	1					1				5		
New Salem	103	37	Twitchell	John	1	2		1		3	3		1	1			12		
Pelham	216	37	Tyler	Daniel	2	1	1			1	2		1				9		
Granby	253	42	Tyler	Gurdon	3			1		1			1				6		
Barnardston	79	31	Tyler	James	1		1			1		3					6		
Barnardston	79	30	Tyler	John	2	2		1		2	1		1				9		
Granby	253	40	Tyler	John				2		2			1	1			6		
Brimfield	269	23	Tyler	Nathan				1		1			1				3		
Leyden	84	18	Tylor	Peter	3	1		1		1	1		1				8		
New Salem	104	5	Tyrell	Jacob		1		1		2	1	1	1				7		
Wilbraham	234	1	Ufford	John	2	1		2		1	1	1					8		
Brimfield	275	9	Underwood	Alpheus	1		1						1				3	South Brimfield	
Brimfield	275	6	Underwood	Eliha	1	2	2		1	1			1	1			9	South Brimfield	
Greenwich	223	16	Underwood	Kingsley	2		1	1		1			1				6		
Monson	267	8	Underwood	Nehemiah	1		1						1				3		
Monson	267	26	Underwood	Reuben	1	1		1		1			1				5		
Monson	262	14	Upham	Benjamin		1		1				1					3		
New Salem	104	11	Upham	Edward	1	2		1		2	2		1				9		
West Springfield	355	25	Upham	James		1			1	1			1	1			5		
Holland	279	31	Upham	Jona	2			1		1			1	1			6		
West Springfield	355	23	Upham	Leonard	1	1		1					1	1			5		
Monson	262	13	Upham	Samuel	1			1		2		1	1	2			8		
Westfield	126	9	Upson	Simeone	3			1		2			1				7		
Charlemont	194	13	Upton	Abiathar			1			3			1				5		
Shutesbury	112	26	Upton	Benjamin		1		1		3	1			1			7		
Charlemont	194	12	Upton	Elias	4		1			1			1				7		
Charlemont	194	11	Upton	Joseph			1	1		1		1					4		
Charlemont	194	14	Upton	Josiah	1	2		1		1	2		1				8		
Charlemont	194	15	Upton	Nathanael	1			1					1				3		
New Salem	104	13	Upton	Stephen		1						1					2		
New Salem	104	12	Upton	Timothy	1	3		1				2	2				9		
Ashfield	345	37	Usher	James	1	1		1		2		1	1				7		
Monson	263	39	Utley	Azel	1	1	1	2		1			2				8		
Southwick	361	4	Utley	Oliver		1	1	1		4			2				9		
Chesterfield	24	7	Utley	Samuel	3	2		1		1		1	1				9		
Wilbraham	233	38	Utley	Stephen	2		1	1					1				5		
Middlefield	156	33	Vaderkin	Henry	2	1			1	1	1		1				7		
Chester	145	29	Vanderburgh	John											1		1		
Springfield	247	19	Vanhorn	Abraham				1						1			2		
Springfield	246	22	Vanhorn	Azariah				1			1		1				3		
Springfield	246	29	Vanhorn	Calvin		1		1		2		1	1				6		
Westfield	123	17	Vanhorn	Derrick	1	1		1		5	1	1	1				11		
Springfield	246	23	Vanhorn	Gad			1			3			1	1			6		
Springfield	247	42	Vanhorn	Gaius	1			1		2			1				5		
Springfield	246	28	Vanhorn	Ruel	1			1		2		1					5		
West Springfield	352	16	Vanhorne	John				2			1			2			5		
Shutesbury	112	28	Vaughan	Ebenezer	1	1		1		2	2		1				8		
Deerfield	55	29	Vaughan	Joseph	1			1					1				3		
New Salem	104	14	Vaughan	Nathan	1	3	3		1	3			1	1			13		
Shutesbury	112	27	Vaughan	Thomas		1						1	1	1			4		
Conway	61	20	Veber	David	3			1		1			1				6		
Westfield	124	8	Veits	John	1			1		2			1				5		
Westfield	124	3	Veits	Seth Junr	1			1				1					3		
Westfield	121	8	Verts	Seth			1	1		1	1		1				6		
West Springfield	355	24	Viets	Simeon	1		2						1	1			5		
Heath	197	29	Vincen	Joshua	4	1		1					1				7		
Ashfield	346	1	Vincent	David	2		1			2			1				6		
Ashfield	346	2	Vincent	Joseph	2		1			1			1				5		
South Brimfield	276	20	Vineka	Andrew	2	1		1		1		1		1			7		
Chesterfield	20	29	Vining	Ebenezer	2	1	1		1	3			1	1			10		
Middlefield	158	22	Vining	Elan		1				1		1					3		
Middlefield	158	21	Vining	Elkanah		1							1				2		
Plainfield	308	34	Vining	George	2	2	2		1	2	1		1				11		
Leyden	84	19	Vining	John		1		1		2	1		1				6		
Chesterfield	23	18	Vinton	Abiather	4	3	1			1			1				10		
South Hadley	251	26	Vinton	Abiather	3	1	2	1		1			1	1			10		
Granby	253	19	Vinton	Abraham			1							1			2		
Monson	265	44	Vinton	Caleb	4		1			1		1	1				8		
Monson	265	42	Vinton	Calvin	1		1	1		1	1	1	1				7		
Goshen	312	21	Vinton	Levi		1		1		3	2	1					9		
Worthington	302	16	Vinton	Mrs								2		1			3		
South Hadley	251	25	Vinton	Samuel Doct				1						1			2		

TOWN	PG#	LN#	LAST NAME	FIRST NAME	FREE WHITE MALES					FREE WHITE FEMALES					TOTAL ALL OTHER	TOTAL SLAVES	TOTALS	DISTRICT/ TOWNSHIP	NOTES
					under 10	10 to 16	16 to 26	26 to 45	45 and over	under 10	10 to 16	16 to 26	26 to 45	45 and over					
New Salem	104	15	Vorce	Asa		1			1			2		1			5		
Northfield	31	2	Vose	Solomon	1		1	1		1		1	1				6		
Ludlow	256	38	Wachburn	Elijah			1	1		2	1	1					6		
Ludlow	256	27	Wackoff	Peter											3		3		
Williamsburg	441	8	Wade	Amasa	1			1		1		1					4		
Buckland	331	18	Wade	Amos Capt.	2	2	1		1	1		1					8		
Buckland	331	19	Wade	Amos Junr	2	2	1		1	1		1					8		
West Springfield	355	29	Wade	James	3	1			1	2	1	1					9		
West Springfield	357	40	Wade	Nathan L.	2			1		2		1					6		
Leyden	84	23	Wadsworth	Amos				1				1					2		
Palmer	261	28	Wadsworth	Ebenezer				1		2			1				4		
Worthington	300	18	Wadsworth	William			1			1		2					4		
Leyden	84	29	Wagner	Elizabeth	1					1			1				3		
Leyden	84	30	Wagner	Francis		1				1		1					3		
Heath	198	7	Wait	Abel	1	1						2					4		
Northampton	9	26	Wait	Abijah		1	4	2	1		1	2		1			12		
Hatfield	11	17	Wait	Benjamin	1	3		1		3			1	1			10		
Whately	68	30	Wait	Benjamin	1		1			2			1				5		
Whately	68	20	Wait	Consider	5			1		1	2		1				10		
Pelham	217	2	Wait	David Ens		1		1			1	1	1				5		
Whately	68	17	Wait	Elihu	2	2	1	1		1	3	1	1				12		
Ashfield	346	13	Wait	Elijah		1		1									2		
Conway	61	47	Wait	Elijah		2											2		
Williamsburg	442	10	Wait	Elijah		3		1						1			5		
Hatfield	14	6	Wait	Elisha			1	1						1			3		
Southampton	130	8	Wait	Elisha		1	1			1	1			1			5		
Hatfield	14	7	Wait	Elisha Jun	2			1					1				4		
Ashfield	346	19	Wait	Gad	5	1		1		1	1		1				10		
Hatfield	14	28	Wait	Gad	2			1		1			1				5		
Whately	68	25	Wait	Jeremiah		1				1			1				3		
Whately	68	28	Wait	Jeremiah				1					1				2		
Whately	68	24	Wait	Joel		1				1				1			4		
Whately	68	21	Wait	Joel Junr	2	2	1		1	1	2			3			12		
Southampton	130	12	Wait	John		1	1	1				1		1			5		
Williamsburg	441	1	Wait	John	1	2	2		1		1	1		1			9		
Whately	68	29	Wait	Jonathan		1				2	1	1					5		
Chester	147	7	Wait	Jonathan	3		1	1			2	2		1			10		
Williamsburg	442	9	Wait	Joseph		1		1		1	1	1		1			6		
Chester	144	37	Wait	Josiah	1			1		1				1			4		
Northampton	9	30	Wait	Josiah	2			1		1	2	2		1			9		
Whately	68	22	Wait	Lemuel	1		3		1	1	1	4		1			12		
Hatfield	11	15	Wait	Lucius	1	2		1		4			1				9		
South Hadley	250	11	Wait	Martin		1		1				2		1			5		
South Hadley	250	10	Wait	Martin Jr	1			1		1			1				4		
Whately	68	26	Wait	Nathan	1			1		2			1				5		
Hatfield	13	29	Wait	Nehemiah		1	1	1				1	1				5		
Whately	68	27	Wait	Nehemiah		1				1		1					3		
Conway	61	44	Wait	Reuben		1				1		1					3		
Williamsburg	441	9	Wait	Salmon		1	1		1	1		1		1			6		
Chester	150	7	Wait	Seth	1		1			2		1					5		
Ashfield	346	14	Wait	Seth Junr	1			1	1	2			1	1			7		
Greenfield	76	1	Wait	William	2		1	1		3	1	1					9		
New Salem	104	22	Waite	Phinehas	1	1			1	?	1			1			7		
Wilbraham	235	20	Walbridge	Joshua	1					1			1				3		
Monson	267	23	Walbridge	William	1			1		1		1		1			5		
Williamsburg	442	24	Walcott	Elijah	2	1		1		3		1					8		
Wilbraham	234	21	Walden	Elisha	3	1	1	1		2		1					9		
Wilbraham	234	22	Walden	Jonathan		2		1				1	1				5		
Blanford	176	30	Wales	Henry	1			1			1	1	1				5		
Westhampton	17	15	Wales	Jonathan	3	1	1			1	1	1	1	1			11		
Brimfield	275	1	Wales	Oliver	2		3		1	1		1	1				9	South Brimfield	
South Brimfield	275	19	Wales	Royal			1			1		1					3		
Brimfield	275	3	Wales	Shubael				1		2				2			5	South Brimfield	
Williamsburg	442	8	Wales	William				1					1	1			3		
Pelham	217	8	Walker	Abel Jr	2			1				1					4		
New Salem	104	17	Walker	Abiathar		2	1	1		1		3					8		
Wilbraham	232	16	Walker	Asa				1		3		1		1			6		
South Brimfield	276	15	Walker	Benja				1				1	1				3		
South Brimfield	276	16	Walker	Benja Jr	1			1				1					3		
Blanford	178	9	Walker	Elisha		1	1	1				1	1				5		
Monson	267	10	Walker	Enos	2		1					1					4		
Belchertown	211	10	Walker	Hezekiah	2	2		1		2		1	1	1			10		
Greenwich	223	20	Walker	James	1	1		1		1	1		1				6		
South Brimfield	276	14	Walker	James		1		1						1			3		
Belchertown	211	13	Walker	James Jr	4	2		1			2			1			10		
Belchertown	211	15	Walker	Jas Capt		1		1						1			3		
Belchertown	211	14	Walker	Jason Lt				1		1			1				3		
New Salem	104	26	Walker	Jesse	2			1		3	1		1				8		
Buckland	331	14	Walker	Job	2			1		1			1				5		
South Brimfield	276	19	Walker	Joseph	3			1									5		

313

TOWN	PG#	LN#	LAST NAME	FIRST NAME	M under 10	M 10 to 16	M 16 to 26	M 26 to 45	M 45 and over	F under 10	F 10 to 16	F 16 to 26	F 26 to 45	F 45 and over	TOTAL ALL OTHER	TOTAL SLAVES	TOTALS	DISTRICT/ TOWNSHIP	NOTES
Belchertown	211	3	Walker	Josiah	3		1						1				5		
Monson	264	1	Walker	Luther				1		2			1				4		
South Brimfield	275	1	Walker	Marshal	3	1	1	1		1		1	1				9		
Belchertown	211	28	Walker	Nathaniel	1			1				1					3		
Belchertown	211	11	Walker	Silas	3			1		1		1					6		
Palmer	261	40	Walker	Silvanus		1	1	1		1			1	1			6		
Heath	197	32	Walker	Thomas	4			1				1					6		
Palmer	261	36	Walkins	Abner	3							1					4		
Greenwich	223	28	Walkins	Thomas	1	2	1	1				2	1				8		
Colrain	189	33	Walkup	George	2			1		2			1				6		
Hadley	286	18	Wallace	Daniel		1			1			1					3		
Colrain	190	1	Wallace	James			1	1	1		1	2	1				7		
Colrain	189	30	Wallace	Seth	3			1		2		1	1				8		
Williamsburg	442	7	Wallcott	Samuel	2	1			1	2				1			7		
Northampton	6	6	Wallcut	Lot	1		1			1		1					4		
Holland	279	32	Wallis	Alanson	1	1		1		1		1	1				6		
Holland	278	12	Wallis	Alfred	2			1		1		1					5		
Holland	278	4	Wallis	David	3	2		1		1		1	1				9		
Northampton	8	38	Wallis	Mary	2	1						1	1				5		
Holland	279	34	Wallis	Renaldo	1			1		2		1					5		
Holland	278	5	Wallis	Thomas Doct.	2		1		1	2			1				7		
Wilbraham	236	20	Wallridge	Peter	2			1		1		1					5		
Gill	88	19	Walmer	William	2		1	1		1		1	1				8		
Chester	145	36	Walton	Andrew			2		1	1		1					5		
Northfield	31	17	Walton	John	2				1	2					1		6		
Palmer	259	42	Walton	Patrick Capt.		1		1	1	1	1	4		1			9		
Palmer	260	37	Ward	Abijah Lt		2		1	1	1	1		2		2		10		
Ashfield	346	16	Ward	Alexander	3			1		3	2		1				11		
Brimfield	271	5	Ward	Amasa				1		2			1				4		
Orange	43	33	Ward	Amos				1		2			1				4		
Russell	138	26	Ward	Amos	1			1		3			1				6		
Palmer	261	1	Ward	Asa		1	1	1		2		1	1				7		
Orange	43	29	Ward	Ashbel	1		1					1					3		
South Brimfield	277	20	Ward	Benjamin		1			1		2		1				5		
Ashfield	346	10	Ward	Caleb	3	2			1	1	2	1					10		
Brimfield	269	6	Ward	Christopher			1		1	1		1					4		
Monson	266	1	Ward	Comfort				1				1	1				3		
Orange	43	34	Ward	Daniel			2			1		1					4		
Worthington	298	11	Ward	David		2	1			4	1	1					9		
Belchertown	207	33	Ward	Ebenzr	3			1			1						5		
Orange	43	23	Ward	Edward	4	1		1		2		1					9		
Ashfield	346	9	Ward	Elijah	2			1		2		1					6		
Wilbraham	232	9	Ward	Jacob	1	3		1			1		1				7		
Buckland	331	6	Ward	Jeremiah	2		1	1	1	1		1	1				8		
Belchertown	207	21	Ward	John		3	1	1	1	1		1		1			8		
Buckland	330	26	Ward	John	1		1	1		3	2		1	1			10		
Middlefield	157	38	Ward	John	1			1		3		1					6		
Russell	137	2	Ward	John	1	1		1		2			1				6		
Buckland	331	17	Ward	John 2d			1										1		
West Springfield	352	29	Ward	Josiah	1			1				1					3		
Buckland	331	4	Ward	Luke	1			1		2	1		1				6		
Ashfield	346	12	Ward	Moses	1			1		2		1					5		
Wilbraham	233	15	Ward	Nehemiah	2			1		3		1					7		
Orange	43	31	Ward	Nemiah		1			1		2		1				5		
Ashfield	346	20	Ward	Phinehas		1	3	1		3	2	1					11		
Ware	228	30	Ward	Reuben	2			1		3	1	1					8		
Belchertown	207	29	Ward	Samuel		1			1			1		2			5		
Granville Mid Soc.	167	13	Ward	Samuel	1		1	1		1	1	1	1				7		
West Springfield	352	17	Ward	Samuel			1	1					1				3		
Brimfield	269	1	Ward	Samuel Dexter			1			2		1					4		
West Springfield	352	30	Ward	Samuel Jr			1			2		1					4		
Brimfield	270	3	Ward	Stephen			1			2			1				4		
Orange	43	28	Ward	Sylvanus	1		2	1		1	1		1	1			8		
Cummington	304	25	Ward	Trowbridge		2				1		1		1			5		
Monson	263	7	Ward	Uriah	2		1	1		2		1	1				8		
Monson	263	8	Ward	William			1	1					1				3		
Shutesbury	112	31	Ward	William			2			1			1				4		
Middlefield	157	14	Ward	Thomas			1			3		1					5		
Springfield	244	13	Wardwell	Benjamin		3		1		1			1				6		
Middlefield	156	42	Wardwell	Dennis	2			1			1						4		
Middlefield	156	41	Wardwell	Eliakim				1					1				2		
Greenfield	76	15	Wardwell	Jotham	4			1		1		1					7		
Springfield	244	14	Wardwell	Samuel			1					1					2		
Buckland	331	16	Ware	Ariel	2			1		1		1					5		
Conway	61	31	Ware	George	1			1			1						3		
Northampton	5	31	Ware	John			1		1		1		1				4		
Conway	61	29	Ware	Jonathan	1	1	1		1	1	2	2	1				10		
Buckland	330	29	Ware	Michael		1		1	1	1		1	1				6		
Buckland	331	1	Ware	Michael Jr	2			1		2		1					6		
Conway	61	36	Ware	Samuel		1	1		1	1	1	2		2			9		

TOWN	PG#	LN#	LAST NAME	FIRST NAME	FREE WHITE MALES					FREE WHITE FEMALES					TOTAL ALL OTHER	TOTAL SLAVES	TOTALS	DISTRICT/ TOWNSHIP	NOTES
					under 10	10 to 16	16 to 26	26 to 45	45 and over	under 10	10 to 16	16 to 26	26 to 45	45 and over					
Rowe	201	9	Wares	Abijah	3		1		1	1	1		1				8		
Middlefield	156	25	Wares	Elias	2	3			1	1			1				8		
Heath	198	8	Warfield	Job					1				1				2		
Heath	197	33	Warfield	Joshua	2	1	1		1	1	1	1	1				9		
Williamsburg	442	20	Warner	Aaron					1	1			1				3		
Plainfield	308	39	Warner	Abel	3	2			1	2		1	1				10		
Wilbraham	233	25	Warner	Azriel	1			1		2		1	1				6		
Rowe	201	13	Warner	Daniel			1						1				2		
Southwick	361	6	Warner	Daniel			1		1				1				3		
Wilbraham	233	12	Warner	Daniel	1			1		1			1				4		
Northampton	4	35	Warner	Daniel Junr	5	1	1		1	1	2	1	1				13		
Amherst	296	7	Warner	David		1			1		1		1				4		
Belchertown	207	35	Warner	Ebenz					1		1		1	1			4		
Granby	253	35	Warner	Eleazer Capt		1		1	1					1			4		
Hadley	288	23	Warner	Elihu	3			1		2	2		1				9		
Chesterfield	23	5	Warner	Elijah	2	2			1	2		3		1			11		
Granby	254	37	Warner	Elijah	1					3			1				5		
Plainfield	308	40	Warner	Elijah	1	1	1		1	2		1	1				8		
Amherst	296	6	Warner	Elisha	1			1					1				3		
Springfield	241	42	Warner	Gerald				1		1				1			3		
Barnardston	79	32	Warner	Ichabod			1		1			1		1			4		
Amherst	293	31	Warner	Jacob					1		2	2		1			6		
Wilbraham	233	13	Warner	Jesse	3	1			1	1	1		1				8		
Barnardston	79	34	Warner	Joel			1			1		1					3		
Chesterfield	20	1	Warner	Joel	4	1		1	1				1	1			9		
Springfield	241	40	Warner	John				1									1		
Springfield	243	2	Warner	John		1	2		1	1							5		
Springfield	241	41	Warner	John Jun	2	1		1			1		1				6		
Amherst	293	12	Warner	Jonathan	1	3	1		1	3	1		1				11		
Hadley	287	7	Warner	Jonathan	1		1			1		1		1			5		
Williamsburg	442	6	Warner	Jonathan		1	1	1	1	2							6		
Barnardston	80	7	Warner	Joseph	2	1			1	2	2	1		1			10		
Cummington	304	26	Warner	Joseph		1	2		1	1	1		1				7		
Northampton	10	8	Warner	Joseph	4	1	2		2	2	1	1	2				15		
Williamsburg	442	11	Warner	Joshua	2		2		1	1			1				7		
Amherst	291	4	Warner	Josiah		1	1	3	2	1			1				9		
Hadley	286	35	Warner	Lemuel		1	1	1	1	1	1	1		2			9		
Springfield	241	43	Warner	Luther	2			1		1	1		1				6		
Williamsburg	442	18	Warner	Mark	2			1		3		1					7		
Worthington	301	40	Warner	Matthew		1	2		1			2		2			8		
Cummington	304	27	Warner	Moses	1			1		2	1	1	1	1			8		
Hatfield	12	21	Warner	Moses	1	1	1		1	2	2						8		
Norwich	152	1	Warner	Moses		1			1			1	1	1			5		
Monson	264	26	Warner	Nathan	2	1		1		2	1	1	1				9		
Williamsburg	441	11	Warner	Nathan	2	1		1					1				5		
Hadley	286	34	Warner	Noadiah		1		1		2			1				5		
West Springfield	357	43	Warner	Noah	2	2		1		1		1	1				8		
Rowe	201	12	Warner	Nodiah		1		1					1				3		
Hadley	288	21	Warner	Oringe		1	1		1	1		1		1			6		
Williamsburg	441	4	Warner	Paul				1		2				1			4		
Belchertown	207	18	Warner	Phinehas	2			1		2			1	1			7		
Barnardston	79	33	Warner	Pliny	?			1				1					4		
Granby	253	25	Warner	Rachel Wid										2			2		
Barnardston	79	35	Warner	Roswell		1				1		1					3		
Wilbraham	234	24	Warner	Samuel				1		1			1	1			4		
Wilbraham	234	25	Warner	Samuel Jr	1	1	1	1		2			1				7		
Norwich	154	9	Warner	Samuel Lieut		1	1		1			1	1				5		
Belchertown	207	19	Warner	Seth					1				1				2		
Williamsburg	442	21	Warner	Seth	1			1				1					3		
Cummington	304	28	Warner	Stephen			2		1		2	1		2			8		
Ashfield	346	3	Warner	Thos Capt.	2	2		1		3	1	1	1				11		
Belchertown	207	20	Warner	Titus	2			1		1			1				5		
Conway	61	21	Warner	William	1		2		1		1	1		1			7		
Springfield	240	5	Warner	Zacha		1		1						1			3		
Hatfield	14	34	Warren	Bevil		1				2		1					4		
Williamsburg	442	15	Warren	Cotton M.	1			1		2			1				5		
Granville West Soc	170	1	Warren	Elisha	1	1	1			3		1	1				9		
Palmer	261	7	Warren	Isaac	2		1		1	1	1	1	1				8		
Shelburne	325	4	Warren	Isaac	4			1		1	1		1				8		
Conway	61	23	Warren	James	4	2			1			1	1				9		
Ashfield	346	4	Warren	Joseph		2		1			1			2			6		
Ashfield	346	5	Warren	Joseph Junr	2	1		1		3	1	1					9		
Williamsburg	442	12	Warren	Mather				1			2			1			4		
Wilbraham	238	9	Warren	Moses Revd	2	1		1		1			1				6		
Deerfield	55	46	Warren	Neverson	2			1						1			4		
Blanford	176	7	Warren	Noah			1		1			1		1			4		
Williamsburg	442	14	Warren	Orange H.	3			1		2			1				7		
Brimfield	271	41	Warren	Philemon	1		2	1		2			2				8		
Wilbraham	238	3	Warren	Seth		1	1	1					1				4		
Ashfield	346	7	Warren	Stephen	1	1			1	3	2	2	1				11		

Census table — heads of household with free white population counts by age, total all other, total slaves, and totals.

TOWN	PG#	LN#	LAST NAME	FIRST NAME	M under 10	M 10 to 16	M 16 to 26	M 26 to 45	M 45 and over	F under 10	F 10 to 16	F 16 to 26	F 26 to 45	F 45 and over	TOTAL ALL OTHER	TOTAL SLAVES	TOTALS	DISTRICT/ TOWNSHIP	NOTES
Ashfield	346	6	Warren	Timothy	2			1		1	2		1				7		
Hawley	335	24	Warrich	Hezekiah		1		1		2	1		1				6		
Wilbraham	233	26	Warriner	Abner	3	1	1	1	1	1	2		1				11		
Springfield	244	37	Warriner	Daniel	1			1		2			1				5		
Wilbraham	234	6	Warriner	David			2		2		1	1		2			8		
Springfield	244	32	Warriner	Ebenezer				1									1		
Springfield	244	33	Warriner	Ebenezer Jr	1	2	1		1			1	1	1			8		
Wilbraham	233	3	Warriner	Ethan			1	2		2			2				7		
West Springfield	355	35	Warriner	Gad		1		1		4	1		2	1			10		
Springfield	240	37	Warriner	Isaac		1		1		1		1		1			5		
West Springfield	355	30	Warriner	Lewis	2	1		1	1	1		1	1				8		
Springfield	244	38	Warriner	Martin	1			1		2			1				5		
Wilbraham	233	29	Warriner	Mary Wd						1	3		1	1			6		
Wilbraham	233	16	Warriner	Moses				1				1					2		
Wilbraham	232	35	Warriner	Samuel		1		1					1				3		
Wilbraham	233	23	Warriner	Solomon	2	1	2	1		1		2		1			10		
Monson	263	43	Warriner	Stephen	1			1		3			1				6		
Palmer	261	12	Warriner	William		2		1		1		2		1			7		
Warwick	40	15	Warwick	Jesse	1		1		1	2	2	2		1			10		
Norwich	153	40	Washborn	Jonathan				1					3	1			5		
Norwich	153	41	Washborn	Josiah			1						1				2		
Colrain	190	15	Washbrn	Experience	2		1			1			1				5		
Pelham	217	18	Washburn	Abram	3			1	1	1	1		1				8		
Greenwich	223	30	Washburn	Cornelius	2		1	1		1	1		1				6		
South Brimfield	277	42	Washburn	Ebenz	3	2		1		1	1		1				9		
Belchertown	207	36	Washburn	Eliab	3			1		1		1					6		
Colrain	190	12	Washburn	Eliab		1		1			1		1				4		
Wendell	108	4	Washburn	Elisha	1		1			1		1	1				5		
Wendell	108	5	Washburn	Elisha Jr			1			1		1					3		
Springfield	241	29	Washburn	Hezekiah			1			1		1					3		
Wendell	108	7	Washburn	Libee	1			1				1					3		
Hadley	285	14	Washburn	Luther	1			1		3		1					6		
Leyden	84	32	Washburn	Nehemiah	4	1		1		1		1					8		
Northampton	10	14	Washburn	Nehemiah				1				1	1	1			4		
Hadley	285	9	Washburn	Salmon		1				1		1					3		
Williamsburg	441	6	Washburn	Stephen			1	1		1			1				4		
Wendell	108	6	Washburn	William	4	1		1		1		1					8		
Leyden	84	31	Waterhouse	Nathan			1				2		1				4		
Blanford	180	5	Waterman	Asael	3		1			2	1		1				8		
Blanford	177	15	Waterman	Ebenezer	1		1		3			1					6		
Northampton	7	2	Waterman	Roger	2			1		1		1					5		
Shelburne	324	29	Waters	John	1		1						1				3		
Longmeadow	95	20	Waters	Nathaniel	2		1			1	1	1					6		
Wendell	108	9	Watkins	Francis	2	1		1		1	1	1		1			8		
Wendell	108	8	Watkins	Stephen	2	1		1		2		2					8		
Chesterfield	24	1	Watkins	Willard	3			1					1				5		
Northfield	31	12	Watrip	Oliver		1	2		1			1		1			6		
Granville East Soc	527	27	Watrous	Benjamin	2			1		2			1	1			7		
West Springfield	352	27	Watrus	Smith	1			1		2			1				5		
Amherst	292	5	Watson	David				1					1				2		
Chesterfield	23	9	Watson	Isaiah	1	1				1		1	1				5		
Shelburne	325	1	Watson	James	1	1	1			1		1	1				6		
Blanford	177	5	Watson	John	1	3	2		1	1	3			1			12		
Colrain	189	31	Watson	John	2			1		1		1					5		
Palmer	262	9	Watson	John				1				1					2		
Amherst	292	3	Watson	Joseph	4			1		1		1					7		
Colrain	190	4	Watson	Robert	2		1	1					1				5		
Leverett	116	30	Watson	Samuel	1			1		2		1					5		
New Salem	104	18	Watson	William		2		1				1					4		
Worthington	299	7	Watt	John	1		1		1	1	1	2		1			8		
Warwick	40	7	Watts	Nicholas		1	1				1	1		1			6		
Hadley	286	14	Way	Ralph											6		6		
Westfield	126	31	Weatherby	Charles	1		1					1					3		
Holland	278	7	Weatherby	Ebenezer	1		1			2		1					5		
Norwich	153	18	Weatherby	Thomas	3			1		1		1					6		
South Brimfield	275	12	Weatherly	Wm			2						1	1			4		
Palmer	258	8	Weaver	Benjamin	1	2		1		2	1		1				8		
Sunderland	283	4	Weaver	Samuel	4			1		2			1	1			9		
Buckland	330	24	Webber	Abner	1			1				1					3		
Brimfield	269	34	Webber	Amasa	1			1		1		1					4		
Holland	279	4	Webber	Andrew				1		1	1	1	1				5		
Holland	280	11	Webber	Benja				1					1				2		
Holland	279	37	Webber	Bradley	1			1		1			1	1			5		
Worthington	300	31	Webber	Ebenezer		1	1						1				3		
Palmer	261	24	Webber	Ebenezer Col.	3	1		1		1	1	1		1			9		
Longmeadow	91	10	Webber	Edward		1	1			1	1	1		1			6		
Holland	278	3	Webber	Ezra		1	1	2					1				5		
Monson	267	4	Webber	Francis	1	1	2		1	1	1			1			8		
Holland	279	23	Webber	Henry				1						2			3		
Buckland	330	25	Webber	John	1		2		1	2	1			1			8		

TOWN	PG#	LN#	LAST NAME	FIRST NAME	FREE WHITE MALES					FREE WHITE FEMALES					TOTAL ALL OTHER	TOTAL SLAVES	TOTALS	DISTRICT/ TOWNSHIP	NOTES
					under 10	10 to 16	16 to 26	26 to 45	45 and over	under 10	10 to 16	16 to 26	26 to 45	45 and over					
Worthington	301	38	Webber	John				1		3			1				5		
Chester	147	6	Webber	Jonatha H.		1		1			2		1				5		
Monson	262	21	Webber	Kimbal			1				1						2		
Holland	279	29	Webber	Prenance		1		1			1		1				4		
Holland	280	7	Webber	Reuben	2	2	2	1		2		1	1				11		
Holland	279	12	Webber	Rinaldo Capt.	1	1		1		1	1		1				6		
Holland	279	25	Webber	S. Edward		1	2		1	2	1		1				8		
Holland	279	11	Webber	Saml Jr Deacn	3		2	1			1		1				8		
Holland	279	21	Webber	Samuel		1		1				1	1				4		
Monson	262	20	Webber	Samuel	1			1		1	2	2		1			8		
Monson	262	15	Webber	Samuel Jr	1			1		3			1				6		
Holland	278	11	Webber	Sewal		1	1	1		1			1	1			6		
Worthington	299	24	Webster	Constant	2	2		1		3		1	1	1			11		
Russell	138	24	Webster	Elezor			1						1				2		
Wilbraham	236	16	Webster	Elijah	3		1						1				5		
Northfield	31	3	Webster	Ezekiel	1	3	1	1		2	1	1	1				11		
Gill	88	23	Webster	Hannah		3					1	1	1	1			7		
Conway	61	45	Webster	Jacob	2			1		2			1				6		
Springfield	243	23	Webster	Joel	4	1		1			1		1				8		
Springfield	243	24	Webster	Joseph		1	1		1	1				1			5		
Barnardston	80	1	Webster	Stephen				1			1			1			3		
Barnardston	80	2	Webster	Stephen Junr	3	1		1		2	1		1				9		
Gill	88	21	Webster	William	2			1		1			1				5		
Blanford	182	13	Webster			1		1				1					3		First name left blank
Leverett	117	2	Wedge	Abijah	3			1		1			1				6		
Leverett	116	29	Wedge	Thomas	2			1		1			1				5		
West Springfield	355	37	Wedger	Ebenezer	1			1		2			1				5		
Greenwich	223	26	Weeks	Amiel	1		1			1	1	1	1				7		
Warwick	40	17	Weeks	Caleb	1		1					1					4		
Ashfield	346	17	Weeks	David				1			1			1			3		
Buckland	331	3	Weeks	Elijah	2			1				1					5		
Norwich	151	5	Weeks	Hezekiah		2		1		1	1			1			6		
Belchertown	207	34	Weeks	Holland	2	1	1			2	1	1					9		
Warwick	40	23	Weeks	John			1			2			1				4		
Norwich	151	6	Weeks	Lemuel		1					1						2		
Warwick	40	3	Weeks	Richard				1					1				2		
Norwich	151	7	Weeks	Samuel	4			1		1		1					7		
Goshen	312	26	Weeks	Thomas				1					1				2		
Northfield	31	19	Weeks	Uriah		1		1					1				3		
Norwich	151	8	Weeks	William	1			1		1		1					4		
Belchertown	203	4	Welch	Solomon	2			1		1			1				5		
Westfield	121	25	Wellar	Aaron			1	1				2		1			5		
Southampton	130	18	Wellar	Ebenezer	1		1	2				1					5		
Westfield	121	24	Wellar	John	1			1		1			1	1			5		
Blanford	177	10	Weller	David		1	1	1					3	1			7		
Westfield	119	30	Weller	Jared	1		1	1		4			1				8		
Norwich	152	17	Weller	Moses	4		2	1	1	2	1	2	1	1			15		
Westfield	119	32	Weller	Oliver	1	2	2	1	1			2		1			10		
Westfield	119	31	Weller	Sarah Wd	1	1	1	1				1		1			6		
South Brimfield	276	42	Welles	Ezekiel	1		1		1	2	2						7		
Greenfield	76	8	Wells	Abner		1	1		1				1				4		
Greenfield	76	3	Wells	Agrippa	4		1	1	1		1		2	1			11		
Hatfield	12	9	Wells	Amasa	3	1		1		1			2	1			9		
Leyden	84	26	Wells	Asa	2	2	1	1					2	1			9		
Conway	61	22	Wells	Benjamin	2	3	1	1		2		2					11		
Hatfield	13	33	Wells	Benjamin			1	1					1				3		
Montague	48	18	Wells	Cornelius			1	1					1				3		
Greenfield	76	9	Wells	Daniel	2	1	1			2	2		1				10		
Deerfield	55	30	Wells	David		1	1			2	2			1			7		
Shelburne	324	23	Wells	David Esq	2	1	1	3	1	1			2	1			12		
Shelburne	324	24	Wells	David Junr	2			1	1	1		1	1	1			7		
Greenfield	76	5	Wells	Eleazer		1	1	1				1		1			6		
Conway	61	37	Wells	Elijah		1							1				2		
Greenfield	76	4	Wells	Elisha	3	1		1	1	1	2	1	1				11		
Hawley	335	27	Wells	Elisha	1	1	1		1		2	2					8		
Williamsburg	442	23	Wells	Elisha	2	1		1		1	1		1				7		
Greenfield	76	16	Wells	Ephraim	1		1	1		2		2		1			8		
Montague	48	17	Wells	Henry		1	1		1		1	3		2			9		
Greenfield	75	36	Wells	Joel	2	1		1		1			1				6		
Rowe	201	11	Wells	John		2	1		1	1		2	1	1			9		
Williamsburg	442	22	Wells	John	1		1	1		2			1				6		
Greenfield	76	6	Wells	Joseph	3	1	1	2	1	2	1	1	1				13		
Leyden	84	28	Wells	Joshua	1	1		1		4			1				8		
Hawley	335	18	Wells	Lemuel		1	1		2	1				2			7		
Deerfield	55	34	Wells	Levi	1			1		4			1				7		
Hatfield	13	10	Wells	Moses			1				2		1				4		
Leyden	84	27	Wells	Nev		2	2	1	1			2	1	1			10		
Greenfield	76	11	Wells	Obed	3	1	1	1		1	3		1				11		
Hatfield	13	14	Wells	Patience										2			2		
Whately	68	23	Wells	Perez	1	1	1	1					1				5		

317

TOWN	PG#	LN#	LAST NAME	FIRST NAME	FREE WHITE MALES under 10	10 to 16	16 to 26	26 to 45	45 and over	FREE WHITE FEMALES under 10	10 to 16	16 to 26	26 to 45	45 and over	TOTAL ALL OTHER	TOTAL SLAVES	TOTALS	DISTRICT/ TOWNSHIP	NOTES
Deerfield	55	32	Wells	Quarters	1		1	1		3			2				8		
Conway	61	30	Wells	Richard		1	2			1		2	1				7		
Whately	68	16	Wells	Rufus	1	1	2		1	1	1	1		1			9		
Conway	61	46	Wells	Ruth			1			1		1		1			4		
Deerfield	55	33	Wells	Samuel	3			1					1				5		
Greenfield	76	14	Wells	Samuel					1		1		1				3		
Hatfield	13	20	Wells	Samuel					1								1		
Greenfield	76	2	Wells	Samuel Junr	5	1		1				1		1	1		10		
Greenfield	76	10	Wells	Silas		1	1	1					1				4		
Leyden	84	22	Wells	Simeon	1			1		3	1		1				7		
Northfield	31	21	Wells	Solomon	2					1		1					4		
Deerfield	55	31	Wells	Thomas	1		1	1		2			1				6		
Leyden	84	20	Wells	Thomas		1	1	1		1	3	1	1				9		
Longmeadow	93	37	Welman	Jacob	4	1		1		1							8		
Colrain	190	7	Weson	Oliver	1		1				1	2	1				6		
Hawley	335	26	West	Asa	1			1		2			1				5		
Hawley	335	29	West	Billy			1			1			1				3		
Hatfield	11	5	West	David		1	1	1		2	3		1				9		
Montague	48	27	West	Jonathan		1											1		
Granville East Soc	533	7	West	Joseph	1		1			1			1				4		
Hawley	335	21	West	Nathan		1		1	1		1			1			5		
Greenwich	223	31	West	Roger Lt.	2	1			2		1		2	1			9		
Middlefield	159	4	West	Russel			1						1				2		
Wilbraham	237	5	West	Stephen	2	1		1			2		1				7		
Warwick	40	2	Westcoat	Richard				1					1				2		
Warwick	40	1	Westcoat	Richard Jr		1		1		3		1	1				7		
New Salem	104	30	Weste	Daniel	1			1		1		1		1			5		
New Salem	104	19	Weste	John	2					1			1				5		
Greenwich	223	17	Whalen	Amos	1		1		1		1	2	1				7		
Chester	146	12	Wharfield	Reuben	3	2			1	2		1	1				10		
Conway	61	38	Wheat	Benjamin	1		1		1	1			1				5		
Westfield	120	21	Wheaton	Marshal	3		1	1		1	1		1				8		
Goshen	312	24	Wheelar	James	1	1			1	2		1	1				7		
Cummington	304	33	Wheelar	Samuel	1	1		1	1	2			1				7		
Worthington	300	37	Wheelar	William	1			1		3			1	1			7		
New Salem	104	20	Wheeler	Benjamin	1	1	2		1	1	2			1			9		
Shutesbury	112	33	Wheeler	Ephraim	2	2	1	1		1		2	1	1			11		
Montgomery	159	19	Wheeler	Fradrick	1		1			1		1					4		
Colrain	189	39	Wheeler	Hezekiah	2			1		1			1				5		
Montgomery	160	2	Wheeler	James		2			1	3		2		1			9		
New Salem	104	25	Wheeler	James				1		3			1				5		
South Brimfield	275	14	Wheeler	James		2			1	2	2	1	1				9		
South Brimfield	277	37	Wheeler	James		2			1	2	2			1			8		
Ware	227	20	Wheeler	Jesse	1	2		1		3	2		1				10		
New Salem	104	29	Wheeler	Joel				1						1			2		
Blanford	175	17	Wheeler	John			1		1	5	3		1				11		
Middlefield	157	12	Wheeler	John	2			1					1				4		
Ware	228	29	Wheeler	John	2	1		1		1			1				6		
Conway	61	40	Wheeler	Joseph	1		1			3			2	1			8		
New Salem	104	21	Wheeler	Joshua	2	1	2		1	4	1	1		1			13		
Greenwich	223	19	Wheeler	Samuel	3		1		1		2	1	1				9		
Montgomery	161	5	Wheeler	Thomas				1		3			1				5		
Charlemont	194	16	Wheelock	Abijah	3	1		1		2			1				8		
Orange	43	26	Wheelock	Alexander	1	2	2			2	1		1				10		
Warwick	40	14	Wheelock	Eleazer	1			1		3	1	1	1				8		
Brimfield	272	39	Wheelock	Henry	4		1	1		1			2	1			10		
Leverett	116	32	Wheelock	John	4	2		1			1	1	1				10		
Orange	43	25	Wheelock	John				1									1		
Warwick	40	21	Wheelock	Jonathan			1					1					2		
Orange	43	32	Wheelock	Noah			1					1					2		
South Hadley	251	13	Wheldon	Jonathan	1			1		2	2		1				7		
Greenfield	75	35	Whipple	Daniel	1			1		1			1	1			5		
Westfield	122	9	Whipple	Joshua				1						1			2		
Westfield	125	33	Whipple	Joshua Jun	1		1			1		1					4		
Wendell	107	39	Whitacker	David	4	2			1		1	2	1				11		
Wendell	108	11	Whitcomb	Dills	2	1		1		2		1	1				8		
Greenwich	223	25	Whitcomb	Ebenezr	2	1	1		1	1	2	1	1				10		
Greenwich	223	22	Whitcomb	James	1			1		2			1				5		
Williamsburg	442	19	Whitcomb	James	1	1				5			1				9		
Montague	48	34	Whitcomb	Jonathan	1			1		4	2		1				9		
Greenwich	223	21	Whitcomb	Nathaniel	1			1		4			1				7		
Shelburne	324	20	White	Aaron		1		1			1	1		1			5		
South Hadley	249	23	White	Aaron	1	1		1				1					5		
West Springfield	352	20	White	Aaron	3	1			2	1		1	1	1			10		
South Hadley	250	46	White	Abigail Wd								2	1				3		
Monson	265	36	White	Asa	1	1	2		1	1	1	1		2			10		
Williamsburg	441	7	White	Asa	2	1			1	2		1	1	1			9		
Heath	198	5	White	Asaph		1	3		1		1						7		
Heath	197	30	White	Benjamin	3	2	2		1		1	1					11		
Plainfield	308	37	White	Caleb	2		1		1			1		2			7		

318

TOWN	PG#	LN#	LAST NAME	FIRST NAME	FREE WHITE MALES under 10	10 to 16	16 to 26	26 to 45	45 and over	FREE WHITE FEMALES under 10	10 to 16	16 to 26	26 to 45	45 and over	TOTAL ALL OTHER	TOTAL SLAVES	TOTALS	DISTRICT/ TOWNSHIP	NOTES
Monson	268	26	White	Calvin	1	1		1		2			1				6		
Chesterfield	20	17	White	Consider			1	1		4	1	1	1				9		
Hatfield	12	5	White	Cotton			5	1				2					8		
Hadley	286	8	White	Daniel		1		1			1	3		1			8		
Hatfield	13	5	White	Daniel		1		1	1		1		1				5		
West Springfield	352	18	White	Daniel				1				1					2		
West Springfield	355	26	White	Daniel Junr			1		2	2	1		1	1			8		
Heath	198	6	White	David				1		1		1					3		
Longmeadow	93	23	White	David		2	1		1	1		1		1			7		
Goshen	312	12	White	Ebenezer	1	2		1		2			1				7		
Hadley	287	8	White	Ebenezer	1		1		1	3		1	1	1			9		
Hatfield	12	31	White	Ebenezer			1			2	1	1	1				6		
Northfield	31	11	White	Ebenezer	1	2		1		1		1	1				7		
South Hadley	250	9	White	Ebenezer	2			1		2		1	1				7		
South Hadley	251	9	White	Eldad	4	1		1		1		1					8		
Norwich	152	29	White	Eleazer			1			3		1					5		
Hatfield	12	35	White	Elihu	1			1	1	2			1				6		
Chester	145	19	White	Elijah				1		1		1		1			4		
Hadley	286	12	White	Elijah	1		1		1			1					4		
Hatfield	14	2	White	Elijah	2			1		3			1				7		
Middlefield	157	4	White	Elijah	2		2		1	3	2		1				11		
Hawley	335	23	White	Eliphalet			2		1		1			1			5		
South Hadley	248	18	White	Enoch Dr		2	1	1	1	1	1	1		2			10		
Goshen	312	14	White	Ezekiel	1	1	1		1		1		1				6		
Williamsburg	442	13	White	Ezekiel		1		1		3			1				6		
West Springfield	352	26	White	Horace		1	2		1		1	1		1	1		8		
Norwich	152	32	White	Jabez	2			1						1			4		
Warwick	40	13	White	Jacob	3	1		1		2	1	1					9		
Colrain	189	37	White	James	4	2		1		1	1	1					10		
Heath	198	3	White	James		2		1			4	1	1				9		
Amherst	294	11	White	Jewel	2			1		1	1		1				6		
Northampton	6	16	White	Job	1	3	1	11	3	1	1	2		1	1		58		
Blanford	178	22	White	Joel			1		1	3	1		1				7		
South Hadley	250	20	White	Joel	1			1				1					4		
Blanford	181	12	White	John	1	1		1		3			1				7		
Monson	262	2	White	John	2	2		1		3		1	1				10		
Monson	266	5	White	John				1				1		1			3		
Northfield	31	22	White	John				1					1				2		
Shutesbury	113	2	White	John	3	1		1		2	1	1	1				10		
Whately	68	19	White	John	1			1		1	1		1				5		
Charlemont	194	16	White	Jonathan				1									1		
Norwich	152	27	White	Joseph			1		1		1	1		1			5		
South Hadley	250	29	White	Joseph	2		1	2		1	1	1	1				9		
West Springfield	352	21	White	Joseph		1	1		1			1		1			5		
Norwich	152	28	White	Joseph Junr	1		1	1		2			1	1			7		
Charlemont	194	17	White	Josiah		1			1	1			1				4		
Goshen	312	13	White	Josiah				1			1			1			3		
South Hadley	251	3	White	Josiah Jr		1	1	1		3	3		1				10		
South Hadley	251	8	White	Josiah Maj		1		1				1	1	1			5		
Colrain	190	5	White	Leonard	3			1		1		1					6		
Buckland	331	10	White	Levi	3	1		1				1					6		
Longmeadow	92	5	White	Lewis Dr		1		1		2			1				5		
Goshen	312	11	White	Louis	1	1	1			1	1			1			6		
Heath	198	4	White	Luke	4	1		1		1	1	1	1				10		
Springfield	242	31	White	Luther	1		1					1					3		
Springfield	242	28	White	Martin	2			1		1			1				5		
Leverett	117	1	White	Matthew	2	2		1		2			1				8		
Hadley	286	20	White	Moses	1	1		1		1			1	2			7		
Rowe	201	7	White	Nahum	1			1			1		1				4		
Brimfield	275	17	White	Nathan Capt	1	1	1	1		1	1	1	1				8	South Brimfield	
Hadley	286	28	White	Nathaniel			1		1	1			1				4		
Easthampton	134	13	White	Nathl	1		2		1	1	1		1				7		
Chesterfield	23	13	White	Noah	2	3		1		2	1		1				10		
West Springfield	352	19	White	Pliny	1			1				1					3		
Springfield	242	30	White	Preserved Jr		1			2	1	1		1				6		
Shelburne	325	6	White	Reuben											4		4		
South Hadley	251	1	White	Reuben		1		1		1	1		1				5		
Gill	88	20	White	Robert	4	1		1			1			1			8		
Whately	68	18	White	Salman				1			1		2	1			5		
Whately	68	15	White	Salman Jun	2	1	1	1		1	2	1	1				10		
Norwich	152	31	White	Samuel		1			1					1			3		
South Hadley	250	18	White	Samuel			1	1		1	2		1				6		
Monson	262	1	White	Sanford				1	1	1	2	2		1			7		
Goshen	310	28	White	Seth			1						2				3		
South Hadley	249	7	White	Simeon	1	1	1	1		1	1		1				7		
Ashfield	346	12	White	Thomas		1	2	1		3		1	1				9		
Norwich	152	30	White	Thomas		2	2		1	3	1	1		1			11		
South Hadley	250	38	White	Thomas				1									1		
Longmeadow	94	10	White	Walter	2		1	1		1			1				6		
Chester	150	6	White	William	2			1		1			1		1		6		

TOWN	PG#	LN#	LAST NAME	FIRST NAME	FREE WHITE MALES under 10	10 to 16	16 to 26	26 to 45	45 and over	FREE WHITE FEMALES under 10	10 to 16	16 to 26	26 to 45	45 and over	TOTAL ALL OTHER	TOTAL SLAVES	TOTALS	DISTRICT/TOWNSHIP	NOTES
Goshen	312	10	White	William		2	2		1			1		1			7		
Springfield	247	25	White	Wm				1						2			3		
Buckland	330	28	White	Zebulon			1				1	1		1			4		
Springfield	240	13	White	Zenas			3					1					4		
Plainfield	308	38	White	Zibee		1		1		1			1				4		
Sunderland	283	29	Whitemore	Daniel	1		2	1			1	1		1			7		
Northfield	31	15	Whiting	Jabez		1	2	1		2	2	1	1				10		
Warwick	40	22	Whiting	John		2		1	1		1	2		1			8		
Southwick	361	7	Whiting	Jonathan				1					1				2		
Cummington	305	26	Whitman	Daniel				1		2		1					4		
Belchertown	211	1	Whitman	James	1	1		1		1	1		1				6		
Goshen	312	25	Whitman	Saml	2	2	2		1	3	2	1					13		
Cummington	304	31	Whitman	Tama	1		1	1						1			4		
Plainfield	308	41	Whitmarsh	Noah			1			3			1				5		
Montague	48	29	Whitmore	Asa	2		1						1				4		
Westfield	120	4	Whitney	Abel	3		3	2		2	2	4	1				17		
Westfield	120	23	Whitney	Charlotte Wd		2	4			1			1				8		
Warwick	40	9	Whitney	Daniel		1	2		1			2		1			7		
Conway	61	27	Whitney	David	1		1	1	1	3		2	1	1			11		
Belchertown	212	2	Whitney	Dorothy	1						1	2		1			5		
Hadley	285	13	Whitney	Ebenezer	1		1	1				1	1				5		
Montague	48	21	Whitney	Ebenezer	3	2		1		1			1				8		
Belchertown	211	12	Whitney	Ebenz	2		1		1		1		1				6		
Conway	61	39	Whitney	Ira	4			1	1	2	1		1	1			11		
Orange	43	30	Whitney	Jabez	2			1		3			1				7		
Buckland	331	7	Whitney	Jacob	1			1			1	1					4		
Warwick	40	8	Whitney	John		1			1		1	3		1			7		
Westhampton	16	27	Whitney	John	2			1		1		1	1				6		
Shelburne	324	19	Whitney	Joseph	1			1		2	2	1		1			8		
Warwick	40	24	Whitney	Joseph		1		1				1		1			4		
Wilbraham	232	1	Whitney	Joseph		1	1		1		1	1		1			6		
Shelburne	325	3	Whitney	Moses	1		1	1		1		1					5		
Warwick	40	12	Whitney	Palmer	1		1		1			2		1			6		
Norwich	154	12	Whitney	Peter	1	3		1		2		1		1			9		
Deerfield	55	48	Whitney	Stephen	1			1		2	2	1	2		1		10		
Granville East Soc	531	4	Whitney	Uriah		2		1					1				4		
Buckland	331	8	Whitney	Willm	2	2		2		1	1		2				10		
Montague	48	20	Whitney	Zachariah				1				1	1				3		
Chesterfield	22	1	Whiton	Abijah		1		1		3	1	2	1				9		
Cummington	304	34	Whiton*	Jacob	2	1	1	1		2	3		1				11		
Chester	146	18	Whitt	Abner	3	2	1	1		1	1		1				10		
Plainfield	308	36	Whitten	David	1			1		2		1	1				6		
Plainfield	308	35	Whitten	Peter	2	2		1		3		1		1			10		
Worthington	301	16	Wibourn	James			1	1			1			3			6		
Northampton	6	34	Wicker	Jacob	2		2	1			1		1				7		
Norwich	154	33	Wickum	Prince											1		1		
Shutesbury	113	5	Wier	William				1			1		1				3		
Greenwich	224	8	Wight	David			1	2				1		1			6		
Greenwich	224	19	Wight	John			1	2				1		1			5		
South Brimfield	275	10	Wight	Polly Wid	2						1	1		1			5		
West Springfield	355	34	Wightman	Jesse	4			1					1				6		
Cummington	303	12	Wilber	David	2			1			1		1				5		
Shutesbury	113	6	Wilber	Elias			1					1					2		
New Salem	104	28	Wilber	Jacob			1	1				1		1			4		
Worthington	302	9	Wilber	Jeddediah		1		1				1		1			4		
Shutesbury	112	32	Wilber	John	1	1		1				1		1			5		
Shutesbury	113	3	Wilber	John Jr			1			1		1					3		
Leyden	84	25	Wilbur	John	1			1		3	1		2				8		
Leyden	84	24	Wilbur	Uriah		1	1		1			3		1			7		
Granville Mid Soc.	167	38	Wilcox	Billy		1	1		1	1				1			5		
Colrain	190	6	Wilcox	Daniel	2	2	3		1			1	1	1			11		
Southwick	361	5	Wilcox	David			1	1				1		1			4		
Granville East Soc	531	34	Wilcox	Eleazer			1		1		2		1				6		
Chester	149	14	Wilcox	James	1						1		1				3		
Hawley	335	22	Wilcox	Josiah		1		1		1				1			4		
Granville Mid Soc.	167	40	Wilcox	Samuel D.	1	1	1	1		2	2			1			9		
Granville East Soc	533	19	Wilcox	Stillman		1	1	1		2			1				6		
Barnardston	80	6	Wilcox	Timothy	2				1		1		1				5		
Williamsburg	442	17	Wild	Jesse			1		2	1			2	1			7		
Leyden	84	21	Wild	John	3			1		3	1		1				9		
Cummington	304	30	Wildair	Abel	1			1		1		1					4		
Cummington	304	29	Wildair	Seth	1	1		1	1	4	1	1		1			11		
Charlemont	194	18	Wilder	Abel	2			1		2	1		1				7		
Chesterfield	20	7	Wilder	Abel	1	1	1	1				1	1				6		
Wendell	108	2	Wilder	Bazeleel	1	2			1		1			1			6		
New Salem	104	23	Wilder	Elijah	1			1				1					3		
Buckland	331	9	Wilder	Gardner	1		3		1		1	3		1			10		
Chesterfield	19	17	Wilder	Jabez		1	1		1			1	1				6		
Ware	228	28	Wilder	John	1	1	2		1		2			1			8		
Chesterfield	24	21	Wilder	Lot	3		1	1		2	2		1				10		

320

TOWN	PG#	LN#	LAST NAME	FIRST NAME	FREE WHITE MALES under 10	10 to 16	16 to 26	26 to 45	45 and over	FREE WHITE FEMALES under 10	10 to 16	16 to 26	26 to 45	45 and over	TOTAL ALL OTHER	TOTAL SLAVES	TOTALS	DISTRICT/ TOWNSHIP	NOTES
Ludlow	256	8	Wilder	Moses Lt				1						1			2		
Wendell	107	40	Wilder	Nathaniel	2	1	2		1			1		1			8		
Wendell	108	1	Wilder	Nathl 2d	1	2		1			1		1				6		
Conway	61	24	Wilder	Samuel	3	1	1		1	2	1	2	1				12		
Northampton	7	12	Wilder	Shubal	1		1	1		3	2		1				9		
Wendell	108	3	Wilder	Silas	1			1				1					3		
Heath	198	2	Wilder	Willis	1		2	1		2	1	2		1			10		
Chesterfield	24	22	Wilder	Zachariah	1	3	2	1		3			1				11		
Leverett	116	25	Wildes	Dolling				1		3			1				5		
Leverett	116	24	Wildes	Samuel	2			1		2			1				6		
Northampton	10	19	Wilds	Elkanah			1					1					2		
Northampton	6	8	Wilds	Jesse		1		1					1				3		
Northampton	10	18	Wilds	Thomas	3	2		1		1	1		1				9		
Worthington	298	6	Wiles	Oliver	2			1					1				4		
Sunderland	283	22	Wiley	Ebenezor	3	1	1	1		1	1		1				9		
Hatfield	13	24	Wilke	Henry	4	1	1		1		2			1			10		
Buckland	331	13	Wilkie	John				1				1	1				3		
Buckland	331	15	Wilkie	John Jun			1			2		1					4		
Deerfield	55	50	Wilkinson	Ebenezer		1	1						1				3		
Amherst	291	35	Wilkinson	George		1	2		1	3		1	1				9		
Conway	61	48	Wilks	John	1			1		1			1				4		
Goshen	312	20	Will	Jesse	3	1	1		1	3	1	2	1				13		
Greenfield	76	7	Willard	Benah	1	1	1		1	1	2	1	2				10		
Norwich	154	1	Willard	Humphrey		1	1	1		3			1				7		
Leverett	116	34	Willard	Josiah	1		1	1		1	1		1				6		
Greenfield	75	37	Willard	Renel	1	3		1		2	1	1	1				10		
South Brimfield	277	4	Willard	Samuel		1		1		3			1				6		
Goshen	312	19	Willcott	Zebulon	4	1	1				1	1	1				10		
Conway	61	43	Willcox	Amos	2	1	1		1	3		2	1				11		
Chester	144	31	Willcox	Elisha Capt	1		2		1		1			2			7		
Colrain	190	16	Willcox	Hiel			2				1						3		
Conway	61	33	Willcox	John				2	1		3	1	1				8		
Conway	61	34	Willcox	Silas		1		1		1			1				4		
Wilbraham	235	19	Willey	Charles	1					1			1				3		
Ludlow	255	12	Willey	Gates			1			1		1					3		
Montague	48	33	William	John	1		1			1		1					4		
Middlefield	158	26	William	Prince											5		5		
Pelham	217	5	William	Silas	3	1		1		3	2	1					11		
Charlemont	194	20	William	William		2	3		1		1	3		1			11		
Montague	48	31	William	Williams	4	1	1		1	3	1			1			12		
Williamsburg	441	10	Williams	Abner	2	1		1		2	1	1					8		
Monson	266	26	Williams	Ambrose	3		1	1		1	2			2			10		
Southampton	128	4	Williams	Amos		1						1					2		
Ashfield	346	11	Williams	Apollos	3		1	1		2			1				8		
Hawley	335	28	Williams	Caleb	1			1		2			1				5		
Amherst	291	27	Williams	Catharine									1				1		
Northfield	31	13	Williams	Charles	2			1				1					4		
Norwich	153	10	Williams	Charles	2	1	2		1	1		1	1				9		
Norwich	154	15	Williams	Daniel 2d	1	1		1		3	1	1	1				9		
Norwich	152	2	Williams	Daniel Jr				1			1	1	1				4		
Ashfield	346	18	Williams	David	1		2					1					4		
Monson	268	8	Williams	David	2	1		1		2	2		1				9		
West Springfield	357	41	Williams	David			1					1	1				3		
Shelburne	325	5	Williams	Dudley	2			1		2			1				6		
Warwick	40	12	Williams	Dudley		1				1			1				3		
Deerfield	55	45	Williams	Eben H.	1			1		2		3	1				8		
Warwick	40	4	Williams	Ebenezer	3	1		1			3	1	1				10		
Westfield	125	32	Williams	Ebenezer	1			1									2		
Worthington	301	7	Williams	Ebenezer	1	2	1		1		1	1		1			8		
South Hadley	250	14	Williams	Eleazer	1					5			1				7		
Springfield	239	6	Williams	Eleazer		1	1					2	1				5		
West Springfield	357	44	Williams	Elijah		2		1		3			1				7		
Ashfield	346	8	Williams	Ephm Esq	3	2	6	1				3	1				16		
Westfield	122	25	Williams	Ephraim	3			1		2			1				7		
Williamsburg	441	3	Williams	Grace				1		2	2						5		
Leverett	116	33	Williams	Henry		1	2		1	1	2		1	1			9		
Granville West Soc	168	26	Williams	Isaac	2	1		1		2	1		1				8		
Norwich	151	13	Williams	Isaac	1			1		1	1		1				5		
Norwich	154	16	Williams	Isaac	2	1		1			1		1				6		
Williamsburg	442	16	Williams	Jacob		2			1	2				1			6		
Amherst	292	36	Williams	John		1	1		1	1		1		1			6		
Blanford	176	15	Williams	John	2			1		1	1		1				6		
Chester	147	26	Williams	John	2			1		2			1	1			7		
Conway	61	41	Williams	John		1	2	1					1				5		
Deerfield	55	43	Williams	John		1	1	1					1				4		
Goshen	312	15	Williams	John	2	1	2	1		3	1	2	1				13		
Heath	197	31	Williams	John	1	2	1		1		1	2		1			9		
Holland	279	19	Williams	John	1		1			2			1				5		
Williamsburg	441	2	Williams	John				1					1				2		
Goshen	312	18	Williams	John 2d	1			1				1					3		

TOWN	PG#	LN#	LAST NAME	FIRST NAME	FREE WHITE MALES					FREE WHITE FEMALES					TOTAL ALL OTHER	TOTAL SLAVES	TOTALS	DISTRICT/TOWNSHIP	NOTES
					under 10	10 to 16	16 to 26	26 to 45	45 and over	under 10	10 to 16	16 to 26	26 to 45	45 and over					
Goshen	312	16	Williams	Jonah	5		1	1					1				8		
Montague	48	32	Williams	Joseph	2			1		2			1				6		
Warwick	40	20	Williams	Joseph	3	1		1		1			1				7		
Williamsburg	441	5	Williams	Joseph	3			1					1				5		
Springfield	242	22	Williams	Joseph Esq		1	1		1		1	1	1				6		
Amherst	292	35	Williams	Justus		1	1	1	1	1	1			1			7		
Belchertown	207	28	Williams	Justus			1					2					3		
Belchertown	203	9	Williams	Moses	1		1			1			1				4		
Westfield	122	17	Williams	Naboth	1		1			3	1		1				7		
Warwick	40	6	Williams	Nathaniel W	2	1	1						1				5		
Brimfield	269	9	Williams	Persis Wd		2	1			1	1		1				6		
Southampton	128	3	Williams	Philip		2				1		1					4		
Westfield	127	23	Williams	Philip			1			2		1					4		
Westfield	120	18	Williams	Reuben		1	1		2		1		1				6		
West Springfield	357	42	Williams	Roger	1		1			1		1					4		
Westfield	124	27	Williams	Roswell	3			1					1				5		
Russell	139	22	Williams	Saml	1	1	3		1	1	2	1	1	1			12		
Granville East Soc	531	22	Williams	Samuel				1					1				2		
Longmeadow	93	22	Williams	Samuel		1	2		1	1	1	2	1				9		
Southampton	129	18	Williams	Saxton		1				1		1					3		
Deerfield	55	42	Williams	Solomon	2	2	1	2				1	1	2			11		
Northampton	5	38	Williams	Solomon	1	2	1		1	3	1	1	1				11		
Conway	61	42	Williams	Statham				1					1		2		4		
Deerfield	55	44	Williams	Stephen	1		1		1	1	1	1	1				7		
Monson	267	24	Williams	Stephen		1				1		1					3		
Brimfield	271	4	Williams	Thomas	2			1		1			1				5		
Westfield	119	14	Williams	Thomas		1		1					1				3		
Warwick	40	11	Williams	Tryphena			1			2	1		1				5		
Deerfield	55	41	Williams	Wm Stodard	2	3		3		1		1	1				11		
Belchertown	211	2	Willis	Abisha	1			1					1	1			4		
Colrain	189	38	Willis	Daniel	1	1		2		1		3					8		
Deerfield	55	49	Willis	Ebenezer	3	1		1			1		1				7		
Colrain	190	8	Willis	Ezra	1	2		1		2	1		1				8		
Colrain	190	13	Willis	Josiah	1		1			1	1		1				5		
Shelburne	324	28	Willis	Josiah	2	2		1		1			1				7		
Leverett	116	31	Willis	Samuel	2			1		4	2		1				10		
Belchertown	210	33	Willis	Solomon		1		1		1		1					4		
Chester	144	17	Williston	Consider	2	1						2					5		
Springfield	241	24	Williston	Godfrey			1					1					4		
West Springfield	352	23	Williston	Israel	1	1		1			2		1				6		
West Springfield	352	25	Williston	John	2	1		1			4		1				9		
West Springfield	352	24	Williston	Nathaniel	3		2	1			1						7		
Easthampton	134	16	Williston	Pason	2			1		2			2				7		
Springfield	239	30	Williston	Thomas				1			1	1	1	1			5		
Orange	43	36	Willmoth	Jotham	1			1		4	2	1	1				10		
Orange	43	35	Willmoth	Nathaniel	2			1		2			1				6		
Chesterfield	20	19	Wills	Josiah	2			1		1	1						5		
Blanford	176	22	Willson	Andrew	4			1		1		1					7		
Colrain	190	3	Willson	David		2	3		2		1	2		1			11		
Colrain	189	41	Willson	David 2d	4			1		1		1	1	1			9		
Rowe	201	6	Willson	Henry	1		1	1		1			1	1			6		
Rowe	201	8	Willson	Henry Jnr	4			1		1		1					7		
Colrain	189	32	Willson	James	2	2		1		2	1	1	1	1			11		
Colrain	189	40	Willson	John	2		1	1			2						6		
Ludlow	257	25	Willson	John	2	1		1				1	1				6		
Warwick	40	19	Willson	John			1							1			2		
Warwick	40	5	Willson	John Junr		1	1	1		1		1					5		
Colrain	189	36	Willson	Jonathan		2	3		1	1	1	1		1			10		
Warwick	40	16	Willson	Jonathan		2	1	1		1			1				6		
Colrain	190	2	Willson	Jonathan 2d		2		1		3			1				7		
Deerfield	55	47	Willson	Samuel		2	1	1	1				1	2			8		
Rowe	201	10	Willson	Warren	1			1			1	1					4		
Worthington	301	34	Willys	Mace		2	1	1			2		1				7		
Springfield	239	36	Wilner	Hendrick	3			1	1				1				6		
Belchertown	207	31	Wilson	Asa	1	2	1	1		3	1		1				10		
Worthington	299	2	Wilson	Benjn	1			1				1		1			4		
Heath	198	1	Wilson	Caleb	2	1		1		1		1					6		
Belchertown	210	25	Wilson	Chester			1										1		
Longmeadow	94	7	Wilson	David	1			1					1				3		
Shelburne	324	22	Wilson	David			2						1				3		
Northfield	31	18	Wilson	Ebenezer	1		1			2		1					5		
Norwich	153	39	Wilson	Elijah	3	2			1			2		1			9		
Shelburne	324	24	Wilson	James	2	1	1		1	2		1	2	1			11		
West Springfield	352	22	Wilson	John		1								1			3		
Belchertown	207	26	Wilson	Nathan	2			1					1				4		
Belchertown	207	32	Wilson	Reuben	1	1		1		3	1		1				8		
Shelburne	324	25	Wilson	Robert			1					1	1				3		
Colrain	190	14	Wilson	Robert Jun			1						1				2		
Worthington	298	33	Wilson	Simeon		1		1		4			1				7		
Shelburne	324	27	Wilson	Thomas	3	1		1			1		1				7		

TOWN	PG#	LN#	LAST NAME	FIRST NAME	FREE WHITE MALES under 10	10 to 16	16 to 26	26 to 45	45 and over	FREE WHITE FEMALES under 10	10 to 16	16 to 26	26 to 45	45 and over	TOTAL ALL OTHER	TOTAL SLAVES	TOTALS	DISTRICT/ TOWNSHIP	NOTES
Belchertown	207	27	Wilson	Thomas Lt		2		1		2	2	1		2			10		
Pelham	217	6	Wilson	William		2		1		2	2			1			8		
Shutesbury	113	4	Winch	John	1			1					1				3		
Chester	148	19	Winchel	Grove	1		1	1		1		1	1				6		
Granville East Soc	529	22	Winchell	Dan				1		2	1		1				5		
West Springfield	355	28	Winchell	David	3			1		1			1				6		
West Springfield	355	33	Winchell	Jacob	1	1	1			1			1	1			6		
West Springfield	355	27	Winchell	John				1		1	1	2	2	1			7		
Granville East Soc	527	6	Winchell	Martin	1			1	1				2				5		
Brimfield	275	5	Winchester	Aaron	4	2		1					1				8		South Brimfield
Northfield	31	20	Winchester	Amasa				1				1	1				3		
South Brimfield	277	19	Winchester	Benjamin	4				1	1	1		1				8		
South Brimfield	276	39	Winchester	Ruth Wid										1			1		
Leverett	116	28	Winchester	Willm			1						1				2		
Greenwich	224	17	Windslow	John	1			1		1	1	1	1				6		
Ware	228	32	Windslow	Thomas		1		1	1	1	1		1	1			7		
Goshen	312	17	Wing	Edward	1	2	3		1	2	1	1		1			12		
Conway	61	26	Wing	Isaiah		2		1		3			1				7		
Conway	61	35	Wing	John	1	2	1		1	2	1		1				9		
New Salem	104	24	Winship	Benjamin	2			1		2			1				6		
Amherst	291	33	Winslow	Amasa	1			1		2			1				5		
Montague	48	30	Winslow	James	1	2	1		1	1	2	1		1			10		
Montague	48	35	Winslow	Josiah				1									1		
Wendell	108	16	Winslow	Josiah	1		1						1				3		
Montague	48	25	Winslow	Nathaniel	1			1						1			3		
Montague	48	28	Winslow	Seth	2			1		3			1				7		
Brimfield	269	32	Winslow	Shubael Dr		1		1		1		2		1			6		
Shutesbury	112	30	Winter	Benja	1	1		1		3	1		1				8		
Pelham	216	5	Winter	David	2			1		1			1				5		
Shelburne	324	21	Winter	Isaac	1	2	1	1			1	1	1	1			9		
Shutesbury	112	29	Winter	Jesse	1	1			1	2				1			6		
Deerfield	55	40	Wise	Joseph	1		1		1	1				1			5		
Montague	48	24	Wise	William Lt	1	1		1		3			1				7		
Orange	43	37	Witherbee	Paul			1					1					2		
Chesterfield	23	23	Witherell	Elihu			2		1			3		1			7		
Warwick	40	10	Witherell	Elijah			1	1				1					3		
Chesterfield	23	22	Witherell	Elisha Jr	1			1		1			1				4		
Chesterfield	23	16	Witherell	John	3	1		1		2	1		2				10		
Palmer	261	27	Withington	Joseph		1			1				1	1			4		
Greenfield	76	12	Witmore	Thomas		1		1		1				1			4		
Belchertown	211	8	Witt	Ivory	4			1		2	2	1	1				11		
Granby	253	15	Witt	John	1			1									2		
Granby	253	16	Witt	Joseph	2	1	1			1		1	1				8		
Monson	266	36	Wittaker	Eddy Doct			1			1		1					3		
Wilbraham	233	31	Witten	Ezra Revd	2		1	1		1	1	1	1				8		
Springfield	245	15	Wolcott	Apaphras				1						1			2		
Longmeadow	93	6	Wolcott	Benjamin				1									1		
West Springfield	357	37	Wolcott	David	4			1				1	1	1			8		
Springfield	245	16	Wolcott	James	2	1		1		1			1				6		
West Springfield	357	36	Wolcott	Jesse	2	1	1		1	2			1				8		
West Springfield	357	39	Wolcott	Noah	1		1	1		3	1		1				8		
West Springfield	357	38	Wolcott	Solomon	1			1		1			1				4		
Monson	264	23	Wolfe	Levi	2			1					1				4		
Hawley	335	20	Wood	Andrews	3	1		1		2			1				8		
Middlefield	155	4	Wood	Artemas	2			1		1			1				5		
Northfield	31	9	Wood	Barzillai	1				1	3		1	1				7		
Greenwich	223	27	Wood	Benjamin		1	1		1	2		2		1			8		
Westhampton	18	14	Wood	David	1		1	1		3	1		1	1			9		
Monson	265	9	Wood	Ebenezer				1						1			2		
Colrain	190	9	Wood	Edmond		2		1		1	1			1			6		
Longmeadow	92	39	Wood	Edward		1				1		1					3		
Wendell	108	14	Wood	Eli	2			1		1		1					5		
Belchertown	207	22	Wood	Ichabod	2			1		2	1		1				7		
Wilbraham	238	2	Wood	Jacob				1		2			1				4		
Chester	146	2	Wood	James	1			1		1	2	1					6		
Buckland	331	11	Wood	John			1	1		1		1	1				5		
New Salem	104	27	Wood	John	2			1		2			1				6		
Monson	265	12	Wood	Jonathan	1	1		1					1				4		
Ware	228	31	Wood	Jonathan	2	2		1		3	1		1				10		
Pelham	217	1	Wood	Levi	1	2			1	2	1		1				8		
Cummington	304	37	Wood	Mary								1		1			2		
Colrain	189	34	Wood	Moses	2	1			1	1	1	1		1			8		
Ludlow	256	5	Wood	Moses	3	1		1		1			1				7		
Chester	147	4	Wood	Nathan	1		1	1				1		1			5		
Ludlow	257	10	Wood	Obadiah Doct			1	1						1			3		
Northfield	31	10	Wood	Samuel	1			1		2			2				6		
Shutesbury	112	34	Wood	Samuel	2	2		1		2			2	1			8		
Middlefield	158	33	Wood	Simeon	1			1				2					4		
Belchertown	207	23	Wood	Solomon				1		3			1				5		
Easthampton	135	10	Wood	Stephen	1	1	1						1				4		

323

TOWN	PG#	LN#	LAST NAME	FIRST NAME	FREE WHITE MALES					FREE WHITE FEMALES					TOTAL ALL OTHER	TOTAL SLAVES	TOTALS	DISTRICT/ TOWNSHIP	NOTES
					under 10	10 to 16	16 to 26	26 to 45	45 and over	under 10	10 to 16	16 to 26	26 to 45	45 and over					
Middlefield	157	33	Wood	Stephen			1		1				1				3		
Monson	265	11	Wood	Stephen	1			1			1	1		1			5		
Longmeadow	92	38	Wood	Submit									1				1		
Belchertown	207	24	Wood	Sylvanus	1			1		1		1					4		
Middlefield	157	17	Wood	Thomas				1				1	1				3		
Greenwich	224	5	Wood	William				1		1		1	1				4		
Belchertown	207	30	Wood	Zeanon		1		1					1				3		
Hawley	335	19	Wood	Zebedee				1				1					3		
Belchertown	211	9	Wood	Zephiniah		1	1					1	2	2			7		
Buckland	331	5	Wood	Amos	2	1	1	1	1	1	1		1	1			10		
Greenwich	223	23	Wood	Aaron	3	1		1		2			1				8		
Conway	61	32	Wood	Ceaser											3		3		
Wendell	108	13	Wood	Thomas			1	1		2			1				5		
Wilbraham	238	1	Wood	William		1	1	1				1		1			5		
Orange	43	24	Woodard	Amos	2	2		1		3	1		1				10		
Buckland	331	2	Woodard	Daniel	2			1		2			1				6		
Buckland	331	12	Woodard	Henry	3	1		1		2	1		1	1			10		
Buckland	330	27	Woodard	James	1	1	1		1		2	1		1			8		
Middlefield	155	12	Woodard	Jonathan				1					1				2		
Orange	43	38	Woodard	Jonathan				1	1	1			1				3		
South Hadley	250	44	Woodbridge	Jahleel		1	1		2		1		1				6		
Norwich	153	42	Woodbridge	John		1	1						1	1			4		
Worthington	297	45	Woodbridge	Jonathan	1	1	1			3	1		1				8		
South Hadley	250	45	Woodbridge	Ruggles Esq		2	2		1			1		1			7		
Southampton	130	30	Woodbridge	Sylvster	1		1		1			1		1			5		
Blanford	181	13	Woodbridge	Wil	3	2		1		1	1	1	1				10		
Leverett	116	23	Woodbury	John	2	1	1		1	1	2	3		1			12		
Leverett	116	27	Woodbury	Knowlton	3			1		2			1				7		
Leverett	116	26	Woodbury	Seth	3	3		1					1	1			10		
Orange	43	27	Woodcock	Nathaniel				1				1		1			3		
Granville Mid Soc.	165	9	Woodruff	Joseph	1	2	1		1	1			1		1		8		
Orange	43	22	Woods	Benjamin		2	1		1				4		1		9		
Worthington	301	36	Woods	David		1			1				1	1			4		
Montague	48	26	Woods	Firman			1		1	1	1	1					5		
Worthington	301	8	Woodward	Daniel		1			1					1			3		
Conway	61	25	Woodward	Ebenezer					1				1	1			3		
Belchertown	211	19	Woodward	Elisha	1			1					1				3		
Wilbraham	233	7	Woodward	Elisha	1			1					1				3		
Belchertown	211	4	Woodward	Ephraim	2			1		2	1		1				7		
Conway	61	28	Woodward	Isaac	4	1	1	1		2		2					11		
Gill	88	22	Woodward	Job		1		1		4	1		1				8		
Greenfield	76	13	Woodward	John					1		1	3		1			6		
Northfield	31	14	Woodward	John	3			1			1		1				6		
Wendell	108	12	Woodward	Jonas	2			1	1				1				5		
Hadley	288	31	Woodward	Samuel		1				1		1					3		
Greenwich	223	24	Woodward	Seth		2	2		1	3	1		1				10		
Greenwich	221	33	Woodward	Solomon				1					1				2		
Wilbraham	236	12	Woodward	Thankful Wd		1								1			2		
Longmeadow	93	16	Woodworth	Azariah	1	1	5	1		2	1		1				12		
Southwick	361	8	Woodworth	Chester		1		1					1				3		
South Hadley	250	36	Woodworth	James	2	1		1		4	1		1				10		
Granville East Soc	529	7	Woolworth	Phinehas	2	2	2		1	3			1				11		
Longmeadow	92	4	Woolworth	Richard		1		2	1				1	1			6		
Longmeadow	92	3	Woolworth	Richard Jr	1	1	1					1	1				6		
Colrain	190	10	Worden	John	2	2		1		2	1		1				9		
Colrain	190	11	Worden	Thomas	1	1	1	1		3	1		1				9		
Colrain	189	35	Workman	Daniel	1	1		1	1	2			2	1			9		
Shutesbury	113	1	Works	Daniel							1	3		1			5		
Wilbraham	232	43	Works	John	4	1	1	1		1		1	1				10		
West Springfield	355	32	Worthington	Amos	1	1							1				3		
Belchertown	211	5	Worthington	David	2			1				3	1				7		
West Springfield	355	39	Worthington	David	2		4	1		1			1				9		
West Springfield	355	38	Worthington	Heman		1		1		2			1				6		
West Springfield	355	36	Worthington	John	2			1		2			1				6		
West Springfield	355	31	Worthington	Jonathan	1		2		1		1	2	1				8		
Springfield	239	20	Worthington	Mary Wd	2		2						2		1		7		
Springfield	244	19	Worthington	Stephen	2			1		1			1				5		
Hawley	335	25	Worthington	Timothy	2	1		1	1	2			1	1			9		
Belchertown	211	6	Worthington	Wm		1			1	1	3		1				7		
West Springfield	352	28	Worthy	Valentine		1	1		1	1	1	1		1			7		
Northampton	5	8	Wright	Aaron				1	1					1			3		
Northampton	5	9	Wright	Aaron Jun	2		1	1		1		1					6		
Ludlow	256	12	Wright	Abel				1		1				1			3		
Ludlow	256	14	Wright	Abel Jr			1			2			1				4		
Barnardston	80	3	Wright	Abner	1	2	3		1				1	1			9		
Montague	48	22	Wright	Abner	1		1	1		1	1	2		1			8		
Sunderland	283	19	Wright	Abner			1			1			1				3		
Northampton	6	38	Wright	Asahel		1		2					1				4		
Northampton	7	10	Wright	Asahel	2	1		1	1	1			1	1			8		
Deerfield	55	36	Wright	Asahel Jun	1	1		1	2	2			1	2			11		

TOWN	PG#	LN#	LAST NAME	FIRST NAME	FREE WHITE MALES					FREE WHITE FEMALES					TOTAL ALL OTHER	TOTAL SLAVES	TOTALS	DISTRICT/ TOWNSHIP	NOTES
					under 10	10 to 16	16 to 26	26 to 45	45 and over	under 10	10 to 16	16 to 26	26 to 45	45 and over					
Chester	150	1	Wright	Bazaleel	1	2	1	1		2			1				8		
Ludlow	256	9	Wright	Benjamin	2	1	1		1	1		1	1				8		
Springfield	246	25	Wright	Calvin	4			1		1			1	2			9		
Springfield	241	33	Wright	Calvin 2d				1		1		1					3		
Deerfield	55	38	Wright	Carnie	1	2	2		1	2	1		1				10		
Montgomery	160	41	Wright	Charles	1	1		1		1			1				5		
Springfield	248	3	Wright	Charles	2			1		1			1				5		
Northampton	4	23	Wright	Daniel		1	2	1		3	1		1				9		
Springfield	244	39	Wright	Daniel	1			1		1		1		1			5		
Springfield	240	35	Wright	Darius			1			1			1				3		
Granville West Soc	169	1	Wright	David		2	1	1					1				5		
Montgomery	161	34	Wright	David			1										1		
Northfield	31	16	Wright	David		2	1		1	1		1	1				7		
Springfield	239	35	Wright	David			1					1		1			3		
Northfield	31	5	Wright	Donaldus			1						1				2		
Northampton	7	20	Wright	Ebenezer				1									1		
Pelham	217	3	Wright	Ebenz		1		1	1	1		2		1			6		
Ludlow	255	13	Wright	Elam	1		1					1					3		
Northfield	31	4	Wright	Eldad	1	1		1		2	1		1				7		
Springfield	245	25	Wright	Eleazer	3	2		1		1	1		1				9		
Easthampton	136	21	Wright	Elijah	1	1	3	2	1			1		2			11		
Northampton	7	17	Wright	Elijah				1				1	1				3		
Easthampton	136	23	Wright	Elijah Junr	1		1	1		1			1				5		
Northfield	31	6	Wright	Eliphaz		1		1	1	1		1		1			5		
Montague	48	23	Wright	Elisha	1	2	1		2	1		1		2			10		
Northampton	7	19	Wright	Enos	2		2		1	1	2		1				9		
Westhampton	15	1	Wright	Ephraim	1	2	1		1	1		2		1			9		
Wilbraham	235	27	Wright	Ezekiel	3			2		1		1	2	1			10		
Springfield	240	34	Wright	George			1						1				2		
Norwich	154	13	Wright	Gideon	2	1	1	1		1			1				7		
Ludlow	256	16	Wright	Goss	2			1					1				44		
Wilbraham	233	2	Wright	Henry		1		1	2		2		1	1			8		
Northampton	7	11	Wright	Israel	1			1					1				3		
Granville West Soc	169	15	Wright	Jabez	1		1						1				3		
Monson	264	20	Wright	Jacob		1		1		1			1				4		
Deerfield	55	51	Wright	James			1						1				2		
Montgomery	160	38	Wright	James	4		1						1				6		
Barnardston	80	4	Wright	Job		1		1		1	3		1				7		
Northampton	6	37	Wright	Jonah	3		1			1		1					6		
Granville West Soc	169	33	Wright	Jonathan	2		1			2	1		1				7		
Chester	148	10	Wright	Joshua	1	1		1	1	2			1	1			8		
Deerfield	55	37	Wright	Judah	2		1	1		1			1	1			7		
Middlefield	156	34	Wright	Jude	1		1	1				1	2				6		
Chester	150	8	Wright	Lewis	1			1		3	2		2	2			11		
Easthampton	134	24	Wright	Luther	1			1		1		1					4		
Deerfield	55	35	Wright	Moses	3			2		1			1				7		
Northampton	7	23	Wright	Moses		1		1	1	1	1		1	1			6		
Middlefield	157	10	Wright	Nathan Capt.	2	1	1		1	1		1	2	1			10		
Barnardston	80	5	Wright	Nehemiah	3		1						1				5		
Northfield	31	8	Wright	Oliver		1	1		1	1	1		1				6		
Westhampton	15	14	Wright	Oliver		1		1		1			1				4		
Northampton	6	36	Wright	Ornass		1		1		1		1	1	2			7		
Hadley	285	6	Wright	Paul			1					1					2		
Westhampton	18	7	Wright	Phineas		2		1				1		1			5		
Northfield	31	7	Wright	Reuben		1		1	1	1		1	1				6		
Westhampton	18	32	Wright	Reuben	1	1		1		1	1		1				6		
Springfield	246	26	Wright	Robert			1			1		1					3		
Westfield	119	36	Wright	Rodrick	1	1	2			3	1		1				10		
Shelburne	325	2	Wright	Saml	1		1						1				3		
Montgomery	160	37	Wright	Samuel		1		2					1	1			5		
Northampton	7	14	Wright	Samuel	1	1	1		1	2		1	1				8		
Westhampton	18	29	Wright	Samuel	2			1		2	1	1	1				8		
Montgomery	160	39	Wright	Samuel Junr	1	1		1		1		2					6		
Northampton	2	6	Wright	Sarah	1							1		1			3		
Wendell	108	10	Wright	Silas	1			1					1				3		
Northampton	7	15	Wright	Solomon			1		1					1			3		
Wilbraham	236	36	Wright	Solomon		1	1		1	1	1			1			6		
Springfield	241	10	Wright	Stephen		1	1		1	1	1	3		1			9		
Easthampton	134	23	Wright	Stephen		1	3	1				1		1			7		
Easthampton	134	3	Wright	Stephen Junr	1	1	1						1				4		
Ludlow	256	10	Wright	Thaddeus	1		1			2		1					5		
Ludlow	256	15	Wright	Timothy		1		1						1			3		
Northampton	5	30	Wright	Timothy				1						1			2		
Northampton	7	13	Wright	Ursula		1	1	1	1			2		1			7		
Deerfield	55	39	Wright	Westwood Cooke	2	2	1	2	1	1		1		1			11		
Wilbraham	235	26	Wright	Zebulon				1		2	2	1					6		
Gill	88	11	Wrisley	Asahel		1	1		1	2	1			1			7		
Gill	88	14	Wrisley	Caleb	2		1			1		1					5		
Gill	88	10	Wrisley	David		1	1		1				1	2			6		
Gill	88	12	Wrisley	David Jun			1			3			1				5		

TOWN	PG#	LN#	LAST NAME	FIRST NAME	FREE WHITE MALES					FREE WHITE FEMALES					TOTAL ALL OTHER	TOTAL SLAVES	TOTALS	DISTRICT/ TOWNSHIP	NOTES
					under 10	10 to 16	16 to 26	26 to 45	45 and over	under 10	10 to 16	16 to 26	26 to 45	45 and over					
Gill	88	15	Wrisley	Eleazer		1			1			1		1			4		
Gill	88	18	Wrisley	Eleazer Jnr			1			1							2		
Gill	88	9	Wrisley	Elijah	2	1	1		1	1	1	2		1			10		
Gill	88	8	Wrisley	Jonathan	1			1		3		1	1				7		
Gill	88	13	Wrisley	Joseph	2	1		1		2			1				7		
Gill	88	16	Wrisley	Obed	1		1			1		1					4		
Montague	48	19	Wrisley	Samuel		1		1		2	2	1	1	1			9		
Gill	88	17	Wrisley	Sylvannus			1					1					2		
New Salem	104	16	Wyart	Joshua	1			1	1	2			1	1			7		
Wendell	108	15	Wyeth	Gad	3			1	1	1		1	1				8		
Greenwich	223	29	Wyot	Stephen					1				1				2		
Colrain	190	17	Yaw	John	1		2						1				4		
Westfield	124	14	Yeoman	Elijah	2	1	2	1		1	1	1	1				10		
Brimfield	275	2	Young	David Doct		1	1	1		1		1	1				6	South Brimfield	
Charlemont	194	21	Young	Henry				1		1		1					3		
Heath	198	9	Young	Henry			2		1		2			1			6		
Shutesbury	113	7	Young	Mercy									1				1		
Charlemont	194	22	Young	Robert	3			1		1			1				6		
Warwick	40	25	Young	Robert		1	1	1		1		2		2			8		
Amherst	291	5	Youngs	Mercy									1				1		
Amherst	294	24	Zale	Elijah	1			1					1				3		

NOTES

www.ingramcontent.com/pod-product-compliance
Lightning Source LLC
Chambersburg PA
CBHW080242290526
45790CB00005B/1670